FINANCIAL
Accounting

Seventh Edition

Walter T. Harrison Jr.
Baylor University

Charles T. Horngren
Stanford University

Pearson Education International

AVP/Executive Editor: Jodi McPherson
VP/Publisher: Natalie Anderson
Director, Product Development: Pamela Hersperger
Editorial Project Manager: Ana Jankowski
Editorial Assistant: Kate Horton
Development Editor: Ralph Moore
Marketing Manager: Andrew Watts
Marketing Assistant: Justin Jacob
Senior Managing Editor, Production: Cynthia Zonneveld
Production Project Manager: Melissa Feimer
Permissions Coordinator: Charles Morris
Senior Operations Supervision: Nick Sklitsis

AV Project Manager: Rhonda Aversa
Senior Art Director: Jonathan Boylan
Cover Design: Jonathan Boylan
Director, Image Resource Center: Melinda Patelli
Manager, Rights and Permissions: Zina Arabia
Manager, Visual Research: Beth Brenzel
Manager, Cover Visual Research & Permissions: Karen Sanatar
Image Permission Coordinator: Jan Marc Quisumbing
Photo Researcher: Teri Stratford
Composition: GEX Publishing Services
Full-Service Project Management: GEX Publishing Services

Pearson Education LTD., London
Pearson Education Singapore, Pte. Ltd
Pearson Education, Canada, Ltd
Pearson Education–Japan

Pearson Education Australia PTY, Limited
Pearson Education North Asia Ltd
Pearson Educación de Mexico, S.A. de C.V.
Pearson Education Malaysia, Pte. Ltd.
Pearson Education, Upper Saddle River, New Jersey

10 9 8 7 6 5 4 3 2 1
ISBN-13: 978-0-13-135557-6
ISBN-10: 0-13-135557-0

For our wives,

Nancy and Joan

Brief Contents

Contents

Chapter 4

Internal Control & Cash 209

Chapter 5

Short-Term Investments & Receivables 257

Chapter 6

Inventory & Cost of Goods Sold 305

Chapter 7

Plant Assets & Intangibles   363

Chapter 8

Liabilities   413

Chapter 9

Stockholders' Equity   473

Chapter 10

Long-Term Investments & International Operations   533

Chapter 11

The Income Statement & the Statement of Stockholders' Equity   579

Chapter 12

The Statement of Cash Flows   615

Chapter 13

Financial Statement Analysis   681

The Accounting Cycle: Key to Success

Note to the Instructor: This financial accounting course builds on the first 3 chapters, which focus on accounting fundamentals and the accounting cycle. You've told us that mastering these chapters will guarantee your students' success as they move through the course. For this reason, *Financial Accounting, 7th edition* is focused on students' success in learning accounting basics. Our goal is for students to be motivated to excel throughout the course.

> Review the inside front cover to see exactly what we offer your students.

Streamlined Design for the 7th Edition

The 7th edition has a streamlined design to aid student learning.

- Shorter chapter openers capture student interest.
- More diagrams and fewer words make the book easy to read.
- Shorter sections keep students from getting bogged down in unnecessary detail.
- 7E has no "boxes" because students skip them.
- All assignment materials list page references that help students use their homework time efficiently.
- Simpler figures in the assignment material enable students to focus on the learning, not on the numbers.

Learning Approach: Focus on Performance

> Student success and performance go hand in hand. That's why we increased opportunities for you and your students to practice accounting throughout the course.

In-Text Practice Material

- **Stop and Think:** At critical junctures in each chapter we ask students to "Stop and Think" about what they've just learned.
- **Decision Guidelines:** This feature summarizes each chapter in terms of the decisions people make as they use accounting information.
- **Summary Problems:** Most chapters have 2 problems—at the mid-point and at the end—with worked-out solutions.
- **Chapter Review Quiz:** At the end of chapter, these multiple-choice questions include answers for quick self-assessment.
- **Practice Quiz:** Multiple-choice questions in the end-of-chapter assignments section have answers in the Check Figures appendix at the end of the book.

Practice Quiz

Test your understanding of the financial statements by answering the following questions. Select the best choice from among the possible answers given.

1. All of the following statements are true except 1. Which statement is false?

   a. Bookkeeping is only a part of accounting.
   b. A proprietorship is a business with several owners.
   c. Professional accountants are held to a high standard of ethical conduct.
   d. The organization that formulates generally accepted accounting principles is the Financial Accounting Standards Board.

2. The valuation of assets on the balance sheet is generally based on:

   a. Historical cost
   b. What it would cost to replace the asset
   c. Current fair market value as established by independent appraisers
   d. Selling price

3. The accounting equation can be expressed as:

   a. Assets + Liabilities = Owners' Equity
   b. Owners' Equity + Assets = Liabilities
   c. Assets = Liabilities – Owners' Equity
   d. Assets – Liabilities = Owners' Equity

Online Practice and Homework Material

■ **Practice Material:** An open-access online practice environment enables students to master chapter material. Selected end-of-chapter problems are available for all learning objectives in Chapters 1–3. The problems (a) are algorithmic, giving students a chance to practice until they have mastery; (b) provide immediate feedback, giving students a chance to see how well they are doing right away; (c) mirror those in the book, giving students a chance to practice before doing "the real thing."

■ **Homework and Quiz Material: My Accounting Lab (MAL)**

> MAL is an online homework and quizzing environment that allows instructors to customize homework and quiz options for their classes.

Selected end-of-chapter (even-numbered) exercises and (A) problems from the text are available. Instructors can post assignments and receive grades. All questions are algorithmically generated so each student session offers different problems and answers while providing immediate feedback and scoring for instructors and their students.

Special Section for Current Users

> Thank you for your continued use of Harrison's *Financial Accounting* in your classroom. To ease your transition, here are highlights of chapter changes for the 7th edition.

Chapter 1.   The Financial Statements
Updated feature company for the book, YUM! Brands
New feature company, Genie Car Wash, for the running example through the accounting cycle
New coverage of the FASB Statement that permits fair-value accounting
New section on limited-liability companies
Accounting Cycle Tutorial

Chapter 2.   Transaction Analysis
Updated chapter opener about Apple Computer
New section on Analyzing Accounts
New transaction explanations
New feature company for the accounting cycle
Accounting Cycle Tutorial

Chapter 3.   Accrual Accounting and Income
New chapter opener on Starbucks Corporation
New exhibit on How Transactions Affect the Ratios
Accounting Cycle Tutorial

Chapter 4.   Internal Control & Cash
New company for the chapter opener, Amex Products
Coverage of the Sarbanes-Oxley Act
New framework for internal control
New material on online banking
New material on ethics

Chapter 5.   Short-Term Investments & Receivables
New chapter opener on PepsiCo
New section on Lending Agreements and the Current Ratio
New section on Writing Off Uncollectible Receivables

Chapter 6.   Inventory & Cost of Goods Sold
Updated chapter opener on Pier 1 Imports
New visuals
Streamlined exhibits
New comparison of FIFO and LIFO
New exhibit comparing Pier 1 Imports, Federated Department Stores, and Home Depot
New section on T-Accounts for Analyzing Plant Asset Transactions

Chapter 7.   Plant Assets & Intangibles
New chapter opener on FedEx Corporation
New coverage of plant-asset accounting errors
New Summary of the Current Liabilities

Chapter 8.   Liabilities
New chapter opener on Southwest Airlines
New section on Partial-Period Interest Amounts

Chapter 9. Stockholders' Equity
Updated chapter opener on IHOP
New section on Authorized, Issued, and Outstanding Stock
New Summary of Treasury Stock Transactions
Expanded exhibits
New coverage of dividends
New section on Analyzing The Stockholders' Equity Accounts

Chapter 10. Long-Term Investments & International Operations
New chapter opener on Intel Corporation
Intel Corporation integrated throughout the chapter
New section: When Should We Sell an Investment?

Chapter 11. The Income Statement & The Statement of Stockholders' Equity
New chapter opener on Pier 1 Imports

Chapter 12. The Statement of Cash Flows
New chapter opener on Google, Inc.
New feature company throughout the chapter, The Roadster Factory
Enhanced visuals

Chapter 13. Financial Statement Analysis
Return to feature company, YUM! Brands, for evaluation and analysis

Teaching And Learning Support

For Instructors
At a Glance Supplements Grid

	Print	Online	IRCD
Instructor's Edition	×	×	×
Test Item File		×	×
Instructor Solutions Manual		×	×
Solution Transparencies	×	×	×
Instructor 508 Compliant PowerPoints		×	×
MyAccountingLab		×	
BlackBoard, WebCT, and CourseCompass		×	
Companion Website		×	
Accounting Cycle Tutorial		×	

Instructor's Resource Center (www.prenhall.com/harrison) This password-protected site is accessible from the catalog page for *Financial Accounting, 7th edition* and hosts the following resources:

■ Instructor PowerPoints, by Courtney Baillie: These are 508-compliant PowerPoints with some worked out, end of chapter exercises and problems.

- Test Item File
- TestGen
- Image Library: Access to most of the images and illustrations featured in the text.
- Excel Application Problems: These problems show when, why, and how people use the accounting guidelines in order to make business decisions. Students can apply the Decision Guidelines to a realistic situation and use the power of Excel to determine a solution.
- **Solutions Manual** by Walter T. Harrison: This manual contains the fully worked-out and accuracy-checked solutions for every question, exercise, and problem in the text.

Instructor's Edition by Helen Brubeck, San Jose State University Each chapter of this comprehensive resource acts as a roadmap to all of the tools available for use by the instructor, including a list of the student learning objectives, a narrative overview of main topics, an outline with teaching tips, a suggested assignment grid for all end-of-chapter questions, problems, 10 minute quizzes, and exercises, and an integration grid that contains the list of exercises and problems available in MyAccountingLab (online homework and assessment tool), Microsoft Excel, and General Ledger.

Test Item File by Calvin Fink This resource features over 1,600 multiple choice and true/false questions written specifically for the 7th edition. All questions are organized by level of difficulty and include the corresponding learning objective number. Additional computational problems are available to instructors on both the instructor resource CD as well as on prenhall.com.

Instructor's Resource CD This CD-ROM contains all the supplements that are hosted on our online Instructor's Resource Center, including the image library.

Solutions Transparencies Every page of the solutions manual has been reproduced in acetate form for use on an overhead projector.

MyAccountingLab (www.myaccountinglab.com) MyAccountingLab is Prentice Hall's online homework and assessment manager to help students "get" accounting through the power of practice. MyAccountingLab features a full e-book, Flash Demo Docs, instructor videos, and additional resources at the student's fingertips to aid learning. With MyAccountingLab, instructors can:

- Deliver all or a portion of the course online, whether the students are in a lab setting or working from home.
- Create and assign online homework and tests that are automatically graded and tightly correlated to the textbook.
- Manage students' results in a powerful online grade book designed specifically for mathematics and statistics.
- Customize the course, depending on the syllabus and the students' needs.

CourseCompass, WebCT, and BlackBoard for Financial Accounting Prentice Hall's course management site is all that instructors and students need for anytime online access to interactive materials that enhance this text.

WebCT, Financial Accounting by Walter T. Harrison © 2008 Prentice Hall's course management site is all instructors and students need for anytime online access to interactive materials that enhance this text.

BlackBoard, Financial Accounting by Walter T. Harrison © 2008 Electronic Book: Prentice Hall's course management site is all instructors and students need for anytime online access to interactive materials that enhance this text.

For Students

Mastering the Accounting Cycle (www.prenhall.com/harrison)

Open Access (no registration or password needed) Companion Website that provides you with:

- Accounting Cycle Tutorial: For practice on material from Chapters 1–3
- Online Practice Environment with algorithmic questions for Chapters 1–3
- Accounting Cycle Pocket Guide: Reference tool that walks you through each step of the accounting cycle
- Self-study quizzes: An interactive study guide for each chapter
- E-Working papers that students can use to complete homework assignments for each chapter
- Student PowerPoints: For use as a study aid or note-taking guide

CourseCompass, Student Access Kit, Financial Accounting

WebCT, Student Access Kit, Financial Accounting

BlackBoard, Student Access Kit, Financial Accounting

MAL-Student Access Card

> Note: All Mastering the Accounting Cycle material can be found within OneKey courses previously listed.

Vango Notes (www.vangonotes.com) Students can study on the go with VangoNotes—chapter reviews from this text in downloadable MP3 format. Students can purchase VangoNotes for the entire textbook or for individual chapters. For each chapter, VangoNotes contains:

- Big Ideas: The "need to know" for each chapter.
- Key Terms: Audio "flashcards" to help students review key concepts and terms.
- Rapid Review: A quick drill session—to use right before taking a test.

Print Study Aids

Accounting Tip Reference Card (A-Tip)
This guide illustrates the key steps in the accounting cycle.

Study Guide Including Demo Docs and E-Working Papers with Flash CD by Helen Brubeck, San Jose State University
This chapter-by-chapter learning aid helps you learn financial accounting and get the maximum benefit from study time. Each chapter contains a Chapter Overview and Review, a Featured Exercise that covers all of the most important chapter material, and

Review Questions and Exercises with Solutions that test your understanding of the material. Demo Docs are available in the study guide—in print and on CD in Flash so students can easily refer to them when they need them. Electronic working papers are included on the accompanying CD.

Acknowledgments

In revising the previous edition of *Financial Accounting*, we had the help of instructors from across the country who have participated in online surveys, chapter reviews, and focus groups. Their comments and suggestions for both the text and the supplements have been a great help in planning and carrying out revisions, and we thank them for their contributions.

Online Reviewers

Lucille Berry, Webster University, MO
Patrick Bouker, North Seattle Community College
Michael Broihahn, Barry University, FL
Kam Chan, Pace University
Hong Chen, Northeastern Illinois University
Charles Coate, St. Bonaventure University, NY
Bryan Church, Georgia Tech at Atlanta
Terrie Gehman, Elizabethtown College, PA
Brian Green, University of Michigan at Dearborn
Chao-Shin Liu, Notre Dame
Herb Martin, Hope College, MI
Bruce Maule, College of San Mateo
Michelle McEacharn, University of Louisiana at Monroe
Bettye Rogers-Desselle, Prairie View A&M University, TX
Norlin Rueschhoff, Notre Dame
William Schmul, Notre Dame
Arnie Schnieder, Georgia Tech at Atlanta
J. B. Stroud, Nicholls State Univesity, LA
Bruce Wampler, Louisiana State University, Shreveport
Myung Yoon, Northeastern Illinois University
Lin Zeng, Northeastern Illinois University

Focus Group Participants

Ellen D. Cook, University of Louisiana at Lafayette
Theodore D. Morrison III, Wingate University, NC
Alvin Gerald Smith, University of Northern Iowa
Carolyn R. Stokes, Frances Marion University, SC
Suzanne Ward, University of Louisiana at Lafayette

Chapter Reviewers

Kim Anderson, Indiana University of Pennsylvania
Peg Beresewski, Robert Morris College, IL
Helen Brubeck, San Jose State University, CA

Mark Camma, Atlantic Cape Community College, NJ
Freddy Choo, San Francisco State University, CA
Laurie Dahlin, Worcester State College, MA
Ronald Guidry, University of Louisiana at Monroe
Ellen Landgraf, Loyola University, Chicago
Nick McGaughey, San Jose State University, CA
Mark Miller, University of San Francisco, CA
Craig Reeder, Florida A&M University
Brian Stanko, Loyola University, Chicago
Marcia Veit, University of Central Florida
Ronald Woan, Indiana University of Pennsylvania

Online Supplement Reviewers

Shawn Abbott, College of the Siskiyous, CA
Sol Ahiarah, SUNY College at Buffalo (Buffalo State)
M. J. Albin, University of Southern Mississippi
Gary Ames, Brigham Young University, Idaho
Walter Austin, Mercer University, Macon GA
Brad Badertscher, University of Iowa
Sandra Bailey, Oregon Institute of Technology
Barbara A. Beltrand, Metropolitan State University, MN
Jerry Bennett, University of South Carolina-Spartanburg
John Bildersee, New York University, Stern School
Candace Blankenship, Belmont University, TN
Charlie Bokemeier, Michigan State University
Scott Boylan, Washington and Lee University, VA
Robert Braun, Southeastern Louisiana University
Linda Bressler, University of Houston Downtown
Carol Brown, Oregon State University
Marcus Butler, University of Rochester, NY
Kay Carnes, Gonzaga University, WA
Brian Carpenter, University of Scranton, PA
Sandra Cereola, James Madison University, VA
Hong Chen, Northeastern Illinois University
Shifei Chung, Rowan University, NJ
Bryan Church, Georgia Tech
Charles Christy, Delaware Tech and Community College, Stanton Campus
Carolyn Clark, Saint Joseph's University, PA
Dianne Conry, University of California State College Extension–Cupertino
John Coulter, Western New England College
Donald Curfman, McHenry County College, IL
Alan Czyzewski, Indiana State University
Bonita Daly, University of Southern Maine
Patricia Derrick, George Washington University
Charles Dick, Miami University
Barbara Doughty, New Hampshire Community Technical College
Carol Dutton, South Florida Community College
James Emig, Villanova University, PA
Ellen Engel, University of Chicago

Alan Falcon, Loyola Marymount University, CA
Janet Farler, Pima Community College, AZ
Andrew Felo, Penn State Great Valley
Ken Ferris, Thunderbird College, AZ
Lou Fowler, Missouri Western State College
Lucille Genduso, Nova Southeastern University, FL
Frank Gersich, Monmouth College, IL
Bradley Gillespie, Saddleback College, CA
Brian Green, University of Michigan–Dearborn
Konrad Gunderson, Missouri Western State College
William Hahn, Southeastern College, FL
Jack Hall, Western Kentucky University
Gloria Halpern, Montgomery College, MD
Kenneth Hart, Brigham Young University, Idaho
Al Hartgraves, Emory University
Thomas Hayes, University of North Texas
Larry Hegstad, Pacific Lutheran University, WA
Candy Heino, Anoka-Ramsey Community College, MN
Anit Hope, Tarrant County College, TX
Thomas Huse, Boston College
Fred R. Jex, Macomb Community College, MI
Beth Kern, Indiana University, South Bend
Hans E. Klein, Babson College, MA
Willem Koole, North Carolina State University
Emil Koren, Hillsborough Community College, FL
Dennis Kovach, Community College of Allegheny County–North Campus
Ellen Landgraf, Loyola University Chicago
Howard Lawrence, Christian Brothers University, TN
Barry Leffkov, Regis College, MA
Chao Liu, Notre Dame University
Barbara Lougee, University of California, Irvine
Heidemarie Lundblad, California State University, Northridge
Anna Lusher, West Liberty State College, WV
Harriet Maccracken, Arizona State University
Carol Mannino, Milwaukee School of Engineering
Aziz Martinez, Harvard University, Harvard Business School
Cathleen Miller, University of Michigan–Flint
Frank Mioni, Madonna University, MI
Bruce L. Oliver, Rochester Institute of Technology
Charles Pedersen, Quinsigamond Community College, MA
George Plesko, Massachusetts Institute of Technology
David Plumlee, University of Utah
Gregory Prescott, University of South Alabama
Craig Reeder, Florida A&M University
Darren Roulstone, University of Chicago
Angela Sandberg, Jacksonville State University, AL
George Sanders, Western Washington University, WA
Betty Saunders, University of North Florida
Arnie Schneider, Georgia Tech

Gim Seow, University of Connecticut
Itzhak Sharav, CUNY–Lehman Graduate School of Business
Gerald Smith, University of Northern Iowa
James Smith, Community College of Philadelphia
Beverly Soriano, Framingham State College, MA
J. B. Stroud, Nicholls State University, LA
Al Taccone, Cuyamaca College, CA
Diane Tanner, University of North Florida
Howard Toole, San Diego State University
Bruce Wampler, Louisiana State University, Shreveport
Frederick Weis, Claremont McKenna College, CA
Frederick Weiss, Virginia Wesleyan College
Allen Wright, Hillsborough Community College, FL
Tony Zordan, University of St. Francis, IL

Supplement Authors and Preparers

Excel templates: Al Fisher, Community College of Southern Nevada
General Ledger templates: Lanny Nelms, The Landor Group
Instructor's Edition: Helen Brubeck, San Jose State University
Interactive Powerpoints: Courtney Baillie
Solutions Manual preparer: Diane Colwyn
Study Guide: Helen Brubeck, San Jose Stete University
Test Item File: Calvin Fink
Working Papers, Essentials of Excel: Dr. L. Murphy Smith, Texas A&M
    University; Dr. Katherine T. Smith
Videos: Beverly Amer, Northern Arizona University; Lanny Nelms, The Landor Group

Prologue

Accounting Careers: Much More Than Counting Things

What kind of career can you have in accounting? Almost any kind you want. A career in accounting lets you use your analytical skills in a variety of ways, and it brings both monetary and personal rewards. According to the Jobs Rated Almanac, "accountant" was the fifth best job in terms of low stress, high compensation, lots of autonomy, and tremendous hiring demand.[1]

Look at what these accountants do:

- Jeffrey S. Sallet is a CPA at the FBI. Sallet investigates the financial side of criminal activities. He conducts surveillance, investigates crime scenes, reviews financial documents, and testifies in court. "My efforts have resulted in the conviction of members and associates of Organized Crime and Union Officials."[2]

- After doing auditing work at KPMG and serving as a controller for a venture-capital-backed firm, David Kupferman started his own CPA practice. He specializes in advising high-net-worth individuals and businesses. Kupferman has a particular interest in bringing foreign technology companies to the United States and works with clients from Australia, Spain, Hungary, England, France, Belarus, Singapore, and Japan.[6]

- Alan Friedman loves music. He plays guitar in a band and knows the music industry inside and out. As a CPA, he helps retailers, musicians, and independent recording labels with accounting and tax services. "My clients appreciate the fact that we are intimately familiar with the . . . music retailing marketplace," Friedman says. Friedman found his niche by combining his hobby with his work.[3]

- Jane Cozzarelli, CPA, is vice president of internal audit at Batelle Memorial Institute, a $1 billion research and development enterprise. Cozzarelli helps Battelle evaluate the risks of multimillion-dollar deals such as joint ventures and acquisitions. By measuring your risks, you can direct capital to them more efficiently. You also are better able to understand the upside and downside of undertaking a risk," Jane says.[4]

- Regine Metellus, CPA, is the CFO for the Germantown Settlement, a charity that empowers over 195,000 elderly and low-to-moderate income residents in Philadelphia. "By making the charity's financial operations more efficient, Metellus helps Germantown Settlement put more money back into the community and truly "make a difference."[5]

And then there is the opportunity for flexible work arrangements:

"I'm probably one of the first people who stayed in public accounting because of quality-of-life advantages," says Eileen Garvey, an audit partner at Ernst & Young in New York. Garvey works a 3-day-a-week schedule. The mother of 2, she made partner as a part-timer. Flexibility works for men, too: Carl Moilienkamp, a manager with a firm in Chicago, took a summer leave to pursue his other career as a chef.

Where Accountants Work

Where can you work as an accountant? There are 4 kinds of employers.

Public Practice

You can work for a public accounting firm, which could be a large international firm such as one of the Big Four where Eileen Garvey works, or a small CPA firm such as Alan Friedman's. Within the CPA firm, you can specialize in areas such as audit, tax, or consulting. In this capacity, you'll be serving as an external accountant to many different clients. Most CPAs start their career at a large CPA firm. From there, they can find themselves in a variety of situations:

■ Jennifer Tufer is a Deloitte & Touche senior manager on assignment in Moscow. As she looks through her incoming mail, she finds a request from a U.S. manufacturer interested in expanding into Russia. "The company wants to know how they would be taxed," she says.

■ Josh Young's first consulting engagement found him on the site of the Northridge earthquake outside Los Angeles. One of his clients was a supermarket chain with 150 damaged stores. Young needed to visit the actual site to determine how much damage had occurred to help prepare the insurance claims.

The highest career level in a CPA firm is partner—becoming a part owner of the firm. Only 2% to 3% of accountants in a Big Four firm make partner.[7] Here are the Big Four:

Deloitte & Touche	Employees: 99,900
Ernst & Young	Employees: 114,300
KPMG	Employees: 113,000
PricewaterhouseCoopers	Employees: 140,000

Managerial Accounting

Instead of working for a wide variety of clients, you can work within 1 corporation or nonprofit enterprise. Your role may be to analyze financial information and communicate that information to managers, who use it to plot strategy and make decisions. You may be called upon to help allocate corporate resources or improve financial performance. For example, you might do a cost-benefit analysis to help decide whether to acquire a company or build a factory. Or you might describe the financial implications of choosing 1 strategy over another. You might work in areas such as internal auditing, financial management, financial reporting, treasury management, and tax planning. The highest position in management accounting is the CFO position, with some CFOs rising to become CEOs.

> Phil Knight, CEO of Nike, and Arthur Blank, cofounder of Home Depot, are CPAs

Government

You can also work as an accountant for the government—federal, state, or local. Like your counterparts in public accounting and business, your role as a government

> Did you know that 15% of FBI new hires in 2004 were CPAs?[8] In fact, 1,400 of the FBI's special agents are accountants, and the number 3 man at the FBI at the time, Assistant Director Thomas Pickard, is a CPA.[9]

accountant includes responsibilities in the areas of auditing, financial reporting, and management accounting. You'll evaluate how government agencies are being managed. You may advise decision makers on how to allocate resources to promote efficiency. You might find yourself working for the IRS, the Securities and Exchange Commission, the Department of Treasury, or even the White House.

Government Accountability Office (GAO)—formerly called the General Accounting Office—is an agency that works for Congress and the American people. Congress asks GAO to study federal government programs and expenditures. GAO studies how the federal government spends taxpayer dollars and advises Congress and the heads of executive agencies (such as the Environmental Protection Agency, Department of Defense, and Health and Human Services) about ways to make government more effective and responsive.

Education

Finally, you can work at a college or university, advancing the thought and theory of accounting and teaching future generations of new accountants. On the research side of education, you might study how companies use accounting information. You might develop new ways of categorizing financial data, or study accounting practices in different countries. You then publish your ideas in journals and books and present them to colleagues at meetings around the world. On the education side, you can help others learn about accounting and give them the tools they need to be their best.

CPA: THREE LETTERS THAT SPEAK VOLUMES

When employers see the CPA designation, they know what to expect about your education, knowledge, abilities, and personal attributes. They value your analytic skills and extensive training. Your CPA credential gives you a distinct advantage in the job market and instant credibility and respect in the workplace. It's a plus when dealing with other professionals such as bankers, attorneys, auditors, and federal regulators. In addition, your colleagues in private industry tend to defer to you when dealing with complex business matters, particularly those involving financial management.[10]

The Hottest Growth Areas in Accounting

Recent legislation, such as the Sarbanes-Oxley Act of 2002, has brought rising demand for accountants of all kinds. In addition to strong overall demand, certain areas of accounting are especially hot.[11]

Sustainability Reporting

Sustainability reporting involves reporting on an organization's performance with respect to health, safety, and environmental (HSE) issues. As businesses take a greater interest in environmental issues, CPAs are getting involved in reporting on such matters as employee health, on-the-job accident rates, emissions of certain pollutants, spills, volumes of waste generated, and initiatives to reduce and minimize such incidents and releases. Utilities, manufacturers, and chemical companies are particularly affected by environmental issues. As a result, they turn to CPAs to set up a preventive system to ensure compliance and avoid future claims or disputes or to provide assistance once legal implications have arisen.

Corporate social responsibility reporting is similar to HSE reporting but with a broadened emphasis on social matters such as ethical labor practices, training, education, and diversity of workforce and corporate philanthropic initiatives. Here's a sampling of companies across industries that provide corporate social responsibility reports:

Company	Primary Industry
Anheuser-Busch	Beverages, theme parks
AT&T	Telecommunications
Bristol-Myers Squibb	Pharmaceuticals
Chiquita Brands	Agribusiness
Conoco	Energy
Dow Chemical	Chemicals
General Motors	Vehicle manufacture
Intel	Microprocessors
Johnson & Johnson	Health-care products and services
McDonald's	Restaurants
Mead	Forest products
Nike	Apparel
PepsiCo	Consumer products
Procter & Gamble	Consumer products
University of Florida	Academic institution

Source: AICPA

Assurance Services

Assurance services are services provided by a CPA that improve the quality of information, or its context, for decision makers. Such information can be financial or non-financial; it can be about past events or about ongoing processes or systems. This broad concept includes audit and attestation services and is distinct from consulting because it focuses primarily on improving information rather than on providing advice or installing systems. You can use your analytical and information-processing expertise by providing assurance services in areas ranging from electronic commerce to elder care, comprehensive risk assessment, business valuations, entity performance measurement, and information systems quality assessment.

Information Technology Services

Companies can't compete effectively if their information technology systems don't have the power or flexibility to perform essential functions. Companies need accountants with strong computer skills who can design and implement advanced systems to fit a company's specific needs and to find ways to protect and insulate data. CPAs skilled in software research and development (including multimedia technology) are also highly valued.

International Accounting

Globalization means that cross-border transactions are becoming commonplace. Countries in Eastern Europe and Latin America, which previously had closed economies, are opening up and doing business with new trading partners. The passage of the North American Free Trade Agreement (NAFTA) and the General Agreement on Tariffs and Trade (GATT) facilitates trade, and the economic growth in areas such as the Pacific Rim further brings greater volumes of trade and financial flows. Organizations need accountants who understand international trade rules, accords, and laws; cross-border merger and acquisition issues; and foreign business customs, languages, cultures, and procedures.

Forensic Accounting

Forensic accounting is in growing demand after scandals such as the collapse of Enron. Forensic accountants look at a company's financial records for evidence of criminal activity. This could be anything from securities fraud to overvaluation of inventory to money laundering and improper capitalization of expenses. Their work is becoming so well known that forensic accountants are appearing in mainstream novels. In The Devil's Banker by best-selling author Christopher Reich, a spy teams up with a forensic accountant to chase down a terrorist ring.

So, whether you seek

- a steady career or a life of international adventure
- a home in a single organization or exposure to the needs of an ever-changing mix of clients
- the personal satisfaction of work for a nonprofit or the financial success in a hot new company

Accounting has a career for you. Every organization, from the smallest mom-and-pop music retailer to the biggest government in the world, needs accountants to help manage its resources. Global trade demands accountability, and ever-more complex tax laws mean an ever-increasing need for the skills and services of accountants.

Endnotes

[1]Alba, Jason, and Manisha Bathija. *Vault Career Guide to Accounting.* (New York: Vault, 2002).
[2]CPA Track. Sponsored by Massachusetts Society of Certified Public Accountants, Inc. http://www.cpatrack.com/cool_cpas/.

[3]http://www.startheregoplaces.com.

[4]Banham, Russ. "Enterprising Views of Risk Management," *Journal of Accountancy*, 197, no. 6 (June 2004): 65–72.

[5]http://www.startheregoplaces.com.

[6]Kahan, Stuart. "Capitalizing on CFO Experiences," *The Practical Accountant*, 37, no. 2 (February 2004): 42–44.

[7]www.careers-in-accounting.com; http://www.deloitte.com; http://www.ey.com; http://www.kpmg.com; http://www.pwc.com.

[8]CPA Letter, January 2004.

[9]Alba, Jason, and Manisha Bathija. *Vault Career Guide to Accounting* (New York. Vault, 2002).

[10]http://www.startheregoplaces.com/news/news_half5.asp.

[11]AICPA, the American Institute of Certified Public Accountants, http://www.aicpa.org.

1 The Financial Statements

YUM! BRANDS

What's your favorite fast food? If it's not a hamburger, it may be a pizza, a taco, or fried chicken. **YUM!** Brands operates **Pizza Hut**, **Taco Bell**, **KFC**, **A&W**, and **Long John Silver's** restaurants.

As you can see, YUM! Brands sells lots of pizza, tacos, and drumsticks—$9,561 million in 2006 (lines 1–3 of YUM! Brands' income statement). On these revenues YUM! Brands earned net income of $824 million in 2006.

These terms—revenues and net income—may be foreign to you now. But after you read this chapter, you'll be able to use these and other business terms. Welcome to the world of accounting!

YUM! Brands, Inc.
Statement of Income (Adapted)
Years Ended December 31, 2006, and 2005

(In millions)	2006	2005
Revenues		
1 Company sales..	$8,365	$8,225
2 Franchise and license fees..	1,196	1,124
3 Total revenues..	9,561	9,349
Expenses		
Company restaurants		
4 Food and paper (Cost of goods sold)......................	2,549	2,584
5 Payroll and employee benefits expense..................	2,142	2,171
6 Occupancy and other operating expenses..............	2,403	2,315
	7,094	7,070
7 General and administrative expenses	1,187	1,158
8 Other operating expenses (income)...........................	18	(32)
9 Total expenses	8,299	8,196
10 Operating profit..	1,262	1,153
11 Interest expense	154	127
12 Income before income taxes......................................	1,108	1,026
13 Income tax expense..	284	264
14 Net income	$ 824	$ 762

Each chapter of this book begins with an actual financial statement.
In this chapter, it's the income statement of YUM! Brands, Inc. The core of financial accounting revolves around the basic financial statements:

- Income statement (the statement of operations)
- Statement of retained earnings
- Balance sheet (the statement of financial position)
- Statement of cash flows

Financial statements are the business documents that companies use to represent their finances to the public. In this chapter we explain all the items that appear in each statement. To learn accounting, focus on decisions. Decisions require information, and accounting provides much of the information for people's decisions, as illustrated in the following diagram:

You take actions every day that require accounting information. For example, the decision to go off for spring break depends on whether you can afford it. The same is true for big companies like **Google** and YUM! Brands. They must weigh what they want to accomplish against what they can afford.

We begin with an overview of how accounting is practiced.

LEARNING OBJECTIVES

1 **Use** accounting vocabulary

2 **Learn** accounting concepts and principles

3 **Apply** the accounting equation to business organizations

4 **Evaluate** business operations

5 **Use** financial statements

For more practice and review of accounting cycle concepts, use ACT, the Accounting Cycle Tutorial, online at www.prenhall.com/harrison. Margin logos like this one, directing you to the appropriate ACT section and material, appear throughout Chapters 1, 2, and 3. When you enter the tutorial, you'll find 3 buttons on the opening page of each chapter module. Here's what the buttons mean: **Tutorial** gives you a review of the major concepts, **Application** gives you practice exercises, and **Glossary** reviews important terms.

BUSINESS DECISIONS

YUM! Brands managers make lots of decisions. Which is selling faster—pizza, fried chicken, or tacos? Is pizza bringing in profits? Should YUM! Brands expand into Asia? Accounting helps companies make these decisions.

Take a look at YUM! Brands' income statement on page 32. Focus on net income (line 14). Net income is profit, the excess of revenues over expenses. You can see that YUM! Brands earned an $824 million profit in 2006. That's good news because it means that YUM had $824 million more revenue (income) than expenses for the year.

YUM's income statement conveys more good news. Net income for 2006 exceeded the net income for 2005. YUM is growing, and investors buy the stocks of growing companies.

Suppose you have $5,000 to invest. What information would you need before investing in YUM! Brands? Let's see how accounting works.

ACCOUNTING IS THE LANGUAGE OF BUSINESS

Accounting is an information system. It measures business activities, processes data into reports, and communicates results to people. Accounting is "the language of business." The better you understand the language, the better you can manage your finances.

Accounting produces **financial statements**, which report information about a business entity. The financial statements measure performance and tell where a business stands in financial terms. In this chapter we focus on YUM! Brands. After completing this chapter, you'll understand financial statements.

OBJECTIVE

1 **Use** accounting vocabulary

Don't confuse bookkeeping and accounting. Bookkeeping is a mechanical part of accounting, just as arithmetic is a part of mathematics. Exhibit 1-1 illustrates accounting's role in business. The process starts and ends with people making decisions.

EXHIBIT 1-1   The Flow of Accounting Information

1. People make decisions.   2. Business transactions occur.   3. Companies report their results.

Who Uses Accounting Information?

Decision makers need information. A banker decides who gets a loan. YUM! Brands decides where to locate a new Pizza Hut. Let's see how some others use accounting information.

- *Individuals.* People like you manage bank accounts and decide whether to rent an apartment or buy a house. Accounting provides the information you need.
- *Investors and Creditors.* Investors and creditors provide the money to finance YUM! Brands. People want to know how much income they can expect to earn on an investment. This requires accounting data.
- *Taxing Authorities.* There are all kinds of taxes. Pizza Hut pays property tax on its assets and income tax on its profits. Taco Bell collects sales tax from you. Taxes are based on accounting data.
- *Nonprofit Organizations.* Nonprofit organizations—churches, hospitals, and charities such as Habitat for Humanity and the Red Cross—base their decisions on accounting data.

Two Kinds of Accounting: Financial Accounting and Management Accounting

There are both *external users* and *internal users* of accounting information. We can therefore classify accounting into 2 branches.

Financial accounting provides information for people outside the firm, such as investors, bankers, government agencies, and the public. This information must meet standards of relevance and reliability.

Management accounting generates inside information for the managers of YUM! Brands. Management information doesn't have to meet external standards of reliability because only company employees use these data.

Ethics in Accounting: Standards of Professional Conduct

Ethical considerations are important to accounting. Companies need money to operate. To attract investors, companies must provide information to the public. Without that information, people won't invest. The United States has laws that require companies to report relevant and reliable information to outsiders. Relevant means "able to affect a decision." Reliable means "verifiable and free of error and bias." The infographic that follows diagrams this process.

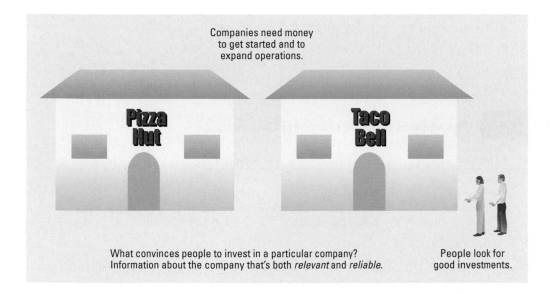

Occasionally, a company will report biased information. It may overstate profits or understate the company's debts. In recent years, several well-known companies reported misleading information. Enron Corporation, once one of the largest companies in the United States, admitted understating its debts. Tyco, WorldCom, and Qwest were accused of overstating profits. These companies' data were unreliable, and their information failed the test of reliability. The results? People invested in them, lost money, and filed lawsuits to recover their losses. Reporting relevant and reliable information to the public is the only ethical course of action.

What are the criteria for ethical judgments in accounting? The *American Institute of Certified Public Accountants (AICPA)*, other professional organizations, and most companies have codes of conduct that require ethical conduct. The AICPA is the country's largest organization of accountants, similar to the American Medical Association for physicians and the American Bar Association for attorneys.

We Need an Audit to Validate the Financial Statements

Each chapter of this book begins with an actual financial statement—Chapter 1 opens with the income statement of YUM! Brands, Inc. YUM! Brands reports that it's profitable. But did the company really sell that many pizzas, tacos, and drumsticks? Were profits really $824 million? Who reports these figures?

YUM's top management is responsible both for (a) company operations and (b) the information YUM *reports* to the public. Can you see the conflict of interest here? A company's *real* performance may differ from what gets *reported* to the public.

How does society deal with this conflict of interest? U.S. law requires all companies that sell their stock to the public to have an annual audit by independent accountants. Audits are intended to protect the public by ensuring that accounting data are relevant and reliable.

Organizing a Business

A business can take 1 of several forms:

- proprietorship
- partnership
- limited-liability company (LLC)
- corporation

Exhibit 1-2 compares ways to organize a business.

EXHIBIT 1-2 The Various Forms of Business Organization

	Proprietorship	Partnership	Corporation	LLC
1. *Owner(s)*	Proprietor—one owner	Partners—2 or more owners	Stockholders—generally many owners	Members
2. *Personal liability of owner(s) for business debts*	Proprietor is personally liable	Partners are personally liable	Stockholders are *not* personally liable	Members are *not* personally liable

Proprietorship. A **proprietorship** has a single owner, called the proprietor. Dell Computer started out in the dorm room of Michael Dell, the owner. Proprietorships tend to be small retail stores or a professional service—a physician, an attorney, or an accountant. Legally, the business *is* the proprietor, and the proprietor is personally liable for all the business's debts. But for accounting, a proprietorship is distinct from its proprietor. Thus, the business records do not include the proprietor's personal finances.

Partnership. A **partnership** has 2 or more persons as co-owners, and each owner is a partner. Many retail establishments and some professional organizations are partnerships. Most partnerships are small or medium-sized, but some are gigantic, with 2,000 or more partners. Like proprietorships, the law views a partnership as the partners. The business is its partners. For this reason, each partner is personally liable for all the partnership's debts. Partnerships are therefore quite risky. This unlimited liability of partners has spawned the creation of limited-liability partnerships (LLPs).

A *limited-liability partnership* is one in which a wayward partner cannot create a large liability for the other partners. Therefore, each partner is liable ony for his or her own actions and those under his or her control.

Limited-Liability Company (LLC). **A limited-liability company** is one in which the business (and not the owner) is liable for the company's debts. An LLC may have 1 owner or many owners, called *members*. Unlike a proprietorship or a basic partnership, the members do *not* have personal liability for the business's debts. Therefore, we say that the members have limited liability—limited to the amount they've invested in the business. Also, an LLC pays no business income tax. Instead, the LLC's income flows through to the members, and they pay personal income tax at their own individual tax rates. Today most proprietorships and partnerships are organized as LLCs or LLPs.

Corporation. A **corporation** is a business owned by the **stockholders**, or **shareholders**. These people own **stock**, which represents shares of ownership in a corporation. Even though proprietorships and partnerships are more numerous, corporations transact much more business and are larger in terms of assets, income, and number of employees. Most well-known companies, such as YUM! Brands, Yahoo!, and Dell Computer, are corporations. Their full names include *Corporation* or *Incorporated* (abbreviated *Corp.* and *Inc.*) to indicate that they are corporations—for example, YUM! Brands, Inc., and Starbucks Corporation. Some bear the name *Company*, such as Ford Motor Company.

A corporation is formed under state law. Unlike proprietorships and partnerships, a corporation is legally distinct from its owners. The corporation is like an artificial person and possesses many of the rights that a person has. The stockholders have no personal obligation for the corporation's debts. So we say the stockholders have limited liability, as do the partners of an LLP and the members of an LLC. Also unlike the other forms of organization, a corporation pays a business income tax.

Ultimate control of a corporation rests with the stockholders, who get 1 vote for each share of stock they own. Stockholders elect the **board of directors**, which sets policy and appoints officers. The board elects a chairperson, who holds the most power in the corporation and often carries the title chief executive officer (CEO). The board also appoints the president as Chief Operating Officer (COO). Corporations have vice presidents in charge of sales, accounting and finance, and other key areas.

ACCOUNTING PRINCIPLES AND CONCEPTS

Accountants follow professional guidelines called **GAAP**, which stands for **generally accepted accounting principles**. In the United States, the *Financial Accounting Standards Board* (*FASB*) formulates GAAP. GAAP is designed to meet the primary objective of financial reporting, which is to provide information useful for making investment and credit decisions.

OBJECTIVE

2 **Learn** accounting concepts and principles

Exhibit 1-3 gives an overview of the conceptual framework of accounting. GAAP, at the bottom, follows the conceptual framework. To be useful, information must be relevant, reliable, comparable, and consistent. This course will expose you to generally accepted accounting. We summarize GAAP in Appendix E. We begin with the basic concepts that form accounting practice.

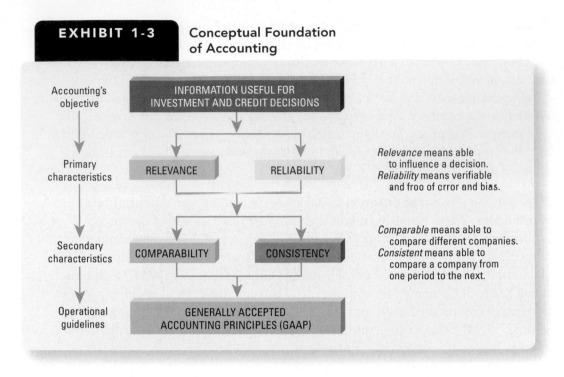

EXHIBIT 1-3 Conceptual Foundation of Accounting

Relevance means able to influence a decision. *Reliability* means verifiable and free of error and bias.

Comparable means able to compare different companies. *Consistent* means able to compare a company from one period to the next.

The Entity Concept

The most basic accounting concept is the **entity**, which is any organization that stands apart as a separate economic unit. Sharp boundaries are drawn around each entity so as not to confuse its affairs with those of others.

Consider David C. Novak, Chairman of the Board of YUM! Brands, Inc. Mr. Novak owns a home and several automobiles. He may owe money on some personal loans. All these assets and liabilities belong to David Novak and have nothing to do with YUM! Brands. Likewise, YUM's cash, computers, and food inventories belong to the company and not to Novak. Why? Because the entity concept draws a sharp boundary around each entity; in this case YUM! Brands is 1 entity, and David Novak is a separate entity.

Let's consider the various restaurant chains that make up YUM! Brands. Top managers evaluate Pizza Hut separately from Taco Bell and KFC. If pizza sales are dropping, YUM can identify the reason. But if sales figures from all the restaurant chains are combined in a single total, managers can't tell how many pizzas and how many tacos the company is selling. To correct the problem, managers need data for each division of the company. Each restaurant chain keeps its own records in order to be evaluated separately.

The Reliability Principle

To ensure relevance and reliability, accounting records are based on the most objective data available. This is the **reliability principle**, also called the **objectivity principle**. Ideally, accounting records are based on information supported by objective evidence. For example, your purchase of a pizza is supported by a paid receipt, which gives objective evidence of the cost of the pizza, say $10. Without the reliability principle, accounting records would be based on opinions and subject to dispute.

Suppose YUM! Brands opens a Taco Bell/Pizza Hut store, and YUM is buying a building. YUM believes the building is worth $185,000. Two real estate professionals appraise the building at $210,000. The owner of the building demands $200,000. Suppose YUM pays $190,000. Beliefs about the building's value and the real-estate appraisals are merely opinions. The accounting value of the building is $190,000 because that amount is supported by a completed transaction. YUM! Brands should, therefore, record the building at its cost of $190,000.

The Cost Principle

The **cost principle** states that assets and services should be recorded at their actual *historical cost*.[1] Suppose a Pizza Hut store purchases kitchen equipment from Domino's Pizza. Assume that YUM gets a good deal on this purchase and pays only $50,000 for equipment that would have cost $70,000 elsewhere. The cost principle requires YUM to record this equipment at its actual cost of $50,000, not the $70,000 that YUM believes it's worth.

The cost principle also holds that accounting records should maintain historical costs for as long as the business holds the asset. Why? Because cost is a reliable measure. Suppose the Taco Bell store holds the equipment for 6 months. Prices increase and the equipment can be sold for $60,000. Should its accounting value be the actual cost of $50,000 or the current market value of $60,000? According to the cost principle, the equipment remains on YUM! Brands' books at a cost of $50,000.

The Going-Concern Concept

The **going-concern concept** assumes that the entity will remain in operation long enough to use existing assets—land, buildings, supplies—for their intended purpose. Consider the alternative to the going-concern concept: going out of business.

A store that is going out of business sells all its assets. In that case, the relevant measure of the assets is their current market value. But going out of business is the exception rather than the rule, and so accounting lists a going concern's assets at their historical cost.

The Stable-Monetary-Unit Concept

In the United States, we record transactions in dollars because that is our medium of exchange. British accountants record transactions in pounds sterling, Japanese in yen, and Europeans in euros.

Unlike a liter or a mile, the value of a dollar changes over time. A rise in the general price level is called *inflation*. During inflation, a dollar will purchase less food, less toothpaste, and less of other goods and services. When prices are stable—there is little inflation—a dollar's purchasing power is also stable.

---

[1]The cost principle may not be as powerful as it once was. Accounting may be moving in the direction of reporting assets and liabilities at their fair value. **Fair value** is the amount that the business could sell the asset for, or the amount that the business could pay to settle the liability. In 2007, the Financial Accounting Standards Board (FASB) issued a statement that *permits* companies to report many financial assets and liabilities at their fair value. Time will tell whether companies will follow this path and whether the FASB will *require* extensive use of fair-value accounting.

Under the **stable-monetary-unit concept**, accountants assume that the dollar's purchasing power is stable. We ignore inflation, and this allows us to add and subtract dollar amounts as though each dollar has the same purchasing power.

THE ACCOUNTING EQUATION

OBJECTIVE

3 **Apply** the accounting equation to business organizations

YUM! Brands' financial statements tell us how the business is performing and where it stands. But how do we arrive at the financial statements? Let's see their building blocks.

Assets and Liabilities

The financial statements are based on the **accounting equation**. This equation presents the resources of a company and the claims to those resources.

- **Assets** are economic resources that are expected to produce a benefit in the future. YUM! Brands' cash, food inventory, equipment, land, and buildings are examples of assets.

Claims on assets come from 2 sources:

- **Liabilities** are "outsider claims." They are debts that are payable to outsiders, called *creditors*. For example, a creditor who has loaned money to YUM! Brands has a claim—a legal right—to a part of YUM's assets until YUM repays the debt.
- **Owners' equity** (also called **capital**) represents the "insider claims" of a business. Equity means ownership, so YUM's stockholders' equity is the stockholders' interest in the assets of the corporation.

The accounting equation shows the relationship among assets, liabilities, and owners' equity. Assets appear on the left side and liabilities and owners' equity on the right. As Exhibit 1-4 shows, the 2 sides must be equal:

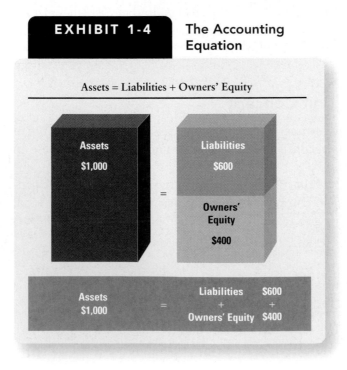

EXHIBIT 1-4   **The Accounting Equation**

Assets = Liabilities + Owners' Equity

Assets		Liabilities
$1,000	=	$600
		Owners' Equity
		$400

Assets		Liabilities	$600
$1,000	=	+	
		Owners' Equity	$400

What are some of YUM! Brands' assets? The first asset is **cash**, the liquid asset that's the medium of exchange. Another important asset is **merchandise inventory** (often called inventories)—the food and paper items—that YUM's restaurants sell. YUM also has assets in the form of property, plant, and equipment. These are the long-lived assets the company uses to do business—kitchen equipment, buildings, computers, and so on. Land, buildings, and equipment are called **property, plant, and equipment** (abbreviated as **PPE**), **plant assets**, or **fixed assets**.

YUM! Brands' liabilities include a number of payables, such as accounts payable and notes payable. The word *payable* always signifies a liability. An **account payable** is a liability for goods or services purchased on credit and supported by the credit standing of the purchaser. A **note payable** is a written promise to pay on a certain date. YUM! Brands calls its notes payble "*short-term borrowings.*" **Long-term debt** is a liability that's payable beyond 1 year from the date of the financial statements.

Owners' Equity

The owners' equity of any business is its assets minus its liabilities. We can write the accounting equation to show that owners' equity is what's left over when we subtract liabilities from assets.

$$\text{Assets} - \text{Liabilities} = \text{Owners' Equity}$$

A corporation's equity—called **stockholders' equity**—has 2 main subparts:

- paid-in capital and
- retained earnings

The accounting equation can be written as

$$\text{Assets} = \text{Liabilities} + \text{Stockholders' Equity}$$
$$\text{Assets} = \text{Liabilities} + \text{Paid-in Capital} + \text{Retained Earnings}$$

Paid-in capital is the amount the stockholders have invested in the corporation. The basic component of paid-in capital is **common stock**, which the corporation issues to the stockholders as evidence of their ownership. All corporations have common stock.

Retained earnings is the amount earned by income-producing activities and kept for use in the business. Two types of transactions affect retained earnings:

- **Revenues** increase retained earnings by delivering goods or services to customers. For example, Pizza Hut's sale of a sausage pizza brings in revenue and increases YUM! Brands' retained earnings.
- **Expenses** decrease retained earnings due to operations. For example, the wages that Pizza Hut pays employees are an expense and decrease retained earnings. Expenses are the cost of doing business; they are the opposite of revenues. Expenses include building rent, salaries, and utility payments. Expenses also include the depreciation of computers and other equipment.

Businesses strive for profits, the excess of revenues over expenses.

- When total revenues exceed total expenses, the result is called **net income**, **net earnings**, or **net profit**.

■ When expenses exceed revenues, the result is a **net loss.**
■ Net income or net loss is the "bottom line" on an income statement. YUM! Brands' bottom line reports 2006 net income of $824 million on page 32 (line 14).

A successful business may pay dividends. **Dividends** are distributions to stockholders of assets (usually cash) generated by net income. Remember: **Dividends are not expenses. Dividends never affect net income.** Exhibit 1-5 shows the relationships among

■ Retained earnings
■ Revenues − Expenses = Net income (or net loss)
■ Dividends

EXHIBIT 1-5	The Components of Retained Earnings

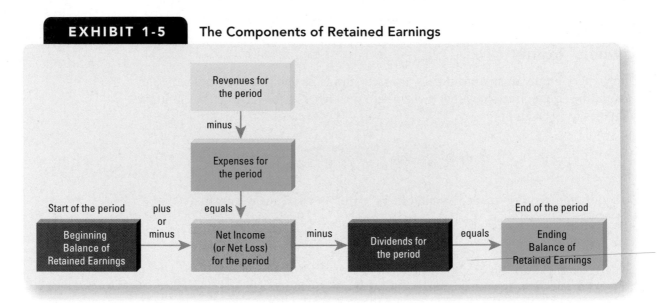

The owners' equity of proprietorships and partnerships is different. Proprietorships and partnerships don't identify paid-in capital and retained earnings. Instead, they use a single heading—Capital—for example, Randall Walker, Capital, for a proprietorship and Pratt, Capital and Salazar, Capital for a partnership.

STOP & think. . .

1. If the assets of a business are $190,000 and the liabilities are $80,000, how much is the owners' equity?
2. If the owners' equity in a business is $60,000 and the liabilities are $30,000, how much are the assets?
3. A company reported monthly revenues of $79,000 and expenses of $81,000. What is the result of operations for the month?

Answers:

1. $110,000 ($190,000 − $80,000)
2. $90,000 ($60,000 + $30,000)
3. Net loss of $2,000 ($79,000 − $81,000); revenues minus expenses

THE FINANCIAL STATEMENTS

The financial statements present a company to the public in financial terms. Each financial statement relates to a specific date or time period. What would investors want to know about YUM! Brands, Inc., at the end of December? Exhibit 1-6 shows 4 questions decision makers may ask. Each answer comes from one of the financial statements.

OBJECTIVE

4 **Evaluate** business operations

EXHIBIT 1-6	Information Reported in the Financial Statements	
Question	**Financial Statement**	**Answer**
1. How well did the company perform during the year?	Income statement (also called the Statement of operations)	Revenues – Expenses Net income (or Net loss)
2. Why did the company's retained earnings change during the year?	Statement of retained earnings	Beginning retained earnings + Net income (or – Net loss) – Dividends Ending retained earnings
3. What is the company's financial position at December 31?	Balance sheet (also called the Statement of financial position)	Assets = Liabilities + Owners' Equity
4. How much cash did the company generate and spend during the year?	Statement of cash flows	Operating cash flows ± Investing cash flows ± Financing cash flows Increase (decrease) in cash

To learn how to use financial statements, let's work through YUM! Brands' statements for the year ended December 31, 2006. The following diagram shows how the data flow from one financial statement to the next. The order is important.

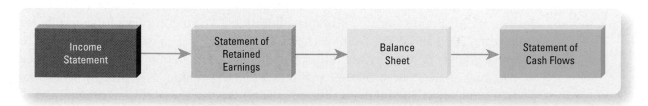

We begin with the income statement in Exhibit 1-7.

The Income Statement Measures Operating Performance

The **income statement**, or **statement of operations**, reports revenues and expenses for the period. The bottom line is net income or net loss *for the period*. At the top of Exhibit 1-7 is the company's name, YUM! Brands, Inc.

EXHIBIT 1-7	Income Statement (Adapted)

YUM! Brands, Inc.
Statement of Income (Adapted)
Years Ended December 31, 2006, and 2005

(In millions)	2006	2005
Revenues		
1 Company sales..	$8,365	$8,225
2 Franchise and license fees..............................	1,196	1,124
3 Total revenues..	9,561	9,349
Expenses		
Company restaurants		
4 Food and paper (Cost of goods sold)......................	2,549	2,584
5 Payroll and employee benefits expense..................	2,142	2,171
6 Occupancy and other operating expenses..............	2,403	2,315
	7,094	7,070
7 General and administrative expenses	1,187	1,158
8 Other operating expenses (income)..........................	18	(32)
9 Total expenses	8,299	8,196
10 Operating profit...	1,262	1,153
11 Interest expense	154	127
12 Income before income taxes............................	1,108	1,026
13 Income tax expense..	284	264
14 Net income	$ 824	$ 762

The date of YUM's income statement is "Years Ended December 31, 2006, and 2005." YUM uses the calendar period as its accounting year, as do around 60% of large companies.[2] Some use a fiscal year, which ends on a date other than December 31. For example, Pier 1 Imports, Wal-Mart, and most other retailers end their accounting year on or around January 31. FedEx's year end falls on May 31. Companies adopt an accounting year that ends at the low point of their operations.

YUM! Brands' income statement in Exhibit 1-7 reports operating results for 2 years, 2006 and 2005, to show trends for revenues, expenses, and net income. To avoid clutter, YUM reports in millions of dollars. During 2006, YUM increased total revenues (line 3) from $9,349 million to $9,561 million. Net income rose from $762 million to $824 million (line 14). YUM! Brands restaurants sold more pizzas, tacos, and fried chicken in 2006, and that boosted profits. Focus on 2006. We show 2005 only for completeness. An income statement reports 2 main categories:

■ Revenues and gains   ■ Expenses and losses

We measure net income as follows:

Net Income = Total Revenues and Gains – Total Expenses and Losses

---

[2]YUM actually reports for the fiscal year that ends on the Saturday nearest December 31. For practical purposes we treat this as the calendar year.

In accounting, the word *net* refers to an amount after a subtraction. *Net* income is the profit left over after subtracting expenses and losses from revenues and gains. **Net income is the single most important item in the financial statements.**

Revenues. Revenues do not always carry the term *revenue* in their titles. For example, net sales revenue is often abbreviated as *net sales*. *Net* sales means sales revenue after subtracting all the goods customers have returned to the company. Wal-Mart, Best Buy, and Gap get some goods back from customers due to product defects. YUM! Brands and other restauranteurs don't have much in the way of sales returns.

YUM! Brands has 2 sources of revenue: company sales (line 1) and fees that YUM earns by licensing its products to others (line 2).

Expenses. Not all expenses have the word *expense* in their title. For example, YUM! Brands' largest expense is for Food and Paper (line 4). Another title of this expense is Cost of goods sold. *Cost of goods sold* (also called *cost of sales*, line 4) represents the cost to YUM of the food it sold to customers. For example, suppose it costs Pizza Hut $3 to make a sausage pizza. Assume Pizza Hut sells the pizza for $10. Sales revenue is $10, and cost of goods sold is $3. Cost of goods sold is the major expense of merchandising entities such as Yum, Best Buy, Wal-Mart, and Safeway (the grocery store chain).

YUM has some other expenses.

- Payroll and Employee Benefits Expense (line 5) is for the salaries, wages, and benefits paid to company employees.
- Occupancy and Other Operating Expenses (line 6) include building rent, utilities, advertising, and depreciation on computers and kitchen equipment.
- General and Administrative Expenses (line 7) are executive salaries and other home-office expenses.
- Other Operating Expenses (line 8) is a catchall label for expenses that don't fit another category. During 2006, YUM had other operating expenses of $18 million. In 2005, YUM had other operating income. Parentheses around the $32 million mean that this amount's category runs opposite the others in its column.
- Interest Expense (line 11) was $154 million for 2006. This is YUM's cost of borrowing money.
- Income Tax Expense (line 13) is the expense levied on YUM! Brands' income by the government.

YUM! Brands reports both Operating Profit (line 10) and Net Income (line 14). Some investors use operating profit to measure operating performance. Others use the "bottom-line" net income.

Now let's move on to the statement of retained earnings in Exhibit 1-8.

Accounting Cycle Tutorial
Income Statement Accounts

The Statement of Retained Earnings Shows What a Company Did with Its Net Income

Retained earnings means exactly what the term implies, that portion of net income the company has kept. Net income flows from the income statement to the **statement of retained earnings** (line 2 in Exhibit 1-8).

Net income increases retained earnings, and dividends decrease retained earnings. Why the decrease? Because the company didn't keep the net income that it gave to its stockholders in the form of dividends.

EXHIBIT 1-8 Statement of Retained Earnings (Adapted)

YUM! Brands, Inc.
Statement of Retained Earnings (Adapted)
Years Ended December 31, 2006, and 2005

(In millions)	2006	2005
Retained earnings:		
1 Balance, beginning of year	$1,619	$1,067
2 Net income	824	762
3 Less: Dividends and other distributions to the stockholders	(850)	(210)
4 Balance, end of year	$1,593	$1,619

YUM's statement of retained earnings needs explanation. Start with 2005. At the beginning of 2005, YUM! Brands had retained earnings of $1,067 million (line 1). During 2005, YUM earned net income of $762 million (line 2) and gave the stockholders dividends of $210 million (line 3). YUM ended 2005 with retained earnings of $1,619 million (line 4).

YUM began 2006 with the ending balance left over from 2005. Then net income added to retained earnings, and dividends decreased retained earnings, as in 2005.

Which item on the statement of retained earnings comes directly from the income statement? It's net income. Line 2 of the retained earnings statement comes directly from line 14 of the income statement. Trace this amount from one statement to the other.

Give yourself a pat on the back. You're already learning how to analyze financial statements!

After a company earns net income, the board of directors decides whether to pay a dividend to the stockholders. In 2006 and 2005, YUM! Brands declared and paid dividends and other distributions to the stockholders (line 3). The dividends decrease retained earnings (the parentheses indicate a subtraction). YUM ended 2006 with retained earnings of $1,593 million (line 4).

Trace retained earnings to the balance sheet in Exhibit 1-9 (line 29). Ending retained earnings from 2006 carries over and becomes the beginning retained earnings of 2007.

The Balance Sheet Measures Financial Position

A company's **balance sheet**, also called the **statement of financial position**, reports 3 items: assets (line 1), liabilities (line 16), and stockholders' equity, which YUM! Brands calls *shareholders' equity* (line 27). The balance sheet is dated at the *moment in time* when the accounting period ends.

Assets. Assets have 2 main categories, current and long-term. **Current assets** are assets that are expected to be converted to cash, sold, or consumed during the next 12 months or within the business's operating cycle if longer than a year. Current assets consist of Cash, Short-Term Investments, Accounts and Notes Receivable, Merchandise Inventory, and Prepaid Expenses (lines 3 to 7). YUM's current assets at

EXHIBIT 1-9	Balance Sheet (Adapted)

YUM! Brands, Inc.
Balance Sheet (Adapted)
December 31, 2006, and 2005

(In millions)	2006	2005
1 ASSETS		
2 **Current Assets**		
3 Cash and cash equivalents	$ 319	$ 158
4 Short-term investments	6	43
5 Accounts and notes receivable	220	236
6 Inventories	93	85
7 Prepaid expenses and other current assets	263	333
8 Total Current Assets	901	855
9 Property, plant and equipment, at cost	$6,777	$6,186
10 Less: Accumulated depreciation	(3,146)	(2,830)
11 Property, plant and equipment, net	3,631	3,356
12 Intangible assets	1,009	868
13 Investments	138	173
14 Other assets	674	545
15 Total Assets	$6,353	$5,797
16 LIABILITIES		
17 **Current Liabilities**		
18 Accounts payable	$ 554	$ 473
19 Income taxes payable	37	79
20 Short-term borrowings (Notes payable)	227	211
21 Salaries and wages payable	302	274
22 Other current liabilities	604	586
23 Total Current Liabilities	1,724	1,623
24 Long-term debt	2,045	1,649
25 Other long-term liabilities	1,147	1,076
26 Total Liabilities	4,916	4,348
27 SHAREHOLDERS' EQUITY		
28 Common stock	27	28
29 Retained earnings	1,593	1,619
30 Other equity	(183)	(198)
31 Total Shareholders' Equity	1,437	1,449
32 Total Liabilities and Shareholders' Equity	$6,353	$5,797

December 31, 2006, total $901 million (line 8). Let's examine each asset that YUM! Brands holds.

- All companies have cash. **Cash** is the liquid asset that's the medium of exchange, and cash equivalents include money-market accounts that are the same as cash.
- **Short-term investments** include stocks and bonds of other companies that YUM intends to sell within the next year.
- **Accounts receivable** are amounts the company expects to collect from customers.

- **Notes receivable** are amounts YUM expects to collect from a party who has signed a promissory note to YUM. These notes receivable come from people to whom YUM has lent money.
- Cash, short-term investments, and current receivables are the most liquid assets, in that order.
- **Merchandise Inventory** (line 6) is the company's most important asset even though it totals only $93 million. *Inventory* is a common abbreviation for *Merchandise inventory*, and the 2 names are used interchangeably.
- **Prepaid Expenses** represent prepayments for advertisements, rent, insurance, and supplies. Prepaid expenses are assets because YUM Brands will benefit from these expenditures in the future.
- **An asset always represents a future benefit**.

The main categories of *long-term assets* are Property, Plant, and Equipment (lines 9–11), Intangibles, and Investments.

- **Property, plant, and equipment (PPE)** includes YUM! Brands' land, buildings, computers, store fixtures, and kitchen equipment. YUM reports PPE on 3 lines. Line 9 shows the company's cost of PPE, which is $6,777 million through December 31, 2006. Cost means the acquisition price to YUM. It does not mean that YUM could sell its PPE for $6,777 million. After all, the company may have acquired the assets several years ago.
- Line 10 shows how much accumulated depreciation YUM has recorded on its PPE. *Depreciation* allocates an asset's cost to expense. Accumulated depreciation is the total amount of depreciation recorded on PPE from acquisition through the end of the year. Accumulated depreciation represents the used-up portion of the asset. We subtract accumulated depreciation from the cost of PPE to determine its book value ($3,631 million on line 11).
- **Intangibles** are assets with no physical form, such as patents and trademarks.
- **Investments** (line 13), with no other words attached, are *long-term* because YUM does not expect to sell them within the next year.
- **Other assets** (line 14) is a catchall category for items difficult to classify.
- Overall, YUM! Brands reports total assets of $6,353 million at December 31, 2006 (line 15).

Liabilities. Liabilities are also divided into current and long-term categories. **Current liabilities** (lines 17–23) are debts payable within 1 year or within YUM's operating cycle if longer than a year. Chief among the current liabilities are Accounts Payable, Income Taxes Payable, Short-Term Borrowing (same as short-term notes Payable), and Salaries and Wages Payable. *Long-term liabilities* are payable after 1 year.

- **Accounts payable** (line 18) represents amounts owed for food and paper inventory.
- **Income taxes payable** are tax debts owed to the government.
- **Short-term borrowings** (line 20) are notes payable that YUM has promised to pay back within 1 year or less.
- **Salaries and wages payable** (line 21) are amounts owed to employees.
- YUM's last current liability is **Other Current Liabilities**. Included in this catch-all category are interest payable on borrowed money, utility payables, and expenses that YUM has not yet paid.

■ At December 31, 2006, YUM's current liabilities total $1,724 million. YUM also owes $2,045 million in long-term debt (line 24). These liabilities include notes payable due after 1 year.

■ At the end of 2006, total liabilities are $4,916 million (line 26). This is high relative to total assets (line 15), and that indicates a not-so-strong financial position.

Owners' Equity. The accounting equation states that

$$\text{Assets} - \text{Liabilities} = \text{Owners' Equity}$$

The assets (resources) and the liabilities (debts) of YUM! Brands are fairly easy to understand. Owners' equity is harder to pin down. Owners' equity is simple to calculate, but what does it *mean*?

YUM! Brands calls its owners' equity *shareholders' equity* (line 27), and this title is descriptive. Remember that a company's owners' equity represents the shareholders' ownership of the business's assets. YUM's equity consists of

■ Common Stock, represented by shares issued to stockholders for $27 million through December 31, 2006 (line 28).

■ Retained earnings at December 31, 2006, is $1,593 million (line 29). A year earlier YUM! Brands had retained earnings of $1,619 million. We saw these figures on the statement of retained earnings in Exhibit 1-8 (line 4). Retained earnings' final resting place is the balance sheet.

■ YUM! Brands' equity holds another item, Other Equity, which is a collection of miscellaneous items. For now, focus on the two main components of stockholders' equity: common stock and retained earnings.

■ At December 31, 2006, YUM! Brands has Total Shareholders' Equity of $1,437 million (line 31). We can now prove that YUM's total assets equal total liabilities and equity (amounts in millions):

**Accounting Cycle Tutorial
Balance Sheet Accounts**

Total assets (line 15)	$6,353	
Total liabilities (line 26)	$4,916	*Must equal*
+ Total shareholders' equity (line 31)	1,437	
Total liabilities and equity (line 32)	$6,353	

The statement of cash flows is the fourth required financial statement.

The Statement of Cash Flows Measures Cash Receipts and Payments

Companies engage in 3 basic types of activities:

1. **Operating activities**   2. **Investing activities**   3. **Financing activities**

The **statement of cash flows** reports cash flows under these 3 categories. Think about the cash flows (receipts and payments) in each category:

■ *Companies* **operate by selling goods and services to customers.** Operating activities result in net income or net loss, and they either increase or decrease cash. The income statement tells whether the company is profitable. The cash-flow statement reports whether operations increased cash. Operating activities are most important, and they should be the company's main source of cash. Negative cash flow from operations can lead to bankruptcy.

- **Companies *invest* in long-term assets.** YUM! Brands buys buildings and equipment, and when these assets wear out, the company sells them. Both purchases and sales of long-term assets are investing cash flows. Investing cash flows are next most important after operations.
- **Companies need money for *financing*.** Financing includes both issuing stock and borrowing. YUM issues stock to its shareholders and borrows from banks. These are cash receipts. The company pays off loans. YUM also pays dividends. These payments are financing cash flows.

Overview. Each category of cash flows—operating, investing, and financing—either increases or decreases cash. In Exhibit 1-10, YUM! Brands' operating activities provided cash of $1,302 million in 2006 (line 4). This signals strong cash flow from operations. 2006's investing activities used cash of $476 million (line 9). That signals expansion. Financing activities used $665 million (line 16). YUM paid off some debt and also paid dividends (lines 13 and 14). On a statement of cash flows, cash receipts appear as positive amounts. Cash payments are negative and enclosed by parentheses.

EXHIBIT 1-10	Statement of Cash Flows (Adapted)

YUM! Brands, Inc.
Statement of Cash Flows (Adapted)
Years Ended December 31, 2006, and 2005

(In millions)	2006	2005
1 Cash Flows—Operating Activities:		
2 Net income	$ 824	$ 762
3 Adjustments to reconcile net income to net cash		
provided by operating activities	478	476
4 Net Cash Provided by Operating Activities	1,302	1,238
5 Cash Flows—Investing Activities:		
6 Purchases of property, plant, and equipment	(614)	(609)
7 Sales of property, plant, and equipment	57	81
8 Other	81	183
9 Net Cash Used in Investing Activities	(476)	(345)
10 Cash Flows—Financing Activities:		
11 Issuance of common stock	–	–
12 Issuance of short-term and long-term debt (Borrowing)	540	160
13 Repayments of short-term and long-term debt	(288)	(48)
14 Payment of dividends and other distributions to stockholders	(850)	(210)
15 Other payments	(67)	(733)
16 Net Cash Used in Financing Activities	(665)	(831)
17 Net Increase in Cash and Cash Equivalents	161	62
18 Cash and Cash Equivalents—Beginning of Year	158	96
19 Cash and Cash Equivalents—End of Year	$ 319	$ 158

Overall, YUM's cash increased by $161 million during 2006 (line 17) and ended the year at $319 million (line 19). Trace ending cash back to the balance sheet in Exhibit 1-9 (line 3). Cash links the statement of cash flows to the balance sheet. You've just performed more financial-statement analysis!

Let's now summarize the relationships that link the financial statements.

RELATIONSHIPS AMONG THE FINANCIAL STATEMENTS

Exhibit 1-11 summarizes the relationships among the financial statements of Barker Company for 2009. Study the exhibit carefully because these relationships apply to all organizations. Specifically, note the following:

OBJECTIVE

5 **Use** financial statements

1. The income statement for the year ended December 31, 2009
   a. Reports revenues and expenses of the year. Revenues and expenses are reported *only* on the income statement.
   b. Reports net income if total revenues exceed total expenses. If expenses exceed revenues, there is a net loss.

2. The statement of retained earnings for the year ended December 31, 2009
   a. Opens with the beginning retained earnings balance.
   b. Adds net income (or subtracts net loss). Net income comes directly from the income statement (arrow ① in Exhibit 1-11).
   c. Subtracts dividends.
   d. Reports the retained earnings balance at the end of the year.

3. The balance sheet at December 31, 2009, end of the accounting year
   a. Reports assets, liabilities, and stockholders' equity at the end of the year. Only the balance sheet reports assets and liabilities.
   b. Reports that assets equal the sum of liabilities plus stockholders' equity. This balancing feature follows the accounting equation and gives the balance sheet its name.
   c. Reports retained earnings, which comes from the statement of retained earnings (arrow ② in Exhibit 1-11).

4. The statement of cash flows for the year ended December 31, 2009
   a. Reports cash flows from operating, investing, and financing activities. Each category results in net cash provided (an increase) or used (a decrease).
   b. Reports whether cash increased (or decreased) during the year. The statement shows the ending cash balance, as reported on the balance sheet (arrow ③ in Exhibit 1-11).

$ac\!\!/t$

Accounting Cycle Tutorial
Glossary

$ac\!\!/t$

Accounting Cycle Tutorial
Glossary Quiz

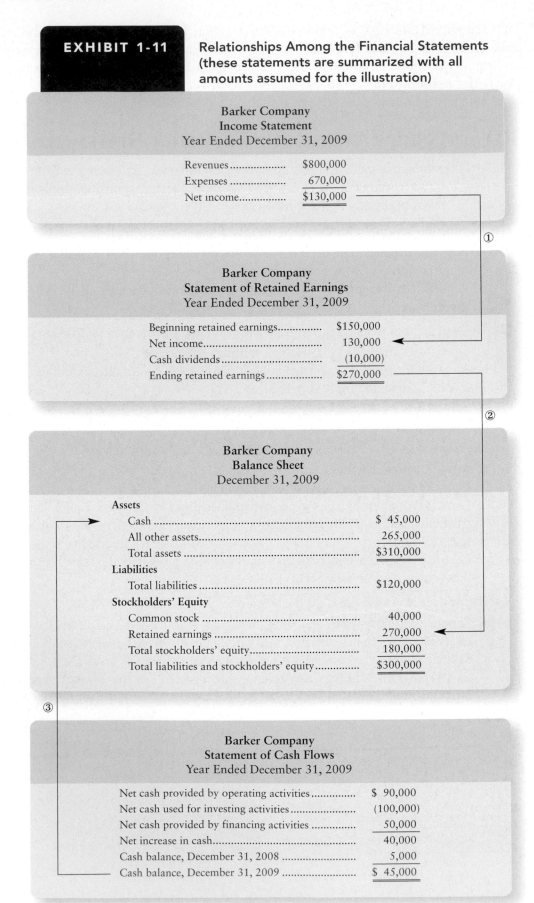

EXHIBIT 1-11 Relationships Among the Financial Statements (these statements are summarized with all amounts assumed for the illustration)

Barker Company
Income Statement
Year Ended December 31, 2009

Revenues..................	$800,000
Expenses	670,000
Net income..............	$130,000

①

Barker Company
Statement of Retained Earnings
Year Ended December 31, 2009

Beginning retained earnings...............	$150,000
Net income.......................................	130,000
Cash dividends.................................	(10,000)
Ending retained earnings..................	$270,000

②

Barker Company
Balance Sheet
December 31, 2009

Assets

Cash	$ 45,000
All other assets...	265,000
Total assets	$310,000

Liabilities

Total liabilities...	$120,000

Stockholders' Equity

Common stock	40,000
Retained earnings	270,000
Total stockholders' equity......................................	180,000
Total liabilities and stockholders' equity..............	$300,000

③

Barker Company
Statement of Cash Flows
Year Ended December 31, 2009

Net cash provided by operating activities...............	$ 90,000
Net cash used for investing activities......................	(100,000)
Net cash provided by financing activities	50,000
Net increase in cash..	40,000
Cash balance, December 31, 2008	5,000
Cash balance, December 31, 2009	$ 45,000

ac↗t

Accounting Cycle Tutorial
Applications Cottage Kitchen

ac↗t

Accounting Cycle Tutorial
Applications Marwood Homes

DECISION GUIDELINES

IN EVALUATING A COMPANY, WHAT DO DECISION MAKERS LOOK FOR?

These Decision Guidelines illustrate how people use financial statements. Decision Guidelines appear throughout the book to show how accounting information aids decision making.

Suppose you are considering an investment in YUM! Brands stock. How do you proceed? Where do you get the information you need? What do you look for?

Question/Decision	What to Look For
1. Can the company sell its products?	1. Sales revenue on the income statement. Are sales growing or falling?
2. What are the main income measures to watch for trends?	2. a. Gross profit (Sales − Cost of goods sold) b. Operating income (Gross profit − Operating expenses) c. Net income (bottom line of the income statement) All 3 income measures should be increasing over time.
3. What percentage of sales revenue ends up as profit?	3. Divide net income by sales revenue. Examine the trend of the net income percentage from year to year.
4. Can the company collect its receivables?	4. From the balance sheet, compare the percentage increase in accounts receivable to the percentage increase in sales. If receivables are growing much faster than sales, collections may be too slow, and a cash shortage may result.
5. Can the company pay its a. Current liabilities? b. Current and long-term liabilities?	5. From the balance sheet, compare a. Current assets to current liabilities. Current assets should be somewhat greater than current liabilities. b. Total assets to total liabilities. Total assets must be somewhat greater than total liabilities.
6. Where is the company's cash coming from? How is cash being used?	6. On the cash-flow statement, operating activities should provide the bulk of the company's cash during most years. Otherwise, the business will fail. Examine investing cash flows to see if the company is purchasing long-term assets—property, plant, and equipment and intangibles (this signals growth). Examine financing cash flows for heavy borrowing (a bad sign) or issuance of stock (a good sign).

Al's Cleaners, Inc., began operations on September 1, 20X9. During September, the business provided services for customers. It is now September 30, and investors wonder how well Al's performed during its first month. The investors also want to know the company's financial position at the end of September and its cash flows during the month.

The following data are listed in alphabetical order. Prepare the Al's Cleaners financial statements at the end of September 20X9.

Accounts payable	$ 1,800	Equipment	$18,000
Accounts receivable	3,000	Payments of cash:	
Adjustments to reconcile net income to net cash provided by operating activities	(3,900)	Acquisition of equipment	40,000
		Dividends	2,100
		Rent expense	1,500
Cash balance at beginning of September	0	Retained earnings at beginning of September	0
Cash balance at end of September	?		
Cash receipts:		Retained earnings at end of September	?
Issuance (sale) of stock to owners	50,000	Salary expense	1,900
Sale of equipment	22,000	Service revenue	10,500
Common stock	51,000	Supplies	3,700
		Interest expense	400

▮ Required

1. Prepare the income statement, the statement of retained earnings, and the statement of cash flows for the month ended September 30, 20X9, and the balance sheet at September 30, 20X9. Draw arrows linking the statements.
2. Answer the following questions:
   a. How well did Al's perform during its first month of operations?
   b. Where does Al's stand financially at the end of September?

Answers

▮ Requirement 1

Financial Statements of Al's Cleaners, Inc.

Al's Cleaners, Inc.
Income Statement
Month Ended September 30, 20X9

Revenue:		
Service revenue		$10,500
Expenses:		
Salary expense	$1,900	
Rent expense	1,500	
Interest expense	400	
Total expenses		3,000
Net income		$ 7,500

①

Al's Cleaners, Inc.
Statement of Retained Earnings
Month Ended September 30, 20X9

Retained earnings, September 1, 20X9	$ 0
Add: Net income for the month	7,500
	7,500
Less: Dividends	(2,100)
Retained earnings, September 30, 20X9	$5,400

②

Al's Cleaners, Inc.
Balance Sheet
September 30, 20X9

Assets		*Liabilities*	
Cash	$33,500	Accounts payable	$ 1,800
Accounts receivable	3,000		
Supplies	3,700	*Stockholders' Equity*	
Equipment	18,000	Common stock	51,000
		Retained earnings	5,400
		Total stockholders' equity	56,400
		Total liabilities and	
Total assets	$58,200	stockholders' equity	$58,200

③

Al's Cleaners, Inc.
Statement of Cash Flows
Month Ended September 30, 20X9

Cash flows from operating activities:		
Net income		$ 7,500
Adjustments to reconcile net income to net cash		
provided by operating activities		(4,900)
Net cash provided by operating activities		2,600
Cash flows from investing activities:		
Acquisition of equipment	$(40,000)	
Sale of equipment	22,000	
Net cash used for investing activities		(18,000)
Cash flows from financing activities:		
Issuance (sale) of stock	$ 51,000	
Payment of dividends	(2,100)	
Net cash provided by financing activities		48,900
Net increase in cash		$33,500
Cash balance, September 1, 20X9		0
Cash balance, September 30, 20X9		$33,500

Requirement 2

2. **a.** Al's Cleaners performed rather well in September. Net income was $7,500—very good in relation to service revenue of $10,500. The company was able to pay cash dividends of $2,100.

   b. Al's Cleaners ended September with cash of $33,500. Total assets of $58,200 far exceed total liabilities of $1,800. Stockholders' equity of $56,400 provides a good cushion for borrowing. The business's financial position at September 30, 20X9, is strong.

REVIEW THE FINANCIAL STATEMENTS

Quick Check (Answers are given on page 77.)

1. All of the following statements are true except one. Which statement is false?
   a. Bookkeeping is only a part of accounting.
   b. A proprietorship is a business with several owners.
   c. Professional accountants are held to a high standard of ethical conduct.
   d. The organization that formulates generally accepted accounting principles is the Financial Accounting Standards Board.
2. The valuation of assets on the balance sheet is generally based on:
   a. Historical cost
   b. What it would cost to replace the asset
   c. Current fair market value as established by independent appraisers
   d. Selling price
3. The accounting equation can be expressed as:
   a. Assets + Liabilities = Owners' Equity
   b. Owners' Equity - Assets = Liabilities
   c. Assets = Liabilities – Owners' Equity
   d. Assets – Liabilities = Owners' Equity
4. The nature of an asset is best described as:
   a. Something with physical form that's valued at cost in the accounting records.
   b. An economic resource representing cash or the right to receive cash in the future.
   c. An economic resource that's expected to benefit future operations.
   d. Something owned by a business that has a ready market value.
5. Which financial statement covers a period of time?
   a. Balance sheet   c. Statement of cash flows
   b. Income statement   d. Both B and C
6. How would net income be most likely to affect the accounting equation?
   a. Increase assets and increase stockholders' equity
   b. Increase liabilities and decrease stockholders' equity
   c. Increase assets and increase liabilities
   d. Decrease assets and decrease liabilities
7. During the year, ChemDry, Inc., has $100,000 in revenues, $40,000 in expenses, and $3,000 in dividend payments. Stockholders' equity changed by:
   a. +$27,000   c. +$12,000
   b. +$57,000   d. –$8,000
8. ChemDry in question 7 had net income (or net loss) of
   a. Net income of $100,000.   c. Net income of $60,000.
   b. Net income of $57,000.   d. Net loss of $40,000.

9. Prestige Corporation holds cash of $5,000 and owes $25,000 on accounts payable. Prestige has accounts receivable of $30,000, inventory of $20,000, and land that cost $50,000. How much are Prestige's total assets and liabilities?

	Total assets	*Liabilities*
a.	$100,000	$25,000
b.	$105,000	$80,000
c.	$105,000	$25,000
d.	$25,000	105,000

10. Which item(s) is (are) reported on the balance sheet?
    a. Retained earnings
    b. Accounts payable
    c. Inventory
    d. All of the above

11. During the year, Brooks Company's stockholders' equity increased from $30,000 to $40,000. Brooks earned net income of $15,000. How much in dividends did Brooks declare during the year?
    a. $6,000
    b. $-0-
    c. $8,000
    d. $5,000

12. Stuebs Company had total assets of $300,000 and total stockholders' equity of $100,000 at the beginning of the year. During the year assets increased by $50,000 and liabilities increased by $40,000. Stockholders' equity at the end of the year is:
    a. $90,000
    b. $110,000
    c. $140,000
    d. $150,000

Accounting Vocabulary

account payable (p. 41) A liability backed by the general reputation and credit standing of the debtor.

accounting (p. 33) The information system that measures business activities, processes that information into reports and financial statements, and communicates the results to decision makers.

accounting equation (p. 40) The most basic tool of accounting: Assets = Liabilities + Owners' Equity.

assets (p. 40) An economic resource that is expected to be of benefit in the future.

balance sheet (p. 46) List of an entity's assets, liabilities, and owners' equity as of a specific date. Also called the *statement of financial position*.

board of directors (p. 37) Group elected by the stockholders to set policy for a corporation and to appoint its officers.

capital (p. 40) Another name for the *owners' equity* of a business.

cash (p. 41) Money and any medium of exchange that a bank accepts at face value.

common stock (p. 41) The most basic form of capital stock.

corporation (p. 37) A business owned by stockholders. A corporation is a legal entity, an "artificial person" in the eyes of the law.

cost principle (p. 39) Principle that states that assets and services should be recorded at their actual cost.

current assets (p. 46) An asset that is expected to be converted to cash, sold, or consumed during the next 12 months, or within the business's normal operating cycle if longer than a year.

current liabilities (p. 48) A debt due to be paid within 1 year or within the entity's operating cycle if the cycle is longer than a year.

dividends (p. 42) Distributions (usually cash) by a corporation to its stockholders.

entity (p. 38) An organization or a section of an organization that, for accounting purposes, stands apart from other organizations and individuals as a separate economic unit.

expenses (p. 41) Decrease in retained earnings that results from operations; the cost of doing business; opposite of revenues.

fair value (p. 39) The amount that a business could sell an asset for, or the amount that a business could pay to settle a liability.

financial accounting (p. 34) The branch of accounting that provides information to people outside the firm.

financial statements (p. 32) Business documents that report financial information about a business entity to decision makers.

financing activities (p. 49) Activities that obtain from investors and creditors the cash needed to launch and sustain the business; a section of the statement of cash flows.

fixed assets (p. 41) Another name for *property, plant, and equipment*.

generally accepted accounting principles (GAAP) (p. 37) Accounting guidelines, formulated by the Financial Accounting Standards Board, that govern how accounting is practiced.

going-concern concept (p. 39) Holds that the entity will remain in operation for the foreseeable future.

income statement (p. 44) A financial statement listing an entity's revenues, expenses, and net income or net loss for a specific period. Also called the *statement of operations*.

investing activities (p. 49) Activities that increase or decrease the long-term assets available to the business; a section of the statement of cash flows.

liabilities (p. 40) An economic obligation (a debt) payable to an individual or an organization outside the business.

limited liability company (p. 37) A business organization in which the business (not the owner) is liable for the company's debts.

long-term debt (p. 41) A liability that falls due beyond 1 year from the date of the financial statements.

management accounting (p. 34) The branch of accounting that generates information for the internal decision makers of a business, such as top executives.

merchandise inventory (p. 41) The merchandise that a company sells to customers, also called *inventory*.

net earnings (p. 41) Another name for *net income*.

net income (p. 41) Excess of total revenues over total expenses. Also called *net earnings* or *net profit*.

net loss (p. 42) Excess of total expenses over total revenues.

net profit (p. 41) Another name for *net income*.

note payable (p. 41) A liability evidenced by a written promise to make a future payment.

objectivity principle (p. 38) Another name for the *reliability principle*.

operating activities (p. 49) Activities that create revenue or expense in the entity's major line of business; a section of the statement of cash flows. Operating activities affect the income statement.

owners' equity (p. 40) The claim of the owners of a business to the assets of the business. Also called *capital, stockholders' equity*, or *net assets*.

paid-in capital (p. 41) The amount of stockholders' equity that stockholders have contributed to the corporation. Also called *contributed capital*.

partnership (p. 36) An association of 2 or more persons who co-own a business for profit.

plant assets (p. 41) Another name for *property, plant, and equipment*.

property, plant, and equipment (p. 41) Long-lived assets, such as land, buildings, and equipment, used in the operation of the business. Also called *plant assets* or *fixed assets*.

proprietorship (p. 36) A business with a single owner.

reliability principle (p. 38) The accounting principle that ensures that accounting records and statements are based on the most reliable data available. Also called the *objectivity principle*.

retained earnings (p. 41) The amount of stockholders' equity that the corporation has earned through profitable operation and has not given back to stockholders.

revenues (p. 41) Increase in retained earnings from delivering goods or services to customers or clients.

shareholder (p. 37) Another name for *stockholder*.

stable-monetary-unit concept (p. 40) The reason for ignoring the effect of inflation in the accounting records, based on the assumption that the dollar's purchasing power is relatively stable.

statement of cash flows (p. 49) Reports cash receipts and cash payments classified according to the entity's major activities: operating, investing, and financing.

statement of financial position (p. 46) Another name for the *balance sheet*.

statement of operations (p. 44) Another name for the *income statement*.

statement of retained earnings (p. 45) Summary of the changes in the retained earnings of a corporation during a specific period.

stock (p. 37) Shares into which the owners' equity of a corporation is divided.

stockholders (p. 37) A person who owns stock in a corporation. Also called a *shareholder*.

stockholders' equity (p. 41) The stockholders' ownership interest in the assets of a corporation.

ASSESS YOUR PROGRESS

Short Exercises

S1-1 (*Learning Objective 1: Using accounting vocabulary*) Suppose you manage a Pizza Hut restaurant. Identify the missing amount for each situation: (pp. 40–42)

Total Assets	=	Total Liabilities	+	Stockholder's Equity
a. $?		$150,000		$150,000
b. 290,000		90,000		?
c. 220,000		?		120,000

S1-2 (*Learning Objective 1: Making ethical judgments*) Accountants follow ethical guidelines in the conduct of their work. What are these standards of professional conduct designed to produce? Why is this goal important? (p. 35)

S1-3 (*Learning Objective 2: Applying accounting concepts*) David Novak is Chairman of the Board of YUM! Brands, Inc. Suppose Mr. Novak has just founded YUM! Brands, and assume that he treats his home and other personal assets as part of YUM! Brands. Answer these questions about the evaluation of YUM! Brands, Inc. (pp. 38–39)

1. Which accounting concept governs this situation?

2. How can the *proper* application of this accounting concept give Novak and others a realistic view of YUM! Brands, Inc.? Explain in detail.

S1-4 (*Learning Objective 3: Using the accounting equation*)

1. Use the accounting equation to show how to determine the amount of a company's owners' equity. How would your answer change if you were analyzing your own household or a single IHOP restaurant? (pp. 40–42)

2. If you know the assets and the owners' equity of a business, how can you measure its liabilities? Give the equation. (pp. 40–42)

S1-5 (*Learning Objective 1: Defining key accounting terms*) Accounting definitions are precise, and you must understand the vocabulary to properly use accounting. Sharpen your understanding of key terms by answering the following questions. (pp. 40–41)

1. How do the *assets* and *owners' equity* of Intel Corporation differ from each other? Which one (assets or owners' equity) must be at least as large as the other? Which one can be smaller than the other?

2. How are Intel's *liabilities* and *owners' equity* similar? How are they different?

S1-6 (*Learning Objective 1: Classifying assets, liabilities, and owners' equity*) Consider Wal-Mart, the world's largest retailer. Classify the following items as an Asset (A), a Liability (L), or an Owners' Equity (E) for Wal-Mart (pp. 40–41):

_____ **a.** Accounts payable 　　_____ **g.** Accounts receivable

_____ **b.** Common stock 　　_____ **h.** Long-term debt

_____ **c.** Supplies 　　_____ **i.** Merchandise inventory

_____ **d.** Retained earnings 　　_____ **j.** Notes payable

_____ **e.** Land 　　_____ **k.** Expenses payable

_____ **f.** Prepaid expenses 　　_____ **l.** Equipment

S1-7 (*Learning Objective 4: Using the income statement*)

1. Identify the 2 basic categories of items on an income statement. (pp. 43–44)

2. What do we call the bottom line of the income statement? (pp. 43–44)

S1-8 (*Learning Objective 4: Preparing an income statement*) Split Second Wireless, Inc., began 2009 with total assets of $110 million and ended 2009 with assets of $160 million. During 2009 Split Second earned revenues of $90 million and had expenses of $20 million. Split Second paid dividends of $10 million in 2009. Prepare the company's income statement for the year ended December 31, 2009, complete with an appropriate heading. (pp. 43–44).

S1-9 (*Learning Objective 4: Preparing a statement of retained earnings*) Nextel Corp. began 2008 with retained earnings of $200 million. Revenues during the year were $400 million and expenses totaled $300 million. Nextel declared dividends of $40 million. What was the company's ending balance of retained earnings? To answer this question, prepare Nextel's statement of retained earnings for the year ended December 31, 2008, complete with its proper heading. (pp. 45–46)

S1-10 (*Learning Objective 4: Preparing a balance sheet*) At December 31, 2008, Womack Travel Services has cash of $13,000, receivables of $2,000, and ticket inventory of $40,000. The company's equipment totals $85,000. Womack owes accounts payable of $10,000, and long-term notes payable of $80,000. Common stock is $15,000.

Prepare Womack's balance sheet at December 31, 2008, complete with its proper heading. Use the accounting equation to compute retained earnings. (pp. 40–42)

S1-11 (*Learning Objective 4 : Preparing a statement of cash flows*) Brazos Medical, Inc., ended 2009 with cash of $24,000. During 2010, Brazos earned net income of $80,000 and had adjustments to reconcile net income to net cash provided by operations totaling $20,000 (this is a negative amount).

Brazos paid $40,000 to purchase equipment during 2010. During 2010, the company paid dividends of $10,000.

Prepare Brazos's statement of cash flows for the year ended December 31, 2010, complete with its proper heading. Follow the format in the summary problem starting on page 55.

S1-12 (*Learning Objective 5: Identifying items with the appropriate financial statement*) Suppose you are analyzing the financial statements of Martin Audiology, Inc. Identify each item with its appropriate financial statement, using the following abbreviations: Income statement (IS), Statement of retained earnings (SRE), Balance sheet (BS), and Statement of cash flows (SCF). Three items appear on 2 financial statements, and one item shows up on 3 statements. (p. 52)

____ **a.** Dividends

____ **b.** Salary expense

____ **c.** Inventory

____ **d.** Sales revenue

____ **e.** Retained earnings

____ **f.** Net cash provided by operating activities

____ **g.** Net income

____ **h.** Cash

____ **i.** Net cash used for financing activities

____ **j.** Accounts payable

____ **k.** Common stock

____ **l.** Interest revenue

____ **m.** Long-term debt

____ **n.** Increase or decrease in cash

Exercises

writing assignment ■

E1-13 (*Learning Objective 1: Organizing a business*) Quality Environmental, Inc., needs funds, and Martha Beard, the president, has asked you to consider investing in the business. Answer the following questions about the different ways that Beard might organize the business. Explain each answer. (p. 37)

a. What forms of organization will enable the owners of Quality Environmental to limit their risk of loss to the amounts they have invested in the business?

b. What form of business organization will give Beard the most freedom to manage the business as she wishes?

c. What form of organization will give creditors the maximum protection in the event that Quality Environmental fails and cannot pay its debts?

E1-14 (*Learning Objective 2: Applying accounting concepts and principles*) Identify the accounting concept or principle that best applies to each of the following situations. (pp. 38–40)

   a. Wendy's, the restaurant chain, sold a store location to Burger King. How can Wendy's determine the sale price of the store—by a professional appraisal, Wendy's cost, or the amount actually received from the sale?

   b. Inflation has been around 6% for some time. Trammel Crow Realtors is considering measuring its land values in inflation-adjusted amounts.

   c. Toyota wants to determine which division of the company—Toyota or Lexus—is more profitable.

   d. You get an especially good buy on a laptop, paying only $399 for a computer that normally costs $799. What is your accounting value for this computer?

E1-15 (*Learning Objective 3: Accounting equation*) Compute the missing amount in the accounting equation for each company (amounts in billions):

	Assets	Liabilities	Owners' Equity
Apple	$?	$ 7	$10
PepsiCo	32	?	14
FedEx	23	11	?

Which company appears to have the strongest financial position? Explain your reasoning. (pp. 40–42)

E1-16 (*Learning Objective 3, 4: Accounting equation*) Krispy Kreme Doughnuts has current assets of $147 million; property, plant, and equipment of $206 million; and other assets totaling $58 million. Current liabilities are $154 million and long-term liabilities total $148 million. (pp. 40–42)

❙ Requirements

   1. Use these data to write Krispy Kreme Doughnuts' accounting equation.

   2. How much in resources does Krispy Kreme have to work with?

   3. How much does Krispy Kreme owe creditors?

   4. How much of the company's assets do the Krispy Kreme stockholders actually own?

E1-17 (*Learning Objective 3: Accounting equation*) Store Front, Inc.'s, comparative balance sheet at January 31, 2009, and 2008, reports (in millions):

	2009	2008
Total assets	$40	$30
Total liabilities	12	10

❙ Required

Three situations about Store Front's issuance of stock and payment of dividends during the year ended January 31, 2009, follow. For each situation, use the accounting equation and the statement of retained earnings to compute the amount of Store Front's net income or net loss during the year ended January 31, 2009. (pp. 40–42, 45–46)

   1. Store Front issued $1 million of stock and paid no dividends.

   2. Store Front issued no stock but paid dividends of $2 million.

   3. Store Front issued $11 million of stock and paid dividends of $1 million.

E1-18 (*Learning Objective 3, 4: Accounting equation*) Answer these questions about 2 companies.

1. Peru, Inc., began the year with total liabilities of $140,000 and total stockholders' equity of $300,000. During the year, total assets increased by 20%. How much are total assets at the end of the year? (pp. 40–42)

2. Social Networking Associates began the year with total assets of $500,000 and total liabilities of $200,000. Net income for the year was $100,000, and dividends were zero. How much is stockholders' equity at the end of the year? (pp. 40–42, 45–46)

E1-19 (*Learning Objective 4: Identifying financial statement information*) Assume MySpace is expanding into Japan. The company must decide where to locate and how to finance the expansion. Identify the financial statement where these decision makers can find the following information about MySpace, Inc. In some cases, more than one statement will report the needed data. (pp. 45–50)

a. Common stock	**i.** Cash spent to acquire the building
b. Income tax payable	**j.** Selling, general, and administrative
c. Dividends	expenses
d. Income tax expense	**k.** Adjustments to reconcile net income
e. Ending balance of retained earnings	to net cash provided by operations
f. Total assets	**l.** Ending cash balance
g. Long-term debt	**m.** Current liabilities
h. Revenue	**n.** Net income

■ **spreadsheet**

E1-20 (*Learning Objective 2, 5: Business organization, balance sheet*) Amounts of the assets and liabilities of Maxwell Banking Company, as of December 31, 2008, are given as follows. Also included are revenue and expense figures for the year ended on that date (amounts in millions):

Property and equipment, net	$ 4	Total revenue	$ 35
Investment assets	72	Receivables.....................................	253
Long-term liabilities	73	Current liabilities	290
Other expenses............................	14	Common stock...................................	12
Cash...	28	Interest expense................................	3
Retained earnings, beginning.......	19	Salary and other employee expenses.....	9
Retained earnings, ending	?	Other assets.....................................	43

❙ *Required*

Prepare the balance sheet of Maxwell Banking Company at December 31, 2008. Use the accounting equation to compute ending retained earnings (pp. 40–41, 45–47)

■ **spreadsheet**

E1-21 (*Learning Objective 2, 5: Income statement*) This exercise should be used with Exercise 1-20. Refer to the data of Maxwell Banking Company in Exercise 1-20.

❙ *Required*

1. Prepare the income statement of Maxwell Banking Company, for the year ended December 31, 2008. (pp. 43–44)

2. What amount of dividends did Maxwell declare during the year ended December 31, 2008? Hint: Prepare a statement of retained earnings. (pp. 45–46)

E1-22 (*Learning Objective 2, 4, 5: Statement of cash flows*) Groovy, Inc., began 2008 with $95,000 in cash. During 2008, Groovy earned net income of $300,000, and adjustments to reconcile net income to net cash provided by operations totaled $60,000, a positive amount. Investing activities used cash of $400,000, and financing activities provided cash of $70,000. Groovy ended 2008 with total assets of $250,000 and total liabilities of $110,000.

I Required

Prepare Groovy, Inc.'s, statement of cash flows for the year ended December 31, 2008. Identify the data items given that do not appear on the statement of cash flows. Also identify the financial statement that reports each unused item. (pp. 46–47)

E1-23 (*Learning Objective 5: Preparing an income statement and a statement of retained earnings*) Assume a Ricoh Copy Center ended the month of July 20X9 with these data:

Payments of cash:		Cash balance, June 30, 20X9	$	0
Acquisition of equipment	$36,000	Cash balance, July 31, 20X9		8,100
Dividends	2,000	Cash receipts:		
Retained earnings,		Issuance (sale) of stock		
June 30, 20X9	0	to owners		35,000
Retained earnings,		Rent expense		700
July 31, 20X9	?	Common stock		35,000
Utilities expense	200	Equipment.................................		36,000
Adjustments to reconcile		Office supplies...........................		1,200
net income to cash provided		Accounts payable		3,200
by operations	2,000	Service revenue..........................		14,000
Salary expense...........................	4,000			

I Required

Prepare the income statement and the statement of retained earnings of Ricoh Copy Center, Inc., for the month ended July 31, 20X9. (pp. 43–44, 45–46)

E1-24 (*Learning Objective 5: Preparing a balance sheet*) Refer to the data in the preceding exercise. Prepare the balance sheet of Ricoh Copy Center, Inc., at July 31, 20X9. (pp. 46–47)

E1-25 (*Learning Objective 5: Preparing a statement of cash flows*) Refer to the data in Exercise 1-23. Prepare the statement of cash flows of Ricoh Copy Center, Inc., for the month ended July 31, 20X9. Draw arrows linking the statements you prepared for Exercises 1-23 through 1-25. (pp. 49–50)

E1-26 (*Learning Objective 4, 5: Advising a business*) This exercise should be used in conjunction with Exercises 1-23 through 1-25.

The owner of Ricoh Copy Center now seeks your advice as to whether he should cease operations or continue the business. Write a report giving him your opinion of net income, dividends, financial position, and cash flows during his first month of operations. Cite specifics from the financial statements to support your opinion. Conclude your memo with advice on whether to stay in business or cease operations. (Challenge)

writing assignment ■

E1-27 (*Learning Objective 2, 5: Applying accounting concepts to explain business activity*) Apply your understanding of the relationships among the financial statements to answer these questions. (Challenge)

writing assignment ■

a. How can a business earn large profits but have a small balance of retained earnings?

b. Give 2 reasons why a business can have a steady stream of net income over a 5-year period and still experience a cash shortage.

c. If you could pick a single source of cash for your business, what would it be? Why?

d. How can a business lose money several years in a row and still have plenty of cash?

Quiz

Test your understanding of the financial statements by answering the following questions. Select the best choice from among the possible answers given.

Q1-28 The *primary* objective of financial reporting is to provide information (p. 37)
a. Useful for making investment and credit decisions.
b. About the profitability of the enterprise.
c. On the cash flows of the company.
d. To the federal government.

Q1-29 For a company of a certain size, which type of business organization provides the least amount of protection for bankers and other creditors of the company? (pp. 36–37)
a. Proprietorship
b. Partnership
c. Both a and b
d. Corporation

Q1-30 Assets are usually reported at their (pp. 39–40)
a. Appraised value.
b. Current market value.
c. Historical cost.
d. None of the above (<u>fill in the blank</u>).

Q1-31 During January, assets increased by $20,000 and liabilities increased by $4,000. Stockholders' equity must have (pp. 40–41)
a. Increased by $16,000.
b. Increased by $24,000.
c. Decreased by $16,000.
d. Decreased by $24,000.

Q1-32 The amount a company expects to collect from customers appears on the (pp. 46–47)
a. Income statement in the expenses section.
b. Balance sheet in the current assets section.
c. Balance sheet in the stockholders' equity section.
d. Statement of cash flows.

Q1-33 All of the following are current assets except (pp. 46–47)
a. Cash.
b. Accounts Receivable.
c. Inventory.
d. Sales Revenue.

Q1-34 Revenues are (p. 41)
a. Increases in paid-in capital resulting from the owners investing in the business.
b. Increases in retained earnings resulting from selling products or performing services.
c. Decreases in liabilities resulting from paying off loans.
d. All of the above.

Q1-35 The financial statement that reports revenues and expenses is called the (pp. 43–44)
a. Statement of retained earnings.
b. Income statement.
c. Statement of cash flows.
d. Balance sheet.

Q1-36 Another name for the balance sheet is the (pp. 46–47)
a. Statement of operations.
b. Statement of earnings.
c. Statement of profit and loss.
d. Statement of financial position.

Q1-37 Baldwin Corporation began the year with cash of $35,000 and a computer that cost $20,000. During the year Baldwin earned sales revenue of $140,000 and had the following expenses: salaries, $59,000; rent, $8,000; and utilities, $3,000. At year end Baldwin's cash balance was down to $16,000. How much net income (or net loss) did Baldwin experience for the year? (pp. 43–44)
a. ($19,000)
b. $70,000
c. $107,000
d. $140,000

Q1-38 Quartz Instruments had retained earnings of $145,000 at December 31, 20X1. Net income for 20X2 totaled $90,000, and dividends for 20X2 were $30,000. How much retained earnings should Quartz report at December 31, 20X2? (pp. 45–46)

a. $205,000
b. $235,000

c. $140,000
d. $175,000

Q1-39 Net income appears on which financial statement(s)? (pp. 43–44)

a. Income statement
b. Statement of retained earnings

c. Both A and B
d. Balance sheet

Q1-40 Cash paid to purchase a building appears on the statement of cash flows among the (pp. 49–50)

a. Operating activities.
b. Financing activities.
c. Investing activities.
d. Stockholders' equity.

Q1-41 The stockholders' equity of Chernasky Company at the beginning and end of 20X0 totaled $15,000 and $18,000, respectively. Assets at the beginning of 20X0 were $25,000. If the liabilities of Chernasky Company increased by $8,000 in 20X0, how much were total assets at the end of 20X0? Use the accounting equation. (pp. 40–42)

a. $36,000
b. $16,000

c. $2,000
d. Some other amount (fill in the blank)

Q1-42 Drexler Company had the following on the dates indicated:

	12/31/X3	12/31/X2
Total assets	$750,000	$520,000
Total liabilities	300,000	200,000

Drexler had no stock transactions in 20X3 and, thus, the change in stockholders' equity for 20X3 was due to net income and dividends. If dividends were $50,000, how much was Drexler's net income for 20X3? Use the accounting equation and the statements of retained earnings. (pp. 40–42, 45–46)

a. $100,000
b. $130,000

c. $180,000
d. Some other amount (fill in the blank)

Problems
(Group A)

Some of these A problems can be found within My Accounting Lab (MAL), an online homework and practice environment. Your instructor may ask you to complete these exercises using MAL.

MyAccountingLab

P1-43A (*Learning Objective 1, 2, 4, 5: Applying accounting vocabulary, concepts, and principles to the income statement*) Assume that the **Kinko's Division of FedEx Corporation** experienced the following transactions during the year ended December 31, 20X5:

a. Suppose Kinko's provided copy services for Microsoft for the discounted price of $250,000. Under normal conditions Kinko's would have provided these services for $280,000. Other revenues totaled $50,000.

b. Salaries cost Kinko's $20,000 to provide these services. Kinko's had to pay employees overtime. Ordinarily the salary cost for these services would have been $18,000.

c. Other expenses totaled $240,000. Income tax expense was 40% of income before tax.

d. Kinko's has 2 operating subdivisions: basic retail and special contracts. Each subdivision is accounted for separately to indicate how well each is performing. At year end, Kinko's combines the statements of all subdivisions to show results for the Kinko's Division as a whole.

e. Inflation affects the amounts that Kinko's must pay for copy machines. To show the effects of inflation, net income would drop by $3,000.

f. If Kinko's were to go out of business, the sale of its assets would bring in $150,000 in cash.

▎Required

1. Prepare the Kinko's Division's income statement for the year ended December 31, 20X5. (pp. 43–44)

2. For items a through f, identify the accounting concept or principle that provides guidance in accounting for the item. State how you have applied the concept or principle in preparing Kinko's income statement.(pp. 48–49)

P1-44A (*Learning Objective 3: Using the accounting equation*) Compute the missing amount (?) for each company—amounts in millions. (pp. 43–47)

	Diamond Corp.	Lance Co.	Berger Inc.
Beginning		(In Millions)	
Assets..................................	$78	$30	$?
Liabilities	47	19	2
Common stock..................	6	1	2
Retained earnings..............	?	10	3
Ending			
Assets..................................	$?	$48	$9
Liabilities	48	30	?
Common stock..................	6	?	2
Retained earnings..............	29	?	?
Income statement			
Revenues............................	$218	$?	$20
Expenses	211	144	?
Net income.........................	?	?	?
Statement of retained earnings			
Beginning RE	$25	$10	$ 3
+ Net income.......................	?	9	1
– Dividends..........................	(3)	(2)	(0)
= Ending RE.........................	$29	$17	$ 4

Which company has the
• Highest net income?
• Highest percent of net income to revenues?

P1-45A (*Learning Objective 2, 5: Balance sheet*) Danielle Stone, the manager of **Image Runner, Inc.**, prepared the company's balance sheet while the accountant was ill. The balance sheet contains some errors. In particular, Stone knew that the balance sheet should balance, so she plugged in the stockholders' equity amount needed to achieve this balance. The stockholders' equity amount is *not* correct. All other amounts are accurate.

Image Runner, Inc.
Balance Sheet
Month Ended October 31, 20X8

Assets		Liabilities	
Cash..	$ 9,100	Notes receivable......................	$ 14,000
Equipment...............................	36,700	Interest expense.....................	2,000
Accounts payable	3,000	Office supplies........................	800
Utilities expense	2,100	Accounts receivable................	2,600
Advertising expense................	300	Note payable...........................	50,000
Land..	80,500	Total	69,400
Salary expense.........................	3,300	**Stockholders' Equity**	
		Stockholders' equity	65,600
Total assets..............................	**$135,000**	Total liabilities	**$135,000**

I Required

1. Prepare the correct balance sheet and date it properly. Compute total assets, total liabilities, and stockholders' equity. (pp. 46–47)

2. Is Image Runner actually in better (or worse) financial position than the erroneous balance sheet reports? Give the reason for your answer. (Challenge)

3. Identify the accounts listed on the incorrect balance sheet that should not be reported on the balance sheet. State why you excluded them from the correct balance sheet you prepared for Requirement 1. On which financial statement should these accounts appear? (pp. 43–44)

P1-46A (*Learning Objective 2, 5: Balance sheet, entity concept*) Heather Hutchison is a realtor. She organized the business as a corporation on March 10, 2008. The business received $50,000 cash from Hutchison and issued common stock. Consider the following facts as of March 31, 2008:

    a. Hutchison has $9,000 in her personal bank account and $16,000 in the business bank account.

    b. Office supplies on hand at the real estate office total $1,000.

    c. Hutchison's business spent $35,000 for a **Keller Williams** franchise, which entitles her to represent herself as an agent. Keller Williams is a national affiliation of independent real estate agents. This franchise is a business asset.

    d. Hutchison's business owes $33,000 on a note payable for some land acquired for a total price of $100,000.

    e. Hutchison owes $65,000 on a personal mortgage on her personal residence, which she acquired in 2002 for a total price of $190,000.

    f. Hutchison owes $300 on a personal charge account with **Sears**.

    g. Hutchison acquired business furniture for $18,000 on March 26. Of this amount, Hutchison's business owes $6,000 on accounts payable at March 31.

I Required

1. Prepare the balance sheet of the real estate business of Heather Hutchison, Realtor, Inc., at March 31, 2008. (pp. 46–47)

2. Does it appear that Hutchison's business can pay its debts? How can you tell? (Challenge)

(*continued*)

3. Identify the personal items given in the preceding facts that should not be reported on the balance sheet of the business. (pp. 46–47)

■ spreadsheet

P1-47A (*Learning Objective 5: Income statement, statement of retained earnings, balance sheet*) The assets and liabilities of Post Oak, Inc., as of December 31, 20X7, and revenues and expenses for the year ended on that date are listed here.

Land	$ 8,000	Equipment	$ 31,000
Note payable	31,000	Interest expense	4,000
Property tax expense	2,000	Interest payable	1,000
Rent expense	14,000	Accounts payable	12,000
Accounts receivable	25,000	Salary expense	34,000
Service revenue	140,000	Building	126,000
Supplies	2,000	Cash	14,000
Utilities expense	3,000	Common stock	10,000

Beginning retained earnings was $111,000, and dividends totaled $42,000 for the year.

❙ Required

1. Prepare the income statement of Post Oak, Inc., for the year ended December 31, 20X7. (pp. 43–44)
2. Prepare the company's statement of retained earnings for the year. (pp. 45–46)
3. Prepare the company's balance sheet at December 31, 20X7. (pp. 46–47)
4. Analyze Post Oak by answering these questions: (Challenge)

   a. Was Post Oak profitable during 20X7? By how much?
   b. Did retained earnings increase or decrease? By how much?
   c. Which is greater, total liabilities or total equity? Who owns more of Post Oak's assets, creditors of the company or the Post Oak stockholders?

P1-48A (*Learning Objective 4: Preparing a statement of cash flows*) The following data come from the financial statements of Kawasaki, Inc., at the end of a recent year (in millions):

Other investing cash payments	$ 200	Purchases of property, plant, and equipment	$ 3,300
Accounts receivable	900	Net income	3,000
Payment of dividends	300	Adjustments to reconcile	
Common stock	5,500	net income to cash	
Issuance of common stock	200	provided by operations	2,900
Sales of property, plant, and equipment	100	Revenues	53,500
		Cash, beginning of year	200
Retained earnings	12,700	end of year	2,600
Cost of goods sold	37,400		

❙ Required

1. Prepare Kawasaki's statement of cash flows for the year ended January 31, 20X3. Follow the format of the summary problem starting on page 55. Not all items given are reported on the statement of cash flows. (pp. 49–50)
2. What was Kawasaki's largest source of cash? Is this a sign of financial strength or weakness? (Challenge)

P1-49A (*Learning Objective 4, 5: Analyzing a company's financial statements*) Summarized versions of Gonzales Company's financial statements are given for 2 recent years.

	20X5	20X4
Income Statement		
Revenues...	$ k	$15,400
Cost of goods sold...	11,000	a
Other expenses..	1,200	1,100
Income before income taxes	900	1,400
Income taxes (40% in 20X5)	l	100
Net income...	$ m	$ b
Statement of Retained Earnings		
Beginning balance	n	$ 2,700
Net income..	o	c
Dividends..	(60)	(50)
Ending balance..	$ p	$ d
Balance Sheet		
Assets:		
Cash...	$ q	$ e
Property, plant, and equipment...........................	1,500	1,700
Other assets...	r	10,100
Total assets	$ s	$12,870
Liabilities:		
Current liabilities	$ t	$ 5,400
Notes payable and long-term debt.......................	2,500	3,100
Other liabilities	70	70
Total liabilities..	$ 8,300	$ f
Shareholders' Equity:		
Common stock...	$ 100	$ 100
Retained earnings..	u	g
Other shareholders' equity	180	250
Total shareholders' equity	v	4,300
Total liabilities and shareholders' equity	$ w	$ h
Statement of Cash Flows		
Net cash provided by operating activities...............	$ x	$ 500
Net cash provided by investing activities................	60	400
Net cash used for financing activities	(700)	(1,000)
Increase (decrease) in cash...................................	310	i
Cash at beginning of year.................................	y	1,170
Cash at end of year	$ z	$ j

I Required

Complete Gonzales' financial statements by determining the missing amounts denoted by the letters. (pp. 43–50)

(Group B)

P1-50B (*Learning Objective 1, 2, 4, 5: Applying accounting vocabulary, concepts, and principles to the income statement*) ABM Corporation experienced the following transactions during the year ended December 31, 20X8:

writing assignment ■

    a. ABM sold products for $53 billion. Company management believes the value of these products is approximately $80 billion. Other revenues totaled $40 billion.

(continued)

b. It cost ABM $36 billion to manufacture the products ABM sold. If ABM had purchased the products instead of manufacturing them, ABM's cost would have been $42 billion.

c. All other expenses, excluding income taxes, totaled $27 billion for the year. Income tax expense was 40% of income before tax.

d. ABM has several operating divisions. Each division is accounted for separately to show how well each division is performing. At year end, ABM combines the statements of all the divisions to report on the company as a whole.

e. Inflation affects ABM's cost to manufacture goods. To show the effects of inflation, the company's net income would drop by $3 billion.

f. If ABM were to go out of business, the sale of company assets should bring in $65 billion in cash.

❚ Required

1. Prepare ABM Corporation's income statement for the year ended December 31, 20X8. (pp. 43–44)

2. For items a through f, identify the accounting concept or principle that tells how to account for the item described. State how you have applied the concept or principle in preparing ABM's income statement. (pp. 38–39)

P1-51B (*Learning Objective 3: Using the accounting equation*) Compute the missing amount (?) for each company—amounts in millions. (pp. 43–47)

	Samurai, Inc.	Peking Co.	Osaka Corp.
		(In Millions)	
Beginning			
Assets.................................	$300	$?	$35
Liabilities	200	10	?
Common stock..................	30	4	8
Retained earnings..............	?	6	10
Ending			
Assets.................................	$?	$24	$36
Liabilities	210	?	17
Common stock..................	30	4	?
Retained earnings..............	100	8	11
Income statement			
Revenues............................	$220	$19	$?
Expenses	180	?	55
Net income........................	?	?	?
Statement of retained earnings			
Beginning RE	$ 70	$ 6	$10
+ Net income.......................	?	5	6
– Dividends..........................	(10)	(3)	?
= Ending RE.........................	$100	$ 8	$11

Which company has the
- Highest net income?
- Highest percent of net income to revenues?

P1-52B (*Learning Objective 2, 5: Balance sheet:*) The manager of Upod, Inc., prepared the balance sheet of the company while the accountant was ill. The balance sheet contains numerous errors. In particular, the manager knew that the balance sheet should balance so he plugged in the stockholders' equity amount needed to achieve this balance. The stockholders' equity amount, however, is *not* correct. All other amounts are accurate.

UPod, Inc.
Balance Sheet
Month Ended July 31, 20X7

Assets		Liabilities	
Cash	$11,000	Accounts payable	$12,000
Office furniture	10,000	Service revenue	50,000
Note payable	16,000	Property tax expense	800
Rent expense	4,000	Accounts payable	5,000
Office supplies	1,000	Total	67,800
Land	44,000	**Stockholders' Equity**	
Advertising expense	2,500	Stockholders' equity	20,700
Total assets	$88,500	Total liabilities	$88,500

Required

1. Prepare the correct balance sheet and date it properly. Compute total assets, total liabilities, and stockholders' equity. (pp. 46–47)
2. Is Upod, Inc., actually in better (or worse) financial position than the erroneous balance sheet reports? Give the reason for your answer. (Challenge)
3. Identify the preceding accounts that should *not* be reported on the balance sheet. State why you excluded them from the correct balance sheet you prepared for Requirement 1. Which financial statement should these accounts appear on? (pp. 43–44)

P1-53B (*Learning Objective 2, 5: Balance sheet, entity concept*) Linda Shriber is a realtor. Shriber organized her business as a corporation on November 14, 2009. The business received $50,000 from Shriber and issued common stock. Consider these facts as of November 30, 2009:

a. Shriber has $10,000 in her personal bank account and $42,000 in the business bank account.
b. Shriber owes $1,800 on a personal charge account with **Macy's**.
c. The business bought furniture for $17,000 on November 25. Of this amount, the business owes $6,000 on accounts payable at November 30.
d. Office supplies on hand at the real estate office total $1,000.
e. The business owes $40,000 on a note payable for some land acquired for a total price of $120,000.
f. The business spent $20,000 for a **Coldwell Banker** real estate franchise, which entitles Shriber to represent herself as a Coldwell Banker agent. Coldwell Banker is a national affiliation of independent real estate agents. This franchise is a business asset.
g. Shriber owes $100,000 on a personal mortgage on her personal residence, which she acquired in 2004 for a total price of $160,000.

Required

1. Prepare the balance sheet of the real estate business of Linda Shriber, Realtor, Inc., at November 30, 2009. (pp. 46–47)
2. Does it appear that Shriber's realty business can pay its debts? How can you tell? (Challenge)
3. Identify the personal items given in the preceding facts that should not be reported on the balance sheet of the business. (pp. 46–47)

P1-54B (*Learning Objective 5: Income statement, statement of retained earnings, balance sheet*) The assets and liabilities of HD Radio Corporation as of December 31, 20X8, and revenues and expenses for the year ended on that date follow.

■ spreadsheet

(continued)

Property tax expense......	$ 4,000	Land..............................	$ 78,000
Accounts receivable........	12,000	Note payable..................	85,000
Advertising expense........	13,000	Accounts payable	19,000
Building..........................	50,000	Rent expense	23,000
Salary expense................	63,000	Cash................................	10,000
Salary payable................	1,000	Common stock................	40,000
Service revenue..............	180,000	Furniture........................	20,000
Supplies..........................	3,000	Interest expense..............	9,000

Beginning retained earnings were $10,000, and dividends totaled $50,000 for the year.

▌Required

1. Prepare the income statement of HD Radio Corporation for the year ended December 31, 20X8. (pp. 43–44)
2. Prepare HD Radio's statement of retained earnings for the year. (pp. 45–46)
3. Prepare HD Radio's balance sheet at December 31, 20X8. (pp. 46–47)
4. Analyze HD Radio Corporation by answering these questions: (Challenge)

   a. Was HD Radio profitable during 20X8? By how much?
   b. Did retained earnings increase or decrease? By how much?
   c. Which is greater, total liabilities or total equity? Who owns more of HD Radio's assets, creditors of the company or the HD Radio stockholders?

P1-55B (*Learning Objective 4: Preparing a statement of cash flows*) The following data are taken from the financial statements of Armstrong Company at the end of 2008 (in millions).

▌Required

Sales of property, plant, and equipment	$ 20	Revenues	$9,100
		Cash, beginning of year.........	200
Adjustments to reconcile net income to net cash provided by operating activities....	(400)	end of year	300
		Purchases of property plant, and equipment	500
Cost of goods sold..........................	5,500	Long-term debt	200
Other investing cash receipts...	80	Net income...........................	700
		Payment of dividends	170
Accounts receivable..........................	1,700	Common stock......................	2,800
Retained earnings..........................	2,900	Issuance of common stock.....	370

1. Prepare Armstrong Company's statement of cash flows for the year ended December 31, 2008. Follow the solution of the summary problem starting on page 55. Not all the items given appear on the statement of cash flows. (pp. 49–50)
2. Which activities provided the largest amount of Armstrong's cash? Is this a sign of financial strength or weakness? (Challenge)

P1-56B (*Learning Objective 4, 5: Analyzing a company's financial statements*) Condensed versions of Mobile Phone Enterprises' financial statements follow for 2 recent years.

	20X6	20X5
Income Statement		
Revenues	$ k	$88,400
Cost of goods sold	74,500	a
Other expenses	15,800	13,500
Income before income taxes	4,000	9,200
Income taxes (40% in 20X6)	l	1,500
Net income	$ m	$ b
Statement of Retained Earnings		
Beginning balance	n	$ 9,900
Net income	o	c
Dividends	(500)	(400)
Ending balance	$ p	$ d
Balance Sheet		
Assets:		
Cash	$ q	$ e
Property, plant, and equipment	23,800	20,800
Other assets	r	16,500
Total assets	$ s	$37,600
Liabilities:		
Current liabilities	$ t	$ 9,900
Long-term debt and other liabilities	11,300	10,100
Total liabilities	22,700	f
Shareholders' Equity:		
Common stock	$ 200	$ 200
Retained earnings	u	g
Other shareholders' equity	100	200
Total shareholders' equity	v	17,600
Total liabilities and shareholders' equity	$ w	$ h
Statement of Cash Flows		
Net cash provided by operating activities	$ x	$ 2,900
Net cash used for investing activities	(3,300)	(3,700)
Net cash provided by financing activities	900	900
Increase (decrease) in cash	100	i
Cash at beginning of year	y	200
Cash at end of year	$ z	$ j

❚ *Required*

Complete Mobile Phone Enterprises' financial statements by determining the missing amounts denoted by the letters. (pp. 43–50)

APPLY YOUR KNOWLEDGE

Decision Cases

Case 1. (*Learning Objective 1, 2: Using financial statements to evaluate a loan request*)
Two businesses, Open Skies Corp., and Roadster, Inc., have sought business loans from you. To decide whether to make the loans, you have requested their balance sheets.

(*continued*)

Open Skies Corp.
Balance Sheet
August 31, 2005

Assets		Liabilities	
Cash..............................	$ 10,000	Accounts payable	$100,000
Accounts receivable..............	20,000	Notes payable	160,000
Furniture.............................	30,000	Total liabilities	260,000
Land....................................	150,000	**Owners' Equity**	
Equipment............................	90,000	Owners' equity..................	40,000
		Total liabilities and	
Total assets...........................	$300,000	owners' equity..................	$300,000

Roadster, Inc.
Balance Sheet
August 31, 2005

Assets		Liabilities	
Cash..............................	$ 10,000	Accounts payable	$ 12,000
Accounts receivable....................	20,000	Note payable...........................	18,000
Merchandise inventory..............	30,000	Total liabilities	30,000
Building.................................	70,000	**Stockholders' Equity**	
		Stockholders' equity................	100,000
		Total liabilities and	
Total assets...............................	$130,000	stockholders' equity..............	$130,000

❚ Required

Using only these balance sheets, to which entity would you be more comfortable lending money? Explain fully, citing specific items and amounts from the respective balance sheets. (Challenge)

Case 2. (*Learning Objective 2, 4, 5: Analyzing a company as an investment*) A year out of college, you have $5,000 to invest. A friend has started Sweepstakes Unlimited, Inc., and she asks you to invest in her company. You obtain the company's financial statements, which are summarized at the end of the first year as follows:

Sweepstakes Unlimited, Inc.
Income Statement
Year Ended Dec. 31, 20X4

Revenues...................	$50,000
Expenses	40,000
Net income...............	$10,000

Sweepstakes Unlimited, Inc.
Balance Sheet
Dec. 31, 20X4

Cash........................	$ 3,000	Liabilities	$30,000
Other assets.............	50,000	Equity	23,000
		Total liabilities	
Total assets..............	$53,000	and equity	$53,000

Visits with your friend turn up the following facts:
   a. Revenues and receivables of $20,000 were overlooked and omitted.

    b. Software costs of $25,000 were recorded as assets. These costs should have been expenses. Sweepstakes Unlimited paid cash for these expenses and recorded the cash payment correctly.

    c. The company owes an additional $5,000 for accounts payable.

❙ Required

1. Prepare corrected financial statements. (pp. 43–47)

2. Use your corrected statements to evaluate Sweepstakes Unlimited's results of operations and financial position. (Challenge)

3. Will you invest in Sweepstakes Unlimited? Give your reason. (Challenge)

Ethical Issue

During 2002, **Enron Corporation** admitted hiding large liabilities from its balance sheet. **WorldCom** confessed to recording expenses as assets. Both companies needed to improve their appearance as reported in their financial statements.

❙ Required

1. What is the fundamental ethical issue in these situations?

2. Use the accounting equation to show how Enron abused good accounting. Use a separate accounting equation to demonstrate WorldCom's error.

3. What can happen when companies report finacial data that are untrue?

Focus on Financials: ■ YUM! Brands

(*Learning Objective 4: Identifying items from a company's financial statements*) This and similar cases in succeeding chapters are based on the financial statements of YUM! Brands, Inc. As you work with YUM! Brands throughout this course, you will develop the ability to use the financial statements of actual companies.

❙ Required

Refer to the YUM! Brands' financial statements in Appendix A at the end of the book.

1. Suppose you own stock in YUM. If you could pick 1 item on the company's income statement to increase year after year, what would it be? Why is this item so important? Did this item increase or decrease during 2006? Is this good news or bad news for the company? (pp. 44–45)

2. What was YUM's largest expense each year? In your own words, explain the meaning of this item. Give specific examples of items that make up this expense. The chapter gives another title for this expense. What is it? (pp. 44–45)

3. Use the balance sheet of YUM in Appendix A to answer these questions: At the end of 2006, how much in total resources did YUM have to work with? How much did the company owe? How much of its assets did the company's stockholders actually own? Use these amounts to write YUM's accounting equation at December 30, 2006. (pp. 44–45)

4. How much cash did YUM have at the beginning of the most recent year? How much cash did YUM have at the end of the year? (pp. 46–47)

Focus on Analysis: ■ Pier 1 Imports

(*Learning Objective 3, 4: Evaluating a leading company*) This and similar cases in each chapter are based on the financial statements of Pier 1 Imports, Inc., given in Appendix B at the end of this book. As you work with Pier 1, you will develop the ability to analyze the financial statements of actual companies.

❙ *Required*

1. Write Pier 1's accounting equation at the end of 2006 (express all items in millions and round to the nearest $1 million). Does Pier 1's financial condition look strong or weak? How can you tell? (pp. 40–41)

2. What was the result of Pier 1's operations during 2006? Identify both the name and the dollar amount of the result of operations for 2006. Does an increase (decrease) signal good news or bad news for the company and its stockholders? (pp. 45–46)

3. Examine retained earnings on the balance sheet and on the statement of stockholders' equity. What caused retained earnings to decrease during 2006? (pp. 45–46)

4. Which statement reports cash as part of Pier 1's financial position? Which statement tells *why* cash increased (or decreased) during the year? What 2 individual items caused Pier 1's cash to increase the most during 2006? (pp. 46–50)

Group Projects

Project 1. As instructed by your professor, obtain the annual report of a well-known company.

❙ *Required*

1. Take the role of a loan committee of Charter Bank, a large banking company headquartered in Charlotte, North Carolina. Assume the company has requested a loan from Charter Bank. Analyze the company's financial statements and any other information you need to reach a decision regarding the largest amount of money you would be willing to lend. Go as deeply into the analysis and the related decision as you can. Specify the following:
   a. The length of the loan period—that is, over what period will you allow the company to pay you back?
   b. The interest rate you will charge on the loan. Will you charge the prevailing interest rate, a lower rate, or a higher rate? Why?
   c. Any restrictions you will impose on the borrower as a condition for making the loan.

   Note: The long-term debt note to the financial statements gives details of the company's existing liabilities.

2. Write your group decision in a report addressed to the bank's board of directors. Limit your report to 2 double-spaced word-processed pages.

3. If your professor directs, present your decision and your analysis to the class. Limit your presentation to 10 to 15 minutes.

Project 2. You are the owner of a company that is about to "go public"—that is, issue its stock to outside investors. You wish to make your company look as attractive as possible to raise $1 million of cash to expand the business. At the same time, you want to give potential investors a realistic picture of your company.

❙ *Required*

1. Design a booklet to portray your company in a way that will enable outsiders to reach an informed decision as to whether to buy some of your stock. The booklet should include the following:
   a. Name and location of your company.
   b. Nature of the company's business (be as detailed as possible).
   c. How you plan to spend the money you raise.
   d. The company's comparative income statement, statement of retained earnings, balance sheet, and statement of cash flows for 2 years: the current year and the preceding year. Make the data as realistic as possible with the intent of receiving $1 million.

2. Word-process your booklet, not to exceed 5 pages.

3. If directed by your professor, make a copy for each member of your class. Distribute copies to the class and present your case with the intent of interesting your classmates in investing in the company. Limit your presentation to 10 to 15 minutes.

For Internet Exercises go to the Web site www.prenhall.com/harrison.

Quick Check Answers

1. *b*
2. *a*
3. *d*
4. *c*
5. *d*
6. *a*
7. *b* *($100,000 – $40,000 – $3,000 = $57,000)*
8. *c* *($100,000 – $40,000 = $60,000)*
9. *c* *Total assets = $105,000 ($5,000 + $30,000 + $20,000 + $50,000). Liabilities = $25,000.*
10. *d*
11. *d* *$30,000 + Net income ($15,000) – Dividends = $40,000; Dividends = $5,000*
12. *b*

	Assets	=	Liabilities	+	Equity
Beginning	$300,000	=	$200,000*	+	$100,000
Increase	50,000	=	40,000	+	10,000*
Ending	$350,000*	=	$240,000*	+	$110,000*

*Must solve for these amounts.

2 Transaction Analysis

APPLE COMPUTER, INC.

How do you manage your music library? You may use **Apple Computer's iTunes**®, which along with the company's iPods® generates lots of income for the company.

How does Apple determine the amount of its revenues, expenses, and net income? Like all other companies, Apple Computer has a comprehensive accounting system. Apple's income statement (statement of operations) is given at the start of this chapter. The income statement shows that during fiscal year 2006, Apple made over $19 billion of sales and earned net income of $2 billion. Where did those figures come from? In this chapter, we'll show you.

Apple Computer, Inc.
Statement of Operations (Adapted)
Fiscal Year Ended September 30, 2006

(In billions)	2006
Net sales	$19.3
Cost of goods sold	13.7
Gross profit	5.6
Operating expenses:	
Research and development expense	0.7
Selling, general, and administrative expense	2.4
Total operating expenses	3.1
Operating income (loss)	2.5
Other income	0.3
Income before income taxes	2.8
Income tax expense	0.8
Net income	$ 2.0

Chapter 1 introduced the financial statements. Chapter 2 will show you how companies actually record the transactions that eventually become part of the financial statements.

LEARNING OBJECTIVES

1 **Analyze** transactions

2 **Understand** how accounting works

3 **Record** transactions in the journal

4 **Use** a trial balance

5 **Analyze** transactions using only T-accounts

For more practice and review of accounting cycle concepts, use ACT, the Accounting Cycle Tutorial, online at www.prenhall.com/harrison. Margin logos like this one, directing you to the appropriate ACT section and material, appear throughout Chapters 1, 2, and 3. When you enter the tutorial, you'll find three buttons on the opening page of each chapter module. Here's what the buttons mean: **Tutorial** gives you a review of the major concepts, **Application** gives you practice exercises, and **Glossary** reviews important terms.

TRANSACTIONS

Business activity is all about transactions. A **transaction** is any event that has a financial impact on the business and can be measured reliably. For example, Apple Computer pays programmers to create iTunes® software. Apple sells computers, borrows money, and repays the loan—three separate transactions.

But not all events qualify as transactions. iTunes® may be featured in *Showtime Magazine* and motivate you to buy an Apple iPod. The magazine article may create lots of new business for Apple. But no transaction occurs until someone actually buys an Apple product. A transaction must occur before Apple records anything.

Transactions provide objective information about the financial impact on a company. Every transaction has two sides:

- You give something, and
- You receive something

In accounting we always record both sides of a transaction. And we must be able to measure the financial impact of the event on the business before recording it as a transaction.

THE ACCOUNT

As we saw in Chapter 1, the accounting equation expresses the basic relationships of accounting:

$$\text{Assets} = \text{Liabilities} + \text{Stockholders' (Owners') Equity}$$

For each asset, each liability, and each element of stockholders' equity, we use a record called the account. An **account** is the record of all the changes in a particular asset, liability, or stockholders' equity during a period. The account is the basic summary device of accounting. Before launching into transaction analysis, let's review the accounts that a company such as Apple Computer uses.

Assets

Assets are economic resources that provide a future benefit for a business. Most firms use the following asset accounts:

Cash. **Cash** means money and any medium of exchange including bank account balances, paper currency, coins, certificates of deposit, and checks.

Accounts Receivable. Apple Computer, like most other companies, sells its goods and services and receives a promise for future collection of cash. The Accounts Receivable account holds these amounts.

Notes Receivable. Apple may receive a note receivable from a customer, who signed the note promising to pay Apple Computer. A note receivable is similar to an account receivable, but a note receivable is more binding because the customer signed the note. Notes receivable usually specify an interest rate.

Inventory. Apple Computer's most important asset is its inventory—the hardware and software Apple sells to customers. Other titles for this account include *Merchandise* and *Merchandise Inventory.*

Prepaid Expenses. Apple Computer pays certain expenses in advance, such as insurance and rent. A **prepaid expense** is an asset because the payment provides a *future* benefit for the business. Prepaid Rent, Prepaid Insurance, and Supplies are prepaid expenses.

Land. The Land account shows the cost of the land Apple uses in its operations.

Buildings. The costs of Apple's office building, manufacturing plant, and the like appear in the Buildings account.

Equipment, Furniture, and Fixtures. Apple has a separate asset account for each type of equipment, for example, Manufacturing Equipment and Office Equipment. The Furniture and Fixtures account shows the cost of these assets, which are similar to equipment.

Liabilities

Recall that a *liability* is a debt. A payable is always a liability. The most common types of liabilities include:

Accounts Payable. The Accounts Payable account is the direct opposite of Accounts Receivable. Apple's promise to pay a debt arising from a credit purchase of inventory or from a utility bill appears in the Accounts Payable account.

Notes Payable. A note payable is the opposite of a note receivable. The Notes Payable account includes the amounts Apple must *pay* because Apple signed notes promising to pay a future amount. Notes payable, like notes receivable, also carry interest.

Accrued Liabilities. An **accrued liability** is a liability for an expense you have not yet paid. Interest Payable and Salary Payable are accrued liability accounts for most companies. Income Tax Payable is another accrued liability.

Stockholders' (Owners') Equity

The owners' claims to the assets of a corporation are called *stockholders' equity, shareholders' equity*, or simply *owners' equity*. A corporation such as Apple Computer uses Common Stock, Retained Earnings, and Dividends accounts to record changes in the company's stockholders' equity. In a proprietorship, there is a single capital account. For a partnership, each partner has a separate owner equity account.

Common Stock. The Common Stock account shows the owners' investment in the corporation. Apple Computer receives cash and issues common stock to its stockholders. A company's common stock is its most basic element of equity. All corporations have common stock.

STOP & think. . .

Name two things that (1) increase Apple Computer's stockholders' equity and (2) decrease Apple's stockholders' equity.

Answer:
(1) Increases in equity: Sale of stock and net income (revenue greater than expenses).
(2) Decreases in equity: Dividends and net loss (expenses greater than revenue).

Retained Earnings. The Retained Earnings account shows the cumulative net income earned by Apple Computer over the company's lifetime, minus its cumulative net losses and dividends.

Dividends. After profitable operations, the board of directors of Apple Computer may (or may not) declare and pay a cash dividend. Dividends are optional; they are decided by the board of directors. The corporation may keep a separate account titled *Dividends*, which indicates a decrease in Retained Earnings.

Revenues. The increase in stockholders' equity from delivering goods or services to customers is called *revenue*. The company uses as many revenue accounts as needed. Apple Computer uses a Sales Revenue account for revenue earned by selling its products. Apple has a Service Revenue account for the revenue it earns by providing services to customers. A lawyer provides legal services for clients and also uses a Service Revenue account. A business that loans money to an outsider needs an Interest Revenue account. If the business rents a building to a tenant, the business needs a Rent Revenue account.

Expenses. The cost of operating a business is called *expense*. Expenses *decrease* stockholders' equity, the opposite effect of revenues. A business needs a separate account for each type of expense, such as Cost of Goods Sold, Salary Expense, Rent Expense, Advertising Expense, Insurance Expense, Utilities Expense, and Income Tax Expense. Businesses strive to minimize expenses and thereby maximize net income.

ACCOUNTING FOR BUSINESS TRANSACTIONS

Example: Super Beauty Salon (SBS), Inc.

To illustrate the accounting for transactions, let's return to SBS, Inc. In Chapter 1's End-of-Chapter Problem, Sandra Morris opened SBS, Inc., in June 20X9.

    We consider 11 events and analyze each in terms of its effect on SBS. We begin by using the accounting equation. In the second half of the chapter, we record transactions using the journal and ledger of accounting.

OBJECTIVE

1 Analyze transactions

Transaction 1. Morris and a few friends invest $60,000 to begin SBS and the business issues common stock to the stockholders. The effect of this transaction on the accounting equation of SBS, Inc., is a receipt of cash and issuance of common stock, as follows:

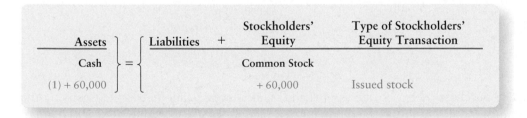

Assets		Liabilities	+	Stockholders' Equity	Type of Stockholders' Equity Transaction
Cash	=			Common Stock	
(1) + 60,000				+ 60,000	Issued stock

Every transaction's net amount on the left side of the equation must equal the net amount on the right side. The first transaction increases both the cash and the common stock of the business. To the right of the transaction we write "Issued stock" to show the reason for the increase in stockholders' equity.

Every transaction affects the financial statements of the business, and we can prepare financial statements after 1, 2, or any number of transactions. For example, SBS could report the company's balance sheet after its first transaction, shown here.

SBS, Inc.
Balance Sheet
June 1, 20X9

Assets		Liabilities	
Cash..........................	$60,000	None	
		Stockholders' Equity	
		Common stock...............................	$60,000
		Total stockholders' equity.............	60,000
		Total liabilities and	
Total assets................	$60,000	stockholders' equity......................	$60,000

This balance sheet shows that the business holds cash of $60,000 and owes no liabilities. The company's equity (ownership) is denoted as *Common Stock* on the balance sheet. A bank would look favorably on this balance sheet because the business has $60,000 cash and no debt—a strong financial position.

As a practical matter, most entities report their financial statements at the end of the accounting period—not after each transaction. But an accounting system can produce statements whenever managers need to know where the business stands.

Transaction 2. Super purchases land for a new location and pays cash of $40,000. The effect of this transaction on the accounting equation is:

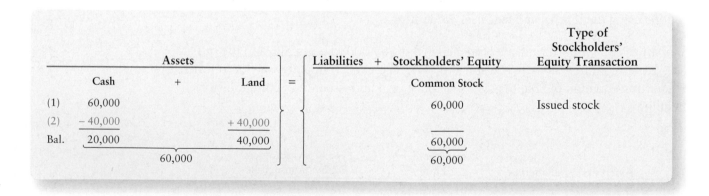

The purchase increases one asset (Land) and decreases another asset (Cash) by the same amount. After the transaction is completed, Super has cash of $20,000, land of $40,000 and no liabilities. Stockholders' equity is unchanged at $60,000. Note that total assets must always equal total liabilities plus equity.

Transaction 3. The business buys supplies on account, agreeing to pay $4,700 within 30 days. This transaction increases both the assets and the liabilities of the business. Its effect on the accounting equation follows.

	Assets				Liabilities	+	Stockholders' Equity
	Cash	+ Supplies	+ Land		Accounts Payable	+	Common Stock
Bal.	20,000		40,000				60,000
(3)		+ 4,700		=	+ 4,700		
Bal.	20,000	4,700	40,000		4,700		60,000
		64,700				64,700	

The new asset is Supplies, and the liability is an Account Payable. Super signs no formal promissory note, so the liability is an account payable, not a note payable.

Transaction 4. Super earns $7,000 of service revenue by providing services for customers. The business collects the cash. The effect on the accounting equation is an increase in the asset Cash and an increase in Retained Earnings, as follows:

	Assets				Liabilities	+	Stockholders' Equity		Type of Stockholders' Equity Transaction
	Cash	+ Supplies	+ Land		Accounts Payable	+	Common Stock	+ Retained Earnings	
Bal.	20,000	4,700	40,000		4,700		60,000		
(4)	+ 7,000			=				+ 7,000	Service revenue
Bal.	27,000	4,700	40,000		4,700		60,000	7,000	
		71,700					71,700		

To the right we record "Service revenue" to show where the $7,000 of increase in Retained Earnings came from.

Transaction 5. Super performs service on account, which means that Super lets some customers pay later. Super earns revenue but doesn't receive the cash immediately. In transaction 5, Super provides beauty services for a wedding party, and the customers promise to pay Super $2,000 within 1 month. This promise is an account receivable—an asset—of SBS. The transaction record follows.

	Assets					Liabilities	+	Stockholders' Equity		Type of Stockholders' Equity Transaction
	Cash	+ Receivable	+ Supplies	+ Land		Accounts Payable	+	Common Stock	+ Retained Earnings	
Bal.	27,000		4,700	40,000		4,700		60,000	7,000	
(5)		+ 2,000			=				+ 2,000	Service revenue
Bal.	27,000	2,000	4,700	40,000		4,700		60,000	9,000	
		73,700						73,700		

It's performing the service that earns the revenue—not collecting the cash. Therefore, Super records revenue when it performs the service—regardless of whether Super receives cash now or later.

Transaction 6. During the month, SBS pays $2,800 for the following expenses: insurance, $1,200; employee salaries, $1,000; and utilities, $600. The effect on the accounting equation is:

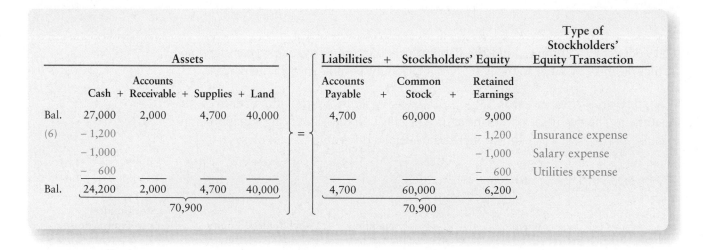

		Assets					Liabilities	+	Stockholders' Equity			Type of Stockholders' Equity Transaction
	Cash	+	Accounts Receivable	+	Supplies	+ Land		Accounts Payable	+	Common Stock	+ Retained Earnings	
Bal.	27,000		2,000		4,700	40,000	=	4,700		60,000	9,000	
(6)	− 1,200										− 1,200	Insurance expense
	− 1,000										− 1,000	Salary expense
	− 600										− 600	Utilities expense
Bal.	24,200		2,000		4,700	40,000		4,700		60,000	6,200	
			70,900							70,900		

The expenses decrease Super's Cash and Retained Earnings. List each expense separately to keep track of its amount.

Transaction 7. Super pays $1,900 on account, which means to pay off an account payable. In this transaction Super pays the store from which it purchased supplies in transaction 3. The transaction decreases Cash and also decreases Accounts Payable as follows:

			Assets							Liabilities	+	Stockholders' Equity		
	Cash	+	Accounts Receivable	+	Supplies	+	Land			Accounts Payable	+	Common Stock	+	Retained Earnings
Bal.	24,200		2,000		4,700		40,000	=		4,700		60,000		6,200
(7)	− 1,900									− 1,900				
Bal.	22,300		2,000		4,700		40,000			2,800		60,000		6,200
			69,000									69,000		

Transaction 8. Sandra Morris, the major stockholder of SBS, paid $30,000 to remodel her home. This event is a personal transaction of the Morris family. It is not recorded by the SBS business. We focus solely on the business entity, not on its owners. This transaction illustrates the entity concept from Chapter 1.

Transaction 9. In transaction 5, Super performed services for customers on account. The business now collects $1,500 from these customers. We say that Super *collects the cash on account*, which means that Super will record an increase in Cash and a decrease in Accounts Receivable. This is not service revenue because Super already recorded the revenue in transaction 5. The effect of collecting cash on account is:

| | Assets | | | | | Liabilities | + | Stockholders' Equity | |
	Cash	+	Accounts Receivable	+	Supplies	+	Land		Accounts Payable	+	Common Stock	+	Retained Earnings
Bal.	22,300		2,000		4,700		40,000	=	2,800		60,000		6,200
(9)	+ 1,500		− 1,500										
Bal.	23,800		500		4,700		40,000		2,800		60,000		6,200
			69,000								59,100		

Transaction 10. Super sells some land for $22,000, which is the same amount that Super paid for the land. Super receives $22,000 cash, and the effect on the accounting equation is:

| | Assets | | | | | | | | Liabilities | + | Stockholders' Equity | |
	Cash	+	Accounts Receivable	+	Supplies	+	Land		Accounts Payable	+	Common Stock	+	Retained Earnings
Bal.	23,800		500		4,700		40,000	=	2,800		60,000		6,200
(10)	+ 22,000						− 22,000						
Bal.	45,800		500		4,700		18,000		2,800		60,000		6,200
			69,000								69,000		

Note that the company did not sell all its land; Super still owns $18,000 worth of land.

Transaction 11. SBS declares a dividend and pays the stockholders $2,000 cash. The effect on the accounting equation is:

| | Assets | | | | Liabilities | + | Stockholders' Equity | | | Type of Stockholders' Equity Transaction |
	Cash	+ Receivable	+ Supplies	+ Land	Accounts Payable	+	Common Stock	+	Retained Earnings	
Bal.	45,800	500	4,700	18,000	= 2,800		60,000		6,200	
(11)	− 2,000								− 2,000	Dividends
Bal.	43,800	500	4,700	18,000	2,800		60,000		4,200	
			67,000					67,000		

The dividend decreases both the Cash and the Retained Earnings of the business. *But dividends are not an expense.*

Transactions and Financial Statements

Exhibit 2-1 summarizes the 11 preceding transactions. Panel A gives the details of the transactions, and Panel B shows the transaction analysis. As you study the exhibit, note that every transaction maintains the equality:

Assets = Liabilities + Stockholders' Equity

Exhibit 2-1 provides the data for SBS's financial statements:

EXHIBIT 2-1 Transaction Analysis: SBS, Inc.

PANEL A—Transaction Details

(1) Received $60,000 cash and issued stock to the owners
(2) Paid $40,000 cash for land
(3) Bought $4,700 of supplies on account
(4) Received $7,000 cash from customers for service revenue earned
(5) Performed services for a customer on account, $2,000
(6) Paid cash expenses: insurance, $1,200; employee salary, $1,000; utilities, $600

(7) Paid $1,900 on the account payable created in transaction 3
(8) Major stockholder paid personal funds to remodel home, *not* a transaction of the business
(9) Received $1,500 on account
(10) Sold land for cash at the land's cost of $22,000
(11) Declared and paid a dividend of $2,000 to the stockholders

PANEL B—Transaction Analysis

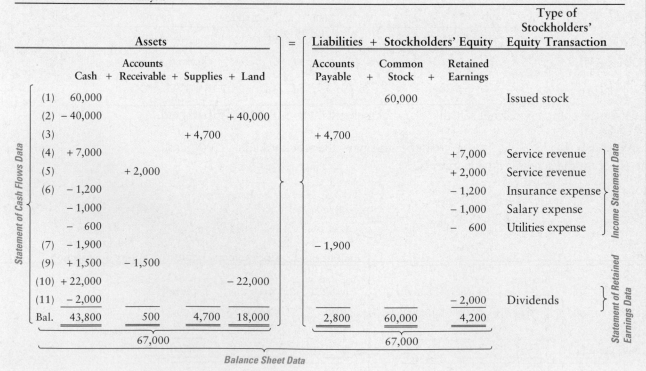

		Assets			=	Liabilities	+	Stockholders' Equity		Type of Stockholders' Equity Transaction
	Cash	Accounts Receivable	Supplies	Land		Accounts Payable	Common Stock	Retained Earnings		
(1)	60,000						60,000		Issued stock	
(2)	– 40,000			+ 40,000						
(3)			+ 4,700			+ 4,700				
(4)	+ 7,000							+ 7,000	Service revenue	
(5)		+ 2,000						+ 2,000	Service revenue	
(6)	– 1,200							– 1,200	Insurance expense	
	– 1,000							– 1,000	Salary expense	
	– 600							– 600	Utilities expense	
(7)	– 1,900					– 1,900				
(9)	+ 1,500	– 1,500								
(10)	+ 22,000			– 22,000						
(11)	– 2,000							– 2,000	Dividends	
Bal.	43,800	500	4,700	18,000		2,800	60,000	4,200		

Statement of Cash Flows Data

Income Statement Data

Statement of Retained Earnings Data

67,000 = 67,000

Balance Sheet Data

- *Income statement* data appear as revenues and expenses under Retained Earnings. The revenues increase retained earnings; the expenses decrease retained earnings.
- The *balance sheet* data are composed of the ending balances of the assets, liabilities, and stockholders' equities shown at the bottom of the exhibit. The accounting equation shows that total assets ($67,000) equal total liabilities plus stockholders' equity ($67,000).
- The *statement of retained earnings* repeats net income (or net loss) from the income statement. Dividends are subtracted. Ending retained earnings is the final result.
- Data for the *statement of cash flows* are aligned under the Cash account. Cash receipts increase cash, and cash payments decrease cash.

Exhibit 2-2 shows SBS financial statements at the end of April, the company's first month of operations. Follow the flow of data to observe the following:

1. The income statement reports revenues, expenses, and either a net income or a net loss for the period. During June, Super earned net income of $6,200. Compare Super's income statement with that of Apple Computer at the beginning of the chapter. The income statement includes only 2 types of accounts: revenues and expenses.

2. The statement of retained earnings starts with the beginning balance of retained earnings, (zero for a new business). Add net income for the period (arrow ①), subtract dividends, and compute the ending balance of retained earnings ($4,200).

3. The balance sheet lists the assets, liabilities, and stockholders' equity of the business at the end of the period. Included in stockholders' equity is retained earnings, which comes from the statement of retained earnings (arrow ②).

Let's put into practice what you have learned thus far.

EXHIBIT 2-2 Financial Statements of SBS, Inc.

SBS, Inc.
Income Statement
Month Ended June 30, 20X9

Revenues		
Service revenue ($7,000 + $3,000)		$9,000
Expenses		
Salary expense..	$1,200	
Insurance expense	1,000	
Utilities expense	600	
Total expenses..		2,800
Net income..		$ 6,200

①

SBS, Inc.
Statement of Retained Earnings
Month Ended June 30, 20X9

Retained earnings, June 1, 20X9..................	$ 0
Add: Net income for the month	6,200
	6,200
Less: Dividends	(2,000)
Retained earnings, June 30, 20X9................	$4,200

②

SBS, Inc.
Balance Sheet
June 30, 20X9

Assets		Liabilities	
Cash..	$43,800	Accounts payable	$ 2,800
Accounts receivable................	500	**Stockholders' Equity**	
Supplies....................................	4,700	Common stock................................	60,000
Land..	18,000	Retained earnings............................	4,200
		Total stockholders' equity.............	64,200
Total assets.............................		Total liabilities and	
	$67,000	stockholders' equity......................	$67,000

MID-CHAPTER SUMMARY PROBLEM

Dawn Blick opens a dog walking service. She names the corporation Walk Your Dog (WYD), Inc. During the first month of operations, May 20X3, the business engages in the following transactions:

a. WYD, Inc., issues its common stock to Dawn Blick, who invests $45,000 to open the business.
b. The company purchases on account office supplies costing $300.
c. WYD pays cash of $50,000 to acquire a lot next to the campus. The company intends to use the land as a building site for a dog park.
d. WYD performs research for clients and receives cash of $1,900.
e. WYD pays $200 on the account payable it created in transaction b.
f. WYD pays $2,000 of personal funds for a vacation.
g. WYD pays cash expenses for salaries ($500) and utilities ($200).
h. The business sells a small parcel of the land for its cost of $10,000.
i. The business declares and pays a cash dividend of $800.

∎ *Required*
1. Analyze the preceding transactions in terms of their effects on the accounting equation of WYD, Inc. Use Exhibit 2-1, Panel B as a guide.
2. Prepare the income statement, statement of retained earnings, and balance sheet of WYD, Inc., after recording the transactions. Draw arrows linking the statements.

Solutions
∎ *Requirement 1*

PANEL B—Analysis of Transactions

	Assets			=	Liabilities	+	Stockholders' Equity			Type of Stockholders' Equity Transaction
	Cash	+	Office Supplies	+	Land	Accounts Payable	+	Common Stock	+	Retained Earnings	
(a)	+ 45,000							+ 45,000			Issued stock
(b)			+ 300			+ 300					
(c)	− 40,000				+ 40,000						
(d)	+ 1,900									+ 1,900	Service revenue
(e)	− 200					− 200					
(f)	Not a transaction of the business										
(g)	− 500									− 500	Salary expense
	− 200									− 200	Utilities expense
(h)	+ 10,000				− 10,000						
(i)	− 800									− 800	Dividends
Bal.	15,200		300		30,000	100		45,000		400	
			45,500					45,500			

WYD, Inc.
Income Statement
Month Ended May 31, 20X3

Revenues		
Service revenue.................		$1,900
Expenses		
Salary expense.................	$500	
Utilities expense	200	
Total expenses.................		700
Net income................................		$1,200

WYD, Inc.
Statement of Retained Earnings
Month Ended May 31, 20X3

Retained earnings, May 1, 20X3...............	$	0
Add: Net income for the month		1,200
		1,200
Less: Dividends		(800)
Retained earnings, May 31, 20X3.............	$	400

WYD, Inc.
Balance Sheet
May 31, 20X3

Assets		Liabilities		
Cash...............................	$15,200	Accounts payable	$	100
Office supplies................	300	**Stockholders' Equity**		
Land..............................	30,000	Common stock.................................		45,000
		Retained earnings............................		400
		Total stockholders' equity.............		45,400
		Total liabilities and		
Total assets....................	$45,500	stockholders' equity......................		$45,500

The analysis in the first half of this chapter can be used, but it is cumbersome. Apple Computer has hundreds of accounts and millions of transactions. The spreadsheet to account for Apple's transactions would be huge! In the second half of this chapter we discuss double-entry accounting as it is actually used in business.

DOUBLE-ENTRY ACCOUNTING

All business transactions include 2 parts:

- You give something.
- You receive something.

Accounting is, therefore, based on a double-entry system, which records the *dual effects* on the entity. *Each transaction affects at least two accounts.* For example, SBS's receipt of $60,000 cash and issuance of stock increased both Cash and Common Stock. It would be incomplete to record only the increase in Cash or only the increase in Common Stock.

The T-Account

An account can be represented by the letter T. We call them *T-accounts.* The vertical line in the letter divides the account into its two sides: left and right. The account title appears at the top of the T. For example, the Cash account can appear as follows:

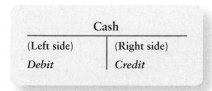

The left side of each account is called the **debit** side, and the right side is called the **credit** side. Often, students are confused by the words *debit* and *credit.* To become comfortable using these terms, remember that for every account

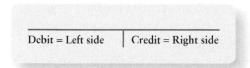

Every business transaction involves both a debit and a credit. The debit side of an account shows what you received. The credit side shows what you gave.

Increases and Decreases in the Accounts: The Rules of Debit and Credit

The type of account determines how we record increases and decreases. *The rules of debit and credit follow* in Exhibit 2-3.

- Increases in *assets* are recorded on the left (debit) side of the account. Decreases in *assets* are recorded on the right (credit) side. You receive cash and debit the Cash account. You pay cash and credit the Cash account.
- Conversely, increases in *liabilities* and *stockholders' equity* are recorded by credits. Decreases in *liabilities* and *stockholders' equity* are recorded by debits.

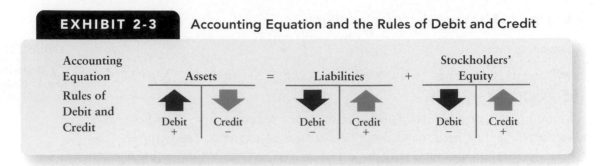

EXHIBIT 2-3 Accounting Equation and the Rules of Debit and Credit

To illustrate the ideas diagrammed in Exhibit 2-3, let's review the first transaction. SBS received $60,000 and issued (gave) stock. Which accounts are affected? The Cash account and the Common Stock account will hold these amounts:

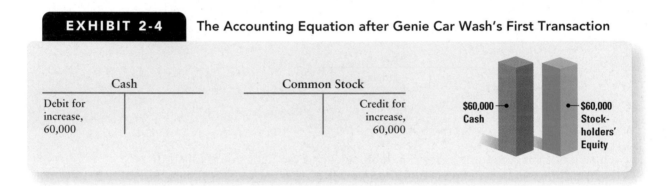

EXHIBIT 2-4 The Accounting Equation after Genie Car Wash's First Transaction

The amount remaining in an account is called its *balance*. This first transaction gives Cash a $60,000 debit balance and Common Stock a $60,000 credit balance. Exhibit 2-4 shows this relationship.

Super's second transaction is a $40,000 cash purchase of land. This transaction decreases Cash with a credit and increases Land with a debit, as shown in the following T-accounts (focus on Cash and Land):

	Cash				Common Stock	
Bal.	60,000	Credit for decrease, 40,000			Bal.	60,000
Bal.	20,000					

	Land	
Debit for increase, 40,000		
Bal.	40,000	

After this transaction, Cash has a $20,000 debit balance, Land has a debit balance of $40,000, and Common Stock has a $60,000 credit balance, as shown in Exhibit 2-5.

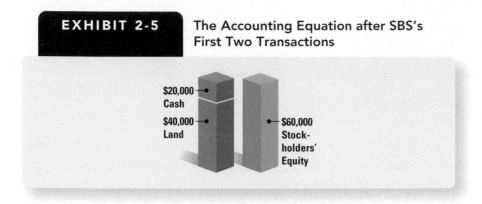

EXHIBIT 2-5 The Accounting Equation after SBS's First Two Transactions

Additional Stockholders' Equity Accounts: Revenues and Expenses

Stockholders' equity also includes the two categories of income statement accounts, Revenues and Expenses:

- *Revenues* are increases in stockholders' equity that result from delivering goods or services to customers.
- *Expenses* are decreases in stockholders' equity due to the cost of operating the business.

Therefore, the accounting equation may be expanded as shown in Exhibit 2-6. Revenues and expenses appear in parentheses because their net effect—revenues minus expenses—equals net income, which increases stockholders' equity. If expenses exceed revenues, there is a net loss, which decreases stockholders' equity.

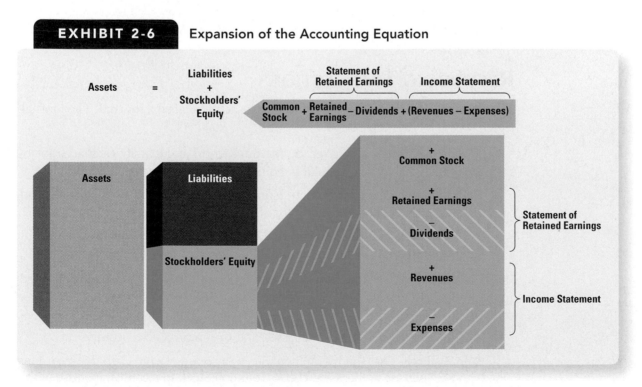

EXHIBIT 2-6 Expansion of the Accounting Equation

We can now express the final form of the rules of debit and credit, as shown in Exhibit 2-7. *You should not proceed until you have learned these rules.* For example, you must remember that

- A debit increases an asset account.
- A credit decreases an asset.

Liabilities and stockholders' equity are the opposite.

- A credit increases a liability account.
- A debit decreases a liability.

Dividends and Expense accounts are exceptions to the rule. Dividends and Expenses are equity accounts that are increased by a debit. Dividends and Expense accounts are negative (or *contra*) equity accounts.

Revenues and Expenses are often treated as separate account categories because they appear on the income statement. Exhibit 2-7 shows Revenues and Expenses below the other equity accounts.

EXHIBIT 2-7   **Final Form of the Rules of Debit and Credit**

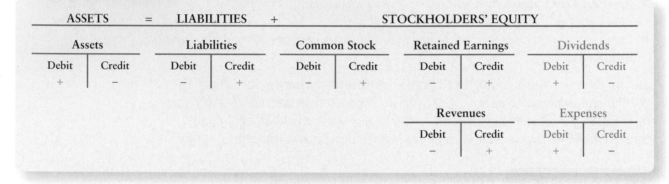

RECORDING TRANSACTIONS

OBJECTIVE

3 **Record** transactions in the journal

Accountants use a chronological record of transactions called a **journal**. The journalizing process follows three steps:

1. Specify each account affected by the transaction and classify each account by type (asset, liability, stockholders' equity, revenue, or expense).

2. Determine whether each account is increased or decreased by the transaction. Use the rules of debit and credit to increase or decrease each account.

3. Record the transaction in the journal, including a brief explanation. The debit side is entered on the left margin, and the credit side is indented to the right.

Step 3 is also called "making the journal entry" or "journalizing the transaction." Let's apply the steps to journalize the first transaction of SBS.

Step 1 The business receives cash and issues stock. Cash and Common Stock are affected. Cash is an asset, and Common Stock is equity.

Step 2 Both Cash and Common Stock increase. Debit Cash to record an increase in this asset. Credit Common Stock to record an increase in this equity account.

Step 3 Journalize the transaction as follows:

JOURNAL

Date	Accounts and Explanation	Debit	Credit
June 2	Cash	60,000	
	Common Stock		60,000
	Issued common stock.		

When analyzing a transaction, first pinpoint the effects (if any) on cash. Did cash increase or decrease? Typically, it is easiest to identify cash effects. Then identify the effects on the other accounts.

Copying Information (Posting) from the Journal to the Ledger

The journal is a chronological record of all company transactions listed by date. But the journal does not indicate how much cash or accounts receivable the business has.

The **ledger** is a grouping of all the T-accounts, with their balances. For example, the balance of the Cash T-account shows how much cash the business has. The balance of Accounts Receivable shows the amount due from customers. Accounts Payable shows how much the business owes suppliers on open account, and so on.

In the phrase "keeping the books," *books* refers to the accounts in the ledger. In most accounting systems, the ledger is computerized. Exhibit 2-8 shows how the asset, liability, and stockholders' equity accounts are grouped in the ledger.

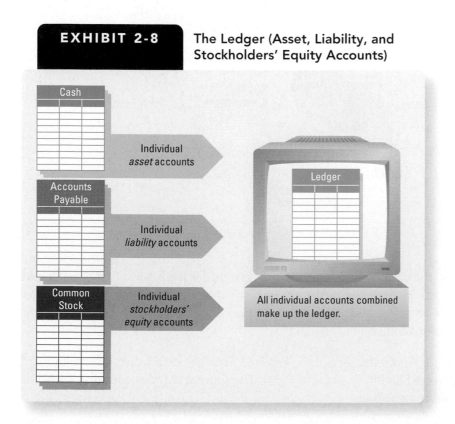

EXHIBIT 2-8 The Ledger (Asset, Liability, and Stockholders' Equity Accounts)

Entering a transaction in the journal does not get the data into the ledger. Data must be copied to the ledger—a process called **posting**. Debits in the journal are always posted as debits in the accounts, and likewise for credits. Exhibit 2-9 shows how SBS's stock issuance transaction is posted to the accounts.

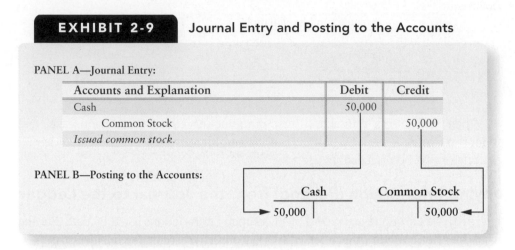

EXHIBIT 2-9   Journal Entry and Posting to the Accounts

PANEL A—Journal Entry:

Accounts and Explanation	Debit	Credit
Cash	50,000	
Common Stock		50,000
Issued common stock.		

PANEL B—Posting to the Accounts:

Cash	Common Stock
50,000	50,000

The Flow of Accounting Data

Exhibit 2-10 summarizes the flow of accounting data from the business transaction to the ledger.

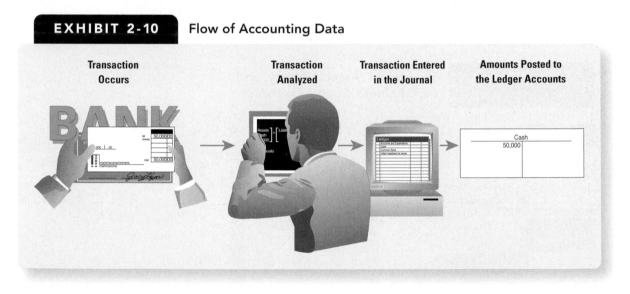

EXHIBIT 2-10   Flow of Accounting Data

Transaction Occurs	Transaction Analyzed	Transaction Entered in the Journal	Amounts Posted to the Ledger Accounts

Let's continue the example of SBS, Inc., and account for the same 11 transactions we illustrated earlier. Here we use the journal and the accounts. Each journal entry posted to the accounts is keyed by date or by transaction number. This linking allows you to locate any information you may need.

Transaction 1 Analysis.   SBS, Inc., received $60,000 cash from the stockholders and in turn issued common stock to them. The journal entry, accounting equation, and ledger accounts follow.

Journal entry	Cash		60,000	
	Common Stock			60,000
	Issued common stock.			

	Assets	=	Liabilities	+	Stockholders' Equity
Accounting equation	60,000	=	0	+	60,000

	Cash		Common Stock
The ledger accounts	(1) 60,000		(1) 60,000

Transaction 2 Analysis. The business paid $40,000 cash for land. The purchase decreased cash; therefore, credit Cash. The purchase increased the asset land; to record this increase, debit Land.

Journal entry	Land	40,000	
	Cash		40,000
	Paid cash for land.		

	Assets	=	Liabilities	+	Stockholders' Equity
Accounting equation	+ 50,000	=	0	+	0
	− 40,000				

	Cash		Land
The ledger accounts	(1) 60,000 | (2) 40,000	(2) 40,000	

Transaction 3 Analysis. The business purchased supplies for $4,700 on account payable. The purchase increased supplies, an asset, and Accounts Payable, a liability.

Journal entry	Supplies	4,700	
	Accounts Payable		4,700
	Purchased office supplies on account.		

	Assets	=	Liabilities	+	Stockholders' Equity
Accounting equation	+ 4,700	=	+ 4,700	+	0

	Supplies		Accounts Payable
The ledger accounts	(3) 4,700		(3) 4,700

Transaction 4 Analysis. The business performed services for clients and received cash of $7,000. The transaction increased cash and service revenue. To record the revenue, credit Service Revenue.

Journal entry	Cash	7,000
	Service Revenue	7,000
	Performed services for cash.	

Accounting equation

Assets	=	Liabilities	+	Stockholders' Equity	+	Revenues
+ 7,000	=	0			+	7,000

The ledger accounts

Cash				Service Revenue	
(1)	60,000	(2)	40,000	(4)	7,000
(4)	7,000				

Transaction 5 Analysis. Super performed services for customers on account. The customers did not pay immediately, so Super billed them for $2,000. The transaction increased accounts receivable; therefore, debit Accounts Receivable. Service revenue also increased, so credit the Service Revenue account.

Journal entry	Accounts Receivable	2,000
	Service Revenue	2,000
	Performed services on account.	

Accounting equation

Assets	=	Liabilities	+	Stockholders' Equity	+	Revenues
+ 2,000	=	0			+	2,000

The ledger accounts

Accounts Receivable		Service Revenue	
(5) 2,000		(4)	7,000
		(5)	2,000

Transaction 6 Analysis. The business paid $2,800 for the following expenses: insurance, $1,200; employee salary, $1,000; and utilities, $600. Credit Cash for the sum of the expense amounts. The expenses increased, so debit each expense account separately.

Journal entry	Insurance Expense	1,200
	Salary Expense	1,000
	Utilities Expense	600
	Cash	2,800
	Paid expenses.	

	Assets	=	Liabilities	+	Stockholders' Equity	−	Expenses
Accounting equation	− 2,800	=	0			−	2,800

	Cash				Insurance Expense		
The ledger accounts	(1)	60,000	(2)	40,000	(6)	1,200	
	(4)	7,000	(6)	2,800			

	Salary Expense				Utilities Expense		
	(6)	1,000			(6)	600	

Transaction 7 Analysis. The business paid $1,900 on the account payable created in transaction 3. Credit Cash for the payment. The payment decreased a liability, so debit Accounts Payable.

Journal entry	Accounts Payable	1,900	
	Cash		1,900
	Paid cash on account.		

	Assets	=	Liabilities	+	Stockholders' Equity
Accounting equation	− 1,900	=	− 1,900	+	0

	Cash				Accounts Payable		
The ledger accounts	(1)	60,000	(2)	40,000	(7)	1,900	(3)	4,700
	(4)	7,000	(6)	2,800				
			(7)	1,900				

Transaction 8 Analysis. Sandra Morris, the major stockholder of SBS, remodeled her personal residence. This is not a transaction of the beauty salon, so the business does not record the transaction.

Transaction 9 Analysis. The business collected $1,500 cash on account from the clients in transaction 5. Cash increased so debit Cash. The asset accounts receivable decreased; therefore, credit Accounts Receivable.

Journal entry	Cash	1,500	
	Accounts Receivable		1,500
	Collected cash on account.		

	Assets	=	Liabilities	+	Stockholders' Equity
Accounting equation	+ 1,500	=	0	+	0
	− 1,500				

	Cash					Accounts Receivable		
The ledger accounts	(1)	60,000	(2)	40,000	(5)	2,000	(9)	1,500
	(4)	7,000	(6)	2,800				
	(9)	1,500	(7)	1,900				

Transaction 10 Analysis. The business sold land for its cost of $22,000, receiving cash. The asset cash increased; debit Cash. The asset land decreased; credit Land.

Journal entry	Cash	22,000	
	Land		22,000
	Sold land.		

	Assets	=	Liabilities	+	Stockholders' Equity
Accounting equation	+ 22,000	=	0	+	0
	− 22,000				

	Cash					Land		
The ledger accounts	(1)	60,000	(2)	40,000	(2)	40,000	(10)	22,000
	(4)	7,000	(6)	2,800				
	(9)	1,500	(7)	1,900				
	(10)	22,000						

Transaction 11 Analysis. SBS paid its stockholders cash dividends of $2,000. Credit Cash for the payment. The transaction also decreased stockholders' equity and requires a debit to an equity account. Therefore, debit Dividends.

Journal entry	Dividends	2,000	
	Cash		2,000
	Declared and paid dividends.		

	Assets	=	Liabilities	+	Stockholders' Equity	−	Dividends
Accounting equation	− 2,000	=	0			−	2,000

The ledger accounts

	Cash				Dividends	
(1)	60,000	(2)	40,000	(11)	2,000	
(4)	7,000	(6)	2,800			
(9)	1,500	(7)	1,900			
(10)	22,000	(11)	2,000			

Accounts After Posting to the Ledger

Exhibit 2-11 shows the accounts after all transactions have been posted to the ledger. Group the accounts under assets, liabilities, and equity.

Each account has a balance, denoted as Bal., which is the difference between the account's total debits and its total credits. For example, the Accounts Payable's balance of $2,800 is the difference between the credit ($4,700) and the debit ($1,900). Cash has a debit balance of $43,800.

A horizontal line separates the transaction amounts from the account balance. If an account's debits exceed its total credits, that account has a debit balance, as for Cash. If the sum of the credits is greater, the account has a credit balance, as for Accounts Payable.

ac̶t

Accounting Cycle Tutorial
Application 1—Xpert Driving School

ac̶t

Accounting Cycle Tutorial
Application 2—Small Business Services

EXHIBIT 2-11 SBS's Ledger Accounts After Posting

Assets	=	Liabilities	+	Stockholders' Equity

	Cash		
(1)	60,000	(2)	40,000
(4)	7,000	(6)	2,800
(9)	1,500	(7)	1,900
(10)	22,000	(11)	2,000
Bal.	43,800		

	Accounts Receivable		
(5)	2,000	(9)	1,500
Bal.	500		

	Supplies
(3)	4,700
Bal.	4,700

	Land		
(2)	40,000	(10)	22,000
Bal.	18,000		

	Accounts Payable		
(7)	1,900	(3)	4,700
		Bal.	2,800

	Common Stock		
		(1)	60,000
		Bal.	60,000

	Revenue

	Service Revenue		
		(4)	7,000
		(5)	2,000
		Bal.	9,000

	Dividends	
(11)	2,000	
Bal.	2,000	

	Expenses

	Insurance Expense	
(6)	1,200	
Bal.	1,200	

	Salary Expense	
(6)	1,000	
Bal.	1,000	

	Utilities Expense	
(6)	600	
Bal.	600	

THE TRIAL BALANCE

A **trial balance** lists all accounts with their balances—assets first, then liabilities and stockholders' equity. The trial balance summarizes all the account balances for the financial statements and shows whether total debits equal total credits. A trial balance

OBJECTIVE

4 Use a trial balance

may be taken at any time, but the most common time is at the end of the period. Exhibit 2-12 is the trial balance of SBS, Inc., after all transactions have been journalized and posted at the end of June.

Accounting Cycle Tutorial Glossary

Accounting Cycle Tutorial Glossary Quiz

EXHIBIT 2-12 — Trial Balance

SBS, Inc.
Trial Balance
June 30, 20X9

Account Title	Balance	
	Debit	Credit
Cash	$43,800	
Accounts receivable	500	
Supplies	4,700	
Land	18,000	
Accounts payable		$ 2,800
Common stock		60,000
Dividends	2,000	
Service revenue		9,000
Insurance expense	1,200	
Salary expense	1,000	
Utilities expense	600	
Total	$71,800	$71,800

Analyzing Accounts

You can often tell what a company did by analyzing its accounts. This is a powerful tool for a manager who knows accounting. For example, if you know the beginning and ending balance of Cash, and if you know total cash receipts, you can compute your total cash payments during the period.

In our chapter example, suppose SBS began August with cash of $1,000. During August Super received cash of $8,000 and ended the month with a cash balance of $3,000. You can compute total cash payments by analyzing Super's Cash account as follows:

Cash				
Beginning balance	1,000			
Cash receipts	8,000	Cash payments		$x = 6,000$
Ending balance	3,000			

Or, if you know Cash's beginning and ending balances and total payments, you can compute cash receipts during the period—for any company!

You can compute either sales on account or cash collections on account by analyzing the Accounts Receivable account as follows (using assumed amounts):

Accounts Receivable			
Beginning balance	6,000		
Sales on account	10,000	Collections on account	11,000
Ending balance	5,000		

Also, you can determine how much you paid on account by analyzing Accounts Payable as follows (using assumed amounts):

Accounts Payable			
		Beginning balance	9,000
Payments on account	4,000	Purchases on account	6,000
		Ending balance	11,000

Please master this powerful technique. It works for any company and for your own personal finances! You will find this tool very helpful when you become a manager.

Correcting Accounting Errors

Accounting errors can occur even in computerized systems. Input data may be wrong, or they may be entered twice or not at all. A debit may be entered as a credit, and vice versa. You can detect the reason or reasons behind many out-of-balance conditions by computing the difference between total debits and total credits. Then perform one or more of the following actions:

1. Search the records for a missing account. Trace each account back and forth from the journal to the ledger. A $200 transaction may have been recorded incorrectly in the journal or posted incorrectly to the ledger. Search the journal for a $200 transaction.

2. Divide the out-of-balance amount by 2. A debit treated as a credit, or vice versa, doubles the amount of error. Suppose SBS added $300 to Cash instead of subtracting $300. The out-of-balance amount is $600, and dividing by 2 identifies $300 as the amount of the transaction. Search the journal for the $300 transaction and trace to the account affected.

3. Divide the out-of-balance amount by 9. If the result is an integer (no decimals), the error may be a

   - *slide* (writing $400 as $40).The accounts would be out of balance by $360 ($400 − $40 = $360). Dividing $360 by 9 yields $40. Scan the trial balance in Exhibit 2-12 for an amount similar to $40. Utilities Expense (balance of $400) is the misstated account.

◼ *transposition* (writing $2,100 as $1,200). The accounts would be out of balance by $900 ($2,100 − $1,200 = $900). Dividing $900 by 9 yields $100. Trace all amounts on the trial balance back to the T-accounts. Dividends (balance of $2,100) is the misstated account.

Chart of Accounts

As you know, the ledger contains the accounts grouped under these headings:

1. **Balance sheet accounts: Assets, Liabilities, and Stockholders' Equity**
2. **Income statement accounts: Revenues and Expenses**

Organizations use a **chart of accounts** to list all their accounts and account numbers. Account numbers usually have 2 or more digits. Asset account numbers may begin with 1, liabilities with 2, stockholders' equity with 3, revenues with 4, and expenses with 5. The second, third, and higher digits in an account number indicate the position of the individual account within the category. For example, Cash may be account number 101, which is the first asset account. Accounts Payable may be number 201, the first liability. All accounts are numbered by using this system.

Organizations with many accounts use lengthy account numbers. For example, the chart of accounts of Apple Computer may use 5-digit account numbers. The chart of accounts for SBS appears in Exhibit 2-13. The gap between account numbers 111 and 141 leaves room to add another category of receivables, for example, Notes Receivable, which may be numbered 121.

EXHIBIT 2-13   Chart of Accounts—SBS, Inc.

Balance Sheet Accounts		
Assets	**Liabilities**	**Stockholders' Equity**
101 Cash	201 Accounts Payable	301 Common Stock
111 Accounts Receivable	231 Notes Payable	311 Dividends
141 Office Supplies		312 Retained Earnings
151 Office Furniture		
191 Land		

Income Statement Accounts (Part of Stockholders' Equity)	
Revenues	**Expenses**
401 Service Revenue	501 Insurance Expense
	502 Salary Expense
	503 Utilities Expense

Appendix D to this book gives two expanded charts of accounts that you will find helpful as you work through this course. The first chart lists the typical accounts that a *service* corporation, such as SBS, would have after a period of growth. The second chart is for a *merchandising* corporation, one that sells a product instead of a service.

The Normal Balance of an Account

An account's *normal balance* falls on the side of the account—debit or credit—where increases are recorded. The normal balance of assets is on the debit side, so assets are *debit-balance accounts.* Conversely, liabilities and stockholders' equity usually have a credit balance, so these are *credit-balance accounts.* Exhibit 2-14 illustrates the normal balances of all the assets, liabilities, and stockholders' equities, including revenues and expenses.

EXHIBIT 2-14   Normal Balances of the Accounts

Assets	Debit	
Liabilities		Credit
Stockholders' Equity—overall		Credit
Common stock..................................		Credit
Retained earnings.............................		Credit
Dividends...	Debit	
Revenues..		Credit
Expenses	Debit	

As explained earlier, stockholders' equity usually contains several accounts. Dividends and expenses carry debit balances because they represent decreases in stockholders' equity. In total, the equity accounts show a normal credit balance.

Account Formats

So far we have illustrated accounts in a 2-column T-account format, with the debit column on the left and the credit column on the right. Another format has 4 *amount* columns, as illustrated for the Cash account in Exhibit 2-15. The first pair of amount columns are for the debit and credit amounts of individual transactions. The last two columns are for the account balance. This 4-column format keeps a running balance in the 2 right columns.

ac
t

Accounting Cycle Tutorial
The Journal, the Ledger, and the Trial Balance

EXHIBIT 2-15   Account in Four-Column Format

Account: Cash   **Account No. 101**

				Balance	
Date	Item	Debit	Credit	Debit	Credit
20X9					
June 2		60,000		60,000	
3			40,000	10,000	

Analyzing Transactions Using Only T-Accounts

OBJECTIVE

5 Analyze transactions using only T-accounts

Businesspeople must often make decisions without the benefit of a complete accounting system. For example, the managers of Apple Computer may consider borrowing $100,000 to buy equipment. To see how the two transactions [(a) borrowing cash and (b) buying equipment] affect Apple, the manager can go directly to T-accounts, as follows:

T-accounts:	Cash	Note Payable	
	(a) 100,000	(a) 100,000	

T-accounts:	Cash	Equipment	Note Payable
	(a) 100,000 | (b) 100,000	(b) 100,000	(a) 100,000

This informal analysis shows immediately that Apple will add $100,000 of equipment and a $100,000 note payable. Assuming that Apple began with zero balances, the equipment and note payable transactions would result in the following balance sheet (date assumed for illustration only):

Apple Computer, Inc.
Balance Sheet
September 12, 20X8

Assets		Liabilities	
Cash.............................	$ 0	Note payable...........................	$100,000
Equipment.....................	100,000		
		Stockholders' Equity	0
		Total liabilities and	
Total assets....................	$100,000	stockholders' equity..............	$100,000

Accounting Cycle Tutorial
Application Constanza Architect

Companies don't actually keep records in this shortcut fashion. But a decision maker who needs information quickly may not have time to journalize, post to the accounts, take a trial balance, and prepare the financial statements. A manager who knows accounting can analyze the transaction and make the decision quickly.

Now apply what you've learned. Study the Decision Guidelines, which summarize the chapter.

DECISION GUIDELINES

HOW TO MEASURE RESULTS OF OPERATIONS AND FINANCIAL POSITION

Any entrepreneur must determine whether the venture is profitable. To do this, he or she needs to know its results of operations and financial position. If Steve Jobs, who founded Apple Computer, Inc., wants to know whether the business is making money, the Guidelines that follow will help him.

Decision	Guidelines
Has a transaction occurred?	If the event affects the entity's financial position and can be reliably recorded—Yes. If either condition is absent—No.
Where to record the transaction?	In the *journal*, the chronological record of transactions
How to record an increase or decrease in the following accounts?	Rules of *debit* and *credit*:

	Increase	Decrease
Assets	Debit	Credit
Liabilities	Credit	Debit
Stockholders' equity	Credit	Debit
Revenues	Credit	Debit
Expenses	Debit	Credit

Decision	Guidelines
Where to store all the information for each account?	In the *ledger*, the book of accounts
Where to list all the accounts and their balances?	In the *trial* balance
Where to report the:	
Results of operations?	In the *income* statement (Revenues – Expenses = Net income or net loss)
Financial position?	In the balance sheet (Assets = Liabilities + Stockholders' equity)

END-OF-CHAPTER SUMMARY PROBLEM

The trial balance of Nambu Consulting, Inc., on October 1, 20X3, lists the entity's assets, liabilities, and stockholders' equity on that date.

	Balance	
Account Title	Debit	Credit
Cash..	$25,000	
Accounts receivable................	5,000	
Accounts payable		$ 2,000
Common stock........................		10,000
Retained earnings...................		18,000
Total	$30,000	$30,000

During October, the business completed the following transactions:

a. Borrowed $50,000 from the bank, with Nambu signing a note payable in the name of the business.
b. Paid cash of $40,000 to a real estate company to acquire land.
c. Performed service for a customer and received cash of $5,000.
d. Purchased supplies on credit, $500.
e. Performed customer service and earned revenue on account, $2,500.
f. Paid $1,400 on account.
g. Paid the following cash expenses: utilities, $3,000; rent, $1,200; and interest, $700.
h. Received $3,000 on account.
i. Received a $200 insurance bill that will be paid next week.
j. Declared and paid dividend of $1,800.

I Required

1. Open the following accounts, with the balances indicated, in the ledger of Calderon Service Center, Inc. Use the T-account format.
   • Assets—Cash, $25,000; Accounts Receivable, $5,000; Supplies, no balance; Land, no balance
   • Liabilities—Accounts Payable, $2,000; Note Payable, no balance
   • Stockholders' Equity—Common Stock, $10,000; Retained Earnings, $18,000; Dividends, no balance
   • Revenues—Service Revenue, no balance
   • Expenses—(none have balances) Utilities Expense, Rent Expense, Interest Expense, Insurance Expense
2. Journalize the preceding transactions. Key journal entries by transaction letter.
3. Post to the ledger and show the balance in each account after all the transactions have been posted.
4. Prepare the trial balance of Nambu Consulting, Inc., at October 31, 20X3.
5. To determine the net income or net loss of the entity during the month of October, prepare the income statement for the month ended October 31, 20X3. List expenses in order from the largest to the smallest.

Answers

Requirement 1

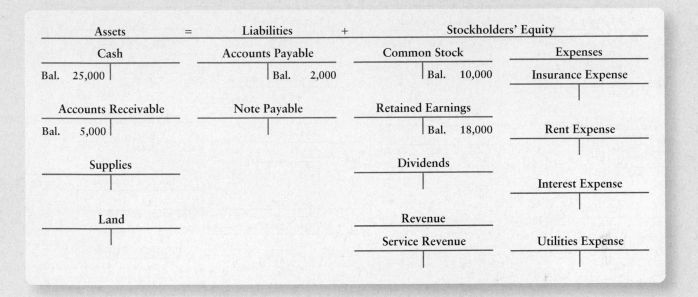

Requirement 2

Accounts and Explanation	Debit	Credit		Accounts and Explanation	Debit	Credit
a. Cash...............................	50,000		g.	Utilities expense	3,000	
Note Payable		50,000		Rent expense	1,200	
Borrowed cash on note payable.				Interest expense............................	700	
b. Land.................................	40,000			Cash		4,900
Cash		40,000		Paid cash expenses.		
Purchased land for cash.			h.	Cash..	3,000	
c. Cash.................................	5,000			Accounts Receivable		3,000
Service Revenue		5,000		Received on account.		
Performed service and received cash.			i.	Insurance expense	200	
d. Supplies.............................	500			Accounts Payable...................		200
Accounts Payable................		500		Received utility bill.		
Purchased supplies on account.			j.	Dividends.....................................	1,800	
e. Accounts Receivable.................	2,500			Cash		1,800
Service Revenue		2,500		Declared and paid dividends.		
Performed service on account.						
f. Accounts Payable	1,200					
Cash		1,200				
Paid on account.						

❙ Requirement 3

Assets	=	Liabilities	+	Stockholders' Equity

Cash

Bal.	25,000	(b)	40,000
(a)	50,000	(f)	1,200
(c)	5,000	(g)	4,900
(h)	3,000	(j)	1,800
Bal.	35,000		

Accounts Receivable

Bal.	5,000	(h)	3,000
(e)	2,500		
Bal.	4,500		

Supplies

(d)	500	
Bal.	500	

Land

(b)	40,000	
Bal.	40,000	

Accounts Payable

(f)	1,200	Bal.	2,000
		(d)	500
		(i)	200
		Bal.	1,500

Note Payable

		(a)	50,000
		Bal.	50,000

Common Stock

	Bal.	10,000

Retained Earnings

	Bal.	18,000

Dividends

(j)	1,800	
Bal.	1,800	

Revenue

Service Revenue

		(c)	5,000
		(e)	2,500
		Bal.	7,500

Expenses

Utilities Expense

(g)	3,000	
Bal.	3,000	

Rent Expense

(g)	1,200	
Bal.	1,200	

Interest Expense

(g)	700	
Bal.	700	

Insurance Expense

(i)	200	
Bal.	200	

❙ Requirement 4

Nambu Consulting, Inc.
Trial Balance
October 31, 20X3

Account Title	Balance Debit	Balance Credit
Cash...	$35,100	
Accounts receivable.................	4,500	
Supplies......................................	500	
Land...	40,000	
Accounts payable		$ 1,500
Note payable...........................		50,000
Common stock......................		10,000
Retained earnings...................		18,000
Dividends..............................	1,800	
Service revenue......................		7,500
Utilities expense	3,000	
Rent expense..........................	1,200	
Interest expense......................	700	
Insurance expense	200	
Total	$87,000	$87,000

Requirement 5

Nambu Consulting, Inc.
Income Statement
Month Ended October 31, 20X3

Revenue		
Service revenue.................		$7,500
Expenses		
Utilities expense	$3,000	
Rent expense...................	1,200	
Interest expense...............	700	
Insurance expense	200	
Total expenses.....................		5,100
Net income..........................		$2,400

REVIEW TRANSACTION ANALYSIS

Quick Check (Answers are given on page 136.)

1. A debit entry to an account:
   a. increases liabilities
   b. increases stockholders' equity
   c. increases assets
   d. both a and c

2. Which account types normally have a credit balance?
   a. liabilities
   b. revenues
   c. expenses
   d. both a and b

3. An attorney performs services of $800 for a client and receives $200 cash with the remainder on account. The journal entry for this transaction would:
   a. debit Cash, credit Accounts Receivable, credit Service Revenue
   b. debit Cash, debit Accounts Receivable, credit Service Revenue
   c. debit Cash, credit Service Revenue
   d. debit Cash, debit Service Revenue, credit Accounts Receivable

4. Accounts Payable had a normal beginning balance of $1,000. During the period, there were debit postings of $400 and credit postings of $600. What was the ending balance?
   a. $800 debit
   b. $800 credit
   c. $1,200 debit
   d. $1,200 credit

5. The list of all accounts with their balances is the:
   a. trial balance
   b. chart of accounts
   c. journal
   d. balance sheet

6. The basic summary device of accounting is the:
   a. ledger
   b. account
   c. journal
   d. trial balance

7. The beginning Cash balance was $5,000. At the end of the period, the balance was $6,000. If total cash paid out during the period was $24,000, the amount of cash receipts was:
   a. $23,000   c. $25,000
   b. $13,000   d. $35,000

8. In a double-entry accounting system
   a. a debit entry is recorded on the left side of a T-account.
   b. half of all the accounts have a normal credit balance.
   c. liabilities, owners' equity, and revenue accounts all have normal debit balances.
   d. both a and c are correct.

9. Which accounts appear on which financial statement?
	Balance sheet	*Income statement*
a.	Cash, revenues, land	Expenses, payables
b.	Receivables, land, payables	Revenues, supplies
c.	Expenses, payables, cash	Revenues, receivables, land
d.	Cash, receivables, payables	Revenues, expenses

10. A doctor purchases medical supplies of $670 and pays $200 cash with the remainder on account. The journal entry for this transaction would be:
    a. Supplies   c. Supplies
       Accounts Payable   Accounts Receivable
       Cash   Cash
    b. Supplies   d. Supplies
       Cash   Accounts Payable
          Accounts Payable   Cash

11. Which is the correct sequence for recording transactions and preparing financial statements?
    a. Journal, ledger, trial balance, financial statements
    b. Ledger, trial balance, journal, financial statements
    c. Financial statements, trial balance, ledger, journal
    d. Ledger, journal, trial balance, financial statements

12. The error of posting $100 as $10 can be detected by
    a. Dividing the out-of-balance amount by 2.
    b. Totalling each account's balance in the ledger.
    c. Dividing the out-of-balance amount by 9.
    d. Examining the chart of accounts.

Accounting Vocabulary

account (p. 81) The record of the changes that have occurred in a particular asset, liability, or stockholders' equity during a period. The basic summary device of accounting.

accrued liability (p. 82) A liability for an expense that has not yet been paid by the company.

cash (p. 81) Money and any medium of exchange that a bank accepts at face value.

chart of accounts (p. 106) List of a company's accounts and their account numbers.

credit (p. 93) The right side of an account.

debit (p. 93) The left side of an account.

journal (p. 96) The chronological accounting record of an entity's transactions.

ledger (p. 97) The book of accounts and their balances.

posting (p. 97) Copying amounts from the journal to the ledger.

prepaid expense (p. 81) A category of miscellaneous assets that typically expire or get used up in the near future. Examples include Prepaid Rent, Prepaid Insurance, and Supplies.

transaction (p. 80) Any event that has a financial impact on the business and can be measured reliably.

trial balance (p. 103) A list of all the ledger accounts with their balances.

ASSESS YOUR PROGRESS

Short Exercises

S2-1 *(Learning Objective 1: Explaining an asset versus an expense)* Lou Ann Staas opened a software consulting firm that immediately paid $9,000 for a computer. Was Staas's payment an expense of the business? Explain your answer. (pp. 81–82)

S2-2 *(Learning Objective 1: Analyzing the effects of transactions)* Hourglass Software began with cash of $10,000. Hourglass then bought supplies for $2,000 on account. Separately, Hourglass paid $5,000 for a computer. Answer these questions.

a. How much in total assets does Hourglass have? (pp. 84–85)
b. How much in liabilities does Hourglass owe? (pp. 84–85)

S2-3 *(Learning Objective 1: Analyzing transactions)* Sandy Lyle, MD, opened a medical practice. The business completed the following transactions:

June 1	Lyle invested $25,000 cash to start her medical practice. The business issued common stock to Lyle.
1	Purchased medical supplies on account totaling $9,000.
2	Paid monthly office rent of $4,000.
3	Recorded $8,000 revenue for service rendered to patients, received cash of $2,000, and sent bills to patients for the remainder.

After these transactions, how much cash does the business have to work with? Use a T-account to show your answer. (pp. 83–86)

S2-4 *(Learning Objective 1: Analyzing transactions)* Refer to Short Exercise S2-3. Which of the transactions of Sandy Lyle, MD, increased the total assets of the business? For each transaction, identify the asset that was increased.

S2-5 *(Learning Objective 2, 3: Recording transactions)* After operating for several months, architect Paul Marciano completed the following transactions during the latter part of October:

October 15	Borrowed $25,000 from the bank, signing a note payable.
22	Performed service for clients on account totaling $9,000.
28	Received $6,000 cash on account from clients.
29	Received a utility bill of $600, an account payable that will be paid during May.
31	Paid monthly salary of $3,000 to employee.

Journalize the transactions of Paul Marciano, Architect. Include an explanation with each journal entry. (pp. 98–102)

S2-6 *(Learning Objective 2, 3: Journalizing transactions; posting)* Adam Lowry, Inc., purchased supplies on account for $5,000. Later Lowry paid $3,000 on account.

1. Journalize the two transactions on the books of Adam Lowry, Inc. Include an explanation for each transaction. (pp. 99–102)

2. Open a T-account for Accounts Payable and post to Accounts Payable. Compute the balance and denote it as Bal. (pp. 99–102)

3. How much does the Lowry business owe after both transactions? In which account does this amount appear? (pp. 99–102)

S2-7 (*Learning Objective 2, 3: Journalizing transactions; posting*) Motion Unlimited performed service for a client who could not pay immediately. Motion expected to collect the $4,000 the following month. A month later, Motion received $2,500 cash from the client.

1. Record the two transactions on the books of Motion Unlimited. Include an explanation for each transaction. (pp. 99–102)

2. Open these T-accounts: Cash, Accounts Receivable, and Service Revenue. Post to all three accounts. Compute each account balance and denote as Bal. (pp. 99–102)

S2-8 (*Learning Objective 4: Preparing and using a trial balance*) Assume that **Old Navy**, reported the following summarized data at December 31, 20X8. Accounts appear in no particular order; dollar amounts are in millions.

Other liabilities	$ 2	Revenues	$36
Cash	8	Other assets	9
Expenses	24	Accounts payable	1
Stockholders' equity	2		

Prepare the trial balance of Old Navy at December 31, 20X8. List the accounts in their proper order, as on page 97. How much was Old Navy's net income or net loss? (pp. 103–104)

S2-9 (*Learning Objective 4: Using a trial balance*) Blackberry's trial balance follows.

Blackberry, Inc.
Trial Balance
June 30, 20X6

	Debit	Credit
Cash	$ 6,000	
Accounts receivable	13,000	
Supplies	4,000	
Equipment	22,000	
Land	50,000	
Accounts payable		$ 19,000
Note payable		20,000
Common stock		10,000
Retained earnings		8,000
Service revenue		70,000
Salary expense	21,000	
Rent expense	10,000	
Utilities expense	1,000	
Total	$127,000	$127,000

Compute these amounts for Blackberry: (pp. 103–104)

1. Total assets

2. Total liabilities

3. Net income or net loss during June

S2-10 (*Learning Objective 4: Using a trial balance*) Refer to Blackberry's trial balance in Short Exercise S2-9. The purpose of this exercise is to help you learn how to correct three common accounting errors. (pp. 105–106)

Error 1. Slide. Suppose the trial balance lists Land as $5,000 instead of $50,000. Recompute column totals, take the difference, and divide by 9. The result is an integer (no decimals), which suggests that the error is either a transposition or a slide.

Error 2. Transposition. Assume the trial balance lists Accounts Receivable as $31,000 instead of $13,000. Recompute column totals, take the difference, and divide by 9. The result is an integer (no decimals), which suggests that the error is either a transposition or a slide.

Error 3. Mislabelling an item. Assume that Blackberry accidentally listed Accounts Receivable as a credit balance instead of a debit. Recompute the trial balance totals for debits and credits. Then take the difference between total debits and total credits, and divide the difference by 2. You get back to the original amount of Accounts Receivable.

S2-11 (*Learning Objective 2: Using key accounting terms*) Accounting has its own vocabulary and basic relationships. Match the accounting terms at left with the corresponding definition or meaning at right. (pp. 81–106)

____ 1. Debit	**A.** The cost of operating a business; a decrease in
____ 2. Expense	stockholders' equity
____ 3. Net income	**B.** Always a liability
____ 4. Ledger	**C.** Revenues – Expenses
____ 5. Posting	**D.** Grouping of accounts
____ 6. Normal balance	**E.** Assets – Liabilities
____ 7. Payable	**F.** Record of transactions
____ 8. Journal	**G.** Always an asset
____ 9. Receivable	**H.** Left side of an account
____ 10. Owners' equity	**I.** Side of an account where increases are recorded
	J. Copying data from the journal to the ledger

S2-12 (*Learning Objective 5: Analyzing transactions without a journal*) Singapore Investments, Inc., began by issuing common stock for cash of $100,000. The company immediately purchased computer equipment on account for $60,000.

1. Set up the following T-accounts of Singapore Investments, Inc.: Cash, Computer Equipment, Accounts Payable, Common Stock. (pp. 107–108)
2. Record the first two transactions of the business directly in the T-accounts without using a journal. (pp. 107–108)
3. Show that total debits equal total credits.

Exercises

E2-13 (*Learning Objective 1: Reporting on business activities*) Assume **J. Crew** opened a store in St. Louis, starting with cash and common stock of $100,000. Monique Farris, the store manager, then signed a note payable to purchase land for $90,000 and a building for $120,000. Farris also paid $60,000 for equipment and $10,000 for supplies to use in the business.

Suppose the home office of J. Crew requires a weekly report from store managers. Write Farris's memo to the home office to report on her purchases. Include the store's balance sheet as the final part of your memo. Prepare a T-account to compute the balance for Cash. (pp. 84–85, 89–90)

E2-14 (*Learning Objective 1: Business transactions and the accounting equation*) **Advanced Design** specializes in imported clothing. During April, Advanced completed a series of transactions. For each of the following items, give an example of a transaction that has the described effect on the accounting equation of Advanced Design. (pp. 83–88)

a. Increase one asset and decrease another asset.
b. Decrease an asset and decrease owners' equity.
c. Decrease an asset and decrease a liability.
d. Increase an asset and increase owners' equity.
e. Increase an asset and increase a liability.

E2-15 (*Learning Objective 1: Transaction analysis*) The following selected events were experienced by either Problem Solvers, Inc., a corporation, or Peter Fleming, the major stock-holder. State whether each event (1) increased, (2) decreased, or (3) had no effect on the total assets of the business. Identify any specific asset affected. (pp. 83–88)

a. Received $9,000 cash from customers on account.
b. Fleming used personal funds to purchase a swimming pool for his home.
c. Sold land and received cash of $60,000 (the land was carried on the company's books at $60,000).
d. Borrowed $50,000 from the bank.
e. Made cash purchase of land for a building site, $85,000.
f. Received $20,000 cash and issued stock to a stockholder.
g. Paid $60,000 cash on accounts payable.
h. Purchased equipment and signed a $100,000 promissory note in payment.
i. Purchased merchandise inventory on account for $15,000.
j. The business paid Fleming a cash dividend of $4,000.

E2-16 (*Learning Objective 1: Transaction analysis; accounting equation*) Randolph Noble opened a medical practice specializing in surgery. During the first month of operation (August), the business, titled Randolph Noble, Professional Corporation (P.C.), experienced the following events:

August	6	Noble invested $50,000 in the business, which in turn issued its common stock to him.
	9	The business paid cash for land costing $30,000. Noble plans to build an office building on the land.
	12	The business purchased medical supplies for $2,000 on account.
	15	Randolph Noble, P.C., officially opened for business.
	15–31	During the rest of the month, Noble treated patients and earned service revenue of $8,000, receiving cash for half the revenue earned.
	15–31	The business paid cash expenses: employee salaries, $1,400; office rent, $1,000; utilities, $300.
	31	The business sold supplies to another physician for the supplies' cost of $500.
	31	The business borrowed $10,000, signing a note payable to the bank.
	31	The business paid $1,000 on account.

❙ Required

1. Analyze the effects of these events on the accounting equation of the medical practice of Randolph Noble, P.C. Use a format similar to that of Exhibit 2-1, Panel B, with headings for Cash, Accounts Receivable, Medical Supplies, Land, Accounts Payable, Note Payable, Common Stock, and Retained Earnings. (pp. 83–88)

2. After completing the analysis, answer these questions about the business.
   a. How much are total assets? (pp. 87–88)
   b. How much does the business expect to collect from patients? (pp. 87–88)
   c. How much does the business owe in total? (pp. 87–88)
   d. How much of the business's assets does Noble really own?
   e. How much net income or net loss did the business experience during its first month of operations? (pp. 89–90)

E2-17 (*Learning Objective 2, 3: Journalizing transactions*) Refer to Exercise 2-16. Record the transactions in the journal of Randolph Noble, P.C. List the transactions by date and give an explanation for each transaction. (pp. 98–103)

E2-18 (*Learning Objective 2, 3: Journalizing transactions*) Double Tree Cellular, Inc., completed the following transactions during April 20X6, its first month of operations:

■ **general ledger**

Apr.	1	Received $25,000 and issued common stock.
	2	Purchased $800 of office supplies on account.
	4	Paid $20,000 cash for land to use as a building site.
	6	Performed service for customers and received cash of $2,000.
	9	Paid $100 on accounts payable.
	17	Performed service for **FedEx** on account totaling $1,200.
	23	Collected $900 from **FedEx** on account.
	30	Paid the following expenses: salary, $1,000; rent, $500.

I Required

Record the transactions in the journal of Double Tree Cellular, Inc. Key transactions by date and include an explanation for each entry, as illustrated in the chapter. (pp. 98–103)

E2-19 (*Learning Objective 3, 4: Posting to the ledger and preparing and using a trial balance*) Refer to Exercise 2-18.

■ **general ledger**

I Required

1. After journalizing the transactions of Exercise 2-18, post the entries to the ledger, using T-accounts. Key transactions by date. Date the ending balance of each account April 30. (pp. 98–103)

2. Prepare the trial balance of Double Tree Cellular, Inc., at April 30, 20X6. (pp. 103–104)

3. How much are total assets, total liabilities, and total stockholders' equity on April 30? Use the accounting equation. (pp. 88–89)

E2-20 (*Learning Objective 2, 3: Journalizing transactions*) The first 7 transactions of Yellow Pages Advertising, Inc., have been posted to the company's accounts as follows:

	Cash				Supplies			Equipment			Land	
(1)	20,000	(3)	8,000	(4)	1,000	(5) 100	(6)	8,000		(3)	31,000	
(2)	7,000	(6)	8,000									
(5)	100	(7)	400									

	Accounts Payable				Note Payable			Common Stock	
(7)	400	(4)	1,000		(2)	7,000		(1)	20,000
					(3)	23,000			

I Required

Prepare the journal entries that served as the sources for the 7 transactions. Include an explanation for each entry. (pp. 98–103) As Yellow Pages moves into the next period, how much cash does the business have? (pp. 103–104) How much does Yellow Pages owe in total liabilities? (pp. 103–104)

■ **spreadsheet**

E2-21 (*Learning Objective 4: Preparing and using a trial balance*) The accounts of Custom Pool Service, Inc., follow with their normal balances at June 30, 20X6. The accounts are listed in no particular order.

Account	Balance	Account	Balance
Dividends...........................	$ 6,000	Common stock...................	$ 8,500
Utilities expense	1,400	Accounts payable	4,300
Accounts receivable..........	15,500	Service revenue.................	22,000
Delivery expense	300	Land.................................	29,000
Retained earnings..............	21,400	Note payable....................	13,000
Salary expense..................	8,000	Cash.................................	9,000

I Required

1. Prepare the company's trial balance at June 30, 20X6, listing accounts in proper sequence, as illustrated in the chapter. For example, Supplies comes before Land. List the expense with the largest balance first, the expense with the next largest balance second, and so on. (pp. 103–104)

2. Prepare the financial statement for the month ended June 30, 20X6, that will tell the company the results of operations for the month. (pp. 89–90)

E2-22 (*Learning Objective 4: Correcting errors in a trial balance*) The trial balance of Haigood, Inc., at September 30, 20X3, does not balance:

Cash......................................	$ 4,200	
Accounts receivable...............	13,000	
Inventory...............................	17,000	
Supplies.................................	600	
Land......................................	55,000	
Accounts payable		$12,000
Common stock.......................		47,900
Service revenue......................		32,100
Salary expense.......................	1,700	
Rent expense.........................	800	
Utilities expense	700	
Total......................................	$93,000	$92,000

The accounting records hold the following errors:
   a. Recorded a $1,000 cash revenue transaction by debiting Accounts Receivable. The credit entry was correct.
   b. Posted a $1,000 credit to Accounts Payable as $100.
   c. Did not record utilities expense or the related account payable in the amount of $200.
   d. Understated Common Stock by $1,100.
   e. Omitted Insurance Expense of $1,000, from the trial balance.

I Required

Prepare the correct trial balance at September 30, 20X3, complete with a heading. Journal entries are not required. (pp. 103–104)

E2-23 (*Learning Objective 5: Recording transactions without a journal*) Set up the following T-accounts: Cash, Accounts Receivable, Office Supplies, Office Furniture, Accounts Payable, Common Stock, Dividends, Service Revenue, Salary Expense, and Rent Expense.

   Record the following transactions directly in the T-accounts without using a journal. Use the letters to identify the transactions. (pp. 107–108)

a. Linda English opened a law firm by investing $10,000 cash and office furniture valued at $5,000. Organized as a professional corporation, the business issued common stock to English.

b. Paid monthly rent of $1,500.

c. Purchased office supplies on account, $800.

d. Paid employees' salaries of $1,800.

e. Paid $400 of the account payable created in transaction c.

f. Performed legal service on account, $8,300.

g. Declared and paid dividends of $2,000.

E2-24 (*Learning Objective 4: Preparing and using a trial balance*) Refer to Exercise 2-23.   **writing assignment ■**

1. After recording the transactions in Exercise 2-23, prepare the trial balance of Linda English, Attorney, at May 31, 20X9. (pp. 103–104)

2. How well did the business perform during its first month? Compute net income (or net loss) for the month. (pp. 89–90)

Serial Exercise

Exercise 2-25 begins an accounting cycle that is completed in Chapter 3.

E2-25 (*Learning Objective 2, 3, 4: Recording transactions and preparing a trial balance*)   **■ general ledger**
Lance Sedberry, Certified Public Accountant, operates as a professional corporation (P.C.). The business completed these transactions during the first part of January:

Jan.	2	Received $5,000 cash from Sedberry, and issued common stock to him.
	2	Paid monthly office rent, $500.
	3	Paid cash for a Dell computer, $3,000, with the computer expected to remain in service for 5 years.
	4	Purchased office furniture on account, $6,000, with the furniture projected to last for 5 years.
	5	Purchased supplies on account, $900.
	9	Performed tax service for a client and received cash for the full amount of $800.
	12	Paid utility expenses, $200.
	18	Performed consulting service for a client on account, $1,700.

I Required

1. Set up T-accounts for Cash, Accounts Receivable, Supplies, Equipment, Furniture, Accounts Payable, Common Stock, Dividends, Service Revenue, Rent Expense, Utilities Expense, and Salary Expense. (pp. 93–103)

2. Journalize the transactions. Explanations are not required. (pp. 98–103)

3. Post to the T-accounts. Key all items by date and denote an account balance on January 18 as Bal. (pp. 98–103)

4. Prepare a trial balance at January 18. In the Serial Exercise of Chapter 3, we add transactions for the remainder of January and will require a trial balance at January 31. (pp. 103–104)

Challenge Exercises

E2-26 (*Learning Objective 5: Computing financial statement amounts*) The manager of Dubois Furniture needs to compute the following amounts.

a. Total cash paid during March. (pp. 103–104)

b. Cash collections from customers during March. Analyze Accounts Receivable. (pp. 103–104)

c. Cash paid on a note payable during March. Analyze Notes Payable. (pp. 103–104)

(*continued*)

Here are the additional data you need to analyze the accounts:

Account	Balance Feb. 28	Balance Mar. 31	Additional Information for the Month of March
1. Cash..............................	$10,000	$ 5,000	Cash receipts, $80,000
2. Accounts Receivable.......	26,000	24,000	Sales on account, $50,000
3. Notes Payable	13,000	21,000	New borrowing, $25,000

Prepare a T-account to compute each amount *a* through *c*.

E2-27 (*Learning Objective 1, 4: Analyzing transactions; using a trial balance*) The trial balance of Loop 340, Inc., at December 31, 20X5, does not balance.

Cash....................................	$ 3,900	Common stock....................	$20,000
Accounts receivable.............	7,200	Retained earnings...............	7,300
Land....................................	34,000	Service revenue....................	9,100
Accounts payable	5,800	Salary expense....................	3,400
Note payable......................	5,000	Advertising expense............	900

❙ Required

1. How much out of balance is the trial balance? Determine the out-of-balance amount. The error lies in the Accounts Receivable account. Add the out-of-balance amount to, or subtract it from, Accounts Receivable to determine the correct balance of Accounts Receivable.

2. After correcting Accounts Receivable, advise the top management of Loop 340, Inc., on the company's
   a. Total assets
   b. Total liabilities
   c. Net income or net loss for December. (pp. 89–90)

E2-28 (*Learning Objective 1: Analyzing transactions*) This question concerns the items and the amounts that 2 entities, Rogers Co., and Providence Hospital, should report in their financial statements.

During June, Providence provided Rogers with medical exams for Rogers employees and sent a bill for $20,000. On July 7 Rogers sent a check to Providence for $15,000. Rogers began June with a cash balance of $25,000; Providence began with cash of $0.

❙ Required

For this situation, show everything that both Rogers and Providence will report on their June and July income statements and on their balance sheets at June 30 and July 31. Use the following format for your answer: (pp. 98–100, 89–90)

Rogers:		
Income statement	June	July
Balance sheet	June 30	July 31
Providence:		
Income statement	June	July
Balance sheet	June 30	July 31

After showing what each company should report, briefly explain how Rogers and the Providence data relate to each other. Be specific. (Challenge)

Quiz

Test your understanding of transaction analysis by answering the following questions. Select the best choice from among the possible answers.

Q2-29 An investment of cash into the business will (pp. 83–84)

a. Decrease total assets.

b. Decrease total liabilities.

c. Increase stockholders' equity.

d. Have no effect on total assets.

Q2-30 Purchasing a computer on account will (pp. 84–85)

a. Increase total assets.

b. Increase total liabilities.

c. Have no effect on stockholders' equity.

d. All of the above.

Q2-31 Performing a service on account will (pp. 85–86)

a. Increase total assets.

b. Increase stockholders' equity.

c. Both a and b.

d. Increase total liabilities.

Q2-32 Receiving cash from a customer on account will (pp. 86–87)

a. Have no effect on total assets.

b. Increase total assets.

c. Decrease liabilities.

d. Increase stockholders equity.

Q2-33 Purchasing computer equipment for cash will (pp. 84–85)

a. Increase both total assets and total liabilities.

b. Decrease both total assets and stockholders' equity.

c. Decrease both total liabilities and stockholders' equity.

d. Have no effect on total assets, total liabilities, or stockholders' equity.

Q2-34 Purchasing a building for $100,000 by paying cash of $20,000 and signing a note payable for $80,000 will (pp. 84–85)

a. Increase both total assets and total liabilities by $100,000.

b. Increase both total assets and total liabilities by $80,000.

c. Decrease total assets and increase total liabilities by $20,000.

d. Decrease both total assets and total liabilities by $20,000.

Q2-35 What is the effect on total assets and stockholders' equity of paying the electric bill as soon as it is received each month? (pp. 85–86)

	Total assets	**Stockholders' equity**
a.	Decrease	No effect
b.	No effect	No effect
c.	Decrease	Decrease
d.	No effect	Decrease

Q2-36 Which of the following transactions will increase an asset and increase a liability? (pp. 84–85)

a. Buying equipment on account.

b. Purchasing office equipment for cash.

c. Issuing stock.

d. Payment of an account payable.

Q2-37 Which of the following transactions will increase an asset and increase stockholders' equity? (pp. 85–86)

a. Collecting cash from a customer on an account receivable.

b. Performing a service on account for a customer.

c. Borrowing money from a bank.

d. Purchasing supplies on account.

Q2-38 Where do we first record a transaction? (pp. 96–97)

a. Ledger

b. Trial balance

c. Account

d. Journal

Q2-39 Which of the following is not an asset account? (pp. 81–82, 89–90)

a. Common Stock

b. Salary Expense

c. Service Revenue

d. None of the above accounts is an asset.

Q2-40 Which statement is false? (pp. 96–97)

a. Revenues are increased by credits.

b. Assets are increased by debits.

c. Dividends are increased by credits.

d. Liabilities are decreased by debits.

Q2-41 The journal entry to record the receipt of land and a building and issuance of common stock (pp. 98–99)

a. Debits Land and Building and credits Common Stock.

b. Debits Land and credits Common Stock.

c. Debits Common Stock and credits Land and Building.

d. Debits Land, Building, and Common Stock.

Q2-42 The journal entry to record the purchase of supplies on account (pp. 99–100)

a. Credits Supplies and debits Cash.

b. Debits Supplies and credits Accounts Payable.

c. Debits Supplies Expense and credits Supplies.

d. Credits Supplies and debits Accounts Payable.

Q2-43 If the credit to record the purchase of supplies on account is not posted, (pp. 99–100)

a. Liabilities will be understated.

b. Expenses will be overstated.

c. Assets will be understated.

d. Stockholders' equity will be understated.

Q2-44 The journal entry to record a payment on account will (pp. 100–102)

a. Debit Accounts Payable and credit Retained Earnings.

b. Debit Cash and credit Expenses.

c. Debit Expenses and credit Cash.

d. Debit Accounts Payable and credit Cash.

Q2-45 If the credit to record the payment of an account payable is not posted, (pp. 100–102)

a. Liabilities will be understated.

b. Expenses will be understated.

c. Cash will be overstated.

d. Cash will be understated.

Q2-46 Which statement is false? (pp. 103–104)

a. A trial balance lists all the accounts with their current balances.

b. A trial balance is the same as a balance sheet.

c. A trial balance can verify the equality of debits and credits.

d. A trial balance can be taken at any time.

Q2-47 A business's purchase of a $100,000 building with an $85,000 mortgage payable and issuance of $15,000 of common stock will (pp. 88–89)

a. Increase stockholders' equity by $15,000.

b. Increase assets by $15,000.

c. Increase assets by $85,000.

d. Increase stockholders' equity by $100,000.

Q2-48 Martex, Inc., a new company, completed these transactions. What will Martex's total assets equal? (pp. 88–89)

(1) Stockholders invested $50,000 cash and inventory worth $25,000.

(2) Sales on account, $12,000.

a. $75,000   c. $63,000
b. $87,000   d. $62,000

Problems
(Group A)

> Some of these A problems can be found within My Accounting Lab (MAL), an online homework and practice environment. Your instructor may ask you to complete these exercises using MAL.

MyAccountingLab

P2-49A (*Learning Objective 1: Analyzing a trial balance*) The trial balance of Amusement Specialties, Inc., follows.

Amusement Specialties, Inc.
Trial Balance
December 31, 20X6

Cash	$ 14,000	
Accounts receivable	11,000	
Prepaid expenses	4,000	
Equipment	171,000	
Building	100,000	
Accounts payable		$ 30,000
Note payable		120,000
Common stock		102,000
Retained earnings		40,000
Dividends	22,000	
Service revenue		86,000
Rent expense	14,000	
Advertising expense	3,000	
Wage expense	32,000	
Supplies expense	7,000	
Total	$378,000	$378,000

Rhonda Ray, your best friend, is considering investing in Amusement Specialties. Rhonda seeks your advice in interpreting this information. Specifically, she asks how to use this trial balance to compute the company's total assets, total liabilities, and net income or net loss for the year.

▌ Required

Write a short note to answer Rhonda's questions. In your note, state the amounts of Amusement Specialties' total assets, total liabilities, and net income or net loss for the year. Also show how you computed each amount. (pp. 103–104, 89–90)

P2-50A *(Learning Objective 1: Analyzing transactions with the accounting equation and preparing the financial statements)* The following amounts summarize the financial position of Ready Resources, Inc., on May 31, 20X8:

			Assets					**= Liabilities**	**+**	**Stockholders' Equity**			
	Cash	+	Accounts Receivable	+	Supplies	+	Land	= Accounts Payable	+	Common Stock	+	Retained Earnings	
Bal.	1,200		1,500				12,000	8,000		4,000		2,700	

During June 20X8, Ready Resources completed these transactions:

a. The business received cash of $5,000 and issued common stock.
b. Performed services for a customer and received cash of $6,700.
c. Paid $5,000 on accounts payable.
d. Purchased supplies on account, $1,000.
e. Collected cash from a customer on account, $500.
f. Consulted on the design of a computer system and billed the customer for services rendered, $2,400.
g. Recorded the following business expenses for the month: (1) paid office rent—$900; (2) paid advertising—$300.
h. Declared and paid a cash dividend of $1,800.

❚ Required

1. Analyze the effects of the preceding transactions on the accounting equation of Ready Resources, Inc. Adapt the format of Exhibit 2-1, Panel B. (pp. 88–89)
2. Prepare the income statement of Ready Resources, Inc., for the month ended June 30, 20X8. List expenses in decreasing order by amount. (pp. 89–90).
3. Prepare the entity's statement of retained earnings for the month ended June 30, 20X8. (pp. 89–90)
4. Prepare the balance sheet of Ready Resources, Inc., at June 30, 20X8. (pp. 89–90)

■ general ledger

P2-51A *(Learning Objective 2, 3: Recording transactions, posting)* This problem can be used in conjunction with Problem 2-50A. Refer to Problem 2-50A.

❚ Required

1. Journalize the transactions of Ready Resources, Inc. Explanations are not required. (pp. 98–103)
2. Set up the following T-accounts: Cash, Accounts Receivable, Supplies, Land, Accounts Payable, Common Stock, Retained Earnings, Dividends, Service Revenue, Rent Expense, and Advertising Expense. Insert in each account its balance as given (example: Cash $1,200). Post the transactions to the accounts. (pp. 98–103)
3. Compute the balance in each account. For each asset account, each liability account, and for Common Stock, compare its balance to the ending balance you obtained in Problem 2-50A. Are the amounts the same or different? (In Chapter 3, we complete the accounting process. There you will learn how the Retained Earnings, Dividends, Revenue, and Expense accounts work together in the processing of accounting information.) (pp. 98–103)

P2-52A *(Learning Objective 1, 2: Analyzing transactions with the accounting equation)* Perry Real Estate Co. experienced the following events during the organizing phase and its first month of operations. Some of the events were personal for the stockholders and did not affect the business. Others were transactions of the business.

Nov.	4	Gaylord Perry, the major stockholder of real estate company, received $50,000 cash from an inheritance.
	5	Perry deposited $50,000 cash in a new business bank account titled Perry Real Estate Co. The business issued common stock to Perry.
	6	The business paid $300 cash for letterhead stationery for the new office.
	7	The business purchased office equipment. The company paid cash of $30,000 and agreed to pay the account payable for the remainder, $7,000, within 3 months.
	10	Perry sold Dell stock, which he had owned for several years, receiving $75,000 cash from his personal stockbroker.
	11	Perry deposited the $75,000 cash from sale of the Dell stock in his personal bank account.
	12	A representative of a large company telephoned Perry and told him of the company's intention to transfer $10,000 of business to Perry.
	18	Perry finished a real estate deal for a client and submitted his bill for services, $10,000. Perry expects to collect from this client within 2 weeks.
	21	The business paid half its account payable for the equipment purchased on November 7.
	25	The business paid office rent of $4,000.
	30	The business declared and paid a cash dividend of $2,000.

I **Required**

1. Classify each of the preceding events as one of the following: (pp. 83–89)
   a. A business-related event but not a transaction to be recorded by Perry Real Estate Co.
   b. A personal transaction for a stockholder, not to be recorded by Perry Real Estate Co.
   c. A business transaction to be recorded by Perry Real Estate Co.

2. Analyze the effects of the preceding events on the accounting equation of Perry Real Estate Co. Use a format similar to that in Exhibit 2-1, Panel B. (pp. 88–89)

3. Record the transactions of the business in its journal. Include an explanation for each entry. (pp. 98–103)

P2-53A (*Learning Objective 2, 3: Analyzing and recording transactions*) During December, Barnett Auction Co. completed the following transactions:

■ **general ledger**

Dec.	1	Barnett received $10,000 cash and issued common stock to the stockholders.
	5	Paid monthly rent, $1,000.
	9	Paid $5,000 cash and signed a $25,000 note payable to purchase land for an office site.
	10	Purchased supplies on account, $1,200.
	19	Paid $600 on account.
	22	Borrowed $15,000 from the bank for business use. Barnett signed a note payable to the bank in the name of the business.
	31	Service revenues earned during the month included $6,000 cash and $5,000 on account.
	31	Paid employees' salaries ($2,000), advertising expense ($1,500), and utilities expense ($1,100).
	31	Declared and paid a cash dividend of $4,000.

(*continued*)

Barnett's business uses the following accounts: Cash, Accounts Receivable, Supplies, Land, Accounts Payable, Notes Payable, Common Stock, Dividends, Service Revenue, Salary Expense, Advertising Expense, and Utilities Expense.

I Required

1. Journalize each transaction of Barnett Auction Co. Explanations are not required. (pp. 98–103)

2. Prepare T-accounts for Cash, Accounts Payable, and Notes Payable. Post to these three accounts. (pp. 102)

3. After these transactions, how much cash does the business have? How much in total liabilities does it owe? (pp. 88–90)

■ **general ledger**

P2-54A *(Learning Objective 2, 3, 4: Journalizing transactions, posting, and preparing and using a trial balance)* During the first month of operations, Double R Heating and Air Conditioning, Inc., completed the following transactions:

Jan.	2	Double R received $30,000 cash and issued common stock to the stockholders.
	3	Purchased supplies, $1,000, and equipment, $2,600, on account.
	4	Performed service for a customer and received cash, $1,500.
	7	Paid cash to acquire land, $22,000.
	11	Performed service for a customer and billed the customer, $800. We expect to collect within 1 month.
	16	Paid for the equipment purchased January 3 on account.
	17	Paid the telephone bill, $100.
	18	Received partial payment from customer on account, $500.
	22	Paid the water and electricity bills, $400.
	29	Received $1,800 cash for servicing the heating unit of a customer.
	31	Paid employee salary, $1,300.
	31	Declared and paid dividends of $2,200.

I Required

Set up the following T-accounts: Cash, Accounts Receivable, Supplies, Equipment, Land, Accounts Payable, Common Stock, Dividends, Service Revenue, Salary Expense, and Utilities Expense.

1. Record each transaction in the journal, using the account titles given. Key each transaction by date. Explanations are not required. (pp. 98–103)

2. Post the transactions to the T-accounts, using transaction dates as posting references. Label the ending balance of each account *Bal.*, as shown in the chapter. (pp. 98–103)

3. Prepare the trial balance of Double R Heating and Air Conditioning, Inc., at January 31 of the current year.

4. The manager asks you how much in total resources the business has to work with, how much it owes, and whether January was profitable (and by how much). (pp. 89–90)

■ **general ledger**

P2-55A *(Learning Objective 3, 4: Recording transactions directly in T-accounts; preparing and using a trial balance)* During the first month of operations (April 20X1), Music Services Corporation completed the following selected transactions:

a. The business received cash of $25,000 and a building valued at $50,000. The corporation issued common stock to the stockholders.

b. Borrowed $50,000 from the bank; signed a note payable.

c. Paid $60,000 for music equipment.

d. Purchased supplies on account, $1,000.

e. Paid employees' salaries, $1,300.

f. Received $500 for service performed for customers.

g. Performed service for customers on account, $1,800.

h. Paid $600 of the account payable created in Transaction d.

i. Received a $500 bill for utility expense that will be paid in the near future.

j. Received cash on account, $1,100.

k. Paid the following cash expenses: (1) rent, $1,000; (2) advertising, $800.

❙ Required

1. Set up the following T-accounts: Cash, Accounts Receivable, Supplies, Music Equipment, Building, Accounts Payable, Note Payable, Common Stock, Service Revenue, Salary Expense, Rent Expense, Advertising Expense, and Utilities Expense. (pp. 107–108)

2. Record the foregoing transactions directly in the T-accounts without using a journal. Use the letters to identify the transactions. (pp. 107–108)

3. Prepare the trial balance of Music Services Corporation at April 30, 20X1. (p. 99)

(Group B)

P2-56B (*Learning Objective 1: Analyzing a trial balance*) Your best friend is considering making an investment in Photometric Tailoring Co. She seeks your advice in interpreting the company's information. Specifically, she asks whether this trial balance provides the data to prepare a balance sheet and an income statement.

writing assignment ▪

Photometric Tailoring Co. Trial Balance December 31, 20X9		
Cash..	$ 12,000	
Accounts receivable................	47,000	
Prepaid expenses	4,000	
Equipment.............................	236,000	
Accounts payable		$105,000
Note payable..........................		92,000
Common stock........................		30,000
Retained earnings...................		32,000
Service revenue......................		139,000
Salary expense........................	63,000	
Rent expense..........................	26,000	
Supplies expense....................	7,000	
Advertising expense...............	3,000	
Total	$398,000	$398,000

❙ Required

Write a memo to answer your friend's questions. State which accounts go on the balance sheet and which accounts go on the income statement. In your memo, state the amount of net income that Photometric Tailoring earned in 20X9, and explain your computation. (pp. 103–104, 89–90)

P2-57B (*Learning Objective 1: Analyzing transactions with the accounting equation and preparing the financial statements*) Donald Healey operates and is the major stockholder of an interior design studio called DH Designers, Inc. The following amounts summarize the business on April 30, 20X1:

		Assets					=	Liabilities	+	Stockholders' Equity		
	Cash	+	Accounts Receivable	+	Supplies	+	Land	=	Accounts Payable	+	Common Stock	+	Retained Earnings
Bal.	1,700		2,200				24,100		5,400		10,000		12,600

(*continued*)

During May 20X1, the business completed these transactions:
a. Healey received $30,000 as a gift and deposited the cash in the business bank account. The business issued common stock to Healey.
b. Paid $1,400 on accounts payable.
c. Performed services for a client and received cash of $4,100.
d. Collected cash from a customer on account, $700.
e. Purchased supplies on account, $800.
f. Consulted on the interior design of a major office building and billed the client for services rendered, $5,000.
g. Received cash of $1,700 and issued common stock to a stockholder.
h. Recorded the following expenses for the month· (1) paid office rent—$1,200; (2) paid advertising—$600.
i. Declared and paid a cash dividend of $2,000.

I Required

1. Analyze the effects of the preceding transactions on the accounting equation of DH Designers, Inc. Adapt the format of Exhibit 2-1, Panel B. (pp. 88–89)

2. Prepare the income statement of DH Designers, Inc., for the month ended May 31, 20X1. List expenses in decreasing order by amount. (pp. 89–90)

3. Prepare the statement of retained earnings of DH Designers, Inc., for the month ended May 31, 20X1. (pp. pp. 89–90)

4. Prepare the balance sheet of DH Designers, Inc., at May 31, 20X1. (pp. pp. 89–90)

■ **general ledger**

P2-58B *(Learning Objective 2, 3: Recording transactions, posting)* This problem can be used in conjunction with Problem 2-57B. Refer to Problem 2-57B.

I Required

1. Journalize the transactions of DH Designers, Inc. Explanations are not required. (pp. 98–103)

2. Set up the following T-accounts: Cash, Accounts Receivable, Supplies, Land, Accounts Payable, Common Stock, Retained Earnings, Dividends, Service Revenue, Rent Expense, and Advertising Expense. Insert in each account its balance as given (example: Cash $1,700). Post to the accounts. (pp. 98–103)

3. Compute the balance in each account. For each asset account, each liability account, and for Common Stock, compare its balance to the ending balance you obtained in Problem 2-57B. Are the amounts the same or different? (In Chapter 3, we complete the accounting process. There you will learn how the Retained Earnings, Dividends, Revenue, and Expense accounts work together in the processing of accounting information.)(pp. 98–103)

P2-59B *(Learning Objective 1, 2: Analyzing transactions with the accounting equation)* Lane Kohler opened a law office, which he operates as a professional corporation. The name of the new entity is Lane Kohler, Attorney and Counselor, Professional Corporation (P.C.). Kohler experienced the following events during the organizing phase of his new business and its first month of operations. Some of the events were personal transactions of the stockholders and did not affect the law practice. Others were transactions that should be accounted for by the business.

March	1	Kohler sold 1,000 shares of **YouTube** stock and received $75,000 cash from his stockbroker.
	2	Kohler deposited in his personal bank account the $75,000 cash from sale of the YouTube stock.
	3	Kohler received $100,000 cash from his former partners in the law firm from which he resigned.
	5	Kohler deposited $50,000 cash in a new business bank account titled Lane Kohler, Attorney and Counselor, P.C. The business issued common stock to Kohler.
	6	A representative of a large company telephoned Kohler and told him of the company's intention to transfer $15,000 of legal business to Kohler.
	7	The business paid $500 cash for letterhead stationery for the law office.
	9	The business purchased office furniture. Kohler paid cash of $10,000 and agreed to pay the account payable for the remainder, $9,500, within 3 months.
	23	Kohler finished court hearings on behalf of a client and submitted his bill for legal services, $3,000. He expected to collect from this client within 1 month.
	29	The business paid $5,000 of its account payable on the furniture purchased on March 9.
	30	The business paid office rent of $1,900.
	31	The business declared and paid a cash dividend of $1,000.

❚ **Required**

1. Classify each of the preceding events as one of the following: (pp. 83–89)
   a. A personal transaction of a stockholder, not to be recorded by the business of Lane Kohler, Attorney and Counselor, P.C.
   b. A business transaction to be recorded by the business of Lane Kohler, Attorney and Counselor, P.C.
   c. A business-related event but not a transaction to be recorded by the business of Lane Kohler, Attorney and Counselor, P.C.

2. Analyze the effects of the preceding events on the accounting equation of the business of Lane Kohler, Attorney and Counselor, P.C. Use a format similar to Exhibit 2-1, Panel B. (pp. 88–89)

3. Record the transactions of the business in its journal. Include an explanation for each entry. (pp. 98–103)

P2-60B (*Learning Objective 2, 3: Analyzing and recording transactions*) Blanton Glass Etching, Inc., owns shops in outlet malls. The business completed the following transactions during June:

■ **general ledger**

June	1	Received cash of $25,000 and issued common stock to the stockholders.
	2	Paid $10,000 cash and signed a $30,000 note payable to purchase land.
	7	Received $15,000 cash from service revenue and deposited that amount in the bank.
	10	Purchased supplies on account, $1,700.
	15	Paid employees' salaries, $2,800, and rent on a shop, $1,800.
	15	Paid advertising expense, $1,200.
	16	Paid $800 on account.
	17	Declared and paid a cash dividend of $3,000.

(continued)

Blanton uses the following accounts: Cash, Supplies, Land, Accounts Payable, Notes Payable, Common Stock, Dividends, Service Revenue, Salary Expense, Rent Expense, and Advertising Expense.

▌ Required

1. Journalize each transaction. Explanations are not required. (pp. 98–103)

2. Prepare T-accounts for Cash, Accounts Payable, and Notes Payable. Post to these 3 accounts.

3. After these transactions, how much cash does the business have? How much does it owe in total liabilities? (pp. 88–90)

■ **general ledger**

P2-61B (*Learning Objective 2, 3, 4: Journalizing transactions, posting, and preparing and using a trial balance*) During the first month of operations, Barron Environmental Services, Inc., completed the following transactions:

Sept.	3	Received $20,000 cash and issued common stock.
	4	Purchased supplies, $800, and furniture, $1,800, on account.
	6	Performed services for a client and received $5,000 cash.
	7	Paid $15,000 cash to acquire land for an office site.
	10	Worked for a client, billed the client, and received her promise to pay the $600 within 1 week.
	14	Paid for the furniture purchased September 4 on account.
	16	Paid the telephone bill, $200.
	17	Received partial payment from client on account, $500.
	24	Paid the water and electricity bills, $400.
	28	Received $1,500 cash for helping a client meet environmental standards.
	30	Paid secretary's salary, $1,200.
	30	Declared and paid dividends of $2,000.

▌ Required

Set up the following T-accounts: Cash, Accounts Receivable, Supplies, Furniture, Land, Accounts Payable, Common Stock, Dividends, Service Revenue, Salary Expense, and Utilities Expense.

1. Record each transaction in the journal, using the account titles given. Key each transaction by date. Explanations are not required. (pp. 98–103)

2. Post the transactions to the T-accounts, using transaction dates as posting references. Label the ending balance of each account Bal., as shown in the chapter (pp. 98–103)

3. Prepare the trial balance of Barron Environmental Services, Inc., at September 30 of the current year. (pp. 89–90)

4. Barron asks you how much in total resources the business has to work with, how much it owes, and whether September was profitable (and by how much). (pp. 89–90)

P2-62B (*Learning Objective 3, 4: Recording transactions directly in T-accounts; preparing and using a trial balance*) During the first month of operations (June 20X3), Walker Consulting Company completed the following selected transactions:

a. Began the business with an investment of $20,000 cash and a building valued at $60,000. The corporation issued common stock to the stockholders.

b. Borrowed $90,000 from the bank; signed a note payable.

c. Purchased supplies on account for $1,300.

d. Paid $35,000 for computer equipment.

e. Paid employees' salaries totaling $2,200.

f. Performed consulting service on account for a client, $2,100.

g. Paid $800 of the account payable created in transaction c.

h. Received a $600 bill for advertising expense that will be paid in the near future.

i. Performed service for clients and received $1,100 in cash.

j. Received $1,200 cash on account.

k. Paid the following cash expenses: (1) rent, $700; (2) utilities, $400.

I *Required*

1. Set up the following T-accounts: Cash, Accounts Receivable, Supplies, Computer Equipment, Building, Accounts Payable, Note Payable, Common Stock, Service Revenue, Salary Expense, Advertising Expense, Rent Expense, and Utilities Expense. (pp. 107–108)

2. Record each transaction directly in the T-accounts without using a journal. Use the letters to identify the transactions. (pp. 107–108)

3. Prepare the trial balance of Walker Consulting Company, at June 30, 20X3. (p. 97)

APPLY YOUR KNOWLEDGE

Decision Cases

Case 1. *(Learning Objective 4, 5: Recording transactions directly in T-accounts, preparing a trial balance, and measuring net income or loss)* A friend named Jay Barlow has asked what effect certain transactions will have on his company. Time is short, so you cannot apply the detailed procedures of journalizing and posting. Instead, you must analyze the transactions without the use of a journal. Barlow will continue the business only if he can expect to earn monthly net income of $10,000. The following transactions occurred this month:

a. Barlow deposited $10,000 cash in a business bank account, and the corporation issued common stock to him.

b. Borrowed $5,000 cash from the bank and signed a note payable due within 1 year.

c. Paid $300 cash for supplies.

d. Purchased advertising in the local newspaper for cash, $800.

e. Purchased office furniture on account, $4,400.

f. Paid the following cash expenses for 1 month: employee salary, $1,700; office rent, $600.

g. Earned revenue on account, $7,000.

h. Earned revenue and received $2,500 cash.

i. Collected cash from customers on account, $1,200.

j. Paid on account, $1,000.

I *Required*

1. Set up the following T-accounts: Cash, Accounts Receivable, Supplies, Furniture, Accounts Payable, Notes Payable, Common Stock, Service Revenue, Salary Expense, Advertising Expense, and Rent Expense. (pp. 107–108)

2. Record the transactions directly in the accounts without using a journal. Key each transaction by letter. (pp. 107–108)

3. Prepare a trial balance for Barlow Networks, Inc., at the current date. List expenses with the largest amount first, the next largest amount second, and so on. (pp. 103–104)

4. Compute the amount of net income or net loss for this first month of operations. Why or why not would you recommend that Barlow continue in business? (pp. 89–90)

Case 2. *(Learning Objective 2: Correcting financial statements; deciding whether to expand a business)* Sophia Loren opened an Italian restaurant. Business has been good, and Loren is considering expanding the restaurant. Loren, who knows little accounting, produced the following financial statements for Little Italy, Inc., at December 31, 20X1, end of the first month of operations:

Little Italy, Inc. Income Statement Month Ended December 31, 20X1			Little Italy, Inc. Balance Sheet December 31, 20X1		
Sales revenue	$36,000		Assets		
Common stock	10,000		Cash	$ 6,000	
Total revenue	46,000		Cost of goods sold (expense)	22,000	
			Food inventory	5,000	
Accounts payable	$ 8,000		Furniture	10,000	
Advertising expense	5,000		Total Assets	43,000	
Rent expense	6,000		Liabilities		
Total expenses	19,000		None		
Net income	$27,000		Owners' Equity	$43,000	

In these financial statements all *amounts* are correct, except for Owners' Equity. Loren heard that total assets should equal total liabilities plus owners' equity, so she plugged in the amount of owners' equity at $43,000 to make the balance sheet come out even.

I *Required*

Sophia Loren has asked whether she should expand the restaurant. Her banker says Loren may be wise to expand if (a) net income for the first month reached $5,000 and (b) total assets are at least $25,000. It appears that the business has reached these milestones, but Loren doubts whether her financial statements tell the true story. She needs your help in making this decision. Prepare a corrected income statement and balance sheet. (Remember that Retained Earnings, which was omitted from the balance sheet, should equal net income for the first month; there were no dividends.) After preparing the statements, give Sophia Loren your recommendation as to whether she should expand the restaurant. (pp. 89–90)

Ethical Issues

Issue 1. Scruffy Murphy is the president and principal stockholder of Scruffy's Bar & Grill, Inc. To expand, the business is applying for a $250,000 bank loan. To get the loan, Murphy is considering two options for beefing up the owners' equity of the business:

> *Option 1.* Issue $100,000 of common stock for cash. A friend has been wanting to invest in the company. This may be the right time to extend the offer.
> *Option 2.* Transfer $100,000 of Murphy's personal land to the business, and issue common stock to Murphy. Then, after obtaining the loan, Murphy can transfer the land back to himself and zero out the common stock.

Journalize the transactions required by each option. Which plan is ethical? Which is unethical and why? (pp. 98–100)

Issue 2. Community Charities has a standing agreement with Empire State Bank. The agreement allows Community Charities to overdraw its cash balance at the bank when donations are running low. In the past, Community Charities managed funds wisely and rarely used this privilege. Recently, however, Douglas Byrd has been named president of Community Charities. To expand operations, Byrd is acquiring equipment and spending a lot for fund-raising. During Byrd's presidency, Community Charities has maintained a negative bank balance of about $3,000.

I *Required*

What is the ethical issue in this situation? Do you approve or disapprove of Byrd's management of Community Charities' and Empire State Bank's funds? Why? (Challenge)

Focus on Financials: ■ YUM! Brands

(*Learning Objective 3, 4: Recording transactions and computing net income*) Refer to YUM! Brands' financial statements in Appendix A at the end of the book. Assume that YUM completed the following selected transactions during 2006.

  a. Made company sales (revenue) and collected cash of $8,365 million.

  b. Earned franchise and license fee revenue on account, $1,196 million.

  c. Purchased inventories, paying cash of $2,557 million.

  d. Incurred food and paper expense of $2,549 million. Credit the Inventories account.

  e. Paid operating and other expenses of $6,188 million.

  f. Collected cash on accounts and notes receivable, $1,212 million.

  g. Paid cash for other assets, $671 million.

I *Required*

1. Set up T-accounts for: Cash (debit balance of $158 million); Accounts and Notes Receivable (debit balance of $236 million); Inventories (debit balance of $85 million); Other Assets ($0 balance); Company Sales (Revenue: $0 balance); Franchise and License Fee Revenue ($0 balance); Food and Paper Expense ($0 balance); Operating and Other Expenses ($0 balance). (pp. 98–103)

2. Journalize YUM's transactions a–g. Explanations are not required. (pp. 98–103)

3. Post to the T-accounts, and compute the balance for each account. Key postings by transaction letters a–g. (pp. 98–103)

4. For each of the following accounts, compare your computed balance to YUM's actual balance as shown on YUM's 2006 income statement or balance sheet in Appendix A. Your amounts should agree to the actual figures. (pp. 103–104)
   a. Cash
   b. Accounts and Notes Receivable
   c. Inventories
   d. Company Sales (Revenue)
   e. Franchise and License Fee Revenue
   f. Food and Paper Expense

5. Use the relevant accounts from requirement 4 to prepare a summary income statement for YUM! Brands, Inc., for 2006. Compare the net income you computed to YUM's actual net income. The 2 amounts should be equal. (p. 53)

Focus on Analysis: ■ Pier 1 Imports

(*Learning Objective 1, 2: Analyzing a leading company's financial statements*) Refer to the **Pier 1 Imports** financial statements in Appendix B at the end of the book. Suppose you are an investor considering buying Pier 1 stock. The following questions are important: **Show amounts in millions and round to the nearest $1 million.**

1. Explain whether Pier 1 had more sales revenue, or collected more cash from customers, during 2006. Combine Pier 1's 2 receivable accounts, and then analyze total receivables to answer this question. (pp. 103–104, Challenge).

2. A major concern of lenders, such as banks, is the amount of "long-term debt" a company owes. How much long-term debt does Pier 1 owe at the end of 2006? at the end of 2005? What must have happened to Pier 1's long-term debt during 2006? (Challenge)

3. Investors are vitally interested in a company's sales and profits, and its trends of sales and profits over time. Consider Pier 1's net sales and net income (net loss) during the period from 2004 through 2006. Compute the percentage increase or decrease in net sales and also in net income (net loss) from 2004 to 2006. Which item grew faster during this 2-year period, net sales or net income (net loss)? (Challenge)

Group Projects

Project 1. You are promoting a rock concert in your area. Your purpose is to earn a profit, so you need to establish the formal structure of a business entity. Assume you organize as a corporation.

▌*Required*

1. Make a detailed list of 10 factors you must consider as you establish the business.

2. Describe 10 of the items your business must arrange to promote and stage the rock concert.

3. Identify the transactions that your business can undertake to organize, promote, and stage the concert. Journalize the transactions, and post to the relevant T-accounts. Set up the accounts you need for your business ledger. Refer to the appendix at the end of book if needed.

4. Prepare the income statement, statement of retained earnings, and balance sheet immediately after the rock concert, that is, before you have had time to pay all the business bills and to collect all receivables.

5. Assume that you will continue to promote rock concerts if the venture is successful. If it is unsuccessful, you will terminate the business within 3 months after the concert. Discuss how to evaluate the success of your venture and how to decide whether to continue in business.

Project 2. Contact a local business and arrange with the owner to learn what accounts the business uses.

▌*Required*

1. Obtain a copy of the business's chart of accounts.

2. Prepare the company's financial statements for the most recent month, quarter, or year. You may use either made-up account balances or balances supplied by the owner.

If the business has a large number of accounts within a category, combine related accounts and report a single amount on the financial statements. For example, the company may have several cash accounts. Combine all cash amounts and report a single Cash amount on the balance sheet.

You will probably encounter numerous accounts that you have not yet learned. Deal with these as best you can. The charts of accounts given in the appendix at the end of the book can be helpful.

For Internet Exercises go to the Web site www.prenhall.com/harrison.

Quick Check Answers

1. *c*   2. *d*   3. *b*   4. *d*   5. *a*   6. *b*   7. *c*   8. *a*   9. *d*   10. *d*   11. *a*   12. *c*

The Way I See It #28

Our schools can be fixed!

It is my belief all children deserve

STARBUCKS COFFEE ®

Careful, the beverage you're about to enjoy is extremely hot.

SPOTLIGHT

STARBUCKS CORPORATION

Starbucks has changed coffee from a breakfast drink to an experience. The corporation began in Seattle, Washington, in 1985 and now has over 10,000 locations in the United States alone, with almost 2,000 more abroad.

As you can see from Starbucks' income statement, the company sold almost $8 billion of coffee and related products during the 2006 fiscal year. How does Starbucks know whether these revenues translated into profit? The income statement reports net income of $564 million. That's a lot of coffee!

Starbucks Corporation
Income Statement (Adapted)
Year Ended September 30, 2006

	Millions
Revenues:	
Net operating revenues	$7,787
Other income	89
Total net revenues	7,876
Expenses:	
Cost of sales (cost of goods sold)	3,179
Store operating expenses	2,688
Other operating expenses	260
Depreciation and amortization expenses	387
General and administrative expenses	473
Total operating expenses	6,987
Income before income tax	889
Income tax expense	325
Net income	$ 564

This chapter completes our coverage of the accounting cycle. It gives the basics of what you need before tackling individual topics such as receivables, inventory, and cash flows.

LEARNING OBJECTIVES

1 Relate accrual accounting and cash flows

2 Apply the revenue and matching principles

3 Adjust the accounts

4 Prepare the financial statements

5 Close the books

6 Use 2 new ratios to evaluate a business

For more practice and review of accounting cycle concepts, use ACT, the accounting Cycle Tutorial, online at www.prenhall.com/harrison. Margin logos like this one, directing you to the appropriate ACT section and material, appear throughout Chapters 1, 2, and 3. When you enter the tutorial, you'll find three buttons on the opening page of each chapter module. Here's what the buttons mean: **Tutorial** gives you a review of the major concepts, **Application** gives you practice exercises, and **Glossary** reviews important terms.

ACCRUAL ACCOUNTING VERSUS CASH-BASIS ACCOUNTING

Managers want to earn a profit. Investors search for companies whose stock prices will increase. Banks seek borrowers who'll pay their debts. Accounting provides the information these people use for decision making. Accounting can be based on either the

- accrual basis, or the
- cash basis

Accrual accounting records the impact of a business transaction as it occurs. When the business performs a service, makes a sale, or incurs an expense, the accountant records the transaction even if it receives or pays no cash.

Cash-basis accounting records only cash transactions—cash receipts and cash payments. Cash receipts are treated as revenues, and cash payments are handled as expenses.

Generally accepted accounting principles (GAAP) require accrual accounting. The business records revenues as the revenues are earned and expenses as the expenses are incurred—not necessarily when cash changes hands. Consider a sale on account. Which transaction increases your wealth—making an $800 sale on account, or collecting the $800 cash? Making the sale increases your wealth by $300 because you gave up inventory that cost you $500 and you got a receivable worth $800. Collecting cash later merely swaps your $800 receivable for $800 cash—no gain on this transaction. Making the sale—not collecting the cash—increases your wealth.

The basic defect of cash-basis accounting is that the cash basis ignores important information. That makes the financial statements incomplete. The result? People using the statements make bad decisions.

Suppose your business makes a sale *on account*. The cash basis does not record the sale because you received no cash. You may be thinking, "Let's wait until we collect cash and then record the sale. After all, we pay the bills with cash, so ignore transactions that don't affect cash."

What's wrong with this argument? There are 2 defects—one on the balance sheet and the other on the income statement.

Balance-Sheet Defect. If we fail to record a sale on account, the balance sheet reports no account receivable. Why is this so bad? The receivable is a real asset, and it should appear on the balance sheet. Without this information, your assets are understated as shown on the balance sheet.

Income-Statement Defect. A sale on account provides revenue that increases the company's wealth. Ignoring the sale understates your revenue and net income on the income statement.

The take-away lessons from this discussion are:

- Watch out for companies that use the cash basis of accounting. Their financial statements omit important information.
- All but the smallest businesses use the accrual basis of accounting.

Accrual Accounting and Cash Flows

Accrual accounting is more complex—and more complete—than cash-basis accounting. Accrual accounting records *cash* transactions, such as

- Collecting cash from customers
- Borrowing money
- Receiving cash from interest earned
- Paying off loans
- Paying salaries, rent, and other expenses
- Issuing stock

Accrual accounting also records *noncash* transactions, such as

- Sales on account
- Depreciation expense
- Purchases of inventory on account
- Usage of prepaid rent, insurance, and supplies
- Accrual of expenses incurred but not yet paid
- Earning of revenue when cash was collected in advance

Accrual accounting is based on a framework of concepts and principles. We turn now to the time-period concept, the revenue principle, and the matching principle.

The Time-Period Concept

The only way for a business to know for certain how well it performed is to shut down, sell the assets, pay the liabilities, and return any leftover cash to the owners. This process, called liquidation, means going out of business. Ongoing companies can't wait until they go out of business to measure income! Instead, they need regular progress reports. Accountants, therefore, prepare financial statements for specific periods. The **time-period concept** ensures that accounting information is reported at regular intervals.

The basic accounting period is 1 year, and virtually all businesses prepare annual financial statements. Around 60% of large companies—including Amazon.com, eBay, and YUM! Brands—use the calendar year from January 1 through December 31.

A *fiscal* year ends on a date other than December 31. Most retailers, including Wal-Mart and JCPenney, use a fiscal year that ends on January 31 because the low point in their business activity falls after Christmas. Starbucks Corporation uses a fiscal year that ends on September 30.

Companies also prepare financial statements for interim periods of less than a year, such as a month, a quarter (3 months), or a semiannual period (6 months). Most of the discussions in this text are based on an annual accounting period.

The Revenue Principle

The **revenue principle** governs two things:

1. When to record revenue (make a journal entry)
2. The amount of revenue to record

When should you record revenue? After it has been earned—and not before. In most cases, revenue is earned when the business has delivered a good or service to a customer. It has done everything required to earn the revenue by transferring the good or service to the customer.

Exhibit 3-1 shows two situations that provide guidance on when to record revenue for Starbucks Corporation. Situation 1 illustrates when not to record revenue. No transaction has occurred, so Starbucks Corporation records nothing. Situation 2 illustrates when revenue should be recorded—after a transaction has occurred.

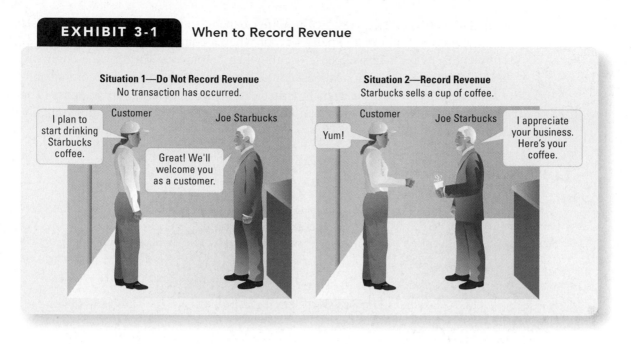

EXHIBIT 3-1 When to Record Revenue

The *amount* of revenue to record is the cash value of the goods or services transferred to the customer. Suppose that in order to promote business, Starbucks runs a promotion and sells coffee for the discount price of $2 per cup. Ordinarily Starbucks would charge $4 for this coffee. How much revenue should Starbucks record? The answer is $2—the cash value of the transaction. The amount of the sale, $2, is the amount of revenue earned—not the regular price of $4.

The Matching Principle

The **matching principle** is the basis for recording expenses. Expenses are the costs of assets used up, and of liabilities created, in the earning of revenue. Expenses have no future benefit to the company. The matching principle includes two steps:

1. Identify all the expenses incurred during the accounting period.
2. Measure the expenses, and match expenses against the revenues earned.

To *match* expenses against revenues means to subtract expenses from revenues to compute net income or net loss. Exhibit 3-2 illustrates the matching principle.

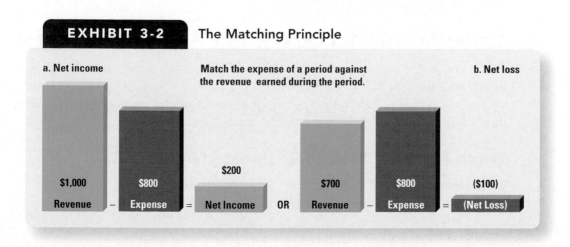

EXHIBIT 3-2 The Matching Principle

Some expenses are paid in cash. Other expenses arise from using up an asset such as supplies. Still other expenses occur when a company creates a liability. For example, Starbucks' salary expense occurs when employees work for the company. Starbucks may pay the salary expense immediately, or Starbucks may record a liability for the salary to be paid later. In either case, Starbucks has salary expense. The critical event for recording an expense is the employees' working for the company, not the payment of cash.

STOP & think. . .

1. A customer pays Starbucks $100 on March 15 for coffee to be served at a party in April. Has Starbucks earned revenue on March 15? When will Starbucks earn the revenue?
2. Starbucks pays $4,500 on July 1 for store rent for the next 3 months. Has Starbucks incurred an expense on July 1?

Answers:

1. No. Starbucks has received the cash but will not deliver the coffee until later. Starbucks earns the revenue when it gives the goods to the customer.
2. No. Starbucks has paid cash for rent in advance. There is no expense. This prepaid rent is an asset because Starbucks has the use of a store location in the future.

Ethical Issues in Accrual Accounting

Accrual accounting provides some ethical challenges that cash accounting avoids. For example, suppose that in 2008, Starbucks Corporation prepays a $3 million advertising campaign to be conducted by a large advertising agency. The advertisements are scheduled to run during December, January, and February. In this case, Starbucks is buying an asset, a prepaid expense.

Suppose Starbucks pays for the advertisements on December 1 and the ads start running immediately. Starbucks should record one-third of the expense ($1 million) during the year ended December 31, 2008, and two-thirds ($2 million) during 2009.

Suppose 2008 is a great year for Starbucks—net income is better than expected. Starbucks' top managers believe that 2009 will not be as profitable. In this case, the company has a strong incentive to expense the full $3 million during 2008 in order to report all the advertising expense in the 2008 income statement. This unethical action would keep $2 million of advertising expense off the 2009 income statement and make 2009's net income look better.

UPDATING THE ACCOUNTS: THE ADJUSTING PROCESS

OBJECTIVE

3 **Adjust** the accounts

At the end of the period, the business reports its financial statements. This process begins with the trial balance introduced in Chapter 2. We refer to this trial balance as unadjusted because the accounts are not yet ready for the financial statements. In most cases the simple label "Trial Balance" means "unadjusted."

Which Accounts Need to Be Updated (Adjusted)?

The stockholders need to know how well Jackson Repair, Inc. is performing. The financial statements report this information, and all accounts must be up-to-date.

That means some accounts must be adjusted. Exhibit 3-3 gives the trial balance of Jackson Repair, Inc., at April 30, 20X9.

This trial balance is unadjusted. That means it's not completely up-to-date. It's not quite ready for preparing the financial statements for presentation to the public.

EXHIBIT 3-3   **Unadjusted Trial Balance**

Jackson Repair, Inc.
Unadjusted Trial Balance
April 30, 20X9

Cash	$24,800	
Accounts receivable	4,200	
Supplies	700	
Prepaid insurance	3,000	
Repair tools	24,000	
Accounts payable		$13,300
Unearned service revenue		600
Common stock		20,000
Retained earnings		20,200
Dividends	3,000	
Service revenue		7,000
Salary expense	900	
Utilities expense	500	
Total	$61,100	$61,100

Cash, Equipment, Accounts Payable, Common Stock, and Dividends are up-to-date and need no adjustment at the end of the period. Why? Because the day-to-day transactions provide all the data for these accounts.

Accounts Receivable, Supplies, Prepaid Insurance, and the other accounts are another story. These accounts are not yet up-to-date on April 30. Why? Because certain transactions have not yet been recorded. Consider Supplies. During April, Jackson Repair used cleaning supplies to wash cars. But Jackson didn't make a journal entry for supplies used every time it washed a car. That would waste time and money. Instead, Jackson waits until the end of the period and then records the supplies used up during the entire month.

The cost of supplies used up is an expense. An adjusting entry at the end of April updates both Supplies (an asset) and Supplies Expense. We must adjust all accounts whose balances are not yet up-to-date.

Categories of Adjusting Entries

Accounting adjustments fall into three basic categories: deferrals, depreciation, and accruals.

Deferrals. A **deferral** is an adjustment for an item that the business paid or received cash in advance. Starbucks purchases supplies for use in its operations. During the period, some supplies (assets) are used up and become expenses. At the end of the period, an adjustment is needed to decrease the Supplies account for the supplies used up. This is Supplies Expense. Prepaid rent, prepaid insurance, and all other prepaid expenses require deferral adjustments.

There are also deferral adjustments for liabilities. Companies such as Starbucks may collect cash from a grocery-store chain in advance of earning the revenue. When Starbucks receives cash up front, Starbucks has a liability to provide coffee for the customer. This liability is called Unearned Sales Revenue. Then, when Starbucks delivers the goods to the customer, it earns Sales Revenue. This earning process requires an adjustment at the end of the period. The adjustment decreases the liability and increases the revenue for the revenue earned. Publishers such as Time, Inc., and your cell-phone company collect cash in advance. They too must make adjusting entries for revenues earned later.

Depreciation. **Depreciation** allocates the cost of a plant asset to expense over the asset's useful life. Depreciation is the most common long-term deferral. Starbucks buys buildings and equipment. As Starbucks uses the assets, it records depreciation for wear-and-tear and obsolescence. The accounting adjustment records Depreciation Expense and decreases the asset's book value over its life. The process is identical to a deferral-type adjustment; the only difference is the type of asset involved.

Accruals. An **accrual** is the opposite of a deferral. For an accrued *expense*, Starbucks records the expense before paying cash. For an accrued *revenue*, Starbucks records the revenue before collecting cash.

Salary Expense can create an accrual adjustment. As employees work for Starbucks Corporation, the company's salary expense accrues with the passage of time. At September 30, 2006, Starbucks owed employees some salaries to be paid after year end. At September 30, Starbucks recorded Salary Expense and Salary Payable for the amount owed. Other examples of expense accruals include interest expense and income tax expense.

An accrued revenue is a revenue that the business has earned and will collect next year. At year end Starbucks must accrue the revenue. The adjustment debits a receivable and credits a revenue. For example, accrual of interest revenue debits Interest Receivable and credits Interest Revenue.

Let's see how the adjusting process actually works for Jackson Repair at April 30. We start with prepaid expenses.

Prepaid Expenses

A **prepaid expense** is an expense paid in advance. Therefore, prepaid expenses are assets because they provide a future benefit for the owner. Let's do the adjustments for prepaid rent and supplies.

Prepaid Rent. Companies pay rent in advance. This prepayment creates an asset for the renter, who can then use the rented item in the future. Suppose Jackson Repair prepays 3 months' insurance ($3,000) on April 1. The entry for the prepayment of 3 months' rent debits Prepaid Insurance as follows:

April 1	Prepaid Insurance ($1,000 × 3)	3,000	
	Cash		3,000
	Paid 3 months' insurance in advance.		

The accounting equation shows that one asset increases and another decreases. Total assets are unchanged.

Assets	=	Liabilities	+	Stockholders' Equity
3,000	=	0	+	0
– 3,000				

After posting, the Prepaid Insurance account appears as follows:

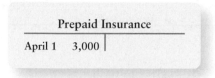

Prepaid Insurance	
April 1 3,000	

Throughout April, the Prepaid Insurance account carries this beginning balance, as shown in Exhibit 3-3 (p. 143). The adjustment transfers $1,000 from Prepaid Insurance to Insurance Expense as follows:*

Adjusting entry a

April 30	Insurance Expense ($3,000 × 1/3)	1,000	
	Prepaid Insurance		1,000
	To record insurance expense.		

Both assets and stockholders' equity decrease.

Assets	=	Liabilities	+	Stockholders' Equity	–	Expenses
– 1,000	=	0				– 1,000

After posting, Prepaid Insurance and Insurance Expense appear as follows:

Prepaid Insurance				Insurance Expense	
April 1 3,000	June 30 1,000 ⟶		April 30 1,000		
Bal. 2,000			Bal. 1,000		

This expense illustrates the matching principle. We record an expense in order to measure net income.

---

*See Exhibit 3-8, page 155, for a summary of adjustments a–g.

Supplies. Supplies are another type of prepaid expense. On April 2, Jackson Repair paid cash of $700 for cleaning supplies:

April 2	Supplies	700	
	Cash		700
	Paid cash for supplies.		

Assets	=	Liabilities	+	Stockholders' Equity
700	=	0	+	0
– 700				

The cost of the supplies Jackson used is supplies expense. To measure April's supplies expense, the business counts the supplies on hand at the end of the month. The count shows that $400 of supplies remain. Subtracting the $400 of supplies on hand from the supplies available ($700) measures supplies expense for the month ($300), as follows:

Asset Available During the Period	–	Asset on Hand at the End of the Period	=	Asset Used (Expense) During the Period
$700	–	$400	=	$300

The April 30 adjusting entry debits the expense and credits the asset, as follows:

Adjusting entry b

April 30	Supplies Expense ($700 – $400)	300	
	Supplies		300
	To record supplies expense.		

Assets	=	Liabilities	+	Stockholders' Equity	–	Expenses
– 300	=	0				– 300

After posting, the Supplies and Supplies Expense accounts appear as follows. The adjustment is highlighted for emphasis.

	Supplies				Supplies Expense	
April 2	700	June 30	300 →	April 30	300	
Bal.	400			Bal.	300	

At the start of May, Supplies has this $400 balance, and the adjustment process is repeated each month.

STOP & think. . .

At the beginning of the month, supplies were $5,000. During the month, $7,000 of supplies were purchased. At month's end, $3,000 of supplies are still on hand. What are the

- adjusting entry
- ending balance in the Supplies account?

Answer:

Supplies Expense ($5,000 + $7,000 − $3,000)	9,000	
Supplies		9,000
Ending balance of supplies = $3,000 (the supplies still on hand)		

Depreciation of Plant Assets

Plant assets are long-lived tangible assets, such as land, buildings, furniture, and equipment. All plant assets but land decline in usefulness, and this decline is an expense. Accountants spread the cost of each plant asset, except land, over its useful life. Depreciation is the process of allocating cost to expense for a long-term plant asset.

To illustrate depreciation, consider Jackson Repair. Suppose that on April 2 Jackson purchased repair tools on account for $24,000:

April 3	Repair Tools	24,000	
	Accounts Payable		24,000
	Purchased Repair Tools on account.		

Assets	=	Liabilities	+	Stockholders' Equity
24,000	=	24,000	+	0

After posting, the Repair Tools account appears as follows:

Repair Tools	
April 3 24,000	

Jackson records an asset when it purchases equipment. Then, as the asset is used, a portion of the asset's cost is transferred to Depreciation Expense. Accounting matches the expense against revenue—this is the matching principle. Computerized systems program the depreciation for automatic entry each period.

Jackson's repair tools will remain useful for 10 years and then be worthless. One way to compute the amount of depreciation for each year is to divide the cost of the asset ($24,000 in our example) by its expected useful life (10 years). This procedure—called the straight-line depreciation method—gives annual depreciation of $2,400. The depreciation amount is an estimate. (Chapter 7 covers plant assets and depreciation in more detail.)

Annual Depreciation = $24,000/10 years = $2,400 per year

Depreciation for April is $200.

Monthly Depreciation = $2,400/12 months = $200 per month

The Accumulated Depreciation Account. Depreciation expense for April is recorded as follows:

			Adjusting entry c
April 30	Depreciation Expense—Repair Tools	200	
	Accumulated Depreciation—Repair Tools		200
	To record depreciation.		

Total assets decrease by the amount of the expense:

Assets	=	Liabilities	+	Stockholders' Equity	–	Expenses
– 200	=	0				– 200

The Accumulated Depreciation account, (not Repair Tools) is credited to preserve the original cost of the asset in the Repair Tools account. Managers can then refer to the Repair Tools account if they ever need to know how much the asset cost.

The **Accumulated Depreciation** account shows the sum of all depreciation expense from using the asset. Therefore, the balance in the Accumulated Depreciation account increases over the asset's life.

Accumulated Depreciation is a contra asset account—an asset account with a normal credit balance. A **contra account** has two distinguishing characteristics:

1. It always has a companion account.

2. Its normal balance is opposite that of the companion account.

In this case, Accumulated Depreciation is the contra account to Repair Tools, so Accumulated Depreciation appears directly after Repair Tools on the balance sheet. A business carries an accumulated depreciation account for each depreciable asset, for example, Accumulated Depreciation—Building and Accumulated Depreciation—Repair Tools.

After posting, the plant asset accounts of Jackson Repair are as follows—with the adjustment highlighted:

Repair Tools			Accumulated Depreciation—Repair Tools			Depreciation Expense—Repair Tools		
April 3	24,000			April 30	200	April 30	200	
Bal.	24,000			Bal.	200	Bal.	200	

Book Value. The net amount of a plant asset (cost minus accumulated depreciation) is called that asset's **book value**, or carrying amount. Exhibit 3-4 shows how Jackson would report the book value of its Repair Tools and building at April 30 (the building data are assumed for this illustration).

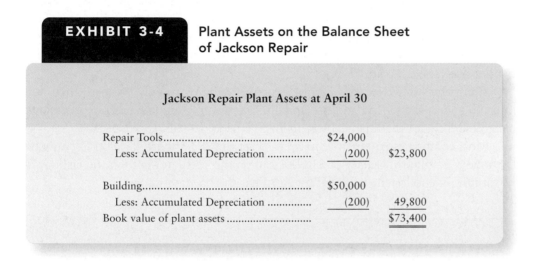

EXHIBIT 3-4	Plant Assets on the Balance Sheet of Jackson Repair

Jackson Repair Plant Assets at April 30

Repair Tools...	$24,000	
Less: Accumulated Depreciation	(200)	$23,800
Building...	$50,000	
Less: Accumulated Depreciation	(200)	49,800
Book value of plant assets		$73,400

At April 30, the book value of Repair Tools is $23,800; the book value of the building is $49,800.

STOP & think. . .

What will be the book value of Jackson's repair tools at the end of May?

Answer:
$24,000 – $200 – $200 = $23,600.

Exhibit 3-5 shows how Starbucks Corporation reports property, plant, and equipment in its annual report. Lines 1 to 6 list specific assets and their cost. Line 7 shows the cost of all Starbucks plant assets. Line 8 gives the amount of accumulated depreciation, and line 9 shows the assets' book value of $2,288 million.

EXHIBIT 3-5	Starbucks Corporation's Reporting of Property, Plant, and Equipment (Adapted, in millions)

1	Land...	$ 32
2	Buildings	109
3	Leasehold improvements.....................................	2,437
4	Store equipment	785
5	Roasting equipment	197
6	Furniture, fixtures, and other	698
7	Property, plant, and equipment, at cost..............	4,258
8	Less: Accumulated depreciation	(1,970)
9	Property, plant, and equipment, net	$2,288

Accrued Expenses

Businesses incur expenses before they pay cash. Consider an employee's salary. Starbucks' expense and payable grow as the employee works, so the liability is said to accrue. Another example is interest expense on a note payable. Interest accrues as the clock ticks. The term **accrued expense** refers to a liability that arises from an expense that has not yet been paid.

Companies don't record accrued expenses daily or weekly. Instead, they wait until the end of the period and use an adjusting entry to update each expense (and related liability) for the financial statements. Let's look at salary expense.

Most companies pay their employees at set times. Suppose Jackson Repair pays its employee a monthly salary of $1,800, half on the 15th and half on the last day of the month. The following calendar for April has the paydays circled:

April						
Sun.	Mon.	Tue.	Wed.	Thur.	Fri.	Sat.
						1
2	3	4	5	6	7	8
9	10	11	12	13	14	(15)
16	17	18	19	20	21	22
23	24	25	26	27	28	29
(30)						

Assume that if a payday falls on a Sunday, Jackson pays the employee on the following Monday. During April, Jackson paid its employees the first half-month salary of $900 and made the following entry:

April 15	Salary Expense	900	
	Cash		900
	To pay salary.		

Assets	=	Liabilities	+	Stockholders' Equity	−	Expenses
− 900	=	0				− 900

After posting, the Salary Expense account is

	Salary Expense	
April 15	900	

The trial balance at April 30 (Exhibit 3-3, p. 143) includes Salary Expense with its debit balance of $900. Because April 30, the second payday of the month, falls on a Sunday, the second half-month amount of $900 will be paid on Monday, May 1. At April 30, therefore, Jackson adjusts for additional salary expense and salary payable of $900 as follows:

Adjusting entry d

April 30	Salary Expense	900	
	Salary Payable		900
	To accrue salary expense.		

An accrued expense increases liabilities and decreases stockholders' equity:

Assets	=	Liabilities	+	Stockholders' Equity	–	Expenses
0	=	900				– 900

After posting, the Salary Payable and Salary Expense accounts appear as follows (adjustment highlighted):

	Salary Payable				Salary Expense	
	April 30	900		April 15	900	
	Bal.	900		April 30	900	
				Bal.	1,800	

The accounts now hold all of April's salary information. Salary Expense has a full month's salary, and Salary Payable shows the amount owed at April 30. All accrued expenses are recorded this way—debit the expense and credit the liability.

Computerized systems contain a payroll module. Accrued salaries can be automatically journalized and posted at the end of each period.

Accrued Revenues

Businesses often earn revenue before they receive the cash. A revenue that has been earned but not yet collected is called an **accrued revenue**.

Assume that FedEx hires Jackson on April 15 to repair delivery trucks each month. Suppose FedEx will pay Jackson $600 monthly, with the first payment on May 15. During April, Jackson will earn half a month's fee, $300, for work done April 15 through April 30. On April 30, Jackson makes the following adjusting entry:

Adjusting entry e

April 30	Accounts Receivable ($600 × 1/2)	300	
	Service Revenue		300
	To accrue service revenue.		

Revenue increases both total assets and stockholders' equity:

Assets	=	Liabilities	+	Stockholders' Equity	+	Revenues
300	=	0				+ 300

Recall that Accounts Receivable has an unadjusted balance of $4,200, and Service Revenue's unadjusted balance is $7,000 (Exhibit 3-3, p. 143). This April 30 adjusting entry has the following effects (adjustment highlighted):

Accounts Receivable			Service Revenue		
	4,200				7,000
April 30	300			April 30	300
Bal.	4,500			Bal.	7,300

All accrued revenues are accounted for similarly—debit a receivable and credit a revenue.

STOP & think. . .

Suppose Jackson Repair holds a note receivable as an investment. At the end of April, $100 of interest revenue has been earned. Journalize the accrued revenue adjustment at April 30.

Answer:

April 30	Interest Receivable	100	
	Interest Revenue		100
	To accrue interest revenue.		

Unearned Revenues

Some businesses collect cash from customers before earning the revenue. This creates a liability called **unearned revenue**. Only when the job is completed does the business earn the revenue. Suppose **Home Depot** engages Jackson Repair to repair Home Depot trucks, agreeing to pay Jackson $600 monthly, beginning immediately. If Jackson collects the first amount on April 15, then Jackson records this transaction as follows:

April 15	Cash	600	
	Unearned Service Revenue		600
	Received cash for revenue in advance.		

	Assets	=	Liabilities	+	Stockholders' Equity
	600	=	600	+	0

After posting, the liability account appears as follows:

Unearned Service Revenue	
	April 15 600

Unearned Service Revenue is a liability because Jackson is obligated to perform services for Home Depot. The April 30 unadjusted trial balance (Exhibit 3-3, p. 143) lists Unearned Service Revenue with a $600 credit balance. During the last 15 days of the month, Jackson will earn one-half of the $600, or $300. On April 30, Jackson makes the following adjustment:

Adjusting entry f

April 30	Unearned Service Revenue ($600 × 1/2)	300	
	Service Revenue		300
	To record unearned service revenue that has been earned.		

	Assets	=	Liabilities	+	Stockholders' Equity	+	Revenues
	0	=	– 300	+			+ 300

This adjusting entry shifts $300 of the total amount received ($600) from liability to revenue. After posting, Unearned Service Revenue is reduced to $300, and Service Revenue is increased by $300, as follows (adjustment highlighted):

Unearned Service Revenue				Service Revenue		
April 30	300	April 15	600			7,000
		Bal.	300		April 30	300
					April 30	300
					Bal.	7,600

All revenues collected in advance are accounted for this way. An unearned revenue is a liability, not a revenue.

One company's prepaid expense is the other company's unearned revenue. For example, Home Depot's prepaid expense is Jackson Repair's liability for unearned revenue.

Exhibit 3-6 diagrams the distinctive timing of prepaids and accruals. Study prepaid expenses all the way across. Then study unearned revenues across, and so on.

EXHIBIT 3-6 Prepaid and Accrual Adjustments

PREPAIDS—Cash First

	First		Later	

Prepaid expenses	*Pay cash and record an asset:*
	Prepaid Expense...... XXX
	    Cash.............. XXX
			Record an expense and decrease the asset:
			Expense............................. XXX
			    Prepaid Expense......... XXX	

Unearned revenues	*Receive cash and record*
	unearned revenue:
	Cash...................... XXX
	    Unearned Revenue XXX
			Record revenue and decrease
			unearned revenue:
			Unearned Revenue XXX
			    Revenue XXX	

ACCRUALS—Cash Later

	First		Later	

Accrued expenses	*Accrue expense and a payable:*
	Expense................... XXX
	    Payable........... XXX
			Pay cash and decrease the payable:
			Payable.............................. XXX
			    Cash.......................... XXX	

Accrued revenues	*Accrue revenue and a receivable:*
	Receivable............... XXX
	    Revenue XXX
			Receive cash and decrease the receivable:
			Cash................................... XXX
			    Receivable.................. XXX	

The authors thank Professors Darrel Davis and Alfonso Oddo for suggesting this exhibit.

Summary of the Adjusting Process

Two purposes of the adjusting process are to

- Measure income
- Update the balance sheet

Therefore, every adjusting entry affects at least one

- Revenue or expense—to measure income
- Asset or liability—to update the balance sheet

Exhibit 3-7 summarizes the standard adjustments.

EXHIBIT 3-7   **Summary of Adjusting Entries**

	Type of Account	
Category of Adjusting Entry	**Debit**	**Credit**
Prepaid expense...................	Expense	Asset
Depreciation.......................	Expense	Contra asset
Accrued expense.................	Expense	Liability
Accrued revenue..................	Asset	Revenue
Unearned revenue...............	Liability	Revenue

Adapted from material provided by Beverly Terry.

Exhibit 3-8 summarizes the adjustments of Jackson Repair, Inc., at April 30—the adjusting entries we've examined over the past few pages.

EXHIBIT 3-8   **The Adjusting Process of Jackson Repair, Inc.**

PANEL A—Information for Adjustments at April 30, 20X9	PANEL B—Adjusting Entries		
(a) Prepaid insurance expired, $1,000.	(a) Insurance Expense...................... Prepaid Insurance................................. To record insurance expense.	1,000	1,000
(b) Supplies used, $300.	(b) Supplies Expense....................... Supplies................................... To record supplies used.	300	300
(c) Depreciation on equipment, $200.	(c) Depreciation Expense—Repair Tools........ Accumulated Depreciation—Repair Tools To record depreciation.	200	200
(d) Accrued salary expense, $900.	(d) Salary Expense........................... Salary Payable....................... To accrue salary expense.	900	900
(e) Accrued service revenue, $300.	(e) Accounts Receivable.................... Service Revenue...................... To accrue service revenue.	300	300
(f) Amount of unearned service revenue that has been earned, $300.	(f) Unearned Service Revenue......................... Service Revenue...................... To record unearned revenue that has been earned.	300	300
(g) Accrued income tax expense, $600.	(g) Income Tax Expense .... Income Tax Payable.............................. To accrue income tax expense.	600	600

PANEL C—Ledger Accounts

Assets	Liabilities	Stockholders' Equity

Assets

Cash

Bal. 24,800	

Accounts Receivable

4,200	
(e) 300	
Bal. 4,500	

Supplies

700	(b) 300
Bal. 400	

Prepaid Insurance

3,000	(a) 1,000
Bal. 2,000	

Repair Tools

Bal. 24,000	

Accumulated Depreciation— Repair Tools

	(c) 200
	Bal. 200

Liabilities

Accounts Payable

	Bal. 13,300

Salary Payable

	(d) 900
	Bal. 900

Unearned Service Revenue

(f) 300	600
	Bal. 300

Income Tax Payable

	(g) 600
	Bal. 600

Stockholders' Equity

Common Stock

	Bal. 20,000

Retained Earnings

	Bal. 20,200

Dividends

Bal. 3,000	

Revenue

Service Revenue

	7,000
	(e) 300
	(f) 300
	Bal. 7,600

Expenses

Insurance Expense

(a) 1,000	
Bal. 1,000	

Salary Expense

900	
(d) 900	
Bal. 1,800	

Supplies Expense

(b) 300	
Bal. 300	

Depreciation Expense—Repair Tools

(c) 200	
Bal. 200	

Utilities Expense

Bal. 500	

Income Tax Expense

(g) 600	
Bal. 600	

- Panel A repeats the data for each adjustment.
- Panel B gives the adjusting entries.
- Panel C shows the accounts after posting the adjusting entries. The adjustments are keyed by letter.

Exhibit 3-8 includes an additional adjusting entry that we have not yet discussed—the accrual of income tax expense. Like individual taxpayers, corporations are subject to income tax. They typically accrue income tax expense and the related income tax payable as the final adjusting entry of the period. Jackson Repair accrues income tax expense with adjusting entry g, as follows:

			Adjusting entry g
April 30	Income Tax Expense	600	
	Income Tax Payable		600
	To accrue income tax expense.		

The income tax accrual follows the pattern for accrued expenses.

The Adjusted Trial Balance

This chapter began with the unadjusted trial balance (see Exhibit 3-3, p. 143). After the adjustments are journalized and posted, the accounts appear as shown in Exhibit 3-8, Panel C. A useful step in preparing the financial statements is to list the accounts, along with their adjusted balances, on an **adjusted trial balance**. This document lists all the accounts and their final balances in a single place. Exhibit 3-9 shows the adjusted trial balance of Jackson Repair.

EXHIBIT 3-9 Adjusted Trial Balance

Jackson Repair, Inc.
Preparation of Adjusted Trial Balance
April 30, 20X9

Account Title	Trial Balance Debit	Trial Balance Credit	Adjustments Debit	Adjustments Credit	Adjusted Trial Balance Debit	Adjusted Trial Balance Credit	
Cash	24,800				24,800		
Accounts receivable	4,200		(e) 300		4,500		
Supplies	700			(b) 300	400		
Prepaid insurance	3,000			(a) 1,000	2,000		
Repair tools	24,000				24,000		
Accumulated depreciation—repair tools				(c) 200		200	Balance Sheet (*Exhibit 3-12*)
Accounts payable		13,300				13,300	
Salary payable				(d) 900		900	
Unearned service revenue		600	(f) 300			300	
Income tax payable				(g) 600		600	
Common stock		20,000				20,000	
Retained earnings		20,200				20,200	Statement of Retained Earnings (*Exhibit 3-11*)
Dividends	3,000				3,000		
Service revenue		7,000		(e) 300		7,600	
				(f) 300			
Insurance expense			(a) 1,000		1,000		
Salary expense	900		(d) 900		1,800		Income Statement (*Exhibit 3-10*)
Supplies expense			(b) 300		300		
Depreciation expense			(c) 200		200		
Utilities expense	500				500		
Income tax expense			(g) 600		600		
	61,100	61,100	3,600	3,600	63,100	63,100	

Note how clearly the adjusted trial balance presents the data. The Account Title and the Trial Balance data come from the trial balance. The two Adjustments columns summarize the adjusting entries. The Adjusted Trial Balance columns then give the final account balances. Each adjusted amount in Exhibit 3-9 is the unadjusted balance plus or minus the adjustments. For example, Accounts Receivable starts with a

ac
t

Accounting Cycle Tutorial Glossary

balance of $4,200. Add the $300 debit adjustment to get Accounts Receivable's ending balance of $4,500. Spreadsheets are designed for this type of analysis.

PREPARING THE FINANCIAL STATEMENTS

OBJECTIVE

4 **Prepare** the financial statements

The April financial statements of Jackson Repair can be prepared from the adjusted trial balance. At the far right, Exhibit 3-9 shows how the accounts are distributed to the financial statements.

■ The income statement (Exhibit 3-10) lists the revenue and expense accounts.
■ The statement of retained earnings (Exhibit 3-11) shows the changes in retained earnings.
■ The balance sheet (Exhibit 3-12) reports assets, liabilities, and stockholders' equity.

The arrows in Exhibits 3-10, 3-11, and 3-12 show the flow of data from one statement to the next.

Why is the income statement prepared first and the balance sheet last?

1. The income statement reports net income or net loss, the result of revenues minus expenses. Revenues and expenses affect stockholders' equity, so net income is then transferred to retained earnings. The first arrow tracks net income.

2. Retained Earnings is the final balancing element of the balance sheet. To solidify your understanding, trace the $20,400 retained earnings figure from Exhibit 3-11 to Exhibit 3-12. Arrow ② tracks retained earnings.

EXHIBIT 3-10 Income Statement

Jackson Repair, Inc.
Income Statement
Month Ended April 30, 20X9

Revenues:		
Service revenue		$7,600
Expenses:		
Salary expense	$1,800	
Insurance expense....................	1,000	
Utilities expense	500	
Depreciation expense..............	200	
Supplies expense	300	3,800
Income before tax		3,800
Income tax expense......................		600
Net income....................................		$3,200

EXHIBIT 3-11 Statement of Retained Earnings

Jackson Repair, Inc.
Statement of Retained Earnings
Month Ended April 30, 20X9

Retained earnings, March 31, 20X9............	$20,200
Add: Net income...	3,200
	23,400
Less: Dividends	(3,000)
Retained earnings, April 30, 20X9..............	$20,400

①

EXHIBIT 3-12 Balance Sheet

Jackson Repair, Inc.
Balance Sheet
April 30, 20X9

Assets			Liabilities		
Cash...............................		$24,800	Accounts payable		$13,300
Accounts receivable........		4,500	Salary payable		900
Supplies..........................		400	Unearned service revenue		300
Prepaid insurance...........		2,000	Income tax payable		600
Repair tools....................	$24,000		Total liabilities		15,200
Less: Accumulated					
depreciation	(200)	23,800	**Stockholders' Equity**		
			Common stock..........................		20,000
			Retained earnings.....................		20,400
			Total stockholders' equity		40,400
			Total liabilities and		
Total assets.....................		$55,500	stockholders' equity...............		$55,500

②

MID-CHAPTER SUMMARY PROBLEM

The trial balance of Regents Company shown below pertains to December 31, 20X5, which is the end of its year-long accounting period. Data needed for the adjusting entries include the following:

a. Supplies on hand at year end, $5,000.

b. Depreciation on furniture and fixtures, $20,000.

c. Depreciation on equipment, $10,000.

d. Salaries owed but not yet paid, $5,000.

e. Accrued service revenue, $12,000.

f. Of the $45,000 balance of unearned service revenue, $30,000 was earned during the year.

g. Accrued income tax expense, $35,000.

❙ Required

1. Open the ledger accounts with their unadjusted balances. Show dollar amounts in thousands, as shown for Accounts Receivable:

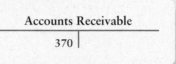

2. Journalize the Regents Company adjusting entries at December 31, 20X5. Key entries by letter, as in Exhibit 3-8, page 155.
3. Post the adjusting entries.
4. Prepare an adjusted trial balance, as shown in Exhibit 3-9, page 157.
5. Prepare the income statement, the statement of retained earnings, and the balance sheet. (At this stage, it is not necessary to classify assets or liabilities as current or long term.) Draw arrows linking these three financial statements.

Regents Company
Trial Balance
December 31, 20X5

Cash	$ 200,000	
Accounts receivable	370,000	
Supplies	6,000	
Furniture and fixtures	100,000	
Accumulated depreciation— furniture and fixtures		$ 40,000
Equipment	250,000	
Accumulated depreciation—equipment		130,000
Accounts payable		380,000
Salary payable		
Unearned service revenue		45,000
Income tax payable		
Common stock		100,000
Retained earnings		198,000
Dividends	65,000	
Service revenue		286,000
Salary expense	175,000	
Supplies expense		
Depreciation expense—furniture and fixtures		
Depreciation expense—building		
Income tax expense		
Miscellaneous expense	13,000	
Total	$1,179,000	$1,179,000

Answers

Requirements 1 and 3

Assets

Cash		Equipment	
Bal.	200	Bal.	250

Accounts Receivable		Accumulated Depreciation—Equipment	
	370		130
(e)	12	(c)	10
Bal.	382	Bal.	140

Supplies		
	6	(a) 4
Bal.	2	

Furniture and Fixtures
Bal. 100

Accumulated Depreciation—Furniture and Fixtures

	40
(b)	20
Bal.	60

Liabilities

Accounts Payable
Bal. 380

Salary Payable	
(d)	5
Bal.	5

Unearned Service Revenue		
(f) 32		45
	Bal.	13

Income Tax Payable	
(g)	35
Bal.	35

Stockholders' Equity

Common Stock
Bal. 100

Retained Earnings
Bal. 198

Dividends
Bal. 65

Revenues

Service Revenue	
	286
(e)	12
(f)	32
Bal.	330

Expenses

Salary Expense	
	175
(d)	5
Bal.	177

Supplies Expense	
(a)	4
Bal.	4

Depreciation Expense—Furniture and Fixtures	
(b)	20
Bal.	20

Depreciation Expense—Equipment	
(c)	10
Bal.	10

Income Tax Expense	
(g)	35
Bal.	35

Miscellaneous Expense	
Bal.	13

Requirements 2

(a)	Dec. 31	Supplies Expense ($6,000 – $5,000)	1,000	
		Supplies		1,000
		To record supplies used.		
(b)	31	Depreciation Expense—Furniture and Fixtures	20,000	
		Accumulated Depreciation—Furniture and Fixtures		20,000
		To record depreciation expense on furniture and fixtures.		
(c)	31	Depreciation Expense—Equipment	10,000	
		Accumulated Depreciation—Equipment		10,000
		To record depreciation expense on equipment.		
(d)	31	Salary Expense	5,000	
		Salary Payable		5,000
		To accrue salary expense.		
(e)	31	Accounts Receivable	12,000	
		Service Revenue		12,000
		To accrue service revenue.		
(f)	31	Unearned Service Revenue	30,000	
		Service Revenue		30,000
		To record unearned service revenue that has been earned.		
(g)	31	Income Tax Expense	35,000	
		Income Tax Payable		35,000
		To accrue income tax expense.		

I *Requirements 4*

Regents Company
Preparation of Adjusted Trial Balance
December 31, 20X5

Account Title	Trial Balance Debit	Trial Balance Credit	Adjustments Debit		Adjustments Credit		Adjusted Trial Balance Debit	Adjusted Trial Balance Credit
Cash	200						200	
Accounts receivable	370		(e)	12			382	
Supplies	6				(a)	1	5	
Furniture and fixtures	100						100	
Accumulated depreciation— furniture and fixtures		40			(b)	20		60
Equipment	250						250	
Accumulated depreciation—equipment		130			(c)	10		140
Accounts payable		380						380
Salary payable					(d)	5		5
Unearned service revenue		45	(f)	30				15
Income tax payable					(g)	35		35
Common stock		100						100
Retained earnings		198						198
Dividends	65						65	
Service revenue		286			(e)	12		328
					(f)	30		
Salary expense	175		(d)	5			180	
Supplies expense			(a)	1			1	
Depreciation expense— furniture and fixtures			(b)	20			20	
Depreciation expense—equipment			(c)	10			10	
Income tax expense			(g)	35			35	
Miscellaneous expense	13						13	
	1,179	1,179	113		113		1,261	1,261

Requirements 5

Regents Company
Income Statement
Year Ended December 31, 20X5

(Amounts in thousands)

Revenue:		
Service revenue		$328
Expenses:		
Salary expense	$180	
Depreciation expense—furniture and fixtures...............	20	
Depreciation expense—equipment	10	
Supplies expense	1	
Miscellaneous expense	13	224
Income before tax		104
Income tax expense		35
Net income..		$ 69

①

Regents Company
Statement of Retained Earnings
Year Ended December 31, 20X5

(Amounts in thousands)

Retained earnings, December 31, 20X4	$198
Add: Net income	69
	267
Less: Dividends	(65)
Retained earnings, December 31, 20X5	$202

②

Regents Company
Balance Sheet
December 31, 20X5

(Amounts in thousands)

Assets			Liabilities		
Cash...		$200	Accounts payable		$380
Accounts receivable.................		382	Salary payable		5
Supplies....................................		5	Unearned service revenue		15
Furniture and fixtures	$100		Income tax payable		35
Less: Accumulated			Total liabilities		435
depreciation..................	(60)	40			
			Stockholders' Equity		
Equipment...............................	$250		Common stock.............................		100
Less: Accumulated			Retained earnings.........................		202
depreciation..................	(140)	110	Total stockholders' equity		302
			Total liabilities and		
Total assets..............................		$737	stockholders' equity...................		$737

Which Accounts Need to Be Closed?

OBJECTIVE

5 **Close** the books

It is now April 30, the end of the month. Van Gray, the manager, will continue Jackson Repair into May, June, and beyond. But wait—the revenue and the expense accounts still hold amounts for April. At the end of each accounting period, it is necessary to close the books.

Closing the books means to prepare the accounts for the next period's transactions. The **closing entries** set the revenue, expense, and dividends balances back to zero at the end of the period. The idea is the same as setting the scoreboard back to zero after a game.

Closing is easily handled by computers. Recall that the income statement reports only one period's income. For example, net income for Starbucks or Jackson Repair for 2008 relates exclusively to 2008. At each year end, Starbucks accountants close the company's revenues and expenses for that year.

Temporary accounts. Because revenues and expenses relate to a limited period, they are called **temporary accounts**. The Dividends account is also temporary. The closing process applies only to temporary accounts (revenues, expenses, and dividends).

Permanent accounts. Let's contrast the temporary accounts with the **permanent accounts**: assets, liabilities, and stockholders' equity. The permanent accounts are not closed at the end of the period because they carry over to the next period. Consider Cash, Receivables, Repair Tools, Accounts Payable, Common Stock, and Retained Earnings. Their ending balances at the end of one period become the beginning balances of the next period.

Closing entries transfer the revenue, expense, and dividends balances to Retained Earnings. Here are the steps to close the books of a company such as Starbucks Corporation or Jackson Repair:

① Debit each revenue account for the amount of its credit balance. Credit Retained Earnings for the sum of the revenues. Now the sum of the revenues is in Retained Earnings.

② Credit each expense account for the amount of its debit balance. Debit Retained Earnings for the sum of the expenses. The sum of the expenses is now in Retained Earnings.

③ Credit the Dividends account for the amount of its debit balance. Debit Retained Earnings. This entry places the dividends amount in the debit side of Retained Earnings. Remember that dividends are not expenses. Dividends never affect net income.

After closing the books, the Retained Earnings account of Jackson Repairs appears as follows (data from page 159):

Retained Earnings			
		Beginning balance	20,200
Expenses	4,400	Revenues	7,600
Dividends	3,000		
		Ending balance	20,400

Assume that Jackson Repairs closes the books at the end of April. Exhibit 3-13 presents the complete closing process for the business. Panel A gives the closing journal entries, and Panel B shows the accounts after closing.

EXHIBIT 3-13 Journalizing and Posting the Closing Entries

PANEL A—Journalizing the Closing Entries   Page 5

Closing Entries

①	April 30	Service Revenue..................................	7,600	
		Retained Earnings		7,600
②	30	Retained Earnings	4,400	
		Insurance Expense....................		1,000
		Salary Expense		1,800
		Supplies Expense......................		300
		Depreciation Expense...............		200
		Utilities Expense.......................		500
		Income Tax Expense		600
③	30	Retained Earnings	3,000	
		Dividends.................................		3,000

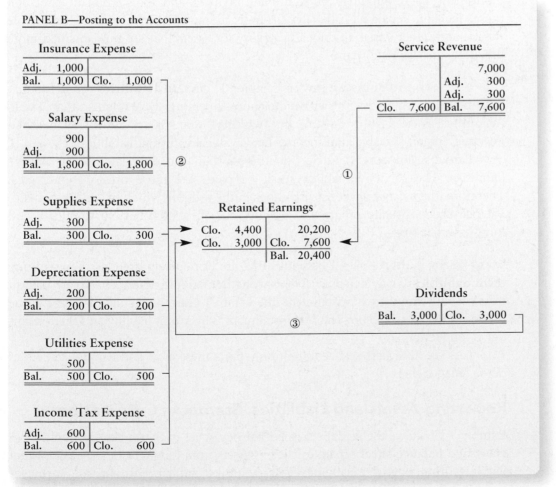

PANEL B—Posting to the Accounts

Adj. = Amount posted from an adjusting entry
Clo. = Amount posted from a closing entry
Bal. = Balance
As arrow ② in Panel B shows, we can make a compound closing entry for all the expenses.

Accounting Cycle Tutorial
Adjusting & Closing the Books

Accounting Cycle Tutorial
Application—Cottage Kitchen

Accounting Cycle Tutorial
Application—Cottage
Kitchen 2

Classifying Assets and Liabilities Based on Their Liquidity

On the balance sheet, assets and liabilities are classified as current or long term to indicate their relative liquidity. **Liquidity** measures how quickly an item can be converted to cash. Cash is the most liquid asset. Accounts receivable are relatively liquid because cash collections usually follow quickly. Inventory is less liquid than accounts receivable because the company must first sell the goods. Equipment and buildings are even less liquid because these assets are held for use and not for sale. A balance sheet lists assets and liabilities in the order of relative liquidity.

Current Assets. As we saw in Chapter 1, **current assets** are the most liquid assets. They will be converted to cash, sold, or consumed during the next 12 months or within the business's normal operating cycle if longer than a year. The **operating cycle** is the time span during which cash is paid for goods and services and these goods and services are sold to bring in cash.

For most businesses, the operating cycle is a few months. Cash, Short-Term Investments, Accounts Receivable, Merchandise Inventory, and Prepaid Expenses are the current assets.

Long-Term Assets. **Long-term assets** are all assets not classified as current assets. One category of long-term assets is plant assets, often labeled Property, Plant, and Equipment. Land, Buildings, Furniture and Fixtures, and Tools are plant assets. Of these, Jackson Repair has only Repair Tools. Long-Term Investments, Intangible Assets, and Other Assets (a catchall category for assets that are not classified more precisely) are also long-term.

Current Liabilities. As we saw in Chapter 1, **current liabilities** are debts that must be paid within 1 year or within the entity's operating cycle if longer than a year. Accounts Payable, Notes Payable due within 1 year, Salary Payable, Unearned Revenue, Interest Payable, and Income Tax Payable are current liabilities.

Bankers and other lenders are interested in the due dates of an entity's liabilities. The sooner a liability must be paid, the more pressure it creates. Therefore, the balance sheet lists liabilities in the order in which they must be paid. Balance sheets usually report two liability classifications, current liabilities and long-term liabilities.

Long-Term Liabilities. All liabilities that are not current are classified as **long-term liabilities**. Many notes payable are long term. Some notes payable are paid in installments, with the first installment due within 1 year, the second installment due the second year, and so on. The first installment is a current liability and the remainder is long term.

Let's see how Starbucks Corporation reports these asset and liability categories on its balance sheet.

Reporting Assets and Liabilities: Starbucks Corporation

Exhibit 3-14 shows the actual classified balance sheet of Starbucks Corporation. A **classified balance sheet** separates current assets from long-term assets and current liabilities from long-term liabilities. You should be familiar with most of Starbucks' accounts. Study the Starbucks balance sheet all the way through—line by line.

EXHIBIT 3-14 Classified Balance Sheet of Starbucks Corporation (Adapted, in millions)

Starbucks Corporation
Balance Sheet (Adapted)
September 30, 2006

(millions)

Assets

Current assets:

Cash and cash equivalents	$ 313
Short-term investments	140
Accounts receivable	224
Inventories	636
Prepaid expenses and other current assets	217
Total current assets	1,530
Long-term investments	225
Property, plant, and equipment, net	2,288
Intangible assets	199
Other assets	187
Total assets	$4,429

Liabilities and Shareholders' Equity

Current liabilities:

Accounts payable	$ 341
Accrued expenses payable	661
Short-term notes payable	700
Current portion of long-term	1
Unearned revenue	232
Total current liabilities	1,935
Long-term debt	2
Other long-term liabilities	263
Total liabilities	2,200

Shareholders' equity:

Common stock	40
Retained earnings	2,151
Other equity	38
Total shareholders' equity	2,229
Total liabilities and shareholders' equity	$4,429

FORMATS FOR THE FINANCIAL STATEMENTS

Companies can format their financial statements in different ways. Both the balance sheet and the income statement can be formatted in two basic ways.

Balance Sheet Formats

The **report format** lists the assets at the top, followed by the liabilities and stockholders' equity below. The balance sheet of Starbucks Corporation in Exhibit 3-14 illustrates the report format. The report format is more popular, with approximately 60% of large companies using it.

The **account format** lists the assets on the left and the liabilities and stockholders' equity on the right in the same way that a T-account appears, with assets (debits) on the left and liabilities and equity (credits) on the right. Exhibit 3-12 (p. 159) shows an account-format balance sheet for Jackson Repair, Inc.. Either format is acceptable.

Income Statement Formats

A **single-step income statement** lists all the revenues together under a heading such as Revenues, or Revenues and Gains. The expenses are listed together in a single category titled Expenses, or Expenses and Losses. There is only one step, the subtraction of Expenses and Losses from the sum of Revenues and Gains, in arriving at net income. Starbucks' income statement (p.138) appears in single-step format.

A **multi-step income statement** reports a number of subtotals to highlight important relationships between revenues and expenses. Exhibit 3-15 shows Starbucks' income statement in multi-step format. Gross profit, income from operations, income before tax, and net income are highlighted for emphasis.

EXHIBIT 3-15	Starbucks Corporation Income Statement in Multi-Step Format

Starbucks Corporation
Income Statement (Adapted)
Year Ended September 30, 2006

		Millions
Net operating revenues..		$7,787
Cost of sales (Cost of goods sold)..........................		3,179
Gross profit...		4,608
Store operating expenses	$2,688	
Other operating expenses......................................	260	
Depreciation and amortization expenses..............	387	
General and administrative expenses....................	473	
Total operating expenses.................................		3,808
Income from operations		800
Other income		89
Income before income taxes		889
Income tax expense		325
Net income..		$ 564

In particular, income from operations ($800 million) is separated from "Other income," which Starbucks did not earn by selling coffee. The other income was mainly interest revenue and other investment income. Most companies consider it important to report their operating income separately from nonoperating income such as interest and dividends.

Most companies' income statements do not conform to either a pure single-step format or a pure multi-step format. Business operations are too complex for all companies to conform to rigid reporting formats.

USING ACCOUNTING RATIOS

As we've seen, accounting provides information for decision making. A bank considering lending money must predict whether the borrower can repay the loan. If the borrower already has a lot of debt, the probability of repayment may be low. If the borrower owes little, the loan may go through. To analyze a company's financial position, decision makers use ratios computed from various items in the financial statements. Let's see how this process works.

OBJECTIVE

6 **Use** 2 new ratios to evaluate a business

Current Ratio

One of the most widely used financial ratios is the **current ratio**, which divides total current assets by total current liabilities, taken from the balance sheet.

$$\text{Current ratio} = \frac{\text{Total current assets}}{\text{Total current liabilities}}$$

For Starbucks Corporation (amounts in millions on page 167):

$$\text{Current ratio} = \frac{\text{Total current assets}}{\text{Total current liabilities}} = \frac{\$1,530}{\$1,935} = 0.79$$

The current ratio measures the company's ability to pay current liabilities with current assets. A company prefers a high current ratio, which means that the business has plenty of current assets to pay current liabilities. An increasing current ratio from period to period indicates improvement in financial position.

As a rule of thumb, a strong current ratio is 1.50, which indicates that the company has $1.50 in current assets for every $1.00 in current liabilities. A company with a current ratio of 1.50 would probably have little trouble paying its current liabilities. Most successful businesses operate with current ratios between 1.20 and 1.50. A current ratio of 1.00 is considered quite low.

Starbucks' current ratio of 0.79 is very low and indicates a weak current position. How does Starbucks survive with so low a current ratio? The company makes most sales for cash, and it has little debt. That leads us to the next ratio.

Debt Ratio

A second aid to decision making is the **debt ratio**, which is the ratio of total liabilities to total assets:

$$\text{Debt ratio} = \frac{\text{Total liabilities}}{\text{Total assets}}$$

For Starbucks (amounts in millions on page 167),

$$\text{Debt ratio} = \frac{\text{Total liabilities}}{\text{Total assets}} = \frac{\$2,200}{\$4,429} = 0.50$$

The debt ratio indicates the proportion of a company's assets that is financed with debt. This ratio measures a business's ability to pay both current and long-term debts (total liabilities).

A low debt ratio is safer than a high debt ratio. Why? Because a company with few liabilities has low required debt payments. This company is unlikely to get into financial difficulty. By contrast, a business with a high debt ratio may have trouble paying its liabilities, especially when sales are low and cash is scarce.

Starbucks' debt ratio of 50% (0.50) is low compared to most companies in the United States. The norm for the debt ratio ranges from 60% to 70%. Starbucks' debt ratio indicates low risk for the company, and that partly offsets Starbucks' risky current ratio.

When a company fails to pay its debts, creditors can take the company away from its owners. Most bankruptcies result from high debt ratios.

How Do Transactions Affect the Ratios?

Companies such as Starbucks are keenly aware of how transactions affect their ratios. Lending agreements often require that a company's current ratio not fall below a certain level. Another loan requirement is that the company's debt ratio may not rise above a threshold, such as 0.70. When a company fails to meet one of these conditions, it is said to violate its lending agreements. The penalty can be severe: The lender can require immediate payment of the loan. Starbucks has so little debt that the company is not in much danger. But many companies are.

Let's use Starbucks Corporation to examine the effects of some transactions on the company's current ratio and debt ratio. As shown in the preceding section, Starbucks' ratios are as follows (dollar amounts in millions):

$$\text{Current ratio} = \frac{\$1,530}{\$1,935} = 0.79 \qquad \text{Debt ratio} = \frac{\$2,200}{\$4,429} = 0.50$$

The managers of any company would be concerned about how inventory purchases, payments on account, expense accruals, and depreciation would affect its ratios. Let's see how Starbucks would be affected by some typical transactions. For each transaction, the journal entry helps identify the effects on the company.

a. Issued stock and received cash of $40 million.

Journal entry:	Cash		40	
	Common Stock			40

Cash, a current asset, affects both the current ratio and the debt ratio as follows:

$$\text{Current ratio} = \frac{\$1,530 + \$40}{\$1,935} = 0.81 \qquad \text{Debt ratio} = \frac{\$2,200}{\$4,429 + \$40} = 0.49$$

The issuance of stock improves both ratios.

b. Paid cash to purchase buildings for $50 million.

Journal entry:

Buildings	50	
Cash		50

Cash, a current asset, decreases, but total assets stay the same. Liabilities are unchanged.

$$\text{Current ratio} = \frac{\$1{,}530 - \$50}{\$1{,}935} = 0.77$$

$$\text{Debt ratio} = \frac{\$2{,}200}{\$4{,}429 + \$50 - \$50} = 0.50; \text{ no change}$$

A cash purchase of a building hurts the current ratio, but doesn't affect the debt ratio.

c. Made a $30 million sale on account to a grocery chain.

Journal entry:

Accounts Receivable	30	
Sales Revenue		30

The increase in Accounts Receivable increases current assets and total assets, as follows:

$$\text{Current ratio} = \frac{\$1{,}530 + \$30}{\$1{,}935} = 0.81$$

$$\text{Debt ratio} = \frac{\$2{,}200}{\$4{,}429 + \$30} = 0.49$$

A sale on account improves both ratios.

d. Collected the account receivable, $30 million.

Journal entry:

Cash	30	
Accounts Receivable		30

This transaction has no effect on total current assets, total assets, or total liabilities. Both ratios are unaffected.

e. Accrued expenses at year end, $40 million.

Journal entry:

Expenses	10	
Expenses Payable		10

$$\text{Current ratio} = \frac{\$1{,}530}{\$1{,}935 + \$40} = 0.78$$

$$\text{Debt ratio} = \frac{\$2{,}200 + \$40}{\$4{,}429} = 0.51$$

Most expenses hurt both ratios.

f. Recorded depreciation, $80 million.

Journal entry:	Depreciation Expense	80	
	Accumulated Depreciation		80

No current accounts are affected, so only the debt ratio is affected.

$$\text{Current ratio} = \frac{\$1,530}{\$1,935} = 0.79 \qquad \text{Debt ratio} = \frac{\$2,200}{\$4,429 - \$80} = 0.51$$

Depreciation decreases total assets and therefore hurts the debt ratio.

g. Earned interest revenue and collected cash, $50 million.

Journal entry:	Cash	50	
	Interest Revenue		50

Cash, a current asset, affects both the current ratio and the debt ratio as follows:

$$\text{Current ratio} = \frac{\$1,530 + \$50}{\$1,935} = 0.82 \qquad \text{Debt ratio} = \frac{\$2,200}{\$4,429 + \$50} = 0.49$$

A revenue improves both ratios.

Now, let's wrap up the chapter by seeing how to use the current ratio and the debt ratio for decision making. The Decision Guidelines feature offers some clues.

DECISION GUIDELINES

USING THE CURRENT RATIO AND THE DEBT RATIO

In general, a *high* current ratio is preferable to a low current ratio. *Increases* in the current ratio improve financial position. By contrast, a *low* debt ratio is preferable to a high debt ratio. Improvement is indicated by a *decrease* in the debt ratio.

     No single ratio gives the whole picture about a company. Therefore, lenders and investors use many ratios to evaluate a company. Let's apply what we have learned. Suppose you are a loan officer at Bank One, and Starbucks Corporation has asked you for a $20 million loan to launch a new blend of coffee. How will you make this loan decision? The Decision Guidelines show how bankers and investors use two key ratios.

USING THE CURRENT RATIO

Decision	Guidelines
How can you measure a company's ability to pay current liabilities with current assets?	$$\text{Current ratio} = \frac{\text{Total current assets}}{\text{Total current liabilities}}$$
Who uses the current ratio for decision making?	*Lenders and other creditors*, who must predict whether a borrower can pay its current liabilities. *Stockholders*, who know that a company that cannot pay its debts is not a good investment because it may go bankrupt. *Managers*, who must have enough cash to pay the company's current liabilities.

What is a good value of the current ratio?	Depends on the industry:
	    A company with strong cash flow can operate successfully with a low current ratio of, say, 1.10–1.20.
	    A company with weak cash flow needs a higher current ratio of, say, 1.30–1.50.
	    Traditionally, a current ratio of 2.00 was considered ideal. Recently, acceptable values have decreased as companies have been able to operate more efficiently; today, a current ratio of 1.50 is considered strong. Cash-rich companies like Starbucks and Yum! Brands can operate with a current ratio below 1.0.

USING THE DEBT RATIO

Decision	Guidelines
How can you measure a company's ability to pay total liabilities?	$$\text{Debt ratio} = \frac{\text{Total liabilities}}{\text{Total assets}}$$
Who uses the debt ratio for decision making?	*Lenders and other creditors*, who must predict whether a borrower can pay its debts. *Stockholders*, who know that a company that cannot pay its debts is not a good investment because it may go bankrupt. *Managers*, who must have enough assets to pay the company's debts.

What is a good value of the debt ratio?	Depends on the industry:
	    A company with strong cash flow can operate successfully with a high debt ratio of, say, 0.70–0.80
	    A company with weak cash flow needs a lower debt ratio of, say, 0.50–0.60.
	    Traditionally, a debt ratio of 0.50 was considered ideal. Recently, values have increased as companies have been able to operate more efficiently; today, a normal value of the debt ratio is around 0.60–0.65.

END-OF-CHAPTER SUMMARY PROBLEM

Refer to the mid-chapter summary problem that begins on page 168.

❙ Required

1. Make Regents Company's closing entries at December 31, 20X5. Explain what the closing entries accomplish and why they are necessary. Show amounts in thousands.
2. Post the closing entries to Retained Earnings and compare Retained Earnings' ending balance with the amount reported on the balance sheet on page 163. The two amounts should be the same.
3. Prepare Regents Company's classified balance sheet to identify the company's current assets and current liabilities. (Regents has no long-term liabilities.) Then compute the company's current ratio and debt ratio at December 31, 20X5.
4. The top management of Regents Company has asked you for a $500,000 loan to expand the business. Regents proposes to pay off the loan over a 10-year period. Recompute Regents's debt ratio assuming you make the loan. Use the company financial statements plus the ratio values to decide whether to grant the loan at an interest rate of 8%, 10%, or 12%. Regents's cash flow is strong. Give the reasoning underlying your decision.

Answers

❙ Requirement 1

20X5		(In thousands)	
Dec. 31	Service Revenue..	328	
	Retained Earnings		328
31	Retained Earnings	259	
	Salary Expense		180
	Depreciation Expense—		
	Furniture and Fixtures...........................		20
	Depreciation Expense—Equipment		10
	Supplies Expense..		1
	Income Tax Expense		35
	Miscellaneous Expense..............................		13
31	Retained Earnings	65	
	Dividends..		65

❙ Explanation of Closing Entries

The closing entries set the balance of each revenue, expense, and Dividends account back to zero for the start of the next accounting period. We must close these accounts because their balances relate only to one accounting period.

❙ Requirement 2

Retained Earnings			
			198
Clo.	259	Clo.	328
Clo.	65		
		Bal.	202

The balance in the Retained Earnings account agrees with the amount reported on the balance sheet, as it should.

Requirement 3

Regents Company
Balance Sheet
December 31, 20X5

(Amounts in thousands)

Assets			Liabilities	
Current assets:			Current liabilities:	
Cash		$200	Accounts payable	$380
Accounts receivable		382	Salary payable	5
Supplies		5	Unearned service revenue	15
Total current assets		587	Income tax payable	35
Furniture and			Total current liabilities	435
fixtures	$100		**Stockholders' Equity**	
Less: Accumulated				
depreciation	(60)	40	Common stock	100
Equipment	$250		Retained earnings	202
Less: Accumulated			Total stockholders' equity	302
depreciation	(140)	110	Total liabilities and	
Total assets		$737	stockholders' equity	$737

$$\text{Current ratio} = \frac{\$587}{\$435} = 1.35 \qquad \text{Debt ratio} = \frac{\$435}{\$737} = 0.59$$

Requirement 4

$$\text{Debt ratio assuming the loan is made} = \frac{\$435 + \$500}{\$737 + \$500} = \frac{\$935}{\$1,237} = .76$$

Decision: Make the loan at 10%.

Reasoning: Prior to the loan, the company's financial position and cash flow are strong. The current ratio is in a middle range, and the debt ratio is not too high. Net income (from the income statement) is high in relation to total revenue. Therefore, the company should be able to repay the loan.

The loan will increase the company's debt ratio from 59% to 76%, which is more risky than the company's financial position at present. On this basis, a midrange interest rate appears reasonable—at least as the starting point for the negotiation between Regents Company and the bank.

REVIEW ACCRUAL ACCOUNTING & INCOME

Quick Check (Answers are given on page 208.)

1. On November 1, Rosewood Apartments received $4,800 from a tenant for three months' rent. The receipt was credited to Unearned Rent Revenue. What adjusting entry is needed on December 31?

   a. Unearned Rent Revenue   3,200
       Rent Revenue   3,200
   b. Rent Revenue   1,600
       Unearned Rent Revenue   1,600
   c. Unearned Rent Revenue   1,600
       Rent Revenue   1,600
   d. Cash   1,600
       Rent Revenue   1,600

2. The following normal balances appear on the *adjusted* trial balance of Augusta National Company:

Equipment..	$90,000
Accumulated depreciation, equipment................	15,000
Depreciation expense, equipment........................	5,000

   The book value of the equipment is
   a. $85,000.   c. $75,000.
   b. $70,000.   d. $60,000.

3. Cadillac, Inc., purchased supplies for $900 during 20X3. At year end Cadillac had $600 of supplies left. The adjusting entry should:
   a. debit Supplies $300.   c. credit Supplies $600.
   b. debit Supplies Expense $300. d. debit Supplies $600.

4. The accountant for Eldorado Corp. failed to make the adjusting entry to record depreciation for the current year. The effect of this error is:
   a. Assets are overstated, stockholders' equity and net income are understated.
   b. Assets and expenses are understated; net income is understated.
   c. Net income is overstated and liabilities are understated.
   d. Assets, net income, and stockholders' equity are all overstated.

5. Interest earned on a note receivable at December 31 equals $125. What adjusting entry is required to accrue this interest?

   a. Interest Payable   125
       Interest Expense   125
   b. Interest Expense   125
       Cash   125
   c. Interest Receivable   125
       Interest Revenue   125
   d. Interest Expense   125
       Interest Payable   125

6. If a real estate company fails to accrue commission revenue,
   a. liabilities are overstated and owners' equity is understated.
   b. assets are understated and net income is understated.
   c. revenues are understated and net income is overstated.
   d. net income is understated and stockholders' equity is overstated.

7. All of the following statements are true except one. Which statement is false?
  a. Adjusting entries are required for a business that uses the cash basis.
  b. Accrual accounting produces better information than cash-basis accounting.
  c. The matching principle directs accountants to identify and measure all expenses incurred and deduct them from revenues earned during the same period.
  d. A fiscal year ends on some date other than December 31.

8. The account Unearned Revenue is a(n):
  a. revenue
  b. expense
  c. asset
  d. liability

9. Adjusting entries:
  a. are needed to measure the period's net income or net loss.
  b. update the accounts.
  c. do not debit or credit cash.
  d. all of the above.

10. An adjusting entry that debits an expense and credits a liability is which type?
  a. accrued expense
  b. depreciation expense
  c. prepaid expense
  d. cash expense

Use the following data for questions 11 and 12.
Here are key figures from the balance sheet of Seville, Inc., at the end of 20X3 (amounts in thousands):

	December 31, 20X3
Total assets (of which 40% are current)	$4,000
Current liabilities	800
Bonds payable (long-term)	1,200
Common stock	1,500
Retained earnings	500
Total liabilities and stockholders' equity	4,000

11. Seville's current ratio at the end of 20X3 is:
  a. 6.25
  b. 2.0
  c. 3.75
  d. 2.24

12. Seville's debt ratio at the end of 20X3 is:
  a. 42% (rounded)
  b. 17% (rounded)
  c. 60%
  d. 50%

13. On a trial balance, which of the following would indicate that an error has been made?
  a. Service Revenue has a debit balance
  b. Salary Expense has a debit balance
  c. Accumulated Depreciation has a credit balance
  d. All of the above indicate errors

14. The entry to close Management Fee Revenue would be:
  a. Management Fee Revenue does not need to be closed out.
  b. Retained Earnings
        Management Fee Revenue
  c. Management Fee Revenue
        Retained Earnings
  d. Management Fee Revenue
        Service Revenue

15. Which of the following accounts is not closed out?
  a. Accumulated Depreciation
  b. Depreciation Expense
  c. Dividends
  d. Interest Revenue

16. FedEx earns service revenue of $500,000. How does this transaction affect FedEx's ratios?
    a. Hurts the current ratio and improves the debt ratio.
    b. Hurts both ratios.
    c. Improves both ratios.
    d. Improves the current ratio and doesn't affect the debit ratio.
17. Suppose Starbucks Corporation borrows $50 million on a 10-year note payable. How does this transaction affect Starbucks' ratios?
    a. Improves both ratios.
    b. Improves the current ratio and hurts the debt ratio.
    c. Hurts both ratios.
    d. Hurts the current ratio and improves the debt ratio.

Accounting Vocabulary

account format (p. 168) A balance-sheet format that lists assets on the left and liabilities and stockholders' equity on the right.

accrual (p. 144) An expense or a revenue that occurs before the business pays or receives cash. An accrual is the opposite of a deferral.

accrual accounting (p. 139) Accounting that records the impact of a business event as it occurs, regardless of whether the transaction affected cash.

accrued expense (p. 150) An expense incurred but not yet paid in cash.

accrued revenue (p. 151) A revenue that has been earned but not yet received in cash.

accumulated depreciation (p. 148) The cumulative sum of all depreciation expense from the date of acquiring a plant asset.

adjusted trial balance (p. 157) A list of all the ledger accounts with their adjusted balances.

book value (of a plant asset) (p. 149) The asset's cost minus accumulated depreciation.

cash-basis accounting (p. 139) Accounting that records only transactions in which cash is received or paid.

classified balance sheet (p. 166) A balance sheet that shows current assets separate from long-term assets, and current liabilities separate from long-term liabilities.

closing the books (p. 164) The process of preparing the accounts to begin recording the next period's transactions. Closing the accounts consists of journalizing and posting the closing entries to set the balances of the revenue, expense, and dividends accounts to zero. Also called closing the accounts.

closing entries (p. 164) Entries that transfer the revenue, expense, and dividends balances from these respective accounts to the Retained Earnings account.

contra account (p. 148) An account that always has a companion account and whose normal balance is opposite that of the companion account.

current assets (p. 166) An asset that is expected to be converted to cash, sold, or consumed during the next 12 months, or within the business's normal operating cycle if longer than a year.

current liabilities (p. 166) A debt due to be paid within one year or within the entity's operating cycle if the cycle is longer than a year.

current ratio (p. 169) Current assets divided by current liabilities. Measures a company's ability to pay current liabilities with current assets.

debt ratio (p. 169) Ratio of total liabilities to total assets. States the proportion of a company's assets that is financed with debt.

deferral (p. 143) An adjustment for which the business paid or received cash in advance. Examples include prepaid rent, prepaid insurance, and supplies.

depreciation (p. 144) the cost of a plant asset over its useful life.

liquidity (p. 166) Measure of how quickly an item can be converted to cash.

long-term assets (p. 166) An asset that is not a current asset.

long-term liabilities (p. 166) A liability that is not a current liability.

matching principle (p. 141) The basis for recording expenses. Directs accountants to identify all expenses incurred during the period, to measure the expenses, and to match them against the revenues earned during that same period.

multi-step income statement (p. 168) An income statement that contains subtotals to highlight important relationships between revenues and expenses.

operating cycle (p. 166) Time span during which cash is paid for goods and services that are sold to customers who pay the business in cash.

permanent accounts (p. 164) Asset, liability, and stockholders' equity accounts that are not closed at the end of the period.

plant assets (p. 147) Long-lived assets, such as land, buildings, and equipment, used in the operation of the business. Also called fixed assets.

prepaid expense (p. 142) A category of miscellaneous assets that typically expire or get used up in the near future. Examples include prepaid rent, prepaid insurance, and supplies.

report format (p. 167) A balance-sheet format that lists assets at the top, followed by liabilities and stockholders' equity below.

revenue principle (p. 140) The basis for recording revenues; tells accountants when to record revenue and the amount of revenue to record.

single-step income statement (p. 168) An income statement that lists all the revenues together under a heading such as Revenues or Revenues and Gains. Expenses appear in a separate category called Expenses or perhaps Expenses and Losses.

temporary accounts (p. 164) The revenue and expense accounts that relate to a limited period and are closed at the end of the period are temporary accounts. For a corporation, the Dividends account is also temporary.

time-period concept (p. 140) Ensures that accounting information is reported at regular intervals.

unearned revenue (p. 153) A liability created when a business collects cash from customers in advance of earning the revenue. The obligation is to provide a product or a service in the future.

ASSESS YOUR PROGRESS

Short Exercises

S3-1 (*Learning Objective 1: Linking accrual accounting and cash flows*) Fleetwood Corporation made sales of $700 million during 20X3. Of this amount, Fleetwood collected cash for all but $30 million. The company's cost of goods sold was $300 million, and all other expenses for the year totaled $350 million. Also during 20X3, Fleetwood paid $400 million for its inventory and $280 million for everything else. Beginning cash was $100 million. Fleetwood's top management is interviewing you for a job and they ask two questions:

a. How much was Fleetwood's net income for 20X3? (p. 159)

b. How much was Fleetwood's cash balance at the end of 20X3? (pp. 103–104)

You will get the job only if you answer both questions correctly.

S3-2 (*Learning Objective 1: Linking accrual accounting and cash flows*) Docker Corporation began 20X9 owing notes payable of $4.0 million. During 20X9 Docker borrowed $2.6 million on notes payable and paid off $2.5 million of notes payable from prior years. Interest expense for the year was $1.0 million, including $0.2 million of interest payable accrued at December 31, 20X9.

Show what Docker should report for these facts on the following financial statements:

- Income statement (p. 159)
  - Interest expence
- Balance sheet (p.159)
  - Notes payable
  - Interest payable

S3-3 (*Learning Objective 2: Applying the revenue and the matching principles*) Ford Motor Company sells large fleets of vehicles to auto rental companies, such as Enterprise and Hertz. Suppose Enterprise is negotiating with Ford to purchase 1,000 Explorers. Write a short paragraph to explain to Ford when Ford should, and should not, record this sales revenue and the related expense for cost of goods sold. Mention the accounting principles that provide the basis for your explanation. (p. 140)

writing assignment ■

S3-4 (*Learning Objective 3: Adjusting prepaid expenses*) Answer the following questions about prepaid expenses:

    a. On November 1, Air & Sea Travel prepaid $3,000 for 6 months' rent. Give the adjusting entry to record rent expense at December 31. Include the date of the entry and an explanation. Then post all amounts to the 2 accounts involved, and show their balances at December 31. Air & Sea Travel adjusts the accounts only at December 31. (pp. 144–145)

    b. On Dec. 1, Air & Sea Travel paid $800 for supplies. At December 31, Air & Sea Travel has $500 of supplies on hand. Make the required journal entry at December 31. Then post all amounts to the accounts and show their balances at December 31. (pp. 145–146)

S3-5 (*Learning Objective 1, 3: Recording depreciation; cash flows*) Suppose that on January 1 **Callaway Golf Company** paid cash of $30,000 for computers that are expected to remain useful for 3 years. At the end of 3 years, the computers' values are expected to be zero.

    1. Make journal entries to record (a) purchase of the computers on January 1 and (b) annual depreciation on December 31. Include dates and explanations, and use the following accounts: Computer Equipment; Accumulated Depreciation—Computer Equipment; and Depreciation Expense—Computer Equipment. (pp. 147–148)

    2. Post to the accounts and show their balances at December 31. (pp. 148–149)

    3. What is the computer equipment's book value at December 31? (pp. 148–149)

S3-6 (*Learning Objective 2: Applying the matching principle and the time-period concept*) During 20X8, Jetway Airlines paid salary expense of $40 million. At December 31, 20X8, Jetway accrued salary expense of $2 million. Jetway then paid $1.9 million to its employees on January 3, 20X9, the company's next payday after the end of the 20X8 year. For this sequence of transactions, show what Jetway would report on its 20X8 income statement and on its balance sheet at the end of 20X8. (p. 159)

S3-7 (*Learning Objective 3: Accruing and paying interest expense*) Mizuno Travel borrowed $100,000 on October 1 by signing a note payable to **Texas First Bank**. The interest expense for each month is $500. The loan agreement requires Mizuno to pay interest on December 31.

    1. Make Mizuno's adjusting entry to accrue monthly interest expense at October 31, at November 30, and at December 31. Date each entry and include its explanation. (pp. 150–151)

    2. Post all three entries to the Interest Payable account. You need not take the balance of the account at the end of each month. (pp. 150–151)

    3. Record the payment of three months' interest at December 31. (Challenge)

S3-8 (*Learning Objective 3: Accruing and receiving cash from interest revenue*) Return to the situation in Short Exercise S3-7. Here you are accounting for the same transactions on the books of Texas First Bank, which lent the money to Mizuno Travel. Perform all three steps of Short Exercise S3-7 for Texas First Bank using the bank's own accounts. (pp. 151–152)

writing assignment ■   **S3-9** (*Learning Objective 3: Explaining unearned revenues*) Write a paragraph to explain why unearned revenues are liabilities instead of revenues. In your explanation, use the following actual example: **The Wall Street Journal** collects cash from subscribers in advance and later delivers newspapers to subscribers over a 1-year period. Explain what happens to the unearned revenue over the course of a year as *The Wall Street Journal* delivers papers to subscribers. Into what account does the earned subscription revenue go as *The Wall Street Journal* delivers papers? Give the journal entries that *The Wall Street Journal* would make to (a) collect $40,000 of subscription revenue in advance and (b) record earning $40,000 of subscription revenue. Include an explanation for each entry, as illustrated in the chapter. (pp. 151–152)

S3-10 (*Learning Objective 4: Reporting prepaid expenses*) Eagle Golf Co. prepaid 3 years' rent ($6,000) on January 1. At December 31, Eagle prepared a trial balance and then made the necessary adjusting entry at the end of the year. Eagle adjusts its accounts once each year—on December 31.

What amount appears for Prepaid Rent on

a. Eagle's *unadjusted* trial balance at December 31? (pp. 156–157)

b. Eagle's *adjusted* trial balance at December 31? (pp. 156–157)

What amount appears for Rent Expense on

c. Eagle's *unadjusted* trial balance at December 31? (pp. 156–157)

d. Eagle's *adjusted* trial balance at December 31? (pp. 156–157)

S3-11 (*Learning Objective 3: Updating the accounts*) Bentley, Inc., collects cash from customers two ways:

a. **Accrued revenue.** Some customers pay Bentley after Bentley has performed service for the customer. During 20X8, Bentley made sales of $50,000 on account and later received cash of $40,000 on account from these customers.

b. **Unearned revenue.** A few customers pay Bentley in advance, and Bentley later performs the service for the customer. During 20X8 Bentley collected $7,000 cash in advance and later earned $6,000 of this amount.

Journalize for Bentley

a. Earning service revenue of $50,000 on account and then collecting $40,000 on account. (pp. 151–152)

b. Receiving $7,000 in advance and then earning $6,000 as service revenue. (pp. 153–154)

Explanations are not required.

S3-12 (*Learning Objective 4: Preparing the financial statements*) Falcon Sporting Goods Company reported the following data at March 31, 20X4, with amounts in thousands:

Retained earnings,		Cost of goods sold..................	$126,000
March 31, 20X3	$ 1,300	Cash.......................................	900
Accounts receivable.......	27,700	Property and equipment,	
Net revenues	174,500	net.......................................	7,200
Total current liabilities..	53,600	Common stock......................	26,000
All other expenses	45,000	Inventories	33,000
Other current assets	4,800	Long-term liabilities	13,500
Other assets..................	24,300	Dividends.............................	0

Use these data to prepare Falcon Sporting Goods Company's income statement for the year ended March 31, 20X4; statement of retained earnings for the year ended March 31, 20X4; and classified balance sheet at March 31, 20X4. Use the report format for the balance sheet. Draw arrows linking the three statements. (pp. 159, 169, 168)

S3-13 (*Learning Objective 5: Making closing entries*) Use the Falcon Sporting Goods data in Short Exercise S3-12 to make the company's closing entries at March 31, 20X4. Then set up a T-account for Retained Earnings and post to that account. Compare Retained Earnings' ending balance to the amount reported on Falcon's statement of retained earnings and balance sheet. What do you find? (pp. 165–166)

S3-14 (*Learning Objective 6: Computing the current ratio and the debt ratio*) Use the Falcon Sporting Goods data in short Exercise S3-12 to compute Falcon's

1. Current ratio (pp. 169–170)

2. Debit ratio (pp. 170–171)

Round to 2 decimal places. Do these ratio values look strong, weak or middle-of-the-road?

S3-15 (*Learning Objective 6: Using the current ratio and the debit ratio*) Use the Falcon Sporting Goods data in Short Exercise S3-12 to compute Falcon's (a) current ratio and (b) debt ratio after each of the following transactions (all amounts in thousands, as in the Falcon financial statements):

1. Falcon earned revenue of $10,000 on account (pp. 171–172)
2. Falcon paid off accounts payable of $10,000. (Challenge)

Round ratios to 2 decimal places.

Exercises

Most of the even-numbered exercises can be found within My Accouting Lab (MAL), an online homework and practice environment. Your instructor may ask you to complete these exercises using MAL.

E3-16 (*Learning Objective 1: Linking accrual accounting and cash flows*) During 20X8 Consolidated Foods Corporation made sales of $4,000 (assume all on account) and collected cash of $4,100 from customers. Operating expenses totaled $800, all paid in cash. At year end, 20X8, Consolidated customers owed the company $400. Consolidated owed creditors $700 on account. All amounts are in millions.

1. For these facts, show what Consolidated reported on the following financial statements (p. 159):

   • Income statement   • Balance sheet

2. Suppose Consolidated had used the cash basis of accounting. What would Consolidated have reported for these facts? (p. 139)

E3-17 (*Learning Objective 1: Linking accrual accounting and cash flows*) During 2009 Valley Sales, Inc., earned revenues of $500,000 on account. Valley collected $510,000 from customers during the year. Expenses totaled $420,000, and the related cash payments were $400,000. Show what Valley would report on its 2009 income statement under the

   a. Cash basis   **b.** Accrual basis

Compute net income under both bases of accounting. Which basis measures net income better? Explain your answer. (p. 139)

E3-18 (*Learning Objective 1, 2: Accrual basis of accounting, applying accounting principles*) During 20X6, Dish Network, Inc., which designs network servers, earned revenues of $700 million. Expenses totaled $540 million. Dish collected all but $20 million of the revenues and paid $550 million on its expenses. Dish's top managers are evaluating 20X6, and they ask you the following questions:

   a. Under accrual accounting, what amount of revenue should Dish Network report for 20X6? Is the revenue the $700 million earned or is it the amount of cash actually collected? How does the revenue principle help to answer these questions? (pp. 139, 140)
   b. Under accrual accounting, what amount of total expense should Dish Network report for 20X6—$540 million or $550 million? Which accounting principle helps to answer this question? (pp. 139–141)
   c. Which financial statement reports revenues and expenses? Which statement reports cash receipts and cash payments? (p. 159)

writing assignment ■

E3-19 (*Learning Objective 2: Applying accounting concepts and principles*) Write a short paragraph to explain in your own words the concept of depreciation as used in accounting. (pp. 147–148)

E3-20 (*Learning Objective 2: Applying accounting concepts and principles*) Identify the accounting concept or principle that gives the most direction on how to account for each of the following situations: (pp. 140–142)

a. Salary expense of $20,000 is accrued at the end of the period to measure income properly.

b. October has been a particularly slow month, and the business will have a net loss for the third quarter of the year. Management is considering not following its customary practice of reporting quarterly earnings to the public.

c. A physician performs a surgical operation and bills the patient's insurance company. It may take 3 months to collect from the insurance company. Should the physician record revenue now or wait until cash is collected?

d. A construction company is building a highway system, and construction will take 3 years. When should the company record the revenue it earns?

e. A utility bill is received on December 30 and will be paid next year. When should the company record utility expense?

writing assignment ■

E3-21 *(Learning Objective 1, 3: Journalizing adjusting entries and analyzing their effects on net income; accrual versus cash basis)* An accountant made the following adjustments at December 31, the end of the accounting period:

a. Prepaid insurance, beginning, $700. Payments for insurance during the period, $2,100. Prepaid insurance, ending, $800.

b. Interest revenue accrued, $900.

c. Unearned service revenue, beginning, $800. Unearned service revenue, ending, $300.

d. Depreciation, $6,200.

e. Employees' salaries owed for 3 days of a 5-day work week; weekly payroll, $9,000.

f. Income before income tax, $20,000. Income tax rate is 40%.

■ general ledger

I *Required*

1. Journalize the adjusting entries. (pp. 144–156)

2. Suppose the adjustments were not made. Compute the overall overstatement or understatement of net income as a result of the omission of these adjustments.

E3-22 *(Learning Objective 2, 3: Allocating supplies cost to the asset and the expense)* Bird-Kultgen, Inc., experienced four situations for its supplies. Compute the amounts indicated by question marks for each situation. For situations 1 and 2, journalize the needed transaction. Consider each situation separately. (pp. 144–146)

■ spreadsheet

	Situation			
	1	2	3	4
Beginning supplies................................	$ 500	$1,000	$300	$ 900
Payments for supplies during the year.......	?	3,100	?	1,100
Total cost to account for...........................	1,300	?	?	2,000
Ending supplies..	400	500	700	?
Supplies expense.....................................	$ 900	$?	$700	$1,400

E3-23 *(Learning Objective 3: Journalizing adjusting entries)* Clark Motor Company faced the following situations. Journalize the adjusting entry needed at December 31, 20X6, for each situation. Consider each fact separately. (pp. 144–156)

■ general ledger

a. The business has interest expense of $9,000 that it must pay early in January 20X7.

b. Interest revenue of $3,000 has been earned but not yet received.

c. On July 1, when we collected $3,000 rent in advance, we debited Cash and credited Unearned Rent Revenue. The tenant was paying us for 2 years' rent.

d. Salary expense is $1,000 per day—Monday through Friday—and the business pays employees each Friday. This year, December 31 falls on a Tuesday.

e. The unadjusted balance of the Supplies account is $3,100. The total cost of supplies on hand is $800.

(continued)

Q3-51 Unadjusted net income equals $5,000. After the following adjustments, net income will be (fill in the blank) $___ (pp. 156, 159, Challenge)
(1) Salaries payable to employees, $500.
(2) Interest due on note payable at the bank, $100.
(3) Unearned revenue that has been earned, $600.
(4) Supplies used, $200.

Q3-52 Salary Payable at the beginning of the month totals $24,000. During the month salaries of $125,000 were accrued as expense. If ending Salary Payable is $10,000, what amount of cash did the company pay for salaries during the month? (Hint: Draw a T-account, as on pp. 103–104.)

a. $129,000

c. $125,000

b. $149,000

d. $139,000

Problems
(Group A)

MyAccountingLab

Some of these A problems can be found within My Accounting Lab (MAL), an online homework and practice environment. Your instructor may ask you to complete these exercises using MAL.

P3-53A (*Learning Objective 1: Linking accrual accounting and cash flows*) Cherokee Corporation earned revenues of $35 million during 20X1 and ended the year with net income of $8 million. During 20X1, Cherokee collected $33 million from customers and paid cash for all of its expenses plus an additional $1 million for amounts payable at December 31, 20X0. Answer these questions about Cherokee's operating results, financial position, and cash flows during 20X1:

❚ *Required*

1. How much were Cherokee's total expenses? Show your work. (pp. 139–140)
2. Identify all the items that Cherokee will report on its 20X1 income statement. Show each amount. (p. 159)
3. Cherokee began 20X1 with receivables of $4 million. All sales are on account. What was the company's receivables balance at the end of 20X1? Identify the appropriate financial statement, and show how Cherokee will report ending receivables in the 20X1 annual report. (pp. 103–104)
4. Cherokee began 20X1 owing accounts payable of $9 million. All expenses are increased on account. During 20X1 Cherokee paid $28 million on account. How much in accounts payable did the company owe at the end of the year? Identify the appropriate financial statement and show how Cherokee will report accounts payable in its 20X1 annual report. (pp. 103–104)

P3-54A (*Learning Objective 1: Cash basis versus accrual basis*) Masters Consulting had the following selected transactions in August:

Aug. 1	Prepaid insurance for August through December, $1,000.
4	Purchased software for cash, $800.
5	Performed service and received cash, $900.
8	Paid advertising expense, $300.
11	Performed service on account, $3,000.
19	Purchased computer on account, $1,600.
24	Collected for the August 11 service.
26	Paid account payable from August 19.
29	Paid salary expense, $900.
31	Adjusted for August insurance expense (see Aug. 1).
31	Earned revenue of $800 that was collected in advance back in July.

I *Required*

1. Show how each transaction would be handled using the cash basis and the accrual basis. Under each column, give the amount of revenue or expense for August. Journal entries are not required. Use the following format for your answer, and show your computations: (pp. 139–140)

	Masters Consulting Amount of Revenue (Expense) for August	
Date	Cash Basis	Accrual Basis

2. Compute August income (loss) before tax under each accounting method. (p. 137)

3. Indicate which measure of net income or net loss is preferable. Use the transactions on August 11 and 24 to explain. (p. 139)

P3-55A *(Learning Objective 1, 2: Applying accounting principles)* Write a memo to explain for a new employee the difference between the cash basis of accounting and the accrual basis. Mention the roles of the revenue principle and the matching principle in accrual accounting. (pp. 139–140)

P3-56A *(Learning Objective 3: Making accounting adjustments)* Journalize the adjusting entry needed on December 31, end of the current accounting period, for each of the following independent cases affecting Callaway Corp. Include an explanation for each entry. (pp. 144–156)

writing assignment ■

a. Details of Prepaid Insurance are shown in the account:

	Prepaid Insurance	
Jan. 1 Bal.	400	
Mar. 31	3,600	

Callaway prepays insurance on March 31 each year. At December 31, $600 is still prepaid.

b. Callaway pays employees each Friday. The amount of the weekly payroll is $6,000 for a 5-day work week. The current accounting period ends on Wednesday.

c. Callaway has a note receivable. During the current year, Callaway has earned accrued interest revenue of $500 that it will collect next year.

d. The beginning balance of supplies was $2,600. During the year, Callaway purchased supplies costing $6,100, and at December 31 supplies on hand total $2,100.

e. Callaway is providing services for Manatee Investments, and the owner of Manatee paid Callaway $12,000 as the annual service fee. Callaway recorded this amount as Unearned Service Revenue. Callaway estimates that it has earned one-third of the total fee during the current year.

f. Depreciation for the current year includes Office Furniture, $1,000 and Equipment, $2,700. Make a compound entry.

P3-57A *(Learning Objective 3, 4, 6: Preparing an adjusted trial balance and the financial statements; using the current ratio to evaluate the business)* The unadjusted trial balance of Princess, Inc., at January 31, 20X2, and the related month-end adjustment data follow.

Princess, Inc.
Trial Balance
January 31, 20X2

Cash	$ 8,000	
Accounts receivable	10,000	
Prepaid rent	3,000	
Supplies	2,000	
Furniture	36,000	
Accumulated depreciation		$ 3,000
Accounts payable		10,000
Salary payable		
Common stock		26,000
Retained earnings (December 31, 20X1)		13,000
Dividends	4,000	
Service revenue		14,000
Salary expense	2,000	
Rent expense		
Utilities expense	1,000	
Depreciation expense		
Supplies expense		
Total	$66,000	$66,000

Adjustment data:
   a. Accrued service revenue at January 31, $2,000.
   b. Prepaid rent expired during the month. The unadjusted prepaid balance of $3,000 relates to the period January through March.
   c. Supplies used during January, $2,000.
   d. Depreciation on furniture for the month. The estimated useful life of the furniture is 3 years.
   e. Accrued salary expense at January 31 for Monday, Tuesday, and Wednesday. The 5-day weekly payroll of $5,000 will be paid on Friday, February 2.

I Required

1. Using Exhibit 3-9, page 157, as an example, prepare the adjusted trial balance of Princess, Inc., at January 31, 20X2. Key each adjusting entry by letter.

2. Prepare the monthly income statement, the statement of retained earnings, and the classified balance sheet. Draw arrows linking the three financial statements. (p. 159)

P3-58A *(Learning Objective 3: Analyzing and recording adjustments)* Peppertree Apartments, Inc.'s, unadjusted and adjusted trial balances at April 30, 20X1, is given on the next page.

	Peppertree Apartments, Inc. Adjusted Trial Balance April 30, 20X1			
	Trial Balance		**Adjusted Trial Balance**	
Account Title	**Debit**	**Credit**	**Debit**	**Credit**
Cash	8,300		8,300	
Accounts receivable	6,300		6,800	
Interest receivable			300	
Note receivable	4,100		4,100	
Supplies	900		200	
Prepaid insurance	2,400		700	
Building	66,400		66,400	
Accumulated depreciation		16,000		18,200
Accounts payable		6,900		6,900
Wages payable				400
Unearned rental revenue		600		100
Common stock		18,000		18,000
Retained earnings		42,700		42,700
Dividends	3,600		3,600	
Rental revenue		9,900		10,900
Interest revenue				300
Wage expense	1,600		2,000	
Insurance expense			1,700	
Depreciation expense			2,200	
Property tax expense	300		300	
Supplies expense			700	
Utilities expense	200		200	
	94,100	94,100	97,500	97,500

Required

1. Make the adjusting entries that account for the differences between the two trial balances. (p. 157)

2. Compute Peppertree's total assets, total liabilities, total equity, and net income. (p. 159)

P3-59A (*Learning Objective 4, 6: Preparing the financial statements and using the debt ratio*) The adjusted trial balance of Snead Corporation, at December 31, 20X6, follows on the next page.

Required

1. Prepare Snead Corporation's 20X6 income statement, statement of retained earnings, and balance sheet. List expenses (except for income tax) in decreasing order on the income statement and show total liabilities on the balance sheet. Draw arrows linking the three financial statements. (p. 159)

■ **general ledger**

■ **spreadsheet**

(continued)

2. Snead's lenders require that the company maintain a debt ratio no higher than 0.60. Compute Snead's debt ratio at December 31, 20X6, to determine whether the company is in compliance with this debt restriction. If not, suggest a way that Snead could have avoided this difficult situation. (pp. 169–170)

Snead Corporation
Adjusted Trial Balance
December 31, 20X6

Cash	$ 1,400	
Accounts receivable	8,900	
Supplies	2,300	
Prepaid rent	1,600	
Equipment	37,100	
Accumulated depreciation		$ 4,300
Accounts payable		3,700
Interest payable		800
Unearned service revenue		600
Income tax payable		2,100
Note payable		18,600
Common stock		5,000
Retained earnings		1,000
Dividends	24,000	
Service revenue		107,900
Depreciation expense	1,600	
Salary expense	39,900	
Rent expense	10,300	
Interest expense	3,100	
Insurance expense	3,800	
Supplies expense	2,900	
Income tax expense	7,100	
Total	$144,000	$144,000

P3-60A (*Learning Objective 5: Closing the books and evaluating retained earnings*) The accounts of Meadowbrook Services, Inc., at March 31, 20X3, are listed in alphabetical order.

Accounts payable	$14,700	Interest expense	$ 600	
Accounts receivable	16,500	Note payable, long-term	6,200	
Accumulated depreciation—		Other assets	14,100	
equipment	7,100	Prepaid expenses	5,300	
Advertising expense	10,900	Retained earnings,		
Cash	7,500	March 31, 20X2	20,200	
Common stock	9,100	Salary expense	17,800	
Current portion of note		Salary payable	2,400	
payable	800	Service revenue	94,100	
Depreciation expense	1,900	Supplies	3,800	
Dividends	31,200	Supplies expense	4,600	
Equipment	43,200	Unearned service revenue	2,800	

Required

1. All adjustments have been journalized and posted, but the closing entries have not yet been made. Journalize Meadowbrook's closing entries at March 31, 20X3. (p. 165)
2. Set up a T-account for Retained Earnings and post to that account. Compute Meadowbrook's net income for the year ended March 31, 20X3. What is the ending balance of Retained Earnings? (pp. 159–165)
3. Did Retained Earnings increase or decrease during the year? What caused the increase or the decrease? (p. 165)

P3-61A (*Learning Objective 4, 6: Preparing a classified balance sheet and using the ratios to evaluate the business*) Refer back to Problem 3-60A.

1. Use the Meadowbrook Services data in Problem 3-60A to prepare the company's classified balance sheet at March 31, 20X3. Show captions for total assets, total liabilities, and total liabilities and stockholders' equity. (p. 167)
2. Compute Meadowbrook's current ratio and debt ratio at March 31, 20X3, rounding to 2 decimal places. At March 31, 20X2, the current ratio was 1.30 and the debt ratio was 0.30. Did Meadbrook's ability to pay both current and total debts improve or deteriorate during 20X3? Evaluate Meadowbrook's debt position as strong or weak and give your reason. (pp. 170–171)

P3-62A (*Learning Objectives 6: Analyzing financial ratios*) This problem demonstrates the effects of transactions on the current ratio and the debt ratio of Hialeah Company. Hialeah's condensed and adapted balance sheet at December 31, 20X6, is:

	(In millions)
Total current assets	$15.5
Properties, plant, equipment, and other assets	15.8
	$31.3
Total current liabilities	$ 9.2
Total long-term liabilities	5.3
Total stockholders' equity	16.8
	$31.3

Assume that during the first quarter of the following year, 20X7, Hialeah completed the following transactions:

a. Paid half the current liabilities.
b. Borrowed $3 million on long-term debt.
c. Earned revenue, $2.5 million, on account.
d. Paid selling expense of $1 million.
e. Accrued general expense of $0.8 million. Credit General Expense Payable, a current liability.
f. Purchased equipment for $4.2 million, paying cash of $1.4 million and signing a long-term note payable for $2.8 million.
g. Recorded depreciation expense of $0.6 million.

Required

1. Compute Hialeah's current ratio and debt ratio at December 31, 20X6. Round to 2 decimal places. (pp. 171–172)
2. Consider each transaction separately. Compute Hialeah's current ratio and debt ratio after each transaction during 20X7, that is, 7 times. Round ratios to 2 decimal places. (pp. 170–172)

(continued)

3. Based on your analysis, you should be able to readily identify the effects of certain transactions on the current ratio and the debt ratio. Test your understanding by completing these statements with either "increase" or "decrease": (pp. 170–172)

   a. Revenues usually _____ the current ratio.
   b. Revenues usually _____ the debt ratio.
   c. Expenses usually _____ the current ratio. (*Note:* Depreciation is an exception to this rule.)
   d. Expenses usually _____ the debt ratio.
   e. If a company's current ratio is greater than 1.0, as it is for Hialeah, paying off a current liability will always _____ the current ratio.
   f. Borrowing money on long term debt will always _____ the current ratio and _____ the debt ratio.

(Group B)

P3-63B (*Learning Objective 1: Linking accural accounting and cash flows*) During 20X1, Schubert, Inc., earned revenues of $19 million from the sale of its products. Schubert ended the year with net income of $4 million. Schubert collected cash of $20 million from customers and paid cash for all 20X1 expenses plus an additional $3 million on account for amounts payable at the end of 20X0. Answer these questions about Schubert's operating results, financial position, and cash flows during 20X1:

1. How much were Schubert's total expenses? Show your work. (pp. 139–140)
2. Identify all the items that Schubert will report on its income statement for 20X1. Show each amount. (p. 150)
3. Schubert began 20X1 with receivables of $6 million. All sales are on account. What was Schubert's receivables balance at the end of 20X1? Identify the appropriate financial statement and show how Schubert will report its ending receivables balance in the company's 20X1 annual report. (pp. 103–104)
4. Schubert began 20X1 owing accounts payable of $9 million. Schubert incurs all expenses on account. During 20X1, Schubert paid $18 million on account. How much in accounts payable did Schubert owe at the end of 20X1? Identify the appropriate financial statement and show how Schubert will report accounts payable in its 20X1 annual report. (pp. 103–104)

P3-64B (*Learning Objective 1: Cash basis versus accrual basis*) Bombay Foods had the following selected transactions during November:

Nov. 1	Received $800 in advance for food to be delivered later.
5	Paid electricity expenses, $700.
9	Received cash for the day's sales, $2,000.
14	Purchased two food warmers, $1,800.
23	Served a banquet, receiving a note receivable, $700.
30	Accrued salary expense, $900.
30	Prepaid building rent for December and January, $3,000.

▌Required

1. Show how each transaction would be handled using the cash basis and the accrual basis. Under each column, give the amount of revenue or expense for November. Journal entries are not required. Use the following format for your answer, and show your computations: (pp. 103–140)

	Amount of Revenue (Expense) for November	
Date	Cash Basis	Accrual Basis

2. Compute income (loss) before tax for November under the two accounting methods. (p. 159)

3. Which method better measures income and assets? Use the last transaction to explain. (p. 139)

P3-65B (*Learning Objective 1, 2: Applying accounting principles*) As the controller of Avon Systems, you have hired a new employee, whom you must train. He objects to making an adjusting entry for accrued salaries at the end of the period. He reasons, "We will pay the salaries soon. Why not wait until payment to record the expense? In the end, the result will be the same." Write a reply to explain to the employee why the adjusting entry is needed for accrued salary expense. (pp. 139–141)

P3-66B (*Learning Objective 3: Making accounting adjustments*) Journalize the adjusting entry needed on December 31, the end of the current accounting period, for each of the following independent cases affecting Chicago Mercantile Services (CMS). Include an explanation for each entry. (pp. 144–156)

    a. Each Friday, CMS pays employees for the current week's work. The amount of the payroll is $2,000 for a 5-day work week. The current accounting period ends on Tuesday.

    b. CMS has received notes receivable from some clients for professional services. During the current year, CMS has earned accrued interest revenue of $1,100, which will be received next year.

    c. The beginning balance of Supplies was $1,800. During the year, CMS purchased supplies costing $12,500, and at December 31 the inventory of supplies on hand is $2,900.

    d. CMS is conducting market research, and the client paid CMS $20,000 at the start of the project. CMS recorded this amount as Unearned Service Revenue. The research will take several months to complete. CMS executives estimate that the company has earned three-fourths of the revenue during the current year.

    e. Depreciation for the current year includes Equipment, $6,300; and Building, $3,700. Make a compound entry.

    f. Details of Prepaid Insurance are shown in the account:

Prepaid Insurance		
Jan. 1 Bal.	1,800	
Sept. 30	3,600	

    CMS pays the annual insurance premium (the payment for insurance coverage is called a *premium*) on September 30 each year. At December 31, $2,700 is still prepaid.

P3-67B (*Learning Objective 3, 4, 6: Preparing an adjusted trial balance and the financial statements; using the current ratio to evaluate the business*) Consider the unadjusted trial balance of Omega Advertising, Inc., at October 31, 20X2, and the related month-end adjustment data.

(*continued*)

Omega Advertising, Inc.
Trial Balance
October 31, 20X2

Cash	$16,300	
Accounts receivable	7,000	
Prepaid rent	4,000	
Supplies	600	
Furniture	36,000	
Accumulated depreciation		$ 3,000
Accounts payable		8,800
Salary payable		
Common stock		15,000
Retained earnings (September 30, 20X2)		21,000
Dividends	4,600	
Advertising revenue		25,400
Salary expense	4,400	
Rent expense		
Utilities expense	300	
Depreciation expense		
Supplies expense		
Total	$73,200	$73,200

Adjustment data:

    a. Accrued advertising revenue at October 31, $2,900.

    b. Prepaid rent expired during the month. The unadjusted prepaid balance of $4,000 relates to the period October 20X2 through January 20X3.

    c. Supplies used during October, $200.

    d. Depreciation on furniture for the month. The furniture's expected useful life is 5 years.

    e. Accrued salary expense at October 31 for Monday through Thursday; the 5-day weekly payroll is $2,000.

❚ Required

1. Using Exhibit 3-9, page 157, as an example, prepare the adjusted trial balance of Omega Advertising at October 31, 20X2. Key each adjusting entry by letter.

2. Prepare the monthly income statement, the statement of retained earnings, and the classified balance sheet. Draw arrows linking the three financial statements. (p. 159)

P3-68B (*Learning Objective 3: Analyzing and recording adjustments*) Valero Sales Company's unadjusted and adjusted trial balances at December 31, 20X7, are given on the next page.

❚ Required

1. Make the adjusting entries that account for the differences between the two trial balances. (p. 157)

2. Compute Valero's total assets, total liabilities, total equity, and net income. (p. 159)

Valero Sales Company
Adjusted Trial Balance
December 31, 20X7

Account Title	Trial Balance		Adjusted Trial Balance	
	Debit	Credit	Debit	Credit
Cash	4,100		4,100	
Accounts receivable	11,200		12,400	
Supplies	1,000		700	
Prepaid insurance	2,600		900	
Office furniture	21,600		21,600	
Accumulated depreciation		8,200		9,300
Accounts payable		6,300		6,300
Salary payable				900
Interest payable				400
Note payable		6,000		6,000
Unearned commission revenue		1,500		1,100
Common stock		5,000		5,000
Retained earnings		3,500		3,500
Dividends	18,300		18,300	
Sales commission revenue		72,800		74,400
Depreciation expense			1,100	
Supplies expense			300	
Utilities expense	4,900		4,900	
Salary expense	26,600		27,500	
Rent expense	12,200		12,200	
Interest expense	800		1,200	
Insurance expense			1,700	
	103,300	103,300	106,900	106,900

P3-69B (*Learning Objective 4, 6: Preparing the financial statements and using the debt ratio*) The adjusted trial balance of Duff & Carson, Inc., at December 31, 20X1, follows on the next page.

❚ *Required*

1. Prepare Duff & Carson's 20X1 income statement, statement of retained earnings, and balance sheet. List expenses in decreasing order on the income statement and show total liabilities on the balance sheet. Draw arrows linking the 3 financial statements. (p. 159)
2. Compute Duff & Carson's debt ratio at December 31, 20X1, rounding to 2 decimal places. Evaluate the company's debt ratio as strong or weak. (pp. 169–170)

Duff & Carson, Inc.
Adjusted Trial Balance
December 31, 20X1

Cash	$ 11,600	
Accounts receivable	41,400	
Prepaid rent	1,300	
Equipment	67,600	
Accumulated depreciation		$ 12,900
Accounts payable		3,600
Unearned service revenue		4,500
Interest payable		2,100
Salary payable		900
Income tax payable		8,800
Note payable		26,200
Common stock		12,000
Retained earnings, Dec. 31, 20X0		20,300
Dividends	48,000	
Service revenue		165,900
Depreciation expense	11,300	
Salary expense	44,000	
Rent expense	12,000	
Interest expense	1,200	
Income tax expense	18,800	
Total	$257,200	$257,200

P3-70B (*Learning Objective 5: Making closing entries and evaluating retained earnings*)
The accounts of Cookie Lapp eTravel, Inc., at December 31, 20X5, are listed in alphabetical order.

Accounts payable	$ 5,100	Note payable, long-term	$10,600
Accounts receivable	6,600	Other assets	3,600
Accumulated depreciation—		Retained earnings,	
furniture	11,600	December 31, 20X4	5,300
Advertising expense	2,200	Salary expense	24,600
Cash	7,300	Salary payable	3,900
Common stock	15,000	Service revenue	93,500
Depreciation expense	1,300	Supplies	7,700
Dividends	47,400	Supplies expense	5,700
Furniture	41,400	Unearned service	
Interest expense	800	revenue	3,600

I *Required*

1. All adjustments have been journalized and posted, but the closing entries have not yet been made. Journalize Lapp's closing entries at December 31, 20X5. (p. 165)
2. Set up a T-account for Retained Earnings and post to that account. Then compute Lapp's net income for 20X5. What is the ending balance of Retained Earnings? (p. 171)
3. Did Retained Earnings increase or decrease during the year? What caused the increase or decrease? (p. 165)

P3-71B (*Learning Objective 4, 6: Preparing a classified balance sheet and using the ratios*)
Refer back to Problem 3-70B.

1. Use the Cookie Lapp eTravel data in Problem 3-70B to prepare the company's classified balance sheet in report form at December 31, 20X5. Label total assets, total liabilities, and stockholders' equity. (p. 165)
2. Compute Cookie Lapp's current ratio and debt ratio at December 31, 20X5. At December 31, 20X4, the current ratio was 1.50 and the debt ratio was 0.45. Did Lapp's ability to pay both current and total liabilities improve or deteriorate during 20X5? (p. 171)

P3-72B (*Learning Objective 6: Analyzing financial ratios*) This problem demonstrates the effects of transactions on the current ratio and the debt ratio of Rockwell Company. Rockwell's condensed balance sheet at March 31, 20X1, follows.

	(In millions)
Total current assets	$3.0
Properties, net, and other assets	3.8
	$6.8
Total current liabilities	$2.2
Total long-term liabilities	2.4
Total stockholders' equity	2.2
	$6.8

During the *following* year, ending March 31, 20X2, Rockwell completed the following transactions:

a. Paid half the current liabilities.
b. Borrowed $3 million on long-term debt.
c. Earned revenue of $2.5 million on account.
d. Paid selling expense of $1 million.
e. Accrued salary expense of $0.8 million. Credit Salary Payable, a current liability.
f. Purchased equipment for $4.2 million, paying cash of $1.4 million and signing a long-term note payable for $2.8 million.
g. Recorded depreciation expense of $0.6 million.

I Required

1. Compute Rockwell's current ratio and debt ratio at March 31, 20X1. Round to 2 decimal places. (p. 171)
2. Consider each transaction separately. Compute Rockwell's current ratio and debt ratio after each transaction during 20X2, that is, 7 times. Round ratios to 2 decimal places. (pp. 172–173)
3. Based on your analysis, you should be able to readily identify the effects of certain transactions on the current ratio and the debt ratio. Test your understanding by completing these statements with either "increase" or "decrease": (pp. 172–173)

   a. Revenues usually _____ the current ratio.
   b. Revenues usually _____ the debt ratio.
   c. Expenses usually _____ the current ratio. (*Note:* Depreciation is an exception to this rule.)
   d. Expenses usually _____ the debt ratio.
   e. If a company's current ratio is greater than 1.0, as for Rockwell, paying off a current liability will always _____ the current ratio.
   f. Borrowing money on long-term debt will always _____ the current ratio and _____ the debt ratio.

APPLY YOUR KNOWLEDGE

Decision Cases

Case 1. *(Learning Objectives 3, 6: Adjusting and correcting the accounts; computing and evaluating the current ratio)* The unadjusted trial balance of Good Times, Inc., at January 31, 20X6, does not balance. In addition, the trial balance needs to be adjusted before the financial statements at January 31, 20X6 can be prepared. The manager of Good Times needs to know the business's current ratio.

Cash	$ 6,000
Accounts receivable	2,200
Supplies	800
Prepaid rent	1,200
Land	41,000
Accounts payable	10,000
Salary payable	0
Unearned service revenue	700
Note payable, due in 3 years	25,400
Common stock	5,000
Retained earnings	7,300
Service revenue	9,100
Salary expense	3,400
Rent expense	0
Advertising expense	900
Supplies expense	0

❚ Required

1. How much *out of balance* is the trial balance? The error is in the Land account. (pp. 156–157)

2. Good Times needs to make the following adjustments at January 31:

   a. Supplies of $600 were used during January.

   b. The balance of Prepaid Rent was paid on January 1 and covers the whole year 20X6. No adjustment was made on January 31.

   c. At January 31, Good Times owes employees $400.

   d. Unearned service revenue of $200 was earned during January.

   Prepare a corrected, adjusted trial balance. Give Land its correct balance. (pp. 156–157)

3. After the error is corrected and after these adjustments are made, compute the current ratio of Good Times, Inc. If your business had this current ratio, could you sleep at night? (p. 171)

Case 2. *(Learning Objectives 4: Preparing financial statements; continue or shut down the business?)* On October 1, Tiger Woods opened Eagle Restaurant, Inc. Woods is now at a crossroads. The October financial statements paint a glowing picture of the business, and Woods has asked you whether he should expand the business. To expand the business, Woods wants to be earning net income of $10,000 per month and have total assets of $35,000. Woods believes he is meeting both goals.

To start the business, Woods invested $20,000, not the $10,000 amount reported as "Common stock" on the balance sheet. The business issued $20,000 of common stock to Woods. The bookkeeper plugged the $10,000 "Common stock" amount into the balance sheet to make it balance. The bookkeeper made some other errors too. Woods shows you the following financial statements that the bookkeeper prepared.

▌*Required*

Prepare corrected financial statements for Eagle Restaurant, Inc.: Income Statement, Statement of Retained Earnings, and Balance Sheet. Then, based on Woods' goals and your corrected statements, recommend to Woods whether he should expand the restaurant. (p. 159)

Eagle Restaurant, Inc.
Income Statement
Month Ended October 31, 20X4

Revenues:		
Investments by owner	$20,000	
Unearned banquet sales revenue	3,000	
		$23,000
Expenses:		
Wages expense	$ 5,000	
Rent expense	4,000	
Dividends	3,000	
Depreciation expense—fixtures	1,000	
		13,000
Net income		$10,000

Eagle Restaurant, Inc.
Balance Sheet
October 31, 20X4

Assets:		Liabilities:	
Cash	$ 6,000	Accounts payable	$ 5,000
Prepaid insurance	1,000	Sales revenue	32,000
Insurance expense	1,000	Acuumulated depreciation—	
Food inventory	3,000	fixtures	1,000
Cost of goods sold (expense)	14,000		38,000
Fixtures (tables, chairs, etc.)	19,000	Owners' equity:	
Dishes and silverware	4,000	Common stock	10,000
	$48,000		$48,000

Case 3. (*Learning Objective 3, 4: Valuing a business on the basis of its net income*) Sherwin Williams has owned and operated SW Advertising, Inc., since its beginning 10 years ago. Recently, Williams mentioned that he would consider selling the company for the right price.

Assume that you are interested in buying this business. You obtain its most recent monthly trial balance, which follows. Revenues and expenses vary little from month to month, and April is a typical month. Your investigation reveals that the trial balance does not include the effects of monthly revenues of $5,000 and expenses totaling $1,100. If you were to buy SW Advertising, you would hire a manager so you could devote your time to other duties. Assume that your manager would require a monthly salary of $6,000.

SW Advertising, Inc.
Trial Balance
June 30, 20XX

Cash	$ 10,000	
Accounts receivable	4,900	
Prepaid expenses	3,200	
Plant assets	115,000	
Accumulated depreciation		$ 76,500
Land	158,000	
Accounts payable		13,800
Salary payable		
Unearned advertising revenue		56,700
Common stock		50,000
Retained earnings		88,000
Dividends	9,000	
Advertising revenue		20,000
Rent expense		
Salary expense	4,000	
Utilities expense	900	
Depreciation expense		
Supplies expense		
Total	$305,000	$305,000

❚ Required

1. Assume that the most you would pay for the business is 20 times the amount of monthly net income *you could expect to earn* from it. Compute this possible price. (p. 159)

2. Williams states that the least he will take for the business is 1.5 times its stockholders' equity on April 30. Compute this amount. (p. 159)

3. Under these conditions, how much should you offer Williams? Give your reason. (Challenge)

Ethical Issues

Issue 1. Cross Timbers Energy Co. is in its third year of operations, and the company has grown. To expand the business, Cross Timbers borrowed $1 million from Bank of Fort Worth. As a condition for making this loan, the bank required that Cross Timbers maintain a current ratio of at least 1.50 and a debt ratio of no more than 0.50.

Business recently has been worse than expected. Expenses have brought the current ratio down to 1.47 and the debt ratio up to 0.51 at December 15. Lane Collins, the general manager, is considering the result of reporting this current ratio to the bank. Collins is considering recording this year some revenue on account that Cross Timbers will earn next year. The contract for this job has been signed, and Cross Timbers will deliver the natural gas during January of next year.

❚ Required

1. Journalize the revenue transaction, and indicate how recording this revenue in December would affect the current ratio and the debt ratio.
2. State whether it is ethical to record the revenue transaction in December. Identify the accounting principle relevant to this situation.
3. Propose for Cross Timbers a course of action that is ethical.

Issue 2. The net income of Accent Photography Company decreased sharply during 2009. Lisa Brown, owner of the company, anticipates the need for a bank loan in 2010. Late in 2009, Brown instructed the accountant to record a $20,000 sale of portraits to the Brown family, even though the photos will not be shot until January 2010. Brown also told the accountant *not* to make the following December 31, 2009, adjusting entries:

> Salaries owed to employees $5,000
> Prepaid insurance that has expired 1,000

I *Required*

1. Compute the overall effect of these transactions on the company's reported income for 2009. Is reported net income overstated or understated?
2. Why did Brown take these actions? Are they ethical? Give your reason, identifying the parties helped and the parties harmed by Brown's action.
3. As a personal friend, what advice would you give the accountant?

Focus on Financials: ■ YUM! Brands

(*Learning Objectives 3, 6: Tracing account balances to the financial statements*) **YUM! Brands, Inc.**—like all other businesses—adjusts accounts prior to year end to get correct amounts for the financial statements. Examine YUM's balance sheet in Appendix A, and pay particular attention to (a) Prepaid Expenses and Other Current Assets and (b) Income Taxes Payable.

I *Required*

1. Why aren't Prepaid Expenses "true" expenses? Why does a company have income taxes payable at year end? (p. 144)
2. Open T-accounts for the two accounts listed above. Insert YUM's balances (in millions) at December 31, 2005. (p. 144)
3. Journalize the following transactions for the year ended December 30, 2006. Key entries by letter, and show amounts in millions. Explanations are not required. (pp. 151–152)

   a. Recorded General Expense for expiration of the beginning balance of Prepaid Expenses.
   b. Paid off the beginning balance of Income Taxes Payable.
   c. Paid the ending balance of Prepaid Expenses.
   d. Recorded Income Tax Expense of $284 million, paying $247 million in cash and accruing the remainder.

4. Post these entries to the 2 accounts and show that the ending balances of Prepaid Expenses and Other Current Assets and of Income Taxes Payable agree with the corresponding amounts reported in YUM's December 30, 2006, balance sheet. (pp. 151–152)
5. Compute the current ratios and debt ratios for YUM! Brands at December 31, 2005, and at December 30, 2006. Did the ratio values improve, deteriorate, or hold steady during 2006? Do YUM's ratio values indicate financial strength or weakness? (pp. 171–172)

Focus on Analysis: ■ Pier 1 Imports

(*Learning Objective 3: Explaining accruals and deferrals*) During 2006, **Pier I Imports** had numerous accruals and deferrals. As a new member of Pier 1's accounting staff, it is your job to explain the effects of accruals and deferrals on Pier 1's net income for 2006. The accrual and deferral data follow, along with questions that Pier 1 stockholders have raised (all amounts in millions):

1. Beginning total receivables for 2006 were $47. Ending receivables for 2006 are $64. Which of these amounts did Pier 1 earn in 2005? Which amount did Pier 1 earn in 2006? Which amount is included in Pier 1's net income for 2006? (pp. 150–151)
2. Accumulated depreciation stood at $383 at the end of 2005 and at $370 at year end 2006. Depreciation expense for 2006 was $56. How can accumulated depreciation decrease during 2006 when the company is adding more depreciation each year? (Challenge) (pp. 146–147)

3. Pier 1 reports an account titled Gift Cards and other Deferred (Unearned) Revenue. This account carried credit balances of $61 at the end of 2005 and $64 at the end of 2006. What type of account is Gift Cards and other Deferred (Unearned) Revenue? Make a single journal entry to show how this account could have increased its balance during 2006. Then explain the event in your own words. (pp. 153–154)

4. Certain income-statement accounts are directly linked to specific balance-sheet accounts other than cash. Examine Pier 1's income statement in Appendix B at the end of this book. For each "Operating cost and expense," each "Nonoperating (income) and expense," and Provision for income taxes, identify the related balance sheet account (other than cash). Use standard account titles, not necessarily the titles Pier 1 uses. (pp. 143–155)

Group Project

Matt Davis formed a lawn service company as a summer job. To start the business on May 1, he deposited $1,000 in a new bank account in the name of the corporation. The $1,000 consisted of an $800 loan from his father and $200 of his own money. The corporation issued 200 shares of common stock to Davis.

Davis rented lawn equipment, purchased supplies, and hired high school students to mow and trim his customers' lawns. At the end of each month, Davis mailed bills to his customers. On August 31, Davis was ready to dissolve the business and return to Duke University for the fall semester. Because he had been so busy, he had kept few records other than his checkbook and a list of amounts owed by customers.

At August 31, Davis's checkbook shows a balance of $1,390, and his customers still owe him $560. During the summer, he collected $5,150 from customers. His checkbook lists payments for supplies totaling $400, and he still has gasoline, weedeater cord, and other supplies that cost a total of $50. He paid his employees wages of $1,900, and he still owes them $200 for the final week of the summer.

Davis rented some equipment from Ludwig Tool Company. On May 1, he signed a 6-month lease on mowers and paid $600 for the full lease period. Ludwig will refund the unused portion of the prepayment if the equipment is in good shape. To get the refund, Davis has kept the mowers in excellent condition. In fact, he had to pay $300 to repair a mower that ran over a hidden tree stump.

To transport employees and equipment to jobs, Davis used a trailer that he bought for $300. He figures that the summer's work used up one-third of the trailer's service potential. The business checkbook lists an expenditure of $460 for dividends paid to Davis during the summer. Also, Davis paid his father back during the summer.

I *Required*

1. Prepare the income statement of Davis Lawn Service, Inc., for the 4 months May through August. The business is not subject to income tax.

2. Prepare the classified balance sheet of Davis Lawn Service, Inc., at August 31.

For Internet Exercises go to the Web site www.prenhall.com/harrison.

Quick Check Answers:

1. *a*	6. *b*	11. *b*	16. *c*
2. *c*	7. *a*	12. *d*	17. *b*
3. *b*	8. *d*	13. *a*	
4. *d*	9. *d*	14. *c*	
5. *c*	10. *a*	15. *a*	

SPOTLIGHT

AMEX PRODUCTS TAKES A HIT

"I've never been so shocked in my life!" exclaimed Lee Grant, manager of the AMEX Products office in Palo Alto, California. "This goes to show how important internal controls are."

Grant just returned from the trial of Marty Popplewell, who was convicted of embezzlement. Popplewell had been the cashier of the AMEX Products office in Palo Alto. As cashier, Popplewell received client cash that came in by mail. Unknown to Grant, Popplewell had been "robbing Peter to pay Paul"—that is transferring client collections to Popplewell's own account and then applying the next client cash receipt to cover the missing amount. With access to client accounts, Popplewell could juggle the books to keep anyone from discovering his scheme. This embezzlement had been going on for 3 years, and the trial proved that Popplewell had stolen $622,000 from the company.

What tipped off Grant to the embezzlement? Popplewell was involved in an auto accident and couldn't work for 2 weeks. The employee covering for Popplewell saw too many irregularities in client accounts. The ensuing investigation pointed to Popplewell, and Grant then turned the case over to the police.

Shortly after the trial, Grant revamped the internal controls at AMEX Products. Now Grant rotates employees from job to job. That way there's always someone checking up on someone else. And now the cashier has no access to client accounting records.

Popplewell's scheme is well known to accountants. It is called lapping—similar to laying shingles on a roof. Lapping takes lots of ingenuity and purpose. The thief has to keep the scheme going or it unravels quickly. That's what happened when Popplewell wasn't on the job to juggle the books.

AMEX Products, Inc.
Balance Sheet (Partial, Adapted)

Assets	December 31, 2007
Cash and cash equivalents	$ 6,260
Cash pledged as collateral	2,000
Accounts receivable	8,290
Inventories	36,200
Prepaid expenses	1,400
Investments	10,000
Equipment and facilities (net of accumulated depreciation of ($2,400)	13,170
Other assets	3,930
Total assets	$81,250

This chapter covers the basics of internal control. It also shows how to account for cash. These 2 topics—internal control and cash—go together because cash is the asset that is stolen most often.

The excerpt from the AMEX Products balance sheet reports the company's assets. Focus on the top line, Cash and cash equivalents. At December 31, 2007, AMEX reported cash of $6,260. If Popplewell's scheme hadn't been detected, the reported cash balance would have been overstated. One purpose of internal control is to produce accurate and reliable accounting records.

LEARNING OBJECTIVES

1 **Set up** an internal control system

2 **Prepare** and **use** a bank reconciliation

3 **Apply** internal controls to cash receipts and payments

4 **Use** a budget to manage your cash

5 **Make** ethical business judgments

INTERNAL CONTROL

A key responsibility of a mananger is to control the operations of the business. Owners and top executives set company goals, they hire managers to lead the way, and employees carry out the plan. **Internal control** is the organizational plan and all the related measures designed to accomplish 5 objectives:

1. **Safeguard assets.** A company must safeguard its assets; otherwise it's throwing away resources. If you fail to safeguard your cash, it will slip away.

2. **Encourage employees to follow company policy.** Everyone in an organization—managers and employees—needs to work toward the same goal. It's also important for managers to develop policies so that the company treats customers and employees fairly.

3. **Promote operational efficiency.** You cannot afford to waste resources. You work hard to make a sale, and you don't want to waste any of the benefits. If the company can buy something for $30, why pay $35? Eliminate waste, and increase your profits.

4. **Ensure accurate, reliable accounting records.** Good records are essential. Without reliable records, you cannot tell which part of the business is profitable and which part needs improvement. You could be losing money on every product you sell—unless you keep good records for the cost of your products.

5. **Comply with legal requirements**, such as the Sarbanes-Oxley Act. Companies, like people, are subject to the law. When companies disobey the law, they must pay fines, or in extreme cases their top executives go to prison.

How critical are internal controls? They're so important that the U.S. Congress passed a law to require public companies—those that sell their stock to the public—to maintain a system of internal controls. Exhibit 4-1 gives AMEX Products' Management Discussion of Financial Responsibility.

EXHIBIT 4-1	AMEX Products, Inc., Management Discussion of Financial Responsibility

Management's Discussion of Financial Responsibility

AMEX Products regularly reviews its framework of internal controls, which includes the company's policies, procedures and organizational structure. Corrective actions are taken to address any control deficiencies, and improvements are implemented as appropriate.

The Sarbanes-Oxley Act (SOX)

The Enron and WorldCom accounting scandals rocked the United States. Enron overstated profits and went out of business almost overnight. WorldCom (now MCI) reported expenses as assets and overstated both profits and assets. The company only recently emerged from bankruptcy. Sadly, the same international accounting firm, Arthur Andersen, had audited both companies' financial statements. Arthur Andersen then closed its doors.

As the scandals unfolded, many people asked, "How can these things happen? Where were the auditors?" To address public concern, Congress passed the Sarbanes-Oxley Act, abbreviated as SOX. SOX revamped corporate governance in the United States and affected the accounting profession. Here are some of the SOX provisions:

1. Public companies must issue an internal control report, and the outside auditor must evaluate the client's internal controls.

2. A new body, the Public Company Accounting Oversight Board, oversees the auditors of public companies.

3. An accounting firm may not both audit a public client and also provide certain consulting services for the same client.

4. Stiff penalties await violators—25 years in prison for securities fraud; 20 years for an executive making false sworn statements.

Recently, the former chief executive of WorldCom was convicted of securities fraud and sentenced to 25 years in prison. The top executives of Enron were also sent to prison. You can see that internal controls and related matters can have serious consequences.

Exhibit 4-2 diagrams the shield that internal controls provide for an organization. Protected by the wall, people do business securely. How does a business achieve good internal control? The next section identifies the components of internal control.

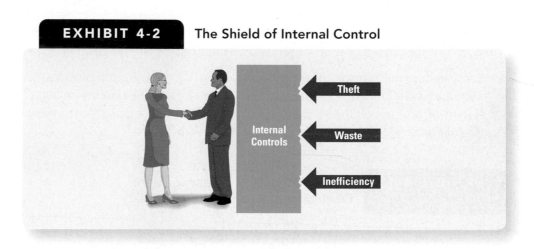

EXHIBIT 4-2 **The Shield of Internal Control**

The Components of Internal Control

OBJECTIVE

1 **Set up** an internal control system

Internal control can be broken down into 5 components:

- Control environment
- Risk assessment
- Control procedures

- Monitoring of controls
- Information system

Control Environment. The control environment is the "tone at the top" of the business. It starts with the owner and the top managers. They must behave honorably to set a good example for company employees. The owner must demonstrate the importance of internal controls if he or she expects employees to take the controls seriously. Former executives of Enron, WorldCom, and Tyco failed to establish a good control environment, and they are in prison as a result.

Risk Assessment. A company must identify its risks. For example, Kraft Foods faces the risk that its food products may harm people. American Airlines planes may crash. And all companies face the risk of bankruptcy. Companies facing difficulties are tempted to falsify the financial statements to make themselves look better than they really are.

Control Procedures. These are the procedures designed to ensure that the business's goals are achieved. Examples include assigning responsibilities, separating duties, and using security devices to protect assets from theft. The next section discusses internal control procedures.

Monitoring of Controls. Companies hire auditors to monitor their controls. Internal auditors monitor company controls to safeguard the company's assets, and external auditors monitor the controls to ensure that the accounting records are accurate.

Information System. As we have seen, the information system is critical. The owner of a business needs accurate information to keep track of assets and measure profits and losses.

Exhibit 4-3 diagrams the components of internal control.

EXHIBIT 4-3   The Components of Internal Control

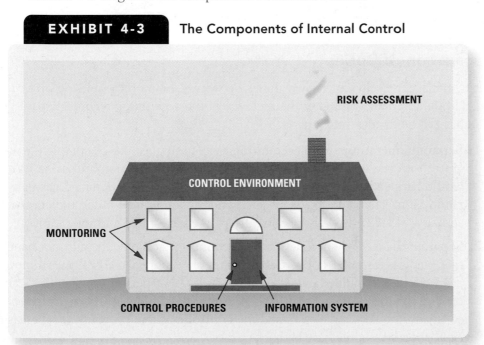

INTERNAL CONTROL PROCEDURES

Whether the business is AMEX Products, Microsoft, or an Exxon gas station, you need the following internal control procedures.

Competent, Reliable, and Ethical Personnel

Employees should be *competent*, *reliable*, and *ethical*. Paying good salaries will attract high-quality employees. You also must train them to do the job, supervise their work, and reward them fairly. This will build a competent staff.

Assignment of Responsibilities

In a business with good internal controls, no important duty is overlooked. Each employee has certain responsibilities. In a company such as AMEX Products, the person in charge of writing checks is called the treasurer. The chief accounting officer is called the **controller**. With clearly assigned responsibilities, all important jobs get done.

Separation of Duties

Smart management divides related duties between 2 or more people. *Separation of duties* limits fraud and promotes the accuracy of the accounting records. Separation of duties can be divided into 2 parts:

1. **Separate operations from accounting.** Accounting should be completely separate from the operating departments, such as production and sales. What would happen if sales personnel recorded the company's revenue? Sales figures could be inflated, and top managers wouldn't know how much the company actually sold. This is why you should separate accounting and sales duties.

2. **Separate the custody of assets from accounting.** Accountants must not handle cash, and cashiers must not have access to the accounting records. If one employee has both cash-handling and accounting duties, that person can steal cash and conceal the theft. This is what happened at AMEX Products. The **treasurer** of a company should handle cash, and the **controller** should account for the cash. Neither person should have both jobs.

Audits

To validate their accounting records, most companies have an audit. An **audit** is an examination of the company's financial statements and accounting system. To evaluate the system, auditors examine the internal controls.

Audits can be internal or external. *Internal auditors* are employees of the business. They ensure that employees are following company policies and operations are running efficiently. Internal auditors also determine whether the company is following legal requirements.

External auditors are completely independent of the business. They are hired to determine that the company's financial statements agree with generally accepted accounting principles. Auditors examine the client's financial statements and the underlying transactions in order to form a professional opinion of the financial statements.

Documents

Documents provide the details of business transactions. Documents include invoices and fax orders. Documents should be prenumbered to prevent theft and inefficiency. A gap in the numbered sequence draws attention.

In a bowling alley a key document is the score sheet. The manager can compare the number of games scored with the amount of cash received. Multiply the number of games by the charge per game and compare the revenue with cash receipts. You can see whether the business is collecting all the revenue.

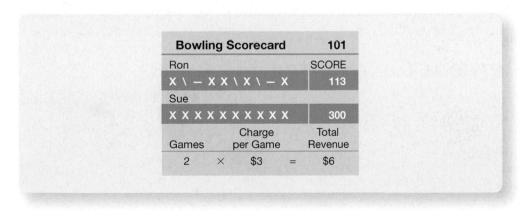

Electronic Devices

Accounting systems are relying less on documents and more on digital storage devices. For example, retailers such as Target Stores and Macy's control inventory by attaching an *electronic sensor* to merchandise. The cashier removes the sensor. If a customer tries to leave the store with the sensor attached, an alarm sounds. According to Checkpoint Systems, these devices reduce theft by as much as 50%.

Bar codes speed checkout at a store, and *surveillance cameras* help identify shoplifters.

Other Controls

Businesses keep important documents in *fireproof vaults*. *Burglar alarms* protect buildings, and *security cameras* protect other property. *Loss-prevention specialists* train employees to spot suspicious activity.

Employees who handle cash are in a tempting position. Many businesses purchase *fidelity bonds* on cashiers. The bond is an insurance policy that reimburses the company for any losses due to employee theft. Before issuing a fidelity bond, the insurance company investigates the employee's background.

Mandatory vacations and *job rotation* improve internal control. Companies move employees from job to job. This improves morale by giving employees a broad view of the business. Also, knowing someone else will do your job next month keeps you honest. AMEX Products didn't rotate employees to different jobs, and it cost the company $622,000.

INTERNAL CONTROLS FOR E-COMMERCE

E-commerce creates its own risks. Hackers may gain access to confidential information such as account numbers and passwords.

Pitfalls

E-commerce pitfalls include:

- Stolen credit-card numbers
- Computer viruses and Trojan Horses
- Phishing expeditions

Stolen Credit-Card Numbers. Suppose you buy CDs from EMusic.com. To make the purchase, your credit-card number must travel through cyberspace. Wireless networks (Wi-Fi) are creating new security hazards.

Amateur hacker Carlos Salgado, Jr., used his home computer to steal 100,000 credit-card numbers with a combined limit exceeding $1 billion. Salgado was caught when he tried to sell the numbers to an undercover FBI agent.

Computer Viruses and Trojan Horses. A **computer virus** is a malicious program that (a) enters program code without consent and (b) performs destructive actions in the victim's computer files or programs. A **Trojan Horse** is a malicious computer program that hides inside a legitimate program and works like a virus. Viruses can destroy or alter data, make bogus calculations, and infect files. Most firms have found a virus in their system.

Suppose the U.S. Department of Defense takes bids for a missile system. Raytheon and Lockheed-Martin are competing for the contract. A hacker infects Raytheon's system and alters Raytheon's design. Then the government labels the Raytheon design as flawed and awards the contract to Lockheed.

Phishing Expeditions. Thieves phish by creating bogus Web sites, such as AOL4Free.com and BankAmerica.com. The neat-sounding Web site attracts lots of visitors, and the thieves obtain account numbers and passwords from unsuspecting people. The thieves then use the data for illicit purposes.

Security Measures

To address the risks posed by e-commerce, companies have devised a number of security measures, including

- Encryption
- Firewalls

Encryption. The server holding confidential information may not be secure. One technique for protecting customer data is encryption. **Encryption** rearranges messages by a mathematical process. The encrypted message can't be read by those who don't know the code. An accounting example uses check-sum digits for account numbers. Each account number has its last digit equal to the sum of the previous digits. For example, consider Customer Number 2237, where $2 + 2 + 3 = 7$. Any account number that fails this test triggers an error message.

Firewalls. **Firewalls** limit access into a local network. Members can access the network but nonmembers can't. Usually several firewalls are built into the system. Think of a fortress with multiple walls protecting the king's chamber in the center. At the point of entry, passwords, PINs (personal identification numbers), and signatures are used. More sophisticated firewalls are used deeper in the network. Start with Firewall 1, and work toward the center.

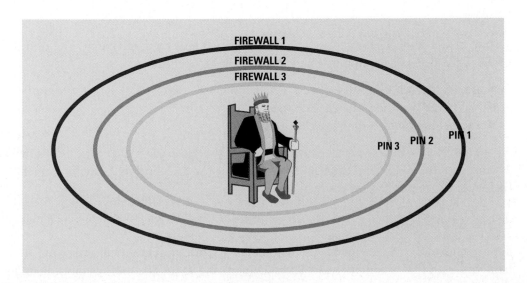

The Limitations of Internal Control—Costs and Benefits

Unfortunately, most internal controls can be overcome. Collusion—2 or more people working together—can beat internal controls. Consider Galaxy Theater. Ralph and Lana can design a scheme in which Ralph sells tickets and pockets the cash from 10 customers. Lana, the ticket taker, admits 10 customers without tickets. Ralph and Lana split the cash. To prevent this situation, the manager must take additional steps, such as matching the number of people in the theater against the number of ticket stubs retained. But that takes time away from other duties.

The stricter the internal control system, the more it costs. A complex system of internal control can strangle the business with red tape. How tight should the controls be? Internal controls must be judged in light of their costs and benefits. An example of a good cost/benefit relationship: A security guard at a **Wal-Mart** store costs about $28,000 a year. On average, each guard prevents about $50,000 of theft. The net savings to Wal-Mart is $22,000.

THE BANK ACCOUNT AS A CONTROL DEVICE

Cash is the most liquid asset because it's the medium of exchange. Cash is easy to conceal and relatively easy to steal. As a result, most businesses create specific controls for cash.

Keeping cash in a bank account helps control cash because banks have established practices for safeguarding customers' money. The documents used to control a bank account include the:

- Signature card
- Deposit ticket
- Check
- Bank statement
- Bank reconciliation

Signature Card

Banks require each person authorized to sign on an account to provide a *signature card*. This protects against forgery.

Deposit Ticket

Banks supply standard forms such as *deposit tickets*. The customer fills in the amount of each deposit. As proof of the transaction, the customer keeps a deposit receipt.

Check

To pay cash, the depositor can write a **check**, which tells the bank to pay the designated party a specified amount. There are 3 parties to a check:

- the maker, who signs the check
- the payee, to whom the check is paid
- the bank on which the check is drawn

Exhibit 4-4 shows a check drawn by AMEX Products, the maker. The check has 2 parts, the check itself and the *remittance advice* below. This optional attachment tells the payee the reason for the payment.

Bank Statement

Banks send monthly statements to customers. A **bank statement** reports what the bank did with the customer's cash. The statement shows the account's beginning and

EXHIBIT 4-4   **Check with Remittance Advice**

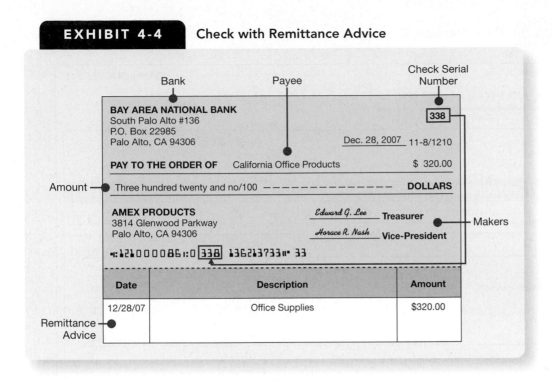

ending balances, cash receipts, and payments. Included with the statement are copies of the maker's *canceled checks* (or the actual paid checks). Exhibit 4-5 is the January bank statement of the Palo Alto office of AMEX Products.

Electronic funds transfer (EFT) moves cash by electronic communication. It is cheaper to pay without having to mail a check, so many people pay their mortgage, rent, utilities, and insurance by EFT.

Bank Reconciliation

There are 2 records of a business's cash:

1. The Cash account in the company's general ledger. Exhibit 4-6 (p. 221) shows that AMEX Product's ending cash balance is $3,340.
2. The bank statement, which shows the cash receipts and payments transacted through the bank. In Exhibit 4-5 (p. 220), the bank shows an ending balance of $5,900 for AMEX.

The books and the bank statement usually show different cash balances. Differences arise because of a time lag in recording transactions—2 examples:

- When you write a check, you immediately deduct it in your checkbook. But the bank does not subtract the check from your account until the bank pays the check a few days later. And you immediately add the cash receipt for all your deposits. But it may take a day or two for the bank to add deposits to your balance.
- Your EFT payments and cash receipts are recorded by the bank before you learn of them.

To ensure accurate cash records, you need to update your cash record—either online or after you receive your bank statement. The result of this updating process creates a **bank reconciliation**, which you must prepare. The bank reconciliation explains all differences between your cash records and your bank balance. The person who prepares the bank reconciliation should have no other cash duties. Otherwise, he or she can steal cash and manipulate the reconciliation to conceal the theft.

EXHIBIT 4-5 Bank Statement

BANK STATEMENT

BAY AREA NATIONAL BANK

SOUTH PALO ALTO #136 P.O. BOX 22985 PALO ALTO, CA 94306

AMEX Products
3814 Glenwood Parkway
Palo Alto, CA 94306

CHECKING ACCOUNT 136–213733

DECEMBER 31, 2007

BEGINNING BALANCE	TOTAL DEPOSITS	TOTAL WITHDRAWALS	SERVICE CHARGES	ENDING BALANCE
6,550	4,370	5,000	20	5,900

——————————— TRANSACTIONS ———————————

DEPOSITS	DATE	AMOUNT
Deposit	12/04	1,150
Deposit	12/08	190
EFT—Receipt of cash dividend	12/17	900
Bank Collection	12/26	2,100
Interest	12/31	30

CHARGES	DATE	AMOUNT
Service Charge	12/31	20

CHECKS

Number	Amount	Number	Amount	Number	Amount
307	100	333	150	335	100
332	3,000	334	100	336	1,100

OTHER DEDUCTIONS	DATE	AMOUNT
NSF	12/04	50
EFT—Insurance	12/20	400

Preparing the Bank Reconciliation

Here are the items that appear on a bank reconciliation. They all cause differences between the bank balance and the book balance. We call your cash record (also known as a "checkbook") the "Books."

Bank Side of the Reconciliation.

1. Items to show on the *Bank* side of the bank reconciliation:

    a. **Deposits in transit** (outstanding deposits). You have recorded these deposits, but the bank has not. Add deposits in transit on the bank reconciliation.

    b. **Outstanding checks.** You have recorded these checks, but the bank has not yet paid them. Subtract outstanding checks.

    c. **Bank errors.** Correct all bank errors on the Bank side of the reconciliation. For example, the bank may erroneously subtract from your account a check written by someone else.

EXHIBIT 4-6 Cash Records of AMEX Products

General Ledger:

ACCOUNT Cash

Date	Item	Debit	Credit	Balance
2007				
Dec. 1	Balance			6,550
2	Cash receipt	1,150		7,700
7	Cash receipt	190		7,890
31	Cash payments		6,150	1,740
31	Cash receipt	1,600		3,340

Cash Payments:

Check No.	Amount	Check No.	Amount
332	$3,000	337	$ 280
333	510	338	320
334	100	339	250
335	100	340	490
336	1,100	Total	$6,150

Book Side of the Reconciliation.

2. Items to show on the *Book* side of the bank reconciliation:

   a. **Bank collections**. Bank collections are cash receipts that the bank has recorded for your account. But you haven't recorded the cash receipt yet. Many businesses have their customers pay directly to their bank. This is called a *lock-box system* and reduces theft. An example is a bank's collecting an account receivable for you. Add bank collections on the bank reconciliation.

   b. **Electronic funds transfers**. The bank may receive or pay cash on your behalf. An EFT may be a cash receipt or a cash payment. Add EFT receipts and subtract EFT payments.

   c. **Service charge**. This cash payment is the bank's fee for processing your transactions. Subtract service charges.

   d. **Interest revenue on your checking account**. You earn interest if you keep enough cash in your account. The bank statement tells you of this cash receipt. Add interest revenue.

   e. **Nonsufficient funds (NSF) checks** are your earlier cash receipts that have turned out to be worthless. NSF checks (sometimes called hot checks) are treated as cash payments on your bank reconciliation. Subtract NSF checks.

   f. **The cost of printed checks**. This cash payment is handled like a service charge. Subtract this cost.

   g. **Book errors**. Correct all book errors on the Book side of the reconciliation. For example, you may have recorded a $150 check that you wrote as $510.

Bank Reconciliation Illustrated. The bank statement in Exhibit 4-5 shows that the December 31 bank balance of AMEX Products is $5,900 (upper right corner). However, the company's Cash account has a balance of $3,340, as shown in Exhibit 4-6. This

OBJECTIVE

2 **Prepare** and **use** a bank reconciliation

situation calls for a bank reconciliation. Exhibit 4-7, panel A, lists the reconciling items for easy reference, and panel B shows the completed reconciliation.

| **EXHIBIT 4-7** | **Bank Reconciliation** |

PANEL A—Reconciling Items

Bank side:

1. Deposit in transit, $1,600.
2. Bank error: The bank deducted $100 for a check written by another company. Add $100 to the bank balance.
3. Outstanding checks—total of $1,340.

Check No.	Amount
337	$280
338	320
339	250
340	490

Book side:

4. EFT receipt of your dividend revenue earned on an investment, $900.
5. Bank collection of your account receivable, $2,100.
6. Interest revenue earned on your bank balance, $30.
7. Book error: You recorded check no. 333 for $510. The amount you actually paid on account was $150. Add $360 to your book balance.
8. Bank service charge, $20.
9. NSF check from a customer, $50. Subtract $50 from your book balance.
10. EFT payment of insurance expense, $400.

PANEL B—Bank Reconciliation

AMEX Products
Bank Reconciliation
December 31, 2007

Bank			Books		
Balance, December 31		$5,900	Balance, December 31		$3,340
Add:			Add:		
1. Deposit in transit		1,600	4. EFT receipt of dividend revenue		900
2. Correction of bank error		100	5. Bank collection of account		
		7,600	receivable		2,100
			6. Interest revenue earned on		
			bank balance		30
			7. Correction of book error—		
			overstated our check no. 333		360
					6,730
Less:					
3. Outstanding checks					
No. 337	$280		Less:		
No. 338	320		8. Service charge	$ 20	
No. 339	250		9. NSF check	50	
No. 340	490	(1,340)	10. EFT payment of insurance expense	400	(470)
Adjusted bank balance		$6,260	Adjusted bank balance		$6,260

These amounts should agree.

SUMMARY OF THE VARIOUS RECONCILING ITEMS:

BANK BALANCE—ALWAYS

- *Add* deposits in transit.
- *Subtract* outstanding checks.
- *Add* or *subtract* corrections of bank errors.

BOOK BALANCE—ALWAYS

- *Add* bank collections, interest revenue, and EFT receipts.
- *Subtract* service charges, NSF checks, and EFT payments.
- *Add* or *subtract* corrections of book errors.

Journalizing Transactions from the Bank Reconciliation. The bank reconciliation is an accountant's tool separate from the journals and ledgers. It does *not* account for transactions in the journal. To get the transactions into the accounts, we must make journal entries and post to the ledger. All items on the *Book* side of the bank reconciliation require journal entries.

The bank reconciliation in Exhibit 4-7 requires AMEX Products to make journal entries to bring the Cash account up-to-date. Numbers in parentheses correspond to the reconciling items listed in Exhibit 4-7, Panel A.

4.	Dec. 31	Cash	900	
		Dividend Revenue		900
		Receipt of dividend revenue earned on investment.		
5.	31	Cash	2,100	
		Accounts Receivable		2,100
		Account receivable collected by bank.		
6.	31	Cash	30	
		Interest Revenue		30
		Interest earned on bank balance.		
7.	31	Cash	360	
		Accounts Payable		360
		Correction of check no. 333.		
8.	31	Miscellaneous Expense[1]	20	
		Cash		20
		Bank service charge.		
9.	31	Accounts Receivable	50	
		Cash		50
		NSF check returned by bank.		
10.	31	Insurance Expense	400	
		Cash		400
		Payment of monthly insurance.		

[1]Miscellaneous Expense is debited for the bank service charge because the service charge pertains to no particular expense category.

The entry for the NSF check (entry 9) needs explanation. Upon learning that a customer's $50 check to us was not good, we must credit Cash to update the Cash account. Unfortunately, we still have a receivable from the customer, so we must debit Accounts Receivable to reinstate our receivable.

Online Banking

Online banking allows you to pay bills and view your account electronically. You don't have to wait until the end of the month to get a bank statement. With online banking you can reconcile transactions at any time and keep your account current whenever you wish. Exhibit 4-8 shows a page from the account history of Toni Anderson's bank account.

The account history—like a bank statement—lists deposits, checks, EFT payments, ATM withdrawals, and interest earned on your bank balance.

EXHIBIT 4-8	Online Banking—Account History (like a Bank Statement)

Account History for Toni Anderson Checking # 5401-632-9
as of Close of Business 07/27/2007

Account Details

Current Balance $4,136.08

Date ↓	Description	Withdrawals	Deposits	Balance
	Current Balance			**$4,136.08**
07/27/07	DEPOSIT		1,170.35	
07/26/07	28 DAYS INTEREST		2.26	
07/25/07	Check #6131 View Image	443.83		
07/24/07	Check #6130 View Image	401.52		
07/23/07	EFT PYMT CINGULAR	61.15		
07/22/07	EFT PYMT CITICARD PAYMENT	3,172.85		
07/20/07	Check #6127 View Image	550.00		
07/19/07	Check #6122 View Image	50.00		
07/16/07	Check #6116 View Image	2,056.75		
07/15/07	Check #6123 View Image	830.00		
07/13/07	Check #6124 View Image	150.00		
07/11/07	ATM 4900 SANGER AVE	200.00		
07/09/07	Check #6119 View Image	30.00		
07/05/07	Check #6125 View Image	2,500.00		
07/04/07	ATM 4900 SANGER AVE	100.00		
07/01/07	DEPOSIT		9,026.37	

FDIC   EQUAL HOUSING LENDER   E-Mail

But the account history doesn't show your beginning balance, so you can't work from your beginning balance to your ending balance.

STOP & think. . .

The bank statement balance is $4,500 and shows a service charge of $15, interest earned of $5, and an NSF check for $300. Deposits in transit total $1,200; outstanding checks are $575. The bookkeeper recorded as $152 a check of $125 in payment of an account payable. This created a book error of $27 (positive amount to correct the error).

1. What is the adjusted bank balance?
2. What was the book balance of cash before the reconciliation?

Answers:

1. $5,125 ($4,500 + $1,200 − $575).
2. $5,408 ($5,125 + $15 − $5 + $300 − $27). The adjusted book and bank balances are the same. The answer can be determined by working backward from the adjusted balance.

Using the Bank Reconciliation to Control Cash. The bank reconciliation can be a powerful control device. Randy Vaughn is a CPA in Houston, Texas. He owns several apartment complexes that are managed by his aunt. His aunt signs up tenants, collects the monthly rents, arranges maintenance work, hires and fires employees, writes the checks, and performs the bank reconciliation. In short, she does it all. This concentration of duties in one person is evidence of weak internal control. Vaughn's aunt could be stealing from him, and as a CPA he is aware of this possibility.

Vaughn trusts his aunt because she is a member of the family. Nevertheless, Vaughn exercises some controls over his aunt's management of his apartments. Vaughn periodically drops by the apartments to see whether the maintenance staff is keeping the property in good condition. To control cash, Vaughn occasionally examines the bank reconciliation that his aunt has performed. Vaughn would know immediately if his aunt is writing checks to herself. By examining the copy of each check, Vaughn establishes control over cash payments.

Vaughn has a simple method for controlling cash receipts. He knows the occupancy level of his apartments. He also knows the monthly rent he charges. Vaughn multiplies the number of apartments—say 20—by the monthly rent (which averages $500 per unit) to arrive at expected monthly rent revenue of $10,000. By tracing the $10,000 revenue to the bank statement, Vaughn can tell if all his rent money went into his bank account. To keep his aunt on her toes, Vaughn lets her know that he periodically audits her work.

Control activities such as these are critical. If there are only a few employees, separation of duties may not be feasible. The manager must control operations, or the assets will slip away.

MID-CHAPTER SUMMARY PROBLEM

The cash account of Baylor Associates at February 28, 2009, follows.

Cash			
Feb. 1	Bal. 3,995	Feb. 3	400
6	800	12	3,100
15	1,800	19	1,100
23	1,100	25	500
28	2,400	27	900
Feb. 28	Bal. 4,095		

Baylor Associates received the bank statement on February 28, 2009 (negative amounts are in parentheses):

Bank Statement for February 2009			
Beginning balance			
Deposits:			$3,995
Feb. 7		$ 800	
15		1,800	
24		1,100	3,700
Checks (total per day):			
Feb. 8		$ 400	
16		3,100	
23		1,100	(4,600)
Other items:			
Service charge			(10)
NSF check from M. E. Crown			(700)
Bank collection of note receivable for the company			1,000
EFT—monthly rent expense			(330)
Interest revenue earned on account balance			15
Ending balance			$3,070

Additional data:
Baylor deposits all cash receipts in the bank and makes all payments by check.

❚ Required
1. Prepare the bank reconciliation of Baylor Associates at February 28, 2009.
2. Journalize the entries based on the bank reconciliation.

Answers

▌Requirement 1

		BAYLOR ASSOCIATES Bank Reconciliation February 28, 2009		
		Bank:		
		Balance, February 28, 2009		$3,070
		Add: Deposit of February 28 in transit		2,400
				5,470
		Less: Outstanding checks issued on Feb. 25 ($500)		
		and Feb. 27 ($900)		(1,400)
		Adjusted bank balance, February 28, 2009		$4,070
		Books:		
		Balance, February 28, 2009		$4,095
		Add: Bank collection of note receivable		1,000
		Interest revenue earned on bank balance		15
				5,110
		Less: Service charge	$ 10	
		NSF check	700	
		EFT—Rent expense	330	(1,040)
		Adjusted book balance, February 28, 2009		$4,070

▌Requirement 2

Feb. 28	Cash		1,000	
	Note Receivable			1,000
	Note receivable collected by bank.			
28	Cash		15	
	Interest Revenue			15
	Interest earned on bank balance.			
28	Miscellaneous Expense		10	
	Cash			10
	Bank service charge.			
28	Accounts Receivable		700	
	Cash			700
	NSF check returned by bank.			
28	Rent Expense		330	
	Cash			330
	Monthly rent expense.			

INTERNAL CONTROL OVER CASH RECEIPTS

OBJECTIVE

3 Apply internal controls to cash receipts and payments

Cash requires some specific internal controls because cash is relatively easy to steal and it's easy to convert to other forms of wealth. Moreover, all transactions ultimately affect cash. That's why cash is called the "eye of the needle." Let's see how to control cash receipts.

All cash receipts should be deposited for safekeeping in the bank—quickly. Companies receive cash over the counter and through the mail. Each source of cash has its own security measures.

Cash Receipts over the Counter

Exhibit 4-9 illustrates a cash receipt over the counter in a department store. The point-of-sale terminal (cash register) provides control over the cash receipts. Consider a Macy's store. For each transaction, Macy's issues a receipt to ensure that each sale is recorded. The cash drawer opens when the clerk enters a transaction, and the machine records it. At the end of the day, a manager proves the cash by comparing the cash in the drawer against the machine's record of sales. This step helps prevent theft by the clerk.

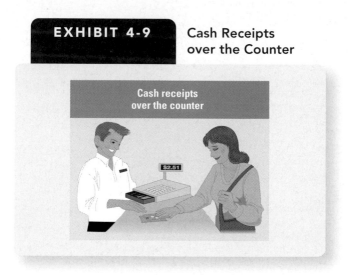

EXHIBIT 4-9 Cash Receipts over the Counter

At the end of the day—or several times a day if business is brisk—the cashier deposits the cash in the bank. The machine tape then goes to the accounting department for the journal entry to record sales revenue. These measures, coupled with oversight by a manager, discourage theft.

Cash Receipts by Mail

Many companies receive cash by mail. Exhibit 4-10 shows how companies control cash received by mail. All incoming mail is opened by a mailroom employee. The mailroom then sends all customer checks to the treasurer, who has the cashier deposit the money in the bank. The remittance advices go to the accounting department for journal entries to Cash and customer accounts receivable. As a final step, the controller compares the following records for the day:

- Bank deposit amount from the treasurer
- Debit to Cash from the accounting department

The debit to Cash should equal the amount deposited in the bank. All cash receipts are safe in the bank, and the company books are up-to-date.

Many companies use a lock-box system. Customers send their checks directly to the company's bank account. Internal control is tight because company personnel never touch incoming cash. The lock-box system puts your cash to work immediately.

EXHIBIT 4-10   Cash Receipts by Mail

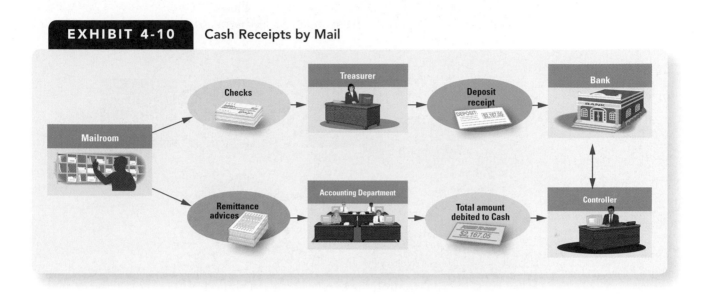

INTERNAL CONTROL OVER CASH PAYMENTS

Companies make most payments by check. Let's see how to control cash payments by check.

Controls over Payment by Check

As we have seen, you need a good separation of duties between (a) operations and (b) writing checks for cash payments. Payment by check is an important internal control, as follows:

- The check provides a record of the payment.
- The check must be signed by an authorized official.
- Before signing the check, the official should study the evidence supporting the payment.

Controls over Purchase and Payment. To illustrate the internal control over cash payments by check, suppose AMEX Products buys some of its inventory from Hanes Textiles. The purchasing and payment process follows these steps, as shown in Exhibit 4-11. Start with the box for AMEX Products on the left side.

1 AMEX faxes a *purchase order* to Hanes Textiles. AMEX says, "Please send us 100 T-shirts."

2 Hanes Textiles ships the goods and faxes an *invoice* back to AMEX. Hanes sent the goods.

3 AMEX receives the *inventory* and prepares a *receiving report* to list the goods received. AMEX got its T-shirts.

4 After approving all documents, AMEX sends a *check* to Hanes. AMEX says, "Okay, we'll pay you."

EXHIBIT 4-11   Cash Payments by Check

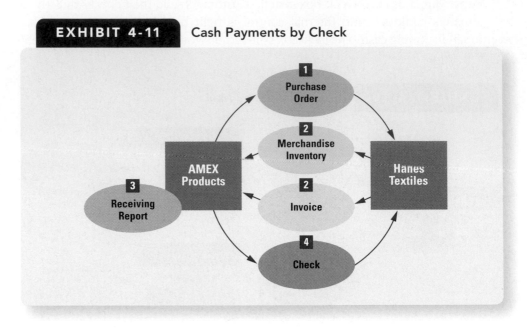

For good internal control, the purchasing agent should neither receive the goods nor approve the payment. If these duties aren't separated, a purchasing agent can buy goods and have them shipped to his or her home. Or a purchasing agent can spend too much on purchases, approve the payment, and split the excess with the supplier. To avoid these problems, companies split the following duties among different employees:

- purchasing goods
- receiving goods
- approving and paying for goods

Exhibit 4-12 shows AMEX's payment packet of documents. Before signing the check, the controller or the treasurer should examine the packet to prove that all the documents agree. Only then does the company know that:

1. It received the goods ordered.
2. It is paying only for the goods received.

EXHIBIT 4-12   Payment Packet

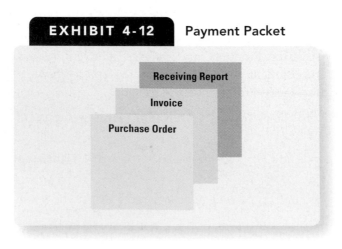

After payment, the check signer punches a hole through the payment packet. Dishonest people have tried to run a bill through twice for payment. This hole shows that the bill has been paid.

Petty Cash. It would be wasteful to write separate checks for an executive's taxi fare, name tags needed right away, or delivery of a package across town. Therefore, companies keep a **petty cash** fund on hand to pay such minor amounts.

The petty cash fund is opened with a particular amount of cash. A check for that amount is then issued to Petty Cash. Assume that on February 28 **Cisco Systems**, the worldwide leader in networks for the Internet, establishes a petty cash fund of $500 in a sales department. The custodian of the petty cash fund cashes the check and places $500 in the fund, which may be a cash box or other device.

For each petty cash payment, the custodian prepares a petty cash ticket to list the item purchased. The sum of the cash in the petty cash fund plus the total of the ticket amounts should equal the opening balance at all times—in this case, $500. The Petty Cash account keeps its $500 balance at all times. Maintaining the Petty Cash account at this balance, supported by the fund (cash plus tickets), is how an **imprest system** works. The control feature is that it clearly identifies the amount for which the custodian is responsible.

Using a Budget to Manage Cash

Managers control operations with a budget. A **budget** is a financial plan that helps coordinate business activities. Cash is budgeted most often.

OBJECTIVE

4 **Use** a budget to manage your cash

How for example does AMEX Products decide when to invest in new inventory-tracking technology? How will AMEX decide how much to spend? Will borrowing be needed, or can AMEX finance the purchase with internally generated cash? Similarly, by what process do you decide how much to spend on your education? On an automobile? On a house? All these decisions depend to some degree on the information that a cash budget provides.

A cash budget helps a company or an individual manage cash by planning receipts and payments during a future period. The company must determine how much cash it will need and then decide whether or not operations will bring in the needed cash. Managers proceed as follows:

1. Start with the entity's cash balance at the beginning of the period. This is the amount left over from the preceding period.

2. Add the budgeted cash receipts and subtract the budgeted cash payments.

3. The beginning balance plus receipts and minus payments equals the expected cash balance at the end of the period.

4. Compare the cash available before new financing to the budgeted cash balance at the end of the period. Managers know the minimum amount of cash they need (the budgeted balance). If the budget shows excess cash, managers can invest the excess. But if the cash available falls below the budgeted balance, the company will need additional financing. The company may need to borrow the shortfall amount. The budget is a valuable tool for helping the company plan for the future.

The budget period can span any length of time—a day, a week, a month, or a year. Exhibit 4-13 shows a cash budget for AMEX Products, Inc., for the year ended December 31, 2008. Study it carefully, because at some point you will use a cash budget.

AMEX Products' cash budget in Exhibit 4-13 begins with $6,260 of cash (line 1). Then add budgeted cash receipts and subtract budgeted payments. In this case, AMEX expects to have $3,900 of cash available at year end (line 10). AMEX managers need to maintain a cash balance of at least $5,000 (line 11). Line 12 shows that AMEX must arrange $1,100 of financing in order to achieve its goals for 2008.

EXHIBIT 4-13   Cash Budget

AMEX Products, Inc.
Cash Budget
For the Year Ended December 31, 2008

(1)	Cash balance, December 31, 2007		$ 6,260
	Budgeted cash receipts:		
(2)	Collections from customers		55,990
(3)	Dividends on investments		1,200
(4)	Sale of store fixtures		5,700
			69,150
	Budgeted cash payments:		
(5)	Purchases of inventory	$33,720	
(6)	Operating expenses	11,530	
(7)	Expansion of store	12,000	
(8)	Payment of long-term debt	5,000	
(9)	Payment of dividends	3,000	65,250
(10)	Cash available (needed) before new financing		$ 3,900
(11)	Budgeted cash balance, December 31, 2008		(5,000)
(12)	Cash available for additional investments, or		
	(New financing needed)		$ (1,100)

Reporting Cash on the Balance Sheet

Most companies have numerous bank accounts, but they usually combine all cash amounts into a single total called "Cash and Cash Equivalents." Cash equivalents include liquid assets such as time deposits and certificates of deposit, which are interest-bearing accounts that can be withdrawn with no penalty. Slightly less liquid than cash, cash equivalents are sufficiently similar to be reported along with cash. The balance sheet of AMEX Products (repeated from page 210) reported the following:

AMEX Products, Inc.
Balance Sheet (Excerpts, adapted)
For the Year Ended December 31, 2007

	(In millions)
Assets	
Cash and cash equivalents	$ 6,260
Cash pledged as collateral	2,000

Compensating Balance Agreements

The Cash account on the balance sheet reports the liquid assets available for day-to-day use. None of the Cash balance is restricted in any way.

Any restricted amount of cash should *not* be reported as Cash on the balance sheet. For example, on the AMEX Products balance sheet, *cash pledged as collateral* (p. 232) is reported separately because that cash is not available for day-to-day use. Instead, AMEX has pledged the cash as security (collateral) for a loan. If AMEX fails to pay the loan, the lender can take the pledged cash. For this reason, the pledged cash is less liquid.

Also, banks often lend money under a compensating balance agreement. The borrower agrees to maintain a minimum balance in a checking account at all times. This minimum balance becomes a long-term asset and is therefore not cash in the normal sense.

Suppose AMEX Products borrowed $10,000 at 8% from First Interstate Bank and agreed to keep 20% ($2,000) on deposit at all times. The net result of the compensating balance agreement is that AMEX actually borrowed only $8,000. And by paying 8% interest on the full $10,000, AMEX's actual interest rate is really 10%, as shown here:

$$\$10,000 \times .08 = \$800 \text{ interest}$$
$$\$800/\$8,000 = .10 \text{ interest rate}$$

Ethics and Accounting

OBJECTIVE

5 **Make** ethical business judgments

Roger Smith, the former chairman of General Motors, said, "Ethical practice is [. . .] good business." Smith knows that unethical behavior doesn't work. Sooner or later it comes back to haunt you. Moreover, ethical behavior wins out in the long run because right triumphs over wrong.

Corporate and Professional Codes of Ethics

Most companies have a code of ethics to encourage employees to behave ethically. But codes of ethics are not enough by themselves. Owners and managers must set a high ethical tone, as we saw in the section on Control Environment. Top managers must make it clear that the company will not tolerate unethical conduct.

As professionals, accountants are expected to maintain higher standards than society in general. Their ability to do business depends entirely on their reputation. Most independent accountants are members of the American Institute of Certified Public Accountants and must abide by the *AICPA Code of Professional Conduct*. Accountants who are members of the Institute of Management Accountants are bound by the *Standards of Ethical Conduct for Management Accountants*.

Ethical Issues in Accounting

In many situations, the ethical choice is easy. For example, stealing cash is both unethical and illegal. In other cases, the choices are more difficult. But in every instance, ethical judgments boil down to a personal decision: What should I do in a given situation? Let's consider 3 ethical issues in accounting.

Situation 1. Brian Bivona is preparing the income tax return of a client who has earned more income than expected. On January 2, the client pays for advertising and asks Bivona to backdate the expense to the preceding year. Backdating the deduction would lower the client's immediate tax payments. After all, there is a difference of only 2 days between January 2 and December 31. This client is important to Bivona. What should Bivona do?

> Bivona should refuse the request because the transaction took place in January of the new year.

What control device could prove that Bivona behaved unethically if he backdated the transaction in the accounting records? An IRS audit could prove that the expense occurred in January rather than in December. Falsifying IRS documents is both unethical and illegal.

Situation 2. Marlene Reed Software Company owes $40,000 to Bank of America. The loan agreement requires Reed's company to maintain a current ratio (current assets divided by current liabilities) of 1.50 or higher. At present, the company's current ratio is 1.40. At this level, Reed is in violation of her loan agreement. She can increase the current ratio to 1.53 by paying off some current liabilities right before year end. Is it ethical to do so?

> Yes, because the action is a real business transaction.

Reed should be aware that paying off the liabilities is only a delaying tactic. It will hold off the bank for now, but the business must improve in order to keep from violating the agreement in the future.

Situation 3. David Duncan, the lead Arthur Anderson auditor of Enron Corporation, thinks Enron may be understating the liabilities on its balance sheet. Enron's transactions are very complex, and outsiders may never figure this out. Duncan asks his firm's Standards Committee how he should handle the situation. They reply, "Require Enron to report all its liabilities." Enron is Duncan's most important client, and Enron is pressuring him to certify the liabilities. Duncan can rationalize that Enron's reported amounts are okay. What should Duncan do? To make his decision, Duncan could follow the framework outlined in the following Decision Guidelines feature.

DECISION GUIDELINES

FRAMEWORK FOR MAKING ETHICAL JUDGMENTS

Weighing tough ethical judgments requires a decision framework. Answering these 4 questions will guide you through tough decisions. Let's apply them to David Duncan's situation. (situation 3 on page 234)

Question	Decision Guidelines
1. What is the ethical issue?	1. *Identify the ethical issue.* The root word of ethical is ethics, which Webster's dictionary defines as "the discipline dealing with what is good and bad and with moral duty and obligation." Duncan's ethical dilemma is to decide what he should do with the information he has uncovered.
2. What are Duncan's options?	2. *Specify the alternatives.* For David Duncan, the alternatives include (a) go along with Enron's liabilities as reported or (b) force Enron to report higher amounts of liabilities.
3. What are the possible consequences?	3. *Assess the possible outcomes.* a. If Duncan certifies Enron's present level of liabilities—and if no one ever objects—Duncan will keep this valuable client. But if Enron's actual liabilities turn out to be higher than reported, Enron investors may lose money and take Duncan to court. That would damage his reputation as an auditor and hurt his firm. b. If Duncan follows his company policy, he must force Enron to increase its reported liabilities. That will anger the company, and Enron may fire Duncan as its auditor. In that case, Duncan will save his reputation, but it will cost him dearly in the short run.
4. What should Duncan do?	4. *Make the decision.* In the end Duncan went along with Enron and certified the company's liabilities. He went directly against his firm's policies. Enron later admitted understating its liabilities, Duncan had to retract his audit opinion, and Duncan's worldwide firm, Arthur Andersen, collapsed quickly. Duncan should have followed company policy. Rarely is one person smarter than a team of experts. Duncan got out from under his firm's umbrella of protection, and it cost him and many others dearly.

END-OF-CHAPTER SUMMARY PROBLEM

Assume the following situation for PepsiCo Inc.: PepsiCo ended 20X3 with cash of $200 million. At December 31, 20X3, Bob Detmer, the CFO of PepsiCo, is preparing the budget for 20X4.

During 20X4, Detmer expects PepsiCo to collect $26,400 million from customers and $80 million from interest earned on investments. PepsiCo expects to pay $12,500 million for its inventories and $5,400 million for operating expenses. To remain competitive, PepsiCo plans to spend $2,200 million to upgrade production facilities and an additional $350 million to acquire other companies. PepsiCo also plans to sell older assets for approximately $300 million and to collect $220 million of this amount in cash. PepsiCo is budgeting dividend payments of $550 million during the year. Finally, the company is scheduled to pay off $1,200 million of long-term debt plus the $6,600 million of current liabilities left over from 20X3.

Because of the growth planned for 20X4, Detmer budgets the need for a minimum cash balance of $300 million.

I *Required*

1. How much must PepsiCo borrow during 20X4 to keep its cash balance from falling below $330 million? Prepare the 20X4 cash budget to answer this important question.

Answer

PepsiCo, Inc.
Cash Budget
For the Year Ended December 31, 20X4

(In millions)

Cash balance, December 31, 20X3..............................		$ 200
Estimated cash receipts:		
Collections from customers.......................................		26,400
Receipt of interest		80
Sales of assets...		220
		26,900
Estimated cash payments:		
Purchases of inventory..	$12,500	
Payment of operating expenses	5,400	
Upgrading of production facilities............................	2,200	
Acquisition of other companies................................	350	
Payment of dividends..	550	
Payment of long-term debt and other		
liabilities ($1,200 + $6,600)	7,800	(28,800)
Cash available (needed) before new financing..............		$ (1,900)
Budgeted cash balance, December 31, 20X4		(300)
Cash available for additional investments, or		
(New financing needed)		$ (2,200)

PepsiCo. must borrow $2,200 million.

REVIEW INTERNAL CONTROL AND CASH

Quick Check (Answers are given on page 256.)

1. Internal control has its own terminology. On the left are some key internal control concepts. On the right are some key terms. Match each internal control concept with its term by writing the appropriate letter in the space provided. Not all letters are used.

____ This procedure limits access to sensitive data.

____ This type of insurance policy covers losses due to employee theft.

____ Trusting your employees can lead you to overlook this procedure.

____ The most basic purpose of internal control.

____ Internal control cannot always safeguard against this problem.

____ Often mentioned as the cornerstone of a good system of internal control.

____ Pay employees enough to require them to do a good job.

a. Competent personnel
b. Encryption
c. Separation of duties
d. Safeguarding assets
e. Fidelity bond
f. Collusion
g. Firewalls
h. Supervision
i. External audits

2. Each of the following is an example of a control procedure, *except*
   a. a sound marketing plan.
   b. sound personnel procedures.
   c. limited access to assets.
   d. separation of duties.

3. Which of the following is an example of poor internal control?
   a. The accounting department compares goods received with the related purchase order
   b. Employees must take vacations
   c. Rotate employees through various jobs
   d. The mailroom clerk records daily cash receipts in the journal

Driver Corporation has asked you to prepare its bank reconciliation at the end of the current month. Answer questions 4–8 using the following code letters to indicate how the item described would be reported on the bank reconciliation.

a. Deduct from the book balance
b. Does not belong on the bank reconciliation
c. Add to the bank balance
d. Deduct from the bank balance
e. Add to the book balance

4. A check for $435 written by Driver during the current month was erroneously recorded as a $354 payment.

5. A $250 deposit made on the last day of the current month did not appear on this month's bank statement.

6. The bank statement showed interest earned of $45.

7. The bank statement included a check from a customer that was marked NSF.

8. The bank statement showed the bank had credited Driver's account for a $600 deposit made by Dover Company.

9. Which of the following reconciling items does not require a journal entry?
   a. NSF check
   b. deposit in transit
   c. bank collection of note receivable
   d. bank service charge

10. A check was written for $628 to purchase supplies. The check was recorded in the journal as $682. The entry to correct this error would:
    a. increase Supplies, $54.
    b. decrease Supplies, $54.
    c. decrease Cash, $54.
    d. a. and c.

11. A cash budget helps control cash by
    a. developing a plan for increasing sales.
    b. ensuring accurate cash records.
    c. helping to determine whether additional cash is available for investments or new financing is needed.
    d. All of the above.

Accounting Vocabulary

audit (p. 213) A periodic examination of a company's financial statements and the accounting systems, controls, and records that produce them.

bank collections (p. 221) Collection of money by the bank on behalf of a depositor

bank reconciliation (p. 219) A document explaining the reasons for the difference between a depositor's records and the bank's records about the depositor's cash.

bank statement (p. 218) Document showing the beginning and ending balances of a particular bank account listing the month's transactions that affected the account.

budget (p. 231) A quantitative expression of a plan that helps managers coordinate the entity's activities.

check (p. 218) Document instructing a bank to pay the designated person or business the specified amount of money.

controller (p. 214) The chief accounting officer of a business.

deposits in transit (p. 220) A deposit recorded by the company but not yet by its bank.

electronic fund transfer (EFT) (p. 221) System that transfers cash by electronic communication rather than by paper documents.

imprest system (p. 231) A way to account for petty cash by maintaining a constant balance in the petty cash account, supported by the fund (cash plus payment tickets) totaling the same amount.

internal control (p. 211) Organizational plan and related measures adopted by an entity to safeguard assets, encourage adherence to company policies, promote operational efficiency, and ensure accurate and reliable accounting records.

nonsufficient funds (NSF) check (p. 221) A "hot" check, one for which the payer's bank account has insufficient money to pay the check. NSF checks are cash receipts that turn out to be worthless.

outstanding checks (p. 220) A check issued by the company and recorded on its books but not yet paid by its bank.

petty cash (p. 231) Fund containing a small amount of cash that is used to pay minor amounts.

treasurer (p. 214) In a large company, the person in charge of writing checks.

ASSESS YOUR PROGRESS

Short Exercises

S4-1 *(Learning Objective 1: Sarbanes-Oxley Act)* What are some of the major requirements of the Sarbanes-Oxley Act? (pp. 211–212)

S4-2 *(Learning Objective 1: Components of internal control)* List the components of internal control. In your own words briefly describe each component. (pp. 211–212)

writing assignment ■

S4-3 *(Learning Objective 1: Characteristics of an effective system of internal control)* Explain in your own words why separation of duties is such an important procedure for safeguarding assets. Describe what can happen if the same person has custody of an asset and also accounts for it. (pp. 213–214)

S4-4 *(Learning Objective 1: Electronic devices and internal control)* Identify 3 electronic control devices used in business. Also show all of the internal control objectives that each electronic device relates to. (pp. 211–212, 215–216)

S4-5 (*Learning Objective 2: Preparing a bank reconciliation*) The Cash account of Reitmeier Corp. reported a balance of $2,500 at August 31. Included were outstanding checks totaling $900 and an August 31 deposit of $500 that did not appear on the bank statement. The bank statement, which came from Synergy Bank, listed an August 31 balance of $3,405. Included in the bank balance was an August 30 collection of $550 on account from a customer who pays the bank directly. The bank statement also shows a $20 service charge, $10 of interest revenue that Reitmeier earned on its bank balance, and an NSF check for $35.

Prepare a bank reconciliation to determine how much cash Reitmeier actually has at August 31. (pp. 222)

S4-6 (*Learning Objective 2: Recording transactions from a bank reconciliation*) After preparing Reitmeier Corp.'s bank reconciliation in Short Exercise S4-5, make the company's journal entries for transactions that arise from the bank reconciliation. Include an explanation with each entry. (pp. 223)

S4-7 (*Learning Objective 2: Using a blank reconciliation as a control device*) Brent Secrest manages Englander Advertising. Secrest fears that a trusted employee has been stealing from the company. This employee receives cash from clients and also prepares the monthly bank reconciliation. To check up on the employee, Secrest prepares his own bank reconciliation, as follows:

Englander Advertising
Bank Reconciliation
August 31, 20X7

Bank		Books	
Balance, August 31......................	$3,300	Balance, August 31......................	$2,820
Add:		Add:	
Deposits in transit	400	Bank collections	800
		Interest revenue	10
Less:		Less:	
Outstanding checks	(1,100)	Service charge...........................	(30)
Adjusted bank balance	$ 2,600	Adjusted book balance...............	$3,600

Does it appear that the employee has stolen from the company? If so, how much? Explain your answer. Which side of the bank reconciliation shows the company's true cash balance? (pp. 222)

writing assignment ■

S4-8 (*Learning Objective 3: Control over cash receipts*) Gina Castillo sells memberships to the Santa Fe Symphony Association in Santa Fe, New Mexico. The Symphony's procedure requires Castillo to write a patron receipt for all memberships sold. The receipt forms are prenumbered. Castillo is having personal financial problems and she stole $500 received from a customer. To hide her theft, Castillo destroyed the company copy of the receipt that she gave the patron. What will alert manager Blaine McCormick that something is wrong? (pp. 228)

S4-9 (*Learning Objective 3: Internal control over cash payments by check*) Answer the following questions about internal control over cash payments:

1. Payment by check carries 2 basic controls over cash. What are they? (pp. 229–230)

2. Suppose a purchasing agent receives the goods that he purchases and also approves payment for the goods. How could a dishonest purchasing agent cheat his company? How do companies avoid this internal control weakness? (pp. 229–230)

S4-10 (*Learning Objective 4: Using a cash budget*) In your own words, briefly explain how a cash budget works and what it accomplishes with its last few lines of data. (p. 230)

writing assignment ■

S4-11 (*Learning Objective 4: Preparing a cash budget*) California Artichoke Growers (CAG) is a major food cooperative. Suppose CAG begins 2008 with cash of $4 million. CAG estimates cash receipts during 2008 will total $97 million. Planned payments will total $95 million. To meet daily cash needs next year, CAG must maintain a cash balance of at least $5 million. Prepare the organization's cash budget for 2008. (p. 232)

writing assignment ■   **S4-12** (*Learning Objective 5: Making an ethical judgment*) Carrie Ford, an accountant for YellowPages.com, discovers that her supervisor Zach McGregor, made several errors last year. In total, the errors overstated Yellow Pages' net income by 20%. It is not clear whether the errors were deliberate or accidental. What should Ford do? (p. 235)

Exercises

E4-13 (*Learning Objective 1: E-Commerce pitfalls*) How do computer viruses, Trojan Horses and phishing expeditions work? How can these E-Commerce pitfalls hurt you? Be specific. (pp. 215–216)

E4-14 (*Learning Objective 1: Explaining the role of internal control*) Answer the following questions on internal control:

a. Separation of duties is an important internal control procedure. Why is this so? (pp. 211–212)
b. Cash may be a small item on the financial statements. Nevertheless, internal control over cash is very important. Why is this true? (p. 228)
c. Crane Company requires that all documents supporting a check be cancelled by punching a hole through the packet. Why is this practice required? What might happen if it were not? (pp. 229–230)

writing assignment ■   **E4-15** (*Learning Objective 1: Identifying internal control weaknesses*) Identify the internal control weakness in the following situations. State how the person can hurt the company.

a. Jerry Miller works as a security guard at ALTEX parking in Denver. Miller has a master key to the cash box where commuters pay for parking. Each night Miller prepares the cash report that shows (a) the number of cars that parked on the lot and (b) the day's cash receipts. Sandra Covington, the ALTEX treasurer, checks Miller's figures by multiplying the number of cars by the parking fee per car. Covington then deposits the cash in the bank. (p. 228)
b. Sharon Fisher is the purchasing agent for Manatee Golf Equipment. Fisher prepares purchase orders based on requests from division managers of the company. Fisher faxes the purchase order to suppliers who then ship the goods to Manatee. Fisher receives each incoming shipment and checks it for agreement with the purchase order and the related invoice. She then routes the goods to the respective division managers and sends the receiving report and the invoice to the accounting department for payment. (pp. 228–233)
c. The external auditor for Mattson Financial Services takes a global view of the audit. To form his professional opinion of Mattson's financial statements, the auditor runs no tests of Mattson's financial statements or of the underlying transactions. Instead, the auditor computes a few ratios and compares the current-year ratio values to the ratio values a year ago. If the ratio values appear reasonable, the auditor concludes that Mattson's financial statements are okay. (pp. 215–216)

E4-16 (*Learning Objective 1: Identifying internal control strengths and weaknesses*) The following situations describe 2 cash payment situations and 2 cash receipt situations. In each pair, one set of internal controls is better than the other. Evaluate the internal controls in each situation as strong or weak, and give the reason for your answer. (pp. 228–233)

Cash payments:

a. Jim McCord Construction policy calls for construction supervisors to request the equipment needed for their jobs. The home office then purchases the equipment and has it shipped to the construction site.

b. Granite & Marble, Inc., policy calls for project supervisors to purchase the equipment needed for jobs. The supervisors then submit the paid receipts to the home office for reimbursement. This policy enables supervisors to get the equipment quickly and keep construction jobs moving.

Cash receipts:

a. At McClaren Chevrolet, cash received by mail goes straight to the accountant, who debits Cash and credits Accounts Receivable to record the collections from customers. The McClaren accountant then deposits the cash in the bank.

b. Cash received by mail at Lone Star Orthopedic Clinic goes to the mail room, where a mail clerk opens envelopes and totals the cash receipts for the day. The mail clerk forwards customer checks to the cashier for deposit in the bank and forwards the remittance slips to the accounting department for posting credits to customer accounts.

E4-17 (*Learning Objective 1: Correcting an internal control weakness*) Spencer Moore served as Executive Director of Downtown Flint, an organization created to revitalize Flint, Michigan. Over the course of 13 years Moore embezzled $352,000. How did Moore do it? By depositing subscriber cash receipts in his own bank account, writing Downtown Flint checks to himself, and creating phony entities that Downtown Flint wrote checks to.

writing assignment ■

Downtown Flint was led by a board of directors comprised of civic leaders. Moore's embezzlement went undetected until Downtown Flint couldn't pay its bills.

Give at least 3 ways Moore's embezzlement could have been prevented. (pp. 228–233)

E4-18 (*Learning Objective 2: Classifying bank reconciliation items*) The following items appear on a bank reconciliation:

1. ___ Outstanding checks

2. ___ Bank error: The bank credited our account for a deposit made by another bank customer

3. ___ Service charge

4. ___ Deposits in transit

5. ___ NSF check

6. ___ Bank collection of a note receivable on our behalf

7. ___ Book error: We debited Cash for $100. The correct debit was $1,000

Classify each item as (a) an addition to the bank balance, (b) a subtraction from the bank balance, (c) an addition to the book balance, or (d) a subtraction from the book balance. (p. 222)

E4-19 (*Learning Objective 2: Preparing a bank reconciliation*) LeAnn Bryant's check book lists the following:

Date	Check No.	Item	Check	Deposit	Balance
Nov. 1					$ 705
4	622	Consolidated Gas Co.	$19		686
9		Dividends		$116	802
13	623	General Tire Co.	43		759
14	624	Exxon Mobil Oil Co.	58		701
18	625	Cash	50		651
26	626	St. Mark's Church	25		626
28	627	Bent Tree Apartments	275		351
30		Paycheck		846	1,197

(*continued*)

The November bank statement shows

Balance			$705
Add: Deposits			116
Deduct checks:	No.	Amount	
	622	$19	
	623	43	
	624	85*	
	625	50	(197)
Other charges:			
NSF check		$ 8	
Service charge		12	(20)
Balance			$604

*This is the correct amount for check number 624.

❙ Required

Prepare Bryant's bank reconciliation at November 30, 20X6. (p. 222)

E4-20 (*Learning Objective 2: Preparing a bank reconciliation*) Tim VanWinkle operates a FedEx Kinko's store. He has just received the monthly bank statement at May 31 from City National Bank, and the statement shows an ending balance of $595. Listed on the statement are an EFT rent collection of $300, a service charge of $12, two NSF checks totaling $120 and a $9 charge for printed checks. In reviewing his cash records, VanWinkle identifies outstanding checks totaling $603 and a May 31 deposit in transit of $1,788. During May, he recorded a $290 check for the salary of a part-time employee as $29. VanWinkle's Cash account shows a May 31 cash balance of $1,882. How much cash does VanWinkle actually have at May 31? (pp. 222)

E4-21 (*Learning Objective 2: Making journal entries from a bank reconciliation*) Use the data from Exercise 4-20 to make the journal entries that VanWinkle should record on May 31 to update his Cash account. Include an explanation for each entry. (p. 223)

E4-22 (*Learning Objective 3: Evaluating internal control over cash receipts*) **Target** stores use point-of-sale terminals as cash registers. The register shows the amount of each sale, the cash received from the customer, and any change returned to the customer. The machine also produces a customer receipt but keeps no record of transactions. At the end of the day, the clerk counts the cash in the register and gives it to the cashier for deposit in the company bank account.

writing assignment ■

Write a memo to convince the store manager that there is an internal control weakness over cash receipts. Identify the weakness that gives an employee the best opportunity to steal cash and state how to prevent such a theft. (p. 228)

E4-23 (*Learning Objective 3: Evaluating internal control over cash payments*) Tee Golf Company manufactures a popular line of golf clubs. Tee Golf employs 140 workers and keeps their employment records on time sheets that show how many hours the employee works each week. On Friday the shop foreman collects the time sheets, checks them for accuracy, and delivers them to the payroll deportment for preparation of paychecks. The treasurer signs the paychecks and returns the checks to the payroll department for distribution to the employees.

Identify the main internal control weakness in this situation, state how the weakness can hurt Tee Golf, and propose a way to correct the weakness. (pp. 229–230)

■ spreadsheet

E4-24 (*Learning Objective 4: Preparing a cash budget*) Cellular Communications, Inc., is preparing its cash budget for 20X8. Cellular ended 20X7 with cash of $81 million, and managers need to keep a cash balance of at least $75 million for operations.

Collections from customers are expected to total $11,284 million during 20X8, and payments for the cost of services and products should reach $6,166 million. Operating expense payments are budgeted at $2,543 million.

During 20X8, Cellular expects to invest $1,825 million in new equipment and sell older assets for $115 million. Debt payments scheduled for 20X8 will total $597 million. The company forecasts net income of $890 million for 20X8 and plans to pay dividends of $338 million.

Prepare Cellular Communications' cash budget for 20X8. Will the budgeted level of cash receipts leave Cellular with the desired ending cash balance of $75 million, or will the company need additional financing? If so, how much? (pp. 232–233)

E4-25 (*Learning Objective 5: Resolving an ethical challenge*). Sunbelt Bank recently appointed the accounting firm of Baker, Jackson, and Trent as the bank's auditor. Sunbelt quickly became one of the Baker, Jackson, and Trent's largest clients. Subject to banking regulations, Sunbelt must provide for any expected losses on notes receivable that Sunbelt may not collect in full.

During the course of the audit, Baker, Jackson, and Trent determined that 3 large notes receivable of Sunbelt seem questionable. Baker, Jackson and Trent discussed these loans with Stephanie Carson, controller of Sunbelt. Carson assured the auditors that these notes were good and that the makers of the notes will be able to pay their notes after the economy improves.

Baker, Jackson, and Trent stated that Sunbelt must record a loss for a portion of these notes receivable to account for the likelihood that Sunbelt may never collect their full amount. Carson objected and threatened to dismiss Baker, Jackson, and Trent if the auditor demands that the bank record the loss. Baker, Jackson, and Trent want to keep Sunbelt as a client. In fact, Baker, Jackson, and Trent were counting on the revenue from the Sunbelt audit to finance an expansion of the firm.

Apply the decision guidelines for ethical judgments outlined on p. 235 to decide how the accounting firm of Baker, Jackson, and Trent should proceed.

writing assignment ■

E4-26 (*Learning Objective 4: Compensating balance agreement*) Assume **Starbucks** borrowed $10 million from Bank of Seattle and agreed to (a) pay an interest rate of 7% and (b) maintain a compensating balance amount equal to 5% of the loan. Determine Starbucks' actual effective interest rate on this loan.

Challenge Exercises

E4-27 (*Learning Objective 3, 5: Internal controls over cash payments, ethical considerations*) Jan Copeland, the owner of Jan's Perfect Presents, has delegated management of the business to Lou Major, a friend. Copeland drops by to meet customers and check up on cash receipts, but Major buys the merchandise and handles cash payments. Business has been very good lately, and cash receipts have kept pace with the apparent level of sales. However, for a year or so, the amount of cash on hand has been too low. When asked about this, Major explains that suppliers are charging more for goods than in the past. During the past year, Major has taken 2 expensive vacations, and Copeland wonders how Major can afford these trips on her $60,000 annual salary and commissions.

List at least 3 ways Major could be defrauding Copeland of cash. In each instance also identify how Copeland can determine whether Major's actions are ethical. Limit your answers to the store's cash payments. The business pays all suppliers by check (no EFTs). (pp. 228–233)

E4-28 (*Learning Objective 4: Preparing and using a cash budget*) Dan Davis, the chief financial officer, is responsible for The Furniture Mart's cash budget for 20X6. The budget will help Davis determine the amount of long-term borrowing needed to end the year with a cash balance of $150 thousand. Davis's assistants have assembled budget data for 20X6, which the computer printed in alphabetical order. Not all the data items reproduced below are used in preparing the cash budget.

(*continued*)

(Assumed Data)	(In thousands)
Actual cash balance, December 31, 20X5	$ 140
Budgeted total assets	22,977
Budgeted total current assets	7,776
Budgeted total current liabilities	4,860
Budgeted total liabilities..	11,488
Budgeted total stockholders' equity..........................	7,797
Collections from customers.......................................	18,527
Dividend payments	237
Issuance of stock	627
Net income...	1,153
Payment of long-term and short-term debt...............	950
Payment of operating expenses	2,349
Purchases of inventory items	14,045
Purchase of property and equipment........................	1,518

❙ Required

1. Prepare the cash budget of The Furniture Mart, Inc., for 20X6. (p. 232)

2. Compute The Furniture Mart's budgeted current ratio and debt ratio at December 31, 20X6. Based on these ratio values, and on the cash budget, would you lend $100 thousand to The Furniture Mart? Give the reason for your decision.

Quiz

Test your understanding of internal control and cash by answering the following questions. Answer each question by selecting the best choice from among the answers given.

Q4-29 All of the following are objectives of internal control except (p. 211)
a. to comply with legal requirements.
b. to safeguard assets.
c. to maximize net income.
d. to ensure accurate and reliable accounting records.

Q4-30 All of the following are internal control procedures except (pp. 213–214)
a. electronic devices.
b. Sarbanes-Oxley reforms.
c. assignment of responsiblities.
d. internal and external audits.

Q4-31 Requiring that an employee with no access to cash do the accounting is an example of which characteristic of internal control: (pp. 213–214)
a. separation of duties
b. competent and reliable personnel
c. competent personnel
d. monitoring of controls

Q4-32 All of the following are controls for cash received over the counter except: (p. 228)
a. the customer should be able to see the amounts entered into the cash register
b. a printed receipt must be given to the customer
c. the cash drawer should open only when the salesclerk enters an amount on the keys
d. the sales clerk must have access to the cash register tape

Q4-33 In a bank reconciliation, an outstanding check is: (p. 222)
a. added to the book balance
b. deducted from the book balance
c. added to the bank balance
d. deducted from the bank balance

Q4-34 In a bank reconciliation, a bank collection of a note receivable is: (p. 222)
a. added to the book balance
b. deducted from the book balance
c. added to the bank balance
d. deducted from the bank balance

Q4-35 In a bank reconciliation, an EFT cash payment is: (p. 222)
a. added to the book balance
c. added to the bank balance
b. deducted from the book balance
d. deducted from the bank balance

Q4-36 If a bookkeeper mistakenly recorded a $58 deposit as $85, the error would be shown on the bank reconciliation as a: (p. 222)
a. $27 addition to the book balance
c. $27 deduction from the book balance
b. $85 deduction from the book balance
d. $85 addition to the book balance

Q4-37 If a bank reconciliation included a deposit in transit of $670, the entry to record this reconciling item would include a: (p. 223)
a. credit to prepaid insurance for $670
c. debit to cash for $670
b. credit to cash for $670
d. no journal entry is required

Q4-38 In a bank reconciliation, interest revenue earned on your bank balance is: (p. 222)
a. added to the book balance
c. added to the bank balance
b. deducted from the book balance
d. deducted from the bank balance

Q4-39 Before paying an invoice for goods received on account, the controller or treasurer should ensure that (pp. 229–230)
a. the company is paying for the goods it ordered.
b. the company is paying for the goods it actually received.
c. the company has not already paid this invoice.
d. All of the above.

Q4-40 La Petite France Bakery is budgeting cash for 20X8. The cash balance at December 31, 20X7, was $10,000. LaPetite budgets 20X8 cash receipts at $85,000. Estimated cash payments include $40,000 for inventory, $30,000 for operating expenses, and $20,000 to expand the store. La Petite needs a minimum cash balance of $10,000 at all times. La Petite expects to earn net income of $40,000 during 20X8. What is the final result of the company's cash budget for 20X8? (pp. 232–236)
a. $10,000 available for additional investments.
b. $5,000 available for additional investments.
c. Must arrange new financing for $5,000.
d. Pay off $10,000 of debt.

Problems
(Group A)

> Some of these A problems can be found within My Accounting Lab (MAL), an online homework and practice environment. Your instructor may ask you to complete these exercises using MAL.

P4-41A (*Learning Objective 1: Idenifying internal control weaknesses*) Avant Garde Imports is an importer of silver, brass, and furniture items from Mexico. Kay Jones is the general manager of Avant Garde Imports. Jones employs 2 other people in the business. Marco Gonzalez serves as the buyer for Avant Garde. In his work Gonzalez travels throughout Mexico to find interesting new products. When Gonzalez finds a new product, he arranges for Avant Garde to purchase and pay for the item. He helps the Mexican artisans prepare their invoices and then faxes the invoices to Jones in the company office.

writing assignment ■

Jones operates out of an office in Tucson, Arizona. The office is managed by Rita Bowden, who handles the mail, keeps the accounting records, makes bank deposits, and prepares the monthly bank reconciliation. Virtually all of Avant Garde's cash receipts arrive by mail—from sales, made to Target, Pier 1 Imports, and Wal-Mart.

Bowden also prepares checks for payment based on invoices that come in from the suppliers who have been contacted by Gonzalez. To maintain control over cash payments, Jones examines the paperwork and signs all checks.

I *Required*

Identify all the major internal control weaknesses in Avant Garde's system and how the resulting action could hurt Avant Garde. Also state how to correct each weakness. (pp. 229–230)

writing assignment ■

P4-42A (*Learning Objective 1, 3: Idenifying internal control weakness*) Each of the following situations reveals an internal control weakness.

a. Accounting firms use paraprofessional employees to perform routine tasks. For example, an accounting paraprofessional might prepare routine tax returns for clients. In the firm of Dunham & Lee, Rodney Lee, one of the partners, turns over a significant portion of his high-level accounting work to his paraprofessional staff. (pp. 213–214)

b. In evaluating the internal control over cash payments of Butler Manufacturing, an auditor learns that the purchasing agent is responsible for purchasing diamonds for use in the company's manufacturing process, approving the invoices for payment, and signing the checks. No supervisor reviews the purchasing agent's work. (pp. 229–230)

c. Charlotte James owns an architecture firm. James's staff consists of 12 professional architects, and James manages the office. Often, James's work requires her to travel to meet with clients. During the past 6 months, James has observed that when she returns from a business trip, the architecture jobs in the office have not progressed satisfactorily. James learns that when she is away, 2 of her senior architects take over office management and neglect their normal duties. One employee could manage the office. (pp. 213–214)

d. B.J. Tanner has been an employee of the City of Marlin for many years. Because the city is small, Tanner performs all accounting duties, plus opening the mail, preparing the bank deposit, and preparing the bank reconciliation. (pp. 213–214)

e. Part of an internal auditor's job is to evaluate how efficiently the company is running. For example, is the company purchasing inventory from the least expensive supplier? After a particularly bad year, Long Photographic Products eliminates its internal audit department to reduce expenses. (pp. 214–215)

I *Required*

1. Identify the missing internal control characteristic in each situation.
2. Identify each firm's possible problem.
3. Propose a solution to the problem.

writing assignment ■

■ spreadsheet

P4-43A (*Learning Objective 2: Using the bank reconciliation as a control device*) The cash data of Alta Vista Toyota for June 20X4 follow:

		Cash			
Date	Item	Jrnl. Ref.	Debit	Credit	Balance
June 1	Balance				5,011
30		CR6	10,578		15,589
30		CP11		10,924	4,665

Cash Receipts (CR)		Cash Payments (CP)	
Date	Cash Debit	Check No.	Cash Credit
June 2	$ 4,174	3113	$ 891
8	407	3114	147
10	559	3115	1,930
16	2,187	3116	664
22	1,854	3117	1,472
29	1,060	3118	1,000
30	337	3119	632
Total	$10,578	3120	1,675
		3121	100
		3122	2,413
		Total	$10,924

Alta Vista received the following bank statement on June 30, 20X4:

Bank Statement for June 20X4

Beginning balance		$ 5,011	
Deposits and other additions:			
June 1............................	$ 326 EFT		
4............................	4,174		
9............................	407		
12............................	559		
17............................	2,187		
22............................	1,701 BC		
23............................	1,854	11,208	
Checks and other deductions:			
June 7............................	$ 891		
13............................	1,390		
14............................	903 US		
15............................	147		
18............................	664		
21............................	219 EFT		
26............................	1,472		
30............................	1,000		
30............................	20 SC	(6,706)	
Ending balance...................		$ 9,513	

Explanation: EFT—electronic funds transfer, BC—bank collection, US—unauthorized signature, SC—service charge.

Additional data for the bank reconciliation include the following:

a. The EFT deposit was a receipt of monthly rent. The EFT debit was a monthly insurance payment.

b. The unauthorized signature check was received from a customer.

c. The correct amount of check number 3115, a payment on account, is $1,390. (Alta Vista's accountant mistakenly recorded the check for $1,930.)

❚ Required

1. Prepare the Alta Vista Toyota bank reconciliation at June 30, 20X4. (p. 222)
2. Describe how a bank account and the bank reconciliation help the general manager control Alta Vista's cash. (p. 233)

P4-44A *(Learning Jobective 4: Preparing a bank reconciliation and the related journal entries)* The May 31 bank statement of Varian Engineering Associates has just arrived from Carolina First Bank. To prepare the Varian bank reconciliation, you gather the following data:

■ **spreadsheet**

a. Varian's Cash account shows a balance of $2,256.14 on May 31.

b. The May 31 bank balance is $3,374.22.

c. The bank statement shows that Varian earned $38.19 of interest on its bank balance during May. This amount was added to Varian's bank balance.

d. Varian pays utilities ($750) and insurance ($290) by EFT.

e. The following Varian checks did not clear the bank by May 31:

(continued)

Check No.	Amount
237	$ 46.10
288	141.00
291	578.05
293	11.87
294	609.51
295	8.88
296	101.63

f. The bank statement includes a deposit of $891.17, collected on account by the bank on behalf of Varian.

g. The bank statement lists a $10.50 bank service charge.

h. On May 31, the Varian treasurer deposited $16.15, which will appear on the June bank statement.

i. The bank statement includes a $300.00 deposit that Varian did not make. The bank added $300 to Varian's account for another company's deposit.

j. The bank statement includes 2 charges for returned checks from customers. One is a $395.00 check received from a customer with the imprint "Unauthorized Signature." The other is a nonsufficient funds check in the amount of $146.67 received from another customer.

❙ Required

1. Prepare the bank reconciliation for Varian Engineering Associates. (p. 222)
2. Journalize the May 31 transactions needed to update Varian's Cash account. Include an explanation for each entry. (p. 223)

writing assignment ■

P4-45A *(Learning Objective 3: Idenifying internal control weakness)* Sun Skin Care makes all sales on credit. Cash receipts arrive by mail, usually within 30 days of the sale. Nancy Brown opens envelopes and separates the checks from the accompanying remittance advices. Brown forwards the checks to another employee, who makes the daily bank deposit but has no access to the accounting records. Brown sends the remittance advices, which show the amount of cash received, to the accounting department for entry in the accounts receivable. Brown's only other duty is to grant allowances to customers. (An *allowance* decreases the amount that the customer must pay.) When Brown receives a customer check for less than the full amount of the invoice, she records the allowance in the accounting records and forwards the document to the accounting department.

❙ Required

You are a new employee of Sun Skin Care. Write a memo to the company president identifying the internal control weakness in this situation. State how to correct the weakness. (p. 228)

writing assignment ■

P4-46A *(Learning Objective 4: Preparing a cash budget and using cash-flow information)* Kenneth Austin, chief financial officer of ReMax Wireless, is responsible for the company's budgeting process. Austin's staff is preparing the ReMax cash budget for 20X7. A key input to the budgeting process is last year's statement of cash flows, which follows (amount in thousands):

ReMax Wireless
Statement of Cash Flows
20X6

(In thousands)	
Cash Flows from Operating Activities	
Collections from customers	$ 60,000
Interest received	100
Purchases of inventory	(44,000)
Operating expenses	(13,900)
Net cash provided by operations	2,200
Cash Flows from Investing Activities	
Purchases of equipment	(4,300)
Purchases of investments	(200)
Sales of investments	400
Net cash used for investing activities	(4,100)
Cash Flows from Financing Activities	
Payment of long-term debt	(300)
Issuance of stock	1,200
Payment of cash dividends	(500)
Net cash provided by financing activities	400
Cash	
Increase (decrease) in cash	(1,500)
Cash, beginning of year	2,700
Cash, end of year	$ 1,200

❚ Required

1. Prepare the ReMax Wireless cash budget for 20X7. Date the budget simply "20X7" and denote the beginning and ending cash balances as "beginning" and "ending." Assume the company expects 20X7 to be the same as 20X6, but with the following changes: (pp. 232–233)
   a. In 20X7, the company expects a 15% increase in collections from customers and a 20% increase in purchases of inventory.
   b. There will be no sales of investments in 20X7.
   c. ReMax plans to issue no stock in 20X7.
   d. ReMax plans to end the year with a cash balance of $2,000 thousand.
2. Does the company's cash budget for 20X7 suggest that ReMax is growing, holding steady, or decreasing in size? (Challenge)

P4-47A *(Learning Objective 5: Making an ethical judgment)* Larry Raborn is executive vice president of Quality Bank. Active in community affairs, Raborn serves on the board of directors of The Salvation Army. The Salvation Army is expanding rapidly and is considering relocating. At a recent meeting, The Salvation Army decided to buy 200 acres of land on the edge of town. The owner of the property is Freda Rader, a major depositor in Quality Bank. Rader is completing a bitter divorce, and Raborn knows that Rader is eager to sell her property. In view of Rader's difficult situation, Raborn believes Rader would accept a low offer for the land. Realtors have appraised the property at $2.2 million.

❚ Required

Apply the ethical judgment framework outlined in the chapter to help Raborn decide what role he should play in The Salvation Army's attempt to buy the land from Rader. (p. 235)

(Group B)

writing assignment ■

P4-48B *(Learning Objective 1: Setting up an effective internal control system)* Trey Osborne, administration of Valley View Clinic, seeks your advice. Valley View Clinic employs 2 people in the office, Jim Bates and Rhonda Clark. Osborne asks you how to assign the various office functions to the 3 people (including Osborne) to achieve good internal control. Here are the duties to be performed by the 2 office workers and Osborne:

a. Record cash payments
b. Record cash receipts
c. Receive incoming cash from patients

d. Reconcile the bank account
e. Deposit cash receipts
f. Sign checks for payment

❙ Required

1 Propose a plan that divides duties a. through f. to Bates, Clark, and Osborne. Your goal is to divide the duties so as to achieve good internal control for the clinic. (pp. 228–233)
2. Identify several combinations of duties that should not be performed by the same person. (pp. 225–230)

writing assignment ■

P4-49B *(Learning Objective 1, 3: Identifying internal control weaknesses)* Each of the following situations has an internal control weakness:

a. Retail stores such as **Target** and **Best Buy** receive a significant portion of their sales revenue in cash. At the end of each day, sales clerks compare the cash in their own register with the record of sales kept within the register. They then forward the cash to a Brinks security officer for deposit in the bank. (p. 228)
b. The office supply company from which Martin Audiology Service purchases cash receipt forms recently notified Martin that the last-shipped sales receipts were not prenumbered. Derek Martin, the owner, replied that he did not use the receipt numbers, so the omission is unimportant to him. (pp. 215–216)
c. Azbell Electronics specializes in programs with musical applications. The company's most popular product prepares musical programs for large gatherings. In the company's early days, the owner and 8 employees wrote the programs, lined up production of the programs, sold the products, and performed the general management of the company. As Azbell has grown, the number of employees has increased dramatically. Recently, the development of a new musical series stopped while the programmers redesigned Azbell's sound system. Azbell could have hired outsiders to do this task. (pp. 213–214)
d. Paul Allen, who has no known sources of outside income, has been a trusted employee of Chapparall Cosmetics for 20 years. Allen performs all cash-handling and accounting duties, including opening the mail, preparing the bank deposit, accounting for cash and accounts receivable, and preparing the bank reconciliation. Allen has just purchased a new Lexus. Linda Altman, owner of the company, wonders how Allen can afford the new car on his salary. (pp. 213–214)
e. Monica Wade employs 3 professional interior designers in her design studio. The studio is located in an area with a lot of new construction, and her business is booming. Ordinarily, Wade does all the purchasing of materials needed to complete jobs. During the summer, Wade takes a long vacation, and in her absence she allows each designer to purchase materials. On her return, Wade reviews operations and observes that expenses are higher and net income is lower than in the past. (pp. 213–214)

❙ Required

1. Identify the missing internal control characteristics in each situation.
2. Identify each firm's possible problem.
3. Propose a solution to the problem.

■ **spreadsheet**

writing assignment ■

P4-50B *(Learning Objective 2: Using the bank reconciliation as a control device)* The cash data of Navajo Products for September 20X5 follow:

Cash					
Date	Item	Jrnl. Ref.	Debit	Credit	Balance
Sept. 1	Balance				7,078
30		CR 10	9,106		16,184
30		CP 16		11,353	4,831

Cash Receipts (CR)		Cash Payments (CP)	
Date	Cash Debit	Check No.	Cash Credit
Sept. 1	$2,716	1413	$ 1,465
9	544	1414	1,004
11	1,655	1415	450
14	896	1416	8
17	367	1417	775
25	890	1418	88
30	2,038	1419	4,126
Total	$9,106	1420	970
		1421	200
		1422	2,267
		Total	$11,353

On September 30, 20X5, Navajo received this bank statement:

Bank Statement for September 20X5

Beginning balance		$ 7,078
Deposits and other additions:		
Sept. 1...........................	$ 625 EFT	
5...........................	2,716	
10...........................	544	
11...........................	1,655	
15...........................	896	
18...........................	367	
25...........................	890	
30...........................	1,400 BC	9,093
Checks and other deductions:		
Sept. 8...........................	$ 441 NSF	
9...........................	1,465	
13...........................	1,004	
14...........................	450	
15...........................	8	
19...........................	340 EFT	
22...........................	775	
29...........................	88	
30...........................	4,216	
30...........................	25 SC	(8,812)
Ending balance...................		$ 7,359

Explanation: BC—bank collection, EFT—electronic funds transfer, NSF—nonsufficient funds check, SC—service charge

(continued)

Additional data for the bank reconciliation:

a. The EFT deposit was for monthly rent revenue. The EFT deduction was for monthly insurance expense.

b. The NSF check was received from a customer.

c. The correct amount of check number 1419, a payment on account, is $4,216. (The Navajo accountant mistakenly recorded the check for $4,126.)

I *Required*

1. Prepare the bank reconciliation of Navajo Products at September 30, 20X5. (p. 222)
2. Describe how a bank account and the bank reconciliation help managers control a firm's cash. (p. 219)

■ **spreadsheet**

writing assignment ■

P4-51B (*Learning Objective 2: Preparing a blank reconciliation and the related journal entries*) The January 31 bank statement of Bed & Bath Accessories has just arrived from First National Bank. To prepare the Bed & Bath bank reconciliation, you gather the following data:

a. The January 31 bank balance is $8,400.82.

b. Bed & Bath's Cash account shows a balance of $7,391.55 on January 31.

c. The following Bed & Bath checks are outstanding at January 31:

Check No.	Amount
616	$403.00
802	74.02
806	36.60
809	161.38
810	229.05
811	48.91

d. The bank statement includes 2 special deposits: $899.14, which is the amount of dividend revenue the bank collected from **IBM** on behalf of Bed & Bath, and $16.86, the interest revenue Bed & Bath earned on its bank balance during January.

e. The bank statement lists a $6.25 bank service charge.

f. On January 31 the Bed & Bath treasurer deposited $381.14, which will appear on the February bank statement.

g. The bank statement includes a $410.00 deduction for a check drawn by Bonjovi Music Company.

h. The bank statement includes 2 charges for returned checks from customers. One is a nonsufficient funds check in the amount of $67.50 received from a customer. The other is a $195.03 check received from another customer. It was returned by the customer's bank with the imprint "Unauthorized Signature."

i. A few customers pay monthly bills by EFT. The January bank statement lists an EFT deposit for sales revenue of $200.23.

I *Required*

1. Prepare the bank reconciliation for Bed & Bath Accessories at January 31. (p.222)
2. Journalize the transactions needed to update the Cash account. Include an explanation for each entry. (p.223)

writing assignment ■

P4-52B (*Learning Objective 3: Identifying an internal control weakness*) Nordhaus Energy Co. makes all sales on credit. Cash receipts arrive by mail, usually within 30 days of the sale. Dan Webster opens envelopes and separates the checks from the accompanying remittance advices. Webster forwards the checks to another employee, who makes the daily bank deposit but has no access to the accounting records. Webster sends the remittance advices, which show the amount of cash received, to the accounting department for entry in the accounts receivable. Webster's only other duty is to grant allowances to customers. (An *allowance* decreases the amount that the customer must pay.) When Webster receives a customer check for less than the full amount of the invoice, he records the allowance in the accounting records and forwards the document to the accounting department.

❙ Required

You are a new employee of Nordhaus Energy Co. Write a memo to the company president identifying the internal control weakness in this situation. Explain how to correct the weakness. (p. 228)

P4-53B *(Learning Objective 1, 3: Preparing a cash budget and using cash–flow information)*
Melissa Becker is chief financial officer of Valero Technology, and is responsible for the company's budgeting process. Becker's staff is preparing the Valero budget for 20X6. The starting point is the statement of cash flows of the current year, 20X5, which follows:

writing assignment ■

Valero Technology Statement of Cash Flows 20X5	
Cash Flows from Operating Activities	
Collections from customers	$ 35,600
Interest received	100
Purchases of inventory	(11,000)
Operating expenses	(16,600)
Net cash provided by operating activities	8,100
Cash Flows from Investing Activities	
Purchases of property and equipment	(5,000)
Purchases of investments	(7,500)
Sales of investments	8,100
Net cash used by investing activities	(4,400)
Cash Flows from Financing Activities	
Payment of dividends	(2,700)
Payment of short-term debt	(1,000)
Long-term borrowings by issuing notes payable	1,200
Issuance of common stock	300
Net cash used by financing activities	(2,200)
Increase (decrease) in Cash	1,500
Cash, beginning of year	2,600
Cash, end of year	$ 4,100

❙ Required

1. Prepare the Valero Technology cash budget for 20X6. Date the budget simply "20X6" and denote the beginning and ending cash balances as "beginning" and "ending." Assume the company expects 20X6 to be the same as 20X5, but with the following changes: (p. 232)

   a. In 20X6, the company expects a 10% increase in collections from customers, a 5% increase in purchases of inventory, and a doubling of additions to property and equipment.

   b. Operating expenses will drop by $2,000.

   c. There will be no sales of investments in 20X6.

   d. Becker plans to end the year with a cash balance of $3,000.

2. Does the company's cash budget for 20X6 suggest that Valero is growing, holding steady, or decreasing in size? (Challenge)

P4-54B (*Learning Objective 5: Making an ethical judgment*) Community Bank has a loan receivable from IMS Chocolates. IMS is 6 months late in making payments to the bank, and Jan French, a Community Bank vice president, is assisting IMS to restructure its debt.

French learns that IMS is depending on landing a contract with Snicker Foods, another Community Bank client. French also serves as Snicker Foods' loan officer at the bank. In this capacity, French is aware that Snicker is considering bankruptcy. No one else outside Snicker Foods knows this. French has been a great help to IMS and IMS's owner is counting on French's expertise in loan workouts to advise the company through this difficult process. To help the bank collect on this large loan, French has a strong motivation to alert IMS of Snicker's financial difficulties.

❙ Required

Apply the ethical judgment framework outlined in the chapter to help Jan French plan her next action. (p. 235)

APPLY YOUR KNOWLEDGE

Decision Cases

Case 1. (*Learning Objective 2: Using a bank reconciliation to detect a theft*) Environmentol Concerns, Inc., has poor internal control. Recently, Oscar Benz, the manager, has suspected the bookkeeper of stealing. Details of the business's cash position at September 30 follow.

a. The Cash account shows a balance of $10,402. This amount includes a September 30 deposit of $3,794 that does not appear on the September 30 bank statement.

b. The September 30 bank statement shows a balance of $8,224. The bank statement lists a $200 bank collection, an $8 service charge, and a $36 NSF check. The accountant has not recorded any of these items.

c. At September 30, the following checks are outstanding:

Check No.	Amount
154	$116
256	150
278	853
291	990
292	206
293	145

d. The bookkeeper receives all incoming cash and makes the bank deposits. He also reconciles the monthly bank statement. Here is his September 30 reconciliation:

Balance per books, September 30..............		$10,402
Add: Outstanding checks		1,460
Bank collection..................................		200
Subtotal...		12,062
Less: Deposits in transit.........................	$3,794	
Service charge	8	
NSF check.......................................	36	(3,838)
Balance per bank, September 30..............		$ 8,224

▌*Required*

Benz has requested that you determine whether the bookkeeper has stolen cash from the business and, if so, how much. He also asks you to explain how the bookkeeper attempted to conceal the theft. To make this determination, you perform a proper bank reconciliation. There are no bank or book errors. Benz also asks you to evaluate the internal controls and to recommend any changes needed to improve them. (p. 222)

Case 2. *(Learning Objective 2: Correcting an internal control weakness)* This case is based on an actual situation experienced by one of the authors. Gilead Construction, headquartered in Topeka, Kansas, built a motel in Kansas City. The construction foreman, Slim Pickins, hired the workers for the project. Pickins had his workers fill out the necessary tax forms and sent the employment documents to the home office.

Work on the motel began on May 1 and ended in December. Each Thursday evening, Pickins filled out a time card that listed the hours worked by each employee during the 5-day work week ended at 5 p.m. on Thursday. Pickins faxed the time sheets to the home office, which prepared the payroll checks on Friday morning. Pickins drove to the home office after lunch on Friday, picked up the payroll checks, and returned to the construction site. At 5 p.m. on Friday, Pickins distributed the paychecks to the workers.

    a. Describe in detail the internal control weakness in this situation. Specify what negative result could occur because of the internal control weakness. (p. 229)

    b. Describe what you would do to correct the internal control weakness. (pp. 228–230)

Ethical Issue

Kurt Hobbs owns apartment complexes in Columbus, Ohio. Each property has a manager who collects rent, arranges for repairs, and runs advertisements in the local newspaper. The property managers transfer cash to Hobbs monthly and prepare their own bank reconciliations. The manager of one property has been stealing large sums of money. To cover the theft, he understates the amount of the outstanding checks on the monthly bank reconciliation. As a result, each monthly bank reconciliation appears to balance. However, the balance sheet reports more cash than Hobbs actually has in the bank. While negotiating the sale of this property, Hobbs shows the balance sheet to prospective investors.

▌*Required*

1. Identify 2 parties other than Hobbs who can be harmed by this theft. In what ways can they be harmed?

2. Discuss the role accounting plays in this situation.

Focus on Financials: ■ Yum! Brands

(Learning Objective 1, 2: Cash and internal control) Refer to the YUM! Brands financial statements in Appendix A at the end of this book. Suppose YUM's year-end bank statement, dated December 30, 2006, has just arrived at company headquarters. Further assume the bank statement shows YUM's cash balance at $324 million and that YUM's Cash and Cash Equivalents account has a balance of $321 million on the books.

1. You must determine how much to report for cash and cash equivalents on the December 30, 2006, balance sheet. Suppose you uncover these reconciling items (all amounts are assumed and in millions):

    a. Interest earned on bank balance, $1.

    b. Outstanding checks, $8.

    c. Bank collections of various items, $2.

    d. Deposits in transit, $3.

    e. Book error—YUM overstated cash by $5.

(continued)

Prepare a bank reconciliation to show how YUM arrived at the correct amount of cash and cash equivalents to report on its December 30, 2006, balance sheet. Prove that your answer is the actual amount YUM reported. Journal entries are not required. (p. 222)

2. Study YUM Brands' Management Responsibility for Financial Statements and indicate how that report links to specific items of internal control discussed in this chapter. (Challenge)

Focus on Analysis: ■ Pier 1 Imports

(*Learning Objective 1, 5: Analyzing internal control and cash flows*) Refer to the **Pier 1 Imports** financial statements in Appendix B at the end of this book.

1. Focus on Cash, Including Temporary Investments (this is the same as cash and cash equivalents). Why did cash change during 2006? The statement of cash flows holds the answer to this question. Analyze the 7 largest *individual* items on the statement of cash flows (not the summary subtotals such as "net cash provided by operating activities"). For each of the 7 individual items, state how Pier 1's action affected cash. Show amounts in millions and round to the nearest 1/10 of $1 million. (Challenge)

2. Pier 1's Report of Management describes the company's internal controls. Show how the management report corresponds to 2 of the 4 elements in the definition of internal control. (Challenge)

Group Project

You are promoting a rock concert in your area. Assume you organize as a corporation, with each member of your group purchasing $10,000 of the corporation's stock. Therefore, each of you is risking some hard-earned money on this venture. Assume it is April 1 and that the concert will be performed on June 30. Your promotional activities begin immediately, and ticket sales start on May 1. You expect to sell all the firm's assets, pay all the liabilities, and distribute all remaining cash to the group members by July 31.

❙ Required

Write an internal control manual that will help to safeguard the assets of the business. The manual should address the following aspects of internal control:

1. Assign responsibilities among the group members.
2. Authorize individuals, including group members and any outsiders that you need to hire to perform specific jobs.
3. Separate duties among the group and any employees.
4. Describe all documents needed to account for and safeguard the business's assets.

For Internet Exercises go to the Web site www.prenhall.com/harrison.

Quick Check Answers

1. *g, e, h, d, f, c, a*	3. *d*	6. *e*	9. *b*
Unused: *b, i*	4. *a*	7. *a*	10. *b*
2. *a*	5. *c*	8. *d*	11. *c*

5 Short-Term Investments & Receivables

RECEIVABLES ARE PEPSICO'S LARGEST CURRENT ASSET

What comes to mind when you think of **PepsiCo**? Do you think of a soft drink or a snack chip? PepsiCo's 2 main products are soft drinks and snack foods. PepsiCo also owns Frito Lay, the snack-food company.

Take a look at PepsiCo's balance sheet. Does it surprise you that receivables are PepsiCo's largest current asset? It turns out that receivables are the largest current asset for lots of companies, including **FedEx** and **Yum! Brands**.

Another category of current asset is short-term investments. As you can see from PepsiCo's balance sheet, PepsiCo had over $1 billion of short-term investments at the end of 2006. You'll notice that short-term investments are listed on the balance sheet immediately after cash and before receivables. Let's see why.

PepsiCo, Inc.
Balance Sheet (Excerpt, Adapted)
December 31, 2006 and 2005

(In millions)	2006	2005
ASSETS		
Current Assets		
Cash and cash equivalents..	$ 1,651	$ 1,716
Short-term investments...	1,171	3,166
Accounts receivable, net of allowance for doubtful		
accounts of $64 in 2006 and $75 in 2005................	3,725	3,261
Inventories	1,926	1,693
Prepaid expenses and other current assets	657	618
Total Current Assets	$9,130	$10,454

This chapter shows how to account for short-term investments and receivables. We cover short-term investments along with receivables to emphasize their relative liquidity. Short-term investments are the next-most-liquid current assets after cash. (Recall that liquid means close to cash.) We begin our discussion with short-term investments.

LEARNING OBJECTIVES

1 **Account** for short-term investments

2 **Apply** internal controls to receivables

3 **Use** the allowance method for uncollectible receivables

4 **Account** for notes receivable

5 **Use** 2 new ratios to evaluate a business

SHORT-TERM INVESTMENTS

OBJECTIVE

1 **Account** for short-term investments

Short-term investments are also called **marketable securities.** These are invest-ments that a company plans to hold for 1 year or less. They allow the company to invest cash for a short period of time and earn a return until the cash is needed.

Short-term investments are the next-most-liquid asset after cash. This is why we report short-term investments immediately after cash and before receivables on the balance sheet. A short-term investment falls into 1 of 3 categories:

Three Categories of Short-Term Investments		
Trading Investment	**Available-for-Sale Investment**	**Held-to-Maturity Investment**
Covered in this section of the chapter	Covered in Chapter 10	Same as accounting for a note receivable, starting on page 274

The investor, such as PepsiCo, expects to sell a trading investment within a very short time—a few months at most. Therefore, all trading investments are current assets. The other 2 categories of investments can be either current or long-term, depending on how long management intends to hold them. Let's begin with trading investments.

Trading Investments

The purpose of owning a **trading investment** is to hold it for a short time and then sell it for more than its cost. Trading investments can be the stock of another company. Suppose PepsiCo purchases **IBM** stock, intending to sell the stock within a few months. If the market value of the IBM stock increases, PepsiCo will have a gain; if IBM's stock price drops, PepsiCo will have a loss. Along the way, PepsiCo will receive dividend revenue from IBM.

Suppose PepsiCo buys the IBM stock on November 18, paying $100,000 cash. PepsiCo records the purchase of the investment at cost:

20X5			
Nov. 18	Short-Term Investments	100,000	
	Cash		100,000
	Purchased investment.		

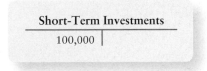

Assume that PepsiCo receives a cash dividend of $4,000 from IBM. PepsiCo records the dividend revenue as follows:

20X5			
Nov. 27	Cash	4,000	
	Dividend Revenue		4,000
	Received cash dividend.		

Assets	=	Liabilities	+	Stockholders' Equity	+	Revenues
+ 4,000	=				+	4,000

Unrealized Gains and Losses. PepsiCo's fiscal year ends on December 31, and PepsiCo prepares financial statements. The IBM stock has risen in value, and on December 31 PepsiCo's investment has a current market value of $102,000. Market value is the amount the owner can sell the investment for. PepsiCo has an *unrealized gain* on the investment:

- *Gain* because the market value ($102,000) is greater than PepsiCo's cost of the investment ($100,000). A gain has the same effect as a revenue.
- *Unrealized gain* because PepsiCo has not yet sold the investment.

Trading investments are reported on the balance sheet at their current market value, because market value is the amount the investor can receive by selling the investment. Prior to preparing financial statements on December 31, PepsiCo adjusts the IBM investment to its current market value with this year-end journal entry:

20X5			
Dec. 31	Short-Term Investments	2,000	
	Unrealized Gain on Investments		2,000
	Adjusted investment to market value.		

Short-Term Investments		Unrealized Gain on Investments	
100,000			2,000
2,000			
102,000			

After the adjustment, PepsiCo's Short-Term Investments account is ready to be reported on the balance sheet—at current market value of $102,000.

If PepsiCo's investment in IBM stock had decreased in value, say to $95,000, then PepsiCo would have reported an unrealized loss. A *loss* has the same effect as an expense. In that case, PepsiCo would have made a different entry at December 31. For an *unrealized* loss of $5,000,

Unrealized Loss on Investments	5,000	
Short-Term Investments		5,000
Adjusted investment to market value.		

Short-Term Investments		Unrealized Loss on Investments	
100,000	5,000	5,000	
95,000			

Reporting on the Balance Sheet and the Income Statement

The Balance Sheet. Short-term investments are current assets. They appear on the balance sheet immediately after cash because short-term investments are almost as liquid as cash. Report trading investments at their *current market value*.

Income Statement. Investments earn interest revenue and dividend revenue. Investments also create gains and losses. For trading investments these items are reported on the income statement as Other revenue, gains, and (losses), as shown in Exhibit 5-1.

EXHIBIT 5-1	Reporting Short-Term Investments and the Related Revenues, Gains, and Losses

Balance sheet			Income statement		
Current assets:........................			Revenues...........................		$ XXX
Cash..................................	$	XXX	Expenses		XXX
Short-term investments, at			Other revenue, gains		
market value		102,000	and (losses):		
Accounts receivable...............		XXX	Interest revenue.............		XXX
			Dividend revenue		4,000
			Unrealized gain on		
			investment...............		2,000
			Net income...................		$ XXX

Realized Gains and Losses. A *realized* gain or loss occurs only when the investor sells an investment. This gain or loss is different from the unrealized gain that we reported for PepsiCo above. The result may be a

- Realized gain = Sale price is *greater than* the Investment carrying amount
- Realized loss = Sale price is *less than* the Investment carrying amount

Suppose PepsiCo sells its IBM stock during 20X6. The sale price is $98,000, and PepsiCo makes this journal entry:

20X6			
Jan. 19	Cash	98,000	
	Loss on Sale of Investments	4,000	
	Short-Term Investments		102,000
	Sold investments at a loss.		

Short-Term Investments		Loss on Sale of Investments	
100,000		4,000	
2,000	102,000		

Accountants rarely use the word "Realized" in the account title. A gain (or a loss) is understood to be a realized gain (or loss) arising from a sale transaction. Unrealized gains and losses are clearly labeled as *unrealized*. PepsiCo would report Gain (or Loss) on Sale of Investments among the "Other" items of the income statement, as shown in Exhibit 5-1.

Lending Agreements and the Current Ratio

Lending agreements often require the borrower to maintain a current ratio at some specified level, say 1.50 or greater. What happens when the borrower's current ratio falls below 1.50? The consequences can be severe:

- The lender can call the loan for immediate payment.
- If the borrower cannot pay, then the lender may take over the company.

Suppose it's December 10 and it looks like Health Corporation of America's (HCA's) current ratio will end the year at a value of 1.48. That would put HCA in default on the lending agreement and create a bad situation. With 3 weeks remaining in the year, how can HCA improve its current ratio?

Recall that the current ratio is computed as

$$\text{Current ratio} = \frac{\text{Total current assets}}{\text{Total current liabilities}}$$

There are several strategies for increasing the current ratio, such as: .

1. Launch a major sales effort. The increase in cash and receivables will more than offset the decrease in Inventory, total current assets will increase, and the current ratio will improve.

2. Pay off some current liabilities before year end. Both current assets in the numerator and current liabilities in the denominator will decrease by the same amount. The proportionate impact on current liabilities in the denominator will be greater than the impact on current assets in the numerator, and the current ratio will increase. This strategy increases the current ratio when the current ratio is already above 1.0, as for HCA and PepsiCo.

3. A third strategy is questionable, and we wish to alert you to one of the accounting games that companies sometimes play. Suppose HCA has some long-term investments (investments that HCA plans to hold for longer than a year—these are long-term assets). Before year end HCA can reclassify these long-term investments as current assets. The investments increase HCA's current assets, and that increases the current ratio. This strategy would be okay if HCA does in fact plan to sell the investments within the next year. But the strategy would be dishonest if HCA plans to keep the investments for longer than a year.

From this example you can see that accounting is not cut-and-dried or all black-and-white. It takes good judgment—and honesty—to become a successful accountant.

MID-CHAPTER SUMMARY PROBLEM

The largest current asset on Waverly Corporation's balance sheet is Short-Term Investments. The investments cost Waverly $8,660, and their market value is $9,000 (amounts in millions):

Suppose Waverly holds the investments in the hope of selling at a profit within a few months. How will Waverly classify the investments? What will Waverly report on the balance sheet at December 31, 20X6? What will Waverly report on its 20X6 income statement? Show a T-account for Short-Term Investments.

Answer

These trading investments are *current assets* as reported on the 20X6 balance sheet, and Waverly's 20X6 income statement will report as follows (amounts in millions):

Balance sheet		Income statement	
Current assets:		Other revenue and expense:	
Cash.....................................	$ XX	Unrealized gain on investments	
Short-term investments,		($9,000 – $8,660)	$ 340
at market value	9,000		

Short-Term Investments	
8,660	
340	

Suppose Waverly sells the investment for $8,700 in 20X7. Journalize the sale and then show the Short-Term Investments T-account as it appears after the sale.

Answer

	(In millions)
Cash..	8,700
Loss on Sale of Investments.........	300
Short-Term Investments..........	9,000
Sold investments at a loss.	

Short-Term Investments	
8,660	
340	9,000

ACCOUNTS AND NOTES RECEIVABLE

Receivables are the third most liquid asset—after cash and short-term investments. Most of the remainder of this chapter shows how to account for receivables.

Types of Receivables

Receivables are monetary claims against others. Receivables are acquired mainly by selling goods and services (accounts receivable) and by lending money (notes receivable). The journal entries to record the receivables can be shown as follows:

Performing a Service on Account			Lending Money on a Note Receivable		
Accounts Receivable....................	XXX		Note Receivable..........................	XXX	
Service Revenue.......................		XXX	Cash..		XXX
Performed a service on account.			*Loaned money to another company.*		

The 2 major types of receivables are accounts receivable and notes receivable. A business's *accounts receivable* are the amounts collectible from customers from the sale of goods and services. Accounts receivable, which are *current assets*, are sometimes called *trade receivables* or merely *receivables*.

The Accounts Receivable account in the general ledger serves as a *control account* that summarizes the total amount receivable from all customers. Companies also keep a *subsidiary record* of accounts receivable with a separate account for each customer, illustrated as follows:

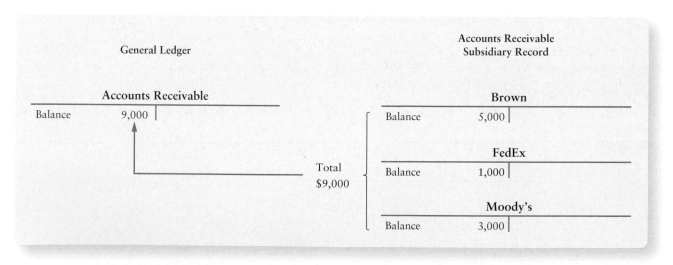

Notes receivable are more formal contracts than accounts receivable. For a note, the borrower signs a written promise to pay the lender a definite sum at the *maturity* date. This is why notes are also called promissory notes. The note may require the borrower to pledge *security* for the loan. This means that the borrower gives the lender permission to claim certain assets, called *collateral*, if the borrower fails to pay the amount due. We cover the details of notes receivable starting on page 274.

Other receivables is a miscellaneous category for all receivables other than accounts receivable and notes receivable. Examples include loans to employees and to related companies.

Internal Controls over Cash Collections on Account

Businesses that sell on credit receive most of their cash receipts on account. Internal control over collections on account is important. Chapter 4 discusses control procedures for cash receipts, but another element of internal control deserves emphasis here—the separation of cash-handling and cash-accounting duties. Consider the following case:

OBJECTIVE

2 **Apply** internal controls to receivables

> **Central Paint Company is a small, family-owned business that takes pride in the loyalty of its workers. Most employees have been with Central for 10 or more years. The company makes 90% of its sales on account and receives most of its cash by mail.**
>
> **The office staff consists of a bookkeeper and an office supervisor. The bookkeeper maintains the general ledger and a subsidiary record of individual customer accounts receivable. The bookkeeper also makes the daily bank deposit.**
>
> **The supervisor prepares monthly financial statements and any special reports the company needs. The supervisor also takes sales orders from customers and serves as office manager.**

Can you identify the internal control weakness here? The problem is that the bookkeeper makes the bank deposit. With this cash-handling duty, the bookkeeper could steal an incoming customer check and write off the customer's account as uncollectible. The customer doesn't complain because the bookkeeper wrote off the customer's account, and Central therefore stops pursuing collection.

How can this weakness be corrected? The supervisor—not the bookkeeper—could open incoming mail and make the daily bank deposit. The bookkeeper should *not* be allowed to handle cash. Only the remittance advices should be forwarded to the bookkeeper to credit customer accounts receivable. Removing cash handling from the bookkeeper and keeping the accounts away from the supervisor separates duties and strengthens internal control.

Using a bank lockbox achieves the same separation of duties. Customers send their payments directly to Central Paint Company's bank, which records cash as the cash goes into Central's bank account. The bank then forwards the remittance advice to Central's bookkeeper, who credits the customer account. No Central Paint employee even touches incoming cash.

How Do We Manage the Risk of Not Collecting?

In Chapters 1 to 4, we use many different companies to illustrate how to account for a business. Chapter 1 began with YUM! Brands, a maker of fast foods. Chapter 2 featured Apple Computer, Inc., Chapter 3 Starbucks Corporation, and Chapter 4 AMEX Products. This chapter features PepsiCo. All these companies hold receivables.

By selling on credit, companies run the risk of not collecting some receivables. Unfortunately, some customers don't pay their debts. The prospect that we may fail to collect from a customer provides the biggest challenge in accounting for receivables. The Decision Guidelines address this challenge.

DECISION GUIDELINES

MANAGING AND ACCOUNTING FOR RECEIVABLES

Here are the management and accounting issues a business faces when the company extends credit to customers. For each issue, the Decision Guidelines propose a plan of action. Let's look at a business situation: Suppose you open a health club near your college. Assume you will let customers use the club and charge bills to their accounts. What challenges will you encounter by extending credit to customers?

The main issues in *managing* receivables, along with plans of action, are:

Issues	Plan of Action
1. What are the benefits and the costs of extending credit to customers?	1. Benefit—Increase in sales. Cost—Risk of not collecting.
2. Extend credit only to creditworthy customers.	2. Run a credit check on prospective customers.
3. Separate cash-handling and accounting duties to keep employees from stealing the cash collected from customers.	3. Design the internal control system to separate duties.
4. Pursue collection from customers to maximize cash flow.	4. Keep a close eye on customer pay habits. Send second, and third, statements to slow-paying customers, if necessary.

The main issues in *accounting* for receivable, and the related plans of action, are (amounts are assumed):

Issues	Plan of Action
1. Measure and report receivables on the balance sheet at their *net realizable value*, the amount we expect to collect. This is the appropriate amount to report for receivables.	Report receivables at their net realizable value: **Balance sheet** Receivables... $1,000 Less: Allowance for uncollectibles.............. (80) Receivables, net... $ 920
2. Measure and report the expense associated with failure to collect receivables. This expense is called *uncollectible-account expense* and is reported on the income statement.	Measure the expense of not collecting from customers: **Income statement** Sales (or service) revenue............................ $8,000 Expenses: Uncollectible-account expense................. 190

These guidelines lead to our next topic, Accounting for Uncollectible Receivables.

ACCOUNTING FOR UNCOLLECTIBLE RECEIVABLES

A company gets an account receivable only when it sells its product or service on credit (on account). You'll recall that the entry to record the earning of revenue on account is (amount assumed)

Accounts Receivable	1,000	
Sales Revenue (or Service Revenue)		1,000
Earned revenue on account.		

Ideally, the company would collect cash for all of its receivables. But unfortunately the entry to record cash collections on account is for only $950.

Cash	950	
Accounts Receivable		950
Collections on account.		

You can see that companies rarely collect all of their accounts receivables. So companies must account for their uncollectible accounts—$50 in this example. Selling on credit creates both a benefit and a cost:

- *Benefit*: Customers who cannot pay cash immediately can buy on credit, so sales and profits increase.
- *Cost*: The company cannot collect from some customers. Accountants label this cost **uncollectible-account expense**, **doubtful-account expense**, or **bad-debt expense**.

PepsiCo reports receivables as follows on its 2006 balance sheet (in millions):

Accounts and notes receivable, net of allowance for doubtful accounts of $64	$3,725

The allowance ($64) represents the amount that PepsiCo does *not* expect to collect. The net amount of the receivables ($3,725 million) is the amount that PepsiCo *does* expect to collect. This is called the *net realizable value* because it's the amount of cash PepsiCo expects to realize in cash receipts.

Uncollectible-account expense is an operating expense along with salaries, depreciation, rent, and utilities. To measure uncollectible-account expense, accountants use the allowance method or, in certain limited cases, the direct write-off method (p. 273).

Allowance Method

The best way to measure bad debts is by the **allowance method.** This method records collection losses based on estimates developed from the company's collection experience. PepsiCo doesn't wait to see which customers will not pay. Instead, PepsiCo records the estimated amount as Uncollectible-Account Expense and also sets up **Allowance for Uncollectible Accounts.** Other titles for this account are **Allowance for Doubtful Accounts** and **Allowance for Bad Debts.** This is a contra

OBJECTIVE

3 Use the allowance method for uncollectible receivables account to Accounts Receivable. The allowance shows the amount of the receivables the business expects *not* to collect.

In Chapter 3 we used the Accumulated Depreciation account to show the amount of a plant asset's cost that has been expensed—the portion of the asset that's no longer a benefit to the company. Allowance for Uncollectible Accounts serves a similar purpose for Accounts Receivable. The allowance shows how much of the receivable has been expensed. You'll find this diagram helpful (amounts are assumed):

Equipment..........................	$100,000	Accounts receivable....................	$10,000
Less: Accumulated		Less: Allowance for	
depreciation	(40,000)	uncollectible accounts	(900)
Equipment, net...................	60,000	Accounts receivable, net............	9,100

Focus on Accounts Receivable. Customers owe this company $10,000, but it expects to collect only $9,100. The *net realizable value* of the receivables is therefore $9,100. Another way to report these receivables is

Accounts receivable, less allowance of $900................ $9,100

You can work backward to determine the full amount of the receivable, $10,000 (net realizable value of $9,100 plus the allowance of $900).

The income statement reports Uncollectible-Account Expense among the operating expenses, as follows (using assumed figures):

Income statement (partial):

Expenses:

    Uncollectible-account expense:................ $2,000

STOP & think. . .

Refer to the PepsiCo balance sheet on page 258. At December 31, 2006, how much did customers owe PepsiCo? How much did PepsiCo expect *not* to collect? How much did PepsiCo expect to collect? What was the net realizable value of PepsiCo's receivables?

Answer:

	Millions
Customers owed PepsiCo..	$3,789
PepsiCo expected not to collect the allowance of	(64)
PepsiCo expected to collect—net realizable value........	$3,725

The best way to estimate uncollectibles uses the company's history of collections from customers. There are 2 basic ways to estimate uncollectibles:

■ Percent-of-sales method   ■ Aging-of-receivables method

Percent-of-Sales. The **percent-of-sales method** computes uncollectible-account expense as a percent of revenue. This method takes an *income-statement approach* because it focuses on the amount of expense to be reported on the income statement. Assume it is December 31, 2006, and PepsiCo's accounts have these balances *before the year-end adjustments* (amounts in millions):

Accounts Receivable	Allowance for Uncollectible Accounts
3,789	29

Customers owe PepsiCo $3,789, and the Allowance amount on the books is $29. But PepsiCo's top managers know that the company will fail to collect more than $29. Suppose PepsiCo's credit department estimates that uncollectible-account expense is 1/10 of 1% (0.001) of total revenues, which were $35,000. The entry that records uncollectible-account expense for the year also updates the allowance as follows (using PepsiCo figures):

2006			
Dec. 31	Uncollectible-Account Expense		
	($35,000 × .001)	35	
	Allowance for Uncollectible Accounts		35
	Recorded expense for the year.		

The expense decreases PepsiCo's assets, as shown by the accounting equation.

Assets	=	Liabilities	+	Stockholders' Equity	–	Expenses
– 35	=	0			–	35

Now PepsiCo's accounts are ready for reporting in the financial statements.

Accounts Receivable	Allowance for Uncollectible Accounts	Uncollectible-Account Expense
3,789	29	35
	Adj. 35	
	End. bal. 64	

Net accounts receivable, $3,725

Compare these amounts to the Stop and Think answer on page 268. They are the same.

Customers owe PepsiCo $3,789, and now the Allowance for Uncollectibles balance is realistic. PepsiCo's balance sheet actually reported accounts receivable at this net realizable value amount of $3,725 ($3,789 − $64).

Aging-of-Receivables. The other popular method for estimating uncollectibles is called **aging-of-receivables.** This method is a *balance-sheet approach* because it focuses on accounts receivable. In the aging method, individual receivables from specific customers are analyzed based on how long they have been outstanding.

Suppose it is December 31, 2006, and PepsiCo's receivables accounts show the following before the year-end adjustment (amounts in millions):

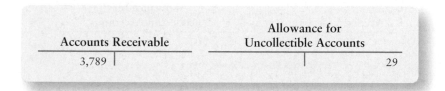

Accounts Receivable		Allowance for Uncollectible Accounts	
3,789			29

These accounts are not yet ready for the financial statements because the allowance balance is not realistic.

PepsiCo's computerized accounting package ages the company's accounts receivable. Exhibit 5-2 shows a representative aging schedule at December 31, 2006. PepsiCo's receivables total $3,789. Of this amount, the aging schedule shows that the company will *not* collect $64 (lower right corner).

EXHIBIT 5-2 Aging the Accounts Receivable of PepsiCo.

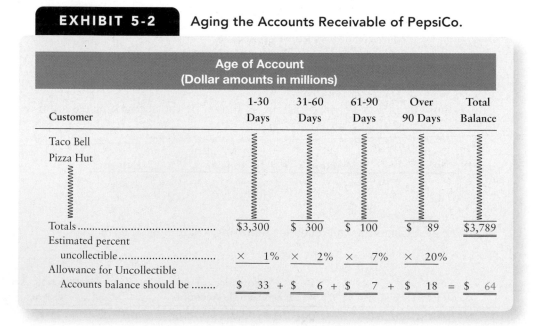

	Age of Account (Dollar amounts in millions)				
Customer	1-30 Days	31-60 Days	61-90 Days	Over 90 Days	Total Balance
Taco Bell					
Pizza Hut					
Totals	$3,300	$ 300	$ 100	$ 89	$3,789
Estimated percent uncollectible	× 1%	× 2%	× 7%	× 20%	
Allowance for Uncollectible Accounts balance should be	$ 33 +	$ 6 +	$ 7 +	$ 18 =	$ 64

The aging method will bring the balance of the allowance account ($29) to the needed amount as determined by the aging schedule ($64). The lower right corner of the aging schedule gives the needed balance in the allowance account. To update the allowance, PepsiCo would make this adjusting entry at year end:

2006			
Dec. 31	Uncollectible-Account Expense	35	
	Allowance for Uncollectible Accounts		
	($64 – $29)		35
	Recorded expense for the year.		

The expense decreases PepsiCo's assets, as shown by the accounting equation.

Assets	=	Liabilities	+	Stockholders' Equity	–	Expenses
– 35	=	0				– 35

Now the balance sheet can report the amount that PepsiCo actually expects to collect from customers: $3,725 ($3,789 – $64). This is the net realizable value of PepsiCo's accounts receivable.

Accounts Receivable		Allowance for Uncollectible Accounts		Uncollectible-Account Expense	
3,789			29	35	
		Adj.	35		
		End. Bal.	64		

Net accounts receivable, $3,725

Writing Off Uncollectible Accounts. Assume that at the beginning of 2007 a division of PepsiCo had these accounts receivable (amounts in thousands):

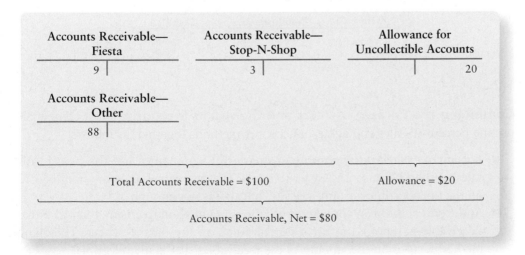

Accounts Receivable— Fiesta	Accounts Receivable— Stop-N-Shop	Allowance for Uncollectible Accounts
9	3	20

Accounts Receivable— Other		
88		

Total Accounts Receivable = $100   Allowance = $20

Accounts Receivable, Net = $80

Suppose that early in 2007, PepsiCo's credit department determines that PepsiCo cannot collect from customers Fiesta and Stop–N–Shop. PepsiCo then writes off the receivables from these 2 customers with the following entry:

2007			
Jan. 31	Allowance for Uncollectible Accounts	12	
	Accounts Receivable—Fiesta		9
	Accounts Receivable—Stop-N-Shop		3
	Wrote off uncollectible receivables.		

After the write-off, PepsiCo's accounts show these amounts:

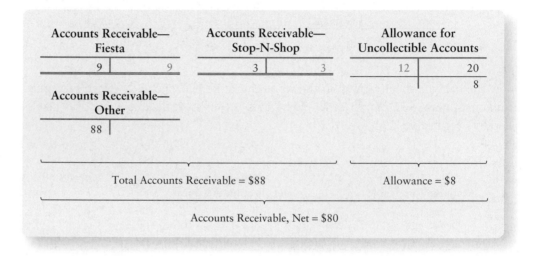

The accounting equation shows that the write-off of uncollectibles has no effect on PepsiCo's total assets. Accounts Receivable, Net is still $80. There is no effect on net income either. Why is there no effect on net income? Net income is unaffected because the write-off of uncollectibles affects no expense account.

Assets	=	Liabilities	+	Stockholders' Equity
+ 12	=	0	+	0
− 12				

Combining the Percent-of-Sales and the Aging Methods. Most companies use the percent-of-sales and aging-of-accounts methods together, as follows:

- For *interim statements* (monthly or quarterly), companies use the percent-of-sales method because it is easier to apply. The percent-of-sales method focuses on the uncollectible-account *expense*, but that is not enough.
- At the end of the year, companies use the aging method to ensure that Accounts Receivable is reported at *net realizable value* on the balance sheet. The aging method focuses on the amount of the receivables that is uncollectible.
- Using the two methods together provides good measures of both the *expense* and the *asset*. Exhibit 5-3 compares the two methods.

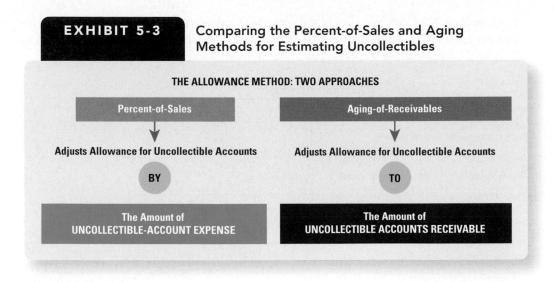

EXHIBIT 5-3 Comparing the Percent-of-Sales and Aging Methods for Estimating Uncollectibles

Direct Write-Off Method

There is another, less preferable, way to account for uncollectible receivables. Under the **direct write-off method**, the company waits until a specific customer's receivable proves uncollectible. Then the accountant writes off the customer's account and records Uncollectible-Account Expense, as follows (using assumed data):

2007			
Jan. 2	Uncollectible-Account Expense	12	
	Accounts Receivable—Fiesta		9
	Accounts Receivable—Stop-N-Shop		3
	Wrote off bad accounts by direct write-off method.		

The direct write-off method is defective for 2 reasons:

1. The direct write-off method uses no allowance for uncollectibles. As a result, receivables are always reported at their full amount, which is more than the business expects to collect. *Assets on the balance sheet are overstated.*

2. The direct write-off method causes a poor matching of uncollectible-account expense against revenue. In this example, PepsiCo made the sales to Fiesta and Stop–N–Shop in 2006 and should have recorded the uncollectible-account expense during 2006, not in 2007 when it wrote off the accounts.

Because of these deficiencies, PepsiCo and virtually all other large companies use the allowance method. The direct write-off method is acceptable only when uncollectibles are so low that there would be no allowance for uncollectible accounts.

Computing Cash Collections from Customers

A company earns revenue and then collects the cash from customers. For PepsiCo and most other companies, there is a time lag between earning the revenue and collecting the cash. Collections from customers are the single most important source of cash for any business. You can compute a company's collections from customers by analyzing its Accounts Receivable account. Receivables typically hold only 5 items, as follows (amounts assumed):

Accounts Receivable			
Beg. balance (left over from last period)	200	Write-offs of uncollectibles	100**
Sales (or service) revenue	1,800*	Collections from customers	X = 1,500†
End. balance (carries over to next period)	400		

*The journal entry that places revenue into the receivable account is

Accounts Receivable	1,800	
Sales (or Service) Revenue		1,800

**The journal entry for write-offs is

Allowance for Uncollectibles	100	
Accounts Receivable		100

†The journal entry that places collections into the receivable account is

Cash	1,500	
Accounts Receivable		1,500

Suppose you know all these amounts expect collections from customers. You can compute collections by solving for X in the T-account.[1] Often write-offs are unknown and must be omitted. Then the computation of collections becomes an approximation.

NOTES RECEIVABLE

OBJECTIVE

4 **Account** for notes receivable

As stated earlier, notes receivable are more formal than accounts receivable. Notes receivable due within 1 year or less are current assets. Notes due beyond 1 year are *long-term receivables* and are reported as long-term assets. Some notes receivable are collected in installments. The portion due within 1 year is a current asset and the remainder is long term. PepsiCo may hold a $20,000 note receivable from a customer, but only the $6,000 the customer must pay within 1 year is a current asset of PepsiCo.

Before launching into the accounting for notes receivable, let's define some key terms:

Creditor. The party to whom money is owed. The creditor is also called the **lender**.

Debtor. The party that borrowed and owes money on the note. The debtor is also called the **maker** of the note or the **borrower**.

Interest. Interest is the cost of borrowing money. The interest is stated in an annual percentage rate.

Maturity date. The date on which the debtor must pay the note.

Maturity value. The sum of principal and interest on the note.

Principal. The amount of money borrowed by the debtor.

Term. The length of time from when the note was signed by the debtor to when the debtor must pay the note.

---

[1]An equation may help you solve for X. The equation is $200 + $1,800 − X − $100 = $400. X = $1,500.

There are 2 parties to a note:

- The *creditor* has a note receivable.
- The *debtor* has a note payable.

Exhibit 5-4 is a typical promissory note.

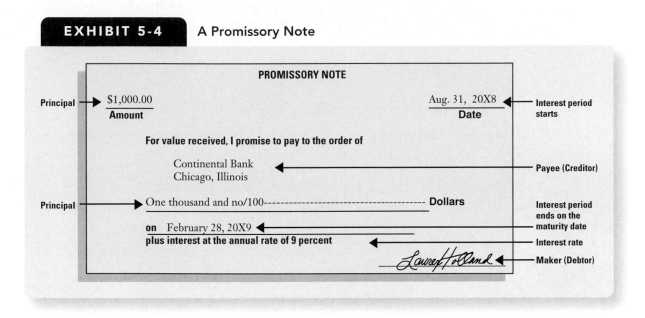

EXHIBIT 5-4   A Promissory Note

The **principal** amount of the note ($1,000) is the amount borrowed by the debtor, lent by the creditor. This 6-month note receivable runs from August 31, 20X8, to February 28, 20X9, when Lauren Holland (the maker) promises to pay Continental Bank (the creditor) the principal of $1,000 plus 9% interest. **Interest** is revenue to the creditor (Continental Bank, in this case).

Accounting for Notes Receivable

Consider the promissory note in Exhibit 5-4. After Lauren Holland signs the note, Continental Bank gives her $1,000 cash. The bank's entries follow, assuming a December 31 year end for Continental Bank:

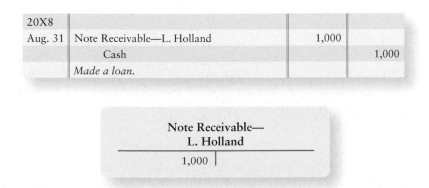

20X8			
Aug. 31	Note Receivable—L. Holland	1,000	
	Cash		1,000
	Made a loan.		

Note Receivable—
L. Holland

| 1,000 | |

The bank gave one asset, cash, in return for another asset, a note receivable, so total assets did not change.

Continental Bank earns interest revenue during September, October, November, and December. At December 31, the bank accrues 9% interest revenue for 4 months as follows:

20X8			
Dec. 31	Interest Receivable ($1,000 × .09 × 4/12)	30	
	Interest Revenue		30
	Accrued interest revenue.		

The bank's assets and revenues increase.

Continental Bank reports these amounts in its financial statements at December 31, 20X8:

Balance sheet
Current assets:
Note receivable $1,000
Interest receivable............... 30
Income statement
Interest revenue.................. $ 30

The bank collects the note on February 28, 20X9, and records

20X9			
Feb. 28	Cash	1,045	
	Note Receivable—L.Holland		1,000
	Interest Receivable		30
	Interest Revenue ($1,000 × .09 × 2/12)		15
	Collected note at maturity.		

This entry zeroes out Note Receivable and Interest Receivable and also records the interest revenue earned in 20X9.

Note Receivable—
L. Holland

1,000	1,000

In its 20X9 financial statements the only item that Continental Bank will report is the interest revenue of $15 that was earned in 20X9. There's no note receivable or interest receivable on the balance sheet because those items were zeroed out when the bank collected the note at maturity.

Two aspects of the interest computation deserve mention:

1. Interest rates are always for an annual period, unless stated otherwise. In this example, the annual interest rate is 9%. At December 31, 20X8, Continental Bank accrues interest revenue for 4 months. The interest computation is

Principal	×	Interest Rate	×	Time	=	Amount of Interest
$1,000	×	.09	×	4/12	=	$30

2. The time element (4/12) is the fraction of the year that the note has been in force during 20X8.

3. Interest is often completed for a number of days. For example, suppose you loaned out $10,000 on April 10. The note receivable runs for 90 days and specifies interest at 8%.

   a. Interest starts accruing on April 11 and runs for 90 days, ending on the due date, July 9, as follows:

Month	Number of Days That Interest Accrues
April	20
May	31
June	30
July	9
Total	90

   b. The interest computation is

   $10,000 × .08 × 90/365 = $197

Some companies sell goods and services on notes receivable (versus selling on accounts receivable). This often occurs when the payment term extends beyond the customary accounts receivable period of 30 to 60 days.

Suppose that on March 20, 20X9, PepsiCo sells a large amount of food to Wal-Mart. PepsiCo gets Wal-Mart's 3-month promissory note plus 10% annual interest. At the outset, PepsiCo would debit Notes Receivable and credit Sales Revenue.

A company may also accept a note receivable from a trade customer whose account receivable is past due. The company then debits Note Receivable and credits Accounts Receivable. We would say the company "received a note receivable on account." Now let's examine some strategies to speed up cash flow.

How to Speed Up Cash Flow

All companies want speedy cash receipts. Rapid cash flow finances new products, research, and development. Thus, companies such as PepsiCo find ways to collect cash quickly. Two common strategies generate cash quickly.

Credit Card or Bankcard Sales. The merchant sells merchandise and lets the customer pay with a credit card, such as Discover or American Express, or with a bankcard, such as VISA or MasterCard. This strategy may dramatically increase sales, but the added revenue comes at a cost. Let's see how credit cards and bankcards work from the seller's perspective.

Suppose Dell, Inc., sells computers for $5,000, and the customer pays with a VISA card. Dell records the sale as follows:

Cash	4,900	
Credit-Card Discount Expense	100	
Sales Revenue		5,000
Recorded bankcard sales.		

Assets	=	Liabilities	+	Stockholders' Equity	+	Revenues	−	Expenses
+ 4,900	=	0	+			+ 5,000	·	− 100

Dell enters the transaction in the credit-card machine. The machine, linked to a VISA server, automatically credits Dell's account for a discounted portion, say $4,900, of the $5,000 sale amount. Two percent ($100) goes to VISA. To Dell, the credit-card discount expense is an operating expense similar to interest expense.

Selling (Factoring) Receivables. PepsiCo makes some large sales to grocery chains on account, debiting Accounts Receivable and crediting Sales Revenue. PepsiCo can then sell these accounts receivable to another business, called a *factor*. The factor earns revenue by paying a discounted price for the receivable and then hopefully collecting the full amount from the customer. The benefit to PepsiCo is the immediate receipt of cash.

To illustrate selling, or *factoring*, accounts receivable, suppose PepsiCo wishes to speed up cash flow and therefore sells $100,000 of accounts receivables, receiving cash of $95,000. PepsiCo would record the sale of the receivables as follows:

Cash	95,000	
Financing Expense	5,000	
Accounting Receivable		100,000
Sold accounts receivable.		

Again, Financing Expense is an operating expense, with the same effect as a loss. Some companies may debit a Loss account. Discounting a note receivable is similar to selling an account receivable. However, the credit is to Notes Receivable (instead of Accounts Receivable).

USING TWO KEY RATIOS TO MAKE DECISIONS

OBJECTIVE

5 Use 2 new ratios to evaluate a business

Investors and creditors use ratios to evaluate the financial health of a company. We introduced the current ratio in Chapter 3. Other ratios, including the quick (or acid-test) ratio and the number of days' sales in receivables, help investors measure liquidity.

Acid-Test (or Quick) Ratio

The balance sheet lists assets in the order of relative liquidity:

1. Cash and cash equivalents
2. Short-term investments
3. Accounts (or notes) receivable

PepsiCo's balance sheet in the chapter-opening story lists these accounts in order.

Managers, stockholders, and creditors care about the liquidity of a company's assets. The current ratio measures ability to pay current liabilities with current assets. A more stringent measure of ability to pay current liabilities is the **acid-test** (or *quick*) **ratio**:

PepsiCo 2006

(Dollars in millions, taken from PepsiCo balance sheet)

$$\text{Acid-test ratio} = \frac{\text{Cash} + \frac{\text{Short-term}}{\text{investments}} + \frac{\text{Net current}}{\text{receivables}}}{\text{Total current liabilities}} = \frac{\$1,651 + \$1,171 + \$3,725}{\$6,860} = 0.95$$

The higher the acid-test ratio, the easier it is to pay current liabilities. PepsiCo's acid-test ratio of 0.95 means that PepsiCo has 95 cents of quick assets to pay each \$1 of current liabilities. This ratio value is close to perfect. Traditionally, companies have wanted an acid-test ratio of 1.0 to be safe. The ratio needs to be high enough for safety, but not too high. After all, cash and the other liquid assets don't earn very high rates of return, as inventory and plant assets do.

What is an acceptable acid-test ratio? The answer depends on the industry. Auto dealers can operate smoothly with an acid-test ratio of 0.20, roughly one-fourth of PepsiCo's ratio value. How can auto dealers survive with so low an acid-test ratio? The auto manufacturers help finance their dealers' inventory. Most dealers, therefore, have a financial safety net. Companies without a big brother like Ford Motor Company need a higher acid-test ratio.

Days' Sales in Receivables

After a business makes a credit sale, the *next* step is collecting the receivable. **Days' sales in receivables**, also called the *collection period*, tells a company how long it takes to collect its average level of receivables. Shorter is better because cash is coming in quickly. The longer the collection period, the less cash is available to pay bills and expand.

Days' sales in receivables can be computed in 2 logical steps. First, compute one day's sales (or total revenues). Then divide one day's sales into average receivables for the period. We show days' sales in receivables for PepsiCo.

(Dollars in millions, taken from PepsiCo's financial statements)

Days' Sales in Receivables		PepsiCo

1. $\text{One day's sales} = \dfrac{\text{Net sales}}{365 \text{ days}}$ $\dfrac{\$35,137}{365 \text{ days}} = \$96 \text{ per day}$

2. $\text{Days' sales in average receivables} = \dfrac{\text{Average receivables *}}{\text{One day's sales}}$ $\dfrac{\$3,493*}{\$96 \text{ per day}} = 36 \text{ days}$

*Average net receivables $= \dfrac{\text{Beginning net receivables} + \text{Ending net receivables}}{2} = \dfrac{\$3,261 + \$3,725}{2} = \$3,493$

Net sales come from the income statement, and the receivables amounts are taken from the balance sheet. Average receivables is the simple average of the beginning and ending balance.

It takes PepsiCo 36 days to collect its average level of receivables. To evaluate PepsiCo's collection period of 36 days, we need to compare 36 days to the credit terms that PepsiCo offers customers when the company makes a sale. Suppose PepsiCo makes sales on net 30 terms, which means that customers should pay PepsiCo within 30 days of the sale. PepsiCo's collection period of 36 days is pretty good in comparison to the ideal measure of 30 days. After all, some customers drag out their payments. And, as we've seen, some customers don't pay at all.

Companies watch their collection periods closely. Whenever collections slow down, the business must find other sources of financing, such as borrowing or selling receivables. During recessions, customers pay more slowly, and a longer collection period may be unavoidable.[2]

REPORTING ON THE STATEMENT OF CASH FLOWS

Receivables and short-term investments appear on the balance sheet as assets. We saw these in PepsiCo's balance sheet at the beginning of the chapter. We've also seen how to report the related revenues, expenses, gains, and losses on the income statement. Because receivable and investment transactions affect cash, their effects must also be reported on the statement of cash flows.

Receivables bring in cash when the business collects from customers. These transactions are reported as *operating activities* on the statement of cash flows because they result from sales. Investment transactions show up as *investing activities* on the statement of cash flows. Chapter 12 shows how companies report their cash flows on the statement of cash flows. In that chapter we will see exactly how to report cash flows related to receivables and investment transactions.

---

[2]Another ratio, **accounts receivable turnover**, captures the same information as days' sales in receivables. Receivable turnover is computed as follows: Net sales ÷ Average net accounts receivable. During 2006, PepsiCo had a receivable turnover rate of 10 times ($35,137/$3,493= 10). The authors prefer days' sales in receivables because days' sales in receivable can be compared directly to the company's credit sale terms.

END-OF-CHAPTER SUMMARY PROBLEM

Superior Technical Resources' (STR's) balance sheet at December 31, 20X2, reported:

	(In millions)
Accounts receivable..................................	$382
Allowance for doubtful accounts................	(52)

STR uses both the percent-of-sales and the aging approaches to account for uncollectible receivables.

I Required

1. How much of the December 31, 20X2, balance of accounts receivables did STR expect to collect? Stated differently, what was the net realizable value of STR's receivables?
2. Journalize, without explanations, 20X3 entries for STR:
   a. Estimated doubtful-account expense of $40 million, based on the percent-of-sales method, all during the year.
   b. Write-offs of uncollectible accounts receivable totaling $58 million. Prepare a T-account for Allowance for Doubtful Accounts and post to this account. Show its unadjusted balance at December 31, 20X3.
   c. December 31, 20X3, aging of receivables, which indicates that $47 million of the total receivables of $409 million is uncollectible at year end. Post to Allowance for Doubtful Accounts, and show its adjusted balance at December 31, 20X3.
3. Show how STR's receivables and the related allowance will appear on the December 31, 20X3, balance sheet.
4. Show what STR's income statement will report for the foregoing transactions.

Answers

I Requirement 1

	(In millions)
Net realizable value of receivables ($382 – $52)	$330

I Requirement 2

		(In millions)	
a.	Doubtful-Account Expense	40	
	Allowance for Doubtful Accounts		40
b.	Allowance for Doubtful Accounts	58	
	Accounts Receivable		58

(continued)

Allowance for Doubtful Accounts

		Dec. 31, 20X2	52
20X3 Write-offs	58	20X3 Expense	40
		Unadjusted balance at Dec. 31, 20X3	34

c.	Doubtful-Account Expense ($47–$34)		13	
	Allowance for Doubtful Accounts			13

Allowance for Doubtful Accounts

	Dec. 31, 20X3 Unadj. bal.	34
	20X3 Expense	13
	Dec. 31, 20X3 Adj. bal.	47

❙ Requirement 3

	(In millions)
Accounts receivable....................................	$409
Allowance for doubtful accounts...............	(47)

❙ Requirement 4

	(In millions)
Expenses: Doubtful-account expense for 20X3 ($40 + $13)	$53

REVIEW RECEIVABLES AND INVESTMENTS

Quick Check (Answers are given on page 304.)

1. **Harvey Penick Golf Academy** held trading investments valued at $55,000 at December 31, 2008. These investments cost Penick $50,000. What is the appropriate amount for Penick to report for these investments on the December 31, 2008, balance sheet?
   a. $50,000
   b. $55,000
   c. $5,000 gain
   d. Cannot be determined from the data given

2. Return to Harvey Penick Golf Academy in question 1. What should appear on the Penick income statement for the year ended December 31, 2008, for the trading investments?
   a. $50,000
   b. $55,000
   c. $5,000 unrealized gain
   d. Cannot be determined from the data given

Use the following information to answer questions 3–7.

Neal Company had the following information relating to credit sales in 20X3:

Accounts receivable12/31/X3	$ 8,000
Allowance for uncollectible accounts 12/31/X3 (before adjustment)	750
Credit sales during 20X3	38,000
Cash sales during 20X3	12,000
Collections from customers on account during 20X3	41,000

3. Uncollectible accounts are determined by the percent-of-sales method to be 2% of credit sales. How much is uncollectible-account expense for 20X3?
   a. $750
   b. $1,000
   c. $750
   d. $10

4. Using the percent-of-sales method, what is the adjusted balance in the Allowance account at year end 20X3?
   a. $750
   b. $760
   c. $1,750
   d. $1,510

5. If uncollectible accounts are determined by the aging-of-receivables method to be $1,140, the uncollectible account expense for 20X3 would be:
   a. $390
   b. $750
   c. $760
   d. $1,140

6. Using the aging-of-receivables method, the balance of the Allowance account after the adjusting entry would be:
   a. $390
   b. $750
   c. $760
   d. $1,140

7. Assuming the aging-of-receivables method is used, the net realizable value of accounts receivable on the 12/31/X3 balance sheet would be:
   a. $6,110
   b. $6,860
   c. $7,250
   d. $8,000

8. Accounts Receivable has a debit balance of $2,300, and the Allowance for Uncollectible Accounts has a credit balance of $200. An $80 account receivable is written off. What is the amount of net receivables (net realizable value) after the write-off?
   a. $2,020
   b. $2,100
   c. $2,180
   d. $2,220

9. Ridgewood Corporation began 20X1 with Accounts Receivable of $500,000. Sales for the year totaled $2,000,000. Ridgewood ended the year with accounts receivable of $600,000. Ridgewood's bad-debt losses are minimal. How much cash did Ridgewood collect from customers in 20X1?
   a. $1,900,000
   b. $1,940,000
   c. $2,000,000
   d. $2,600,000

10. Saturn Company received a 2-month, 8%, $1,500 note receivable on December 1. The adjusting entry on December 31 will:
    a. debit Interest Receivable $10
    b. credit Interest Revenue $10
    c. Both a and b
    d. credit Interest Revenue $120

11. What is the maturity value of a $30,000, 10%, 6-month note?
    a. $25,000
    b. $30,000
    c. $31,500
    d. $33,000

12. If the adjusting entry to accrue interest on a note receivable is omitted, then:
    a. assets, net income, and stockholders' equity are overstated.
    b. assets, net income, and stockholders' equity are understated.
    c. liabilities are understated, net income is overstated, and stockholders' equity is overstated.
    d. assets are overstated, net income is understated, and stockholders' equity is understated.

13. Net sales total $730,000. Beginning and ending accounts receivable are $62,000 and $58,000, respectively. Calculate days' sales in receivables.
    - **a.** 32 days
    - **b.** 23 days
    - **c.** 43 days
    - **d.** 30 days

14. From the following list of accounts, calculate the quick ratio.

Cash	$ 3,000	Accounts payable	$ 8,000
Accounts receivable	6,000	Salary payable	3,000
Inventory	10,000	Notes payable (due in 2 years)	8,000
Prepaid insurance	2,000	Short-term investments	2,000

- **a.** 2.1
- **b.** 1.3
- **c.** 1.0
- **d.** 1.4

Accounting Vocabulary

acid-test ratio (p. 280) Ratio of the sum of cash plus short-term investments plus net current receivables to total current liabilities. Tells whether the entity can pay all its current liabilities if they come due immediately. Also called the *quick ratio*.

accounts receivable turnover (p. 280) Net sales divided by average net accounts receivable.

aging-of-accounts receivable (p. 267) A way to estimate bad debts by analyzing individual accounts receivable according to the length of time they have been receivable from the customer.

Allowance for Doubtful Accounts (p. 267) Another name for *Allowance for Uncollectible Accounts*.

Allowance for Uncollectible Accounts (p. 267) A contra account, related to accounts receivable, that holds the estimated amount of collection losses. Another name for *Allowance for Doubtful Accounts*.

allowance method (p. 267) A method of recording collection losses based on estimates of how much money the business will not collect from its customers.

bad-debt expense (p. 267) Another name for *uncollectible-account expense*.

creditor (p. 274) The party to whom money is owed.

days' sales in receivables (p. 279) Ratio of average net accounts receivable to one day's sales. Indicates how many days' sales remain in Accounts Receivable awaiting collection. Also called the *collection period*.

debtor (p. 274) The party who owes money.

direct write-off method (p. 273) A method of accounting for bad debts in which the company waits until a customer's account receivable proves uncollectible and then debits Uncollectible-Account Expense and credits the customer's Account Receivable.

doubtful-account expense (p. 267) Another name for *uncollectible-account expense*.

interest (p. 274) The borrower's cost of renting money from a lender. Interest is revenue for the lender and expense for the borrower.

marketable securities (p. 258) Another name for *short-term investments*.

maturity (p. 274) The date on which a debt instrument must be paid.

percent-of-sales method (p. 269) Computes uncollectible-account expense as a percentage of net sales. Also called the income statement approach because it focuses on the amount of expense to be reported on the income statement.

principal (p. 274) The amount borrowed by a debtor and lent by a creditor.

quick ratio (p. 280) Another name for *acid-test ratio*.

receivables (p. 264) Monetary claims against a business or an individual, acquired mainly by selling goods or services and by lending money.

short-term investments (p. 258) Investments that a company plans to hold for one year or less. Also called *marketable securities*.

term (p. 274) The length of time from inception to maturity.

trading investments (p. 259) Stock investments that are to be sold in the near future with the intent of generating profits on the sale.

uncollectible-account expense (p. 267) Cost to the seller of extending credit. Arises from the failure to collect from credit customers. Also called doubtful-account expense or bad-debt expense.

ASSESS YOUR PROGRESS

Short Exercises

S5-1 (*Learning Objective 1: Reporting trading investments*) Answer these questions about investments. (p. 259)

1. Why is a trading investment always a current asset? Explain.

2. What is the amount to report on the balance sheet for a trading investment?

S5-2 (*Learning Objective 1: Accounting for a trading investment*) Bannister Corp. holds short-term trading investments. On November 16, Bannister paid $80,000 for a short-term trading investment in **Intel stock**. At December 31, the market value of Intel stock is $84,000. For this situation, show everything that Bannister would report on its December 31 balance sheet and on its income statement for the year ended December 31. (p. 259)

S5-3 (*Learning Objective 1: Accounting for a trading investment*) Beckham Investments paid $104,000 for a short-term trading investment in **IBM** stock.

1. Suppose the IBM stock decreased in value to $98,000 at December 31. Make the Beckham journal entry to adjust the Short-Term Investment account to market value. (p. 260)

2. Show how Beckham would report the short-term investment on its balance sheet and the unrealized gain or loss on its income statement. (p. 260)

S5-4 (*Learning Objective 2: Internal control over the collection of receivables*) Don Roose keeps the Accounts Receivable T-account of Zachary & Polk, a partnership. What duty will a good internal control system withhold from Roose? Why? (p. 265)

Short Exercises S5-5 through S5-7 should be used together.

S5-5 (*Learning Objective 3: Applying the allowance method (percent-of-sales) to account for uncollectibles*) During its first year of operations, Scottish Products, Inc., had sales of $900,000, all on account. Industry experience suggests that Scottish Products' uncollectibles will amount to 2% of credit sales. At December 31, 20X4, Scottish Products' accounts receivable total $80,000. The company uses the allowance method to account for uncollectibles.

writing assignment ■

1. Make Scottish Products' journal entry for uncollectible-account expense using the percent-of-sales method. (p. 269)

2. Show how Scottish Products should report accounts receivable on its balance sheet at December 31, 20X4. Follow the reporting format illustrated in the middle of page 268.

S5-6 (*Learning Objective 3: Applying the allowance method (percent-of-sales) to account for uncollectibles*) This exercise continues the situation of Short Exercise S5-5, in which Scottish Products ended the year 20X4 with accounts receivable of $80,000 and an allowance for uncollectible accounts of $18,000. During 20X5, Scottish Products completed the following transactions:

1. Credit sales, $1,000,000 (p. 267)
2. Collections on account, $880,000. (p. 267)
3. Write-offs of uncollectibles, $16,000 (p. 271)
4. Uncollectible-account expense, 1.5% of credit sales (p. 269)

Journalize the 20X5 transactions for Scottish Products. Explanations are not required.

S5-7 (*Learning Objective 3: Applying the allowance method (percent-of-sales) to account for uncollectibles*) Use the solution to Short Exercise S5-6 to answer these questions about Scottish Products, Inc., for 20X5.

1. Start with Accounts Receivable's beginning balance ($80,000) and then post to the Accounts Receivable T-account. How much do Scottish Products customers owe the company at December 31, 20X5? (p. 274)

2. Start with the Allowance account's beginning credit balance ($18,000) and then post to the Allowance for Uncollectible Accounts T-account. How much of the receivables at December 31, 20X5, does the company expect *not* to collect? (p. 271)

3. At December 31, 20X5, what is the net realizable value of the company's accounts receivable? (p. 267)

S5-8 (*Learning Objective 3: Applying the allowance method (aging-of-accounts-receivable) to account for uncollectibles*) Gulig and Durham, a law firm, started 20X8 with accounts receivable of $60,000 and an allowance for uncollectible accounts of $8,000. The 20X8 service revenue on account was $400,000, and cash collections on account totaled $410,000. During 20X8, Gulig & Durham wrote off uncollectible accounts receivable of $7,000. At December 31, 20X8, the aging of accounts receivable indicated that Gulig & Durham will *not* collect $10,000 of its accounts receivable.

Journalize Gulig & Durham's (a) service revenue, (b) cash collections on account, (c) write-offs of uncollectible receivables, and (d) uncollectible-account expense for the year. Explanations are not required. Prepare a T-account for Allowance for Uncollectible Accounts to show your computation of uncollectible-account expense for the year. (pp. 267–272)

S5-9 (*Learning Objective 3: Applying the allowance method (aging-of-accounts-receivable) to account for uncollectibles*) Perform the following accounting for the receivables of **Patillo, Brown & Hill**, an accounting firm, at December 31, 20X7.

1. Start with the beginning balances for these T-accounts:

   - Accounts Receivable, $80,000
   - Allowance for Uncollectible Accounts, $9,000

   Post the following 20X7 transactions to the T-accounts:
   a. Service revenue of $700,000, all on account (p. 268)
   b. Collections on account, $720,000 (p. 268)
   c. Write-offs of uncollectible accounts, $7,000 (p. 267)
   d. Uncollectible-account expense (allowance method), $8,000 (p. 267)

2. What are the ending balances of Accounts Receivable and Allowance for Uncollectible Accounts? (p. 267)

3. Show how Patillo, Brown & Hill will report accounts receivable on its balance sheet at December 31, 20X7. Follow the reporting format near the middle of page 268.

S5-10 (*Learning Objective 4: Accounting for a note receivable*) **Synergy Bank** loaned $100,000 to David Mann on a 6-month, 8% note. Record the following for Synergy Bank: (p. 275)

   a. Lending the money on March 6.
   b. Collecting the principal and interest at maturity. Specify the date.

Explanations are not required.

S5-11 (*Learning Objective 4: Computing note receivable amounts*)

1. Compute the amount of interest during 20X7, 20X8, and 20X9 for the following note receivable: On April 30, 20X7, Centennial Credit Union loaned $100,000 to Heather Hutchison on a 2-year 9% note. (p. 275)

2. Which party has a (an)
   a. Note receivable? (p. 274)   c. Interest revenue? (p. 276)
   b. Note payable? (Challenge)   d. Interest expense? (Challenge)

3. How much in total would Centennial Credit Union collect if Hutchison paid off the note early—say, on October 30, 20X7? (p. 275)

S5-12 (*Learning Objective 4: Accruing interest receivable and collecting a note receivable*) On May 31, 20X5, Nancy Thomas borrowed $6,000 from 1ˢᵗ Interstate Bank. Thomas signed a note payable, promising to pay the bank principal plus interest on May 31, 20X6. The interest rate on the note is 8%. The accounting year of 1ˢᵗ Interstate Bank ends on December 31, 20X5. Journalize 1ˢᵗ Interstate Bank's (a) lending money on the note receivable at May 31, 20X5, (b) accrual of interest at December 31, 20X5, and (c) collection of principal and interest at May 31, 20X6, the maturity date of the note. (p. 274)

S5-13 (*Learning Objective 4: Reporting receivables amounts*) Using your answers to Short Exercise S5-12, show how the 1ˢᵗ Interstate Bank will report the following. (p. 276)

    a. Whatever needs to be reported on the bank's classified balance sheet at December 31, 20X5. Ignore cash.

    b. Whatever needs to be reported on the bank's income statement for the year ended December 31, 20X5.

    c. Whatever needs to be reported on the bank's classified balance sheet at December 31, 20X6. Ignore Cash.

    d. Whatever needs to be reported on the bank's income statement for the year ended December 31, 20X6.

S5-14 (*Learning Objective 5: Evaluating the acid-test ratio and days' sales in receivables*) Botany Clothiers reported the following amounts in its 20X6 financial statements. The 20X5 figures are given for comparison.

		20X6		20X5
Current assets:				
Cash..		$ 9,000		$ 9,000
Short-term investments................		15,000		11,000
Accounts receivable.....................	$80,000		$74,000	
Less allowance for				
uncollectibles......................	(7,000)	73,000	(6,000)	68,000
Inventory.....................................		188,000		189,000
Prepaid insurance........................		2,000		2,000
Total current assets		287,000		279,000
Total current liabilities....................		101,000		107,000
Net sales...		803,000		732,000

❚ Required

1. Compute Botany's acid-test ratio at the end of 20X6. Round to 2 decimal places. How does the acid-test ratio compare with the industry average of 0.95? (p. 280)

2. Compare Botany's days' sales in receivables measure for 20X6 with the company's credit terms of net 30 days. (p. 279)

S5-15 (*Learning Objective 5: Reporting receivables and other accounts in the financial statements*) Victoria Medical Service reported the following selected items (amounts in thousands):

Unearned revenues (current)...............	$ 207	Service revenue....................................	$8,613
Allowance for		Other assets...	767
doubtful accounts............................	109	Property, plant, and equipment...........	3,316
Other expenses....................................	2,569	Operating expense...............................	1,620
Accounts receivable.............................	817	Cash...	239
Accounts payable	385	Notes payable (long-term)..................	719

(continued)

1. Classify each item as (a) income statement or balance sheet and as (b) debit balance or credit balance. (p. 96)

2. How much net income (or net loss) did Victoria earn for the year? (pp. 280)

3. Compute Victoria's current ratio. Round to 2 decimal places. (p. 280).

Exercises

E5-16 (*Learning Objective 1: Accounting for a trading investment*) **Merrill Lynch**, the investment banking company, often has extra cash to invest. Suppose Merrill Lynch buys 1,000 shares of **Microsoft Corporation** stock at $55 per share. Assume Merrill Lynch expects to hold the Microsoft stock for 1 month and then sell it. The purchase occurs on December 15, 20X4. At December 31, the market price of a share of Microsoft stock is $63 per share.

❙ Required

1. What type of investment is this to Merrill Lynch? Give the reason for your answer. (p. 259)

2. Record Merrill Lynch's purchase of the Microsoft stock on December 15 and the adjustment to market value on December 31. (p. 259)

3. Show how Merrill Lynch would report this investment on its balance sheet at December 31 and any gain or loss on its income statement for the year ended December 31, 20X4. (p. 260)

E5-17 (*Learning Objective 1: Reporting a trading investment*) On November 16, Edward Jones Co. paid $98,000 for trading investment in the stock of **Yahoo.com**. On December 12, Edward Jones received a $500 cash dividend from Yahoo. It is now December 31, and the market value of the Yahoo stock is $91,000. For this investment, show what Edward Jones should report in its income statement and balance sheet. (p. 260)

E5-18 (*Learning Objective 1: Accounting for a trading investment*) **PepsiCo** reports short-term investments on its balance sheet. Suppose a division of PepsiCo completed the following short-term investment transactions during 20X8:

20X8	
Nov. 6	Purchased 1,000 shares of Starbucks stock for $35,000. PepsiCo plans to sell the stock at a profit in the near future.
27	Received a cash dividend of $0.85 per share on the Starbucks stock.
Dec. 31	Adjusted the investment in Starbucks stock. Current market value is $33,000. PepsiCo still plans to sell the stock in early 20X9.
20X9	
Jan. 11	Sold the Starbucks stock for $36,000.

❙ Required

1. Prepare T-accounts for Cash; Short-Term Investment; Dividend Revenue; Unrealized Loss on Investment or Unrealized Gain on Investment; and Gain on Sale of Investment. Show the effects of PepsiCo's investment transactions. Start with a cash balance of $55,000; all the other accounts start at zero. (p. 259)

writing assignment ■ **E5-19** (*Learning Objective 2: Controlling cash receipts from customers*) As a recent college graduate, you land your first job in the customer collections department of Backroads Publishing. Shawn Dugan, the manager, asked you to propose a system to ensure that cash received from customers by mail is handled properly. Draft a short memorandum to explain the essential element in your proposed plan. State why this element is important. Refer to Chapter 4 if necessary. (p. 265)

E5-20 *(Learning Objective 3: Reporting bad debts by the allowance method)* At December 31, 20X8, Delaware Valley Nissan has an accounts receivable balance of $101,000. Allowance for Doubtful Accounts has a credit balance of $2,000 before the year-end adjustment. Service revenue for 20X8 was $800,000. Delaware Valley estimates that doubtful-account expense for the year is 1% of sales. Make the December 31 entry to record doubtful-account expense. Show how the accounts receivable and the allowance for doubtful accounts are reported on the balance sheet. Use the reporting format of PepsiCo on page 258.

E5-21 *(Learning Objective 3: Using the allowance method for bad debts)* On September 30, Google Party Planners had a $40,000 balance in Accounts Receivable and a $3,000 credit balance in Allowance for Uncollectible Accounts. During October, Google made credit sales of $100,000. October collections on account were $94,000, and write-offs of uncollectible receivables totaled $1,700. Uncollectible-account expense is estimated as 2% of revenue.

I Required

1. Journalize sales, collections, write-offs of uncollectibles, and uncollectible-account expense by the allowance method during October. Explanations are not required. (pp. 267–274)

2. Show the ending balances in Accounts Receivable, Allowance for Uncollectible Accounts, and *Net* Accounts Receivable at October 31. How much does Google expect to collect? (p. 271)

3. Show how Google will report Accounts Receivable on its October 31 balance sheet. Use the PepsiCo format on page 258.

E5-22 *(Learning Objective 3: Using the direct write-off method for bad debts)* Refer to Exercise E5-21.

I Required

1. Record uncollectible-account expense for October by the direct write-off method. (p. 273)

2. What amount of accounts receivable would Google Party Planners report on its October 31 balance sheet under the direct write-off method? Does Google expect to collect the full amount? (p. 273)

E5-23 *(Learning Objective 3: Using the aging approach to estimate bad debts)* At December 31, 20X7, before any year-end adjustments, the accounts receivable balance of Sunset Hills Clinic is $235,000. The allowance for doubtful accounts has a $7,400 credit balance. Sunset Hills prepares the following aging schedule for accounts receivable:

■ **spreadsheet**

		Age of Accounts		
Total Balance	1–30 Days	31–60 Days	61–90 days	Over 90 Days
$235,000	$110,000	$60,000	$50,000	$15,000
Estimated uncollectible	0.5%	1.0%	6.0%	40%

I Required

1. Based on the aging of accounts receivable, is the unadjusted balance of the allowance account adequate? Too high? Too low? (p. 271)

2. Make the entry required by the aging schedule. Prepare a T-account for the allowance. (p. 271)

3. Show how Sunset Hills Clinic will report Accounts Receivable on its December 31 balance sheet. Include the 2 accounts that come before receivables on the balance sheet, using assumed amounts. (pp. 270, 267)

E5-24 (*Learning Objective 3: Measuring and accounting for uncollectibles*) University Travel experienced the following revenue and accounts receivable write-offs.

Month	Service Revenue	Accounts Receivable Write-Offs in Month			
		January	February	March	Total
January	$ 6,800	$53	$ 86		$139
February	7,000		105	$ 33	138
March	7,500			115	115
	$21,300	$53	$191	$148	$392

University Travel estimates that 2% of revenues will become uncollectible.

Journalize service revenue (all on account), bad-debt expense, and write-offs during March. Include explanations. (pp. 267–273)

■ **general ledger**

E5-25 (*Learning Objective 4: Recording notes receivable and accruing interest revenue*) Record the following note receivable transactions in the journal of Town & Country Realty. How much interest revenue did Town & Country earn this year? Use a 365-day year for interest computations, and round interest amounts to the nearest dollar.

Nov. 1	Loaned $50,000 cash to Springfield Co. on a 1-year, 9% note.
Dec. 3	Performed service for Joplin Corporation, receiving a 90-day, 12% note for $10,000.
16	Received a $2,000, 6-month, 12% note on account from Afton, Inc.
31	Accrued interest revenue for the year.

E5-26 (*Learning Objective 4: Reporting the effects of note receivable transactions on the balance sheet and income statement*) Mattson Loan Company completed these transactions:

20X8		
Apr.	1	Loaned $20,000 to Charlene Baker on a 1-year, 8% note.
Dec.	31	Accrued interest revenue on the Baker note.
20X9		
Apr.	1	Collected the maturity value of the note from Baker (principal plus interest).

Show what Mattson would report for these transactions on its 20X8 and 20X9 balance sheets and income statements. Mattson's accounting year ends on December 31. (p. 276)

E5-27 (*Learning Objective 3, 4: Practical questions about receivables*) Answer these questions about receivables and uncollectibles. For the true-false questions, explain any answers that turn out to be false.

1. True or false? Credit sales increase receivables. Collections and write-offs decrease receivables. (p. 273)

2. Which receivables figure, the *total* amount that customers *owe* the company, or the *net* amount the company expects to collect, is more interesting to investors as they consider buying the company's stock? Give your reason. (Challenge)

3. Show how to determine net accounts receivable. (p. 267)

4. True or false? The direct write-off method of accounting for uncollectibles understates assets. (p. 273)

5. Ohio Bank lent $100,000 to Cincinnati Company on a 6-month, 6% note. Which party has interest receivable? Which party has interest payable? Interest expense? Interest revenue? How much interest will these organizations record 1 month after Cincinnati Company signs the note? (p. 275)

6. When Ohio Bank accrues interest on the Cincinnati Company note, show the directional effects on the bank's assets, liabilities, and equity (increase, decrease, or no effect). (p. 275)

E5-28 (*Learning Objective 5: Using the acid-test ratio and days' sales in receivables to evaluate a company*) **Bullock & Masters, Inc.**, reported the following items at December 31, 20X6 (amounts in millions):

Balance Sheets (Summarized)

	Year End 20X6	Year End 20X5		Year End 20X6	Year End 20X5
Current assets:			**Current liabilities:**		
Cash	$137	$136	Accounts payable	$ 48	$ 48
Marketable securities	30	83	Other current liabilities	158	277
Accounts receivable, net	37	42	Long-term liabilities	11	10
Inventories	29	44			
Other current assets	19	59	Stockholders' equity	172	246
Long-term assets	137	217			
Total assets	$389	$581	Total liabilities and equity	$389	$581

Income Statement (partial):	20X6
Sales revenue	$450

Compute Bullock & Masters' (a) acid-test ratio and (b) days' sales in average receivables for 20X6. Evaluate each ratio value as strong or weak. Bullock & Masters sells on terms of net 30 days. (pp. 279, 280)

E5-29 (*Learning Objective 5: Analyzing a company's financial statements*) **Best Buy Co., Inc.,** the electronics and appliance chain, reported these figures in millions of dollars:

	2006	2005
Net sales..	$30,848	$27,433
Receivables at end of year..............	506	375

❙ Required

1. Compute Best Buy's average collection period during 2006. (p. 279)

2. Is Best Buy's collection period long or short? **Hewlett Packard** takes 41 days to collect its average level of receivables. **FedEx**, the overnight shipper, takes 38 days. What causes Best Buy's collection period to be so different? (Challenge)

Challenge Exercises

E5-30 (*Learning Objective 2: Determining whether to sell on bankcards*) Ripley Shirt Company sells on credit and manages its own receivables. Average experience for the past 3 years has been as follows:

	Cash	Credit	Total
Sales....................................	$300,000	$300,000	$600,000
Cost of goods sold...........................	165,000	165,000	330,000
Uncollectible-account expense...........	—	10,000	10,000
Other expenses................................	84,000	84,000	168,000

John Ripley, the owner, is considering whether to accept bankcards (VISA, MasterCard). Ripley expects total sales to increase by 10% but cash sales to remain unchanged. If Ripley switches to bankcards, the business can save $8,000 on other expenses, but VISA and MasterCard charge 2% on bankcard sales. Ripley figures that the increase in sales will be due to the increased volume of bankcard sales.

❙ Required

Should Ripley Shirt Company start selling on bankcards? Show the computations of net income under the present plan and under the bankcard plan. (Challenge)

E5-31 (*Learning Objective 3: Reconstructing receivables and bad-debt amounts*) **PepsiCo Inc.** reported net receivables of $3,725 million and $3,261 million at December 31, 2006, and 2005, after subtracting allowances of $64 million and $75 million at these respective dates. PepsiCo earned total revenue of $35,137 million (all on account) and recorded doubtful-account expense of $10 million for the year ended December 31, 2006. (All amounts are adapted from PepsiCo financial statements.)

❙ Required

Use this information to measure the following amounts for the year ended December 31, 2006. (p. 273)
a. Write-offs of uncollectible receivables.   b. Collections from customers.

Quiz

Test your understanding of receivables by answering the following questions. Select the best choice from among the possible answers given.

Q5-32 CitiBank, the nationwide banking company, owns lots of investments. Assume that CitiBank paid $600,000 for trading investments on December 3. Two weeks later CitiBank received a $45,000 cash dividend. At December 31, these trading investments were quoted at a market price of $603,000. CitiBank's December income statement should report (p. 260)
a. Dividend revenue of $45,000.   c. Both a and b.
b. Unrealized loss of $3,000.   d. None of the above.

Q5-33 Refer to the CitiBank data in Question Q5-32. At December 31, CitiBank's balance sheet should report (p. 260)
a. Dividend revenue of $45,000.   c. Short-term investment of $603,000.
b. Unrealized gain of $3,000.   d. Short-term investment of $600,000.

Q5-34 Under the allowance method for uncollectible receivables, the entry to record uncollectible-account expense has what effect on the financial statements? (p. 269)
a. Increases expenses and increases owners' equity.
b. Decreases assets and has no effect on net income.
c. Decreases owners' equity and increases liabilities.
d. Decreases net income and decreases assets.

Q5-35 Snead Company uses the aging method to adjust the allowance for uncollectible accounts at the end of the period. At December 31, 20X1, the balance of accounts receivable is $210,000 and the allowance for uncollectible accounts has a credit balance of $3,000 (before adjustment). An analysis of accounts receivable produced the following age groups:

Current	$150,000
60 days past due........................	50,000
Over 60 days past due................	10,000
	$210,000

Based on past experience, Snead estimates that the percentage of accounts that will prove to be uncollectible within the 3 age groups is 2%, 8%, and 20%, respectively. Based on these facts, the adjusting entry for uncollectible accounts should be made in the amount of (p. 270)

a. $3,000.
b. $6,000.
c. $9,000.
d. $13,000.

Q5-36 Refer to Question Q5-35. The net receivables on the balance sheet is _____.

Q5-37 Linus Company uses the percent-of-sales method to estimate uncollectibles. Net credit sales for the current year amount to $100,000 and management estimates 2% will be uncollectible. Allowance for doubtful accounts prior to adjustment has a credit balance of $2,000. The amount of expense to report on the income statement will be: (p. 269)

a. $30,000
b. $32,000
c. $28,000
d. $2,000

Q5-38 Refer to Question Q5-37. The balance of Allowance for Doubtful Accounts, after adjustment, will be: (p. 269)

a. $2,000
b. $4,000
c. $6,000
d. $12,000
e. Cannot be determined from the information given

Q5-39 Draw a T-account to illustrate the information in Questions Q5-37 and Q5-38. Then early the following year, Linus wrote off $3,000 of old receivables as uncollectible. The balance in the Allowance account is now _____. (p. 271)

The next four questions use the following data:

On August 1, 20X7, Azores, Inc., sold equipment and accepted a 6-month, 9%, $10,000 note receivable. Azores' year-end is December 31.

Q5-40 How much interest revenue should Azores accrue on December 31, 20X7? (p. 276)

a. $225
b. $450
c. $375
d. some other amount _____

Q5-41 If Azores, Inc., fails to make an adjusting entry for the accrued interest, (p. 276)

a. net income will be understated and liabilities will be overstated.
b. net income will be understated and assets will be understated.
c. net income will be overstated and liabilities will be understated.
d. net income will be overstated and assets will be overstated.

Q5-42 How much interest does Azores, Inc., expect to collect on the maturity date (February 1, 20X8)? (p. 275)

a. $450
b. $280
c. $75
d. some other amount _____

Q5-43 Which of the following accounts will Azores credit in the journal entry at maturity on February 1, 20X8, assuming collection in full? (p. 275)

a. Interest Receivable
b. Note Payable

c. Interest Payable
d. Cash

Q5-44 Write the journal entry for Question Q5-43. (p. 275)

Q5-45 Which of the following is included in the calculation of the acid-test ratio? (p. 279)

a. cash and accounts receivable
b. prepaid expenses and cash
c. inventory and short-term investment
d. inventory and prepaid expenses

Q5-46 A company with net sales of $1,217,000, beginning net receivables of $90,000, and ending net receivables of $110,000, has a days' sales in accounts receivable of: (pp. 278–280)

a. 50 days
b. 55 days

c. 30 days
d. 33 days

Q5-47 The company in question Q5-46 sells on credit terms of "net 30 days." Its days' sales in receivables is (p. 279)

a. Too high.
b. Too low.

c. About right.
d. Cannot be evaluated from the data given.

Problems
(Group A)

MyAccountingLab

Some of these A problems can be found within My Accounting Lab (MAL), an online homework and practice environment. Your instructor may ask you to complete these problems using MAL.

P5-48A (*Learning Objective 1: Accounting for a trading investment*) During the fourth quarter of 20X6, Cablevision, Inc., generated excess cash, which the company invested in securities, as follows:

Nov. 12	Purchased 1,000 shares of common stock as a trading investment, paying $9 per share.	
Dec. 14	Received cash dividend of $0.32 per share on the trading investment.	
31	Adjusted the trading investment to its market value of $7.50 per share	

❙ Required

1. Prepare T-accounts for: Cash, balance of $20,000; Short-Term Investment; Dividend Revenue; Unrealized Gain on Investment (or Unrealized Loss on Investment). (pp. 259–261)
2. Journalize the foregoing transactions and post to the T-accounts.
3. Show how to report the short-term investment on the Cablevision balance sheet at December 31.
4. Show how to report whatever should appear on Cablevision's income statement.
5. Cablevision sold the trading investment for $8,000 on January 10, 20X7. Journalize the sale.

writing assignment ■

P5-49A (*Learning Objective 2: Controlling cash receipts from customers*) Computer Giant, Inc., makes all sales on account. Susan Phillips, accountant for the company, receives and opens incoming mail. Company procedure requires Phillips to separate customer checks from the remittance slips, which list the amounts that Phillips posts as credits to customer accounts receivable. Phillips deposits the checks in the bank. At the end of each day she computes the day's total amount posted to customer accounts and matches this total to the bank deposit slip. This procedure ensures that all receipts are deposited in the bank.

I Required

As a consultant hired by Computer Giant, Inc., write a memo to management evaluating the company's internal controls over cash receipts from customers. If the system is effective, identify its strong features. If the system has flaws, propose a way to strengthen the controls. (p. 265)

P5-50A (*Learning Objective 3: Accounting for revenue, collections, and uncollectibles; percent-of-sales method*) This problem takes you through the accounting for sales, receivables, and uncollectibles for **FedEx Corporation**, the overnight shipper. By selling on credit, FedEx cannot expect to collect 100% of its accounts receivable. At May 31, 20X6, and 20X5, respectively, FedEx reported the following on its balance sheet (adapted and in millions of dollars):

writing assignment ■

	May 31,	
	20X6	20X5
Accounts receivable......................................	$3,660	$3,422
Less: Allowance for uncollectibles..............	(144)	(125)
Accounts receivable, net............................	$3,516	$3,297

During the year ended May 31, 20X6, FedEx earned service revenue and collected cash from customers. Assume uncollectible-account expense for the year was 1% of service revenue and that FedEx wrote off uncollectible receivables. At year end FedEx ended with the foregoing May 31, 20X6, balances.

I Required
1. Prepare T-accounts for Accounts Receivable and Allowance for Uncollectibles and insert the May 31, 20X5, balances as given. (pp. 267–270)
2. Journalize the following assumed transactions of FedEx, Inc., for the year ended May 31, 20X6 (explanations are not required).
   a. Service revenue on account, $32,300 million.
   b. Collections on account, $31,758 million.
   c. Uncollectible-account expense, 1% of service revenue.
   d. Write-offs of uncollectible accounts receivable, $304 million.
3. Post your entries to the Accounts Receivable and the Allowance for Uncollectibles T-accounts.
4. Compute the ending balances for the two T-accounts and compare your balances to the actual May 31, 20X6, amounts. They should be the same.
5. Show what FedEx would report on its *income statement* for the year ended May 31, 20X6.

P5-51A (*Learning Objective 3: Using the aging approach for uncollectibles*) The September 30, 20X7, records of First Data Communications include these accounts:

■ general ledger

Accounts Receivable......................................	$230,000
Allowance for Doubtful Accounts...............	(8,500)

During the year, First Data estimates doubtful-account expense at 1% of credit sales. At year end, the company ages its receivables and adjusts the balance in Allowance for Doubtful

(continued)

Accounts to correspond to the aging schedule. During the last quarter of 20X7, the company completed the following selected transactions:

20X7	
Nov. 30	Wrote off as uncollectible the $1,100 account receivable from Rainbow Carpets and the $600 account receivable from Show-N-Tell Antiques.
Dec. 31	Adjusted the Allowance for Doubtful Accounts and recorded Doubtful-Account Expense at year end, based on the aging of receivables, which follows.

		Age of Accounts		
Total Balance	1–30 Days	31–60 Days	61–90 days	Over 90 Days
$230,000	$150,000	$40,000	$14,000	$26,000
Estimated uncollectible	0.2%	0.5%	5.0%	30.0%

❙ Required

1. Record the transactions in the journal. Explanations are not required. (pp. 267–271)
2. Prepare a T-account for Allowance for Doubtful Accounts and post to that account.
3. Show how First Data will report its accounts receivable on a comparative balance sheet for 20X7 and 20X6. Use the reporting format on page 268. At December 31, 20X6, the company's Accounts Receivable balance was $212,000 and the Allowance for Doubtful Accounts stood at $4,200.

P5-52A (*Learning Objective 1, 3, 5: Short-term investments, uncollectibles, and the ratios*) Assume **Deloitte & Touche**, the accounting firm, advises Pappadeaux Seafood that Pappadeaux's financial statements must be changed to conform to GAAP. At December 31, 20X7, Pappadeaux's accounts include the following:

Cash	$ 51,000
Short-term trading investments, at cost	19,000
Accounts receivable	37,000
Inventory	61,000
Prepaid expenses	14,000
Total current assets	$182,000
Accounts payable	$ 62,000
Other current liabilities	41,000
Total current liabilities	$103,000

Deloitte & Touche advised Pappadeaux that

- Cash includes $20,000 that is deposited in a compensating balance account that is tied up until 20X9.
- The market value of the short-term trading investments is $17,000. Pappadeaux purchased the investments a couple of weeks ago.
- Pappadeaux has been using the direct write-off method to account for uncollectible receivables. During 20X7, Pappadeaux wrote off bad receivables of $7,000. Deloitte & Touche determines that uncollectible-account expense should be 2.5% of sales revenue, which totaled $600,000 in 20X7. The aging of Pappadeaux's receivables at year end indicated uncollectibles of $5,000.
- Pappadeaux reported net income of $92,000 in 20X7.

I *Required*

1. Restate Pappadeaux's current accounts to conform to GAAP. (Challenge)
2. Compute Pappadeaux's current ratio and acid-test ratio both before and after your corrections. (pp. 262, 280)
3. Determine Pappadeaux's correct net income for 20X7. (Challenge)

P5-53A *(Learning Objective 4: Notes receivable and accrued interest revenue)* Assume that **Kraft Foods**, famous for cheese, Jell-O, and Planters nuts, completed the following selected transactions.

■ general ledger

20X7	
Nov. 30	Sold goods to Safeway, Inc., receiving a $50,000, 3-month, 6% note.
Dec. 31	Made an adjusting entry to accrue interest on the Safeway note.
20X8	
Feb. 28	Collected the Safeway note.
Mar. 1	Received a 90-day, 7%, $6,000 note from Pete's Catering on account.
1	Sold the Pete's Catering note to Lakewood Bank, receiving cash of $5,900.
Dec. 16	Loaned $25,000 cash to Nabisco Brands, receiving a 90-day, 12% note.
31	Accrued the interest on the Nabisco note.

I *Required*

1. Record the transactions in Kraft's journal. Round interest amounts to the nearest dollar. Explanations are not required. (pp. 274–276)
2. Show what Kraft will report on its comparative classified balance sheet at December 31, 20X8, and December 31, 20X7. (p. 276)

P5-54A *(Learning Objective 5: Using ratio data to evaluate a company's financial position)* The comparative financial statements of Sunset Pools, Inc., for 2009, 2008, and 2007 included the following selected data.

writing assignment ■

	2009	2008	2007
		(In millions)	
Balance sheet:			
Current assets:			
Cash	$ 86	$ 80	$ 60
Short-term investments	140	154	122
Receivables, net of allowance for doubtful accounts of $27, $21, and $15, respectively	247	245	278
Inventories	319	381	342
Prepaid expenses	21	27	46
Total current assets	813	887	848
Total current liabilities	403	498	413
Income statement:			
Net sales	$2,898	$2,727	$2,206

I *Required*

1. Compute these ratios for 2009 and 2008: (pp. 262, 279–280)
   a. Current ratio   b. Acid-test ratio   c. Days' sales in receivables

(continued)

2. Write a memo explaining to top management which ratio values improved from 2008 to 2009 and which ratio values deteriorated. State whether the overall trend is favorable or unfavorable and give the reason for your evaluation. (pp. 169, 279, 280)

(Group B)

P5-55B (*Learning Objective 1: Accounting for a trading investment*) During the fourth quarter of 20X8, the operations of Norris Carpet Center generated excess cash, which the company invested in securities, as follows:

Dec. 10	Purchased 2,000 shares of common stock as a trading investment, paying $15 per share.
17	Received cash dividend of $0.60 per share on the trading investment.
31	Adjusted the trading investment to its market value of $34,000.

❚ Required

1. Prepare T-accounts for Cash, balance of $85,000; Short-Term Investment; Dividend Revenue; and Unrealized Gain on Investment (or Unrealized Loss on Investment). (pp. 259–262)
2. Journalize the foregoing transactions and post to the T-accounts.
3. Show how to report the short-term investment on Norris's balance sheet at December 31.
4. Show how to report whatever should appear on Norris's income statement.
5. On January 6, 20X9, Norris sold the trading investment for $29,000. Journalize the sale.

writing assignment ■

P5-56B (*Learning Objective 2: Controlling cash receipts from customers*) Mountainview Software Sales makes all sales on credit, so virtually all cash receipts arrive in the mail. Linda Holcomb, the company president, has just returned from a trade association meeting with new ideas for the business. Among other things, Holcomb plans to institute stronger internal controls over cash receipts from customers.

❚ Required

Take the role of Linda Holcomb, the company president. Write a memo to employees outlining procedures to ensure that all cash receipts are deposited in the bank and that the total amounts of each day's cash receipts are posted to customer accounts receivable. (pp. 228–229)

P5-57B (*Learning Objective 3: Accounting for revenue, collections, and uncollectibles; percent-of-sales method*) Oakley Service Company sells for cash and on account. By selling on credit, Oakley cannot expect to collect 100% of its accounts receivable. At December 31, 20X6, and 20X5, respectively, Oakley reported the following on its balance sheet (in thousands of dollars):

	December 31,	
	20X6	20X5
Accounts receivable....................................	$500	$400
Less: Allowance for uncollectibles...............	(95)	(60)
Accounts receivable, net.............................	$405	$340

During the year ended December 31, 20X6, Oakley earned service revenue and collected cash from customers. Uncollectible-account expense for the year was 5% of service revenue and Oakley wrote off uncollectible accounts receivable. At year end, Oakley ended with the foregoing December 31, 20X6, balances.

I *Required*

1. Prepare T-accounts for Accounts Receivable and Allowance for Uncollectibles, and insert the December 31, 20X5, balances as given. (pp. 267–270)
2. Journalize the following transactions of Oakley for the year ended December 31, 20X6 (explanations are not required):
   a. Service revenue on account, $6,700 thousand.
   b. Collections from customers on account, $6,300 thousand.
   c. Uncollectible-account expense, 5% of service revenue.
   d. Write-offs of uncollectible accounts receivable, $300 thousand.
3. Post to the Accounts Receivable and Allowance for Uncollectibles T-accounts.
4. Compute the ending balances for the 2 T-accounts and compare to the Oakley Tire amounts at December 31, 20X6. They should be the same.
5. Show what Oakley should report on its *income statement* for the year ended December 31, 20X6.

P5-58B (*Learning Objective 3: Using the aging approach for uncollectibles*) The September 30, 20X4, records of Synetics Computers include these accounts:

■ general ledger

Accounts Receivable....................................	$109,000
Allowance for Doubtful Accounts..............	(4,100)

At year end, Synetics ages its receivables and adjusts the balance in Allowance for Doubtful Accounts to correspond to the aging schedule. During the last quarter of 20X4, Synetics completed the following selected transactions:

20X4		
Oct. 31	Wrote off the following accounts receivable as uncollectible:	
	Cisco Foods $300; Tindall Storage, $400; and Tiffany Energy, $1,100.	
Dec. 31	Adjusted the Allowance for Doubtful Accounts and recorded	
	doubtful-account expense at year end, based on the aging of	
	receivables, which follows.	

		Age of Accounts		
Total Balance	**1–30 Days**	**31–60 Days**	**61–90 days**	**Over 90 Days**
$114,000	$80,000	$20,000	$4,000	$10,000
Estimated uncollectible	0.5%	1.0%	5.0%	40.0%

I *Required*

1. Record the transactions in the journal. Explanations are not required. (pp. 267–271)
2. Prepare a T-account for Allowance for Doubtful Accounts and post to that account.
3. Show how Synetics Computers will report its accounts receivable in a comparative balance sheet for 20X4 and 20X3. Use the reporting format on page 268. At December 31, 20X3, the company's Accounts Receivable balance was $111,000 and the Allowance for Doubtful Accounts stood at $3,700.

P5-59B (*Learning Objective 1, 3, 5: Short-term investments, uncollectibles, and the ratios*) The top managers of Hobby Horse Stores seek the counsel of **Ernst & Young**, the accounting firm, and learn that Hobby Horse must make some changes to bring its financial statements

(continued)

into conformity with generally accepted accounting principles (GAAP). At December 31, 20X1, Hobby Horse's accounts include the following:

Cash	$ 18,000
Short-term trading investments, at cost	34,000
Accounts receivable	49,000
Inventory	54,000
Prepaid expenses	8,000
Total current assets	$163,000
Accounts payable	46,000
Other current liabilities	69,000
Total current liabilities	$115,000

Assume Ernst & Young drew the following conclusions:

- Cash includes $6,000 that is deposited in a compensating balance account that will be tied up until 20X4.
- The market value of the short-term trading investments is $32,000. Hobby Horse purchased the investments in early December.
- Hobby Horse has been using the direct write-off method to account for uncollectibles. During 20X1, the company wrote off bad receivables of $7,000. Ernst & Young determines that uncollectible-account expense should be 3% of sales, which for 20X1 totaled $400,000. An aging of receivables at year end indicated uncollectibles of $5,000.
- Hobby Horse reported net income of $81,000 for 20X1.

I Required

1. Restate all current accounts to conform to GAAP. (Challenge)
2. Compute Hobby Horse's current ratio and acid-test ratio both before and after your corrections. (pp. 262, 280)
3. Determine Hobby Horse's correct net income for 20X1. (Challenge)

■ **general ledger**

P5-60B (*Learning Objective 4: Notes receivable and accrued interest revenue*) Lilley & Taylor, CPAs completed the following selected transactions:

20X7		
Oct. 31	Performed service for Lifeway Catholic School, receiving a $30,000, 3-month, 8% note.	
Dec. 31	Made an adjusting entry to accrue interest on the Lifeway note.	
20X8		
Jan. 31	Collected the Lifeway note.	
Feb. 18	Received a 90-day, 10%, $10,000 note from Fishbowl, Inc., on account.	
19	Sold the Fishbowl note to First State Bank, receiving cash of $9,700.	
Nov. 11	Loaned $20,000 cash to Diaz Insurance Agency, receiving a 90-day, 9% note.	
Dec. 31	Accrued the interest on the Diaz note.	

I Required

1. Record the transactions in Lilley & Taylor's journal. Round all amounts to the nearest dollar. Explanations are not required. (pp. 274–275)
2. Show what Lilley & Taylor will report on its comparative classified balance sheet at December 31, 20X8, and December 31, 20X7. (p. 276)

P5-61B (*Learning Objective 5: Using ratio data to evaluate a company's financial position*) The comparative financial statements of New World Piano Company for 20X3, 20X2, and 20X1 included the following selected data:

writing assignment ■

■ **spreadsheet**

	20X3	20X2	20X1
	(In millions)		
Balance sheet:			
Current assets:			
Cash	$ 67	$ 66	$ 62
Short-term investments	93	101	69
Receivables, net of allowance for doubtful accounts of $7, $6 and $4, respectively	206	154	197
Inventories	408	383	341
Prepaid expenses	32	31	25
Total current assets	806	735	694
Total current liabilities	440	416	388
Income statement:			
Net sales	$2,071	$2,005	$1,944

▌ *Required*

1. Compute these ratios for 20X3 and 20X2: (pp. 262, 278–280)

   a. Current ratio   **b.** Acid-test ratio   **c.** Days' sales in receivables

2. Write a memo explaining to top management which ratio values showed improvement from 20X2 to 20X3 and which ratio values deteriorated. State whether the overall trend is favorable or unfavorable for the company and give the reason for your evaluation. (pp. 169, 279, 280)

APPLY YOUR KNOWLEDGE

Decision Cases

Case 1. (*Learning Objective 3: Revenues, collections, and bad debts on receivables*) A fire during 2008 destroyed most of the accounting records of Clearview Cablevision, Inc. The only accounting data for 2008 that Clearview can come up with are the following balances at December 31, 2008. The general manager also knows that bad-debt expense should be 5% of service revenue.

Accounts receivable	$180,000
Less: Allowance for bad debts.................................	(22,000)
Total expenses, excluding bad-debt expense............	670,000
Collections from customers......................................	840,000
Write-offs of bad receivables....................................	30,000
Accounts receivable, December 31, 2007................	110,000

(continued)

Prepare a summary income statement for Clearview Cablevision, Inc., for the year ended December 31, 2008. The stockholders want to know whether the company was profitable in 2008. Use a T-account for Accounts Receivable to compute service revenue. (pp. 159, 274)

Case 2. (*Learning Objective 3: Estimating the collectibility of accounts receivable*) Suppose you work in the loan department of Superior Bank. Dean Young, owner of Dean Young Beauty Aids, has come to you seeking a loan for $500,000 to expand operations. Young proposes to use accounts receivable as collateral for the loan and has provided you with the following information from the company's most recent financial statements:

	20X7	20X6	20X5
	(In thousands)		
Sales	$1,475	$1,001	$902
Cost of goods sold	876	647	605
Gross profit	599	354	297
Other expenses	518	287	253
Net profit or (loss) before taxes	$ 81	$ 67	$ 44
Accounts receivable	$ 128	$ 107	$ 94
Allowance for doubtful accounts	13	11	9

I *Required*

Analyze the trends of sales, days' sales in receivables, and cash collections from customers for 20X7 and 20X6. Would you make the loan to Young? Support you decision with facts and figures. (pp. 279, 280)

Ethical Issue

Sunnyvale Loan Company is in the consumer loan business. Sunnyvale borrows from banks and loans out the money at higher interest rates. Sunnyvale's bank requires Sunnyvale to submit quarterly financial statements to keep its line of credit. Sunnyvale's main asset is Notes Receivable. Therefore, Uncollectible-Account Expense and Allowance for Uncollectible Accounts are important accounts for the company.

Kimberly Burnham, the company's owner, prefers for net income to increase in a smooth pattern, rather than increase in some periods and decrease in other periods. To report smoothly increasing net income, Burnham underestimates Uncollectible-Account Expense in some periods. In other periods, Burnham overestimates the expense. She reasons that the income overstatements roughly offset the income understatements over time.

I *Required*

Is Sunnyvale Loans' practice of smoothing income ethical? Why or why not?

Focus on Financials: ■ YUM! Brands

(*Learning Objective 1, 3, 4: Short-term investments and accounts receivable*) Refer to YUM! Brands financial statements in Appendix A at the end of this book.

1. Assume that YUM! Brands purchased no short-term investments and had no market-value write-downs during 2006. The statement of cash flows reports that YUM sold short-term investments during 2006. Also the balance sheet shows that short-term investments decreased during 2006. How much gain or loss did YUM have on the sale of short-term investments? (p. 261)

2. How much did customers owe YUM at the end of 2005 and at the end of 2006? As of these dates, how much did YUM expect to collect from customers? (p. 267)

3. How much cash did YUM collect from customers and franchisees during 2006? Assume that write-offs of uncollectibles totaled $14 million during 2006. Show your work. (p. 273)

Focus on Analysis: ■ Pier 1 Imports

(*Learning Objective 3: Analyzing accounts receivable*) This case is based on the Pier 1 Imports financial statements in Appendix B at the end of this book.

1. Consider only Pier 1's "Other accounts receivable." How much did Pier 1's customers owe the company at the end of 2006? Of this amount, how much did Pier 1 expect to collect? How much did Pier 1 expect *not* to collect? (p. 267)

2. Were Pier 1's "Other accounts receivable" of higher quality at the end of 2006 or at the end of 2005? How can you tell? (p. 267, Challenge)

3. Would you predict that Pier 1's doubtful-account expense increased or decreased during 2006 as compared to 2005? Indicate how you formed your opinion. (Challenge)

Group Project

Jillian Michaels and Dee Childress worked for several years as sales representatives for Xerox Corporation. During this time, they became close friends as they acquired expertise with the company's full range of copier equipment. Now they see an opportunity to put their expertise to work and fulfill lifelong desires to establish their own business. Navarro Community College, located in their city, is expanding, and there is no copy center within 5 miles of the campus. Business in the area is booming, office buildings and apartments are springing up, and the population of the Navarro section of the city is growing.

Michaels and Childress want to open a copy center, similar to **FedEx Kinko's**, near the Navarro campus. A small shopping center across the street from the college has a vacancy that would fit their needs. Michaels and Childress each have $35,000 to invest in the business, but they forecast the need for $200,000 to renovate the store and purchase some of the equipment they will need. Xerox Corporation will lease 2 large copiers to them at a total monthly rental of $6,000. With enough cash to see them through the first 6 months of operation, they are confident they can make the business succeed. The two women work very well together, and both have excellent credit ratings. Michaels and Childress must borrow $130,000 to start the business, advertise its opening, and keep it running for its first 6 months.

❙ *Required*

Assume 2 roles: (1) Michaels and Childress, the partners who will own Navarro Copy Center; and (2) loan officers at Synergy Bank.

1. As a group, visit a copy center to familiarize yourselves with its operations. If possible, interview the manager or another employee. Then write a loan request that Michaels and Childress will submit to Synergy Bank with the intent of borrowing $130,000 to be paid back over 3 years. The loan will be a personal loan to the partnership of Michaels and Childress, not to Navarro Copy Center. The request should specify all the details of Michaels' and Childress's plan that will motivate the bank to grant the loan. Include a budget for each of the first 6 months of operation of the proposed copy center.

2. As a group, interview a loan officer in a bank. Write Synergy Bank's reply to the loan request. Specify all the details that the bank should require as conditions for making the loan.

3. If necessary, modify the loan request or the bank's reply in order to reach agreement between the 2 parties.

For Internet Exercises go to the Web site www.prenhall.com/harrison.

Quick Check Answers

1. *b*
2. *c*
3. *a* ($38,000 × .02)
4. *d* ($750 + $760)
5. *a* ($1,140 − $750)
6. *d*
7. *b* ($8,000 − $1,140)
8. *b* ($2,300 − $80) − ($200 − $80)
9. *a* ($500,000 + $2,000,000 − $600,000)
10. *c* ($1,500 × .08 × 1/12)
11. *c* $30,000 + ($30,000 × .10 × 6/12)
12. *b*
13. *d* [($62,000 + $58,000)/2] ÷ ($730,000/365)
14. *c* ($3,000 + $6,000 + $2,000) ÷ ($8,000 + $3,000)

6 Inventory & Cost of Goods Sold

PIER 1 IMPORTS

You've just graduated from college, taken a job, and you're moving into an apartment. The place is unfurnished, so you'll need a sofa, a table, and a few chairs. Where will you find these things? Pier 1 Imports may get some of your business.

Pier 1 is known for featuring stylish home furnishings at popular prices—just about right for a new graduate. The company operates 1,100 stores in the U.S., plus 43 Pier 1 Kids stores that sell children's furniture and accessories.

Pier 1's balance sheet is summarized here. You can see that the merchandise inventory (labeled simply as Inventories) is Pier 1's largest asset. That's not surprising since Pier 1, like other retailers, attracts customers with goods that they can purchase and take home immediately.

Pier 1 Imports, Inc.
Balance Sheets (Adapted)

(In millions)

	2006	2005
Assets		
Current assets:		
Cash and cash equivalents	$ 246	$ 186
Receivables, net of allowance for doubtful account of $1 and $1, respectively	64	47
Inventories	369	366
Prepaid expenses and other current assets	96	80
Total current assets	775	679
Properties, net	299	320
Other noncurrent assets	96	77
	$1,170	$1,076
Liabilities and Shareholders' Equity		
Current liabilities	$ 289	$ 292
Long-term debt	184	19
Other noncurrent liabilities	107	101
Shareholders' equity	590	664
	$1,170	$1,076

We also present Pier 1's income statement. Fiscal 2006 was a tough year—Pier 1 had a net loss of $40 million. Sales dropped from the preceding year, and expenses increased.

Pier 1 Imports, Inc.
Statements of Operations (Adapted)

(In millions)

	Year Ended	
	2006	2005
Net sales	$1,777	$1,825
Operating costs and expenses:		
Cost of sales (Cost of goods sold)	1,175	1,122
Operating expenses	645	605
Operating income (loss)	(43)	98
Nonoperating income	1	1
Income (loss) before income taxes	(42)	99
Income tax expense (income tax saving in 2006)	(14)	37
Income (loss) from continuing operations	(28)	62
(Loss) from discontinued operations	(12)	(2)
Net income (loss)	$ (40)	$ 60

You can see that the cost of sales (another name for cost of goods sold) is by far Pier 1's largest expense. The account titled *Cost of Goods Sold* perfectly describes that expense. In short,

■ Pier 1 buys inventory, an asset carried on the books at cost.
■ The goods that Pier 1 sells are no longer Pier 1's asset. The cost of inventory that's sold gets shifted into the expense account, Cost of Goods Sold.

Merchandise inventory is the heart of a merchandising business, and cost of goods sold is the most important expense for a company that sells goods rather than services. This chapter covers the accounting for inventory and cost of goods sold. It also shows you how to analyze financial statements. Here we focus on inventory, cost of goods sold, and gross profit.

We begin by showing how the financial statements of a merchandiser such as Pier 1 Imports or Ford Motor Company differ from those of service entities such as FedEx and Wells Fargo Bank. The financial statements in Exhibit 6-1 (p. 308) highlight how service entities differ from merchandisers (dollar amounts are assumed).

LEARNING OBJECTIVES

1 **Account** for inventory

2 **Understand** the various inventory methods

3 **Use** gross profit percentage and inventory turnover to evaluate operations

4 **Estimate** inventory by the gross profit method

5 **Show** how inventory errors affect the financial statements

ACCOUNTING FOR INVENTORY

The basic concept of accounting for merchandise inventory can be illustrated with an example. Suppose Pier 1 Imports has in stock 3 chairs that cost $300 each. Pier 1 marks the chairs up by $200 and sells 2 of the chairs for $500 each.

■ Pier 1's balance sheet reports the 1 chair that the company still holds in inventory.
■ The income statement reports the cost of the 2 chairs sold, as shown in Exhibit 6-2.

Here is the basic concept of how we identify inventory, the asset, from cost of goods sold, the expense.

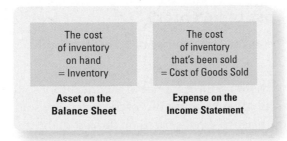

The cost of inventory on hand = Inventory	The cost of inventory that's been sold = Cost of Goods Sold
Asset on the Balance Sheet	**Expense on the Income Statement**

Inventory's cost shifts from asset to expense when the seller delivers the goods to the buyer.

EXHIBIT 6-1 Contrasting a Service Company with a Merchandiser

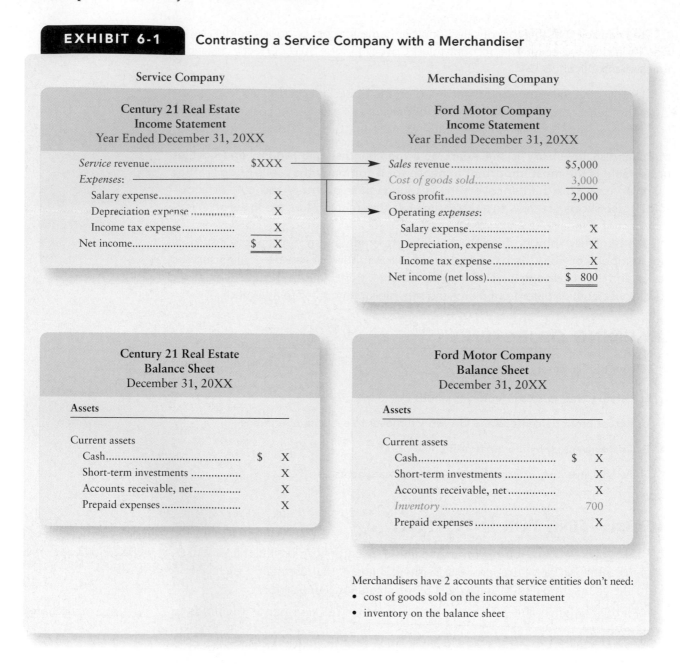

Merchandisers have 2 accounts that service entities don't need:
- cost of goods sold on the income statement
- inventory on the balance sheet

Sale Price vs. Cost of Inventory

Note the difference between the sale price of inventory and the cost of inventory. In our example,

- Sales revenue is based on the *sale price* of the inventory sold ($500 per chair).
- Cost of goods sold is based on the *cost* of the inventory sold ($300 per chair).
- Inventory on the balance sheet is based on the *cost* of the inventory still on hand ($300 per chair).

Exhibit 6-2 shows these items.

EXHIBIT 6-2 Inventory and Cost of Goods Sold When Inventory Cost Is Constant

Balance Sheet (partial)		Income Statement (partial)	
Current assets		Sales revenue	
Cash..	$XXX	(2 chairs @ sale price of $500)	$1,000
Short-term investments	XXX	Cost of goods sold	
Accounts receivable...............................	XXX	(2 chairs @ cost of $300).......................	600
Inventory (1 chair @ cost of $300).........	300	Gross profit..	$ 400
Prepaid expenses	XXX		

Gross profit, also called *gross margin*, is the excess of sales revenue over cost of goods sold. It is called *gross* profit because operating expenses have not yet been subtracted. Exhibit 6-3 shows actual inventory and cost of goods sold data adapted from the financial statements of Pier 1 Imports.

EXHIBIT 6-3 Pier 1 Imports Inventory and Cost of Goods Sold (Cost of Sales)

Pier 1 Imports, Inc.
Balance Sheet (Adapted)
February 28, 2006

Assets (In millions)

Current assets	
Cash and cash equivalents.................	$246
Receivables, net................................	64
Inventories	369

Pier 1 Imports, Inc.
Statements of Income (Adapted)
Year Ended February 28, 2006

(In millions)

Net sales	$1,777
Cost of sales (same as Cost of goods sold)..............	1,175
Gross profit...	$ 602

Pier 1's inventory of $369 million represents

$$\text{Inventory} \atop \text{(balance sheet)} = {\text{Number of units of} \atop \text{inventory } on \ hand} \times {\text{Cost per unit} \atop \text{of inventory}}$$

Pier 1's cost of goods sold ($1,175 million) represents

$$\text{Cost of goods sold (income statement)} = \text{Number of units of inventory } \textit{sold} \times \text{Cost per unit of inventory}$$

Let's see what "units of inventory" and "cost per unit" mean.

Number of Units of Inventory. The number of inventory units on hand is determined from the accounting records, backed up by a physical count of the goods at year end. Companies do not include in their inventory any goods they hold on *consignment* because those goods belong to another company. But they do include their own inventory that is out on consignment and held by another company.

Cost Per Unit of Inventory. The cost per unit of inventory poses a challenge because companies purchase goods at different prices throughout the year. Which unit costs go into ending inventory? Which unit costs go to cost of goods sold?

The next section shows how different accounting methods determine amounts on the balance sheet and the income statement. First, however, you need to understand how inventory accounting systems work.

<table>
<tr><td>OBJECTIVE</td></tr>
<tr><td>1 Account for inventory</td></tr>
</table>

Accounting for Inventory in the Perpetual System

There are 2 main types of inventory accounting systems: the periodic system and the perpetual system. The **periodic inventory system** is used for inexpensive goods. A fabric store or a lumber yard won't keep a running record of every bolt of fabric or every two-by-four. Instead, these stores count their inventory periodically—at least once a year—to determine the quantities on hand. Businesses such as restaurants and hometown nurseries also use the periodic system because the accounting cost of a periodic system is low.

A **perpetual inventory system** uses computer software to keep a running record of inventory on hand. This system achieves control over goods such as Pier 1 Imports furniture, Ford automobiles, jewelry, and most other types of inventory. Most businesses use the perpetual inventory system.

Even with a perpetual system, the business still counts the inventory on hand annually. The physical count establishes the correct amount of ending inventory for the financial statements and also serves as a check on the perpetual records. Here is a quick summary of the 2 main inventory accounting systems.

Perpetual Inventory System	**Periodic Inventory System**
• Used for all types of goods	• Used for inexpensive goods
• Keeps a running record of all goods bought, sold, and on hand	• Does *not* keep a running record of all goods bought, sold, and on hand
• Inventory counted at least once a year	• Inventory counted at least once a year

How the Perpetual System Works. Let's use an everyday situation to show how a perpetual inventory system works. When you check out of a Foot Locker, a Best Buy, or a Pier 1 store, the clerk scans the bar codes on the labels of the items you buy.

Exhibit 6-4 illustrates a typical bar code. Suppose you are buying a desk lamp from Pier 1 Imports. The bar code on the product label holds lots of information. The optical scanner reads the bar code, and the computer records the sale and updates the inventory records.

EXHIBIT 6-4 | **Bar Code for Electronic Scanner**

Recording Transactions in the Perpetual System. All accounting systems record each purchase of inventory. When Pier 1 makes a sale, 2 entries are needed in the perpetual system:

- The company records the sale—debits Cash or Accounts Receivable and credits Sales Revenue for the sale price of the goods.
- Pier 1 also debits Cost of Goods Sold and credits Inventory for the cost of the inventory sold.

Exhibit 6-5, page 313, shows the accounting for inventory in a perpetual system. Panel A gives the journal entries and the T-accounts, and Panel B shows the income statement and the balance sheet. All amounts are assumed. (The chapter's Appendix 6A illustrates the accounting for these same transactions in a periodic inventory system.)

In Exhibit 6-5, the first entry to Inventory summarizes a lot of detail. The cost of the inventory, $560,000, is the *net* amount of the purchases, determined as follows (using assumed amounts):

Purchase price of the inventory	$600,000
+ **Freight-in** (the cost to transport the goods from the seller to the buyer)	4,000
− **Purchase returns** for unsuitable goods returned to the seller	(25,000)
− **Purchase allowances** granted by the seller	(5,000)
− **Purchase discounts** for early payment by the buyer	(14,000)
= Net purchases of inventory—Cost to the buyer	$560,000

Freight-in is the transportation cost, paid by the buyer, to move goods from the seller to the buyer. Freight-in is accounted for as part of the cost of inventory. A **purchase return** is a decrease in the cost of inventory because the buyer returned the goods to the seller. A **purchase allowance** also decreases the cost of inventory because the buyer got an allowance (a deduction) from the amount owed. Throughout this book, we often refer to net purchases simply as Purchases.

EXHIBIT 6-5   **Recording and Reporting Inventory—Perpetual System (Amounts Assumed)**

PANEL A—Recording Transactions and the T-accounts (All amounts are assumed)

Journal Entry

1.	Inventory	560,000	
	Accounts Payable		560,000
	Purchased inventory on account.		
2.	Accounts Receivable	900,000	
	Sales Revenue		900,000
	Sold inventory on account.		
	Cost of Goods Sold	540,000	
	Inventory		540,000
	Recorded cost of goods sold.		

Inventory

Beginning balance	100,000*		
Purchases	560,000	Cost of goods sold	540,000
Ending balance	120,000		

*Beginning inventory was $100,000

Cost of Goods Sold

Cost of goods sold	540,000

PANEL B—Reporting in the Financial Statements

Income Statement (partial)		Ending Balance Sheet (partial)	
Sales revenue	$900,000	Current assets:	
Cost of goods sold	540,000	Cash	$ XXX
Gross profit	$360,000	Short-term investments	XXX
		Accounts receivable	XXX
		Inventory	120,000
		Prepaid expenses	XXX

A **purchase discount** is a decrease in the buyer's cost of inventory earned by paying quickly. Many companies offer payment terms of "2/10 n/30." This means the buyer can take a 2% discount for payment within 10 days, with the final amount due within 30 days. Another common credit term is "net 30," which tells the customer to pay the full amount within 30 days. In summary,

> Net purchases = Purchases
>   − Purchase returns and allowances
>   − Purchase discounts
>   + Freight-in

Net sales are computed exactly the same as net purchases, but with no freight-in, as follows:

> Net sales = Sales revenue
>   − Sales returns and allowances
>   − Sales discounts

Freight-out paid by the *seller* is not part of the cost of inventory. Instead, freight-out is delivery expense. It's the seller's expense of delivering merchandise to customers. (Appendix 6A shows the accounting for these same transactions in a periodic accounting system.) Now study Exhibit 6-5. This exhibit illustrates all the inventory transactions in the perpetual system.

INVENTORY COSTING

Inventory is the first asset for which a manager can decide which accounting method to use. The accounting method selected affects the profits to be reported, the amount of income tax to be paid, and the values of the ratios derived from the balance sheet.

What Goes into Inventory Cost?

The cost of inventory on Pier 1's balance sheet represents all the costs that Pier 1 incurred to bring its inventory to the point of sale. The following cost principle applies to all assets:

> **The cost of any asset, such as inventory, is the sum of all the costs incurred to bring the asset to its intended use, less any discounts.**

As we have seen, inventory's cost includes its basic purchase price, plus freight-in, insurance while in transit, and any fees or taxes paid to get the inventory ready to sell, less returns, allowances, and discounts.

After a Pier 1 chair is sitting in the showroom, other costs, such as advertising and sales commissions, are *not* included as the cost of inventory. Advertising, sales commissions, and delivery costs are expenses.

The Various Inventory Costing Methods

Determining the cost of inventory is easy when the unit cost remains constant, as in Exhibit 6-2. But the unit cost usually changes. For example, prices often rise. The desk lamp that cost Pier 1 $10 in January may cost $14 in June and $18 in October. Suppose Pier 1 sells 1,000 lamps in November. How many of those lamps cost $10, how many cost $14, and how many cost $18?

To compute cost of goods sold and the cost of ending inventory still on hand, we must assign unit cost to the items. Accounting uses 4 generally accepted inventory methods:

OBJECTIVE

2 **Understand** the various inventory methods

1. Specific unit cost
2. Average cost
3. First-in, first-out (FIFO) cost
4. Last-in, first-out (LIFO) cost

A company can use any of these methods. The methods can have very different effects on reported profits, income taxes, and cash flow. Therefore, companies select their inventory method with great care.

Specific Unit Cost. Some businesses deal in unique inventory items, such as automobiles, antique furniture, jewels, and real estate. These businesses cost their inventories at the specific cost of the particular unit. For instance, a Toyota dealer may have 2 vehicles in the showroom—a "stripped-down" model that cost the dealer $19,000 and a "loaded" model that cost the dealer $24,000. If the dealer sells the loaded model, the cost of goods sold is $24,000. The stripped-down auto will be the only unit left in inventory, and so ending inventory is $19,000.

The **specific-unit-cost method** is also called the *specific identification method*. This method is too expensive to use for inventory items that have common characteristics, such as bushels of wheat, gallons of paint, or auto tires.

The other inventory accounting methods—average, FIFO, and LIFO—are fundamentally different. These other methods do not use the specific cost of a particular unit. Instead, they assume different flows of inventory costs. To illustrate average, FIFO, and LIFO costing, we use a common set of data, given in Exhibit 6-6.

EXHIBIT 6-6   Inventory Data Used to Illustrate the Various Inventory Costing Methods

Inventory					
Begin. bal.	(10 units @ $10)	100			
Purchases:			Cost of goods sold		
No. 1	(25 units @ $14)	350		(40 units @ ?)	?
No. 2	(25 units @ $18)	450			
Ending balance	(20 units @ ?)	?			

In Exhibit 6-6, Pier 1 began the period with 10 lamps that cost $10 each; the beginning inventory was therefore $100. During the period Pier 1 bought 50 more lamps, sold 40 lamps, and ended the period with 20 lamps, summarized in the T-account as follows:

Goods Available		Number of Units	Total Cost
Goods available	=	10 + 25 + 25 = 60 units	$100 + $350 + $450 = $900
Cost of goods sold	=	40 units	?
Ending inventory	=	20 units	?

The big accounting questions are

1. What is the cost of goods sold for the income statement?
2. What is the cost of the ending inventory for the balance sheet?

It all depends on which inventory method Pier 1 uses. Pier 1 actually uses the average-cost method, so let's look at average costing first.

Average Cost. The **average-cost method**, sometimes called the *weighted-average method*, is based on the average cost of inventory during the period. Average cost per unit is determined as follows (data from Exhibit 6-6):

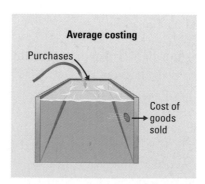

Average costing

Purchases

Cost of goods sold

$$\text{Average cost per unit} = \frac{\text{Cost of goods available*}}{\text{Number of units available*}} = \frac{\$900}{60} = \$15$$

*Goods available = Beginning inventory + Purchases

Cost of goods sold =	Number of units sold	× Average cost per unit	
=	40 units	× $15	= $600

Ending inventory =	Number of units on hand	× Average cost per unit	
=	20 units	× $15	= $300

The following T-account shows the effects of average costing:

Inventory (at Average Cost)

Begin. bal.	(10 units @ $10)	100		
Purchases:				
No. 1	(25 units @ $14)	350		
No. 2	(25 units @ $18)	450	Cost of goods sold (40 units @ average cost of $15 per unit)	600
Ending balance	(20 units @ average cost of $15 per unit)	300		

FIFO Cost. Under the FIFO method, the first costs into inventory are the first costs assigned to cost of goods sold—hence, the name *first-in, first-out*. The diagram near the bottom of the page shows the effect of FIFO costing. The following T-account shows how to compute FIFO cost of goods sold and ending inventory for the Pier 1 lamps (data from Exhibit 6-6):

Inventory (at FIFO cost)

Begin. bal.	(10 units @ $10)	100	Cost of goods sold (40 units):		
Purchases:					
No. 1	(25 units @ $14)	350	(10 units @ $10)	100	
No. 2	(25 units @ $18)	450	(25 units @ $14)	350	} 540
			(5 units @ $18)	90	
Ending bal.	(20 units @ $18)	360			

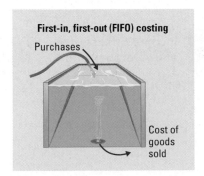

First-in, first-out (FIFO) costing

Purchases

Cost of goods sold

Under FIFO, the cost of ending inventory is always based on the latest costs incurred—in this case $18 per unit.

LIFO Cost. LIFO costing is the opposite of FIFO. Under LIFO, the last costs into inventory go immediately to cost of goods sold, as shown in the diagram. Compare LIFO and FIFO, and you will see a vast difference.

The following T-account shows how to compute the LIFO inventory amounts for the Pier 1 lamps (data from Exhibit 6-6).

Inventory (at LIFO cost)					
Begin. bal.	(10 units @ $10)	100			
Purchases:			Cost of goods sold (40 units):		
No. 1	(25 units @ $14)	350	(25 units @ $18)	450	} 660
No. 2	(25 units @ $18)	450	(15 units @ $14)	210	
Ending bal.	(10 units @ $10) (10 units @ $14) }	240			

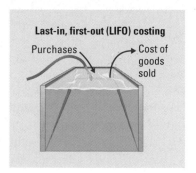

Last-in, first-out (LIFO) costing

Under LIFO, the cost of ending inventory is always based on the oldest costs—from beginning inventory plus the early purchases of the period—$10 and $14 per unit.

The Effects of FIFO, LIFO and Average Cost on Cost of Goods Sold, Gross Profit, and Ending Inventory

In our Pier 1 example, the cost of inventory rose from $10 to $14 to $18. When inventory unit costs change this way, the various inventory methods produce different cost-of-goods sold figures. Exhibit 6-7 summarizes the income effects (sales − cost of goods sold = gross profit) of the 3 inventory methods (remember that prices are rising). Study Exhibit 6-7 carefully, focusing on cost of goods sold and gross profit.

EXHIBIT 6-7 Income Effects of the FIFO, LIFO, and Average Inventory Methods

	FIFO	LIFO	Average
Sales revenue (assumed)	$1,000	$1,000	$1,000
Cost of goods sold.......................	540 (lowest)	660 (highest)	600
Gross profit.................................	$ 460 (highest)	$ 340 (lowest)	$ 400

Exhibit 6-8 graphs the flow of costs under FIFO and LIFO during both increasing costs (Panel A) and decreasing costs (Panel B). Study this exhibit carefully; it will help you *really* understand FIFO and LIFO.

EXHIBIT 6-8 Cost of Goods Sold and Ending Inventory— FIFO and LIFO; Increasing Costs and Decreasing Costs

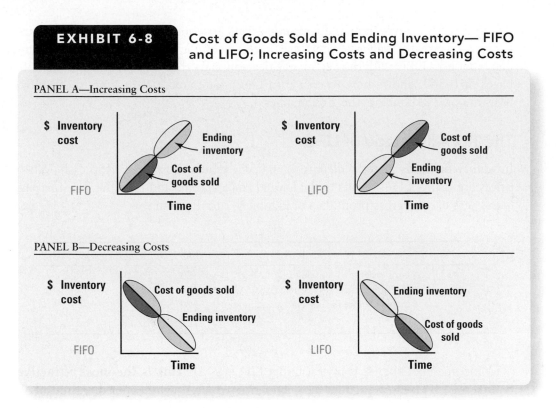

When inventory costs are increasing,

	Cost of Goods Sold (COGS)	Ending Inventory (EI)
FIFO	FIFO COGS is lowest because it's based on the oldest costs, which are low. Gross profit is, therefore, the highest.	FIFO EI is highest because it's based on the most recent costs, which are high.
LIFO	LIFO COGS is highest because it's based on the most recent costs, which are high. Gross profit is, therefore, the lowest.	LIFO EI is lowest because it's based on the oldest costs, which are low.

When inventory costs are decreasing,

	Cost of Goods Sold (COGS)	Ending Inventory (EI)
FIFO	FIFO COGS is highest because it's based on the oldest costs, which are high. Gross profit is, therefore, the lowest.	FIFO EI is lowest because it's based on the most recent costs, which are low.
LIFO	LIFO COGS is lowest because it's based on the most recent costs, which are low. Gross profit is, therefore, the highest.	LIFO EI is highest because it's based on the oldest costs, which are high.

Financial analysts search the stock markets for companies with good prospects for income growth. Analysts sometimes need to compare the net income of a company that uses LIFO with the net income of a company that uses FIFO. Appendix 6B, pages 361–362, shows how to convert a LIFO company's net income to the FIFO basis in order to compare the 2 companies.

The Tax Advantage of LIFO

Inventory methods directly affect income taxes, which must be paid in cash. When prices are rising, LIFO results in the *lowest taxable income* and thus the *lowest income taxes*. Let's use the gross profit data of Exhibit 6-7 to illustrate.

	FIFO	LIFO
Gross profit (from Exhibit 6-7)	$460	$340
Operating expenses (assumed)...............	260	260
Income before income tax	$200	$ 80
Income tax expense (40%)....................	$ 80	$ 32

Income tax expense is lowest under LIFO ($32). **This is the most attractive feature of LIFO—low income tax payments**, which is why about one-third of all companies use LIFO. During periods of inflation, many companies switch to LIFO for its tax and cash-flow advantage. Exhibit 6-9, based on an American Institute of Certified Public Accountants (AICPA) survey of 600 companies, indicates that FIFO remains the most popular inventory method.

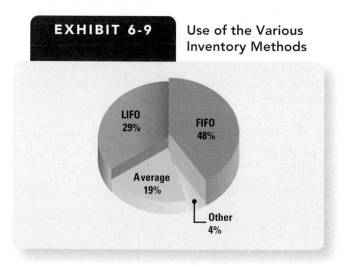

EXHIBIT 6-9 Use of the Various Inventory Methods

LIFO 29%

FIFO 48%

Average 19%

Other 4%

Comparison of the Inventory Methods

Let's compare the average, FIFO, and LIFO inventory methods.

1. Measuring Cost of Goods Sold. How well does each method match inventory expense—cost of goods sold—against revenue? LIFO results in the most realistic net income figure because LIFO assigns the most recent inventory costs to expense. In contrast, FIFO matches old inventory costs against revenue—a poor measure of expense. FIFO income is therefore less realistic than LIFO income.

2. Measuring Ending Inventory. Which method reports the most up-to-date inventory cost on the balance sheet? FIFO. LIFO can value inventory at very old costs because LIFO leaves the oldest prices in ending inventory.

LIFO and Managing Reported Income. LIFO allows managers to manipulate net income by timing their purchases of inventory. When inventory prices are rising rapidly and a company wants to show less income (in order to pay less taxes), managers can buy a large amount of inventory near the end of the year. Under LIFO, these high inventory costs go straight to cost of goods sold. As a result, net income is decreased.

If the business is having a bad year, management may wish to report higher income. The company can delay the purchase of high-cost inventory until next year. This avoids decreasing current-year income. In the process, the company draws down inventory quantities, a practice known as *LIFO inventory liquidation*.

LIFO Liquidation. When LIFO is used and inventory quantities fall below the level of the previous period, the situation is called a *LIFO liquidation*. To compute cost of goods sold, the company must dip into older layers of inventory cost. Under LIFO, and when prices are rising, that action shifts older, lower costs into cost of goods sold. The result is higher net income. Managers try to avoid a LIFO liquidation because it increases income taxes.

International Perspective. Many U.S. companies that use LIFO must use another method in foreign countries. Why? LIFO is not allowed in Australia, the United Kingdom, and some other British commonwealth countries. Virtually all countries permit FIFO and the average cost method.

MID-CHAPTER SUMMARY PROBLEM

Suppose a division of **Texas Instruments** that handles computer microchips has these inventory records for January 20X9:

Date	Item	Quantity	Unit Cost	Total cost
Jan. 1	Beginning inventory	100 units	$ 8	$ 800
6	Purchase	60 units	9	540
21	Purchase	150 units	9	1,350
27	Purchase	90 units	10	900

Company accounting records show sales of 310 units for revenue of $6,770. Operating expense for January was $1,900.

❚ *Required*

1. Prepare the January income statement, showing amounts for FIFO, LIFO, and average cost. Label the bottom line "Operating income." Round average cost per unit to 3 decimal places and all other figures to whole-dollar amounts. Show your computations.

2. Suppose you are the financial vice president of Texas Instruments. Which inventory method will you use if your motive is to
   a. Minimize income taxes?
   b. Report the highest operating income?
   c. Report operating income between the extremes of FIFO and LIFO?
   d. Report inventory on the balance sheet at the most current cost?
   e. Attain the best measure of net income for the income statement?
   State the reason for each of your answers.

Answers

Requirement 1

Texas Instruments Incorporated
Income Statement for Microchip
Month Ended January 31, 20X9

	FIFO	LIFO	Average
Sales revenue.........................	$6,770	$6,770	$6,770
Cost of goods sold.................	2,870	2,782	2,690
Gross profit...........................	3,900	3,988	4,080
Operating expenses	1,900	1,900	1,900
Operating income..................	$2,000	$2,088	$2,180

Cost of goods sold computations:
FIFO: (100 @ $8) + (60 @ $9) + (150 @ $9) = $2,690
LIFO: (90 @ $10) + (150 @ $9) + (60 @ $9) + (10 @ $8) = $2,870
Average: 310 × $8.975* = $2,782

$$*\frac{(\$800 + \$540 + \$1,350 + \$900)}{(100 + 60 + 150 + 90)} = \$8.975$$

Requirement 2

a. Use LIFO to minimize income taxes. Operating income under LIFO is lowest when inventory unit costs are increasing, as they are in this case (from $8 to $10). (If inventory costs were decreasing, income under FIFO would be lowest.)
b. Use FIFO to report the highest operating income. Income under FIFO is highest when inventory unit costs are increasing, as in this situation.
c. Use the average cost method to report an operating income amount between the FIFO and LIFO extremes. This is true in this situation and in others when inventory unit costs are increasing or decreasing.
d. Use FIFO to report inventory on the balance sheet at the most current cost. The oldest inventory costs are expensed as cost of goods sold, leaving in ending inventory the most recent (most current) costs of the period.
e. Use LIFO to attain the best measure of net income. LIFO produces the best matching of current expense with current revenue. The most recent (most current) inventory costs are expensed as cost of goods sold.

ACCOUNTING PRINCIPLES RELATED TO INVENTORY

Several accounting principles have special relevance to inventories:

- ■ Consistency ■ Disclosure ■ Conservatism

Consistency Principle

The **consistency principle** states that businesses should use the same accounting methods and procedures from period to period. Consistency enables investors to compare a company's financial statements from one period to the next.

Suppose you are analyzing Interfax Corporation's net income pattern over a 2-year period. Interfax switched from LIFO to FIFO during that time. Its net income increased dramatically but only because of the change in inventory method. If you did not know of the accounting change, you might believe that Interfax's income increased due to improved operations, but that's not the case.

The consistency principle does not mean that a company is not permitted to change its accounting methods. However, a company making an accounting change must disclose the effect of the change on net income. American-Saudi Oil Company, Inc., disclosed the following in a note to its annual report:

> **EXCERPT FROM NOTE 6 OF THE FINANCIAL STATEMENTS**
> . . . American-Saudi changed its method of accounting for the cost of crude oil . . . from the FIFO method to the LIFO method. The company believes that the LIFO method better matches current costs with current revenues. . . . The change decreased the Company's 2007 net income . . . by $3 million. . . .

Disclosure Principle

The **disclosure principle** holds that a company's financial statements should report enough information for outsiders to make informed decisions about the company. The company should report *relevant*, *reliable*, and *comparable* information about itself. That means disclosing inventory accounting methods. Without knowledge of the accounting method, a banker could make an unwise lending decision. Suppose the banker is comparing two companies—one using LIFO and the other, FIFO. The FIFO company reports higher net income but only because it uses FIFO. Without knowing this, the banker could loan money to the wrong business.

Accounting Conservatism

Conservatism in accounting means reporting financial statement amounts that paint the gloomiest immediate picture of the company. What advantage does conservatism give a business? Many accountants regard conservatism as a brake on management's optimistic tendencies. The goal of accounting conservatism is to present reliable data.

Conservatism appears in accounting guidelines such as "anticipate no gains, but provide for all probable losses" and "if in doubt, record an asset at the lowest reasonable amount and report a liability at the highest reasonable amount." Conservatism directs accountants to decrease the accounting value of an asset if it appears unrealistically high. Assume that **Texas Instruments** paid $35,000 for inventory that has become outdated and whose current value is only $12,000. Conservatism dictates that Texas Instruments must record a $23,000 loss immediately and write the inventory down to $12,000.

Lower-of-Cost-or-Market Rule

The **lower-of-cost-or-market rule** (abbreviated as **LCM**) is based on accounting conservatism. LCM requires that inventory be reported in the financial statements at whichever is lower—the inventory's historical cost or its market value. Applied to inventories, *market value* generally means *current replacement cost* (that is, how much the business would have to pay now to replace its inventory). If the replacement cost of inventory falls below its historical cost, the business must write down the value of its goods to market value. **The business reports ending inventory at its LCM value on the balance sheet**. All this can be done automatically by a computerized accounting system. How is the write-down accomplished?

Suppose Pier 1 Imports paid $3,000 for inventory on September 26. By December 31, the inventory can be replaced for $2,000. Pier 1's December 31 balance sheet must report this inventory at LCM value of $2,000. Exhibit 6-10 presents the effects of LCM on the balance sheet and the income statement. Before any LCM effect, cost of goods sold is $9,000. An LCM write-down decreases Inventory and increases Cost of Goods Sold, as follows:

Cost of Goods Sold	1,000	
Inventory		1,000
Wrote inventory down to market value.		

EXHIBIT 6-10	Lower-of-Cost-or-Market (LCM) Effects on Inventory and Cost of Goods Sold

Balance Sheet

Current assets:	
Cash	$ XXX
Short-term investments	XXX
Accounts receivable	XXX
Inventories, at market	
(which is lower than $3,000 cost)	2,000
Prepaid expenses	XXX
Total current assets	$X,XXX

Income Statement

Sales revenue	$21,000
Cost of goods sold ($9,000 + $1,000)	10,000
Gross profit	$11,000

If the market value of Pier 1's inventory had been above cost, Pier 1 would have made no adjustment for LCM. In that case, simply report the inventory at cost, which is the lower of cost or market.

Companies disclose LCM in notes to their financial statements, as shown on the following page for Pier 1 Imports:

NOTE 1: ACCOUNTING POLICIES
■ *Inventories.* Inventories are . . . stated at the *lower of average cost or market.* [Emphasis added.]

LCM is not optional. It is required by GAAP.

INVENTORY AND THE FINANCIAL STATEMENTS

Detailed Income Statement

Exhibit 6-11 provides an example of a detailed income statement, complete with all the discounts and expenses in their proper places. Study it carefully.

EXHIBIT 6-11 Detailed Income Statment

New Jersey Technology, Inc.
Income Statement
Year Ended December 31, 20X7

Sales revenue	$100,000	
Less: Sales discounts	(2,000)	
Sales returns and allowances	(3,000)	
Net sales		$95,000*
Cost of goods sold		45,000
Gross profit		50,000
Operating expenses:		
Selling:		
Sales commission expense	$ 5,000	
Freight-out (delivery expense)	1,000	
Other expenses (detailed)	6,000	12,000
Administrative:		
Salary expense	$ 2,000	
Depreciation expense	2,000	
Other expenses (detailed)	4,000	8,000
Income before income tax		30,000
Income tax expense (40%)		12,000
Net income		$18,000

*Most companies report only the net sales figure, $95,000.

Analyzing Financial Statements

Owners, managers, and investors use ratios to evaluate a business. Two ratios relate directly to inventory: gross profit percentage and the rate of inventory turnover.

Gross Profit Percentage. Gross profit—sales minus cost of goods sold—is a key indicator of a company's ability to sell inventory at a profit. Merchandisers strive to increase **gross profit percentage**, also called the *gross margin percentage.* Gross profit percentage is markup stated as a percentage of sales. Gross profit percentage is computed as follows for Pier 1 Imports. Data (in millions) for 2006 are taken from Exhibit 6-3, page 309.

OBJECTIVE

3 **Use** gross profit percentage and inventory turnover to evaluate operations

$$\text{Gross profit percentage} = \frac{\text{Gross profit}}{\text{Net sales revenue}} = \frac{\$602}{\$1,777} = 0.339 = 33.9\%$$

The gross profit percentage is watched carefully by managers and investors. A 33.9% gross margin means that each dollar of sales generates about 34 cents of gross profit. On average, cost of goods sold consumes 66 cents of each sales dollar for Pier 1. For most firms, the gross profit percentage changes little from year to year, so a small downturn may signal trouble.[1]

Pier 1's gross profit percentage of 34% is similar to that of Home Depot (33%), but much lower than the gross profit percentage of Federated Department Stores (40.6%). Exhibit 6-12 graphs the gross profit percentages for these 3 companies.

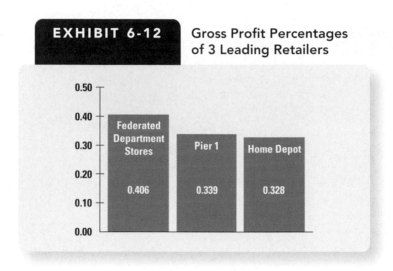

EXHIBIT 6-12 Gross Profit Percentages of 3 Leading Retailers

Inventory Turnover. Pier 1 Imports strives to sell its inventory as quickly as possible because the goods generate no profit until they're sold. The faster the sales, the higher the income, and vice versa for slow-moving goods. Ideally, a business could operate with zero inventory, but most businesses, especially retailers, must keep some goods on hand. **Inventory turnover**, the ratio of cost of goods sold to average inventory, indicates how rapidly inventory is sold. The 2006 computation for Pier 1 Imports follows (data in millions from Exhibit 6-3, page 309):

$$\text{Inventory turnover} = \frac{\text{Cost of goods sold}}{\text{Average inventory}} = \frac{\text{Cost of goods sold}}{\left(\dfrac{\text{Beginning}}{\text{inventory}} + \dfrac{\text{Ending}}{\text{inventory}}\right) \div 2}$$

$$= \frac{\$1,175}{(\$369 + \$366)/2} = \begin{array}{l}\text{3.2 times per year}\\\text{(every 114 days)}\end{array}$$

The inventory turnover statistic shows how many times the company sold (or turned over) its average level of inventory during the year. Inventory turnover varies from industry to industry.

Exhibit 6-13 graphs the rates of inventory turnover for the same 3 companies. Let's compare Pier 1 and Home Depot because their gross profit percentages are so similar. You can see that Home Depot turns inventory over much faster than Pier 1. As a

---

[1]Recall from the chapter-opening story that Pier 1 had a net loss in 2006. The loss may have resulted from a declining gross profit percentage. As recently as 2003, Pier 1's gross profit percentage was 43%.

result, Home Depot is much more profitable than Pier 1. Federated Department Stores sells its inventory more slowly because Federated stores (Macy's and Bloomingdale's) sell more expensive goods that take longer to sell.

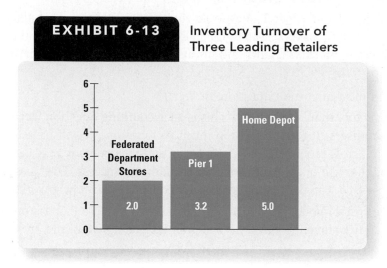

EXHIBIT 6-13   Inventory Turnover of Three Leading Retailers

STOP & think. . .

Examine Exhibits 6-12 and 6-13. What do those ratio values say about the merchandising (pricing) strategies of Federated Department Stores and Home Depot?

Answer:
It's obvious that Federated sells high-end merchandise. Federated's gross profit percentage is much higher than Home Depot's. Home Depot has a much faster rate of inventory turnover. The lower the price, the faster the turnover, and vice versa.

ADDITIONAL INVENTORY ISSUES

Using the Cost-of-Goods-Sold Model

Exhibit 6-14 presents the **cost-of-goods-sold model.** Some may view this model as related to the periodic inventory system. But the cost-of-goods-sold model is used by all companies, regardless of their accounting system. The model is extremely powerful because it captures all the inventory information for an entire accounting period. Study this model carefully (all amounts are assumed).

EXHIBIT 6-14   The Cost-of-Goods-Sold Model

Cost-of-goods sold:

Beginning inventory	$1,200
+ Purchases	6,300
= Goods available.....................	7,500
− Ending inventory....................	(1,500)
= Cost of goods sold.................	$6,000

Pier 1 Imports uses a perpetual inventory accounting system. Let's see how Pier 1 can use the cost-of-goods-sold model to manage the business effectively.

1. What's the single most important question for Pier 1 to address?
   - What merchandise should Pier 1 offer to its customers? This is a *marketing* question that requires market research. If Pier 1 continually stocks up on the wrong merchandise, sales will suffer and profits will drop. This is what happened in 2006.

2. What's the second most important question for Pier 1?
   - How much inventory should Pier 1 buy? **This is an accounting question faced by all merchandisers**. If Pier 1 buys too much merchandise, it will have to lower prices, the gross profit percentage will suffer, and the company may lose money. Buying the right quantity of inventory is critical for success. This question can be answered with the cost-of-goods-sold model. Let's see how it works.

We must rearrange the cost-of-goods-sold formula. Then we can help a Pier 1 store manager know how much inventory to buy, as follows (using amounts from Exhibit 6-14):

1	Cost of goods sold (based on the plan for the next period).....................	$6,000
2 +	Ending inventory (based on the plan for the next period).......................	1,500
3 =	Goods available as planned...	7,500
4 −	Beginning inventory (actual amount left over from the prior period)......	(1,200)
5 =	Purchases (how much inventory the manager needs to buy)...................	$6,300

In this case the manager should buy $6,300 of merchandise to work his plan for the upcoming period.

Estimating Inventory by the Gross Profit Method

Often a business must *estimate* the value of its goods. A fire may destroy inventory, and the insurance company requires an estimate of the loss. In this case, the business must estimate the cost of ending inventory because it was destroyed.

The **gross profit method**, also known as the *gross margin method*, is widely used to estimate ending inventory. This method uses the familiar cost-of-goods-sold model (amounts are assumed):

Beginning inventory	$ 4,000
+ Purchases	16,000
= Goods available.......................................	20,000
− Ending inventory......................................	(5,000)
= Cost of goods sold....................................	$15,000

For the gross-profit method, we rearrange *ending inventory* and *cost of goods sold* as follows:

Beginning inventory	$ 4,000
+ Purchases	16,000
= Goods available.......................................	20,000
− Cost of goods sold....................................	(15,000)
= Ending inventory......................................	$ 5,000

Suppose a fire destroys some of Pier 1's inventory. To collect insurance, Pier 1 must estimate the cost of the ending inventory lost. Using Pier 1's *actual gross profit rate* of 34%, you can estimate the cost of goods sold. Then subtract cost of goods sold from goods available to estimate ending inventory. Exhibit 6-15 shows the calculations for the gross profit method, with new amounts assumed for the illustration.

EXHIBIT 6-15 | Gross Profit Method of Estimating Inventory

Beginning inventory		$18,000
Purchases		72,000
Goods available		90,000
Estimated cost of goods sold:		
Net sales revenue	$100,000	
Less estimated gross profit of 34%	(34,000)	
Estimated cost of goods sold		66,000
Estimated cost of *ending inventory*		$24,000

You can also use the gross profit method to test the overall reasonableness of an ending inventory amount. This method also helps to detect large errors.

STOP & think. . .

Beginning inventory is $70,000, net purchases total $365,000, and net sales are $500,000. With a normal gross profit rate of 40% of sales (cost of goods sold = 60%), how much is ending inventory?

Answer:

$$\$135,000 = [\$70,000 + \$365,000 - (0.60 \times \$500,000)]$$

Effects of Inventory Errors

Inventory errors sometimes occur. An error in ending inventory creates errors for 2 accounting periods. In Exhibit 6-16 start with period 1, in which ending inventory is *overstated* by $5,000 and cost of goods sold is therefore *understated* by $5,000. Then compare period 1 with period 3, which is correct. *Period 1 should look exactly like period 3.*

Inventory errors counterbalance in 2 consecutive periods. Why? Recall that period 1's ending inventory becomes period 2's beginning amount. Thus, the period 1 error carries over into period 2. Trace the ending inventory of $15,000 from period 1 to period 2. Then compare periods 2 and 3. *All 3 periods should look exactly like period 3.* The Exhibit 6-16 amounts in color are incorrect.

OBJECTIVE

5 Show how inventory errors affect the financial statements

EXHIBIT 6-16 Inventory Errors: An Example

	Period 1 Ending Inventory Overstated by $5,000		Period 2 Beginning Inventory Overstated by $5,000		Period 3 Correct
Sales revenue.....................................		$100,000		$100,000	$100,000
Cost of goods sold:					
Beginning inventory	$10,000		$15,000		$10,000
Purchases.....................................	50,000		50,000		50,000
Cost of goods available	60,000		65,000		60,000
Ending inventory.........................	(15,000)		(10,000)		(10,000)
Cost of goods sold		45,000		55,000	50,000
Gross profit..................................		$ 55,000		$ 45,000	$ 50,000
			100,000		

The authors thank Professor Carl High for this example.

Beginning inventory and ending inventory have opposite effects on cost of goods sold (beginning inventory is added; ending inventory is subtracted). Therefore, after two periods, an inventory error washes out (counterbalances). Notice that total gross profit is correct for periods 1 and 2 combined ($100,000) even though each year's gross profit is off by $5,000. The correct gross profit is $50,000 for each period, as shown in Period 3.

We must have accurate information for all periods. Exhibit 6-17 summarizes the effects of inventory accounting errors.

EXHIBIT 6-17 Effects of Inventory Errors

Inventory Error	Period 1		Period 2	
	Cost of Goods Sold	Gross Profit and Net Income	Cost of Goods Sold	Gross Profit and Net Income
Period 1				
Ending inventory **overstated**	Understated	Overstated	Overstated	Understated
Period 1				
Ending inventory **understated**	Overstated	Understated	Understated	Overstated

The Decision Guidelines feature summarizes the situations that call for (a) a particular inventory system and (b) the motivation for using each costing method.

DECISION GUIDELINES

ACCOUNTING FOR INVENTORY

Suppose a Pier 1 store stocks 2 basic categories of merchandise:

- Furniture pieces, such as tables and chairs
- Small items of low value, near the checkout stations, such as cupholders and breath mints

Jacob Stiles, the store manager, is considering how accounting will affect the business. Let's examine several decisions Stiles must make to properly account for the store's inventory.

Decision	Guidelines	System or Method
Which inventory system to use?	• Expensive merchandise • Cannot control inventory by visual inspection	→ Perpetual system for the furniture
	• Can control inventory by visual inspection	→ Periodic system for the small, low-value items
Which costing method to use?	• Unique inventory items	→ Specific unit cost for art objects because they are unique
	• Most current cost of ending inventory • Maximizes reported income when costs are rising	→ FIFO
	• Most current measure of cost of goods sold and net income • Minimizes income tax when costs are rising	→ LIFO
	• Middle-of-the-road approach for income tax and reported income	→ Average

END-OF-CHAPTER SUMMARY PROBLEM

Town & Country Gift Ideas began 20X6 with 60,000 units of inventory that cost $36,000. During 20X6, Town & Country purchased merchandise on account for $352,500 as follows:

Purchase 1	(100,000 units costing)	$ 65,000
Purchase 2	(270,000 units costing)	175,500
Purchase 3	(160,000 units costing)	112,000

Cash payments on account totaled $326,000 during the year.

Town & Country's sales during 20X6 consisted of 520,000 units of inventory for $660,000, all on account. The company uses the FIFO inventory method.

Cash collections from customers were $630,000. Operating expenses totaled $240,500, of which Town & Country paid $211,000 in cash. Town & Country credited Accrued Liabilities for the remainder. At December 31, Town & Country accrued income tax expense at the rate of 35% of income before tax.

I Required

1. Make summary journal entries to record Town & Country's transactions for the year, assuming the company uses a perpetual inventory system.
2. Determine the FIFO cost of Town & Country's ending inventory at December 31, 20X6 2 ways:
   a. Use a T-account.
   b. Multiply the number of units on hand by the unit cost.
3. Show how Town & Country would compute cost of goods sold for 20X6. Follow the FIFO example on page 315.
4. Prepare Town & Country's income statement for 20X6. Show totals for the gross profit and income before tax.
5. Determine Town & Country's gross profit percentage, rate of inventory turnover, and net income as a percentage of sales for the year. In Town & Country's industry, a gross profit percentage of 40%, an inventory turnover of 6 times per year, and a net income percentage of 7% are considered excellent. How well does Town & Country compare to these industry averages?

Answers

I Requirement 1

Inventory ($65,000 + $175,500 + $112,000)	$352,500	
Accounts Payable		352,500
Accounts Payable	326,000	
Cash		326,000
Accounts Receivable	660,000	
Sales Revenue		660,000
Cost of Goods Sold (see Requirement 3)	339,500	
Inventory		339,500
Cash	630,000	
Accounts Receivable		630,000
Operating Expenses	240,500	
Cash		211,000
Accrued Liabilities		29,500
Income Tax Expense (see Requirement 4)	28,000	
Income Tax Payable		28,000

❚ Requirement 2

Inventory			
Beginning bal.	36,000		
Purchases	352,500	Cost of goods sold	339,500
Ending bal.	49,000		

Number of units in ending inventory (60,000 + 100,000 + 270,000 + 160,000 − 520,000)		70,000
Unit cost of ending inventory at FIFO ($112,000 ÷ 160,000 from Purchase 3).....	×	$ 0.70
FIFO cost of ending inventory.......................		$49,000

❚ Requirement 3

Cost of goods sold (520,000 units):	
60,000 units costing....................................	$ 36,000
100,000 units costing...................................	65,000
270,000 units costing...................................	175,500
90,000 units costing $0.70 each*	63,000
Cost of goods sold..	$339,500

*From Purchase 3: $112,000/160,000 units = $0.70 per unit.

❚ Requirement 4

Town & Country Gift Ideas
Income Statement
Year Ended December 31, 20X6

Sales revenue	$660,000
Cost of goods sold..	339,500
Gross profit..	320,500
Operating expenses	240,500
Income before tax	80,000
Income tax expense (35%)...	28,000
Net income..	$ 52,000

❚ Requirement 5

		Industry Average
Gross profit percentage:	$320,500 ÷ $660,000 = 48.6%	40%
Inventory turnover:	$\dfrac{\$339,500}{(\$36,000 + \$49,000)/2} = 8$ times	6 times
Net income as a percent of sales:	$52,000 ÷ $660,000 = 7.9%	7%

Town & Country's statistics are better than the industry averages.

REVIEW INVENTORY & COST OF GOODS SOLD

Quick Check (Answers are given on page 356.)

1. Which statement is true?
   a. The Sales account is used to record only sales on account.
   b. The invoice is the purchaser's request for collection from the customer.
   c. Gross profit is the excess of sales revenue over cost of goods sold.
   d. A service company purchases products from suppliers and then sells them.

2. Sales discounts should appear in the financial statements:
   a. As an addition to inventory
   b. As an addition to sales
   c. As an operating expense
   d. Among the current liabilities
   e. As a deduction from sales

3. How is inventory classified in the financial statements?
   a. as an asset
   b. as a liability
   c. as an expense
   d. as a revenue
   e. as a contra account to Cost of Goods Sold

Questions 4–6 use the following data of Manatee, Inc.

	Units	Unit Cost	Total Cost	Units Sold
Beginning inventory	20	$6	$120	
Purchase on May 23	30	7	210	
Purchase on Nov. 5	15	8	120	
Sales	50	?	?	

4. Manatee uses a FIFO inventory system. Cost of goods sold for the period is:
   a. $330
   b. $347
   c. $355
   d. $365

5. Manatee's LIFO cost of ending inventory would be:
   a. $161
   b. $90
   c. $208
   d. $225

6. Manatee's average cost of ending inventory is:
   a. $161
   b. $90
   c. $104
   d. $225

7. When applying lower-of-cost-or-market to inventory, "market" generally means
   a. resale value.
   b. original cost.
   c. replacement cost.
   d. original cost, less physical deterioration.

8. During a period of rising prices, the inventory method that will yield the highest net income and asset value is:
   a. Specific identification
   b. Average cost
   c. LIFO
   d. FIFO

9. Which statement is true?
   a. The inventory method that best matches current expense with current revenue is FIFO.
   b. Application of the lower-of-cost-or-market rule often results in a lower inventory value.
   c. An error overstating ending inventory in 20X1 will understate 20X1 net income.
   d. When prices are rising, the inventory method that results in the lowest ending inventory value is FIFO.

10. The ending inventory of Bar Harbor Co. is $44,000. If beginning inventory was $50,000 and goods available totaled $104,000, the cost of goods sold is:
   a. $112,000   d. $50,000
   b. $198,000   e. none of the above ($ fill in the blank).
   c. $60,000

11. Bell Company had cost of goods sold of $130,000. The beginning and ending inventories were $10,000 and $20,000, respectively. Purchases for the period must have been:
   a. $82,000   d. $140,000
   b. $94,000   e. $138,000
   c. $132,000

Use the following information for questions 12–14.

12. Tee Company had a $20,000 beginning inventory and a $24,000 ending inventory. Net sales were $160,000; purchases, $80,000; purchase returns and allowances, $5,000 and freight-in, $6,000. Cost of goods sold for the period is
   a. $69,000.   d. $85,000.
   b. $49,000.   e. none of the above.
   c. $77,000.

13. What is Tee's gross profit percentage (rounded to the nearest percentage)?
   a. 52%   c. 47%
   b. 88%   d. none of the above

14. What is Tee's rate of inventory turnover?
   a. 3.4 times   c. 6.4 times
   b. 3.5 times   d. 6.2 times

15. Beginning inventory is $60,000, purchases are $180,000 and sales total $300,000. The normal gross profit is 30%. Using the gross profit method, how much is ending inventory?
   a. $120,000   d. $30,000
   b. $106,400   e. None of the above; $(fill in the blank).
   c. $244,000

16. An overstatement of ending inventory in one period results in:
   a. no effect on net income of the next period
   b. an understatement of net income of the next period
   c. an overstatement of net income of the next period
   d. an understatement of the beginning inventory of the next period

Accounting Vocabulary

average-cost method (p. 314) Inventory costing method based on the average cost of inventory during the period. Average cost is determined by dividing the cost of goods available by the number of units available. Also called the *weighted-average method*.

conservatism (p. 321) The accounting concept by which the least favorable figures are presented in the financial statements.

consistency principle (p. 321) A business must use the same accounting methods and procedures from period to period.

cost of goods sold (p. 307) Cost of the inventory the business has sold to customers.

cost-of-goods-sold model (p. 325) Formula that brings together all the inventory data for the entire accounting period: Beginning inventory + Purchases = Goods available.

Then, Goods available – Ending inventory = Cost of goods sold.

disclosure principle (p. 321) A business's financial statements must report enough information for outsiders to make knowledgeable decisions about the business. The company should report relevant, reliable, and comparable information about its economic affairs.

first-in, first-out (FIFO) cost (method) (p. 321) Inventory costing method by which the first costs into inventory are the first costs out to cost of goods sold. Ending inventory is based on the costs of the most recent purchases.

gross margin (p. 309) Another name for *gross profit*.

gross margin method (p. 326) Another name for the *gross profit method*.

gross margin percentage (p. 323) Another name for the *gross profit percentage*.

gross profit (p. 309) Sales revenue minus cost of goods sold. Also called *gross margin*.

gross profit method (p. 326) A way to estimate inventory based on a rearrangement of the cost-of-goods-sold model: Beginning inventory + Net purchases = Goods available − Cost of goods sold = Ending inventory. Also called the *gross margin method*.

gross profit percentage (p. 333) Gross profit divided by net sales revenue. Also called the *gross margin percentage*.

inventory (p. 307) The merchandise that a company sells to customers.

inventory turnover (p. 324) Ratio of cost of goods sold to average inventory. Indicates how rapidly inventory is sold.

last-in, first-out (LIFO) cost (method) (p. 324) Inventory costing method by which the last costs into inventory are the first costs out to cost of goods sold. This method leaves the oldest costs—those of beginning inventory and the earliest purchases of the period—in ending inventory.

lower-of-cost-or-market (LCM) rule (p. 322) Requires that an asset be reported in the financial statements at whichever is lower—its historical cost or its market value (current replacement cost for inventory).

periodic inventory system (p. 310) An inventory system in which the business does not keep a continuous record of the inventory on hand. Instead, at the end of the period, the business makes a physical count of the inventory on hand and applies the appropriate unit costs to determine the cost of the ending inventory.

perpetual inventory system (p. 310) An inventory system in which the business keeps a continuous record for each inventory item to show the inventory on hand at all times.

purchase allowance (p. 311) A decrease in the cost of purchases because the seller has granted the buyer a subtraction (an allowance) from the amount owed.

purchase discount (p. 312) A decrease in the cost of purchases earned by making an early payment to the vendor.

purchase return (p. 311) A decrease in the cost of purchases because the buyer returned the goods to the seller.

specific-unit-cost method (p. 313) Inventory cost method based on the specific cost of particular units of inventory.

weighted-average method (p. 314) Another name for the *average-cost method*.

ASSESS YOUR PROGRESS

Short Exercises

S6-1 (*Learning Objective 1: Accounting for inventory transactions*) Journalize the following assumed transactions for **The Coca-Cola Company.** Show amounts in billions. (p. 312)

- Cash purchases of inventory, $3.9 billion
- Sales on account, $19.4 billion
- Cost of goods sold (perpetual inventory system), $4.2 billion
- Collections on account, $18.9 billion

S6-2 (*Learning Objective 1: Accounting for inventory transactions*) Riley Kilgo, Inc., purchased inventory costing $100,000 and sold 80% of the goods for $240,000. All purchases and sales were on account. Kilgo later collected 20% of the accounts receivable.

1. Journalize these transactions for Kilgo, which uses the perpetual inventory system. (p. 312)

2. For these transactions, show what Kilgo will report for inventory, revenues, and expenses on its financial statements. Report gross profit on the appropriate statement. (p. 320)

S6-3 (*Learning Objective 2: Applying the average, FIFO, and LIFO methods*) Allstate Sporting Goods started April with an inventory of 10 sets of golf clubs that cost a total of $1,500. During April Allstate purchased 20 sets of clubs for $3,200. At the end of the month, Allstate had 6 sets of golf clubs on hand. The store manager must select an inventory costing method, and he asks you to tell him both cost of goods sold and ending inventory under these 3 accounting methods: (pp. 314–318)

    a. Average Cost   **b.** FIFO   **c.** LIFO

S6-4 (*Learning Objective 2: Applying the average, FIFO, and LIFO methods*) Pinkie's Copy Center uses laser printers. Pinkie's started the year with 100 containers of ink (average cost of $9.20 each, FIFO cost of $9 each, LIFO cost of $8 each). During the year, Pinkie's purchased 700 containers of ink at $10 and sold 600 units for $20 each. Pinkie's paid operating expenses throughout the year, a total of $3,000. Pinkie's is not subject to income tax.

Prepare Pinkie's income statement for the current year ended December 31 under the average, FIFO, and LIFO inventory costing methods. Include a complete statement heading. (p. 320)

S6-5 (*Learning Objective 2: Income tax effects of the inventory costing methods*) This exercise should be used in conjunction with Short Exercise S6-4. Now assume that Pinkie's Copy Center in Short Exercise 6-4 is a corporation subject to a 40% income tax. Compute Pinkie's income tax expense under the average, FIFO, and LIFO inventory costing methods. Which method would you select to (a) maximize income before tax and (b) minimize income tax expense? Format your answer as shown on page 316.

S6-6 (*Learning Objective 2: Income and tax effects of LIFO*) Microdot.com uses the LIFO method to account for inventory. Microdot is having an unusually good year, with net income well above expectations. The company's inventory costs are rising rapidly. What can Microdot do immediately before the end of the year to decrease net income? Explain how this action decreases reported income, and tell why Microdot might want to decrease its net income. (pp. 316–317)

writing assignment ■

S6-7 (*Learning Objective 2: Applying the lower-of-cost-or-market-rule to inventory*) It is December 31, end of the year and the controller of Garcia Corporation is applying the lower-of-cost-or-market (LCM) rule to inventories. Before any year-end adjustments Garcia has these data:

Cost of goods sold:...	$410,000
Historical cost of ending inventory,	
as determined by a physical count..............	60,000

Garcia determines that the replacement cost of ending inventory is $49,000. Show what Garcia should report for ending inventory and for cost of goods sold. Identify the financial statement where each item appears. (pp. 321–323)

S6-8 (*Learning Objective 3: Using ratio data to evaluate operations*) **PepsiCo** made sales of $35,137 million during 2006. Cost of goods sold for the year totaled $15,762 million. At the end of 2005, PepsiCo's inventory stood at $1,693 million, and PepsiCo ended 2006 with inventory of $1,926 million.

Compute PepsiCo's gross profit percentage and rate of inventory turnover for 2006. (pp. 321–323)

S6-9 (*Learning Objective 4: Estimating ending inventory by the gross profit method*) Federal Technology began the year with inventory of $300,000 and purchased $1,600,000 of goods during the year. Sales for the year are $3,000,000, and Federal's gross profit percentage is 40% of sales. Compute Federal's estimated cost of ending inventory by using the gross profit method. (pp. 325–327)

S6-10 (*Learning Objective 5: Assessing the effect of an inventory error—1 year only*) CWD, Inc., reported these figures for its fiscal year (amounts in millions):

Net sales...............................	$ 1,700
Cost of goods sold...............	1,180
Ending inventory..................	360

(*continued*)

Suppose CWD later learns that ending inventory was overstated by $10 million. What are CWD's correct amounts for (a) net sales, (b) ending inventory, (c) cost of goods sold, and (d) gross profit? (pp. 327–328)

S6-11 (*Learning Objective 5: Assessing the effect of an inventory error on 2 years*) OfficeMax's $5 million cost of inventory at the end of last year was understated by $1.6 million.

1. Was last year's reported gross profit of $4 million overstated, understated, or correct? What was the correct amount of gross profit last year? (p. 328)

2. Is this year's gross profit of $4.8 million overstated, understated, or correct? What is the correct amount of gross profit for the current year? (p. 328)

writing assignment ■

S6-12 (*Learning Objective 2, 4: Ethical implications of inventory actions*) Determine whether each of the following actions in buying, selling, and accounting for inventories is ethical or unethical. Give your reason for each answer.

1. In applying the lower-of-cost-or-market rule to inventories, Terre Haute Industries recorded an excessively low market value for ending inventory. This allowed the company to pay less income tax for the year.(p. 322)

2. Laminated Photo Film purchased lots of inventory shortly before year end to increase the LIFO cost of goods sold and decrease reported income for the year.(p. 318)

3. Madison, Inc., delayed the purchase of inventory until after December 31, 20X4, to keep 20X3's cost of goods sold from growing too large. The delay in purchasing inventory helped net income of 20X3 to reach the level of profit demanded by the company's investors. (p. 318)

4. Dover Sales Company deliberately overstated ending inventory in order to report higher profits (net income). (p. 328)

5. Brazos Corporation deliberately overstated purchases to produce a high figure for cost of goods sold (low amount of net income). The real reason was to decrease the company's income tax payments to the government. (p. 328)

Exercises

■ general ledger

E6-13 (*Learning Objective 1, 2: Accounting for inventory transactions*) Accounting records for Allegheny Corporation yield the following data for the year ended December 31, 20X8 (amounts in thousands):

Inventory, December 31, 20X7	$ 370
Purchases of inventory (on account)...	1,200
Sales of inventory—80% on account; 20% for cash (cost $900).............	2,000
Inventory at FIFO cost, December 31, 20X8...	670

I *Required*

1. Journalize Allegheny's inventory transactions for the year under the perpetual system. Show all amounts in thousands. Use Exhibit 6-5 as a model, page 312.

2. Report ending inventory, sales, cost of goods sold, and gross profit on the appropriate financial statement (amounts in thousands). (p. 312)

E6-14 (*Learning Objective 1, 2: Analyzing inventory transactions*) McKinley, Inc., inventory records for a particular development program show the following at October 31:

Oct.	1	Beginning inventory	5 units @ 160	=	$ 800
	15	Purchase...............................	11 units @ 170	=	1,870
	26	Purchase...............................	5 units @ 180	=	900

At October 31, 8 of these programs are on hand. *Journalize for McKinley*:

1. Total October purchases in one summary entry. All purchases were on credit. (p. 312)

2. Total October sales and cost of goods sold in 2 summary entries. The selling price was $500 per unit and all sales were on credit. McKinley uses the FIFO inventory method. (pp. 312, 315–316)

3. Under FIFO, how much gross profit would McKinley earn on these transactions? What is the FIFO cost of McKinley's ending inventory? (p. 316)

E6-15 (*Learning Objective 2: Determining ending inventory and cost of goods sold by 4 methods*) Use the data for McKinely Inc. in Exercise E6-14 to answer the following. (pp. 314–316)

■ **spreadsheet**

I *Required*

1. Compute cost of goods sold and ending inventory, using each of the following methods:
   a. Specific unit cost, with three $160 units and five $180 units still on hand at the end
   b. Average cost
   c. First-in, first-out
   d. Last-in, first-out

2. Which method produces the highest cost of goods sold? Which method produces the lowest cost of goods sold? What causes the difference in cost of goods sold?

E6-16 (*Learning Objective 2: Computing the tax advantage of LIFO over FIFO*) Use the data in Exercise E6-14 to illustrate McKinley's income tax advantage from using LIFO over FIFO. Sales revenue is $6,000, operating expenses are $1,100, and the income tax rate is 40%. How much in taxes would McKinley save by using the LIFO method versus FIFO? (p. 316)

E6-17 (*Learning Objective 2: Determining ending inventory and cost of goods sold—FIFO vs. LIFO*) MusicBiz.net specializes in sound equipment. Because each inventory item is expensive, MusicBiz uses a perpetual inventory system. Company records indicate the following data for a line of speakers:

Date		Item	Quantity	Unit Cost	Sale Price
June	1	Balance	5	$90	
	6	Purchase	12	95	
	8	Sale	3		$150
	30	Sale	8		155

I *Required*

1. Determine the amounts that MusicBiz should report for cost of goods sold and ending inventory 2 ways: (pp. 315–316)
   a. FIFO   b. LIFO

2. MusicBiz uses the FIFO method. Prepare MusicBiz's income statement for the month ended June 30, 20X5, reporting gross profit. Operating expenses totaled $320, and the income tax rate was 40%. (pp. 316–320)

E6-18 (*Learning Objective 2: Measuring gross profit—FIFO vs. LIFO; Falling prices*) Suppose a **Best Buy** store in Orlando, Florida, ended May 20X6 with 800,000 units of merchandise that cost an average of $7 each. Suppose the store then sold 600,000 units for $5.0 million during June. Further, assume the store made 2 large purchases during June as follows:

June	6	100,000 units @ $6 =	$ 600,000
	21	400,000 units @ $5 =	2,000,000

(continued)

1. At June 30, the store manager needs to know the store's gross profit under both FIFO and LIFO. Supply this information. (pp. 315–318)

2. What caused the FIFO and LIFO gross profit figures to differ? (Challenge).

E6-19 (*Learning Objective 2: Managing income taxes under the LIFO method*) Deitrick Guitar Company is nearing the end of its worst year ever. With 3 weeks until year end, it appears that net income for the year will have decreased by 20% from last year. Jim Deitrick, the president and principal stockholder, is distressed with the year's results.

writing assignment ■

Deitrick asks you, the financial vice president, to come up with a way to increase the business's net income. Inventory quantities are a little higher than normal because sales have been slow during the last few months. Deitrick uses the LIFO inventory method, and inventory costs have risen dramatically during the latter part of the year.

▌ Required

Write a memorandum to Jim Deitrick to explain how the company can increase its net income for the year. Explain your reasoning in detail. Deitrick is a man of integrity, so your plan must be completely ethical. (pp. 318–319)

E6-20 (*Learning Objective 2: Identifying income, tax, and other effects of the inventory methods*) This exercise tests your understanding of the various inventory methods. In the space provided, write the name of the inventory method that best fits the description. Assume that the cost of inventory is rising. (pp. 313–316, 321–322)

_____ 1. Generally associated with saving income taxes.

_____ 2. Results in a cost of ending inventory that is close to the current cost of replacing the inventory.

_____ 3. Used to account for automobiles, jewelry, and art objects.

_____ 4. Provides a middle-ground measure of ending inventory and cost of goods sold.

_____ 5. Maximizes reported income.

_____ 6. Matches the most current cost of goods sold against sales revenue.

_____ 7. Results in an old measure of the cost of ending inventory.

_____ 8. Writes inventory down when replacement cost drops below historical cost.

_____ 9. Enables a company to buy high-cost inventory at year end and thereby decrease reported income and income tax.

_____ 10. Enables a company to keep reported income from dropping lower by liquidating older layers of inventory.

E6-21 (*Learning Objective 2: Applying the lower-of-cost-or-market rule to inventories*) Sloan, Inc., uses a perpetual inventory system. Sloan has these account balances at December 31, 20X4, prior to making the year-end adjustments:

Inventory		Cost of Goods Sold		Sales Revenue	
Beg. bal. 12,400					
End bal. 14,000		Bal. 78,000		Bal. 125,000	

A year ago, the replacement cost of Sloan's ending inventory was $13,000, which exceeded cost of $12,400. Sloan has determined that the replacement cost of the December 31, 20X4, ending inventory is $12,000.

▌ Required

Prepare Sloan Inc.'s 20X4 income statement through gross profit to show how the company would apply the lower-of-cost-or-market rule to its inventories. (p. 322)

I Required

E6-22 (*Learning Objective 2: Determining amounts for the income statement; using the cost-of-goods-sold model*) Supply the missing income statement amounts for each of the following companies (amounts adapted, in millions or billions): (pp. 323-326)

Company	Net Sales	Beginning Inventory	Purchases	Ending Inventory	Cost of Goods Sold	Gross Profit
Krispy Kreme	$543	$29	$470	$24	(a)	(b)
Hewlitt-Packard	74	7	(c)	8	(d)	19
PepsiCo	(e)	(f)	16	2	16	19
Best Buy	31	2	24	(g)	23	(h)

Prepare the income statement for Krispy Kreme Doughnuts, Inc., in millions of dollars—for the year ended January 31, 2006. Use the cost-of-goods-sold model to compute cost of goods sold. Krispy Kreme's operating and other expenses, as adapted, for the year were $2,040. Ignore income tax. (pp. 307–308, 325–326)

Note: Exercise E6-23 builds on Exercise E6-22 with a profitability analysis of these actual companies.

E6-23 (*Learning Objective 3: Measuring profitability*) Refer to the data in Exercise E6-22. Compute all ratio values to answer the following questions:

- Which company has the highest, and which company has the lowest, gross profit percentage?
- Which company has the highest, and the lowest rate of inventory turnover?

Based on your figures, which company appears to be the most profitable? (pp. 322–325)

■ **general ledger**

E6-24 (*Learning Objective 3: Gross profit percentage and inventory turnover*) Turner & Taft, a partnership, had these inventory data:

	20X3	20X4
Ending inventory at:		
FIFO cost...............	$18,000	$ 20,000
LIFO cost...............	14,000	18,000
Cost of goods sold at:		
FIFO cost...............		$ 85,500
LIFO cost...............		92,800
Sales revenue...............		138,000

Turner & Taft need to know the company's gross profit percentage and rate of inventory turnover for 20X4 under (pp. 315–316, 322–325)

  1. FIFO   **2.** LIFO

Which method makes the business look better on (pp. 322–325)

  3. Gross profit percentage?   **4.** Inventory turnover?

E6-25 (*Learning Objective 2: Budgeting inventory purchases*) **Pier 1 Imports** prepares budgets to help manage the company. Suppose Pier 1 is budgeting for the fiscal year ended January 31, 20X4. During preceding fiscal year 20X3, sales totaled $1,777 million and cost of goods sold was $1,175 million. At January 31, 20X3, inventory stood at $366 million.

During the upcoming 20X4 year, suppose Pier 1 expects cost of goods sold to increase by 8%. The company budgets next year's ending inventory at $369 million.

(continued)

I *Required*

One of the most important decisions a manager makes is how much inventory to buy. How much inventory should Pier 1 purchase during the upcoming year to reach its budgeted figures? (p. 325)

■ **spreadsheet**

E6-26 *(Learning Objective 4: Estimating inventory by the gross profit method)* Vacation Properties began January with concession inventory of $48,000. The business made net purchases of concessions for $106,000 and had net sales of $200,000 before a fire destroyed its concession inventory. For the past several years, Vacation Properties' gross profit percentage has been 40%. Estimate the cost of the concession inventory destroyed by the fire. Identify another reason managers use the gross profit method to estimate ending inventory. (pp. 325–326)

E6-27 *(Learning Objective 5: Correcting an inventory error)* Dijon Mustard, Inc., reported the following comparative income statement for the years ended September 30, 20X5, and 20X4:

Dijon Mustard, Inc.
Income Statement
Years Ended September 30, 20X5, and 20X4

	20X5		20X4	
Sales revenue..........................		$149,000		$122,000
Cost of goods sold				
Beginning inventory.........	$ 18,000		$ 12,000	
Purchases.........................	72,000		66,000	
Goods available	90,000		78,000	
Ending inventory.............	(16,000)		(18,000)	
Cost of goods sold		74,000		60,000
Gross profit.........................		75,000		62,000
Operating expenses		20,000		20,000
Net income..........................		$ 55,000		$ 42,000

Dijon's shareholders are thrilled by the company's boost in sales and net income during 20X5. Then they discover that ending 20X4 inventory was understated by $9,000. Prepare the corrected comparative income statement for the 2-year period. How well did Dijon really perform in 20X5, as compared with 20X4? (pp. 326–328)

Challenge Exercises

E6-28 *(Learning Objective 2: Inventory policy decisions)* For each of the following situations, identify the inventory method that you would use or, given the use of a particular method, state the strategy that you would follow to accomplish your goal: (pp. 314–319)

   a. Inventory costs are increasing. Your company uses LIFO and is having an unexpectedly good year. It is near year end, and you need to keep net income from increasing too much in order to save on income tax.

   b. Suppliers of your inventory are threatening a labor strike, and it may be difficult for your company to obtain inventory. This situation could increase your income taxes.

   c. Company management, like that of **IBM** and **Pier 1 Imports**, prefers a middle-of-the-road inventory policy that avoids extremes.

d. Inventory costs are *decreasing*, and your company's board of directors wants to minimize income taxes.

e. Inventory costs are *increasing*, and the company prefers to report high income.

f. Inventory costs have been stable for several years, and you expect costs to remain stable for the indefinite future. (Give the reason for your choice of method.)

E6-29 (*Learning Objective 2: Measuring the effect of a LIFO liquidation*) Suppose **Saks Fifth Avenue**, the specialty retailer, had these records for ladies' evening gowns during 20X9.

Beginning inventory (40 @ $1,000)	$ 40,000
Purchase in February (20 @ $1,100)	22,000
Purchase in June (50 @ $1,200)	60,000
Purchase in December (30 @ $1,300)................	39,000
Goods available...	$161,000

Assume sales of evening gowns totaled 120 units during 20X9 and that Saks uses the LIFO method to account for inventory. The income tax rate is 40%.

❚ *Required*

1. Compute Sak's cost of goods sold for evening gowns in 20X9. (pp. 314–319)

2. Compute what cost of goods sold would have been if Saks had purchased enough inventory in December—at $1,300 per evening gown—to keep year-end inventory at the same level it was at the beginning of the year, 40 units. (Challenge).

E6-30 (*Learning Objective 3: Evaluating a company's profitability*) Z Mart, Inc., declared bankruptcy. Let's see why. Z Mart reported these figures:

Z Mart, Inc.
Statement of Income
Years Ended December 30, 20X7, 20X6, and 20X5

Millions	20X7	20X6	20X5	20X4
Sales..	$37.0	$35.9	$33.7	
Cost of sales............................	29.7	28.1	26.3	
Selling expenses.......................	7.4	6.5	6.2	
Other expenses........................	0.1	0.9	0.7	
Net income (net loss)...............	$ (0.2)	$ 0.4	$ 0.5	
Additional data:				
Ending inventory..................	8.4	7.8	7.0	6.4

❚ *Required*

Evaluate the trend of Z Mart's results of operations during 20X5 through 20X7. Consider the trends of sales, gross profit, and net income. Track the gross profit percentage (to 3 decimal places) and the rate of inventory turnover (to 1 decimal place) in each year—20X5, 20X6, and 20X7. Also discuss the role that selling expenses must have played in Z Mart's difficulties. (pp. 322–324)

Quiz

Test your understanding of accounting for inventory by answering the following questions. Select the best choice from among the possible answers given.

Q6-31 Riverside Software began January with $3,500 of merchandise inventory. During January, Riverside made the following entries for its inventory transactions:

Inventory		6,000	
Accounts Payable			6,000
Accounts Receivable		7,200	
Sales Revenue			7,200
Cost of Goods Sold		5,500	
Inventory			5,500

How much was Riverside's inventory at the end of January? (pp. 312–314)
a. Zero
b. $4,000
c. $4,500
d. $5,000

Q6-32 Use the data in question 6-31. What is Riverside's gross profit for January? (pp. 308–309)
a. Zero
b. $1,700
c. $5,500
d. $7,200

Q6-33 When does the cost of inventory become an expense? (p. 307)
a. When cash is collected from the customer.
b. When inventory is purchased from the supplier.
c. When payment is made to the supplier.
d. When inventory is delivered to a customer.

The next 2 questions use the following facts. Leading Edge Frame Shop wants to know the effect of different inventory costing methods on its financial statements. Inventory and purchases data for April follow.

			Units	Unit Cost	Total Cost
April	1	Beginning inventory	2,000	$10.00	$20,000
	4	Purchase	1,000	10.60	10,600
	9	Sale	(1,500)		

Q6-34 If Leading Edge uses the FIFO method, the *cost of the ending inventory* will be (pp. 315–316)
a. $10,600.
b. $15,000.
c. $15,300.
d. $15,600.

Q6-35 If Leading Edge uses the LIFO method, *cost of goods sold* will be (pp. 315–316)
a. $10,600.
b. $15,000.
c. $15,300.
d. $15,600.

Q6-36 In a period of rising prices, (p. 316–318)
a. Gross profit under FIFO will be higher than under LIFO.
b. LIFO inventory will be greater than FIFO inventory.
c. Cost of goods sold under LIFO will be less than under FIFO.
d. Net income under LIFO will be higher than under FIFO.

Q6-37 The income statement for Heritage Health Foods shows gross profit of $144,000, operating expenses of $130,000, and cost of goods sold of $216,000. What is the amount of net sales revenue? (pp. 316–318)

a. $274,000   c. $360,000
b. $246,000   d. $490,000

Q6-38 The word "market" as used in "the lower of cost or market" generally means (pp. 321–322)

a. Original cost.   c. Retail market price.
b. Replacement cost.   d. Liquidation price.

Q6-39 The sum of (a) ending inventory and (b) cost of goods sold is

a. Goods available.   c. Gross profit.
b. Net purchases.   d. Beginning inventory.

Q6-40 The following data come from the inventory records of Dodge Company:

Net sales revenue	$620,000
Beginning inventory	60,000
Ending inventory	40,000
Net purchases	400,000

Based on these facts, the gross profit for Dodge Company is (p. 326)

a. $150,000.   c. $190,000.
b. $220,000.   d. Some other amount (*enter here*).

Q6-41 Elizabeth Baker Cosmetics ended the month of May with inventory of $20,000. Elizabeth Baker expects to end June with inventory of $15,000 after cost of goods sold of $90,000. How much inventory must Elizabeth Baker purchase during June in order to accomplish these results? (p. 326)

a. $85,000   c. $105,000
b. $95,000   d. Cannot be determined from the data given.

Q6-42 Two financial ratios that clearly distinguish a discount chain such as **Wal-Mart** from a high-end retailer such as **Neiman Marcus** are the gross profit percentage and the rate of inventory turnover. Which set of relationships is most likely for Neiman Marcus? (p. 324)

	Gross profit percentage	Inventory turnover
a.	High	High
b.	Low	Low
c.	Low	High
d.	High	Low

Q6-43 Sales are $500,000 and cost of goods sold is $300,000. Beginning and ending inventories are $25,000 and $35,000, respectively. How many times did the company turn its inventory over during this period? (pp. 323–325)

a. 16.7 times   c. 8 times
b. 6.7 times   d. 10 times

Q6-44 Tulsa, Inc., reported the following data:

Freight in	$ 20,000	Sales returns	$ 10,000
Purchases	205,000	Purchase returns	6,000
Beginning inventory	50,000	Sales revenue	490,000
Purchase discounts	4,000	Ending inventory	40,000

(continued)

Tulsa's gross profit percentage is (pp. 323–324)

a. 47.9%.   c. 53.1%.
b. 52.1%.   d. 54.0%.

Q6-45 Sherman Tank Company had the following for the first quarter of 20X8:

Beginning inventory, $50,000   Net purchases, $75,000
Net sales revenue, $90,000   Gross profit rate, 30%

By the gross profit method, the ending inventory should be (pp. 326–327)

a. $62,000.   c. $64,000.
b. $63,000.   d. $65,000.

Q6-46 An error understated Rice Corporation's December 31, 20X8, ending inventory by $40,000. What effect will this error have on total assets and net income for 20X8? (p. 328)

	Assets	**Net income**
a.	No effect	No effect
b.	No effect	Overstate
c.	Understate	Understate
d.	Understate	Understate

Q6-47 What is the effect of Rice Corporation's 20X8 inventory error on net income for 20X9? (p. 328)

a. No effect
b. Understate
c. Overstate

Problems
(Group A)

MyAccountingLab

> Most of these A problems can be found within My Accounting Lab (MAL), an online homework and practice environment. Your instructor may ask you to complete these problems using MAL.

■ **general ledger**

P6-48A (*Learning Objective 1, 2: Accounting for inventory in a perpetual system*) **Best Buy** purchases inventory in crates of merchandise; each crate of inventory is a unit. The fiscal year of Best Buy ends each February 28.

Assume you are dealing with a single Best Buy store in Nashville, Tennessee, and that the store experienced the following: The Nashville store began fiscal year 20X5 with an inventory of 20,000 units that cost a total of $1,000,000. During the year, the store purchased merchandise on account as follows:

April (30,000 units @ cost of $60)	$1,800,000
August (50,000 units @ cost of $64)	3,200,000
November (60,000 units @ cost of $70)...............	4,200,000
Total purchases...	$9,200,000

Cash payments on account totaled $8,800,000.

During fiscal year 20X5, the store sold 150,000 units of merchandise for $14,400,000, of which $5,000,000 was for cash and the balance was on account. Best Buy uses the average cost method for inventories.

Operating expenses for the year were $4,000,000. The store paid 80% in cash and accrued the rest as accrued liabilities. The store accrued income tax at the rate of 40%.

I Required

1. Make summary journal entries to record the store's transactions for the year ended February 28, 20X5. Best Buy uses a perpetual inventory system. (p. 312)
2. Prepare a T-account to show the activity in the Inventory account. (p. 315).
3. Prepare the store's income statement for the year ended February 28, 20X5. Show totals for gross profit, income before tax, and net income. (pp. 316, 318)

P6-49A *(Learning Objective 2: Measuring cost of goods sold and ending inventory—perpetual system)* Assume a **Nike** outlet store began August 20X0 with 40 pairs of running shoes that cost the store $40 each. The sale price of these shoes was $70. During August, the store completed these inventory transactions:

		Units	Unit Cost	Unit Sale Price
Aug. 3	Sale	16	$40	$70
8	Purchase......	80	41	
11	Sale	24	40	70
19	Sale	9	41	72
24	Sale	30	41	72
30	Purchase......	18	42	

I Required

1. The preceding data are taken from the store's perpetual inventory records. Which cost method does the store use? Explain how you arrived at your answer. (pp. 314–318)
2. Determine the store's cost of goods sold for August. Also compute gross profit for August. (pp. 318–319)
3. What is the cost of the store's August 31 inventory of running shoes? (pp. 316–318)

P6-50A *(Learning Objective 2: Computing inventory by 3 methods—perpetual system)* Army-Navy Surplus began March with 70 tents that cost $20 each. During the month, Army-Navy made the following purchases at cost:

March 4	100 tents @ $22 = $2,200
19	160 tents @ 24 = 3,840
25	40 tents @ 25 = 1,000

Army-Navy Surplus sold 320 tents, and at March 31 the ending inventory consists of 50 tents. The sale price of each tent was $45.

I Required

1. Determine the cost of goods sold and ending inventory amounts for March under (1) average cost, (2) FIFO cost, and (3) LIFO cost. Round average cost per unit to 4 decimal places, and round all other amounts to the nearest dollar. (p. 312)
2. Explain why cost of goods sold is highest under LIFO. Be specific. (p. 316)
3. Prepare Army-Navy Surplus's income statement for March. Report gross profit. Operating expenses totaled $4,000. Army-Navy uses average costing for inventory. The income tax rate is 40%. (p. 318)

writing assignment ■

P6-51A (*Learning Objective 2: Applying the different inventory costing methods—perpetual system*) The records of Armstrong Aviation include the following accounts for inventory of aviation fuel at December 31 of the current year:

Inventory			
Jan. 1	Balance	700 units @ $7.00	4,900
Mar. 6	Purchase	300 units @ 7.05	2,115
June 22	Purchase	8,400 units @ 7.50	63,000
Oct. 4	Purchase	500 units @ 8.50	4,250

Sales Revenue			
	Dec. 31	9,000 units	127,800

❚ Required

1. Prepare a partial income statement through gross profit under the average, FIFO, and LIFO methods. Round average cost per unit to 4 decimal places and all other amounts to the nearest dollar. (p. 318)
2. Which inventory method would you use to minimize income tax? Explain why this method causes income tax to be the lowest. (p. 318)

writing assignment ■

P6-52A (*Learning Objective 2: Applying the lower-of-cost-or-market rule to inventories—perpetual system*) AMC Trade Mart has recently had lackluster sales. The rate of inventory turnover has dropped, and the merchandise is gathering dust. At the same time, competition has forced AMC's suppliers to lower the prices that AMC will pay when it replaces its inventory. It is now December 31, 20X6, and the current replacement cost of AMC's ending inventory is $80,000 below what AMC actually paid for the goods, which was $190,000. Before any adjustments at the end of the period, the Cost of Goods Sold account has a balance of $780,000.

What accounting action should AMC take in this situation? Give any journal entry required. At what amount should AMC report Inventory on the balance sheet? At what amount should the company report Cost of Goods Sold on the income statement? Discuss the accounting principle or concept that is most relevant to this situation. (p. 322)

P6-53A (*Learning Objective 3: Using gross profit percentage and inventory turnover to evaluate two companies*) **Krispy Kreme Doughnuts** and **Starbucks** are both specialty food chains. The 2 companies reported these figures, in millions:

Krispy Kreme Doughnuts, Inc.
Statement of Operations (Adapted)

	Fiscal Year	
	2006	2005
Revenues:		
Net sales	$543	$708
Costs and Expenses:		
Cost of goods sold	475	598
General and administrative expenses	68	55

Krispy Kreme Doughnuts, Inc.
Balance Sheet (Adapted)

	January 31,	
	2006	2005
Assets		
Current assets:		
Cash and cash equivalents	$17	$28
Receivables	27	30
Inventories	24	29

Starbucks Corporation
Statement of Earnings (Adapted)

	Fiscal Year	
	2006	2005
Net sales	$7,787	$6,369
Cost of goods sold	3,179	2,605
Sellings, general and administrative expenses	2,948	2,363

Starbucks Corporation
Balance Sheet (Adapted)

	Year End	
	2006	2005
Assets		
Current assets:		
Cash and temporary investments	$313	$174
Receivables, net	224	191
Inventories	636	546

(continued)

▌Required

1. Compute the gross profit percentage and the rate of inventory turnover for Krispy Kreme and for Starbucks for 2006. (pp. 323–325)
2. Based on these statistics, which company looks more profitable? Why? What other expense category should we consider in evaluating these 2 companies? (Challenge)

■ **spreadsheet**

P6-54A (*Learning Objective 4: Estimating inventory by the gross profit method; preparing the income statement*) Assume **Amazon.com** lost some video inventory in a fire. To file an insurance claim, Amazon must estimate its inventory by the gross profit method. Assume that for the past 2 years, Amazon's gross profit has averaged 40% of net sales. Suppose Amazon's inventory records reveal the following data:

Inventory, July 1	$ 360,000
Transactions during July:	
Purchases	2,780,000
Purchase discounts	20,000
Purchase returns..................	40,000
Sales revenue.......................	4,430,000
Sales returns........................	750,000

▌Required

1. Estimate the cost of the lost inventory, using the gross profit method.(pp. 326–327)
2. Prepare the July income statement for this product through gross profit. Show the detailed computation of cost of goods sold in a separate schedule. (p. 328)

P6-55A (*Learning Objective 1: Determining the amount of inventory to purchase*) Here are condensed versions of Pontiac Convenience Store's most recent income statement and balance sheet. Because the business is organized as a proprietorship, it pays no corporate income tax.

Pontiac Convenience Store
Income Statement
Year Ended December 31, 20X2

Sales	$900,000
Cost of sales	700,000
Gross profit	200,000
Operating expenses.............	80,000
Net income	$120,000

Pontiac Convenience Store
Balance Sheet
December 31, 20X2

Assets		Liabilities and Capital	
Cash	$ 70,000	Accounts payable	$ 35,000
Inventories	35,000	Note payable.................	280,000
Land and		Total liabilities	315,000
buildings, net	360,000	Owner, capital..............	150,000
		Total liabilities	
Total assets....................	$465,000	and capital	$465,000

The owner is budgeting for 20X3. She expects sales and cost of goods sold to increase by 8%. To meet customer demand for the increase in sales, ending inventory will need to be $50,000 at December 31, 20X3. The owner hopes to earn a net income of $160,000 next year.

I *Required*

1. One of the most important decisions a manager makes is the amount of inventory to purchase. Compute the amount of inventory to purchase in 20X3. (p. 326)
2. Prepare the store's budgeted income statement for 20X3 to reach the target net income of $160,000. To reach this goal, operating expenses must decrease by $24,000. (Challenge)

P6-56A (*Learning Objective 5: Correcting inventory errors over a 3-year period*) Columbia Video Sales reported these data (adapted, in millions). The shareholders are very happy with Columbia's steady increase in net income.

	20X6		20X5		20X4	
Net sales revenue..............................		$36		$33		$30
Cost of goods sold:						
Beginning inventory...................	$ 6		$ 5		$ 4	
Purchases	26		24		22	
Goods available	32		29		26	
Less: Ending inventory...............	(7)		(6)		(5)	
Cost of goods sold		25		23		21
Gross profit......................................		11		10		9
Total operating expenses		8		8		8
Net income.......................................		$ 3		$ 2		$ 1

Auditors discovered that the ending inventory for 20X4 was understated by $1 million and that the ending inventory for 20X5 was also understated by $1 million. The ending inventory for 20X6 was correct.

I *Required*

1. Show corrected income statements for each of the 3 years. (p. 328)
2. How much did these assumed corrections add to or take away from Columbia's total net income over the 3-year period? How did the corrections affect the trend of net income? (p. 328)
3. Will Columbia's shareholders still be happy with the company's trend of net income? Give the reason for your answer. (Challenge)

(Group B)

P6-57B (*Learning Objective 1, 2: Accounting for inventory in a perpetual system*) Italian Leather Goods began 20X6 with an inventory of 50,000 units that cost $1,500,000. During the year the store purchased merchandise on account as follows:

■ **general ledger**

March (40,000 units @ cost of $32).....................	$1,280,000
August (40,000 units @ cost of $34)	1,360,000
October (180,000 units @ cost of $35)	6,300,000
Total purchases...	$8,940,000

Cash payments on account totaled $8,610,000.

(continued)

During 20X6, the company sold 260,000 units of merchandise for $12,900,000, of which $4,700,000 was for cash and the balance was on account. Italian Leather Goods uses the LIFO method for inventories.

Operating expenses for the year were $2,080,000. Italian Leather Goods paid 60% in cash and accrued the rest as accrued liabilities. The company accrued income tax at the rate of 40%.

❚ Required

1. Make summary journal entries to record the Italian Leather Goods transactions for the year ended December 31, 20X6. The company uses a perpetual inventory system. (p. 312)
2. Prepare a T-account to show the activity in the Inventory account. (pp. 314–315)
3. Prepare the Italian Leather Goods income statement for the year ended December 31, 20X6. Show totals for gross profit, income before tax, and net income. (pp. 316–318)

P6-58B (*Learning Objective 2: Measuring cost of goods sold and ending inventory—perpetual system*) Whitewater Sports began July with 50 backpacks that cost $19 each. The sale price of each backpack was $36. During July, Whitewater completed these inventory transactions:

		Units	Unit Cost	Unit Sale Price
July 2	Purchase	12	$20	
8	Sale	37	19	$36
13	Sale	13	19	36
	Sale	4	20	37
17	Purchase	24	20	
22	Sale	15	20	37

❚ Required

1. The preceding data are taken from Whitewater's perpetual inventory records. Which cost method does Whitewater use? How can you tell? (pp. 314–318)
2. Determine Whitewater's cost of goods sold for July. Also compute gross profit for July. (pp. 314–318)
3. What is the cost of Whitewater's July 31 inventory of backpacks? (pp. 314–318)

P6-59B (*Learning Objective 2: Computing inventory by 3 methods—perpetual system*) Spice, Inc., began October with 100 shirts that cost $76 each. During October, the store made the following purchases at cost:

Oct. 3	200 @ $81 =	$16,200
12	90 @ 82 =	7,380
24	240 @ 85 =	20,400

Spice sold 500 shirts and ended October with 130 shirts. The sale price of each shirt was $130.

❚ *Required*

1. Determine the cost of goods sold and ending inventory amounts by the average, FIFO, and LIFO cost methods. Round average cost per unit to 3 decimal places, and round all other amounts to the nearest dollar. (pp. 314–318)
2. Explain why cost of goods sold is highest under LIFO. Be specific. (p. 318)
3. Prepare Spice's income statement for October. Report gross profit. Operating expenses totaled $10,000. Spice uses the LIFO method for inventory. The income tax rate is 40%. (pp. 316, 323)

P6-60B (*Learning Objective 2: Applying the different inventory costing methods— perpetual system*) The records of Sonic Sound Systems include the following for cases of compact discs at December 31 of the current year:

writing assignment ■

		Inventory		
Jan. 1	Balance ⎰300 cases @ $300	121,500		
	⎱100 cases @ 315			
May 19	Purchase 600 cases @ 335	201,000		
Aug. 12	Purchase 400 cases @ 350	140,000		
Oct. 4	Purchase 700 cases @ 370	259,000		

		Sales Revenue		
	Dec. 31	1,800 cases		910,000

❚ *Required*

1. Prepare a partial income statement through gross profit under the average, FIFO, and LIFO cost methods. Round average cost per unit to 4 decimal places and all other amounts to the nearest dollar. (p. 316)
2. Which inventory method would you use to report the highest net income? Explain why this method produces the highest reported income. (p. 316)

P6-61B (*Learning Objective 2: Applying the lower-of-cost-or-market rule to inventories— perpetual system*) Westside Copiers has recently been plagued with lackluster sales. The rate of inventory turnover has dropped, and some of the company's merchandise is gathering dust. At the same time, competition has forced some of Westside's suppliers to lower the prices that Westside will pay when it replaces its inventory. It is now December 31, 20X7. The current replacement cost of Westside's ending inventory is $6,800,000, which is far less than Westside paid for the goods, $8,900,000. Before any adjustments at the end of the period, Westside's Cost of Goods Sold account has a balance of $36,400,000.

writing assignment ■

What accounting action should Westside Copiers take in this situation? Give any journal entry required. At what amount should Westside report Inventory on the balance sheet? At what amount should Westside report Cost of Goods Sold on the income statement? Discuss the accounting principle or concept that is most relevant to this situation. (p. 322)

P6-62B *(Learning Objective 3: Using gross profit percentage and inventory turnover to evaluate two leading companies)* **Hewlett Packard** and **Apple Computer** are competitors. The companies reported these amounts, in billions:

Hewlett-Packard Company
Statement of Earnings (Adapted)

	Fiscal Years	
	2006	2005
Net sales	$73.6	$68.9
Cost of sales	55.2	52.6
Selling, general, and administrative expenses	11.3	11.2

Hewlett-Packard Company
Balance Sheet (Adapted)

	Year End	
	2006	2005
Assets		
Cash and cash equivalents	$16.4	$13.9
Accounts receivable	10.9	9.9
Inventories	7.8	6.9

Apple Computer, Inc.
Statement of Operations (Adapted)

	Fiscal Years	
	2006	2005
Net sales	$19.3	$13.9
Cost of sales	13.7	9.9
Selling, general, and administrative expenses	2.4	1.9

Apple Computer, Inc.
Balance Sheet (Adapted)

	Year End	
	2006	2005
Assets		
Cash and cash equivalents	$6.4	$3.5
Accounts receivable	1.3	0.9
Inventories	0.3	0.2

❙ Required

1. Compute both companies' gross profit percentage and their rate of inventory turnover during 2006. (pp. 323–325)

2. Can you tell from these statistics which company should be more profitable in percentage terms? Why? What other important category of expenses do the gross profit percentage and the inventory turnover ratio fail to consider? (Challenge)

P6-63B (*Learning Objective 4: Estimating inventory by the gross profit method; preparing the income statement*) Assume **FedEx Kinko's,** the copy center, lost some inventory in a fire. To file an insurance claim, FedEx Kinko's must estimate its ending inventory by the gross profit method. Assume for the past 2 years, FedEx Kinko's gross profit has averaged 40% of net sales. Suppose the company's inventory records reveal the following data at June 15, date of the fire.

■ **spreadsheet**

Inventory, January 1	$1,200,000
Transactions during the year:	
Purchases	6,500,000
Purchase discounts	100,000
Purchase returns...................	10,000
Sales revenue	8,600,000
Sales returns........................	20,000

❙ Required

1. Estimate the cost of the ending inventory lost in the fire using the gross profit method. (pp. 326–327)

2. Prepare FedEx Kinko's income statement through gross profit for the period up to the date of the fire. Date the statement "For the Period Up to the Fire." Show the detailed computations of cost of goods sold in a separate schedule. (p. 328)

P6-64B (*Learning Objective 1: Determining the amount of inventory to purchase*) A Pay Less convenience store's income statement and balance sheet reported the following. The business is organized as a proprietorship, so it pays no corporate income tax.

The owner is budgeting for 20X6. He expects sales and cost of goods sold to increase by 10%. To meet customer demand, ending inventory will need to be $80,000 at December 31, 20X6. The owner can lower operating expenses by $6,000 by doing some of the work himself. He hopes to earn a net income of $160,000 next year.

Pay Less Store
Income Statement
Year Ended December 31, 20X5

Sales	$960,000
Cost of goods sold	720,000
Gross profit	240,000
Operating expenses.............	110,000
Net income	$130,000

Pay Less Store
Balance Sheet
December 31, 20X5

Assets		Liabilities and Capital	
Cash	$ 40,000	Accounts payable	$ 30,000
Inventories	70,000	Note payable................	190,000
Land and		Total liabilities	220,000
buildings, net	270,000	Owner, capital...............	160,000
		Total liabilities	
Total assets....................	$380,000	and capital	$380,000

(continued)

❙ *Required*

1. One of the most important decisions a business owner makes is the amount of inventory to purchase. Compute the amount of inventory to purchase in 20X6. (p. 326)
2. Prepare the store's budgeted income statement for 20X6 to reach the target net income of $160,000. To reach this goal, Pay Less must decrease operating expenses by $6,000. (Challenge)

P6-65B (*Learning Objective 5: Correcting inventory errors over a 3-year period*) The accounting records of Oriental Rugs show these data (in thousands):

Auditors discovered that the ending inventory for 2005 was overstated by $100 thousand and that the ending inventory for 2006 was understated by $50 thousand. The ending inventory at December 31, 2007, was correct.

Oriental Rugs

(Amounts in thousands)	2007		2006		2005	
Net sales revenue.................		$1,400		$1,200		$1,100
Cost of goods sold:						
Beginning inventory........	$ 400		$ 300		$ 200	
Purchases	800		700		600	
Goods available	1,200		1,000		800	
Less ending inventory......	(500)		(400)		(300)	
Cost of goods sold		700		600		500
Gross profit.........................		700		600		600
Total operating expenses		500		430		450
Net income.........................		$ 200		$ 170		$ 150

❙ *Required*

1. Show correct income statements for each of the 3 years.
2. How much did these corrections add to, or take away from, Oriental Rugs' total net income over the 3-year period? How did the corrections affect the trend of net income? (p. 328)

APPLY YOUR KNOWLEDGE

Decision Cases

writing assignment ■

Case 1. (*Learning Objective 1, 2: Assessing the impact of a year-end purchase of inventory*) Duracraft Corporation is nearing the end of its first year of operations. Duracraft made inventory purchases of $745,000 during the year, as follows:

January	1,000 units @	$100.00 =	$100,000
July	4,000	121.25	485,000
November	1,000	160.00	160,000
Totals	6,000		$745,000

Sales for the year are 5,000 units for $1,200,000 of revenue. Expenses other than cost of goods sold and income taxes total $200,000. The president of the company is undecided about whether to adopt the FIFO method or the LIFO method for inventories. The income tax rate is 40%.

❚ Required

1. To aid company decision making, prepare income statements under FIFO and under LIFO. (pp. 306, 320)
2. Compare the net income under FIFO with net income under LIFO. Which method produces the higher net income? What causes this difference? Be specific. (pp. 318, 319)

Case 2. (*Learning Objective 2: Assessing the impact of the inventory costing method on the financial statements*) The inventory costing method a company chooses can affect the financial statements and thus the decisions of the people who use those statements.

writing assignment ■

❚ Required

1. Company A uses the LIFO inventory method and discloses its use of the LIFO method in notes to the financial statements. Company B uses the FIFO method to account for its inventory. Company B does *not* disclose which inventory method it uses. Company B reports a higher net income than Company A. In which company would you prefer to invest? Give your reason. (p. 321)
2. Conservatism is an accepted accounting concept. Would you want management to be conservative in accounting for inventory if you were a shareholder or a creditor of a company? Give your reason. (p. 321)

Ethical Issue

During 20X8, Vanguard, Inc., changed to the LIFO method of accounting for inventory. Suppose that during 20X9, Vanguard changes back to the FIFO method and the following year Vanguard switches back to LIFO again.

❚ Required

1. What would you think of a company's ethics if it changed accounting methods every year?
2. What accounting principle would changing methods every year violate?
3. Who can be harmed when a company changes its accounting methods too often? How?

Focus on Financials: ■ YUM! Brands

(*Learning Objective 2, 3: Analyzing inventories*) The notes are part of the financial statements. They give details that would clutter the statements. This case will help you learn to use a company's inventory notes. Refer to **YUM! Brands'** statements and related notes in Appendix A at the end of the book and answer the following questions:

1. How much was YUM's merchandise inventory at December 30, 2006? At December 30, 2005? (p. 306)
2. How does YUM *value* its inventories? Which *cost* method does the company use? (p. 313)
3. How much were Yum's purchases of food and paper inventory during the year ended December 30, 2006? (p. 326)
4. Did YUM's gross profit percentage on company sales improve or deteriorate in 2006 compared to 2005? (p. 323)
5. Would you rate YUM's rate of inventory turnover as fast or slow in comparison to most other companies? Explain your answer. (pp. 324–325)

Focus on Analysis: ■ Pier 1 Imports

(*Learning Objective 1, 2, 3: Measuring critical inventory amounts*) Refer to the **Pier 1 Imports** financial statements in Appendix B at the end of this book. Show amounts in millions and round to the nearest $1 million.

1. Three important pieces of inventory information are (a) the cost of inventory on hand, (b) the cost of goods sold, and (c) the cost of inventory purchases. Identify or compute each of these items for Pier 1 at the end of 2006. (p. 326)
2. Which item in requirement 1 is most directly related to cash flow? Why? (Challenge)
3. Assume that all inventory purchases were made on account, and that only inventory purchases increased Accounts Payable. Compute Pier 1's cash payments for inventory during 2006. (p. 105)
4. How does Pier 1 *value* its inventories? Which *costing* method does Pier 1 use? (pp. 313–316)
5. Did Pier 1's gross profit percentage and rate of inventory turnover improve or deteriorate in 2006 (versus 2005)? Consider the overall effect of these 2 ratios. Did Pier 1 improve during 2006? How did these factors affect the net loss for 2006? Pier 1's inventories totaled $374 million at the end of 2004. Round decimals to 3 places. (pp. 323–325)

Group Project

(*Learning Objective 3: Comparing companies' inventory turnover ratios*) Obtain the annual reports of 10 companies, 2 from each of 5 different industries. Most companies' financial statements can be downloaded from their Web sites.

writing assignment ■

1. Compute each company's gross profit percentage and rate of inventory turnover for the most recent 2 years. If annual reports are unavailable or do not provide enough data for multiple-year computations, you can gather financial statement data from *Moody's Industrial Manual*.
2. For the industries of the companies you are analyzing, obtain the industry averages for gross profit percentage and inventory turnover from Robert Morris Associates, *Annual Statement Studies*; Dun and Bradstreet, *Industry Norms and Key Business Ratios*; or Leo Troy, *Almanac of Business and Industrial Financial Ratios*.
3. How well does each of your companies compare to the other company in its industry? How well do your companies compare to the average for their industry? What insight about your companies can you glean from these ratios?
4. Write a memo to summarize your findings, stating whether your group would invest in each of the companies it has analyzed.

For Internet Exercises go to the Web site www.prenhall.com/harrison.

Quick Check Answers

1. *c*
2. *e*
3. *a*
4. *a* [(20 × $6) + (30 × $7) = $330]
5. *b* (15 × $6 =$90)
6. *c* 15 × [($120 + $210 + $120) ÷ 65] = $103.85
7. *c*
8. *d*
9. *b*
10. *c* ($104,000 − $44,000 = $60,000)

11. *d* ($10,000 + X − $20,000 = $130,000; X = $140,000)
12. *c* ($20,000 + $80,000 − $5,000 + $6,000 − $24,000 = $77,000)
13. *a* ($160,000 − $77,000)/$160,000 = .519
14. *b* [$77,000 ÷ ($20,000 + $24,000)/2 = 3.5]
15. *d* $60,000 + $180,000 − [$300,000 × (1 − .30)] = $30,000
16. *b*

APPENDIX A TO CHAPTER 6

Accounting for Inventory in the Periodic System

In the periodic inventory system, the business keeps no running record of the merchandise. Instead, at the end of the period, the business counts inventory on hand and applies the unit costs to determine the cost of ending inventory. This inventory figure appears on the balance sheet and is used to compute cost of goods sold.

Recording Transactions in the Periodic System

In the periodic system, throughout the period the Inventory account carries the beginning balance left over from the preceding period. The business records purchases of inventory in the Purchases account (an expense). Then, at the end of the period, the Inventory account must be updated for the financial statements. A journal entry removes the beginning balance by crediting Inventory and debiting Cost of Goods Sold. A second journal entry sets up the ending inventory balance, based on the physical count. The final entry in this sequence transfers the amount of Purchases to Cost of Goods Sold. These end-of-period entries can be made during the closing process.

Exhibit 6A-1 illustrates the accounting in the periodic system. After the process is complete, Inventory has its correct ending balance of $120,000, and Cost of Goods Sold shows $540,000.

| EXHIBIT 6-A1 | Recording and Reporting Inventories—Periodic System (Amounts Assumed) |

PANEL A—Recording Transactions and the T-accounts (All amounts are assumed)

1.	Purchases	560,000	
	Accounts Payable		560,000
	Purchased inventory on account.		
2.	Accounts Receivable	900,000	
	Sales Revenue		900,000
	Sold inventory on account.		
3.	End-of-period entries to update Inventory and record Cost of Goods Sold:		
a.	Cost of Goods Sold	100,000	
	Inventory (beginning balance)		100,000
	Transferred beginning inventory to COGS.		
b.	Inventory (ending balance)	120,000	
	Cost of Goods Sold		120,000
	Set up ending inventory based on physical count.		
c.	Cost of Goods Sold	560,000	
	Purchases		560,000
	Transferred purchases to COGS.		

The T-accounts show the following:

Inventory			Cost of Goods Sold	
100,000*	100,000		100,000	120,000
120,000			560,000	
			540,000	

*Beginning inventory was $100,000

PANEL B—Reporting in the Financial Statements

Income Statement (Partial)			Ending Balance Sheet (Partial)	
Sales revenue		$900,000	Current assets:	
Cost of goods sold:			Cash	$ XXX
Beginning inventory	$ 100,000		Short-term investments	XXX
Purchases	560,000		Accounts receivable	XXX
Goods available	660,000		Inventory	120,000
Ending inventory	(120,000)		Prepaid expenses	XXX
Cost of goods sold		540,000		
Gross profit		$360,000		

Appendix Assignments

Short Exercises

S6A-1 (*Recording inventory transactions in the periodic system*) Parkland Technologies began the year with inventory of $20,000. During the year, Parkland purchased inventory costing $100,000 and sold goods for $140,000, with all transactions on account. Parkland ended the year with inventory of $30,000. Journalize all the necessary transactions under the periodic inventory system.

S6A-2 (*Computing cost of goods sold and preparing the income statement—periodic system*) Use the data in Short Exercise S6A-1 to do the following for Parkland Technologies:

1. Post to the Inventory and Cost of Goods Sold accounts.

2. Compute cost of goods sold by the cost-of-goods-sold model.

3. Prepare the income statement of Parkland Technologies through gross profit.

Exercises

E6A-3 (*Computing amounts for the GAAP inventory methods—periodic system*) Suppose **Intel Corporation's** inventory records for a particular computer chip indicate the following at October 31:

Oct. 1	Beginning inventory	5 units @ $160 =	$ 800
8	Purchase..............................	4 units @ 160 =	640
15	Purchase..............................	11 units @ 170 =	1,870
26	Purchase..............................	5 units @ 180 =	900

The physical count of inventory at October 31 indicates that 8 units of inventory are on hand.

❙ Required
Compute ending inventory and cost of goods sold, using each of the following methods. Round all amounts to the nearest dollar:

1. Specific unit cost, assuming four $160 units and four $170 units are on hand

2. Average cost

3. First-in, first-out

4. Last-in, first-out

E6A-4 (*Journalizing inventory transactions in the periodic system; computing cost of goods sold*) Use the data in Exercise E6A-3 to journalize the following for the periodic system:

1. Total October purchases in 1 summary entry. All purchases were on credit.

2. Total October sales in a summary entry. Assume that the selling price was $300 per unit and that all sales were on credit.

3. October 31 entries for inventory. Intel uses LIFO. Post to the Cost of Goods Sold T-account to show how this amount is determined. Label each item in the account.

4. Show the computation of cost of goods sold by the cost-of-goods-sold model.

Problems

P6A-5 (*Computing cost of goods sold and gross profit on sales—periodic system*) Assume a **Ralph Lauren Polo** outlet store began August 20X4 with 50 units of inventory that cost $40 each. The sale price of these units was $70. During August, the store completed these inventory transactions:

		Units	Unit Cost	Unit Sale Price
Aug. 3	Sale	16	$40	$70
8	Purchase......	80	41	72
11	Sale	34	40	70
19	Sale	9	41	72
24	Sale	35	41	72
30	Purchase......	18	42	73
31	Sale	10	41	72

(*continued*)

I *Required*

1. Determine the store's cost of goods sold for August under the periodic inventory system. Assume the FIFO method.

2. Compute gross profit for August.

P6A-6 (*Recording transactions in the periodic system; reporting inventory items in the financial statements*) Accounting records for Total Desserts, Inc., yield the following data for the year ended December 31, 20X5 (amounts in thousands):

Inventory, December 31, 20X4	$ 370
Purchases of inventory (on account)	2,900
Sales of inventory—80% on account; 20% for cash	4,390
Inventory at the lower of FIFO cost or market, December 31, 20X5	560

I *Required*

1. Journalize Total Desserts' inventory transactions for the year under the periodic system. Show all amounts in thousands. Use Exhibit 6A-1 as a model.

2. Report ending inventory, sales, cost of goods sold, and gross profit on the appropriate financial statement (amounts in thousands). Show the computation of cost of goods sold.

APPENDIX B TO CHAPTER 6

The LIFO Reserve—Converting a LIFO Company's Net Income to the FIFO Basis

Suppose you are a financial analyst, and it is your job to recommend stocks for your clients to purchase as investments. You have narrowed your choice to **Wal-Mart Stores, Inc.**, and **Gap, Inc.** Wal-Mart uses the LIFO method for inventories and the GAP uses FIFO. The 2 companies' net incomes are not comparable because they use different inventory methods. To compare the 2 companies, you need to place them on the same footing.

The Internal Revenue Service allows companies to use LIFO for income tax purposes only if they use LIFO for financial reporting, but companies may also report an alternative inventory amount in the financial statements. Doing so presents a rare opportunity to convert a company's net income from the LIFO basis to what the income would have been if the business had used FIFO. Fortunately, you can convert Wal-Mart's income from the LIFO basis, as reported in the company's financial statements, to the FIFO basis. Then you can compare Wal-Mart and Gap.

Like many other companies that use LIFO, Wal-Mart reports the FIFO cost, a LIFO Reserve, and the LIFO cost of ending inventory. The LIFO Reserve[1] is the difference between the LIFO cost of an inventory and what the cost of that inventory would be under FIFO. Assume that Wal-Mart reported the following amounts:

Wal-Mart Uses LIFO		
	(In millions)	
	20X3	**20X2**
From the Wal-Mart balance sheet:		
Inventories (approximate FIFO cost)...............	$ 25,056	$22,749
Less LIFO reserve..	(165)	(135)
LIFO cost..	24,891	22,614
From the Wal-Mart income statement:		
Cost of goods sold..	$191,838	
Net income..	8,039	
Income tax rate	35%	

Converting Wal-Mart's 20X3 net income to the FIFO basis focuses on the LIFO Reserve because the reserve captures the difference between Wal-Mart's ending inventory costed at LIFO and at FIFO. Observe that during each year, the FIFO cost of ending inventory exceeded the LIFO cost. During 20X3, the LIFO Reserve increased by $30 million ($165 million – $135 million). *The LIFO Reserve can increase only when inventory costs are rising.* Recall that during a period of rising costs, LIFO produces the highest cost of goods sold and the lowest net income. Therefore, for 20X3, Wal-Mart's cost of goods sold would have been lower if the company had used the FIFO method for inventories. Wal-Mart's net income would have been higher, as the following computations show:

---

[1]The LIFO Reserve account is widely used in practice even though the term *reserve* is poor terminology.

If Wal-Mart Had Used FIFO in 20X3	
	(In millions)
Cost of goods sold, as reported under LIFO..	$191,838
− Increase in LIFO Reserve ($165 − $135)	(30)
= Cost of goods sold, if Wal-Mart had used FIFO.......................................	$191,808
Lower cost of goods sold → Higher pretax income by................................	$ 30
Minus income taxes (35%)	11
Higher net income under FIFO........................	19
Net income as reported under LIFO...............	8,039
Net income Wal-Mart would have reported for 20X3 if using FIFO	$ 8,058

Now you can compare Wal-Mart's net income with that of Gap, Inc. All the ratios used for the analysis—current ratio, inventory turnover, and so on—can be compared between the 2 companies as though they both used the FIFO inventory method.

The LIFO Reserve provides another opportunity for managers and investors to answer a key question about a company.

How much income tax has the company saved over its lifetime by using the LIFO method to account for inventory?

Using Wal-Mart as an example, the computation at the end of 20X3 is (amounts in millions):

Income tax saved by using LIFO = LIFO Reserve × Income tax rate
$58   = $165   ×   .35

With these price changes, by the end of 20X3 Wal-Mart has saved a total of $58 million by using the LIFO method to account for its merchandise inventory. Had Wal-Mart used the FIFO method, Wal-Mart would have almost $58 million less cash to invest in the opening of new stores.

In recent years many companies have experienced decreases in the cost of their inventories. When prices decline, cost of goods sold under FIFO is greater (LIFO cost of goods sold is less). This makes gross profit and net income less under FIFO.

7 Plant Assets & Intangibles

SPOTLIGHT

FEDEX CORPORATION

If you need a document delivered across the country overnight, FedEx can handle it. FedEx Corporation sets the standard for quick delivery. As you can see from the company's balance sheet, FedEx moves packages using aircraft, package-handling equipment, computers, and vehicles. These are FedEx's most important assets (lines 9–13).

This chapter covers long-term plant assets to complete our coverage of assets, except for investments in Chapter 10. Let's begin by examining the various types of long-term assets.

FedEx Corporation
Consolidated Balance Sheets (Partial, Adapted)

(In millions)	May 31, 2006	May 31, 2005
1 ASSETS		
2 CURRENT ASSETS		
3 Cash and cash equivalents......................................	$ 1,937	$ 1,039
4 Receivables, less allowances of $144 and $125	3,516	3,297
5 Spare parts, supplies and fuel	308	250
6 Prepaid expenses and other	703	683
7 Total current assets...	6,464	5,269
8 PROPERTY AND EQUIPMENT, AT COST		
9 Aircraft	8,611	7,610
10 Package handling and ground support equipment....	3,558	3,366
11 Computer and electronic equipment..................	4,331	3,893
12 Vehicles..	2,203	1,994
13 Facilities and other...	5,371	5,154
14 Total cost...	24,074	22,017
15 Less: Accumulated depreciation	(13,304)	(12,374)
16 Net property and equipment...........................	10,770	9,643
17 OTHER LONG-TERM ASSETS		
18 Goodwill..	2,825	2,835
19 Prepaid pension cost...	1,349	1,272
20 Intangible and other assets	1,282	1,385
21 Total other long-term assets...........................	5,456	5,492
22 TOTAL ASSETS	$ 22,690	$ 20,404

LEARNING OBJECTIVES

1 **Determine** the cost of a plant asset

2 **Account** for depreciation

3 **Select** the best depreciation method

4 **Analyze** the effect of a plant asset disposal

5 **Account** for natural resources and depletion

6 **Account** for intangible assets and amortization

7 **Report** plant asset transactions on the statement of cash flows

TYPES OF ASSETS

Businesses use several types of long-lived assets, as shown in Exhibit 7-1. We also show the expense that applies to each asset. For example, buildings, airplanes, and equipment depreciate. Natural resources deplete, and intangible assets are amortized.

- **Plant assets**, or *fixed assets*, are long-lived assets that are tangible—for instance, land, buildings, and equipment. The expense associated with plant assets is called *depreciation*. Of the plant assets, land is unique. Land is not expensed over time because its usefulness does not decrease. Most companies report plant assets as Property, plant, and equipment on the balance sheet. **FedEx** uses the heading Property and Equipment (lines 8–16).
- **Intangible assets** are useful because of the special rights they carry. They have no physical form. Patents, copyrights, and trademarks are intangible assets; so is goodwill. Accounting for intangibles is similar to accounting for plant assets. FedEx reports Goodwill and Intangible Assets on its balance sheet (lines 18 and 20). Prepaid pension cost (line 19) is a type of long-term prepaid expense that's covered in later courses.

Accounting for plant assets and intangibles has its own terminology. Different names apply to the individual plant assets and their corresponding expenses, as shown in Exhibit 7-1.

EXHIBIT 7-1 **Plant Assets Terminology**

Asset Account (Balance Sheet)	Related Expense Account (Income Statement)
Plant Assets	
Land	None
Buildings, Machinery and Equipment	Depreciation
Furniture and Fixtures	Depreciation
Land Improvements	Depreciation
Natural Resources	Depletion
Intangibles	Amortization

Unless stated otherwise, we describe accounting that follows generally accepted accounting principles for the financial statements. Later, we cover depreciation for income-tax purposes. Before examining the various types of plant assets, let's see how to value them.

Measuring the Cost of a Plant Asset

Here is a basic working rule for determining the cost of an asset:

The cost of any asset is the sum of all the costs incurred to bring the asset to its intended use. The cost of a plant asset includes purchase price, plus any taxes, commissions, and other amounts paid to make the asset ready for use. Because the specific costs differ for the various types of plant assets, we discuss the major groups individually.

OBJECTIVE

1 **Determine** the cost of a plant asset

Land

The cost of land includes its purchase price (cash plus any note payable given), brokerage commission, survey fees, legal fees, and any back property taxes that the purchaser pays. Land cost also includes expenditures for grading and clearing the land and for removing unwanted buildings.

The cost of land does *not* include the cost of fencing, paving, security systems, and lighting. These are separate plant assets—called *land improvements*—and they are subject to depreciation.

Suppose FedEx signs a $300,000 note payable to purchase 20 acres of land for a new shipping site. FedEx also pays $10,000 for real estate commission, $8,000 of back property tax, $5,000 for removal of an old building, a $1,000 survey fee, and $260,000 to pave the parking lot—all in cash. What is FedEx's cost of this land?

Purchase price of land......................		$300,000
Add related costs:		
Real estate commission	$10,000	
Back property tax.........................	8,000	
Removal of building....................	5,000	
Survey fee....................................	1,000	
Total related costs.......................		24,000
Total cost of land...........................		$324,000

Note that the cost to pave the parking lot, $260,000, is *not* included in the land's cost, because the pavement is a land improvement. FedEx would record the purchase of this land as follows:

Land	324,000	
Note Payable		300,000
Cash		24,000

Assets	=	Liabilities	+	Stockholders' Equity
+ 324,000 − 24,000	=	+ 300,000	+	0

This purchase of land increases both assets and liabilities. There is no effect on equity[1].

Buildings, Machinery, and Equipment

The cost of constructing a building includes architectural fees, building permits, contractors' charges, and payments for material, labor, and overhead. If the company constructs its own building, the cost will also include the cost of interest on money borrowed to finance the construction.

When an existing building (new or old) is purchased, its cost includes the purchase price, brokerage commission, sales and other taxes paid, and all expenditures to repair and renovate the building for its intended purpose.

The cost of FedEx's is package-handling equipment includes its purchase price (less any discounts), plus transportation from the seller to FedEx, insurance while in transit, sales and other taxes, purchase commission, installation costs, and any expenditures to test the asset before it's placed in service. The equipment cost will also include the cost of any special platforms. Then after the asset is up and running, insurance, taxes, and maintenance costs are recorded as expenses, not as part of the asset's cost.

---

[1]We show the accounting equation along with each journal entry—where the accounting equation aids your understanding of the transaction.

Land Improvements and Leasehold Improvements

For a FedEx shipping terminal, the cost to pave a parking lot ($260,000) would be recorded in a separate account entitled Land Improvements. This account includes costs for such other items as driveways, signs, fences, and sprinkler systems. Although these assets are located on the land, they are subject to decay, and their cost should therefore be depreciated.

FedEx may lease some of its airplanes and other assets. The company customizes these assets for its special needs. For example, FedEx paints its red, white, and blue logo on delivery trucks. These improvements are assets of FedEx even though the company may not own the truck. The cost of leasehold improvements should be depreciated over the term of the lease. Most companies call the depreciation on lease-hold improvements *amortization*, which is the same concept as *depreciation*.

Lump-Sum (or Basket) Purchases of Assets

Businesses often purchase several assets as a group, or a "basket," for a single lump-sum amount. For example, FedEx may pay one price for land and a building. The company must identify the cost of each asset. The total cost is divided among the assets according to their relative sales (or market) values. This technique is called the *relative-sales-value method*.

Suppose FedEx purchases land and a building in Denver. The building sits on 2 acres of land, and the combined purchase price of land and building is $2,800,000. An appraisal indicates that the land's market value is $300,000 and that the building's market value is $2,700,000.

FedEx first figures the ratio of each asset's market value to the total market value. Total appraised value is $2,700,000 + $300,000 = $3,000,000. Thus, the land, valued at $300,000, is 10% of the total market value. The building's appraised value is 90% of the total. These percentages are then used to determine the cost of each asset, as follows:

Asset	Market (Sales) Value		Total Market Value		Percentage of Total Market Value		Total Cost	Cost of Each Asset
Land	$ 300,000	÷	$3,000,000	=	10%	×	$2,800,000	$ 280,000
Building	2,700,000	÷	3,000,000	=	90%	×	$2,800,000	2,520,000
Total	$3,000,000				100%			$2,800,000

If FedEx pays cash, the entry to record the purchase of the land and building is

	Land	280,000	
	Building	2,520,000	
	Cash		2,800,000

Assets	=	Liabilities	+	Stockholders' Equity
+ 280,000	=			
+ 2,520,000	=	0	+	0
− 2,800,000	=			

Total assets don't change—merely the makeup of FedEx's assets.

STOP & think. . .

How would FedEx divide a $120,000 lump-sum purchase price for land, building, and equipment with estimated market values of $40,000, $95,000, and $15,000, respectively?

Answer:

	Estimated Market Value	Percentage of Total Market Value	×	Total Cost	=	Cost of Each Asset
Land..................	$ 40,000	26.7%*	×	$120,000	=	$ 32,040
Building,.............	95,000	63.3%	×	$120,000	=	75,960
Equipment.........	15,000	10.0%	×	$120,000	=	12,000
Total................	$150,000	100.0%				$120,000

*$40,000/$150,000 units = 0.267, and so on

Capital Expenditure vs. Immediate Expense

When a company spends money on a plant asset, it must decide whether to record an asset or an expense. Examples of these expenditures range from FedEx's purchase of an airplane to replacing the tires on a FedEx truck.

Expenditures that increase the asset's capacity or extend its useful life are called **capital expenditures**. For example, the cost of a major overhaul that extends the useful life of a FedEx truck is a capital expenditure. Capital expenditures are said to be *capitalized, which means the cost is added to an asset account* and not expensed immediately. A major decision in accounting for plant assets is whether to capitalize or to expense a certain cost.

Costs that do not extend the asset's capacity or its useful life, but merely maintain the asset or restore it to working order, are recorded as expenses. For example, Repair Expense is reported on the income statement and matched against revenue. The costs of repainting a FedEx delivery truck, repairing a dented fender, and replacing tires are also expensed immediately. Exhibit 7-2 shows the distinction between capital expenditures and immediate expenses for delivery truck expenditures.

EXHIBIT 7-2 Capital Expenditure or Immediate Expense for Costs Associated with a Delivery Truck

Record an Asset for Capital Expenditures	Record Repair and Maintenance Expense (Not an Asset) for an Expense
Extraordinary repairs:	**Ordinary repairs:**
Major engine overhaul	Repair of transmission or other mechanism
Modification of body for new use of truck	Oil change, lubrication, and so on
Addition to storage capacity of truck	Replacement of tires and windshield, or a paint job

The distinction between a capital expenditure and an expense requires judgment: Does the cost extend the asset's usefulness or its useful life? If so, record an asset. If the cost merely repairs the asset or returns it to its prior condition, then record an expense.

Most companies expense all small costs, say, below $1,000. For higher costs, they follow the rule we gave above: capitalize costs that extend the asset's usefulness or its useful life, and expense all other costs. A conservative policy is one that avoids overstating assets and profits. A company that overstates its assets may get into trouble and have to defend itself in court. Whenever investors lose money because a company overstated its profits or its assets, the investors file a lawsuit. The courts tend to be sympathetic to investor losses caused by shoddy accounting.

Accounting errors sometimes occur for plant asset costs. For example, a company may

- expense a cost that should have been capitalized. This error overstates expenses and understates net income in the year of the error.
- capitalize a cost that should have been expensed. This error understates expenses and overstates net income in the year of the error.

MEASURING DEPRECIATION ON PLANT ASSETS

As we've seen in previous chapters, plant assets are reported on the balance sheet at book value, which is

Book Value of a Plant Asset = Cost − Accumulated Depreciation

Plant assets wear out, grow obsolete, and lose value over time. To account for this process we allocate a plant asset's cost to expense over its life—a process called *depreciation*. The depreciation process matches the asset's expense against revenue to measure income, as the matching principle directs. Exhibit 7-3 illustrates the accounting for a Boeing 737 jet by FedEx.

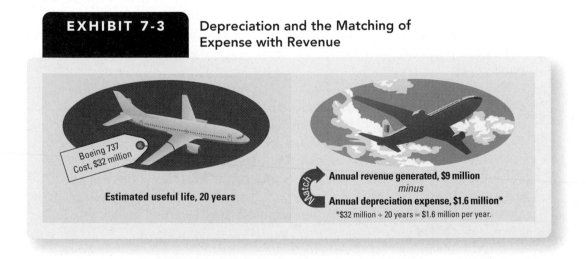

EXHIBIT 7-3 Depreciation and the Matching of Expense with Revenue

Boeing 737
Cost, $32 million

Estimated useful life, 20 years

Match

Annual revenue generated, $9 million
minus
Annual depreciation expense, $1.6 million*
*$32 million ÷ 20 years = $1.6 million per year.

Recall that depreciation expense (not accumulated depreciation) is reported on the income statement.

Only land has an unlimited life and is not depreciated for accounting purposes. For most plant assets, depreciation is caused by:

- *Physical wear and tear.* For example, physical deterioration takes its toll on the usefulness of FedEx airplanes, equipment, delivery trucks, and buildings.
- *Obsolescence.* Computers and other electronic equipment may become *obsolete* before they deteriorate. An asset is obsolete when another asset can do the job more efficiently. An asset's useful life may be shorter than its physical life. FedEx and other companies depreciate their computers over a short period of time— perhaps 4 years—even though the computers will remain in working condition much longer.

Suppose FedEx buys a computer for use in tracking packages. FedEx believes it will get 4 years of service from the computer, which will then be worthless. Under straight-line depreciation, FedEx expenses one-quarter of the asset's cost in each of its 4 years of use.

You've just seen what depreciation is. Let's see what depreciation is *not*.

1. *Depreciation is not a process of valuation.* Businesses do *not* record depreciation based on changes in the market value of their plant assets. Instead, businesses allocate the asset's *cost* to the period of its useful life.

2. *Depreciation does not mean setting aside cash to replace assets as they wear out.* Any cash fund is entirely separate from depreciation.

How to Measure Depreciation

To measure depreciation for a plant asset, we must know 3 things about the asset:

    1. Cost   **2.** Estimated useful life   **3.** Estimated residual value

We have discussed cost, which is a known amount. The other 2 factors must be estimated.

Estimated useful life is the length of service expected from using the asset. Useful life may be expressed in years, units of output, miles, or some other measure. For example, the useful life of a building is stated in years. The useful life of a FedEx airplane or delivery truck may be expressed as the number of miles the vehicle is expected to travel. Companies base estimates on their experience and trade publications.

Estimated residual value—also called *scrap value* or *salvage value*—is the expected cash value of an asset at the end of its useful life. For example, FedEx may believe that a package-handling machine will be useful for 7 years. After that time, FedEx may expect to sell the machine as scrap metal. The amount FedEx believes it can get for the machine is the estimated residual value. In computing depreciation, the estimated residual value is *not* depreciated because FedEx expects to receive this amount from selling the asset. If there's no expected residual value, the full cost of the asset is depreciated. A plant asset's **depreciable cost** is measured as follows:

> Depreciable Cost = Asset's cost – Estimated residual value

Depreciation Methods

There are 3 main depreciation methods:

- Straight-line
- Units-of-production
- Double-declining-balance—an accelerated depreciation method

These methods allocate different amounts of depreciation to each period. However, they all result in the same total amount of depreciation, which is the asset's depreciable cost. Exhibit 7-4 presents the data we use to illustrate depreciation computations for a FedEx truck.

EXHIBIT 7-4 Data for Depreciation Computations—A FedEx Truck

Data Item	Amount
Cost of truck	$41,000
Less: Estimated residual value	(1,000)
Depreciable cost	$40,000
Estimated useful life:	
Years	5 years
Units of production	100,000 units [miles]

Straight-Line Method. In the **straight-line (SL) method**, an equal amount of depreciation is assigned to each year (or period) of asset use. Depreciable cost is divided by useful life in years to determine the annual depreciation expense. Applied to the FedEx truck data from Exhibit 7-4, SL depreciation is

$$\text{Straight-line depreciation per year} = \frac{\text{Cost} - \text{Residual value}}{\text{Useful life, in years}}$$

$$= \frac{\$41,000 - \$1,000}{5}$$

$$= \$8,000$$

The entry to record depreciation is

Depreciation Expense		8,000	
Accumulated Depreciation			8,000

Assets	=	Liabilities	+	Stockholders' Equity	−	Expenses
− 8,000	=	0				− 8,000

Observe that depreciation decreases the asset (through Accumulated Depreciation) and also decreases equity (through Depreciation Expense). Let's assume that FedEx purchased this truck on January 1, 20X3. Assume that FedEx's accounting year ends on December 31. Exhibit 7-5 gives a *straight-line depreciation schedule* for the truck.

The final column of the exhibit shows the *asset's book value*, which is cost less accumulated depreciation.

EXHIBIT 7-5	Straight-Line Depreciation for a FedEx Truck

Date	Asset Cost	Depreciation for the Year			Accumulated Depreciation	Asset Book Value
		Depreciation Rate	Depreciable Cost	Depreciation Expense		
1- 1-20X3	$41,000					$41,000
12-31-20X3		0.20* ×	$40,000 =	$8,000	$ 8,000	33,000
12-31-20X4		0.20 ×	40,000 =	8,000	16,000	25,000
12-31-20X5		0.20 ×	40,000 =	8,000	24,000	17,000
12-31-20X6		0.20 ×	40,000 =	8,000	32,000	9,000
12-31-20X7		0.20 ×	40,000 =	8,000	40,000	1,000

*⅕ year = .20 per year

As an asset is used in operations,

- accumulated depreciation increases.
- the book value of the asset decreases.

An asset's final book value is its *residual value* ($1,000 in Exhibit 7-5). At the end of its useful life, the asset is said to be *fully depreciated*.

STOP & think. . .

A FedEx sorting machine that cost $10,000, has a useful life of 5 years, and residual value of $2,000, was purchased on January 1. What is SL depreciation for each year?

Answer:

$1,600 = ($10,000 − $2,000)/5

Units-of-Production Method. In the **units-of-production (UOP) method**, a fixed amount of depreciation is assigned to each *unit of output*, or service, produced by the asset. Depreciable cost is divided by useful life—in units of production—to determine this amount. This per-unit depreciation expense is then multiplied by the number of units produced each period to compute depreciation. The UOP depreciation for the FedEx truck data in Exhibit 7-4 (p. 371) is

$$\text{Units-of-production depreciation per unit of output} = \frac{\text{Cost} - \text{Residual value}}{\text{Useful life, in units of production}}$$

$$= \frac{\$41,000 - \$1,000}{100,000 \text{ miles}} = \$0.40 \text{ per mile}$$

Assume that FedEx expects to drive the truck 20,000 miles during the first year, 30,000 during the second, 25,000 during the third, 15,000 during the fourth, and 10,000 during the fifth. Exhibit 7-6 shows the UOP depreciation schedule.

| EXHIBIT 7-6 | | Units-of-Production Depreciation for a FedEx Truck | | | | | |

Date	Asset Cost	Depreciation for the Year			Accumulated Depreciation	Asset Book Value
		Depreciation Per Unit	Number of Units	Depreciation Expense		
1- 1-20X3	$41,000					$41,000
12-31-20X3		$0.40* ×	20,000	= $ 8,000	$ 8,000	33,000
12-31-20X4		0.40 ×	30,000	= 12,000	20,000	21,000
12-31-20X5		0.40 ×	25,000	= 10,000	30,000	11,000
12-31-20X6		0.40 ×	15,000	= 6,000	36,000	5,000
12-31-20X7		0.40 ×	10,000	= 4,000	40,000	1,000

*($41,000 – $1,000)/100,000 miles = $0.40 per mile.

The amount of UOP depreciation varies with the number of units the asset produces. In our example, the total number of units produced is 100,000. UOP depreciation does not depend directly on time, as do the other methods.

Double-Declining-Balance Method. An **accelerated depreciation method** writes off a larger amount of the asset's cost near the start of its useful life than the straight-line method does. Double-declining-balance is the main accelerated depreciation method. **Double-declining-balance (DDB) depreciation** computes annual depreciation by multiplying the asset's declining book value by a constant percentage, which is 2 times the straight-line depreciation rate. DDB amounts are computed as follows:

- *First*, compute the straight-line depreciation rate per year. A 5-year truck has a straight-line depreciation rate of 1/5, or 20% each year. A 10-year asset has a straight-line rate of 1/10, or 10%, and so on.
- *Second*, multiply the straight-line rate by 2 to compute the DDB rate. For a 5-year asset, the DDB rate is 40% (20% × 2). A 10-year asset has a DDB rate of 20% (10% × 2).
- *Third*, multiply the DDB rate by the period's beginning asset book value (cost less accumulated depreciation). Under the DDB method, ignore the residual value of the asset in computing depreciation, except during the last year. The DDB rate for the FedEx truck in Exhibit 7-4 (p. 371) is

$$\text{DDB depreciation rate per year} = \frac{1}{\text{Useful life, in years}} \times 2$$

$$= \frac{1}{5 \text{ years}} \times 2$$

$$= 20\% \times 2 = 40\%$$

- *Fourth*, determine the final year's depreciation amount—that is, the amount needed to reduce asset book value to its residual value. In Exhibit 7-7, the fifth and final year's DDB depreciation is $4,314—book value of $5,314 less the $1,000 residual value. *The residual value should not be depreciated* but should remain on the books until the asset is disposed of.

EXHIBIT 7-7	Double-Declining-Balance Depreciation for a FedEx Truck

Date	Asset Cost	DDB Rate	Asset Book Value		Depreciation Expense	Accumulated Depreciation	Asset Book Value
			Depreciation for the Year				
1- 1-20X3	$41,000						$41,000
12-31-20X3		0.40 ×	$41,000	=	$16,400	$16,400	24,600
12-31-20X4		0.40 ×	24,600	=	9,840	26,240	14,760
12-31-20X5		0.40 ×	14,760	=	5,904	32,144	8,856
12-31-20X6		0.40 ×	8,856	=	3,542	35,686	5,314
12-31-20X7					4,314*	40,000	1,000

*Last-year depreciation is the "plug" amount needed to reduce asset book value (far right column) to the residual amount ($5,314 − $1,000 = $4,314).

The DDB method differs from the other methods in 2 ways:

1. Residual value is ignored initially; first-year depreciation is computed on the asset's full cost.

2. Depreciation expense in the final year is the "plug" amount needed to reduce the asset's book value to the residual amount.

STOP & think. . .

What is the DDB depreciation each year for the asset in the Stop and Think on page 372?

Answers:

    Yr. 1: $4,000 ($10,000 × 40%)
    Yr. 2: $2,400 ($6,000 × 40%)
    Yr. 3: $1,440 ($3,600 × 40%)
    Yr. 4: $160 ($10,000 − $4,000 − $2,400 − $1,440 − $2,000 = $160)*
    Yr. 5: $0

    *The asset is not depreciated below residual value of $2,000.

Comparing Depreciation Methods

Let's compare the 3 methods in terms of the yearly amount of depreciation. The yearly amount varies by method, but the total $40,000 depreciable cost is the same under all methods.

			Accelerated Method
Year	Straight-Line	Units-of-Production	Double-Declining Balance
		Amount of Depreciation Per Year	
1	$ 8,000	$ 8,000	$16,400
2	8,000	12,000	9,840
3	8,000	10,000	5,904
4	8,000	6,000	3,542
5	8,000	4,000	4,314
Total	$40,000	$40,000	$40,000

Generally accepted accounting principles (GAAP) say to match an asset's depreciation against the revenue the asset produces. For a plant asset that generates revenue evenly over time, the straight-line method best meets the matching principle. The units-of-production method best fits those assets that wear out because of physical use rather than obsolescence. The accelerated method (DDB) applies best to assets that generate more revenue earlier in their useful lives and less in later years.

Exhibit 7-8 graphs annual depreciation amounts for the straight-line, units-of-production, and accelerated depreciation (DDB) methods. The graph of straight-line depreciation is flat through time because annual depreciation is the same in all periods. Units-of-production depreciation follows no particular pattern because annual depreciation depends on the use of the asset. Accelerated depreciation is greatest in the first year and less in the later years.

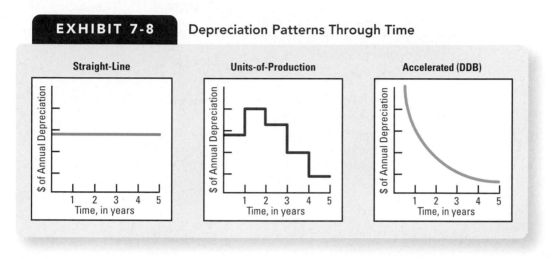

EXHIBIT 7-8 Depreciation Patterns Through Time

Exhibit 7-9 shows the percentage of companies that use each depreciation method from a survey of 600 companies by the American Institute of CPAs.

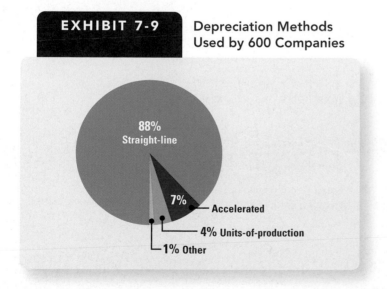

EXHIBIT 7-9 Depreciation Methods Used by 600 Companies

88% Straight-line
7% Accelerated
4% Units-of-production
1% Other

For reporting in the financial statements, straight-line depreciation is most popular. As we shall see, however, accelerated depreciation is most popular for income-tax purposes.

MID-CHAPTER SUMMARY PROBLEM

Suppose FedEx purchased equipment on January 1, 20X7, for $44,000. The expected useful life of the equipment is 10 years or 100,000 units of production, and its residual value is $4,000. Under 3 depreciation methods, the annual depreciation expense and the balance of accumulated depreciation at the end of 20X7 and 20X8 are as follows:

	Method A		Method B		Method C	
Year	Annual Depreciation Expense	Accumulated Depreciation	Annual Depreciation Expense	Accumulated Depreciation	Annual Depreciation Expense	Accumulated Depreciation
20X7	$4,000	$4,000	$8,800	$ 8,800	$1,200	$1,200
20X8	4,000	8,000	7,040	15,840	5,600	6,800

I *Required*

1. Identify the depreciation method used in each instance, and show the equation and computation for each. (Round to the nearest dollar.)
2. Assume continued use of the same method through year 20X9. Determine the annual depreciation expense, accumulated depreciation, and book value of the equipment for 20X7 through 20X9 under each method, assuming 12,000 units of production in 20X9.

Answers

I *Requirement 1*

Method A: Straight-Line

Depreciable cost = $40,000($44,000 – $4,000)

Each year: $40,000/10 years = $4,000

Method B: Double-Declining-Balance

$$\text{Rate} = \frac{1}{10 \text{ years}} \times 2 = 10\% \times 2 = 20\%$$

20X7: 0.20 × $44,000 = $8,800

20X8: 0.20 × ($44,000 – $8,800) = $7,040

Method C: Units-of-Production

$$\text{Depreciation per unit} = \frac{\$44,000 - \$4,000}{100,000 \text{ units}} = \$0.40$$

20X7: $0.40 × 3,000 units = $1,200

20X8: $0.40 × 14,000 units = $5,600

❙ Requirement 2

Method A: Straight-Line

Year	Annual Depreciation Expense	Accumulated Depreciation	Book Value
Start			$44,000
20X7	$4,000	$ 4,000	40,000
20X8	4,000	8,000	36,000
20X9	4,000	12,000	32,000

Method B: Double-Declining-Balance

Year	Annual Depreciation Expense	Accumulated Depreciation	Book Value
Start			$44,000
20X7	$8,800	$ 8,800	35,200
20X8	7,040	15,840	28,160
20X9	5,632	21,472	22,528

Method C: Units-of-Production

Year	Annual Depreciation Expense	Accumulated Depreciation	Book Value
Start			$44,000
20X7	$1,200	$ 1,200	42,800
20X8	5,600	6,800	37,200
20X9	4,800	11,600	32,400

Computations for 20X9

Straight-line	$40,000/10 years = $4,000
Double-declining-balance	$28,160 × 0.20 = $5,632
Units-of-production	12,000 units × $0.40 = $4,800

OTHER ISSUES IN ACCOUNTING FOR PLANT ASSETS

Plant assets are complex because

- they have long lives.
- depreciation affects income taxes.
- companies may have gains or losses when they sell plant assets.

OBJECTIVE

3 Select the best depreciation method

Depreciation for Tax Purposes

FedEx and most other companies use straight-line depreciation for reporting to stockholders and creditors on their financial statements. But for their income taxes they also keep a separate set of depreciation records. For tax purposes, FedEx and most other companies use an accelerated depreciation method. This is legal, ethical, and honest. U.S. law permits it.

Suppose you are a business manager, and the IRS allows an accelerated depreciation method. Why do FedEx managers prefer accelerated over straight-line depreciation for income-tax purposes? Accelerated depreciation provides the fastest tax deductions, thus decreasing immediate tax payments. FedEx can reinvest the tax savings back in the business. FedEx has a choice—pay taxes or buy equipment. This choice is easy.

To understand the relationships between cash flow, depreciation, and income tax, recall our depreciation example of a FedEx truck:

- First-year depreciation is $8,000 under straight-line and $16,400 under double-declining-balance (DDB).
- DDB is permitted for income tax purposes.

Assume that this FedEx office has $400,000 in revenue and $300,000 in cash operating expenses during the truck's first year and an income tax rate of 30%. The cash-flow analysis appears in Exhibit 7-10.

EXHIBIT 7-10 The Cash-Flow Advantage of Accelerated Depreciation over Straight-Line Depreciation for Income Tax Purposes

		SL	Accelerated
1	Cash revenue..	$400,000	$400,000
2	Cash operating expenses	300,000	300,000
3	Cash provided by operations before income tax...............	100,000	100,000
4	Depreciation expense (a noncash expense)............................	8,000	16,400
5	Income before income tax	$ 92,000	$ 83,600
6	Income tax expense (30%)...	$ 27,600	$ 25,080
	Cash-flow analysis:		
7	Cash provided by operations before tax	$100,000	$100,000
8	Income tax expense	27,600	25,080
9	Cash provided by operations..	$ 72,400	$ 74,920
10	Extra cash available for investment if DDB is used ($74,920 – $72,400)...........................		$ 2,520

You can see that, for income-tax purposes, accelerated depreciation helps conserve cash for the business. That's why virtually all companies use accelerated depreciation to compute their income tax.

There is a special depreciation method—used only for income tax purposes—called the **Modified Accelerated Cost Recovery System (MACRS)**. Under MACRS assets are grouped into 1 of 8 classes identified by asset life (Exhibit 7-11). Depreciation for the first 4 classes is computed by the double-declining-balance method. Depreciation for 15-year assets and 20-year assets is computed by the 150%-declining-balance method. Under 150% DB, annual depreciation is computed by multiplying the straight-line rate by 1.50 (instead of 2.00, as for DDB).

> For a 20-year asset, the straight-line rate is 0.05 per year (1/20 = 0.05), so the annual MACRS depreciation rate is 0.075 (0.05 × 1.50 = 0.075). The taxpayer computes annual depreciation by multiplying asset book value by 0.075, in a manner similar to how DDB works.

Most real estate is depreciated by the straight-line method (see the last 2 categories in Exhibit 7-11).

EXHIBIT 7-11	**MACRS Depreciation Method**	

Class Identified by Asset Life (years)	Representative Assets	Depreciation Method
3	Race horses	DDB
5	Automobiles, light trucks	DDB
7	Equipment	DDB
10	Equipment	DDB
15	Sewage-treatment plants	150% DDB
20	Certain real estate	150% DDB
27½	Residential rental property	SL
39	Nonresidential rental property	SL

Depreciation for Partial Years

Companies purchase plant assets whenever they need them, not just at the beginning of the year. Therefore, companies must compute *depreciation for partial years*. Suppose UPS purchases a warehouse building on April 1 for $500,000. The building's estimated life is 20 years, and its estimated residual value is $80,000. UPS's accounting year ends on December 31. Let's consider how UPS computes depreciation for April through December:

- First, compute depreciation for a full year.
- Second, multiply full-year depreciation by the fraction of the year that you held the asset—in this case, 9/12. Assuming the straight-line method, the year's depreciation for this UPS building is $15,750, as follows:

$$\text{Full-year depreciation} \quad \frac{\$500,000 - \$80,000}{20} = \$21,000$$

$$\text{Partial year depreciation} \quad \$21,000 \times 9/12 = \$15,750$$

What if UPS bought the asset on April 18? Many businesses record no monthly depreciation on assets purchased after the 15th of the month, and they record a full month's depreciation on an asset bought on or before the 15th.

Most companies use computerized systems to account for fixed assets. Each asset has a unique identification number, and the system will automatically calculate the asset's depreciation expense. Accumulated Depreciation is automatically updated.

Changing the Useful Life of a Depreciable Asset

After an asset is in use, managers may change its useful life on the basis of experience and new information. **The Walt Disney Company** made such a change, called a *change in accounting estimate*. Disney recalculated depreciation on the basis of revised useful lives of several of its theme park assets. The following note in Walt Disney's financial statements reports this change in accounting estimate:

> **Note 5**
> ...[T]he Company extended the estimated useful lives of certain theme park ride and attraction assets based upon historical data and engineering studies. The effect of this change was to decrease depreciation by approximately $8 million (an increase in net income of approximately $4.2 million...).

Assume that a Disney hot dog stand cost $50,000 and that the company originally believed the asset had a 10-year useful life with no residual value. Using the straight-line method, the company would record $5,000 depreciation each year ($50,000/10 years = $5,000). Suppose Disney used the asset for 4 years. Accumulated depreciation reached $20,000, leaving a remaining depreciable book value (cost *less* accumulated depreciation *less* residual value) of $30,000 ($50,000 – $20,000). From its experience, management believes the asset will remain useful for an additional 10 years. The company would spread the remaining depreciable book value over the asset's remaining life as follows:

$$\frac{\text{Asset's remaining depreciable book value}}{} \div \frac{\text{(New) Estimated useful life remaining}}{} = \frac{\text{(New) Annual depreciation}}{}$$

$$\$30,000 \div 10 \text{ years} = \$3,000$$

The yearly depreciation entry based on the new estimated useful life is

Depreciation Expense—Hot Dog Stand	3,000	
Accumulated Depreciation—Hot Dog Stand		3,000

Depreciation decreases both assets and equity.

Assets	=	Liabilities	+	Stockholders' Equity	–	Expenses
– 3,000	=	0				– 3,000

Fully Depreciated Assets

A *fully depreciated asset* is one that has reached the end of its estimated useful life. Suppose FedEx has fully depreciated equipment with zero residual value (cost was $60,000). FedEx accounts will appear as follows:

Equipment	–	Accumulated Depreciation		Book value
60,000			60,000	= $0

The equipment's book value is zero, but that doesn't mean the equipment is worthless. FedEx may use the equipment for a few more years, but FedEx will not record any more depreciation on a fully depreciated asset.

When FedEx disposes of the equipment, FedEx will remove both the asset's cost ($60,000) and its accumulated depreciation ($60,000) from the books. The next section shows how to account for plant asset disposals.

Accounting for Disposal of Plant Assets

Eventually, a plant asset ceases to serve a company's needs. The asset may wear out or become obsolete. Before accounting for the disposal of the asset, the business should bring depreciation up to date to

■ measure the asset's final book value and
■ record the expense up to the date of sale.

To account for disposal, remove the asset and its related accumulated depreciation from the books. Suppose the final year's depreciation expense has just been recorded for a machine that cost $60,000 and is estimated to have zero residual value. The machine's accumulated depreciation thus totals $60,000. Assuming that this asset is junked, the entry to record its disposal is:

OBJECTIVE

4 **Analyze** the effect of a
plant asset disposal

Accumulated Depreciation—Machinery	60,000	
Machinery		60,000
To dispose of a fully depreciated machine.		

Assets	=	Liabilities	+	Stockholders' Equity
+ 60,000 − 60,000	=	0	+	0

There is no gain or loss on this disposal, and there's no effect on total assets, liabilities, or equity.

If assets are junked before being fully depreciated, the company incurs a loss on the disposal. Suppose FedEx disposes of equipment that cost $60,000. This asset's accumulated depreciation is $50,000, and book value is, therefore, $10,000. Junking this equipment results in a loss equal to the book value of the asset, as follows:

Accumulated Depreciation—Equipment	50,000	
Loss on Disposal of Equipment	10,000	
Equipment		60,000
To dispose of equipment.		

Assets	=	Liabilities	+	Stockholders' Equity	−	Losses
+ 50,000 − 60,000	=	0				− 10,000

FedEx got rid of an asset with $10,000 book value and received nothing. The result is a $10,000 loss, which decreases both total assets and equity.

The Loss on Disposal of Equipment is reported as Other income (expense) on the income statement. Losses decrease net income exactly as expenses do. Gains increase net income the same as revenues.

Selling a Plant Asset. Suppose FedEx sells equipment on September 30, 20X4, for $7,000 cash. The equipment cost $10,000 when purchased on January 1, 20X1, and has been depreciated straight-line. FedEx estimated a 10-year useful life and no residual value. Prior to recording the sale, FedEx accountants must update the asset's depreciation. Assume that FedEx uses the calendar year as its accounting period. Partial-year depreciation must be recorded for the asset's depreciation from January 1, 20X4, to the sale date. The straight-line depreciation entry at September 30, 20X4, is

Sept. 30	Depreciation Expense ($10,000/10 years × 9/12)	750	
	Accumulated Depreciation—Equipment		750
	To *update depreciation.*		

The Equipment account and the Accumulated Depreciation account appear as follows. Observe that the equipment's book value is $6,250 ($10,000 – $3,750).

	Equipment			Accumulated Depreciation		
Jan.1, 20X1	10,000			Dec. 31, 20X1	1,000	
				Dec. 31, 20X2	1,000	= Book value
		–		Dec. 31, 20X3	1,000	$6,250
				Sept. 30, 20X4	750	
				Balance	3,750	

Suppose FedEx sells the equipment for $7,300 cash. The gain on the sale is $1,050, computed as follows:

Cash received from sale of the asset		$7,300
Book value of asset sold:		
Cost	$10,000	
Less: Accumulated depreciation	(3,750)	6,250
Gain on sale of the asset................................		$1,050

The entry to record sale of the equipment for $7,300 cash is

Sept. 30	Cash	7,300	
	Accumulated Depreciation—Equipment	3,750	
	Equipment		10,000
	Gain on Sale of Equipment		1,050
	To *sell equipment.*		

Total assets increase, and so does equity—by the amount of the gain.

Assets	=	Liabilities	–	Stockholders' Equity	+	Gains
+ 7,300						
+ 3,750	=	0				+ 1,050
−10,000						

Gains are recorded as credits, as revenues are. Gains and losses on asset disposals appear on the income statement as Other Income (Expense), or Other Gains (Losses).

Exchanging Plant Assets. Managers often trade in old assets for new ones. For example, a pizzeria may trade in a 5-year-old delivery car for a newer model. In many cases, the business simply transfers the book value of the old asset plus any cash payment into the new asset account. For example, assume Mazzio Pizzeria's

- old delivery car cost $9,000 and has accumulated depreciation of $8,000. The old car's book value is $1,000.

If Mazzio trades in the old automobile and pays cash of $10,000,

- the cost of the new delivery car is $11,000 (book value of the old asset, $1,000, plus cash given, $10,000).

The pizzeria records the exchange transaction as follows:

DeliveryAuto (new)	11,000	
Accumulated Depreciation (old)	8,000	
Delivery Auto (old)		9,000
Cash		10,000
Traded in old delivery car for new auto.		

Assets	=	Liabilities	+	Stockholders' Equity
+11,000				
+ 8,000	=	0	+	0
− 9,000				
−10,000				

There was no effect on total assets, liabilities or equity—because there was no gain or loss on the exchange.

T-Accounts for Analyzing Plant Asset Transactions

You can perform quite a bit of analysis if you know how transactions affect the plant asset accounts. Here are the accounts with descriptions of the activity in each account.

Building (or Equipment)				Accumulated Depreciation		
Beginning balance Cost of assets purchased		Cost of assets disposed of		Accum. deprec. of assets disposed of		Beginning balance Depreciation expense for the current period
Ending balance						Ending balance

Depreciation Expense			Gain on Sale of Building (or Equipment)		
Depreciation expense for the current period					Gain on sale
			Loss on Sale of Building (or Equipment)		
			Loss on sale		

Example: Suppose you started the year with buildings that cost $100,000. During the year you bought another building for $150,000 and ended the year with buildings that cost $180,000. What was the cost of the building you sold?

Building				
Beginning balance	100,000			
Cost of assets purchased	150,000	Cost of assets sold		? = $70,000
Ending balance	180,000			

You can perform similar analyses to answer other interesting questions about what the business did during the period.

ACCOUNTING FOR NATURAL RESOURCES

OBJECTIVE

5 **Account** for natural
resources and depletion

Natural resources are plant assets of a special type, such as iron ore, petroleum (oil), and timber. As plant assets are expensed through depreciation, so natural resource assets are expensed through *depletion*. **Depletion expense** is that portion of the cost of a natural resource that is used up in a particular period. Depletion expense is computed in the same way as units-of-production depreciation.

An oil lease may cost **ExxonMobil** $100,000 and contain an estimated 10,000 barrels of oil. The depletion rate would be $10 per barrel ($100,000/10,000 barrels). If 3,000 barrels are extracted, depletion expense is $30,000 (3,000 barrels × $10 per barrel). The depletion entry is

Depletion Expense (3,000 barrels × $10)		30,000	
Accumulated Depletion—Oil			30,000

This entry is almost identical to a depreciation entry.

If 4,500 barrels are removed the next year, that period's depletion is $45,000 (4,500 barrels × $10 per barrel). Accumulated Depletion is a contra account similar to Accumulated Depreciation.

Natural resource assets can be reported on ExxonMobil's balance sheet as follows (amounts assumed):

Property, Plant, and Equipment:		
Equipment...	$960,000	
Less: Accumulated depreciation	(410,000)	$550,000
Oil..	$340,000	
Less: Accumulated depletion	(140,000)	200,000
Total property, plant, and equipment...............		$750,000

ACCOUNTING FOR INTANGIBLE ASSETS

As we've seen, *intangible assets* are long-lived assets with no physical form. Intangibles are valuable because they carry special rights from patents, copyrights, trademarks, franchises, leaseholds, and goodwill. Like buildings and equipment, an intangible asset is recorded at its acquisition cost. Intangibles are the most valuable assets of high-tech companies and those that depend on research and development. The residual value of most intangibles is zero.

Intangible assets fall into 2 categories:

■ Intangibles with *finite lives* that can be measured. We record amortization for these intangibles. **Amortization expense** is the title of the expense associated with intangibles. Amortization works like depreciation and is usually computed on a straight-line basis. Amortization can be credited directly to the asset account, as we shall see.

■ Intangibles with *indefinite lives*. Record no amortization for these intangibles. Instead, check them annually for any loss in value, and record a loss when it occurs. Goodwill is the most prominent example of an intangible asset with an indefinite life.

In the following discussions, we illustrate the accounting for both categories of intangibles.

Accounting for Specific Intangibles

Each type of intangible asset is unique, and the accounting can vary from one asset to another.

Patents. **Patents** are federal government grants that give the holder the exclusive right for 20 years to produce and sell an invention. The invention may be a product or a process—for example, Sony compact disc players and the Dolby noise-reduction process. Like any other asset, a patent may be purchased. Suppose a company pays $170,000 to acquire a patent on January 1, and the business believes the expected useful life of the patent is 5 years—not the entire 20-year period. Amortization expense is $34,000 per year ($170,000/5 years). Sony records the acquisition and amortization for this patent as follows:

Jan. 1	Patents	170,000	
	Cash		170,000
	To acquire a patent.		

Dec. 31	Amortization Expense—Patents ($170,000/5)	34,000	
	Patents		34,000
	To amortize the cost of a patent.		

You can see that we credited the Patents account directly (no Accumulated Amortization account).

Assets	=	Liabilities	+	Stockholders' Equity	–	Expenses
– 34,000	=	0				– 34,000

Amortization for an intangible decreases both assets and equity exactly as depreciation does for equipment or a building.

Copyrights. **Copyrights** are exclusive rights to reproduce and sell a book, musical composition, film, or other work of art. Copyrights also protect computer software programs, such as **Microsoft's** Windows® and Excel. Issued by the federal government, copyrights extend 70 years beyond the author's (composer's, artist's, or programmer's) life. The cost of obtaining a copyright from the government is low, but a company may pay a large sum to purchase an existing copyright from the owner. For example, a publisher may pay the author of a popular novel $1 million or more for the book copyright. Because the useful life of a copyright is usually no longer than 2 or 3 years, each period's amortization amount is a high proportion of the copyright cost.

Trademarks and Trade Names. **Trademarks** and **trade names** (or *brand names*) are distinctive identification of a product or service. The "eye" symbol that flashes across our television screens is the trademark that identifies the **CBS** television network. You are probably also familiar with **NBC's** peacock. Advertising slogans that are legally protected include **United Airlines**' "Fly the friendly skies®" and **Avis Rental Car's** "We try harder®." These are distinctive identifications of products or services, marked with the symbol ™ or ®.

Some trademarks may have a definite useful life set by contract. We should amortize this trademark's cost over its useful life. But a trademark or a trade name may have an indefinite life and not be amortized.

Franchises and Licenses. **Franchises** and **licenses** are privileges granted by a private business or a government to sell a product or service in accordance with specified conditions. The Chicago Cubs baseball organization is a franchise granted to its owner by the National League. **McDonald's** restaurants and **Holiday Inns** are popular franchises. The useful lives of many franchises and licenses are indefinite and, therefore, are not amortized.

Goodwill. In accounting, **goodwill** has a very specific meaning.

> **Goodwill is defined as the excess of the cost of purchasing another company over the sum of the market values of the acquired company's net assets (assets minus liabilities).**

A purchaser is willing to pay for goodwill when the purchaser buys another company that has abnormal earning power.

FedEx operates in several foreign countries. Suppose FedEx acquires Europa Company at a cost of $10 million. Europa's assets have a market value of $9 million, and its liabilities total $2 million so Europa's *net* assets total $7 million at current market value. In this case, FedEx paid $3 million for goodwill, computed as follows:

Purchase price paid for Europa Company		$10 million
Sum of the market values of Europa Company's assets	$9 million	
Less: Europa Company's liabilities	(2 million)	
Market value of Europa Company's net assets		7 million
Excess is called *goodwill*		$ 3 million

FedEx's entry to record the acquisition of Europa Company, including its goodwill, would be

Assets (Cash, Receivables, Inventories, Plant Assets, all at market value)		9,000,000	
Goodwill		3,000,000	
Liabilities			2,000,000
Cash			10,000,000

Goodwill in accounting has special features, as follows:

1. Goodwill is recorded *only* when it is purchased in the acquisition of another company. A purchase transaction provides objective evidence of the value of goodwill. Companies never record goodwill that they create for their own business.

2. According to generally accepted accounting principles (GAAP), goodwill is not amortized because the goodwill of many entities increases in value.

Accounting for the Impairment of an Intangible Asset

Some intangibles—such as goodwill, licenses, and some trademarks—have indefinite lives and therefore are not subject to amortization. But all intangibles are subject to a write-down when their value decreases. **PepsiCo** is a major company with vast amounts of purchased goodwill due to its acquisition of other companies.

Each year, PepsiCo determines whether the goodwill it has purchased has increased or decreased in value. If PepsiCo's goodwill is worth more at the end of the year than at the beginning, no increase in the asset is permitted. But if PepsiCo's goodwill has decreased in value, say from $500 million to $470 million, then

PepsiCo will record a $30 million loss and write down the book value of the goodwill, as follows (in millions):

20X9			
Dec. 31	Loss on Goodwill ($500–$470)	30	
	Goodwill		30

Both assets (Goodwill) and equity decrease (through the Loss account).

Assets	=	Liabilities	+	Stockholders' Equity	–	Losses
– 30	=	0				– 30

PepsiCo's financial statements will report the following (in millions):

	20X6	20X5
Balance sheet		
Intangible assets:		
Goodwill..........................	$470	$500
Income statement		
(Loss) on goodwill...............	(30)	—

Accounting for Research and Development Costs

Accounting for research and development (R&D) costs is one of the most difficult issues in accounting. R&D is the lifeblood of companies such as **Procter & Gamble**, **General Electric**, **Intel**, and **Boeing**. R&D is one of these companies' most valuable (intangible) assets. But, in general, companies do not report R&D assets on their balance sheets.

GAAP requires companies to expense R&D costs as they incur them. Only in limited circumstances may the company capitalize R&D cost as an asset. For example, a company may incur R&D cost under a contract guaranteeing that the company will recover R&D costs from a customer. This R&D cost is an asset, and the company records an intangible R&D asset when it incurs the cost. But this is the exception to the general rule.

REPORTING PLANT ASSET TRANSACTIONS ON THE STATEMENT OF CASH FLOWS

OBJECTIVE

7 **Report** plant asset transactions on the statement of cash flows

Three main types of plant asset transactions appear on the statement of cash flows:

■ acquisitions
■ sales
■ depreciation (including amortization and depletion).

Acquisitions and sales are *investing* activities. A company invests in plant assets. The payments for equipment and buildings are investing activities that appear on the statement of cash flows. The sale of plant assets results in a cash receipt, as illustrated in Exhibit 7-12, which excerpts data from the cash-flow statement of FedEx

Corporation. Depreciation, acquisitions, and sales of plant assets are denoted in color (lines 2, 5, and 6).

EXHIBIT 7-12 **Reporting Plant Asset Transactions on FedEx's Statement of Cash Flows**

FedEx Corporation
Statement of Cash Flows (partial, adapted)
Year Ended May 31, 2006

		Millions
Cash Flows from Operating Activities:		
1	Net income..	$1,806
	Adjustments to reconcile net income to net cash provided by operating activities:	
2	Depreciation and amortization..............................	1,548
3	Other items (summarized).....................................	322
4	Cash provided by operating activities....................	3,676
Cash Flows from Investing Activities:		
5	Capital expenditures	(2,518)
6	Proceeds from asset dispositions...........................	64
7	Cash (used in) investing activities.........................	(2,454)
Cash Flows from Financing Activities:		
8	Cash (used in) financing activities	(324)
9	Net increase in cash and cash equivalents.............	898
10	Cash and cash equivalents, beginning of period	1,039
11	Cash and cash equivalents, end of period.........................	$1,937

Let's examine FedEx's investing activities first. During 2006, FedEx paid $2,518 million for plant assets (line 5). FedEx also sold property and equipment, receiving cash of $64 million (line 6). FedEx labels the cash received as Proceeds from asset dispositions. The $64 million is the amount of cash FedEx received from the sale of plant assets.

FedEx's statement of cash flows reports Depreciation and amortization (line 2). Observe that "Depreciation and amortization" is listed as a positive item under Adjustments to reconcile net income to Cash provided by operating activities. You may be wondering why depreciation appears on the cash-flow statement. After all, depreciation does not affect cash.

In this format, the operating activities section of the cash-flow statement starts with net income (line 1) and reconciles to cash provided by operating activities (line 4). Depreciation decreases net income but does not affect cash. Depreciation is therefore added back to net income to measure cash flow from operations. The add-back of depreciation to net income offsets the earlier subtraction of the expense. The sum of net income plus depreciation, therefore, helps to reconcile net income (on the accrual basis) to cash flow from operations (a cash-basis amount). We revisit this topic in the full context of the statement of cash flows in Chapter 12.

Incidentally, FedEx's cash flows are exceptionally strong. Operations generated $3,676 million of cash, and FedEx spent $2,518 million on new property and equipment. FedEx is growing.

DECISION GUIDELINES

PLANT ASSETS AND RELATED EXPENSES

FedEx Corporation, like all other companies, must make some decisions about how to account for its plant assets and intangibles. Let's review some of these decisions.

Decision	Guidelines
Capitalize or expense a cost?	General rule: Capitalize all costs that provide *future* benefit for the business such as a new package-handling system. Expense all costs that provide no *future* benefit, such as a repair to an airplane.
Capitalize or expense: • Cost associated with a new asset?	Capitalize all costs that bring the asset to its intended use, including asset purchase price, transportation charges, and taxes paid to acquire the asset.
• Cost associated with an existing asset?	Capitalize only those costs that add to the asset's usefulness or to its useful life. Expense all other costs as maintenance or repairs.
Which depreciation method to use: • For financial reporting?	Use the method that best matches depreciation expense against the revenues produced by the asset. Most companies use the straight-line method.
• For income tax?	Use the method that produces the fastest tax deductions (MACRS). A company can use different depreciation methods for financial reporting and for income-tax purposes. In the United States, this practice is both legal and ethical.
• How to account for natural resources?	Capitalize the asset's acquisition cost and all later costs that add to the natural resource's future benefit. Then record depletion expense, as computed by the units-of-production method.
• How to account for intangibles?	Capitalize acquisition cost and all later costs that add to the asset's future benefit. For intangibles with finite lives, record amortization expense. For intangibles with indefinite lives, do not record amortization. But if an intangible asset loses value, then record a loss in the amount of the decrease in asset value.

END-OF-CHAPTER SUMMARY PROBLEM

1. The figures that follow appear in the *Answers to the Mid-Chapter Summary Problem,* Requirement 2, on page 377.

	Method A: Straight-Line			Method B: Double-Declining-Balance		
Year	Annual Depreciation Expense	Accumulated Depreciation	Book Value	Annual Depreciation Expense	Accumulated Depreciation	Book Value
Start			$44,000			$44,000
20X7	$4,000	$ 4,000	40,000	$8,800	$ 8,800	35,200
20X8	4,000	8,000	36,000	7,040	15,840	28,160
20X9	4,000	12,000	32,000	5,632	21,472	22,528

❚ Required

1. Suppose the income tax authorities permitted a choice between these 2 depreciation methods. Which method would FedEx select for income-tax purposes? Why?
2. Suppose FedEx purchased the equipment described in the table on January 1, 20X7. Management has depreciated the equipment by using the double-declining-balance method. On July 1, 20X9, FedEx sold the equipment for $27,000 cash.

❚ Required

Record depreciation for 20X9 and the sale of the equipment on July 1, 20X9.

Answers

1. For tax purposes, most companies select the accelerated method because it results in the most depreciation in the earliest years of the asset's life. Accelerated depreciation minimizes income tax payments in the early years of the asset's life. That maximizes the business's cash at the earliest possible time.
2. Entries to record depreciation to date of sale, and then the sale of the equipment:

20X9			
July 1	Depreciation Expense—Equipment ($5,632 × 1/2 year)	2,816	
	Accumulated Depreciation—Equipment		2,816
	To update depreciation.		
July 1	Cash	27,000	
	Accumulated Depreciation—Equipment		
	($15,840 + $2,816)	18,656	
	Equipment		44,000
	Gain on Sale of Equipment		1,656
	To record sale of equipment.		

REVIEW PLANT ASSETS AND INTANGIBLES

Quick Check (Answers are given on page 412.)

1. Burleson, Inc. purchased a tract of land, a small office building, and some equipment for $1,500,000. The appraised value of the land was $850,000, the building $675,000, and the equipment $475,000. What is the cost of the land?
   - a. $481,667
   - b. $850,000
   - c. $637,500
   - d. None of the above.

2. Which statement is false?
   - a. Depreciation creates a fund to repace the asset at the end of its useful life.
   - b. The cost of a plant asset minus accumulated depreciation equals the asset's book value.
   - c. Depreciation is a process of allocating the cost of a plant asset over its useful life.
   - d. Depreciation is based on the matching principle because it matches the cost of the asset with the revenue generated over the asset's useful life.

Use the following data for questions 3–6.
On September 1, 20X3, Grande Communications purchased a new piece of equipment that cost $25,000. The estimated useful life is 5 years and estimated residual value is $2,500.

3. What is depreciation expense for 20X3 if Grande uses the straight-line method?
   - a. $1,875
   - b. $1,500
   - c. $2,083
   - d. $4,500

4. Assume Grande purchased the equipment on January 1, 20X3. If Grande uses the straight-line method for depreciation, what is the asset's book value at the end of 20X4?
   - a. $13,500
   - b. $15,000
   - c. $18,625
   - d. $16,000

5. Assume Grande purchased the equipment on January 1, 20X3. If Grande uses the double-declining-balance method, what is depreciation for 20X4?
   - a. $5,400
   - b. $6,000
   - c. $8,333
   - d. $15,000

6. Return to Grande's original purchase date of September 1, 20X3. Assume that Grande uses the straight-line method of depreciation and sells the equipment for $11,500 on September 1, 20X7. The result of the sale of the equipment is a gain (loss) of
   - a. $4,500.
   - b. $13,500.
   - c. $(9,000).
   - d. $0.

7. A company bought a new machine for $17,000 on January 1. The machine is expected to last 4 years and have a residual value of $2,000. If the company uses the double-declining-balance method, accumulated depreciation at the end of year 2 will be:
   - a. $10,880
   - b. $11,250
   - c. $12,750
   - d. $15,000

8. Which of the following is *not* a capital expenditure:
   - a. The addition of a building wing.
   - b. A complete overhaul of an air-conditioning system.
   - c. A tune-up of a company vehicle.
   - d. Replacement of an old motor with a new one in a piece of equipment.
   - e. The cost of installing a piece of equipment.

9. Which of the following assets is *not* subject to a decreasing book value through depreciation, depletion, or amortization:
   - a. Goodwill
   - b. Intangibles
   - c. Land improvements
   - d. Natural resources

10. Why would a business select an accelerated method of depreciation for tax purposes?
    - a. MACRS depreciation follows a specific pattern of depreciation.
    - b. Accelerated depreciation generates a greater amount of depreciation over the life of the asset than does straight-line depreciation.
    - c. Accelerated depreciation is easier to calculate because salvage value is ignored.
    - d. Accelerated depreciation generates higher depreciation expense immediately, and therefore lower tax payments in the early years of the asset's life.

11. A company purchased an oil well for $200,000. It estimates that the well contains 50,000 barrels, has a 10-year life, and no salvage value. If the company extracts and sells 6,000 barrels of oil in the first year, how much depletion expense should be recorded?

    a. $16,000   c. $20,000

    b. $24,000   d. $100,000

12. Which item among the following is *not* an intangible asset:

    a. A trademark   d. Goodwill

    b. A copyright   e. All of the above are intagible assets

    c. A patent

Accounting Vocabulary

accelerated depreciation method (p. 373) A depreciation method that writes off a relatively larger amount of the asset's cost nearer the start of its useful life than the straight-line method does.

amortization (p. 385) The systematic reduction of a lump-sum amount. Expense that applies to intangible assets in the same way depreciation applies to plant assets and depletion applies to natural resources.

capital expenditure (p. 368) Expenditure that increases an asset's capacity or efficiency or extends its useful life. Capital expenditures are debited to an asset account.

copyright (p. 386) Exclusive right to reproduce and sell a book, musical composition, film, other work of art, or computer program. Issued by the federal government, copyrights extend 70 years beyond the author's life.

depletion expense (p. 384) That portion of a natural resource's cost that is used up in a particular period. Depletion expense is computed in the same way as units-of-production depreciation.

depreciable cost (p. 370) The cost of a plant asset minus its estimated residual value.

double-declining-balance (DDB) method (p. 373) An accelerated depreciation method that computes annual depreciation by multiplying the asset's decreasing book value by a constant percentage, which is 2 times the straight-line rate.

estimated residual value (p. 370) Expected cash value of an asset at the end of its useful life. Also called *residual value, scrap value,* or *salvage value.*

estimated useful life (p. 370) Length of service that a business expects to get from an asset. May be expressed in years, units of output, miles, or other measures.

franchises and licenses (p. 386) Privileges granted by a private business or a government to sell a product or service in accordance with specified conditions.

goodwill (p. 387) Excess of the cost of an acquired company over the sum of the market values of its net assets (assets minus liabilities).

intangible assets (p. 365) An asset with no physical form, a special right to current and expected future benefits.

Modified Accelerated Cost Recovery System (MACRS) (p. 378) A special depreciation method used only for income-tax purposes. Assets are grouped into classes, and for a given class depreciation is computed by the double-declining-balance method, the 150%-declining balance method, or, for most real estate, the straight-line method.

patent (p. 385) A federal government grant giving the holder the exclusive right for 20 years to produce and sell an invention.

plant assets (p. 365) Long-lived assets, such as land, buildings, and equipment, used in the operation of the business. Also called *fixed assets.*

straight-line (SL) method (p. 371) Depreciation method in which an equal amount of depreciation expense is assigned to each year of asset use.

trademark, trade name (p. 386) A distinctive identification of a product or service. Also called a *brand name.*

units-of-production (UOP) method (p. 372) Depreciation method by which a fixed amount of depreciation is assigned to each unit of output produced by the plant asset.

ASSESS YOUR PROGRESS

Short Exercises

S7-1 (*Learning Objective 1: Cost and book value of a company's plant assets*) Examine **FedEx's** assets at the beginning of this chapter. Answer these questions about the company: (p. 364)

1. What is FedEx's largest category of assets? List all 2006 assets and their amounts as reported by FedEx.

2. What was FedEx's cost of property and equipment at May 31, 2006? What was the book value of property and equipment on this date? Why is book value less than cost?

writing assignment ■

S7-2 (*Learning Objective 1: Measuring the cost of a plant asset*) Page 365–366 of this chapter lists the costs included for the acquisition of land. First is the purchase price of the land, which is obviously part of the cost of the land. The reasons for including the other costs are not so obvious. For example, property tax is ordinarily an expense, not part of the cost of an asset. State why the other costs listed on page 366 are included as part of the cost of the land. After the land is ready for use, will these other costs be capitalized or expensed?

S7-3 (*Learning Objective 1: Lump-sum purchase of assets*) Suppose you get a good buy on land, a building, and some equipment. At the time of your acquisition, the land has a current market value of $80,000, the building's market value is $80,000, and the equipment's market value is $40,000. Journalize your lump-sum purchase of the 3 assets for a total cost of $150,000. You sign a note payable for this amount. (p. 367)

S7-4 (*Learning Objective 1: Capitalizing versus expensing plant asset costs*) Assume **United Airlines** repaired a Boeing 777 aircraft at a cost of $1.6 million, which United paid in cash. Further, assume the United accountant erroneously capitalized this expense as part of the cost of the plane.

   Show the effects of the accounting error on United Airlines' income statement. To answer this question, determine whether revenues, total expenses, and net income were overstated or understated by the accounting error. (p. 369)

S7-5 (*Learning Objective 2: Computing depreciation by 3 methods—first year only*) Assume that at the beginning of 20X0, **UPS**, a FedEx competitor, purchased a used Boeing 737 aircraft at a cost of $25,000,000. UPS expects the plane to remain useful for 5 years (5 million miles) and to have a residual value of $5,000,000. UPS expects to fly the plane 750,000 miles the first year, 1,250,000 miles each year 2 through 4, and 500,000 miles the last year. (pp. 372–373)

1. Compute UPS's first-year depreciation on the plane using the following methods:

   a. Straight-line   **b.** Units-of-production   **c.** Double-declining-balance

2. Show the airplane's book value at the end of the first year under each depreciation method.

S7-6 (*Learning Objective 2: Computing depreciation by 3 methods—third year only*) Use the UPS data in Short Exercise S7-5 to compute UPS's third-year depreciation on the plane using the following methods: (pp. 372–373)

   a. Straight-line   **b.** Units-of-production   **c.** Double-declining balance

writing assignment ■

S7-7 (*Learning Objective 3: Selecting the best depreciation method for income tax purposes*) This exercise uses the assumed UPS data from Short Exercise S7-5. Assume UPS is trying to decide which depreciation method to use for income tax purposes. (pp. 377–378)

1. Which depreciation method offers the tax advantage for the first year? Describe the nature of the tax advantage.

2. How much income tax will UPS save for the first year of the airplane's use as compared with using the straight-line depreciation method? The income tax rate is 40%. Ignore any earnings from investing the extra cash.

S7-8 (*Learning Objective 2: Partial-year depreciation*) Assume that on September 30, 20X4, **Swissair**, the national airline of Switzerland, purchased an Airbus aircraft at a cost of €40,000,000 (€ is the symbol for the euro). Swissair expects the plane to remain useful for 7 years (5,000,000 miles) and to have a residual value of €5,000,000. Swissair will fly the plane 400,000 miles during the remainder of 20X4. Compute Swissair's depreciation on the plane for the year ended December 31, 20X4, using the following methods: (pp. 371, 372, 299)

  a. Straight-line   **b.** Units-of-production **c.** Double-declining-balance

Which method would produce the highest net income for 20X4? Which method produces the lowest net income? (pp. 379–380)

S7-9 (*Learning Objective 2: Computing and recording depreciation after a change in useful life of the asset*) **Six Flags over Georgia** paid $60,000 for a concession stand. Six Flags started out depreciating the building straight-line over 10 years with zero residual value. After using the concession stand for 4 years, Six Flags determines that the building will remain useful for only 2 more years. Record Six Flags' depreciation on the concession stand for year 5 by the straight-line method. (pp. 379–380)

S7-10 (*Learning Objective 4: Recording a gain or loss on disposal*) On January 1, 20X4, JetBlue purchased an airplane for $25,000,000. JetBlue expects the plane to remain useful for 5 years and to have a residual value of $5,000,000. JetBlue uses the straight-line method to depreciate its airplanes. JetBlue flew the plane for 4 years and sold it on January 1, 20X8, for $8,000,000.

1. Compute accumulated depreciation on the airplane at January 1, 20X8 (same as Decembere 31, 20X7). (p. 372)
2. Record the sale of the plane on January 1, 20X8. (p. 382)

S7-11 (*Learning Objective 5: Accounting for the depletion of a company's natural resources*) **ChevronTexaco**, the giant oil company, holds reserves of oil and gas assets. At the end of 20X4, assume the cost of ChevronTexaco's mineral assets totaled $150 billion, representing 12 billion barrels of oil in the ground. (pp. 384–385)

1. Which depreciation method do ChevronTexaco's and other oil companies use to compute their annual depletion expense for the minerals removed from the ground?
2. Suppose ChevronTexaco removed 0.6 billion barrels of oil during 20X5. Record depletion expense for the year. Show amounts in billions.
3. At December 31, 20X4, ChevronTexaco's Accumulated Depletion account stood at $85.0 billion. Report Mineral Assets and Accumulated Depletion at December 31, 20X5. Do ChevronTexaco's Mineral Assets appear to be plentiful or mostly used up? Give your reason.

S7-12 (*Learning Objective 6: Measuring and recording goodwill*) **PepsiCo, Inc.**, dominates the snack-food industry with its Frito-Lay brand. Assume that PepsiCo, Inc., purchased Taco Chips, Inc., for $8.5 million cash. The market value of Taco Chips' assets is $14 million, and Taco Chips has liabilities of $9 million. (pp. 386–387)

❙ *Required*

1. Compute the cost of the goodwill purchased by PepsiCo.
2. Explain how PepsiCo will account for goodwill in future years.

S7-13 (*Learning Objective 6: Accounting for patents and research and development cost*) This exercise summarizes the accounting for patents, which like copyrights, trademarks, and franchises, provide the owner with a special right or privilege. It also covers research and development costs.

 Suppose Jaguar Automobiles Limited paid $500,000 to research and develop a new global positioning system. Jaguar also paid $1,200,000 to acquire a patent on a new motor. After readying the motor for production, Jaguar's sales revenue for the first year totaled $6,500,000. Cost of goods sold was $3,200,000, and selling expenses totaled $300,000. All these transactions occurred during 20X4. Jaguar expects the patent to have a useful life of 3 years.

(*continued*)

Prepare Jaguar Automobiles' income statement for the year ended December 31, 20X4, complete with a heading. Ignore income tax. (pp. 385–388)

S7-14 *(Learning Objective 7: Reporting investing activities on the statement of cash flows)* During 20X5, Imperial Sugar Co. purchased 2 other companies for $180 million. Also during 20X5, Imperial made capital expenditures of $45 million to expand its market share. During the year, Imperial sold its South American operations, receiving cash of $110 million. Overall, Imperial reported a net income of $1.4 million during 20X5.

Show what Imperial Sugar Co. would report for cash flows from investing activities on its statement of cash flows for 20X5. Report a total amount for net cash provided by (used for) investing activities. (p. 389)

Exercises

E7-15 *(Learning Objective 1: Determining the cost of plant assets)* Afton Self Storage purchased land, paying $150,000 cash as a down payment and signing a $150,000 note payable for the balance. Afton also had to pay delinquent property tax of $2,000, title insurance costing $2,500, and $6,000 to level the land and remove an unwanted building. The company paid $50,000 to add soil for the foundation and then constructed an office building at a cost of $1,000,000. It also paid $65,000 for a fence around the property, $10,400 for the company sign near the property entrance, and $6,000 for lighting of the grounds. Determine the cost of Afton's land, land improvements, and building. (pp. 366–367)

E7-16 *(Learning Objective 1, 4: Allocating costs to assets acquired in a lump-sum purchase; disposing of a plant asset)* Haley-Davis Inc. bought 3 used machines in a $100,000 lump-sum purchase. An independent appraiser valued the machines as follows:

Machine No.	Appraised Value
1	$27,000
2	45,000
3	36,000

What is each machine's individual cost? Immediately after making this purchase, Haley-Davis sold machine 2 for its appraised value. What is the result of the sale? Round decimals to 3 places. (p. 367)

E7-17 *(Learning Objective 1: Distinguishing capital expenditures from expenses)* Assume **M&M Mars** purchased conveyor-belt machinery. Classify each of the following expenditures as a capital expenditure or an immediate expense related to machinery: (a) sales tax paid on the purchase price, (b) transportation and insurance while machinery is in transit from seller to buyer, (c) purchase price, (d) installation, (e) training of personnel for initial operation of the machinery, (f) special reinforcement to the machinery platform, (g) income tax paid on income earned from the sale of products manufactured by the machinery, (h) major overhaul to extend the machinery's useful life by 3 years, (i) ordinary repairs to keep the machinery in good working order, (j) lubrication of the machinery before it is placed in service and (k) periodic lubrication after the machinery is placed in service. (p. 368)

E7-18 *(Learning Objective 1, 2: Measuring, depreciating, and reporting plant assets)* During 20X4, Golden Book Store paid $480,000 for land and built a store in Chicago. Prior to construction, the city of Chicago charged Golden $1,000 for a building permit, which Golden paid. Golden also paid $15,000 for architect's fees. The construction cost of $660,000 was financed by a long-term note payable, with interest cost of $39,000 paid at completion of the project. The building was completed September 30, 20X4. Golden depreciates the building by the straight-line method over 35 years, with estimated residual value of $330,000. (pp. 366, 371)

1. Journalize transactions for
    a. Purchase of the land
    b. All the costs chargeable to the building in a single entry
    c. Depreciation on the building

Explanations are not required.

2. Report Golden Book Store's plant assets on the company's balance sheet at December 31, 20X4. (p. 364)

3. What will Golden's income statement for the year ended December 31, 20X4, report for this situation? (pp. 369–370)

E7-19 (*Learning Objective 2, 3: Determining depreciation amounts by three methods*) **Little Caesar's Pizza** bought a used Nissan delivery van on January 2, 20X1, for $15,000. The van was expected to remain in service 4 years (100,000 miles). At the end of its useful life, Little Caesar's officials estimated that the van's residual value will be $3,000. The van traveled 34,000 miles the first year, 28,000 the second year, 18,000 the third year, and 20,000 in the fourth year. Prepare a schedule of *depreciation expense* per year for the van under the 3 depreciation methods. Show your computations. (pp. 371–374)

Which method best tracks the wear and tear on the van? Which method would Little Caesar's prefer to use for income tax purposes? Explain in detail why Little Caesar's prefers this method. (p. 377)

writing assignment ■

■ **spreadsheet**

E7-20 (*Learning Objective 1, 2, 7: Reporting plant assets, depreciation, and investing cash flows*) Assume that in January 20X6, an **IHOP** restaurant purchased a building, paying $50,000 cash and signing a $100,000 note payable. The restaurant paid another $60,000 to remodel the building. Furniture and fixtures cost $50,000, and dishes and supplies—a current asset—were obtained for $9,000.

IHOP is depreciating the building over 20 years by the straight-line method, with estimated residual value of $50,000. The furniture and fixtures will be replaced at the end of 5 years and are being depreciated by the double-declining-balance method, with zero residual value. At the end of the first year, the restaurant still has dishes and supplies worth $2,000.

Show what the restaurant will report for supplies, plant assets, and cash flows at the end of the first year on its (pp. 364, 369–370, 389)

- Income statement
- Balance sheet
- Statement of cash flows

Show all computations.   (investing only)

Note: The purchase of dishes and supplies is an operating cash flow because supplies are a current asset.

E7-21 (*Learning Objective 3: Selecting the best depreciation method for income tax purposes*) On June 30, 20X6, Holtkamp Corp. paid $210,000 for equipment that is expected to have a 7-year life. In this industry, the residual value of equipment is approximately 10% of the asset's cost. Holtkamp's cash revenues for the year are $100,000 and cash expenses total $60,000.

Select the appropriate MACRS depreciation method for income tax purposes (pp. 378–379). Then determine the extra amount of cash that Holtkamp. can invest by using MACRS depreciation, versus straight-line, for the year ended December 31, 20X6. The income tax rate is 35%. (pp. 376–377)

E7-22 (*Learning Objective 2: Changing a plant asset's useful life*) Assume **United Van Lines** purchased a building for $900,000 and depreciated it on a straight-line basis over 40 years. The estimated residual value was $100,000. After using the building for 20 years, United realized that the building will remain useful only 15 more years. Starting with the 21st year, United began depreciating the building over the newly revised total life of 35 years and decreased the estimated residual value to $50,000. Record depreciation expense on the building for years 20 and 21. (pp. 379–380)

E7-23 (*Learning Objective 4: Analyzing the effect of a sale of a plant asset; DDB depreciation*) Assume that on January 2, 20X4, Insurors of Pennsylvania purchased fixtures for $8,700 cash, expecting the fixtures to remain in service 5 years. Insurors has depreciated the fixtures on a double-declining-balance basis, with $1,000 estimated residual value. On September 30, 20X5, Insurors sold the fixtures for $2,500 cash. Record both the depreciation expense on the fixtures for 20X5 and then the sale of the fixtures. Apart from your journal entry, also show how to compute the gain or loss on Insurors' disposal of these fixtures. (p. 382)

E7-24 (*Learning Objective 1, 2, 4: Measuring a plant asset's cost, using UOP depreciation, and trading in a used asset*) Celadon is a large trucking company that operates throughout the United States. Celadon uses the units-of-production (UOP) method to depreciate its trucks.

Celadon trades in trucks often to keep driver morale high and to maximize fuel economy. Consider these facts about one **Volvo** truck in the company's fleet: When acquired in 20X2, the tractor-trailer rig cost $285,000 and was expected to remain in service for 5 years or 1,000,000 miles. Estimated residual value was $35,000. During 20X2, the truck was driven 75,000 miles; during 20X3, 120,000 miles; and during 20X4, 210,000 miles. After 35,000 miles in 20X5, the company traded in the Volvo truck for a **Mack** rig. Celadon paid cash of $150,000. Determine Celadon's cost of the new truck. Journal entries are not required. (p. 383)

E7-25 (*Learning Objective 5: Recording natural resource assets and depletion*) Colorado Mines paid $498,500 for the right to extract ore from a 200,000-ton mineral deposit. In addition to the purchase price, Colorado Mines also paid a $500 filing fee, a $1,000 license fee to the state of Colorado, and $60,000 for a geologic survey of the property. Because the company purchased the rights to the minerals only, it expected the asset to have zero residual value when fully depleted. During the first year of production, Colorado Mines removed 80,000 tons of ore. Make journal entries to record (a) purchase of the mineral rights, (b) payment of fees and other costs, and (c) depletion for first-year production. What is the mineral asset's book value at the end of the year? (pp. 334–335)

E7-26 (*Learning Objective 6: Recording intangibles, amortization, and a change in the asset's useful life*) **(Part 1.)** **Holze Music Company** purchased for $600,000 a patent for a new sound system. Although the patent gives legal protection for 20 years, it is expected to provide Holze with a competitive advantage for only 6 years. Assuming the straight-line method of amortization, make journal entries to record (a) the purchase of the patent and (b) amortization for year 1.

(Part 2.) After using the patent for 2 years, Holze learns at a professional meeting that **BOSE** is designing a more powerful system. On the basis of this new information, Holze determines that the patent's total useful life is only 4 years. Record amortization for year 3. (pp. 379–380, 384–385)

writing assignment ■   **E7-27** (*Learning Objective 6: Computing and accounting for goodwill*) Assume Google paid $18 million to purchase MySpace.com. Assume further that MySpace had the following summarized data at the time of the Google acquisition (amounts in millions):

MySpace.com			
Assets		**Liabilities and Equity**	
Current assets	$10	Total liabilities	$24
Long-term assets	20	Stockholders' equity	6
	$30		$30

MySpace's long-term assets had a current market value of only $15 million.

I *Required*

1. Compute the cost of goodwill purchased by Google. (pp. 386–387)
2. Journalize Google's purchase of MySpace. (pp. 386–387)
3. Explain how Google will account for goodwill in the future. (pp. 387–388)

E7-28 (*Learning Objective 7: Reporting cash flows for property and equipment*) Assume **Starbucks Corporation** completed the following transactions. For each transaction, show what Starbucks would report for investing activities on its statement of cash flows. Show negative amounts in parentheses. (pp. 387–389)

    a. Sold a store building for $600,000. The building had cost Starbucks $1,000,000, and at the time of the sale its accumulated depreciation totaled $400,000.

    b. Lost a store building in a fire. The building cost $300,000 and had accumulated depreciation of $180,000. The insurance proceeds received by Starbucks totaled $120,000.

    c. Renovated a store at a cost of $100,000.

    d. Purchased store fixtures for $50,000. The fixtures are expected to remain in service for 10 years and then be sold for $15,000. Starbucks uses the straight-line depreciation method.

Challenge Exercises

E7-29 (*Learning Objective 2: Units-of-production depreciation*) Atlas Gym purchased exercise equipment at a cost of $100,000. In addition, Atlas paid $2,000 for a special platform on which to stabilize the equipment for use. Freight costs of $1,200 to ship the equipment were borne by the seller. Atlas will depreciate the equipment by the units-of-production method, based on an expected useful life of 50,000 hours of exercise. The estimated residual value of the equipment is $10,000. How many hours did Atlas Gym use the machine if depreciation expense is $3,680? (p. 372)

E7-30 (*Learning Objective 4: Determining the sale price of property and equipment*) **FedEx Corporation** reported the following for property and equipment (in millions, adapted):

	Year End	
	20X6	20X5
Property and equipment..................	$24,074	$22,017
Accumulated depreciation...............	(13,304)	(12,080)

During 20X6, FedEx paid $2,518 million for new property and equipment. Depreciation for the year totaled $1,548 million. During 20X6, FedEx sold property and equipment for cash of $64 million. How much was FedEx's gain or loss on the sale of property and equipment during 20X6? (p. 382)

E7-31 (*Learning Objective 2: Determining net income after a change in depreciation method*) Amanda, Inc., has a popular line of sunglasses. Amanda reported net income of $68 million for 20X1. Depreciation expense for the year totaled $18 million. Amanda, Inc., depreciates plant assets over 8 years using the straight-line method and no residual value.

    Amanda, Inc., paid $160 million for plant assets at the beginning of 20X1. Then at the start of 20X2, Amanda switched over to double-declining-balance (DDB) depreciation. 20X2 is expected to be the same as 20X1 except for the change in depreciation method. If Amanda had been using DDB depreciation all along, how much net income can Amanda, Inc. expect to earn during 20X2? Ignore income tax. (pp. 371–375)

E7-32 (*Learning Objective 1: Capitalizing versus expensing; measuring the effect of an error*) **Agence France Press (AFP)** is a major French telecommunication conglomerate. Assume that early in year 1, AFP purchased equipment at a cost of 6 million euros (€6 million). Management expects the equipment to remain in service 4 years and estimated residual value to be negligible. AFP uses the straight-line depreciation method. *Through an accounting error, AFP expensed the entire cost of the equipment at the time of purchase.* Because AFP is operated as a partnership, it pays no income tax.

❙ Required

Prepare a schedule to show the overstatement or understatement in the following items at the end of each year over the 4-year life of the equipment: (p. 369, Challenge)

> 1. Total current assets   2. Equipment, net   3. Net income

Quiz

Test your understanding of accounting for plant assets, natural resources, and intangibles by answering the following questions. Select the best choice from among the possible answers given.

Q7-33 A capital expenditure (p. 368)

a. is expensed immediately.
b. records additional capital.

c. adds to an asset.
d. is a credit like capital (owners' equity).

Q7-34 Which of the following items should be accounted for as a capital expenditure? (p. 368)

a. Taxes paid in conjunction with the purchase of office equipment.
b. The monthly rental cost of an office building.
c. Costs incurred to repair leaks in the building roof.
d. Maintenance fees paid with funds provided by the company's capital.

Q7-35 Suppose you buy land for $3,000,000 and spend $1,000,000 to develop the property. You then divide the land into lots as follows:

Category	Sale price per lot
10 Hilltop lots................	$500,000
10 Valley lots.................	300,000

How much did each hilltop lot cost you? (p. 367)

a. $171,429
b. $228,571

c. $250,000
d. $400,000

Q7-36 Which statement about depreciation is false? (pp. 369–370)

a. Depreciation is a process of allocating the cost of an asset to expense over its useful life.
b. Depreciation should not be recorded in years that the market value of the asset has increased.
c. A major objective of depreciation accounting is to match the cost of using an asset with the revenues it helps to generate.
d. Obsolescence as well as physical wear and tear should be considered when determining the period over which an asset should be depreciated.

Use the following information to answer questions 37 and 38:

Madison Corporation acquired a machine for $26,000 and has recorded depreciation for 3 years using the straight-line method over a 6-year life and $2,000 residual value. At the start of the fourth year of use, Madison revised the estimated useful life to a total of 10 years. Estimated residual value declined to $0.

Q7-37 What is the book value of the machine at the end of 3 full years of use? (p. 372)
a. $10,000
c. $13,000
b. $12,000
d. $14,000

Q7-38 How much depreciation should Madison record in each of the asset's last 7 years (that is, year 4 through year 10), following the revision? (pp. 379–380)
a. $2,000
c. $2,800
b. $2,600
d. Some other amount

Q7-39 Kramer Company failed to record depreciation of equipment. How does this omission affect Kramer's financial statements? (p. 369)
a. Net income is overstated and assets are understated.
b. Net income is understated and assets are understated.
c. Net income is understated and assets are overstated.
d. Net income is overestated and assets are overstated.

Q7-40 Jack's Stereo, Inc., uses the double-declining-balance method for depreciation on its computers. Which item is not needed to compute depreciation for the first year? (p. 373)
a. Original cost
c. Expected useful life in years
b. Estimated residual value
d. All the above are needed.

Q7-41 Which of the following costs is reported on a company's income statement? (pp. 368–370)
a. Accumulated depreciation
b. Land
c. Accounts payable
d. Depreciation expense

Q7-42 Which of the following items is reported on the balance sheet? (Challenge)
a. Net sales revenue
c. Gain on disposal of equipment
b. Accumulated depreciation
d. Cost of goods sold

Q7-43 Hamilton Company purchased a machine for $8,800 on January 1, 20X6. The machine has been depreciated using the straight-line method over an 8-year life and $800 residual value. Hamilton sold the machine on January 1, 20X8, for $7,500. What gain or loss should Hamilton record on the sale? (p. 382)
a. Gain, $500
c. Loss, $1,300
b. Gain, $700
d. Gain, $1,500

Q7-44 Journalize Hamilton's sale of the machine.

Q7-45 Same information as for question 43, except the machine was purchased on April 2, 20X6. What is straight-line depreciation for the year ended December 31, 20X6, and what is the book value on December 31, 20X7 (fill in the blanks)? (p. 372)
Depreciation for 20X6 _____   Book value at December 31, 20X7 _____

Q7-46 A company purchased mineral assets costing $850,000, with estimated residual value of $50,000, and holding approximately 400,000 tons of ore. During the first year, 45,000 tons are extracted and sold. What is the amount of depletion for the first year? (pp. 384–385)
a. $13,913
c. $90,000
b. $70,000
d. Cannot be determined from the data given

Q7-47 Suppose **FedEx** pays $60 million to buy Lone Star Overnight. Lone Star's assets are valued at $70 million, and its liabilities total $20 million. How much goodwill did FedEx purchase in its acquisition of Lone Star Overnight? (pp. 386–387)
a. $10 million
c. $30 million
b. $20 million
d. $40 million

Problems
(Group A)

P7-48A (*Learning Objective 1, 2: Identifying the elements of a plant asset's cost*) Assume **Google Inc.** opened an office in Orlando, Florida. Further assume that Google incurred the following costs in acquiring land, making land improvements, and constructing and furnishing the new sales building.

a. Purchase price of land, including an old building that will be used for a garage (land market value is $320,000; building market value is $80,000)	$350,000
b. Landscaping (additional dirt and earth moving)	8,100
c. Fence around the land	31,600
d. Attorney fee for title search on the land	600
e. Delinquent real estate taxes on the land to be paid by Google	5,900
f. Company signs at entrance to the property	1,800
g. Building permit for the sales building	300
h. Architect fee for the design of the sales building	19,800
i. Masonry, carpentry, and roofing of the sales building	516,000
j. Renovation of the garage building	41,800
k. Interest cost on construction loan for sales building	9,000
l. Landscaping (trees and shrubs)	6,400
m. Parking lot and concrete walks on the property	52,300
n. Lights for the parking lot and walkways	7,300
o. Salary of construction supervisor (85% to sales building; 9% to land improvements; and 6% to garage building renovation)	40,000
p. Office furniture for the sales building	79,400
q. Transportation and installation of furniture	1,800

Assume Google depreciates buildings over 40 years, land improvements over 20 years, and furniture over 8 years, all on a straight-line basis with zero residual value.

❙ Required

1. Set up columns for Land, Land Improvements, Sales Building, Garage Building, and Furniture. Show how to account for each of Google's costs by listing the cost under the correct account. Determine the total cost of each asset. (pp. 366–367)

2. All construction was complete and the assets were placed in service on May 2. Record depreciation for the year ended December 31. Round to the nearest dollar. (p. 371)

3. How will what you learned in this problem help you manage a business?

■ **general ledger**

P7-49A (*Learning Objective 2: Recording plant asset transactions; reporting on the balance sheet*) Highland Lakes Resort reported the following on its balance sheet at December 31, 20X5:

Property, plant, and equipment, at cost:	
Land	$ 140,000
Buildings	700,000
Less: Accumulated depreciation	(340,000)
Equipment	400,000
Less: Accumulated depreciation	(260,000)

In early July 20X6, the resort expanded operations and purchased additional equipment at a cost of $100,000. The company depreciates buildings by the straight-line method over 20 years with residual value of $80,000. Due to obsolescence, the equipment has a useful life of only 10 years and is being depreciated by the double-declining-balance method with zero residual value.

❚ Required

1. Journalize Highland Lakes Resort's plant asset purchase and depreciation transactions for 20X6. (pp. 368, 373)

2. Report plant assets on the December 31, 20X6, balance sheet. (p. 364)

P7-50A (*Learning Objective 1, 2, 4: Recording plant asset transactions, exchanges, and changes in useful life*) **Lamborghini, Inc.,** has the following plant asset accounts: Land, Buildings, and Equipment, with a separate accumulated depreciation account for each of these except land. Lamborghini completed the following transactions:

■ **general ledger**

Jan. 2	Traded in equipment with accumulated depreciation of $67,000 (cost of $130,000) for similar new equipment with a cash cost of $176,000. Received a trade-in allowance of $70,000 on the old equipment and paid $106,000 in cash. (p. 383)
June 30	Sold a building that had a cost of $650,000 and had accumulated depreciation of $145,000 through December 31 of the preceding year. Depreciation is computed on a straight-line basis. The building has a 40-year useful life and a residual value of $250,000. Lamborghini received $100,000 cash and a $400,000 note receivable. (p. 382)
Oct. 29	Purchased land and a building for a single price of $420,000. An independent appraisal valued the land at $150,000 and the building at $300,000. (p. 367)
Dec. 31	Recorded depreciation as follows: (p. 373)
	Equipment has an expected useful life of 6 years and an estimated residual value of 5% of cost. Depreciation is computed on the double-declining-balance method.
	Depreciation on buildings is computed by the straight-line method. The new building carries a 40-year useful life and a residual value equal to 10% of its cost.

❚ Required

Record the transactions in Lamborghini, Inc's., journal.

P7-51A (*Learning Objective 2: Explaining the concept of depreciation*) The board of directors of Fiberglass Structures, Inc., is reviewing the 20X7 annual report. A new board member—a wealthy woman with little business experience—questions the company accountant about the depreciation amounts. The new board member wonders why depreciation expense has decreased from $200,000 in 20X6 to $184,000 in 20X7 to $172,000 in 20X8. She states that she could understand the decreasing annual amounts if the company had been disposing of properties each year, but that has not occurred. Further, she notes that growth in the city is increasing the values of company properties. Why is the company recording depreciation when the property values are increasing?

writing assignment ■

❚ Required

Write a paragraph or 2 to explain the concept of depreciation to the new board member and to answer her questions. (pp. 369–370)

P7-52A (*Learning Objective 2, 3: Computing depreciation by 3 methods and the cash-flow advantage of accelerated depreciation for tax purposes*) On January 3, 20X2, J.B. Weld Co. paid $224,000 for a computer system. In addition to the basic purchase price, the company paid a setup fee of $6,200, $6,700 sales tax, and $3,100 for a special platform on which to

■ **spreadsheet**

(continued)

place the computer. J.B. Weld management estimates that the computer will remain in service 5 years and have a residual value of $20,000. The computer will process 50,000 documents the first year, with annual processing decreasing by 5,000 documents during each of the next 4 years (that is, 45,000 documents in 20X3; 40,000 documents in 20X4; and so on). In trying to decide which depreciation method to use, the company president has requested a depreciation schedule for each of 3 depreciation methods (straight-line, units-of-production, and double-declining-balance).

❙ Required

1. For each of the generally accepted depreciation methods, prepare a depreciation schedule showing asset cost, depreciation expense, accumulated depreciation, and asset book value. (pp. 372–373)

2. J.B. Weld reports to stockholders and creditors in the financial statements using the depreciation method that maximizes reported income in the early years of asset use. For income tax purposes, the company uses the depreciation method that minimizes income tax payments in those early years. Consider the first year J.B. Weld Co. uses the computer. Identify the depreciation methods that meet Weld's objectives, assuming the income tax authorities permit the use of any of the methods. (pp. 377–378)

3. Cash provided by operations before income tax is $150,000 for the computer's first year. The income tax rate is 40%. For the 2 depreciation methods identified in Requirement 2, compare the net income and cash provided by operations (cash flow). Show which method gives the net-income advantage and which method gives the cash-flow advantage. (p. 378)

P7-53A *(Learning Objective 2, 4, 7: Analyzing plant asset transactions from a company's financial statements)* **Best Buy Inc.** sells electronics and appliances. The excerpts that follow are adapted from Best Buy's financial statements for 2006.

Balance Sheet (dollars in millions)	February 28, 2006	2005
Assets		
Total current assets	$7,985	$6,903
Property, plant, and equipment	4,836	4,192
Less: Accumulated depreciation	2,124	1,728
Goodwill...	557	513

Statement of Cash Flows (dollars in millions)	Year Ended February 28, 2006	2005
Operating activities:		
Net income	$1,140	$984
Noncash items affecting net income:		
Depreciation	456	459
Investing activities:		
Additions to property, plant, and equipment...............	723	619

❙ Required

Answer these questions about Best Buy's plant assets and goodwill:

1. How much was Best Buy's cost of plant assets at February 28, 2006? How much was the book value of plant assets? Show computations. (pp. 364, 369)

2. The financial statements give 3 evidences that Best Buy purchased plant assets and goodwill during 2006. What are they? (pp. 386–387, 389)

3. Prepare T-accounts for Property, Plant, and Equipment; Accumulated Depreciation, and Goodwill. Then show all the activity in these accounts during 2006. Label each increase or decrease and give its dollar amount. During 2006, Best Buy sold plant assets that had cost the company $79 million (accumulated depreciation on these assets was $60 million). Assume there were no losses on goodwill during 2006. (pp. 385–386)

P7-54A (*Learning Objective 5: Accounting for natural resources, and the related expense*) Atlantic Energy Company's balance sheet includes the asset Iron Ore. Atlantic Energy paid $2.6 million cash for a lease giving the firm the right to work a mine that contained an estimated 200,000 tons of ore. The company paid $60,000 to remove unwanted buildings from the land and $70,000 to prepare the surface for mining. Atlantic Energy also signed a $30,000 note payable to a landscaping company to return the land surface to its original condition after the lease ends. During the first year, Atlantic Energy removed 40,000 tons of ore, which it sold on account for $32 per ton. Operating expenses for the first year totaled $240,000, all paid in cash. In addition, the company accrued income tax at the tax rate of 40%.

❙ Required

1. Record all of Atlantic Engery's transactions for the year. (pp. 384–385)

2. Prepare the company's income statement for its iron ore operations for the first year. Evaluate the profitability of the company's operations. (p. 80)

P7-55A (*Learning Objective 7: Reporting plant asset transactions on the statement of cash flows*) At the end of 20X0, Solar Power Associates (SPA) had total assets of $17.3 billion and total liabilities of $9.5 billion. Included among the assets were property, plant, and equipment with a cost of $4.8 billion and accumulated depreciation of $3.4 billion.

SPA completed the following selected transactions during 20X1: The company earned total revenues of $26.5 billion and incurred total expenses of $21.3 billion, which included depreciation of $1.7 billion. During the year, SPA paid $1.4 billion for new property, plant, and equipment and sold old plant assets for $0.3 billion. The cost of the assets sold was $0.8 billion, and their accumulated depreciation was $0.4 billion.

❙ Required

1. Explain how to determine whether SPA had a gain or loss on the sale of old plant assets during the year. What was the amount of the gain or loss, if any? (p. 382)

2. Show how SPA would report property, plant, and equipment on the balance sheet at December 31, 20X1, after all the year's activity. What was the book value of property, plant, and equipment? (p. 364)

3. Show how SPA would report its operating activities and investing activities on its statement of cash flows for 20X1. Ignore gains and losses. (p. 389)

(Group B)

P7-56B (*Learning Objective 1, 2: Identifying the elements of a plant asset's cost*) Scissors Salons operate in several states. The home office incurred the following costs to acquire land and a garage, make land improvements, and construct and furnish the office building.

(*continued*)

a.	Purchase price of land, including a building that will be used as a garage (land market value is $150,000; building market value is $50,000)	$180,000
b.	Delinquent real estate taxes on the land to be paid by Scissors	3,700
c.	Landscaping (additional dirt and earth moving)	3,550
d.	Title insurance on the land acquisition	1,000
e.	Fence around the land	26,000
f.	Building permit for the office building	200
g.	Architect fee for the design of the office building	45,000
h.	Company signs at near front and rear approaches to company property	53,550
i.	Renovation of the garage	16,400
j.	Concrete, wood, and other materials used in the office building	322,000
k.	Masonry, carpentry, and roofing to construct the office building	234,000
l.	Interest cost on construction loan for office building	3,400
m.	Parking lots and concrete walks on the property	17,450
n.	Lights for the parking lot, walkways, and company signs	8,900
o.	Salary of construction supervisor (90% to office building, 6% to land improvements, and 4% to garage renovation)	55,000
p.	Furniture for the office building	61,500
q.	Transportation of furniture from seller to the office building	1,300
r.	Landscaping (trees and shrubs)	9,100

Scissors Salons depreciates buildings over 40 years, land improvements over 20 years, and furniture over 8 years, all on a straight-line basis with zero residual value.

❚ Required

1. Set up columns for Land, Land Improvements, Office Building, Garage, and Furniture. Show how to account for each of Scissors' costs by listing the cost under the correct account. Determine the total cost of each asset. (pp. 366–367)

2. All construction was complete and the assets were placed in service on March 29. Record depreciation for the year ended December 31. Round figures to the nearest dollar. (pp. 371–372).

3. How will what you learned in this problem help you manage a business? (Challenge)

■ general ledger

P7-57B (*Learning Objective 2: Recording plant asset transactions; reporting on the balance sheet*) **Ambold Lock & Key, Inc.** has a hefty investment in security equipment, as reported in the company's balance sheet at December 31, 20X5:

Property, plant, and equipment, at cost:	
Land	$ 200,000
Buildings	310,000
Less: Accumulated depreciation	(40,000)
Security equipment	620,000
Less: Accumulated depreciation	(370,000)

In early July 20X6, Ambold purchased additional security equipment at a cost of $80,000. Ambold depreciates buildings by the straight-line method over 20 years with residual value of $70,000. Due to obsolescence, security equipment has a useful life of only 8 years and is being depreciated by the double-declining-balance method with zero residual value.

❚ Required

1. Journalize Ambold's plant asset purchase and depreciation transactions for 20X6. (pp. 368, 373).

2. Report plant assets on the company's December 31, 20X6, balance sheet. (p. 364)

■ **general ledger**

P7-58B (*Learning Objective 1, 2, 4: Recording plant asset transactions, exchanges, and changes in useful life*) Schmaltz Cable Company's balance sheet reports the following assets under Property and Equipment: Land, Buildings, Office Furniture, Communication Equipment, and Televideo Equipment. The company has a separate accumulated depreciation account for each of these assets except land. Assume that Schmaltz completed the following transactions:

Jan. 3	Traded in communication equipment with accumulated depreciation of $85,000 (cost of $96,000) for similar new equipment with a quoted price of $118,000. The seller gave Schmaltz a trade-in allowance of $18,000 on the old equipment, and Schmaltz paid $100,000 in cash. (p. 383)
June 30	Sold a building that had cost of $495,000 and had accumulated depreciation of $255,000 through December 31 of the preceding year. Depreciation is computed on a straight-line basis. The building has a 40-year life and a residual value of $95,000. Schmaltz received $50,000 cash and a $250,000 note receivable. (p. 382)
Nov. 4	Purchased used communication and televideo equipment from **Time Warner Cable**. Total cost was $80,000 paid in cash. An independent appraisal valued the communication equipment at $75,000 and the televideo equipment at $25,000. (p. 367)
Dec. 31	Recorded depreciation as follows: Equipment is depreciated by the double-declining-balance method over a 5-year life with zero residual value. Record depreciation separately on the equipment purchased on January 3 and on November 4. (p. 373)

❚ *Required*

Record the transactions in the journal of Schmaltz Cable Company.

writing assignment ■

P7-59B (*Learning Objective 2: Explaining the concept of depreciation*) The board of directors of Gemstar Instruments is having its quarterly meeting. Accounting policies are on the agenda, and depreciation is being discussed. A new board member has some strong opinions. Jeffrey Hatton, an environmental engineer, argues that depreciation must be coupled with a fund to replace company assets. Otherwise, there is no substance to depreciation, he argues. He also challenges the 3-year estimated life over which Gemstar Instruments is depreciating company computers. He notes that the computers will last at least 5 years. Hatton argues for depreciating computers over 5 years instead of 3.

❚ *Required*

Write a paragraph or 2 to explain the accounting concept of depreciation to Jeffrey Hatton and to answer his arguments. (pp. 369–370)

■ **spreadsheet**

P7-60B (*Learning Objective 2, 3: Computing depreciation by 3 methods and the cash-flow advantage of accelerated depreciation for tax purposes*) On January 2, 20X1, St. Paul Vision Center purchased equipment at a cost of $63,000. Before placing the equipment in service, St. Paul spent $2,200 for special chips, $800 for a platform, and $4,000 to customize the equipment. St. Paul management estimates that the equipment will remain in service for 6 years and have a residual value of $16,000. The equipment can be expected to process 18,000 examinations in each of the first 4 years and 14,000 tests in each of the next 2 years. In trying to decide which depreciation method to use, Lana Rich, the general manager, requests a depreciation schedule for each method (straight-line, units-of-production, and double-declining-balance).

❚ *Required*

1. Prepare a depreciation schedule for each of the depreciation methods, showing asset cost, depreciation expense, accumulated depreciation, and asset book value. (pp. 372–373).

(*continued*)

2. St. Paul reports to creditors in the financial statements using the depreciation method that maximizes reported income in the early years of asset use. For income tax purposes, however, the company uses the depreciation method that minimizes income-tax payments in those early years. Consider the first year that St. Paul uses the equipment. Identify the depreciation methods that meet the general manager's objectives, assuming the income tax authorities would permit the use of any of the methods. (pp. 377–378)

3. Cash provided by operations before income tax is $100,000 for the equipment's first year. The income tax rate is 35%. For the 2 depreciation methods identified in Requirement 2, compare the net income and cash provided by operations (cash flow). Show which method gives the net-income advantage and which method gives the cash-flow advantage. (p. 378)

P7-61B (*Learning Objective 2, 4, 7: Analyzing plant asset transactions from a company's financial statements*) **Hewlett-Packard Company (HP)** is the leading computer company in the world. The excerpts that follow are adapted from HP's financial statements for fiscal year 2006.

Balance Sheet (dollars in millions)	October 31, 2006	2005
Assets		
Total current assets	$48,264	$43,334
Property, plant, and equipment	15,024	13,880
Less: Accumulated depreciation	8,561	7,429
Goodwill	16,853	16,441

Statement of Cash Flows (dollars in millions)	Year Ended October 31, 2006	2005
Cash Flows from Operating Activities:		
Net income	$ 6,198	$ 2,398
Noncash items affecting net income:		
Depreciation	2,353	2,344
Cash Flows from Investing Activities:		
Capital expenditures	$(2,536)	$(1,995)
Acquisition of businesses	(855)	(641)

❙ Required

Answer these questions about Hewlett-Packard's plant assets and goodwill:

1. How much was HP's cost of plant assets at October 31, 2006? How much was the book value of plant assets? Show computations. (pp. 364, 369)

2. The financial statements give 4 evidences that HP purchased plant assets and goodwill during 2006. What are they? (pp. 386-387, 389)

3. Prepare T-accounts for Property, Plant, and Equipment; Accumulated Depreciation; and Goodwill. Then show all the activity in each account during 2006. Label each increase or decrease and give its dollar amount. During 2006, HP sold plant assets that had cost the company $1,392 million (accumulated depreciation on these assets was $1,221 million). Assume there was no loss on goodwill during 2006. (p. 384)

P7-62B (*Learning Objective 5: Accounting for natural resources and the related expense*)
Mainstay Pipeline Company operates a pipeline that provides natural gas to several East Coast cities. Mainstay's balance sheet includes the asset Oil Properties.

Mainstay paid $5 million cash for petroleum reserves that contained an estimated 500,000 barrels of oil. The company paid $350,000 for additional geologic tests of the property and $110,000 to prepare the surface for drilling. Prior to production, the company signed a $40,000 note payable to have a building constructed on the property. Because the building provides on-site headquarters for the drilling effort and will be abandoned when the oil is depleted, its cost is debited to the Oil Properties account and included in depletion charges. During the first year of production, Mainstay removed 80,000 barrels of oil, which it sold on credit for $38 per barrel. Operating expenses related to this project totaled $660,000 for the first year, all paid in cash. In addition, Mainstay accrued income tax at the rate of 40%.

I Required

1. Record all of Mainstay's transactions for the year. (pp. 384–385)

2. Prepare the company's income statement for this oil and gas project for the first year. Evaluate the profitability of the project. (p. 80)

writing assignment ■

P7-63B (*Learning Objective 7: Reporting plant asset transactions on the statement of cash flows*) Assume that at the end of 20X2, **Verizon**, the telecommunications company, had total assets of $15.2 billion and total liabilities of $10.5 billion. Included among the assets were property, plant, and equipment with a cost of $17.1 billion and accumulated depreciation of $10.2 billion.

Assume that Verizon completed the following selected transactions during 20X3: The company earned total revenues of $16.9 billion and incurred total expenses of $13.2 billion, which included depreciation of $1.7 billion. During the year, Verizon paid $2.8 billion for new property, plant, and equipment and sold old plant assets for $1.0 billion. The cost of the assets sold was $1.6 billion, and their accumulated depreciation was $0.4 billion.

I Required

1. Explain how to determine whether Verizon had a gain or a loss on the sale of old plant assets. What was the amount of the gain or loss, if any? (p. 382)

2. Show how Verizon would report property, plant, and equipment on the balance sheet at December 31, 20X3, after all the year's activity. (p. 364)

3. Show how Verizon would report operating activities and investing activities on its statement of cash flows for 20X3. Ignore gains and losses. (p. 389).

APPLY YOUR KNOWLEDGE

Decision Cases

writing assignment ■

Case 1. (*Learning Objective 2, 3: Measuring profitability based on different inventory and depreciation methods*) Suppose you are considering investing in 2 businesses, La Petite France Bakery and Burgers Ahoy!. The 2 companies are virtually identical, and both began operations at the beginning of the current year. During the year, each company purchased inventory as follows:

Jan. 4	10,000 units at $4 =	40,000
Apr. 6	5,000 units at 5 =	25,000
Aug. 9	7,000 units at 6 =	42,000
Nov. 27	10,000 units at 7 =	70,000
Totals	32,000	$177,000

(continued)

During the first year, both companies sold 25,000 units of inventory.

In early January, both companies purchased equipment costing $150,000 that had a 10-year estimated useful life and a $20,000 residual value. La Petite France uses the inventory and depreciation methods that maximize reported income. By contrast, Burgers uses the inventory and depreciation methods that minimize income tax payments. Assume that both companies' trial balances at December 31 included the following:

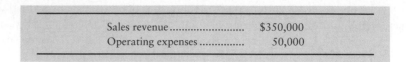

Sales revenue	$350,000
Operating expenses	50,000

The income tax rate is 40%.

I Required

1. Prepare both companies' income statements. (pp. 372, 374)

2. Write an investment newsletter to address the following questions: Which company appears to be more profitable? Which company has more cash to invest in promising projects? If prices continue rising over the long term, which company would you prefer to invest in? Why? (Challenge)

writing assignment ■

Case 2. *(Learning Objective 1, 6: Plant assets and intangible assets)* The following questions are unrelated except that they all apply to plant assets and intangible assets:

1. The manager of Carpet World regularly debits the cost of repairs and maintenance of plant assets to Plant and Equipment. Why would she do that, since she knows she is violating GAAP? (p. 368)

2. The manager of Horizon Software regularly buys plant assets and debits the cost to Repairs and Maintenance Expense. Why would he do that, since he knows this action violates GAAP? (p. 368)

3. It has been suggested that because many intangible assets have no value except to the company that owns them, they should be valued at $1.00 or zero on the balance sheet. Many accountants disagree with this view. Which view do you support? Why? (pp. 384–385)

Ethical Issue

writing assignment ■

United Jersey Bank of Princeton purchased land and a building for the lump sum of $6.0 million. To get the maximum tax deduction, the bank's managers allocated 80% of the purchase price to the building and only 20% to the land. A more realistic allocation would have been 60% to the building and 40% to the land.

I Required

1. Explain the tax advantage of allocating too much to the building and too little to the land.

2. Was United Jersey Bank's allocation ethical? If so, state why. If not, why not? Identify who was harmed.

Focus on Financials: ■ YUM! Brands

(Learning Objective 2, 3, 6: Analyzing plant assets) Refer to **YUM! Brands'** financial statements in Appendix A at the end of the book, and answer the following questions:

1. Which depreciation method does YUM use for reporting to stockholders and creditors in the financial statements? What type of depreciation method does the company probably use for income tax purposes? Why is this method preferable for tax purposes? (pp. 371–374, 377–380)

2. Depreciation expense is embedded in the expense amounts listed on the income statement. It is reported on the statement of cash flows. How much was YUM's depreciation and amortization expense during fiscal year 2006? How much was YUM's accumulated depreciation and amortization at the end of 2006? Explain why accumulated depreciation and amortization exceeds depreciation and amortization expense for the current year. (Challenge, pp. 148–149)

3. How much did YUM spend on property, plant, and equipment during 2006? In 2005? Evaluate the trend in these capital expenditures as to whether it conveys good news or bad news for YUM. Explain (p. 368)

4. YUM reports 2 separate intangible assets. What are they? How does YUM account for each of these intangibles over its lifetime? (pp. 384–385)

Focus on Analysis: ■ Pier 1 Imports

(*Learning Objective 2, 4, 7: Explaining plant asset activity*) Refer to the **Pier 1 Imports** financial statements in Appendix B at the end of this book. This case leads you through a comprehensive analysis of Pier 1's long-term assets. Its purpose is to show you how to account for plant asset (properties) transactions in summary form.

1. On the statement of cash flows, how much did Pier 1 pay for capital expenditures during 2006? How much cash did Pier 1 receive from the disposition of properties (fixed assets) during 2006? Consider the loss on disposal of fixed assets reported under Cash Flow from Operating Activities, and determine the book value of plant assets that Pier 1 sold during 2006. Do not round these amounts. (pp. 364–385)

2. Use the answer to requirement 1, plus the amount of depreciation and amortization reported on the statement of cash flows, to explain all the activity in the Properties, Net account during 2006. Of the total depreciation and amortization for 2006, assume that $10 million related to Other Noncurrent Assets and not to Properties. Use either a T-account or an equation for your analysis. For this requirement, show amounts in millions and round to the nearest $1 million. (pp. 384–385)

3. Which depreciation method does Pier 1 use? Over what useful life does Pier 1 depreciate buildings, equipment, furniture, and fixtures?

4. Were Pier 1's plant assets proportionately newer or older at the end of 2006 (versus 2005)? Explain your answer. (Challenge)

Group Project

Visit a local business.

❙ Required

1. List all its plant assets.

2. If possible, interview the manager. Gain as much information as you can about the business's plant assets. For example, try to determine the assets' costs, the depreciation method the company is using, and the estimated useful life of each asset category. If an interview is impossible, then develop your own estimates of the assets' costs, useful lives, and book values, assuming an appropriate depreciation method.

3. Determine whether the business has any intangible assets. If so, list them and gain as much information as possible about their nature, cost, and estimated useful lives.

4. Write a detailed report of your findings and be prepared to present your results to the class.

For Internet Exercises go to the Web site www.prenhall.com/harrison.

Quick Check Answers:

1. *c* {[$850,000/($850,000 + $675,000 + $475,000)] × $1,500,000 = $637,500}
2. *a*
3. *b* ($25,000 − $2,500)/5 × 4/12 = $1,500)
4. *d* [($25,000 − $2,500)/5 × 2 = $9,000; $25,000 − $9,000 = $16,000]
5. *b* [$25,000 × 2/5 − $10,000; ($25,000 − $10,000) × 2/5 = $6,000]
6. *a* [($25,000 − $2,500)/5 × 4 = $18,000; $25,000 − $18,000 = $7,000; $11,500 − $7,000 = gain of $4,500]
7. *c* [$17,000 × 2/4 = $8,500; ($17,000 − $8,500) × 2/4 = $4,250; $8,500 + $4,250 = $12,750]
8. *c*
9. *a*
10. *d*
11. *b* [$200,000 × (6,000/50,000) = $24,000]
12. *e*

8 Liabilities

SOUTHWEST AIRLINES: A SUCCESS STORY

Southwest Airlines has been a maverick in the airline industry from the start. Most recently, Southwest has churned out profits while other airlines have been in bankruptcy.

The airlines have some interesting liabilities. Southwest's Rapid Rewards program provides free flights to the company's frequent fliers. Southwest accrues frequent-flier liability for this program and reports "Accrued Liabilities" on the company balance sheet.

Southwest collects cash in advance and then provides flights for customers later. This creates unearned revenue that Southwest can report as "Unearned Ticket Revenue." The company also has notes payable and bonds payable that it reports under "Long-Term Debt."

Southwest Airlines Co.
Balance Sheet (Adapted)
December 31, 2006

(In millions)

Assets		Liabilities and Stockholders' Equity	
Current Assets		**Current Liabilities**	
Cash	$ 1,390	Accounts payable	$ 643
Other current assets	1,211	Accrued liabilities	1,323
Total current assets	2,601	Unearned ticket revenue	799
Equipment and		Current maturities of	
property, net	10,094	long-term debt	122
Other assets	765	Total current liabilities	2,887
		Long-term debt	1,567
		Other long-term liabilities	2,557
		Stockholders' Equity	6,449
Total assets	$13,460	Total liabilities and equity	$13,460

This chapter shows how to account for liabilities—both current and long-term. We begin with current liabilities.

LEARNING OBJECTIVES

1 **Account** for current liabilities and contingent liabilities

2 **Account** for bonds payable

3 **Measure** interest expense

4 **Understand** the advantages and disadvantages of borrowing

5 **Report** liabilities on the balance sheet

CURRENT LIABILITIES

OBJECTIVE

1 Account for current liabilities and contingent liabilities

Current liabilities are obligations due within 1 year or within the company's normal operating cycle if longer than a year. Obligations due beyond that period of time are classified as *long-term liabilities*.

Current liabilities are of 2 kinds:

■ known amounts.
■ estimated amounts.

We look first at current liabilities of a known amount.

Current Liabilities of Known Amount

Current liabilities of known amount include accounts payable, short-term notes payable, sales tax payable, accrued liabilities, payroll liabilities, unearned revenues, and current portion of long-term debt.

Accounts Payable. Amounts owed for products or services purchased on account are *accounts payable*. For example, Southwest Airlines purchases soft drinks and napkins on accounts payable. We have seen many other accounts payable examples in preceding chapters. One of a merchandiser's most common transactions is the credit purchase of inventory. **Best Buy** and **Wal-Mart** buy their inventory on account.

Short-Term Notes Payable. **Short-term notes payable**, a common form of financing, are notes payable due within 1 year. **Starbucks** lists its short-term notes payable as *short-term borrowings*. Starbucks may issue short-term notes payable to borrow cash or to purchase assets. On its notes payable, Starbucks must accrue interest expense and interest payable at the end of the period. The following sequence of entries covers the purchase of inventory, accrual of interest expense, and payment of a 10% short-term note payable that's due in 1 year.

20X5			
Jan. 1	Inventory	8,000	
	Note Payable, Short-Term		8,000
	Purchase of inventory by issuing a note payable		

This transaction increases both an asset and a liability.

Assets	=	Liabilities	+	Stockholders' Equity
+ 8,000	=	+ 8,000	+	0

The Starbucks fiscal year ends each September 30. At year end, Starbucks must accrue interest expense at 10% for January through September:

Sept. 30	Interest Expense ($8,000 × .10 × 9/12)	600	
	Interest Payable		600
	Accrual of interest expense at year end.		

Liabilities increase and equity decreases because of the expense.

Assets	=	Liabilities	+	Stockholders' Equity	−	Expenses
0	=	+ 600				− 600

The balance sheet at year end will report the Note Payable of $8,000 and the related Interest Payable of $600 as current liabilities. The income statement will report interest expense of $600.

The following entry records the note's payment at maturity on January 1, 20X6:

20X6			
Jan. 1	Note Payable, Short-Term	8,000	
	Interest Payable	600	
	Interest Expense ($8,000 × .10 × 3/12)	200	
	Cash [$8,000 + ($8,000 × .10)]		8,800
	Payment of a note payable and interest at maturity.		

The debits zero out the payables and also record Starbuck's interest expense for October, November, and December.

Sales Tax Payable. Most states levy a sales tax on retail sales. Retailers collect the tax from customers and thus owe the state for sales tax collected. Suppose one Saturday's sales at a Home Depot store totaled $200,000. Home Depot collected an additional 5% ($10,000) of sales tax. The store would record that day's sales as follows:

Cash ($200,000 × 1.05)	210,000	
Sales Revenue		200,000
Sales Tax Payable ($200,000 × .05)		10,000
To record cash sales and the related sales tax.		

Assets, liabilities, and equity all increase—equity because of the revenues.

Assets	=	Liabilities	+	Stockholders' Equity	+	Revenues
+ 210,000	=	+ 10,000				+ 200,000

Accrued Liabilities (Accrued Expenses). An **accrued liability** usually results from an expense the business has incurred but not yet paid. Therefore, an accrued expense creates a liability, which explains why it is also called an *accrued expense.*

For example, Southwest Airlines' salary expense and salary payable occur as employees work for the company. Interest expense accrues with the passage of time. There are several categories of accrued expenses:

- Salaries and Wages Payable
- Interest Payable
- Income Taxes Payable

Salaries and Wages Payable is the liability for payroll expenses not yet paid at the end of the period. This category includes salaries, wages, and payroll taxes withheld from employee paychecks. *Interest Payable* is the company's interest payable on notes payable. *Income Taxes Payable* is the amount of income tax the company still owes at year end.

Payroll Liabilities. **Payroll**, also called *employee compensation*, is a major expense. For service organizations—such as law firms, real estate companies, and travel agencies—compensation is *the* major expense, just as cost of goods sold is the largest expense for a merchandising company.

Employee compensation takes many different forms. A *salary* is employee pay stated at a monthly or yearly rate. A *wage* is employee pay stated at an hourly rate. Sales employees earn a *commission*, which is a percentage of the sales the employee has made. A *bonus* is an amount over and above regular compensation. Accounting for all forms of compensation follows the pattern illustrated in Exhibit 8-1 (using assumed figures).

EXHIBIT 8-1	Accounting for Payroll Expenses and Liabilities		
Salary Expense		10,000	
Employee Income Tax Payable			1,200
FICA Tax Payable			800
Salary Payable to Employees [take-home pay]			8,000
To record salary expense.			

Every expense accrual has the same effect: Liabilities increase and equity decreases because of the expense. The accounting equation shows these effects.

Assets	=	Liabilities	+	Stockholders' Equity	–	Expenses
		+ 1,200				– 10,000
0	=	+ 800				
		+ 8,000				

Salary expense represents *gross pay* (that is, employee pay before subtractions for taxes and other deductions). Salary expense creates several payroll liabilities:

- *Employee Income Tax Payable* is the employees' income tax that has been withheld from paychecks.
- *FICA Tax Payable* includes the employees' Social Security tax and Medicare tax, which also are withheld from paychecks. (FICA stands for the Federal Insurance Contributions Act, which created the Social Security tax.)
- *Salary Payable* to employees is their net (take-home) pay.

Companies must also pay some *employer* payroll taxes and expenses for employee benefits. Accounting for these expenses is similar to the illustration in Exhibit 8-1.

Unearned Revenues. *Unearned revenues* are also called *deferred revenues* and *revenues collected in advance.* For all unearned revenue the business has received cash from customers before earning the revenue. The company has a liability—an obligation to provide goods or services to the customer. Let's consider an example.

Southwest Airlines sells tickets and collects cash in advance. Southwest therefore reports Unearned Ticket Revenue for airline tickets sold in advance*. At December 31, 2006, Southwest owed customers $799 million of air travel (see page 414). Let's see how Southwest accounts for unearned ticket revenue.

---

*Some airlines call this liability "Air Traffic Liability."

Assume that Southwest collects $300 for a round-trip ticket from Dallas to Los Angeles and back. Southwest records the cash collection and related liability as follows:

20X8			
Dec. 15	Cash	300	
	Unearned Ticket Revenue		300
	Received cash in advance for ticket sales.		

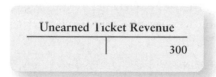

Suppose the customer flies to Los Angeles late in December. Southwest records the revenue earned as follows:

20X8			
Dec. 28	Unearned Ticket Revenue	150	
	Ticket Revenue ($300 × 1/2)		150
	Earned revenue that was collected in advance.		

The liability decreases and the revenue goes up.

Unearned Ticket Revenue		
150	300	
	Bal.	150

Ticket Revenue	
	150

At year end, Southwest reports

∎ $150 of unearned ticket revenue (a liability) on the balance sheet
∎ $150 of ticket revenue on the income statement

The customer returns to Dallas in January 20X9, and Southwest records the revenue earned with this journal entry:

20X9			
Jan. 4	Unearned Ticket Revenue	150	
	Ticket Revenue ($300 × 1/2)		150
	Earned revenue that was collected in advance.		

Now the liability balance is zero because Southwest has earned all the revenue it collected in advance.

```
              Unearned Ticket Revenue
                    150  |          300
                    150  |
                         | Bal.       0
```

Current Portion of Long-Term Debt. Some long-term debt must be paid in installments. The **current portion of long-term debt** (also called *current maturity* or *current installment*) is the amount of the principal that is payable within 1 year. At the end of each year, a company reclassifies (from long-term debt to a current liability) the amount of its long-term debt that must be paid next year.

Southwest Airlines reports Current Maturities of Long-Term Debt as a current liability. Southwest also reports a long-term liability for Long-Term Debt, which excludes the current maturities. *Long-term debt* refers to long-term notes payable and bonds payable, which we cover in the second half of this chapter.

Current Liabilities That Must Be Estimated

A business may know that a liability exists but not know its exact amount. The business must report the liability on the balance sheet. Estimated liabilities vary among companies. Let's look first at Estimated Warranty Payable, a liability account that most merchandisers have.

Estimated Warranty Payable. Many companies guarantee their products under *warranty* agreements. The warranty period may extend for 90 days to a year for consumer products. Automobile companies—General Motors, BMW, and Toyota—accrue liabilities for vehicle warranties.

Whatever the warranty's life, the matching principle demands that the company record the *warranty expense* in the same period that the business records sales revenue. After all, the warranty motivates customers to buy products, so the company must record warranty expense. At the time of the sale, however, the company doesn't know which products are defective. The exact amount of warranty expense cannot be known with certainty, so the business must estimate warranty expense and the related liability.

Assume that **Black & Decker**, which manufactures power tools, made sales of $100,000 subject to product warranties. Assume that in past years between 2% and 4% of products proved defective. Black & Decker could estimate that 3% of sales will require repair or replacement. In this case Black & Decker would estimate warranty expense of $3,000 ($100,000 × 0.03) for the year and make the following entry:

Warranty Expense	3,000	
Estimated Warranty Payable		3,000
To accrue warranty expense.		

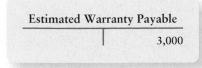

```
              Estimated Warranty Payable
                          |        3,000
```

Assume that defects add up to $2,800, and Black & Decker will replace the defective products. Black & Decker then records the following:

Estimated Warranty Payable	2,800	
Inventory		2,800
To replace defective products sold under warranty.		

Estimated Warranty Payable		
2,800		3,000
	Bal.	200

At the end of the year Black & Decker will report Estimated Warranty Payable of $200 as a current liability. The income statement reports Warranty Expense of $3,000 for the year. Then, next year Black & Decker will repeat this process. The Estimated Warranty Payable account probably won't ever zero out.

If Black & Decker paid cash to satisfy the warranty, then the credit would be to Cash rather than to Inventory. Vacation pay is another expense that must be estimated. And income taxes must be estimated because the final amount isn't determined until early the next year.

Contingent Liabilities

A *contingent liability* is not an actual liability. Instead, it's a potential liability that depends on a *future* event arising out of past events. The Financial Accounting Standards Board (FASB) provides these guidelines to account for contingent liabilities:

1. Record an actual liability if it's *probable* that the loss (or expense) will occur **and** the *amount can be reasonably estimated*. Warranty expense is an example.

2. Report the contingency in a financial statement note if it's *reasonably possible* that a loss (or expense) will occur. Lawsuits in progress are a prime example. Southwest Airlines includes a note in its financial statements to report contingent liabilities.

> **Note 17, Contingencies**
> The Company is subject to various legal proceeding [...] including [...] examinations by the Internal Revenue Service (IRS). The IRS regularly examines the Company's federal income tax returns and, in the course thereof, proposes adjustments to the Company's federal income tax liability reported on such returns.
> The Company's management does not expect that [...] any of its currently ongoing legal proceedings or [...] any proposed adjustments [...] by the IRS [...] will have a material adverse effect on the Company's financial condition, results of operations or cash flow.

3. There is no need to report a contingent loss that is unlikely to occur. Instead, wait until an actual transaction clears up the situation. For example, suppose **Del Monte Foods** grows vegetables in Nicaragua, and the Nicaraguan government threatens to confiscate the assets of all foreign companies. Del Monte will report nothing about the contingency if the probability of a loss is considered remote.

A contingent liability may arise from lawsuits that claim wrongdoing by the company. The plaintiff may seek damages through the courts. If the court or the IRS rules in favor of Southwest, there is no liability. But if the ruling favors the plaintiff, then Southwest will have an actual liability. It would be unethical to omit these disclosures from the financial statements because investors need this information to properly evaluate a company.

Are All Your Liabilities Reported on the Balance Sheet?

The big danger with liabilities is that you may fail to report a large debt on your balance sheet. What is the consequence of missing a large liability? You will definitely understate your liabilities and your debt ratio. You'll probably overstate your net income. In short, your financial statements will make you look better than you really are. Any such error, if significant, hurts a company's credibility.

Contingent liabilities are very easy to overlook because they aren't actual debts. How would you feel if you owned stock in a company that failed to report a contingency that put the company out of business. If you had known of the contingency, you could have sold the stock and avoided the loss. In this case, you would hire a lawyer to file suit against the company for negligent financial reporting.

SUMMARY OF THE CURRENT LIABILITIES

Let's summarize what we've covered thus far. A company can report its current liabilities on the balance sheet as follows:

Accounting, Inc.
Balance Sheet
December 31, 20X1

Assets	Liabilities
Current Assets:	Current liabilities:
Cash	Accounts payable
Short-term investments	Salary payable*
Etc.	Interest payable*
	Income tax payable*
Property, plant, and equipment:	Unearned revenue
Land	Estimated warranty payable*
Etc.	Notes payable, short-term
	Current portion of long-term debt
Other assets	Total current liabilities
	Long-term liabilities
	Stockholder's Equity
	Common stock
	Retained earnings
Total assets $XXX	Total liabilities and stockholders equity $XXX

*These items are often combined and reported in a single total as "Accrued Liabilities" or "Accrued Expenses Payable."

On its income statement this company would report

- *Expenses* related to some of the current liabilities. Examples include Salary Expense, Interest Expense, Income Tax Expense, and Warranty Expense.
- *Revenue* related to the unearned revenue. Examples include Service Revenue and Sales Revenue that were collected in advance.

MID-CHAPTER SUMMARY PROBLEM

Assume that the **Estée Lauder Companies, Inc.**, faced the following liability situations at June 30, 20X4, the end of the company's fiscal year. Show how Estée Lauder would report these liabilities on its balance sheet at June 30, 20X4.

a. Salary expense for the last payroll period of the year was $900,000. Of this amount, employees' withheld income tax totaled $88,000 and FICA taxes were $61,000. These payroll amounts will be paid in early July.

b. On fiscal-year 20X4 sales of $400 million, management estimates warranty expense of 2%. One year ago, at June 30, 20X3, Estimated Warranty Payable stood at $3 million. Warranty payments were $9 million during the year ended June 30, 20X4.

c. The company pays royalties on its purchased trademarks. Royalties for the trademarks are equal to a percentage of Estée Lauder's sales. Assume that sales in 20X4 were $400 million and were subject to a royalty rate of 3%. At June 30, 20X4, Estée Lauder owes two-thirds of the year's royalty, to be paid in July.

d. Long-term debt totals $100 million and is payable in annual installments of $10 million each. The interest rate on the debt is 7%, and the interest is paid each December 31.

Answer

Liabilities at June 30, 20X4:

a. Current liabilities:

Salary payable ($900,000 − $88,000 − $61,000)...............	$ 751,000
Employee income tax payable	88,000
FICA tax payable	61,000

b. Current liabilities:

Estimated warranty payable...	2,000,000
[$3,000,000 + ($400,000,000 × 0.02) − $9,000,000]	

c. Current liabilities:

Royalties payable ($400,000,000 × 0.03 × 2/3).................	8,000,000

d. Current liabilities:

Current installment of long-term debt.................................	10,000,000
Interest payable ($100,000,000 × 0.07 × 6/12).................	3,500,000
Long-term debt ($100,000,000 − $10,000,000)....................	90,000,000

LONG-TERM LIABILITIES: BONDS AND NOTES PAYABLE

Large companies such as Southwest Airlines, Home Depot, and **Toyota** cannot borrow billions from a single lender. So how do corporations borrow huge amounts? They issue (sell) bonds to the public. **Bonds payable** are groups of notes payable issued to multiple lenders, called *bondholders*. Southwest Airlines needs airplanes and can borrow large amounts by issuing bonds to thousands of individual investors, who each lend Southwest a modest amount. Southwest receives the cash it needs, and each investor limits risk by diversifying investments—not putting all the investor's "eggs in one basket." Here we treat bonds payable and notes payable together because their accounting is the same.

Bonds: An Introduction

Each bond payable is, in effect, a note payable. Bonds payable are debts of the issuing company.

Purchasers of bonds receive a bond's certificate, which carries the issuing company's name. The certificate also states the *principal*, which is typically stated in units of $1,000; principal is also called the bond's *face value*, *maturity value*, or *par value*. The bond obligates the issuing company to pay the debt at a specific future time called the *maturity date*.

Interest is the rental fee on borrowed money. The bond certificate states the interest rate that the issuer will pay the holder and the dates that the interest payments are due (generally twice a year). Exhibit 8-2, shows an actual bond certificate.

EXHIBIT 8-2	Bond (Note) Certificate (Adapted)

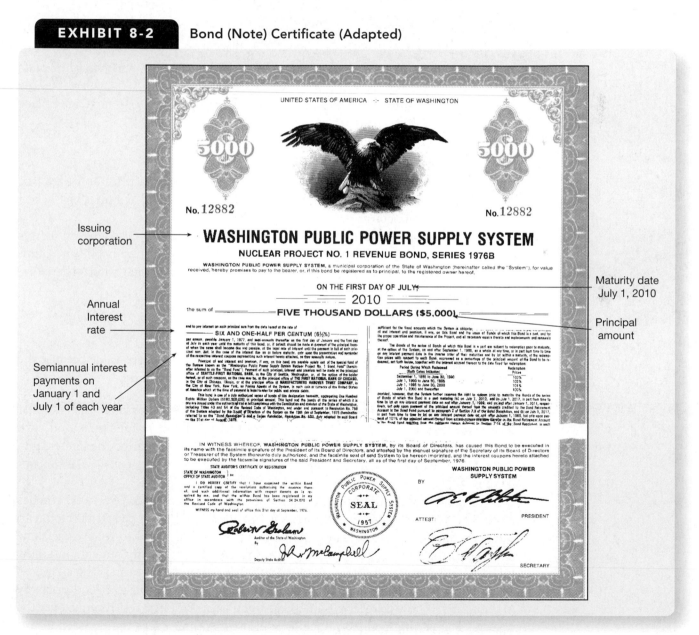

Issuing corporation

Annual Interest rate

Semiannual interest payments on January 1 and July 1 of each year

Maturity date July 1, 2010

Principal amount

Issuing bonds usually requires the services of a securities firm, such as Merrill Lynch, to act as the underwriter of the bond issue. The **underwriter** purchases the bonds from the issuing company and resells them to its clients, or it may sell the bonds to its clients and earn a commission on the sale.

Types of Bonds. All the bonds in a particular issue may mature at the same time (**term bonds**) or in installments over a period of time (**serial bonds**). Serial bonds are like installment notes payable. Some of Southwest Airlines' long-term debts are serial in nature because they are payable in installments.

Secured, or *mortgage*, *bonds* give the bondholder the right to take specified assets of the issuer if the company *defaults*—that is, fails to pay interest or principal. *Unsecured bonds*, called **debentures**, are backed only by the good faith of the borrower. Debentures carry a higher rate of interest than secured bonds because debentures are riskier investments.

Bond Prices. Investors may buy and sell bonds through bond markets. Bond prices are quoted at a percentage of their maturity value. For example,

- A $1,000 bond quoted at 100 is bought or sold for $1,000, which is 100% of its face value.
- The same bond quoted at 101.5 has a market price of $1,015 (101.5% of face value = $1,000 × 1.015).
- A $1,000 bond quoted at 88.375 is priced at $883.75 ($1,000 × 0.88375).

Bond Premium and Bond Discount. A bond issued at a price above its face (par) value is said to be issued at a **premium**, and a bond issued at a price below face (par) value has a **discount**.

Premium on Bonds Payable has a *credit* balance and Discount on Bonds Payable carries a *debit* balance. Bond Discount is therefore a contra liability account.

As a bond nears maturity, its market price moves toward par value. Therefore, the price of a bond issued at a

- premium decreases toward maturity value.
- discount increases toward maturity value.

On the maturity date, a bond's market value exactly equals its face value because the company that issued the bond pays that amount to retire the bond.

The Time Value of Money. A dollar received today is worth more than a dollar to be received in the future. You can invest today's dollar immediately and earn income from it. But if you must wait to receive the dollar, you forgo the interest revenue. Money earns income over time, a fact called the *time value of money*. Let's examine how the *time value of money* affects the pricing of bonds.

Assume that a Southwest Airlines bond with a face value of $1,000 reaches maturity 3 years from today and carries no interest. Would you pay $1,000 today to purchase this bond? No, because the payment of $1,000 today to receive the same amount in the future provides you with no income on the investment. Just how much would you pay today to receive $1,000 at the end of 3 years? The answer is some amount *less* than $1,000. Let's suppose that you feel $750 is a good price. By investing $750 now to receive $1,000 later, you earn $250 interest revenue over the 3 years. The issuing company such as Southwest Airlines, sees the transaction this way: Southwest will pay you $250 interest to use your $750 for 3 years.

The amount to invest *now* to receive more later is called the **present value** of a future amount. In our example, $750 is the present value, and $1,000 is the future amount.

Our $750 bond price is a reasonable estimate. The exact present value of any future amount depends on

1. The amount of the future payment ($1,000 in our example)
2. The length of time from the investment date to the date when the future amount is to be collected (3 years)
3. The interest rate during the period (say 10%)

In this case the present value is very close to $750. Present value is always less than the future amount. We discuss how present value is computed in Appendix C at the end of the book (pp. 805–814).

Bond Interest Rates Determine Bond Prices. Bonds are always sold at their *market price*, which is the amount investors will pay for the bond. **Market price is the bond's present value**, which equals the present value of the principal payment plus the present value of the cash interest payments. Interest is usually paid semiannually (twice a year). Some companies pay interest annually or quarterly.

Two interest rates work to set the price of a bond:

■ The **stated interest rate**, also called the coupon rate, is the interest rate printed on the bond certificate. The stated interest rate determines the amount of cash interest the borrower pays—and the investor receives—each year. Suppose Southwest Airlines bonds have a stated interest rate of 9%. Southwest would pay $9,000 of interest annually on each $100,000 bond. Each semiannual payment would be $4,500 ($100,000 × 0.09 × 6/12).

■ The **market interest rate**, or *effective interest rate*, is the rate that investors demand for loaning their money. The market interest rate varies by the minute.

A company may issue bonds with a stated interest rate that differs from the prevailing market interest rate. In fact, the 2 interest rates often differ.

Exhibit 8-3 shows how the stated interest rate and the market interest rate interact to determine the issue price of a bond payable for 3 separate cases.

EXHIBIT 8-3 How the Stated Interest Rate and the Market Interest Rate Interact to Determine the Price of a Bond

Issue Price of Bonds Payable

Case A:

Stated interest rate on a bond payable	equals	Market interest rate	Therefore,	Price of face (par, or maturity) value
Example: 9%	=	9%	→	Par: $1,000 bond issued for $1,000

Case B:

Stated interest rate on a bond payable	less than	Market interest rate	Therefore,	Discount price (price below face value)
Example: 9%	<	10%	→	Discount: $1,000 bond issued for a price below $1,000

Case C:

Stated interest rate on a bond payable	greater than	Market interest rate	Therefore,	Premium price (price above face value)
Example: 9%	>	8%	→	Premium: $1,000 bond issued for a price above $1,000

Southwest Airlines may issue 9% bonds when the market rate has risen to 10%. Will the Southwest 9% bonds attract investors in this market? No, because investors can earn 10% on other bonds of similar risk. Therefore, investors will purchase Southwest bonds only at a price less than their face value. The difference between the lower price and face value is a *discount* (Exhibit 8-3). Conversely, if the market interest rate is 8%, Southwest's 9% bonds will be so attractive that investors will pay more than face value to purchase them. The difference between the higher price and face value is a *premium*.

Issuing Bonds Payable at Par (Face Value)

OBJECTIVE

2 **Account** for bonds payable

We start with the most straightforward situation—issuing bonds at their par value. There is no premium or discount on these bonds payable.

Suppose Southwest Airlines has $50,000 of 9% bonds payable that mature in 5 years. Assume that Southwest issued these bonds at par on January 1, 2008. The issuance entry is

2008			
Jan. 1	Cash	50,000	
	Bonds Payable		50,000
	To issue bonds at par.		

Bonds Payable	
	50,000

Assets and liabilities increase when a company issues bonds payable.

Assets	=	Liabilities	+	Stockholders' Equity
+ 50,000	=	+ 50,000	+	0

Southwest, the borrower, makes a one-time entry to record the receipt of cash and the issuance of bonds. Afterward, investors buy and sell the bonds through the bond markets. These later buy-and-sell transactions between outside investors do *not* involve Southwest at all.

Interest payments occur each January 1 and July 1. Southwest's entry to record the first semiannual interest payment is:

2008			
July 1	Interest Expense ($50,000 × 0.09 × 6/12)	2,250	
	Cash		2,250
	To pay semiannual interest.		

The payment of interest expense decreases assets and equity. Bonds payable are not affected.

Assets	=	Liabilities	+	Stockholders' Equity	−	Expenses
− 2,250	=	0	+			− 2,250

At year end, Southwest accrues interest expense and interest payable for 6 months (July through December), as follows:

2008			
Dec. 31	Interest Expense ($50,000 × 0.09 × 6/12)	2,250	
	Interest Payable		2,250
	To accrue interest.		

Liabilities increase, and equity decreases.

Assets	=	Liabilities	+	Stockholders' Equity	−	Expenses
0	=	+ 2,250	+			− 2,250

On January 1, Southwest will pay the interest, debiting Interest Payable and crediting Cash. Then, at maturity, Southwest pays off the bonds as follows:

2013			
Jan. 1	Bonds Payable	50,000	
	Cash		50,000
	To pay bonds payable at maturity.		

Bonds Payable	
50,000	50,000
	Bal. 0

Assets	=	Liabilities	+	Stockholders' Equity
− 50,000	=	− 50,000		

Issuing Bonds Payable at a Discount

Market conditions may force a company to issue bonds at a discount. Suppose Southwest Airlines issued $100,000 of 9%, 5-year bonds when the market interest rate is 10%. The market price of the bonds drops, and Southwest receives $96,149[1] at issuance. The transaction is recorded as follows:

2008			
Jan. 1	Cash	96,149	
	Discount on Bonds Payable	3,851	
	Bonds Payable		100,000
	To issue bonds at a discount.		

---

[1]Appendix C at the end of this book shows how to determine the price of this bond.

The accounting equation shows that Southwest has a net liability of $96,149—not $100,000.

Assets	=	Liabilities	+	Stockholders' Equity
+ 96,149	=	− 3,851	+	0
		+ 100,000		

The bonds payable accounts have a net balance of $96,149 as follows:

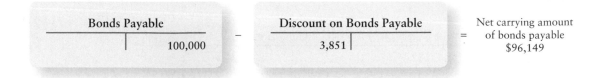

Bonds Payable | 100,000 — Discount on Bonds Payable | 3,851 = Net carrying amount of bonds payable $96,149

Southwest's balance sheet immediately after issuance of the bonds would report the following:

Total current liabilities....................................		$ XXX
Long-term liabilities:		
Bonds payable, 9%, due 2013....................	$100,000	
Less: Discount on bonds payable................	(3,851)	96,149

Discount on Bonds Payable is a contra account to Bonds Payable, a decrease in the company's liabilities. Subtracting the discount from Bonds Payable yields the *carrying amount* of the bonds. Thus, Southwest's liability is $96,149, which is the amount the company borrowed.

What Is the Interest Expense on These Bonds Payable?

OBJECTIVE

3 Measure interest expense

Southwest pays interest on bonds semiannually, which is common practice. Each semiannual *interest payment* is set by the bond contract and therefore remains the same over the life of the bonds:

$$\text{Semiannual interest payment} = \$100,000 \times 0.09 \times 6/12$$
$$= \$4,500$$

But Southwest's *interest expense* increases as the bonds march toward maturity. Remember: These bonds were issued at a discount.

Panel A of Exhibit 8-4 repeats the Southwest Airlines bond data we've been using. Panel B provides an amortization table that does 2 things:

- Determines the periodic interest expense (column B)
- Shows the bond carrying amount (column E)

Study the exhibit carefully because the amounts we'll be using come directly from the amortization table. This exhibit shows the *effective-interest method of amortization*, which is the correct way to measure interest expense.

EXHIBIT 8-4 Debt Amortization for a Bond Discount

Panel A—Bond Data

Issue date—January 1, 2008	Maturity date—January 1, 2013
Face (par or *maturity*) value—$100,000	Market interest rate at time of issue—10% annually, 5% semiannually
Stated interest rate—9%	Issue price—$96,149
Interest paid—4½% semiannually, $4,500 = $100,000 × 0.09 × 6/12	

Panel B—Amortization Table

	A	B	C	D	E
Semiannual Interest Date	Interest Payment (4 1/2% of Maturity Value)	Interest Expense (5% of Preceding Bond Carrying Amount)	Discount Amortization (B – A)	Discount Account Balance (Preceding D – C)	Bond Carrying Amount ($100,000 – D)
Jan. 1, 2008				$3,851	$ 96,149
July 1	$4,500	$4,807	$307	3,544	96,456
Jan. 1, 2009	4,500	4,823	323	3,221	96,779
July 1	4,500	4,839	339	2,882	97,118
Jan. 1, 2010	4,500	4,856	356	2,526	97,474
July 1	4,500	4,874	374	2,152	97,848
Jan. 1, 2011	4,500	4,892	392	1,760	98,240
July 1	4,500	4,912	412	1,348	98,652
Jan. 1, 2012	4,500	4,933	433	915	99,085
July 1	4,500	4,954	454	461	99,539
Jan. 1, 2013	4,500	4,961*	461	-0-	100,000

*Adjusted for effect of rounding

Notes
- Column A   The semiannual interest payments are constant—fixed by the bond contract.
- Column B   The interest expense each period = the preceding bond carrying amount × the market interest rate.
    Interest expense increases as the bond carrying amount (E) increases.
- Column C   The discount amortization (C) is the excess of interest expense (B) over interest payment (A).
- Column D   The discount balance (D) decreases when amortized.
- Column E   The bond carrying amount (E) increases from $96,149 at issuance to $100,000 at maturity.

Interest Expense on Bonds Issued at a Discount

In Exhibit 8-4, Southwest Airlines borrowed $96,149 cash but must pay $100,000 when the bonds mature. What happens to the $3,851 balance of the discount account over the life of the bond issue?

The $3,851 is additional interest expense to Southwest over and above the stated interest that Southwest pays each 6 months. Exhibit 8-5 graphs the interest expense and the interest payment on the Southwest bonds over their lifetime. Observe that the semiannual interest payment is fixed—by contract—at $4,500. But the amount of interest expense increases as the discount bond marches upward toward maturity.

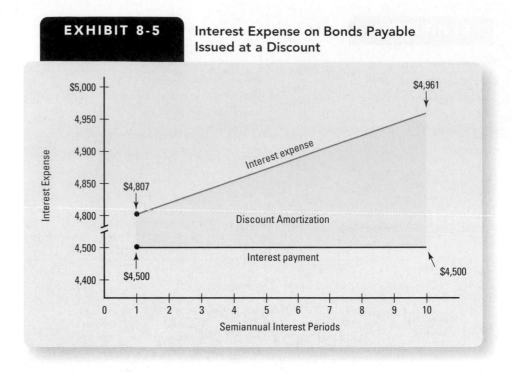

EXHIBIT 8-5 Interest Expense on Bonds Payable Issued at a Discount

The discount is allocated to interest expense through amortization over the term of the bonds. Exhibit 8-6 illustrates the amortization of the bonds from $96,149 at the start to $100,000 at maturity. These amounts come from Exhibit 8-4, column E (p. 429).

Now let's see how Southwest would account for these bonds issued at a discount. In our example, Southwest issued its bonds on January 1, 2008. On July 1, Southwest made the first semiannual interest payment. But Southwest's interest expense is greater than its payment of $4,500. Southwest's journal entry to record interest expense and the interest payment for the first 6 months follows (with all amounts taken from Exhibit 8-4, page 429:

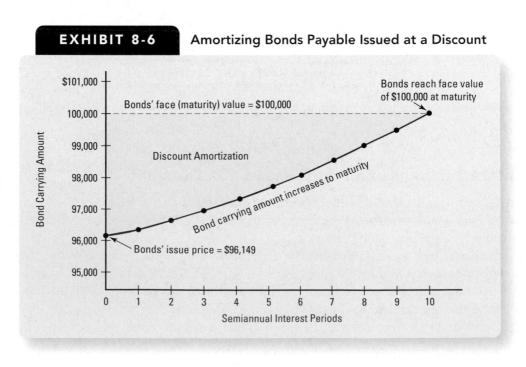

EXHIBIT 8-6 Amortizing Bonds Payable Issued at a Discount

2008			
July 1	Interest Expense	4,807	
	Discount on Bonds Payable		307
	Cash		4,500
	To pay semiannual interest and amortize bond discount.		

The credit to Discount on Bonds Payable accomplishes 2 purposes:

- It amortizes the bonds as they march upward toward maturity value.
- It amortizes the discount to interest expense.

At December 31, 2008, Southwest accrues interest and amortizes the bonds for July through December with this entry (amounts from Exhibit 8-4, page 429:

2008			
Dec. 31	Interest Expense	4,823	
	Discount on Bonds Payable		323
	Interest Payable		4,500
	To accrue semiannual interest and amortize bond discount.		

At December 31, 2008, Southwest's bond accounts appear as follows:

Bonds Payable		**Discount on Bonds Payable**	
	100,000	3,851	307
			323
		Bal. 3,221	

Bond carrying amount, $96,779 = $100,000 − $3,221 from Exhibit 8-4, page 429.

STOP & think. . .

What would Southwest Airlines' 2008 income statement and year-end balance sheet report for these bonds?

Answer:

Income Statement for 2008

Interest expense ($4,807 + $4,823)	$ 9,630

Balance Sheet at December 31, 2008

Current liabilities:		
Interest payable...		$ 4,500
Long-term liabilities:		
Bonds payable..	$100,000	
Less: Discount on bonds payable...............	(3,221)	96,779

At maturity on January 1, 2013, the discount will have been amortized to zero, and the bonds' carrying amount will be face value of $100,000. Southwest will retire the bonds by paying $100,000 to the bondholders.

Partial-Period Interest Amounts

Companies don't always issue bonds at the beginning or the end of their accounting year. They issue bonds when market conditions are most favorable, and that may be on May 16, August 1, or any other date. To illustrate partial-period interest, assume **Google Inc.** issues $100,000 of 8% bonds payable at 96 on August 31, 2009. The market rate of interest was 9%, and these bonds pay semiannual interest on February 28 and August 31 each year. The first few lines of Google's amortization table are

Semiannual Interest Date	4% Interest Payment	4 ½% Interest Expense	Discount Amortization	Discount Account Balance	Bond Carrying Amount
Aug. 31, 2009				$4,000	$96,000
Feb. 28, 2010	$4,000	$4,320	$320	3,680	96,320
Aug. 31, 2010	4,000	4,334	334	3,346	96,654

Google's accounting year ends on December 31, so at year end Google must accrue interest and amortize bond discount for 4 months (September through December). At December 31, 2009, Google will make this entry:

2009			
Dec. 31	Interest Expense ($4,320 × 4/6)	2,880	
	Discount on Bonds Payable ($320 × 4/6)		213
	Interest Payable ($4,000 × 4/6)		2,667
	To accrue interest and amortize discount at year end.		

The year-end entry at December 31, 2009, uses 4/6 of the upcoming semiannual amounts at February 28, 2010. This example clearly illustrates the benefit of an amortization schedule.

Issuing Bonds Payable at a Premium

Let's modify the Southwest Airlines bond example to illustrate issuance of the bonds at a premium. Assume that Southwest issues $100,000 of 5-year, 9% bonds that pay interest semiannually. If the 9% bonds are issued when the market interest rate is 8%, their issue price is $104,100.[2] The premium on these bonds is $4,100, and Exhibit 8-7 shows how to amortize the bonds by the effective-interest method. In practice, bond premiums are rare because few companies issue their bonds to pay cash interest above the market interest rate. We cover bond premiums for completeness.

Southwest's entries to record issuance of the bonds on January 1, 2008, and to make the first interest payment and amortize the bonds on July 1, are as follows:

2008			
Jan. 1	Cash	104,100	
	Bonds Payable		100,000
	Premium on Bonds Payable		4,100
	To issue bonds at a premium.		

---

[2]Appendix C at the end of this book shows how to determine the price of this bond.

At the beginning, Southwest's liability is $104,000—not $100,000. The accounting equation makes this clear.

Assets	=	Liabilities	+	Stockholders' Equity
+ 104,100	=	+ 100,000	+	0
		+ 4,100		

2008			
July 1	Interest Expense (from Exhibit 8-7)	4,164	
	Premium on Bonds Payable	336	
	Cash		4,500
	To pay semiannual interest and amortize bond premium.		

EXHIBIT 8-7   Debt Amortization for a Bond Premium

Panel A—Bond Data

Issue date—January 1, 2008	Maturity date—January 1, 2013
Face (par or *maturity*) value—$100,000	Market interest rate at time of issue—8% annually, 4% semiannually
Stated interest rate—9%	Issue price—$104,100
Interest paid—4½% semiannually, $4,500 = $100,000 × 0.09 × 6/12	

Panel B—Amortization Table

	A	B	C	D	E
Semiannual Interest Date	Interest Payment (4 1/2% of Maturity Value)	Interest Expense (4% of Preceding Bond Carrying Amount)	Premium Amortization (A – B)	Premium Account Balance (Preceding D – C)	Bond Carrying Amount ($100,000 + D)
Jan. 1, 2008				$4,100	$ 104,100
July 1	$4,500	$4,164	$336	3,764	103,764
Jan. 1, 2009	4,500	4,151	349	3,415	103,415
July 1	4,500	4,137	363	3,052	103,052
Jan. 1, 2010	4,500	4,122	378	2,674	102,674
July 1	4,500	4,107	393	2,281	102,281
Jan. 1, 2011	4,500	4,091	409	1,872	101,872
July 1	4,500	4,075	425	1,447	101,447
Jan. 1, 2012	4,500	4,058	442	1,005	101,005
July 1	4,500	4,040	460	545	100,545
Jan. 1, 2013	4,500	3,955*	545	-0-	100,000

*Adjusted for effect of rounding

Notes
- Column A   The semiannual interest payments are constant—fixed by the bond contract.
- Column B   The interest expense each period = the preceding bond carrying amount × the market interest rate. Interest expense decreases as the bond carrying amount (E) decreases.
- Column C   The premium amortization (C) is the excess of interest payment (A) over interest expense (B).
- Column D   The premium balance (D) decreases when amortized.
- Column E   The bond carrying amount (E) decreases from $104,100 at issuance to $100,000 at maturity.

Immediately after issuing the bonds at a premium on January 1, 2008, Southwest would report the bonds payable on the balance sheet as follows:

Total current liabilities............................	$	XXX
Long-term liabilities:		
Bonds payable.......................................	$100,000	
Premium on bonds payable..................	4,100	104,100

A premium is *added* to the balance of bonds payable to determine the carrying amount.

In Exhibit 8-7 Southwest borrowed $104,100 cash but must pay back only $100,000 at maturity. The $4,100 premium is a reduction in Southwest's interest expense over the term of the bonds. Exhibit 8-8 graphs Southwest's interest payments (column A from Exhibit 8-7) and interest expense (column B).

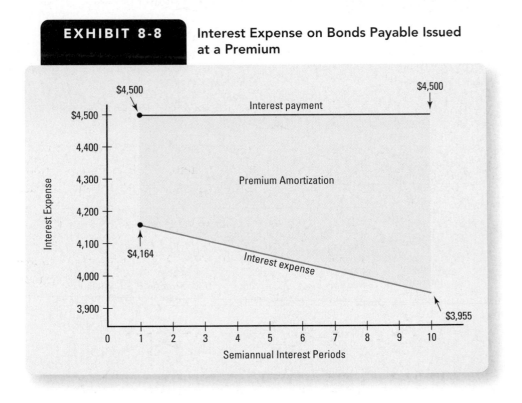

EXHIBIT 8-8 **Interest Expense on Bonds Payable Issued at a Premium**

Through amortization the premium decreases interest expense each period over the term of the bonds. Exhibit 8-9 diagrams the amortization of the bonds from the issue price of $104,100 to maturity value of $100,000. All amounts are taken from Exhibit 8-7.

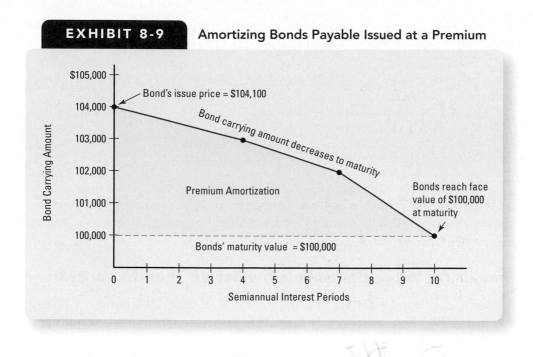

EXHIBIT 8-9   Amortizing Bonds Payable Issued at a Premium

The Straight-Line Amortization Method: A Quick and Dirty Way to Measure Interest Expense

There's a less precise way to amortize bond discount or premium. The *straight-line amortization method* divides a bond discount (or premium) into equal periodic amounts over the bond's term. The amount of interest expense is the same for each interest period.

Let's apply the straight-line method to the Southwest Airlines bonds issued at a discount and illustrated in Exhibit 8-4 (p. 429). Suppose Southwest's financial vice president is considering issuing the 9% bonds at $96,149. To estimate semiannual interest expense on the bonds, the executive can use the straight-line amortization method for the bond discount, as follows:

Semiannual cash interest payment ($100,000 × 0.09 × 6/12)...............	$4,500
+ Semiannual amortization of discount ($3,851 ÷ 10)............................	385
= Estimated semiannual interest expense...	$4,885

The straight-line amortization method uses these same amounts every period over the term of the bonds.

Southwest's entry to record interest and amortization of the bond discount under the straight-line amortization method would be

2008			
July 1	Interest Expense	4,885	
	Discount on Bonds Payable		385
	Cash		4,500
	To pay semiannual interest and amortize bond discount.		

Generally accepted accounting principles (GAAP) permit the straight-line amortization method only when its amounts differ insignificantly from the amounts determined by the effective-interest method.

Should We Retire Bonds Payable Before Their Maturity?

Normally, companies wait until maturity to pay off, or *retire*, their bonds payable. But companies sometimes retire bonds early. The main reason for retiring bonds early is to relieve the pressure of making high interest payments. Also, the company may be able to borrow at a lower interest rate.

Some bonds are **callable**, which means that the issuer may *call*, or pay off, those bonds at a prearranged price (this is the *call price*) whenever the issuer chooses. The call price is often a percentage point or 2 above the par value, perhaps 101 or 102. Callable bonds give the issuer the benefit of being able to pay off the bonds whenever it is most favorable to do so. The alternative to calling the bonds is to purchase them in the open market at their current market price.

Southwest Airlines has $300 million of debenture bonds outstanding. Assume the unamortized discount is $30 million. Lower interest rates may convince management to pay off these bonds now. Assume that the bonds are callable at 101. If the market price of the bonds is 99, will Southwest call the bonds at 101 or purchase them for 99 in the open market? Market price is the better choice because the market price is lower than the call price. Let's see how to account for an early retirement of bonds payable. Retiring the bonds at 99 results in a loss of $27 million, computed as follows:

	Millions
Par value of bonds being retired...............................	$300
Less: Unamortized discount......................................	(30)
Carrying amount of the bonds being retired............	270
Market price ($300 × .99)..	297
Loss on retirement of bonds payable......................	$ 27

Gains and losses on early retirement of bonds payable are reported as Other income (loss) on the income statement.

Convertible Bonds and Notes

Some corporate bonds may be converted into the **issuing** company's common stock. These bonds are called **convertible bonds** (or **convertible notes**). For investors these bonds combine the safety of (a) assured receipt of interest and principal on the bonds with (b) the opportunity for gains on the stock. The conversion feature is so attractive that investors usually accept a lower interest rate than they would on non-convertible bonds. The lower cash interest payments benefit the issuer. If the market price of the issuing company's stock gets high enough, the bondholders will convert the bonds into stock.

Suppose Southwest Airlines has convertible notes payable of $100 million. If Southwest's stock price rises high enough, the noteholders will convert the notes into the company's common stock. Conversion of the notes payable into stock will decrease Southwest's liabilities and increase its equity.

Assume the noteholders convert the notes into 4 million shares of Southwest Airlines common stock ($1 par) on May 14. Southwest makes the following entry in its accounting records:

May 14	Notes Payable	100,000,000	
	Common Stock (4,000,000 × $1 par)		4,000,000
	Paid-in Capital in Excess of		
	Par—Common		96,000,000
	To record conversion of notes payable.		

The accounting equation shows that liabilities decrease and equity goes up.

Assets	=	Liabilities	+	Stockholders' Equity
0	=	– 100,000,000		+ 4,000,000 + 96,000,000

The carrying amount of the notes ($100 million) ceases to be debt and becomes stockholders' equity. Common Stock is recorded at its *par value*, which is a dollar amount assigned to each share of stock. In this case, the credit to Common Stock is $4,000,000 (4,000,000 shares × $1 par value per share). The extra carrying amount of the notes payable ($96,000,000) is credited to another stockholders' equity account, Paid-in Capital in Excess of Par—Common. We'll be using this account in various ways in the next chapter.

Financing Operations with Bonds or Stock?

OBJECTIVE

4 **Understand** the advantages and disadvantages of borrowing

Managers must decide how to get the money they need to pay for assets. There are 3 main ways to finance operations:

- By retained earnings
- By issuing stock
- By issuing bonds (or notes) payable

Each strategy has its advantages and disadvantages.

1. *Financed by retained earnings* means that the company already has enough cash to purchase the needed assets. There's no need to issue more stock or to borrow money. This strategy is low-risk to the company.

2. *Issuing stock* creates no liabilities or interest expense and is less risky to the issuing corporation. But issuing stock is more costly, as we shall see.

3. *Issuing bonds or notes payable* does not dilute control of the corporation. It often results in higher earnings per share because the earnings on borrowed money usually exceed interest expense. But creating more debt increases the risk of the company.

Earnings per share (EPS) is the amount of a company's net income for each share of its stock. EPS is the single most important statistic for evaluating companies because EPS is a standard measure of operating performance that applies to companies of different sizes and from different industries.

Suppose Southwest Airlines needs $500,000 for expansion. Assume Southwest has net income of $300,000 and 100,000 shares of common stock outstanding. Management is considering 2 financing plans. Plan 1 is to issue $500,000 of 6% bonds payable, and plan 2 is to issue 50,000 shares of common stock for $500,000. Management believes the new cash can be invested in operations to earn income of $200,000 before interest and taxes.

Exhibit 8-10 shows the earnings-per-share advantage of borrowing. As you can see, Southwest's EPS amount is higher if the company borrows by issuing bonds (compare lines 9 and 10). Southwest earns more on the investment ($102,000) than the interest it pays on the bonds ($30,000). This is called **trading on the equity**, or using **leverage**. It is widely used to increase earnings per share of common stock.

EXHIBIT 8-10   Earnings-Per-Share Advantage of Borrowing

	Plan 1		Plan 2	
	Borrow $500,000 at 6%		Issue 50,000 Shares of Common Stock for $500,000	
1 Net income before expansion		$300,000		$300,000
2 Expected project income before interest and income tax	$200,000		$200,000	
3 Less interest expense ($500,000 × .06)	(30,000)		0	
4 Expected project income before income tax	170,000		200,000	
5 Less income tax expense (40%)	(68,000)		(80,000)	
6 Expected project net income		102,000		120,000
7 Total company net income		$402,000		$420,000
8 Earnings per share after expansion:				
9 Plan 1 Borrow ($402,000/100,000 shares)		$4.02		
10 Plan 2 Issue Stock ($420,000/150,000 shares)				$2.80

In this case borrowing results in higher earnings per share than issuing stock. Borrowing has its disadvantages, however. Interest expense may be high enough to eliminate net income and lead to losses. Also, borrowing creates liabilities that must be paid during bad years as well as good years. In contrast, a company that issues stock can omit its dividends during a bad year. The Decision Guidelines provide some help in deciding how to finance operations.

DECISION GUIDELINES

FINANCING WITH DEBT OR WITH STOCK

El Chico is the leading chain of Tex-Mex restaurants in the United States, begun by the Cuellar family in the Dallas area. Suppose El Chico is expanding into neighboring states. Take the role of Miguel Cuellar and assume you must make some key decisions about how to finance the expansion.

Decision	Guidelines
How will you finance El Chico's expansion?	Your financing plan depends on El Chico's ability to generate cash flow, your willingness to give up some control of the business, the amount of financing risk you are willing to take, and El Chico's credit rating.
Do El Chico's operations generate enough cash to meet all its financing needs?	If yes, the business needs little outside financing. There is no need to borrow. If no, the business will need to issue additional stock or borrow the money.
Are you willing to give up some of your control of the business?	If yes, then issue stock to other stockholders, who can vote their shares to elect the company's directors. If no, then borrow from bondholders, who have no vote in the management of the company.
How much financing risk are you willing to take?	If much, then borrow as much as you can, and you may increase El Chico's earnings per share. But this will increase the business's debt ratio and the risk of being unable to pay its debts. If little, then borrow sparingly. This will hold the debt ratio down and reduce the risk of default on borrowing agreements. But El Chico's earnings per share may be lower than if you were to borrow.
How good is the business's credit rating?	The better the credit rating, the easier it is to borrow on favorable terms. A good credit rating also makes it easier to issue stock. Neither stockholders nor creditors will entrust their money to a company with a bad credit rating.

The Times-Interest-Earned Ratio

We have just seen how borrowing can increase EPS. But too much debt can lead to bankruptcy if the business cannot pay liabilities as they come due. UAL Inc., the parent company of United Airlines, fell into the debt trap.

The **debt ratio** measures the effect of debt on the company's *financial position* but says nothing about the ability to pay interest expense. Analysts use a second ratio—the **times-interest-earned ratio**—to relate income to interest expense. To compute this ratio, we divide *income from operations* (also called *operating income*) by interest expense. This ratio measures the number of times that operating income can *cover* interest expense. The times-interest-earned ratio is also called the **interest-coverage ratio**. A high times-interest-earned ratio indicates ease in paying interest expense; a low value suggests difficulty. Let's see how competing airlines, Southwest and United (UAL), compare on the times-interest-earned ratio (dollar amounts in millions taken from the companies' 2006 financial statements):

Times–interest earned ratio	=	Operating income / Interest expense
Southwest		$\dfrac{\$934}{\$128} = 7.3$ times
United		$\dfrac{\$499}{\$728} = 0.7$ times

Southwest's income from operations covers its interest expense 7.3 times. UAL's times-interest-earned ratio is less than 1.0 times. UAL is much more risky on this ratio than Southwest.

STOP & think. . .

Which company, Southwest or UAL, would you expect to have the higher debt ratio? Compute the 2 companies' debt ratios to confirm your opinion. Summarized balance sheets follow at December 31, 2006.

	Millions	
	Southwest	**UAL**
Total assets	$13,460	$25,369
Total liabilities	$ 7,011	$23,221
Stockholders' equity	6,449	2,148
Total liabilities and equity	$13,460	$25,369

Answer:
As expected, UAL has a much higher debt ratio than Southwest, as follows (dollar amounts in millions):

	Southwest	**UAL**
Debit Ratio $= \dfrac{\text{Total liabilities}}{\text{Total assets}} =$	$\dfrac{\$ 7,011}{\$13,460}$	$\dfrac{\$23,221}{\$25,369}$
	$= 0.521$	$= 0.915$

LONG-TERM LIABILITIES: LEASES AND PENSIONS

A **lease** is a rental agreement in which the tenant (**lessee**) agrees to make rent payments to the property owner (**lessor**) in exchange for the use of the asset. Leasing allows the lessee to acquire the use of a needed asset without having to make the large up-front payment that purchase agreements require. Accountants distinguish between 2 types of leases: operating leases and capital leases.

Types of Leases

Operating leases are often short-term or cancelable. They give the lessee the right to use the asset but provide no continuing rights to the asset. The lessor retains the usual risks and rewards of owning the leased asset. To account for an operating lease, the lessee debits Rent Expense (or Lease Expense) and credits Cash for the amount of the lease payment. Operating leases require the lessee to make rent payments, so an operating lease creates a liability even though that liability does not appear on the lessee's balance sheet.

Capital leases. Most businesses use capital leasing to finance the acquisition of some assets. A **capital lease** is a long-term noncancelable debt. How do we distinguish a capital lease from an operating lease? *FASB Statement No. 13* provides the guidelines. To be classified as a capital lease, the lease must meet any *1* of the following criteria:

1. The lease transfers title of the leased asset to the lessee at the end of the lease term. Thus, the lessee becomes the legal owner of the leased asset.

2. The lease contains a *bargain purchase option*. The lessee can be expected to purchase the leased asset and become its legal owner.

3. The lease term is 75% or more of the estimated useful life of the leased asset. The lessee uses up most of the leased asset's service potential.

4. The present value of the lease payments is 90% or more of the market value of the leased asset. In effect, the lease payments are the same as installment payments for the leased asset.

Accounting for a capital lease is much like accounting for the purchase of an asset. The lessee enters the asset into the lessee's accounts and records a lease liability at the beginning of the lease term. Thus, the lessee capitalizes the asset even though the lessee may never take legal title to the asset.

Most companies lease some of their plant assets. Southwest Airlines leases airplanes under capital leases. At December 31, 2006, Southwest Airlines reported its capital leases in Note 8 of its financial statements, excerpted as follows:

Note 8 Leases (partial)
Southwest's "future minimum lease payments under capital leases [...] December 31, 2006, were" (in millions):

Year Ending December 31	Capital Lease Payments	
2007	$ 16	
2008	16	
2009	16	
2010	15	
2011	12	
after 2011	–	
	75	*This is Southwest's*
Less amount representing interest	(12)	*liability under its*
Present value of...lease payments	$ 63 ◄———	*capital leases.*

The note shows that Southwest must pay a total of $75 million on its capital leases. The present value of this liability is $63 million. The present value is the amount that's included in the liability figures reported on Southwest's balance sheet.

Do Lessees Prefer Operating Leases or Capital Leases?

Suppose you were the chief financial officer (CFO) of Southwest Airlines. Southwest leases some of its planes. The lease can be structured either as an operating lease or as a capital lease. Which type of lease would you prefer for Southwest? Why? Computing Southwest's debt ratio 2 ways (new lease as an *operating* lease versus new lease as a *capital* lease) will make your decision clear (using Southwest's actual figures in millions):

		New Lease is an Operating Lease	New Lease is a Capital Lease	
Debt ratio $=$	$\dfrac{\text{Total liabilities}}{\text{Total assets}}$ $=$	$\dfrac{\$\ 7{,}011}{\$13{,}460}$	$\dfrac{\$7{,}011 + \$63}{\$13{,}460 + \$63}$ $=$	$\dfrac{\$\ 7{,}074}{\$13{,}523}$
	$=$	0.521	$=$	0.523

You can see that a capital lease increases the debt ratio—only a bit for Southwest, but a lot for UAL and AMR (parent company of American Airlines). By contrast, operating leases don't affect the debt ratio that's reported on the balance sheet. For this reason, companies prefer operating leases.

Pensions and Postretirement Liabilities

Most companies have retirement plans for their employees. A **pension** is employee compensation that will be received during retirement. Companies also provide postretirement benefits, such as medical insurance for retired former employees. Because employees earn these benefits by their service, the company records pension and retirement-benefit expense while employees work for the company.

Pensions are one of the most complex areas of accounting. As employees earn their pensions and the company pays into the pension plan, the plan's assets grow. The obligation for future pension payments to employees also accumulates. At the end of each period, the company compares

- The fair market value of the assets in the retirement plans—cash and investments—with
- The plans' *accumulated benefit obligation*, which is the present value of promised future payments to retirees.

If the plan assets exceed the accumulated benefit obligation, the plan is said to be *overfunded*. In this case, the asset and obligation amounts are to be reported only in the notes to the financial statements. However, if the accumulated benefit obligation (the liability) exceeds plan assets, the plan is *underfunded*, and the company must report the excess liability amount as a long-term liability on the balance sheet.

Southwest Airlines' retirement plans don't create large liabilities for Southwest. To illustrate pension liabilities let's see the pension plan of AMR Corp., the parent company of American Airlines.

At December 31, 2006, the retirement plans of AMR Corporation were under-funded. They had

- Assets with a fair market value of $8,767 million
- Accumulated benefit obligations totaling $13,409 million

AMR's balance sheet, therefore, included a Pension and Post-Retirement Liability of $4,642 million ($13,409 − $8,767). This liability was reported among Other Long-Term Liabilities.

REPORTING LIABILITIES

Reporting on the Balance Sheet

OBJECTIVE

5 Report liabilities on the balance sheet

This chapter began with the liabilities reported on the balance sheets of Southwest Airlines. Exhibit 8-11 shows a standard way for Southwest to report its long-term debt.

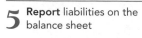 **EXHIBIT 8-11** Reporting the Liabilities of Southwest Airlines Co.

Southwest Airlines Co. Balance Sheet (Partial, adapted)		Note 10 Financial Instruments (adapted) Long-term debt consists of (in millions);	
Liabilities (in millions)		7⅞% notes due 2007	$ 100
Current Liabilities:		French credit agreements due 2012	37
Accounts payable	$ 643	6½% notes due 2012	369
Accrued liabilities	1,323	5¼% notes due 2014	336
Unearned ticket revenue	799	5¾% notes due 2016	300
Current maturities of long-term debt	122 ◄	5⅛% notes due 2017	300
Total current liabilities	2,887	French credit agreements due 2017	100
Long-term debt	1,567 ◄	Other long-term debt	147
Other long-term liabilities	2,557	Total long-term debt	1,689
		Less current maturities	(122)
		Long-term debt	$1,567

Exhibit 8-11 includes Note 10 from Southwest's financial statements. The note gives additional details about the company's liabilities. Note 10 shows the interest rates and the maturity dates of Southwest's long-term debt. Investors need these data to evaluate the company. The note also reports

- Current maturities of long-term debt ($122 million) as a current liability
- Long-term debt (excluding current maturities) of $1,567 million

Trace these amounts from the Note to the balance sheet. Working back and forth between the financial statements and the related notes is an important part of financial analysis. You now have the tools to understand the liabilities reported on an actual balance sheet.

Reporting the Fair Market Value of Long-Term Debt

FASB Statement No. 107 requires companies to report the fair market value of their long-term debt. At December 31, 2006, Southwest Airlines' Note 10 could have included this excerpt:

> **The estimated fair values of the Company's long-term debt was $1,678 million.**

Overall, the fair market value of Southwest's long-term debt is about $11 million less than its carrying amount on books ($1,689).

Reporting Financing Activities on the Statement of Cash Flows

The Southwest Airlines balance sheet (p. 414) shows that the company finances about half of its operations with debt. In fact, Southwest's debt ratio is 52%. Let's examine Southwest's financing activities as reported on its statement of cash flows. Exhibit 8-12 is an excerpt from Southwest's cash-flow statement.

EXHIBIT 8-12	Statement of Cash Flows (partial; adapted) for Southwest Airlines Co.

Southwest Airlines Co.
Statement of Cash Flows

(In millions)	Year Ended December 31, 2006
Cash Flow from Operating Activities:	
Net cash provided by operating activities	$ 1,406
Cash Flow from Investing Activities:	
Net cash used for investing activities	$(1,495)
Cash Flow from Financing Activities:	
Issuance of long-term debt	$ 300
Payments of long-term debt	(607)

During 2006, Southwest borrowed $300 million and paid off $607 million. You can see that Southwest is decreasing its debt position. This may be one reason the company is more profitable than its competitors.

END-OF-CHAPTER SUMMARY PROBLEM

The **Cessna Aircraft Company** has outstanding an issue of 8% convertible bonds that mature in 2018. Suppose the bonds are dated October 1, 2008, and pay interest each April 1 and October 1.

❙ Required

1. Complete the following effective-interest amortization table through October 1, 2010.

   Bond Data

   Maturity (face) value—$100,000

   Stated interest rate—8%

   Interest paid—4% semiannually, $4,000 ($100,000 × 0.08 × 6/12)

   Market interest rate at the time of issue—9% annually, 4 1/2% semiannually

   Issue price—93.5

| | Amortization Table | | | | |
	A	B	C	D	E
Semiannual Interest Date	Interest Payment (4% of Maturity Amount)	Interest Expense (4½% of Preceding Bond Carrying Amount)	Discount Amortization (B – A)	Discount Account Balance (Preceding D – C)	Bond Carrying Amount ($100,000 – D)
10-1-08					
4-1-09					
10-1-09					
4-1-10					
10-1-10					

2. Using the amortization table, record the following transactions:
   a. Issuance of the bonds on October 1, 2008.
   b. Accrual of interest and amortization of the bonds on December 31, 2008.
   c. Payment of interest and amortization of the bonds on April 1, 2009.
   d. Conversion of one-third of the bonds payable into no-par stock on October 2, 2010. For no-par stock, transfer the bond carrying amount into the Common Stock account. There is no Additional Paid-in Capital account.
   e. Retirement of two-thirds of the bonds payable on October 2, 2010. Purchase price of the bonds was based on their call price of 102.

Answers

❙ Requirement 1

	A	B	C	D	E
Semiannual Interest Date	Interest Payment (4% of Maturity Amount)	Interest Expense (4½% of Preceding Bond Carrying Amount)	Discount Amortization (B – A)	Discount Account Balance (Preceding D – C)	Bond Carrying Amount ($100,000 – D)
10-1-08				$6,500	$93,500
4-1-09	$4,000	$4,208	$208	6,292	93,708
10-1-09	4,000	4,217	217	6,075	93,925
4-1-10	4,000	4,227	227	5,848	94,152
10-1-10	4,000	4,237	237	5,611	94,389

❘ Requirement 2

a.	2008			
	Oct. 1	Cash ($100,000 × 0.935)	93,500	
		Discount on Bonds Payable	6,500	
		Bonds Payable		100,000
		To issue bonds at a discount.		
b.	Dec. 31	Interest Expense ($4,208 × 3/6)	2,104	
		Discount on Bonds Payable ($208 × 3/6)		104
		Interest Payable ($4,000 × 3/6)		2,000
		To accrue interest and amortize the bonds.		
c.	2009			
	Apr. 1	Interest Expense	2,104	
		Interest Payable	2,000	
		Discount on Bonds Payable ($208 × 3/6)		104
		Cash		4,000
		To pay semiannual interest, part of which was		
		accrued, and amortize the bonds.		
d.	2010			
	Oct. 2	Bonds Payable ($100,000 × 1/3)	33,333	
		Discount on Bonds Payable (5,611 × 1/3)		1,870
		Common Stock ($94,389 × 1/3)		31,463
		To record conversion of bonds payable.		
e.	Oct. 2	Bonds Payable ($100,000 × 2/3)	66,667	
		Loss on Retirement of Bonds	5,074	
		Discount on Bonds Payable ($5,611 × 2/3)		3,741
		Cash ($100,000 × 2/3 × 1.02)		68,000
		To retire bonds payable before maturity.		

REVIEW LIABILITIES

Quick Check (Answers are given on page 471.)

1. Which of the following is *not* an estimated liability?
   - **a.** Allowance for bad debts
   - **b.** Product warranties
   - **c.** Income taxes
   - **d.** Vacation pay

2. Recording estimated warranty expense in the current year *best* follows which accounting principle?
   - **a.** Consistency
   - **b.** Materiality
   - **c.** Full disclosure
   - **d.** Historical cost
   - **e.** Matching

3. Lotta Sound grants a 90-day warranty on all stereos. Historically, approximately 2 1/2% of all sales prove to be defective. Sales in July are $200,000. In July, $2,900 of defective units are returned for replacement. What entry must Lotta Sound make at the end of July to record the warranty expense?
   - **a.** Debit Warranty Expense and credit Estimated Warranty Payable, $2,900.
   - **b.** Debit Warranty Expense and credit Cash, $4,865.

(*continued*)

    c. Debit Warranty Expense and credit Estimated Warranty Payable, $5,000.

    d. No entry is needed at July 31.

4. Outback Camera Co. was organized to sell a single product that carries a 60-day warranty against defects. Engineering estimates indicate that 5% of the units sold will prove defective and require an average repair cost of $40 per unit. During Outback's first month of operations, total sales were 400 units; by the end of the month, 6 defective units had been repaired. The liability for product warranties at month-end should be:

    a. $270   **d.** $810

    b. $530   **e.** None of these

    c. $560

5. A contingent liability should be recorded in the accounts:

    a. if the related future event will probably occur.

    b. if the amount is due in cash within 1 year.

    c. if the amount can be reasonably estimated.

    d. Both a and b.

    e. Both a and c.

6. An unsecured bond is a

    a. registered bond.   **d.** serial bond.

    b. mortgage bond.   **e.** debenture bond.

    c. term bond.

7. The Discount on Bonds Payable account

    a. is a contra account to Bonds Payable.   **d.** is expensed at the bond's maturity.

    b. is a miscellaneous revenue account.   **e.** has a normal credit balance.

    c. is an expense account.

8. The discount on a bond payable becomes

    a. additional interest expense the year the bonds are sold.

    b. additional interest expense over the life of the bonds.

    c. a reduction in interest expense the year the bonds mature.

    d. a reduction in interest expense over the life of the bonds.

    e. a liability in the year the bonds are sold.

9. A bond that matures in installments is called a

    a. secured bond.   **d.** term bond.

    b. zero coupon.   **e.** callable bond.

    c. serial bond.

10. The carrying value of Bonds Payable equals

    a. Bonds Payable – Premium on Bonds Payable.

    b. Bonds Payable – Discount on Bonds Payable.

    c. Bonds Payable + Discount on Bonds Payable.

    d. Bonds Payable + Accrued Interest.

11. A corporation issues bonds that pay interest each March 1 and September 1. The corporation's December 31 adjusting entry may include a

    a. debit to Cash.   **d.** debit to Interest Payable.

    b. credit to Cash.   **e.** credit to Discount on Bonds Payable.

    c. credit to Interest Expense.

Use this information to answer questions 12–16.

McLennan Corporation issued $200,000 of 9 1/2% 5-year bonds. The bonds are dated and sold on 1/1/X2. Interest payment dates are 1/1 and 7/1. The bonds are issued for $196,140 to yield the market interest rate of 10%. Use the effective-interest method for questions 12–15.

12. What is the amount of interest expense that McLennan Corporation will record on 7/1/X2, the first semiannual interest payment date?

    a. $9,807   **c.** $10,000

    b. $9,926   **d.** $19,000

13. What is the amount of discount amortization that McLennan Corporation will record on 7/1/X2, the first semiannual interest payment date?

    a. $0   **c.** $193

    b. $74   **d.** $307

14. What is the total cash payment for interest for each 12-month period?
    a. $10,000   **c.** $19,614
    b. $19,000   **d.** $20,000

15. What is the carrying amount of the bonds on the 12/31/X2 balance sheet?
    a. $196,140   **c.** $196,769
    b. $196,526   **d.** $196,912

16. Using straight-line amortization, the carrying amount of McLennan Corporation's bonds at 12/31/X2 is
    a. $196,140.   **c.** $196,769.
    b. $196,526.   **d.** $196,912.

Accounting Vocabulary

accrued expense (p. 416) An expense incurred but not yet paid in cash. Also called *accrued liability*.

accrued liability (p. 416) A liability for an expense that has not yet been paid. Also called *accrued expense*.

bonds payable (p. 422) issued to multiple lenders called *bondholders*.

callable bonds (p. 436) at a specified price whenever the issuer wants.

capital lease (p. 442) Lease agreement that meets any 1 of 4 criteria: (1) The lease transfers title of the leased asset to the lessee. (2) The lease contains a bargain purchase option. (3) The lease term is 75% or more of the estimated useful life of the leased asset. (4) The present value of the lease payments is 90% or more of the market value of the leased asset.

convertible bonds (or **notes**) (p. 437) Bonds or notes that may be converted into the issuing company's common stock at the investor's option.

current installment of long-term debt (p. 419) The amount of the principal that is payable within one year.

debentures (p. 424) Unsecured bonds—bonds backed only by the good faith of the borrower.

discount (**on a bond**) (p. 424) Excess of a bond's face (par) value over its issue price.

earnings per share (**EPS**) (p. 438) Amount of a company's net income per share of its outstanding common stock.

interest-coverage ratio (p. 441) Another name for the *times-interest-earned ratio*.

lease (p. 442) Rental agreement in which the tenant (lessee) agrees to make rent payments to the property owner (lessor) in exchange for the use of the asset.

lessee (p. 442) Tenant in a lease agreement.

lessor (p. 442) Property owner in a lease agreement.

leverage (p. 438) Earning more income on borrowed money than the related interest expense, thereby increasing the earnings for the owners of the business. Also called *leverage*.

market interest rate (p. 425) Interest rate that investors demand for loaning their money. Also called *effective interest rate*.

operating lease (p. 442) Usually a short-term or cancelable rental agreement.

payroll (p. 416) Employee compensation, a major expense of many businesses.

pension (p. 443) Employee compensation that will be received during retirement.

premium (**on a bond**) (p. 424) Excess of a bond's issue price over its face (par) value.

present value (p. 424) Amount a person would invest now to receive a greater amount at a future date.

serial bonds (p. 424) Bonds that mature in installments over a period of time.

short-term notes payable (p. 415) Note payable due within 1 year.

stated interest rate (p. 425) Interest rate that determines the amount of cash interest the borrower pays and the investor receives each year.

term bonds (p. 424) Bonds that all mature at the same time for a particular issue.

times-interest-earned ratio (p. 441) Ratio of income from operations to interest expense. Measures the number of times that operating income can cover interest expense. Also called the *interest-coverage ratio*.

trading on the equity (p. 438) Earning more income on borrowed money than the related interest expense, thereby increasing the earnings for the owners of the business. Also called *leverage*.

underwriter (p. 423) Organization that purchases the bonds from an issuing company and resells them to its clients or sells the bonds for a commission, agreeing to buy all unsold bonds.

ASSESS YOUR PROGRESS

Short Exercises

S8-1 (*Learning Objective 1: Accounting for a note payable*) Malibu Sports Authority purchased inventory costing $10,000 by signing a 10% short-term note payable. The purchase occurred on March 31, 20X7. Malibu pays annual interest each year on March 31. Journalize Malibu's (a) purchase of inventory, (b) accrual of interest expense on December 31, 20X7, and (c) payment of the note plus interest on March 31, 20X8. (p. 415)

S8-2 (*Learning Objective 1: Reporting a short-term note payable and the related interest in the financial statements*) This short exercise works with Short Exercise S8-1.

1. Refer to the data in Short Exercise S8-1. Show what the company would report on its balance sheet at December 31, 20X7, and on its income statement for the year ended on that date. (pp. 421, 376–377)

2. What 1 item will the financial statements for the year ended December 31, 20X8 report? Identify the financial statement, the item, and its amount. (p. 421)

S8-3 (*Learning Objective 1: Accounting for warranty expense and estimated warranty payable*) **Nissan USA** guarantees automobiles against defects for 4 years or 50,000 miles, whichever comes first. Suppose Nissan can expect warranty costs during the 4-year period to add up to 3% of sales.

Assume that Lakeland Nissan in Lakeland, Florida, made sales of $500,000 during 20X0. Lakeland Nissan received cash for 10% of the sales and took notes receivable for the remainder. Payments to satisfy customer warranty claims totaled $12,000 during 20X0.

1. Record the sales, warranty expense, and warranty payments for Lakeland Nissan. Ignore any reimbursement that Lakeland Nissan may receive from Nissan USA. (pp. 419–420)

2. Post to the Estimated Warranty Payable T-account. The beginning balance was $10,000. At the end of 20X0, how much in estimated warranty payable does Lakeland Nissan owe its customers? (pp. 419–420)

S8-4 (*Learning Objective 1: Applying GAAP; reporting warranties in the financial statements*) Refer to the data given in Short Exercise S8-3. What amount of warranty expense will Lakeland Nissan report during 20X0? Which accounting principle addresses this situation? Does the warranty expense for the year equal the year's cash payments for warranties? Explain the relevant accounting principle as it applies to measuring warranty expense. (pp. 419–420)

S8-5 (*Learning Objective 1: Interpreting a company's contingent liabilities*) **Harley-Davidson, Inc.**, the motorcycle manufacturer, included the following note in its annual report:

NOTES TO CONSOLIDATED FINANCIAL STATEMENTS
7 (In Part): Commitments and Contingencies

The Company self-insures its product liability losses in the United States up to $3 million (catastrophic coverage is maintained for individual claims in excess of $3 million up to $25 million). Outside the United States, the Company is insured for product liability up to $25 million per individual claim and in the aggregate.

1. Why are these *contingent* (versus *real*) liabilities? (pp. 419–420)

2. In the United States, how can the contingent liability become a real liability for Harley-Davidson? What are the limits to the company's product liabilities in the United States? Explain how these limits work. (p. 421)

3. How can a contingency outside the United States become a real liability for the company? How does Harley-Davidson's potential liability differ for claims outside the United States? (p. 421)

S8-6 (*Learning Objective 2: Pricing bonds*) Compute the price of the following bonds (p. 424):

a. $1,000,000 quoted at 89.75   c. $100,000 quoted at 97.50
b. $500,000 quoted at 110.375   d. $400,000 quoted at 102.625

S8-7 (*Learning Objective 2: Determining bond prices at par, discount, or premium*) Determine whether the following bonds payable will be issued at par value, at a premium, or at a discount (p. 429):

a. The market interest rate is 9%. Chevy, Inc., issues bonds payable with a stated rate of 8 1/2%.
b. Charger Corporation issued 7 1/2% bonds payable when the market rate was 7 1/2%.
c. Explorer Corporation issued 8% bonds when the market interest rate was 6 7/8%.
d. Tundra Company issued bonds payable that pay cash interest at the stated interest rate of 7%. At the date of issuance, the market interest rate was 8 1/4%.

S8-8 (*Learning Objective 2: Journalizing basic bond payable transactions; bonds issued at par*) Suppose **Washington Public Power Supply System (WPPSS)** issued the 10-year bond in Exhibit 8-2, page 423, when the market interest rate was 6 1/2%. Assume that the accounting year of WPPSS ends on December 31. Journalize the following transactions for WPPSS, including an explanation for each entry (pp. 429–430)

a. Issuance of the bond payable on July 1, 2000.
b. Accrual of interest expense on December 31, 2000 (rounded to the nearest dollar).
c. Payment of cash interest on January 1, 2001.
d. Payment of the bonds payable at maturity. (Give the date.)

S8-9 (*Learning Objective 2: Issuing bonds payable and amortizing bonds by the effective-interest method*) Edgewood Nurseries, Inc., issued $100,000 of 7%, 10-year bonds payable at a price of 87 on January 31, 20X8. The market interest rate at the date of issuance was 9%, and the Edgewood bonds pay interest semiannually.

1. Prepare an effective-interest amortization table for the bonds through the first 3 interest payments. Use Exhibit 8-4, page 429, as a guide and round amounts to the nearest dollar. (p. 428)

2. Record Edgewood's issuance of the bonds on January 31, 20X8, and payment of the first semiannual interest amount and amortization of the bonds on July 31, 20X8. Explanations are not required. (p. 431)

S8-10 (*Learning Objective 3: Analyzing data on long-term debt*) Use the amortization table that you prepared for Edgewood Nurseries in Short Exercise S8-9 to answer these questions about the company's long-term debt: (p. 428)

1. How much cash did Edgewood borrow on January 31, 20X8? How much cash will Edgewood pay back at maturity on January 31, 20X8?

2. How much cash interest will Edgewood pay each 6 months?

3. How much interest expense will Edgewood report on July 31, 20X8, and on January 31, 20X9? Why does the amount of interest expense increase each period? Explain in detail.

S8-11 (*Learning Objective 3: Determining bonds payable amounts; amortizing bonds by the straight-line method*) WPPSS borrowed money by issuing the bond payable in Exhibit 8-2, page 423. Assume the issue price was 94 on July 1, 2000. (pp. 422–423, 428)

1. How much cash did WPPSS receive when it issued the bond payable?

2. How much must WPPSS pay back at maturity? When is the maturity date?

3. How much cash interest will WPPSS pay each 6 months? Carry the interest amount to the nearest cent.

4. How much interest expense will WPPSS report each 6 months? Assume the straight-line amortization method and carry the interest amount to the nearest cent.

S8-12 (*Learning Objective 3: Issuing bonds payable, accruing interest, and amortizing bonds by the straight-line method*) Return to the WPPSS bond in Exhibit 8-2, page 423.

(*continued*)

Assume that WPPSS issued the bond payable on July 1, 2000, at a price of 90. Also assume that WPPSS's accounting year ends on December 31. Journalize the following transactions for WPPSS, including an explanation for each entry (pp. 431, 435–436):

a. Issuance of the bonds on July 1, 2000.

b. Accrual of interest expense and amortization of bonds on December 31, 2000. (Use the straight-line amortization method, and round amounts to the nearest dollar.)

c. Payment of the first semiannual interest amount on January 1, 2001.

S8-13 *(Learning Objective 4: Earnings-per-share effects of financing with bonds versus stock)* Assume that **YouTube, Inc.**, needs $1 million to expand the company. YouTube is considering the issuance of either

- $1,000,000 of 7% bonds payable to borrow the money, or

- 100,000 shares of common stock at $10 per share

Before any new financing, YouTube expects to earn net income of $400,000, and the company already has 200,000 shares of common stock outstanding. YouTube believes the expansion will increase income before interest and income tax by $200,000. YouTube's income tax rate is 30%.

Prepare an analysis similar to Exhibit 8-10, page 439, to determine which plan is likely to result in the higher earnings per share. Based solely on the earnings-per-share comparison, which financing plan would you recommend for YouTube?

writing assignment ■   **S8-14** *(Learning Objective 4: Computing the times-interest-earned ratio)* Zigzag International reported the following data in 20X8 (in millions):

Net operating revenues..............	$29.2
Operating expenses	25.3
Operating income......................	3.9
Nonoperating items:	
Interest expense......................	(1.4)
Other	(0.2)
Net income...............................	$ 2.3

Compute Zigzag's times-interest-earned ratio, and write a sentence to explain what the ratio value means. Would you be willing to lend Zigzag $1 million? State your reason. (p. 440)

S8-15 *(Learning Objective 5: Reporting liabilities, including capital lease obligations)* Trinidad Industries has the following selected accounts at December 31, 20X7:

Bonds payable................................	$300,000
Equipment......................................	114,000
Current portion of	
bonds payable.........................	50,000
Notes payable, long-term	60,000
Interest payable	
(due March 1, 20X8)..............	7,000
Accounts payable	44,000
Discount on bonds payable	
(all long-term).........................	10,000
Accounts receivable.......................	31,000

Prepare the liabilities section of Trinidad's balance sheet at December 31, 20X7, to show how Trinidad would report these items. Report total current liabilities and total liabilities. (pp. 421, 414)

Exercises

E8-16 (*Learning Objective 1: Accounting for warranty expense and the related liability*) The accounting records of Audio-Video, Inc., included the following balances before the year-end adjustments:

Estimated Warranty Payable	Sales Revenue	Warranty Expense
Beg. bal 8,000	150,000	

In the past, Audio-Video's warranty expense has been 6% of sales. During the current period, the business paid $9,400 to satisfy the warranty claims of customers.

I *Required*

1. Record Audio-Video's warranty expense for the period and the company's cash payments to satisfy warranty claims. Explanations are not required. (pp. 419–440)

2. Show everything Audio-Video will report on its income statement and balance sheet for this situation. (p. 421)

3. Which data item from requirement 2 will affect Audio-Video's current ratio? Will Audio-Video's current ratio increase or decrease as a result of this item? (p. 169)

E8-17 (*Learning Objective 1: Recording and reporting current liabilities*) Yankee Traveler Magazine completed the following transactions during 20X6:

Aug. 31	Sold 1-year subscriptions, collecting cash of $1,500, plus sales tax of 4%.
Dec. 31	Remitted (paid) the sales tax to the state of New York.
31	Made the necessary adjustment at year end.

Journalize these transactions (explanations not required). Then report any liability on the company's balance sheet at December 31. (pp. 417–418).

E8-18 (*Learning Objective 1: Reporting payroll expense and liabilities*) Penske Talent Search has an annual payroll of $150,000. In addition, the company incurs payroll tax expense of 9%. At December 31, Penske owes salaries of $7,600 and FICA and other payroll tax of $900. The company will pay these amounts early next year.

Show what Penske will report for the foregoing on its income statement and year-end balance sheet. (pp. 417, 421)

E8-19 (*Learning Objective 1: Recording note payable transactions*) Joy's Lahaina Grill completed the following note-payable transactions.

(*continued*)

20X6	
July 1	Purchased kitchen equipment costing $60,000 by issuing a 1-year, 8% note payable.
Dec. 31	Accrued interest on the note payable.
20X7	
July 1	Paid the note payable at maturity.

Answer these questions for Joy's Lahaina Grill (pp. 415–416):

1. How much interest expense must be accrued at December 31, 20X6?

2. Determine the amount of Joy's final payment on July 1, 20X7.

3. How much interest expense will Joy's report for 20X6 and for 20X7?

E8-20 (*Learning Objective 1: Accounting for income tax*) At December 31, 20X4, Young Real Estate reported a current liability for income tax payable of $200,000. During 20X5, Young earned income of $900,000 before income tax. The company's income tax rate during 20X5 was 35%. Also during 20X5, Young paid income taxes of $350,000.

How much income tax payable did Young Real Estate report on its balance sheet at December 31, 20X5? How much income tax expense did Young report on its 20X5 income statement? (p. 421)

writing assignment ■

E8-21 (*Learning Objective 1, 5: Analyzing liabilities*) Geodesic Domes, Inc., builds environmentally sensitive structures. The company's 20X8 revenues totaled $360 million, and at December 31, 20X8, the company had $65 million in current assets. The December 31, 20X8, balance sheet reported the liabilities and stockholders' equity as follows.

At year end (In millions)	20X8	20X7
Liabilities and Shareholders' Equity		
Current Liabilities		
Accounts payable	$ 29	$ 26
Accrued expenses	16	20
Employee compensation and benefits	9	11
Current portion of long-term debt	5	—
Total Current Liabilities	59	57
Long-Term Debt	115	115
Postretirement Benefits Payable	31	27
Other Liabilities	21	17
Shareholders' Equity	73	70
Total Liabilities and Shareholders' Equity	$299	$286

❙ Required

1. Describe each of Geodesic Domes, Inc.'s, liabilities and state how the liability arose. (pp. 414, 419–420, 424, 443)

2. What were the company's total assets at December 31, 20X8? Was the company's debt ratio at the end of 20X8 high, low, or in a middle range? (p. 169)

E8-22 (*Learning Objective 1: Reporting a contingent liability*) **L&M Electronics'** revenues for 20X3 totaled $25.9 million. As with most companies, L&M is a defendant in lawsuits related to its products. Note 14 of the L&M Annual Report for 20X3 reported:

14. Contingencies

The company is involved in various legal proceedings. . . . It is the Company's policy to accrue for amounts related to these legal matters if it is probable that a liability has been incurred and an amount is reasonably estimable.

❚ Required

1. Suppose L&M's lawyers believe that a significant legal judgment against the company is reasonably possible. How should L&M report this situation in its financial statements? (pp. 419–420)

2. Suppose L&M's lawyers believe it is probable that a $2 million judgment will be rendered against the company. Report this situation in L&M's financial statements. Journalize any entry required by GAAP. Explanations are not required. (pp. 419–420)

E8-23 (*Learning Objective 1, 5: Reporting current and long-term liabilities*) Assume that **Pinnacle Golf Equipment** completed these selected transactions during December 20X7.

a. Sales of $2,000,000 are subject to estimated warranty cost of 3%. The estimated warranty payable at the beginning of the year was $30,000, and warranty payments for the year totaled $55,000.

b. On December 1, Pinnacle signed a $100,000 note payable that requires annual payments of $20,000 plus 9% interest on the unpaid balance each December 1.

c. **Academy Sports**, a chain of sporting goods stores, ordered $100,000 of golf equipment. With its order, Academy Sports sent a check for $100,000, and Pinnacle shipped $85,000 of the goods. Pinnacle will ship the remainder of the goods on January 3, 20X8.

d. The December payroll of $100,000 is subject to employee withheld income tax of 9% and FICA tax of 8%. On December 31, Pinnacle pays employees their take-home pay and accrues all tax amounts.

❚ Required

Classify each liability as current or long-term and report the liability and its amount that would appear on the Pinnacle Golf Equipment balance sheet at December 31, 20X7. Show a total for current liabilities. (pp. 416–418)

E8-24 (*Learning Objective 2: Issuing bonds payable, paying and accruing interest, and amortizing the bonds by the straight-line method*) On January 31, Triumph Sports Cars issued 10-year, 7% bonds payable with a face value of $100,000. The bonds were issued at 98 and pay interest on January 31 and July 31. Triumph amortizes bonds by the straight-line method. Record (a) issuance of the bonds on January 31, (b) the semiannual interest payment and discount amortization on July 31, and (c) the interest accrual and discount amortization on December 31. (pp. 427, 436)

E8-25 (*Learning Objective 2, 3: Measuring cash amounts for a bond; amortizing the bonds by the straight-line method*) City Bank has $200,000 of 8% debenture bonds outstanding. The bonds were issued at 102 in 2004 and mature in 2024.

❚ Required

1. How much cash did City Bank receive when it issued these bonds? (pp. 431–432)

2. How much cash in *total* will City Bank pay the bondholders through the maturity date of the bonds? (Challenge)

3. Take the difference between your answers to Requirements 1 and 2. This difference represents City Bank's total interest expense over the life of the bonds. (Challenge)

4. Compute City Bank's annual interest expense by the straight-line amortization method. Multiply this amount by 20. Your 20-year total should be the same as your answer to Requirement 3. (pp. 435–436, Challenge)

E8-26 (*Learning Objective 2, 3: Issuing bonds payable (discount); recording interest payments and the related bond amortization*) Family General Stores, Inc., is authorized to issue $500,000 of 7%, 10-year bonds payable. On December 31, 2008, when the market interest rate is 8%, the company issues $400,000 of the bonds and receives cash of $372,660. Family General amortizes bonds by the effective-interest method. The semiannual interest dates are June 30 and December 31.

▌Required

1. Prepare a bond amortization table for the first 4 semiannual interest periods. (p. 428)

2. Record issuance of the bonds payable on December 31, 20X8 and the semiannual interest payments on June 30, 2009, and on December 31, 2009. (p. 431)

E8-27 (*Learning Objective 2, 3: Issuing bonds payable (premium); recording interest accrual and payment and the related bond amortization*) On June 30, 2008, the market interest rate is 7%. Dellaca Enterprises issues $300,000 of 8%, 20-year bonds payable at 110.625. The bonds pay interest on June 30 and December 31. Dellaca amortizes bonds by the effective-interest method.

▌Required

1. Prepare a bond amortization table for the first 4 semiannual interest periods. (p. 428)

2. Record issuance of the bonds on June 30, 2008, the payment of interest at December 31, 2008, and the semiannual interest payment on June 30, 2009. (p. 431)

E8-28 (*Learning Objective 3: Debt payment and bond amortization schedule*) Carlson Candies issued $600,000 of 8 3/8% (.08375), 5-year bonds payable on January 1, 20X1, when the market interest rate was 9 1/2% (.095). The company pays interest annually at year end. The issue price of the bonds was $574,082.

▌Required

Create a spreadsheet model to prepare a schedule to amortize the bonds. Use the effective-interest method of amortization. Round to the nearest dollar and format your answer as shown here. (p. 428)

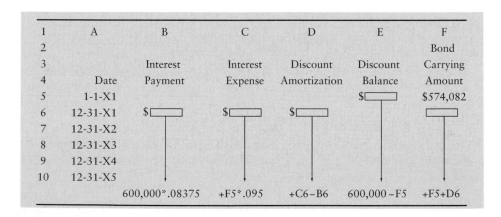

E8-29 (*Learning Objective 2: Recording conversion of notes payable*) Montrose Corporation issued $400,000 of 8 1/2% notes payable on December 31, 20X4, at a price of 98.5. The notes' term to maturity is 10 years. After 3 years, the notes may be converted into Montrose common stock. Each $1,000 face amount of notes is convertible into 50 shares of $1 par stock. On December 31, 20X9, noteholders exercised their right to convert all the notes into common stock.

┃ Required

1. Without making journal entries, compute the carrying amount of the notes payable at December 31, 20X9, immediately before the conversion. Montrose uses the straight-line method to amortize bonds. (pp. 435–436)

2. All amortization has been recorded properly. Journalize the conversion transaction at December 31, 20X9. (p. 436)

E8-30 (*Learning Objective 4: Measuring the times-interest-earned ratio*) Companies that operate in different industries may have very different financial ratio values. These differences may grow even wider when we compare companies located in different countries.

Compare 3 leading companies on their current ratio, debt ratio, and times-interest-earned ratio. Compute 3 three ratios for **Kroger** (the U.S. grocery chain), **Sony** (the Japanese electronics manufacturer), and **Daimler** (the German auto company). (p. 441)

Income data

(Amounts in millions or billions)	Kroger	Sony	Daimler
Total revenues	$66,111	¥7,475	€151,589
Operating income	2,236	191	2,072
Interest expense	488	29	913
Net income	1,115	124	3,227

Asset and liability data

(Amounts in millions or billions)	Kroger	Sony	Daimler
Total current assets	$ 6,755	¥3,770	€93,131
Long-term assets	14,460	6,838	96,891
Total current liabilities	7,581	3,200	59,977
Long-term liabilities	8,711	4,204	95,890
Stockholders' equity	4,923	3,204	34,155

Note: ¥ is the symbol for a Japanese yen; € for a euro.

Based on your computed ratio values, which company looks the least risky? (Challenge)

writing assignment ■

E8-31 (*Learning Objective 4: Analyzing alternative plans for raising money*) Altman & Associates is considering 2 plans for raising $500,000 to expand operations. Plan A is to borrow at 8%, and plan B is to issue 100,000 shares of common stock. Before any new financing, Altman has net income of $500,000 and 100,000 shares of common stock outstanding. Assume you own most of Altman's existing stock. Management believes the company can use the new funds to earn additional income of $420,000 before interest and taxes. Altman's income tax rate is 30%.

┃ Required

1. Analyze Altman's situation to determine which plan will result in higher earnings per share. Use Exhibit 8-10 (p. 439) as a model.

2. Which plan results in the higher earnings per share? Which plan allows you to retain control of the company? Which plan creates more financial risk for the company? Which plan do you prefer? Why? Present your conclusion in a memo to Altman's board of directors. (p. 439)

Challenge Exercises

E8-32 *(Learning Objective 1, 5: Reporting current liabilities)* Assume the top management of **Best Buy Co., Inc.**, examines company accounting records at February 7, three weeks before the end of the fiscal year (amounts in billions):

Total current assets	$ 8.0
Noncurrent assets	3.9
	$11.9
Total current liabilities	6.0
Noncurrent liabilities	0.6
Owners' equity	5.3
	$11.9

Suppose Best Buy's top management wants to achieve a current ratio of 1.4. How much in current liabilities should Best Buy pay off within the next 3 weeks to achieve its goal? (Challenge)

E8-33 *(Learning Objective 2, 3, 5: Refinancing old bonds payable with new bonds)* United Products completed one of the most famous debt refinancings in history. A debt refinancing occurs when a company issues new bonds payable to retire old bonds. The company debits the old bonds payable and credits the new bonds payable.

United had $125 million of 5 1/2% bonds payable outstanding, with 20 years to maturity. United retired these old bonds by issuing $75 million of new 9% bonds payable to the holders of the old bonds and paying the bondholders $13 million in cash. United issued both groups of bonds at par so there was no bond premium or discount. At the time of the debt refinancing, United had total assets of $600 million and total liabilities of $450 million. Net income for the most recent year was $6.5 million on sales of $1 billion.

❙ Required

1. Journalize the debt refinancing transaction. (Challenge)

2. Compute annual interest expense for both the old and the new bond issues. (Challenge)

3. Why did United Products refinance the old 5 1/2% bonds payable with the new 9% bonds? Consider interest expense, net income, and the debt ratio. (Challenge)

writing assignment ■

E8-34 *(Learning Objective 2, 3: Analyzing bond transactions)* This (adapted) advertisement appeared in *The Wall Street Journal*. (*Note:* A *subordinated debenture* is an unsecured bond payable whose rights are less than the rights of other bondholders.)

❚ Required

Answer these questions.

1. Journalize Mark IV's issuance of these bonds payable on March 15, 2007. No explanation is required, but describe the transaction in detail, indicating who received cash, who paid cash, and how much. (p. 430)
2. Why is the stated interest rate on these bonds so high? (p. 424)
3. Compute the semi-annual cash interest payment on the bonds. (pp. 428–429)
4. Compute the semi-annual interest expense under the straight-line amortization method. (pp. 435–436)
5. Compute both the first-year (from March 15, 2007, to March 15, 2008) and the second-year interest expense (March 15, 2008, to March 15, 2009) under the effective-interest amortization method. The market rate of interest at the date of issuance was 14%. Why is interest expense greater in the second year? (p. 428)

Quiz

Test your understanding of accounting for liabilities by answering the following questions. Select the best choice from among the possible answers given.

Q8-35 For the purpose of classifying liabilities as current or noncurrent, the term *operating cycle* refers to (p. 166)
a. a period of 1 year.
b. the time period between date of sale and the date the related revenue is collected.
c. the time period between purchase of merchandise and the conversion of this merchandise back to cash.
d. the average time period between business recessions.

Q8-36 Failure to accrue interest expense results in (p. 421)
a. an overstatement of net income and an overstatement of liabilities.
b. an understatement of net income and an overstatement of liabilities.
c. an understatement of net income and an understatement of liabilities.
d. an overstatement of net income and an understatement of liabilities.

Q8-37 Sportscar Warehouse operates in a state with a 6% sales tax. For convenience, Sportscar Warehouse credits Sales Revenue for the total amount (selling price plus sales tax) collected from each customer. If Sportscar Warehouse fails to make an adjustment for sales taxes (p. 415),
a. net income will be overstated and liabilities will be overstated.
b. net income will be overstated and liabilities will be understated.
c. net income will be understated and liabilities will be overstated.
d. net income will be understated and liabilities will be understated.

Q8-38 What kind of account is *Unearned Revenue*? (p. 417)
a. Asset account
b. Liability account
c. Revenue account
d. Expense account

Q8-39 An end-of-period adjusting entry that debits Unearned Revenue most likely will credit (p. 418)
a. a revenue.
b. an asset.
c. an expense.
d. a liability.

Q8-40 Adrian, Inc. manufactures and sells computer monitors with a 3-year warranty. Warranty costs are expected to average 8% of sales during the warranty period. The following table shows the sales and actual warranty payments during the first 2 years of operations:

Year	Sales	Warranty Payments
20X1	$500,000	$ 4,000
20X2	700,000	32,000

(continued)

Based on these facts, what amount of warranty liability should Adrian, Inc. report on its balance sheet at December 31, 20X2? (pp. 419–420)

a. $32,000

b. $36,000

c. $60,000

d. $96,000

Q8-41 Today's Fashions has a debt that has been properly reported as a long-term liability up to the present year (20X8). Some of this debt comes due in 20X8. If Today's Fashions continues to report the current position as a long-term liability, the effect will be to (p. 416)

a. overstate the current ratio.

b. overstate net income.

c. understate total liabilities.

d. understate the debt ratio.

Q8-42 A bond with a face amount of $10,000 has a current price quote of 102.875. What is the bond's price? (p. 424)

a. $1,028,750

b. $10,200.88

c. $10,028.75

d. $10,287.50

Q8-43 Bond carrying value equals Bonds Payable (pp. 427, 434)

a. minus Premium on Bonds Payable.

b. plus Discount on Bonds Payable.

c. plus Premium on Bonds Payable.

d. minus Discount on Bonds Payable.

e. both a and b.

f. both c and d.

Q8-44 What type of account is *Discount on Bonds Payable* and what is its normal balance? (p. 424)

	Type of account	Normal balance
a.	Contra liability	Debit
b.	Reversing account	Debit
c.	Adjusting amount	Credit
d.	Contra liability	Credit

Questions 45–48 use the following data:

Q8-45 Sweetwater Company sells $100,000 of 10%, 15-year bonds for 97 on April 1, 20X1. The market rate of interest on that day is 10 1/2%. Interest is paid each year on April 1. The entry to record the sale of the bonds on April 1 would be. (pp. 426–427)

a.	Cash	97,000	
	Bonds Payable		97,000
b.	Cash	100,000	
	Bonds Payable		100,000
c.	Cash	97,000	
	Discount on Bonds Payable	3,000	
	Bonds Payable		100,000
d.	Cash	100,000	
	Discount on Bonds Payable		3,000
	Bonds Payable		97,000

Q8-46 Sweetwater Company uses the straight-line amortization method. The sale price of the bonds was $97,000. The amount of interest expense on April 1 of each year will be: (pp. 426–427)

a. $4,080

b. $4,000

c. $4,200

d. $10,200

e. None of these. The interest expense is _____.

Q8-47 Write the adjusting entry required at December 31, 20X1 (pp. 431, 435–436)

Q8-48 Write the journal entry required at April 1, 20X2. (pp. 431, 435–436)

Q8-49 McPherson Corporation issued $100,000 of 10%, 5-year bonds payable on January 1, 20X4, for $92,280. The market interest rate when the bonds were issued was 12%. Interest is paid semiannually on January 1 and July 1. The first interest payment is July 1, 20X4. Using the effective-interest amortization method, how much interest expense will McPherson record on July 1, 20X4? (p. 428)

a. $6,000

b. $5,228

c. $6,772

d. $5,000

e. Some other amount ____

Q8-50 Using the facts in the preceding question, McPherson's journal entry to record the interest expense on July 1, 20X4 will include a (p. 431)

a. debit to Bonds Payable.

b. credit to Interest Expense.

c. debit to Premium on Bonds Payable.

d. credit to Discount on Bonds Payable.

Q8-51 Amortizing the discount on bonds payable (pp. 424, 428)

a. increases the recorded amount of interest expense.

b. is necessary only if the bonds were issued at more than face value.

c. reduces the semiannual cash payment for interest.

d. reduces the carrying value of the bond liability.

Q8-52 The journal entry on the maturity date to record the payment of $1,000,000 of bonds payable that were issued at a $70,000 discount includes (pp. 427, 431–432)

a. a debit to Discount on Bonds Payable for $70,000.

b. a credit to Cash for $1,070,000.

c. a debit to Bonds Payable for $1,000,000.

d. all of the above.

Q8-53 Is the payment of the face amount of a bond on its maturity date regarded as an operating activity, an investing activity, or a financing activity? (pp. 445–446)

a. Operating activity

b. Investing activity

c. Financing activity

Problems

(Group A)

Some of these A problems can be found within My Accounting Lab (MAL), an online homework and practice environment. Your instructor may ask you to complete these exercises using MAL.

MyAccountingLab

P8-54A (*Learning Objective 1: Measuring current liabilities*) Sea Spray Marine experienced these events during the current year.

a. December revenue totaled $110,000, and in addition, Sea Spray collected sales tax of 5%. The tax amount will be sent to the state of Maine early in January. (p. 415)

b. On October 31, Sea Spray signed a 6-month, 7% note payable to purchase a boat costing $90,000. The note requires payment of principal and interest at maturity. (p. 415)

c. On August 31, Sea Spray received cash of $1,800 in advance for service revenue. This revenue will be earned evenly over 6 months. (p. 417)

(continued)

d. Revenues of $900,000 were covered by Sea Spray's service warranty. At January 1, estimated warranty payable was $11,300. During the year, Sea Spray recorded warranty expense of $31,000 and paid warranty claims of $34,700. (p. 418).

e. Sea Spray owes $100,000 on a long-term note payable. At December 31, 6% interest for the year plus $20,000 of this principal are payable within 1 year. (p. 416)

▌Required

For each item, indicate the account and the related amount to be reported as a *current* liability on the Sea Spray Marine balance sheet at December 31.

P8-55A (*Learning Objective 1: Recording liability-related transactions*) The following transactions of Smooth Sounds Music Company occurred during 20X5 and 20X6:

20X5	
Mar. 3	Purchased a Steinway piano (inventory) for $40,000, signing a 6-month, 8% note payable.
Apr. 30	Borrowed $50,000 on a 9% note payable that calls for annual installment payments of $25,000 principal plus interest. Record the short-term note payable in a separate account from the long-term note payable.
Sept. 3	Paid the 6-month, 8% note at maturity.
Dec. 31	Accrued warranty expense, which is estimated at 2% of sales of $190,000.
31	Accrued interest on the outstanding note payable.
20X6	
Apr. 30	Paid the first installment plus interest for 1 year on the outstanding note payable.

▌Required

Record the transactions in Smooth Sounds' journal. Explanations are not required. (pp. 415–416)

P8-56A (*Learning Objective 2: Recording bond transactions (at par) and reporting bonds payable on the balance sheet*) The board of directors of Circuits Plus authorizes the issue of $1 million of 7%, 10-year bonds payable. The semiannual interest dates are May 31 and November 30. The bonds are issued on May 31, 20X5, at par.

▌Required

1. Journalize the following transactions: (pp. 429–430)
   a. Issuance of half of the bonds on May 31, 20X5.
   b. Payment of interest on November 30, 20X5.
   c. Accrual of interest on December 31, 20X5.
   d. Payment of interest on May 31, 20X6.
2. Report interest payable and bonds payable as they would appear on the Circuits Plus balance sheet at December 31, 20X5. (pp. 432–433)

writing assignment ■

P8-57A (*Learning Objective 2, 5: Issuing bonds at a discount, amortizing by the straight-line method, and reporting bonds payable on the balance sheet*) On February 28, 20X4, ETrade Inc., issues 8 1/2%, 20-year bonds payable with a face value of $200,000. The bonds pay interest on February 28 and August 31. ETrade amortizes bonds by the straight-line method.

▌Required

1. If the market interest rate is 7 5/8% when ETrade issues its bonds, will the bonds be priced at par, at a premium, or at a discount? Explain. (pp. 425–426)
2. If the market interest rate is 9% when ETrade issues its bonds, will the bonds be priced at par, at a premium, or at a discount? Explain. (pp. 425–426)
3. Assume that the issue price of the bonds is 97. Journalize the following bond transactions. (pp. 429–431, 435–436)

a. Issuance of the bonds on February 28, 20X4.
b. Payment of interest and amortization of the bonds on August 31, 20X4.
c. Accrual of interest and amortization of the bonds on December 31, 20X4.
d. Payment of interest and amortization of the bonds on February 28, 20X5.

4. Report interest payable and bonds payable as they would appear on the ETrade balance sheet at December 31, 20X4. (pp. 431–433)

P8-58A *(Learning Objective 2: Accounting for bonds payable at a discount and amortizing by the straight-line method)*

writing assignment ■

1. Journalize the following transactions of Trekker Boot Company: (pp. 426–427, 435–436)

2007		
Jan. 1	Issued $500,000 of 8%, 10-year bonds payable at 97.	
July 1	Paid semiannual interest and amortized bonds by the straight-line method on the 8% bonds payable.	
Dec. 31	Accrued semiannual interest expense and amortized bonds by the straight-line method on the 8% bonds payable.	
2008		
Jan. 1	Paid semiannual interest.	
2017		
Jan. 1	Paid the 8% bonds at maturity.	

2. At December 31, 2007, after all year-end adjustments, determine the carrying amount of Trekker's bonds payable, net.(pp. 431–433)

3. For the 6 months ended July 1, 2007, determine for Trekker: (pp. 436–437)
   a. Interest expense   b.   Cash interest paid

What causes interest expense on the bonds to exceed cash interest paid? (p. 430)

P8-59A *(Learning Objective 2, 3, 5: Analyzing a company's long-term debt and reporting long-term debt on the balance sheet (effective-interest method))* Notes to the E-Z-Boy Recliners financial statements reported the following data on December 31, Year 1 (the end of the fiscal year):

Note 6. Indebtedness		
Bonds payable, 5%, due in Year 6	$600,000	
Less: Discount..	(25,274)	$574,726
Notes payable, 8.3%, payable in $50,000		
annual installments starting in Year 5..............		250,000

E-Z-Boy amortizes bonds by the effective-interest method.

▌*Required*

1. Answer the following questions about E-Z-Boy's long-term liabilities: (pp. 428–429)
   a. What is the maturity value of the 5% bonds?
   b. What are E-Z-Boy's annual cash interest payments on the 5% bonds?
   c. What is the carrying amount of the 5% bonds at December 31, year 1?

2. Prepare an amortization table through December 31, Year 4, for the 5% bonds. The market interest rate for these bonds was 6%. E-Z-Boy pays interest annually on December 31. How much is E-Z-Boy's interest expense on the 5% bonds for the year ended December 31, Year 4? (pp. 428–429)

3. Show how E-Z-Boy Recliners, would report the bonds payable and notes payable at December 31, Year 4. (pp. 427, 431–433)

P8-60A (*Learning Objective 2, 3, 5: Issuing convertible bonds at a discount, amortizing by the effective-interest method, retiring bonds early, converting bonds, and reporting the bonds payable on the balance sheet*) On December 31, 20X7, Digital Connections issued 8%, 10-year convertible bonds payable with a maturity value of $500,000. The semiannual interest dates are June 30 and December 31. The market interest rate is 9%, and the issue price of the bonds is 94. Digital Connections amortizes bonds by the effective-interest method.

❚ Required

1. Prepare an effective-interest-method amortization table for the first 4 semiannual interest periods. (p. 428)
2. Journalize the following transactions: (pp. 432–433, 437)
    a. Issuance of the bonds on December 31, 20X7. Credit Convertible Bonds Payable.
    b. Payment of interest and amortization of the bonds on June 30, 20X8.
    c. Payment of interest and amortization of the bonds on December 31, 20X8.
    d. Conversion by the bondholders on July 1, 20X9, of bonds with face value of $200,000 into 10,000 shares of Digital Connections' $1-par common stock. (p. 437)
3. Show how Digital Connections would report the remaining bonds payable on its balance sheet at December 31, 20X9. (pp. 432–433)

writing assignment ■

P8-61A (*Learning Objective 4: Financing operations with debt or with stock*) Outback Sporting Goods is embarking on a massive expansion. Assume plans call for opening 20 new stores during the next 2 years. Each store is scheduled to be 50% larger than the company's existing locations, offering more items of inventory, and with more elaborate displays. Management estimates that company operations will provide $1 million of the cash needed for expansion. Outback must raise the remaining $6 million from outsiders. The board of directors is considering obtaining the $6 million either through borrowing or by issuing common stock.

❚ Required

Write a memo to Outback's management discussing the advantages and disadvantages of borrowing and of issuing common stock to raise the needed cash. Which method of raising the funds would you recommend? (p. 438)

P8-62A (*Learning Objective 5: Reporting liabilities on the balance sheet; times-interest-earned ratio*) The accounting records of Pacer Foods, Inc., include the following items at December 31, 20X8:

Mortgage note payable, current	$ 50,000	Accumulated depreciation, equipment	$219,000
Accumulated pension benefit obligation	463,000	Discount on bonds payable (all long-term)	7,000
Bonds payable, long-term...........	490,000	Operating income................	291,000
Mortgage note payable, long-term	150,000	Equipment..........................	487,000
Bonds payable, current portion ...	70,000	Pension plan assets (market value)................	382,000
Interest expense.........................	67,000	Interest payable..................	9,000

❚ Required

1. Show how each relevant item would be reported on the Pacer Foods, Inc., classified balance sheet, including headings and totals for current liabilities and long-term liabilities. (pp. 421, 434)

2. Answer the following questions about Pacer's financial position at December 31, 20X8:
   a. What is the carrying amount of the bonds payable (combine the current and long-term amounts)? (p. 434)
   b. Why is the interest-payable amount so much less than the amount of interest expense? (Challenge)
3. How many times did Pacer cover its interest expense during 20X8? (p. 441)

(Group B)

P8-63B (*Learning Objective 1: Measuring current liabilities*) Goldwater Corporation experienced these 5 events during the current year:
   a. December sales totaled $50,000, and Goldwater collected an additional state sales tax of 6%. This amount will be sent to the state of Indiana early in January. (p. 415)
   b. On November 30, Goldwater received rent of $6,000 in advance for a lease on unused store space. This rent will be earned evenly over 3 months. (p. 417)
   c. On September 30, Goldwater signed a 6-month, 9% note payable to purchase store fixtures costing $12,000. The note requires payment of principal and interest at maturity. (p. 415)
   d. Sales of $400,000 were covered by Goldwater's product warranty. At January 1, estimated warranty payable was $12,400. During the year, Goldwater recorded warranty expense of $22,300 and paid warranty claims of $24,600. (pp. 418–419)
   e. Goldwater owes $100,000 on a long-term note payable. At December 31, 6% interest since July 31 and $20,000 of this principal are payable within 1 year. (p. 416)

❙ Required

For each item, indicate the account and the related amount to be reported as a *current* liability on the Goldwater Corporation balance sheet at December 31.

P8-64B (*Learning Objective 1: Recording liability-related transactions*) Assume that the following transactions of **Mardell Book Stores** occurred during 20X8 and 20X9.

❙ Required

Record the transactions in the company's journal. Explanations are not required. (pp. 415–416)

20X8	
Jan. 9	Purchased store fixtures at a cost of $50,000, signing an 8%, 6-month note payable for that amount.
June 30	Borrowed $200,000 on a 9% note payable that calls for annual installment payments of $50,000 principal plus interest. Record the short-term note payable in a separate account from the long-term note payable.
July 9	Paid the 6-month, 8% note at maturity.
Dec. 31	Accrued warranty expense, which is estimated at 3% of sales of $600,000.
31	Accrued interest on the outstanding note payable.
20X9	
June 30	Paid the first installment and interest for 1 year on the outstanding note payable.

P8-65B (*Learning Objective 2: Recording bond transactions (at par) and reporting bonds payable on the balance sheet*) Assume the board of directors of **Fiesta Bowl Arizona Corporation** authorizes the issue of $1 million of 8%, 20-year bonds payable. The semiannual interest dates are March 31 and September 30. The bonds are issued on March 31, 20X8, at par.

❙ Required

1. Journalize the following transactions: (pp. 426–427)
   a. Issuance of the bonds on March 31, 20X8.
   b. Payment of interest on September 30, 20X8.
   c. Accrual of interest on December 31, 20X8.
   d. Payment of interest on March 31, 20X9.
2. Report interest payable and bonds payable as they would appear on the Fiesta Bowl Arizona Corporation balance sheet at December 31, 20X8. (pp. 431–433)

P8-66B (*Learning Objective 2, 5: Issuing notes at a discount, amortizing by the straight-line method, and reporting notes payable on the balance sheet*) On February 28, 20X8, Kids R Us, Inc., issues 7%, 10-year notes payable with a face value of $300,000. The notes pay interest on February 28 and August 31, and Kids R Us amortizes bonds by the straight-line method.

❙ Required

1. If the market interest rate is 6% when Kids R Us issues its notes, will the notes be priced at par, at a premium, or at a discount? Explain. (p. 426)
2. If the market interest rate is 8% when Kids R Us issues its notes, will the notes be priced at par, at a premium, or at a discount? Explain. (p. 426)
3. Assume that the issue price of the notes is 96. Journalize the following note payable transactions: (pp. 427–428, 435–436)
   a. Issuance of the notes on February 28, 20X8.
   b. Payment of interest and amortization of the bonds on August 31, 20X8.
   c. Accrual of interest and amortization of the bonds on December 31, 20X8.
   d. Payment of interest and amortization of the bonds on February 28, 20X9.
4. Report interest payable and notes payable as they would appear on the Kids R Us balance sheet at December 31, 20X8. (pp. 431–433)

writing assignment ■

P8-67B (*Learning Objective 2: Accounting for bonds payable at a discount and amortizing by the straight-line method*)

1. Journalize the following transactions of Ski Boats Unlimited: (pp. 427–428, 435–436)

20X4		
Jan. 1	Issued $100,000 of 8%, 5-year bonds payable at 94.	
July 1	Paid semiannual interest and amortized the bonds by the straight-line method on our 8% bonds payable.	
Dec. 31	Accrued semiannual interest expense and amortized the bonds by the straight-line method on our 8% bonds payable.	
20X5		
Jan. 1	Paid semiannual interest.	
20X9		
Jan. 1	Paid the 8% bonds at maturity.	

2. At December 31, 20X4, after all year-end adjustments, determine the carrying amount of Ski Boats Unlimited's bonds payable, net. (pp. 431–433)
3. For the 6 months ended July 1, 20X4, determine the following for Ski Boats Unlimited: (pp. 436–437)
   a. Interest expense   b. Cash interest paid
   What causes interest expense on the bonds to exceed cash interest paid? (p. 430)

P8-68B (*Learning Objective 2, 3, 5: Analyzing a company's long-term debt and reporting the long-term debt on the balance sheet (effective-interest method)*) The notes to the Christian Charities financial statements reported the following data on December 31, Year 1 (end of the fiscal year):

Note D—Long-Term Debt	
7% bonds payable, due in Year 7.............................. $500,000	
Less: Discount.. (26,032) $473,968	
6½% notes payable; principal due in annual	
amounts of $50,000 in Years 5 through 10...............	300,000

Christian Charities amortizes bonds by the effective-interest method and pays all interest amounts at December 31.

❚ *Required*

1. Answer the following questions about Christian Charities' long-term liabilities: (p. 428)
   a. What is the maturity value of the 7% bonds?
   b. What is Christian Charities' annual cash interest payment on the 7% bonds?
   c. What is the carrying amount of the 7% bonds at December 31, Year 1?
2. Prepare an amortization table through December 31, Year 4, for the 7% bonds. The market interest rate on the bonds was 8%. Round all amounts to the nearest dollar. How much is Christian Charities' interest expense on the 7% bonds for the year ended December 31, Year 4? (p. 428)
3. Show how Christian Charities would report the 7% bonds payable and the 6 1/2% notes payable at December 31, Year 4. (pp. 428, 431–433)

P8-69B (*Learning Objective 2, 3, 5: Issuing convertible bonds at a premium, by the effective-interest method, retiring bonds early, converting bonds, and reporting the bonds payable on the balance sheet*) On December 31, 20X6, Caribbean Cruise Lines (CCL) issues 9%, 10-year convertible bonds payable with a maturity value of $300,000. The semiannual interest dates are June 30 and December 31. The market interest rate is 8%, and the issue price of the bonds is 106. CCL amortizes bonds by the effective-interest method.

❚ *Required*

1. Prepare an effective-interest-method amortization table for the first 4 semiannual interest periods. (p. 434)
2. Journalize the following transactions. (pp. 431–437)
   a. Issuance of the bonds on December 31, 20X6. Credit Convertible Bonds Payable.
   b. Payment of interest and amortization of the bonds on June 30, 20X7.
   c. Payment of interest and amortization of the bonds on December 31, 20X7.
   d. Conversion by the bondholders on July 1, 20X8, of bonds with face value of $150,000 into 10,000 shares of CCL's $1-par common stock.
3. Show how Caribbean Cruise Lines would report the remaining bonds payable on its balance sheet at December 31, 20X8. (pp. 431–433)

P8-70B (*Learning Objective 4: Financing operations with debt or with stock*) Two businesses in very different circumstances are pondering how to raise $2 million.

writing assignment ■

Pizzazz.com has fallen on hard times. Net income has been low for the last 3 years, even falling by 10% from last year's level of profits, and cash flow also took a nose dive. Top management has experienced some turnover and has stabilized only recently. To become competitive again, Pizzazz.com needs $2 million to invest in new technology.

MeToo Personals is in the midst of its most successful period since it began operations in 2005. Net income has increased by 25%. The outlook for the future is bright with new markets opening up and competitors unable to compete with MeToo Personals. As a result MeToo is planning a large-scale expansion.

(continued)

❚ Required

Propose a plan for each company to raise the needed cash. Which company should borrow? Which company should issue stock? Consider the advantages and the disadvantages of raising money by borrowing and by issuing stock and discuss them in your answer. (p. 438)

P8-71B *(Learning Objective 5: Reporting liabilities on the balance sheet, times-interest-earned ratio)* The accounting records of Hartford Financial Services include the following items at December 31, 20X6:

Premium on bonds payable(all long-term)...............	$ 13,000
Interest payable...	3,900
Pension plan assets(market value)	402,000
Operating income..	104,000
Accumulated pension benefit obligation..................	436,000
Interest expense..	39,000
Bonds payable, current portion	50,000
Accumulated depreciation, building........................	70,000
Mortgage note payable, long-term	215,000
Bonds payable, long-term.......................................	250,000
Building..	160,000

❚ Required

1. Show how each relevant item would be reported on Hartford Financial Services' classified balance sheet. Include headings and totals for current liabilities and long-term liabilities. (pp. 421, 434)
2. Answer the following questions about the financial position of Hartford Financial Services at December 31, 20X6:
   a. What is the carrying amount of the bonds payable (combine the current and long-term amounts)? (p. 434)
   b. Why is the interest payable amount so much less than the amount of interest expense? (Challenge)
3. How many times did Hartford cover its interest expense during 20X6? (pp. 440–441)

APPLY YOUR KNOWLEDGE

Decision Cases

Case 1. *(Learning Objective 2: Exploring an actual bankruptcy)* In 20X2, **Enron Corporation** filed for Chapter 11 bankruptcy protection, shocking the business community: How could a company this large and this successful go bankrupt? This case explores the causes and the effects of Enron's bankruptcy.

At December 31, 20X0, and for the 4 years ended on that date, Enron reported the following (amounts in millions):

Balance Sheet (summarized)				
Total assets				$65,503
Total liabilities..				54,033
Total stockholders' equity..				11,470
Income Statements (excerpts)				
	20X0	19X9	19X8	19X7
Net income	$979*	$893	$703	$105

*Operating income = $1,953
Interest expense = $838

Unknown to investors and lenders, Enron also controlled hundreds of partnerships that owed vast amounts of money. These special-purpose entities (SPEs) did not appear on the Enron financial statements. Assume that the SPEs' assets totaled $7,000 million and their liabilities stood at $6,900 million; assume a 10% interest rate on these liabilities.

During the 4-year period up to 20X0, Enron's stock price shot up from $17.50 to $90.56. Enron used its escalating stock price to finance the purchase of the SPEs by guaranteeing lenders that Enron would give them Enron stock if the SPEs could not pay their loans.

In 20X1, the SEC launched an investigation into Enron's accounting practices. It was alleged that Enron should have been including the SPEs in its financial statements all along. Enron then restated net income for years up to 20X0, wiping out nearly $600 million of total net income (and total assets) for this 4-year period. Enron's stock price tumbled, and the guarantees to the SPEs' lenders added millions to Enron's liabilities (assume the full amount of the SPEs' debt). To make matters worse, the assets of the SPEs lost much of their value; assume that their market value is only $500 million.

▌ Required

1. Compute the debt ratio that Enron reported at the end of 20X0. Recompute this ratio after including the SPEs in Enron's financial statements. Also compute Enron's times-interest-earned ratio both ways for 20X0. Assume that the changes to Enron's financial position occurred during 20X0. (pp. 169, 440)

2. Why does it appear that Enron failed to include the SPEs in its financial statements? How do you view Enron after including the SPEs in the company's financial statements? (Challenge)

Case 2. *(Learning Objective 4: Analyzing alternative ways of raising $5 million)* Business is going well for **Park 'N Fly**, the company that operates remote parking lots near major airports. The board of directors of this family-owned company believes that Park 'N Fly could earn an additional $1.5 million income before interest and taxes by expanding into new markets. However, the $5 million that the business needs for growth cannot be raised within the family. The directors, who strongly wish to retain family control of the company, must consider issuing securities to outsiders. The directors are considering 3 financing plans.

Plan A is to borrow at 6%. Plan B is to issue 100,000 shares of common stock. Plan C is to issue 100,000 shares of nonvoting, $3.75 preferred stock ($3.75 is the annual dividend paid on each share of preferred stock).* Park 'N Fly presently has net income of $3.5 million and 1 million shares of common stock outstanding. The company's income tax rate is 35%.

▌ Required

1. Prepare an analysis to determine which plan will result in the highest earnings per share of common stock. (pp. 438–439)

2. Recommend 1 plan to the board of directors. Give your reasons. (pp. 438–439)

---

*For a discussion of preferred stock, see Chapter 9.

Ethical Issues

Issue 1. Microsoft Corporation is the defendant in numerous lawsuits claiming unfair trade practices. Microsoft has strong incentives not to disclose these contingent liabilities. However, GAAP requires that companies report their contingent liabilities.

I *Required*

1. Why would a company prefer not to disclose its contingent liabilities?

2. Describe how a bank could be harmed if a company seeking a loan did not disclose its contingent liabilities.

3. What is the ethical tightrope that companies must walk when they report their contingent liabilities?

Issue 2. The top managers of Medtech.com borrowed heavily to develop a prescription-medicine distribution system. Medtech's outlook was bright, and investors poured millions into the company. Sadly, Medtech never lived up to its potential, and the company is in bankruptcy. It can't pay about half of its liabilities.

I *Required*

Is it unethical for managers to saddle a company with a high level of debt? Or is it just risky? Who could be hurt by a company's taking on too much debt? Discuss.

Focus on Financials: ■ YUM! Brands

(*Learning Objective 1, 2, 5: Analyzing current and contingent liabilities*) Refer to **YUM! Brands'** financial statements in Appendix A at the end of this book.

1. YUM's balance sheet reports a combined total for Accounts payable and other current liabilities. Give the breakdown of the reported total at the end of 2006. (Challenge)

2. Income tax provision is another title for income tax expense. Why is YUM's income tax provision larger than income taxes payable at the end of each year? (Challenge)

3. Did YUM borrow more or pay off more short-term and long-term debt during 2006? How can you tell? (Challenge)

4. How would experienced analysts rate YUM's overall debt position—risky, safe, or average? Compute the ratio at December 30, 2006 that answers this question. (p. 169)

Focus on Analysis: ■ Pier 1 Imports

(*Learning Objective 1, 2, 3, 5: Analyzing current liabilities and long-term debt*) **Pier 1 Imports'** financial statements in Appendix B at the end of this book report a number of liabilities. Show amounts in thousands.

1. How would experienced analysts rate Pier 1's overall debt position at year end 2006—risky, safe, or average? Compute the ratio that enables you to answer this question. (pp. 169–170)

2. The statement of cash flow reports that Pier 1 completed 2 notes payable transactions and 1 long-term debt transaction during 2006. Journalize those transactions. (pp. 415, 426)

3. Use the data on the faces of Pier 1's 2006 income statement and balance sheet to estimate Pier 1's average interest rate during 2006 on all company borrowings. Use the beginning balance of long-term debt for 2006. (Challenge)

Group Projects

Project 1. Consider 3 different businesses:

1. A bank

2. A magazine publisher

3. A department store

For each business, list all of its liabilities—both current and long-term. Then compare the 3 lists to identify the liabilities that the 3 businesses have in common. Also identify the liabilities that are unique to each type of business.

Project 2. Alcenon Corporation leases the majority of the assets that it uses in operations. Alcenon prefers operating leases (versus capital leases) in order to keep the lease liability off its balance sheet and maintain a low debt ratio.

Alcenon is negotiating a 10-year lease on an asset with an expected useful life of 15 years. The lease requires Alcenon to make 10 annual lease payments of $20,000 each, with the first payment due at the beginning of the lease term. The leased asset has a market value of $135,180. The lease agreement specifies no transfer of title to the lessee and includes no bargain purchase option.

Write a report for Alcenon's management to explain what conditions must be present for Alcenon to be able to account for this lease as an operating lease.

For Internet Exercises go to the Web site www.prenhall.com/harrison.

Quick Check Answers

1. *a*

2. *e*

3. *c* ($200,000 × 0.025 = $5,000)

4. *c* [400 × 0.05 × $40 = warranty expense of $800; repaired $40 × 6 = $240; year-end liability = $560 ($800 - $240)]

5. *e*

6. *e*

7. *a*

8. *b*

9. *c*

10. *b*

11. *e*

12. *a* ($196,140 × .10 × 6/12 = $9,807)

13. *d* [Int. exp. = $9,807 Int. payment = $9,500 ($200,000 × .095 × 6/12)
     $9,807 – $9,500 = $307]

14. *b* ($200,000 × .095 = $19,000)

15. *c* (See Amortization Schedule)

Date	Interest Payment	Interest Expense	Discount Amortiz.	Bond Carry Amt.
1/1/X2				$196,140
7/1/X2	$9,500	$9,807	$307	196,447
1/1/X3	9,500	9,822	322	196,769

16. *d* {$196,140 + [($200,000 – $196,140) × 1/5] = $196,912}

9 Stockholders' Equity

IHOP: THE BEST PANCAKES IN TOWN

It's late and you have a history exam tomorrow morning at 8. Where do you go for a quick bite? **IHOP** may be your choice, because IHOP locates near college campuses.

IHOP started in 1958 and first offered the company's stock to the public in 1991. Now IHOP operates 1,302 restaurant and racks up annual sales of $350 million.

In this chapter we'll show you how to account for IHOP's issuance of stock to investors. We'll also cover the other elements of stockholders' equity—Additional Paid-in Capital, Retained Earnings, and Treasury Stock, plus dividends and stock splits. By the time you finish this chapter, you may be hungry for a stack of IHOP pancakes. Or you may go out and buy some IHOP stock.

IHOP Corp.
Consolidated Balance Sheet (Adapted)
December 31, 2006

(In thousands, except number of shares)

Assets

Current assets:

Total current assets	$ 78,393
Long-term receivables	302,088
Property and equipment, net	309,737
Other assets...	78,652
Total assets..	$ 768,870

Liabilities and Stockholders' Equity

Current liabilities:

Total current liabilities	$ 64,105
Long-term debt	94,468
Other long-term liabilities	321,084
1 Stockholders' equity:	
2 Preferred stock, $1 par value, 10,000,000 shares authorized; shares issued and outstanding: none...................................	—
3 Common stock, $.01 par value, 40,000,000 shares authorized; 22,718,007 shares issued and 17,873,548 shares outstanding	227
4 Additional paid-in capital	131,748
5 Retained earnings..	358,975
6 Treasury stock, at cost (4,844,459 shares)............................	(201,604)
7 Other equity..	(133)
8 Total stockholders' equity..	289,213
Total liabilities and stockholders' equity	$ 768,870

Chapters 4 to 8 discussed accounting for assets and liabilities. By this time, you should be familiar with all the assets and liabilities listed on IHOP's balance sheet. Let's focus now on IHOP's stockholders' equity. In this chapter we discuss some of the decisions a company faces when:

■ paying dividends
■ issuing stock
■ buying back its stock

Let's begin with the organization of a corporation.

LEARNING OBJECTIVES

1 **Explain** the features of a corporation

2 **Account** for the issuance of stock

3 **Describe** how treasury stock affects a company

4 **Account** for dividends

5 **Use** stock values in decision making

6 **Compute** return on assets and return on equity

7 **Report** equity transactions on the statement of cash flows

WHAT'S THE BEST WAY TO ORGANIZE A BUSINESS?

Anyone starting a business must decide how to organize the company. Corporations differ from proprietorships and partnerships in several ways.

Separate Legal Entity. A corporation is a business entity formed under state law. It is a distinct entity, an artificial person that exists apart from its owners, the **stockholders**, or **shareholders**. The corporation has many of the rights that a person has. For example, a corporation may buy, own, and sell property. Assets and liabilities in the business belong to the corporation and not to its owners. The corporation may enter into contracts, sue, and be sued.

Nearly all large companies, such as **IHOP**, **Toyota**, and **Wal-Mart**, are corporations. Their full names may include *Corporation* or *Incorporated* (abbreviated *Corp.* and *Inc.*) to indicate that they are corporations, for example, IHOP Corp. and Pier 1 Imports, Inc. Corporations can also use the word *Company*, such as Ford Motor Company.

Continuous Life and Transferability of Ownership. Corporations have *continuous lives* regardless of changes in their ownership. The stockholders of a corporation may buy more of the stock, sell the stock to another person, give it away, or bequeath it in a will. The transfer of the stock from one person to another does not affect the continuity of the corporation. In contrast, proprietorships and partnerships terminate when their ownership changes.

Limited Liability. Stockholders have **limited liability** for the corporation's debts. They have no personal obligation for corporate liabilities. The most that a stockholder can lose on an investment in a corporation's stock is the cost of the investment. Limited liability is one of the most attractive features of the corporate form of organization. It enables corporations to raise more capital from a wider group of investors than proprietorships and partnerships can. By contrast, proprietors and partners are personally liable for all the debts of their businesses.[1]

Separation of Ownership and Management. Stockholders own the corporation, but the *board of directors*—elected by the stockholders—appoints officers to manage the business. Thus, stockholders may invest $1,000 or $1 million in the corporation without having to manage it.

Management's goal is to maximize the firm's value for the stockholders. But the separation between owners and managers may create problems. Corporate officers may run the business for their own benefit and not for the stockholders. For example, the CEO of **Tyco Corporation** was accused of looting Tyco of $600 million. The CFO of **Enron Corporation** set up outside partnerships and paid himself millions to manage the partnerships—unknown to Enron stockholders. Both men went to prison.

Corporate Taxation. Corporations are separate taxable entities. They pay several taxes not borne by proprietorships or partnerships, including an annual franchise tax levied by the state. The franchise tax keeps the corporate charter in force. Corporations also pay federal and state income taxes.

Corporate earnings are subject to **double taxation** on their income.

---

[1]Unless the business is organized as a limited-liability company (LLC) or a limited-liability partnership (LLP).

- First, corporations pay income taxes on their corporate income.
- Then stockholders pay personal income tax on the cash dividends received from corporations. Proprietorships and partnerships pay no business income tax. Instead, the business's tax falls solely on the owners.

Government Regulation. Because stockholders have only limited liability for corporation debts, outsiders doing business with the corporation can look no further than the corporation if it fails to pay. To protect a corporation's creditors and stockholders, both federal and state governments monitor corporations. The regulations mainly ensure that corporations disclose the information that investors and creditors need to make informed decisions. Accounting provides much of this information.

Exhibit 9-1 summarizes the advantages and disadvantages of the corporate form of business organization.

EXHIBIT 9-1 Advantages and Disadvantages of a Corporation

Advantages	Disadvantages
1. Can raise more capital than a proprietorship or partnership can	1. Separation of ownership and management
2. Continuous life	2. Corporate taxation
3. Ease of transferring ownership	3. Government regulation
4. Limited liability of stockholders	

Organizing a Corporation

The creation of a corporation begins when its organizers, called the *incorporators*, obtain a charter from the state. The charter includes the authorization for the corporation to issue a certain number of shares of stock. A share of stock is the basic unit of ownership for a corporation. The incorporators

- pay fees
- sign the charter
- file documents with the state
- agree to a set of **bylaws**, which act as the constitution for governing the company.

The corporation then comes into existence.

Ultimate control of the corporation rests with the stockholders who elect a **board of directors** that sets company policy and appoints officers. The board elects a **chairperson**, who usually is the most powerful person in the organization. The chairperson of the board of directors has the title chief executive officer (CEO). The board also designates the **president**, who is the chief operating officer (COO) in charge of day-to-day operations. Most corporations also have vice presidents in charge of sales, manufacturing, accounting and finance (the chief financial officer, or CFO), and other key areas. Exhibit 9-2 shows the authority structure in a corporation.

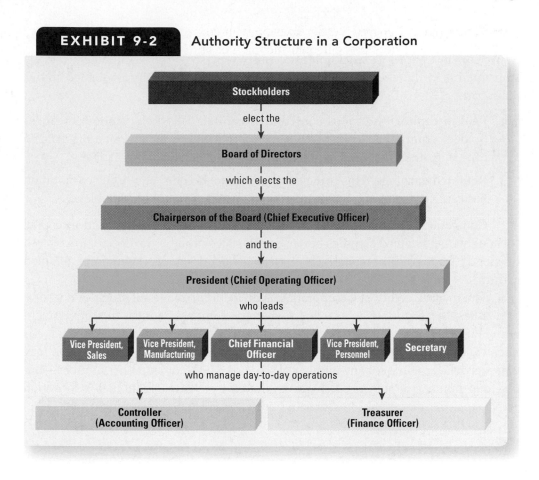

EXHIBIT 9-2 Authority Structure in a Corporation

Stockholders' Rights

Ownership of stock entitles stockholders to 4 basic rights, unless a specific right is withheld by agreement with the stockholders:

1. *Vote.* The right to participate in management by voting on matters that come before the stockholders. This is the stockholder's sole voice in the management of the corporation. A stockholder gets 1 vote for each share of stock owned.

2. *Dividends.* The right to receive a proportionate part of any dividend. Each share of stock in a particular class receives an equal dividend.

3. *Liquidation.* The right to receive a proportionate share of any assets remaining after the corporation pays its liabilities in liquidation. Liquidation means to go out of business, sell the assets, pay all liabilities, and distribute any remaining cash to the owners.

4. *Preemption.* The right to maintain one's proportionate ownership in the corporation. Suppose you own 5% of a corporation's stock. If the corporation issues 100,000 new shares, it must offer you the opportunity to buy 5% (5,000) of the new shares. This right, called the *preemptive right*, is usually withheld from the stockholders.

Stockholders' Equity

As we saw in Chapter 1, **stockholders' equity** represents the stockholders' ownership interest in the assets of a corporation. Stockholders' equity is divided into 2 main parts:

1. **Paid-in capital**, also called **contributed capital**. This is the amount of stockholders' equity the stockholders have contributed to the corporation. Paid-in capital includes the stock accounts and any additional paid-in capital.

2. **Retained earnings.** This is the amount of stockholders' equity the corporation has earned through profitable operations and has not used for dividends.

Companies report stockholders' equity by source. They report paid-in capital separately from retained earnings because most states prohibit the declaration of cash dividends from paid-in capital. Thus, cash dividends are declared from retained earnings.

The owners' equity of a corporation is divided into shares of **stock**. A corporation issues *stock certificates* to its owners when the company receives their investment in the business—usually cash. Because stock represents the corporation's capital, it is often called *capital stock*. The basic unit of capital stock is 1 *share*. A corporation may issue a stock certificate for any number of shares—1, 100, or any other number—but the total number of *authorized* shares is limited by charter. Exhibit 9-3 shows an actual stock certificate for 288 shares of Central Jersey Bancorp common stock.

EXHIBIT 9-3   **Stock Certificate**

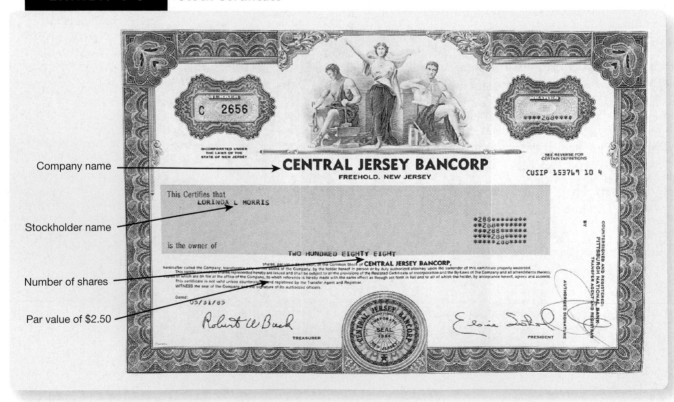

Stock in the hands of a stockholder is said to be **outstanding**. The total number of shares of stock outstanding at any time represents 100% ownership of the corporation.

Classes of Stock

Corporations issue different types of stock to appeal to a variety of investors. The stock of a corporation may be either

- Common or preferred
- Par or no-par

Common and Preferred. Every corporation issues **common stock**, the basic form of capital stock. Unless designated otherwise, the word *stock* is understood to mean "common stock." Common stockholders have the 4 basic rights of stock ownership, unless a right is specifically withheld. The common stockholders are the owners of the corporation. They stand to benefit the most if the corporation succeeds because they take the most risk by investing in common stock.

Preferred stock gives its owners certain advantages over common stockholders. Preferred stockholders receive dividends before the common stockholders and they also receive assets before the common stockholders if the corporation liquidates. Owners of preferred stock also have the 4 basic stockholder rights, unless a right is specifically denied. Companies may issue different classes of preferred stock (Class A and Class B or Series A and Series B, for example). Each class of stock is recorded in a separate account. The most preferred stockholders can expect to earn is their fixed dividend.

Preferred stock is a hybrid between common stock and long-term debt. Like debt, preferred stock pays a fixed dividend. But like stock, the dividend is not required to be paid unless the board of directors declares the dividend. Also, companies have no obligation to pay back true preferred stock. Preferred stock that must be redeemed (paid back) by the corporation is a liability masquerading as a stock.

Preferred stock is rare. A recent survey of 600 corporations revealed that only 9% of them had preferred stock (Exhibit 9-4). All corporations have common stock. The balance sheet of IHOP Corp. (p. 474, line 2) shows that IHOP is authorized to issue preferred stock. To date, however, IHOP has issued none of the preferred.

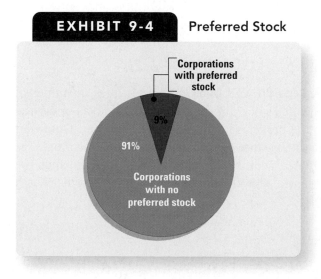

EXHIBIT 9-4   Preferred Stock

Exhibit 9-5 shows some of the similarities and differences among common stock, preferred stock, and long-term debt.

EXHIBIT 9-5	Comparison of Common Stock, Preferred Stock, and Long-Term Debt		
	Common Stock	Preferred Stock	Long-Term Debt
1. Obligation to repay principal	No	No	Yes
2. Dividends/interest	Dividends are not tax-deductible	Dividends are not tax-deductible	Interest expense is tax-deductible
3. Obligation to pay dividends/interest	Only after declaration	Only after declaration	At fixed rates and dates

Par Value and No-Par. Stock may be par-value stock or no-par stock. **Par value** is an arbitrary amount assigned by a company to a share of its stock. Most companies set the par value of their common stock low to avoid legal difficulties from issuing their stock below par. Most states require companies to maintain a minimum amount of stockholders' equity for the protection of creditors, and this minimum is often called the corporation's legal capital. For corporations with par-value stock, **legal capital** is the par value of the shares issued.

The par value of **PepsiCo** common stock is 1 2/3 cents per share. **Best Buy** common stock carries a par value of $1 per share, and **Pier 1 Imports'** common stock has par value of $1 per share. Par value of preferred stock is sometimes higher.

No-par stock does not have par value. But some no-par stock has a **stated value**, which makes it similar to par-value stock. The stated value is an arbitrary amount similar to par value. In a recent survey, only 9% of the companies had no-par stock outstanding. Apple Computer, Krispy Kreme Doughnuts, and Sony have no-par stock.

Issuing Stock

OBJECTIVE

2 **Account** for the issuance of stock

Large corporations such as **IHOP**, **PepsiCo**, and **Microsoft** need huge quantities of money to operate. Corporations may sell stock directly to the stockholders or use the service of an *underwriter*, such as the brokerage firms **Merrill Lynch** and **Goldman Sachs**. Companies often advertise the issuance of their stock to attract investors. *The Wall Street Journal* is the most popular medium for such advertisements, which are also called *tombstones*. Exhibit 9-6 is a reproduction of IHOP's tombstone, which appeared in *The Wall Street Journal*.

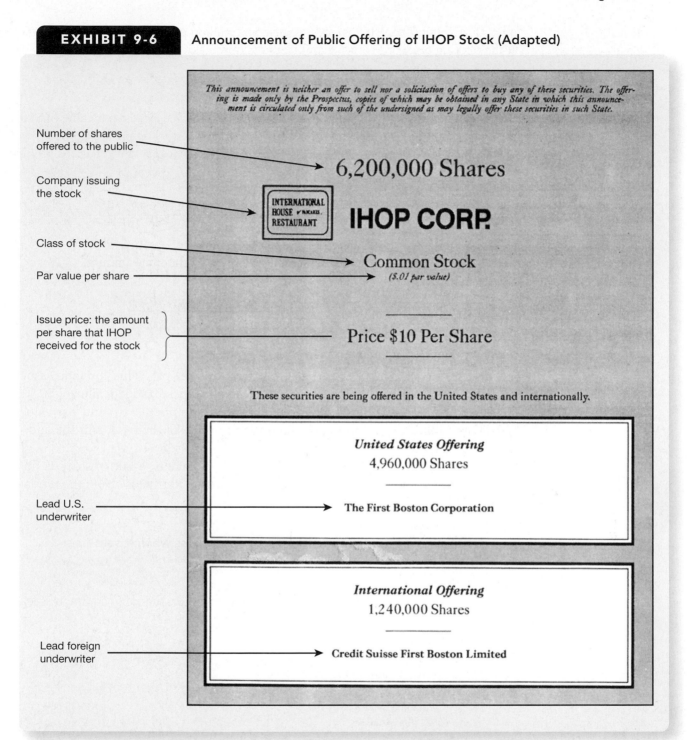

EXHIBIT 9-6   Announcement of Public Offering of IHOP Stock (Adapted)

The lead underwriter of IHOP's public offering was First Boston. Outside the United States, Credit Suisse First Boston led the way. Several other domestic brokerage firms and investment bankers sold IHOP stock to their clients. In its initial public offering (Exhibit 9-6), IHOP sought to raise $62 million of capital (6.2 million shares at the offering price of $10 per share). Let's see how a stock issuance works.

Common Stock

Common Stock at Par. Suppose IHOP's common stock carried a par value of $10 per share. The entry for issuance of 6.2 million shares of stock at par would be

Jan. 8	Cash (6,200,000 × $10)	62,000,000	
	Common Stock		62,000,000
	To issue common stock.		

IHOP's assets and stockholders' equity increase by the same amount.

Assets	=	Liabilities	+	Stockholders' Equity
+ 62,000,000	=	0		+ 62,000,000

Common Stock Above Par. Most corporations set par value low and issue common stock for a price above par. IHOP's common stock has a par value of $0.01 (1 cent) per share. The $9.99 difference between issue price ($10) and par value ($0.01) is additional paid-in capital. Both the par value of the stock and the additional amount are part of paid-in capital.

Because the entity is dealing with its own stockholders, a sale of stock is not gain, income, or profit to the corporation. This situation illustrates one of the fundamentals of accounting:

> **A company neither earns a profit nor incurs a loss when it sells its stock to, or buys its stock from, its own stockholders.**

With par value of $0.01, IHOP's actual entry to record the issuance of common stock looked something like this:

July 23	Cash (6,200,000 × $10)	62,000,000	
	Common Stock (6,200,000 × $0.01)		62,000
	Paid-in Capital in Excess of Par—Common		
	(6,200,000 × $9.99)		61,938,000
	To issue common stock.		

Both assets and equity increase by the same amount.

Assets	=	Liabilities	+	Stockholders' Equity
+ 62,000,000	=	0		+ 62,000
				+ 61,938,000

Another title for Paid-in Capital in Excess of Par—Common is Additional Paid-in Capital, as used by IHOP Corporation (p. 474, line 4). At the end of the year, IHOP could report stockholders' equity on its balance sheet as follows:

Stockholders' Equity	
Common stock, $0.01 par, 40 million shares authorized, 6.2 million shares issued..............	$ 62,000
Paid-in capital in excess of par............................	61,938,000
Total paid-in capital..	62,000,000
Retained earnings...	358,975
Total stockholders' equity....................................	$62,358,975

All the transactions in this section include a receipt of cash by the corporation as it issues *new* stock. The transactions we illustrate are different from those reported in the daily news. In those transactions, one stockholder sold stock to another investor. The corporation doesn't record those transactions because they were between 2 outside parties.

STOP & think. . .

Examine IHOP's balance sheet at December 31, 2006 (p. 474). Answer these questions about IHOP's actual stock transactions (amounts in thousands, except per share):

1. What was IHOP's total paid-in capital at December 31, 2006?
2. How many shares of common stock had IHOP issued through the end of 2006 (in thousands)?
3. What was the average issue price of the IHOP stock that the company had issued through the end of 2006?

Answers:

		December 31, 2006
1.	Total paid-in capital...	$227 + $131,748 = $131,975
2.	Number of shares issued	22,718

3. $$\frac{\text{Average issue price of stock}}{\text{through the end of 2006}} = \frac{\text{Total received from issuance of stock}}{\text{Shares issued}} = \frac{\$131,975}{22,718}$$

$$= \$5.81 \text{ per share}$$

IHOP has issued its stock at an average price of $5.81 per share.

No-Par Common Stock. To record the issuance of no-par stock, the company debits the asset received and credits the stock account for the cash value of the asset received. Suppose Apple Computer issues 855 million shares of no-par common stock for $4,355 million. Apple's stock issuance entry is (in millions)

Aug. 14	Cash	4,355	
	Common Stock		4,355
	To issue no-par common stock.		

Assets	=	Liabilities	+	Stockholders' Equity
+ 4,355	=	0		+ 4,355

Apple's charter authorizes the company to issue 1,800 million shares of no-par stock, and the company has approximately $5,629 in retained earnings. Apple Computer, Inc., reports stockholders' equity on the balance sheet as follows (in millions)

Stockholders' Equity

Common stock, no par, 1,800 shares authorized, 855 shares issued..................	$4,355
Retained earnings..	5,629
Total stockholders' equity	$9,984

You can see that a company with true no-par stock has no Additional Paid-in Capital account.

No-Par Common Stock with a Stated Value. Accounting for no-par stock with a stated value is identical to accounting for par-value stock. The excess over stated value is credited to Additional Paid-in Capital.

Common Stock Issued for Assets Other Than Cash. When a corporation issues stock and receieves assets other than cash, the company records the assets received at their current market value and credits the stock and additional paid-in capital accounts accordingly. The assets' prior book value isn't relevant because the stockholder will demand stock equal to the market value of the asset given. Kahn Corporation issued 15,000 shares of its $1 par common stock for equipment worth $4,000 and a building worth $120,000. Kahn's entry is

Nov. 12	Equipment	4,000	
	Building	120,000	
	Common Stock (15,000 × $1)		15,000
	Paid-in Capital in Excess of Par—Common		
	($124,000 – $15,000)		109,000
	To issue no-par common stock in exchange for equipment		
	and a building.		

Assets and equity both increase by $124,000.

Assets	=	Liabilities	+	Stockholders' Equity
+ 4,000 + 120,000	=	0		+ 15,000 + 109,000

A Stock Issuance for Other Than Cash Can Create an Ethical Challenge

Generally accepted accounting principles require a company to record its stock at the fair market value of whatever the corporation receives in exchange for the stock. When the corporation receives cash, there is clear evidence of the value of the stock because cash is worth its face amount. But when the corporation receives an asset other than cash, the value of the asset can create an ethical challenge.

A computer whiz may start a new company by investing computer software. The software may be market-tested or it may be new. The software may be worth millions or worthless. The corporation must record the asset received and the stock given with a journal entry such as the following:

Software	500,000	
Common Stock		500,000
Issued stock in exchange for software.		

If the software is really worth $500,000, the accounting records are okay. But if the software is new and untested, the assets and equity may be overstated.

Suppose your computer-whiz friend invites you to invest in the new business and shows you this balance sheet:

Gee-Whiz Computer Solutions, Inc.
Balance Sheet
December 31, 20X8

Assets		Liabilities	
Computer software	$500,000		$ -0-
		Stockholders' Equity	
		Common stock.............................	500,000
Total assets............................	$500,000	Total liabilities and equity............	$500,000

Companies like to report large asset and equity amounts on their balance sheets. That makes them look prosperous and creditworthy. Gee-Whiz looks debt-free and appears to have a valuable asset. Will you invest in this new business? Here are 2 takeaway lessons:

- Some accounting values are more solid than others.
- Not all financial statements mean exactly what they say—unless they are audited by independent CPAs.

Preferred Stock

Accounting for preferred stock follows the pattern we illustrated for common. When a company issues preferred stock, it credits Preferred Stock at its par value, with any excess credited to Paid-in Capital in Excess of Par—Preferred. This is an entirely separate account from Paid-in-Capital in Excess of Par—Common. Accounting for no-par preferred follows the pattern for no-par common stock. When reporting stockholders' equity on the balance sheet, a corporation lists its accounts in this order:

- preferred stock
- common stock
- retained earnings

as illustrated for IHOP on page 474.

In Chapter 8 we saw how to account for convertible bonds payable (p. 437). Companies also issue convertible preferred stock. The preferred stock is usually convertible into the company's common stock and always at the discretion of the preferred stockholders. Whenever the common stock's market price gets high enough—or the preferred's market price gets low enough—holders of convertible preferred will convert their stock into common. Here are some representative journal entries for convertible preferred stock, using assumed amounts:

2008	Cash	50,000	
	Convertible Preferred Stock		50,000
	Issued convertible preferred stock.		

2010	Convertible Preferred Stock	50,000	
	Common Stock		8,000
	Paid-in Capital in Excess of Par—Common		42,000
	Investors converted preferred into common.		

As you can see, we merely remove Preferred Stock from the books and give the new Common Stock the prior book value of the preferred.

MID-CHAPTER SUMMARY PROBLEM

1. Test your understanding of the first half of this chapter by deciding whether each of the following statements is true or false.
   a. The policy-making body in a corporation is called the board of directors.
   b. The owner of 100 shares of preferred stock has greater voting rights than the owner of 100 shares of common stock.
   c. Par-value stock is worth more than no-par stock.
   d. Issuance of 1,000 shares of $5 par-value stock at $12 increases contributed capital by $12,000.
   e. The issuance of no-par stock with a stated value is fundamentally different from issuing par-value stock.
   f. A corporation issues its preferred stock in exchange for land and a building with a combined market value of $200,000. This transaction increases the corporation's owners' equity by $200,000 regardless of the assets' prior book values.
   g. Preferred stock is a riskier investment than common stock.

2. Adolfo Company has 2 classes of common stock. Only the Class A common stockholders are entitled to vote. The company's balance sheet included the following presentation:

Stockholders' Equity	
Capital stock:	
Class A common stock, voting, $1 par value,	
authorized and issued 1,260,000 shares..................	$ 1,260,000
Class B common stock, nonvoting, no par value,	
authorized and issued 46,200,000 shares...............	11,000,000
	12,260,000
Additional paid-in capital..	2,011,000
Retained earnings..	872,403,000
	$886,674,000

❙ Required

a. Record the issuance of the Class A common stock. Use the Adolfo account titles.
b. Record the issuance of the Class B common stock. Use the Adolfo account titles.
c. How much of Adolfo's stockholders' equity was contributed by the stockholders? How much was provided by profitable operations? Does this division of equity suggest that the company has been successful? Why or why not?
d. Write a sentence to describe what Adolfo's stockholders' equity means.

Answers

1.a. True   b. False   c. False   d. True   e. False   f. True   g. False

2.a.

Cash		3,271,000	
Class A Common Stock			1,260,000
Additional Paid-in Capital			2,011,000
To record issuance of Class A common stock.			

b.

Cash	11,000,000	
Class B Common Stock		11,000,000
To record issuance of Class B common stock.		

c. Contributed by the stockholders: $14,271,000 ($12,260,000 + $2,011,000). Provided by profitable operations: $872,403,000.

This division suggests that the company has been successful because most of its stockholders' equity has come from profitable operations.

d. Adolfo stockholders' equity of $886,674,000 means that the company's stockholders own $886,674,000 of the business's assets.

AUTHORIZED, ISSUED, AND OUTSTANDING STOCK

It's important to distinguish among 3 distinctly different numbers of a company's stock. The following examples use IHOP's actual data from page 474.

- **Authorized stock** is the maximum number of shares the company can issue under its present charter. IHOP is authorized to issue 40 million shares of common stock.
- **Issued stock** is the number of shares the company has issued to its stockholders. This is a cumulative total from the company's beginning up through the current date. As of December 31, 2006, IHOP had issued 22,718,007 shares of its common stock.
- **Outstanding stock** is the number of shares that the stockholders own (that is, the number of shares outstanding in the hands of the stockholders). Outstanding stock is issued stock minus treasury stock. At December 31, 2006, IHOP had 17,873,548 shares of common stock outstanding, computed as follows:

Issued shares (line 3)	22,718,007
Less: Treasury shares (line 6)................	(4,844,459)
Outstanding shares (line 3)....................	17,873,548

Now let's learn about treasury stock.

TREASURY STOCK

OBJECTIVE

3 **Describe** how treasury stock affects a company

A company's own stock that it has issued and later reacquired is called **treasury stock**.[2] In effect, the corporation holds this stock in its treasury. Corporations purchase their own stock for several reasons:

1. The company has issued all its authorized stock and needs some stock for distributions to employees under stock purchase plans.

2. The business wants to increase net assets by buying its stock low and hoping to resell it for a higher price.

3. Management wants to avoid a takeover by an outside party.

---

[2]In this text, we illustrate the *cost* method of accounting for treasury stock because it is used most widely. Other methods are presented in intermediate accounting courses.

Should a Company Buy Back Its Own Stock?

Let's illustrate the accounting for treasury stock for IHOP Corp. We use rounded amounts, as adapted, and stated in thousands. If IHOP had not purchased any treasury stock, the company could have reported the following stockholders' equity at December 31, 2006 (amounts in thousands):

(Before Purchase of Treasury Stock)	
Common stock...............................	$ 227
Additional paid-in capital...............	131,748
Retained earnings...........................	358,975
Other equity....................................	(133)
Total stockholders' equity..............	$490,817

Assume that during 2007, IHOP paid $201,604 to purchase some of its common stock as treasury stock. IHOP would record the purchase of treasury stock as follows (in thousands):

2007			
Nov. 12	Treasury Stock	201,604	
	Cash		201,604
	Purchased treasury stock.		

Assets	=	Liabilities	+	Stockholders' Equity
− 201,604	=	0		− 201,604

Treasury stock is recorded at cost—without regard to the par value of the stock.

Treasury Stock has a debit balance, the opposite of the other equity accounts. Therefore, *Treasury Stock is contra stockholders' equity*, reported beneath Retained Earnings on the balance sheet. Treasury Stock's balance is subtracted from equity as shown for IHOP (amounts in thousands):

(After Purchase of Treasury Stock)	
Common stock..	$ 227
Paid-in capital in excess of par—common..............	131,748
Retained earnings..	358,975
Less Treasury stock (at cost)..................................	(201,604)
Other equity...	(133)
Total stockholders' equity......................................	$289,213

Compare IHOP's total equity before the purchase of treasury stock ($490,817) and after ($289,213). IHOP's total equity decreased by $201,604, the cost of the treasury stock. The purchase of treasury stock has the opposite effect of issuing stock:

- Issuing stock *grows* assets and equity.
- Purchasing treasury stock *shrinks* assets and equity.

Treasury stock is so named because it is held in the company treasury awaiting resale. Now let's see how to account for the sale of treasury stock.

Sale of Treasury Stock

Selling treasury stock grows assets and equity exactly as issuing new stock does. Suppose IHOP resells its treasury stock in 2008 for $250,000. The sale increases assets and equity by the full amount of cash received. IHOP would record this sale of treasury stock as follows (in thousands):

2008			
July 22	Cash	250,000	
	Treasury Stock		201,604
	Paid-in Capital from Treasury Stock Transactions		
	(or Additional Paid-in Capital—Common)		48,396
	Sold treasury stock.		

Assets	=	Liabilities	+	Stockholders' Equity
+ 250,000	=	0		+ 201,604
				+ 48,396

If IHOP had sold the treasury stock for a price below cost, then IHOP could have debited Retained Earnings for the difference.

Summary of Treasury-Stock Transactions

There are only 2 types of treasury-stock transactions:

- Buying treasury stock. Assets and equity *decrease* by an amount equal to the cost of treasury stock purchased.
- Selling treasury stock. Assets and equity *increase* by an amount equal to the sale price of the treasury stock sold.

Retirement of Stock

A corporation may purchase its own stock and *retire* it by canceling the stock certificates. Companies retire their preferred stock to avoid paying dividends on the preferred stock. The retired stock cannot be reissued. When a company retires its stock, the journal entry credits Cash and debits the stock account and any additional paid-in capital on the stock. Retirements of common stock are rare.

RETAINED EARNINGS, DIVIDENDS, AND SPLITS

The Retained Earnings account carries the balance of the business's net income, less its net losses and less any declared dividends that have been accumulated over the corporation's lifetime. *Retained* means "held onto." Successful companies grow by reinvesting back into the business the assets they generate through profitable operations. IHOP Corp. is an example; the vast majority of IHOP's equity comes from retained earnings.

The Retained Earnings account is not a reservoir of cash for paying dividends to the stockholders. In fact, the corporation may have a large balance in Retained Earnings but not have enough cash to pay a dividend. Cash and Retained Earnings are 2 entirely separate accounts with no particular relationship. Retained Earnings says nothing about the company's Cash balance.

A *credit* balance in Retained Earnings is normal, indicating that the corporation's lifetime earnings exceed lifetime losses and dividends. A *debit* balance in Retained Earnings arises when a corporation's lifetime losses and dividends exceed lifetime earnings. Called a **deficit**, this amount is subtracted to determine total stockholders' equity. In a recent survey, 15.5% of companies had a retained earnings deficit (Exhibit 9-7).

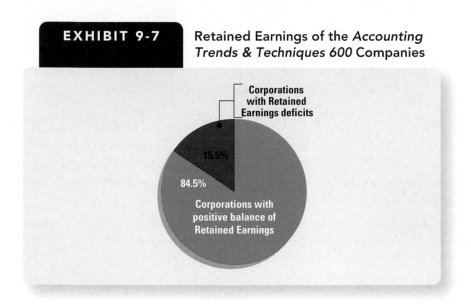

EXHIBIT 9-7 Retained Earnings of the *Accounting Trends & Techniques 600* Companies

Should the Company Declare and Pay Cash Dividends?

A **dividend** is a corporation's return to its stockholders of the benefits of earnings. Dividends usually take 1 of 3 forms:

- Cash
- Stock
- Noncash assets

In this section we focus on cash dividends and stock dividends because noncash dividends are rare. For a noncash asset dividend, debit Retained Earnings and credit the asset (for example, Long-Term Investment) for the current market value of the asset given.

Cash Dividends

Most dividends are cash dividends. Finance courses discuss how a company decides on its dividend policy. Accounting tells a company if it can pay a dividend. To do so, a company must have both

- Enough Retained Earnings   and   ■ Enough Cash to *pay*
  to *declare* the dividend   the dividend

A corporation declares a dividend before paying it. Only the board of directors has the authority to declare a dividend. The corporation has no obligation to pay a dividend until the board declares one, but once declared, the dividend becomes a legal liability of the corporation. There are 3 relevant dates for dividends (using assumed amounts):

1. *Declaration date, June 19.* On the declaration date, the board of directors announces the dividend. Declaration of the dividend creates a liability for the corporation. Declaration is recorded by debiting Retained Earnings and crediting Dividends Payable. Assume a $50,000 dividend.

June 19	Retained Earnings[3]	50,000	
	Dividends Payable		50,000
	Declared a cash dividend.		

Liabilities increase, and equity goes down.

Assets	=	**Liabilities**	+	**Stockholders' Equity**
0	=	+ 50,000		− 50,000

2. *Date of record, July 1.* As part of the declaration, the corporation announces the record date, which follows the declaration date by a few weeks. The stockholders on the record date will receive the dividend. There is no journal entry for the date of record.

3. *Payment date, July 10.* Payment of the dividend usually follows the record date by a week or 2. Payment is recorded by debiting Dividends Payable and crediting Cash.

July 10	Dividends Payable	50,000	
	Cash		50,000
	Paid cash dividend.		

Both assets and liabilities decrease. The corporation shrinks.

Assets	=	**Liabilities**	+	**Stockholders' Equity**
− 50,000	=	− 50,000		

Analyzing The Stockholder's Equity Accounts

By knowing accounting you can look at a company's comparative year-to-year financial statements and tell a lot about what the company did during the current year. For example, IHOP reported the following for Retained Earnings (in thousands):

| | December 31, | |
	2006	2005
Retained earnings................	$358,975	$332,560

---

[3]In the early part of this book, we debited a Dividends account to clearly identify the purpose of the payment. From here on, we follow the more common practice of debiting the Retained Earnings account for dividend declarations.

What do these figures tell you about IHOP's results of operations during 2006—was it a net income or a net loss? How can you tell? IHOP had a net income. This is for certain, because

- Retained Earnings increased in 2006.
- Net income is the only item that increases Retained Earnings.

Was IHOP's net income the full $26,415 ($358,975 – $332,560 = $26,415)? Not necessarily. IHOP may have declared a dividend, and dividends decrease Retained Earnings.

If you know accounting—if you know IHOP's net income ($44,553 from IHOP's income statement), you can compute IHOP's dividend declarations during 2006, as follows (in thousands):

Retained Earnings			
		Begin. bal.	332,560
Dividends	?	Net income	44,553
		Ending bal.	358,975

Dividends (x) were $18,138 ($332,560 + $44,553 – x = $358,975; x = $18,138). It really helps to know accounting!

Dividends on Preferred Stock

When a company has issued both preferred and common stock, the preferred stockholders receive their dividends first. The common stockholders receive dividends only if the total dividend is large enough to pay the preferred stockholders first.

Avant Garde, Inc., has 100,000 shares of $1.50 preferred stock outstanding in addition to its common stock. The $1.50 designation means that the preferred stockholders receive an annual cash dividend of $1.50 per share. In 20X6, Avant Garde declares an annual dividend of $500,000. The allocation to preferred and common stockholders is:

Preferred dividend (100,000 shares × $1.50 per share)............	$150,000
Common dividend (remainder: $500,000 – $150,000)	350,000
Total dividend..	$500,000

If Avant Garde declares only a $200,000 dividend, preferred stockholders receive $150,000, and the common stockholders get the remainder, $50,000 ($200,000 – $150,000).

Two Ways to Express the Dividend Rate on Preferred Stock. Dividends on preferred stock are stated either as a

- Percent of par value   or   ■ Dollar amount per share

For example, preferred stock may be "6% preferred," which means that owners of the preferred stock receive an annual dividend equal to 6% of the stock's par value. If par value is $100 per share, preferred stockholders receive an annual cash dividend of

$6 per share (6% of $100). Alternatively, the preferred stock may be "$3 preferred," which means that the preferred stockholders receive an annual dividend of $3 per share regardless of the stock's par value. The dividend rate on no-par preferred stock is stated in a dollar amount per share.

Dividends on Cumulative and Noncumulative Preferred Stock. The allocation of dividends may be complex if the preferred stock is *cumulative*. Corporations sometimes fail to pay a dividend to preferred stockholders. This is called *passing the dividend*, and the passed dividends are said to be *in arrears*. The owners of **cumulative preferred stock** must receive all dividends in arrears plus the current year's dividend before any dividends go to the common stockholders. *In most states preferred stock is cumulative unless it is specifically labeled as noncumulative.* Therefore, most preferred stock is cumulative.

The preferred stock of Avant Garde, Inc., is cumulative. Suppose Avant Garde passed the preferred dividend of $150,000 in 20X6. Before paying dividends to common in 20X7, Avant Garde must first pay preferred dividends of $150,000 for both 20X6 and 20X7, a total of $300,000. In 20X7, Avant Garde declares a $500,000 dividend. The entry to record the declaration is

Sept. 6	Retained Earnings	500,000	
	Dividends Payable, Preferred ($150,000 × 2)		300,000
	Dividends Payable, Common ($500,000 – $300,000)		200,000
	To declare a cash dividend.		

If the preferred stock is *noncumulative*, the corporation is not obligated to pay dividends in arrears—until the board of directors declares the dividend.

Stock Dividends

A **stock dividend** is a proportional distribution by a corporation of its own stock to its stockholders. Stock dividends increase the stock account and decrease Retained Earnings. Total equity is unchanged, and no asset or liability is affected.

The corporation distributes stock dividends to stockholders in proportion to the number of shares they already own. If you own 300 shares of IHOP common stock and IHOP distributes a 10% common stock dividend, you get 30 (300 × .10) additional shares. You would then own 330 shares of the stock. All other IHOP stockholders would also receive 10% more shares, leaving all stockholders' ownership unchanged.

In distributing a stock dividend, the corporation gives up no assets. Why, then, do companies issue stock dividends? A corporation may choose to distribute stock dividends for these reasons:

1. *To continue dividends but conserve cash.* A company may need to conserve cash and yet wish to continue dividends in some form. So the corporation may distribute a stock dividend. Stockholders pay no income tax on stock dividends.

2. *To reduce the per-share market price of its stock.* Distribution of a stock dividend usually causes the stock's market price to fall because of the increased supply of the stock. The objective is to make the stock less expensive and therefore attractive to more investors.

Generally accepted accounting principles (GAAP) label a stock dividend of 25% or less as *small* and suggest that the dividend be recorded at the market value of the shares distributed. Suppose IHOP declared a 10% stock dividend in 2008. At the time, assume IHOP had 20,000,000 shares of common stock outstanding, and IHOP's stock is trading for $60 per share. IHOP would record this stock dividend as follows:

2008			
May 19	Retained Earnings[4] (20,000,000 shares of common outstanding × 0.10 stock dividend × $60 market value per share of common)	120,000,000	
	Common Stock (20,000,000 × 0.10 × $0.01 per value per share)		20,000
	Paid-in Capital in Excess of Par—Common		119,980,000
	Distributed a 10% stock dividend.		

The accounting equation clearly shows that a stock dividend has no effect on total assets, liabilities, or equity. The increases in equity offset the decreases, and the net effect is zero.

Assets	=	**Liabilities**	+	**Stockholders' Equity**
0				− 120,000,000
	=	0		+ 20,000
				+ 119,980,000

GAAP identifies stock dividends above 25% as *large* and permits large stock dividends to be recorded at par value. For a large stock dividend, therefore, IHOP would debit Retained Earnings and credit Common Stock for the par value of the shares distributed in the dividend.

Stock Splits

A **stock split** is an increase in the number of shares of stock authorized, issued, and outstanding, coupled with a proportionate reduction in the stock's par value. For example, if the company splits its stock 2 for 1, the number of outstanding shares is doubled and each share's par value is halved. A stock split, like a large stock dividend, decreases the market price of the stock—with the intention of making the stock more attractive in the market. Most leading companies in the United States—including **IBM, PepsiCo,** and **Best Buy**—have split their stock.

The market price of a share of **Best Buy** common stock has been approximately $50. Assume that Best Buy wishes to decrease the market price to approximately $25 per share. Best Buy can split its common stock 2 for 1, and the stock price will fall to around $25. A 2-for-1 stock split means that

- the company will have twice as many shares of stock authorized, issued, and outstanding after the split as it had before.
- each share's par value will be cut in half.

---

[4]Many companies debit Additional Paid-in Capital for their stock dividends.

Before the split, Best Buy had approximately 500 million shares of $0.10 (10 cents) par common stock issued and outstanding. Compare Best Buy's stockholders' equity before and after a 2-for-1 stock split:

Best Buy Co., Inc., Stockholders' Equity (Adapted)

Before 2-for-1 Stock Split	(In millions)		After 2-for-1 Stock Split	(In millions)	
Common stock, $0.10 par, 1,000 shares			Common stock, $0.05 par, 2,000 shares		
authorized, 500 shares issued.........	$	50	authorized, 1,000 shares issued......	$	50
Additional paid in capital....................		643	Additional paid-in capital...................		643
Retained earnings...............................		4,304	Retained earnings...............................		4,304
Other equity.......................................		260	Other...		260
Total stockholders' equity..................		$5,257	Total stockholders' equity..................		$5,257

All account balances are the same after the stock split as before. Only 3 Best Buy items are affected:

- Par value per share drops from 10 cents to 5 cents.
- Shares *authorized* double from 1,000 to 2,000.
- Shares *issued* double from 500 to 1,000.

Total equity doesn't change, nor do any assets or liabilities.

Summary of the Effects on Assets, Liabilities, and Stockholders' Equity

We've seen how to account for the basic stockholders' equity transactions:

- Issuance of stock—common and preferred (pp. 480–486)
- Purchase and sale of treasury stock (pp. 488–490)
- Cash dividends (pp. 491–494)
- Stock dividends and stock splits (pp. 494–496)

How do these transactions affect assets, liabilities, and equity? Exhibit 9-8 provides a helpful summary.

EXHIBIT 9-8 **Effects on Assets, Liabilities, and Equity**

	Effect on Total		
Transaction	Assets =	Liabilities +	Stockholders' Equity
Issuance of stock—common and preferred.................................	Increase	No effect	Increase
Purchase of treasury stock.................	Decrease	No effect	Decrease
Sale of treasury stock	Increase	No effect	Increase
Declaration of cash dividend.............	No effect	Increase	Decrease
Payment of cash dividend..................	Decrease	Decrease	No effect
Stock dividend—large and small	No effect	No effect	No effect*
Stock split	No effect	No effect	No effect

*The stock accounts increase and retained earnings decrease by offsetting amounts that net to zero.

MEASURING THE VALUE OF STOCK

The business community measures *stock values* in various ways, depending on the purpose of the measurement. These values include market value, redemption value, liquidation value, and book value.

Market, Redemption, Liquidation, and Book Value

A stock's **market value**, or *market price*, is the price a person can buy or sell 1 share of the stock for. Market value varies with the corporation's net income, financial position, and future prospects, and with general economic conditions. *In almost all cases, stockholders are more concerned about the market value of a stock than any other value.*

IHOP's stock price has been quoted recently at $59 per share. Therefore, if IHOP were issuing 1,000 shares of its common stock, IHOP would receive cash of $59,000 (1,000 shares × $59 per share). This is the market value of the stock IHOP issued.

Preferred stock that requires the company to redeem the stock at a set price is called *redeemable preferred stock*. The company is *obligated* to redeem (pay to retire) the preferred stock. Therefore, redeemable preferred stock is really not stockholders' equity. Instead it's a liability. The price the corporation agrees to pay for the stock, set when the stock is issued, is called the **redemption value**. **Liquidation value** is the amount that a company must pay a preferred stockholder in the event the company liquidates (sells out) and goes out of business.

The **book value** per share of common stock is the amount of owners' equity on the company's books for each share of its stock. If the company has only common stock outstanding, its book value is computed by dividing total equity by the number of shares of common *outstanding*. Recall that *outstanding* stock is *issued* stock minus *treasury* stock. For example, a company with stockholders' equity of $150,000 and 5,000 shares of common stock outstanding has a book value of $30 per share ($150,000 ÷ 5,000 shares).

If the company has both preferred and common outstanding, the preferred stockholders have the first claim to owners' equity. Preferred stock often has a specified redemption value. The preferred equity is its redemption value plus any cumulative preferred dividends in arrears. Book value per share of common is then computed as follows:

$$\text{Book value per share of common stock} = \frac{\text{Total stockholders' equity} - \text{Preferred equity}}{\text{Number of shares of common stock outstanding}}$$

Crusader Corporation's balance sheet reports the following amounts:

Stockholders' Equity	
Preferred stock, 5%, $100 par, 400 shares issued, redemption value $130 per share	$ 40,000
Common stock, $10 par, 5,500 shares issued	55,000
Additional paid-in capital—common	72,000
Retained earnings	88,000
Treasury stock—common, 500 shares at cost	(15,000)
Total stockholders' equity	$240,000

Cumulative preferred dividends are in arrears for 4 years (including the current year). Crusader's preferred stock has a redemption value of $130 per share. The book-value-per-share computations for Crusader Corporation are:

Preferred Equity	
Redemption value (400 shares × $130)	$52,000
Cumulative dividends ($40,000 × 0.05 × 4 years)	8,000
Preferred equity	$60,000*
Common Equity	
Total stockholders' equity	$240,000
Less preferred equity	(60,000)
Common equity	$180,000
Book value per share [$180,000 ÷ 5,000 shares outstanding (5,500 shares issued minus 500 treasury shares)]	$ 36.00

*If the preferred stock had no redemption value, then preferred equity would be $40,000 + preferred dividends in arrears.

Some investors search for stocks whose market price is below book value. They believe this indicates a good buy. Financial analysts often shy away from companies with a stock price at or below book value. To these investors, such a company is in trouble. As you can see, not all investors agree on a stock value. In fact, wise investors base their decisions on more than a single ratio. In Chapter 13 you'll see the full range of financial ratios, plus a few more analytical techniques.

Relating Profitability to a Company's Stock

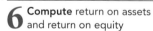

OBJECTIVE

6 **Compute** return on assets and return on equity

Investors search for companies whose stocks are likely to increase in value. They're constantly comparing companies. But a comparison of IHOP with a new restaurant chain is not meaningful. IHOP's profits run into the millions, which far exceed a new company's net income. Does this automatically make IHOP a better investment? Not necessarily. To compare companies of different size, investors use some standard profitability measures, including

- return on assets
- return on equity

Return on Assets. The **rate of return on total assets**, or simply **return on assets (ROA)**, measures a company's use of its assets to earn income for the 2 groups who finance the business:

- Creditors to whom the corporation owes money. Creditors want interest.
- Stockholders who own the corporation's stock. Stockholders want net income.

The sum of interest expense and net income is the return to the 2 groups who finance a corporation. This sum is the numerator of the return-on-assets ratio. The denominator is average total assets. ROA is computed as follows, using actual data from the 2006 annual report of IHOP Corp. (dollars in millions):

$$\text{Rate of return on total assets} = \frac{\text{Net income} + \text{Interest expense}}{\text{Average total assets}}$$
$$= \frac{\$45 + \$12}{(\$769 + \$771)/2} = \frac{\$57}{\$770} = 0.074$$

Net income and interest expense come from the income statement. Average total assets is computed from the beginning and ending balance sheets.

What is a good rate of return on total assets? Ten percent is considered strong in most industries. However, rates of return vary by industry. Some high-technology companies earn much higher returns than do utility companies, groceries, and manufacturers of consumer goods such as toothpaste and paper towels. IHOP's return on assets (7.4%) is low.

Return on Equity. **Rate of return on common stockholders' equity**, often called **return on equity (ROE)**, shows the relationship between net income available to common and average common stockholders' equity. Return on equity is computed only on common stock because the return to preferred stockholders is the specified dividend (for example, 5%).

The numerator of return on equity is net income minus preferred dividends. The denominator is *average common stockholders' equity*—total stockholders' equity minus preferred equity. IHOP Corp.'s ROE for 2006 is computed as follows (dollars in millions):

$$\text{Rate of return on common stockholder's equity} = \frac{\text{Net income} - \text{Preferred dividends}}{\text{Average common stockholders' equity}}$$
$$= \frac{\$45 - \$0}{(\$289^5 + \$294^5)/2} = \frac{\$45}{\$291.5} = 0.154$$

Because IHOP Corp. has no preferred stock, preferred dividends are zero, and average *common* equity is the same as average *total* equity—the average of the beginning and ending amounts.

IHOP's return on equity (15.4%) is more than double IHOP's return on assets (7.4%). ROE is always higher than ROA for a successful company. Stockholders take a lot more investment risk than bondholders, so the stockholders demand that ROE exceed ROA. If ROA were higher, that would mean that the return on debt—interest—is higher than the return on equity—net income. If that were true, there wouldn't be any stockholders. Everyone would be investing in bonds!

Investors and creditors use ROE in much the same way they use ROA—to compare companies. The higher the rate of return, the more successful the company. In most industries, 15% is considered a good ROE. Therefore, IHOP's 15.4% return on common stockholders' equity compares well with most companies.

---

[5] Ending equity comes from page 474. Beginning equity comes from the 2005 balance sheet.

The Decision Guidelines feature (p. 502) offers suggestions for what to consider when investing in stock.

REPORTING STOCKHOLDERS' EQUITY TRANSACTIONS

Statement of Cash Flows

OBJECTIVE

7 **Report** equity transactions on the statement of cash flows

Many of the transactions we've covered are reported on the statement of cash flows. Equity transactions are *financing activities* because the company is dealing with its owners. Financing transactions that affect both cash and equity fall into 3 main categories:

- issuance of stock
- treasury stock
- dividends

Issuances of Stock. During 2006, IHOP Corp. issued common stock. This is as a financing activity, as shown in Exhibit 9-9

EXHIBIT 9-9	IHOP Corp's Financing Activities (Adapted)

Cash Flows from Financing Activities	(In thousands)
Issuance of common stock............................	$5,944
Purchase of treasury stock...........................	(42,695)
Payment of dividends	(18,138)

Treasury Stock. During 2006, IHOP purchased treasury stock and reported the payment as a financing activity.

Dividends. Most companies, including IHOP, pay cash dividends to their stockholders. Dividend payments are a type of financing transaction because the company is paying its stockholders for the use of their money. Stock dividends are not reported on the statement of cash flows because the company pays no cash.

In Exhibit 9-9, cash receipts appear as positive amounts and cash payments as negative amounts, denoted by parentheses.

Reporting Stockholders' Equity on the Balance Sheet

Businesses may report stockholders' equity in a way that differs from our examples. We use a detailed format in this book to help you learn all the components of stockholders' equity.

One of the most important skills you will take from this course is the ability to understand the financial statements of real companies. Exhibit 9-10 presents a side-by-side comparison of our general teaching format and the format you are likely to encounter in real-world balance sheets, such as IHOP's. All amounts are assumed for this illustration.

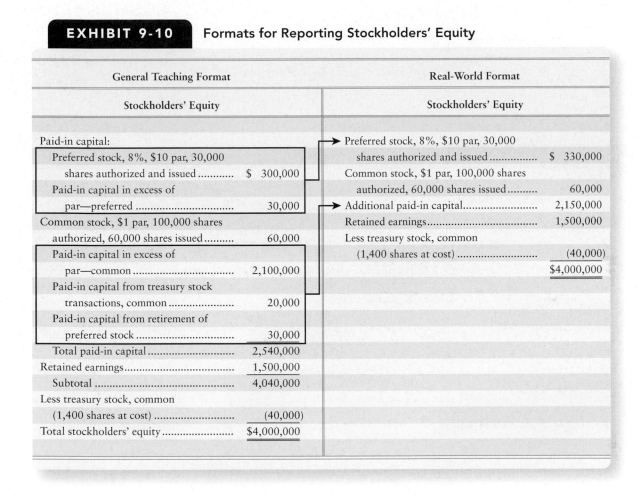

EXHIBIT 9-10 Formats for Reporting Stockholders' Equity

General Teaching Format	Real-World Format
Stockholders' Equity	**Stockholders' Equity**
Paid-in capital:	Preferred stock, 8%, $10 par, 30,000
Preferred stock, 8%, $10 par, 30,000	shares authorized and issued .... $ 330,000
shares authorized and issued .... $ 300,000	Common stock, $1 par, 100,000 shares
Paid-in capital in excess of	authorized, 60,000 shares issued 60,000
par—preferred 30,000	Additional paid-in capital......................... 2,150,000
Common stock, $1 par, 100,000 shares	Retained earnings.................................... 1,500,000
authorized, 60,000 shares issued 60,000	Less treasury stock, common
Paid-in capital in excess of	(1,400 shares at cost) .... (40,000)
par—common.................................. 2,100,000	$4,000,000
Paid-in capital from treasury stock	
transactions, common 20,000	
Paid-in capital from retirement of	
preferred stock 30,000	
Total paid-in capital............................ 2,540,000	
Retained earnings..................................... 1,500,000	
Subtotal 4,040,000	
Less treasury stock, common	
(1,400 shares at cost) .... (40,000)	
Total stockholders' equity........................ $4,000,000	

In general:

- Preferred Stock comes first and is usually reported as a single amount
- Common Stock lists par value per share, the number of shares authorized and the number of shares issued. The balance of the Common Stock account is determined as follows:

> Common stock = Number of shares *issued* × Par value per share

- Additional paid-in capital combines Paid-in Capital in Excess of Par plus Paid-in Capital from Treasury Stock Transactions plus Paid-in Capital from Retirement of Preferred Stock. Additional paid-in capital belongs to the common stockholders.
- Outstanding stock equals issued stock minus treasury stock.
- Retained Earnings comes after the paid-in capital accounts.
- Treasury Stock can come last, as a subtraction in arriving at total stockholders' equity.

DECISION GUIDELINES

INVESTING IN STOCK

Suppose you've saved $5,000 to invest. You visit a nearby **Edward Jones** office, where the broker probes for your risk tolerance. Are you investing mainly for dividends or for growth in the stock price? You must make some key decisions.

Investor Decision	Guidelines
Which category of stock to buy for:	
• A safe investment?	Preferred stock is safer than common, but for even more safety, invest in high-grade corporate bonds or government securities.
• Steady dividends?	Cumulative preferred stock. However, the company is not obligated to declare preferred dividends, and the dividends are unlikely to increase.
• Increasing dividends?	Common stock, as long as the company's net income is increasing and the company has adequate cash flow to pay a dividend after meeting all obligations and other cash demands.
• Increasing stock price?	Common stock, but again only if the company's net income and cash flow are increasing.
How to identify a good stock to buy?	There are many ways to pick stock investments. One strategy that works reasonably well is to invest in companies that consistently earn higher rates of return on assets and on equity than competing firms in the same industry. Also, select industries that are expected to grow.

END-OF-CHAPTER SUMMARY PROBLEM

1. The balance sheet of Trendline Corp. reported the following at December 31, 20X6.

Stockholders' Equity

Preferred stock, 4%, $10 par, 10,000 shares authorized and issued (redemption value, $110,000).................	$100,000
Common stock, no-par, $5 stated value, 100,000 shares authorized, 50,000 shares issued............................	250,000
Paid-in capital in excess of par or stated value:	
Common stock	239,500
Retained earnings...	395,000
Less: Treasury stock, common (1,000 shares)................	(8,000)
Total stockholders' equity	$976,500

Required

a. Is the preferred stock cumulative or noncumulative? How can you tell?

b. What is the total amount of the annual preferred dividend?

c. How many shares of common stock are outstanding?

d. Compute the book value per share of the common stock. No preferred dividends are in arrears, and Trendline has not yet declared the 20X6 dividend.

2. Use the following accounts and related balances to prepare the classified balance sheet of Whitehall, Inc., at September 30, 20X7. Use the account format of the balance sheet.

Common stock, $1 par,		Long-term note payable	80,000
50,000 shares authorized,		Inventory.......................................	85,000
20,000 shares issued...................	20,000	Property, plant, and	
Dividends payable.........................	4,000	equipment, net	226,000
Cash..	9,000	Accounts receivable, net	23,000
Accounts payable	28,000	Preferred stock, $3.75, no-par,	
Paid-in capital in excess		10,000 shares authorized,	
of par—common	115,000	2,000 shares issued...................	24,000
Treasury stock, common,		Accrued liabilities.........................	3,000
1,000 shares at cost...................	6,000	Retained earnings.........................	75,000

Answers

1. a. The preferred stock is cumulative because it is not specifically labeled otherwise.

b. Total annual preferred dividend: $4,000 ($100,000 × 0.04).

c. Common shares outstanding: 49,000 (50,000 issued – 1,000 treasury).

d. Book value per share of common stock:

Common:	
Total stockholders' equity	$976,500
Less stockholders' equity allocated to preferred	(114,000)*
Stockholders' equity allocated to common	$862,500
Book value per share ($862,500 ÷ 49,000 shares)	$17.60

*Redemption value	$110,000
Cumulative dividend ($100,000 × 0.04)	4,000
Stockholders' equity allocated to preferred	$114,000

2.

Whitehall, Inc.
Balance Sheet
September 30, 20X7

Assets		Liabilities	
Current		**Current**	
Cash	$ 9,000	Account payable	$ 28,000
Accounts receivable, net	23,000	Dividends payable	4,000
Inventory	85,000	Accrued liabilities	3,000
Total current assets	117,000	Total current liabilities	35,000
Property, plant, and equipment, net	226,000	Long-term note payable	80,000
		Total liabilities	115,000
		Stockholders' Equity	
		Preferred stock, $3.75, no par, 10,000 shares authorized, 2,000 shares issued	$ 24,000
		Common stock, $1 par, 50,000 shares authorized, 20,000 shares issued	20,000
		Paid-in capital in excess of par—common	115,000
		Retained earnings	75,000
		Treasury stock, common, 1,000 shares at cost	(6,000)
		Total stockholders' equity	228,000
Total assets	$343,000	Total liabilities and stockholders' equity	$343,000

REVIEW STOCKHOLDERS' EQUITY

Quick Check (Answers are given on page 532.)

1. Copeland Company is authorized to issue 40,000 shares of $10 par common stock. On January 15, 20X8, Copeland issued 10,000 shares at $15 per share. Copeland's journal entry to record these facts should include a
   a. credit to Common Stock for $100,000.
   b. credit to Paid-in Capital in Excess of Par for $150,000.
   c. debit to Common Stock for $150,000.
   d. both a and b.

Questions 2–5 use the following account balances of Casio Co. at March 31, 20X7:

Dividends Payable	$ 22,000	Cash	$ 74,000
Preferred Stock, $100 par	100,000	Common Stock, $1 par	180,000
Paid-in Capital in Excess of Par—		Retained Earnings	200,000
Common	45,000		

2. Casio has issued _____ shares of common stock.
   a. 74,000
   c. 225,000
   b. 180,000
   d. Some other amount _____
3. Casio's total paid-in capital at March 31, 20X7, is
   a. $495,000.
   c. $1,175,000.
   b. $680,000.
   d. Some other amount _____.
4. Casio's total stockholders' equity as of March 31, 20X7, is
   a. $1,406,000.
   c. $525,000.
   b. $1,249,000.
   d. $1,480,000.
5. What would Casio's total stockholders' equity be if Casio had $5,000 of Treasury Stock?
   a. $420,000
   c. $430,000
   b. $425,000
   d. $520,000
6. Woodstock Corporation purchased treasury stock in 20X2 at a price of $30 per share and resold the treasury stock in 20X3 at a price of $40 per share. What amount should Woodstock report on its income statement for 20X3?
   a. $40
   c. $10
   b. $30
   d. $0
7. The stockholders' equity section of a corporation's balance sheet reports

	Treasury Stock	Discount on Bonds Payable
a.	Yes	No
b.	No	Yes
c.	Yes	Yes
d.	No	No

8. The purchase of treasury stock
   a. increases one asset and decreases another asset.
   b. decreases total assets and decreases total stockholder's equity.
   c. has no effect on total assets, total liabilities, or total stockholders' equity.
   d. decreases total assets and increases total stockholders' equity.
9. When does a cash dividend become a legal liability?
   a. On date of payment.
   c. On date of declaration.
   b. On date of record.
   d. It never becomes a liability because it is paid.
10. When do dividends increase stockholders' equity?
    a. Never.
    c. On date of record.
    b. On date of declaration.
    d. On date of payment.

11. Willow Run Mall, Inc., has 5,000 shares of 5%, $20 par cumulative preferred stock and 100,000 shares of $1 par common stock outstanding. At the beginning of the current year, preferred dividends were 3 years in arrears. Willow Run's board of directors wants to pay a $1.25 cash dividend on each share of outstanding common stock. To accomplish this, what total amount of dividends must Willow Run declare?

    a. $170,000   **c.** $145,000

    b. $185,000   **d.** Some other amount $_____

12. Stock dividends

    a. have no effect on total stockholders' equity.

    b. are distributions of cash to stockholders.

    c. reduce the total assets of the company.

    d. increase the corporation's total liabilities.

13. What is the effect of a stock split and a stock dividend on total assets?

	Stock split	Stock dividend
a.	Decrease	No effect
b.	Decrease	Decrease
c.	No effect	Decrease
d.	No effect	No effect

14. A 2-for-1 stock split has the same effect on the number of shares being issued as a

    a. 20% stock dividend.   **c.** 100% stock dividend.

    b. 50% stock dividend.   **d.** 200% stock dividend.

15. The numerator for computing the rate of return on total assets is

    a. net income.

    b. net income minus interest expense.

    c. net income plus interest expense.

    d. net income minus preferred dividends.

16. The numerator for computing the rate of return on common equity is

    a. net income minus preferred dividends.

    b. net income minus interest expense.

    c. net income plus preferred dividends.

    d. net income.

Accounting Vocabulary

Board of directors (p. 476) Group elected by the stockholders to set policy for a corporation and to appoint its officers.

Book value (of a stock) (p. 497) Amount of owners' equity on the company's books for each share of its stock.

Bylaws (p. 476) Constitution for governing a corporation.

Chairperson (p. 476) Elected by a corporation's board of directors, usually the most powerful person in the corporation.

Common stock (p. 479) The most basic form of capital stock. The common stockholders own a corporation.

Contributed capital (p. 478) The amount of stockholders' equity that stockholders have contributed to the corporation. Also called *contributed capital*.

Cumulative preferred stock (p. 494) Preferred stock whose owners must receive all dividends in arrears before the corporation can pay dividends to the common stockholders.

Deficit (p. 491) Debit balance in the Retained Earnings account.

Dividends (p. 491) Distribution (usually cash) by a corporation to its stockholders.

Double taxation (p. 476) Corporations pay income taxes on corporate income. Then, the stockholders pay personal income tax on the cash dividends that they receive from corporations.

Legal capital (p. 480) Minimum amount of stockholders' equity that a corporation must maintain for the protection of creditors. For corporations with par-value stock, legal capital is the par value of the stock issued.

Limited liability (p. 475) No personal obligation of a stockholder for corporation debts. A stockholder can lose no more on an investment in a corporation's stock than the cost of the investment.

Market value (of a stock) (p. 497) Price for which a person could buy or sell a share of stock.

Outstanding stock (p. 479) Stock in the hands of stockholders.

Paid-in capital (p. 478) The amount of stockholders' equity that stockholders have contributed to the corporation. Also called *contributed capital*.

Par value (p. 480) Arbitrary amount assigned by a company to a share of its stock.

Preferred stock (p. 479) Stock that gives its owners certain advantages, such as the priority to receive dividends before the common stockholders and the priority to receive assets before the common stockholders if the corporation liquidates.

President (p. 476) Chief operating officer in charge of managing the day-to-day operations of a corporation.

Rate of return on common stockholders' equity (p. 499) Net income minus preferred dividends, divided by average common stockholders' equity. A measure of profitability. Also called *return on equity*.

Rate of return on total assets (p. 498) Net income plus interest expense divided by average total assets. This ratio measures a company's success in using its assets to earn income for the persons who finance the business. Also called *return on assets*.

Retained earnings (p. 478) The amount of stockholders' equity that the corporation has earned through profitable operation of the business and has not given back to stockholders.

Return on assets (p. 498) Another name for *rate of return on total assets*.

Return on equity (p. 499) Another name for *rate of return on common stockholders' equity*.

Shareholders (p. 475) A person who owns stock in a corporation. Also called a *shareholder*.

Stated value (p. 480) An arbitrary amount assigned to no-par stock; similar to par value.

Stock (p. 478) Shares into which the owners' equity of a corporation is divided.

Stock dividend (p. 494) A proportional distribution by a corporation of its own stock to its stockholders.

Stockholders (p. 475) A person who owns stock in a corporation. Also called a *shareholder*.

Stockholders' equity (p. 478) The stockholders' ownership interest in the assets of a corporation.

Stock split (p. 495) An increase in the number of authorized, issued, and outstanding shares of stock coupled with a proportionate reduction in the stock's par value.

Treasury stock (p. 488) A corporation's own stock that it has issued and later reacquired.

ASSESS YOUR PROGRESS

Short Exercises

S9-1 (*Learning Objective 1: Advantages and disadvantages of a corporation*) What are 2 main advantages that a corporation has over a proprietorship and a partnership? What are 2 main disadvantages of a corporation? (pp. 475–476)

S9-2 (*Learning Objective 1: Authority structure in a corporation*) Consider the authority structure in a corporation, as diagrammed in Exhibit 9-2, page 477.

1. What group holds the ultimate power in a corporation?
2. Who is the most powerful person in the corporation? What's the abbreviation of this person's title?
3. Who's in charge of day-to-day operations? What's the abbreviation of this person's title?
4. Who's in charge of accounting and finance? What's the abbreviation of this person's title?

S9-3 (*Learning Objective 1: Characteristics of preferred and common stock*) Answer the following questions about the characteristics of a corporation's stock: (pp. 476–480)

1. Who are the real owners of a corporation?
2. What privileges do preferred stockholders have over common stockholders?
3. Which class of stockholders reap greater benefits from a highly profitable corporation? Explain?

S9-4 (*Learning Objective 2: Effect of a stock issuance on paid-in capital*) IHOP received $62,000,000 for the issuance of its stock on July 23. The par value of the IHOP stock was only $62,000. Was the excess amount of $61,938,000 a profit to IHOP? If not, what was it? (pp. 482–483)

Suppose the par value of the IHOP stock had been $1 per share, $5 per share, or $10 per share. Would a change in the par value of the company's stock affect IHOP's total paid-in capital? Give the reason for your answer. (pp. 481–483)

S9-5 (*Learning Objective 2: Issuing stock—par value stock and no-par stock*) At fiscal year end 2006, Hewlett-Packard and Krispy Kreme Doughnuts reported these adapted amounts on their balance sheets (all amounts in millions):

Hewlett-Packard:		
Common stock, 1 cent par value, 2,700 shares issued		$ 27
Additional paid-in capital		17,966

Krispy Kreme Doughnuts:		
Common stock, no par value, 62 shares issued		$298

Assume each company issued its stock in a single transaction. Journalize each company's issuance of its stock, using its actual account titles. Explanations are not required. (pp. 482–485)

S9-6 (*Learning Objective 2: Issuing stock to finance the purchase of assets*) This Short Exercise demonstrates the similarity and the difference between 2 ways to acquire plant assets. (pp. 482, 485)

Case A—Issue stock and buy the assets in separate transactions:	Case B—Issue stock to acquire the assets in a single transaction:
Longview Corporation issued 10,000 shares of its $5 par common stock for cash of $200,000. In a separate transaction, Longview used the cash to purchase a building for $160,000 and equipment for $40,000. Journalize the 2 transactions. (pp. 482–483)	Tyler Corporation issued 10,000 shares of its $5 par common stock to acquire a building valued at $160,000 and equipment worth $40,000. Journalize this transaction. (pp. 484–485)

Compare the balances in all the accounts after making both sets of entries. Are the account balances the same or different?

S9-7 (*Learning Objective 2: Preparing the stockholders' equity section of a balance sheet*) The financial statements of Eppley Employment Services, Inc., reported the following accounts (adapted, with dollar amounts in thousands except for par value):

Paid-in capital in excess of par	$198	Total revenues	$1,390
Other stockholders' equity (negative)	(29)	Accounts payable	420
Common stock $0.01 par;		Retained earnings	646
600 shares issued	6	Other current liabilities	2,566
Long-term debt	25	Total expenses	805

Prepare the stockholders' equity section of Eppley's balance sheet. Net income has already been closed to Retained Earnings. (pp. 482–483)

S9-8 (*Learning Objective 2: Using stockholders' equity data*) Use the Eppley Employment Services data in Short Exercises 9-7 to compute Eppley's

    a. Net income (pp. 43–44)
    b. Total liabilities (pp. 46–47)
    c. Total assets (use the accounting equation) (pp. 41–42)

S9-9 (*Learning Objective 3: Accounting for the purchase and sale of treasury stock*)
General Marketing Corporation reported the following stockholders' equity at December 31.
(adapted and in millions):

Common stock...............................	$ 243
Additional paid-in capital.................	297
Retained earnings............................	2,159
Treasury stock.................................	(691)
Total stockholders' equity................	$2,008

During the next year, General Marketing purchased treasury stock at a cost of $28 million and
resold treasury stock for $7 million (this treasury stock had cost General Marketing $3 million).

Record the purchase and resale of General Marketing's treasury stock. Overall, how much
did stockholders' equity increase or decrease as a result of the 2 treasury stock transactions?
(pp. 489–490)

CP9-10 (*Learning Objective 4: Accounting for cash dividends*) Gleneagles Corporation
earned net income of $70,000 during the year ended December 31, 20X6. On December 15,
Gleneagles declared the annual cash dividend on its 5% preferred stock (10,000 shares with
total par value of $100,000) and a $0.60 per share cash dividend on its common stock (25,000
shares with total par value of $50,000). Gleneagles then paid the dividends on January 4, 20X7.

writing assignment ■

Journalize for Gleneagles Corporation: (pp. 491–493)

a. Declaring the cash dividends on December 15, 20X6.
b. Paying the cash dividends on January 4, 20X7.

Did Retained Earnings increase or decrease during 20X6? By how much? (Challenge)

S9-11 (*Learning Objective 4: Dividing cash dividends between preferred and common
stock*) Refer to the allocation of dividends for Avant Garde, Inc., on page 493. Answer these
questions about Avant Garde's cash dividends. (pp. 493–494)

1. How much in dividends must Avant Garde declare each year before the common stockholders receive any cash dividends for the year?
2. Suppose Avant Garde declares cash dividends of $300,000 for 20X6. How much of the
   dividends go to preferred? How much goes to common?
3. Is Avant Garde's preferred stock cumulative or noncumulative? How can you tell?
4. Avant Garde passed the preferred dividend in 20X5 and 20X6. Then in 20X7, Avant
   Garde declares cash dividends of $800,000. How much of the dividends go to preferred?
   How much goes to common?

S9-12 (*Learning Objective 4: Recording a small stock dividend*) Fidelity Bancshares has
60,000 shares of $1 par common stock outstanding. Suppose Fidelity distributes a 10% stock
dividend when the market value of its stock is $11.50 per share.

1. Journalize Fidelity's distribution of the stock dividend on May 11. An explanation is not
   required. (pp. 494–495)
2. What was the overall effect of the stock dividend on Fidelity's total assets? On total liabilities? On total stockholders' equity? (p. 495)

S9-13 (*Learning Objective 5: Computing book value per share*) Refer to the Real-World
Format of Stockholders' Equity in Exhibit 9-10, page 501. That company has passed its preferred dividends for 3 years including the current year. Compute the book value of a share of
the company's common stock. (pp. 497–498, 500–501)

S9-14 (*Learning Objective 6: Computing and explaining return on assets and return on
equity*) Give the formula for computing (a) rate of return on total assets (ROA) and (b) rate
of return on common stockholders' equity (ROE). Then answer these questions about the
rate-of-return computations. (pp. 498–500)

writing assignment ■

(continued)

1. Why is interest expense added to net income in the computation of ROA?
2. Why are preferred dividends subtracted from net income to compute ROE?

S9-15 (*Learning Objective 6: Computing return on assets and return on equity for a leading company*) **Sony Corpration's** 2006 financial statements reported the following items, with 2005 figures given for comparison (adapted and in millions). Compute Sony's return on assets and return on common equity for 2006. Evaluate the rates of return as strong or weak. ¥ is the symbol for the Japanese yen. (pp. 498–500)

	2006	2005
Balance sheet		
Total assets	¥10,608	¥9,499
Total liabilities	¥ 7,404	¥6,629
Total stockholders' equity (all common)	3,204	2,870
Total liabilities and equity	¥10,608	¥9,499
Income statement		
Revenues and other income	¥ 7,629	
Operating expense	7,284	
Interest expense	29	
Other expense	192	
Net income	¥ 124	

S9-16 (*Learning Objective 7: Measuring cash flows from financing activities*) During 2006, **PepsiCo** earned net income of $5.6 billion and paid off $2.7 billion of long-term notes payable. PepsiCo raised $1.2 billion by issuing common stock, paid $3.0 billion to purchase treasury stock, and paid cash dividends of $1.9 billion. Report PepsiCo's *cash flows from financing activities* on the statement of cash flows for 2006. (pp. 445, 500–501)

Exercises

writing assignment ■

E9-17 (*Learning Objective 1: Organizing a corporation*) Lance Brown and Monica Kobelsky are opening a **Schlotzky's** deli. Brown and Kobelsky need outside capital, so they plan to organize the business as a corporation. They come to you for advice. Write a memorandum informing them of the steps in forming a corporation. Identify specific documents used in this process, and name the different parties involved in the ownership and management of a corporation. (pp. 475–476)

■ general ledger

E9-18 (*Learning Objective 2: Issuing stock and reporting stockholders' equity*) Burgers & Fries, Inc., is authorized to issue 100,000 shares of common stock and 5,000 shares of preferred stock. During its first year, the business completed the following stock issuance transactions:

July 19	Issued 10,000 shares of $2.50 par common stock for cash of $6.50 per share.
Oct. 3	Issued 500 shares of $1.50 no-par preferred stock for $50,000 cash.
11	Received inventory valued at $11,000 and equipment with market value of $8,500 for 3,300 shares of the $2.50 par common stock.

❚ *Required*

1. Journalize the transactions. Explanations are not required.

2. Prepare the stockholders' equity section of Burgers & Fries' balance sheet. The ending balance of retained earnings is a deficit of $42,000.

E9-19 (*Learning Objective 2: Stockholders' equity section of a balance sheet*) Citadel Sporting Goods is authorized to issue 5,000 shares of preferred stock and 10,000 shares of common stock. During a 2-month period, Citadel completed these stock-issuance transactions:

June	23	Issued 1,000 shares of $1 par common stock for cash of $16 per share.
July	2	Issued 300 shares of $4.50, no-par preferred stock for $20,000 cash.
	12	Received inventory valued at $15,000 and equipment with market value of $43,000 for 3,000 shares of the $1 par common stock.

❚ *Required*

Prepare the stockholders' equity section of the Citadel Sporting Goods balance sheet for the transactions given in this exercise. Retained earnings has a balance of $49,000. Journal entries are not required. (pp. 482–485)

E9-20 (*Learning Objective 2: Measuring the paid-in capital of a corporation*) Trans World Publishing was recently organized. The company issued common stock to an attorney who provided legal services of $20,000 to help organize the corporation. Trans World also issued common stock to an inventor in exchange for his patent with a market value of $80,000. In addition, Trans World received cash both for the issuance of 5,000 shares of its preferred stock at $110 per share and for the issuance of 20,000 shares of its common stock at $15 per share. During the first year of operations, Trans World earned net income of $55,000 and declared a cash dividend of $26,000. Without making journal entries, determine the total paid-in capital created by these transactions. (pp. 288–291)

E9-21 (*Learning Objective 2, 3: Stockholders' equity section of a balance sheet*) Sagebrush Software had the following selected account balances at December 31, 20X6 (in thousands, except par value per share). Prepare the stockholders' equity section of Sagebrush Software's balance sheet (in thousands). (pp. 489–490)

■ **spreadsheet**

Inventory...	$ 653	Common stock, $0.25 par	
Property, plant, and		per share, 800 shares	
equipment, net	857	authorized, 360 shares	
Paid-in capital in excess of par	901	issued	$ 90
Treasury stock,		Retained earnings...............	2,202
120 shares at cost......................	1,380	Accounts receivable, net......	600
Other stockholders' equity	(729)*	Notes payable	1,122

*Debit balance

How can Sagebrush have a larger balance of treasury stock than the sum of Common Stock and Paid-in Capital in Excess of Par? (pp. 489–490 and Challenge)

■ general ledger

E9-22 (*Learning Objective 2, 3: Recording treasury stock transactions and measuring their effects on stockholders' equity*) Journalize the following transactions of **Concilio Video Productions**:

Apr. 19	Issued 2,000 shares of $1 par common stock at $5 per share.	
July 22	Purchased 900 shares of treasury stock at $7 per share.	
Nov. 11	Sold 800 shares of treasury stock at $12 per share.	

What was the overall effect of these transactions on Concilio's stockholders' equity?

E9-23 (*Learning Objective 2, 3, 4: Recording stock issuance, treasury stock, and dividend transactions*) At December 31, 20X7, Blumenthall Corporation reported the stockholders' equity accounts shown here (as adapted, with dollar amounts in millions, except share amounts).

Common stock $1.50 par value per share, 1,800 million shares issued................	$ 2,700
Capital in excess of par value................	8,100
Retained earnings.................................	1,200
Treasury stock, at cost	-0-
Total stockholders' equity.................	$12,000

Blumenthall's 20X8 transactions included the following:
a. Net income, $440 million.
b. Issuance of 6 million shares of common stock for $12.50 per share.
c. Purchase of 1 million shares of treasury stock for $14 million.
d. Declaration and payment of cash dividends of $30 million.

Journalize Blumenthall's transactions in b, c, and d. Explanations are not required. (pp. 482–483, 489–493)

E9-24 (*Learning Objective 2, 3, 4: Reporting stockholders' equity after a sequence of transactions*) Use the Blumenthall Corporation data in Exercise 9-23 to prepare the stockholders' equity section of the company's balance sheet at December 31, 20X8. (pp. 482–483, 489–493)

E9-25 (*Learning Objective 2, 3, 4, 5: Inferring transactions from a company's stockholders' equity*) OPTICAL PRODUCTS COMPANY reported the following shareholders' equity on its balance sheet:

Shareholders' Equity (Dollars and shares in millions)	December 31, 20X9	December 31, 20X8
Preferred stock—$1 per share par value; authorized 20 shares; Convertible Preferred Stock; issued and outstanding: 20X9 and 20X8—6 and 12 shares, respectively.................	$ 6	$ 12
Common stock—$1 per share par value; authorized 1,000 shares; issued: 20X9 and 20X8—564 and 364 shares, respectively.................................	564	364
Additional paid-in capital..	2,706	1,536
Retained earnings..	6,280	5,006
Treasury stock, common—at cost 20X9—49 shares; 20X8—9 shares	(1,235)	(215)
Total shareholders' equity......................................	8,321	6,703
Total liabilities and shareholders' equity	$48,918	$45,549

I Required

1. What caused OPTICAL PRODUCTS' preferred stock to decrease during 20X9? Cite all the possible causes. (pp. 486, 490–491)

2. What caused OPTICAL PRODUCTS' common stock to increase during 20X9? Identify all the possible causes. (pp. 482–483, 486, 494–495)

3. How many shares of OPTICAL PRODUCTS' common stock were outstanding at December 31, 20X9? (p. 488)

4. OPTICAL PRODUCTS' net income during 20X9 was $1,410 million. How much were OPTICAL PRODUCTS' dividends during the year? (pp. 492–493)

5. During 20X9, OPTICAL PRODUCTS sold no treasury stock. What average price per share did OPTICAL PRODUCTS pay for the treasury stock the company purchased during 20X9? (pp. 492–493 and Challenge)

E9-26 (*Learning Objective 4: Computing dividends on preferred and common stock*) Great Lakes Manufacturing, Inc., reported the following:

Stockholders' Equity	
Preferred stock, cumulative, $1 par, 5%, 60,000 shares issued..........	$ 60,000
Common stock, $0.10 par, 9,130,000 shares issued.....................	913,000

Great Lakes Manufacturing has paid all preferred dividends through 20X1.

I Required

Compute the total amounts of dividends to both preferred and common for 20X4 and 20X5 if total dividends are $50,000 in 20X4 and $100,000 in 20X5. (pp. 493–494)

E9-27 (*Learning Objective 4: Recording a stock dividend and reporting stockholders' equity*) The stockholders' equity for Dairy Queen Drive-Ins (DQ) on December 31, 2009, follows (adapted).

Stockholders' Equity	
Common stock, $0.10 par, 2,000,000 shares	
authorized, 500,000 shares issued.....................	$ 50,000
Paid-in capital in excess of par—common..............	962,000
Retained earnings..	7,122,000
Other equity..	(195,000)
Total stockholders' equity...............................	$7,939,000

On April 15, 2010, the market price of DQ common stock was $17 per share. Assume DQ distributed a 10% stock dividend on this date.

I Required

1. Journalize the distribution of the stock dividend. (pp. 494–495)

2. Prepare the stockholders' equity section of the balance sheet after the stock dividend. (Challenge)

(continued)

3. Why is total stockholders' equity unchanged by the stock dividend? (p. 495)

4. Suppose DQ had a cash balance of $540,000 on April 16, 2010. What is the maximum amount of cash dividends DQ can declare? (pp. 494–495)

E9-28 (*Learning Objective 2, 3, 4: Measuring the effects of stock issuance, dividends, and treasury stock transactions*) Identify the effects—both the direction and the dollar amount—of these assumed transactions on the total stockholders' equity of **FedEx Corporation**. Each transaction is independent. (p. 496)

    a. Declaration of cash dividends of $80 million.

    b. Payment of the cash dividend in *a*.

    c. 10% stock dividend. Before the dividend, 69 million shares of $1 par common stock were outstanding; the market value was $7.625 at the time of the dividend.

    d. A 50% stock dividend. Before the dividend, 69 million shares of $1 par common stock were outstanding; the market value was $13.75 at the time of the dividend.

    e. Purchase of 2,000 shares of treasury stock (par value $1) at $4.25 per share.

    f. Sale of 600 shares of the treasury stock for $5.00 per share. Cost of the treasury stock was $4.25 per share.

    g. A 3-for-1 stock split. Prior to the split, 69 million shares of $1 par common were outstanding.

E9-29 (*Learning Objective 4: Reporting stockholders' equity after a stock split*) Solartech Corp. had the following stockholders' equity at January 31 (dollars in millions, except par value per share):

Common stock, $0.10 par, 500 million shares authorized, 440 million shares issued	$ 44
Additional paid-in capital	318
Retained earnings	2,393
Other equity	(149)
Total stockholders' equity	$2,606

On March 7, Solartech split its $0.10 par common stock 2 for 1. Prepare the stockholders' equity section of the balance sheet immediately after the split. (pp. 495–497)

E9-30 (*Learning Objective 5: Measuring the book value per share of common stock*) The balance sheet of Oriental Rug Company reported the following:

Redeemable preferred stock, 6%, $60 par value, redemption value $10,000; outstanding 100 shares	$ 6,000
Common stockholders' equity:	
8,000 shares issued and outstanding	87,200
Total stockholders' equity	$93,200

❙ Required

1. Compute the book value per share for the common stock, assuming all preferred dividends are fully paid up (none in arrears). (pp. 497–498)

2. Compute the book value per share of the common stock, assuming that 3 years' preferred dividends including the current year, are in arrears. (pp. 497–498)

3. Oriental Rug's common stock recently traded at market price of $7.75 per share. Does this mean that Oriental Rug's stock is a good buy at $7.75? (pp. 498–499)

writing assignment ■

E9-31 (*Learning Objective 6: Evaluating profitability*) Lexington Inns reported these figures for 20X4 and 20X3 (in millions):

	20X4	20X3
Balance sheet		
Total assets	$15,695	$13,757
Common stock and additional paid-in capital	43	388
Retained earnings	11,519	16,510
Other equity	(2,914)	(9,294)
Income statement		
Operating income	$ 4,021	$ 3,818
Interest expense	219	272
Net income	1,486	1,543

Compute Lexington's return on assets and return on common stockholders' equity for 20X4. Do these rates of return suggest strength or weakness? Give your reason. (pp. 498–500)

E9-32 (*Learning Objective 6: Evaluating profitability*) Carolina Atlantic Company included the following items in its financial statements for 20X7, the current year (amounts in millions):

writing assignment ■

Payment of long-term debt	$17,055	Dividends paid	$ 225	
Proceeds from issuance		Interest expense:		
of common stock.....................	8,425	Current year.....................	1,437	
Total liabilities:		Preceding year	597	
Current year end	32,320	Net income:		
Preceding year end	38,023	Current year.....................	1,882	
Total stockholders' equity:		Preceding year	2,001	
Current year end	23,478	Operating income:		
Preceding year end	14,048	Current year.....................	4,884	
Borrowings.................................	6,582	Preceding year.................	4,012	

Compute Carolina Atlantic's return on assets and return on common equity during 20X7 (the current year). Carolina Atlantic has no preferred stock outstanding. Do the company's rates of return look strong or weak? Give your reason. (pp. 498–500)

E9-33 (*Learning Objective 7: Reporting cash flows from financing activities*) Use the Carolina Atlantic data in Exercise E9-32 to show how the company reported cash flows from financing activities during 20X7 (the current year). List items in descending order from largest to smallest dollar amount. (pp. 445, 500–501)

Challenge Exercises

E9-34 (*Learning Objective 2, 3, 4: Reconstructing transactions from the financial statements*) A-1 Networking Solutions began operations on January 1, 20X7, and immediately issued its stock, receiving cash. A-1's balance sheet at December 31, 20X7, reported the following stockholders' equity:

Common stock, $1 par......................	$ 50,000
Additional paid-in capital.................	200,600
Retained earnings.............................	38,000
Treasury stock, 500 shares................	(2,000)
Total stockholders' equity.................	$286,600

(continued)

During 20X7, A-1
  a. Issued stock for $5 per share. (pp. 482–483)
  b. Purchased 800 shares of treasury stock, paying $4 per share. (pp. 489–490)
  c. Resold some of the treasury stock. (pp. 489–490)
  d. Earned net income of $56,000 and declared and paid cash dividends. Revenues were $171,000 and expenses totaled $115,000.

I Required

Journalize all of A-1's stockholders' equity transactions during the year. A-1's entry *d.* to close net income to Retained Earnings was:

Revenues	171,000	
Expenses		115,000
Retained Earnings		56,000

E9-35 (*Learning Objective 7: Reporting financing activities on the statement of cash flows*) Use the data in Exercise E9-34 to report all of A-1 Networking Solutions' financing activities on the company's statement of cash flows for 20X7 (Journal entries and/or T-accounts may aid your approach to a solution). (pp. 500–501)

writing assignment ■

E9-36 (*Learning Objective 2, 3, 4: Explaining the changes in stockholders' equity*) Apollo Corporation reported the following stockholders' equity data (all dollars in millions except par value per share):

	December 31,	
	20X2	20X1
Preferred stock	$ 604	$ 740
Common stock, $1 par value	900	891
Additional paid-in capital.....................	1,490	1,468
Retained earnings..................................	20,661	19,108
Treasury stock, common	(2,758)	(2,643)

Apollo earned net income of $2,960 during 20X2. For each account except Retained Earnings, 1 transaction explains the change from the December 31, 20X1, balance to the December 31, 20X2, balance. Two transactions affected Retained Earnings. Give a full explanation, including the dollar amount, for the change in each account. (pp. 492–493)

■ spreadsheet

E9-37 (*Learning Objective 2, 3, 4: Accounting for changes in stockholders' equity*) Fun City, Inc., ended 20X5 with 8 million shares of $1 par common stock issued and outstanding. Beginning additional paid-in capital was $13 million, and retained earnings totaled $40 million.

  ■ In March 20X6, Fun City issued 2 million shares of common stock at a price of $2 per share.
  ■ In May, the company distributed a 10% stock dividend at a time when Fun City's common stock had a market value of $3 per share.
  ■ Then in October, Fun City's stock price dropped to $1 per share and the company purchased 2 million shares of treasury stock.
  ■ For the year, Fun City earned net income of $26 million and declared cash dividends of $17 million.

  Complete the following tabulation to show what Fun City should report for stockholders' equity at December 31, 20X6. Journal entries are not required. (Challenge)

(Amounts in millions)	Common Stock	+	Additional Paid-In Capital	+	Retained Earnings	−	Treasury Stock	=	Total Equity
Balance, Dec. 31, 20X5.....................	$8		$13		$40		$0		$61
Issuance of stock									
Stock dividend.................................									
Purchase of treasury stock................									
Net income.....................................									
Cash dividends................................									
Balance, Dec. 31, 20X6...................	$		$		$		$		$

Quiz

Test your understanding of stockholders' equity by answering the following questions. Select the best choice from among the possible answers given.

Q9-38 Which of the following is a characteristic of a corporation? (pp. 474–475)
a. mutual agency
b. no income tax
c. limited liability of stockholders
d. both a and b

Q9-39 Team Spirit, Inc., issues 240,000 shares of no-par common stock for $5 per share. The journal entry is: (pp. 483–484)

a.	Cash	240,000	
	Common Stock		240,000
b.	Cash	1,200,000	
	Common Stock		240,000
	Gain on the Sale of Stock		960,000
c.	Cash	1,200,000	
	Common Stock		1,200,000
d.	Cash	1,200,000	
	Common Stock		480,000
	Paid-in Capital in Excess of Stated Value—Common		720,000

Q9-40 Par value (pp. 479–480)
a. represents what a share of stock is worth.
b. represents the original selling price for a share of stock.
c. is established for a share of stock after it is issued.
d. is an arbitrary amount that establishes the legal capital for each share.
e. may exist for common stock but not for preferred stock.

Q9-41 The paid-in capital portion of stockholders' equity does not include (pp. 477–478)
a. Preferred Stock.
b. Paid-in Capital in Excess of Par Value.
c. Retained Earnings.
d. Common Stock.

Q9-42 Preferred stock is *least* likely to have which of the following characteristics? (pp. 478–479)
a. Preference as to assets on liquidation of the corporation
b. Extra liability for the preferred stockholders
c. The right of the holder to convert to common stock
d. Preference as to dividends

Q9-43 Which of the following classifications represents the *most* shares of common stock? (p. 488)

a. Issued shares
b. Outstanding shares
c. Treasury shares
d. Unissued shares
e. Authorized shares

Use the following information for Questions Q9-44 to Q9-46:

These account balances at December 31 relate to Sportaid, Inc.:

Accounts Payable	$ 51,700	Paid-in Capital in Excess of Par—Common	$280,000
Accounts Receivable	81,350	Preferred Stock, 10%, $100 Par	89,000
Common Stock	313,000	Retained Earnings	71,800
Treasury Stock	5,000	Notes Receivable	12,500
Bonds Payable	3,400		

Q9-44 What is total paid-in capital for Sportaid, Inc.? (pp. 477–478, 500–501)

a. $682,000
b. $701,345
c. $694,445
d. $753,800
e. None of the above.

Q9-45 What is total stockholders' equity for Sportaid, Inc.? (pp. 500–501)

a. $753,800
b. $758,800
c. $748,800
d. $764,735
e. None of the above.

Q9-46 Sportaid's net income for the period is $119,600 and beginning common stockholders' equity is $681,400. Calculate Sportaid's return on common stockholders' equity. (pp. 449–500)

a. 15.7%
b. 16.5%
c. 17.5%
d. 18.6%

Q9-47 A company paid $20 per share to purchase 500 shares of its common stock as treasury stock. The stock was originally issued at $15 per share. The journal entry to record the purchase of the treasury stock is: (pp. 489–490)

a.	Treasury Stock	10,000	
	Cash		10,000
b.	Treasury Stock	7,500	
	Retained Earnings	2,500	
	Cash		10,000
c.	Treasury Stock	5,000	
	Paid-in Capital in Excess of Par	5,000	
	Cash		10,000
d.	Common Stock	10,000	
	Cash		10,000

Q9-48 When treasury stock is sold for less than its cost, the entry should include a debit to: (pp. 489–490)

a. Gain on Sale of Treasury Stock.
b. Loss on Sale of Treasury Stock.
c. Paid-in Capital in Excess of Par.
d. Retained Earnings.

Q9-49 A company purchased 200 shares of its common stock at $55 per share. It then sells 30 of the treasury shares at $58 per share. The entry to sell the treasury stock includes a (pp. 489–490)

a. credit to Cash for $1,740.
b. credit to Treasury Stock for $1,740.
c. credit to Retained Earnings for $240.

d. debit to Retained Earnings for $90.

e. credit to Paid-in Capital, Treasury Stock for $90.

Q9-50 Stockholders are eligible for a dividend if they own the stock on the date of: (pp. 491–493)

a. declaration.

b. record.

c. payment.

d. issuance.

Q9-51 Mario's Foods has outstanding 500 shares of 7% preferred stock, $100 par value, and 1,200 shares of common stock, $20 par value. Mario's declares dividends of $14,300. The correct entry is: (pp. 493–494)

a.	Retained Earnings	14,300	
	Dividends Payable, Preferred		3,500
	Dividends Payable, Common		10,800
b.	Dividends Expense	14,300	
	Cash		14,300
c.	Retained Earnings	14,300	
	Dividends Payable, Preferred		7,150
	Dividends Payable, Common		7,150
d.	Dividends Payable, Preferred	3,500	
	Dividends Payable, Common	10,800	
	Cash		14,300

Q9-52 A corporation has 20,000 shares of 8% preferred stock outstanding. Also, there are 20,000 shares of common stock outstanding. Par value for each is $100. If a $350,000 dividend is paid, how much goes to the preferred stockholders? (pp. 493–494)

a. None

b. $350,000

c. $160,000

d. $120,000

e. $320,000

Q9-53 Assume the same facts as in question 52. What is the amount of dividends per share on common stock? (pp. 493–494, Challenge)

a. $9.50

b. $8.00

c. $17.50

d. $1.50

e. None of these.

Q9-54 Which of the following is *not* true about a 10% stock dividend? (pp. 494–495)

a. Par value decreases.

b. Paid-in Capital increases.

c. Retained Earnings decreases.

d. The market value of the stock is needed to record the stock dividend.

e. Total stockholders' equity remains the same.

Q9-55 A company declares a 5% stock dividend. The debit to Retained Earnings is an amount equal to: (pp. 494–495)

a. the par value of the shares to be issued.

b. the excess of the market price over the original issue price of the shares to be issued.

c. the book value of the shares to be issued.

d. the market value of the shares to be issued.

Q9-56 Which of the following statements is *not* true about a 3-for-1 stock split? (pp. 495–497)

a. Par value is reduced to one-third of what it was before the split.

b. Total stockholders' equity increases.

c. The market price of each share of stock will decrease.

d. A stockholder with 10 shares before the split owns 30 shares after the split.

e. Retained Earnings remains the same.

Q9-57 Franco Company's net income and interest expense are $44,000 and $4,000, respectively, and average total assets are $384,000. How much is Franco's retun on assets? (pp. 498–499)

a. 10.4%   c. 12.5%

b. 11.5%   d. 13.1%

Problems
(Group A)

MyAccountingLab

Some of these A problems can be found within My Accounting Lab (MAL), an online homework and practice environment. Your instructor may ask you to complete these problems using MAL.

writing assignment ■

P9-58A (*Learning Objective 1, 2, 5: Explaining the features of a corporation's stock*) Reinhart Corporation is conducting a special meeting of its board of directors to address some concerns raised by the stockholders. Stockholders have submitted the following questions. Answer each question.

1. Why are common stock and retained earnings shown separately in the shareholders' equity section of the balance sheet? (pp. 477–478)
2. Lou Harris, a Reinhart shareholder, proposes to give some land she owns to the company in exchange for shares of the company stock. How should Reinhart Corporation determine the number of shares of our stock to issue for the land? (pp. 489–490)
3. Preferred shares generally are preferred with respect to dividends and in the event of our liquidation. Why would investors buy our *common* stock when *preferred* stock is available? (pp. 478–479)
4. What does the redemption value of our preferred stock require us to do? (p. 495)
5. One of our stockholders owns 100 shares of Reinhart stock and someone has offered to buy her shares for their book value. Our stockholder asks us the formula for computing the book value of her stock. (pp. 497–498)

P9-59A (*Learning Objective 2: Recording corporate transactions and preparing the stockholders' equity section of the balance sheet*) The partners who own Bassett Furniture Co. wished to avoid the unlimited personal liability of the partnership form of business, so they incorporated as BFC Inc. The charter from the state of Florida authorizes the corporation to issue 10,000 shares of $6 no-par preferred stock and 250,000 shares of $5 par common stock. In its first month, BFC completed the following transactions:

Jan.	3	Issued 1,000 shares of common stock to the promoter for assistance with issuance of the common stock. The promotional fee was $10,000. Debit Organization Expense.
	6	Issued 5,000 shares of common stock to Jo Bassett and 3,800 shares to Mel Bassett in return for cash equal to the stock's market value of $11 per share. The Bassetts were partners in Bassett Furniture Co.
	12	Issued 1,000 shares of preferred stock to acquire a patent with a market value of $110,000.
	22	Issued 1,500 shares of common stock for $12 cash per share.

▌Required

1. Record the transactions in the journal. (pp. 482–486)

2. Prepare the stockholders' equity section of the BFC Inc. balance sheet at January 31. The ending balance of Retained Earnings is $89,000. (pp. 482–483, 500–501)

P9-60A (*Learning Objective 2, 4: Preparing the stockholders' equity section of the balance sheet*) Lima Corp. has the following stockholders' equity information:

Lima's charter authorizes the company to issue 10,000 shares of 5% preferred stock with par value of $100 and 400,000 shares of no-par common stock. The company issued 1,000 shares of the preferred stock at $100 per share. It issued 100,000 shares of the common stock for a total of $370,000. The company's retained earnings balance at the beginning of 20X8 was $40,000, and net income for the year was $90,000. During 20X8, Lima declared the specified dividend on preferred and a $0.50 per-share dividend on common. Preferred dividends for 20X7 were in arrears.

❙ Required

Prepare the stockholders' equity section of Lima Corp.'s balance sheet at December 31, 20X8. Show the computation of all amounts. Journal entries are not required. (pp. 500–501)

P9-61A (*Learning Objective 3: Purchasing treasury stock to fight off a takeover of the corporation*) Gary Swan Imports, Inc., is located in Jacksonville, Florida. Swan is the only company with reliable sources for its imported gifts. The company does a brisk business with specialty stores such as **Macy's**. Swan's recent success has made the company a prime target for a takeover. An investment group from Miami is attempting to buy 51% of Swan's outstanding stock against the wishes of Swan's board of directors. Board members are convinced that the Miami investors would sell the most desirable pieces of the business and leave little of value.

writing assignment ■

At the most recent board meeting, several suggestions were advanced to fight off the hostile takeover bid. The suggestion with the most promise is to purchase a huge quantity of treasury stock. Swan has the cash to carry out this plan.

❙ Required

1. Suppose you are a significant stockholder of Gary Swan Imports, Inc. Write a memorandum to explain to the board how the purchase of treasury stock would make it difficult for the Miami group to take over Swan. Include in your memo a discussion of the effect that purchasing treasury stock would have on stock outstanding and on the size of the corporation. (pp. 489–490)
2. Suppose Swan management is successful in fighting off the takeover bid and later sells the treasury stock at prices greater than the purchase price. Explain what effect these sales will have on assets, stockholders' equity, and net income. (pp. 489–490)

P9-62A (*Learning Objective 2, 3, 4: Measuring the effects of stock issuance, treasury stock, and dividend transactions on stockholders' equity*) Federal Exchange Corporation is authorized to issue 500,000 shares of $1 par common stock.

In its initial public offering during 20X2, Federal Exchange issued 200,000 shares of its $1 par common stock for $12 per share. Over the next year, Federal Exchange's common stock price increased, and the company issued 100,000 more shares at an average price of $14.50.

During 20X4, the price of Federal Exchange's common stock dropped to $8, and Federal Exchange purchased 30,000 shares of its common stock for the treasury. After the market price of the common stock increased in 20X5, Federal Exchange sold 20,000 shares of the treasury stock for $11 per share.

During the 5 years 20X2 to 20X6, Federal Exchange earned net income of $295,000 and declared and paid cash dividends of $119,000. Stock dividends of $110,000 were distributed to the stockholders in 20X3, with $14,000 credited to common stock and $96,000 credited to additional paid-in capital. At December 31, 20X6, total assets of the company are $7,030,000, and liabilities add up to $3,024,000.

(continued)

▌Required

Show the computation of Federal Exchange Corporation's total stockholders' equity at December 31, 20X6. Present a detailed computation of each element of stockholders' equity. (pp. 482–483, 489–490, 493–495, 500–501)

writing assignment ■

P9-63A (*Learning Objective 2, 4: Analyzing the stockholders' equity and dividends of a corporation*) Teak Outdoor Furniture Company included the following stockholders' equity on its year-end balance sheet at February 28:

Stockholders' Equity	
Preferred stock, 5.5% cumulative—par value $20 per share; authorized 100,000 shares in each class;	
Class A—issued 75,000 shares	$ 1,500,000
Class B—issued 92,000 shares	1,840,000
Common stock—par value $5 per share; authorized 1,000,000 shares;	
issued 280,000 shares	1,400,000
Additional paid-in capital, common	5,540,000
Retained earnings	8,330,000
	$18,610,000

▌Required

1. Identify the different issues of stock Teak Outdoor Furniture Company has outstanding. (pp. 481–486)
2. Give the summary entries to record issuance of all the Teak stock. Assume that all the stock was issued for cash. Explanations are not required. (pp. 482–483, 485–486)
3. Suppose Teak passed its preferred dividends for 3 years. Would the company have to pay those dividends in arrears before paying dividends to the common stockholders? Give your reason. (pp. 493–494)
4. What amount of preferred dividends must Teak declare and pay each year to avoid having preferred dividends in arrears? (pp. 493–494)
5. Assume that preferred dividends are in arrears for 20X8. Record the declaration of an $800,000 dividend on February 28, 20X9. An explanation is not required. (pp. 493–494)

P9-64A (*Learning Objective 2, 3, 4: Accounting for stock issuance, dividends, and treasury stock*) Boston Enterprises reported the following summarized balance sheet at December 31, 20X7:

Assets	
Current assets	$18,200
Property and equipment, net	34,700
Total assets	$52,900
Liabilities and Equity	
Liabilities	$ 6,200
Stockholders' equity:	
$5 cumulative preferred stock, $10 par, 180 shares issued	1,800
Common stock, $1 par, 2,400 shares issued	2,400
Paid-in capital in excess of par, common	23,500
Retained earnings	19,000
Total liabilities and equity	$52,900

During 20X8, Boston completed these transactions that affected stockholders' equity:

Feb. 22	Issued 1,000 shares of common stock for $16 per share.
May 4	Declared the regular cash dividend on the preferred stock.
24	Paid the cash dividend.
July 9	Distributed a 10% stock dividend on the common stock. Market price of the common stock was $18 per share.
Nov. 19	Reacquired 800 shares of common stock as treasury stock, paying $14 per share.
Dec. 8	Sold 600 shares of the treasury stock for $15 per share.

❙ Required

1. Journalize Boston's transactions. Explanations are not required. (pp. 482–483, 489–493)
2. Report Boston's stockholders' equity at December 31, 20X8. Net income for 20X8 was $62,000. (pp. 500–501)

P9-65A (*Learning Objective 3, 4: Measuring the effects of dividend and treasury stock transactions on a company*) Dairy Freeze of Texas, Inc., completed the following transactions during 20X6, the company's tenth year of operations:

Feb. 2	Issued 10,000 shares of company stock ($5 par) for cash of $250,000.
Mar. 18	Purchased 2,000 shares of the company's own common stock at $22 per share.
Apr. 22	Sold 700 shares of treasury common stock for $26 per share.
Aug. 6	Declared a cash dividend on the 10,000 shares of $0.60 no-par preferred stock.
Sept. 1	Paid the cash dividends.
Nov. 18	Distributed a 10% stock dividend on the 30,000 shares of $1 par common stock outstanding. The market value of the common stock was $25 per share.

❙ Required

Analyze each transaction in terms of its effect on the accounting equation of Dairy Freeze of Texas, Inc. (p. 496)

P9-66A (*Learning Objective 3, 6: Preparing a corporation's balance sheet; measuring profitability*) The following accounts and related balances of Bluebird Designers, Inc., as of December 31, 20X8, are arranged in no particular order.

Cash	$41,000	Interest expense	$ 16,100
Accounts receivable, net	24,000	Property, plant, and	
Paid-in capital in excess		equipment, net	357,000
of par—common	19,000	Common stock, $1 par,	
Accrued liabilities	26,000	500,000 shares authorized,	
Long-term note payable	98,000	115,000 shares issued	115,000
Inventory	99,000	Prepaid expenses	10,000
Dividends payable	9,000	Common stockholders'	
Retained earnings	?	equity, December 31, 20X7	222,000
Accounts payable	131,000	Net income	31,000
Trademark, net	9,000	Total assets,	
Preferred stock, $0.50,		December 31, 20X7	494,000
no-par, 10,000 shares		Treasury stock,	
authorized and issued	27,000	18,000 shares at cost	22,000
Goodwill	14,000		

(*continued*)

❙ Required

1. Prepare the company's classified balance sheet in the account format at December 31, 20X8. (pp. 159, 500–501)
2. Compute rate of return on total assets and rate of return on common stockholders' equity for the year ended December 31, 20X8. (pp. 498–500)
3. Do these rates of return suggest strength or weakness? Give your reason. (pp. 499–500)

P9-67A (*Learning Objective 7: Analyzing the statement of cash flows*) The statement of cash flows of **PepsiCo, Inc.**, reported the following (adapted) for the year ended December 31, 2006:

Cash flows from financing activities—*amounts in millions:*	
Cash dividends paid	$(1,854)
Issuance of common stock at par value	1,194
Proceeds from issuance of long-term notes payable	51
Purchases of treasury stock	(3,010)
Payments of long-term notes payable	(157)

❙ Required

Make the journal entry that PepsiCo would use to record each of these transactions. (pp. 425–428, 482–483, 489–493)

(Group B)

writing assignment ■

P9-68B (*Learning Objective 1, 3, 4: Explaining the features of a corporation's stock*) The board of directors of Freestroke Swim Centers, Inc., is meeting to address the concerns of stockholders. Stockholders have submitted the following questions for discussion at the board meeting. Answer each question.

1. Why did Freestroke organize as a corporation if a corporation must pay an additional layer of income tax? (pp. 474–475)
2. How is preferred stock similar to common stock? How is preferred stock similar to debt? (pp. 478–479)
3. Freestroke purchased treasury stock for $50,000 and a year later sold it for $65,000. Explain to the stockholders whether the $15,000 excess is profit to be reported on the company's income statement. Explain your answer. (pp. 489–490)
4. Would Freestroke investors prefer to receive cash dividends or stock dividends? Explain your reasoning. (pp. 491–495)

P9-69B (*Learning Objective 2: Recording corporate transactions and preparing the stockholders' equity section of the balance sheet*) The charter from the state of Utah authorizes Challenger Canoes, Inc., to issue 10,000 shares of 6%, $100 par preferred stock and 100,000 shares of $1 par common stock. In its first month, Challenger completed the following transactions:

Oct.	6	Issued 300 shares of common stock to the lawyer for assistance with chartering the corporation. The lawyer's fee was $1,500. Debit Organization Expense.
	9	Issued 9,000 shares of common stock to Jerry Grant and 12,000 shares to Sheila Hoffman in return for cash equal to the stock's market value of $5 per share. Grant and Hoffman are executives of the company.
	10	Issued 400 shares of preferred stock to acquire a patent with a market value of $40,000.
	26	Issued 2,000 shares of common stock for cash of $12,000.

I *Required*

1. Record the transactions in the journal. (pp. 482–483, 485–486)
2. Prepare the stockholders' equity section of the Challenger balance sheet at October 31. The ending balance of Retained Earnings is $49,000. (pp. 482–483, 500–501)

P9-70B (*Learning Objective 2, 4: Preparing the stockholders' equity section of the balance sheet*) The charter of Samuells' Sportswear authorizes the company to issue 5,000 shares of 5%, $100 par preferred stock and 500,000 shares of no-par common stock. Samuells' issued 1,000 shares of the preferred stock at $100 per share. It issued 100,000 shares of the common stock for $427,000. The company's retained earnings balance at the beginning of 20X6 was $61,000. Net income for 20X6 was $80,000, and the company declared a 5% cash dividend on preferred stock for 20X6.

I *Required*

Prepare the stockholders' equity section of Samuells' Sportswear, Inc.'s, balance sheet at December 31, 20X6. Show the computation of all amounts. Journal entries are not required. (pp. 500–501)

P9-71B (*Learning Objective 3: Fighting off a takeover of the corporation*) Calpak Outdoor Sports is positioned ideally in the water sports business. Located in Denver, Colorado, Calpak is the only company with a distribution network for its imported goods. The company does a brisk business with specialty stores such as **Cabella's**, **REI**, and **Academy Sports**. Calpak's recent success has made the company a prime target for a takeover. Against the wishes of Calpak's board of directors, an investment group from Los Angeles is attempting to buy 51% of Calpak's outstanding stock. Board members are convinced that the Los Angeles investors would sell off the most desirable pieces of the business and leave little of value. At the most recent board meeting, several suggestions were advanced to fight off the hostile takeover bid.

writing assignment ▪

I *Required*

Suppose you are a significant stockholder of Calpak Outdoor Sports. Write a short memo to the board to propose an action that would make it difficult for the investor group to take over Calpak. Include in your memo a discussion of the effect your proposed action would have on the company's assets, liabilities, and total stockholders' equity. (pp. 488–489)

P9-72B (*Learning Objective 2, 3, 4: Measuring the effects of stock issuance, treasury stock, and dividend transactions on stockholders' equity*) Wholegrain Health Foods, Inc., is authorized to issue 5,000,000 shares of $1 par common stock.

In its initial public offering during 20X4, Wholegrain issued 500,000 shares of its $1 par common stock for $7.00 per share. Over the next year, Wholegrain's stock price increased and the company issued 400,000 more shares at an average price of $8.50.

During 20X6, the price of Wholegrain's common stock dropped to $7, and the company purchased 60,000 shares of its common stock for the treasury. After the market price of the common stock rose in 20X7, Wholegrain sold 40,000 shares of the treasury stock for $8 per share.

During the 5 years 20X4 through 20X8, Wholegrain earned net income of $620,000 and declared and paid cash dividends of $140,000. Stock dividends of $280,000 were distributed to the stockholders in 20X7, with $35,000 credited to common stock and $245,000 credited to additional paid-in capital. At December 31, 20X8, the company has total assets of $14,200,000 and total liabilities of $6,920,000.

I *Required*

Show the computation of Wholegrain's total stockholders' equity at December 31, 20X8. Present a detailed computation of each element of stockholders' equity. (pp. 482–483, 489–490, 493–495, 500–501)

P9-73B (*Learning Objective 2, 4: Analyzing the stockholders' equity and dividends of a corporation*) Steeltrap Security included the following stockholders' equity on its balance sheet:

Stockholders' Equity	($ Millions)
Preferred stock—	
Authorized 20,000 shares in each class:	
$5.00 Cumulative Convertible Preferred Stock,	
$50.00 par value, 2,500 shares issued	$ 125,000
$2.50 Cumulative Convertible Preferred Stock,	
$25.00 par value, 4,000 shares issued	100,000
Common stock—$2 par value:	
Authorized 80,000 shares, issued 48,000 shares................	96,000
Additional paid-in capital—common	288,000
Retained earnings..	529,000
	$1,138,000

❙ Required

1. Identify the different issues of stock Steeltrap Security has outstanding. (pp. 480–486)
2. Which class of stock did Steeltrap issue at par value, and which class did it issue above par value? (pp. 481–486)
3. Suppose Steeltrap passed its preferred dividends for 1 year. Would the company have to pay these dividends in arrears before paying dividends to the common stockholders? Why? (pp. 491–494)
4. What amount of preferred dividends must Steeltrap declare and pay each year to avoid having preferred dividends in arrears? (pp. 493–494)
5. Assume preferred dividends are in arrears for 20X7. Journalize the declaration of a $50,000 cash dividend for 20X8. No explanation is needed. (pp. 493–494)

P9-74B (*Learning Objective 2, 3, 4: Accounting for stock issuance, dividends, and treasury stock*) Madrid Jewelry Company reported the following summarized balance sheet at December 31, 20X8:

Assets	
Current assets...	$33,400
Property and equipment, net	51,800
Total assets	$85,200
Liabilities and Equity	
Liabilities	$37,800
Stockholders' equity:	
$0.50 cumulative preferred stock, $5 par,	
400 shares issued..	2,000
Common stock, $1 par, 6,000 shares issued...............	6,000
Paid-in capital in excess of par, common....................	17,400
Retained earnings..	22,000
Total liabilities and equity...	$85,200

During 20X9, Madrid completed these transactions that affected stockholders' equity:

Feb.	13	Issued 5,000 shares of common stock for $4 per share.
June	7	Declared the regular cash dividend on the preferred stock.
	24	Paid the cash dividend.
Aug.	9	Distributed a 10% stock dividend on the common stock. Market price of the common stock was $5 per share.
Oct.	26	Reacquired 500 shares of common stock as treasury stock, paying $6 per share.
Nov.	20	Sold 200 shares of the treasury stock for $8 per share.

❚ Required

1. Journalize Madrid's transactions. Explanations are not required. (pp. 482–483, 489–495)
2. Report Madrid Jewelry Company's stockholders' equity at December 31, 20X9. Net income for 20X9 was $27,000. (pp. 500–501)

P9-75B (*Learning Objective 3, 4: Measuring the effects of dividend and treasury stock transactions on a company*) Niles Corporation completed the following selected transactions during the current year:

Mar.	3	Distributed a 10% stock dividend on the 90,000 shares of common stock outstanding ($2.50 par). The market value of the common stock was $25 per share.
May	16	Declared a cash dividend on the 5%, $100 par preferred stock (5,000 shares outstanding).
	30	Paid the cash dividends.
Oct.	26	Purchased 1,500 shares of treasury stock at $24 per share.
Dec.	8	Sold all of the treasury stock for $27 per share.
	19	Issued 10,000 shares of common stock ($2.50 par) for $28 per share.

❚ Required

Analyze each transaction in terms of its effect on the accounting equation of Niles Corporation. (p. 496)

P9-76B (*Learning Objective 3, 6: Preparing a corporation's balance sheet; measuring profitability*) The following accounts and related balances of Kingston Appliances, Inc., are arranged in no particular order.

■ **general ledger**

Dividends payable	$ 3,000	Accounts payable	$ 31,000
Total assets, December 31, 20X6	461,000	Retained earnings	?
Net income	36,200	Common stock, $1 par; 100,000 shares authorized, 42,000 shares issued	42,000
Common stockholders' equity, December 31, 20X6	283,000	Inventory	93,000
Interest expense	3,800	Property, plant, and equipment, net	181,000
Treasury stock, common, 1,600 shares at cost	11,000	Goodwill	6,000
Prepaid expenses	13,000	Preferred stock, 4%, $10 par, 25,000 shares authorized, 3,700 shares issued	37,000
Patent, net	31,000		
Accrued liabilities	17,000		
Long-term note payable	79,000	Additional paid-in capital— common	140,000
Accounts receivable, net	71,000		
Cash	44,000		

(continued)

❙ Required

1. Prepare Kingston's classified balance sheet in the account format at December 31, 20X7. (pp. 159, 500–501)
2. Compute rate of return on total assets and rate of return on common stockholders' equity for the year ended December 31, 20X7. (pp. 498–500)
3. Do these rates of return suggest strength, weakness, or a mid range? Give your reason. (pp. 500–501)

writing assignment ■

P9-77B (*Learning Objective 7: Analyzing the statement of cash flows*) The statement of cash flows of Picture Perfect Photography reported the following for the year ended December 31, 20X8.

Cash flows from financing activities:	
Dividends [declared and] paid	$ (8,300)
Proceeds from issuance of common stock at par value	14,100
Payments of short-term notes payable	(6,900)
Payments of long-term notes payable	(1,300)
Proceeds from issuance of long-term notes payable	2,100
Purchases of treasury stock	(6,300)

❙ Required

Make the journal entry that Picture Perfect used to record each of these transactions. (pp. 415–416, 427–428, 482–483, 489–493, 500–501)

APPLY YOUR KNOWLEDGE

Decision Cases

writing assignment ■

Case 1. (*Learning Objective 2: Evaluating alternative ways of raising capital*) Nate Smith and Darla Jones have written a computer program for a video game that may rival Playstation and Xbox. They need additional capital to market the product, and they plan to incorporate their business. Smith and Jones are considering alternative capital structures for the corporation. Their primary goal is to raise as much capital as possible without giving up control of the business. Smith and Jones plan to receive 50,000 shares of the corporation's common stock in return for the net assets of their old business. After the old company's books are closed and the assets adjusted to current market value, Smith's and Jones's capital balances will each be $25,000.

The corporation's plans for a charter include an authorization to issue 10,000 shares of preferred stock and 500,000 shares of $1 par common stock. Smith and Jones are uncertain about the most desirable features for the preferred stock. Prior to incorporating, Smith and Jones are discussing their plans with 2 investment groups. The corporation can obtain capital from outside investors under either of the following plans:

- **Plan 1.** Group 1 will invest $80,000 to acquire 800 shares of 6%, $100 par nonvoting, preferred stock.
- **Plan 2.** Group 2 will invest $55,000 to acquire 500 shares of $5, no-par preferred stock and $35,000 to acquire 35,000 shares of common stock. Each preferred share receives 50 votes on matters that come before the stockholders.

❙ Required

Assume that the corporation is chartered.

1. Journalize the issuance of common stock to Smith and Jones. Debit each person's capital account for its balance. (pp. 482–483)

2. Journalize the issuance of stock to the outsiders under both plans. (pp. 482–483)

3. Assume that net income for the first year is $120,000 and total dividends are $30,000. Prepare the stockholders' equity section of the corporation's balance sheet under both plans. (pp. 500–501)

4. Recommend one of the plans to Smith and Jones. Give your reasons. (Challenge)

Case 2. (*Learning Objective 4: Analyzing cash dividends and stock dividends*) **United Parcel Service (UPS), Inc.** had the following stockholders' equity amounts on December 31, 20X5 (adapted, in millions):

writing assignment ■

Common stock and additional paid-in capital; 1,135 shares issued...............	$ 278
Retained earnings..	9,457
Total stockholders' equity..	$9,735

During 20X5, UPS paid a cash dividend of $0.715 per share. Assume that, after paying the cash dividends, UPS distributed a 10% stock dividend. Assume further that the following year UPS declared and paid a cash dividend of $0.65 per share.

Suppose you own 10,000 shares of UPS common stock, acquired 3 years ago, prior to the 10% stock dividend. The market price of UPS stock was $61.02 per share before the stock dividend.

I Required

1. How does the stock dividend affect your proportionate ownership in UPS? Explain. (pp. 493–496)

2. What amount of cash dividends did you receive last year? What amount of cash dividends will you receive after the above dividend action? (pp. 491–493)

3. Assume that immediately after the stock dividend was distributed, the market value of UPS's stock decreased from $61.02 per share to $55.473 per share. Does this decrease represent a loss to you? Explain. (Challenge)

4. Suppose UPS announces at the time of the stock dividend that the company will continue to pay the annual $0.715 *cash* dividend per share, even after distributing the *stock* dividend. Would you expect the market price of the stock to decrease to $55.473 per share as in Requirement 3? Explain. (pp. 490–494)

Case 3. (*Learning Objective 2, 3, 4, 5: Evaluating financial position and profitability*) At December 31, 20X4, **Enron Corporation** reported the following data (condensed in millions):

writing assignment ■

Total assets	$65,503
Total liabilities	54,033
Stockholders' equity.......................................	11,470
Net income, as reported, for 20X4...............	979

During 20X5, Enron restated company financial statements for 20X1 to 20X4, after reporting that some data had been omitted from those prior-year statements. Assume that the startling events of 20X5 included the following:

- Several related companies should have been, but were not, included in the Enron statements for 20X4. These companies had total assets of $5,700 million, liabilities totaling $5,600 million, and net losses of $130 million.
- In January 20X5, Enron's stockholders got the company to give them $2,000 million of 12% long-term notes payable in return for their giving up their common stock. Interest is accrued at year end.

(continued)

Take the role of a financial analyst. It is your job to analyze Enron Corporation and rate the company's long-term debt.

❙ Required

1. Measure Enron's expected net income for 20X5 two ways:
   a. Assume 20X5's net income should be the same as the amount of net income that Enron actually reported for 20X4. (Given)
   b. Recompute expected net income for 20X5 taking into account the new developments of 20X5. (Challenge)
   c. Evaluate Enron's likely trend of net income for the future. Discuss *why* this trend is developing. Ignore income tax. (Challenge)

2. Write Enron's accounting equation two ways:
   a. As actually reported at December 31, 20X4. (pp. 40–41)
   b. As adjusted for the events of 20X5. (pp. 40–41, Challenge)

3. Measure Enron's debt ratio as reported at December 31, 20X4, and again after making the adjustments for the events of 20X5. (pp. 169–170)

4. Based on your analysis, make a recommendation to the Debt-Rating Committee of Moody's Investor Services. Would you recommend upgrading, downgrading, or leaving Enron's debt rating undisturbed (currently, it is "high-grade"). (Challenge)

Ethical Issues

writing assignment ■

Ethical Issue 1. *Note: This case is based on a real situation.*

George Campbell paid $50,000 for a franchise that entitled him to market Success Associates software programs in the countries of the European Union. Campbell intended to sell individual franchises for the major language groups of western Europe—German, French, English, Spanish, and Italian. Naturally, investors considering buying a franchise from Campbell asked to see the financial statements of his business.

Believing the value of the franchise to be greater than $50,000, Campbell sought to capitalize his own franchise at $500,000. The law firm of McDonald & LaDue helped Campbell form a corporation chartered to issue 500,000 shares of common stock with par value of $1 per share. Attorneys suggested the following chain of transactions:

a. A third party borrows $500,000 and purchases the franchise from Campbell.

b. Campbell pays the corporation $500,000 to acquire all its stock.

c. The corporation buys the franchise from the third party, who repays the loan.

In the final analysis, the third party is debt-free and out of the picture. Campbell owns all the corporation's stock, and the corporation owns the franchise. The corporation balance sheet lists a franchise acquired at a cost of $500,000. This balance sheet is Campbell's most valuable marketing tool.

❙ Required

1. What is unethical about this situation?

2. Who can be harmed in this situation? How can they be harmed? What role does accounting play here?

writing assignment ■

Ethical Issue 2. St. Genevieve Petroleum Company is an independent oil producer in Baton Parish, Louisiana. In February, company geologists discovered a pool of oil that tripled the company's proven reserves. Prior to disclosing the new oil to the public, St. Genevieve quietly bought most of its stock as treasury stock. After the discovery was announced, the company's stock price increased from $6 to $27.

❚ *Required*

1. Did St. Genevieve managers behave ethically? Explain your answer.
2. Identify the accounting principle relevant to this situation.
3. Who was helped and who was harmed by management's action?

Focus on Financials: ■ YUM! Brands

(Learning Objective 2, 3, 6: Analyzing common stock, retained earnings, return on equity, and return on assets) **YUM! Brands'** financial statements appear in Appendix A at the end of this book.

1. YUM reports common stock in a single total. Why is there no paid-in capital in excess of par? (pp. 483–484)
2. YUM's common stock balance appears to be 0. Does the company really have no common stock outstanding? Explain. (Challenge)
3. Examine YUM's statement of shareholders' equity. Explain why YUM's retained earnings balance decreased during 2006. (pp. 490–493)
4. Compute YUM's return on equity and return on assets for 2006. Which is larger? Is this a sign of financial strength or weakness? Explain. (pp. 498–500)

Focus on Analysis: ■ Pier 1 Imports

(Learning Objective 2, 3, 4: Analyzing treasury stock and retained earnings) This case is based on the financial statements of **Pier 1 Imports**, given in Appendix B at the end of this book. In particular, this case uses Pier 1's statement of shareholders' equity for the year 2006.

1. During 2006, Pier 1 purchased treasury stock and also sold treasury stock under the company's stock option plan and stock purchase plan. Was Pier 1's average price per share higher for the treasury stock the company purchased or for the treasury stock sold under the stock option plan and the stock purchase plan? What was the difference in price per share between the 2 transactions? Ignore the "Restricted stock grant and amortization." (pp. 488–489, Challenge)
2. Journalize the purchase of treasury stock and the sale of treasury stock under the stock option plan and the stock purchase plan during the year ended February 25, 2006. (pp. 489–490, Challenge)
3. Prepare a T-account to show the beginning and ending balances, plus all the activity in Retained Earnings for the year ended February 25, 2006. (p. 492)

Group Project

Competitive pressures are the norm in business. **Lexus** automobiles (made in Japan) have cut into the sales of **Mercedes-Benz** (a German company), **Jaguar Motors** (a British company), **General Motors Cadillac Division**, and **Ford Lincoln Division** (both U.S. companies). **Dell**, **Gateway**, and **Compaq** computers have siphoned business away from **Apple** and **IBM**. Foreign steelmakers have reduced the once-massive U.S. steel industry to a fraction of its former size.

writing assignment ■

Indeed, corporate downsizing has occurred on a massive scale. Each company or industry mentioned here has pared down plant and equipment, laid off employees, or restructured operations.

(continued)

❙ *Required*

1. Identify all the stakeholders of a corporation. A *stakeholder* is a person or a group who has an interest (that is, a stake) in the success of the organization.

2. Identify several measures by which a company may be considered deficient and in need of downsizing. How can downsizing help to solve this problem?

3. Debate the downsizing issue. One group of students takes the perspective of the company and its stockholders, and another group of students takes the perspective of the other stakeholders of the company (the community in which the company operates and society at large).

For Internet Exercises go to the Web site www.prenhall.com/harrison.

Quick Check Answers:

1. *a* (10,000 shares × $10 = $100,000)
2. *b* $180,000/$1 par = 180,000 shares
3. *d* ($180,000 + $100,000 + $45,000 = $325,000)
4. *c* ($180,000 + $200,000 + $100,000 + $45,000 = $525,000)
5. *d* ($525,000 − $5,000 = $520,000)
6. *d* [No gain or loss (for the income statement) on treasury stock transactions]
7. *a*
8. *b*
9. *c*
10. *a*
11. *c* [First, annual preferred dividend = $5,000 (5,000 × $20 × .05)]
    [($5,000 × 4) + (100,000 × $1.25) = $145,000]
12. *a*
13. *d*
14. *c*
15. *c*
16. *a*

10 Long-Term Investments & International Operations

INTEL HOLDS SEVERAL DIFFERENT TYPES OF INVESTMENTS

After college you'll start investing through a plan at work, and you may make some investments on your own. The reasons people invest are for current income (interest and dividends) and appreciation of the investment's value (stocks, bonds, and real estate, for example).

Businesses like **Intel**, **General Electric**, and **Coca-Cola** invest for the same reasons. In this chapter you'll learn how to account for investments of all types. We use Intel Corporation as our example company because Intel has so many interesting investments.

Intel Corporation
Consolidated Balance Sheets (partial; adapted)
December 31, 2006

(In millions)	2006
1 Assets	
2 Current assets:	
3 Cash and cash equivalents......................................	$ 6,598
4 Short-term investments...	2,270
5 Trading assets..	1,134
6 Accounts receivable, net of allowance for	
doubtful accounts of $32 ($64 in 2005)................	2,709
7 Inventories...	4,314
8 Other current assets...	1,255
9 Total current assets..	18,280
10 Property, plant and equipment, net	17,602
11 Marketable strategic equity securities	398
12 Other long-term investments...................................	4,023
13 Goodwill...	3,861
14 Other long-term assets..	4,204
15 Total assets	$48,368

What comes to mind when you think of Intel? Computer processors and microchips? Yes, Intel produces processors and computer chips. But, interestingly, 27.5% of Intel's assets are tied up in investments of various types. The Assets section of Intel's 2006 balance sheet reports investments on lines 4, 5, 11, and 12. Some of Intel's other asset categories also include investments.

Throughout this course, you've become increasingly familiar with the financial statements of companies such as **Intel, Southwest Airlines**, and **IHOP**. You've seen most of the items that appear in a set of financial statements. One of your learning goals should be to develop the ability to analyze whatever you encounter in real-company statements. This chapter will help you advance toward that goal.

The first half of this chapter shows how to account for long-term investments, including a brief overview of consolidated financial statements. The second half of the chapter covers accounting for international operations.

LEARNING OBJECTIVES

1 **Account** for available-for-sale investments

2 **Use** the equity method for investments

3 **Understand** consolidated financial statements

4 **Account** for long-term investments in bonds

5 **Account** for international operations

6 **Report** investing transactions on the statement of cash flows

STOCK INVESTMENTS: AN OVERVIEW

Investments come in all sizes and shapes—from a few shares of stock to the acquisition of an entire company. In earlier chapters, we discussed stocks and bonds from the perspective of the company that issued the securities. In this chapter, we examine *long-term* investments.

To consider investments, we need to define 2 key terms. The entity that owns the stock of a corporation is the *investor*. The corporation that issued the stock is the *investee*. If you own some shares of Intel common stock, you are an investor and Intel is the investee.

Stock Prices

You can log onto the Internet to learn Intel's current stock price. Exhibit 10-1 presents information on Intel. During the previous 52 weeks, Intel common stock had a high price of $22.50 and a low of $16.75 per share. The annual cash dividend is $0.45 per share. During the previous day, 49.5 million shares of Intel common stock were traded. At day's end the price of the stock closed at $22.15, up $0.19 from the closing price of the preceding day.

EXHIBIT 10-1	Stock Price Information for Intel Corporation

52-Week Hi	52-Week Lo	Stock (sym)	Div	Volume	Close	Net Change
$22.50	$16.75	INTC	$0.45	49,542,200	$22.15	+ $0.19

Reporting Investments on the Balance Sheet

An investment is an asset to the investor. The investment may be short-term or long-term. **Short-term investments**—also called *marketable securities*—are current assets. To be listed as short-term on the balance sheet,

- the investment must be *liquid* (readily convertible to cash).
- the investor must intend either to convert the investment to cash within 1 year or to use it to pay a current liability.

We saw how to account for short-term investments in Chapter 5.

Investments that aren't short-term are listed as **long-term investments**, a category of noncurrent assets. Long-term investments include stocks and bonds that the investor expects to hold for longer than 1 year. Exhibit 10-2 shows where short-term and long-term investments appear on the balance sheet.

EXHIBIT 10-2	Reporting Investments on the Balance Sheet		
Current Assets:			
Cash		$X	
Short-term investments		X	
Accounts receivable		X	
Inventories		X	
Prepaid expenses		X	
Total current assets			X
Long-term investments [or simply Investments]			X
Property, plant, and equipment			X
Intangible assets			X
Other assets			X

Assets are listed in order of liquidity. Long-Term Investments are less liquid than Current Assets but more liquid than Property, Plant, and Equipment. Intel also reports short-term investments immediately after cash (p. 534).

The accounting rules for investments in stock depend on the percentage of ownership by the investor. The closer the relationship, the tighter is the accounting, as shown in Exhibit 10-3.[1]

EXHIBIT 10-3	Accounting Methods for Long-Term Investments Based on Level of Ownership

Percentage Ownership by the Investor	Similar to a Man/Woman Relationship	GAAP Accounting Method
Up to 20% ⟶	Dating Relationship ⟶	Available-for-Sale
20–50% ⟶	Girlfriend/Boyfriend ⟶	Equity
Greater than 50% ⟶	Married ⟶	Consolidation

An investment up to 20% is casual because the investor usually has almost no influence on the investee. This is like a dating relationship. Ownership between 20% and 50% provides the investor with the opportunity to significantly influence the investee, similar to a girlfriend/boyfriend arrangement. An investment above 50% of the investee's stock is like a marriage. The investor has lots of influence—perhaps control—over the investee company. Let's see how these methods apply to long-term investments in stock.

AVAILABLE-FOR-SALE INVESTMENTS

OBJECTIVE

1 **Account** for available-for-sale investments

Available-for-sale investments are stock investments other than trading securities. They are classified as current assets if the business expects to sell them within the next year. All other available-for-sale investments are classified as long term (Exhibit 10-2).

---

[1]Professor Mark Miller suggested this characterization of investments.

Accounting for Available-for-Sale Investments

Available-for-sale investments are accounted for at market value because the company expects to sell the investment at its market price. *Cost* is used only as the initial amount for recording the investments. These investments are reported on the balance sheet at **current market value**.

Suppose Intel purchases 1,000 shares of **Hewlett-Packard** common stock at the market price of $44.00. Intel intends to hold this investment for longer than a year and therefore treats it as an available-for-sale investment. Intel's entry to record the investment is:

20X7			
Oct. 23	Long-Term Investment (1,000 × $44)	44,000	
	Cash		44,000
	Purchased investment.		

Assets	=	Liabilities	+	Stockholders' Equity
+ 44,000 − 44,000	=	0	+	0

Assume that Intel receives a $0.20 cash dividend on the Hewlett-Packard stock. Intel's entry to record receipt of the dividend is

20X7			
Nov. 14	Cash (1,000 × $0.20)	200	
	Dividend Revenue		200
	Received cash dividend.		

Assets	=	Liabilities	+	Stockholders' Equity	+	Revenues
+200	=	0	+			+200

Receipt of a *stock* dividend is different from receipt of a cash dividend. For a stock dividend, the investor records no dividend revenue. Instead, the investor makes a memorandum entry in the accounting records to denote the new number of shares of stock held as an investment. Because the number of shares of stock held has increased, the investor's cost per share decreases. To illustrate, suppose Intel receives a 10% stock dividend from Hewlett-Packard Company. Intel would receive 100 shares (10% of 1,000 shares previously held) and make this memorandum entry in its accounting records:

> **MEMORANDUM—Receipt of stock dividend: Received 100 shares of Hewlett-Packard common stock in 10% stock dividend. New cost per share is $40.00 (cost of $44,000 ÷ 1,100 shares).**

In all future transactions affecting this investment, Intel's cost per share is now $40.00.

What Value of an Investment Is Most Relevant?

Market value is the amount that you can buy or sell an investment for. Because of the relevance of market values for decision making, available-for-sale investments in stock are reported on the balance sheet at their market value. On the balance-sheet date we therefore adjust available-for-sale investments from their last carrying amount to current market value. Assume that the market value of the Hewlett-Packard common stock is $46,500 on December 31, 20X7. In this case, Intel makes the following entry to bring the investment to market value.

20X7			
Dec. 31	Allowance to Adjust Investment to Market		
	($46,500 − $44,000)	2,500	
	Unrealized Gain on Investment		2,500
	Adjusted investment to market value.		

The increase in the investment's market value creates additional equity for the investor.

Assets	=	Liabilities	+	Stockholders' Equity
+ 2,500	=	0		+ 2,500

Allowance to Adjust Investment to Market is a companion account to Long-Term Investment. In this case, the investment's cost ($44,000) plus the Allowance ($2,500) equals the investment carrying amount ($46,500), as follows:

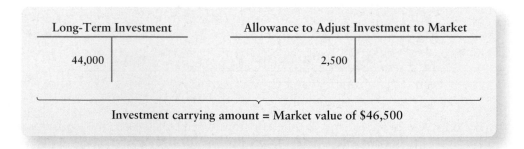

Long-Term Investment	Allowance to Adjust Investment to Market
44,000	2,500

Investment carrying amount = Market value of $46,500

Here the Allowance has a debit balance because the market value of the investment increased. If the investment's market value declines, the Allowance is credited. In that case the carrying amount is its cost minus the Allowance.

The other side of the adjustment entry (top of this page) is a credit to Unrealized Gain on Investment. If the market value of the investment declines, the company debits Unrealized Loss on Investment. *Unrealized* gains and losses result from changes in market value, not from sales of investments. For available-for-sale investments, the

Unrealized Gain account or the Unrealized Loss account is reported in 2 places in the financial statements:

- *Other comprehensive income*, which can be reported on the *income statement* in a separate section below net income
- *Accumulated other comprehensive income*, which is a separate section of stockholders' equity, below retained earnings, on the *balance sheet*

The following display shows how Intel could report its investment and the related unrealized gain in its financial statements at the end of 20X7 (all other figures are assumed for this illustration):

Balance sheet		Income statement		
Assets:				
Total current assets	$ XXX	Revenues		$50,000
Long-term investments—		Expenses, including		
at market value		income tax		36,000
($44,000 + $2,500)	46,500	Net income		$14,000
Property, plant, and equipment,		Other comprehensive income:		
net	XXX	Unrealized gain on		
Stockholders' equity:		investments	$ 2,500	
Common stock	1,000	Less Income tax		
Retained earnings	2,000	40%	(1,000)	1,500
Accumulated other		Comprehensive income		$15,500
comprehensive income:				
Unrealized gain on investments	2,500			
Total stockholders' equity	$ 5,500			

Selling an Available-for-Sale Investment

The sale of an available-for-sale investment usually results in a *realized* gain or loss. Realized gains and losses measure the difference between the amount received from the sale and the cost of the investment.

Suppose Intel sells its investment in Hewlett-Packard stock for $43,000 during 20X9. Intel would record the sale as follows:

20X9	Cash	43,000	
May 19	Loss on Sale of Investment	1,000	
	Long-Term Investment (cost)		44,000
	Sold investment.		

Assets	=	Liabilities	+	Stockholders' Equity	−	Losses
+ 43,000	=	0			−	1,000
− 44,000						

Intel would report Loss on Sale of Investments as an "Other" item on the income statement. Then at December 31, 20X9, Intel must update the Allowance to Adjust

Investment to Market and the Unrealized Gain on Investment accounts to their current balances. These adjustments are covered in intermediate accounting courses.

STOP & think...

Suppose **Intel Corporation** holds the following available-for-sale securities as long-term investments at December 31, 20X9:

Stock	Cost	Current Market Value
The Coca-Cola Company.........	$ 85,000	$71,000
Eastman Kodak Company........	16,000	12,000
	$101,000	$83,000

Show how Intel will report long-term investments on its December 31, 20X9, balance sheet.

Answer:

Assets	
Long-term investments, at market value................	$83,000

When Should We Sell an Investment?

Companies control when they sell investments, and that helps them control when they record gains and losses. Suppose a bad year hits and Intel holds an investment that has appreciated in value. Intel can sell the investment, record the gain, and boost reported income.

The cost principle of accounting provides this opportunity to "manage" earnings. If companies had to account for all investments at pure market value, there would be no gain or loss on the sale. Instead, all gains and losses would be recorded when the market value of the asset changes. That would eliminate part of management's ability to "manage" earnings. But the business community may not be ready to fully embrace market-value accounting.

EQUITY-METHOD INVESTMENTS

We use the **equity method** to account for investments in which the investor owns 20% to 50% of the investee's stock.

Buying a Large Stake in Another Company

An investor with a stock holding between 20% and 50% of the investee's voting stock may significantly influence the investee (as in a girlfriend/boyfriend relationship). Such an investor can probably affect dividend policy, product lines, and other important matters.

Intel holds equity-method investments in IM Flash Technologies and Clearwire Corporation. These investee companies are often referred to as *affiliates*; thus Clearwire is an affiliate of Intel. And because Intel has a voice in shaping the policy and operations of Clearwire, some measure of Clearwire's profits and losses should be included in Intel's income.

Accounting for Equity-Method Investments

Investments accounted for by the equity method are recorded initially at cost. Suppose Intel pays $400 million for 30% of the common stock of Clearwire Corporation. Intel's entry to record the purchase of this investment follows (in millions):

Jan. 6	Long-Term Investment	400	
	Cash		400
	To purchase equity–method investment.		

Assets	=	Liabilities	+	Stockholders' Equity
+ 400	=	0	+	0
− 400				

The Investor's Percentage of Investee Income. Under the equity method, Intel, as the investor, applies its percentage of ownership—30%, in our example—in recording its share of the investee's net income and dividends. If Clearwire reports net income of $250 million for the year, Intel records 30% of this amount as follows (in millions):

Dec. 31	Long-Term Investment ($250 × 0.30)	75	
	Equity-Method Investment Revenue		75
	To record investment revenue.		

Assets	=	Liabilities	+	Stockholders' Equity
+ 75	=	0		+ 75

Because of the close relationship between Intel and Clearwire, Intel the investor, increases the Investment account and records Investment Revenue when Clearwire the investee, reports income. As Clearwire's owners' equity increases, so does the Investment account on Intel's books.

Receiving Dividends under the Equity Method. Intel records its proportionate part of cash dividends received from Clearwire. When Clearwire declares and pays a cash dividend of $100 million, Intel receives 30% of this dividend and records this entry (in millions):

Dec. 31	Cash ($100 × 0.30)	30	
	Long-Term Investment		30
	To receive cash dividend on equity-method investment.		

Assets	=	Liabilities	+	Stockholders' Equity
+ 30	=	0	+	0
− 30				

The Investment account is *decreased* for the receipt of a dividend on an equity-method investment. Why? Because the dividend decreases the investee's owners' equity and thus the investor's investment.

After the preceding entries are posted, Intel's Investment account shows Intel's equity in the net assets of Clearwire (in millions):

Long-Term Investment			
Jan. 6 Purchase	400	Dec. 31 Dividends	30
Dec. 31 Net income	75		
Dec. 31 Balance	445		

Intel would report the long-term investment on the balance sheet and the equity-method investment revenue on the income statement as follows:

	Millions
Balance sheet (partial):	
Assets	
Total current assets..	$XXX
Long-term investments, at equity.......................	445
Property, plant, and equipment, net...................	XXX
Income statement (partial):	
Income from operations......................................	$XXX
Other revenue:	
Equity-method investment revenue................	75
Net income..	$XXX

Gain or loss on the sale of an equity-method investment is measured as the difference between the sale proceeds and the carrying amount of the investment. For example, Intel's sale of 20% of the Clearwire common stock for $81 million would be recorded as follows:

Feb. 13	Cash	81	
	Loss on Sale of Investment	8	
	Long-Term Investment ($445,000 × 0.20)		89
	Sold 20% of investment.		

Assets	=	Liabilities	+	Stockholders' Equity	−	Losses
+ 81	=	0			−	8
− 89						

Summary of the Equity Method. The following T-account illustrates the accounting for equity-method investments:

Equity-Method Investment	
Original cost	Share of losses
Share of income	Share of dividends
Balance	

CONSOLIDATED SUBSIDIARIES

Companies buy a significant stake in another company in order to *influence* the other company's operations. In this section we cover the situation in which a corporation buys enough of another company to actually *control* that company. Intel's ownership of Intel Capital is an example.

OBJECTIVE

3 **Understand** consolidated financial statements

Why Buy Another Company?

Most large corporations own controlling interests in other companies. A **controlling** (or **majority**) **interest** is the ownership of more than 50% of the investee's voting stock. Such an investment enables the investor to elect a majority of the members of the investee's board of directors and thus control the investee. The investor is called the **parent company**, and the investee company is called the **subsidiary**. For example, **Intel Capital** is a subsidiary of Intel Corporation, the parent. Therefore, the stockholders of Intel control Intel Capital, as diagrammed in Exhibit 10-4.

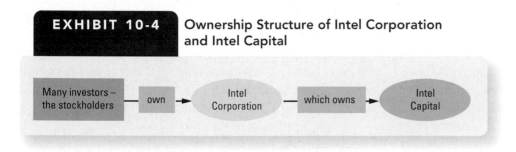

EXHIBIT 10-4 Ownership Structure of Intel Corporation and Intel Capital

Exhibit 10-5 shows some of the subsidiaries of Intel Corporation.

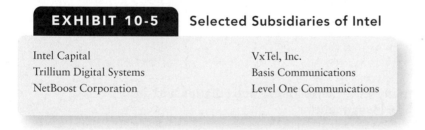

EXHIBIT 10-5 Selected Subsidiaries of Intel

Intel Capital	VxTel, Inc.
Trillium Digital Systems	Basis Communications
NetBoost Corporation	Level One Communications

Consolidation Accounting

Consolidation accounting is a method of combining the financial statements of all the companies controlled by the same stockholders. Consolidation can be likened to marriage. This method reports a single set of financial statements for the consolidated entity, which carries the name of the parent company. Exhibit 10-6 summarizes the accounting methods used for stock investments.

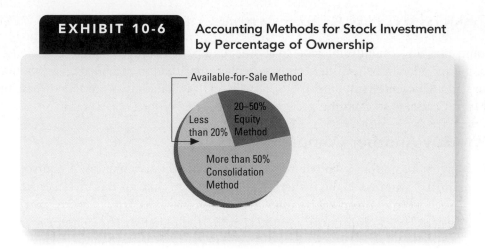

EXHIBIT 10-6 Accounting Methods for Stock Investment by Percentage of Ownership

Consolidated statements combine the balance sheets, income statements, and cash-flow statements of the parent company with those of its subsidiaries. The result is a single set of statements as if the parent and its subsidiaries were one company. Investors can gain a better perspective on total operations than they could by examining the reports of the parent and each individual subsidiary.

In consolidated statements the assets, liabilities, revenues, and expenses of each subsidiary are added to the parent's accounts. For example, the balance in Intel Capital's Cash account is added to the balance in the Intel Corporation Cash account. The sum of the 2 amounts is presented as a single amount in the Intel consolidated balance sheet. Each account balance of a subsidiary, such as Intel Capital or Net Boost Corporation loses its identity in the consolidated statements, which bear the name of the parent, Intel Corporation. When a subsidiary's financial statements get consolidated into the parent company's statements, the subsidiary's statements are no longer available to the public.

Exhibit 10-7 diagrams a corporate structure for a parent corporation that owns controlling interests in 5 subsidiaries and an equity-method investment in another investee company.

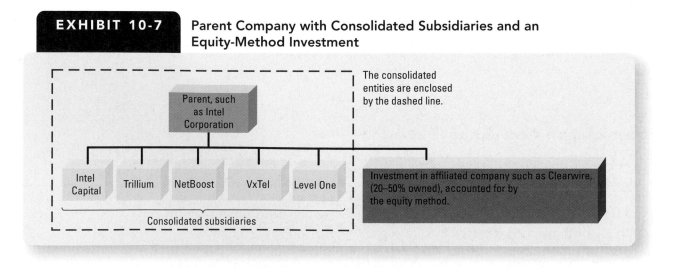

EXHIBIT 10-7 Parent Company with Consolidated Subsidiaries and an Equity-Method Investment

The Consolidated Balance Sheet and the Related Work Sheet

Intel owns all (100%) the outstanding common stock of Intel Capital. Both Intel and Intel Capital keep separate sets of books. Intel, the parent company, uses a work sheet to prepare the consolidated statements of Intel and its consolidated subsidiaries. Then Intel's consolidated balance sheet shows the combined assets and liabilities of both Intel and all its subsidiaries.

Exhibit 10-8 shows the work sheet for consolidating the balance sheets of Parent Corporation and Subsidiary Corporation. We use these hypothetical entities to illustrate the consolidation process. Consider elimination entry (a) for the parent-subsidiary ownership accounts. Entry (a) credits the parent's Investment account to eliminate its debit balance. Entry (a) also eliminates the subsidiary's stockholders' equity accounts by debiting the subsidiary's Common Stock and Retained Earnings for their full balances. Without this elimination, the consolidated financial statements would include both the parent company's investment in the subsidiary and the subsidiary company's equity. But these accounts represent the same thing—Subsidiary's equity—and so they must be eliminated from the consolidated totals. If they weren't, the same resources would be counted twice.

EXHIBIT 10-8 Work Sheet for a Consolidated Balance Sheet

	Parent Corporation	Subsidiary Corporation	Eliminations Debit	Eliminations Credit	Parent and Subsidiary Consolidated Amounts
Assets					
Cash	12,000	18,000			30,000
Note receivable from Subsidiary	80,000	—		(b) 80,000	—
Inventory	104,000	91,000			195,000
Investment in Subsidiary	150,000	—		(a) 150,000	—
Other assets	218,000	138,000			356,000
Total	564,000	247,000			581,000
Liabilities and Stockholders' Equity					
Accounts payable	43,000	17,000			60,000
Notes payable	190,000	80,000	(b) 80,000		190,000
Common stock	176,000	100,000	(a) 100,000		176,000
Retained earnings	155,000	50,000	(a) 50,000		155,000
Total	564,000	247,000	230,000	230,000	581,000

The resulting Parent and Subsidiary consolidated balance sheet (far-right column) reports no Investment in Subsidiary account. Moreover, the consolidated totals for Common Stock and Retained Earnings are those of Parent Corporation only. Study the final column of the consolidation work sheet.

In this example, Parent Corporation has an $80,000 note receivable from Subsidiary, and Subsidiary has a note payable to Parent. The parent's receivable and the subsidiary's payable represent the same resources—all entirely within the consolidated entity. Both, therefore, must be eliminated and entry (b) accomplishes this.

- The $80,000 credit in the Elimination column of the work sheet zeros out Parent's Note Receivable from Subsidiary.
- The $80,000 debit in the Elimination column zeros out the Subsidiary's Note Payable to Parent.

■ The resulting consolidated amount for notes payable is the amount owed to creditors outside the consolidated entity, which is appropriate.

After the work sheet is complete, the consolidated amount for each account represents the total asset, liability, and equity amounts controlled by Parent Corporation.

STOP & think. . .

Examine Exhibit 10-8. Why does the consolidated stockholders' equity ($176,000 + $155,000) *exclude* the equity of Subsidiary Corporation?

Answer:

The stockholders' equity of the consolidated entity is that of the parent only.

Goodwill and Minority Interest

Goodwill and Minority Interest are 2 accounts that only a consolidated entity can have. *Goodwill*, which we studied in Chapter 7, arises when a parent company pays more to acquire a subsidiary company than the market value of the subsidiary's net assets. As we saw in Chapter 7, goodwill is the intangible asset that represents the parent company's excess payment to acquire the subsidiary. GE reports goodwill on its balance sheet.

Minority interest arises when a parent company owns less than 100% of the stock of a subsidiary. For example, General Electric (GE) owns less than 100% of some of the companies it controls. The remainder of the subsidiaries' stock is minority interest to GE. Minority Interest can be included along with the liabilities on the balance sheet of the parent company.[2] GE reports minority interest on its balance sheet. By contrast, Intel reports no minority interest, so that suggests that Intel owns 100% of all its subsidiaries.

Income of a Consolidated Entity

The income of a consolidated entity is the net income of the parent plus the parent's proportion of the subsidiaries' net income. Suppose Parent Company owns all the stock of Subsidiary S-1 and 60% of the stock of Subsidiary S-2. During the year just ended, Parent earned net income of $330,000, S-1 earned $150,000, and S-2 had a net loss of $100,000. Parent Company would report net income of $420,000, computed as follows:

	Net Income (Net Loss) of Each Company		Parent's Ownership of Each Company		Parent's Consolidated Net Income (Net Loss)
Parent Company	$330,000	×	100%	=	$330,000
Subsidiary S-1	150,000	×	100%	=	150,000
Subsidiary S-2	(100,000)	×	60%	=	(60,000)
Consolidated net income					$420,000

---

[2]The FASB is considering classifying minority interest as a special category of stockholders' equity.

LONG-TERM INVESTMENTS IN BONDS

The major investors in bonds are financial institutions—pension plans, mutual funds, and insurance companies such as Intel Capital. The relationship between the issuing corporation and the investor (bondholder) may be diagrammed as follows:

OBJECTIVE

4 **Account** for long-term investments in bonds

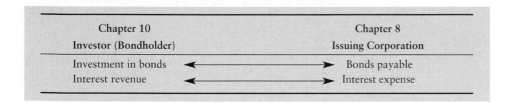

Chapter 10		Chapter 8
Investor (Bondholder)		Issuing Corporation
Investment in bonds	⟷	Bonds payable
Interest revenue	⟷	Interest expense

An investment in bonds is classified either as short-term (a current asset) or as long-term. Short-term investments in bonds are rare. Here, we focus on long-term investments called **held-to-maturity investments**.

Bond investments are recorded at cost. Years later, at maturity, the investor will receive the bonds' face value. Often bond investments are purchased at a premium or a discount. When there is a premium or discount, held-to-maturity investments are amortized to account for interest revenue and the bonds' carrying amount. Held-to-maturity investments are reported by the **amortized cost method**, which determines the carrying amount.

Suppose Intel Capital purchases $10,000 of 6% CBS bonds at a price of 95.2 on April 1, 20X5. The investor intends to hold the bonds as a long-term investment until their maturity. Interest dates are April 1 and October 1. Because these bonds mature on April 1, 20X9, they will be outstanding for 4 years (48 months). In this case the investor paid a discount price for the bonds (95.2% of face value). Intel Capital must amortize the bonds' carrying amount from cost of $9,520 up to $10,000 over their term to maturity. Assume amortization of the bonds by the straight-line method. The following are the entries for this long-term investment:

20X5			
Apr. 1	Long-Term Investment in Bonds ($10,000 × 0.952)	9,520	
	Cash		9,520
	To purchase bond investment.		
Oct. 1	Cash ($10,000 × 0.06 × 6/12)	300	
	Interest Revenue		300
	To receive semiannual interest.		
Oct. 1	Long-Term Investment in Bonds [($10,000 − $9,520)/48] × 6	60	
	Interest Revenue		60
	To amortize bond investment.		

At December 31, Intel Capital's year-end adjustments are

20X5			
Dec. 31	Interest Receivable ($10,000 × 0.06 × 3/12)	150	
	Interest Revenue		150
	To accrue interest revenue.		
Dec. 31	Long-Term Investment in Bonds [($10,000 − $9,520)/48] × 3	30	
	Interest Revenue		30
	To amortize bond investment.		

This amortization entry has 2 effects:

- It increases the Long-Term Investment account on its march toward maturity value.
- It records the interest revenue earned from the increase in the carrying amount of the investment.

The financial statements of Intel Capital at December 31, 20X5, would report the following for this investment in bonds:

Balance sheet at December 31, 20X5:
Current assets:
Interest receivable.. $ 150
Long-term investments in bonds ($9,520 + $60 + $30)   9,610
Property, plant, and equipment..   X,XXX

Income statement for the year ended December 31, 20X5:
Other revenues:
Interest revenue ($300 + $60 + $150 + $30)........................... $ 540

DECISION GUIDELINES

ACCOUNTING METHODS FOR LONG-TERM INVESTMENTS

These guidelines show which accounting method to use for each type of long-term investment. Intel has all types of investments—stocks, bonds, 25% interests, and controlling interests. How should Intel account for its various investments?

Type of Long-Term Investment	Accounting Method
Intel owns less than 20% of investee stock	Available-for-sale
Intel owns between 20% and 50% of investee/affiliate stock	Equity
Intel owns more than 50% of investee stock	Consolidation
Intel owns long-term investment in bonds (held-to-maturity investment)	Amortized cost

MID-CHAPTER SUMMARY PROBLEMS

1. Identify the appropriate accounting method for each of the following situations:
   a. Investment in 25% of investee's stock
   b. 10% investment in stock
   c. Investment in more than 50% of investee's stock
2. At what amount should the following available-for-sale investment portfolio be reported on the December 31 balance sheet? All the investments are less than 5% of the investee's stock.

Stock	Investment Cost	Current Market Value
DuPont	$ 5,000	$ 5,500
ExxonMobil	61,200	53,000
Procter & Gamble	3,680	6,230

Journalize any adjusting entry required by these data.

3. Investor paid $67,900 to acquire a 40% equity-method investment in the common stock of Investee. At the end of the first year, Investee's net income was $80,000, and Investee declared and paid cash dividends of $55,000. What is Investor's ending balance in its Equity-Method Investment account? Use a T-account to answer.
4. Parent company paid $85,000 for all the common stock of Subsidiary Company, and Parent owes Subsidiary $20,000 on a note payable. Complete the consolidation work sheet below.

	Parent Company	Subsidiary Company	Eliminations Debit	Eliminations Credit	Consolidated Amounts
Assets					
Cash	7,000	4,000			
Note receivable from Parent	—	20,000			
Investment in Subsidiary	85,000	—			
Other assets	108,000	99,000			
Total	200,000	123,000			
Liabilities and Stockholders' Equity					
Accounts payable	15,000	8,000			
Notes payable	20,000	30,000			
Common stock	120,000	60,000			
Retained earnings	45,000	25,000			
Total	200,000	123,000			

Answers
1. a. Equity   b. Available-for-sale   c. Consolidation
2. Report the investments at market value: $64,730, as follows:

(continued)

Stock	Investment Cost	Current Market Value
DuPont	$ 5,000	$ 5,500
ExxonMobil	61,200	53,000
Procter & Gamble	3,680	6,230
Totals	$69,880	$64,730

Adjusting entry:

Unrealized Loss on Investments ($69,880 – $64,730)	5,150	
Allowance to Adjust Investment to Market		5,150
To adjust investments to current market value.		

3.

Equity-Method Investment

Cost	67,900	Dividends	22,000**
Income	32,000*		
Balance	77,900		

*$80,000 × .40 = $32,000
**$55,000 × .40 = $22,000

4. Consolidation work sheet:

	Parent Company	Subsidiary Company	Eliminations Debit	Eliminations Credit	Consolidated Amounts
Assets					
Cash	7,000	4,000			11,000
Note receivable from Parent ...	—	20,000		(a) 20,000	—
Investment in Subsidiary.........	85,000	—		(b) 85,000	—
Other assets	108,000	99,000			207,000
Total	200,000	123,000			218,000
Liabilities and Stockholders' Equity					
Accounts payable....................	15,000	8,000			23,000
Notes payable.........................	20,000	30,000	(a) 20,000		30,000
Common stock	120,000	60,000	(b) 60,000		120,000
Retained earnings	45,000	25,000	(b) 25,000		45,000
Total......................................	200,000	123,000	105,000	105,000	218,000

ACCOUNTING FOR INTERNATIONAL OPERATIONS

Many U.S. companies do a large part of their business abroad. **Intel**, **General Electric**, and **PepsiCo**, among others, are very active in other countries. In fact, Intel earns 84% of its revenue outside the United States. Exhibit 10-9 shows the percentages of international revenues for these companies.

EXHIBIT 10-9 Extent of International Business

Company	Percentage of International Revenues
Intel	84%
General Electric	87
PepsiCo	41%

Accounting for business activities across national boundaries is called *international accounting*. Electronic communication makes international accounting important because investors around the world need the same data to make decisions. Therefore, the accounting in Australia needs to be the same as in Brazil and the United Kingdom. The International Accounting Standards Board (IASB) is working on a uniform set of accounting standards for the whole world.

Foreign Currencies and Exchange Rates

Most countries use their own national currency. An exception is the European Union nations—France, Germany, Italy, Belgium, and others use a common currency, the *euro*, whose symbol is €. If Intel, a U.S. company, sells computer processors to software developers in France, will Intel receive U.S. dollars or euros? If the transaction is in dollars, the company in France must buy dollars to pay Intel in U.S. currency. If the transaction is in euros, then Intel will collect euros and must sell euros for dollars.

The price of one nation's currency can be stated in terms of another country's monetary unit. This measure of one currency against another is called the **foreign-currency exchange rate**. In Exhibit 10-10, the dollar value of a euro is $1.35. This means that 1 euro can be bought for $1.35. Other currencies are also listed in Exhibit 10-10.

EXHIBIT 10-10 Foreign-Currency Exchange Rates

Country	Monetary Unit	U.S. Dollar Value	Country	Monetary Unit	U.S. Dollar Value
Brazil	Real (R)	$0.49	United Kingdom	Pound (£)	$1.99
Canada	Dollar ($)	0.91	Italy	Euro (€)	1.35
France	Euro (€)	1.35	Japan	Yen (¥)	0.0083
Germany	Euro (€)	1.35	Mexico	Peso (P)	0.092

Source: *The Wall Street Journal* (May 9, 2007), p. C14.

We can convert the cost of an item stated in one currency to its cost in a second currency. We call this conversion a *translation*. Suppose an item costs 200 euros. To compute its cost in dollars, we multiply the euro amount by the conversion rate: 200 euros × $1.35 = $270.

Two main factors affect the price (the exchange rate) of a particular currency:

1. The ratio of a country's imports to its exports.

2. The rate of return available in the country's capital markets.

The Import/Export Ratio. Japanese exports often exceed Japan's imports. Customers of Japanese companies must buy yen (the Japanese unit of currency) to pay for their purchases. This strong demand drives up the price of the yen. In contrast, the United States imports more goods than it exports. Americans must sell dollars to buy the foreign currencies needed to pay for the foreign goods. As the supply of the dollar increases, the price of a dollar falls.

The Rate of Return. The rate of return available in a country's capital markets affects the amount of investment funds flowing into the country. When rates of return are high in a politically stable country such as the United States, international investors buy stocks, bonds, and real estate in that country. This activity increases the demand for the nation's currency and drives up its exchange rate.

Currencies are often described as "strong" or "weak." The exchange rate of a **strong currency** is rising relative to other nations' currencies. The exchange rate of a **weak currency** is falling relative to other currencies.

The Wall Street Journal listed the exchange rate for the British pound as $1.99 on May 9. On May 10, that rate may rise to $2.00. We would say that the dollar has weakened against the pound. The pound has become more expensive, and that makes travel in England more expensive for Americans.

Managing Cash in International Transactions. International transactions are common. **D.E. Shipp Belting**, a family-owned company in Waco, Texas, provides an example. Shipp Belting makes conveyor belts used in a variety of industries. Farmers along the Texas–Mexico border use Shipp conveyor belts to process vegetables. Some of these customers are in Mexico, so Shipp makes sales in pesos, the Mexican monetary unit. Shipp Belting purchases inventory from Swiss companies, and some of these transactions are in Swiss francs.

Do We Collect Cash in Dollars or in Foreign Currency? Do We Pay in Dollars or in Foreign Currency?

Consider Shipp Belting's sale of conveyor belts to Artes de Mexico, a vegetable grower in Matamoros, Mexico. The sale can be conducted in dollars or in pesos. If Artes de Mexico agrees to pay in dollars, Shipp avoids the complication of dealing in a foreign currency, and the transaction is the same as selling to M&M Mars across town. But suppose Artes de Mexico orders 1 million pesos (approximately $90,000) worth of conveyor belts from Shipp. Further suppose Artes demands to pay in pesos and Shipp agrees to receive pesos instead of dollars.

Shipp will need to convert the pesos to dollars, so the transaction poses a challenge. What if the peso weakens before Shipp collects from Artes? In that case, Shipp will not collect as many dollars as expected. The following example shows how to account for international sales stated in a foreign currency.

Shipp Belting sells goods to Artes de Mexico for a price of 1 million pesos on July 28. On that date, a peso is worth $0.086. One month later, on August 28, the peso has weakened against the dollar so that a peso is worth only $0.083. Shipp receives 1 million pesos from Artes on August 28, but the dollar value of Shipp's cash receipt is $3,000 less than expected. Shipp ends up earning less than hoped for on the transaction. The following journal entries show how Shipp would account for these transactions:

July 28	Accounts Receivable—Artes (1,000,000 pesos × $0.086)	86,000	
	Sales Revenue		86,000
	Sale on account.		

Aug. 28	Cash (1,000,000 pesos × $0.083)	83,000	
	Foreign-Currency Transaction Loss	3,000	
	Accounts Receivable—Artes		86,000
	Collection on account.		

If Shipp had required Artes to pay at the time of the sale, Shipp would have received pesos worth $86,000. But by selling on account, Shipp exposed itself to *foreign-currency exchange risk.* Shipp therefore had a $3,000 foreign-currency transaction loss when it received $3,000 less cash than expected. If the peso had increased in value, Shipp would have had a foreign-currency transaction gain.

When a company holds a receivable denominated in a foreign currency, it wants the foreign currency to strengthen so that it can be converted into more dollars. Unfortunately, that did not occur for Shipp Belting.

Purchasing in a foreign currency also exposes a company to foreign-currency exchange risk. To illustrate, assume Shipp Belting buys inventory from Gesellschaft Ltd., a Swiss company. The price is 20,000 Swiss francs. On September 15 Shipp receives the goods, and the Swiss franc is quoted at $0.80. When Shipp pays 2 weeks later, the Swiss franc has weakened against the dollar—to $0.78. Shipp would record the purchase and payment as follows:

Sept. 15	Inventory (20,000 Swiss francs × $0.80)	16,000	
	Accounts Payable—Gesellschaft Ltd		16,000
	Purchase on account.		

Sept. 29	Accounts Payable—Gesellschaft Ltd	16,000	
	Cash (20,000 Swiss francs × $0.78)		15,600
	Foreign-Currency Transaction Gain		400
	Payment on account.		

The Swiss franc could have strengthened against the dollar, and Shipp would have had a foreign-currency transaction loss. A company with a payable denominated in a foreign currency wants the dollar to get stronger: The payment then costs fewer dollars.

Reporting Gains and Losses on the Income Statement

The Foreign-Currency Transaction Gain account holds gains on transactions settled in a foreign currency. Likewise, the Foreign-Currency Transaction Loss account holds losses on transactions conducted in foreign currencies. Report the *net amount* of these 2 accounts on the income statement as Other Revenues and Gains, or Other Expenses and Losses, as the case may be. For example, Shipp Belting would combine its $3,000 foreign-currency loss and the $400 gain and report the net loss of $2,600 on the income statement as follows:

Other Expenses and Losses:	
Foreign-currency transaction loss, net	$2,600

These gains and losses fall into the "Other" category because they arise from buying and selling foreign currencies, not from the company's main business (in the case of D.E. Shipp Belting, selling conveyor belts).

Should We Hedge Our Foreign-Currency-Transaction Risk?

One way for U.S. companies to avoid foreign-currency transaction losses is to insist that international transactions be settled in dollars. This requirement puts the burden of currency translation on the foreign party. But this approach may alienate customers and decrease sales. Another way for a company to protect itself is by hedging. **Hedging** means to protect oneself from losing money in 1 transaction by engaging in a counterbalancing transaction.

A U.S. company selling goods to be collected in Mexican pesos expects to receive a fixed number of pesos. If the peso is losing value, the U.S. company would expect the pesos to be worth fewer dollars than the amount of the receivable—an expected loss situation, as we saw for Shipp Belting.

The U.S. company may have accumulated payables in a foreign currency, such as Shipp's payable to the Swiss company. Losses on pesos may be offset by gains on Swiss francs. Most companies do not have equal amounts of receivables and payables in foreign currency. To obtain a more precise hedge, companies can buy *futures contracts*. These are contracts for foreign currencies to be received in the future. Futures contracts can create a payable to exactly offset a receivable, and vice versa. Many companies that do business internationally use hedging techniques.

Consolidation of Foreign Subsidiaries

A U.S. company with a foreign subsidiary must consolidate the subsidiary's financial statements into its own statements for reporting to the public. The consolidation of a foreign subsidiary poses 2 special challenges:

1. Many foreign countries require accounting treatments that differ from American accounting principles. For reporting to the American public, the subsidiary's statements must conform to American generally accepted accounting principles (GAAP).

2. The subsidiary's statements may be expressed in a foreign currency. First, we must translate the subsidiary's statements into dollars. Then the 2 companies' financial statements can be consolidated as illustrated in Exhibit 10-8.

The process of translating a foreign subsidiary's financial statements into dollars usually creates a *foreign-currency translation adjustment*. This item appears in the financial statements of most multinational companies and is reported as part of other comprehensive income on the income statement and as part of stockholders' equity on the consolidated balance sheet.

A translation adjustment arises due to changes in the foreign exchange rate over time. In general,

- *assets* and *liabilities* are translated into dollars at the current exchange rate on the date of the statements.
- *Stockholders' equity* is translated into dollars at older, historical exchange rates.

This difference in exchange rates creates an out-of-balance condition on the balance sheet. The translation adjustment brings the balance sheet back into balance. Let's see how the translation adjustment works.

Suppose Intel has an Italian subsidiary whose financial statements are expressed in euros (the European currency). Intel must consolidate the Italian subsidiary's financials into its own statements. When Intel acquired the Italian company in 20X6, a euro was worth $1.35. When the Italian firm earned its retained income during 20X6–20X9, the average exchange rate was $1.30. On the balance sheet date in 20X9, a euro is worth only $1.20. Exhibit 10-11 shows how to translate the Italian company's balance sheet into dollars.

EXHIBIT 10-11   Translation of a Foreign-Currency Balance Sheet into Dollars

Italian Imports, Inc., Accounts	Euros	Exchange Rate	Dollars
Assets	800,000	$1.20	$960,000
Liabilities	500,000	1.20	$600,000
Stockholders' equity			
Common stock	100,000	1.35	135,000
Retained earnings	200,000	1.30	260,000
Accumulated other comprehensive income:			
Foreign-currency translation adjustment			(35,000)
	800,000		$960,000

The **foreign-currency translation adjustment** is the balancing amount that brings the dollar amount of liabilities and equity of a foreign subsidiary into agreement with the dollar amount of total assets (in Exhibit 10-11, total assets equal $960,000). Only after the translation adjustment of $35,000 do total liabilities and equity equal total assets stated in dollars.

What caused the negative translation adjustment? The euro weakened after the acquisition of the Italian company.

- When Intel acquired the foreign subsidiary in 20X6, a euro was worth $1.35.
- When the Italian company earned its income during 20X6 through 20X9, the average exchange rate was $1.30.
- On the balance sheet date in 20X9, a euro is worth only $1.20.
- Thus, the Italian company's equity (assets minus liabilities) are translated into only $360,000 ($960,000 − $600,000).
- To bring stockholders' equity to $360,000 requires a $35,000 negative adjustment.

In a sense, a negative translation adjustment is like a loss, reported as a contra item in the stockholders' equity section of the balance sheet, as in Exhibit 10-11. The Italian firm's dollar figures in Exhibit 10-11 are what Intel would include in its consolidated balance sheet. The consolidation procedures would follow those illustrated beginning on page 543.

International Accounting Standards

In this text, we focus on the accounting principles that are generally accepted in the United States. Most accounting methods are consistent throughout the world. Double-entry accounting, the accrual system, and the basic financial statements are used worldwide. Differences, however, do exist among countries, as shown in Exhibit 10-12.

EXHIBIT 10-12 Some International Accounting Differences

Country	Inventories	Goodwill	Research and Development Costs
United States	Specific unit cost, FIFO, LIFO, and average cost	Record any loss in value of goodwill	Expensed as incurred
Germany	Similar to U.S.	Amortized over 5 years	Expensed as incurred
Japan	Similar to U.S.	Amortized over 5 years	May be capitalized and amortized over 5 years
United Kingdom	LIFO is unacceptable for tax purposes and is not widely used.	Amortized over useful life or not amortized if life is indefinite.	Expense research costs. Some development costs may be capitalized.

In discussing depreciation (Chapter 7), we emphasized that in the United States, the accounting methods used for reporting to tax authorities differ from the methods used for reporting to shareholders. However, tax reporting and shareholder reporting are identical in many countries.

Several organizations are working to achieve worldwide harmony of accounting standards. Chief among these is the *IASB*, which operates much as the Financial

Accounting Standards Board (FASB) in the United States. It has the support of the accounting professions in the United States, most of the British Commonwealth countries, Japan, France, Germany, the Netherlands, and Mexico. However, the IASB has no authority to require compliance. It must rely on cooperation by the various national accounting professions.

INVESTING ACTIVITIES ON THE STATEMENT OF CASH FLOWS

Investing activities include many types of transactions. In Chapter 7, we covered the purchase and sale of long-term assets such as plant and equipment. In this chapter, we examine investments in stocks and bonds.

Exhibit 10-13 provides excerpts from Intel's statement of cash flows. During 2006, Intel sold available-for-sale investments and received $7.1 billion of cash. Intel bought available-for-sale investments for $5.3 billion and equity-method investments for $1.7 billion. These actual investing activities relate directly to the topics you studied in this chapter.

OBJECTIVE

6 **Report** investing transactions on the statement of cash flows

EXHIBIT 10-13	**Intel Corporation Statement of Cash Flows (Partial, Adapted)**

Intel Corporation
Statement of Cash Flows

(In billions)	2006
Cash flows provided by (used for) investing activities:	
Sales of available-for-sale investments	$ 7.1
Purchases of available-for-sale investments	(5.3)
Additions to property, plant, and equipment	(5.8)
Purchases of equity-method investments	(1.7)
Proceeds from selling subsidiary companies	0.8
Net cash (used for) investing activities	$(4.9)

END-OF-CHAPTER SUMMARY PROBLEM

Translate the balance sheet of the Brazilian subsidiary of **Wrangler Corporation**, a U.S. company, into dollars. When Wrangler acquired this subsidiary, the exchange rate of the Brazilian currency, the real, was $0.40. The average exchange rate applicable to retained earnings is $0.41. The real's current exchange rate is $0.43.

Before performing the translation, predict whether the translation adjustment will be positive or negative. Does this situation generate a foreign-currency translation gain or loss? Give your reasons.

	Reals
Assets	900,000
Liabilities	600,000
Stockholders' equity:	
Common stock	30,000
Retained earnings	270,000
	900,000

Answer

Translation of foreign-currency balance sheet:

This situation will generate a *positive* translation adjustment, which is like a gain. The gain occurs because the real's current exchange rate, which is used to translate net assets (assets minus liabilities), exceeds the historical exchange rates used for stockholders' equity.

The calculation follows.

	Reals	Exchange Rate	Dollars
Assets	900,000	0.43	$387,000
Liabilities	600,000	0.43	$258,000
Stockholders' equity:			
Common stock	30,000	0.40	12,000
Retained earnings	270,000	0.41	110,700
Accumulated other comprehensive income: Foreign-currency translation adjustment	—		6,300
	900,000		$387,000

REVIEW LONG-TERM INVESTMENTS AND INTERNATIONAL OPERATIONS

Quick Check (Answers are given on page 578.)

1. Intel's investment in less than 1% of GE's stock, which Intel expects to hold for 2 years and then sell, is which type of investment?
   a. Trading
   b. Equity
   c. Available-for-sale
   d. Consolidation

2. DuBois Corporation purchased an available-for-sale investment in 1,000 shares of Microsoft stock for $31 per share. On the next balance-sheet date, Microsoft stock is quoted at $35 per share. DuBois' *balance sheet* should report
   a. unrealized loss of $4,000.
   b. unrealized gain of $31,000.
   c. investments of $31,000.
   d. investments of $35,000.

3. Use the DuBois Corporation data in question 2. DuBois' *income statement* should report
   a. unrealized gain of $4,000.
   b. unrealized loss of $4,000.
   c. investments of $31,000.
   d. nothing because DuBois hasn't sold the investment.

4. Use the DuBois Corporation data in question 2. DuBois sold the Microsoft stock for $40,000 2 years later. DuBois' *income statement* should report
   a. unrealized gain of $4,000.
   b. gain on sale of $9,000.
   c. gain on sale of $5,000.
   d. investments of $40,000.

5. Alexander Moving & Storage Co. paid $100,000 for 20% of the common stock of Sellers Co. Sellers earned net income of $50,000 and paid dividends of $25,000. The carrying value of Alexander's investment in Sellers is
   a. $100,000.
   b. $105,000.
   c. $125,000.
   d. $150,000.

6. Tarrant, Inc., owns 80% of Rockwall Corporation, and Rockwall owns 80% of Kaufman Company. During 20X6, these companies' net incomes are as follows before any consolidations:
   - Tarrant $100,000
   - Rockwall $68,000
   - Kaufman $40,000

   How much net income should Tarrant report for 20X6?
   a. $100,000
   b. $164,000
   c. $180,000
   d. $204,000

7. **iPod, Inc.**, holds an investment in Coca-Cola bonds that pay interest each June 30. iPod's *balance sheet* at December 31 should report
   a. Interest receivable.
   b. Interest payable.
   c. Interest revenue.
   d. Interest expense.

8. You are taking a vacation to France, and you buy euros for $1.35. On your return you cash in your unused euros for $1.29. During your vacation
   a. the dollar lost value.
   b. the euro rose against the dollar.
   c. the euro gained value.
   d. the dollar rose against the euro.

9. Wood County, Texas, purchased earth-moving equipment from a Canadian company. The cost was $1,000,000 Canadian, and the Canadian dollar was quoted at $0.93. A month later, Wood County paid its debt, and the Canadian dollar was quoted at $0.95. What was Wood County's cost of the equipment?
   a. $20,000
   b. $930,000
   c. $950,000
   d. $1,020,000

10. Intel owns numerous foreign subsidiary companies. When Intel consolidates its British subsidiary, Intel should translate the subsidiary's assets into dollars at the
    a. historical exchange rate when Intel purchased the British company.
    b. average exchange rate during the period Intel owned the British subsidiary.
    c. current exchange rate.
    d. none of the above. There's no need to translate the subsidiary's assets into dollars.

Accounting Vocabulary

Available-for-sale investments (p. 536) All investments not classified as held-to-maturity or trading securities.

Consolidated statements (p. 544) Financial statements of the parent company plus those of majority-owned subsidiaries as if the combination were a single legal entity

Controlling interest (p. 543) Ownership of more than 50% of an investee company's voting stock.

Equity method (p. 540) The method used to account for investments in which the investor has 20–50% of the investee's voting stock and can significantly influence the decisions of the investee.

Foreign-currency exchange rate (p. 551) The measure of one country's currency against another country's currency.

Foreign-currency translation adjustment (p. 555) The balancing figure that brings the dollar amount of the total liabilities and stockholders' equity of the foreign subsidiary into agreement with the dollar amount of its total assets.

Hedging (p. 554) To protect oneself from losing money in one transaction by engaging in a counterbalancing transaction.

Held-to-maturity investments (p. 547) Bonds and notes that an investor intends to hold until maturity.

Long-term investments (p. 535) Any investment that does not meet the criteria of a short-term investment; any investment that the investor expects to hold longer than a year or that is not readily marketable.

Majority interest (p. 543) Ownership of more than 50% of an investee company's voting stock.

Marketable securities (p. 535) Investment that a company plans to hold for 1 year or less. Also called *marketable securities.*

Minority interest (p. 546) A subsidiary company's equity that is held by stockholders other than the parent company.

Parent company (p. 543) An investor company that owns more than 50% of the voting stock of a subsidiary company.

Short-term investments (p. 535) Investment that a company plans to hold for 1 year or less. Also called *marketable securities.*

Strong currency (p. 552) A currency whose exchange rate is rising relative to other nations' currencies.

Subsidiary company (p. 543) An investee company in which a parent company owns more than 50% of the voting stock.

Weak currency (p. 552) A currency whose exchange rate is falling relative to that of other nations.

ASSESS YOUR PROGRESS

Short Exercises

S10-1 (*Learning Objective 1: Accounting for an available-for-sale investment; unrealized gain or loss*) Assume **UPS** completed these long-term available-for-sale investment transactions during 20X7:

20X7	
Apr. 10	Purchased 300 shares of **Sysco** stock, paying $20 per share. UPS intends to hold the investment for the indefinite future.
July 22	Received a cash dividend of $1.25 per share on the Sysco stock.
Dec. 31	Adjusted the Sysco investment to its current market value of $5,100.

1. Journalize UPS's investment transactions. Explanations are not required. (pp. 537–539)
2. Show how to report the investment and any unrealized gain or loss on UPS's balance sheet at December 31, 20X8. Ignore income tax. (pp. 538–539)

S10-2 (*Learning Objective 1: Accounting for the sale of an available-for-sale investment*) Use the data given in Short Exercise S10-1. On May 19, 20X9, UPS sold its investment in Sysco stock for $22 per share.

1. Journalize the sale. No explanation is required. (pp. 539–540)
2. How does the gain or loss that you recorded here differ from the gain or loss that was recorded at December 31, 20X7? (pp. 539–540)

S10-3 (*Learning Objective 2: Accounting for a 40% investment in another company*) Suppose on February 1, 20X8, **General Motors** paid $410 million for a 40% investment in **Isuzu Motors**. Assume Isuzu earned net income of $60 million and paid cash dividends of $20 million during 20X8.

1. What method should General Motors use to account for the investment in Isuzu? Give your reason. (p. 540)
2. Journalize these 3 transactions on the books of General Motors. Show all amounts in millions of dollars and include an explanation for each entry. (p. 541)
3. Post to the Long-Term Investment T-account. What is its balance after all the transactions are posted? (p. 542)

S10-4 (*Learning Objective 2: Accounting for the sale of an equity-method investment*) Use the data given in Short Exercise S10-3. Assume that in November 20X9, General Motors sold half its investment in Isuzu to Toyota. The sale price was $140 million. Compute General Motors' gain or loss on the sale. (p. 542)

S10-5 (*Learning Objective 3: Understanding consolidated financial statements*) Answer these questions about consolidation accounting: (pp. 543–544)

1. Define *parent company*. Define *subsidiary company*.
2. How do consolidated financial statements differ from the financial statements of a single company?
3. Which company's name appears on the consolidated financial statements? How much of the subsidiary's stock must the parent own before reporting consolidated statements?

S10-6 (*Learning Objective 3: Understanding goodwill and minority interest*) Two accounts that arise from consolidation accounting are goodwill and minority interest. (p. 546)

writing assignment ■

1. What is goodwill, and how does it arise? Which company reports goodwill, the parent or the subsidiary? Where is goodwill reported?
2. What is minority interest, and which company reports it, the parent or the subsidiary? Where is minority interest reported?

S10-7 (*Learning Objective 4: Working with a bond investment*) **Prudential Bache (PB)** owns vast amounts of corporate bonds. Suppose PB buys $1,000,000 of **CitiCorp** bonds at a price of 101. The CitiCorp bonds pay cash interest at the annual rate of 7% and mature at the end of 5 years. (pp. 547–548)

1. How much did PB pay to purchase the bond investment? How much will PB collect when the bond investment matures?
2. How much cash interest will PB receive each year from CitiCorp?
3. Will PB's annual interest revenue on the bond investment be more or less than the amount of cash interest received each year? Give your reason.
4. Compute PB's annual interest revenue on this bond investment. Use the straight-line method to amortize the investment.

S10-8 (*Learning Objective 4: Recording bond investment transactions*) Return to Short Exercise S10-7, the **Prudential Bache (PB)** investment in **CitiCorp** bonds. Journalize on PB's books: (pp. 547–548)

    a. Purchase of the bond investment on June 30, 20X1. PB expects to hold the investment to maturity.
    b. Receipt of semiannual cash interest on December 31, 20X1.
    c. Amortization of the bonds on December 31, 20X1. Use the straight-line method.
    d. Collection of the investment's face value at the maturity date on January 2, 20X6. (Assume the receipt of 20X5 interest and the amortization of bonds for 20X5 have already been recorded, so ignore these entries.)

S10-9 (*Learning Objective 5: Accounting for transactions stated in a foreign currency*) Suppose **Dr. Pepper** sells soft drink syrup to a Russian company on September 14. Dr. Pepper agrees to accept 200,000 Russian rubles. On the date of sale, the ruble is quoted at $0.34. Dr. Pepper collects

(continued)

half the receivable on October 19, when the ruble is worth $0.30. Then on November 10, when the foreign-exchange rate of the ruble is $0.35, Dr. Pepper collects the final amount.

Journalize these 3 transactions for Dr. Pepper. (pp. 552–553)

S10-10 (*Learning Objective 5: Accounting for transactions stated in a foreign currency*) **Shipp Belting** sells goods for 1,000,000 Mexican pesos. The foreign-exchange rate for a peso is $0.090 on the date of sale. Shipp Belting then collects cash on August 28, when the exchange rate for a peso is $0.092. Record Shipp's cash collection.

Shipp Belting buys inventory for 20,000 Swiss francs. A Swiss franc costs $0.81 on the purchase date. Record Shipp Belting's payment of cash on September 29, when the exchange rate for a Swiss Franc is $0.85.

In these two scenarios, which currencies strengthened? Which currencies weakened? (pp. 551–552)

writing assignment ■

S10-11 (*Learning Objective 5: International accounting differences*) Exhibit 10-11, page 555, outlines some differences between accounting in the United States and accounting in other countries. American companies transact a lot of business with British companies. But there are important differences between American and British accounting. In your own words, describe these differences for inventories, goodwill, and research and development.

S10-12 (*Learning Objective 6: Reporting cash flows*) Companies divide their cash flows into 3 categories for reporting on the statement of cash flows. (p. 557)

1. List the 3 categories of cash flows in the order they appear on the statement of cash flows. Which category of cash flows is most closely related to this chapter?

2. Identify 2 types of transactions that companies report as cash flows from investing activities.

Exercises

■ general ledger

E10-13 (*Learning Objective 1: Journalizing transactions for an available-for-sale investment*) Journalize the following long-term available-for-sale investment transactions of Solomon Brothers Department Stores: (pp. 537–539)

    a. Purchased 400 shares of **Kraft Foods** common stock at $32 per share, with the intent of holding the stock for the indefinite future.

    b. Received cash dividend of $1 per share on the Kraft investment.

    c. At year end, adjusted the investment account to current market value of $38 per share.

    d. Sold the Kraft stock for the market price of $23 per share.

E10-14 (*Learning Objective 1: Accounting for long-term investments*) Dow-Smith Co. bought 3,000 shares of **Hong Kong** common stock at $37; 600 shares of **Beijing** stock at $46.75; and 1,400 shares of **Shanghai** stock at $79—all as available-for-sale investments. At December 31, **Hoover's Online** reports Hong Kong stock at $29.125, Beijing at $48.50, and Shanghai at $68.25.

I *Required*

1. Determine the cost and the market value of the long-term investment portfolio at December 31. (pp. 537–538)

2. Record Dow-Smith's adjusting entry at December 31. (pp. 538–539)

3. What would Dow-Smith report on its income statement and balance sheet for the information given? Make the necessary disclosures. Ignore income tax. (pp. 538–539)

E10-15 (*Learning Objective 2: Accounting for transactions under the equity method*) **Intel Corporation** owns equity-method investments in several companies. Suppose Intel paid $1,000,000 to acquire a 25% investment in Thai Software Company. Thai Software reported net income of $640,000 for the first year and declared and paid cash dividends of $420,000.

1. Record the following in Intel's journal: (a) purchase of the investment, (b) Intel's proportion of Thai Software's net income, and (c) receipt of the cash dividends.

2. What is the ending balance in Intel's investment account? (p. 541)

E10-16 (*Learning Objective 2: Measuring gain or loss on the sale of an equity-method investment*) Without making journal entries, record the transactions of Exercise 10-15 directly in the **Intel** account, Long-Term Investment in Thai Software. Assume that after all the noted transactions took place, Intel sold its entire investment in Thai Software for cash of $2,700,000. How much is Intel's gain or loss on the sale of the investment? (p. 542)

E10-17 (*Learning Objective 2: Applying the appropriate accounting method for a 30% investment*) Oaktree Financial paid $500,000 for a 25% investment in the common stock of eTrav, Inc. For the first year, eTrav reported net income of $200,000 and at year end declared and paid cash dividends of $100,000. On the balance-sheet date, the market value of Oaktree's investment in eTrav stock was $384,000.

I **Required**

1. Which method is appropriate for Oaktree Financial to use in accounting for its investment in eTrav? Why? (p. 540)

2. Show everything that Oaktree would report for the investment and any investment revenue in its year-end financial statements. (p. 542)

E10-18 (*Learning Objective 3: Preparing a consolidated balance sheet*) Alfa, Inc., owns Romeo Corp. The 2 companies' individual balance sheets follow:

■ **spreadsheet**

	Alfa	Romeo
Assets		
Cash	$ 49,000	$ 14,000
Accounts receivable, net	82,000	53,000
Note receivable from Alfa	—	42,000
Inventory	55,000	77,000
Investment in Romeo	100,000	—
Plant assets, net	286,000	99,000
Other assets	22,000	8,000
Total	$594,000	$293,000
Liabilities and Stockholders' Equity		
Accounts payable	$ 44,000	$ 26,000
Notes payable	147,000	36,000
Other liabilities	82,000	131,000
Common stock	210,000	80,000
Retained earnings	111,000	20,000
Total	$594,000	$293,000

I **Required**

1. Prepare the consolidated balance sheet of Alfa, Inc. It is sufficient to complete the consolidation work sheet. (p. 545)

2. What is the amount of stockholders' equity for the consolidated entity? (p. 546)

E10-19 (*Learning Objective 4: Recording bond investment transactions*) Assume that on September 30, 20X3, **Fiat, Inc.**, paid 97 for 6 1/2% bonds of Skoda Corporation as a long-term held-to-maturity investment. The maturity value of the bonds will be $20,000 on September 30, 20X8. The bonds pay interest on March 31 and September 30.

I **Required**

1. What method should Fiat use to account for its investment in the Skoda bonds? (pp. 547–548)

2. Using the straight-line method of amortizing the bonds, journalize all of Fiat's transactions on the bonds for 20X3. (pp. 547–548)

3. Show how Fiat would report everything related to the bond investment on its balance sheet at December 31, 20X3. (p. 548)

E10-20 (*Learning Objective 5: Managing and accounting for foreign-currency transactions*)
Assume that **Circuit City Stores** completed the following foreign-currency transactions:

Mar. 17	Purchased DVD players as inventory on account from **Sony**. The price was 300,000 yen, and the exchange rate of the yen was $0.0086.
Apr. 16	Paid Sony when the exchange rate was $0.0082.
19	Sold merchandise on account to **BonTemps**, a French company, at a price of 60,000 euros. The exchange rate was $1.20
30	Collected from BonTemps when the exchange rate was $1.15.

1. Journalize these transactions for Circuit City. Focus on the gains and losses caused by changes in foreign-currency rates. (pp. 552–553)

2. On March 18, immediately after the purchase, and on April 20, immediately after the sale, which currencies did Circuit City want to strengthen? Which currencies did in fact strengthen? Explain your reasoning in detail. (pp. 552–553)

E10-21 (*Learning Objective 5: Translating a foreign-currency balance sheet into dollars*)
Translate into dollars the balance sheet of California Leather Goods' Spanish subsidiary. When California Leather Goods acquired the foreign subsidiary, a euro was worth $1.01. The current exchange rate is $1.35. During the period when retained earnings were earned, the average exchange rate was $1.15 per euro (pp. 554–555)

	Euros
Assets.....................................	500,000
Liabilities	300,000
Stockholders' equity:	
Common stock....................	50,000
Retained earnings...............	150,000
	500,000

During the period covered by this situation, which currency was stronger, the dollar or the euro? (pp. 552–553)

E10-22 (*Learning Objective 6: Preparing and using the statement of cash flows*) During fiscal year 20X6, **Krispy Kreme Doughnuts** reported net loss of $135.8 million. Krispy Kreme received $1.0 million from the sale of other businesses. Krispy Kreme made capital expenditures of $10.4 million and sold property, plant, and equipment for $7.3 million. The company purchased long-term investments at a cost of $12.2 million and sold other long-term investments for $2.5 million.

▌*Required*
Prepare the investing activities section of Krispy Kreme's statement of cash flows. Based solely on Krispy Kreme's investing activities, does it appear that the company is growing or shrinking? How can you tell? (pp. 557, 619, 639)

E10-23 (*Learning Objective 6: Using the statement of cash flows*) At the end of the year, Blue Chip Properties' statement of cash flows reported the following for investment activities:

Blue Chip Properties
Consolidated Statement of Cash Flows (Partial)

Cash flows from Investing Activities	
Notes receivable collected	$ 3,110,000
Purchases of short-term investments...	(3,457,000)
Proceeds from sales of equipment...	1,409,000*
Proceeds from sales of investments (cost of $450,000)..............	461,000
Expenditures for property and equipment.................................	(1,761,000)
Net cash used by investing activities...	$ (238,000)

*Cost $5,100,000; Accumulated depreciation, $3,691,000.

I *Required*

For each item listed, make the journal entry that placed the item on Blue Chip's statement of cash flows. (pp. 97, 99, 259, 382, 539)

Challenge Exercises

E10-24 (*Learning Objective 1, 2, 3, 5: Accounting for various types of investments*) This exercise summarizes the accounting for investments. Suppose **YouTube.com** owns the following investments at December 31, 20X1:

  a. 100% of the common stock of YouTube United Kingdom, which holds assets of £800,000 and owes a total of £600,000. At December 31, 20X1, the current exchange rate of the pound (£) is £1 = $2.00. The translation rate of the pound applicable to stockholders' equity is £1 = $1.60. During 20X1, YouTube United Kingdom earned net income of £100,000 and the average exchange rate for the year was £1 = $1.95. YouTube United Kingdom paid cash dividends of £40,000 during 20X1.
  b. Investments that YouTube is holding to sell. These investments cost $900,000 and declined in value by $400,000 during 20X1, but they paid cash dividends of $16,000 to YouTube. One year ago, at December 31, 20X0, the market value of these investments was $1,100,000.
  c. 25% of the common stock of YouTube Financing Associates. During 20X1, YouTube Financing earned net income of $300,000 and declared and paid cash dividends of $80,000. The carrying amount of this investment was $700,000 at December 31, 20X0.

I *Required*

  1. Which method is used to account for each investment? (pp. 536–537, 540, 543–544)
  2. By how much did each of these investments increase or decrease YouTube's net income during 20X1? (pp. 539, 542, 546)
  3. For investments b and c, show how YouTube would report these investments on its balance sheet at December 31, 20X1. (pp. 536–537, 542)

E10-25 (*Learning Objective 1, 6: Explaining and analyzing accumulated other comprehensive income*) Big-Box Retail Corporation reported stockholders' equity on its balance sheet at December 31, as follows:

Big-Box Retail Balance Sheet (Partial)	
Shareholders' Equity:	Millions
Common stock, $0.10 par value—	
800 million shares authorized,	
300 million shares issued	$ 30
Additional paid-in capital	1,088
Retained earnings...	6,250
Accumulated other comprehensive (loss)...............	(?)
Less Treasury stock, at cost....................................	(50)

I Required

1. Identify the 2 components that typically make up Accumulated other comprehensive income. (pp. 539, 555–556)

2. For each component of Accumulated other comprehensive income, describe the event that can cause a *positive* balance. Also describe the events that can cause a *negative* balance for each component. (pp. 539, 555–556)

3. At December 31, 20X2, Big-Box's Accumulated other comprehensive loss was $53 million. Then during 20X3, Big-Box had a positive foreign-currency translation adjustment of $29 million and an unrealized loss of $16 million on available-for-sale investments. What was Big-Box's balance of Accumulated other comprehensive income (loss) at December 31, 20X3? (pp. 555–556)

Quiz

Test your understanding of long-term investments and international operations by answering the following questions. Select the best choice from among the possible answers given.

Questions 26–28 use the following data:
Assume that Fox Networks owns the following long-term available-for-sale investments:

Company	Number of Shares	Cost Per Share	Current Market Value Per Share	Dividend Per Share
Airbus Corp.	1,000	$60	$71	$2
Whole Grains, Inc.	200	9	11	1.50
MySpace Ltd.	500	20	24	1

Q10-26 Fox's balance sheet should report (p. 539)
a. investments of $85,200.
b. investments of $81,200.
c. dividend revenue $2,800.
d. unrealized loss of $13,400.

Q10-27 Fox's income statement should report (pp. 538–539)
a. investments of $71,800.   c. unrealized gain of $13,400.
b. gain on sale of investment of $13,400.   d. dividend revenue of $2,800.

Q10-28 Suppose Fox sells the Airbus stock for $68 per share. Journalize the sale. (p. 539)

Q10-29 Dividends received on an equity-method investment (p. 541)
a. increase the investment account.   c. increase dividend revenue.
b. decrease the investment account.   d. increase owners' equity.

Q10-30 The starting point in accounting for all investments is (pp. 536–537, 541)
a. market value on the balance-sheet date.   c. cost.
b. equity value.   d. cost minus dividends.

Q10-31 Consolidation accounting (pp. 543–544)
a. combines the accounts of the parent company and those of the subsidiary companies.
b. eliminates all liabilities.
c. reports the receivables and payables of the parent company only.
d. all of the above.

Q10-32 On January 1, 20X1, Microloft, Inc., purchased $100,000 face value of the 7% bonds of Mail Frontier, Inc., at 105. The bonds mature on January 1, 20X6. For the year ended December 31, 20X4, Microloft received cash interest of (pp. 547–548)
a. $5,000.   c. $6,400.
b. $6,000.   d. $7,000.

Q10-33 Return to Microloft, Inc.'s, bond investment in the preceding question. For the year ended December 31, 20X1, Microloft earned interest revenue of (p. 548)
a. $5,000.   c. $7,000.
b. $6,000.   d. $8,000.

Q10-34 Yukon Systems purchased inventory on account from **Panasonic**. The price was ¥100,000, and a yen was quoted at $0.0090. Yukon paid the debt in yen a month later, when the price of a yen was $0.0092. Yukon (pp. 552–554)
a. debited Inventory for $900.
b. debited Inventory for $920.
c. recorded a Foreign-Currency Transaction Loss of $80.
d. None of the above.

Q10-35 One way to hedge a foreign-currency transaction loss is to (pp. 553–554)
a. pay in the foreign currency.   c. offset foreign-currency inventory and
b. collect in your own currency.   plant assets.
                                              d. pay debts as late as possible.

Q10-36 Foreign-currency transaction gains and losses are reported on the (pp. 553–554)
a. balance sheet.   c. statement of cash flows.
b. consolidation work sheet.   d. income statement.

Q10-37 Consolidation of a foreign subsidiary usually results in a (pp. 555–556)
a. gain or loss on consolidation.   c. foreign-currency translation adjustment.
b. LIFO/FIFO difference.   d. foreign-currency transaction gain or loss.

Problems
(Group A)

MyAccountingLab

> Some of these A problems can be found within My Accounting Lab (MAL), an online homework and practice environment. Your instructor may ask you to complete these exercises using MAL.

P10-38A (*Learning Objective 1, 2: Reporting investments on the balance sheet and the related revenue on the income statement*) Washington Exchange Company completed the following long-term investment transactions during 20X6.

20X6	
May 12	Purchased 20,000 shares, which make up 35% of the common stock of Fellingham Corporation at total cost of $370,000.
July 9	Received annual cash dividend of $1.26 per share on the Fellingham investment.
Sept. 16	Purchased 800 shares of Tomassini, Inc., common stock as an available-for-sale investment, paying $41.50 per share.
Oct. 30	Received cash dividend of $0.30 per share on the Tomassini investment.
Dec. 31	Received annual report from Fellingham Corporation. Net income for the year was $510,000.

At year end the current market value of the Tomassini stock is $30,600. The market value of the Fellingham stock is $652,000.

❚ Required

1. For which investment is current market value used in the accounting? Why is market value used for 1 investment and not the other? (pp. 537–538, 541)
2. Show what Washington would report on its year-end balance sheet and income statement for these investment transactions. It is helpful to use a T-account for the Long-Term Investment in Fellingham Stock account. Ignore income tax. (pp. 538–539, 542)

■ general ledger

P10-39A (*Learning Objective 1, 2: Accounting for available-for-sale and equity-method investments*) The beginning balance sheet of NASDOQ Corporation included the following:

Long-Term Investment in MSC Software (equity-method investment)	$619,000

NASDOQ completed the following investment transactions during the year:

Mar. 16	Purchased 2,000 shares of ATI, Inc., common stock as a long-term available-for-sale investment, paying $12.25 per share.
May 21	Received cash dividend of $0.75 per share on the ATI investment.
Aug. 17	Received cash dividend of $81,000 from MSC Software.
Dec. 31	Received annual report from MSC Software; net income for the year was $550,000. Of this amount, NASDOQ's proportion is 22%.

At year end, the market values of NASDOQ's investments are: ATI, $25,700; MSC, $700,000.

I *Required*

1. Record the transactions in the journal of NASDOQ Corporation. (pp. 537–542)
2. Post entries to the T-account for Long-Term Investment in MSC and determine its balance at December 31. (p. 542)
3. Show how to report the Long-Term Available-for-Sale Investments and the Long-Term Investment in MSC accounts on NASDOQ's balance sheet at December 31. (pp. 538–539, 542)

P10-40A (*Learning Objective 3: Analyzing consolidated financial statements*) This problem demonstrates the dramatic effect that consolidation accounting can have on a company's ratios. **Ford Motor Company (Ford)** owns 100% of **Ford Motor Credit Corporation (FMCC)**, its financing subsidiary. Ford's main operations consist of manufacturing automotive products. FMCC mainly helps people finance the purchase of automobiles from Ford and its dealers. The 2 companies' individual balance sheets are adapted and summarized as follows (amounts in billions):

	Ford (Parent)	FMCC (Subsidiary)
Total assets	$89.6	$170.5
Total liabilities	$65.1	$156.9
Total stockholders' equity	24.5	13.6
Total liabilities and equity	$89.6	$170.5

Assume that FMCC's liabilities include $1.6 billion owed to Ford, the parent company.

I *Required*

1. Compute the debt ratio of Ford Motor Company considered alone. (p. 169)
2. Determine the consolidated total assets, total liabilities, and stockholders' equity of Ford Motor Company after consolidating the financial statements of FMCC into the totals of Ford, the parent company. (pp. 544–545)
3. Recompute the debt ratio of the consolidated entity. Why do companies prefer not to consolidate their financing subsidiaries into their own financial statements? (p. 169)

P10-41A (*Learning Objective 3: Consolidating a wholly-owned subsidiary*) Razorback Express, Inc., paid $266,000 to acquire all the common stock of Sooner Corporation, and Sooner owes Razorback $81,000 on a note payable. Immediately after the purchase on September 30, 20X8, the 2 companies' balance sheets follow.

■ spreadsheet

	Razorback	Sooner
Assets		
Cash	$ 24,000	$ 20,000
Accounts receivable, net	91,000	42,000
Note receivable from Sooner	81,000	—
Inventory	19,000	214,000
Investment in Sooner	266,000	—
Plant assets, net	278,000	219,000
Total	$759,000	$495,000
Liabilities and Stockholders' Equity		
Accounts payable	$ 57,000	$ 49,000
Notes payable	175,000	149,000
Other liabilities	129,000	31,000
Common stock	150,000	118,000
Retained earnings	248,000	148,000
Total	$759,000	$495,000

(continued)

❙ *Required*

Prepare the consolidated balance sheet of Razorback Express (It is sufficient to complete a consolidation work sheet.) (pp. 544–545)

P10-42A *(Learning Objective 4: Accounting for a bond investment purchased at a premium)* Insurance companies and pension plans hold large quantities of bond investments. Wolverine Insurance Corp. purchased $600,000 of 6% bonds of Eaton, Inc., for 106 on March 1, 20X4. These bonds pay interest on March 1 and September 1 each year. They mature on March 1, 20X8. At December 31, 20X4, the market price of the bonds is 103.5.

❙ *Required*

1. Journalize Wolverine's purchase of the bonds as a long-term investment on March 1, 20X4 (to be held to maturity), receipt of cash interest, and amortization of the bond investment at December 31, 20X4. The straight-line method is appropriate for amortizing the bond investment. (pp. 547–548)
2. Show all financial statement effects of this long-term bond investment on Wolverine Insurance Corp.'s balance sheet and income statement at December 31, 20X4. (p. 548)

■ **general ledger**

P10-43A *(Learning Objective 5: Recording foreign-currency transactions and reporting the transaction gain or loss)* Suppose **Bridgestone Corporation** completed the following international transactions:

May	1	Sold inventory on account to **Fiat**, the Italian automaker, for €82,000. The exchange rate of the euro is $1.30, and Fiat demands to pay in euros.
	10	Purchased supplies on account from a Canadian company at a price of Canadian $50,000. The exchange rate of the Canadian dollar is $0.70, and payment will be in Canadian dollars.
	17	Sold inventory on account to an English firm for 100,000 British pounds. Payment will be in pounds, and the exchange rate of the pound is $1.90.
	22	Collected from Fiat. The exchange rate is €1 = $1.33.
June	18	Paid the Canadian company. The exchange rate of the Canadian dollar is $0.69.
	24	Collected from the English firm. The exchange rate of the British pound is $1.87.

❙ *Required*

1. Record these transactions in Bridgestone's journal and show how to report the transaction gain or loss on the income statement. (pp. 552–554)
2. How will what you learned in this problem help you structure international transactions? (Challenge)

P10-44A *(Learning Objective 5: Measuring and explaining the foreign-currency translation adjustment)* Assume that **Intel** has a subsidiary company based in Japan.

❙ *Required*

1. Translate into dollars the foreign-currency balance sheet of the Japanese subsidiary of Intel.

	Yen
Assets	300,000,000
Liabilities	80,000,000
Stockholders' equity:	
Common stock	20,000,000
Retained earnings	200,000,000
	300,000,000

When Intel acquired this subsidiary, the Japanese yen was worth $0.0064. The current exchange rate is $0.0083. During the period when the subsidiary earned its income, the average exchange rate was $0.0070 per yen. (pp. 555–556)

Before you perform the foreign-currency translation calculations, indicate whether Intel has experienced a positive or a negative translation adjustment. State whether the adjustment is a gain or a loss, and show where it is reported in the financial statements. (pp. 551–552, 555–556)

2. To which company does the foreign-currency translation adjustment "belong"? In which company's financial statements will the translation adjustment be reported? (pp. 555–556)

P10-45A (*Learning Objective 6: Using a cash-flow statement*) Excerpts from Smart Pro, Inc.'s, statement of cash flows appear as follows:

writing assignment ■

Smart Pro, Inc.
Consolidated Statement of Cash Flows (Adapted, partial)
Years Ended December 31,

(In millions)	20X8	20X7
Cash and cash equivalents, beginning of year	$ 2,976	$ 3,695
Net cash provided by operating activities	8,654	12,827
Cash flows provided by (used for) investing activities:		
Additions to property, plant, and equipment	(7,309)	(6,674)
Acquisitions of other companies	(883)	(2,317)
Purchases of available-for-sale investments	(7,141)	(17,188)
Sales of available-for-sale investments	15,138	16,144
Net cash (used for) investing activities	(195)	(10,035)
Cash flows provided by (used for) financing activities:		
Borrowing	329	215
Retirement of long-term debt	(10)	(46)
Proceeds from issuance of stock	762	797
Repurchase and retirement of common stock	(4,008)	(4,007)
Payment of dividends to stockholders	(538)	(470)
Net cash (used for) financing activities	(3,465)	(3,511)
Net increase (decrease) in cash and cash equivalents	4,994	(719)
Cash and cash equivalents, end of year	$ 7,970	$ 2,976

❙ Required

As the chief executive officer of Smart Pro, Inc., your duty is to write the management letter to your stockholders to explain Smart Pro's investing activities during 20X8. Compare the company's level of investment with preceding years and indicate the major way the company financed its investments during 20X8. Net income for 20X8 was $1,291 million. (p. 557)

(Group B)

P10-46B (*Learning Objective 1, 2: Reporting investments on the balance sheet and the related revenue on the income statement*) Homestead Financial Corporation owns numerous investments in the stock of other companies. Homestead Financial completed the following long-term investment transactions:

20X4	
May 1	Purchased 8,000 shares, which make up 25% of the common stock of Mars Company at total cost of $450,000.
Sep. 15	Received a cash dividend of $1.40 per share on the Mars investment.
Oct. 12	Purchased 1,000 shares of Mercury Corporation common stock as an available-for-sale investment paying $22.50 per share.
Dec. 14	Received a cash dividend of $0.75 per share on the Mercury investment.
31	Received annual report from Mars Company. Net income for the year was $350,000.

At year end the current market value of the Mercury stock is $19,200. The market value of the Mars stock is $740,000.

I Required

1. For which investment is current market value used in the accounting? Why is market value used for 1 investment and not the other? (pp. 537–538, 541)
2. Show what Homestead Financial will report on its year-end balance sheet and income statement for these investments. (It is helpful to use a T-account for the Long-Term Investment in Mars Stock account.) Ignore income tax. (pp. 538–539, 542)

■ **general ledger**

P10-47B (*Learning Objective 1, 2: Accounting for available-for-sale and equity-method investments*) The beginning balance sheet of Dealmaker Securities included the following:

Long-Term Investments in Affiliates (equity-method investments)	$409,000

Dealmaker completed the following investment transactions during the year:

Feb. 16	Purchased 10,000 shares of BCM Software common stock as a long-term available-for-sale investment, paying $9.25 per share.
May 14	Received cash dividend of $0.82 per share on the BCM investment.
Oct. 15	Received cash dividend of $29,000 from an affiliated company.
Dec. 31	Received annual reports from affiliated companies. Their total net income for the year was $620,000. Of this amount, Dealmaker's proportion is 25%.

The market values of Dealmaker's investments are BCM, $89,000; affiliated companies, $947,000.

I Required

1. Record the transactions in the journal of Dealmaker Securities. (pp. 537–542)
2. Post entries to the Long-Term Investments in Affiliates T-account and determine its balance at December 31. (p. 542)

3. Show how to report Long-Term Available-for-Sale Investments and Long-Term Investments in Affiliates on Dealmaker's balance sheet at December 31. (pp. 538–539, 542)

P10-48B (*Learning Objective 3: Analyzing consolidated financial statements*) This problem demonstrates the dramatic effect that consolidation accounting can have on a company's ratios. **General Motors Corporation (GM)** owns 100% of **General Motors Acceptance Corporation (GMAC)**, its financing subsidiary. GM's main operations consist of manufacturing automotive products. GMAC mainly helps people finance the purchase of automobiles from GM and its dealers. The 2 companies' individual balance sheets are summarized as follows (amounts in billions):

	General Motors (Parent)	GMAC (Subsidiary)
Total assets	$132.6	$94.6
Total liabilities	$109.3	$86.3
Total stockholders' equity	23.3	8.3
Total liabilities and equity	$132.6	$94.6

Assume that GMAC's liabilities include $5.1 billion owed to General Motors, the parent company.

❙ *Required*

1. Compute the debt ratio of GM Corporation considered alone. (p. 169)
2. Determine the consolidated total assets, total liabilities, and stockholders' equity of GM after consolidating the financial statements of GMAC into the totals of GM, the parent company. (pp. 544–545)
3. Recompute the debt ratio of the consolidated entity. Why do companies prefer not to consolidate their financing subsidiaries into their own financial statements? (p. 169)

P10-49B (*Learning Objective 3: Consolidating a wholly-owned subsidiary*) Murdoch Corporation paid $179,000 to acquire all the common stock of Newswire, Inc., and Newswire owes Murdoch $55,000 on a note payable. Immediately after the purchase on June 30, 20X6, the 2 companies' balance sheets were as follows:

■ spreadsheet

	Murdoch	Newswire
Assets		
Cash	$ 48,000	$ 32,000
Accounts receivable, net	264,000	43,000
Note receivable from Newswire	55,000	—
Inventory	193,000	153,000
Investment in Newswire	179,000	—
Plant assets, net	105,000	138,000
Total	$844,000	$366,000
Liabilities and Stockholders' Equity		
Accounts payable	$ 76,000	$ 37,000
Notes payable	118,000	123,000
Other liabilities	174,000	27,000
Common stock	82,000	90,000
Retained earnings	394,000	89,000
Total	$844,000	$366,000

❙ *Required*

Prepare Murdoch's consolidated balance sheet. (It is sufficient to complete a consolidation work sheet.) (pp. 544–545)

P10-50B (*Learning Objective 4: Accounting for a bond investment purchased at a discount*)
Financial institutions hold large quantities of bond investments. Suppose **Morgan Stanley**
purchases $500,000 of 6% bonds of General Components Corporation for 96 on January 31,
20X0. These bonds pay interest on January 31 and July 31 each year. They mature on July 31,
20X8. At December 31, 20X0, the market price of the bonds is 93.

I *Required*

1. Journalize Morgan Stanley's purchase of the bonds as a long-term investment on January
   31, 20X0 (to be held to maturity), receipt of cash interest and amortization of the bond
   investment on July 31, 20X0, and accrual of interest revenue and amortization at
   December 31, 20X0. The straight-line method is appropriate for amortizing the bond
   investment. (pp. 547–548)
2. Show all financial statement effects of this long-term bond investment on Morgan
   Stanley's balance sheet and income statement at December 31, 20X0. (p. 548)

■ **general ledger**

P10-51B (*Learning Objective 5: Recording foreign-currency transactions and reporting the
transaction gain or loss*) Sun Power Drinks, Inc.(SPD) completed the following international
transactions:

Apr.	4	Sold soft-drink syrup on account to a Mexican company for $81,000. The exchange rate of the Mexican peso is $0.101, and the customer agrees to pay in dollars.
	13	Purchased inventory on account from a Canadian company at a price of Canadian $100,000. The exchange rate of the Canadian dollar is $0.65, and payment will be in Canadian dollars.
	20	Sold goods on account to an English firm for 70,000 British pounds. Payment will be in pounds, and the exchange rate of the pound is $1.96.
	27	Collected from the Mexican company.
May	21	Paid the Canadian company. The exchange rate of the Canadian dollar is $0.62.
June	17	Collected from the English firm. The exchange rate of the British pound is $2.00.

I *Required*

1. Record these transactions in Sun's journal and show how to report the transaction gain or
   loss on the income statement. (pp. 552–554)
2. How will what you learned in this problem help you structure international transactions?
   (Challenge)

P10-52B (*Learning Objective 5: Measuring and explaining the foreign-currency translation adjustment*) Amex Fabrics owns a subsidiary based in France.

I *Required*

1. Translate the foreign-currency balance sheet of the French subsidiary of Amex Fabrics
   into dollars. When Amex acquired this subsidiary, the euro was worth $1.17. The current
   exchange rate is $1.35 per euro. During the period when the subsidiary earned its
   income, the average exchange rate was $1.26 per euro. (pp. 555–556)

	Euros
Assets...................................	3,000,000
Liabilities	1,000,000
Stockholders' equity:	
Common stock....................	300,000
Retained earnings................	1,700,000
	3,000,000

Before you perform the foreign-currency translation calculation, indicate whether Amex Fabrics has experienced a positive or a negative foreign-currency translation adjustment. State whether the adjustment is a gain or loss, and show where it is reported in the financial statements. (pp. 551–552, 555–556)

2. To which company does the translation adjustment "belong"? In which company's financial statements will the translation adjustment be reported? (pp. 555–556)

P10-53B (*Learning Objective 6: Using a cash-flow statement*) Excerpts from **The Coca-Cola Company** statement of cash flows, as adapted, appear as follows:

writing assignment ■

The Coca-Cola Company and Subsidiaries Consolidated Statements of Cash Flows (Adapted)		
	Years Ended December 31,	
(In millions)	20X4	20X3
Operating Activities		
Net cash provided by operating activities.......	$ 4,110	$ 1,165
Investing Activities		
Purchases of property, plant, and equipment......	(769)	(733)
Acquisitions and investments, principally		
trademarks and bottling companies	(651)	(397)
Purchases of investments..................................	(456)	(508)
Proceeds from disposals of investments..............	455	290
Proceeds from disposals of property, plant,		
and equipment	91	45
Other investing activities.....................................	142	138
Net cash used in investing activities	(1,188)	(1,165)
Financing activities		
Issuances of debt (borrowing)	3,011	3,671
Payments of debt...	(3,937)	(4,256)
Issuances of stock..	164	331
Purchases of stock for treasury..........................	(277)	(133)
Dividends...	(1,791)	(1,685)
Net cash used in financing activities...............	(2,830)	(2,072)

(continued)

❙ Required

As the chief executive officer of The Coca-Cola Company, your duty is to write the management letter to your stockholders explaining Coca-Cola's major investing activities during 20X4. Compare the company's level of investment with previous years and indicate how the company financed its investments during 20X4. Net income for 20X4 was $3,969 million. (p. 557)

APPLY YOUR KNOWLEDGE

Decision Cases

Case 1. (*Learning Objective 1, 5: Making an investment decision*) Infografix Corporation's consolidated sales for 20X6 were $26.6 billion, and expenses totaled $24.8 billion. Infografix operates worldwide and conducts 37% of its business outside the United States. During 20X6, Infografix reported the following items in its financial statements (amounts in billions):

Foreign-currency translation adjustments..	$(202)
Unrealized holding _____ on available-for-sale investments.............	(328)

As you consider an investment in Infografix stock, some concerns arise. Answer each of the following questions:

1. What do the parentheses around the two dollar amounts signify? (pp. 538–539, 557)

2. Are these items reported as assets, liabilities, stockholders' equity, revenues, or expenses? Are they normal-balance accounts, or are they contra accounts? (pp. 538–539, 557)

3. Are these items reason for rejoicing or sorrow at Infografix? Are Infografix's emotions about these items deep or only moderate? Why? (Challenge)

4. Did Infografix include these items in net income? in retained earnings? In the final analysis, how much net income did Infografix report for 20X6? (pp. 538–539, 557)

5. Should these items scare you away from investing in Infografix stock? Why or why not? (Challenge)

Case 2. (*Learning Objective 1, 2, 4: Making an investment sale decision*) Cathy Talbert is the general manager of Barham Company, which provides data-management services for physicians in the Columbus, Ohio, area. Barham Company is having a rough year. Net income trails projections for the year by almost $75,000. This shortfall is especially important. Barham plans to issue stock early next year and needs to show investors that the company can meet its earnings targets.

Barham holds several investments purchased a few years ago. Even though investing in stocks is outside Barham's core business of data-management services, Talbert thinks these investments may hold the key to helping the company meet its net income goal for the year. She is considering what to do with the following investments:

1. Barham owns 50% of the common stock of Ohio Office Systems, which provides the business forms that Barham uses. Ohio Office Systems has lost money for the past 2 years but still has a retained earnings balance of $550,000. Talbert thinks she can get Ohio's treasurer to declare a $160,000 cash dividend, half of which would go to Barham. (pp. 540, 541)

2. Barham owns a bond investment purchased 8 years ago for $250,000. The purchase price represents a discount from the bonds' maturity value of $400,000. These bonds mature 2 years from now, and their current market value is $380,000. Ms. Talbert has checked with a

Charles Schwab investment representative, and Talbert is considering selling the bonds. Schwab would charge a 1% commission on the sale transaction. (pp. 547–548)

3. Barham owns 5,000 shares of **Microsoft** stock valued at $53 per share. One year ago, Microsoft stock was worth only $28 per share. Barham purchased the Microsoft stock for $37 per share. Talbert wonders whether Barham should sell the Microsoft stock. (p. 539)

❙ Required

Evaluate all 3 actions as a way for Barham Company to generate the needed amount of income. Recommend the best way for Barham to achieve its net income goal.

Ethical Issue

writing assignment ■

Media One owns 18% of the voting stock of Web Talk, Inc. The remainder of the Web Talk stock is held by numerous investors with small holdings. Austin Cohen, president of Media One and a member of Web Talk's board of directors, heavily influences Web Talk's policies.

Under the market value method of accounting for investments, Media One's net income increases as it receives dividend revenue from Web Talk. Media One pays President Cohen a bonus computed as a percentage of Media One's net income. Therefore, Cohen can control his personal bonus to a certain extent by influencing Web Talk's dividends.

A recession occurs in 20X4, and Media One's income is low. Cohen uses his power to have Web Talk pay a large cash dividend. The action requires Web Talk to borrow in order to pay the dividend.

❙ Required

1. In getting Web Talk to pay the large cash dividend, is Cohen acting within his authority as a member of the Web Talk board of directors? Are Cohen's actions ethical? Whom can his actions harm?

2. Discuss how using the equity method of accounting for investment would decrease Cohen's potential for manipulating his bonus.

Focus on Financials: ■ YUM! Brands

(*Learning Objective 2, 3, 5: Analyzing investments, consolidated subsidiaries, and international operations*) The financial statements of **YUM! Brands, Inc.** are given in Appendix A at the end of this book.

1. YUM accounts for its investments in unconsolidated affiliates by the equity method. During 2006, YUM made additional equity-method investments and sold no equity-method investments. Assume YUM received no dividends from unconsolidated affiliates. What was the overall result of operations for YUM's unconsolidated affiliates during 2006? State the reason underlying your answer. (p. 777)

2. What is YUM's percentage ownership of its consolidated subsidiaries? How can you tell? Which financial statement provides the evidence? (p. 778)

3. Does YUM have any foreign subsidiaries? What evidence answers this question? Which financial statement provides the evidence? (p. 779)

4. Which monetary currency was stronger, the U.S. dollar or YUM's foreign currencies, during 2004, 2005, and 2006? Give the basis for your answers. (pp. 554–556, 779)

Focus on Analysis: ■ Pier 1 Imports

(*Learning Objective 3, 5: Analyzing consolidated statements and international operations*) This case is based on the financial statements of **Pier 1 Imports, Inc.** given in Appendix B at the end of this book.

1. What indicates that Pier 1 Imports owns foreign subsidiaries? Identify the item that proves your point and the financial statement on which the item appears. (p. 797)

(*continued*)

2. Which currency, the U.S. dollar, or Pier 1's foreign currencies, was stronger in each fiscal year 2004, 2005, and 2006? Give the evidence to support each answer. Ignore the minimum pension liability adjustment. (p.797)

3. At February 25, 2006, did Pier 1 Imports have a cumulative net gain or a cumulative net loss from translating its foreign subsidiaries' financial statements into dollars? How can you tell? Ignore the beginning balance of Cumulative Other Comprehensive Income at March 1, 2003. (p. 797, Challenge)

Group Project

Pick a stock from *The Wall Street Journal* or other database or publication. Assume that your group purchases 1,000 shares of the stock as a long-term investment and that your 1,000 shares are less than 20% of the company's outstanding stock. Research the stock in *Value Line*, *Moody's Investor Record*, or other source to determine whether the company pays cash dividends and, if so, how much and at what intervals.

I *Required*

1. Track the stock for a period assigned by your professor. Over the specified period, keep a daily record of the price of the stock to see how well your investment has performed. Each day, search the Corporate Dividend News in *The Wall Street Journal* to keep a record of any dividends you've received. End the period of your analysis with a month end, such as September 30 or December 31.

2. Journalize all transactions that you have experienced, including the stock purchase, dividends received (both cash dividends and stock dividends), and any year-end adjustment required by the accounting method that is appropriate for your situation. Assume you will prepare financial statements on the ending date of your study.

3. Show what you will report on your company's balance sheet, income statement, and statement of cash flows as a result of your investment transactions.

For Internet Exercises go to the Web site www.prenhall.com/harrison.

Quick Check Answers

1. *c*
2. *d* (1,000 shares × $35 = $35,000)
3. *a* ($35,000 − $31,000 = $4,000)
4. *b* [$40,000 − (1,000 shares × $31) = $9,000]
5. *b* [$100,000 + 0.20 ($50,000 − $25,000) = $105,000]
6. *c* {$100,000 + 0.80 [$68,000 + 0.80($40,000)] = $180,000}
7. *a*
8. *d*
9. *b* ($1,000,000 Canadian × $0.93 = $930,000)
10. *c*

11 The Income Statement & the Statement of Stockholders' Equity

PIER 1 IMPORTS HAD A TOUGH YEAR

Marvin J. Girouard, Chairman and CEO, begins Pier 1 Imports' 2006 annual report with these words, "Fiscal 2006 was a difficult year for Pier 1 Imports." Indeed it was a tough year, as you can see from Pier 1's income statement.

Sales in 2006 were down from 2005 (line1), and Pier 1 actually lost money in 2006 (line 15). But there's more to this story. Pier 1's income statement includes some new items:

- continuing operations (line 10)
- discontinued operations (lines 11 through 14)
- income tax saving (line 13)

Pier 1 Imports, Inc.
Consolidated Statements of Operations (Adapted)
(In thousands except per share amounts)

		Year Ended	
	2006	2005	2004
1 Net sales	$1,776,701	$1,825,343	$1,806,092
Operating costs and expenses:			
2 Cost of sales (including buying and store occupancy costs)	1,175,011	1,121,697	1,045,180
3 Selling, general and administrative expenses	588,273	549,635	526,060
4 Depreciation and amortization	56,229	55,762	48,869
	1,819,513	1,727,094	1,620,109
5 Operating income (loss)	(42,812)	98,249	185,983
Nonoperating (income) and expenses:			
6 Interest and investment income	(3,510)	(2,635)	(2,724)
7 Interest expense	2,610	1,735	1,688
	(900)	(900)	(1,036)
8 Income (loss) from continuing operations before income taxes	(41,912)	99,149	187,019
9 Provision (benefit) for income taxes	(14,441)	36,384	69,315
10 Income (loss) from continuing operations	(27,471)	62,765	117,704
11 Discontinued operations:			
12 Income (loss) from discontinued operations (including write down of assets held for sale of $7,441 in 2006)	(17,583)	(2,308)	297
13 Income tax saving	(5,250)	—	—
14 Income (loss) from discontinued operations	(12,333)	(2,308)	297
15 Net income (loss)	$ (39,804)	$ 60,457	$ 118,001
16 Earnings (loss) per share from continuing operations:			
Basic	$ (.32)	$ .72	$ 1.32
17 Earnings (loss) per share from disconinuted operations:			
Basic	$ (.14)	$ (.03)	$ .00
18 Earnings (loss) per share:			
Basic	$ (.46)	$ .69	$ 1.32

This chapter rounds out your coverage of the corporate income statement. After studying this material, you will have seen all the types of items that appear on an income statement. You'll also learn about earnings per share (lines 16 through 18), the most often-mentioned statistic in business. Finally, you'll learn about the statement of stockholders' equity, which is like an expanded version of the statement of retained earnings. Your new learning will help you analyze financial statements and use the information in decision making.

Net income. Income from continuing operations. Which number measures a company's progress? This chapter will help you make that decision. We begin with a basic question: how to evaluate the quality of earnings. The term *quality of earnings* refers to the characteristics of an earnings number that make it most useful for decision making.

LEARNING OBJECTIVES

1 **Analyze** a corporate income statement

2 **Account** for a corporation's income tax

3 **Analyze** a statement of stockholders' equity

4 **Understand** managers' and auditors' responsibilities for the financial statements

EVALUATING THE QUALITY OF EARNINGS

A corporation's net income (including earnings per share) receives more attention that any other item in the financial statements. To stockholders, the larger the net income, the greater the likelihood of dividends. To creditors, the better the ability to pay debts.

Suppose you are considering investing in the stock of **Pier 1 Imports** or Brand X Superstore. The 2 companies are similar but they generate profits in different ways:

- Brand X's profits come from continuing operations.
- Pier 1 Imports is better known, but the company is struggling to turn a profit.

Do you go with the known company (Pier 1), or do you follow the numbers (Brand X)?

To explore the makeup and the quality of earnings, let's examine its various sources. Exhibit 11-1 provides a comprehensive example that we will use throughout the chapter. It is the income statement of Allied Electronics Corporation, which produces electronic-control instruments.

Continuing Operations

In Exhibit 11-1, the topmost section of the income statement reports the results of continuing operations (lines 1 to 10). This part of the business is expected to continue from period to period. **We use this information to predict that Allied Electronics will earn income of approximately $54,000 next year.**

The continuing operations of Allied Electronics include 3 new items:

- During 20X9, Allied *restructured* operations at a loss of $8,000 (line 6). Restructuring costs include severance pay to laid-off workers and moving expenses for employees transferred to other locations. The restructuring loss is part of continuing operations because Allied Electronics is remaining in the electronics business. But the restructuring loss is an "Other" item because restructuring falls outside Allied's core activity.
- Allied had a *gain on the sale of machinery* (line 7), also outside the company's core business. This explains why the gain isn't part of operating income (lines 1 to 5).
- *Income tax expense* (line 9) is subtracted in arriving at income from continuing operations. Corporate income tax is a significant expense. The current maximum federal income tax rate for corporations is 35%. State income taxes run about 5% in many states. Thus, we use an income tax rate of 40% in our illustrations. The $36,000 income tax expense in Exhibit 11-1 equals the pretax income from continuing operations multiplied by the tax rate ($90,000 × 0.40 = $36,000).

OBJECTIVE

1 **Analyze** a corporate income statement

EXHIBIT 11-1   Allied Electronics Corporation
Income Statement

Allied Electronics Corporation
Income Statement
Year Ended December 31, 20X9

	1 Sales revenue..	$500,000
	2 Cost of goods sold	240,000
	3 Gross profit	260,000
	4 Operating expenses (detailed)	181,000
	5 Operating income	79,000
	Other gains (losses):	
	6 Loss on restructuring operations	(8,000)
	7 Gain on sale of machinery...	19,000
	8 Income from continuing operations before income tax	90,000
	9 Income tax expense..	36,000
	10 Income from continuing operations	54,000
	11 Discontinued operations, $35,000, less income tax of $14,000	21,000
	12 Income before extraordinary item and cumulative effect of	
	change in inventory method...	75,000
	13 Extraordinary flood loss, $20,000, less income tax saving of $8,000.....	(12,000)
	14 Cumulative effect of change in inventory method, $10,000,	
	less income tax of $4,000	6,000
	15 Net income	$ 69,000
	Earnings per share of common stock (20,000 shares outstanding):	
	16 Income from continuing operations...	$ 2.70
	17 Income from discontinued operations	1.05
	18 Income before extraordinary item and cumulative effect of	
	change in inventory method	3.75
	19 Extraordinary loss...	(0.60)
	20 Cumulative effect of change in inventory method......................	0.30
	21 Net income..	$ 3.45

Labels along the left margin: Continuing Operations (lines 1–10), Special Items (lines 11–14), Earnings per Share (lines 16–21).

Which Income Number Predicts Future Profits?

How is income from continuing operations used in investment analysis? Suppose Margaret Blume, an analyst with First Charter Bank in Tallahassee, Florida, is estimating the value of Allied Electronics' common stock. Blume believes that Allied Electronics can earn annual income each year equal to its income from continuing operations—$54,000 for Allied Electronics.

To estimate the value of Allied's common stock, financial analysts determine the present value (present value means the value *today*) of Allied's stream of future income. Blume must use some interest rate to compute the present value. Assume that an appropriate interest rate (*i*) for the valuation of Allied Electronics is 12%. This rate is based on the risk that Allied might not be able to earn annual income of $54,000 for the indefinite future. The rate is also called the **investment capitalization rate** because it is used to estimate the value of an investment. The higher the risk, the higher the rate, and vice versa. The computation of the estimated value of a stock such as Allied Electronics or Pier 1 Imports is

$$\text{Estimated value of Allied Electronics common stock} = \frac{\text{Estimated annual income in the future}}{\text{Investment capitalization rate}} = \frac{\$54,000}{0.12} = \$450,000^{1}$$

Blume thus estimates that Allied Electronics Corporation is worth $450,000. She would then compare this estimate to the current market value of Allied Electronics' stock, which is $513,000. Allied Electronics' balance sheet reports that Allied has 20,000 shares of common stock outstanding, and *Hoover's Online* reports that Allied common stock is selling for $4.75 per share. The current value of Allied stock is thus

Current market value of the company	=	Number of shares of common stock outstanding	×	Current market price per share
$513,000	=	20,000	×	$25.65

The investment decision rule may be:

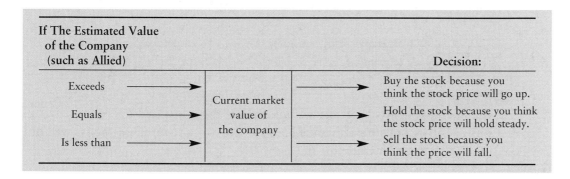

In this case,

			Decision:
Estimated Value of Allied $450,000	Is less than	Current market value of Allied $513,000	→ Sell the stock
$22.50 per share*	Is less than	$25.65 per share	

*$450,000/20,000 shares = $22.50 per share

Blume believes Allied's stock price should fall below its current market value of $513,000 to somewhere in a range near $450,000. Based on this analysis, First Charter Bank would recommend that investors holding Allied stock should sell it.

Investors often value a single share of stock. They can estimate the value of 1 share of stock by using earnings per share (EPS) of common stock, as follows:

$$\text{Estimated value of one share of common stock} = \frac{\text{Estimated annual earnings per share}}{\text{Investment capitalization rate}} = \frac{\$2.70}{0.12} = \$22.50$$

[1]This valuation model has many forms, which are covered in finance classes. Here we introduce the basic form.

The analysis based on 1 share of stock follows the pattern illustrated for the company as a whole.

Discontinued Operations

Most large companies engage in several lines of business. For example, Pier 1 Imports has its basic stores in addition to Pier 1 Kids stores. **General Electric** makes household appliances and jet engines and owns **NBC**, the media network. We call each identifiable part of a company a segment of the business.

A company may sell a segment of its business. During fiscal year 2006 Pier 1 sold its operations in the United Kingdom and Ireland, called "The Pier." The sale of a business segment is viewed as a one time transaction. Pier 1's income statement reports on the segment of the business that has been disposed of under the heading Discontinued Operations (line 11 through 14 on page 580).

Let's return to the Allied Electronics example in Exhibit 11-1 (p. 582). Allied faces an income tax rate of 40%, so the discontinued operations are taxed at the 40% rate. Discontinued operations are reported along with their income tax by Allied Electronics Corporation as follows (line 11, p. 580).

Discontinued operations, $35,000, less ancome tax of $14,000 .... $21,000

Financial analysts typically do *not* include discontinued operations in predictions of future corporate income because the discontinued segments will not continue to generate income for the company.

Gains and losses on the sales of plant assets are *not* reported as discontinued operations. These items are not so unusual, and they recur from time to time, so they appear in the "Other" section of the income statement (Exhibit 11-1, lines 6 and 7).

Extraordinary Gains and Losses (Extraordinary Items)

Extraordinary gains and losses, also called *extraordinary items*, are both *unusual* for the company and *infrequent*. Losses from natural disasters (such as earthquakes, floods, and tornadoes) and the expropriation of company assets by a foreign government (expropriation) are extraordinary. Pier 1 Imports had no extraordinary items on its income statement.

Extraordinary items are reported along with their income tax effects. During 20X9, Allied Electronics Corporation suffered a $20,000 flood loss (Exhibit 11-1, line 13). This extraordinary item reduced income and therefore reduced Allied's income tax. Taxes decrease the net amount of a loss the same way they reduce net income. Another way to report an extraordinary loss along with its tax effect is as follows:

Extraordinary flood loss..................................	$(20,000)
Less Income tax saving................................	8,000
Extraordinary flood loss, net of tax................	(12,000)

Trace this item to the income statement in Exhibit 11-1 (line 13). An extraordinary gain is reported in the same way, net of its income tax.

On page 580, Pier 1 Imports reports an income tax saving resulting from its loss on discontinued operations. Gains and losses due to lawsuits, restructuring, and the sale of plant assets are *not* extraordinary items. These gains and losses are considered normal business occurrences and are reported as Other Gains and Losses. Exhibit 11-1 (p. 582, lines 6 and 7) provides an example.

Cumulative Effect of a Change in Accounting Method

Companies sometimes change from one accounting method to another, such as from double-declining-balance (DDB) to straight-line depreciation, or from first-in, first-out (FIFO) to average cost for inventory. An accounting change makes it difficult to compare one period with preceding periods. Without detailed information, investors can be misled into thinking that the current year is better or worse than the preceding year, when in fact the only difference is a change in accounting method.

Companies report accounting changes in a special section of the income statement. This section usually appears after extraordinary items. Exhibit 11-1, line 14 gives an example for Allied Electronics.

Allied Electronics Corporation changed from average costing to FIFO for inventory at the beginning of 20X9. How did this accounting change affect 20X9? First, it decreased cost of goods sold for 20X9 and thereby increased 20X9 income from continuing operations. Second, the change affected previous years. If Allied had been using FIFO in all previous years, cost of goods sold would have been less, and net income would have been $6,000 higher ($10,000 minus the additional income tax of $4,000). Exhibit 11-1 reports the cumulative effect of this accounting change on line 14.

Watch Out for Voluntary Accounting Changes That Increase Reported Income

Investment analysts follow companies to see if they meet their forecasted earnings targets. And managers sometimes take drastic action to increase reported earnings. Assume it's late in November and our earnings may fall *below* the target for the year. A reasonable thing to do is to try to increase sales and net income. Managers can also cut expenses. These actions are ethical and honest. Profits earned by these actions are real. Managers can take another action that is honest and legal, but its ethics are questionable. Suppose the company has been using the double-declining-balance method for depreciation. Changing to straight-line depreciation can increase reported income.

Accounting changes are a quick-and-dirty way to create reported profits when the company can't earn enough from continuing operations. This is why GAAP requires companies to report changes in accounting methods, along with their effects on earnings—to let investors know where the income came from. Moreover, for voluntary accounting changes, the companies must restate all prior-year financial statements to show how they would have appeared if the new accounting method had been in effect all along.[2] This helps investors compare all periods' profits and losses on the same accounting basis.

---

[2]FASB Statement No. 154, "Accounting Changes and Error Corrections," May 2005.

Earnings per Share of Common Stock

The final segment of the income statement reports earnings per share. **Earnings per share (EPS)** is the amount of a company's net income per share of its *outstanding common stock*. EPS is a key measure of a business's success because it shows how much income the company earned for each share of stock. Stock prices are quoted at an amount per share, and investors buy a certain number of shares. EPS is used to help determine the value of a share of stock. EPS is computed as follows:

$$\text{Earnings per share} = \frac{\text{Net income} - \text{Preferred dividends}}{\text{Average number of shares of common stock outstsanding}}$$

The corporation lists its various sources of income separately: continuing operations, discontinued operations, and so on. It also lists the EPS figure for each element of net income. Consider the EPS of Allied Electronics Corporation. The final section of Exhibit 11-1 (lines 16 to 21) shows how companies report EPS. Allied Electronics has 20,000 shares of common stock outstanding.

	Earnings per share of common stock (20,000 shares outstanding):	
16	Income from continuing operations ($54,000/20,000)	$2.70
17	Income from discontinued operations ($21,000/20,000)	1.05
18	Income before extraordinary item and cumulative effect of change in inventory method ($75,000/20,000)...........................	3.75
19	Extraordinary loss ($12,000/20,000)	(0.60)
20	Cumulative effect of change in inventory method ($6,000/20,000)	0.30
21	Net income ($69,000/20,000)	$3.45

Effect of Preferred Dividends on Earnings Per Share. Recall that EPS is earnings per share of *common* stock. But the holders of preferred stock have first claim on dividends. Therefore, preferred dividends must be subtracted from net income to compute EPS. Preferred dividends are not subtracted from discontinued operations, extraordinary items, or the cumulative effect of accounting changes.

Suppose Allied Electronics Corporation had 10,000 shares of preferred stock outstanding, each with a $1.00 dividend. Allied's annual preferred dividends would be $10,000 (10,000 × $1.00). The $10,000 is subtracted from each income subtotal, resulting in the following EPS amounts (recall that Allied has 20,000 shares of common stock outstanding):

Earnings per share of common stock (20,000 shares outstanding):	
Income from continuing operations ($54,000 − $10,000)/20,000	$2.20
Income from discontinued operations ($21,000/20,000)...............................	1.05
Income before extraordinary item and cumulative effect of change in inventory method ($75,000 − $10,000)/20,000.........................	3.25
Extraordinary loss ($12,000/20,000)	(0.60)
Cumulative effect of change in inventory method ($6,000/20,000)	0.30
Net income ($69,000 − $10,000)/20,000	$2.95

Earnings Per Share Dilution. Some corporations have convertible preferred stock, which may be exchanged for common stock. When preferred is converted to common, the EPS is *diluted*—reduced—because more common shares are divided into net income. Corporations with complex capital structures present 2 sets of EPS figures:

- EPS based on actual outstanding common shares (*basic* EPS)
- EPS based on outstanding common shares plus the additional shares that can arise from conversion of the preferred stock into common (*diluted* EPS)

Reporting Comprehensive Income

All companies report net income or net loss on their income statements. As we saw in Chapter 10, companies with unrealized gains and losses on certain investments and foreign-currency translation adjustments also report another income figure. **Comprehensive income** is the company's change in total stockholders' equity from all sources other than from the owners of the business. Comprehensive income includes net income plus:

- Unrealized gains (losses) on available-for-sale investments
- Foreign-currency translation adjustments

These items do not enter into the determination of net income or of earnings per share. They can be reported as Other comprehensive income, as shown in Exhibit 11-2. All amounts are assumed for this illustration.

EXHIBIT 11-2 Reporting Comprehensive Income

Allied Electronics Corporation
Statement of Comprehensive Income (Partial)
Year Ended December 31, 20X9

Net income...			$69,000
Other comprehensive income:			
Unrealized gain on investment	$ 6,500		
Less income tax (40%)	2,600	$ 3,900	
Foreign-currency translation adjustment (loss)..............	$(9,000)		
Less income tax saving (40%)....................................	3,600	(5,400)	
Other comprehensive income (loss).............................			(1,500)
Comprehensive income			$67,500

What Should You Analyze to Gain an Overall Picture of a Company?

Two key figures used in financial analysis are

- Net income (or income from continuing operations)
- Cash flow from operations

For any 1 period, Allied Electronics' net income and net cash flow from operating activities may chart different paths. Accounting income arises from the accrual process as follows:

Total revenues and gains − Total expenses and losses = Net income (or Net loss)

As we have seen, revenues and gains are recorded when they occur, regardless of when the company receives or pays cash.

Net cash flow, on the other hand, is based solely on cash receipts and cash payments. During 2009, a company may have lots of revenues and expenses and a hefty net income. But the company may have weak cash flow because it cannot collect from customers. The reverse may also be true: The company may have abundant cash but little income.

The income statement and the cash-flow statement often paint different pictures of the company. Which statement provides better information? Neither: Both statements are needed, along with the balance sheet and statement of stockholders' equity, for an overall view of the business. In Chapter 12 we'll cover the statement of cash flows in detail.

ACCOUNTING FOR CORPORATE INCOME TAXES

OBJECTIVE

2 **Account** for a corporation's income tax

Corporations pay income tax as individuals do, but corporate and personal tax rates differ. The current federal tax rate on most corporate income is 35%. Most states also levy income taxes on corporations, so most corporations have a combined federal and state income tax rate of approximately 40%.

To account for income tax, the corporation measures

- *Income tax expense*, an expense on the income statement. Income tax expense helps measure net income.
- *Income tax payable*, a current liability on the balance sheet. Income tax payable is the amount of tax to pay the government in the next period.

Accounting for income tax follows the principles of accrual accounting. Suppose in 20X7 Pier 1 Imports reported income before tax (also called **pretax accounting income**) of $100 million. Pier 1's combined income tax rate is close to 40%. To start this discussion, assume income tax expense and income tax payable are the same. Then Pier 1 would record income tax for the year as follows (amounts in millions):

20X7			
Dec. 31	Income Tax Expense ($100 × 0.40)	40	
	Income Tax Payable		40
	Recorded income tax for the year.		

Pier 1's 20X7 financial statements would report these figures (partial, in millions):

Income statement		Balance sheet	
Income before income tax	$100	Current liabilities:	
Income tax expense	(40)	Income tax payable	$40
Net income................................	$ 60		

In general, income tax expense and income tax payable can be computed as follows:*

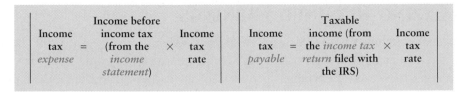

*The authors thank Jean Marie Hudson for suggesting this presentation.

The income statement and the income tax return are entirely separate documents:

- The *income statement* reports the results of operations.
- The *income tax return* is filed with the Internal Revenue Service (IRS) to measure how much tax to pay the government in the current period.

For most companies, tax expense and tax payable differ. Some revenues and expenses affect income differently for accounting and for tax purposes. The most common difference between accounting income and **taxable income** occurs when a corporation uses straight-line depreciation in its financial statements and accelerated depreciation for the tax return.

Continuing with the Pier 1 Imports illustration, suppose for 20X8 that Pier 1 had:

- Pretax accounting income of $100 million on its income statement
- Taxable income of $80 million on its income tax return

Taxable income is less than accounting income because Pier 1 uses

- straight-line depreciation for accounting purposes (say $30 million)
- accelerated depreciation for tax purposes (say $10 million).

Pier 1 would record income tax for 20X8 as follows (dollar amounts in millions and an income tax rate of 40%):

20X8			
Dec. 31	Income Tax Expense ($100 × 0.40)	40	
	Income Tax Payable ($80 × 0.40)		32
	Deferred Tax Liability		8
	Recorded income tax for the year.		

Deferred Tax Liability is usually long-term.

Pier 1's financial statements for 20X8 will report the following:

Income statement		Balance sheet	
Income before income tax	$100	Current liabilities:	
Income tax expense	(40)	Income tax payable	$32
Net income	$ 60	Long-term liabilities:	
		Deferred tax liability	8*

*The beginning balance of Deferred tax liability was zero.

Early in 20X9, Pier 1 would pay income tax payable of $32 million because this is a current liability. The deferred tax liability can be paid later.

For a given year, Income Tax Payable can exceed Income Tax Expense. When that occurs, the company debits a Deferred Tax Asset.

ANALYZING RETAINED EARNINGS

Occasionally a company records a revenue or an expense incorrectly. If the error is corrected in a later period, the balance of Retained Earnings is wrong until corrected. Corrections to Retained Earnings for errors of an earlier period are called **prior-period adjustments**. The prior-period adjustment appears on the statement of retained earnings.

Assume that NPR Corporation recorded 20X6 income tax expense as $30,000, but the correct amount was $40,000. This error understated expenses by $10,000 and overstated net income by $10,000. The government sent a bill in 20X7 for the additional $10,000, and this alerted NPR to the mistake.

This accounting error requires a prior-period adjustment. Prior-period adjustments are not reported on the income statement because they relate to an earlier accounting period. This prior-period adjustment would appear on the statement of retained earnings, as shown in Exhibit 11-3, with all amounts assumed:

EXHIBIT 11-3 **Reporting a Prior-Period Adjustment on the Statement of Retained Earnings**

NPR Corporation Statement of Retained Earnings Year Ended December 31, 20X7	
Retained earnings balance, December 31, 20X6, as originally reported	$390,000
Prior-period adjustment—debit to correct error in recording income tax expense of 20X6	(10,000)
Retained earnings balance, December 31, 20X6, as adjusted	380,000
Net income for 20X7	110,000
	490,000
Dividends for 20X7..	(40,000)
Retained earnings balance, December 31, 20X7...	$450,000

ANALYZING THE STATEMENT OF STOCKHOLDERS' EQUITY

Companies report a statement of stockholders' equity, which includes retained earnings. The statement of stockholders' equity is formatted like a statement of retained earnings but with a column for each element of stockholders' equity. The **statement of stockholders' equity** thus reports the reasons for all the changes in equity during the period.

Exhibit 11-4 is the 20X9 statement of stockholders' equity for Allied Electronics Corporation. Study its format. There is a column for each element of equity, starting with Common Stock on the left. The far-right column reports the total. The top row (line 1) reports beginning balances, taken from last period's balance sheet. The rows then report the various transactions that affected equity, starting with Issuance of stock (line 2). The statement ends with the December 31, 20X9, balances (line 10). All the amounts on the bottom line appear on the ending balance sheet, given in Exhibit 11-5.

OBJECTIVE

3 Analyze a statement of stockholders' equity

EXHIBIT 11-4 Reporting a Prior-Period Adjustment on the Statement of Stockholders' Equity

Allied Electronics Corporation
Statement of Stockholders' Equity
Year Ended December 31, 20X9

	Common Stock $1 Par	Additional Paid-in Capital	Retained Earnings	Treasury Stock	Unrealized Gain (Loss) on Investments	Foreign-Currency Translation Adjustment	Total Stockholders' Equity
1 Balance, December 31, 20X8........	$10,000	$160,000	$130,000	$(25,000)	$6,000	$(10,000)	$271,000
2 Issuance of stock............................	20,000	500,000					520,000
3 Net income			69,000				69,000
4 Cash dividends..............................			(21,000)				(21,000)
5 Stock dividend—10%...................	3,000	72,000	(75,000)				0
6 Purchase of treasury stock				(9,000)			(9,000)
7 Sale of treasury stock....................		7,000		4,000			11,000
8 Unrealized gain on investments..........................					1,000		1,000
9 Foreign-currency translation adjustment						3,000	3,000
10 Balance, December 31, 20X9........	$33,000	$739,000	$103,000	$(30,000)	$7,000	$ (7,000)	$845,000

Let's examine Allied Electronics' stockholders' equity during 20X9.

Issuance of Stock (Line 2). During 20X9, Allied issued common stock for $520,000. Of this total, $20,000 (par value) went into the Common Stock account, and $500,000 increased Additional Paid-in Capital. Total equity increased by $520,000.

Net Income (Line 3). During 20X9, Allied Electronics earned net income of $69,000, which increased Retained Earnings. Trace net income from the income statement (Exhibit 11-1, p. 582) to the statement of stockholders' equity (Exhibit 11-4).

Declaration of Cash Dividends (Line 4). Allied Electronics declared cash dividends of $21,000. Exhibit 11-4 reports the decrease in retained earnings from the declaration of the cash dividends.

Distribution of Stock Dividends (Line 5). During 20X9, Allied Electronics distributed a stock dividend to its stockholders. Prior to the stock dividend, Allied's Common Stock account had a balance of $30,000 (beginning balance of $10,000 + new issue of $20,000). The 10% stock dividend then added 3,000 shares of $1-par common stock, or $3,000, to the Common Stock account.

Allied decreased (debited) Retained Earnings for the market value of this "small" stock dividend. The difference between the market value of the dividend ($75,000) and its par value ($3,000) was credited to Additional Paid-in Capital ($72,000).

Purchase and Sale of Treasury Stock (Lines 6 and 7). Recall from Chapter 9 that treasury stock is recorded at cost. During 20X9, Allied Electronics paid $9,000 to buy treasury stock (line 6). This transaction decreased stockholders' equity. Allied later sold some treasury stock (line 7). The sale of treasury stock brought in $11,000 cash and increased total stockholders' equity by $11,000. The treasury stock that Allied sold had cost the company $4,000, and the extra $7,000 was added to Additional Paid-in Capital. At year end (line 10), Allied still owned treasury stock that cost the company $30,000. The parentheses around the treasury stock figures in Exhibit 11-4 mean that treasury stock is a negative element of stockholders' equity. Trace treasury stock's ending balance to the balance sheet in Exhibit 11-5.

EXHIBIT 11-5 Stockholders' Equity Section of the Balance Sheet

Allied Electronic Corporation
Balance Sheet (Partial)
December 31, 20X9

Total assets...	$1,500,000
Total liabilities	$ 655,000
Stockholders' equity:	
Common stock, $1 par, shares issued—33,000..................	$ 33,000
Additional paid-in capital...	739,000
Retained earnings	103,000
Treasury stock	(30,000)
Accumulated other comprehensive income:	
Unrealized gain on investments......................................	7,000
Foreign-currency translation adjustment........................	(7,000)
Total stockholders' equity..	845,000
Total liabilities and stockholders' equity	$1,500,000

Accumulated Other Comprehensive Income (Lines 8 and 9). Two categories of other comprehensive income are unrealized gains and losses on available-for-sale investments and the foreign-currency translation adjustment.

At December 31, 20X8, Allied Electronics held available-for-sale investments with an unrealized gain of $6,000. This explains the beginning balance. Then, during 20X9, the market value of the investments increased by another $1,000 (line 8). At December 31, 20X9, Allied's portfolio of investments had an unrealized gain of $7,000 (line 10). An unrealized loss on investments would appear as a negative amount.

At December 31, 20X8, Allied had a negative foreign-currency translation adjustment of $10,000 (line 1). During 20X9, the foreign-currency translation adjustment increased by $3,000 (line 9), and at December 31, 20X9, Allied's cumulative foreign-currency translation adjustment stood at $7,000—a negative amount that resembles an unrealized loss (line 10).

RESPONSIBILITY FOR THE FINANCIAL STATEMENTS

Management's Responsibility

Management issues a report on internal control over financial reporting, along with the company's financial statements. Exhibit 11-6 is an excerpt from the report of management for Pier 1 Imports.

Management declares its responsibility for the internal controls over financial reporting in accordance with GAAP. As we've seen throughout this book, GAAP is the standard for preparing the financial statements. GAAP is designed to produce relevant, reliable, and useful information for making investment and credit decisions.

OBJECTIVE

4 **Understand** managers' and auditors' responsibilities for the financial statements

---

EXHIBIT 11-6   **Excerpt from Management's Responsibility for Financial Reporting—Pier 1 Imports, Inc.**

REPORT OF MANAGEMENT ON INTERNAL CONTROL OVER FINANCIAL REPORTING

Management is responsible for establishing and maintaining a system of internal control over financial reporting designed to provide reasonable assurance that transactions are executed in accordance with management authorization and that such transactions are properly recorded and reported in the financial statements, and that records are maintained so as to permit preparation of the financial statements in accordance with U.S. generally accepted accounting principles....

Auditor Report

The Securities Exchange Act of 1934 requires companies that issue their stock publicly to file audited financial statements with the Securities and Exchange Commission (SEC), a governmental agency. Companies engage outside auditors who are certified public accountants to examine their statements. The independent auditors decide whether the company's financial statements comply with GAAP and then issue an audit report. Exhibit 11-7 is the audit report on the financial statements of Pier 1 Imports, Inc.

| **EXHIBIT 11-7** | **Excerpt from the Audit Report on the Financial Statements of Pier 1 Imports, Inc.** |

REPORT OF INDEPENDENT REGISTERED PUBLIC ACCOUNTING FIRM

To the Board of Directors of Pier 1 Imports, Inc.

We have audited the accompanying consolidated balance sheets of Pier 1 Imports, Inc. as of February 25, 2006 and February 26, 2005, and the related consolidated statements of operations, shareholders' equity, and cash flows for each of the three years in the period ended February 25, 2006. These financial statements are the responsibility of the Company's management. Our responsibility is to express an opinion on these financial statements based on our audits.

We conducted our audits in accordance with the standards of the Public Company Accounting Oversight Board (United States).... We believe that our audits provide a reasonable basis for our opinion.

In our opinion, the financial statements referred to above present fairly, in all material respects, the consolidated financial position of Pier 1 Imports, Inc. at February 25, 2006 and February 26, 2005, and the consolidated results of its operations and its cash flows for each of the three years in the period ended February 25, 2006, in conformity with U.S. generally accepted accounting principles.

/s/ Ernst & Young LLP

Fort Worth, Texas
April 25, 2006

The audit report is addressed to the board of directors of the company. The auditing firm signs its name, in this case the Fort Worth office of **Ernst & Young LLP** (LLP is the abbreviation for limited liability partnership).

The audit report typically contains 3 paragraphs:

- The first paragraph identifies the audited statements.
- The second paragraph describes how the audit was performed, mentioning that generally accepted auditing standards are the benchmark for evaluating audit quality.
- The third paragraph states Ernst & Young's opinion that Pier 1's financial statements conform to GAAP and that people can rely on them for decision making. Pier 1's audit report contains a **clean opinion**, more properly called an **unqualified opinion**. Audit reports usually fall into one of four categories:

1. **Unqualified (clean).** The statements are reliable.
2. **Qualified.** The statements are reliable, except for 1 or more items for which the opinion is said to be qualified.
3. **Adverse.** The statements are unreliable.
4. **Disclaimer.** The auditor was unable to reach a professional opinion.

The independent audit adds credibility to the financial statements. It is no accident that financial reporting and auditing are more advanced in the United States than anywhere else in the world and that U.S. capital markets are the envy of the world.

DECISION GUIDELINES

USING THE INCOME STATEMENT AND RELATED NOTES IN INVESTMENT ANALYSIS

Suppose you've completed your studies, taken a job, and been fortunate to save $10,000. Now you are ready to start investing. These guidelines provide a framework for using accounting information for investment analysis.

Decision	Factors to Consider		Decision Variable or Model
Which measure of profitability should be used for investment analysis?	Are you interested in accounting income? →	Income, including all revenues, expenses, gains, and losses?	Net income (bottom line)
		Income that can be expected to repeat from year to year?	Income from continuing operations
	Are you interested in cash flows?	→	Cash flows from operating activities (Chapter 12)

Note: A conservative strategy may use both income and cash flows and compare the 2 sets of results.

What is the estimated value of the stock?	If you believe the company can earn the income (or cash flow) indefinitely →	$\text{Estimated value} = \dfrac{\text{Annual income}}{\text{Investment capitalization rate}}$	
	If you believe the company can earn the income (or cash flow) for a finite number of years →	$\text{Estimated value} = \text{Annual income} \times \dfrac{\text{Present value of annuity}}{\text{(See Appendix C)}}$	
How does risk affect the value of the stock?	If the investment is high risk → Increase the investment capitalization rate		
	If the investment is low risk → Decrease the investment capitalization rate		

END-OF-CHAPTER SUMMARY PROBLEM

The following information was taken from the ledger of Maxim, Inc.:

Prior-period adjustment— credit to Retained Earnings	$ 5,000	Treasury stock, common (5,000 shares at cost)	$ 25,000
Gain on sale of plant assets	21,000	Selling expenses	78,000
Cost of goods sold	380,000	Common stock, no par, 45,000 shares issued	180,000
Income tax expense (saving):		Sales revenue	620,000
Continuing operations	32,000	Interest expense	30,000
Discontinued operations	8,000	Extraordinary gain	26,000
Extraordinary gain	10,000	Income from discontinued operations	20,000
Cumulative effect of change in inventory method	(4,000)	Loss due to lawsuit	11,000
Preferred stock, 8%, $100 par,		General expenses	62,000
500 shares issued	50,000	Retained earnings, beginning, as originally reported	103,000
Dividends	16,000	Cumulative effect of change in inventory method (debit)	(10,000)

❙ Required

Prepare a single-step income statement (with all revenues and gains grouped together) and a statement of retained earnings for Maxim, Inc., for the current year ended December 31, 20XX. Include the earnings-per-share presentation and show computations. Assume no changes in the stock accounts during the year.

Answers

Maxim, Inc.
Income Statement
Year Ended December 31, 20XX

Revenue and gains:		
Sales revenue..		$620,000
Gain on sale of plant assets...		21,000
Total revenues and gains		641,000
Expenses and losses:		
Cost of goods sold	$380,000	
Selling expenses	78,000	
General expenses	62,000	
Interest expense	30,000	
Loss due to lawsuit	11,000	
Income tax expense...	32,000	
Total expenses and losses		593,000
Income from continuing operations..		48,000
Discontinued operations, $20,000, less income tax, $8,000..............		12,000
Income before extraordinary item and		
cumulative effect of change in depreciation method.....................		60,000
Extraordinary gain, $26,000, less income tax, $10,000		16,000
Cumulative effect of change in inventory		
method, $10,000, less income tax saving, $4,000........................		(6,000)
Net income..		$ 70,000
Earnings per share:*		
Income from continuing operations		
[($48,000 – $4,000)/40,000 shares]......................................		$ 1.10
Income from discontinued operations		
($12,000/40,000 shares)...		0.30
Income before extraordinary item and cumulative		
effect of change in inventory method		
[($60,000 – $4,000)/40,000 shares]		1.40
Extraordinary gain ($16,000/40,000 shares)...............................		0.40
Cumulative effect of change in inventory		
method ($6,000/40,000 shares)...		(0.15)
Net income [($70,000 – $4,000)/40,000 shares].........................		$ 1.65

*Computations:

$$EPS = \frac{Income - Preferred\ dividends}{Common\ shares\ outstanding}$$

Preferred dividends: $50,000 × 0.08 = $4,000
Common shares outstanding:
   45,000 shares issued – 5,000 treasury shares = 40,000 shares outstanding

Maxim, Inc.
Statement of Retained Earnings
Year Ended December 31, 20XX

Retained earnings balance, beginning, as originally reported................	$103,000
Prior-period adjustment—credit	5,000
Retained earnings balance, beginning, as adjusted...............................	108,000
Net income for current year...	70,000
	178,000
Dividends for current year..	(16,000)
Retained earnings balance, ending...	$162,000

REVIEW THE INCOME STATEMENT

Quick Check (Answers are given on page 614.)

1. The quality of earnings suggests that:
   a. Net income is the best measure of the results of operations.
   b. Income from continuing operations is better than income from one-time transactions.
   c. Continuing operations and one-time transactions are of equal importance.
   d. Stockholders want the corporation to earn enough income to be able to pay its debts.

2. Which statement is true?
   a. Discontinued operations are a separate category on the income statement.
   b. Extraordinary items are part of discontinued operations.
   c. Cumulative effect of accounting changes is combined with continuing operations on the income statement.
   d. All of the above are true.

3. **FedEx Corporation** earned $5.94 per share of its common stock. Suppose you capitalize FedEx's income at 6%. How much are you willing to pay for a share of FedEx stock?
   a. $32.17
   b. $5.17
   c. $165.00
   d. Some other amount _____

4. Return to Pier 1 Imports' income statement on page 580. Pier 1 has no preferred stock outstanding. How many shares of common stock did Pier 1 have outstanding during fiscal year 2006? Focus on the bottom line, net loss.
   a. 99 million
   b. 320 million
   c. 86.5 million
   d. 31 million

5. Why is it important for companies to report their accounting changes to the public?
   a. Accounting changes affect dividends, and investors want dividends.
   b. Some accounting changes are more extraordinary than others.
   c. Most accounting changes increase net income, and investors need to know why the increase in net income occurred.
   d. Without the reporting of accounting changes, investors could believe all the company's income came from continuing operations.

6. Other comprehensive income
   a. affects earnings per share.
   b. includes extraordinary gains and losses.
   c. includes unrealized gains and losses on investments.
   d. has no effect on income tax.

7. Onstar GPS Systems earned income before tax of $50,000. Taxable income was $40,000, and the income tax rate was 40%. Onstar recorded income tax with this journal entry:

a.	Income Tax Expense	20,000	
	Income Tax Payable		16,000
	Deferred Tax Liability		4,000
b.	Income Tax Expense	20,000	
	Income Tax Payable		20,000
c.	Income Tax Payable	16,000	
	Income Tax Expense		16,000
d.	Income Tax Payable	20,000	
	Income Tax Expense		16,000
	Deferred Tax Liability		4,000

8. Deferred Tax Liability is usually

	Type of Account	Reported on the
a.	Short-term	Income statement
b.	Short-term	Statement of stockholders' equity
c.	Long-term	Income statement
d.	Long-term	Balance statement

9. The main purpose of the statement of stockholders' equity is to report
   a. financial position.
   b. reasons for changes in the equity accounts.
   c. results of operations.
   d. comprehensive income.

10. An auditor report by independent accountants
   a. ensures that the financial statements are error-free.
   b. gives investors assurance that the company's stock is a safe investment.
   c. gives investors assurance that the company's financial statements conform to GAAP.
   d. is ultimately the responsibility of the management of the client company.

Accounting Vocabulary

adverse opinion (p. 594) An audit opinion stating that the financial statements are unreliable.

clean opinion (p. 594) An *unqualified opinion*.

comprehensive income (p. 587) A company's change in total stockholder's equity from all sources other than from the owners of the business.

disclaimer (p. 594) An audit opinion stating that the auditor was unable to reach a professional opinion regarding the quality of the financial statements.

earnings per share (EPS) (p. 586) Amount of a company's net income per share of its outstanding common stock.

extraordinary gains and losses (p. 584) Also called *extraordinary items*, these gains and losses are both unusual for the company and infrequent.

extraordinary items (p. 584) An *extraordinary gain or loss*.

investment capitalization rate (p. 582) An earnings rate used to estimate the value of an investment in stock.

pretax accounting income (p. 588) Income before tax on the income statement.

prior-period adjustment (p. 590) A correction to beginning balance of retained earnings for an error of an earlier period.

qualified opinion (p. 594) An audit opinion stating that the financial statements are reliable, except for one or more items for which the opinion is said to be qualified.

statement of stockholders' equity (p. 590) Reports the changes in all categories of stockholders' equity during the period.

taxable income (p. 589) The basis for computing the amount of tax to pay the government.

unqualified (clean) opinion (p. 594) An audit opinion stating that the financial statements are reliable.

ASSESS YOUR PROGRESS

Short Exercises

S11-1 (*Learning Objective 1: Preparing a complex income statement*) List the major parts of a complex corporate income statement for Oneida Corporation for the year ended March 31, 20X9. Include all the major parts of the income statement, starting with net sales revenue and ending with net income (net loss). You may ignore dollar amounts and earnings per share. (p. 582)

S11-2 (*Learning Objective 1: Explaining the items on a complex income statement*) Study the 2005 (not 2006) income statement of **Pier 1 Imports** (p. 580) and answer these questions about the company: (pp. 580–582)

    writing assignment ■

1. How much gross profit did Pier 1 earn on the sale of its products? How much was income from continuing operations? Net income? (p. 309)

2. At the end of 2005, what dollar amount of net income would most sophisticated investors use to predict Pier 1's net income for 2006 and beyond? Name this item, give its amount, and state your reason. (p. 582)

S11-3 (*Learning Objective 1: Preparing a complex income statement*) Financial Resources, Inc., reported the following items, listed in no particular order at December 31, 20X7 (in thousands):

Other gains (losses)	$ (2,000)	Extraordinary gain	$ 5,000
Net sales revenue	182,000	Cost of goods sold	71,000
Loss on discontinued		Operating expenses	64,000
operations	15,000	Accounts receivable	19,000

Income tax of 40% applies to all items.

    Prepare Financial Resources' income statement for the year ended December 31, 20X7. Omit earnings per share. (p. 582)

S11-4 (*Learning Objective 1: Reporting earnings per share*) Return to the Financial Resources data in Short Exercise S11-3. Financial Resources had 10,000 shares of common stock outstanding during 20X7. Financial Resources declared and paid preferred dividends of $6,000 during 20X7.

    Report Financial Resources' earnings per share on the income statement. (p. 586)

S11-5 (*Learning Objective 1: Reporting comprehensive income*) Use the Financial Resources data in Short Exercise S11-3. In addition, Financial Resources had unrealized gains of $1,000 on investments and a $2,000 foreign-currency translation adjustment (a gain) during 20X7. Both amounts are net of tax. Start with Financial Resources' net income from S11-3 and show how the company could report other comprehensive income on its 20X7 income statement. (pp. 587–588)

    Should Financial Resources report earnings per share for other comprehensive income? State why or why not.

S11-6 (*Learning Objective 1: Valuing a company's stock*) For fiscal year 2006, **Apple Computer, Inc.**, reported net sales of $19,315 million, net income of $1,989 million, and no significant discontinued operations, extraordinary items, or accounting changes.

    Earnings per share was $2.36. At a capitalization rate of 6%, how much should 1 share of Apple stock be worth? Compare your estimated stock price to Apple's actual stock price as quoted in *The Wall Street Journal*, in your newspaper, or on the Internet. Based on your estimated market value, should you buy, hold, or sell Apple stock? (pp. 582–584)

writing assignment ■

S11-7 (*Learning Objective 1: Interpreting earnings-per-share data*) Marstaller Motor Company has preferred stock outstanding and issued additional common stock during the year. (p. 586)

1. Give the basic equation to compute earnings per share of common stock for net income.
2. List the income items for which Marstaller must report earnings-per-share data.
3. What makes earnings per share so useful as a business statistic?

S11-8 (*Learning Objective 2: Accounting for a corporation's income tax*) Pensacola Marine, Inc., had income before income tax of $110,000 and taxable income of $90,000 for 20X8, the company's first year of operations. The income tax rate is 40%.

1. Make the entry to record Pensacola Marine's income taxes for 20X8. (pp. 589–590)
2. Show what Pensacola Marine will report on its 20X8 income statement starting with income before income tax. Also show what Pensacola Marine will report for current and long-term liabilities on its December 31, 20X8, balance sheet. (pp. 589–590)

S11-9 (*Learning Objective 3: Reporting a prior-period adjustment*) iFlash, Inc., was set to report the following statement of retained earnings for the year ended December 31, 20X1.

iFlash, Inc. Statement of Retained Earnings Year Ended December 31, 20X1	
Retained earnings, December 31, 20X0	$140,000
Net income for 20X1	91,000
Dividends for 20X1...	(14,000)
Retained earnings, December 31, 20X1	$217,000

Before issuing its 20X1 financial statements, iFlash learned that net income of 20X0 was overstated by $16,000. Prepare iFlash's 20X1 statement of retained earnings to show the correction of the error—that is, the prior-period adjustment. (pp. 589–590)

S11-10 (*Learning Objective 4: Using the statement of stockholders' equity*) Use the statement of stockholders' equity in Exhibit 11-4 (p. 591) to answer the following questions about Allied Electronics Corporation:

1. How much cash did the issuance of common stock bring in during 20X9? (p. 483)
2. What was the effect of the stock dividends on Allied's retained earnings? on total paid-in capital? on total stockholders' equity? on total assets? (pp. 494–496)
3. What was the cost of the treasury stock that Allied purchased during 20X9? What was Allied's cost of the treasury stock that Allied sold during the year? For how much did Allied sell the treasury stock during 20X9? (pp. 489, 490)

Exercises

E11-11 (*Learning Objective 1: Preparing and using a complex income statement*) Outback Cycles, Inc., reported a number of special items on its income statement. The following data, listed in no particular order, came from Outback's financial statements (amounts in thousands):

Income tax expense (saving):		Net sales...	$13,800
Continuing operations..................	$610	Foreign-currency translation	
Discontinued operations..............	50	adjustment	360
Extraordinary loss.......................	(3)	Extraordinary loss................................	13
Unrealized gain on		Income from discontinued operations	270
available-for-sale investments.......	40	Dividends declared and paid	680
Short-term investments....................	35	Total operating expenses.......................	12,250

▮ Required

Show how the Outback Cycles, Inc., income statement for the year ended September 30, 20X8 should appear. Omit earnings per share. (p. 582)

E11-12 (*Learning Objective 1: Preparing and using a complex income statement*) The Golden Books Company accounting records include the following for 20X6 (in thousands):

■ spreadsheet

Other revenues	$ 1,800
Income tax expense — extraordinary gain	500
Income tax expense — income from continuing operations	2,800
Extraordinary gain	1,300
Sales revenue	104,000
Total operating expenses	97,900

▮ Required

1. Prepare Golden Books' single-step income statement for the year ended December 31, 20X6, including EPS. Golden Books had 1,600 thousand shares of common stock and no preferred stock outstanding during the year. (pp. 138, 586)

2. Assume investors capitalize Golden Books earnings at 7%. Estimate the price of 1 share of the company's stock. (pp. 582–584)

E11-13 (*Learning Objective 1: Using an income statement*) High Seas Cruise Lines, Inc., reported the following income statement for the year ended December 31, 2006.

writing assignment ■

	Millions
Operating revenues	$70,752
Operating expenses	60,258
Operating income	10,494
Other revenue (expense), net	985
Income from continuing operations	11,479
Discontinued operations, net of tax	935
Cumulative effect of accounting change, net of tax	(503)
Net income	$11,911

▮ Required

1. Were High Seas' discontinued operations and cumulative effect of the accounting change more like an expense or a revenue? How can you tell? (p. 582)

2. Should the discontinued operations and the cumulative effect of High Seas' accounting change be included in or excluded from net income? State your reason. (pp. 584–585)

3. Suppose you are working as a financial analyst and your job is to predict High Seas' net income for 2007 and beyond. Which item from the income statement will you use for your prediction? Identify its amount. Why will you use this item? (p. 582)

E11-14 (*Learning Objective 1: Using income data for investment analysis*) During 20X6, **PepsiCo, Inc.**, had sales of $35.1 billion, operating profit of $6.4 billion, and net income of $5.6 billion. Earnings per share (EPS) were $3.42. On May 15, 20X7, of a share of PepsiCo's common stock was priced at $67.26 on the New York Stock Exchange.

What investment capitalization rate did investors appear to be using to determine the value of 1 share of PepsiCo stock? The formula for the value of 1 share of stock uses EPS in the calculation. (pp. 582–584, 586)

E11-15 (*Learning Objective 1: Computing earnings per share*) Tennyson Loan Company's balance sheet reports the following:

Preferred stock, $50 par value, 6%, 10,000 shares issued	$500,000
Common stock, $0.50 par, 1,200,000 shares issued.....................	600,000
Treasury stock, common, 100,000 shares at cost	800,000

During 20X7 Tennyson earned net income of $5,800,000. Compute Tennyson's EPS for 20X7. (p. 586)

E11-16 (*Learning Objective 1: Computing and using earnings per share*) Midtown Holding Company operates numerous businesses, including motel, auto rental, and real estate companies. Year 20X6 was interesting for Midtown, which reported the following on its income statement (in millions):

Net revenues	$3,930
Total expenses and other..	3,354
Income from continuing operations.............................	576
Discontinued operations, net of tax............................	84
Income before extraordinary item and cumulative effect of accounting change, net of tax...............	660
Extraordinary gain, net of tax	8
Net income...	$ 668

During 20X6, Midtown had the following (in millions, except for par value per share):

Common stock, $0.01 par value, 900 shares issued	$ 9
Treasury stock, 180 shares at cost..	(3,568)

❙ Required

Show how Midtown should report earnings per share for 20X6. (p. 586)

E11-17 (*Learning Objective 2: Accounting for income tax by a corporation*) For 20X9, its first year of operations, Smartpages Advertising earned pretax accounting income (on the income statement) of $600,000. Taxable income (on the tax return filed with the Internal Revenue Service) is $550,000. The income tax rate is 40%. Record Smartpages' income tax for the year. Show what Smartpages will report on its 20X9 income statement and balance sheet for this situation. Start the income statement with income before tax. (pp. 588–589)

E11-18 (*Learning Objective 2: Accounting for income tax by a corporation*) During 20X6, the Castle Heights Corp. income statement reported income of $300,000 before tax. The company's income tax return filed with the IRS showed taxable income of $250,000. During 20X6, Castle Heights was subject to an income tax rate of 40%.

❙ Required

1. Journalize Castle Heights' income taxes for 20X6. (pp. 589–590)
2. How much income tax did Castle Heights have to pay currently for the year 20X6? (pp. 589–590)
3. At the beginning of 20X6, Castle Heights' balance of Deferred Tax Liability was $40,000. How much Deferred Tax Liability did Castle Heights report on its balance sheet at December 31, 20X6? (pp. 589–590)

E11-19 (*Learning Objective 3: Reporting a prior-period adjustment on the statement of retained earnings*) Roy Beaty Products, Inc., a household products chain, reported a prior-period adjustment in 20X2. An accounting error caused net income of 20X1 to be understated by $13 million. Retained earnings at December 31, 20X1, as previously reported, stood at $344 million. Net income for 20X2 was $92 million, and 20X2 dividends were $48 million.

❙ Required

Prepare the company's statement of retained earnings for the year ended December 31, 20X2. How does the prior-period adjustment affect Roy Beaty's net income for 20X2? (pp. 589–590)

E11-20 (*Learning Objective 3: Preparing a staement of stockholders' equity*) At December 31, 20X4, Lake Air Mall, Inc., reported stockholders' equity as follows:

Common stock, $1 par, 500,000 shares authorized, 320,000 shares issued	$ 320,000
Additional paid-in capital.......................................	600,000
Retained earnings..	680,000
	$1,600,000

During 20X5, Lake Air Mall completed these transactions (listed in chronological order):

a. Declared and issued a 5% stock dividend on the outstanding stock. At the time, Lake Air Mall stock was quoted at a market price of $10 per share.
b. Issued 20,000 shares of common stock at the price of $12 per share.
c. Net income for the year, $340,000.
d. Declared cash dividends of $100,000.

❙ Required

Prepare Lake Air Mall, Inc.'s, statement of stockholders' equity for 20X5, using the format of Exhibit 11-4 (p. 591) as a model.

E11-21 (*Learning Objective 3: Using a company's statement of stockholders' equity*) Spring Water Company reported the following items on its statement of shareholders' equity for the year ended December 31, 20X9 (in thousands):

	$1 Par Common Stock	Capital in Excess of Par Value	Retained Earnings	Accumulated Other Comprehensive Income	Total Shareholders' Equity
Balance, Dec. 31, 20X8.....................	$380	$1,590	$3,500	$9	$5,479
Net earnings..			1,020		
Unrealized gain on investments					
Issuance of stock	110	560		1	
Cash dividends.................................			(220)		
Balance, Dec.31, 20X9......................					

❙ Required

1. Determine the December 31, 20X9, balances in Spring Water's shareholders' equity accounts and total shareholders' equity on this date. (pp. 590–591)
2. Spring Water's total liabilities on December 31, 20X9 are $5,000 thousand. What is Spring Water's debt ratio on this date? (p. 169)
3. Was there a profit or a loss for the year ended December 31, 20X9? How can you tell? (pp. 592–593)
4. At what price per share did Spring Water issue common stock during 20X9? (pp. 590–591)

E11-22 (*Learning Objective 4: Identifying responsibility and standards for the financial statements*) The annual report of **Apple Computer, Inc.**, included the following:

Management's Annual Report on Internal Control over Financial Reporting

The Company's management is responsible for establishing and maintaining adequate control over financial reporting [....] Management conducted an evaluation of the effectiveness of the Company's internal control over financial reporting [....] Based on this evaluation, management has concluded that the company's internal control over financial reporting was effective as of September 30, 2006....

Report of Independent Registered Public Accounting Firm
The Board of Directors and Shareholders
Apple Computer, Inc.:

We have audited the accompanying consolidated balance sheets of Apple Computer, Inc. and subsidiaries (the Company) as of September 30, 2006 and September 24, 2005, and the related consolidated statements of operations, shareholders' equity and cash flows for each of the years in the three-year period ended September 30, 2006. These consolidated financial statements are the responsibility of the Company's management. Our responsibility is to express an opinion on these consolidated financial statements based on our audits.

We conducted our audits in accordance with the standards of the Public Company Accounting Oversight Board (United States)....

In our opinion, the consolidated financial statements referred to above present fairly, in all material respects, the financial position of the Company as of September 30, 2006 and September 24, 2005, and the results of their operations and their operations and their cash flows for each of the years in the three-year period ended September 30, 2006, in conformity with accounting principles generally accepted in the United States of America.

/S/ KPMG LLP

Mountain View, California
December 29, 2006

---

1. Who is responsible for Apple's financial statements? (pp. 593–594)
2. By what accounting standard are the financial statements prepared? (pp. 593–594)
3. Identify 1 concrete action that Apple management takes to fulfill its responsibility for the reliability of the company's financial information. (p. 593)
4. Which entity gave an outside, independent opinion on the Apple financial statements? Where was this entity located, and when did it release its opinion to the public? (p. 594)
5. Exactly what did the audit cover? Give names and dates. (p. 594)
6. By what standard did the auditor conduct the audit? (p. 594)
7. What was the auditor's opinion of Apple's financial statements? (p. 594)

Quiz

Test your understanding of the corporate income statement and the statement of stockholders equity by answering the following questions. Select the best choice from among the possible answers given.

Q11-23 What is the best source of income for a corporation? (p. 582)
a. Prior-period adjustments
b. Continuing operations
c. Extraordinary items
d. Discontinued operations

Jergens Lotion Company reports several earnings numbers on its current-year income statement (parentheses indicate a loss):

Gross profit	$ 140,000	Income from continuing operations	$ 35,000
Net income	41,000	Extraordinary gains	14,000
Income before income tax	60,000	Discontinued operations	(8,000)

Q11-24 How much net income would most investment analysts predict for Jurgen's to earn next year? (p. 582)
a. $14,000
b. $35,000
c. $49,000
d. $41,000

Q11-25 Return to the preceding question. Suppose you are evaluating Jergens Lotion Company stock as an investment. You require a 10% rate of return on investments, so you capitalize Jergen's earnings at 10%. How much are you willing to pay for all of Jergens' stock? (pp. 582–584)
a. $1,400,000
b. $600,000
c. $410,000
d. $350,000

Q11-26 Hi-Valu Corporation had the following extraordinary items:

Extraordinary flood loss	$ 90,000
Extraordinary gain on lawsuit	110,000

Net income before income tax and before extraordinary items totals $260,000, and the income tax rate is 40%. Hi-Valu's net income is (pp. 582, 584–585)
a. $168,000.
b. $280,000.
c. $380,000.
d. $460,000.

Q11-27 Hi-Valu Corporation in question 26 has 10,000 shares of 5%, $100 par preferred stock and 100,000 shares of common stock outstanding. Earnings per share for net income is (p. 586)
a. $1.02.
b. $1.18.
c. $1.68.
d. $2.02.

Q11-28 Earnings per share is *not* reported for (pp. 587–588)
a. continuing operations.
b. discontinued operations.
c. comprehensive income.
d. extraordinary items.

Q11-29 Copystar Corporation has income before income tax of $150,000 and taxable income of $100,000. The income tax rate is 40%. Copystar's income statement will report net income of (pp. 589–590)
a. $40,000.
b. $60,000.
c. $90,000.
d. $120,000.

Q11-30 Copystar Corporation in the preceding question must immediately pay income tax of (pp. 589–590)
a. $60,000.
b. $8,000.
c. $32,000.
d. $40,000.

Q11-31 Use the Copystar Corporation data in question 29. At the end of its first year of operations, Copystar's deferred tax liability is (pp. 589–590)
a. $20,000.
b. $28,000.
c. $32,000.
d. $40,000.

Q11-32 Which of the following items is most closely related to prior-period adjustments? (pp. 589–590)
a. Earnings per share
b. Retained earnings
c. Accounting changes
d. Preferred stock dividends

Q11-33 Examine the statement of stockholders' equity of Allied Electronics Corporation in Exhibit 11-4, page 591. What was the market value of each share of the stock that Allied gave its stockholders in the stock dividend? (pp. 495, 590–591)

a. $8   c. $34,000
b. $8,000   d. $25

Q11-34 Which statement is true? (pp. 593–594)
a. Management audits the financial statements.
b. Independent auditors prepare the financial statements.
c. GAAP governs the form and content of the financial statements.
d. The Public Company Oversight Board evaluates internal controls.

Problems
(Group A)

MyAccountingLab

> Some of these problems A can be found within My Accounting Lab (MAL), an online homework and practice environment. Your instructor may ask you to complete these problems using MAL.

P11-35A (*Learning Objective 1: Preparing a complex income statement*) The following information was taken from the records of Filner Cosmetics, Inc., at December 31, 20X8.

Prior-period adjustment—		Dividends on common stock	$37,000
debit to Retained Earnings.............	$ 4,000	Interest expense.................................	23,000
Income tax expense (saving):		Gain on lawsuit settlement................	8,000
Continuing operations...................	28,000	Dividend revenue	11,000
Income from discontinued		Treasury stock, common	
operations.....................................	2,000	(2,000 shares at cost)...............	28,000
Extraordinary loss	(10,800)	General expenses.............................	71,000
Cumulative effect of change		Sales revenue	567,000
in inventory method	3,000	Retained earnings, beginning,	
Loss on sale of plant assets....................	10,000	as originally reported..............	63,000
Income from discontinued		Selling expenses.................................	87,000
operations.....................................	7,000	Common stock, no par,	
Preferred stock, 6%, $25 par,		22,000 shares authorized	
4,000 shares issued........................	100,000	and issued..............................	350,000
Cumulative effect of change in		Extraordinary loss............................	27,000
inventory method (credit)	7,600	Cost of goods sold............................	319,000

❙ Required
1. Prepare Filner Cosmetics' single-step income statement, which lists all revenues together and all expenses together, for the fiscal year ended December 31, 20X8. Include earnings-per-share data. (pp. 138, 582)
2. Evaluate income for the year ended December 31, 20X8. Filner's top managers hoped to earn income from continuing operations equal to 10% of sales. (Challenge)

P11-36A (*Learning Objective 3: Preparing a statement of retained earnings*) Use the data in Problem P11-35A to prepare the Filner Cosmetics statement of retained earnings for the year ended December 31, 20X8. (pp. 589–590)

P11-37A (*Learning Objective 1: Using income data to make an investment decision*) Filner Cosmetics in Problem P11-35A holds significant promise for carving a niche in its industry. A group of Canadian investors is considering purchasing the company's outstanding common stock. Filner's stock is currently selling for $32 per share.

A *Financial Markets Magazine* story predicted the company's income is bound to grow. It appears that Filner can earn at least its current level of income for the indefinite future. Based on this information, the investors think that an appropriate investment capitalization rate for estimating the value of Filner's common stock is 8%. How much will this belief lead the investors to offer for Filner Cosmetics? Will Filner's existing stockholders be likely to accept this offer? Explain your answers. (pp. 582–584)

P11-38A *(Learning Objective 1: Computing earnings per share and estimating the price of a stock)* Turnaround Specialists, Ltd., (TSL) specializes in taking underperforming companies to a higher level of performance. TSL's capital structure at December 31, 20X7 included 10,000 shares of $2.50 preferred stock and 120,000 shares of common stock. During 20X8, TSL issued common stock and ended the year with 127,000 shares of common stock outstanding. Average common shares outstanding during 20X8 were 123,500. Income from continuing operations during 20X8 was $219,000. The company discontinued a segment of the business at a loss of $69,000, and an extraordinary item generated a gain of $49,500. All amounts are after income tax.

❙ *Required*

1. Compute TSL's earnings per share. Start with income from continuing operations. (p. 586)
2. Analysts believe TSL can earn its current level of income for the indefinite future. Estimate the market price of a share of TSL common stock at investment capitalization rates of 6%, 8%, and 10%. Which estimate presumes an investment in TSL is the most risky? How can you tell? (pp. 582–584)

P11-39A *(Learning Objective 1: Preparing a corrected income statement, including comprehensive income)* Richard Wright, accountant for Sweetie Pie Foods, Inc., was injured in an auto accident. Another employee prepared the following income statement for the fiscal year ended June 30, 20X7:

Sweetie Pie Foods, Inc.
Income Statement
June 30, 20X7

Revenue and gains:		
Sales		$733,000
Paid-in capital in excess of par—common		100,000
Total revenues and gains		833,000
Expenses and losses:		
Cost of goods sold	$383,000	
Selling expenses	103,000	
General expenses	74,000	
Sales returns	22,000	
Unrealized loss on available-for-sale investments	4,000	
Dividends paid	15,000	
Sales discounts	10,000	
Income tax expense	56,400	
Total expenses and losses		667,400
Income from operations		165,600
Other gains and losses:		
Extraordinary gain	30,000	
Loss on discontinued operations	(15,000)	
Total other gains (losses)		15,000
Net income		$180,600
Earnings per share		$4.52

(continued)

The individual *amounts* listed on the income statement are correct. However, some *accounts* are reported incorrectly, and some accounts do not belong on the income statement at all. Also, income tax (40%) has not been applied to all appropriate figures. Sweetie Pie Foods issued 44,000 shares of common stock back in 20X1 and held 4,000 shares as treasury stock all during the fiscal year 20X7.

I Required

Prepare a corrected statement of income (single-step, which lists all revenues together and all expenses together), including comprehensive income, for fiscal year 20X7. Include earnings per share. (p. 582)

P11-40A (*Learning Objective 2: Accounting for a corporation's income tax*) The accounting (not the income tax) records of Haynes Publications, Inc., provide the comparative income statement for 20X1 and 20X2, respectively:

	20X1	20X2
Total revenue	$600,000	$720,000
Expenses:		
Cost of goods sold.............................	$290,000	$310,000
Operating expenses	180,000	190,000
Total expenses before tax...................	470,000	500,000
Pretax accounting income	$130,000	$220,000

Taxable income for 20X1 includes these modifications from pretax accounting income:
   a. Additional taxable income of $10,000 for rent revenue earned in 20X2 but taxed in 20X1.
   b. Additional depreciation expense of $20,000 for MACRS tax depreciation.

The income tax rate is $40%.

I Required

1. Compute Haynes' taxable income for 20X1. (Challenge, p. 589)
2. Journalize the corporation's income taxes for 20X1. (pp. 589–590)
3. Prepare the corporation's income statement for 20X1. (pp. 589–590)

P11-41A (*Learning Objective 3: Using a statement of stockholders' equity*) Asian Food Specialties, Inc., reported the following statement of stockholders' equity for the year ended June 30, 20X7:

Asian Food Specialties, Inc.
Statement of Stockholders' Equity
Year Ended June 30, 20X7

(In millions)	Common Stock	Additional Paid-in Capital	Retained Earnings	Treasury Stock	Total
Balance, June 30, 20X6...............	$175	$2,118	$1,702	$(18)	$3,977
Net income.................................			540		540
Cash dividends............................			(117)		(117)
Issuance of stock (5 shares)..........	5	46			51
Stock dividend.............................	18	180	(198)		—
Sale of treasury stock		14		6	20
Balance, June 30, 20X7...............	$198	$2,358	$1,927	$(12)	$4,471

▌ Required

Answer these questions about Asian Food Specialties' stockholders' equity transactions.

1. The income tax rate is 40%. How much income before income tax did Asian Food Specialties report on the income statement? (pp. 588–590)
2. What is the par value of the company's common stock? (pp. 482–483)
3. At what price per share did Asian Food Specialties issue its common stock during the year? (p. 482)
4. What was the cost of treasury stock sold during the year? What was the total selling price of the treasury stock sold? What was the increase in total stockholders' equity? (p. 489)
5. Asian Food Specialties' statement of stockholders' equity lists the stock transactions in the order in which they occurred. What was the percentage of the stock dividend? Round to the nearest percentage. (p. 495)

(Group B)

P11-42B (*Learning Objective 1: Preparing a complex income statement*) The following information was taken from the records of Kendall Corporation at April 30, 20X3. Kendall manufactures electronic controls for model airplanes.

Dividends	$ 15,000	Treasury stock, common	
Interest revenue	4,000	(1,000 shares at cost)	$ 11,000
Extraordinary gain	30,000	Prior-period adjustment—	
Income form discontinued operations	5,000	credit to Retained Earnings	6,000
Loss on insurance settlement	12,000	Interest expense	11,000
General expenses	113,000	Cost of goods sold	424,000
Preferred stock—5%, $40 par,		Cumulative effect of change in	
10,000 shares authorized,		inventory method (debit)	(18,000)
5,000 shares issued	200,000	Loss on sale of plant assets	8,000
Retained earnings, beginning,		Income tax expense (saving):	
as originally reported	88,000	Continuing operations	72,000
Selling expenses	136,000	Discontinued operations	2,000
Common stock, $10 par,		Extraordinary gain	12,000
25,000 shares authorized and issued	250,000	Cumulative effect of change	
Sales revenue	833,000	in inventory method	(7,000)

▌ Required

1. Prepare Kendall's single-step income statement, which lists all revenues together and all expenses together, for the fiscal year ended April 30, 20X3. Include earnings-per-share data. (pp. 138, 582)
2. Evaluate income for the year ended April 30, 20X3. Kendall's top managers hoped to earn income from continuing operations equal to 10% of sales. (Challenge)

P11-43B (*Learning Objective 3: Preparing a statement of retained earnings*) Use the data in Problem P11-42B to prepare Kendall Corporation's statement of retained earnings for the year ended April 30, 20X3. (pp. 589–590)

P11-44B (*Learning Objective 1: Using income data to make an investment decision*) Kendall Corporation in Problem P11-42B holds significant promise for carving a niche in the electronic controls industry, and a group of Swiss investors is considering purchasing Kendall's outstanding common stock. Kendall's common stock is currently selling for $50 per share.

A *Business Today* magazine story predicts that Kendall's income is bound to grow. It appears that the company can earn at least its current level of income for the indefinite future.

(*continued*)

Based on this information, the investors think an appropriate investment capitalization rate for estimating the value of Kendall common stock is 6%. How much will this belief lead the investors to offer for Kendall Corporation? Will the existing stockholders of Kendall be likely to accept this offer? Explain your answers. (pp. 582–584)

P11-45B *(Learning Objective 1: Computing earnings per share and estimating the price of a stock)* The capital structure of AMEX Products at December 31, 20X5, included 20,000 shares of $1.25 preferred stock and 44,000 shares of common stock. During 20X6, AMEX issued common stock and ended the year with 58,000 shares. The average number of common shares outstanding for the year was 51,000. Income from continuing operations during 20X6 was $81,100. The company discontinued a segment of the business at a gain of $6,630, and an extraordinary item generated a loss of $16,000. All amounts are after income tax.

I Required

1. Compute AMEX's earnings per share. Start with income from continuing operations. (p. 586)
2. Analysts believe AMEX can earn its current level of income for the indefinite future. Estimate the market price of a share of AMEX common stock at investment capitalization rates of 7%, 9%, and 11%. Which estimate presumes an investment in AMEX stock is the most risky? How can you tell? (pp. 582–584)

P11-46B *(Learning Objective 1: Preparing a corrected income statement, including comprehensive income)* Rhonda Sparks, accountant for Canon Pet Supplies, was injured in a skiing accident. Another employee prepared the accompanying income statement for the year ended December 31, 20X1.

The individual *amounts* listed on the income statement are correct. However, some *accounts* are reported incorrectly, and 1 account does not belong on the income statement at all. Also, income tax (40%) has not been applied to all appropriate figures. Canon issued 52,000 shares of common stock in 20X0 and held 2,000 shares as treasury stock all during 20X1.

Canon Pet Supplies Income Statement 20X1		
Revenue and gains:		
Sales		$362,000
Unrealized gain on available-for-sale investments		10,000
Paid-in capital in excess of par—common		80,000
Total revenues and gains		452,000
Expenses and losses:		
Cost of goods sold	$103,000	
Selling expenses	56,000	
General expenses	61,000	
Sales returns	11,000	
Dividends paid	7,000	
Sales discounts	6,000	
Income tax expense	50,000	
Total expenses and losses		294,000
Income from operations		158,000
Other gains and losses:		
Extraordinary loss	$(20,000)	
Loss on discontinued operations	(3,000)	
Total other losses		(23,000)
Net income		$135,000
Earnings per share		$2.70

I Required

Prepare a corrected statement of income (single-step, which lists all revenues together and all expenses together), including comprehensive income for 20X1. Include earnings per share. (p. 582)

P11-47B (*Learning Objective 2: Accounting for a corporation's income tax*) The accounting (not the income tax) records of Colorado Rafting, Inc., provide the following comparative income statement for 20X4 and 20X5, respectively.

	20X4	20X5
Total revenue	$900,000	$990,000
Expenses:		
Cost of goods sold	$430,000	$460,000
Operating expenses	270,000	280,000
Total expenses before tax	700,000	740,000
Pretax accounting income	$200,000	$250,000

Taxable income for 20X4 includes these modifications from pretax accounting income:

a. Additional taxable income of $15,000 for accounting income earned in 20X5 but taxed in 20X4.
b. Additional depreciation expense of $30,000 for MACRS tax depreciation.

The income tax rate is $40%.

I Required

1. Compute Colorado Rafting's taxable income for 20X4. (Challenge, p. 589)
2. Journalize the corporation's income taxes for 20X4. (pp. 589–590)
3. Prepare the corporation's income statement for 20X4. (pp. 589–590)

P11-48B (*Learning Objective 3: Using a statement of stockholders' equity*) Datacom Services, Inc., reported the following statement of stockholders' equity for the year ended October 31, 20X7.

Datacom Services, Inc.
Statement of Stockholders' Equity
Year Ended October 31, 20X7

(In millions)	Common Stock	Additional Paid-in Capital	Retained Earnings	Treasury Stock	Total
Balance, Oct. 31, 20X6	$427	$1,622	$904	$(117)	$2,836
Net income			360		360
Cash dividends			(194)		(194)
Issuance of stock (13 shares)	13	36			49
Stock dividend	44	122	(166)		–
Sale of treasury stock		11		9	20
Balance, Oct. 31, 20X7	$484	$1,791	$904	$108	$3,071

I Required

Answer these questions about Datacom Services' stockholders' equity transactions:

1. The income tax rate is 40%. How much income before income tax did Datacom report on the income statement? (pp. 588–590)
2. What is the par value of the company's common stock? (pp. 482–483)

(continued)

3. At what price per share did Datacom Services issue its common stock during the year? (pp. 482–483)
4. What was the cost of treasury stock sold during the year? What was the selling price of the treasury stock sold? What was the increase in total stockholders' equity? (pp. 489–490)
5. Datacom Services' statement lists the stock transactions in the order they occurred. What was the percentage of the stock dividend? (p. 495)

APPLY YOUR KNOWLEDGE

Decision Cases

writing assignment ▪

Case 1. (*Learning Objective 1: Evaluating the components of income*) Prudhoe Bay Oil Co. is having its initial public offering (IPO) of company stock. To create public interest in its stock, Prudhoe Bay's chief financial officer has blitzed the media with press releases. One, in particular, caught your eye. On November 19, Prudhoe Bay announced unaudited earnings per share (EPS) of $1.19, up 89% from last year's EPS of $0.63. An 89% increase in EPS is outstanding!

Before deciding to buy Prudhoe Bay stock, you investigated further and found that the company omitted several items from the determination of unaudited EPS, as follows:

- Unrealized loss on available-for-sale investments, $0.06 per share
- Gain on sale of building, $0.05 per share
- Cumulative effect of change in method of recognizing revenue, increase in retained earnings $1.10 per share
- Restructuring expenses, $0.29 per share
- Loss on settlement of lawsuit begun 5 years ago, $0.12 per share
- Lost income due to employee labor strike, $0.24 per share
- Income from discontinued operations, $0.09 per share

Wondering how to treat these "special items," you called your stockbroker at **Merrill Lynch**. She thinks that these items are nonrecurring and outside Prudhoe Bay's core operations. Furthermore, she suggests that you ignore the items and consider Prudhoe Bay's earnings of $1.19 per share to be a good estimate of long-term profitability.

❙ Required

What EPS number will you use to predict Prudhoe Bay's future profits? Show your work, and explain your reasoning for each item. (pp. 580–586)

writing assignment ▪

Case 2. (*Learning Objective 1: Using the financial statements in investment analysis*) Mike Magid Toyota is an automobile dealership. Magid's annual report includes Note 1— Summary of Significant Accounting Policies as follows:

> **Income Recognition**
>
> **Sales are recognized when cash payment is received or, in the case of credit sales, which represent the majority of . . . sales, when a down payment is received and the customer enters into an installment sales contract. These installment sales contracts . . . are normally collectible over 36 to 60 months. . . .**
>
> **Revenue from auto insurance policies sold to customers are recognized as income over the life of the contracts.**

Bay Area Nissan, a competitor of Mike Magid Toyota, includes the following note in its Summary of Significant Accounting Policies:

> **Accounting Policies for Revenues**
>
> Sales are recognized when cash payment is received or, in the case of credit sales, which represent the majority of . . . sales, when the customer enters into an installment sales contract. Customer down payments are rare. Most of these installment sales contracts are normally collectible over 36 to 60 months. . . . Revenue from auto insurance policies sold to customers are recognized when the customer signs an insurance contract. Expenses are recognized over the life of the insurance contracts.

Suppose you have decided to invest in an auto dealership and you've narrowed your choices to Magid and Bay Area. Which company's earnings are of higher quality? Why? Will their accounting policies affect your investment decision? If so, how? Mention specific accounts in the financial statements that will differ between the 2 companies. (pp. 580–581, Challenge)

Ethical Issue

The income statement of Royal Bank of Singapore reported the following results of operations:

Earnings before income taxes, extraordinary gain, and cumulative effect of accounting change	$187,046
Income tax expense	72,947
Earnings before extraordinary gain and cumulative effect of accounting change	114,099
Extraordinary gain, net of income tax	419,557
Cumulative effect of change in accounting, net of income tax	(39,196)
Net earnings	$494,460

Suppose Royal Bank's management had reported the company's results of operations in this manner:

Earnings before income taxes	$847,111
Income tax expense	352,651
Net earnings	$494,460

I *Required*

1. Does it really matter how a company reports its operating results? Why? Who could be helped by management's action? Who could be hurt?

2. Suppose Royal Bank's management decides to report its operating results in the second manner. Evaluate the ethics of this decision.

Focus on Financials: ■ YUM! Brands

(*Learning Objective 1: Analyzing income and investments*) Refer to the **YUM! Brands, Inc.** financial statements in Appendix A at the end of this book.

1. YUM's income statement does not mention income from continuing operations. Why not? (pp. 580–585)

(continued)

2. Take the role of an investor, and suppose you are determining the price to pay for a share of YUM stock. Assume you are considering 3 investment capitalization rates that depend on the risk of an investment in YUM: 5%, 6%, and 7%. Compute your estimated value of a share of YUM stock using each of the 3 capitalization rates. Which estimated value would you base your investment strategy on if you rate YUM risky? If you consider YUM a safe investment? Use basic earnings per share for 2006. (pp. 582–584, 586)

3. Go to YUM! Brands Web site and compare your computed estimates to YUM's actual stock price. Which of your prices is most realistic? (Challenge)

Focus on Analysis: ■ Pier 1 Imports

(Learning Objective 1, 3: Evaluating the quality of earnings, valuing investments, and analyzing stock outstanding) This case is based on the **Pier 1 Imports** financial statements in Appendix B at the end of this book.

1. Pier 1's income statement reports only 1 special item. What is it, and what is its amount for 2006? (pp. 580–585)

2. What is your evaluation of the quality of Pier 1's earnings? State how you formed your opinion. (pp. 580–585)

3. At the end of 2005, how much would you have been willing to pay for 1 share of Pier 1 stock if you had rated the investment as high risk? as low risk? Use even-numbered investment capitalization rates in the range of 6%–12% for your analysis, and use basic earnings per share for continuing operations. (pp. 582–584)

4. Go to Pier 1's Web site and get the current price of a share of Pier 1 Imports' common stock. Which value that you estimated in requirement 2 is closest to Pier 1's actual stock price? (Challenge)

Group Project

Select a company and research its business. Search the business press for articles about this company. Obtain its annual report by requesting it directly from the company or from the company's Web site or from *Moody's Industrial Manual* (the exercise will be most meaningful if you obtain an actual copy and do not have to use *Moody's*).

I *Required*

1. Based on your group's analysis, come to class prepared to instruct the class on 6 interesting facts about the company that can be found in its financial statements and the related notes. Your group can mention only the obvious, such as net sales or total revenue, net income, total assets, total liabilities, total stockholders' equity, and dividends, in conjunction with other terms. Once you use an obvious item, you may not use that item again.

2. The group should write a paper discussing the facts that it has uncovered. Limit the paper to 2 double-spaced word-processed pages.

For Internet Exercises go to the Web site www.prenhall.com/harrison.

Quick Check Answers

12 The Statement of Cash Flows

SPOTLIGHT

GOOGLE: THE ULTIMATE ANSWER MACHINE

What do you use to find Web sites on the Internet? It's probably Google, the world's largest search engine. Google was created by Larry Page and Sergey Brin when they were students at Stanford University. These guys have done well. Recently the market value of Google stock surpassed that of Wal-Mart, the world's largest retailer.

The beauty of Google is that it's so easy to use. Access the Internet at www.google.com, and you can simply enter what you want to find in the search box. You get a whole list of helpful Web sites. Google may be the ultimate answer machine.

Google Inc.
Consolidated Statement of Cash Flows (Adapted; in millions)
Year Ended December 31, 2006

Cash Flows from Operating Activities		
Net income	$ 3,077	
Adjustments to reconcile net income to net cash		
provided by operating activities:		
Depreciation and amortization...	572	
Change in assets and liabilities, net of acquired businesses:		
Accounts receivable	(624)	
Other current assets...	(289)	
Accounts payable...	95	
Accrued expenses and other liabilities........................	292	
Unearned revenue	31	
Income taxes payable..	398	
Other, net..	29	
Net cash provided by operating activities..........................		$ 3,581
Cash Flows from Investing Activities		
Purchases of property and equipment	$ (1,903)	
Purchases of investments...	(27,701)	
Sales of investments	23,107	
Acquisitions of other companies	(402)	
Net cash used in investing activities		(6,899)
Cash Flows from Financing Activities		
Proceeds from issuance of common stock, net.......................	$ 2,384	
Other, net...	582	
Net cash provided by financing activities		2,966
Other, net...		20
Net increase (decrease) in cash and cash equivalents		(332)
Cash and cash equivalents at beginning of year.....................		3,877
Cash and cash equivalents at end of year.............................		$ 3,545

In preceding chapters, we covered cash flows as they related to various topics: receivables, plant assets, and so on. In this chapter, we show you how to prepare and use the statement of cash flows. We begin with the statement format used by the vast majority (98.7%) of companies, called the *indirect approach*. We end with the alternate format of the statement of cash flows, the *direct approach*, used by 1.3% of companies in a recent survey. After working through this chapter, you can analyze the cash flows of actual companies.

This chapter has 3 distinct sections:

- Introduction, beginning on this page
- Preparing the Statement of Cash Flows: Indirect Method, page 620
- Preparing the Statement of Cash Flows: Direct Method, page 634

The introduction applies to all the cash-flow topics. Professors who wish to cover only the indirect method can assign the first 2 parts of the chapter. Those interested only in the direct method can proceed from the introduction, which ends on page 620, to the direct method, on page 634.

LEARNING OBJECTIVES

1 **Identify** the purposes of the statement of cash flows

2 **Distinguish** among operating, investing, and financing cash flows

3 **Prepare** a statement of cash flows by the indirect method

4 **Prepare** a statement of cash flows by the direct method

BASIC CONCEPTS: THE STATEMENT OF CASH FLOWS

The balance sheet reports financial position, and balance sheets from two periods show whether cash increased or decreased. But that doesn't tell *why* the cash balance changed. The income statement reports net income and offers clues about cash, but the income statement doesn't tell *why* cash increased or decreased. We need a third financial statement.

The **statement of cash flows** reports **cash flows**—cash receipts and cash payments—in other words, where cash came from (receipts) and how it was spent (payments). The statement covers a span of time and therefore is dated "Year Ended December 31, 2008" or "Month Ended June 30, 2009." Exhibit 12-1 illustrates the relative timing of the 4 basic statements.

OBJECTIVE

1 **Identify** the purposes of the statement of cash flows

EXHIBIT 12-1 Timing of the Financial Statements

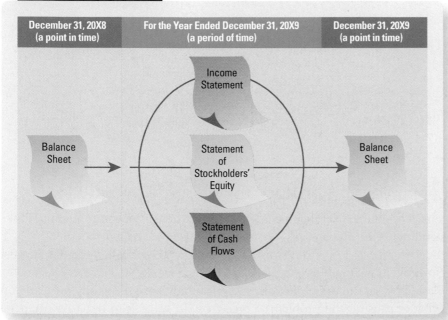

The statement of cash flows serves these purposes:

1. ***Predicts future cash flows.*** Past cash receipts and payments are reasonably good predictors of future cash flows.

2. ***Evaluates management decisions.*** Businesses that make wise decisions prosper, and those that make unwise decisions suffer losses. The statement of cash flows reports how managers got cash and how they used cash to run the business.

3. *Determines ability to pay dividends and interest.* Stockholders want dividends on their investments. Creditors demand interest and principal on their loans. The statement of cash flows reports on the ability to make these payments.

4. *Shows the relationship of net income to cash flows.* Usually, high net income leads to an increase in cash, and vice versa. But cash flow can suffer even when net income is high.

On a statement of cash flows, *cash* means more than just cash in the bank. It includes **cash equivalents**, which are highly liquid short-term investments that can be converted into cash immediately. Examples include money-market accounts and investments in U.S. Government securities. Throughout this chapter, the term cash refers to cash and cash equivalents.

How's Your Cash Flow? Telltale Signs of Financial Difficulty

Companies want to earn net income because profit measures success. Without net income, a business sinks. There will be no dividends, and the stock price suffers. High net income attracts investors, but you can't pay bills with net income. That requires cash.

A company needs both net income and strong cash flow. Income and cash flow usually move together because net income generates cash. Sometimes, however, net income and cash flow take different paths. To illustrate, consider Fastech Company:

Fastech Company
Income Statement
Year Ended December 31, 20X7

Sales revenue...............	$100,000
Cost of goods sold........	30,000
Operating expenses......	10,000
Net income..................	$ 60,000

Fastech Company
Balance Sheet
December 31, 20X7

Cash........................	$ 3,000	Total current liabilities............	$ 50,000
Receivables.............	37,000	Long-term liabilities................	20,000
Inventory.................	40,000		
Plant assets, net.......	60,000	Stockholders' equity................	70,000
Total assets..............	$140,000	Total liabilities and equity........	$140,000

What can we glean from Fastech's income statement and balance sheet?

■ Fastech is profitable. Net income is 60% of revenue. Fastech's profitability looks outstanding.

■ The current ratio is 1.6, and the debt ratio is only 50%. These measures suggest little trouble in paying bills.

■ But Fastech is on the verge of bankruptcy. Can you spot the problem? Can you see what is causing the problem? Three trouble spots leap out to a financial analyst.

1. The cash balance is very low. Three thousand dollars isn't enough cash to pay the bills of a company with sales of $100,000.

2. Fastech isn't selling inventory fast enough. Fastech turned over its inventory only 0.75 times during the year. As we saw in Chapter 6, inventory turnover

rates of 3–8 times a year are common. A turnover ratio of 0.75 times means it takes Fastech far too long to sell its inventory, and that delays cash collections.

3. Fastech's days' sales in receivables ratio is 135 days. Very few companies can wait that long to collect from customers.

The takeaway lesson from this discussion is this:

■ You need both net income and strong cash flow to succeed in business.

Let's turn now to the different categories of cash flows.

Operating, Investing, and Financing Activities

A business engages in 3 types of business activities:

■ Operating activities   ■ Investing activities   ■ Financing activities

OBJECTIVE

2 **Distinguish** among operating, investing, and financing cash flows

Google's statement of cash flows reports cash flows under these 3 headings, as shown for Google on page 616.

Operating activities create revenues, expenses, gains, and losses—*net income*, which is a product of accrual-basis accounting. The statement of cash flows reports on operating activities. Operating activities are the most important of the 3 categories because they reflect the core of the organization. *A successful business must generate most of its cash from operating activities.*

Investing activities increase and decrease *long-term assets*, such as computers, land, buildings, equipment, and investments in other companies. Purchases and sales of these assets are investing activities. Investing activities are important, but they are less critical than operating activities.

Financing activities obtain cash from investors and creditors. Issuing stock, borrowing money, buying and selling treasury stock, and paying cash dividends are financing activities. Paying off a loan is another example. Financing cash flows relate to *long-term liabilities* and *owners' equity*. They are the least important of the 3 categories of cash flows, and that's why they come last. Exhibit 12-2 shows how operating, investing, and financing activities relate to the various parts of the balance sheet.

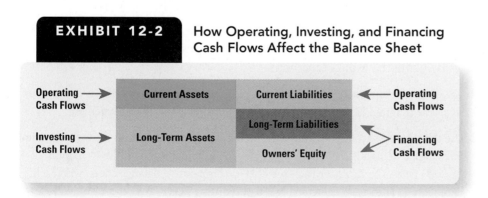

EXHIBIT 12-2 How Operating, Investing, and Financing Cash Flows Affect the Balance Sheet

Examine Google's statement of cash flows on page 616. Focus on the final line of each section: Operating, Investing, and Financing. Google has very strong cash flows.

During 2006, Google's operating activities provided $3.6 billion of cash. Google invested almost $7 billion and received $3 billion in financing. These figures show that

- *Operations* are Google's largest source of cash.
- The company is *investing* in the future.
- People are willing to *finance* Google.

Two Formats for Operating Activities

There are 2 ways to format operating activities on the statement of cash flows:

- **Indirect method**, which reconciles from net income to net cash provided by operating activities. (pp. 620–634)
- **Direct method**, which reports all cash receipts and cash payments from operating activities. (pp. 634–645)

The 2 methods use different computations, but they produce the same figure for cash from *operating activities*. The 2 methods do not affect *investing* or *financing activities*. The following table summarizes the differences between the 2 approaches:

Indirect Method		Direct Method	
Net income............................	$600	Collections from customers..........	$2,000
Adjustments:		*Deductions:*	
Depreciation, etc.	300	Payments to suppliers, etc.	(1,100)
Net cash provided by		Net cash provided by	
operating activities	$900	operating activities	$ 900

─────────── same ───────────

We begin with the indirect method because 98 out of 100 companies use it.

PREPARING THE STATEMENT OF CASH FLOWS: INDIRECT METHOD

OBJECTIVE

3 **Prepare** a statement of cash flows by the indirect method

To illustrate the statement of cash flows, we use **The Roadster Factory, Inc. (TRF)**, a dealer in auto parts for sports cars. Proceed as follows to prepare the statement of cash flows by using the indirect method:

Step 1 Lay out the template as shown in Part 1 of Exhibit 12-3. The exhibit is comprehensive. The diagram in Part 2 (p. 622) gives a visual picture of the statement.

Step 2 Use the balance sheet to determine the increase or decrease in cash during the period. The change in cash is the "check figure" for the statement of cash flows. Exhibit 12-4 (p. 623) gives The Roadster Factory's (TRF's) comparative balance sheet, with cash highlighted. TRF's cash decreased by $8,000 during 20X9. *Why* did cash decrease? The statement of cash flows will provide the answer.

Step 3 From the income statement, take net income, depreciation, depletion, and amortization expense, and any gains or losses on the sale of long-term assets. Print these items on the statement of cash flows. Exhibit 12-5 (p. 623) gives TRF's income statement, with relevant items highlighted.

Step 4 Use the income statement and balance sheet data to prepare the statement of cash flows. The statement of cash flows is complete only after you have explained the year-to-year changes in all the balance sheet accounts.

EXHIBIT 12-3 **Part 1: Template of the Statement of Cash Flows: Indirect Method**

The Roadster Factory, Inc. (TRF)
Statement of Cash Flows
Year Ended December 31, 20X9

Cash flows from operating activities
  Net income
    Adjustments to reconcile net income to net cash provided by operating activities:
    + Depreciation/depletion/amortization expense
    + Loss on sale of long-term assets
    − Gain on sale of long-term assets
    − Increases in current assets other than cash
    + Decreases in current assets other than cash
    + Increases in current liabilities
    − Decreases in current liabilities
        Net cash provided by (used for) operating activities
Cash flows from investing activities:
  Sales of long-term assets (investments, land, building, equipment, and so on)
  − Purchases of long-term assets
  + Collections of notes receivable
  − Loans to others
        Net cash provided by (used for) investing activities
Cash flows from financing activities:
  Issuance of stock
  + Sale of treasury stock
  − Purchase of treasury stock
  + Borrowing (issuance of notes or bonds payable)
  − Payment of notes or bonds payable
  − Payment of dividends
        Net cash provided by (used for) financing activities
Net increase (decrease) in cash during the year
  + Cash at December 31, 20X8
  = Cash at December 31, 20X9

Go to "Cash Flows from Operating Activities" on page 624.

EXHIBIT 12-3   Part 2: Positive and Negative Items on the
Statement of Cash Flows: Indirect Method

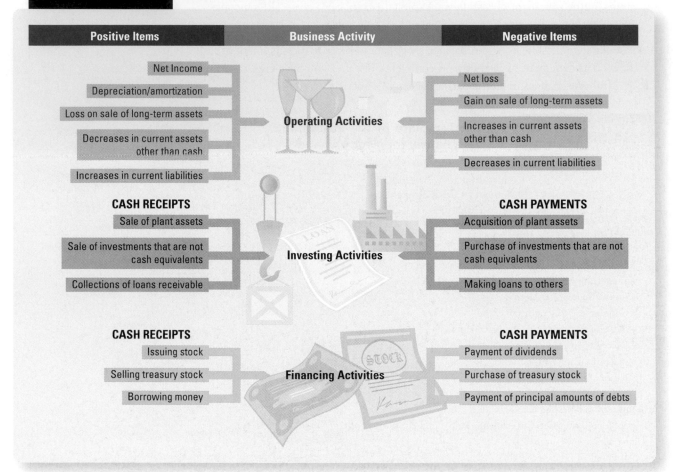

Positive Items	Business Activity	Negative Items

Operating Activities

Positive Items:
- Net Income
- Depreciation/amortization
- Loss on sale of long-term assets
- Decreases in current assets other than cash
- Increases in current liabilities

Negative Items:
- Net loss
- Gain on sale of long-term assets
- Increases in current assets other than cash
- Decreases in current liabilities

Investing Activities

CASH RECEIPTS:
- Sale of plant assets
- Sale of investments that are not cash equivalents
- Collections of loans receivable

CASH PAYMENTS:
- Acquisition of plant assets
- Purchase of investments that are not cash equivalents
- Making loans to others

Financing Activities

CASH RECEIPTS:
- Issuing stock
- Selling treasury stock
- Borrowing money

CASH PAYMENTS:
- Payment of dividends
- Purchase of treasury stock
- Payment of principal amounts of debts

EXHIBIT 12-4 Comparative Balance Sheet

The Roadster Factory, Inc. (TRF)
Comparative Balance Sheet
December 31, 20X9 and 20X8

(In thousands)	20X9	20X8	Increase (Decrease)	
Assets				
Current:				
Cash	$ 34	$ 42	$ (8)	⎫
Accounts receivable	96	81	15	⎬ Changes in current assets—*Operating*
Inventory	35	38	(3)	⎬
Prepaid expenses	8	7	1	⎭
Notes receivable	21	—	21	⎫ Changes in noncurrent assets—*Investing*
Plant assets, net of depreciation	343	219	124	⎬
Total	$537	$387	$150	
Liabilities				
Current:				
Accounts payable	$ 91	$ 57	$ 34	⎫
Salary and wage payable	4	6	(2)	⎬ Changes in current liabilities—*Operating*
Accrued liabilities	1	3	(2)	⎭
Long-term debt	160	77	83	⎫ Changes in long-term liabilities and paid-in capital accounts—*Financing*
Stockholders' Equity				⎬
Common stock	162	158	4	⎭
Retained earnings	119	86	33	⎬ Changes due to net income—*Operating* Change due to dividends—*Financing*
Total	$537	$387	$150	

EXHIBIT 12-5 Income Statement

The Roadster Factory, Inc. (TRF)
Income Statement
Year Ended December 31, 20X9

	(In thousands)	
Revenues and gains:		
Sales revenue	$303	
Interest revenue	2	
Gain on sale of plant assets	8	
Total revenues and gains		$313
Expenses:		
Cost of goods sold	$150	
Salary and wage expense	56	
Depreciation expense	18	
Other operating expense	17	
Income tax expense	15	
Interest expense	7	
Total expenses		263
Net income		$ 50

EXHIBIT 12-6	Statement of Cash Flows—Operating Activities by the Indirect Method

The Roadster Factory, Inc. (TRF)
Statement of Cash Flows (Indirect Method)
For the Year Ended December 31, 20X9

		(In thousands)
Cash flows from operating activities:		
Net income		$50
Adjustments to reconcile net income to net cash		
provided by operating activities:		
Ⓐ Depreciation	$ 18	
Ⓑ Gain on sale of plant assets	(8)	
Increase in accounts receivable	(15)	
Decrease in inventory	3	
Increase in prepaid expenses	(1)	
Ⓒ Increase in accounts payable	34	
Decrease in salary and wage payable	(2)	
Decrease in accrued liabilities	(2)	27
Net cash provided by operating activities		$77

Cash Flows from Operating Activities

Operating activities are related to the transactions that make up net income.[1]

The operating section begins with the net income, taken from the income statement, (Exhibit 12-5) and is followed by "Adjustments to reconcile net income to net cash provided by operating activities." Let's discuss these adjustments.

Ⓐ **Depreciation, Depletion, and Amortization Expenses.** These expenses are added back to net income to convert net income to cash flow. Let's see why. Depreciation is recorded as follows:

Depreciation Expense	18,000	
Accumulated Depreciation		18,000

Depreciation has no effect on cash. But depreciation, like all other expenses, decreases net income. Therefore, to convert net income to cash flows, we add depreciation back to net income. The add-back cancels the earlier deduction.

[1]The authors thank Professor Alfonso Oddo for suggesting this summary.

Example: Suppose you had only 2 transactions, a $1,000 cash sale and depreciation expense of $300. Cash flow from operations is $1,000, and net income is $700 ($1,000 – $300). To go from net income ($700) to cash flow ($1,000), we add back the depreciation ($300). Depletion and amortization are treated like depreciation.

Gains and Losses on the Sale of Assets. Sales of long-term assets are *investing* Ⓑ activities and there's often a gain or loss on the sale. On the statement of cash flows, the gain or loss is an adjustment to net income. Exhibit 12-6 includes an adjustment for a gain. During 20X9, The Roadster Factory sold equipment for $62,000. The book value was $54,000, so there was a gain of $8,000.

The $62,000 cash received from the sale is an investing activity, and the $62,000 includes the $8,000 gain. Net income also includes the gain, so we must subtract the gain from net cash provided by operations, as shown in the statement of cash flows (Exhibit 12-7). (We explain investing activities in the next section.)

A loss on the sale of plant assets also creates an adjustment in the operating section. Losses are *added back* to net income to compute cash flow from operations.

Changes in the Current Asset and Current Liability Accounts. Most cur- Ⓒ rent assets and current liabilities result from operating activities. For example, accounts receivable result from sales, inventory relates to cost of goods sold, and so on. Changes in the current accounts are adjustments to net income on the cash-flow statement. The reasoning follows:

1. **An increase *in another current asset decreases cash*.** It takes cash to acquire assets. Suppose you make a sale on account. Accounts receivable are increased, but cash isn't affected yet. Exhibit 12-4 (p. 623) reports that during 20X9, The Roadster Factory's Accounts Receivable increased by $15,000. To compute cash flow from operations, we must subtract the $15,000 increase in Accounts Receivable, as shown in Exhibit 12-6. The reason is this: We have *not* collected this $15,000 in cash. The same logic applies to all the other current assets. If they increase, cash decreases.

2. **A decrease *in another current asset increases cash*.** Suppose TRF's Accounts Receivable balance decreased by $4,000. Cash receipts caused Accounts Receivable to decrease, so we add decreases in Accounts Receivable and the other current assets to net income.

3. **A decrease *in a current liability decreases cash*.** Payment of a current liability decreases both cash and the liability, so we subtract decreases in current liabilities from net income. In Exhibit 12-6, the $2,000 decrease in Accrued Liabilities is *subtracted* to compute net cash provided by operations.

4. **An increase *in a current liability increases cash*.** The Roadster Factory's Accounts Payable increased. That can occur only if cash was not spent to pay this debt. Cash payments are therefore less than expenses and TRF has more cash on hand. Thus, increases in current liabilities increase cash.

| EXHIBIT 12-7 | Statement of Cash Flows—Indirect Method |

The Roadster Factory, Inc. (TRF)
Statement of Cash Flows (Indirect Method)
For the Year Ended December 31, 20X9

		(In thousands)
Cash flows from operating activities:		
Net income		$ 50
Adjustments to reconcile net income to net cash provided by operating activities:		
(A) Depreciation	18	
(B) Gain on sale of plant assets	(8)	
Increase in accounts receivable	(15)	
Decrease in inventory	3	
Increase in prepaid expenses	(1)	
(C) Increase in accounts payable	34	
Decrease in salary and wage payable	(2)	
Decrease in accrued liabilities	(2)	27
Net cash provided by operating activities		77
Cash flows from investing activities:		
Acquisition of plant assets	$(196)	
Loan to another company	(21)	
Proceeds from sale of plant assets	62	
Net cash used for investing activities		(155)
Cash flows from financing activities:		
Proceeds from issuance of long-term debt	$ 94	
Proceeds from issuance of common stock	4	
Payment of long-term debt	(11)	
Payment of dividends	(17)	
Net cash provided by financing avctivities		70
Net (decrease) in cash		$ (8)
Cash balance, December 31, 20X8		42
Cash balance, December 31, 20X9		$ 34

Evaluating Cash Flows from Operating Activities. Let's step back and evaluate The Roadster Factory's operating cash flows during 20X9. TRF's operations provided net cash flow of $77,000. This amount exceeds net income, and it should because of the add-back of depreciation. Now let's examine TRF's investing and financing activities, as reported in Exhibit 12-7.

Cash Flows from Investing Activities

Investing activities affect long-term assets, such as Plant Assets, Investments, and Notes Receivable.

Most of the data come from the balance sheet.

Computing Purchases and Sales of Plant Assets. Companies keep a separate account for each plant asset. But for computing cash flows, it is helpful to combine all the plant assets into a single summary account. Also, we subtract accumulated depreciation and use the net figure. It's easier to work with a single plant asset account.

To illustrate, observe that The Roadster Factory's

- balance sheet reports beginning plant assets, net of accumulated depreciation, of $219,000. The ending balance is $343,000 (Exhibit 12-4).
- income statement shows depreciation expense of $18,000 and an $8,000 gain on sale of plant assets (Exhibit 12-5).

TRF's purchases of plant assets total $196,000 (take this amount as given; see Exhibit 12-7). How much, then, are the proceeds from the sale of plant assets? First, we must determine the book value of the plant assets sold, as follows:

Plant Assets, Net								
Beginning balance	+	Acquisitions	−	Depreciation	−	Book value of assets sold	=	Ending balance
$219,000	+	$196,000	−	$18,000		−X	=	$343,000
						−X	=	$343,000 − $219,000 − $196,000 + $18,000
						X	=	$54,000

The sale proceeds are $62,000, determined as follows:

	Sale proceeds	=	Book value of assets sold	+	Gain	−	Loss
	X	=	$54,000	+	$8,000	−	$0
	X	=	$62,000				

Trace the sale proceeds of $62,000 to the statement of cash flows in Exhibit 12-7. The Plant Assets T-account provides another look at the computation of the book value of the assets sold.

Plant Assets, Net

Beginning balance	219,000	Depreciation	18,000
Acquisitions	196,000	Book value of assets sold	54,000
Ending balance	343,000		

If the sale resulted in a loss of $3,000, the sale proceeds would be $51,000 ($54,000 − $3,000), and the statement of cash flows would report $51,000 as a cash receipt from this investing activity.

Computing Purchases and Sales of Investments, and Loans and Collections. The cash amounts of investment transactions can be computed in the manner illustrated for plant assets. Investments are easier because there is no depreciation, as shown in the following equation:

Investments (amounts assumed for illustration only)						
Beginning balance	+	Purchases	−	Book value of investments sold	=	Ending balance
$100,000	+	$50,000		−X	=	$140,000
				−X	=	$140,000 − $100,000 − $50,000
				X	=	$10,000

The investments T-account provides another look (amounts assumed).

Investments			
Beginning balance	100		
Purchases	50	Book value of investments sold	10
Ending balance	140		

The Roadster Factory has a long-term receivable, and the cash flows from loan transactions on notes receivable can be determined as follows (data from Exhibit 12-4):

Notes Receivable							
Beginning balance	+	New loans made	−	Collections	=	Ending balance	
$0	+	X		−0	=	$21,000	
		X			=	$21,000	

Notes Receivable			
Beginning balance	0		
New loans made	21	Collections	0
Ending balance	21		

Exhibit 12-8 summarizes the cash flows from investing activities, highlighted in color.

EXHIBIT 12-8	Computing Cash Flows from Investing Activities

Receipts

From sale of plant assets	Beginning plant assets, net	+	Acquisition cost	−	Depreciation	−	Book value of assets sold	=	Ending plant assets, net
	Cash received	=	Book value of assets sold	+ or −	Gain on sale Loss on sale				
From sale of investments	Beginning investments	+	Purchase cost of investments	−	Cost of investments sold	=	Ending investments		
	Cash received	=	Cost of investments sold	+ or −	Gain on sale Loss on sale				
From collection of notes receivable	Beginning notes receivable	+	New loans made	−	Collections	=	Ending notes receivable		

Payments

For acquisition of plant assets	Beginning plant assets, net	+	Acquisition cost	−	Depreciation	−	Book value of assets sold	=	Ending plant assets, net
For purchase of investments	Beginning investments	+	Purchase cost of investments	−	Cost of investments sold	=	Ending investments		
For new loans made	Beginning notes receivable	+	New loans made	−	Collections	=	Ending notes receivable		

Cash Flows from Financing Activities

Financing activities affect liabilities and stockholders' equity, such as Notes Payable, Bonds Payable, Long-Term Debt, Common Stock, Paid-in Capital in Excess of Par, and Retained Earnings. Most of the data come from the balance sheet.

Computing Issuances and Payments of Long-Term Debt. The beginning and ending balances of Long-Term Debt, Notes Payable, or Bonds Payable come from the balance sheet. If either new issuances or payments are known, the other amount can be computed. The Roadster Facory's new debt issuances total $94,000 (take this amount as given; Exhibit 12-7). Debt payments are computed from the Long-Term Debt account (see Exhibit 12-4).

Long-Term Debt (Notes Payable, Bonds Payable)

Beginning balance	+	Issuance of new debt	−	Payments of debt	=	Ending balance
$77,000	+	$94,000		−X	=	$160,000
				−X	=	$160,000 − $77,000 − $94,000
				X	=	$11,000

Long-Term Debt

		Beginning balance	77,000
Payments	11,000	Issuance of new debt	94,000
		Ending balance	160,000

Computing Issuances of Stock and Purchases of Treasury Stock. These cash flows can be determined from the stock accounts. For example, cash received from issuing common stock is computed from Common Stock and Capital in Excess of Par. We use a single summary Common Stock account as we do for plant assets. The Roadster Factory data are

Common Stock

Beginning balance	+	Issuance of new stock	=	Ending balance
$158,000	+	$4,000	=	$162,000

Common Stock

	Beginning balance	158,000
	Issuance of new stock	4,000
	Ending balance	162,000

The Roadster Factory has no treasury stock, but cash flows from purchasing treasury stock can be computed as follows (using assumed amounts):

Treasury Stock (amounts assumed for illustration only)				
Beginning balance	+	Purchase of treasury stock	=	Ending balance
$16,000	+	$3,000	=	$19,000

Treasury Stock		
Beginning balance	16,000	
Purchase of treasury stock	3,000	
Ending balance	19,000	

Computing Dividend Payments. If dividend payments are not given elsewhere, they can be computed. The Roadster Factory's dividend payments are

Retained Earnings						
Beginning balance	+	Net income	−	Dividend declarations and payments	=	Ending balance
$86,000	+	$50,000		−X	=	$119,000
				−X	=	$119,000 − $86,000 − $50,000
				X	=	$17,000

The T-accounts also show the dividend computation.

Retained Earnings			
Dividend declarations and payments	17,000	Beginning balance	86,000
		Net income	50,000
		Ending balance	119,000

Exhibit 12-9 summarizes the cash flows from financing activities, highlighted in color.

EXHIBIT 12-9   Computing Cash Flows from Financing Activities

Receipts

From borrowing—issuance of long-term debt (notes payable)	Beginning long-term debt (notes payable)	+	Cash received from issuance of long-term debt	− Payment of debt =	Ending long-term debt (notes payable)
From issuance of stock	Beginning stock	+	Cash received from issuance of new stock	= Ending stock	

Payments

Of long-term debt	Beginning long-term debt (notes payable)	+	Cash received from issuance of long-term debt	− Payment of debt =	Ending long-term debt (notes payable)
To purchase treasury stock	Beginning treasury stock + Purchase cost of treasury stock = Ending treasury stock				
Of dividends	Beginning retained earnings + Net income − Dividend declarations and payments = Ending retained earnings				

STOP & think. . .

Classify each of the following as an operating activity, an investing activity, or a financing activity as reported on the statement of cash flows prepared by the *indirect* method.

a. Issuance of stock
b. Borrowing
c. Sales revenue
d. Payment of dividends
e. Purchase of land
f. Purchase of treasury stock

g. Paying bonds payable
h. Interest expense
i. Sale of equipment
j. Cost of goods sold
k. Purchase of another company
l. Making a loan

Answer:

a. Financing
b. Financing
c. Operating
d. Financing

e. Investing
f. Financing
g. Financing
h. Operating

i. Investing
j. Operating
k. Investing
l. Investing

Noncash Investing and Financing Activities

Companies make investments that do not require cash. They also obtain financing other than cash. Our examples have included none of these transactions. Now suppose The Roadster Factory issued common stock valued at $300,000 to acquire a warehouse. TRF would journalize this transaction as follows:

| Warehouse Building | 300,000 | |
| Common Stock | | 300,000 |

This transaction would not be reported as a cash payment because TRF paid no cash. But the investment in the warehouse and the issuance of stock are important. These noncash investing and financing activities can be reported in a separate schedule under the statement of cash flows. Exhibit 12-10 illustrates noncash investing and financing activities (all amounts are assumed).

EXHIBIT 12-10 Noncash Investing and Financing Activities (All Amounts Assumed)

	Thousands
Noncash Investing and Financing Activities:	
Acquisition of building by issuing common stock	$300
Acquisition of land by issuing note payable	70
Payment of long-term debt by issuing common stock	100
Total noncash investing and financing activities	$470

Now let's apply what you've learned about the statement of cash flows prepared by the indirect method.

MID-CHAPTER SUMMARY PROBLEM

Lucas Corporation reported the following income statement and comparative balance sheet, along with transaction data for 20X5:

Lucas Corporation
Income Statement
Year Ended December 31, 20X5

Sales revenue		$662,000
Cost of goods sold		560,000
Gross profit		102,000
Operating expenses		
Salary expenses	$46,000	
Depreciation expense— equipment	7,000	
Amortization expense— patent	3,000	
Rent expense	2,000	
Total operating expenses		58,000
Income from operations		44,000
Other items:		
Loss on sale of equipment		(2,000)
Income before income tax		42,000
Income tax expense		16,000
Net income		$ 26,000

Lucas Corporation
Balance Sheet
December 31, 20X5 and 20X4

Assets	20X5	20X4	Liabilities	20X5	20X4
Current:			Current:		
Cash and equivalents	$ 19,000	$ 3,000	Accounts payable	$ 35,000	$ 26,000
Accounts receivable	22,000	23,000	Accrued liabilities	7,000	9,000
Inventories	34,000	31,000	Income tax payable	10,000	10,000
Prepaid expenses	1,000	3,000	Total current liabilities	52,000	45,000
Total current assets	76,000	60,000	Long-term note payable	44,000	—
Long-term investments	18,000	10,000	Bonds payable	40,000	53,000
Equipment, net	67,000	52,000	**Owners' Equity**		
Patent, net	44,000	10,000	Common stock	52,000	20,000
			Retained earnings	27,000	19,000
			Less: Treasury stock	(10,000)	(5,000)
Total assets	$205,000	$132,000	Total liabilities and equity	$205,000	$132,000

Transaction Data for 20X5:

Purchase of equipment	$ 98,000	Issuance of long-term note payable to purchase patent	$ 37,000
Payment of cash dividends	18,000		
Issuance of common stock to retire bonds payable	13,000	Issuance of long-term note payable to borrow cash	7,000
Purchase of long-term investment	8,000	Issuance of common stock for cash	19,000
Purchase of treasury stock	5,000	Sale of equipment (book value, 76,000)	74,000

❙ Required

Prepare Lucas Corporation's statement of cash flows (indirect method) for the year ended December 31, 20X5. Follow the 4 steps outlined below. For Step 4, prepare a T-account to show the transaction activity in each long-term balance sheet account. For each plant asset, use a single account, net of accumulated depreciation (for example: Equipment, Net).

❙ Requirement 1

Step 1 Lay out the template of the statement of cash flows.

Step 2 From the comparative balance sheet, determine the increase in cash during the year, $16,000.

Step 3 From the income statement, take net income, depreciation, amortization, and the loss on sale of equipment, to the statement of cash flows.

Step 4 Complete the statement of cash flows. Account for the year-to-year change in each balance sheet account.

Answer

Lucas Corporation
Statement of Cash Flows
Year Ended December 31, 20X5

Cash flows from operating activities:		
Net income		$ 26,000
Adjustments to reconcile net income to		
net cash provided by operating activities:		
Depreciation	$ 7,000	
Amortization..	3,000	
Loss on sale of equipment	2,000	
Decrease in accounts receivable.................................	1,000	
Increase in inventories...	(3,000)	
Decrease in prepaid expenses	2,000	
Increase in accounts payable	9,000	
Decrease in accrued liabilities....................................	(2,000)	19,000
Net cash provided by operating activities.............		45,000
Cash flows from investing activities:		
Purchase of equipment	$(98,000)	
Sale of equipment...	74,000	
Purchase of long-term investment	(8,000)	
Net cash used for investing activities....................		(32,000)
Cash flows from financing activities:		
Issuance of common stock	$ 19,000	
Payment of cash dividends	(18,000)	
Issuance of long-term note payable	7,000	
Purchase of treasury stock..	(5,000)	
Net cash provided by financing activities.............		3,000
Net increase in cash..		**$ 16,000**
Cash balance, December 31, 20X4		3,000
Cash balance, December 31, 20X5		$ 19,000
Noncash investing and financing activities:		
Issuance of long-term note payable to purchase patent...		$ 37,000
Issuance of common stock to retire bonds payable.........		13,000
Total noncash investing and financing activities.........		$ 50,000

Long-Term Investments		
Bal.	10,000	
	8,000	
Bal.	18,000	

Equipment, Net		
Bal.	52,000	
	98,000	76,000
		7,000
Bal.	67,000	

Patent, Net		
Bal.	10,000	
	37,000	3,000
Bal.	44,000	

Long-term Note Payable		
	Bal.	0
		37,000
		7,000
	Bal.	44,000

Bonds Payable		
	Bal.	53,000
13,000		
	Bal.	40,000

Common Stock		
	Bal.	20,000
		13,000
		19,000
	Bal.	52,000

Retained Earnings		
	Bal.	19,000
18,000		26,000
	Bal.	27,000

Treasury Stock		
Bal.	5,000	
Bal.	5,000	
Bal.	10,000	

PREPARING THE STATEMENT OF CASH FLOWS: DIRECT METHOD

OBJECTIVE

4 **Prepare** a statement of cash flows by the direct method

The Financial Accounting Standards Board (FASB) prefers the direct method of reporting operating cash flows because it provides clearer information about the sources and uses of cash. But only about 1% of companies use this method because it takes more computations than the indirect method. Investing and financing cash flows are unaffected by the operating cash flows.

To illustrate the statement of cash flows, we use The Roadster Factory, Inc. (TRF), a dealer in auto parts for sports cars. To prepare the statement of cash flows by the direct method, proceed as follows:

Step 1 Lay out the template of the statement of cash flows by the direct method, as shown in Part 1 of Exhibit 12-11. Part 2 (p. 636) gives a visual picture of the statement.

Step 2 Use the balance sheet to determine the increase or decrease in cash during the period. The change in cash is the "check figure" for the statement of cash flows. The Roadster Factory's comparative balance sheet shows that cash decreased by $8,000 during 20X9 (Exhibit 12-4, p. 623). *Why* did cash fall during 20X9? The statement of cash flows explains.

EXHIBIT 12-11 **Part 1: Template of the Statement of Cash Flows—Direct Method**

The Roadster Factory, Inc. (TRF)
Statement of Cash Flows
Year Ended December 31, 20X9

Cash flows from operating activities:

Receipts:

    Collections from customers

    Interest received on notes receivable

    Dividends received on investments in stock

        Total cash receipts

Payments:

    To suppliers

    To employees

    For interest

    For income tax

        Total cash payments

Net cash provided by (used for) operating activities

Cash flows from investing activities:

    Sales of long-term assets (investments, land, building, equipment, and so on)

   − Purchases of long-term assets

   + Collections of notes receivable

   − Loans to others

Net cash provided by (used for) investing activities

Cash flows from financing activities:

    Issuance of stock

   + Sale of treasury stock

   − Purchase of treasury stock

   + Borrowing (issuance of notes or bonds payable)

   − Payment of notes or bonds payable

   − Payment of dividends

Net cash provided by (used for) financing activities

Net increase (decrease) in cash during the year

   + Cash at December 31, 20X8

   = Cash at December 31, 20X9

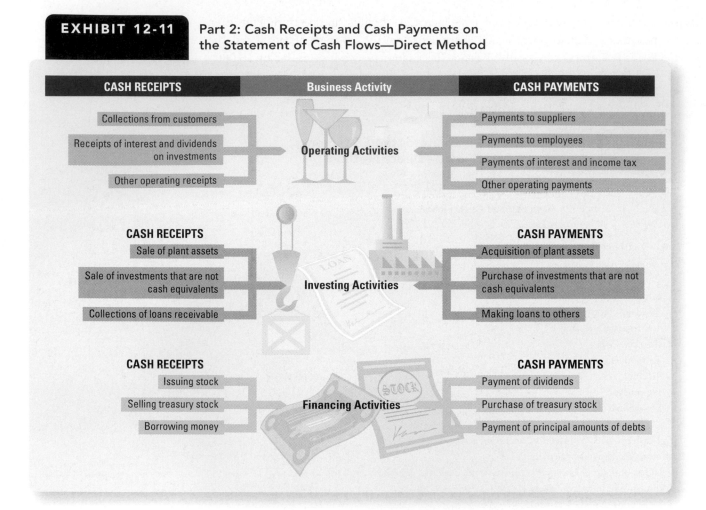

Step 3 Use the available data to prepare the statement of cash flows. The Roadster Factory's transaction data appear in Exhibit 12-12. These transactions affected both the income statement (Exhibit 12-5, p. 623) and the statement of cash flows. Some transactions affect one statement and some affect the other. For example, sales (item 1) are reported on the income statement. Cash collections (item 2) go on the statement of cash flows. Other transactions, such as interest expense and payments (item 11) affect both statements. *The statement of cash flows reports only those transactions with cash effects* (those with an asterisk in Exhibit 12-12). Exhibit 12-13 gives The Roadster Factory's statement of cash flows for 20X9.

Cash Flows from Operating Activities. Operating cash flows are listed first because they are most important. Exhibit 12-13 shows that The Roadster Factory is sound; operating activities were the largest source of cash.

Cash Collections from Customers. Both cash sales and collections of accounts receivable are reported on the statement of cash flows as "Collections from customers . . . $288,000" in Exhibit 12-13.

Cash Receipts of Interest and Dividends. The income statement reports interest revenue and dividend revenue. Only the cash receipts of interest and dividends appear on the statement of cash flows—$2,000 of interest received in Exhibit 12-13.

EXHIBIT 12-12	Summary of The Roadster Factory's 20X9 Transactions

Operating Activities
1. Sales on credit, $303,000
*2. Collections from customers, $288,000
*3. Interest revenue and receipts, $2,000
4. Cost of goods sold, $150,000
5. Purchases of inventory on credit, $147,000
*6. Payments to suppliers, $133,000
7. Salary and wage expense, $56,000
*8. Payments of salary and wages, $58,000
9. Depreciation expense, $18,000
10. Other operating expense, $17,000
*11. Income tax expense and payments, $15,000
*12. Interest expense and payments, $7,000

Investing Activities
*13. Cash payments to acquire plant assets, $196,000
*14. Loan to another company, $21,000
*15. Proceeds from sale of plant assets, $62,000, including $8,000 gain

Financing Activities
*16. Proceeds from issuance of long-term debt, $94,000
*17. Proceeds from issuance of common stock, $4,000
*18. Payment of long-term debt, $11,000
*19. Declaration and payment of cash dividends, $17,000

*Indicates a cash flow to be reported on the statement of cash flows.
Note: Income statement data are taken from Exhibit 12-16, page 641.

Payments to Suppliers. Payments to suppliers include all expenditures for inventory and operating expenses except employee pay, interest, and income taxes. *Suppliers* are those entities that provide inventory and essential services. For example, a clothing store's suppliers may include **Tommy Hilfiger, Adidas,** and **Ralph Lauren.** Other suppliers provide advertising, utilities, and office supplies. Exhibit 12-13 shows that The Roadster Factory paid suppliers $133,000.

Payments to Employees. This category includes salaries, wages, and other forms of employee pay. Accrued amounts are excluded because they have not yet been paid. The statement of cash flows reports only the cash payments ($58,000).

Payments for Interest Expense and Income Tax Expense. Interest and income tax payments are reported separately. The Roadster Factory paid cash for all its interest and income taxes. Therefore, the same amount goes on the income statement and the statement of cash flows. These payments are operating cash flows because the interest and income tax are expenses.

EXHIBIT 12-13 Statement of Cash Flows—
Direct Method

The Roadster Factory, Inc. (TRF)
Statement of Cash Flows (Direct Method)
For Year Ended December 31, 20X9

	(In thousands)	
Cash flows from operating activities:		
Receipts:		
Collections from customers	$ 288	
Interest received	2	
Total cash receipts		$ 290
Payments:		
To suppliers	$(133)	
To employees	(58)	
For income tax	(15)	
For interest	(7)	
Total cash payments		(213)
Net cash provided by operating activities		77
Cash flows from investing activities:		
Acquisition of plant assets	$(196)	
Loans to another company	(21)	
Proceeds from sale of plant assets	62	
Net cash used for investing activities		(155)
Cash flows from financing activities:		
Proceeds from issuance of long-term debt	$ 94	
Proceeds from issuance of common stock	4	
Payment of long-term debt	(11)	
Payment of dividends	(17)	
Net cash provided by financing activities		70
Net (decrease) in cash		$ (8)
Cash balance, December 31, 20X8		42
Cash balance, December 31, 20X9		$ 34

Depreciation, Depletion, and Amortization Expense. These expenses are *not* listed on the direct-method statement of cash flows because they do not affect cash.

Cash Flows from Investing Activities

Investing is critical because a company's investments affect the future. Large purchases of plant assets signal expansion. Meager investing activity means the business is not growing.

Purchasing Plant Assets and Investments and Making Loans to Other Companies. These cash payments acquire long-term assets. The Roadster Factory's first investing activity in Exhibit 12-13 is the purchase of plant assets ($196,000). TRF also made a $21,000 loan and thus got a note receivable.

Proceeds from Selling Plant Assets and Investments and from Collecting Notes Receivable. These cash receipts are also investing activities. The sale of the plant assets needs explanation. The Roadster Factory received $62,000 cash from the sale of plant assets, and there was an $8,000 gain on this transaction. What is the appropriate amount to show on the cash-flow statement? It is $62,000, the cash received from the sale, not the $8,000 gain.

Investors are often critical of a company that sells large amounts of its plant assets. That may signal an emergency. For example, problems in the airline industry have caused some companies to sell airplanes to generate cash.

Cash Flows from Financing Activities

Cash flows from financing activities include the following:

Proceeds from Issuance of Stock and Debt (Notes and Bonds Payable). Issuing stock and borrowing money are 2 ways to finance a company. In Exhibit 12-13, The Roadster Factory received $4,000 when it issued common stock. TRF also received $94,000 cash when it issued long-term debt (such as a note payable) to borrow money.

Payment of Debt and Purchasing the Company's Own Stock. Paying debt (notes payable) is the opposite of borrowing. TRF reports long-term debt payments of $11,000. The purchase of treasury stock is another example of a use of cash.

Payment of Cash Dividends. Paying cash dividends is a financing activity, as shown by The Roadster Factory's $17,000 payment in Exhibit 12-13. A *stock* dividend has no effect on Cash and is *not* reported on the cash-flow statement.

Noncash Investing and Financing Activities

Companies make investments that do not require cash. They also obtain financing other than cash. Our examples thus far have included none of these transactions. Now suppose that The Roadster Factory issued common stock valued at $300,000 to acquire a warehouse. TRF would journalize this transaction as follows:

Warehouse Building	300,000	
Common Stock		300,000

This transaction would not be reported as a cash payment because TRF paid no cash. But the investment in the warehouse and the issuance of stock are important. These noncash investing and financing activities can be reported in a separate schedule under the statement of cash flows. Exhibit 12-14 illustrates noncash investing and financing activities (all amounts are assumed).

EXHIBIT 12-14 Noncash Investing and Financing Activities (All Amounts Assumed)

	Thousands
Noncash Investing and Financing Activities:	
Acquisition of building by issuing common stock	$300
Acquisition of land by issuing note payable	70
Payment of long-term debt by issuing common stock	100
Total noncash investing and financing activities	$470

STOP & think. . .

Classify each of the following as an operating activity, an investing activity, or a financing activity. Also identify those items that are not reported on the statement of cash flows prepared by the *direct* method.

a. Net income
b. Payment of dividends
c. Borrowing
d. Payment of cash to suppliers
e. Making a loan
f. Sale of treasury stock
g. Depreciation expense
h. Purchase of equipment

i. Issuance of stock
j. Purchase of another company
k. Payment of a note payable
l. Payment of income taxes
m. Collections from customers
n. Accrual of interest revenue
o. Expiration of prepaid expense
p. Receipt of cash dividends

Answer:

a. Not reported
b. Financing
c. Financing
d. Operating

e. Investing
f. Financing
g. Not reported
h. Investing

i. Financing
j. Investing
k. Financing
l. Operating

m. Operating
n. Not reported
o. Not reported
p. Operating

Now let's see how to compute the operating cash flows by the direct method.

Computing Operating Cash Flows by the Direct Method

To compute operating cash flows by the direct method, we use the income statement and the *changes* in the balance sheet accounts. Exhibit 12-15 diagrams the process. Exhibit 12-16 is The Roadster Factory's income statement, and Exhibit 12-17 is the comparative balance sheet.

EXHIBIT 12-15   Direct Method of Computing Cash Flows from Operating Activities

RECEIPTS / PAYMENTS	Income Statement Account	Change in Related Balance Sheet Account	
RECEIPTS:			
From customers	Sales Revenue	+ Decrease in Accounts Receivable − Increase in Accounts Receivable	
Of interest	Interest Revenue	+ Decrease in Interest Receivable − Increase in Interest Receivable	
PAYMENTS:			
To suppliers	Cost of Goods Sold	+ Increase in Inventory − Decrease in Inventory	+ Decrease in Accounts Payable − Increase in Accounts Payable
	Operating Expense	+ Increase in Prepaids − Decrease in Prepaids	+ Decrease in Accrued Liabilities − Increase in Accrued Liabilities
To employees	Salary (Wage) Expense	+ Decrease in Salary (Wage) Payable − Increase in Salary (Wage) Payable	
For interest	Interest Expense	+ Decrease in Interest Payable − Increase in Interest Payable	
For income tax	Income Tax Expense	+ Decrease in Income Tax Payable − Increase in Income Tax Payable	

*We thank Professor Barbara Gerrity for suggesting this exhibit.

EXHIBIT 12-16 Income Statement

The Roadster Factory, Inc. (TRF)
Income Statement
Year Ended December 31, 20X9

(In thousands)

Revenues and gains:

Sales revenue	$303	
Interest revenue	2	
Gain on sale of plant assets	8	
Total revenues and gains		$313

Expenses:

Cost of goods sold	$150	
Salary and wage expense	56	
Depreciation expense	18	
Other operating expense	17	
Income tax expense	15	
Interest expense	7	
Total expenses		263
Net income		$ 50

EXHIBIT 12-17 Comparative Balance Sheet

The Roadster Factory, Inc. (TRF)
Comparative Balance Sheet
December 31, 20X9 and 20X8

(In thousands)	20X9	20X8	Increase (Decrease)	
Assets				
Current:				
Cash	$ 34	$ 42	$ (8)	
Accounts receivable	96	81	15	Changes in current assets—*Operating*
Inventory	35	38	(3)	
Prepaid expenses	8	7	1	
Notes receivable	21	—	21	Changes in noncurrent assets—*Investing*
Plant assets, net of depreciation	343	219	124	
Total	$537	$387	$150	
Liabilities				
Current:				
Accounts payable	$ 91	$ 57	$ 34	
Salary and wage payable	4	6	(2)	Changes in current liabilities—*Operating*
Accrued liabilities	1	3	(2)	
Long-term debt	160	77	83	Changes in long-term liabilities and paid-in capital accounts—*Financing*
Stockholders' Equity				
Common stock	162	158	4	
Retained earnings	119	86	33	Changes due to net income—*Operating* Change due to dividends—*Financing*
Total	$537	$387	$150	

Computing Cash Collections from Customers. Collections start with sales revenue (an accrual-basis amount). The Roadster Factory's income statement (Exhibit 12-16) reports sales of $303,000. Accounts receivable increased from $81,000 at the beginning of the year to $96,000 at year end, a $15,000 increase (Exhibit 12-17). Based on those amounts, Cash Collections equal $288,000, as follows. We must solve for cash collections (X):

Accounts Receivable					
Beginning balance	+	Sales	− Collections	=	Ending balance
$81,000	+	$303,000	−X	=	$96,000
			−X	=	$96,000 − $81,000 − $303,000
			X	=	$288,000

The T-account for Accounts Receivable provides another view of the same computation.

Accounts Receivable

Beginning balance	81,000		
Sales	303,000	Collections	288,000
Ending balance	96,000		

Accounts Receivable increased, so collections must be less than sales.

All collections of receivables are computed this way. Let's turn now to cash receipts of interest revenue. In our example, The Roadster Factory earned interest revenue and collected cash of $2,000. The amounts of interest revenue and cash receipts of interest often differ and exhibit 12-15 shows how to make this computation.

Computing Payments to Suppliers. This computation includes 2 parts:

- Payments for inventory
- Payments for operating expenses (other than interest and income tax)

Payments for inventory are computed by converting cost of goods sold to the cash basis. We use Cost of Goods Sold, Inventory, and Accounts Payable. First, we must solve for purchases. All the amounts come from Exhibits 12-16 and 12-17.

Cost of Goods Sold					
Beginning inventory	+	Purchases	− Ending inventory	=	Cost of goods sold
$38,000	+	X	− $35,000	=	$150,000
		X		=	$150,000 − $38,000 + $35,000
		X		=	$147,000

Now we can compute cash payments for inventory (Y), as follows:

Accounts Payable					
Beginning balance	+	Purchases	− Payments for inventory	=	Ending balance
$57,000	+	$147,000	−Y	=	$91,000
			−Y	=	$91,000 − $57,000 − $147,000
			Y	=	$113,000

The T-accounts show where the data come from. Start with Cost of Goods Sold.

Cost of Goods Sold			
Beg. inventory	38,000	End. inventory	35,000
Purchases	147,000		
Cost of goods sold	150,000		

Accounts Payable			
Payments for inventory	113,000	Beg. bal.	57,000
		Purchases	147,000
		End. bal.	91,000

Accounts Payable increased, so payments for inventory are less than purchases.

Computing Payments for Operating Expenses. Payments for operating expenses other than interest and income tax are computed from three accounts: Prepaid Expenses, Accrued Liabilities, and Other Operating Expenses. All The Roadster Factory data come from Exhibits 12-16 and 12-17.

Prepaid Expenses

Beginning balance	+	Payments	−	Expiration of prepaid expense (assumed)	=	Ending balance
$7,000	+	X	−	$7,000	=	$8,000
		X			=	$8,000 − $7,000 + $7,000
		X			=	$8,000

Accrued Liabilities

Beginning balance	+	Accrual of expense at year end (assumed)	−	Payments	=	Ending balance
$3,000	+	$1,000		−X	=	$1,000
				−X	=	$1,000 − $3,000 − $1,000
				X	=	$3,000

Other Operating Expenses

Accrual of expense at year end	+	Expiration of prepaid expense	−	Payments	=	Ending balance
$1,000	+	$7,000		X	=	$17,000
				X	=	$17,000 − $1,000 − $7,000
				X	=	$9,000
		Total payments for operating expenses			=	$8,000 + $3,000 + $9,000
					=	$20,000

The T-accounts give another picture of the same data.

Prepaid Expenses			
Beg. bal.	7,000	Expiration of prepaid expense	7,000
Payments	8,000		
End. bal.	8,000		

Accrued Liabilities			
Payment	3,000	Beg. bal.	3,000
		Accrual of expense at year end	1,000
		End. bal.	1,000

Other Operating Expenses		
Accrual of expense at year end	1,000	
Expiration of prepaid expense	7,000	
Payments	9,000	
End. bal.	17,000	

Total payments for operating expenses = $20,000($8,000 + $3,000 + $9,000)

Now we can compute Payments to Suppliers as follows:

Payments to Suppliers	=	Payments for Inventory	+	Payments for Operating Expenses
$133,000	=	$113,000	+	$20,000

Computing Payments to Employees. It is convenient to combine all payments to employees into 1 account, Salary and Wage Expense. We then adjust the expense for the change in Salary and Wage Payable, as shown here:

Salary and Wage Payable

Beginning balance	+	Salary and wage expense	−	Payments	=	Ending balance
$6,000	+	$56,000		−X	=	$4,000
				−X	=	$4,000 − $6,000 − $56,000
				X	=	$58,000

Salary and Wage Payable

		Beginning balance	6,000
Payments to employees	58,000	Salary and wage expense	56,000
		Ending balance	4,000

Computing Payments of Interest and Income Taxes. The Roadster Factory's expense and payment amounts are the same for interest and income tax, so no analysis is required. If the expense and the payment differ, the payment can be computed as shown in Exhibit 12-15.

Computing Investing and Financing Cash Flows

Investing and financing activities are explained on pages 626–630. These computations are the same for both the direct and the indirect methods.

STOP & think. . .

Fidelity Company reported the following for 2006 and 2005 (in millions):

At December 31,	2006	2005
Receivables, net	$3,500	$3,900
Inventory	5,200	5,000
Accounts payable	900	1,200
Income taxes payable	600	700

Year Ended December 31,	2006
Revenues..	$23,000
Cost of goods sold.........................	14,100
Income tax expense.......................	900

Based on these figures, how much cash did
- Fidelity collect from customers during 2006?
- Fidelity pay for inventory during 2006?
- Fidelity pay for income taxes during 2006?

		Beginning Receivables	+	Revenues	−	Collections	=	Ending Receivables
Collections from customers	= $23,400:	$3,900	+	$23,000	−	$23,400	=	$3,500

		Cost of Goods Sold	+	Increase in Inventory	+	Decrease in Accounts Payable	=	Payments
Payments for inventory	= $14,600:	$14,100	+	($5,200 − $5,000)	+	($1,200 − $900)	=	$14,600

		Beginning Income Taxes Payable	+	Income Tax Expense	−	Payment	=	Ending Income Taxes Payable
Payment of income taxes	= $1,000:	$700	+	$900	−	$1,000	=	$600

MEASURING CASH ADEQUACY: FREE CASH FLOW

Throughout this chapter, we have focused on cash flows from operating, investing, and financing activities. Some investors want to know how much cash a company can "free up" for new opportunities. **Free cash flow** is the amount of cash available from operations after paying for planned investments in plant assets. Free cash flow can be computed as follows:

$$\text{Free cash flow} = \frac{\text{Net cash provided}}{\text{by operating activities}} - \frac{\text{Cash payments earmarked for}}{\text{investments in plant assets}}$$

PepsiCo, Inc., uses free cash flow to manage its operations. Suppose PepsiCo expects net cash inflow of $2.3 billion from operations. Assume PepsiCo plans to spend $1.9 billion to modernize its bottling plants. In this case, PepsiCo's free cash flow would be $0.4 billion ($2.3 billion - $1.9 billion). If a good investment opportunity comes along, PepsiCo should have $0.4 billion to invest in the other company. **Shell Oil Company** also uses free-cash-flow analysis. A large amount of free cash flow is preferable because it means that a lot of cash is available for new investments. The Decision Guidelines that follow shows some ways to use cash-flow and income data for investment and credit analysis.

DECISION GUIDELINES

INVESTORS' AND CREDITORS' USE OF CASH-FLOW AND RELATED INFORMATION

Jan Childres is a private investor. Through years of experience she has devised some guidelines for evaluating both stock investments and bond investments. Childres uses a combination of accrual-accounting data and cash-flow information. Here are her decision guidelines for both investors and creditors.

INVESTORS

Questions	Factors to Consider*	Financial Statement Predictor/Decision Model*
1. How much in dividends can I expect to receive from an investment in stock?	Expected future net income	Income from continuing operations**
	Expected future cash balance	Net cash flows from (in order): • Operating activities • Investing activities • Financing activities
	Future dividend policy	Current and past dividend policy
2. Is the stock price likely to increase or decrease?	Expected future net income	Income from continuing operations**
	Expected future cash flows from operating activities	Income from continuing operations** Net cash flow from operating activities
3. What is the future stock price likely to be?	Expected future income from • continuing operations, *and* • net cash flow from operating activities	$$\text{Expected future price of a share of stock} = \frac{\text{Expected future earnings per share**}}{\text{Investment capitalization rate**}}$$ $$\text{Expected future price of a share of stock} = \frac{\text{Net cash flow from operations per share}}{\text{Investment capitalization rate**}}$$

CREDITORS

Questions	Factors to Consider	Financial Statement Predictor
Can the company pay the interest and principal at the maturity of a loan?	Expected future net cash flow from operating activities	Income from continuing operations** Net cash flow from operating activities

*There are many other factors to consider in making these decisions. These are some of the more common.
**See Chapter 11.

END-OF-CHAPTER SUMMARY PROBLEM

Adeva Health Foods, Inc., reported the following comparative balance sheet and income statement for 20X6.

Adeva Health Foods, Inc.
Comparative Balance Sheet
December 31, 20X6 and 20X5

	20X6	20X5
Cash	$ 19,000	$ 3,000
Accounts receivable	22,000	23,000
Inventories	34,000	31,000
Prepaid expenses	1,000	3,000
Equipment, net	90,000	79,000
Intangible assets	9,000	9,000
	$175,000	$148,000
Accounts payable	$ 14,000	$ 9,000
Accrued liabilities	16,000	19,000
Income tax payable	14,000	12,000
Notes payable	45,000	50,000
Common stock	31,000	20,000
Retained earnings	64,000	40,000
Treasury stock	(9,000)	(2,000)
	$175,000	$148,000

Adeva Health Foods, Inc.
Income Statement
Year Ended December 31, 20X6

Sales revenue	$190,000
Gain on sale of equipment	6,000
Total revenue and gains	$196,000
Cost of goods sold	$ 85,000
Depreciation expense	19,000
Other operating expenses	36,000
Total expenses	140,000
Income before income tax	56,000
Income tax expense	18,000
Net income	$ 38,000

Assume that **Berkshire Hathaway** is considering buying Adeva. Berkshire Hathaway requests the following cash-flow data for 20X6. There were no noncash investing and financing activities.

a. Collections from customers
b. Cash payments for inventory
c. Cash payments for operating expenses

d. Cash payment for income tax
e. Cash received from the sale of equipment. Adeva paid $40,000 for new equipment during the year.
f. Issuance of common stock
g. Issuance of notes payable. Adeva paid off $20,000 during the year.
h. Cash dividends. There were no stock dividends.

Provide the requested data. Show your work.

Answer

a. Analyze Accounts Receivable (let X = Collections from customers):

Beginning	+	Sales	−	Collections	=	Ending
+ 23,000	+	190,000	−	X	=	$22,000
				X	=	$191,000

b. Analyze Inventory and Accounts Payable (let X = Purchases, and let Y = Payments for inventory):

Beginning Inventory	+	Purchases	−	Ending inventory	=	Cost of Goods Sold
$31,000	+	X	−	$34,000	=	$85,000
		X			=	$88,000

Beginning Accounts Payable	+	Purchases	−	Payments	=	Ending Accounts Payable
$9,000	+	$88,000	−	Y	=	$14,000
				Y	=	$83,000

c. Start with Other Operating Expenses, and adjust for the changes in Prepaid Expenses and Accrued Liabilities:

Other Operating Expenses	− Decrease in Prepaid Expenses	+ Decrease in Accrued Liabilities	=	Payments for Operating Expenses
$36,000	− $2,000	+ $3,000	=	$37,000

d. Analyze Income Tax Payable (let X = Payment of income tax):

Beginning	+	Income Tax Expense	−	Payments	=	Ending
$12,000	+	$18,000	−	X	=	$14,000
				X	=	$16,000

e. Analyze Equipment, Net (let X = Book value of equipment sold. Then combine with the gain or loss to compute cash received from the sale.)

Beginning	+	Aquisitions	–	Depreciation	–	Book Value Sold	=	Ending
$79,000	+	$40,000	–	$19,000	–	X	=	$90,000
						X	=	$10,000

Cash Received from Sale	=	Book Value Sold	+	Gain on Sale
$16,000	=	$10,000	+	$6,000

f. Analyze Common Stock (let X = issuance)

Beginning	+	Issuance	=	Ending
$20,000	+	X	=	$31,000
		X	=	$11,000

g. Analyze Notes Payable (let X = issuance):

Beginning	+	Issuance	–	Payment	=	Ending
$50,000	+	X	–	$20,000	=	$45,000
		X			=	$15,000

h. Analyze Retained Earnings (let X = dividends)

Beginning	+	Net Income	–	Dividends	=	Ending
$40,000	+	$38,000	–	X	=	$64,000
				X	=	$14,000

REVIEW STATEMENT OF CASH FLOWS

Quick Check (Answers are given on page 680.)

1. All of the following activities are reported on the statement of cash flows except:
   - a. operating activities.
   - b. investing activities.
   - c. financing activities.
   - d. marketing activities.
2. Activities that create long-term liabilities are usually
   - a. operating activities.
   - b. investing activities.
   - c. financing activities.
   - d. noncash investing and financing activities.

3. Activities affecting long-term assets are
  a. operating activities.   **c.** financing activities.
  b. investing activities.   **d.** marketing activities.

4. In 20X9, IMC Corporation borrowed $50,000, paid dividends of $12,000, issued 2,000 shares of stock for $30 per share, purchased land for $24,000, and received dividends of $6,000. Net income was $80,000, and depreciation for the year totaled $5,000. How much should be reported as net cash provided by operating activities by the indirect method?
  a. $85,000   **c.** $110,000
  b. $98,000   **d.** $104,000

5. Activities that obtain the cash needed to launch and sustain a company are
  a. income activities   **c.** financing activities.
  b. investing activities.   **d.** marketing activities.

6. The exchange of stock for land would be reported as
  a. Exchanges are not reported on   **c.** investing activities.
     the statement of cash flows.   **d.** financing activities.
  b. noncash investing and
     financing activities.

Use the following Carolina Company information for questions 7–10.

Net income...............................	$47,000	Increase in accounts payable	$ 7,000
Depreciation expense	8,000	Acquisition of equipment	24,000
Payment of dividends	2,000	Sale of treasury stock	3,000
Increase in accounts receivable	4,000	Payment of long-term debt.........	9,000
Collection of notes receivable...........	6,000	Proceeds from sale of land..........	36,000
Loss on sale of land........................	12,000	Decrease in inventories..............	2,000

7. Under the indirect method, net cash provided by operating activities would be:
  a. $72,000   **c.** $83,000
  b. $76,000   **d.** $84,000

8. Net cash provided by (used for) investing activities would be:
  a. $18,000   **c.** $(6,000)
  b. $(12,000)   **d.** $24,000

9. Net cash provided by (used for) financing activities would be:
  a. $4,000   **c.** $(8,000)
  b. $2,000   **d.** $(11,000)

10. The cost of land must have been
  a. $30,000.   **c.** $54,000.
  b. $48,000.   **d.** Cannot be determined from the data given.

11. Blue Bunny Ice Cream began the year with $45,000 in accounts receivable and ended the year with $31,000 in accounts receivable. If sales for the year were $650,000, the cash collected from customers during the year amounted to:
  a. $664,000   **c.** $733,000
  b. $672,000   **d.** $655,000

12. Hampshire Farms, Ltd., made sales of $690,000 and had cost of goods sold of $390,000. Inventory decreased by $15,000 and accounts payable decreased by $9,000. Operating expenses were $175,000. How much was Hampshire Farms' net income for the year?
  a. $110,000   **c.** $125,000
  b. $116,000   **d.** $300,000

13. Use the Hampshire Farms data from question 12. How much cash did Hampshire Farms pay for inventory during the year?
  a. $374,000   **c.** $396,000
  b. $390,000   **d.** (Some other amount_____).

Accounting Vocabulary

cash equivalents (p. 618) Highly liquid short-term investments that can be converted into cash immediately.

cash flows (p. 617) Cash receipts and cash payments (disbursements).

direct method (p. 620) Format of the operating activities section of the statement of cash flows; lists the major categories of operating cash receipts (collections from customers and receipts of interest and dividends) and cash disbursements (payments to suppliers, to employees, for interest and income taxes).

financing activities (p. 619) Activities that obtain from investors and creditors the cash needed to launch and sustain the business; a section of the statement of cash flows.

free cash flow (p. 645) The amount of cash available from operations after paying for planned investments in plant assets.

indirect method (p. 620) Format of the operating activities section of the statement of cash flows; starts with net income and reconciles to cash flows from operating activities.

investing activities (p. 619) Activities that increase or decrease the long-term assets available to the business; a section of the statement of cash flows.

operating activities (p. 619) Activities that create revenue or expense in the entity's major line of business; a section of the statement of cash flows. Operating activities affect the income statement.

statement of cash flows (p. 617) Reports cash receipts and cash payments classified according to the entity's major activities: operating, investing, and financing.

ASSESS YOUR PROGRESS

Short Exercises

S12-1 (*Learning Objective 1: Purposes of the statement of cash flows*) State how the statement of cash flows helps investors and creditors perform each of the following functions. (pp. 616–617)

    a. Predict future cash flows.
    b. Evaluate management decisions.

S12-2 (*Learning Objective 2: Evaluating operating cash flows—indirect method*) Examine the **Google** cash-flow statement on page 616. Suppose Google's operating activities *used*, rather than *provided*, cash. Identify 3 things under the indirect method that could cause operating cash flows to be negative. (pp. 616, 620–621)

S12-3 (*Learning Objective 3: Reporting cash flows from operating activities—indirect method*) Majestic America Transportation (MAT) began 20X6 with accounts receivable, inventory, and prepaid expenses totaling $65,000. At the end of the year MAT had a total of $78,000 for these current assets. At the beginning of 20X6, MAT owed current liabilities of $42,000, and at year end current liabilities totaled $40,000.

    Net income for the year was $80,000. Included in net income were a $4,000 gain on the sale of land and depreciation expense of $9,000.

    Show how MAT should report cash flows from operating activities for 20X6. MAT uses the *indirect* method. Use Exhibit 12-6 (p. 624) as a guide.

S12-4 (*Learning Objective 2: Identifying items for reporting cash flows from operations—indirect method*) Cooper Clinic, Inc., is preparing its statement of cash flows (indirect method) for the year ended September 30, 20X7. Consider the following items in preparing the company's statement of cash flows. Identify each item as an operating activity—addition to net income (O+), or subtraction from net income (O-); an investing activity (I); a financing activity (F); or an activity that is not used to prepare the cash-flow statement by the indirect method (N). Place the appropriate symbol in the blank space. (pp. 620–631).

(continued)

__	a. Loss on sale of land	__	h. Increase in accounts payable
__	b. Depreciation expense	__	i. Net income
__	c. Increase in inventory	__	j. Payment of dividends
__	d. Decrease in prepaid expense	__	k. Decrease in accrued liabilities
__	e. Decrease in accounts receivable	__	l. Issuance of common stock
__	f. Purchase of equipment	__	m. Gain on sale of building
__	g. Collection of cash from customers	__	n. Retained earnings

S12-5 (*Learning Objective 3. Computing operating cash flows—indirect method*) (Short Exercise S12-6 is an alternate exercise.) Edwards Corporation accountants have assembled the following data for the year ended June 30, 20X8.

Net income.............................	$?	Cost of goods sold...................	$100,000
Payment of dividends...............	6,000	Other operating expenses.........	35,000
Proceeds from issuance		Purchase of equipment.............	40,000
of common stock............	20,000	Decrease in current liabilities....	5,000
Sales revenue...........................	224,000	Payment of note payable..........	30,000
Increase in current		Proceeds from sale of land........	60,000
assets other than cash	30,000	Depreciation expense	8,000
Purchase of treasury stock........	5,000		

Prepare the *operating activities section* of Edwards' statement of cash flows for the year ended June 30, 20X8. Edwards uses the *indirect* method for operating cash flows. (pp. 623–624)

S12-6 (*Learning Objective 3: Preparing a statement of cash flows—indirect method*) Use the data in Short Exercise S12-5 to prepare Edwards Corporations' statement of cash flows for the year ended June 30, 20X8. Edwards uses the *indirect* method for operating activities. Use Exhibit 12-7, page 626, as a guide, but you may stop after determining the net increase (or decrease) in cash.

S12-7 (*Learning Objective 3: Computing investing cash flows*) Motorcars of Phoenix, Inc., reported the following financial statements for 20X6:

Motorcars of Phoenix, Inc.
Income Statement
Year Ended December 31, 20X6

(In thousands)

Sales revenue............................	$710
Cost of goods sold....................	$340
Salary expense..........................	70
Depreciation expense	20
Other expenses.........................	130
Total expenses..........................	560
Net income	$150

Motorcars of Phoenix, Inc.
Comparative Balance Sheet
December 31, 20X6 and 20X5

(In thousands)

Assets	20X6	20X5	Liabilities	20X6	20X5
Current:			Current:		
Cash	$ 19	$ 16	Accounts payable..........	$ 47	$ 42
Accounts receivable	59	48	Salary payable	23	21
Inventory.....................	75	84	Accrued liabilities	8	11
Prepaid expenses...........	3	2	Long-term notes payable........	68	58
Long-term investments...........	55	75			
Plant assets, net.....................	225	185	**Stockholders' Equity**		
			Common stock......................	40	32
			Retained earnings..................	250	246
Total	$436	$410	Total	$436	$410

Compute the following investing cash flows. (p. 628):

  a. Acquisitions of plant assets (all were for cash). Motorcars of Phoenix sold no plant assets.
  b. Proceeds from the sale of investments. Motorcars of Phoenix purchased no investments.

S12-8 (*Learning Objective 3: Computing financing cash flows*) Use the Motorcars of Phoenix data in Short Exercise S12-7 to compute. (pp. 630–631)

  a. New borrowing or payment of long-term notes payable. Motorcars of Phoenix had only 1 long-term note payable transaction during the year.
  b. Issuance of common stock or retirement of common stock. Motorcars of Phoenix had only 1 common stock transaction during the year.
  c. Payment of cash dividends (same as dividends declared).

S12-9 (*Learning Objective 4: Preparing a statement of cash flows—direct method*) Tally-Ho Horse Farm, Inc., began 20X6 with cash of $44,000. During the year, Tally-Ho earned service revenue of $500,000 and collected $510,000 from customers. Expenses for the year totaled $420,000, with $400,000 paid in cash to suppliers and employees. Tally-Ho also paid $100,000 to purchase equipment and a cash dividend of $50,000 to stockholders. During 20X6 Tally-Ho borrowed $20,000 by issuing a note payable.

Prepare the company's statement of cash flows for the year. Format operating activities by the direct method. (pp. 637–638)

S12-10 (*Learning Objective 4: Computing operating cash flows—direct method*) Short Exercise S12-11 is an alternate. Millbrook Golf Club, Inc., provides the following data for the year ended June 30, 20X9.

Cost of goods sold............................	$100,000	Payment of dividends	$ 6,000
Payments to suppliers.......................	87,000	Proceeds from issuance	
Purchase of equipment......................	40,000	of common stock	20,000
Payments to employees.....................	70,000	Sales revenue	210,000
Payment of note payable	30,000	Collections from customers................	180,000
Proceeds from sale of land...............	60,000	Payment of income tax.......................	10,000
Depreciation expense	8,000	Purchase of treasury stock.................	5,000

(*continued*)

Prepare the *operating activities section* of Millbrook Golf Club, Inc.'s, statement of cash flows for the year ended June 30, 20X9. Millbrook uses the *direct* method for operating cash flows. (pp. 637–638)

S12-11 (*Learning Objective 4: Preparing a statement of cash flows—direct method*) Use the data in Short Exercise S12-10 to prepare Millbrook Golf Club, Inc.'s, statement of cash flows for the year ended June 30, 20X9. Millbrook uses the *direct* method for operating activities. Use Exhibit 12-13, page 638, as a guide, but you may stop after determining the net increase (or decrease) in cash.

S12-12 (*Learning Objective 4: Computing operating cash flows—direct method*) Use the Motorcars of Phoenix data in Short Exercise S12-7 to compute the following:

    a. Collections from customers (pp. 640–641) **b.** Payments for inventory (pp. 642–643)

S12-13 (*Learning Objective 4: Computing operating cash flows—direct method*) Use the Motorcars of Phoenix data in Short Exercise S12-7 to compute the following:

    a. Payments to employees (pp. 643–644)   **b.** Payments of other expenses (pp. 643–644)

Exercises

writing assignment ■

E12-14 (*Learning Objective 1: Identifying the purposes of the statement of cash flows*) U.S. Plating, Inc., has experienced an unbroken string of 10 years of growth in net income. Nevertheless, the company is facing bankruptcy. Creditors are calling all of U.S. Plating's loans for immediate payment, and the cash is simply not available. It is clear that the company's top managers overemphasized profits and gave too little attention to cash flows.

❙ Required

Write a brief memo, in your own words, to explain to the managers of U.S. Plating, Inc., the purposes of the statement of cash flows. (pp. 616–617)

E12-15 (*Learning Objective 2: Identifying activities for the statement of cash flows—indirect method*) Tyler-Bolton Investments specializes in low-risk government bonds. Identify each of Tyler-Bolton's transactions as operating (O), investing (I), financing (F), noncash investing and financing (NIF), or a transaction that is not reported on the statement of cash flows (N). Indicate whether each item increases (+) or decreases (–) cash. The indirect method is used for operating activities. (pp. 620–631)

___	a. Net income		___	k. Acquisition of equipment by issuance of note payable
___	b. Payment of cash dividend			
___	c. Sale of long-term investment		___	l. Payment of long-term debt
___	d. Loss on sale of equipment		___	m. Acquisition of building by cash payment
___	e. Amortization of intangible assets		___	n. Accrual of salary expense
___	f. Issuance of long-term note payable to borrow cash		___	o. Purchase of long-term investment
___	g. Depreciation of equipment		___	p. Decrease in merchandise inventory
___	h. Purchase of treasury stock			
___	i. Issuance of common stock for cash		___	q. Increase in prepaid expenses
			___	r. Cash sale of land
___	j. Increase in accounts payable		___	s. Decrease in accrued liabilities

E12-16 (*Learning Objective 2: Classifying transactions for the statement of cash flows—indirect method*) Indicate whether each of the following transactions records an operating activity, an investing activity, a financing activity, or a noncash investing and financing activity. The statement of cash flows is prepared by the *indirect* method. (pp. 620–631)

a.	Equipment	18,000			h.	Cash	81,000	
	Cash		18,000			Common Stock		12,000
b.	Cash	7,200				Capital in Excess of Par		69,000
	Long-Term Investment		7,200		i.	Treasury Stock	13,000	
c.	Bonds Payable	45,000				Cash		13,000
	Cash		45,000		j.	Cash	60,000	
d.	Building	164,000				Accounts Receivable	10,000	
	Note Payable, Long-Term		164,000			Service Revenue		70,000
e.	Loss on Disposal of Equipment	1,400			k.	Salary Expense	22,000	
	Equipment, Net		1,400			Cash		22,000
f.	Dividends Payable	16,500			l.	Land	87,000	
	Cash		16,500			Cash		87,000
g.	Furniture and Fixtures	22,100			m.	Depreciation Expense	9,000	
	Cash		22,100			Accumulated Depreciation		9,000

E12-17 (*Learning Objective 3: Computing cash flows from operating activities—indirect method*) The accounting records of North Central Distributors, Inc., reveal the following:

writing assignment ■

Net income............................	$35,000	Depreciation................................	$18,000
Collection of dividend		Decrease in current	
revenue	7,000	liabilities	20,000
Payment of interest.................	16,000	Increase in current assets	
Sales revenue	9,000	other than cash	27,000
Loss on sale of land...............	5,000	Payment of dividends	7,000
Acquisition of land	37,000	Payment of income tax...............	13,000

❙ *Required*

Compute cash flows from operating activities by the indirect method. Use the format of the operating activities section of Exhibit 12-6 (p. 624). Also evaluate the operating cash flow of North Central Distributors. Give the reason for your evaluation.

E12-18 (*Learning Objective 3: Computing cash flows from operating activities—indirect method*) The accounting records of Saskatoon Fur Traders include these accounts:

Cash

Mar. 1	5,000		
Receipts	447,000	Payments	448,000
Mar. 31	4,000		

Accounts Receivable

Mar. 1	18,000		
Receipts	443,000	Collections	447,000
Mar. 31	14,000		

Inventory

Mar. 1	19,000		
Purchases	337,000	Cost of sales	335,000
Mar. 31	21,000		

Equipment

Mar. 1	93,000		
Acquisition	6,000		
Mar. 31	99,000		

Accumulated Depreciation—Equipment

		Mar. 1	52,000
		Depreciation	3,000
		Mar. 31	55,000

Accounts Payable

		Mar. 1	14,000
Payments	332,000	Purchases	337,000
		Mar. 31	19,000

Accrued Liabilities

		Mar. 1	9,000
Payments	14,000	Receipts	11,000
		Mar. 31	6,000

Retained Earnings

Quarterly		Mar. 1	64,000
dividend	18,000	Net income	41,000
		Mar. 31	87,000

(continued)

Compute Saskatoon's net cash provided by (used for) operating activities during March. Use the indirect method. Does Saskatoon have trouble collecting receivables or selling inventory? How can you tell? (pp. 623–624)

writing assignment ■   **E12-19** (*Learning Objective 3: Preparing the statement of cash flows—indirect method*) The income statement and additional data of Noel Travel Products, Inc., follow:

Noel Travel Products, Inc.
Income Statement
Years Ended December 31, 20X6

Revenues:		
Sales revenue	$229,000	
Dividend revenue	8,000	$237,000
Expenses:		
Cost of goods sold	$ 91,000	
Salary expense	45,000	
Depreciation expense	29,000	
Advertising expense	4,000	
Interest expense	2,000	
Income tax expense	9,000	180,000
Net income		$ 57,000

Additional data:

  a. Acquisition of plant assets was $150,000. Of this amount, $100,000 was paid in cash and $50,000 by signing a note payable.
  b. Proceeds from sale of land totaled $24,000.
  c. Proceeds from issuance of common stock totaled $30,000.
  d. Payment of long-term note payable was $15,000.
  e. Payment of dividends was $11,000.
  f. From the balance sheet:

	December 31,	
	20X6	20X5
Current Assets:		
Cash	$47,000	$20,000
Accounts receivable	43,000	58,000
Inventory	83,000	77,000
Prepaid expenses	9,000	8,000
Current Liabilities:		
Accounts payable	$35,000	$22,000
Accrued liabilities	13,000	21,000

❙ Required

  1. Prepare Noel's statement of cash flows for the year ended December 31, 20X6, using the indirect method. (p. 626)

  2. Evaluate Noel's cash flows for the year. In your evaluation, mention all 3 categories of cash flows and give the reason for your evaluation. (pp. 618–619)

E12-20 (*Learning Objective 3: Interpreting a cash-flow statement—indirect method*)
Consider 3 independent cases for the cash flows of 827 Boulevard Shoes. For each case, identify from the cash-flow statement how 827 Boulevard Shoes generated the cash to acquire new plant assets. Rank the 3 cases from the most healthy financially to the least healthy. (p. 626)

	Case A	Case B	Case C
Cash flows from operating activities:			
Net income	$ 30,000	$ 30,000	$ 30,000
Depreciation and amortization	11,000	11,000	11,000
Increase in current assets	(1,000)	(19,000)	(7,000)
Decrease in current liabilities	0	(6,000)	(8,000)
	$ 40,000	$ 16,000	$ 26,000
Cash flows from investing activities:			
Acquisition of plant assets	$(91,000)	$(91,000)	$ (91,000)
Sales of plant assets	8,000	97,000	4,000
	$(83,000)	$ 6,000	$ (87,000)
Cash flows from financing activities:			
Issuance of stock............................	$ 50,000	$ 16,000	$104,000
Payment of debt.............................	(9,000)	(21,000)	(29,000)
	$ 41,000	$ (5,000)	$ 75,000
Net increase (decrease) in cash	$ (2,000)	$ 17,000	$ 14,000

E12-21 (*Learning Objective 3: Computing investing and financing amounts for the statement of cash flows*) Compute the following items for the statement of cash flows:

   a. Beginning and ending Plant Assets, Net, are $103,000 and $107,000, respectively. Depreciation for the period was $21,500, and purchases of new plant assets were $27,000. Plant assets were sold at a $1,000 loss. What were the cash proceeds of the sale? (pp. 626–628)
   b. Beginning and ending Retained Earnings are $45,000 and $73,000, respectively. Net income for the period was $47,000, and stock dividends were $8,000. How much were cash dividends? (pp. 630–632)

E12-22 (*Learning Objective 4: Identifying activities for the statement of cash flows—direct method*) Identify each of the following transactions as operating (O), investing (I), financing (F), noncash investing and financing (NIF), or not reported on the statement of cash flows (N). Indicate whether each transaction increases (+) or decreases (–) cash. The *direct* method is used for operating activities. (pp. 634–640)

__	a. Purchase of treasury stock	__	k. Acquisition of equipment by
__	b. Issuance of common stock		issuance of note payable
	for cash	__	l. Payment of long-term debt
__	c. Payment of accounts payable	__	m. Acquisition of building by
__	d. Issuance of preferred stock		payment of cash
	for cash	__	n. Accrual of salary expense
__	e. Payment of cash dividend	__	o. Purchase of long-term
__	f. Sale of long-term investment		investment
__	g. Amortization of patent	__	p. Payment of wages to
__	h. Collection of accounts		employees
	receivable	__	q. Collection of cash interest
__	i. Issuance of long-term note	__	r. Cash sale of land
	payable to borrow cash	__	s. Distribution of stock
__	j. Depreciation of equipment		dividend

E12-23 (*Learning Objective 4: Classifying transactions for the statement of cash flows—direct method*) Indicate where, if at all, each of the following transactions would be reported on a statement of cash flows prepared by the *direct* method and the accompanying schedule of noncash investing and financing activities. (pp. 634–640)

a.	Equipment	18,000			h.	Retained Earnings	36,000	
	Cash		18,000			Common Stock		36,000
b.	Cash	7,200			i.	Cash	2,000	
	Long-Term Investment		7,200			Interest Revenue		2,000
c.	Bonds Payable	45,000			j.	Land	87,700	
	Cash		45,000			Cash		87,700
d.	Building	164,000			k.	Accounts Payable	8,300	
	Cash		164,000			Cash		8,300
e.	Cash	1,400			l.	Salary Expense	4,300	
	Accounts Receivable		1,400			Cash		4,300
f.	Dividends Payable	16,500			m.	Cash	81,000	
	Cash		16,500			Common Stock		12,000
g.	Furniture and Fixtures	22,100				Capital in Excess of Par		69,000
	Note Payable, Short-Term		22,100	n.		Treasury Stock	13,000	
						Cash		13,000

writing assignment ■

E12-24 (*Learning Objective 4: Computing cash flows from operating activities—direct method*) The accounting records of Jasmine Pharmaceuticals, Inc., reveal the following:

Payment of salaries and wages.................................	$34,000	Net income..................................	$34,000	
Depreciation..............................	22,000	Payment of income tax..............	13,000	
Decrease in current liabilities...........................	20,000	Collection of dividend revenue	7,000	
Increase in current assets other than cash	27,000	Payment of interest....................	16,000	
		Cash sales..................................	38,000	
		Loss on sale of land	5,000	
Payment of dividends................	12,000	Acquisition of land	37,000	
Collection of accounts receivable.........................	93,000	Payment of accounts payable	54,000	

❚ Required

Compute cash flows from operating activities by the *direct* method. Use the format of the operating activities section of Exhibit 12-13 (pp. 637–638). Also evaluate Jasmine's operating cash flow. Give the reason for your evaluation. (pp. 618–619, 637–638)

E12-25 (*Learning Objective 4: Identifying items for the statement of cash flows—direct method*) Selected accounts of Fishbowl Antiques show the following:

Salary Payable

		Beginning balance	9,000
Payments	40,000	Salary expense	38,000
		Ending balance	7,000

Buildings

Beginning balance	90,000	Depreciation	18,000
Acquisitions	145,000	Book value of building sold	109,000*
Ending balance	108,000		

*Sale price was 140,000.

Notes Payable

		Beginning balance	273,000
Payments	69,000	Issuance of note payable for cash	83,000
		Ending balance	287,000

▌*Required*

For each account, identify the item or items that should appear on a statement of cash flows prepared by the *direct* method. State where to report the item. (pp. 635–640)

E12-26 (*Learning Objective 4: Preparing the statement of cash flows—direct method*) The income statement and additional data of Floral World, Inc., follow:

writing assignment ■

Floral World, Inc.
Income Statement
Year Ended June 30, 20X6

Revenues:		
Sales revenue	$229,000	
Dividend revenue	15,000	$244,000
Expenses:		
Cost of goods sold	$103,000	
Salary expense	45,000	
Depreciation expense	29,000	
Advertising expense	11,000	
Interest expense	2,000	
Income tax expense	9,000	199,000
Net income		$ 45,000

Additional data:
  a. Collections from customers are $30,000 more than sales.
  b. Payments to suppliers are $1,000 more than the sum of cost of goods sold plus advertising expense.

(continued)

    c. Payments to employees are $1,000 more than salary expense.

    d. Dividend revenue, interest expense, and income tax expense equal their cash amounts.

    e. Acquisition of plant assets is $150,000. Of this amount, $101,000 is paid in cash and $49,000 by signing a note payable.

    f. Proceeds from sale of land total $24,000.

    g. Proceeds from issuance of common stock total $30,000.

    h. Payment of long-term note payable is $15,000.

    i. Payment of dividends is $11,000.

    j. Cash balance, June 30, 20X5, was $20,000.

❙ Required

1. Prepare Floral World, Inc.'s, statement of cash flows and accompanying schedule of non-cash investing and financing activities. Report operating activities by the *direct* method. (pp. 637–640)

2. Evaluate Floral World's cash flows for the year. In your evaluation, mention all 3 categories of cash flows and give the reason for your evaluation. (pp. 618–619)

E12-27 (*Learning Objective 4: Computing amounts for the statement of cash flows—direct method*) Compute the following items for the statement of cash flows:

    a. Beginning and ending Accounts Receivable are $22,000 and $32,000, respectively. Credit sales for the period total $60,000. How much are cash collections from customers? (pp. 640–641)

    b. Cost of goods sold is $111,000. Beginning Inventory was $25,000, and ending Inventory is $21,000. Beginning and ending Accounts Payable are $14,000 and $8,000, respectively. How much are cash payments for inventory? (pp. 642–643)

Challenge Exercises

E12-28 (*Learning Objective 3, 4: Computing cash-flow amounts*) 500 Broad Street, Inc., reported the following in its financial statements for the year ended August 31, 20X9 (in thousands):

	20X9	20X8
Income Statement		
Net sales	$24,623	$21,207
Cost of sales	18,048	15,466
Depreciation	269	230
Other operating expenses	3,883	4,248
Income tax expense	537	486
Net income	$ 1,886	$ 777
Balance Sheet		
Cash and equivalents	$ 17	$ 13
Accounts receivable	601	615
Inventory	3,100	2,831
Property and equipment, net	4,345	3,428
Accounts payable	1,547	1,364
Accrued liabilities	938	631
Income tax payable	201	194
Long-term liabilities	478	464
Common stock	519	446
Retained earnings	4,380	3,788

Determine the following cash receipts and payments for 500 Broad Street, Inc., during 20X9:

a. Collections from customers (pp. 640–641)

b. Payments for inventory (pp. 642–643)

c. Payments for other operating expenses (pp. 642–643)

d. Payment of income tax (pp. 643–644)

e. Proceeds from issuance of common stock (p. 629)

f. Payment of cash dividends (pp. 630–631)

E12-29 (*Learning Objective 3: Using the balance sheet and the cash-flow statement together*) Crown Specialties reported the following at December 31, 20X8 (in thousands):

	20X8	20X7
From the comparative balance sheet:		
Property and equipment, net...	$11,150	$9,590
Long-term notes payable...	4,400	3,080
From the statement of cash flows:		
Depreciation	$ 1,920	
Capital expenditures..	(4,130)	
Proceeds from sale of		
property and equipment	770	
Proceeds from issuance of long-term note payable.......	1,190	
Payment of long-term note payable.............................	(110)	
Issuance of common stock	383	

Determine the following items for Crown Specialties during 20X8:

1. Gain or loss on the sale of property and equipment (p. 627)

2. Amount of long-term debt issued for something other than cash (pp. 629, 631–632)

Quiz

Test your understanding of the statement of cash flows by answering the following questions. Select the best choice from among the possible answers given.

Q12-30 Paying off bonds payable is reported on the statement of cash flows under (pp. 620–621)

a. operating activities.

b. investing activities.

c. financing activities.

d. noncash investing and financing activities.

Q12-31 The sale of inventory for cash is reported on the statement of cash flows under (pp. 620–621, 626)

a. operating activities.

b. investing activities.

c. financing activities.

d. noncash investing and financing activities.

Q12-32 Selling equipment is reported on the statement of cash flows under (pp. 620–621)

a. operating activities.

b. investing activities.

c. financing activities.

d. noncash investing and financing activities.

Q12-33 Which of the following terms appears on a statement of cash flows—indirect method? (pp. 620–621)

a. Payments to suppliers

b. Depreciation expense

c. Collections from customers

d. Cash receipt of interest revenue

Q12-34 On an indirect method statement of cash flows, an increase in a prepaid insurance would be: (pp. 620–621)

a. included in payments to suppliers.

b. added to net income.

c. added to increases in current assets.

d. deducted from net income.

Q12-35 On an indirect method statement of cash flows, an increase in accounts payable would be: (pp. 620–621)
a. reported in the investing activities section.
b. reported in the financing activities section.
c. added to net income in the operating activities section.
d. deducted from net income in the operating activities section.

Q12-36 On an indirect method statement of cash flows, a gain on the sale of plant assets would be (pp. 620–621)
a. ignored, since the gain did not generate any cash.
b. reported in the investing activities section.
c. deducted from net income in the operating activities section.
d. added to net income in the operating activities section.

Q12-37 Paying cash dividends is a/an _____ activity. (pp. 620–621)

Receiving cash dividends is a/an _____ activity. (pp. 637–638)

Q12-38 Matlock Camera Co. sold equipment with a cost of $20,000 and accumulated depreciation of $8,000 for an amount that resulted in a gain of $3,000. What amount should Matlock report on the statement of cash flows as "proceeds from sale of plant assets"? (p. 627)
a. $9,000   c. $15,000
b. $17,000   d. Some other amount (fill in the blank)

Questions 39–47 use the following data. Taft Corporation formats operating cash flows by the *indirect* method.

Taft's Income Statement for 20X3

Sales revenue	$180,000	
Gain on sale of equipment	8,000*	$188,000
Cost of goods sold	$110,000	
Depreciation	6,000	
Other operating expenses	25,000	141,000
Net income		$ 47,000

*The book value of equipment sold during 20X3 was $20,000.

Taft's Comparative Balance Sheet at the end of 20X3

	20X3	20X2		20X3	20X2
Cash	$ 4,000	$ 1,000	Accounts payable	$ 6,000	$ 7,000
Accounts receivable	7,000	11,000	Accrued liabilities	7,000	3,000
Inventory	10,000	9,000	Common stock	20,000	10,000
Plant and equipment, net	93,000	69,000	Retained earnings	81,000	70,000
	$114,000	$90,000		$114,000	$90,000

Q12-39 How many items enter the computation of Taft's net cash provided by operating activities? (pp. 620–621)

a. 2

b. 3

c. 5

d. 7

Q12-40 How do Taft's accrued liabilities affect the company's statement of cash flows for 20X3? (pp. 620–621)

a. They don't because the accrued liabilities are not yet paid.

b. Increase in cash provided by operating activities.

c. Increase in cash used by investing activities.

d. Increase in cash used by financing activities

Q12-41 How do accounts receivable affect Taft's cash flows from operating activities for 20X3? (pp. 620–621)

a. Increase in cash provided by operating activities.

b. Decrease in cash provided by operating activities

c. They don't because accounts receivable result from investing activities.

d. Decrease in cash used by investing activities.

Q12-42 Taft's net cash provided by operating activities during 20X3 was: (pp. 623–624)

a. $3,000

b. $47,000

c. $51,000

d. $58,000

Q12-43 How many items enter the computation of Taft's net cash flow from investing activities for 20X3? (pp. 620–621)

a. 2

b. 3

c. 5

d. 7

Q12-44 The book value of equipment sold during 20X3 was $20,000. Taft's net cash flow from investing activities for 20X3 was: (pp. 627)

a. net cash used of $22,000.

b. net cash used of $28,000.

c. net cash used of $50,000.

d. net cash used of $28,000.

Q12-45 How many items enter the computation of Taft's net cash flow from financing activities for 20X3? (pp. 620–621)

a. 2

b. 3

c. 5

d. 7

Q12-46 Taft's largest financing cash flow for 20X3 resulted from: (p. 626)

a. sale of equipment.

b. purchase of equipment.

c. issuance of common stock.

d. payment of dividends.

Q12-47 Taft's net cash flow from financing activities for 20X3 was: (p. 626)

a. net cash used of $25,000.

b. net cash used of $20,000.

c. net cash provided of $10,000.

d. net cash used of $26,000.

Q12-48 Sales totaled $800,000, accounts receivable increased by $40,000, and accounts payable decreased by $35,000. How much cash did the company collect from customers? (pp. 640–641)

a. $760,000

b. $795,000

c. $800,000

d. $840,000

Q12-49 Income Tax Payable was $5,000 at the end of the year and $2,800 at the beginning. Income tax expense for the year totaled $59,100. What amount of cash did the company pay for income tax during the year? (pp. 643–644)

a. $56,900

b. $59,100

c. $61,300

d. $61,900

Problems
(Group A)

MyAccountingLab

> Some of these A problems can be found within My Accounting Lab (MAL), an online homework and practice environment. Your instructor may ask you to complete these exercises using PHGA.

writing assignment ■

P12-50A (*Learning Objective 1, 2: Using cash-flow data to evaluate performance*) Top managers of Relax Inns are reviewing company performance for 20X9. The income statement reports a 20% increase in net income over 20X8. However, most of the increase resulted from an extraordinary gain on insurance proceeds from storm damage to a building. The balance sheet shows a large increase in receivables. The cash-flow statement, in summarized form, reports the following:

Net cash used for operating activities	$(80,000)
Net cash provided by investing activities	40,000
Net cash provided by financing activities	50,000
Increase in cash during 20X9	$ 10,000

I Required

Write a memo giving Relax Inns' managers your assessment of 20X9 operations and your outlook for the future. Focus on the information content of the cash-flow data. (pp. 618–619)

P12-51A (*Learning Objective 2, 3: Preparing an income statement, balance sheet, and statement of cash flows—indirect method*) Vintage Automobiles of Philadelphia, Inc., was formed on January 1, 20X8, when Vintage issued its common stock for $300,000. Early in January, Vintage made the following cash payments:

   a. $150,000 for equipment
   b. $120,000 for inventory (4 cars at $30,000 each)
   c. $20,000 for 20X8 rent on a store building

In February, Vintage purchased 6 cars for inventory on account. Cost of this inventory was $260,000 ($43,333.33 each). Before year end, Vintage paid $208,000 of this debt. Vintage uses the FIFO method to account for inventory.

During 20X8, Vintage sold 8 vintage autos for a total of $500,000. Before year end, Vintage collected 80% of this amount.

The business employs 3 people. The combined annual payroll is $95,000, of which Vintage owes $4,000 at year end. At the end of the year, Vintage paid income tax of $10,000.

Late in 20X8, Vintage declared and paid cash dividends of $11,000.

For equipment, Vintage uses the straight-line depreciation method, over 5 years, with zero residual value.

I Required

1. Prepare Vintage Automobiles of Philadelphia, Inc.'s, income statement for the year ended December 31, 20X8. Use the single-step format, with all revenues listed together and all expenses together. (pp. 623–624)
2. Prepare Vintage's balance sheet at December 31, 20X8. (pp. 621–622)
3. Prepare Vintage's statement of cash flows for the year ended December 31, 20X8. Format cash flows from operating activities by using the *indirect* method. (p. 626)

P12-52A (*Learning Objective 2, 3: Preparing the statement of cash flows—indirect method*) Primrose Software Corp. has assembled the following data for the year ended December 31, 20X7.

	December 31,	
	20X7	20X6
Current Accounts:		
Current assets:		
Cash and cash equivalents	$38,700	$22,700
Accounts receivable	69,700	64,200
Inventories..	88,600	83,000
Prepaid expenses..............................	5,300	4,100
Current liabilities:		
Accounts payable.............................	$57,200	$55,800
Income tax payable...........................	18,600	16,700
Accrued liabilities	15,500	27,200

Transaction Data for 20X7:

Acquisition of land by issuing		Purchase of treasury stock	$14,300
long-term note payable	$95,000	Loss on sale of equipment	11,700
Stock dividends	31,800	Payment of cash dividends	18,300
Collection of loan..................	8,700	Issuance of long-term note	
Depreciation expense	21,800	payable to borrow cash.....	34,400
Purchase of building..............	125,300	Net income...........................	45,100
Retirement of bonds payable		Issuance of common stock	
by issuing common stock	65,000	for cash	41,200
Purchase of long-term		Procedes from sale of	
investment.........................	31,600	equipment	58,000
		Amortization expense..........	5,300

I *Required*

Prepare Primrose Software Corp.'s statement of cash flows using the *indirect* method to report operating activities. Include an accompanying schedule of noncash investing and financing activities. (pp. 626, 631–632)

P12-53A (*Learning Objective 2, 3: Preparing the statement of cash flows—indirect method*) The comparative balance sheet of Northern Movie Theater Company at March 31, 20X9, reported the following:

writing assignment ■

■ **spreadsheet**

	March 31,	
	20X9	20X8
Current assets:		
Cash and cash equivalents	$ 9,900	$14,000
Accounts receivable	14,900	21,700
Inventories..	63,200	60,600
Prepaid expenses..............................	1,900	1,700
Current liabilities:		
Accounts payable.............................	$30,300	$27,600
Accrued liabilities	10,700	11,100
Income tax payable...........................	8,000	4,700

Northern's transactions during the year ended March 31, 20X9, included the following:

Acquisition of land by issuing note payable	$101,000	Sale of long-term investment.	$13,700
Amortization expense............	2,000	Depreciation expense	15,300
Payment of cash dividend......	30,000	Cash purchase of building.....	47,000
Cash purchase of equipment	78,700	Net income...........................	50,000
		Issuance of common stock for cash	11,000
Issuance of long-term note payable to borrow cash	50,000	Stock dividend.......................	18,000

I *Required*

1. Prepare Northern Movie Theater Company's statement of cash flows for the year ended March 31, 20X9, using the *indirect* method to report cash flows from operating activities. Report non-cash investing and financing activities in an accompanying schedule. (pp. 626, 631–632)
2. Evaluate Northern's cash flows for the year. Mention all 3 categories of cash flows and give the reason for your evaluation. (pp. 618–619)

P12-54A (*Learning Objective 2, 3: Preparing the statement of cash flows—indirect method*) The 20X8 comparative balance sheet and income statement of 4 Seasons Supply Corp. follow. 4 Seasons had no noncash investing and financing transactions during 20X8. During the year, there were no sales of land or equipment, no issuance of notes payable, no retirements of stock, and no treasury stock transactions.

I *Required*

1. Prepare the 20X8 statement of cash flows, formatting operating activities by using the *indirect* method. (p. 626)
2. How will what you learned in this problem help you evaluate an investment? (Challenge)

4 Season Supply Corp.
Comparative Balance Sheet

	December 31, 20X8	December 31, 20X7	Increase (Decrease)
Current assets:			
Cash and cash equivalents	$ 17,600	$ 5,300	$ 12,300
Accounts receivable	27,200	27,600	(400)
Inventories....................................	83,600	87,200	(3,600)
Prepaid expenses...........................	2,500	1,900	600
Plant assets:			
Land.......................................	89,000	60,000	29,000
Equipment,net	53,500	49,400	4,100
Total assets................................	$273,400	$231,400	$ 42,000
Current liabilities:			
Accounts payable...........................	$ 35,800	$ 33,700	$ 2,100
Salary payable	3,100	6,600	(3,500)
Other accrued liabilities.................	22,600	23,700	(1,100)
Long-term liabilities:			
Notes payable.............................	75,000	100,000	(25,000)
Stockholders' equity:			
Common stock, no-par..................	88,300	64,700	23,600
Retained earnings	48,600	2,700	45,900
Total liabilities and stockholders' equity.....	$273,400	$231,400	$ 42,000

4 Season Supply Corp.
Income Statement for 20X8

Revenues:		
Sales revenue		$228,700
Expenses:		
Cost of goods sold	$70,600	
Salary expense	27,800	
Depreciation expense.....................	4,000	
Other operating expense...............	10,500	
Interest expense	11,600	
Income tax expense	29,100	
Total expenses		153,600
Net income		$ 75,100

P12-55A (*Learning Objective 2, 4: Preparing the statement of cash flows—direct method*)   **writing assignment ■**
Ethan Allen Furniture Gallery, Inc., provided the following data from the company's records
for the year ended April 30, 20X7:

a. Credit sales, $583,900

b. Loan to another company, $12,500

c. Cash payments to purchase plant assets, $59,400

d. Cost of goods sold, $382,600

e. Proceeds from issuance of common stock, $8,000

f. Payment of cash dividends, $48,400

g. Collection of interest, $4,400

h. Acquisition of equipment by issuing short-term note payable, $16,400

i. Payments of salaries, $93,600

j. Proceeds from sale of plant assets, $22,400, including $6,800 loss

k. Collections on accounts receivable, $428,600

l. Interest revenue, $3,800

m. Cash receipt of dividend revenue, $4,100

n. Payments to suppliers, $368,500

o. Cash sales, $171,900

p. Depreciation expense, $59,900

q. Proceeds from issuance of note payable, $19,600

r. Payments of long-term notes payable, $50,000

s. Interest expense and payments, $13,300

t. Salary expense, $95,300

u. Loan collections, $12,800

v. Proceeds from sale of investments, $9,100, including $2,000 gain

w. Payment of short-term note payable by issuing long-term note payable, $63,000

x. Amortization expense, $2,900

y. Income tax expense and payments, $37,900

z. Cash balance: April 30, 20X6, $39,300; April 30, 20X7, $36,600

Required

1. Prepare Ethan Allen Furniture Gallery, Inc.'s, statement of cash flows for the year ended April 30, 20X7. Use the *direct* method for cash flows from operating activities. Follow the format of Exhibit 12-13 (p. 638), but do *not* show amounts in thousands. Include an accompanying schedule of noncash investing and financing activities. (pp. 637–638, 639–640)

2. Evaluate 20X7 from a cash-flow standpoint. Give your reasons. (pp. 618–619)

P12-56A (*Learning Objective 2, 4: Preparing an income statement, balance sheet, and statement of cash flows—direct method*) Use the Vintage Automobiles of Philadelphia, Inc., data from Problem P12-51A.

(continued)

❚ Required

1. Prepare Vintage's income statement for the year ended December 31, 20X8. Use the single-step format, with all revenues listed together and all expenses together. (pp. 641–642)
2. Prepare Vintage's balance sheet at December 31, 20X8. (pp. 641–642)
3. Prepare Vintage's statement of cash flows for the year ended December 31, 20X8. Format cash flows from operating activities by using the *direct* method. (pp. 637–638)

P12-57A (*Learning Objective 2, 4: Preparing the statement of cash flows—direct method*) Use the 4 Seasons Supply Corp. data from Problem P12-54A.

❚ Required

writing assignment ■

1. Prepare the 20X8 statement of cash flows by using the *direct* method. (pp. 637–638)
2. How will what you learned in this problem help you evaluate an investment? (Challenge)

■ spreadsheet

P12-58A (*Learning Objective 3, 4: Preparing the statement of cash flows—direct and indirect methods*) To prepare the statement of cash flows, accountants for Franklin Electric Company have summarized 20X8 activity in 2 accounts as follows:

Cash			
Beginning balance	53,600	Payments on accounts payable	399,100
Sale of long-term investment	21,200	Payments of dividends	27,200
Collections from customers	661,700	Payments of salaries and wages	143,800
Issuance of common stock	47,300	Payments of interest	26,900
Receipts of dividends	17,100	Purchase of equipment	31,400
		Payments of operating expenses	34,300
		Payment of long-term note payable	41,300
		Purchase of treasury stock	26,400
		Payment of income tax	18,900
Ending balance	51,600		

Common Stock			
		Beginning balance	84,400
		Issuance for cash	47,300
		Issuance to acquire land	80,100
		Issuance to retire note payable	19,000
		Ending balance	230,800

❚ Required

1. Prepare the statement of cash flows of Franklin Electric Company for the year ended December 31, 20X8, using the *direct* method to report operating activities. Also prepare the accompanying schedule of noncash investing and financing activities. (pp. 637–640)
2. Use the following data from Franklin's 20X8 income statement and balance sheet to prepare a supplementary schedule of cash flows from operating activities by using the *indirect* method. (pp. 623–624)

Franklin Electric Company
Income Statement
Year Ended December 31, 20X8

Revenues:

Sales revenue		$689,300
Dividend revenue		17,100
Total revenue		706,400

Expenses and losses:

Cost of goods sold	$402,600	
Salary and wage expense	150,800	
Depreciation expense	19,300	
Other operating expense	44,100	
Interest expense	28,800	
Income tax expense	16,200	
Loss on sale of investments	1,100	
Total expenses and losses		662,900
Net income		$ 43,500

Franklin Electric Company
Selected Balance Sheet Data

	20X8 Increase (Decrease)
Current assets:	
Cash and cash equivalents	$ (2,000)
Accounts receivable	27,600
Inventories	(11,800)
Prepaid expenses	600
Long-term investments	(22,300)
Equipment, net	12,100
Land	80,100
Current liabilities:	
Accounts payable	$ (8,300)
Interest payable	1,900
Salary payable	7,000
Other accrued liabilities	10,400
Income tax payable	(2,700)
Long-term note payable	(60,300)
Common stock	146,400
Retained earnings	16,300
Treasury stock	(26,400)

P12-59A (*Learning Objective 3, 4: Preparing the statement of cash flows—indirect and direct methods*) The comparative balance sheet of Graphic Design Studio, Inc., at June 30, 20X9, included these amounts.

Graphic Design Studio
Balance Sheet
June 30, 20X9 and 20X8

	20X9	20X8	Increase (Decrease)
Current assets:			
Cash	$ 28,600	$ 8,600	$ 20,000
Accounts receivable	48,800	51,900	(3,100)
Inventories	68,600	60,200	8,400
Prepaid expenses	3,700	2,800	900
Long-term investment	10,100	5,200	4,900
Equipment, net	74,500	73,600	900
Land	42,400	96,000	(53,600)
	$276,700	$298,300	$(21,600)
Current liabilities:			
Notes payable, short-term	$ 13,400	$18,100	$(4,700)
Accounts payable	42,400	40,300	2,100
Income tax payable	13,800	14,500	(700)
Accrued liabilities	8,200	9,700	(1,500)
Interest payable	3,700	2,900	800
Salary payable	900	2,600	(1,700)
Long-term note payable	47,400	94,100	(46,700)
Common stock	59,800	51,200	8,600
Retained earnings	87,100	64,900	22,200
	$276,700	$298,300	$(21,600)

Transaction data for the year ended June 30, 20X9:

a. Net income, $60,300
b. Depreciation expense on equipment, $13,400
c. Purchased long-term investment, $4,900
d. Sold land for $46,900, including $6,700 loss
e. Acquired equipment by issuing long-term note payable, $14,300
f. Paid long-term note payable, $61,000
g. Received cash for issuance of common stock, $3,900
h. Paid cash dividends, $38,100
i. Paid short-term note payable by issuing common stock, $4,700

❙ *Required*

1. Prepare the statement of cash flows of Graphic Design Studio, Inc., for the year ended June 30, 20X9, using the *indirect* method to report operating activities. Also prepare the accompanying schedule of noncash investing and financing activities. All current accounts except short-term notes payable result from operating transactions. (pp. 626, 631–632)
2. Prepare a supplementary schedule showing cash flows from operations by the *direct* method. The accounting records provide the following: collections from customers

$261,800; interest received, $1,300; payments to suppliers, $133,500; payments to employees, $40,500; payments for income tax, $10,600; and payment of interest, $5,300. (pp. 637–638)

(Group B)

writing assignment ■

P12-60B (*Learning Objective 1, 2: Using cash-flow information to evaluate performance*) Top managers of Culinary Imports are reviewing company performance for 20X7. The income statement reports a 15% increase in net income, the fifth consecutive year showing an income increase above 10%. The income statement includes a nonrecurring loss without which net income would have increased by 16%. The balance sheet shows modest increases in assets, liabilities, and stockholders' equity. The assets posting the largest increases are plant and equipment because the company is halfway through a 5-year expansion program. No other asset and no liabilities are increasing dramatically. A summarized version of the cash-flow statement reports the following:

Net cash provided by operating activities	$ 310,000
Net cash used for investing activities	(290,000)
Net cash provided by financing activities	50,000
Increase in cash during 20X7	$ 70,000

▌Required

Write a memo giving top managers of Culinary Imports your assessment of 20X7 operations and your outlook for the future. Focus on the net income and the cash-flow data. (pp. 618–619)

P12-61B (*Learning Objective 2, 3: Preparing an income statement, balance sheet, and statement of cash flows—indirect method*) Cruise America Motorhomes, Inc. (CAM), was formed on January 1, 20X8, when the company issued its common stock for $200,000. Early in January, CAM made the following cash payments:

  a. For store fixtures, $50,000
  b. For inventory 2 motorhomes at $60,000 each, a total of $120,000
  c. For rent on a store building, $12,000

In February, CAM purchased 3 motorhomes on account. Cost of this inventory was $160,000 ($53,333.33 each). Before year end, CAM paid $140,000 of this debt. CAM uses the FIFO method to account for inventory.

During 20X8, CAM sold 4 motorhomes for a total of $560,000. Before year end, CAM collected 90% of this amount.

The store employs 3 people. The combined annual payroll is $90,000, of which CAM owes $3,000 at year end. At the end of the year, CAM paid income tax of $64,000.

Late in 20X8, CAM declared and paid cash dividends of $40,000.

For store fixtures, CAM uses the straight-line depreciation method, over 5 years, with zero residual value.

▌Required

1. Prepare Cruise America Motorhomes, Inc.'s, income statement for the year ended December 31, 20X8. Use the single-step format, with all revenues listed together and all expenses together. (pp. 623–624)
2. Prepare CAM's balance sheet at December 31, 20X8. (p. 622)
3. Prepare CAM's statement of cash flows for the year ended December 31, 20X8. Format cash flows from operating activities by the indirect method. (p. 626)

P12-62B (*Learning Objective 2, 3: Preparing the statement of cash flows—indirect method*) Accountants for Crowne Plaza Products, Inc., have assembled the following data for the year ended December 31, 20X4:

	December 31,	
	20X4	20X3
Current Accounts:		
Current assets:		
Cash and cash equivalents	$29,100	$34,800
Accounts receivable	70,100	73,700
Inventories	90,600	96,500
Prepaid expenses	3,200	2,100
Current liabilities:		
Accounts payable	$71,600	$67,500
Income tax payable	5,900	6,800
Accrued liabilities	28,300	23,200

Transaction Data for 20X4:

Payment of cash dividends	$48,300	Stock dividends	$ 12,600
Issuance of long-term note		Collection of loan	10,300
payable to borrow cash	71,000	Depreciation expense	29,200
Net income	31,000	Purchase of equipment	69,000
Issuance of preferred stock		Payment of note payable	
for cash	36,200	by issuing common stock	89,400
Sale of long-term investment	12,200	Purchase of long-term	
Amortization expense	1,100	investment	44,800
Payment of long-term		Acquisition of building by	
note payable	47,800	issuing long-term note	
Gain on sale of investment	3,500	payable	201,000

❙ Required

Prepare Crowne Plaza Products' statement of cash flows using the *indirect* method to report operating activities. Include an accompanying schedule of noncash investing and financing activities. (pp. 626, 631–632)

writing assignment ■

■ spreadsheet

P12-63B (*Learning Objective 2, 3: Preparing the statement of cash flows—indirect method*) The comparative balance sheet of Crossbow Novelties Corp. at December 31, 20X5, reported the following:

	December 31,	
	20X5	20X4
Current Assets:		
Cash and cash equivalents	$28,800	$12,500
Accounts receivable	28,600	29,300
Inventories	51,600	53,000
Prepaid expenses	4,200	3,700
Current Liabilities:		
Accounts payable	$31,100	$28,000
Accrued liabilities	14,300	16,800
Income tax payable	11,000	14,300

Crossbow's transactions during 20X5 included the following:

Cash purchase of building	$124,000	Amortization expense	5,000
Net income	52,000	Payment of cash dividends	17,000
Issuance of common		Cash purchase of equipment	55,000
stock for cash	105,600	Issuance of long-term note	
Stock dividend	13,000	payable to borrow cash	32,000
Sale of long-term		Retirement of note payable	
investment	6,000	by issuing common stock	30,000
		Depreciation expense	12,800

▌*Required*

1. Prepare the statement of cash flows of Crossbow Novelties Corp. for the year ended December 31, 20X5. Use the *indirect* method to report cash flows from operating activities. Report noncash investing and financing activities in an accompanying schedule. (pp. 626, 631–632)
2. Evaluate Crossbow's cash flows for the year. Mention all 3 categories of cash flows and give the reason for your evaluation.

P12-64B (*Learning Objective 2, 3: Preparing the statement of cash flows—indirect method*) The 20X8 comparative balance sheet and income statement of Riverbend Pools, Inc., follows. Riverbend had no noncash investing and financing transactions during 20X8. During the year, there were no sales of land or equipment, no issuances of notes payable, no retirements of stock, and no treasury stock transactions.

writing assignment ■

■ **spreadsheet**

▌*Required*

1. Prepare the statement of cash flows of Riverbend Pools, Inc., for the year ended December 31, 20X8. Format operating activities by the indirect method. (p. 626)
2. How will what you learned in this problem help you evaluate an investment? (Challenge)

Riverbend Pools, Inc.
Comparative Balance Sheet
December 31, 20X8 and 20X7

	20X8	20X7	Increase (Decrease)
Current assets:			
Cash and cash equivalents	$ 28,700	$ 15,600	$13,100
Accounts receivable	47,100	44,000	3,100
Inventories	94,300	89,900	4,400
Prepaid expenses	1,700	2,200	(500)
Plant assets:			
Land	35,100	10,000	25,100
Equipment, net	100,900	93,700	7,200
Total assets	$307,800	$255,400	$52,400
Current liabilities:			
Accounts payable	$ 22,700	$ 24,600	$ (1,900)
Salary payable	2,100	1,400	700
Other accrued liabilities	24,400	22,500	1,900
Long-term liabilities:			
Notes payable	55,000	65,000	(10,000)
Stockholders' equity:			
Common stock, no-par	131,100	122,300	8,800
Retained earnings	72,500	19,600	52,900
Total liabilities and stockholders' equity	$307,800	$255,400	$52,400

(continued)

Riverbend Pools, Inc.
Income Statement for 20X8

Revenues:

Sales revenue		$438,000
Interest revenue		11,700
Total revenues		449,700

Expenses:

Cost of goods sold	$185,200	
Salary expense	76,400	
Depreciation expense.....................	15,300	
Other operating expense...............	49,700	
Interest expense	24,600	
Income tax expense	16,900	
Total expenses........................		368,100
Net income...		$ 81,600

writing assignment ■

P12-65B (*Learning Objective 2, 4: Preparing the statement of cash flows—direct method*)
Rocco's Gourmet Foods, Inc., provides the following data from the company's records for the
year ended July 31, 20X5:

a. Salary expense, $105,300
b. Cash payments to purchase plant assets, $181,000
c. Proceeds from issuance of note payable, $44,100
d. Payments of long-term note payable, $18,800
e. Proceeds from sale of plant assets, $59,700, including $10,600 gain
f. Interest revenue, $12,100
g. Cash receipt of dividend revenue on stock investments, $2,700
h. Payments to suppliers, $673,300
i. Interest expense and payments, $37,800
j. Cost of goods sold, $481,100
k. Collection of interest revenue, $11,700
l. Acquisition of equipment by issuing short-term note payable, $35,500

m. Payments of salaries, $104,000
n. Credit sales, $768,100
o. Loan to another company, $35,000
p. Income tax expense and payments, $56,400
q. Depreciation expense, $27,700
r. Collections on accounts receivable, $741,100
s. Loan collections, $74,400
t. Proceeds from sale of investments, $34,700, including $3,800 loss
u. Payment of long-term note payable by issuing preferred stock, $107,300
v. Amortization expense, $23,900
w. Cash sales, $146,000
x. Proceeds from issuance of common stock, $50,000
y. Payment of cash dividends, $50,500
z. Cash balance: July 31, 20X4—$23,800; July 31, 20X5—$31,400

❚ *Required*

1. Prepare Rocco's Gourmet Foods, Inc.'s, statement of cash flows for the year ended July 31, 20X5. Use the *direct* method for cash flows from operating activities. Follow the format of Exhibit 12-13, but do *not* show amounts in thousands. Include an accompanying schedule of noncash investing and financing activities. (pp. 637–640)
2. Evaluate 20X5 in terms of cash flow. Give your reasons. (pp. 618–619)

P12-66B (*Learning Objective 2, 4: Preparing an income statement, balance sheet, and statement of cash flows—direct method*) Use the Cruise America Motorhomes, Inc. (CAM), data from Problem P12-61B.

❙ Required

1. Prepare CAM's income statement for the year ended December 31, 20X8. Use the single-step format, with all the revenues listed together and all expenses together. (pp. 641–642)
2. Prepare CAM's balance sheet at December 31, 20X8. (pp. 641–642)
3. Prepare CAM's statement of cash flows for the year ended December 31, 20X8. Format cash flows from operating activities by using the *direct* method. (pp. 637–638)

P12-67B (*Learning Objective 2, 4: Preparing the statement of cash flows—direct method*) Use the Riverbend Pools, Inc., data from Problem P12-64B.

writing assignment ■

■ spreadsheet

❙ Required

1. Prepare the 20X8 statement of cash flows by using the *direct* method. (pp. 637–638)
2. How will what you learned in this problem help you evaluate an investment? (Challenge)

P12-68B (*Learning Objective 3, 4: Preparing the statement of cash flows—direct and indirect methods*) To prepare the statement of cash flows, accountants for Powers Art Gallery, Inc., have summarized 20X6 activity in 2 accounts as follows:

Cash

Beginning balance	87,100	Payments of operating expenses	46,100
Issuance of common stock	34,600	Payment of long-term note payable	78,900
Receipts of dividends	1,900	Purchase of treasury stock	10,400
Collection of loan	18,500	Payment of income tax	8,000
Sale of long-term investments	9,900	Payments on accounts payable	101,600
Receipts of interest	12,200	Payments of dividends	1,800
Collections from customers	308,100	Payments of salaries and wages	67,500
Sale of treasury stock	26,200	Payments of interest	21,800
		Purchase of equipment	79,900
Ending balance	82,500		

Common Stock

		Beginning balance	103,500
		Issuance for cash	34,600
		Issuance to acquire land	62,100
		Issuance to retire long-term note payable	21,100
		Ending balance	221,300

❙ Required

1. Prepare Powers' statement of cash flows for the year ended December 31, 20X6, using the *direct* method to report operating activities. Also prepare the accompanying schedule of noncash investing and financing activities. Powers' 20X6 income statement and selected balance sheet data follow. (pp. 637–640)
2. Prepare a supplementary schedule showing cash flows from operating activities by the *indirect* method. (pp. 623–624)

(continued)

Powers Art Gallery, Inc.
Income Statement
Year Ended December 31, 20X6

Revenues and gains:		
Sales revenue		$291,800
Interest revenue		12,200
Dividend revenue		1,900
Gain on sale of investments		700
Total revenues and gains		306,600
Expenses:		
Cost of goods sold	$103,600	
Salary and wage expense	66,800	
Depreciation expense	20,900	
Other operating expense	44,700	
Interest expense	24,100	
Income tax expense	2,600	
Total expenses		262,700
Net income		$ 43,900

Power Art Gallery, Inc.
Selected Balance Sheet Data

	20X6 Increase (Decrease)
Current assets:	
Cash and cash equivalents	$ (4,600)
Accounts receivable	(16,300)
Inventories	5,700
Prepaid expenses	(1,900)
Loan receivable	(18,500)
Long-term investments	(9,200)
Equipment, net	59,000
Land	62,100
Current liabilities:	
Accounts payable	$ 7,700
Interest payable	2,300
Salary payable	(700)
Other accrued liabilities	(3,300)
Income tax payable	(5,400)
Long-term note payable	(100,000)
Common stock	117,800
Retained earnings	42,100
Treasury stock	15,800

P12-69B (*Learning Objective 3, 4: Preparing the statement of cash flows—indirect and direct method*) Artes de Mexico, Inc.'s, comparative balance sheet at September 30, 20X9 included the following balances:

Artes de Mexico, Inc.
Balance Sheet
September 30, 20X9 and 20X8

	20X9	20X8	Increase (Decrease)
Current assets:			
Cash	$ 21,700	$ 17,600	$ 4,100
Accounts receivable	46,000	46,800	(800)
Inventories....................................	121,700	116,900	4,800
Prepaid expenses...........................	8,600	9,300	(700)
Long-term investments...........................	51,100	13,800	37,300
Equipment, net..	131,900	92,100	39,800
Land	47,100	74,300	(27,200)
	$428,100	$370,800	$ 57,300
Current liabilities:			
Notes payable, short-term	$ 22,000	$ 0	$ 22,000
Accounts payable..........................	88,100	98,100	(10,000)
Accrued liabilities	17,900	29,100	(11,200)
Salary payable	1,500	1,100	400
Long-term note payable	123,000	121,400	1,600
Common stock..	113,900	62,000	51,900
Retained earnings..................................	61,700	59,100	2,600
	$428,100	$370,800	$ 57,300

Transaction data for the year ended September 30, 20X9:

- a. Net income, $66,900
- b. Depreciation expense on equipment, $8,500
- c. Purchased long-term investments, $37,300
- d. Sold land for $38,100, including $10,900 gain
- e. Acquired equipment by issuing long-term note payable, $26,300
- f. Paid long-term note payable, $24,700
- g. Received cash of $51,900 for issuance of common stock
- h. Paid cash dividends, $64,300
- i. Acquired equipment by issuing short-term note payable, $22,000

▌*Required*

1. Prepare Artes de Mexico's statement of cash flows for the year ended September 30, 20X9, using the *indirect* method to report operating activities. Also prepare the accompanying schedule of noncash investing and financing activities. All current accounts except short-term notes payable result from operating transactions. (pp. 626, 631–632)
2. Prepare a supplementary schedule showing cash flows from operations by using the *direct* method. The accounting records provide the following: collections from customers, $343,100; interest received, $8,600; payments to suppliers, $216,400; payments to employees, $63,000; payment of income tax, $21,200; payment of interest, $10,700. (pp. 637–638)

APPLY YOUR KNOWLEDGE

Decision Cases

Case 1. (*Learning Objective 3: Preparing and using the statement of cash flows to evaluate operations*) The 20X8 income statement and the 20X8 comparative balance sheet of T-Bar-M Camp, Inc., have just been distributed at a meeting of the camp's board of directors. The

writing assignment ▪

directors raise a fundamental question: Why is the cash balance so low? This question is especially troublesome since 20X8 showed record profits. As the controller of the company, you must answer the question.

T–Bar–M Camp, Inc.
Comparative Income Statement
Year Ended December 31, 20X8

(In thousands)	
Revenues:	
Sales revenue	$436
Expenses:	
Cost of goods sold	$221
Salary expense	48
Depreciation expense	46
Interest expense	13
Amortization expense	11
Total expenses.......................................	339
Net income	$ 97

T–Bar–M Camp, Inc.
Comparative Balance Statement
December 31, 20X8 and 20X7

(In thousands)	20X8	20X7
Assets		
Cash	$ 17	$ 63
Accounts receivable, net	72	61
Inventories...	194	181
Long-term investments	31	0
Property, plant and equipment................	369	259
Accumulated depreciation	(244)	(198)
Patents..	177	188
Totals..	$ 616	$ 554
Liabilities and Owners' Equity		
Accounts payable.....................................	$ 63	$ 56
Accrued liabilities	12	17
Notes payable, long-term........................	179	264
Common stock, no par............................	149	61
Retained earnings	213	156
Totals..	$ 616	$ 554

❙ *Required*

1. Prepare a statement of cash flows for 20X8 in the format that best shows the relationship between net income and operating cash flow. The company sold no plant assets or long-term investments and issued no notes payable during 20X8. There were *no* noncash investing and financing transactions during the year. Show all amounts in thousands. (pp. 626, 631–632)

2. Answer the board members' question: Why is the cash balance so low? Point out the 2 largest cash payments during 20X8. (Challenge)

3. Considering net income and the company's cash flows during 20X8, was it a good year or a bad year? Give your reasons. (pp. 618–619)

Case 2. (*Learning Objective 1, 2: Using cash-flow data to evaluate an investment*) Applied Technology, Inc., and Four-Star Catering are asking you to recommend their stock to your clients. Because Applied and Four-Star earn about the same net income and have similar financial positions, your decision depends on their cash-flow statements, summarized as follows:

writing assignment ■

	Applied		Four–Star	
Net cash provided by operating activities:...............		$ 30,000		$ 70,000
Cash provided by (used for) investing activities:				
Purchase of plant assets.......................	$(20,000)		$(100,000)	
Sale of plant assets.............................	40,000	20,000	10,000	(90,000)
Cash provided by (used for) financing activities:				
Issuance of common stock		—		30,000
Paying off long-term debt		(40,000)		—
Net increase in cash.......................		$ 10,000		$10,000

Based on their cash flows, which company looks better? Give your reasons. (Challenge)

Ethical Issue

Columbia Motors is having a bad year. Net income is only $37,000. Also, 2 important overseas customers are falling behind in their payments to Columbia, and Columbia's accounts receivable are ballooning. The company desperately needs a loan. The Columbia board of directors is considering ways to put the best face on the company's financial statements. Columbia's bank closely examines cash flow from operations. Daniel Peavey, Columbia's controller, suggests reclassifying as long-term the receivables from the slow-paying clients. He explains to the board that removing the $80,000 rise in accounts receivable from current assets will increase net cash provided by operations. This approach may help Columbia get the loan.

writing assignment ■

I *Required*

1. Using only the amounts given, compute net cash provided by operations, both without and with the reclassification of the receivables. Which reporting makes Columbia look better?

2. Under what condition would the reclassification of the receivables be ethical? Unethical?

Focus on Financials: ■ YUM! Brands

(*Learning Objective 1, 2, 3, 4: Using the statement of cash flows*) Use **YUM! Brands, Inc.'s**, statement of cash flows along with the company's other financial statements, all in Appendix A at the end of the book, to answer the following questions.

I *Required*

1. By which method does YUM report cash flows from *operating* activities? How can you tell (pp. 619–621)?

writing assignment ■

2. Suppose YUM reported net cash flows from operating activities by using the direct method. Compute these amounts for the year ended December 30, 2006 (ignore the statement of cash flows, and use only YUM's income statement and balance sheet).
   a. Collections from customers, franchises, and licenses. (p. 629)
   b. Payments for inventory. YUM calls its Cost of Goods Sold "Food and Paper Expense." Note 11 gives the Accounts Payable balance. (pp. 642–643)

3. Prepare a T-account for Property, Plant, and Equipment, Net and show all activity in this account for 2006. Use the depreciation amount in note 9 and assume that YUM (a) sold property, plant, and equipment with book value of $53 million and (b) acquired $180 million of property, plant, and equipment as part of YUM's acquisitions of other companies. (p. 627)

4. Evaluate 2006 in terms of net income, total assets, stockholders' equity, cash flows from operating activities, and overall results. Be specific. (Challenge)

Focus on Analysis: ■ Pier 1 Imports

(*Learning Objective 1, 2, 3, 4: Analyzing cash flows*) Refer to the **Pier 1 Imports** financial statements in Appendix B at the end of this book. Focus on 2006.

1. What is Pier 1's main source of cash? Is this good news or bad news to Pier 1 managers, stockholders, and creditors? What is Pier 1's main use of cash? Good news or bad news? Explain all answers in detail. (pp. 618–619)

2. Explain in detail the 3 main reasons why net cash provided by operations differs from net income. (pp. 620–621)

3. Did Pier 1 buy more fixed assets or sell more fixed assets during 2006? How can you tell? (pp. 620–621)

4. Identify the sale price, the book value, and the gain or loss from selling fixed assets during 2006. *Fixed assets* is another name of property, plant, and equipment. (p. 627)

5. How much cash in total did Pier 1 return to stockholders during 2006? (pp. 629–631)

Group Projects

Project 1. Each member of the group should obtain the annual report of a different company. Select companies in different industries. Evaluate each company's trend of cash flows for the most recent 2 years. In your evaluation of the companies' cash flows, you may use any other information that is publicly available—for example, the other financial statements (income statement, balance sheet, statement of stockholders' equity, and the related notes) and news stories from magazines and newspapers. Rank the companies' cash flows from best to worst and write a 2-page report on your findings.

Project 2. Select a company and obtain its annual report, including all the financial statements. Focus on the statement of cash flows and, in particular, the cash flows from operating activities. Specify whether the company uses the direct method or the indirect method to report operating cash flows. As necessary, use the other financial statements (income statement, balance sheet, and statement of stockholders' equity) and the notes to prepare the company's cash flows from operating activities by using the *other* method.

For Internet Exercises go to the Web site www.prenhall.com/harrison.

Quick Check Answers

1. *d*
2. *c*
3. *b*
4. *a* ($80,000 + $5,000 = $85,000)
5. *c*
6. *b*
7. *a* ($47,000 + $8,000 − $4,000 + $12,000 + $7,000 + $2,000 = $72,000)
8. *a* ($6,000 − $24,000 + $36,000 = $18,000)
9. *c* (−$2,000 + $3,000 − $9,000 = −$8,000)
10. *b* ($12,000 + $36,000 = $48,000)
11. *a* [$650,000 + ($45,000 − $31,000) = $664,000]
12. *c* ($690,000 − $390,000 − $175,000 = $125,000)
13. *d* ($390,000 −$15,000 + $9,000 = $384,000)

13 Financial Statement Analysis

HOW WELL IS YUM! BRANDS DOING?

This book began with the financial statements of **YUM! Brands, Inc.**, the company that owns **Pizza Hut**, **Taco Bell**, **A&W**, **KFC**, and **Long John Silver** restaurants. Throughout the book we have shown how to account for companies such as **YUM! Brands, Pier 1 Imports**, and **Google**. Only one aspect of the course remains: the overall analysis of financial statements.

We begin with the analysis of YUM! Brands' income statement. In 2006 YUM had revenues of $9,561 million, and the company earned net income of $824 million. These numbers look pretty good, but *how* good are they? We need to compare 2006 with prior years to see if YUM made progress during 2006. It could turn out that 2006 was worse than 2005. We also need to compare YUM to its competitors.

YUM! Brands, Inc.
Statements of Income (Adapted)
Years Ended December 31, 2006 and 2005

In millions	2006	2005
Revenues	$9,561	$9,349
Expenses:		
Food and paper (Cost of goods sold)	2,549	2,584
Payroll and employee benefits	2,142	2,171
Occupancy and other operating expenses	2,403	2,315
General and administrative expenses	1,187	1,158
Interest expense	154	127
Other expense (income), net	18	(32)
Income before income taxes	1,108	1,026
Income tax expense	284	264
Net income	$ 824	$ 762

This chapter covers the basic tools of financial analysis. The first part of the chapter shows how to evaluate YUM! Brands from year to year and how to compare YUM! Brands to other companies. For this comparison we use 2 leading fast-food chains, **YUM! Brands** and **McDonald's**. The second part of the chapter discusses the most widely used financial ratios. You have seen many of these ratios in earlier chapters—the current ratio, days' sales in receivables, and inventory turnover, return on assets, and return on equity.

By studying all these ratios together,

■ You will learn the basic tools of financial analysis.
■ You will enhance your business education.

Regardless of your chosen field—marketing, management, finance, entrepreneurship, or accounting—you will find these analytical tools useful as you move through your career.

LEARNING OBJECTIVES

1 **Perform** a horizontal analysis of financial statements

2 **Perform** a vertical analysis of financial statements

3 **Prepare** common-size financial statements

4 **Use** the statement of cash flows for decisions

5 **Compute** the standard financial ratios

6 **Use** ratios in decision making

7 **Measure** the economic value added by operations

HOW DOES AN INVESTOR EVALUATE A COMPANY?

Investors and creditors cannot evaluate a company by examining only 1 year's data. This is why most financial statements cover at least 2 periods, like the **YUM! Brands** income statement that begins this chapter. In fact, most financial analysis covers trends of 3 to 5 years. The goal of financial analysis is to predict the future.

The graphs in Exhibit 13-1 show YUM! Brands' 3-year trend of revenues and net income.

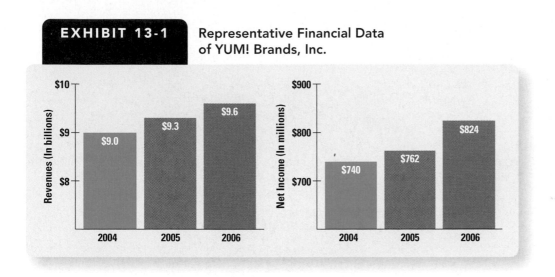

EXHIBIT 13-1 Representative Financial Data of YUM! Brands, Inc.

Both YUM's revenues and net income increased during 2005 and 2006. These are good signs. How would you predict YUM's revenues and net income for 2007 and beyond? Based on the recent past, you would probably extend the revenue line and the net income line upward. Let's examine some financial analysis tools. We begin with horizontal analysis.

HORIZONTAL ANALYSIS

Many decisions hinge on the trend of revenues, expenses, net income, and so on. Have revenues increased from last year? By how much? Suppose sales have increased by $50,000. Considered alone this fact is not very helpful, but the *percentage change* in sales helps a lot. It's better to know that sales have increased by 20% than to know that the increase is $50,000.

The study of percentage changes from year to year is called **horizontal analysis**. Computing a percentage change takes 2 steps:

1. Compute the dollar amount of the change from one period (the base period) to the next.
2. Divide the dollar amount of change by the base-period amount.

OBJECTIVE

1 **Perform** a horizontal analysis of financial statements

Illustration: YUM! Brands

Horizontal analysis is illustrated for YUM! Brands as follows (dollars in millions):

	2006	2005	Increase (Decrease)	
			Amount	Percentage
Revenue	$9,561	$9,349	$212	2.3%

YUM's revenues increased by 2.3% during 2006, computed as follows:

STEP 1 Compute the dollar amount of change from 2005 to 2006:

2006		2005		Increase
$9,561	–	$9,349	=	$212

STEP 2 Divide the dollar amount of change by the base-period amount. This computes the percentage change for the period:

$$\text{Percentage change} = \frac{\text{Dollar amount of change}}{\text{Base-year amount}}$$

$$= \frac{\$212}{\$9,349} = 2.3\%$$

Exhibits 13-2 and 13-3 are detailed horizontal analysis for YUM! Brands. The income statements show that revenues increased by 2.3% during 2006. But net income on the bottom line grew by 8.1%. Why the difference? YUM's revenues grew faster than expenses.

EXHIBIT 13-2   Comparative Income Statement—Horizontal Analysis

YUM! Brands, Inc.
Statement of Income (Adapted)
Years Ended December 31, 2006 and 2005

Dollars in millions	2006	2005	Increase (Decrease)	
			Amount	Percentage
Revenues..	$9,561	$9,349	$212	2.3 %
Expenses:				
Food and paper (Cost of goods sold)	2,549	2,584	(35)	(1.4)
Payroll and employee benefits..................................	2,142	2,171	(29)	(1.3)
Occupancy and other operating expenses	2,403	2,315	88	3.8
General and administrative expenses	1,187	1,158	29	2.5
Interest expense	154	127	27	21.3
Other expense, net...	18	(32)	50	156.3
Income before income taxes	1,108	1,026	82	8.0
Income tax expense..	284	264	20	7.6
Net income..	$ 824	$ 762	$ 62	8.1 %

EXHIBIT 13-3 Comparative Balance Sheet—Horizontal Analysis

YUM! Brands, Inc.
Balance Sheet (Adapted)
December 31, 2006 and 2005

(Dollars in millions)	2006	2005	Increase (Decrease) Amount	Percentage
Assets				
Current Assets:				
Cash and cash equivalents	$ 319	$ 158	$161	101.9 %
Short-term investments	6	43	(37)	(86.0)
Receivables, net	220	236	(16)	(6.8)
Inventories...	93	85	8	9.4
Prepaid expenses and other...	263	333	(70)	(21.0)
Total current assets	901	855	46	5.4
Property, plant, and equipment, net	3,631	3,356	275	8.2
Intangible assets...	1,009	868	141	16.2
Other assets	812	718	94	13.1
Total assets..	$6,353	$5,797	$556	9.6 %
Liabilities and Shareholders' Equity				
Current Liabilities:				
Accounts payable...	$1,386	$1,256	$130	10.4 %
Income tax payable..	37	79	(42)	(53.2)
Short-term debt..	227	211	16	7.6
Other...	74	77	(3)	(3.9)
Total current liabilities	1,724	1,623	101	6.2
Long-term debt..	2,045	1,649	396	24.0
Other liabilities..	1,147	1,076	71	6.6
Total liabilities	4,916	4,348	568	13.1
Shareholders' Equity				
Common stock	—*	—*	—	
Retained earnings	1,593	1,619	(26)	(1.6)
Accumulated other comprehensive (loss)	(156)	(170)	14	8.2
Total shareholders' equity	1,437	1,449	(12)	(0.8)
Total liabilities and shareholders' equity	$6,353	$5,797	$556	9.6 %

*Amount rounds to 0.

STOP & think...

Examine Exhibit 13-2. Which item had the largest percentage increase during 2006? Should this increase cause alarm? Explain your reasoning.

Answer:

Other expense had the largest percentage increase (156.3%). This increase would *not* cause alarm because the dollar amount of the expense is low. This illustrates the materiality concept, which says to give major consideration to big items and less attention to small (immaterial) items. In this case, other expense is immaterial to the analysis of YUM! Brands.

The comparative balance sheets in Exhibit 13-3 show that total assets grew by 9.6% and total liabilities increased by 13.1%. Shareholders' equity therefore decreased by 0.8%. YUM! Brands' growth during 2006 is modest.

Trend Percentages

Trend percentages are a form of horizontal analysis. Trends indicate the direction a business is taking. How have revenues changed over a 5-year period? What trend does net income show? These questions can be answered by trend percentages over a representative period, such as the most recent 5 years.

Trend percentages are computed by selecting a base year whose amounts are set equal to 100%. The amount for each following year is stated as a percentage of the base amount. To compute a trend percentage, divide an item for a later year by the base-year amount.

$$\text{Trend \%} = \frac{\text{Any year \$}}{\text{Base year \$}}$$

YUM! Brands showed net income for the past 6 years as follows:

(In millions)	2006	2005	2004	2003	2002	Base 2001
Net income...............	$824	$762	$740	$617	$583	$492

We want trend percentages for the 5-year period 2002 to 2006. The base year is 2001. Trend percentages are computed by dividing each year's amount by the 2001 amount. The resulting trend percentages follow (2001 = 100%):

	2006	2005	2004	2003	2002	Base 2001
Net income...............	167	155	150	125	118	100

Net income rose sharply in 2002 and in 2004, and grew steadily in the other years.

You can perform a trend analysis on any item you consider important. Trend analysis is widely used for predicting the future.

Horizontal analysis highlights changes over time. However, no single technique gives a complete picture of a business.

VERTICAL ANALYSIS

OBJECTIVE

2 **Perform** a vertical analysis of financial statements

Vertical analysis shows the relationship of a financial-statement item to its base, which is the 100% figure. All items on the statement are reported as a percentage of the base. For the income statement, total revenue is usually the base. Suppose under normal conditions a company's net income is 8% of revenue. A drop to 6% may cause the company's stock price to fall.

Illustration: YUM! Brands

Exhibit 13-4 shows the vertical analysis of YUM! Brands' income statement as a percentage of revenue. In this case,

$$\text{Vertical analysis } \% = \frac{\text{Each income statement item}}{\text{Total revenue}}$$

EXHIBIT 13-4	Comparative Income Statement—Vertical Analysis

YUM! Brands, Inc.
Statements of Income (Adapted)
Years Ended December 31, 2006 and 2005

(Dollars in millions)	2006 Amount	2006 Percentage of Total	2005 Amount	2005 Percentage of Total
Revenues	$9,561	100.0%	$9,349	100.0 %
Expenses:				
Food and paper (Cost of goods sold)	2,549	26.7	2,584	27.6
Payroll and employee benefits	2,142	22.4	2,171	23.2
Occupancy and other operating expenses	2,403	25.1	2,315	24.8
General and administrative expenses	1,187	12.4	1,158	12.4
Interest expense	154	1.6	127	1.3
Other expense (income), net	18	0.2	(32)	(0.3)
Income before income taxes	1,108	11.6	1,026	11.0
Income tax expense	284	3.0	264	2.8
Net income	$ 824	8.6%	$ 762	8.2 %

For YUM! Brands in 2006, the vertical-analysis percentage for cost of goods sold is 26.7% ($2,549/$9,561 = .267). YUM's major expenses decreased in 2006. Net income's percentage of revenue (8.6%) is a little higher than the year earlier.

Exhibit 13-5 shows the vertical analysis of YUM's balance sheet. The base amount (100%) is total assets. The vertical analysis of YUM! Brands' balance sheet reveals several things about YUM's financial position at December 31, 2006:

■ Cash increased nicely in 2006.

■ Current assets make up a small percentage of total assets (only 14.2%), and prepaid expenses are the second largest current asset. It makes sense that inventory is a small percentage because food spoils quickly.

■ Total liabilities make up 77.4% of YUM's total assets. This is a heavy debt load. YUM's financial position improved modestly during 2006.

How Do We Compare One Company to Another?

OBJECTIVE

3 **Prepare** common-size
financial statements

Exhibits 13-4 and 13-5 can be modified to report only percentages (no dollar amounts). Such a statement is called a **common-size statement**. Envision these statements with only the percentages.

EXHIBIT 13-5   Comparative Balance Sheet—Vertical Analysis

YUM! Brands, Inc.
Balance Sheet (Adapted)
December 31, 2006 and 2005

	2006		2005	
(Dollars in millions)	Amount	Percentage of Total	Amount	Percentage of Total
Assets				
Current Assets:				
Cash and cash equivalents	$ 319	5.0 %	$ 158	2.7 %
Short-term investments	6	0.1	43	0.7
Receivables, net	220	3.5	236	4.1
Inventories	93	1.5	85	1.5
Prepaid expenses and other	263	4.1	333	5.7
Total current assets	901	14.2	855	14.7
Property, plant, and equipment, net	3,631	57.1	3,356	57.9
Intangible assets	1,009	15.9	868	15.0
Other assets	812	12.8	718	12.4
Total assets	$6,353	100.0 %	$5,797	100.0 %
Liabilities and Shareholders' Equity				
Current Liabilities:				
Accounts payable	$1,386	21.8 %	$1,256	21.7 %
Income tax payable	37	0.6	79	1.4
Short-term debt	227	3.5	211	3.6
Other	74	1.2	77	1.3
Total current liabilities	1,724	27.1	1,623	28.0
Long-term debt	2,045	32.2	1,649	28.4
Other liabilities	1,147	18.1	1,076	18.6
Total liabilities	4,916	77.4	4,348	75.0
Shareholders' Equity				
Common stock	—*		—*	
Retained earnings	1,593	25.1	1,619	27.9
Accumulated other comprehensive (loss)	(156)	(2.5)	(170)	(2.9)
Total shareholders' equity	1,437	22.6	1,449	25.0
Total liabilities and shareholders' equity	$6,353	100.0 %	$5,797	100.0 %

*Amount rounds to zero.

On a common-size income statement, each item is expressed as a percentage of the revenue amount. Total revenue is therefore the *common size*. In the balance sheet, the common size is total assets. A common-size statement aids the comparison of different companies because all amounts are stated in percentages.

STOP & think. . .

Calculate the common-size percentages for the following income statement:

Net sales..................................	$150,000
Cost of goods sold..................	60,000
Gross profit............................	90,000
Operating expense..................	40,000
Operating income...................	50,000
Income tax expense...............	15,000
Net income............................	$ 35,000

Answer:

Net sales..................................	100%	(= $150,000 ÷ $150,000)
Cost of goods sold..................	40	(= $ 60,000 ÷ $150,000)
Gross profit............................	60	(= $ 90,000 ÷ $150,000)
Operating expense..................	27	(= $ 40,000 ÷ $150,000)
Operating income...................	33	(= $ 50,000 ÷ $150,000)
Income tax expense...............	10	(= $ 15,000 ÷ $150,000)
Net income............................	23%	(= $ 35,000 ÷ $150,000)

BENCHMARKING

Benchmarking compares a company to some standard set by others. The goal of benchmarking is improvement. Suppose you are a financial analyst for **Edward Jones Company**. You are considering investing in a fast-food company, say, YUM! Brands or McDonald's. A direct comparison of their financial statements is not meaningful because McDonald's is larger. But you can convert both companies' income statements to common size and compare the percentages. This comparison is meaningful, as we shall see.

Benchmarking Against a Key Competitor

Exhibit 13-6 presents the common-size income statements of YUM! Brands and McDonald's. McDonald's is the fast-food market leader. In this comparison, McDonald's comes out the winner. McDonald's seems to control expenses better than YUM! Brands. Net income is a higher percentage of revenue at The Golden Arches.

EXHIBIT 13-6 **Common-Size Income Statement Compared with a Key Competitor**

YUM! Brands, Inc.
Common-Size Income Statement for Comparison with Key Competitor
Year Ended During 2006

	YUM! Brands	McDonald's
Revenues	100.0%	100.0%
Cost of goods sold	26.7	24.8
Payroll expenses	22.4	19.4
Occupancy and other operating expenses	25.1	18.6
General and administrative expenses	12.4	10.8
Other expenses (income), net	4.8	10.0
Net income	8.6%	16.4%

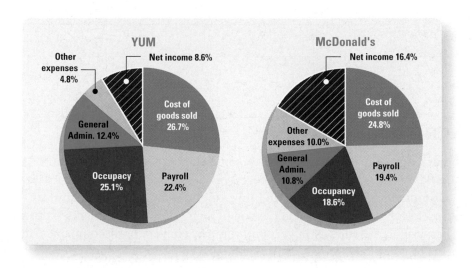

Using the Statement of Cash Flows

This chapter has focused on the income statement and balance sheet. We may also perform horizontal and vertical analyses on the statement of cash flows. To continue our discussion of its role in decision making, let's use Exhibit 13-7, the statement of cash flows of Unix Corporation.

EXHIBIT 13-7 Statement of Cash Flows

Unix Corporation
Statement of Cash Flows
Year Ended June 30, 2006

		Millions
Operating activities:		
Net income		$ 35,000
Adjustments for noncash items:		
Depreciation	$ 14,000	
Net increase in current assets other than cash	(24,000)	
Net increase in current liabilities	8,000	(2,000)
Net cash provided by operating activities		33,000
Investing activities:		
Sale of property, plant, and equipment	$ 91,000	
Net cash provided by investing activities		91,000
Financing activities:		
Borrowing	$ 22,000	
Payment of long-term debt	(90,000)	
Purchase of treasury stock	(9,000)	
Payment of dividends	(23,000)	
Net cash used for financing activities		(100,000)
Increase (decrease) in cash		$ 24,000

Analysts find the statement of cash flows more helpful for spotting weakness than for gauging success. Why? Because a *shortage* of cash can throw a company into bankruptcy, but lots of cash doesn't ensure success. The statement of cash flows in Exhibit 13-7 reveals the following:

- Unix's operations provide less cash than net income. That's strange. Ordinarily, cash provided by operations exceeds net income because of the add-back of depreciation. The increases in current assets and current liabilities should cancel out over time. For Unix Corporation, current assets increased far more than current liabilities during the year. This may be harmless. But it may signal difficulty in collecting receivables or selling inventory. Either event will cause trouble.
- The sale of plant assets is Unix's major source of cash. This is okay if this is a one-time situation. Unix may be shifting from one line of business to another, and it may be selling off old assets. But if the sale of plant assets is the major source of cash for several periods, Unix will face a cash shortage. A company can't sell off its plant assets forever. Soon it will go out of business.
- The only strength shown by the statement of cash flows is that Unix paid off more long-term debt than it did new borrowing. This will improve the debt ratio and Unix's credit standing.

Here are some cash-flow signs of a healthy company:

- Operations are the major *source* of cash (not a *use* of cash).
- Investing activities include more purchases than sales of long-term assets.
- Financing activities are not dominated by borrowing.

MID-CHAPTER SUMMARY PROBLEM

Perform a horizontal analysis and a vertical analysis of the comparative income statement of Hard Rock Products, Inc., which makes metal detectors. State whether 20X6 was a good year or a bad year, and give your reasons.

Hard Rock Products, Inc.
Comparative Income Statement
Years Ended December 31, 20X6 and 20X5

	20X6	20X5
Total revenues	$275,000	$225,000
Expenses:		
Cost of goods sold	194,000	165,000
Engineering, selling, and administrative expenses	54,000	48,000
Interest expense	5,000	5,000
Income tax expense	9,000	3,000
Other expense (income)	1,000	(1,000)
Total expenses	263,000	220,000
Net income	$ 12,000	$ 5,000

Answer

The horizontal analysis shows that total revenues increased 22.2%. This was greater than the 19.5% increase in total expenses, resulting in a 140% increase in net income.

Hard Rock Products, Inc.
Horizontal Analysis of Comparative Income Statement
Years Ended December 31, 20X6 and 20X5

	20X6	20X5	Increase (Decrease) Amount	Increase (Decrease) Percent
Total revenues	$275,000	$225,000	$50,000	22.2%
Expenses:				
Cost of goods sold	194,000	165,000	29,000	17.6
Engineering, selling, and administrative expenses	54,000	48,000	6,000	12.5
Interest expense	5,000	5,000	—	—
Income tax expense	9,000	3,000	6,000	200.0
Other expense (income)	1,000	(1,000)	2,000	—*
Total expenses	263,000	220,000	43,000	19.5
Net income	$ 12,000	$ 5,000	$ 7,000	140.0%

*Percentage changes are typically not computed for shifts from a negative to a positive amount and vice versa.

The vertical analysis on the next page shows decreases in the percentages of net sales consumed by the cost of goods sold (from 73.3% to 70.5%) and by the engineering, selling, and administrative expenses (from 21.3% to 19.6%). Because these 2 items are Hard Rock's largest dollar expenses, their percentage decreases are quite important. The relative reduction in expenses raised 20X6 net income to 4.4% of sales, compared with 2.2% the preceding year. The overall analysis indicates that 20X6 was significantly better than 20X5.

Hard Rock Products, Inc.
Vertical Analysis of Comparative Income Statement
Years Ended December 31, 20X6 and 20X5

	20X6		20X5	
	Amount	Percent	Amount	Percent
Total revenues	$275,000	100.0 %	$225,000	100.0 %
Expenses:				
Cost of goods sold	194,000	70.5	165,000	73.3
Engineering, selling, and				
administrative expenses	54,000	19.6	48,000	21.3
Interest expense	5,000	1.8	5,000	2.2
Income tax expense	9,000	3.3	3,000	1.4**
Other expense (income)	1,000	0.4	(1,000)	(0.4)
Total expenses	263,000	95.6	220,000	97.8
Net income	$ 12,000	4.4 %	$ 5,000	2.2 %

**Number rounded up.

USING RATIOS TO MAKE BUSINESS DECISIONS

Ratios are a major tool of financial analysis. A ratio expresses the relationship of one number to another. Suppose your balance sheet shows current assets of $100,000 and current liabilities of $50,000. The ratio of current assets to current liabilities is $100,000 to $50,000. We can express this ratio as 2 to 1, or 2:1. The current ratio is 2.0.

Many companies include ratios in a special section of their annual reports. RubberMate Corporation displays ratio data in the Summary section. Exhibit 13-8 shows data from that summary section. Investment services—**Moody's, Standard & Poor's, Risk Management Association**, and others—report these ratios.

OBJECTIVE

5 **Compute** the standard financial ratios

EXHIBIT 13-8 Financial Summary of RubberMate Corporation (Dollar Amounts in Millions Except per-share Amounts)

Year Ended December 31	20X6	20X5	20X4
Operating Results			
Net income	$ 218	$ 164	$ 163
Per common share	$1.32	$1.02	$1.02
Percent of sales	10.8%	9.1%	9.8%
Return on average shareholders' equity	20.0%	17.5%	19.7%
Financial Position			
Current assets	$ 570	$ 477	$ 419
Current liabilities	$ 359	$ 323	$ 345
Working capital	$ 211	$ 154	$ 74
Current ratio	1.59	1.48	1.21

The ratios we discuss in this chapter are classified as follows:

1. Ability to pay current liabilities
2. Ability to sell inventory and collect receivables
3. Ability to pay long-term debt
4. Profitability
5. Analyze stock as an investment

How much can a computer help in analyzing financial statements for investment purposes? Time yourself as you complete the problems in this chapter. Multiply your efforts by 10 as though you were comparing 10 companies. Now rank these 10 companies on the basis of 4 or 5 ratios.

Measuring Ability to Pay Current Liabilities

Working capital is defined as follows:

$$\text{Working capital} = \text{Current assets} - \text{Current liabilities}$$

Working capital measures the ability to pay current liabilities with current assets. In general, the larger the working capital, the better the ability to pay debts. Recall that capital is total assets minus total liabilities. Working capital is like a "current" version of total capital. Consider 2 companies with equal working capital:

	Company	
	Jones	Smith
Current assets.....................	$100,000	$200,000
Current liabilities	50,000	150,000
Working capital	$ 50,000	$ 50,000

Both companies have working capital of $50,000, but Jones's working capital is as large as its current liabilities. Smith's working capital is only one-third as large as current liabilities. Jones is in a better position because its working capital is a higher percentage of current liabilities. Two decision-making tools based on working-capital data are the *current ratio* and the *acid-test ratio*.

Current Ratio. The most common ratio evaluating current assets and current liabilities is the **current ratio**, which is current assets divided by current liabilities. The current ratio measures the ability to pay current liabilities with current assets. Exhibit 13-9, page 695, gives the income statement and balance sheet data of Palisades Furniture.

The current ratios of Palisades Furniture, Inc., at December 31, 20X8 and 20X7, follow, along with the average for the retail furniture industry:

	Formula	Palisades' Current Ratio		Industry Average
		20X8	20X7	
Current ratio =	$\dfrac{\text{Current assets}}{\text{Current liabilities}}$	$\dfrac{\$262,000}{\$142,000} = 1.85$	$\dfrac{\$236,000}{\$126,000} = 1.87$	1.50

EXHIBIT 13-9   Comparative Financial Statements

Palisades Furniture, Inc.
Comparative Income Statement
Years Ended December 31, 20X8 and 20X7

	20X8	20X7
Net sales	$858,000	$803,000
Cost of goods sold...............................	513,000	509,000
Gross profit..	345,000	294,000
Operating expenses:		
Selling expenses	126,000	114,000
General expenses	118,000	123,000
Total operating expenses................	244,000	237,000
Income from operations	101,000	57,000
Interest revenue	4,000	—
Interest (expense)	(24,000)	(14,000)
Income before income taxes	81,000	43,000
Income tax expense	33,000	17,000
Net income..	$ 48,000	$ 26,000

Palisades Furniture, Inc.
Comparative Balance Sheet
December 31, 20X8 and 20X7

	20X8	20X7
Assets		
Current Assets:		
Cash..	$ 29,000	$ 32,000
Accounts receivable, net............................	114,000	85,000
Inventories	113,000	111,000
Prepaid expenses	6,000	8,000
Total current assets	262,000	236,000
Long-term investments..................................	18,000	9,000
Property, plant, and equipment, net	507,000	399,000
Total assets...	$787,000	$644,000
Liabilities		
Current Liabilities:		
Notes payable	$ 42,000	$ 27,000
Accounts payable	73,000	68,000
Accrued liabilities.....................................	27,000	31,000
Total current liabilities.........................	142,000	126,000
Long-term debt	289,000	198,000
Total liabilities	431,000	324,000
Stockholders' Equity		
Common stock, no par................................	186,000	186,000
Retained earnings	170,000	134,000
Total stockholders' equity	356,000	320,000
Total liabilities		
and stockholders' equity.......................	$787,000	$644,000

The current ratio was virtually unchanged during 20X8. In general, a higher current ratio indicates a stronger financial position. The business has sufficient current assets to maintain its operations. Palisades Furniture's current ratio of 1.85 compares favorably with the current ratios of some well-known companies:

Company	Current Ratio
YUM! Brands..	0.52
Hewlett-Packard Company................	1.35
eBay	2.14

Note: These figures show that ratio values vary widely from one industry to another.

What is an acceptable current ratio? The answer depends on the industry. The norm for companies in most industries is around 1.50, as reported by the Risk Management Association. Palisades Furniture's current ratio of 1.85 is better than average.

The Limitations of Ratio Analysis

Business decisions are made in a world of uncertainty. As useful as ratios are, they aren't a cure-all. Consider a physician's use of a thermometer. A reading of 102.0° Fahrenheit tells a doctor something is wrong with the patient, but that doesn't indicate what the problem is or how to cure it.

In financial analysis, a sudden drop in the current ratio signals that *something* is wrong, but that doesn't identify the problem. A manager must analyze the figures to learn what caused the ratio to fall. A drop in current assets may mean a cash shortage or that sales are slow. The manager must evaluate all the ratios in the light of factors such as increased competition or a slowdown in the economy.

Legislation, international affairs, scandals, and other factors can turn profits into losses. To be useful, ratios should be analyzed over a period of years to consider all relevant factors. Any 1 year, or even any 2 years, may not represent the company's performance over the long term.

Acid-Test Ratio. The **acid-test** (or *quick*) **ratio** tells us whether the entity could pass the acid test of paying all its current liabilities if they came due immediately. The acid-test ratio uses a narrower base to measure liquidity than the current ratio does.

To compute the acid-test ratio, we add cash, short-term investments, and net current receivables (accounts and notes receivable, net of allowances) and divide by current liabilities. Inventory and prepaid expenses are excluded because they are less liquid. A business may be unable to convert inventory to cash immediately.

Palisades Furniture's acid-test ratios for 20X8 and 20X7 follow.

Formula	Palisades' Acid-Test Ratio		Industry Average
	20X8	20X7	
Acid-test ratio = $\dfrac{\text{Cash + Short-term investments} + \text{Net current receivables}}{\text{Current liabilities}}$	$\dfrac{\$29,000 + \$0 + \$114,000}{\$142,000} = 1.01$	$\dfrac{\$32,000 + \$0 + \$85,000}{\$126,000} = 0.93$	0.40

The company's acid-test ratio improved during 20X8 and is significantly better than the industry average. Compare Palisades' acid test ratio with the values of some leading companies.

Company	Acid-Test Ratio
Best Buy	0.70
IHOP	1.02
Pier 1 Imports	1.08

An acid-test ratio of 0.90 to 1.00 is acceptable in most industries. How can a company such as Best Buy function with such a low acid-test ratio? Best Buy prices its inventory to turn it over quickly. And most of Best Buy's sales are for cash or credit cards, so the company collects cash quickly. This points us to the next two ratios.

Measuring Ability to Sell Inventory and Collect Receivables

The ability to sell inventory and collect receivables is critical. In this section, we discuss 3 ratios that measure this ability.

Inventory Turnover. Companies generally strive to sell their inventory as quickly as possible. The faster inventory sells, the sooner cash comes in.

Inventory turnover measures the number of times a company sells its average level of inventory during a year. A fast turnover indicates ease in selling inventory; a low turnover indicates difficulty. A value of 6 means that the company's average level of inventory has been sold 6 times during the year, and that's usually better than a turnover of 3 times. But too high a value can mean that the business is not keeping enough inventory on hand, which can lead to lost sales if the company can't fill orders. Therefore, a business strives for the most *profitable* rate of turnover, not necessarily the *highest* rate.

To compute inventory turnover, divide cost of goods sold by the average inventory for the period. We use the cost of goods sold—*not sales*—in the computation because both cost of goods sold and inventory are stated *at cost*. Palisades Furniture's inventory turnover for 20X8 is

Formula	Palisades' Inventory Turnover	Industry Average
Inventory turnover = $\dfrac{\text{Cost of goods sold}}{\text{Average inventory}}$	$\dfrac{\$513,000}{\$112,000} = 4.6$	1.50

Cost of goods sold comes from the income statement (Exhibit 13-9). Average inventory is the average of beginning ($111,000) and ending inventory ($113,000). (See the balance sheet, Exhibit 13-9.) If inventory levels vary greatly from month to month, you should compute the average by adding the 12 monthly balances and dividing the sum by 12.

Inventory turnover varies widely with the nature of the business. For example, YUM! Brands has an inventory turnover ratio of 29 times per year because food spoils so quickly. **Pier 1 Imports**, on the other hand, turns over its furniture only around 3 times per year. Pier 1 keeps enough inventory on hand for customers to make their selections.

To evaluate inventory turnover, compare the ratio over time. A sharp decline suggests the need for corrective action.

Accounts Receivable Turnover. **Accounts receivable turnover** measures the ability to collect cash from customers. In general, the higher the ratio, the better. However, a receivable turnover that is too high may indicate that credit is too tight, and that may cause you to lose sales to good customers.

To compute accounts receivable turnover, divide net sales by average net accounts receivable. The ratio tells how many times during the year average receivables were turned into cash. Palisades Furniture's accounts receivable turnover ratio for 20X8 is

Formula		Palisades' Accounts Receivable Turnover	Industry Average
Accounts receivable turnover	$= \dfrac{\text{Net sales}}{\text{Average net accounts receivable}}$	$\dfrac{\$858,000}{\$99,500} = 8.6$	51.0

Average net accounts receivable is figured by adding beginning ($85,000) and ending receivables ($114,000), then dividing by 2. If accounts receivable vary widely during the year, compute the average by using the 12 monthly balances.

Palisades' receivable turnover of 8.6 times per year is much slower than the industry average. Why the slow collection? Palisades is a hometown store that sells to local people who pay bills over a period of time. Many larger furniture stores sell their receivables to other companies called *factors*. This practice keeps receivables low and receivable turnover high. But companies that factor (sell) their receivables receive less than face value of the receivables. Palisades Furniture follows a different strategy.

Days' Sales in Receivables. Businesses must convert accounts receivable to cash. All else being equal, the lower the receivable balance, the better the cash flow.

The **days'-sales-in-receivables** ratio shows how many days' sales remain in Accounts Receivable. Compute the ratio by a 2-step process:

1. Divide net sales by 365 days to figure average sales per day.

2. Divide average net receivables by average sales per day.

The data to compute this ratio for Palisades Furniture, Inc., are taken from the 20X8 income statement and the balance sheet (Exhibit 13-9):

Formula		Palisades' Days' Sales in Accounts Receivable	Industry Average
Days' Sales in Average Accounts Receivable:			
1. One day's sales $=\dfrac{\text{Net sales}}{365 \text{ days}}$		$\dfrac{\$858,000}{365 \text{ days}} = \$2,351$	
2. Days' sales in average accounts receivable $=\dfrac{\text{Average net accounts receivable}}{\text{One day's sales}}$		$\dfrac{\$99,500}{\$2,351} = 42 \text{ days}$	7 days

Days' sales in average receivables can also be computed in a single step: $99,500/($858,000/365 days) = 42 days.

Measuring Ability to Pay Debts

The ratios discussed so far relate to current assets and current liabilities. They measure the ability to sell inventory, collect receivables, and pay current bills. Two indicators of the ability to pay total liabilities are the *debt ratio* and the *times-interest-earned ratio*.

Debt Ratio. Suppose you are a bank loan officer and you have received $500,000 loan applications from 2 similar companies. The first firm already owes $600,000, and the second owes only $250,000. Which company gets the loan? Company 2, because it owes less.

This relationship between total liabilities and total assets is called the **debt ratio**. It tells us the proportion of assets financed with debt. A debt ratio of 1 reveals that debt has financed all the assets. A debt ratio of 0.50 means that debt finances half the assets. The higher the debt ratio, the greater the pressure to pay interest and principal. The lower the ratio, the lower the risk.

The debt ratios for Palisades Furniture in 20X8 and 20X7 follow.

		Palisades' Debt Ratio		Industry
	Formula	20X8	20X7	Average
Debt ratio =	$\dfrac{\text{Total liabilities}}{\text{Total assets}}$	$\dfrac{\$431,000}{\$787,000} = 0.55$	$\dfrac{\$324,000}{\$644,000} = 0.50$	0.64

Risk Management Association reports that the average debt ratio for most companies ranges around 0.62, with relatively little variation from company to company. Palisades' 0.55 debt ratio indicates a fairly low-risk debt position compared with the retail furniture industry average of 0.64.

Times-Interest-Earned Ratio. Analysts use a second ratio—the **times-interest-earned ratio**—to relate income to interest expense. To compute the times-interest-earned ratio, divide income from operations (operating income) by interest expense. This ratio measures the number of times operating income can *cover* interest expense and is also called the *interest-coverage ratio*. A high ratio indicates ease in paying interest; a low value suggests difficulty.

Palisades' times-interest-earned ratios are

		Palisades' Times-Interest-Earned Ratio		Industry
	Formula	20X8	20X7	Average
Times-interest-earned ratio =	$\dfrac{\text{Income from operations}}{\text{Interest expense}}$	$\dfrac{\$101,000}{\$24,000} = 4.21$	$\dfrac{\$57,000}{\$14,000} = 4.07$	2.80

The company's times-interest-earned ratio increased in 20X8. This is a favorable sign.

Measuring Profitability

The fundamental goal of business is to earn a profit, and so the ratios that measure profitability are reported widely.

Rate of Return on Sales. In business, *return* refers to profitability. Consider the **rate of return on net sales**, or simply *return on sales*. (The word *net* is usually omitted for convenience.) This ratio shows the percentage of each sales dollar earned as net income. The return-on-sales ratios for Palisades Furniture are

	Formula	Palisades' Rate of Return on Sales		Industry Average
		20X8	20X7	
Rate of return on sales	$= \dfrac{\text{Net income}}{\text{Net sales}}$	$\dfrac{\$48,000}{\$858,000} = 0.056$	$\dfrac{\$26,000}{\$803,000} = 0.032$	0.008

Companies strive for a high rate of return. The higher the percentage, the more profit is being generated by sales dollars. Palisades Furniture's return on sales is higher than the average furniture store. Compare Palisades' rate of return on sales to the rates of some leading companies:

Company	Rate of Return on Sales
FedEx	0.056
PepsiCo	0.125
Intel	0.143

Rate of Return on Total Assets. The **rate of return on total assets**, or simply *return on assets*, measures a company's success in using assets to earn a profit. Creditors have loaned money, and the interest they receive is their return on investment. Shareholders have bought the company's stock, and net income is their return. The sum of interest expense and net income is the return to the 2 groups that have financed the company. This sum is the numerator of the ratio. Average total assets is the denominator. The return-on-assets ratio for Palisades Furniture is

	Formula	Palisades' 20X8 Rate of Return on Total Assets	Industry Average
Rate of return on assets	$= \dfrac{\text{Net income} + \text{Interest expense}}{\text{Average total assets}}$	$\dfrac{\$48,000 + \$24,000}{\$715,500} = 0.101$	0.078

To compute average total assets, add the beginning and ending balances and divide by 2. Compare Palisades Furniture's rate of return on assets to the rates of these leading companies:

Company	Rate of Return on Assets
General Electric	0.059
Starbucks	0.145
Google	0.214

Rate of Return on Common Stockholders' Equity. A popular measure of profitability is **rate of return on common stockholders' equity**, often shortened to *return on equity*. This ratio shows the relationship between net income and common stockholders' investment in the company—how much income is earned for every $1 invested.

To compute this ratio, first subtract preferred dividends from net income to measure income available to the common stockholders. Then divide income available to common by average common equity during the year. Common equity is total equity minus preferred equity. The 20X8 return on common equity for Palisades Furniture is

Formula		Palisades' 20X8 Rate of Return on Common Stockholders' Equity	Industry Average
Rate of return on common stockholders' equity	$= \dfrac{\text{Net income} - \text{Preferred dividends}}{\text{Average common stockholders' equity}}$	$\dfrac{\$48,000 - \$0}{\$338,000} = 0.142$	0.121

Average equity uses the beginning and ending balances [($320,000 + $356,000)/2 = $338,000].

Observe that Palisades' return on equity (0.142) is higher than its return on assets (0.101). This is a good sign. The difference results from borrowing at one rate—say, 8%—and investing the funds to earn a higher rate, such as the firm's 14.2% return on equity. This practice is called using **leverage**, or **trading on the equity**. The higher the debt ratio, the higher the leverage. Companies that finance operations with debt are said to *leverage* their positions.

For Palisades Furniture, leverage increases profitability. This is not always the case, because leverage can hurt profits. If revenues drop, debts still must be paid. Therefore, leverage is a double-edged sword. It increases profits during good times but compounds losses during bad times.

Palisades Furniture's rate of return on equity lags behind those of GE, Google, and Starbucks.

Company	Rate of Return on Common Equity
General Electric.................	0.188
Google	0.233
Starbucks	0.261

Earnings per Share of Common Stock. *Earnings per share of common stock*, or simply **earnings per share (EPS)**, is the amount of net income earned for each share of outstanding *common* stock. EPS is the most widely quoted of all financial statistics. It's the only ratio that appears on the income statement.

Earnings per share is computed by dividing net income available to common stockholders by the average number of common shares outstanding during the year. Preferred dividends are subtracted from net income because the preferred stockholders have a prior claim to their dividends. Palisades Furniture has no preferred stock and thus has no preferred dividends. The firm's EPS for 20X8 and 20X7 follows (Palisades has 10,000 shares of common stock outstanding).

		Palisades' Earnings per Share	
	Formula	20X8	20X7
Earnings per share of common stock	$= \dfrac{\text{Net income} - \text{Preferred dividends}}{\text{Average number of shares of common stock outstanding}}$	$\dfrac{\$48,000 - \$0}{10,000} = \$4.80$	$\dfrac{\$26,000 - \$0}{10,000} = \$2.60$

Palisades Furniture's EPS increased 85% during 20X8, and that's good news. The Palisades stockholders should not expect such a significant boost every year. Most companies strive to increase EPS by 10% to 15% annually.

Analyzing Stock Investments

OBJECTIVE

6 Use ratios in decision making

Investors buy stock to earn a return on their investment. This return consists of 2 parts: (1) gains (or losses) from selling the stock and (2) dividends.

Price/Earnings Ratio. The **price/earnings ratio** is the ratio of common stock price to earnings per share. This ratio, abbreviated P/E, appears in *The Wall Street Journal* stock listings and online. It shows the market price of $1 of earnings.

Calculations for the P/E ratios of Palisades Furniture, Inc., follow. The market price of Palisades' common stock was $60 at the end of 20X8 and $35 at the end of 20X7. Stock prices can be obtained from a company's Web site, a financial publication, or a stockbroker.

		Palisades' Price/Earnings Ratio	
	Formula	20X8	20X7
P/E ratio $=$	$\dfrac{\text{Market price per share of common stock}}{\text{Earnings per share}}$	$\dfrac{\$60.00}{\$4.80} = 12.5$	$\dfrac{\$35.00}{\$2.60} = 13.5$

Given Palisades Furniture's 20X8 P/E ratio of 12.5, we would say that the company's stock is selling at 12.5 times earnings. Each $1 of Palisades' earnings is worth $12.50 to the stock market.

Dividend Yield. **Dividend yield** is the ratio of dividends per share of stock to the stock's market price. This ratio measures the percentage of a stock's market value returned annually to the stockholders as dividends. *Preferred* stockholders pay special attention to this ratio because they invest primarily to receive dividends.

Palisades Furniture paid annual cash dividends of $1.20 per share in 20X8 and $1.00 in 20X7. The market prices of the company's common stock were $60 in 20X8 and $35 in 20X7. The firm's dividend yields on common stock are

		Dividend Yield on Palisades' Common Stock	
	Formula	20X8	20X7
Dividend yield on common stock* $=$	$\dfrac{\text{Dividend per share of common stock}}{\text{Market price per share of common stock}}$	$\dfrac{\$1.20}{\$60.00} = 0.020$	$\dfrac{\$1.00}{\$35.00} = 0.029$

*Dividend yields may also be calculated for preferred stock.

An investor who buys Palisades Furniture common stock for $60 can expect to receive around 2% of the investment annually in the form of cash dividends. Dividend yields vary widely, from 5% to 8% for older, established firms (such as **Procter & Gamble** and **General Motors**) down to the range of 0% to 3% for young, growth-oriented companies. **Google**, **Starbucks**, and **eBay** pay no cash dividends.

Book Value per Share of Common Stock. **Book value per share of common stock** is simply common stockholders' equity divided by the number of shares of common stock outstanding. Common equity equals total equity less preferred equity. Palisades Furniture has no preferred stock outstanding. Calculations of its book value per share of common follow. Recall that 10,000 shares of common stock were outstanding.

	Formula	Book Value per Share of Palisades' Common Stock	
		20X8	20X7
Book value per share of common stock	$= \dfrac{\text{Total stockholders' equity} - \text{Preferred equity}}{\text{Number of shares of common stock outstanding}}$	$\dfrac{\$356,000 - \$0}{10,000} = \$35.60$	$\dfrac{\$320,000 - \$0}{10,000} = \$32.00$

Book value indicates the recorded accounting amount for each share of common stock outstanding. Many experts believe book value is not useful for investment analysis because it bears no relationship to market value and provides little information beyond what's reported on the balance sheet. But some investors base their investment decisions on book value. For example, some investors rank stocks by the ratio of market price to book value. The lower the ratio, the more attractive the stock. These investors are called "value" investors, as contrasted with "growth" investors, who focus more on trends in net income.

OTHER MEASURES

Economic Value Added (EVA®)

The top managers of **Coca-Cola, Quaker Oats**, and other leading companies use **economic value added (EVA®)** to evaluate operating performance. EVA® combines accounting and finance to measure whether operations have increased stockholder wealth. EVA® can be computed as follows:

$$\text{EVA}^® = \text{Net income} + \text{Interest expense} - \text{Capital charge}$$

$$\text{Capital charge} = \left(\begin{array}{c} \text{(Beginning balances)} \\ \text{Notes payable} + \begin{array}{c}\text{Current maturities of long-term debt}\end{array} + \begin{array}{c}\text{Long-term debt}\end{array} + \begin{array}{c}\text{Stockholders' equity}\end{array} \end{array} \right) \times \begin{array}{c}\text{Cost of capital}\end{array}$$

All amounts for the EVA® computation, except the cost of capital, come from the financial statements. The **cost of capital** is a weighted average of the returns

OBJECTIVE

7 **Measure** the economic value added by operations

demanded by the company's stockholders and lenders. Cost of capital varies with the company's level of risk. For example, stockholders would demand a higher return from a start-up company than from YUM! Brands because the new company is untested and therefore more risky. Lenders would also charge the new company a higher interest rate because of its greater risk. Thus, the new company has a higher cost of capital than YUM! Brands.

The cost of capital is a major topic in finance classes. In the following discussions we assume a value for the cost of capital (such as 10%, 12%, or 15%) to illustrate the computation of EVA®.

The idea behind EVA® is that the returns to the company's stockholders (net income) and to its creditors (interest expense) should exceed the company's capital charge. The **capital charge** is the amount that stockholders and lenders *charge* a company for the use of their money. A positive EVA® amount suggests an increase in stockholder wealth, and so the company's stock should remain attractive to investors. If EVA® is negative, stockholders will probably be unhappy with the company and sell its stock, resulting in a decrease in the stock's price. Different companies tailor the EVA® computation to meet their own needs.

Let's apply EVA® to YUM! Brands. The company's EVA® for 2006 can be computed as follows, assuming a 10% cost of capital (dollars in millions):

$$
\begin{aligned}
\text{YUM! Brand's EVA}^{\circledR} &= \frac{\text{Net}}{\text{income}} + \frac{\text{Interest}}{\text{expense}} - \left(\left[\frac{\text{Short-term}}{\text{borrowings}} + \frac{\text{Long-term}}{\text{debt}} + \frac{\text{Stockholders'}}{\text{equity}} \right] \times \frac{\text{Cost of}}{\text{capital}} \right) \\
&= \$824 + \$154 - [(\$74 + \$2{,}045 + \$1{,}437) \times 0.10] \\
&= \$978 - \$3{,}556 \times 0.10 \\
&= \$978 - \$356 \\
&= \$622
\end{aligned}
$$

(Beginning balances)

By this measure, YUM! Brands' operations added $622 million of value to its stockholders' wealth after meeting the company's capital charge. This performance is very strong.

Red Flags in Financial Statement Analysis

Recent accounting scandals have highlighted the importance of *red flags* in financial analysis. The following conditions may mean a company is very risky.

- **Earnings Problems.** Have income from continuing operations and net income decreased for several years in a row? Has income turned into a loss? This may be okay for a company in a cyclical industry, such as an airline or a home builder, but a company such as YUM! Brands may be unable to survive consecutive loss years.
- **Decreased Cash Flow.** Cash flow validates earnings. Is cash flow from operations consistently lower than net income? Are the sales of plant assets a major source of cash? If so, the company may be facing a cash shortage.

- **Too Much Debt.** How does the company's debt ratio compare to that of major competitors and to the industry average? If the debt ratio is much higher than average, the company may be unable to pay debts during tough times. As we saw earlier, YUM! Brands' debt ratio of 77% is quite high.[1]
- **Inability to Collect Receivables.** Are days' sales in receivables growing faster than for other companies in the industry? A cash shortage may be looming. YUM's cash collections are very strong.
- **Buildup of Inventories.** Is inventory turnover slowing down? If so, the company may be unable to move products, or it may be overstating inventory as reported on the balance sheet. Recall from the cost-of-goods-sold model that one of the easiest ways to overstate net income is to overstate ending inventory. YUM! Brands has no problem here.
- **Trends of Sales, Inventory, and Receivables.** Sales, receivables, and inventory generally move together. Increased sales lead to higher receivables and require more inventory in order to meet demand. Strange movements among these items may spell trouble. YUM's relationships look normal.

Efficient Markets

An **efficient capital market** is one in which market prices fully reflect all information available to the public. Because stock prices reflect all publicly accessible data, it can be argued that the stock market is efficient. Market efficiency has implications for management action and for investor decisions. It means that managers cannot fool the market with accounting gimmicks. If the information is available, the market as a whole can set a "fair" price for the company's stock.

Suppose you are the president of Anacomp Corporation. Reported earnings per share are $4, and the stock price is $40—so the P/E ratio is 10. You believe Anacomp's stock is underpriced. To correct this situation, you are considering changing your depreciation method from accelerated to straight-line. The accounting change will increase earnings per share to $5. Will the stock price then rise to $50? Probably not; the company's stock price will probably remain at $40 because the market can understand the accounting change. After all, the company merely changed its method of computing depreciation. There is no effect on Anacomp's cash flows, and the company's economic position is unchanged: An efficient market interprets data in light of their true underlying meaning.

In an efficient market, the search for "underpriced" stock is fruitless unless the investor has relevant *private* information. But it is unlawful to invest on the basis of *inside* information. An appropriate strategy seeks to manage risk, diversify investments, and minimize transaction costs. Financial analysis helps mainly to identify the risks of various stocks and then to manage the risk.

The Decision Guidelines feature summarizes the most widely used ratios.

---

[1] In 2003, YUM's debt ratio was 89%, and we stated, "YUM's debt ratio needs to shrink over the next several years." The company has made significant progress—with a 77% debt ratio at the end of 2006.

DECISION GUIDELINES

USING RATIOS IN FINANCIAL STATEMENT ANALYSIS

Lane and Kay Collins operate a financial services firm. They manage other people's money and do most of their own financial-statement analysis. How do they measure companies' ability to pay bills, sell inventory, collect receivables, and so on? They use the standard ratios we have covered throughout this book.

Ratio	Computation	Information Provided
Measuring ability to pay current liabilities:		
1. Current ratio	$\dfrac{\text{Current assets}}{\text{Current liabilities}}$	Measures ability to pay current liabilities with current assets
2. Acid-test (quick) ratio	$\dfrac{\text{Cash} + \text{Short-term investments} + \text{Net current receivables}}{\text{Current liabilities}}$	Shows ability to pay all current liabilities if they come due immediately
Measuring ability to sell inventory and collect receivables:		
3. Inventory turnover	$\dfrac{\text{Cost of goods sold}}{\text{Average inventory}}$	Indicates saleability of inventory— the number of times a company sells its average level of inventory during a year.
4. Accounts receivable turnover	$\dfrac{\text{Net credit sales}}{\text{Average net accounts receivable}}$	Measures ability to collect cash from credit customers
5. Days' sales in receivables	$\dfrac{\text{Average net accounts receivable}}{\text{One day's sales}}$	Shows how many days' sales remain in Accounts Receivable— how many days it takes to collect the average level of receivables.
Measuring ability to pay long-term debt:		
6. Debt ratio	$\dfrac{\text{Total liabilities}}{\text{Total assets}}$	Indicates percentage of assets financed with debt
7. Times-interest-earned ratio	$\dfrac{\text{Income from operations}}{\text{Interest expense}}$	Measures the number of times operating income can cover interest expense
Measuring profitability:		
8. Rate of return on net sales	$\dfrac{\text{Net income}}{\text{Net sales}}$	Shows the percentage of each sales dollar earned as net income
9. Rate of return on total assets	$\dfrac{\text{Net income} + \text{Interest expense}}{\text{Average total assets}}$	Measures how profitably a company uses its assets
10. Rate of return on common stockholders' equity	$\dfrac{\text{Net income} - \text{Preferred dividends}}{\text{Average common stockholders' equity}}$	Gauges how much income is earned with the money invested by the common shareholders

Ratio	Computation	Information Provided
11. Earnings per share of common stock	$$\frac{\text{Net income} - \text{Preferred dividends}}{\text{Average number of shares of common stock outstanding}}$$	Gives the amount of net income earned for each share of the company's common stock outstanding

Analyzing stock as an investment:

Ratio	Computation	Information Provided
12. Price/earnings ratio	$$\frac{\text{Market price per share of common stock}}{\text{Earnings per share}}$$	Indicates the market price of $1 of earnings
13. Dividend yield	$$\frac{\text{Dividend per share of common (or preferred) stock}}{\text{Market price per share of common (or preferred) stock}}$$	Shows the percentage of a stock's market value returned as dividends to stockholders each period
14. Book value per share of common stock	$$\frac{\text{Total stockholders' equity} - \text{Preferred equity}}{\text{Number of shares of common stock outstanding}}$$	Indicates the recorded accounting amount for each share of common stock outstanding

END-OF-CHAPTER SUMMARY PROBLEM

The following financial data are adapted from the annual reports of Lampeer Corporation.

Lampeer Corporation
Four-Year Selected Financial Data
Years Ended January 31, 2008, 2007, 2006 and 2005

Operating Results*	2008	2007	2006	2005
Net Sales	$13,848	$13,673	$11,635	$9,054
Cost of goods sold and occupancy expenses excluding depreciation and amortization	9,704	8,599	6,775	5,318
Interest expense	109	75	45	46
Income from operations	338	1,445	1,817	1,333
Net earnings (net loss)	(8)	877	1,127	824
Cash dividends	76	75	76	77
Financial Position				
Merchandise inventory	1,677	1,904	1,462	1,056
Total assets	7,591	7,012	5,189	3,963
Current ratio	1.48:1	0.95:1	1.25:1	1.20:1
Stockholders' equity	3,010	2,928	2,630	1,574
Average number of shares of common stock outstanding (in thousands)	860	879	895	576

*Dollar amounts are in thousands.

❙ Required

Compute the following ratios for 2006 through 2008, and evaluate Lampeer's operating results. Are operating results strong or weak? Did they improve or deteriorate during the 3-year period? Your analysis will reveal a clear trend.

1. Gross profit percentage*
2. Net income as a percentage of sales
3. Earnings per share
4. Inventory turnover
5. Times-interest-earned ratio
6. Rate of return on stockholders' equity

---

*Refer to Chapter 6 if necessary.

Answer

	2008	2007	2006
1. Gross profit percentage	$\dfrac{\$13,848 - \$9,704}{\$13,848} = 29.9\%$	$\dfrac{\$13,673 - \$8,599}{\$13,673} = 37.1\%$	$\dfrac{\$11,635 - \$6,775}{\$11,635} = 41.8\%$
2. Net income as a percentage of sales	$\dfrac{\$(8)}{\$13,848} = (0.06)\%$	$\dfrac{\$877}{\$13,673} = 6.4\%$	$\dfrac{\$1,127}{\$11,635} = 9.7\%$
3. Earnings per share	$\dfrac{\$(8)}{860} = \$(0.01)$	$\dfrac{\$877}{879} = \$1.00$	$\dfrac{\$1,127}{895} = \$1.26$
4. Inventory turnover	$\dfrac{\$9,704}{(\$1,677 + \$1,904)/2} = 5.4 \text{ times}$	$\dfrac{\$8,599}{(\$1,904 + \$1,462)/2} = 5.1 \text{ times}$	$\dfrac{\$6,775}{(\$1,462 + \$1,056)/2} = 5.4 \text{ times}$
5. Times-interest-earned ratio	$\dfrac{\$338}{\$109} = 3.1 \text{ times}$	$\dfrac{\$1,445}{\$75} = 19.3 \text{ times}$	$\dfrac{\$1,817}{\$45} = 40.4 \text{ times}$
6. Rate of return on stockholders' equity	$\dfrac{\$(8)}{(\$3,010 + \$2,928)/2} = (0.3\%)$	$\dfrac{\$877}{(\$2,928 + \$2,630)/2} = 31.6\%$	$\dfrac{\$1,127}{(\$2,630 + \$1,574)/2} = 53.6\%$

Evaluation: During this period, Lampeer's operating results deteriorated on all these measures except inventory turnover. The gross profit percentage is down sharply, as are the times-interest-earned ratio and all the return measures. From these data it is clear that Lampeer could sell its merchandise, but not at the markups the company enjoyed in the past. The final result, in 2008, was a net loss for the year.

REVIEW FINANCIAL STATEMENT ANALYSIS

Quick Check (Answers are given on page 740.)

Analyze the Donaldson Company financial statements by answering the questions that follow. Donaldson owns a chain of restaurants.

Donaldson Company
Consolidated Statement of Income (Adapted)
Years Ended December 31, 2008, 2007, and 2006

In Millions, Except per Share Data	2008	2007	2006
Revenues			
Sales by Company-operated restaurants	$12,795.4	$11,499.6	$11,040.7
Revenues from franchised and affiliated restaurants	4,345.1	3,906.1	3,829.3
Total revenues	17,140.5	15,405.7	14,870.0
Operating Expenses			
Company-operated restaurant expenses			
Food & paper (Cost of goods sold)	4,314.8	3,917.4	3,802.1
Payroll & employee benefits	3,411.4	3,078.2	2,901.2
Occupancy & other operating expenses	3,279.8	2,911.0	2,750.4
Franchised restaurants—occupancy expenses	937.7	840.1	800.2
Selling, general & administrative expenses	1,833.0	1,712.8	1,661.7
Other operating expense, net	531.6	833.3	257.4
Total operating expenses	14,308.3	13,292.8	12,173.0
Operating income	2,832.2	2,112.9	2,697.0
Interest expense	388.0	374.1	452.4
Gain on sale of subsidiary			(137.1)
Nonoperating expense, net	97.8	76.7	52.0
Income before income taxes and			
cumulative effect of accounting changes	2,346.4	1,662.1	2,329.7
Income tax expense	838.2	670.0	693.1
Income before cumulative effect of accounting changes	1,508.2	992.1	1,636.6
Cumulative effect of accounting changes, net of tax benefits of $9.4 and $17.6	(36.8)	(98.6)	
Net income	$ 1,471.4	$ 893.5	$ 1,636.6
Per common share–basic:			
Income before cumulative effect of accounting changes	$ 1.19	$ 0.78	$ 1.27
Cumulative effect of accounting changes	(0.03)	(0.08)	
Net income	$ 1.16	$ 0.70	$ 1.27
Dividends per common share	$ 0.40	$ 0.24	$ 0.23

Donaldson Company
Consolidated Balance Sheet
Years Ended December 31, 2008 and 2007

In Millions, Except per Share Data	2008	2007
Assets		
Current assets		
Cash and equivalents	$ 492.8	$ 330.4
Accounts and notes receivable	734.5	855.3
Inventories, at cost, not in excess of market	129.4	111.7
Prepaid expenses and other current assets	528.7	418.0
Total current assets	1,885.4	1,715.4
Other assets		
Investments in affiliates	1,089.6	1,037.7
Goodwill, net	1,665.1	1,558.5
Miscellaneous	960.3	1,075.5
Total other assets	3,715.0	3,671.7
Property and equipment		
Property and equipment, at cost	28,740.2	26,218.6
Accumulated depreciation and amortization	(8,815.5)	(7,635.2)
Net property and equipment	19,924.7	18,583.4
Total assets	$25,525.1	$23,970.5
Liabilities and Shareholders' Equity		
Current liabilities		
Accounts payable	$ 577.4	$ 635.8
Income taxes	71.5	16.3
Other taxes	222.0	191.8
Accrued interest	193.1	199.4
Accrued restructuring and restaurant closing costs	115.7	328.5
Accrued payroll and other liabilities	918.1	774.7
Current maturities of long-term debt	388.0	275.8
Total current liabilities	2,485.8	2,422.3
Long-term debt	9,342.5	9,703.6
Other long-term liabilities and minority interests	699.8	560.0
Deferred income taxes	1,015.1	1,003.7
Shareholders' equity		
Preferred stock, no par value; authorized—165.0 million shares; issued—none		
Common stock, $.01 par value; authorized—3.5 billion shares;		
issued—1,660.6 million shares	16.6	16.6
Additional paid-in capital	1,837.5	1,747.3
Unearned ESOP compensation	(90.5)	(98.4)
Retained earnings	20,172.3	19,204.4
Accumulated other comprehensive income (loss)	(635.5)	(1,601.3)
Common stock in treasury, at cost; 398.7 and 392.4 million shares	(9,318.5)	(8,987.7)
Total shareholders' equity	11,981.9	10,280.9
Total liabilities and shareholders' equity	$25,525.1	$23,970.5

1. Horizontal analysis of Donaldson's income statement for 2008 would show which of the following for Selling, general, & administrative expenses? (pp. 683–684)
   - **a.** 1.14
   - **b.** 1.10
   - **c.** 1.07
   - **d.** None of the above (<u>fill in the blank</u>).

2. Vertical analysis of Donaldson's income statement for 2008 would show which of the following for Selling, general, & administrative expenses? (pp. 687–688)
   - **a.** 1.144
   - **b.** 0.143
   - **c.** 0.107
   - **d.** None of the above (<u>fill in the blank</u>).

3. Which item on Donaldson's income statement has the most favorable trend during 2007–2008? (pp. 686–687)
   - **a.** Total revenues
   - **b.** Net income
   - **c.** Food and paper costs
   - **d.** Payroll & employee benefits

4. On Donaldson's common-size balance sheet, Goodwill would appear as (pp. 689–690)
   - **a.** 0.065.
   - **b.** up by 6.8%.
   - **c.** $1,665.1 million.
   - **d.** 9.7% of total revenues.

5. A good benchmark for Donaldson Company would be (pp. 689–690)
   - **a.** Whataburger.
   - **b.** Boeing.
   - **c.** Intel.
   - **d.** All of the above.

6. Donaldson's inventory turnover for 2008 was (pp. 697–698)
   - **a.** 91 times.
   - **b.** 62 times.
   - **c.** 21 times.
   - **d.** 36 times.

7. Donaldson's acid-test ratio at the end of 2008 was (pp. 697–698)
   - **a.** 1.49.
   - **b.** 0.49.
   - **c.** 0.30.
   - **d.** 0.20.

8. Donaldson's average collection period for accounts and notes receivables is (pp. 697–699)
   - **a.** 1 day.
   - **b.** 2 days.
   - **c.** 30 days.
   - **d.** 17 days.

9. Donaldson's total debt position looks (p. 699)
   - **a.** safe.
   - **b.** middle-ground.
   - **c.** risky.
   - **d.** Cannot tell from the financials.

10. Donaldson's return on total revenues for 2008 was (p. 700)
    - **a.** 13.2%.
    - **b.** $1.16.
    - **c.** 5.9%.
    - **d.** 8.6%.

11. Donaldson's return on stockholders' equity for 2008 was (pp. 701–702)
    - **a.** 13.2%.
    - **b.** 8.6%.
    - **c.** 5.9%.
    - **d.** $1,471.4 million.

12. On June 30, 2009, Donaldson's common stock sold for $26 per share. At that price, how much did investors say $1 of the company's net income was worth? (pp. 702–703)
    - **a.** $1.00
    - **b.** $22.41
    - **c.** $21.85
    - **d.** $26.00

13. Use Donaldson's financial statements and the data in question 12 to compute Donaldson's dividend yield during 2008. (pp. 702–703)
    - **a.** 3.1%
    - **b.** 2.4%
    - **c.** 2.2%
    - **d.** 1.5%

14. How much EVA® did Donaldson generate for investors during 2008? Assume the cost of capital was 8%. (pp. 703–704)
    - **a.** $973 million
    - **b.** $1,471 million
    - **c.** $239 million
    - **d.** $1,859 million

Accounting Vocabulary

accounts receivable turnover (p. 698) Measures a company's ability to collect cash from credit customers. To compute accounts receivable turnover, divide net credit sales by average net accounts receivable.

acid-test ratio (p. 696) Ratio of the sum of cash plus short-term investments plus net current receivables to total current liabilities. Tells whether the entity can pay all its current liabilities if they come due immediately. Also called the *quick ratio*.

benchmarking (p. 689) The comparison of a company to a standard set by other companies, with a view toward improvement.

book value per share of common stock (p. 703) Common stockholders' equity divided by the number of shares of common stock outstanding. The recorded amount for each share of common stock outstanding.

capital charge (p. 704) The amount that stockholders and lenders charge a company for the use of their money. Calculated as (Notes payable + Loans payable + Long-term debt + Stockholders' equity) × Cost of capital.

common-size statement (p. 688) A financial statement that reports only percentages (no dollar amounts).

cost of capital (p. 703) A weighted average of the returns demanded by the company's stockholders and lenders.

current ratio (p. 694) Current assets divided by current liabilities. Measures a company's ability to pay current liabilities with current assets.

days' sales in receivables (p. 698) Ratio of average net accounts receivable to 1 day's sales. Indicates how many days' sales remain in Accounts Receivable awaiting collection. Also called the *collection period*.

debt ratio (p. 699) Ratio of total liabilities to total assets. States the proportion of a company's assets that is financed with debt.

dividend yield (p. 702) Ratio of dividends per share of stock to the stock's market price per share. Tells the percentage of a stock's market value that the company returns to stockholders as dividends.

earnings per share (EPS) (p. 701) Amount of a company's net income earned for each share of its outstanding common stock.

economic value added (EVA®) (p. 703) Used to evaluate a company's operating performance. EVA combines the concepts of accounting income and corporate finance to measure whether the company's operations have increased stockholder wealth. EVA = Net income + Interest expense – Capital charge.

efficient capital market (p. 705) A capital market in which market prices fully reflect all information available to the public.

horizontal analysis (p. 684) Study of percentage changes in comparative financial statements.

inventory turnover (p. 697) Ratio of cost of goods sold to average inventory. Indicates how rapidly inventory is sold.

leverage (p. 701) Earning more income on borrowed money than the related interest expense, thereby increasing the earnings for the owners of the business. Also called *trading on the equity*.

price/earnings ratio (p. 702) Ratio of the market price of a share of common stock to the company's earnings per share. Measures the value that the stock market places on $1 of a company's earnings.

quick ratio (p. 696) Another name for the *acid-text ratio*.

rate of return on common stockholders' equity (p. 701) Net income minus preferred dividends, divided by average common stockholders' equity. A measure of profitability. Also called *return on equity*.

rate of return on net sales (p. 700) Ratio of net income to net sales. A measure of profitability. Also called *return on sales*.

rate of return on total assets (p. 700) Net income plus interest expense, divided by average total assets. This ratio measures a company's success in using its assets to earn income for the persons who finance the business. Also called *return on assets*.

return on equity (p. 701) Another name for *rate of return on common stockholders' equity*.

times-interest-earned ratio (p. 699) Ratio of income from operations to interest expense. Measures the number of times that operating income can cover interest expense. Also called the *interest-coverage ratio*.

trading on the equity (p. 701) Another name for *leverage*.

trend percentages (p. 686) A form of horizontal analysis that indicates the direction a business is taking.

vertical analysis (p. 694) Analysis of a financial statement that reveals the relationship of each statement item to a specified base, which is the 100% figure.

working capital (p. 694) Current assets minus current liabilities; measures a business's ability to meet its short-term obligations with its current assets.

ASSESS YOUR PROGRESS

Short Exercises

S13-1 (*Learning Objective 1: Horizontal analysis of revenues and net income*) Cannes Corporation, reported the following amounts on its 2008 comparative income statement.

writing assignment ■

(In thousands)	2008	2007	2006
Revenues........................	$10,889	$10,095	$9,777
Total expenses...............	5,985	5,604	5,194

Perform a horizontal analysis of revenues and net income—both in dollar amounts and in percentages—for 2008 and 2007. (pp. 683–684)

S13-2 (*Learning Objective 1: Trend analysis of sales and net income*) Zoobilee, Inc., reported the following sales and net income amounts:

(In thousands)	2009	2008	2007	2006
Sales..........................	$9,180	$8,990	$8,770	$8,550
Net income................	520	500	460	400

Show Zoobilee's trend percentages for sales and net income. Use 2006 as the base year. (pp. 686–687)

S13-3 (*Learning Objective 2: Vertical analysis to correct a cash shortage*) Vision Software reported the following amounts on its balance sheets at December 31, 20X4, 20X3, and 20X2.

writing assignment ■

	20X4	20X3	20X2
Cash....................................	$ 6,000	$ 6,000	$ 5,000
Receivables, net....................	30,000	22,000	19,000
Inventory.............................	148,000	106,000	74,000
Prepaid expenses.................	2,000	2,000	1,000
Property, plant, and equipment, net	96,000	88,000	87,000
Total assets	$282,000	$224,000	$186,000

Sales and profits are high. Nevertheless, Vision is experiencing a cash shortage. Perform a vertical analysis of Vision Software's assets at the end of years 20X4, 20X3, 20X2. Use the analysis to explain the reason for the cash shortage. (pp. 688–689)

S13-4 (*Learning Objective 3: Common-size income statements of 2 companies*) (pp. 687–688) Porterfield, Inc., and Beasley Corporation are competitors. Compare the 2 companies by converting their condensed income statements to common size.

(In millions)	Porterfield	Beasley
Net sales...	$9,489	$19,536
Cost of goods sold..	5,785	14,101
Selling and administrative expenses................	2,690	3,846
Interest expense...	59	16
Other expense	34	38
Income tax expense...	331	597
Net income..	$ 590	$ 938

(continued)

Which company earned more net income? Which company's net income was a higher percentage of its net sales? Which company is more profitable? Explain your answer. (p. 700)

S13-5 *(Learning Objective 5, 6: Evaluating the trend in a company's current ratio)* Examine the financial data of RubberMate Corporation in Exhibit 13-8 (p. 693). Show how to compute RubberMate's current ratio for each year 20X4 through 20X6. Is the company's ability to pay its current liabilities improving or deteriorating? (p. 696)

S13-6 *(Learning Objective 5, 6: Evaluating a company's acid-test ratio)* Use the **YUM! Brands** balance sheet data in Exhibit 13-3, page 694.

1. Compute YUM's acid-test ratio at December 31, 2006 and 2005. (pp. 697–698)

2. Compare YUM's ratio values to those of **Best Buy**, **IHOP**, and **Pier 1 Imports** on page 697. Is YUM's acid-test ratio strong or weak? Explain. (pp. 697–698)

S13-7 *(Learning Objective 5: Computing inventory turnover and days' sales in receivables)* Use the YUM! Brands 2006 income statement (p. 682) and balance sheet (p. 685) to compute the following:

    a. YUM's rate of inventory turnover for 2006. (pp. 697–698)

    b. Days' sales in average receivables during 2006. (Round dollar amounts to 1 decimal place.) (pp. 698–699)

Do these measures look strong or weak? Give the reason for your answer. (pp. 697–699)

S13-8 *(Learning Objective 5, 6: Measuring ability to pay long-term debt)* Use the financial statements of YUM! Brands (pp. 682, 685).

1. Compute the company's debt ratio at December 31, 2006. In which text exhibit does this ratio value appear? (p. 699)

2. Compute the company's times-interest-earned ratio for 2006. For operating income, use income before both interest expense and income taxes. You can simply add interest expense back to income before taxes. (p. 699)

3. Is YUM's ability to pay liabilities and interest expense strong or weak? Comment on the value of each ratio computed for requirements 1 and 2. (p. 699)

S13-9 *(Learning Objective 5, 6: Measuring profitability)* Use the financial statements of YUM! Brands (p. 682, 685) to locate or, if necessary, to compute these profitability measures for 2006. Show each computation.

    a. Rate of return on sales. (p. 700)

    b. Rate of return on total assets. (p. 700)

    c. Rate of return on common stockholders' equity. (pp. 701–702)

Are these rates of return strong or weak? Explain. (pp. 701–702)

S13-10 *(Learning Objective 5: Computing EPS and the price/earnings ratio)* The annual report of Classic Cars, Inc., for the year ended December 31, 2007, included the following items (in millions):

Preferred stock outstanding, 4%	$500
Net income	$990
Number of shares of common stock outstanding	200

1. Compute earnings per share (EPS) and the price/earnings ratio for Classic Cars' stock. Round to the nearest cent. The price of a share of Classic Car stock is $77.60. (pp. 701–704)

2. How much does the stock market say $1 of Classic Cars' net income is worth? (pp. 702–703)

S13-11 (*Learning Objective 5: Using ratio data to reconstruct an income statement*) A skeleton of Hill Country Florist's income statement appears as follows (amounts in thousands):

	Income Statement	
Net sales	$7,278
Cost of goods sold	(a)
Selling expenses	1,510
Administrative expenses	326
Interest expense	(b)
Other expenses	151
Income before taxes	1,042
Income tax expense	(c)
Net income	$ (d)

Use the following ratio data to complete Hill Country Florist's income statement:

a. Inventory turnover was 5 (beginning inventory was $787; ending inventory was $755). (pp. 697–698)

b. Rate of return on sales is 0.12. (p. 700)

S13-12 (*Learning Objective 5: Using ratio data to reconstruct a balance sheet*) A skeleton of Hill Country Florist's balance sheet appears as follows (amounts in thousands):

	Balance Sheet		
Cash	$ 253	Total current liabilities	$1,164
Receivables	(a)	Long-term debt	(e)
Inventories	555	Other long-term liabilities	826
Prepaid expenses	(b)		
Total current assets	(c)		
Plant assets, net	(d)	Common stock	185
Other assets	1,150	Retained earnings	2,846
Total assets	$6,315	Total liabilities and equity	$ (f)

Use the following ratio data to complete Hill Country Florist's balance sheet: (pp. 696–699)
a. Debt ratio is 0.52.   **b.** Current ratio is 1.20.   **c.** Acid-test ratio is 0.70.

S13-13 (*Learning Objective 7: Measuring economic value added*) Compute economic value added (EVA®) for Mainstream Software. The company's cost of capital is 12%. Net income was $695 thousand, interest expense $394 thousand, beginning long-term debt $1,294 thousand, and beginning stockholders' equity was $3,031 thousand. Round all amounts to the nearest thousand dollars. (pp. 703–704)

Should the company's stockholders be happy with the EVA®? (pp. 703–704)

Exercises

E13-14 (*Learning Objective 1: Computing year-to-year changes in working capital*) What were the dollar amount of change and the percentage of each change in Rocky Mountain Lodge's working capital during 2008 and 2007? Is this trend favorable or unfavorable? (pp. 686–687)

	2008	2007	2006
Total current assets	$326,000	$290,000	$280,000
Total current liabilities	170,000	167,000	150,000

■ **spreadsheet**

E13-15 (*Learning Objective 1: Horizontal analysis of an income statement*) Prepare a horizontal analysis of the comparative income statement of Stamps Music Co. Round percentage changes to the nearest one-tenth percent (3 decimal places). (pp. 683–684)

Stamps Music Co.
Comparative Income Statement
Years Ended December 31, 2007 and 2006

	2007	2006
Total revenue	$403,000	$430,000
Expenses:		
Cost of goods sold	$188,000	$202,000
Selling and general expenses	93,000	90,000
Interest expense	4,000	10,000
Income tax expense	37,000	42,000
Total expenses	322,000	344,000
Net income	$ 81,000	$ 86,000

E13-16 (*Learning Objective 1: Computing trend percentages*) Compute trend percentages for Carmel Valley Sales & Service's total revenue, and net income for the following 5-year period, using year 0 as the base year. Round to the nearest full percent (pp. 686–687).

(In thousands)	Year 4	Year 3	Year 2	Year 1	Year 0
Total revenue	$1,418	$1,287	$1,106	$1,009	$1,043
Net income	125	104	93	81	85

Which grew faster during the period, total revenue or net income?

E13-17 (*Learning Objective 2: Vertical analysis of a balance sheet*) Cobra Golf Company has requested that you perform a vertical analysis of its balance sheet to determine the component percentages of its assets, liabilities, and stockholders' equity. (pp. 688–689)

Cobra Golf Company
Balance Sheet
December 31, 20X8

Assets

Total current assets	$ 92,000
Property, plant, and equipment, net	247,000
Other assets	35,000
Total assets	$374,000

Liabilities

Total current liabilities	$ 48,000
Long-term debt	108,000
Total liabilities	156,000

Stockholders' Equity

Total stockholders' equity	218,000
Total liabilities and stockholders' equity	$374,000

E13-18 (*Learning Objective 3: Preparing a common-size income statement*) Prepare a comparative common-size income statement for Stamps Music Co., using the 2007 and 2006 data of Exercise 13-15 and rounding percentages to one-tenth percent (3 decimal places). (pp. 687–688)

■ spreadsheet

E13-19 (*Learning Objective 4: Analyzing the statement of cash flows*) Identify any weaknesses revealed by the statement of cash flows of Florida Citrus Growers, Inc. (pp. 619–631, 639)

writing assignment ■

Florida Citrus Growers, Inc.
Statement of Cash Flows
For the Current Year

Operating activities:		
Income from operations		$ 42,000
Add (subtract) noncash items:		
Depreciation	$ 23,000	
Net increase in current assets other than cash	(45,000)	
Net decrease in current liabilities exclusive of short-term debt	(7,000)	(29,000)
Net cash provided by operating activities		13,000
Investing activities:		
Sale of property, plant, and equipment		101,000
Financing activities:		
Issuance of bonds payable	$ 102,000	
Payment of short-term debt	(159,000)	
Payment of long-term debt	(79,000)	
Payment of dividends	(42,000)	
Net cash used for financing activities		(178,000)
Increase (decrease) in cash		$ (64,000)

■ spreadsheet

E13-20 *(Learning Objective 5: Computing 5 ratios)* The financial statements of National News, Inc., include the following items:

	Current Year	Preceding Year
Balance Sheet:		
Cash	$ 17,000	$ 22,000
Short-term investments	11,000	26,000
Net receivables	64,000	73,000
Inventory	77,000	71,000
Prepaid expenses	16,000	8,000
Total current assets	185,000	200,000
Total current liabilities	111,000	91,000
Income Statement:		
Net credit sales	$654,000	
Cost of goods sold	327,000	

❙ Required

Compute the following ratios for the current year: (pp. 696–699)

a. Current ratio   d. Accounts receivable turnover

b. Acid-test ratio   e. Days' sales in average receivables

c. Inventory turnover

writing assignment ■

■ spreadsheet

E13-21 *(Learning Objective 5, 6: Analyzing the ability to pay current liabilities)* Patio Furniture Company has asked you to determine whether the company's ability to pay its current liabilities and long-term debts improved or deteriorated during 20X9. To answer this question, compute the following ratios for 20X9 and 20X8. (pp. 696–699)

a. Current ratio   c. Debt ratio

b. Acid-test ratio   d. Times-interest-earned ratio

Summarize the results of your analysis in a written report.

	20X9	20X8
Cash	$ 61,000	$ 47,000
Short-term investments	28,000	—
Net receivables	142,000	116,000
Inventory	286,000	263,000
Prepaid expenses	11,000	9,000
Total assets	643,000	489,000
Total current liabilities	255,000	221,000
Long-term debt	46,000	52,000
Income from operations	165,000	158,000
Interest expense	40,000	39,000

E13-22 (*Learning Objective 5, 6: Analyzing profitability*) Compute 4 ratios that measure ability to earn profits for PGI Decor, Inc., whose comparative income statement follows: (pp. 700–702)

PGI Decor, Inc.
Comparative Income Statement
Years Ended December 31, 20X8 and 20X7

Dollars in thousands	20X8	20X7
Net sales	$174,000	$158,000
Cost of goods sold	93,000	86,000
Gross profit	81,000	72,000
Selling and general expenses	46,000	41,000
Income from operations	35,000	31,000
Interest expense	9,000	10,000
Income before income tax	26,000	21,000
Income tax expense	9,000	8,000
Net income	$ 17,000	$ 13,000

Additional data:

	20X8	20X7	20X6
Total assets	$204,000	$191,000	$171,000
Common stockholders' equity	$ 96,000	$ 89,000	$ 79,000
Preferred dividends	$ 3,000	$ 3,000	$ 0
Common shares outstanding during the year	21,000	20,000	18,000

Did the company's operating performance improve or deteriorate during 20X8?

E13-23 (*Learning Objective 5, 6: Evaluating a stock as an investment*) Evaluate the common stock of Phillips Distributing Company as an investment. Specifically, use the 3 common stock ratios to determine whether the common stock increased or decreased in attractiveness during the past year. (pp. 701–703)

writing assignment ■

	20X7	20X6
Net income	$112,000	$ 96,000
Dividends to common	25,000	20,000
Total stockholders' equity at year end (includes 80,000 shares of common stock)	580,000	500,000
Preferred stock, 8%	100,000	100,000
Market price per share of common stock at year end	$ 22.50	$ 16.75

E13-24 (*Learning Objective 7: Using economic value added to measure corporate performance*) Two companies with different economic-value-added (EVA®) profiles are **Amazon.com** and **eBay**. Adapted versions of the 2 companies' financial statements are presented here (in millions):

	Amazon.com	eBay
Balance sheet data:		
Total assets	$ 4,363	$13,494
Interest-bearing debt	$ 1,247	$ 0
All other liabilities...........................	2,685	2,589
Stockholders' equity	431	10,905
Total liabilities and equity...............	$ 4,363	$13,494
Income statement data:		
Total revenue	$10,711	$ 3,271
Interest expense...............................	78	9
Net income.......................................	$ 190	$ 778

❙ *Required*

1. Before performing any calculations, which company do you think represents the better investment? Give your reason. (Challenge)

2. Compute the EVA® for each company and then decide which company's stock you would rather hold as an investment. Assume both companies' cost of capital is 10%. (pp. 703–704)

Challenge Exercises

E13-25 (*Learning Objective 2, 3, 5: Using ratio data to reconstruct a company's balance sheet*) The following data (dollar amounts in millions) are taken from the financial statements of Phase 1 Industries, Inc.

Total liabilities	$11,800
Preferred stock	$ 0
Total current assets	$10,200
Accumulated depreciation................	$ 1,400
Debt ratio...	59%
Current ratio	1.50

❙ *Required*

Complete the following condensed balance sheet. Report amounts to the nearest million dollars. (pp. 696, 699)

Current assets		$?
Property, plant, and equipment	$?	
Less Accumulated depreciation	(?)	?
Total assets		$?
Current liabilities		$?
Long-term liabilities		?
Stockholders' equity		?
Total liabilities and stockholders' equity		$?

E13-26 (*Learning Objective 2, 3, 5: Using ratio data to reconstruct a company's income statement*) The following data (dollar amounts in millions) are from the financial statements of Federal Corporation:

Average stockholders' equity	$3,600
Interest expense	$ 400
Preferred stock	$ 0
Operating income as a percent of sales	25%
Rate of return on stockholders' equity	20%
Income tax rate	40%

I Required

Complete the following condensed income statement. Report amounts to the nearest million dollars. (pp. 700–702)

Sales	$?
Operating expense	?
Operating income	?
Interest expense	?
Pretax income	?
Income tax expense	?
Net income	$?

Practice Quiz

Use the Miami Bell Corporation *financial statements to answer the questions that follow.*

(continued)

Miami Bell Corporation
Consolidated Statements of Financial Position
(In millions)

	December 31, 20X4	December 31, 20X3
Assets		
Current assets:		
Cash and cash equivalents...................................	$ 4,317	$ 4,232
Short-term investments.....................................	835	406
Accounts receivable, net....................................	3,635	2,586
Inventories	327	306
Other	1,519	1,394
Total current assets	10,633	8,924
Property, plant, and equipment, net	1,517	913
Investments..	6,770	5,267
Other noncurrent assets.......................................	391	366
Total assets..	$19,311	$15,470
Liabilities and Stockholders' Equity		
Current liabilities:		
Accounts payable	$ 7,316	$ 5,989
Accrued and other	3,580	2,944
Total current liabilities....................................	10,896	8,933
Long-term debt..	505	506
Other noncurrent liabilities....................................	1,630	1,158
Commitments and contingent liabilities (Note 7)......	—	—
Total liabilities	13,031	10,597
Stockholders' equity:		
Preferred stock and capital in excess of $0.01 par value; shares issued and outstanding: none	—	—
Common stock and capital in excess of $0.01 par value; shares authorized: 7,000; shares issued: 2,721 and 2,681, respectively...........	6,823	6,018
Treasury stock, at cost; 165 and 102 shares, respectively...	(6,539)	(4,539)
Retained earnings...	6,131	3,486
Other comprehensive loss...................................	(83)	(33)
Other...	(52)	(59)
Total stockholders' equity	6,280	4,873
Total liabilities and stockholders' equity	$19,311	$15,470

Miami Bell Corporation
Consolidated Statements of Income
(In millions, except per share amounts)

| | Year ended December 31, | | |
	20X4	20X3	20X2
Net revenue..	$41,444	$35,404	$31,168
Cost of goods sold..	33,892	29,055	25,661
Gross profit	7,552	6,349	5,507
Operating expenses:			
Selling, general, and administrative......	3,544	3,050	2,784
Research, development, and			
engineering	464	455	452
Special charges.....................................	—	—	482
Total operating expenses	4,008	3,505	3,718
Operating income...........................	3,544	2,844	1,789
Investment and other income (loss), net	180	183	(58)
Income before income taxes.................	3,724	3,027	1,731
Income tax expense......................................	1,079	905	485
Net income...	$ 2,645	$ 2,122	$ 1,246
Earnings per common share:			
Basic...	$ 1.03	$ 0.82	$ 0.48

Q13-27 During 20X4, Miami Bell's total assets (pp. 683–684)
a. increased by $8,341 million.
b. increased by 24.8%.
c. Both a and b.
d. increased by 19.9%.

Q13-28 Miami Bell's current ratio at year end 20X4 is closest to (p. 696)
a. 1.2.
b. 1.1.
c. 1.0.
d. 0.80.

Q13-29 Miami Bell's acid-test ratio at year end 20X4 is closest to (pp. 697–698)
a. $0.80.
b. $0.65.
c. 0.47.
d. $8,787 million.

Q13-30 What is the largest single item included in Miami Bell's debt ratio at December 31, 20X4? (p. 699)
a. Cash and cash equivalents
b. Accounts payable
c. Investments
d. Common stock

Q13-31 Using the earliest year available as the base year, the trend percentage for Miami Bell's net revenue during 20X4 was (pp. 686–687)
a. 117%.
b. up by $10,276 million.
c. up by 17.1%.
d. 133%.

Q13-32 Miami Bell's common-size income statement for 20X4 would report cost of goods sold as (pp. 687–688)
a. $33,892 million.
b. Up by 16.6%.
c. 81.8%.
d. 132.1%.

Q13-33 Miami Bell's days' sales in average receivables during 20X4 was (pp. 698–699)
a. 22 days.
b. 27 days.
c. 32 days.
d. 114 days.

Q13-34 Miami Bell's inventory turnover during fiscal year 20X4 was (pp. 697–698)
a. very slow.   c. 107 times.
b. 54 times.   d. 129 times.

Q13-35 Miami Bell's long-term debt bears interest at 6%. During the year ended December 31, 20X4, Bell's times-interest-earned ratio was (p. 699)
a. 117 times.   c. 100 times.
b. 110 times.   d. 125 times.

Q13-36 Miami Bell's trend of return on sales is (p. 700)
a. improving.   c. stuck at 6%.
b. declining.   d. worrisome.

Q13-37 How many shares of common stock did Miami Bell have outstanding, on average, during 20X4? Hint: Compute earnings per share. (pp. 701–702)
a. 2,721 million   c. 2,645 million
b. 2,701 million   d. 2,568 million

Q13-38 Book value per share of Miami Bell's common stock outstanding at December 31, 20X4, was (pp. 703–704)
a. $2.72.   c. $6,280.
b. $4.37.   d. $2.46.

Problems
(Group A)

MyAccountingLab

> Some of these A problems can be found within My Accounting Lab (MAL), an online homework and practice environment. Your instructor may ask you to complete these exercises using MAL.

P13-39A (*Learning Objective 1, 5, 6: Trend percentages, return on sales, and comparison with the industry*) Net sales, net income, and total assets for Container Shipping, Inc., for a 5-year period follow:

(In thousands)	20X8	20X7	20X6	20X5	20X4
Net sales.....................	$367	$313	$266	$281	$197
Net income.................	27	11	11	18	16
Total assets	286	254	209	197	185

❚ *Required*

1. Compute trend percentages for each item for 20X5 through 20X8. Use 20X4 as the base year and round to the nearest percent. (pp. 686–687)
2. Compute the rate of return on net sales for 20X6 through 20X8, rounding to 3 decimal places. (p. 700)
3. How does Container Shipping's return on net sales compare with that of the industry? (p. 700) In the shipping industry, rates above 5% are considered good, and rates above 7% are outstanding. (p. 700)

P13-40A (*Learning Objective 2, 3, 5, 6: Common-size statements, analysis of profitability, and comparison with the industry*) Top managers of Medical Products, Inc., have asked for your help in comparing the company's profit performance and financial position with the average for the industry. The accountant has given you the company's income statement and balance sheet and also the following data for the industry:

Medical Products, Inc.
Income Statement Compared with Industry Average
Year Ended December 31, 20X5

	Medical Products	Industry Average
Net sales.................................	$957,000	100.0%
Cost of goods sold..................	652,000	55.9
Gross profit............................	305,000	44.1
Operating expenses	200,000	28.1
Operating income...................	105,000	16.0
Other expenses.......................	3,000	2.4
Net income	$102,000	13.6%

Medical Products, Inc.
Balance Sheet Compared with Industry Average
December 31, 20X5

	Medical Products	Industry Average
Current assets............................	$486,000	74.4%
Fixed assets, net	117,000	20.0
Intangible assets, net	24,000	0.6
Other assets..............................	3,000	5.0
Total	$630,000	100.0%
Current liabilities	$245,000	45.6%
Long-term liabilities	114,000	19.0
Stockholders' equity.................	271,000	35.4
Total	$630,000	100.0%

I Required

1. Prepare a common-size income statement and balance sheet for Medical Products. The first column of each statement should present Medical Products' common-size statement, and the second column should show the industry averages. (pp. 687–689)

2. For the profitability analysis, compute Medical Products' (a) ratio of gross profit to net sales (b) ratio of operating income to net sales, and (c) ratio of net income to net sales. Compare these figures with the industry averages. Is Medical Products' profit performance better or worse than the average for the industry? (p. 700)

3. For the analysis of financial position, compute Medical Products' (a) ratios of current assets and current liabilities to total assets and (b) ratio of stockholders' equity to total assets. Compare these ratios with the industry averages. Is Medical Products' financial position better or worse than the average for the industry? (pp. 688–689)

writing assignment ■

P13-41A (*Learning Objective 4: Using the statement of cash flows for decision making*) You are evaluating 2 companies as possible investments. The 2 companies, similar in size, are commuter airlines that fly passengers up and down the East Coast. All other available information has been analyzed and your investment decision depends on the cash-flow statement.

writing assignment ■

(continued)

Commonwealth Airlines (Comair)
Statement of Cash Flows
Years Ended November 30, 20X9 and 20X8

	20X9	20X8
Operating activities:		
Net income (net loss)	$ (67,000)	$154,000
Adjustments for noncash items:		
Total	84,000	(23,000)
Net cash provided by operating activities	17,000	131,000
Investing activities:		
Purchase of property, plant, and		
equipment...	$ (50,000)	$ (91,000)
Sale of long-term investments	52,000	4,000
Net cash provided by (used for)		
investing activities.................................	2,000	(87,000)
Financing activities:		
Issuance of short-term notes payable	$ 122,000	$143,000
Payment of short-term notes payable........	(179,000)	(134,000)
Payment of cash dividends........................	(45,000)	(64,000)
Net cash used for financing activities........	(102,000)	(55,000)
Increase (decrease) in cash.................................	$ (83,000)	$ (11,000)
Cash balance at beginning of year......................	92,000	103,000
Cash balance at the end of year..........................	$ 9,000	$ 92,000

Jetway, Inc.
Statement of Cash Flows
Years Ended November 30, 20X9 and 20X8

	20X9	20X8
Operating activities:		
Net income	$ 184,000	$ 131,000
Adjustments for noncash items:		
Total..	64,000	62,000
Net cash provided by operating activities	248,000	193,000
Investing activities:		
Purchase of property, plant,		
and equipment......................................	$(303,000)	$(453,000)
Sale of property, plant, and equipment	46,000	72,000
Net cash used for investing activities	(257,000)	(381,000)
Financing activities:		
Issuance of long-term notes payable..........	$ 174,000	$ 118,000
Payment of short-term notes payable........	(66,000)	(18,000)
Net cash provided by financing activities......	108,000	100,000
Increase (decrease) in cash.................................	$ 99,000	$ (88,000)
Cash balance at beginning of year......................	116,000	204,000
Cash balance at end of year................................	$ 215,000	$ 116,000

Required

Discuss the relative strengths and weaknesses of Comair and Jetway. Conclude your discussion by recommending 1 of the companies' stocks as an investment. (pp. 690–691)

P13-42A (*Learning Objective 5, 6: Effects of business transactions on selected ratios*)
Financial statement data of Metroplex Engineering include the following items:

Cash	$ 47,000	Accounts payable	$142,000
Short-term investments	21,000	Accrued liabilities	50,000
Accounts receivable, net	102,000	Long-term notes payable	146,000
Inventories	274,000	Other long-term liabilities	78,000
Prepaid expenses	15,000	Net income	104,000
Total assets	933,000	Number of common	
Short-term notes payable	72,000	shares outstanding	22,000

Required

1. Compute Metroplex's current ratio, debt ratio, and earnings per share. Use the following format for your answer: (pp. 696, 699, 701–702)

Requirement 1

Current ratio	Debt ratio	Earnings per share

2. Compute the 3 ratios after evaluating the effect of each transaction that follows. Consider each transaction *separately*.
   a. Borrowed $27,000 on a long-term note payable.
   b. Issued 10,000 shares of common stock, receiving cash of $108,000.
   c. Paid short-term notes payable, $51,000.
   d. Purchased merchandise of $48,000 on account, debiting Inventory.
   e. Received cash on account, $6,000.

Format your answer as follows:

Requirement 2

Transaction (letter)	Current ratio	Debt ratio	Earnings per share

P13-43A (*Learning Objective 5, 6: Using ratios to evaluate a stock investment*) Comparative financial statement data of Crest Optical Mart follow:

Crest Optical Mart
Comparative Income Statement
Years Ended December 31, 20X6 and 20X5

	20X6	20X5
Net sales	$667,000	$599,000
Cost of goods sold	378,000	313,000
Gross profit	289,000	286,000
Operating expenses	129,000	147,000
Income from operations	160,000	139,000
Interest expense	37,000	41,000
Income before income tax	123,000	98,000
Income tax expense	44,000	43,000
Net income	$ 79,000	$ 55,000

(continued)

Crest Optical Mart
Comparative Balance Sheet
December 31, 20X6 and 20X5

	20X6	20X5	20X4*
Current assets:			
Cash	$ 37,000	$ 40,000	
Current receivables, net	208,000	151,000	$138,000
Inventories	152,000	186,000	144,000
Prepaid expenses	5,000	20,000	
Total current assets	402,000	397,000	
Property, plant, and equipment, net	287,000	256,000	
Total assets	$689,000	$653,000	607,000
Total current liabilities	$286,000	$217,000	
Long-term liabilities	145,000	185,000	
Total liabilities	431,000	402,000	
Preferred stockholders' equity, 4%, $20 par	50,000	50,000	
Common stockholders' equity, no par	208,000	201,000	198,000
Total liabilities and stockholders' equity	$689,000	$653,000	

*Selected 20X4 amounts.

Other information:

1. Market price of Crest common stock: $61 at December 31, 20X6, and $45.50 at December 31, 20X5.
2. Common shares outstanding: 15,000 during 20X6 and 14,000 during 20X5.
3. All sales on credit.

▮ Required

1. Compute the following ratios for 20X6 and 20X5:
   a. Current ratio (p. 696)
   b. Inventory turnover (pp. 697–698)
   c. Times-interest-earned ratio (p. 699)
   d. Return on assets (p. 700)
   e. Return on common stockholders' equity (pp. 701–702)
   f. Earnings per share of common stock (pp. 701–702)
   g. Price/earnings ratio (pp. 702–703)
2. Decide whether (a) Crest's financial position improved or deteriorated during 20X6 and (b) the investment attractiveness of Crest's common stock appears to have increased or decreased. (Challenge)
3. How will what you learned in this problem help you evaluate an investment? (Challenge)

writing assignment ■

P13-44A (*Learning Objective 5, 6, 7: Using ratios to decide between 2 stock investments; measuring economic value added*) Assume that you are considering purchasing stock as an investment. You have narrowed the choice to Video.com and On-Line Express and have assembled the following data:

Selected income statement data for current year:

	Video	Express
Net sales (all on credit).................	$603,000	$519,000
Cost of goods sold.........................	454,000	387,000
Income from operations	93,000	72,000
Interest expense............................	—	12,000
Net income...................................	56,000	38,000

Selected balance sheet and market price data at *end* of current year:

	Video	Express
Current assets:		
Cash	$ 25,000	$ 39,000
Short-term investments	6,000	13,000
Current receivables, net	189,000	164,000
Inventories..	211,000	183,000
Prepaid expenses...	19,000	15,000
Total current assets	450,000	414,000
Total assets..	974,000	938,000
Total current liabilities	366,000	338,000
Total liabilities	667,000*	691,000*
Preferred stock, 4%, $100 par		25,000
Common stock, $1 par (150,000 shares)................	150,000	
$5 par (20,000 shares)...................		100,000
Total stockholders' equity	307,000	247,000
Market price per share of common stock	$ 9	$ 47.50

*Includes Long-term debt: Video $-0-, and Express $350,000

Selected balance sheet data at *beginning* of current year:

	Video	Express
Current receivables, net...	$142,000	$193,000
Inventories	209,000	197,000
Total assets..	842,000	909,000
Long-term debt	—	303,000
Preferred stock, 4%, $100 par		25,000
Common stock, $1 par (150,000 shares)................	150,000	
$5 par (20,000 shares).................		100,000
Total stockholders' equity.......................................	263,000	215,000

Your strategy is to invest in companies that have low price/earnings ratios but appear to be in good shape financially. Assume that you have analyzed all other factors and that your decision depends on the results of ratio analysis.

(*continued*)

I *Required*

1. Compute the following ratios for both companies for the current year and decide which company's stock better fits your investment strategy.
   a. Acid-test ratio (pp. 697–698)
   b. Inventory turnover (pp. 697–698)
   c. Days' sales in average receivables (pp. 698–699)
   d. Debt ratio (p. 699)
   e. Times-interest-earned ratio (p. 699)
   f. Return on common stockholders' equity (pp. 701–702)
   g. Earnings per share of common stock (pp. 701–702)
   h. Price/earnings ratio (pp. 702–703)

2. Compute each company's economic-value-added (EVA®) measure and determine whether the companies' EVA®s confirm or alter your investment decision. Each company's cost of capital is 10%. (pp. 703–704)

writing assignment ■

P13-45A *(Learning Objective 6: Analyzing a company based on its ratios)* Take the role of an investment analyst at **Merrill Lynch**. It is your job to recommend investments for your client. The only information you have is the following ratio values for 2 companies in the graphics software industry.

Ratio	Omicron.net	Data Miners
Days' sales in receivables	51	43
Inventory turnover	9	7
Gross profit percentage	62%	71%
Net income as a percent of sales	16%	14%
Times interest earned	12	18
Return on equity	29%	36%
Return on assets	19%	14%

Write a report to the Merrill Lynch investment committee. Recommend 1 company's stock over the other. State the reasons for your recommendation. (pp. 697–702)

(Group B)

P13-46B *(Learning Objective 1, 5, 6: Trend percentages, return on common equity, and comparison with the industry)* Net revenues, net income, and common stockholders' equity for Accenté Corporation for a 5-year period follow.

(In thousands)	2008	2007	2006	2005	2004
Net revenues	$781	$714	$681	$662	$581
Net income	41	35	32	28	20
Ending common stockholders' equity	386	354	330	296	263

I *Required*

1. Compute trend percentages for each item for 2005 through 2008. Use 2004 as the base year. Round to the nearest percent. (pp. 686–687)
2. Compute the rate of return on common stockholders' equity for 2006 through 2008, rounding to 3 decimal places. (pp. 701–702)

3. In this industry, rates of return on common stockholders' equity of 13% are average, rates above 16% are good, and rates above 20% are outstanding. Accenté has no preferred stock outstanding. How does Accenté's return on common stockholders' equity compare with the industry? (pp. 701–702)

P13-47B (*Learning Objective 2, 3, 5, 6: Common-size statements, analysis of profitability, and comparison with the industry*) Pathfinder, Inc., has asked you to compare the company's profit performance and financial position with the industry average. The proprietor has given you the company's income statement and balance sheet as well as the industry average data for retailers.

writing assignment ■

Pathfinder, Inc.
Income Statement Compared with Industry Average
Year Ended December 31, 20X6

	Pathfinder	Industry Average
Net sales..................................	$700,000	100.0%
Cost of goods sold..................	497,000	65.8
Gross profit............................	203,000	34.2
Operating expenses	163,000	19.7
Operating income..................	40,000	14.5
Other expenses.......................	3,000	0.4
Net income	$ 37,000	14.1%

Pathfinder, Inc.
Balance Sheet Compared with Industry Average
December 31, 20X6

	Pathfinder	Industry Average
Current assets............................	$300,000	70.9%
Fixed assets, net	74,000	23.6
Intangible assets, net	4,000	0.8
Other assets..............................	22,000	4.7
Total	$400,000	100.0%
Current liabilities	$206,000	48.1%
Long-term liabilities	64,000	16.6
Stockholders' equity................	130,000	35.3
Total	$400,000	100.0%

I *Required*

1. Prepare a common-size income statement and balance sheet for Pathfinder. The first column of each statement should present Pathfinder's common-size statement, and the second column, the industry averages. (pp. 687–688)

(*continued*)

2. For the profitability analysis, compute Pathfinder's (a) ratio of gross profit to net sales, (b) ratio of operating income to net sales, and (c) ratio of net income to net sales. Compare these figures with the industry averages. Is Pathfinder's profit performance better or worse than the industry average? (p. 700)

3. For the analysis of financial position, compute Pathfinder's (a) ratio of current assets to total assets, and (b) ratio of stockholders' equity to total assets. Compare these ratios with the industry averages. Is Pathfinder's financial position better or worse than the industry averages? (pp. 688–689)

writing assignment ■

P13-48B (*Learning Objective 4: Using the statement of cash flows for decision making*) You have been asked to evaluate 2 companies as possible investments. The 2 companies, Norfolk Southern Corp. and Stafford Crystal Company, are similar in size. Assume that all other available information has been analyzed, and the decision concerning which company's stock to purchase depends on their cash-flow data.

I *Required*

Discuss the relative strengths and weaknesses of each company. Conclude your discussion by recommending 1 company's stock as an investment. (pp. 690–691)

Norfolk Southern Corp.
Statement of Cash Flows
Years Ended September 30, 20X7 and 20X6

	20X7		20X6	
Operating activities:				
Net income		$ 17,000		$44,000
Adjustments for noncash items:				
Total		(14,000)		(4,000)
Net cash provided by operating activities		3,000		40,000
Investing activities:				
Purchase of property, plant, and				
equipment	$ (13,000)		$ (3,000)	
Sale of property, plant, and equipment	86,000		79,000	
Net cash provided by investing activities		73,000		76,000
Financing activities:				
Issuance of short-term notes payable	$ 43,000		$ 19,000	
Payment of short-term notes payable	(101,000)		(108,000)	
Net cash used for financing activities		(58,000)		(89,000)
Increase in cash		$ 18,000		$ 27,000
Cash balance at beginning of year		31,000		4,000
Cash balance at end of year		$ 49,000		$ 31,000

Strafford Crystal Company
Statement of Cash Flows
Years Ended September 30, 20X7 and 20X6

	20X7	20X6
Operating activities:		
Net income	$ 89,000	$ 71,000
Adjustments for noncash items:		
Total	19,000	—
Net cash provided by operating activities.	108,000	71,000
Investing activities:		
Purchase of property, plant, and equipment	$(121,000)	$(91,000)
Net cash used for investing activities	(121,000)	(91,000)
Financing activities:		
Issuance of long-term notes payable	$ 46,000	$ 43,000
Payment of short-term notes payable	(15,000)	(40,000)
Payment of cash dividends	(12,000)	(9,000)
Net cash provided by (used for)		
financing activities	19,000	(6,000)
Increase (decrease) in cash	6,000	$(26,000)
Cash balance at beginning of year	54,000	80,000
Cash balance at end of year	$ 60,000	$ 54,000

P13-49B (*Learning Objective 5, 6: Effects of business transactions on selected ratios*) Financial statement data of HiFlite Electronics include the following items (dollars in thousands):

Cash	$ 22,000
Short-term investments	39,000
Accounts receivable, net	83,000
Inventories	141,000
Prepaid expenses	8,000
Total assets	677,000
Short-term notes payable	49,000
Accounts payable	103,000
Accrued liabilities	38,000
Long-term notes payable	160,000
Other long-term liabilities	31,000
Net income	91,000
Number of common shares outstanding	40,000

I Required

1. Compute HiFlite's current ratio, debt ratio, and earnings per share. Use the following format for your answer: (pp. 696, 699, 701–702)

Requirement 1
Current ratio   Debt ratio   Earnings per share

(continued)

2. Compute the 3 ratios after evaluating the effect of each transaction that follows. Consider each transaction *separately*.

   a. Purchased store supplies of $46,000 on account.
   b. Borrowed $125,000 on a long-term note payable.
   c. Issued 5,000 shares of common stock, receiving cash of $120,000.
   d. Paid short-term notes payable, $32,000.
   e. Received cash on account, $19,000.

   Format your answer as follows:

Requirement 2 Transaction (letter)	Current ratio	Debt ratio	Earnings per share

writing assignment ■

P13-50B (*Learning Objective 5, 6: Using ratios to evaluate a stock investment*) Comparative financial statement data of Mira TV Sales follow.

Mira TV Sales
Comparative Income Statement
Years Ended December 31, 20X9 and 20X8

	20X9	20X8
Net sales	$662,000	$527,000
Cost of goods sold	429,000	318,000
Gross profit	233,000	209,000
Operating expenses	136,000	134,000
Income from operations	97,000	75,000
Interest expense	9,000	8,000
Income before income tax	88,000	67,000
Income tax expense	30,000	27,000
Net income	$ 58,000	$ 40,000

Mira TV Sales
Comparative Balance Sheet
December 31, 20X9 and 20X8

	20X9	20X8	20X7*
Current assets:			
Cash	$ 96,000	$ 97,000	
Current receivables, net	162,000	116,000	$103,000
Inventories	147,000	162,000	207,000
Prepaid expenses	16,000	7,000	
Total current assets	421,000	382,000	
Property, plant, and equipment, net	214,000	178,000	
Total assets	$635,000	$560,000	598,000
Total current liabilities	$206,000	$223,000	
Long-term liabilities	119,000	117,000	
Total liabilities	325,000	340,000	
Preferred stockholders' equity, 6%, $100 par	100,000	100,000	
Common stockholders' equity, no par	210,000	120,000	90,000
Total liabilities and stockholders' equity	$635,000	$560,000	

*Selected 20X7 amounts.

Other information:

1. Market price of Mira's common stock: $83 at December 31, 20X9, and $62.50 at December 31, 20X8.
2. Common shares outstanding: 10,000 during 20X9 and 9,000 during 20X8.
3. All sales on credit.

▌Required

1. Compute the following ratios for 20X9 and 20X8:
   a. Current ratio (p. 696)
   b. Inventory turnover (pp. 697–698)
   c. Times-interest-earned ratio (p. 699)
   d. Return on common stockholders' equity (pp. 701–702)
   e. Earnings per share of common stock (pp. 701–702)
   f. Price/earnings ratio (pp. 702–703)
2. Decide (a) whether Mira's financial position improved or deterioriated during 20X9 and (b) whether the investment attractiveness of Mira's common stock appears to have increased or decreased. (Challenge)
3. How will what you learned in this problem help you evaluate an investment? (Challenge)

P13-51B (*Learning Objective 5, 6, 7: Using ratios to decide between 2 stock investments; measuring economic value added*) Assume that you are purchasing an investment and have decided to invest in a company in the publishing business. You have narrowed the choice to Thrifty Nickel Corp. and The Village Cryer and have assembled the following data:

writing assignment ■

Selected income statement data for the current year:

	Thrifty Nickel	Village Cryer
Net sales (all on credit).................	$371,000	$497,000
Cost of goods sold........................	209,000	258,000
Income from operations	79,000	138,000
Interest expense............................	—	19,000
Net income	48,000	72,000

Selected balance sheet data at *beginning* of the current year:

	Thrifty Nickel	Village Cryer
Current receivables, net..	$ 40,000	$ 48,000
Inventories	93,000	88,000
Total assets...	259,000	270,000
Long-term debt	—	86,000
Preferred stock, 5%, $100 par	—	20,000
Common stock, $1 par (10,000 shares).................	10,000	
$2.50 par (5,000 shares)..............		12,500
Total stockholders' equity.....................................	118,000	126,000

(*continued*)

Selected balance sheet and market price data at *end* of the current year:

	Thrifty Nickel	Village Cryer
Current assets:		
Cash	$ 22,000	$ 19,000
Short-term investments	20,000	18,000
Current receivables, net	42,000	46,000
Inventories	87,000	100,000
Prepaid expenses	2,000	3,000
Total current assets	173,000	186,000
Total assets	265,000	328,000
Total current liabilities	108,000	98,000
Total liabilities	108,000*	131,000*
Preferred stock: 5%, $100 par		20,000
Common stock, $1 par (10,000 shares)	10,000	
$2.50 par (5,000 shares)		12,500
Total stockholders' equity	157,000	197,000
Market price per share of common stock	$ 51	$ 112

* Includes Long-term debt: Thrifty Nickel $-0- and Village Cryer $86,000

Your strategy is to invest in companies that have low price/earnings ratios but appear to be in good shape financially. Assume that you have analyzed all other factors and your decision depends on the results of ratio analysis.

▌Required

1. Compute the following ratios for both companies for the current year, and decide which company's stock better fits your investment strategy.
   a. Acid-test ratio (pp. 697–698)
   b. Inventory turnover (pp. 697–698)
   c. Days' sales in average receivables (pp. 698–699)
   d. Debt ratio (p. 699)
   e. Times-interest-earned ratio (p. 699)
   f. Return on common stockholders' equity (pp. 701–702)
   g. Earnings per share of common stock (pp. 701–702)
   h. Price/earnings ratio (pp. 702–703)
2. Compute each company's economic-value-added (EVA®) measure and determine whether the companies' EVA®s confirm or alter your investment decision. Each company's cost of capital is 12%. (pp. 703–704)

P13-52B (*Learning Objective 6: Analyzing a company based on its ratios*) Take the role of an investment analyst at **Solomon Brothers**. It is your job to recommend investments for your clients. The only information you have is the following ratio values for 2 companies in the pharmaceuticals industry.

Ratio	MONY Group	Pegasus, Inc.
Days' sales in receivables............................	36	42
Inventory turnover......................................	6	8
Gross profit percentage	49%	51%
Net income as a percent of sales................	7.2%	8.3%
Times interest earned	16	9
Return on equity..	32.3%	21.5%
Return on assets...	12.1%	16.4%

Write a report to Solomon Brothers investment committee. Recommend 1 company's stock over the others'. State the reasons for your recommendation. (pp. 697–702)

APPLY YOUR KNOWLEDGE

Decision Cases

Case 1. (*Learning Objective 5, 6: Assessing the effects of transactions on a company*) **AOL Time Warner Inc.** had a bad year in 20X1; the company suffered a $4.9 billion net loss. The loss pushed most of the return measures into the negative column and the current ratio dropped below 1.0. The company's debt ratio is still only 0.27. Assume top management of AOL Time Warner is pondering ways to improve the company's ratios. In particular, management is considering the following transactions:

1. Sell off the cable television segment of the business for $30 million (receiving half in cash and half in the form of a long-term note receivable). Book value of the cable television business is $27 million.
2. Borrow $100 million on long-term debt.
3. Purchase treasury stock for $500 million cash.
4. Write off one-fourth of goodwill carried on the books at $128 million.
5. Sell advertising at the normal gross profit of 60%. The advertisements run immediately.
6. Purchase trademarks from **NBC**, paying $20 million cash and signing a 1-year note payable for $80 million.

❙ Required

1. Top management wants to know the effects of these transactions (increase, decrease, or no effect) on the following ratios of AOL Time Warner:
   a. Current ratio (p. 696)
   b. Debt ratio (p. 699)
   c. Times-interest-earned ratio (measured as [net income + interest expense]/interest expense) (p. 699)
   d. Return on equity (pp. 701–702)
   e. Book value per share of common stock (pp. 703–704)
2. Some of these transactions have an immediately positive effect on the company's financial condition. Some are definitely negative. Others have an effect that cannot be judged as clearly positive or negative. Evaluate each transaction's effect as positive, negative, or unclear. (Challenge)

Case 2. (*Learning Objective 5, 6: Analyzing the effects of an accounting difference on the ratios*) **Gap Inc.** uses the first-in, first-out (FIFO) method to account for its inventory, and **Lands' End** uses last-in, first-out (LIFO). Analyze the effect of this difference in accounting method on the 2 companies' ratio values. For each ratio discussed in this chapter, indicate which company will have the higher (and the lower) ratio value. Also identify those ratios that are unaffected by the FIFO/LIFO difference. Ignore the effects of income taxes, and assume inventory costs are increasing. Then, based on your analysis of the ratios, summarize your conclusions as to which company looks better overall. (pp. 315, 319, 696–704).

Case 3. (*Learning Objective 2, 5, 6: Identifying action to cut losses and establish profitability*) Suppose you manage Outward Bound, Inc., a Vermont sporting goods store that lost money during the past year. To turn the business around, you must analyze the company and industry data for the current year to learn what is wrong. The company's data follow:

Outward Bound, Inc.
Common-Size Balance Sheet Data

	Outward Bound	Industry Average
Cash and short-term investments	3.0%	6.8%
Trade receivables, net	15.2	11.0
Inventory	64.2	60.5
Prepaid expenses	1.0	0.0
Total current assets	83.4%	78.3%
Fixed assets, net	12.6	15.2
Other assets	4.0	6.5
Total assets	100.0%	100.0%
Notes payable, short-term, 12%	17.1%	14.0%
Accounts payable	21.1	25.1
Accrued liabilities	7.8	7.9
Total current liabilities	46.0	47.0
Long-term debt, 11%	19.7	16.4
Total liabilities	65.7	63.4
Common stockholders' equity	34.3	36.6
Total liabilities and stockholders' equity	100.0%	100.0%

Outward Bound, Inc.
Common-Size Income Statement Data

	Outward Bound	Industry Average
Net sales	100.0%	100.0%
Cost of sales	(68.2)	(64.8)
Gross profit	31.8	35.2
Operating expense	(37.1)	(32.3)
Operating income (loss)	(5.3)	2.9
Interest expense	(5.8)	(1.3)
Other revenue	1.1	0.3
Income (loss) before income tax	(10.0)	1.9
Income tax (expense) saving	4.4	(0.8)
Net income(loss)	(5.6)%	1.1%

❙ Required

On the basis of your analysis of these figures, suggest 4 courses of action Outward Bound might take to reduce its losses and establish profitable operations. Give your reason for each suggestion. (Challenge)

Ethical Issue

Turnberry Golf Corporation's long-term debt agreements make certain demands on the business. For example, Turnberry may not purchase treasury stock in excess of the balance of retained earnings. Also, long-term debt may not exceed stockholders' equity, and the current ratio may not fall below 1.50. If Turnberry fails to meet any of these requirements, the company's lenders have the authority to take over management of the company.

    Changes in consumer demand have made it hard for Turnberry to attract customers. Current liabilities have mounted faster than current assets, causing the current ratio to fall to 1.47. Before releasing financial statements, Turnberry management is scrambling to improve the current ratio. The controller points out that an investment can be classified as either long-term or short-term, depending on management's intention. By deciding to convert an investment to cash within 1 year, Turnberry can classify the investment as short-term—a current asset. On the controller's recommendation, Turnberry's board of directors votes to reclassify long-term investments as short-term.

❙ Required

1. What effect will reclassifying the investments have on the current ratio? Is Turnberry's financial position stronger as a result of reclassifying the investments?   **writing assignment ■**

2. Shortly after the financial statements are released, sales improve; so, too, does the current ratio. As a result, Turnberry management decides not to sell the investments it had reclassified as short term. Accordingly, the company reclassifies the investments as long term. Has management behaved unethically? Give the reasoning underlying your answer.

Focus on Financials: ■ YUM! Brands

(*Learning Objective 1, 6: Measuring profitability and analyzing stock as an investment*)   **writing assignment ■**
Use the financial statements and the data in **YUM! Brands'** 5-year summary of selected financial data (Appendix A at the end of the book) to answer the following questions.

❙ Required

1. Using 2003 as the base year, perform a trend analysis of YUM's selected Financial Data for total revenue, operating profit, net income, and net cash provided by operating activities for each year 2004 through 2006. (pp. 686–687)

2. Evaluate YUM's operating performance during 2004 through 2006. Comment on each item computed. (Challenge)

Focus on Analysis: ■ Pier 1 Imports

(*Learning Objective 1, 6: Analyzing trend data*) Use the **Pier 1 Imports** financial statements in Appendix B at the end of this book to address the following questions. Study the Financial Summary that precedes the financial statements.   **writing assignment ■**

1. During 2006, Pier 1's sales decreased and the company suffered a net loss. Perform a trend analysis of Pier 1's Financial Summary data for net sales, gross profit, operating income, and net income. Use 2002 as the base year, and compute trend figures for 2003, 2004, 2005, and 2006. (pp. 686–687)

2. Discuss the results of Pier 1's operations based on your trend analysis during 2003–2006. (Challenge)

3. What in your opinion is the company's outlook for the future? (Challenge)

Group Projects

writing assignment ■

Project 1. Select an industry you are interested in, and use the leading company in that industry as the benchmark. Then select 2 other companies in the same industry. For each category of ratios in the Decision Guidelines feature on pages 706 and 707, compute at least 2 ratios for all 3 companies. Write a 2-page report that compares the 2 companies with the benchmark company.

Project 2. Select a company and obtain its financial statements. Convert the income statement and the balance sheet to common size and compare the company you selected to the industry average. **Risk Management Association's** *Annual Statement Studies,* **Dun & Bradstreet's** *Industry Norms & Key Business Ratios,* and **Prentice Hall's** *Almanac of Business and Industrial Financial Ratios* by Leo Troy, publish common-size statements for most industries.

For Internet Exercises go to the Web site www.prenhall.com/harrison.

Quick Check Answers

1. *c* ($1,833/$1,712.8 = 1.070)
2. *c* ($1,833/$17,140.5 = 0.107)
3. *b* (Net income: $1,471.4 − $893.5 = $577.9; $577.9/$893.5 = Increase of 64.7%)
4. *a* ($1,665.1/$25,525.1 = 0.065)
5. *a*
6. *d* $\left[\dfrac{\$4,314.8}{(\$129.4 + \$111.7)/2}\right] = 35.8 \approx 36$ times
7. *b* [($492.8 + $734.5)/ $2,485.8 = 0.49]
8. *d* $\left[\dfrac{\$734.5 + \$855.3/2}{\$17,140.5/365}\right] = 16.9 \approx 17$ days
9. *a* (Debt ratio is ($25,525.1 − $11,981.9)/$25,525.1 = 0.53. This debt ratio is lower than the average for most companies, given in the chapter as 0.62.)
10. *d* ($1,471.4/$17,140.5 = 0.086)
11. *a* $\left[\dfrac{\$1,471.4}{(\$11,981.9 + \$10,280.9)/2}\right] = 0.132$
12. *b* ($26/$1.16 = 22.41)
13. *d* ($0.40/$26.00 = 0.015)
14. *c* ($1,471.4 + $388 − ($275.8 + $9,703.6 + $10,280.9) × 0.08 = $238.6 ≈ $239

Demo Doc for Chapter 1

The Accounting Equation and Financial Statement Preparation

Demo Doc: To make sure you understand this material, work through the following demonstration "Demo Doc" with detailed comments to help you see the concept within the framework of a worked-through problem.

Learning Objectives 3, 4, 5

David Richardson is the only shareholder of DR Painting Inc., a painting business near an historical housing district. At March 31, 2009, DR Painting had the following information:

Cash	$27,300
Accounts receivable	1,400
Supplies	1,800
Truck	20,000
Accounts payable	1,000
Common stock	40,000
Retained earnings (March 1)	5,000
Retained earnings (March 31)	?
Dividends	1,500
Service revenue	7,000
Salary expense	1,000

Requirements

1. Prepare the income statement and statement of retained earnings for the month of March 2009 and the balance sheet of the business at March 31, 2009. Use Exhibits 1-7, 1-8, and 1-9 (pp. 44, 46, and 47) in the text as a guide.

2. Write the accounting equation of the business.

Demo Doc Solutions

Requirement 1

Prepare the income statement, statement of retained earnings, and balance sheet of the business. Use Exhibits 1-7, 1-8, and 1-9 (pp. 44, 46, and 47) in the text as a guide.

Part 1	Part 2	Part 3	Part 4	Demo Doc Complete

Income Statement

The income statement is the first statement to prepare because the other financial statements rely upon the net income number calculated on the income statement.

The income statement reports the profitability of the business. To prepare an income statement, begin with the proper heading. A proper heading includes the name of the company (DR Painting, Inc.), the name of the statement (Income Statement), and the time period covered (Month Ended March 31, 2009). Notice that we are reporting income for a period of time, rather than at a single date.

The income statement lists all revenues and expenses. It uses the following formula to calculate net income:

$$\text{Revenues} - \text{Expenses} = \text{Net income}$$

First, you should list revenues. Second, list the expenses. After you have listed and totaled the revenues and expenses, subtract the total expenses from total revenues to determine net income or net loss. A positive number means you earned net income (revenues exceeded expenses). A negative number indicates that expenses exceeded revenues, and this is a net loss.

DR Painting's total Service Revenue for the month was $7,000. The only expense is Salary Expense of $1,000. On the income statement, these would be reported as follows:

DR PAINTING, INC.
Income Statement
Month Ended March 31, 2009

Revenue:		
Service revenue		$7,000
Expenses:		
Salary expense	$1,000	
Total expenses		1,000
Net income		$6,000

Note that the result is a net income of $6,000 ($7,000 − $1,000 = $6,000). You will also report net income on the statement of retained earnings, which comes next.

Statement of Retained Earnings

Part 1	Part 2	Part 3	Part 4	Demo Doc Complete

The statement of retained earnings shows the changes in Retained Earnings for a period of time. To prepare a statement of retained earnings, begin with the proper heading. A proper heading includes the name of the company (DR Painting, Inc.), the name of the statement (Statement of Retained Earnings), and the time period covered (Month Ended March 31, 2009). As with the income statement, we are reporting the changes in Retained Earnings for a period of time, rather than at a single date.

Net income is used on the statement of retained earnings to calculate the new balance in Retained Earnings. This calculation uses the following formula:

> Beginning Retained Earnings
> + Net Income (or − Net Loss)
> − Dividends
> = Ending Retained Earnings

Start the body of the statement of retained earnings with the Retained Earnings at the beginning of the period (March 1). Then list net income. Observe that the amount of net income comes directly from the income statement. Following net income you will list the dividends declared, which reduce Retained Earnings. Finally, total all amounts and compute the Retained Earnings at the end of the period.

The beginning Retained Earnings of $5,000 was given in the problem. Net income of $6,000 comes from the income statement and is added. Dividends of $1,500 amounts are deducted. On the statement of retained earnings, these amounts are reported as follows:

DR PAINTING, INC.
Statement of Retained Earnings
Month Ended March 31, 2009

Beginning retained earnings	$ 5,000
Add: Net income	6,000
	11,000
Less: Dividends	(1,500)
Retained earnings, March 31, 2009	$ 9,500

Note that Retained Earnings has a balance of $9,500 at March 31, 2009. You will also report Retained Earning's ending balance on the balance sheet, which you prepare last.

Balance Sheet

Part 1	Part 2	Part 3	Part 4	Demo Doc Complete

The balance sheet reports the financial position of the business at a moment in time. To prepare a balance sheet, begin with the proper heading. A proper heading includes the name of the company (DR Painting, Inc.), the name of the statement (Balance Sheet), and the time of the ending balances (March 31, 2009). Unlike the income statement and statement of retained earnings, we are reporting the financial position of the company at a specific date rather than for a period of time.

The balance sheet lists all assets, liabilities, and equity of the business, with the accounting equation verified at the bottom.

To prepare the body of the balance sheet, begin by listing assets. Then list all the liabilities and stockholders' equity. Notice that the balance sheet is organized in the same order as the accounting equation. The amount of Retained Earnings comes directly from the ending balance on your statement of retained earnings. You should then total both sides of the balance sheet to make sure that they are equal. If they are not equal, then you must correct an error.

In this case, assets accounts include cash of $27,300, accounts receivable of $1,400, $1,800 worth of supplies, and the truck, valued at $20,000. The only liability is accounts payable of $1,000. Stockholders' equity consists of common stock of $40,000, and the updated retained earnings of $9,500, from the statement of retained earnings.

DR PAINTING, INC.
Balance Sheet
March 31, 2009

Assets		Liabilities	
Cash	$27,300	Accounts payable	$ 1,000
Accounts receivable	1,400		
Supplies	1,800	**Stockholders' Equity**	
Truck	20,000	Common stock	40,000
		Retained earnings	9,500
		Total stockholders' equity	49,500
		Total liabilities and	
Total assets	$50,500	stockholders' equity	$50,500

Assets = Liabilities + Stockholders' Equity

Requirement 2

Write the accounting equation of the business

In this case, asset accounts total $50,500. Liabilities total $1,000—the balance of Accounts Payable, and stockholder's equity is $49,500. This gives us a total for liabilities and equity of $50,500 ($1,000 + $49,500).

The accounting equation is:

Assets of $50,500 = Liabilities of $1,000 + Stockholders' Equity of $49,500

Part 1	Part 2	Part 3	Part 4	Demo Doc Complete

For Internet Exercises, go to the Web site www.prenhall.com/harrison.

Demo Doc for Chapter 2

Debit/Credit Transaction Analysis

Demo Doc: To make sure you understand this material, work through the following demonstration "demo doc" with detailed comments to help you see the concept within the framework of a worked-through problem.

Learning Objectives 1, 2, 3, 4

On September 1, 2008, Michael Moe incorporated Moe's Mowing, Inc., a company that provides mowing and landscaping services. During the month of September, the business incurred the following transactions:

a. To begin operations, Michael deposited $10,000 cash in the business's bank account. The business received the cash and issued common stock to Michael.

b. The business purchased equipment for $3,500 on account.

c. The business purchased office supplies for $800 cash.

d. The business provided $2,600 of services to a customer on account.

e. The business paid $500 cash toward the equipment previously purchased on account in transaction b.

f. The business received $2,000 in cash for services provided to a new customer.

g. The business paid $200 cash to repair equipment.

h. The business paid $900 cash in salary expense.

i. The business received $2,100 cash from a customer on account.

j. The business paid cash dividends of $1,500.

Requirements

1. Create blank T-accounts for the following accounts: Cash, Accounts Receivable, Supplies, Equipment, Accounts Payable, Common Stock, Dividends, Service Revenue, Salary Expense, Repair Expense.

2. Journalize the transactions and then post to the T-accounts. Use the table in Exhibit 2-16 to help with the journal entries.

EXHIBIT 2-16	The Rules of Debit and Credit

	Increase	Decrease
Assets	debit	credit
Liabilities	credit	debit
Stockholders' Equity	credit	debit
Revenues	credit	debit
Expenses	debit	credit
Dividends	debit	credit

3. Total each T-account to determine its balance at the end of the month.

4. Prepare the trial balance of Moe's Mowing, Inc., at September 30, 2008.

Demo Doc Solutions

Requirement 1

Create blank T-accounts for the following accounts: Cash, Accounts Receivable, Supplies, Equipment, Accounts Payable, Common Stock, Dividends, Service Revenue, Salary Expense, Repair Expense.

Part 1	Part 2	Part 3	Part 4	Demo Doc Complete

Opening a T-account means drawing a blank account that looks like a capital "T" and putting the account title across the top. T-accounts show the additions and subtractions made to each account. For easy reference, the accounts are grouped into assets, liabilities, stockholders' equity, revenue, and expenses (in that order).

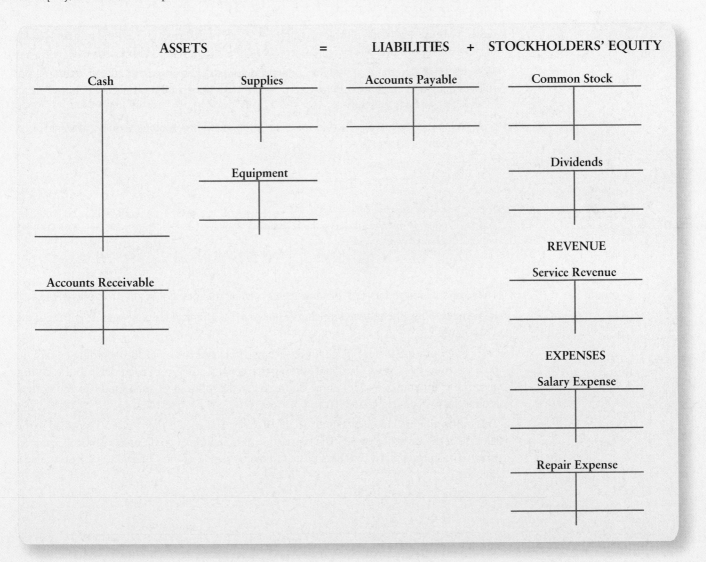

Requirement 2

Journalize the transactions and show how they are recorded in T-accounts.

Part 1	**Part 2**	Part 3	Demo Doc Complete

a. To begin operations, Michael deposited $10,000 cash in the business's bank account. The business received the cash and issued common stock to Michael.

First, we must determine which accounts are affected by the transaction.

The business received $10,000 cash from its principal stockholder (Michael Moe). In exchange, the business issued common stock to Michael. So, the accounts involved are Cash and Common Stock.

Remember that we are recording the transactions of Moe's Mowing, Inc., not the transactions of Michael Moe, the person. Michael and his business are 2 entirely separate accounting entities.

The next step is to determine what type of accounts these are. Cash is an asset, Common Stock is part of equity.

Next, we must determine if these accounts increased or decreased. From the business's point of view, Cash (an asset) has increased. Common Stock (equity) has also increased.

Now we must determine if these accounts should be debited or credited. According to the rules of debit and credit (see Exhibit 2-16 on p. 746), an increase in assets is a debit, while an increase in equity is a credit.

So, Cash (an asset) increases, which requires a debit. Common Stock (equity) also increases, which requires a credit.

The journal entry follows.

a.		Cash (Asset ↑; debit)	10,000	
		Common Stock (Equity ↑; credit)		10,000
		Issued common stock.		

The total dollar amounts of debits must always equal the total dollar amounts of credits.

Remember to use the transaction letters as references. This will help as we post entries to the T-accounts.

Each T-account has 2 sides—one for recording debits and the other for recording credits. To post the transaction to a T-account, simply transfer the amount of each debit to the correct account as a debit (left-side) entry, and transfer the amount of each credit to the correct account as a credit (right-side) entry.

This transaction includes a debit of $10,000 to cash. This means that $10,000 is posted to the left side of the Cash T-account. The transaction also includes a credit of $10,000 to Common Stock. This means that $10,000 is posted to the right side of the Common Stock account, as follows:

	Cash			Common Stock	
a.	10,000			a.	10,000

Now the first transaction has been journalized and posted. We repeat this process for every journal entry. Let's proceed to the next transaction.

b. The business purchased equipment for $3,500 on account.

The business received equipment in exchange for a promise to pay for the $3,500 cost at a future date. So the accounts involved in the transaction are Equipment and Accounts Payable.

Equipment is an asset and Accounts Payable is a liability.

The asset Equipment has increased. The liability Accounts Payable has also increased.

Looking at Exhibit 2-16 (p. 746), an increase in assets (in this case, the increase in Equipment) is a debit, while an increase in liabilities (in this case, Accounts Payable) is a credit.

The journal entry follows.

b.	Equipment (Asset ↑; debit)	3,500	
	Accounts Payable (Liability ↑; credit)		3,500
	Purchased equipment on account.		

$3,500 is then posted to the debit (left) side of the Equipment T-account. $3,500 is posted to the credit (right) side of Accounts Payable, as follows:

Equipment		Accounts Payable	
b. 3,500		b. 3,500	

c. The business purchased office supplies for $800 cash.

The business purchased supplies, paying cash of $800. So the accounts involved in the transaction are Supplies and Cash.

Supplies and Cash are both assets.

Supplies (an asset) has increased. Cash (an asset) has decreased.

Looking at Exhibit 2-16 (p. 746), an increase in assets is a debit, while a decrease in assets is a credit.

So the increase to Supplies (an asset) is a debit, while the decrease to Cash (an asset) is a credit.

The journal entry follows:

c.	Supplies (Asset ↑; debit)	800	
	Cash (Asset ↓; credit)		800
	Purchased supplies for cash.		

$800 is then posted to the debit (left) side of the Supplies T-account. $800 is posted to the credit (right) side of the Cash account, as follows:

	Cash				Supplies
a.	10,000			c.	800
		c.	800		

Notice the $10,000 already on the debit side of the Cash account. This came from transaction a.

d. The business provided $2,600 of services to a customer on account.

The business rendered service for a customer and received a promise from the customer to pay us $2,600 cash next month. So the accounts involved in the transaction are Accounts Receivable and Service Revenue.

Accounts Receivable is an asset and Service Revenue is revenue.

Accounts Receivable (an asset) has increased. Service Revenue (revenue) has also increased.

Looking at Exhibit 2-16 (p. 746), an increase in assets is a debit, while an increase in revenue is a credit.

So the increase to Accounts Receivable (an asset) is a debit, while the increase to Service Revenue (revenue) is a credit.

The journal entry follows.

d.		Accounts Receivable (Asset ↑; debit)	2,600	
		Service Revenue (Revenue ↑; credit)		2,600
		Provided services on account.		

$2,600 is posted to the debit (left) side of the Accounts Receivable T-account. $2,600 is posted to the credit (right) side of the Service Revenue account, as follows:

	Accounts Receivable			Service Revenue	
d.	2,600			d.	2,600

e. The business paid $500 cash toward the equipment previously purchased on account in transaction b.

The business paid some of the money that it owed on the purchase of equipment in transaction b. The accounts involved in the transaction are Accounts Payable and Cash.

Accounts Payable is a liability that has decreased. Cash is an asset that has also decreased.

Remember that Accounts Payable shows the amount the business must pay in the future (a liability). When the business pays these creditors, Accounts Payable will decrease because the business will then owe less (in this case, Accounts Payable drops from $3,500—in transaction b—to $3,000).

Looking at Exhibit 2-16 (p. 746), a decrease in liabilities is a debit, while a decrease in assets is a credit.

So Accounts Payable (a liability) decreases, which is a debit. Cash (an asset) decreases, which is a credit.

e.		Accounts Payable (Liability ↓; debit)	500	
		Cash (Asset ↓; credit)		500
		Partial payment on account.		

$500 is posted to the debit (left) side of the Accounts Payable T-account. $500 is posted to the credit (right) side of the Cash account, as follows:

	Cash					Accounts Payable		
a.	10,000						b.	3,500
		c.	800		e.	500		
		e.	500					

Again notice the amounts already in the T-accounts from previous transactions. The reference letters show which transaction caused each amount to appear in the T-account.

f. The business received $2,000 in cash for services provided to a new customer.

The business received $2,000 cash in exchange for mowing and landscaping services rendered to a customer. The accounts involved in the transaction are Cash and Service Revenue.

Cash is an asset that has increased and Service Revenue is revenue, which has also increased.

Looking at Exhibit 2-16 (p. 746), an increase in assets is a debit, while an increase in revenue is a credit.

So the increase to Cash (an asset) is a debit. The increase to Service Revenue (revenue) is a credit.

f.		Cash (Asset ↑; debit)	2,000	
		Service Revenue (Revenue ↑; credit)		2,000
		Provided services for cash.		

$2,000 is then posted to the debit (left) side of the Cash T-account. $2,000 is posted to the credit (right) side of the Service Revenue account, as follows:

	Cash					Service Revenue		
a.	10,000						d.	2,600
		c.	800				f.	2,000
		e.	500					
f.	2,000							

Notice how we keep adding onto the T-accounts. The values from previous transactions remain in their places.

g. The business paid $200 cash to repair equipment.

The business paid $200 cash to have equipment repaired. Because the benefit of the repairs has already been used, the repairs are recorded as Repair Expense. Because the repairs were paid in cash, the Cash account is also involved.

Repair Expense is an expense that has increased and Cash is an asset that has decreased.

Looking at Exhibit 2-16 (p. 746), an increase in expenses calls for a debit, while a decrease in an asset requires a credit.

So Repair Expense (an expense) increases, which is a debit. Cash (an asset) decreases, which is a credit.

g.	Repair Expense (Expense ↑ ; debit)	200	
	Cash (Asset ↓ ; credit)		200
	Paid for repairs.		

$200 is then posted to the debit (left) side of the Repair Expense T-account. $200 is posted to the credit (right) side of the Cash account, as follows:

	Cash					Repair Expense	
a.	10,000				g.	200	
		c.	800				
		e.	500				
f.	2,000						
		g.	200				

h. The business paid $900 cash for salary expense.

The business paid employees $900 in cash. Because the benefit of the employees' work has already been used, their salaries are recorded as Salary Expense. Because the salaries were paid in cash, the Cash account is also involved.

Salary Expense is an expense that has increased and Cash is an asset that has decreased.

Looking at Exhibit 2-16 (p. 746), an increase in expenses is a debit, while a decrease in an asset is a credit.

In this case, Salary Expense (an expense) increases, which is a debit. Cash (an asset) decreases, which is a credit.

h.	Salary Expense (Expense ↑ ; debit)	900	
	Cash (Asset ↓ ; credit)		900
	Paid salary.		

$900 is posted to the debit (left) side of the Salary Expense T-account. $900 is posted to the credit (right) side of the Cash account, as follows:

	Cash						Salary Expense		
a.	10,000					h.	900	
		c.	800					
		e.	500					
f.	2,000							
		g.	200					
		h.	900					

i. The business received $2,100 cash from a customer on account.

The business received cash of $2,100 from a customer for services previously provided in transaction **d**. The accounts affected by this transaction are Cash and Accounts Receivable.

Cash and Accounts Receivable are both assets.

The asset Cash has increased, and the asset Accounts Receivable has decreased.

Remember, Accounts Receivable shows the amount of cash the business has coming from customers. When the business receives cash from these customers, Accounts Receivable will decrease, because the business will have less to receive in the future (in this case, it reduces from $2,600—in transaction d—to $500).

Looking at Exhibit 2-16 (p. 746), an increase in assets is a debit, while a decrease in assets is a credit.

So Cash (an asset) increases, which is a debit. Accounts Receivable (an asset) decreases, which is a credit.

i.	Cash (Asset ↑; debit)	2,100	
	Accounts Receivable (Asset ↓; credit)		2,100
	Received cash on account.		

$2,100 is posted to the debit (left) side of the Cash T-account. $2,100 is posted to the credit (right) side of the Accounts Receivable account, as follows:

	Cash						Accounts Receivable		
a.	10,000					d.	2,600		
		c.	800					i.	2,100
		e.	500						
f.	2,000								
		g.	200						
		h.	900						
i.	2,100								

j. The business declared and paid cash dividends of $1,500.

The business paid Michael dividends from the earnings it had retained on his behalf. This caused Michael's ownership interest (equity) to decrease. The accounts involved in this transaction are Dividends and Cash.

Dividends have increased and Cash is an asset that has decreased.

Looking at Exhibit 2-16 (p. 746), an increase in dividends is a debit, while a decrease in an asset is a credit.

Remember that Dividends are a negative element of stockholders' equity. Therefore, when Dividends increase, stockholders' equity decreases. So in this case, Dividends decrease equity with a debit. Cash (an asset) decreases with a credit.

j.	Dividends (Dividends ↑; debit)	1,500	
	Cash (Asset ↓; credit)		1,500
	Paid dividends.		

$1,500 is posted to the debit (left) side of the Dividends T-account. $1,500 is posted to the credit (right) side of the Cash account, as follows:

	Cash					Dividends	
a.	10,000				j.	1,500	
		c.	800				
		e.	500				
f.	2,000						
		g.	200				
		h.	900				
i.	2,100						
		j.	1,500				

Now we can summarize all of the journal entries during the month:

Requirement 3

Total each T-account to determine its balance at the end of the month.

Part 1	Part 2	**Part 3**	Demo Doc Complete

Ref.		Accounts and Explanation	Debit	Credit
a.		Cash	10,000	
		Common Stock		10,000
		Issued common stock.		
b.		Equipment	3,500	
		Accounts Payable		3,500
		Purchased equipment on account.		
c.		Supplies	800	
		Cash		800
		Purchased supplies for cash.		
d.		Accounts Receivable	2,600	
		Service Revenue		2,600
		Provided services on account.		
e.		Accounts Payable	500	
		Cash		500
		Partial payment on account.		
f.		Cash	2,000	
		Service Revenue		2,000
		Provided services for cash.		
g.		Repair Expense	200	
		Cash		200
		Paid for repairs.		
h.		Salary Expense	900	
		Cash		900
		Paid salary.		
i.		Cash	2,100	
		Accounts Receivable		2,100
		Received cash on account.		
j.		Dividends	1,500	
		Cash		1,500
		Paid dividends.		

To compute the balance in a T-account (total the T-account), add up the numbers on the debit/left side of the account and (separately) add the credit/right side of the account. The difference between the total debits and the total credits is the account's balance, which is placed on the side that holds the larger total. This gives the balance in the T-account.

For example, for the Cash account, the numbers on the debit/left side total $10,000 + $2,000 + $2,100 = $14,100. The credit/right side = $800 + $500 + $200 + $900 + $1,500 = $3,900. The difference is $14,100 − $3,900 = $10,200. At the end of the period Cash has a debit balance of $10,200. We put the $10,200 at the bottom of the debit side because that was the side that showed the bigger total ($14,100). This is called a debit balance.

An easy way to think of totaling T-accounts is:

> Beginning balance in a T-account
> + Increases to the T-account
> − Decreases to the T-account
> T-account balance (net total)

T-accounts after posting all transactions and totaling each account:

| | | | ASSETS | | | = | | LIABILITIES | + | STOCKHOLDERS' EQUITY | |

Cash

a.	10,000		
		c.	800
		e.	500
f.	2,000		
		g.	200
		h.	900
i.	2,100		
		j.	1,500
Bal.	10,200		

Accounts Receivable

d.	2,600		
		i.	2,100
Bal.	500		

Supplies

c.	800	
Bal.	800	

Equipment

b.	3,500	
Bal.	3,500	

Accounts Payable

		b.	3,500
e.	500		
		Bal.	3,000

Common Stock

		a.	10,000
		Bal.	10,000

Dividends

j.	1,500	
Bal.	1,500	

REVENUE

Service Revenue

		d.	2,600
		f.	2,000
		Bal.	4,600

EXPENSES

Salary Expense

h.	900	
Bal.	900	

Repair Expense

g.	200	
Bal.	200	

Requirement 4

The trial balance lists all the accounts along with their balances. This listing is helpful because it summarizes all the accounts in one place. Otherwise one must plow through all the T-accounts to find the balance of Accounts Payable, Salary Expense, or any other account.

The trial balance is an *internal* accounting document that accountants and managers use to prepare the financial statements. It's not like the income statement and balance sheet, which are presented to the public.

Data for the trial balance come directly from the T-accounts that we prepared in Requirement 3. A debit balance in a T-account remains a debit in the trial balance, and likewise for credits. For example, the T-account for Cash shows a debit balance of $10,200, and the trial balance lists Cash the same way. The Accounts Payable T-account shows a $3,000 credit balance, and the trial balance lists Accounts Payable correctly.

The trial balance or Moe's Mowing at September 30, 2008, appears as follows. Notice that we list the accounts in their proper order—assets, liabilities, stockholder's equity, revenues, and expenses.

Moe's Mowing, Inc.
Trial Balance
September 30, 2008

		Balance	
		Debit	Credit
Assets	Cash	$10,200	
	Accounts receivable	500	
	Supplies	800	
	Equipment	3,500	
Liabilities	Accounts payable		$ 3,000
Equity	Common stock		10,000
	Dividends	1,500	
Revenues	Service revenue		4,600
Expenses	Salary expense	900	
	Repair expense	200	
	Total	$17,600	$17,600

You should trace each account from the T-accounts to the trial balance.

Part 1	Part 2	Part 3	**Demo Doc Complete**

Demo Doc for Chapter 3

Preparation of Adjusting Entries, Closing Entries, and Financial Statements

Demo Doc: To make sure you understand this material, work through the following demonstration "Demo Doc" with detailed comments to help you see the concept within the framework of a worked-through problem.

Learning Objectives 2–5

Cloud Break Consulting, Inc., has the following information at June 30, 2008:

CLOUD BREAK CONSULTING, INC.
Unadjusted Trial Balance
June 30, 2008

Account Title	Balance Debit	Balance Credit
Cash	$131,000	
Accounts receivable	104,000	
Supplies	4,000	
Prepaid rent	27,000	
Land	45,000	
Building	300,000	
Accumulated depreciation—building		$155,000
Accounts payable		159,000
Unearned service revenue		40,000
Common stock		50,000
Retained earnings		52,000
Dividends	7,000	
Service revenue		450,000
Salary expense	255,000	
Rent expense	25,000	
Miscellaneous expense	8,000	
Total	$906,000	$906,000

June 30 is Cloud Break's fiscal year end; accordingly, it must make adjusting entries for the following items:

a. **Supplies on hand at year-end, $1,000.**

b. **Nine months of rent totaling $27,000 were paid in advance on April 1, 2008. Cloud Break has recorded no rent expense yet.**

c. **Depreciation expense has not been recorded on the building for the 2008 fiscal year. The building has a useful life of 25 years.**

d. **Employees work Monday through Friday. The weekly payroll is $5,000 and is paid every Friday. June 30, 2008, falls on a Thursday.**

(continued)

e. Service revenue of $15,000 must be accrued.

f. Cloud Break received $40,000 in advance for consulting services to be provided evenly from January 1, 2008 through August 31, 2008. Cloud Break has recorded none of this revenue.

Requirements

1. Open the T-accounts with their unadjusted balances.

2. Journalize Cloud Break's adjusting entries at June 30, 2008, and post the entries to the T-accounts.

3. Total each T-account in the ledger.

4. Journalize and post Cloud Break's closing entries.

5. Prepare Cloud Break's income statement and statement of retained earnings for the year ended June 30, 2008, and the balance sheet at June 30, 2008. Draw arrows linking the 3 financial statements.

Demo Doc Solutions

Requirement 1

Open the T-accounts with their unadjusted balances.

Part 1	Part 2	Part 3	Part 4	Part 5	Part 6	Part 7	Demo Doc Complete

Remember from Chapter 2 that opening a T-account means drawing a blank account that looks like a capital "T" and putting the account title across the top. To help find the accounts later, they are grouped into assets, liabilities, stockholders' equity, revenues, and expenses (in that order). If the account has a starting balance, it **must** appear on the correct side.

Remember that debits are always on the left side of the T-account and credits are always on the right side. This is true for *every* account.

The correct side to enter each account's starting balance is the side of *increase* in the account. This is because we expect all accounts to have a *positive* balance (that is, more increases than decreases).

For assets, an increase is a debit, so we would expect all assets (except contra assets such as Accumulated Depreciation) to have a debit balance. For liabilities and stockholders' equity, an increase is a credit, so we would expect all liabilities and equities (except Dividends) to have a credit balance. By the same reasoning, we expect revenues to have credit balances and expenses and dividends to have debit balances.

The unadjusted balances appearing in the T-accounts are simply the amounts from the starting trial balance.

ASSETS		STOCKHOLDERS' EQUITY	EXPENSES

ASSETS

Cash
Bal. 131,000

Accounts Receivable
Bal. 104,000

Supplies
Bal. 4,000

Prepaid Rent
Bal. 27,000

Land
Bal. 45,000

Building
Bal. 300,000

Accumulated Depreciation—Building
Bal. 155,000

LIABILITIES

Accounts Payable
Bal. 159,000

Unearned Service Revenue
Bal. 40,000

STOCKHOLDERS' EQUITY

Common Stock
Bal. 50,000

Retained Earnings
Bal. 52,000

Dividends
Bal. 7,000

REVENUE

Service Revenue
Bal. 450,000

EXPENSES

Salary Expense
Bal. 255,000

Rent Expense
Bal. 25,000

Miscellaneous Expense
Bal. 8,000

Requirement 2

Journalize Cloud Break's adjusting entries at June 30, 2008, and post the entries to the T-accounts.

Part 1	**Part 2**	Part 3	Part 4	Part 5	Part 6	Part 7	Demo Doc Complete

a. Supplies on hand at year end, $1,000.

On June 30, 2008, the unadjusted balance in the Supplies account was $4,000. However, a count shows that only $1,000 of supplies actually remains on hand. The supplies that are no longer there have been used. When assets/benefits are used, an expense is created.

Cloud Break will need to make an adjusting journal entry in order to report the correct amount of supplies on the balance sheet.

Looking at the Supplies T-account:

Supplies			
4,000			
		Used up	X
Bal.	1,000		

The supplies have decreased because they have been used up. The amount of the decrease is **X. X** = $4,000 − $1,000 = $3,000.

$3,000 of supplies expense must be recorded to show the value of supplies that have been used.

a.	June 30	Supplies Expense ($4,000 – $1,000) (Expense ↑; debit)	3,000	
		Supplies (Asset ↓; credit)		3,000
		To record supplies expense.		

After posting, Supplies and Supplies Expense hold their correct ending balances:

ASSETS				EXPENSES		
Supplies				Supplies Expense		
4,000				a.	3,000	
		a.	3,000	Bal.	3,000	
Bal.	1,000					

b. Nine months of rent (totalling $27,000) were paid in advance on April 1, 2008. Cloud Break has recorded no rent expense yet.

A prepayment for something, such as for rent or insurance, creates a *future* benefit (an asset) because the business is now entitled to receive the prepaid goods or services. Once those goods or services are received (in this case, once Cloud Break has occupied the building being rented), the benefit expires, and the prepaid cost becomes an expense.

Cloud Break prepaid $27,000 for 9 months of rent on April 1. This means that Cloud Break pays $27,000/9 = $3,000 a month for rent. At June 30, Prepaid Rent is adjusted for the amount of the asset that has been used up. Because Cloud Break has occupied the building being rented for 3 months (April, May, and June), 3 months of the prepayment have been used. The amount of rent used is $3 \times \$3,000 = \$9,000$. Because that portion of the past benefit (asset) has expired, it becomes an expense (in this case, the adjustment transfers $9,000 from Prepaid Rent to Rent Expense).

This means that Rent Expense must be increased (a debit) and Prepaid Rent (an asset) must be decreased (a credit), with the following journal entry:

b.	June 30	Rent Expense (Expense ↑; debit)	9,000	
		Prepaid Rent (Asset ↓; credit)		9,000
		To record rent expense.		

Posting places $9,000 in each account, as follows:

	ASSETS				EXPENSES	
	Prepaid Rent				**Rent Expense**	
	27,000				25,000	
		b.	9,000	b.	9,000	
Bal.	18,000			Bal.	34,000	

c. Depreciation expense has not been recorded on the building for the 2008 fiscal year. The building has a useful life of 25 years.

Depreciation expense per year is calculated as:

$$\text{Depreciation expense per year} = \frac{\text{Original cost of asset}}{\text{Useful life of asset (in years)}}$$

The cost principle compels us to keep the original cost of a plant asset in that asset account. Because there is $300,000 in the Building account, we know that this is the original cost of the building. We are told in the question that the building's useful life is 25 years.

$$\text{Depreciation expense per year} = \$300,000/25 \text{ years} = \$12,000 \text{ per year}$$

We will record depreciation of $12,000 in an adjusting journal entry. The journal entry for depreciation expense is *always* the same. Only the dollar amount changes. There is always an increase to Depreciation Expense (a debit) and an increase to the contra-asset account of Accumulated Depreciation (a credit).

c.	June 30	Depreciation Expense—Building (Expense ↑; debit)	12,000	
		Accumulated Depreciation—Building		
		(Contra Asset ↑; credit)		12,000
		To record depreciation on building.		

ASSETS				EXPENSES	
ASSET		**CONTRA ASSET**			
Building		**Accumulated Depreciation— Building**		**Depreciation Expense— Building**	
300,000			155,000	c.	12,000
		c.	12,000		
Bal.	300,000	Bal.	167,000	Bal.	12,000

The book value of the building is its original cost (the amount in the Building T-account) minus the accumulated depreciation on the building.

Book value of plant assets:	
Building..	$300,000
Less: Accumulated depreciation	(167,000)
Book value of the building	$133,000

d. Employees work Monday through Friday. The weekly payroll is $5,000 and is paid every Friday. June 30, 2008, falls on a Thursday.

Salary is an accrued expense. That is, it's a liability that comes from an *expense* that hasn't been paid yet. Most employers pay their employees *after* the work has been done, so the work is a past benefit to the employer. This expense (Salary Expense, in this case) grows until payday.

Cloud Break's employees are paid $5,000 for 5 days of work. That means they earn $5,000/5 = $1,000 per day. By the end of the day on Thursday, June 30, they have earned $1,000/day × 4 days = $4,000 of salary.

If the salaries have not been paid, then they are pay*able* (or in other words, they are *owed*) and must be recorded as some kind of payable account. You might be tempted to use Accounts Payable, but this account is usually reserved for *bills* received. But employees don't bill employers for their paychecks. The appropriate payable account for salaries is Salary Payable.

The accrual of salary expense creates an increase to Salary Expense (a debit) and an increase to the liability Salary Payable (a credit) of $4,000.

d.	June 30	Salary Expense (Expense ↑; debit)	4,000	
		Salary Payable (Liability ↑; credit)		4,000
		To accrue salary expense.		

EXPENSES			LIABILITIES		
Salary Expense			**Salary Payable**		
	255,000		d.		4,000
d.	4,000				
Bal.	259,000		Bal.		4,000

e. Service revenue of $15,000 must be accrued.

Accrued revenue is another way of saying "accounts receivable" (or receipt in the future). When *accrued* revenue is recorded, it means that accounts receivable are also recorded (that is, the business gave goods or services to customers, but the business has not yet received the cash). The business is entitled to these receivables because the revenue has been earned.

Service Revenue must be increased by $15,000 (a credit) and the Accounts Receivable asset must be increased by $15,000 (a debit).

e.	June 30	Accounts Receivable (Asset ↑; debit)	15,000	
		Service Revenue (Revenue ↑; credit)		15,000
		To accrue service revenue.		

ASSETS			REVENUES		
Accounts Receivable			**Service Revenue**		
	104,000				450,000
e.	15,000			e.	15,000
Bal.	119,000			Bal.	465,000

f. Cloud Break received $40,000 in advance for consulting services to be provided evenly from January 1, 2008, through August 31, 2008. Cloud Break has recorded none of this revenue.

Cloud Break received cash in advance for work to be performed in the future. By accepting the cash, Cloud Break also accepted the obligation to perform that work (or provide a refund). In accounting, an obligation is a liability. We call this liability "unearned revenue" because it *will* be revenue (after the work is performed) but it is not revenue *yet*.

The $40,000 collected in advance is still in the Unearned Service Revenue account. However, some of the revenue has been earned as of June 30. Six months of the earnings period have passed (January through June), so Cloud Break has earned 6 months of the revenue.

The entire revenue-earning period is 8 months (January through August), so the revenue earned per month is $40,000/8 = $5,000. The 6 months of revenue that Cloud Break has earned through the end of June totals $30,000 (6 × $5,000).

So Unearned Service Revenue, a liability, must be decreased by $30,000 (a debit). Because that portion of the revenue is now earned, Service Revenue is increased by $30,000 (a credit).

f.	June 30	Unearned Service Revenue (Liability ↓; debit)	30,000	
		Service Revenue (Revenue ↑; credit)		30,000
		To record the earning of service revenue that was *collected in advance.*		

Essentially, the $30,000 has been shifted from "unearned revenue" to "earned" revenue.

	LIABILITIES			REVENUES	
	Unearned Service Revenue			**Service Revenue**	
		40,000			450,000
f.	30,000		e.		15,000
			f.		30,000
	Bal.	10,000		Bal.	495,000

Now we can summarize all of the adjusting journal entries:

Ref.	Date	Accounts and Explanation	Debit	Credit
	2008			
a.	June 30	Supplies Expense ($4,000 – $1,000)	3,000	
		Supplies		3,000
		To record supplies expense.		
b.	30	Rent Expense	9,000	
		Prepaid Rent		9,000
		To record rent expense.		
c.	30	Depreciation Expense—Building	12,000	
		Accumulated Depreciation—Building		12,000
		To record depreciation on building.		
d.	30	Salary Expense	4,000	
		Salary Payable		4,000
		To accrue salary expense.		
e.	30	Accounts Receivable	15,000	
		Service Revenue		15,000
		To accrue service revenue.		
f.	30	Unearned Service Revenue	30,000	
		Service Revenue		30,000
		To record the earning of service revenue that was *collected in advance.*		

Requirement 3

Total each T-account in the ledger.

Part 1	Part 2	**Part 3**	Part 4	Part 5	Part 6	Part 7	Demo Doc Complete

After posting all of these entries and totaling all of the T-accounts, we have:

ASSETS

Cash

Bal. 131,000	

Accounts Receivable

104,000	
e. 15,000	
Bal. 119,000	

Supplies

4,000		
	a.	3,000
Bal. 1,000		

Prepaid Rent

27,000		
	b.	9,000
Bal. 18,000		

Land

Bal. 45,000	

Building

Bal. 300,000	

Accumulated Depreciation—Building

		155,000
	c.	12,000
	Bal.	167,000

LIABILITIES

Accounts Payable

	Bal. 159,000

Salary Payable

	d.	4,000
	Bal.	4,000

Unearned Service Revenue

		40,000
f. 30,000		
	Bal.	10,000

STOCKHOLDERS' EQUITY

Common Stock

	Bal.	50,000

Retained Earnings

	Bal.	52,000

Dividends

Bal. 7,000	

REVENUE

Service Revenue

		450,000
	e.	15,000
	f.	30,000
	Bal.	495,000

EXPENSES

Salary Expense

255,000	
d. 4,000	
Bal. 259,000	

Supplies Expense

a. 3,000	
Bal. 3,000	

Rent Expense

25,000	
b. 9,000	
Bal. 34,000	

Depreciation Expense— Building

c. 12,000	
Bal. 12,000	

Miscellaneous Expense

Bal. 8,000	

Requirement 4

Journalize and post Cloud Break's closing entries.

Part 1	Part 2	Part 3	**Part 4**	Part 5	Part 6	Part 7	Demo Doc Complete

We prepare closing entries to (1) clear out the revenue, expense, and dividends accounts to a zero balance in order to get them ready for the next period. They must begin the next period empty so that we can evaluate each period's income separately from all other periods. We also need to (2) update the Retained Earnings account by transferring all revenues, expenses, and dividends into it.

The Retained Earnings balance is calculated each year using the following formula:

Beginning retained earnings
+ Net income (or − Net loss)
− Dividends declared
= Ending retained earnings

You can see this in the Retained Earnings T-account as well:

Retained Earnings	
	Beginning retained earnings
	Net income
Dividends	
	Ending retained earnings

This formula is the key to preparing the closing entries. We will use this formula, but we will do it *inside* the Retained Earnings T-account.

From the trial balance given in the problem, we know that beginning Retained Earnings is $52,000. The first component of the formula is already in the T-account.

The next component is net income, which is *not* yet in the Retained Earnings account. There is no T-account with net income in it, but we can place all the components of net income into the Retained Earnings account and come out with the net income number at the bottom. Remember:

Revenues − Expenses = Net income

This means that we need to get all of the revenues and expenses into the Retained Earnings account.

We start with our revenue T-account:

Service Revenue		
	Bal.	495,000

In order to clear out all the income statement accounts so that they are empty to begin the next year, the first step is to debit each revenue account for the amount of its credit balance. Service Revenue has a *credit* balance of $495,000, so to bring that to zero, we need to *debit* Service Revenue for $495,000.

This means that we have part of our first closing entry:

1.	Service Revenue	495,000	
	???		495,000

What is the credit side of this entry? The reason we started with Service Revenue was to help calculate net income in the Retained Earnings account. So the other side of the entry must go to Retained Earnings:

1.	Service Revenue	495,000	
	Retained Earnings		495,000

Part 1	Part 2	Part 3	Part 4	**Part 5**	Part 6	Part 7	Demo Doc Complete

The second step is to *credit* each expense account for the amount of its *debit* balance to bring each expense account to zero. In this case, we have 5 different expenses:

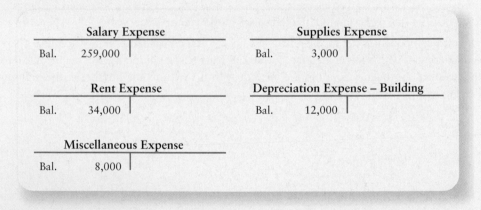

	Salary Expense			Supplies Expense	
Bal.	259,000		Bal.	3,000	

	Rent Expense			Depreciation Expense – Building	
Bal.	34,000		Bal.	12,000	

	Miscellaneous Expense	
Bal.	8,000	

The sum of all the expenses will go to the debit side of the Retained Earnings account:

2.	Retained Earnings	316,000	
	Salary Expense		259,000
	Supplies Expense		3,000
	Rent Expense		34,000
	Depreciation Expense—Building		12,000
	Miscellaneous Expense		8,000

The last component of the Retained Earnings formula is dividends. There is a Dividends account:

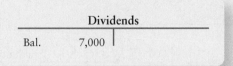

	Dividends	
Bal.	7,000	

The final step in the closing process is to transfer Dividends to the debit side of the Retained Earnings account. The Dividends account has a *debit* balance of $7,000, so to bring that to zero, we need to *credit* Dividends by $7,000. The balancing debit will go to Retained Earnings:

3.	Retained Earnings		7,000	
	Dividends			7,000

This entry subtracts Dividends from Retained Earnings. Retained Earnings now holds the following data:

Retained Earnings

				52,000	**Beginning retained earnings**
Expenses	2.	316,000	1.	495,000	Revenue } Net income
Dividends	3.	7,000			
			Bal.	224,000	**Ending retained earnings**

The formula to update Retained Earnings has now been re-created inside the Retained Earnings T-account.

The following accounts are included in the closing process:

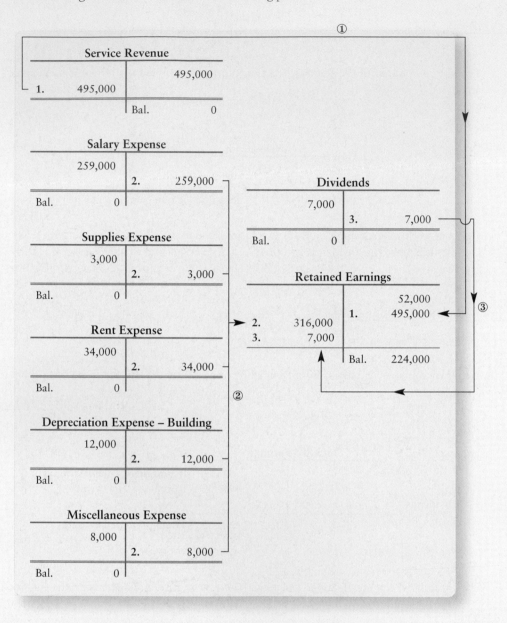

Notice that each temporary account (the revenues, the expenses, and Dividends), now has a zero balance.

Requirement 5

Prepare Cloud Break's income statement and the statement of retained earnings for the year ended June 30, 2008, and the balance sheet at June 30, 2008. Draw arrows linking the 3 financial statements.

| Part 1 | Part 2 | Part 3 | Part 4 | Part 5 | Part 6 | **Part 7** | Demo Doc Complete |

CLOUD BREAK CONSULTING, INC.
Income Statement
Year Ended June 30, 2008

Revenue:		
Service revenue		$495,000
Expenses:		
Salary expense	$259,000	
Rent expense	34,000	
Depreciation expense—building	12,000	
Supplies expense	3,000	
Miscellaneous expense	8,000	
Total expenses		316,000
Net income		$179,000

CLOUD BREAK CONSULTING, INC.
Statement of Retained Earnings
Year Ended June 30, 2008

Retained earnings, June 30, 2007	$ 52,000
Add: Net income	179,000
	231,000
Less: Dividends	(7,000)
Retained earnings, June 30, 2008	$224,000

CLOUD BREAK CONSULTING, INC.
Balance Sheet
June 30, 2008

Assets			Liabilities	
Cash		$131,000	Accounts payable	$159,000
Accounts receivable		119,000	Salary payable	4,000
Supplies		1,000	Unearned service revenue	10,000
Prepaid rent		18,000	Total liabilities	173,000
Land		45,000		
Building	$300,000		**Stockholders' Equity**	
Less: Accumulated			Common stock	50,000
depreciation	(167,000)	133,000	Retained earnings	224,000
			Total stockholders' equity	274,000
			Total liabilities and	
Total assets		$447,000	stockholders' equity	$447,000

RELATIONSHIPS AMONG THE FINANCIAL STATEMENTS

The arrows in these statements show how the financial statements relate to each other. Follow the arrow that takes the ending balance of Retained Earnings to the balance sheet.

1. Net income from the income statements is reported as an increase to Retained Earnings on the statement of retained earnings. A net loss would be reported as a decrease to Retained Earnings.

2. Ending Retained Earnings from the statement of retained earnings is transferred to the balance sheet. The ending Retained Earnings is the final balancing amount for the balance sheet.

| Part 1 | Part 2 | Part 3 | Part 4 | Part 5 | Part 6 | Part 7 | Demo Doc Complete |

Report of Independent Registered Public Accounting Firm

The Board of Directors and Shareholders
YUM! Brands, Inc.:

We have audited the accompanying consolidated balance sheets of YUM! Brands, Inc. and Subsidiaries ("YUM") as of December 30, 2006 and December 31, 2005, and the related consolidated statements of income, cash flows and shareholders' equity and comprehensive income for each of the years in the three-year period ended December 30, 2006. These consolidated financial statements are the responsibility of YUM's management. Our responsibility is to express an opinion on these consolidated financial statements based on our audits.

We conducted our audits in accordance with the standards of the Public Company Accounting Oversight Board (United States). Those standards require that we plan and perform the audit to obtain reasonable assurance about whether the financial statements are free of material misstatement. An audit includes examining, on a test basis, evidence supporting the amounts and disclosures in the financial statements. An audit also includes assessing the accounting principles used and significant estimates made by management, as well as evaluating the overall financial statement presentation. We believe that our audits provide a reasonable basis for our opinion.

In our opinion, the consolidated financial statements referred to above present fairly, in all material respects, the financial position of YUM as of December 30, 2006 and December 31, 2005, and the results of its operations and its cash flows for each of the years in the three-year period ended December 30, 2006, in conformity with U.S. generally accepted accounting principles.

We also have audited, in accordance with the standards of the Public Company Accounting Oversight Board (United States), the effectiveness of YUM's internal control over financial reporting as of December 30, 2006, based on criteria established in *Internal Control—Integrated Framework* issued by the Committee of Sponsoring Organizations of the Treadway Commission (COSO), and our report dated February 28, 2007 expressed an unqualified opinion on management's assessment of, and the effective operation of, internal control over financial reporting.

As discussed in Notes 2 and 16 to the consolidated financial statements, YUM adopted the provisions of the Financial Accounting Standards Board's Statement of Financial Accounting Standards No. 123R (Revised 2004), "Share-Based Payment," and changed its method for accounting for share-based payments in 2005.

As discussed in Note 2 to the consolidated financial statements, YUM changed its method of quantifying errors in 2006. Also, as discussed in Notes 2 and 15 to the consolidated financial statements, YUM adopted the provisions of the Financial Accounting Standards Board's Statement of Financial Accounting Standards No. 158, "Employers' Accounting for Defined Benefit Pension and Other Postretirement Plans—an amendment of FASB Statements No. 87, 88, 106 and 132 (R)," in 2006.

KPMG LLP

KPMG LLP
Louisville, Kentucky
February 28, 2007

Management's Report on Internal Control Over Financial Reporting

Our management is responsible for establishing and maintaining adequate internal control over financial reporting, as such term is defined in Rule 13a-15(f) under the Securities Exchange Act of 1934. Under the supervision and with the participation of our management, including our principal executive officer and principal financial officer, we conducted an evaluation of the effectiveness of our internal control over financial reporting based on the framework in *Internal Control — Integrated Framework* issued by the Committee of Sponsoring Organizations of the Treadway Commission. Based on our evaluation under the framework in *Internal Control — Integrated Framework*, our management concluded that our internal control over financial reporting was effective as of December 30, 2006. Our management's assessment of the effectiveness of our internal control over financial reporting as of December 30, 2006 has been audited by KPMG LLP, an independent registered public accounting firm, as stated in their report which is included herein.

Supplement to Yum! Brands, Inc. Annual Report to Shareholders

On June 12, 2006, David Novak, Yum Brands, Inc. Chairman and Chief Executive Officer submitted a certification to the New York Stock Exchange (the NYSE) as required by Section 303A.12(a) of the NYSE Listed Company Manual. This certification indicated that Mr. Novak was not aware of any violations by the Company of NYSE Corporate Governance listing standards.

In connection with the filing of the Company's Form 10-K for the year ended December 30, 2006, the Company has included as exhibits certifications signed by Mr. Novak and Mr. Richard Carucci, Chief Financial Officer, pursuant to Rule 13a-14(a) of Securities Exchange Act of 1934, as adopted pursuant to Section 302 of the Sarbanes-Oxley Act of 2002.

These statements are required by the NYSE as part of the Company's Annual Report to Shareholders.

Consolidated Statements of Income
YUM! Brands, Inc. and Subsidiaries

Fiscal years ended December 30, 2006,
December 31, 2005 and December 25, 2004
(in millions, except per share data)

	2006	2005	2004
Revenues			
Company sales	$ 8,365	$ 8,225	$ 7,992
Franchise and license fees	1,196	1,124	1,019
Total revenues	9,561	9,349	9,011
Costs and Expenses, Net			
Company restaurants			
Food and paper	2,549	2,584	2,538
Payroll and employee benefits	2,142	2,171	2,112
Occupancy and other operating expenses	2,403	2,315	2,183
	7,094	7,070	6,833
General and administrative expenses	1,187	1,158	1,056
Franchise and license expenses	35	33	26
Closures and impairment expenses	59	62	38
Refranchising (gain) loss	(24)	(43)	(12)
Other (income) expense	(51)	(80)	(55)
Wrench litigation (income) expense	—	(2)	(14)
AmeriServe and other charges (credits)	(1)	(2)	(16)
Total costs and expenses, net	8,299	8,196	7,856
Operating Profit	1,262	1,153	1,155
Interest expense, net	154	127	129
Income before Income Taxes	1,108	1,026	1,026
Income tax provision	284	264	286
Net Income	$ 824	$ 762	$ 740
Basic Earnings Per Common Share	$ 3.02	$ 2.66	$ 2.54
Diluted Earnings Per Common Share	$ 2.92	$ 2.55	$ 2.42
Dividends Declared Per Common Share	$ 0.865	$ 0.445	$ 0.30

See accompanying Notes to Consolidated Financial Statements.

Consolidated Statements of Cash Flows

YUM! Brands, Inc. and Subsidiaries

Fiscal years ended December 30, 2006,
December 31, 2005 and December 25, 2004
(in millions)

	2006	2005	2004
Cash Flows — Operating Activities			
Net income	$ 824	$ 762	$ 740
Adjustments to reconcile net income to net cash provided by operating activities:			
Depreciation and amortization	479	469	448
Closures and impairment expenses	59	62	38
Refranchising (gain) loss	(24)	(43)	(12)
Contributions to defined benefit pension plans	(43)	(74)	(55)
Deferred income taxes	(30)	(101)	142
Equity income from investments in unconsolidated affiliates	(51)	(51)	(54)
Distributions of income received from unconsolidated affiliates	32	44	55
Excess tax benefits from share-based compensation	(62)	(87)	—
Share-based compensation expense	65	62	3
Other non-cash charges and credits, net	101	78	83
Changes in operating working capital, excluding effects of acquisitions and dispositions:			
Accounts and notes receivable	24	(1)	(39)
Inventories	(3)	(4)	(7)
Prepaid expenses and other current assets	(33)	78	(5)
Accounts payable and other current liabilities	(46)	(10)	(20)
Income taxes payable	10	54	(131)
Net change in operating working capital	(48)	117	(202)
Net Cash Provided by Operating Activities	1,302	1,238	1,186
Cash Flows — Investing Activities			
Capital spending	(614)	(609)	(645)
Proceeds from refranchising of restaurants	257	145	140
Acquisition of remaining interest in unconsolidated affiliate, net of cash assumed	(178)	—	—
Acquisition of restaurants from franchisees	(7)	(2)	(38)
Short-term investments	39	12	(36)
Sales of property, plant and equipment	57	81	52
Other, net	(30)	28	(14)
Net Cash Used in Investing Activities	(476)	(345)	(541)
Cash Flows — Financing Activities			
Proceeds from issuance of long-term debt	300	—	—
Repayments of long-term debt	(211)	(14)	(371)
Short-term borrowings by original maturity			
More than three months — proceeds	236	—	—
More than three months — payments	(54)	—	—
Three months or less, net	4	(34)	—
Revolving credit facilities, three months or less, net	(23)	160	19
Repurchase shares of common stock	(983)	(1,056)	(569)
Excess tax benefit from share-based compensation	62	87	—
Employee stock option proceeds	142	148	200
Dividends paid on common shares	(144)	(123)	(58)
Other, net	(2)	—	—
Net Cash Used in Financing Activities	(673)	(832)	(779)
Effect of Exchange Rate on Cash and Cash Equivalents	8	1	4
Net (Decrease) Increase in Cash and Cash Equivalents	161	62	(130)
Net Increase in Cash and Cash Equivalents of Mainland China for December 2004	—	34	—
Cash and Cash Equivalents — Beginning of Year	158	62	192
Cash and Cash Equivalents — End of Year	$ 319	$ 158	$ 62

See accompanying Notes to Consolidated Financial Statements.

Consolidated Balance Sheets
YUM! Brands, Inc. and Subsidiaries

December 30, 2006 and December 31, 2005
(in millions)

	2006	2005
ASSETS		
Current Assets		
Cash and cash equivalents	$ 319	$ 158
Short-term investments	6	43
Accounts and notes receivable, less allowance: $18 in 2006 and $23 in 2005	220	236
Inventories	93	85
Prepaid expenses and other current assets	132	75
Deferred income taxes	57	181
Advertising cooperative assets, restricted	74	77
Total Current Assets	901	855
Property, plant and equipment, net	3,631	3,356
Goodwill	662	538
Intangible assets, net	347	330
Investments in unconsolidated affiliates	138	173
Other assets	369	320
Deferred income taxes	305	225
Total Assets	$ 6,353	$ 5,797
LIABILITIES AND SHAREHOLDERS' EQUITY		
Current Liabilities		
Accounts payable and other current liabilities	$ 1,386	$ 1,256
Income taxes payable	37	79
Short-term borrowings	227	211
Advertising cooperative liabilities	74	77
Total Current Liabilities	1,724	1,623
Long-term debt	2,045	1,649
Other liabilities and deferred credits	1,147	1,076
Total Liabilities	4,916	4,348
Shareholders' Equity		
Preferred stock, no par value, 250 shares authorized; no shares issued	—	—
Common stock, no par value, 750 shares authorized; 265 shares and 278 shares issued in 2006 and 2005, respectively	—	—
Retained earnings	1,593	1,619
Accumulated other comprehensive loss	(156)	(170)
Total Shareholders' Equity	1,437	1,449
Total Liabilities and Shareholders' Equity	$ 6,353	$ 5,797

See accompanying Notes to Consolidated Financial Statements.

Consolidated Statements of Shareholders' Equity and Comprehensive Income

YUM! Brands, Inc. and Subsidiaries

Fiscal years ended December 30, 2006, December 31, 2005 and December 25, 2004 (in millions, except per share data)	Issued Common Stock		Retained Earnings	Accumulated Other Comprehensive Income (Loss)	Total
	Shares	Amount			
Balance at December 27, 2003	292	$ 916	$ 414	$ (210)	$ 1,120
Net income			740		740
Foreign currency translation adjustment arising during the period				73	73
Minimum pension liability adjustment (net of tax impact of $3 million)				6	6
Comprehensive Income					819
Dividends declared on common shares ($0.30 per common share)			(87)		(87)
Repurchase of shares of common stock	(14)	(569)			(569)
Employee stock option exercises (includes tax impact of $102 million)	12	302			302
Compensation-related events		10			10
Balance at December 25, 2004	290	$ 659	$ 1,067	$ (131)	$ 1,595
Net income			762		762
Foreign currency translation adjustment arising during the period				(31)	(31)
Foreign currency translation adjustment included in net income				6	6
Minimum pension liability adjustment (net of tax impact of $8 million)				(15)	(15)
Net unrealized gain on derivative instruments (net of tax impact of $1 million)				1	1
Comprehensive Income					723
Dividends declared on common shares ($0.445 per common share)			(129)		(129)
China December 2004 net income			6		6
Repurchase of shares of common stock	(21)	(969)	(87)		(1,056)
Employee stock option exercises (includes tax impact of $94 million)	9	242			242
Compensation-related events		68			68
Balance at December 31, 2005	278	$ —	$ 1,619	$ (170)	$ 1,449
Adjustment to initially apply SAB No. 108			**100**		**100**
Net income			**824**		**824**
Foreign currency translation adjustment arising during the period (includes tax impact of $13 million)				**59**	**59**
Minimum pension liability adjustment (net of tax impact of $11 million)				**17**	**17**
Net unrealized gain on derivative instruments (net of tax impact of $3 million)				**5**	**5**
Comprehensive Income					**905**
Adjustment to initially apply SFAS No. 158 (net of tax impact of $37 million)				**(67)**	**(67)**
Dividends declared on common shares ($0.865 per common share)			**(234)**		**(234)**
Repurchase of shares of common stock	**(20)**	**(284)**	**(716)**		**(1,000)**
Employee stock option exercises (includes tax impact of $68 million)	**7**	**210**			**210**
Compensation-related events		**74**			**74**
Balance at December 30, 2006	**265**	**$ —**	**$ 1,593**	**$ (156)**	**$ 1,437**

See accompanying Notes to Consolidated Financial Statements.

Notes to Consolidated Financial Statements
(Tabular amounts in millions, except share data)

Description of Business

YUM! Brands, Inc. and Subsidiaries (collectively referred to as "YUM" or the "Company") comprises the worldwide operations of KFC, Pizza Hut, Taco Bell and since May 7, 2002, Long John Silver's ("LJS") and A&W All-American Food Restaurants ("A&W") (collectively the "Concepts"), which were added when we acquired Yorkshire Global Restaurants, Inc. ("YGR"). YUM is the world's largest quick service restaurant company based on the number of system units, with more than 34,000 units of which approximately 42% are located outside the U.S. in more than 100 countries and territories. YUM was created as an independent, publicly-owned company on October 6, 1997 (the "Spin-off Date") via a tax-free distribution by our former parent, PepsiCo, Inc. ("PepsiCo"), of our Common Stock (the "Spin-off") to its shareholders. References to YUM throughout these Consolidated Financial Statements are made using the first person notations of "we," "us" or "our."

Through our widely-recognized Concepts, we develop, operate, franchise and license a system of both traditional and non-traditional quick service restaurants. Each Concept has proprietary menu items and emphasizes the preparation of food with high quality ingredients as well as unique recipes and special seasonings to provide appealing, tasty and attractive food at competitive prices. Our traditional restaurants feature dine-in, carryout and, in some instances, drive-thru or delivery service. Non-traditional units, which are principally licensed outlets, include express units and kiosks which have a more limited menu and operate in non-traditional locations like airports, gasoline service stations, convenience stores, stadiums, amusement parks and colleges, where a full-scale traditional outlet would not be practical or efficient. We also operate multibrand units, where two or more of our Concepts are operated in a single unit. In addition, we continue to pursue the multibrand combination of Pizza Hut and WingStreet, a flavored chicken wings concept we have developed.

In 2005, we began reporting information for our international business in two separate operating segments as a result of changes to our management reporting structure. The China Division includes mainland China ("China"), Thailand and KFC Taiwan, and the International Division includes the remainder of our international operations. While this reporting change did not impact our consolidated results, segment information for 2004 was restated to be consistent with the current period presentation.

Beginning in 2005, we also changed the China business reporting calendar to more closely align the timing of the reporting of its results of operations with our U.S. business. Previously our China business, like the rest of our international businesses, closed one month (or one period for certain of our international businesses) earlier than YUM's period end date to facilitate consolidated reporting. To maintain comparability of our consolidated results of operations, amounts related to our China business for December 2004 have not been reflected in our Consolidated Statements of Income and net income for the China business for the one month period ended December 31, 2004 was recognized as an adjustment directly to consolidated retained earnings in the year ended December 31, 2005. Our consolidated results of operations for the years ended December 30, 2006 and December 31, 2005 both include the results of operations of the China business for the months of January through December. Our consolidated results of operations for the year ended December 25, 2004 continue to include the results of operations of the China business for the months of December 2003 through November 2004 as previously reported.

For the month of December 2004 the China business had revenues of $79 million and net income of $6 million. As mentioned previously, neither of these amounts is included in our Consolidated Statement of Income for the year ended December 31, 2005 and the net income figure was credited directly to retained earnings in the first quarter of 2005. Net income for the month of December 2004 was negatively impacted by costs incurred in preparation of opening a significant number of new stores in early 2005 as well as increased advertising expense, all of which was recorded in December's results of operations. Additionally, the net increase in cash for the China business in December 2004 has been presented as a single line item on our Consolidated Statement of Cash Flows for the year ended December 31, 2005. The $34 million net increase in cash was primarily attributable to short-term borrowings for working capital purposes, a majority of which were repaid prior to the end of the China business' first quarter of 2006.

Summary of Significant Accounting Policies

Our preparation of the accompanying Consolidated Financial Statements in conformity with accounting principles generally accepted in the United States of America requires us to make estimates and assumptions that affect reported amounts of assets and liabilities, disclosure of contingent assets and liabilities at the date of the financial statements, and the reported amounts of revenues and expenses during the reporting period. Actual results could differ from these estimates.

PRINCIPLES OF CONSOLIDATION AND BASIS OF PREPARATION Intercompany accounts and transactions have been eliminated. Certain investments in businesses that operate our Concepts are accounted for by the equity method. Our lack of majority voting rights precludes us from controlling these affiliates, and thus we do not consolidate these affiliates. Our share of the net income or loss of those unconsolidated affiliates is included in other (income) expense.

We participate in various advertising cooperatives with our franchisees and licensees established to collect and administer funds contributed for use in advertising and promotional programs designed to increase sales and enhance the reputation of the Company and its franchise owners. Contributions to the advertising cooperatives are required for both company operated and franchise restaurants and are generally based on a percent of restaurant sales. In certain of these cooperatives we possess majority voting rights, and thus control and consolidate the cooperatives. We report all assets and liabilities of these advertising cooperatives that we consolidate as advertising cooperative assets, restricted and advertising cooperative liabilities in the Consolidated Balance Sheet. The advertising cooperatives assets, consisting primarily of cash received from franchisees and accounts receivable from franchisees, can only be used for selected purposes and are considered restricted. The advertising cooperative liabilities represent the corresponding obligation arising from the receipt of the contributions to purchase advertising and promotional programs. As the contributions to these cooperatives are designated and segregated for advertising, we act as an agent for the franchisees and licensees with regard to these contributions. Thus, in accordance with Statement of Financial Accounting Standards ("SFAS") No. 45, "Accounting for Franchise Fee Revenue," we do not reflect franchisee and licensee contributions to these cooperatives in our Consolidated Statements of Income or Consolidated Statements of Cash Flows.

In 2004, we adopted Financial Accounting Standards Board ("FASB") Interpretation No. 46 (revised December 2003), "Consolidation of Variable Interest Entities, an interpretation of ARB No. 51" ("FIN 46R"). FIN 46R addresses the consolidation of an entity whose equity holders either (a) have not provided sufficient equity at risk to allow the entity to finance its own activities or (b) do not possess certain characteristics of a controlling financial interest. FIN 46R requires the consolidation of such an entity, known as a variable interest entity ("VIE"), by the primary beneficiary of the entity. The primary beneficiary is the entity, if any, that is obligated to absorb a majority of the risk of loss from the VIE's activities, entitled to receive a majority of the VIE's residual returns, or both. FIN 46R excludes from its scope businesses (as defined by FIN 46R) unless certain conditions exist.

The principal entities in which we possess a variable interest include franchise entities, including our unconsolidated affiliates described above. We do not possess any ownership interests in franchise entities except for our investments in various unconsolidated affiliates accounted for under the equity method. Additionally, we generally do not provide financial support to franchise entities in a typical franchise relationship.

We also possess variable interests in certain purchasing cooperatives we have formed along with representatives of the franchisee groups of each of our Concepts. These purchasing cooperatives were formed for the purpose of purchasing certain restaurant products and equipment in the U.S. Our equity ownership in each cooperative is generally proportional to our percentage ownership of the U.S. system units for the Concept. We account for our investments in these purchasing cooperatives using the cost method, under which our recorded balances were not significant at December 30, 2006 or December 31, 2005.

As a result of the adoption of FIN 46R, we have not consolidated any franchise entities, purchasing cooperatives or other entities.

FISCAL YEAR Our fiscal year ends on the last Saturday in December and, as a result, a 53rd week is added every five or six years. Fiscal year 2005 included 53 weeks. The first three quarters of each fiscal year consist of 12 weeks and the fourth quarter consists of 16 weeks in fiscal years with 52 weeks and 17 weeks in fiscal years with 53 weeks. In fiscal year 2005, the 53rd week added $96 million to total revenues and $23 million to total operating profit in our Consolidated Statement of Income. Our subsidiaries operate on similar fiscal calendars with period or month end dates suited to their businesses. The subsidiaries' period end dates are within one week of YUM's period end date with the exception of all of our international businesses except China. The international businesses except China close one period or one month earlier to facilitate consolidated reporting.

RECLASSIFICATIONS We have reclassified certain items in the accompanying Consolidated Financial Statements and Notes thereto for prior periods to be comparable with the classification for the fiscal year ended December 30, 2006. These reclassifications had no effect on previously reported net income.

The most significant reclassification we made was related to the presentation of deferred taxes on our Consolidated Balance Sheet at December 31, 2005. Previously, deferred tax assets and liabilities were netted for all tax jurisdictions outside of the U.S. Due to the implementation of new tax accounting software, we netted our deferred tax assets and liabilities at the individual tax jurisdiction level outside the U.S. at December 30, 2006. We reclassified certain amounts on our Consolidated Balance Sheet at December 31, 2005 to be consistent with this presentation which resulted in an increase to both current deferred income tax assets and liabilities of $18 million and an increase to both long term deferred income tax assets and liabilities of $87 million.

FRANCHISE AND LICENSE OPERATIONS We execute franchise or license agreements for each unit which set out the terms of our arrangement with the franchisee or licensee. Our franchise and license agreements typically require the franchisee or licensee to pay an initial, non-refundable fee and continuing fees based upon a percentage of sales. Subject to our approval and their payment of a renewal fee, a franchisee may generally renew the franchise agreement upon its expiration.

We incur expenses that benefit both our franchise and license communities and their representative organizations and our Company operated restaurants. These expenses, along with other costs of servicing of franchise and license agreements are charged to general and administrative ("G&A") expenses as incurred. Certain direct costs of our franchise and license operations are charged to franchise and license expenses. These costs include provisions for estimated uncollectible fees, franchise and license marketing funding, amortization expense for franchise related intangible assets and certain other direct incremental franchise and license support costs.

We monitor the financial condition of our franchisees and licensees and record provisions for estimated losses on receivables when we believe that our franchisees or licensees are unable to make their required payments. While we use the best information available in making our determination, the ultimate recovery of recorded receivables is also dependent upon future economic events and other conditions that may be beyond our control. Net provisions for uncollectible franchise and license receivables of $2 million, $3 million and $1 million were included in franchise and license expense in 2006, 2005 and 2004, respectively.

REVENUE RECOGNITION Our revenues consist of sales by Company operated restaurants and fees from our franchisees and licensees. Revenues from Company operated restaurants are recognized when payment is tendered at the time of sale. We recognize initial fees received from a franchisee or licensee as revenue when we have performed substantially all initial services required by the franchise or license agreement, which is generally upon the opening of a store. We recognize continuing fees based upon a percentage of franchisee and licensee sales as earned. We recognize renewal fees when a renewal agreement with a franchisee or licensee becomes effective. We include initial fees collected upon the sale of a restaurant to a franchisee in refranchising (gain) loss.

DIRECT MARKETING COSTS We charge direct marketing costs to expense ratably in relation to revenues over the year in which incurred and, in the case of advertising production costs, in the year the advertisement is first shown. Deferred direct marketing costs, which are classified as prepaid expenses, consist of media and related advertising production costs which will generally be used for the first time in the next fiscal year and have historically not been significant. To the extent we participate in advertising cooperatives, we expense our contributions as incurred. Our advertising expenses were $492 million, $497 million and $458 million in 2006, 2005 and 2004, respectively. We report substantially all of our direct marketing costs in occupancy and other operating expenses.

RESEARCH AND DEVELOPMENT EXPENSES Research and development expenses, which we expense as incurred, are reported in G&A expenses. Research and development expenses were $33 million, $33 million and $26 million in 2006, 2005 and 2004, respectively.

IMPAIRMENT OR DISPOSAL OF LONG-LIVED ASSETS In accordance with SFAS No. 144, "Accounting for the Impairment or Disposal of Long-Lived Assets" ("SFAS 144"), we review our long-lived assets related to each restaurant to be held and used in the business, including any allocated intangible assets subject to amortization, semi-annually for impairment, or whenever events or changes in circumstances indicate that the carrying amount of a restaurant may not be recoverable. We evaluate restaurants using a "two-year history of operating losses" as our primary indicator of potential impairment. Based on the best information available, we write down an impaired restaurant to its estimated fair market value, which becomes its new cost basis. We generally measure estimated fair market value by discounting estimated future cash flows. In addition, when we decide to close a restaurant it is reviewed for impairment and depreciable lives are adjusted based on the expected disposal date. The impairment evaluation is based on the estimated cash flows from continuing use through the expected disposal date plus the expected terminal value.

We account for exit or disposal activities, including store closures, in accordance with SFAS No. 146, "Accounting for Costs Associated with Exit or Disposal Activities" ("SFAS 146"). Store closure costs include costs of disposing of the assets as well as other facility-related expenses from previously closed stores. These store closure costs are generally expensed as incurred. Additionally, at the date we cease using a property under an operating lease, we record a liability for the net present value of any remaining lease obligations, net of estimated sublease income, if any. Any subsequent adjustments to that liability as a result of lease termination or changes in estimates of sublease income are recorded in store closure costs. To the extent we sell assets, primarily land, associated with a closed store, any gain or loss upon that sale is also recorded in store closure costs (income).

Refranchising (gain) loss includes the gains or losses from the sales of our restaurants to new and existing franchisees and the related initial franchise fees, reduced by transaction costs. In executing our refranchising initiatives, we most often offer groups of restaurants. We classify restaurants as held for sale and suspend depreciation and amortization when (a) we make a decision to refranchise; (b) the stores can be immediately removed from operations; (c) we have begun an active program to locate a buyer; (d) significant changes to the plan of sale are not likely; and (e) the sale is probable within one year. We recognize estimated losses on refranchisings when the restaurants are classified as held for sale. We also recognize as refranchising loss impairment associated with stores we have offered to refranchise for a price less than their carrying value, but do not believe have met the criteria to be classified as held for sale. We recognize gains on restaurant refranchisings when the sale transaction closes, the franchisee has a minimum amount of the purchase price in at-risk equity, and we are satisfied that the franchisee can meet its financial obligations. If the criteria for gain recognition are not met, we defer the gain to the extent we have a remaining financial exposure in connection with the sales transaction. Deferred gains are recognized when the gain recognition criteria are met or as our financial exposure is reduced. When we make a decision to retain a store, or group of stores, previously held for sale, we revalue the store at the lower of its (a) net book value at our original sale decision date less normal depreciation and amortization that would have been recorded during the period held for sale or (b) its current fair market value. This value becomes the store's new cost basis. We record any difference between the store's carrying amount and its new cost basis to refranchising gain (loss).

Considerable management judgment is necessary to estimate future cash flows, including cash flows from continuing use, terminal value, sublease income and refranchising proceeds. Accordingly, actual results could vary significantly from our estimates.

IMPAIRMENT OF INVESTMENTS IN UNCONSOLIDATED AFFILIATES We record impairment charges related to an investment in an unconsolidated affiliate whenever events or circumstances indicate that a decrease in the fair value of an investment has occurred which is other than temporary. In addition, we evaluate our investments in unconsolidated affiliates for impairment when they have experienced two consecutive years of operating losses. We recorded no impairment associated with our investments in unconsolidated affiliates during the years ended December 30, 2006, December 31, 2005 and December 25, 2004.

Considerable management judgment is necessary to estimate future cash flows. Accordingly, actual results could vary significantly from our estimates.

GUARANTEES We account for certain guarantees in accordance with FASB Interpretation No. 45, "Guarantor's Accounting and Disclosure Requirements for Guarantees, Including Indirect Guarantees of Indebtedness to Others, an interpretation of FASB Statements No. 5, 57 and 107 and a rescission of FASB Interpretation No. 34" ("FIN 45"). FIN 45 elaborates on the disclosures to be made by a guarantor in its interim and annual financial statements about its obligations under guarantees issued. FIN 45 also clarifies that a guarantor is required to recognize, at inception of a guarantee, a liability for the fair value of certain obligations undertaken.

We have also issued guarantees as a result of assigning our interest in obligations under operating leases as a condition to the refranchising of certain Company restaurants. Such guarantees are subject to the requirements of SFAS No. 145, "Rescission of FASB Statements No. 4, 44, and 64, Amendment of FASB Statement No. 13, and Technical Corrections" ("SFAS 145"). We recognize a liability for the fair value of such lease guarantees under SFAS 145 upon refranchising and upon any subsequent renewals of such leases when we remain contingently liable. The related expense in both instances is included in refranchising gain (loss).

CASH AND CASH EQUIVALENTS Cash equivalents represent funds we have temporarily invested (with original maturities not exceeding three months) as part of managing our day-to-day operating cash receipts and disbursements.

INVENTORIES We value our inventories at the lower of cost (computed on the first-in, first-out method) or net realizable value.

PROPERTY, PLANT AND EQUIPMENT We state property, plant and equipment at cost less accumulated depreciation and amortization and valuation allowances. We calculate depreciation and amortization on a straight-line basis over the estimated useful lives of the assets as follows: 5 to 25 years for buildings and improvements, 3 to 20 years for machinery and equipment and 3 to 7 years for capitalized software costs. As discussed above, we suspend depreciation and amortization on assets related to restaurants that are held for sale.

LEASES AND LEASEHOLD IMPROVEMENTS We account for our leases in accordance with SFAS No. 13, "Accounting for Leases" and other related authoritative guidance. When determining the lease term, we often include option periods for which failure to renew the lease imposes a penalty on the Company in such an amount that a renewal appears, at the inception of the lease, to be reasonably assured. The primary penalty to which we are subject is the economic detriment associated with the existence of leasehold improvements which might be impaired if we choose not to continue the use of the leased property.

In 2004, we recorded an adjustment to correct instances where our leasehold improvements were not being depreciated over the shorter of their useful lives or the term of the lease, including options in some instances, over which we were recording rent expense, including escalations, on a straight line basis. The cumulative adjustment, primarily through increased U.S. depreciation expense, totaled $11.5 million ($7 million after tax). The portion of this adjustment that related to 2004 was approximately $3 million. As the portion of the adjustment recorded that was a correction of errors of amounts reported in our prior period financial statements was not material to any of those prior period financial statements, the entire adjustment was recorded in the 2004 Consolidated Financial Statements and no adjustment was made to any prior period financial statements.

We record rent expense for leases that contain scheduled rent increases on a straight-line basis over the lease term, including any option periods considered in the determination of that lease term. Contingent rentals are generally based on sales levels in excess of stipulated amounts, and thus are not considered minimum lease payments and are included in rent expense as they accrue. We generally do not receive leasehold improvement incentives upon opening a store that is subject to a lease.

Prior to fiscal year 2006, we capitalized rent while we were constructing a restaurant even if such construction period was subject to a rent holiday. Such capitalized rent was then expensed on a straight-line basis over the remaining term of the lease upon opening of the restaurant. Effective January 1, 2006 as required by FASB Staff Position No. 13-1, "Accounting for Rental Costs Incurred during a Construction Period" ("FSP 13-1"), we began expensing rent associated with leased land or buildings for construction periods whether rent was paid or we were subject to a rent holiday. The adoption of FSP 13-1 did not significantly impact our results of operations in 2006 and we do not anticipate significant future impact.

INTERNAL DEVELOPMENT COSTS AND ABANDONED SITE COSTS We capitalize direct costs associated with the site acquisition and construction of a Company unit on that site, including direct internal payroll and payroll-related costs. Only those site-specific costs incurred subsequent to the time that the site acquisition is considered probable are capitalized. If we subsequently make a determination that a site for which internal development costs have been capitalized will not be acquired or developed, any previously capitalized internal development costs are expensed and included in G&A expenses.

GOODWILL AND INTANGIBLE ASSETS The Company accounts for acquisitions of restaurants from franchisees and other acquisitions of businesses that may occur from time to time in accordance with SFAS No. 141, "Business Combinations" ("SFAS 141"). Goodwill in such acquisitions represents the excess of the cost of a business acquired over the net of the amounts assigned to assets acquired, including identifiable intangible assets, and liabilities assumed. SFAS 141 specifies criteria to be used in determining whether intangible assets acquired in a business combination must be recognized and reported separately from goodwill. We base amounts assigned to goodwill and other identifiable intangible assets on independent appraisals or internal estimates.

The Company accounts for recorded goodwill and other intangible assets in accordance with SFAS No. 142, "Goodwill and Other Intangible Assets" ("SFAS 142"). In accordance with SFAS 142, we do not amortize goodwill and indefinite-lived intangible assets. We evaluate the remaining useful life of an intangible asset that is not being amortized each reporting period to determine whether events and circumstances continue to support an indefinite useful life. If an intangible asset that is not being amortized is subsequently determined to have a finite useful life, we amortize the intangible asset prospectively over its estimated remaining useful life. Amortizable intangible assets are amortized on a straight-line basis.

In accordance with the requirements of SFAS 142, goodwill has been assigned to reporting units for purposes of impairment testing. Our reporting units are our operating segments in the U.S. (see Note 21) and our business management units internationally (typically individual countries). We evaluate goodwill and indefinite-lived assets for impairment on an annual basis or more often if an event occurs or circumstances change that indicate impairments might exist. Goodwill impairment tests consist of a comparison of each reporting unit's fair value with its carrying value. The fair value of a reporting unit is an estimate of the amount for which the unit as a whole could be sold in a current transaction between willing parties. We generally estimate fair value based on discounted cash flows. If the carrying value of a reporting unit exceeds its fair value, goodwill is written down to its implied fair value. We have selected the beginning of our fourth quarter as the date on which to perform our ongoing annual impairment test for goodwill. For 2006, 2005 and 2004, there was no impairment of goodwill identified during our annual impairment testing.

For indefinite-lived intangible assets, our impairment test consists of a comparison of the fair value of an intangible asset with its carrying amount. Fair value is an estimate of the price a willing buyer would pay for the intangible asset and is generally estimated by discounting the expected future cash flows associated with the intangible asset. We also perform our annual test for impairment of our indefinite-lived intangible assets at the beginning of our fourth quarter. No impairment of indefinite-lived intangible assets was recorded in 2006, 2005 or 2004.

Our amortizable intangible assets are evaluated for impairment whenever events or changes in circumstances indicate that the carrying amount of the intangible asset may not be recoverable. An intangible asset that is deemed impaired is written down to its estimated fair value, which is based on discounted cash flows. For purposes of our impairment analysis, we update the cash flows that were initially used to value the amortizable intangible asset to reflect our current estimates and assumptions over the asset's future remaining life.

SHARE-BASED EMPLOYEE COMPENSATION In the fourth quarter 2005, the Company adopted SFAS No. 123 (Revised 2004), "Share-Based Payment" ("SFAS 123R"), which replaced SFAS No. 123 "Accounting for Stock-Based Compensation" ("SFAS 123"), superseded APB 25, "Accounting for Stock Issued to Employees" and related interpretations and amended SFAS No. 95, "Statement of Cash Flows." The provisions of SFAS 123R are similar to those of SFAS 123, however, SFAS 123R requires all new, modified and unvested share-based payments to employees, including grants of employee stock options and stock appreciation rights ("SARs"), be recognized in the financial statements as compensation cost over the service period based on their fair value on the date of grant. Compensation cost is recognized over the service period on a straight-line basis for the fair value of awards that actually vest.

We adopted SFAS 123R using the modified retrospective application transition method effective September 4, 2005, the beginning of our 2005 fourth quarter. As permitted by SFAS 123R, we applied the modified retrospective application transition method to the beginning of the fiscal year of adoption (our fiscal year 2005). As such, the results for the first three fiscal quarters of 2005 were required to be adjusted to recognize the compensation cost previously reported in the pro forma footnote disclosures under the provisions of SFAS 123. However, years prior to 2005 were not restated.

The adoption of SFAS 123R resulted in a decrease in operating profit, the associated income tax benefits and a decrease in net income as shown below. Additionally, cash flows from operating activities decreased $62 million and $87 million in 2006 and 2005, respectively, and cash flows from financing activities increased $62 million and $87 million in 2006 and 2005, respectively.

	2006	2005
Payroll and employee benefits	$ 9	$ 10
General and administrative expense	51	48
Operating profit	60	58
Income tax benefit	(21)	(20)
Net income impact	$ 39	$ 38

Prior to 2005, all share-based payments were accounted for under the recognition and measurement principles of APB 25 and its related interpretations. Accordingly, no expense was reflected in the Consolidated Statements of Income for stock options, as all stock options granted had an exercise price equal to the market value of our underlying common stock on the date of grant. The following table illustrates the pro forma effect on net income and earnings per share if the Company had applied the fair value recognition provisions of SFAS 123 to all share-based payments for 2004.

	2004
Net Income, as reported	$ 740
Add: Compensation expense included in reported net income, net of related tax	3
Deduct: Total stock-based employee compensation expense determined under fair value based method for all awards, net of related tax effects	(40)
Net income, pro forma	703
Basic Earnings per Common Share	
As reported	$ 2.54
Pro forma	2.42
Diluted Earnings per Common Share	
As reported	$ 2.42
Pro forma	2.30

DERIVATIVE FINANCIAL INSTRUMENTS We do not use derivative instruments for trading purposes and we have procedures in place to monitor and control their use. Our use of derivative instruments has included interest rate swaps and collars, treasury locks and foreign currency forward contracts. These derivative contracts are entered into with financial institutions.

We account for these derivative financial instruments in accordance with SFAS No. 133, "Accounting for Derivative Instruments and Hedging Activities" ("SFAS 133") as amended by SFAS No. 149, "Amendment of Statement 133 on Derivative Instruments and Hedging Activities" ("SFAS 149"). SFAS 133 requires that all derivative instruments be recorded on the Consolidated Balance Sheet at fair value. The accounting for changes in the fair value (i.e., gains or losses) of a derivative instrument is dependent upon whether the derivative has been designated and qualifies as part of a hedging relationship and further, on the type of hedging relationship. For derivative instruments that are designated and qualify as a fair value hedge, the gain or loss on the derivative instrument as well as the offsetting gain or loss on the hedged item attributable to the hedged risk are recognized in the results of operations. For derivative instruments that are designated and qualify as a cash flow hedge, the effective portion of the gain or loss on the derivative instrument is reported as a component of other comprehensive income (loss) and reclassified into earnings in the same period or periods during which the hedged transaction affects earnings. Any ineffective portion of the gain or loss on the derivative instrument is recorded in the results of operations immediately. For derivative instruments not designated as hedging instruments, the gain or loss is recognized in the results of operations immediately. See Note 14 for a discussion of our use of derivative instruments, management of credit risk inherent in derivative instruments and fair value information.

COMMON STOCK SHARE REPURCHASES From time to time, we repurchase shares of our Common Stock under share repurchase programs authorized by our Board of Directors. Shares repurchased constitute authorized, but unissued shares under the North Carolina laws under which we are incorporated. Additionally, our Common Stock has no par or stated value. Accordingly, we record the full value of share repurchases against Common Stock except when to do so would result in a negative balance in our Common Stock account. In such instances, on a period basis, we record the cost of any further share repurchases as a reduction in retained earnings. Due to the large number of share repurchases and the increase in our Common Stock market value over the past several years, our Common Stock balance is frequently zero at the end of any period. Accordingly, $716 million and $87 million in share repurchases were recorded as a reduction in retained earnings in 2006 and 2005, respectively. We have no legal restrictions on the payment of dividends. See Note 19 for additional information.

PENSION AND POSTRETIREMENT MEDICAL BENEFITS In the fourth quarter of 2006, we adopted the recognition and disclosure provisions of SFAS No. 158, "Employers' Accounting for Defined Benefit Pension and Other Postretirement Plans—an amendment of FASB Statements No. 87, 88, 106 and 132(R)" ("SFAS 158"). SFAS 158 amends SFAS No. 87, "Employers' Accounting for Pensions" ("SFAS 87"), SFAS No. 88, "Employers' Accounting for Settlements and Curtailments of Defined Benefit Plans and for Termination Benefits" ("SFAS 88"), SFAS No. 106, "Employers' Accounting for Postretirement Benefits Other Than Pensions" ("SFAS 106") and SFAS No. 132(R), "Employers' Disclosures about Pensions and Other Postretirement Benefits."

SFAS 158 required the Company to recognize the funded status of its pension and postretirement plans in the December 30, 2006 Consolidated Balance Sheet, with a corresponding adjustment to accumulated other comprehensive income, net of tax. Gains or losses and prior service costs or credits that arise in future years will be recognized as a component of other comprehensive income to the extent they have not been recognized as a component of net periodic benefit cost pursuant to SFAS 87 or SFAS 106.

The incremental effects of adopting the provisions of SFAS 158 on the Company's Consolidated Balance Sheet at December 30, 2006 are presented as follows. The adoption of SFAS 158 had no impact on the Consolidated Statement of Income.

	Before Application of SFAS 158	Adjustments	After Application of SFAS 158
Intangible assets, net	$ 350	$ (3)	$ 347
Deferred income taxes	268	37	305
Total assets	6,319	34	6,353
Accounts payable and other current liabilities	1,384	2	1,386
Other liabilities and deferred credits	1,048	99	1,147
Total liabilities	4,815	101	4,916
Accumulated other comprehensive loss	(89)	(67)	(156)
Total stockholders' equity	1,504	(67)	1,437

SFAS 158 also requires measurement of the funded status of pension and postretirement plans as of the date of a Company's fiscal year end effective in the year ended 2008. Certain of our plans currently have measurement dates that do not coincide with our fiscal year end and thus we will be required to change their measurement dates in 2008.

QUANTIFICATION OF MISSTATEMENTS In September 2006, the Securities and Exchange Commission (the "SEC") issued Staff Accounting Bulletin No. 108, "Considering the Effects of Prior Year Misstatements when Quantifying Misstatements in Current Year Financial Statements" ("SAB 108"). SAB 108 provides interpretive guidance on how the effects of the carryover or reversal of prior year misstatements should be considered in quantifying a current year misstatement for the purpose of a materiality assessment. SAB 108 requires that registrants quantify a current year misstatement using an approach that considers both the impact of prior year misstatements that remain on the balance sheet and those that were recorded in the current year income statement. Historically, we quantified misstatements and assessed materiality based on a current year income statement approach. We were required to adopt SAB 108 in the fourth quarter of 2006.

The transition provisions of SAB 108 permit uncorrected prior year misstatements that were not material to any prior periods under our historical income statement approach but that would have been material under the dual approach of SAB 108 to be corrected in the carrying amounts of assets and liabilities at the beginning of 2006 with the offsetting adjustment to retained earnings for the cumulative effect of misstatements. We have adjusted certain balances in the accompanying Consolidated Financial Statements at the beginning of 2006 to correct the misstatements discussed below which we considered to be immaterial in prior periods under our historical approach. The impact of the January 1, 2006 cumulative effect adjustment, net of any income tax effect, was an increase to retained earnings as follows:

Deferred tax liabilities adjustments	$ 79
Reversal of unallocated reserve	6
Non-GAAP conventions	15
Net increase to January 1, 2006 retained earnings	$ 100

DEFERRED TAXES   Our opening Consolidated Balance Sheet at Spin-off included significant deferred tax assets and liabilities. Over time we have determined that deferred tax liability amounts were recorded in excess of those necessary to reflect our temporary differences.

UNALLOCATED RESERVES   A reserve was established in 1999 equal to certain out of year corrections recorded during that year such that there was no misstatement under our historical approach. No adjustments have been recorded to this reserve since its establishment and we do not believe the reserve is required.

NON-GAAP ACCOUNTING CONVENTIONS   Prior to 2006, we used certain non-GAAP conventions to account for capitalized interest on restaurant construction projects, the leases of our Pizza Hut United Kingdom unconsolidated affiliate and certain state tax benefits. The net income statement impact on any given year from the use of these non-GAAP conventions was immaterial both individually and in the aggregate under our historical approach. Below is a summary of the accounting policies we adopted effective the beginning of 2006 and the impact of the cumulative effect adjustment under SAB 108, net of any income tax effect. The impact of these accounting policy changes was not significant to our results of operations in 2006.

INTEREST CAPITALIZATION   SFAS No. 34, "Capitalization of Interest Cost" requires that interest be capitalized as part of an asset's acquisition cost. We traditionally have not capitalized interest on individual restaurant construction projects. We increased our 2006 beginning retained earnings balance by approximately $12 million for the estimated capitalized interest on existing restaurants, net of accumulated depreciation.

LEASE ACCOUNTING BY OUR PIZZA HUT UNITED KINGDOM UNCON-SOLIDATED AFFILIATE   Prior to our fourth quarter acquisition of the remaining fifty percent interest in our Pizza Hut United Kingdom unconsolidated affiliate, we accounted for our ownership under the equity method. The unconsolidated affiliate historically accounted for all of its leases as operating and we made no adjustments in recording equity income. We decreased our 2006 beginning retained earnings balance by approximately $4 million to reflect our fifty percent share of the cumulative equity income impact of properly recording certain leases as capital.

RECOGNITION OF CERTAIN STATE TAX BENEFITS   We have historically recognized certain state tax benefits on a cash basis as they were recognized on the respective state tax returns instead of in the year the benefit originated. We increased our 2006 beginning retained earnings by approximately $7 million to recognize these state tax benefits as deferred tax assets.

NEW ACCOUNTING PRONOUNCEMENTS NOT YET ADOPTED In July 2006, the FASB issued FASB Interpretation No. 48, "Accounting for Uncertainty in Income Taxes" ("FIN 48"), an interpretation of FASB Statement No. 109, "Accounting for Income Taxes." FIN 48 is effective for fiscal years beginning after December 15, 2006, the year beginning December 31, 2006 for the Company. FIN 48 requires that a position taken or expected to be taken in a tax return be recognized in the financial statements when it is more likely than not (i.e., a likelihood of more than fifty percent) that the position would be sustained upon examination by tax authorities. A recognized tax position is then measured at the largest amount of benefit that is greater than fifty percent likely of being realized upon ultimate settlement. Upon adoption, the cumulative effect of applying the recognition and measurement provisions of FIN 48, if any, shall be reflected as an adjustment to the opening balance of retained earnings. We do not currently anticipate that the adjustment to the opening balance of retained earnings we will record upon adoption of FIN 48 will materially impact our financial condition.

FIN 48 requires that subsequent to initial adoption a change in judgment that results in subsequent recognition, derecognition or change in a measurement of a tax position taken in a prior annual period (including any related interest and penalties) be recognized as a discrete item in the period in which the change occurs. Currently, we record such changes in judgment, including audit settlements, as a component of our annual effective rate. Thus, our reported quarterly income tax rate may become more volatile upon adoption of FIN 48. This change will not impact the manner in which we record income tax expense on an annual basis.

FIN 48 also requires expanded disclosures including identification of tax positions for which it is reasonably possible that total amounts of unrecognized tax benefits will significantly change in the next twelve months, a description of tax years that remain subject to examination by major tax jurisdiction, a tabular reconciliation of the total amount of unrecognized tax benefits at the beginning and end of each annual reporting period, the total amount of unrecognized tax benefits that, if recognized, would affect the effective tax rate and the total amounts of interest and penalties recognized in the statements of operations and financial position.

In September 2006, the FASB issued SFAS No. 157, "Fair Value Measures" ("SFAS 157"). SFAS 157 defines fair value, establishes a framework for measuring fair value and enhances disclosures about fair value measures required under other accounting pronouncements, but does not change existing guidance as to whether or not an instrument is carried at fair value. SFAS 157 is effective for fiscal years beginning after November 15, 2007, the year beginning December 30, 2007 for the Company. We are currently reviewing the provisions of SFAS 157 to determine any impact for the Company.

In February 2007, the FASB issued SFAS No. 159 "The Fair Value Option for Financial Assets and Financial Liabilities," ("SFAS 159"). SFAS 159 provides companies with an option to report selected financial assets and financial liabilities at fair value. Unrealized gains and losses on items for which the fair value option has been elected are reported in earnings at each subsequent reporting date. SFAS 159 is effective for fiscal years beginning after November 15, 2007, the year beginning December 30, 2007 for the Company. We are currently reviewing the provisions of SFAS 159 to determine any impact for the Company.

3.

Earnings Per Common Share ("EPS")

	2006	2005	2004
Net income	**$ 824**	$ 762	$ 740
Weighted-average common shares outstanding (for basic calculation)	**273**	286	291
Effect of dilutive share-based employee compensation	**9**	12	14
Weighted-average common and dilutive potential common shares outstanding (for diluted calculation)	**282**	298	305
Basic EPS	**$ 3.02**	$ 2.66	$ 2.54
Diluted EPS	**$ 2.92**	$ 2.55	$ 2.42
Unexercised employee stock options and stock appreciation rights (in millions) excluded from the diluted EPS computation[a]	**0.1**	0.5	0.4

(a) These unexercised employee stock options and stock appreciation rights were not included in the computation of diluted EPS because their exercise prices were greater than the average market price of our Common Stock during the year.

Items Affecting Comparability of Net Income

FACILITY ACTIONS   Refranchising (gain) loss, store closure (income) costs and store impairment charges by reportable segment are as follows:

	2006	2005	2004
U.S.			
Refranchising net (gain) loss[a][b]	**$ (20)**	$ (40)	$ (14)
Store closure costs (income)	**(1)**	2	(3)
Store impairment charges	**38**	44	17
Closure and impairment expenses	**$ 37**	$ 46	$ 14
International Division			
Refranchising net (gain) loss[a][b]	**$ (4)**	$ (3)	$ 3
Store closure costs (income)	**1**	(1)	1
Store impairment charges	**15**	10	19
Closure and impairment expenses	**$ 16**	$ 9	$ 20
China Division			
Refranchising net (gain) loss[a]	**$ —**	$ —	$ (1)
Store closure costs (income)	**(1)**	(1)	(1)
Store impairment charges	**7**	8	5
Closure and impairment expenses	**$ 6**	$ 7	$ 4
Worldwide			
Refranchising net (gain) loss[a][b]	**$ (24)**	$ (43)	$ (12)
Store closure costs (income)	**(1)**	—	(3)
Store impairment charges	**60**	62	41
Closure and impairment expenses	**$ 59**	$ 62	$ 38

(a) Refranchising (gain) loss is not allocated to segments for performance reporting purposes.
(b) Includes initial franchise fees in the U.S. of $11 million in 2006, $7 million in 2005 and $2 million in 2004, and in the International Division of $6 million in 2006, $3 million in 2005 and $8 million in 2004. See Note 7.

The following table summarizes the 2006 and 2005 activity related to reserves for remaining lease obligations for closed stores.

	Beginning Balance	Amounts Used	New Decisions	Estimate/ Decision Changes	Other	Ending Balance
2005 Activity	$ 43	(13)	14	—	—	$ 44
2006 Activity	**$ 44**	**(17)**	**8**	**1**	**—**	**$ 36**

Assets held for sale at December 30, 2006 and December 31, 2005 total $13 million and $11 million, respectively, of U.S. property, plant and equipment, primarily land, on which we previously operated restaurants and are included in prepaid expenses and other current assets on our Consolidated Balance Sheets.

WRENCH LITIGATION   In fiscal year 2003, we recorded a charge of $42 million related to a lawsuit filed against Taco Bell Corp. (the "Wrench litigation"). Income of $14 million was recorded for 2004 reflecting settlements associated with the Wrench litigation for amounts less than previously accrued as well as related insurance recoveries. We recorded income of $2 million in 2005 from a settlement with an insurance carrier related to the Wrench litigation. We continue to pursue additional recoveries which, if any, will be recorded as realized.

AMERISERVE AND OTHER CHARGES (CREDITS)   AmeriServe Food Distribution Inc. ("AmeriServe") was the primary distributor of food and paper supplies to our U.S. stores when it filed for protection under Chapter 11 of the U.S. Bankruptcy Code on January 31, 2000. A plan of reorganization for AmeriServe (the "POR") was approved on November 28, 2000, which resulted in, among other things, the assumption of our distribution agreement, subject to certain amendments, by McLane Company, Inc. During the AmeriServe bankruptcy reorganization process, we took a number of actions to ensure continued supply to our system. Those actions resulted in significant expense for the Company, primarily recorded in 2000. Under the POR, we are entitled to proceeds from certain residual assets, preference claims and other legal recoveries of the estate.

Income of $1 million, $2 million and $16 million was recorded as AmeriServe and other charges (credits) for 2006, 2005 and 2004, respectively. These amounts primarily resulted from cash recoveries related to the AmeriServe bankruptcy reorganization process.

Supplemental Cash Flow Data

	2006	2005	2004
Cash Paid For:			
Interest	**$ 185**	$ 132	$ 146
Income taxes	**304**	232	276
Significant Non-Cash Investing and Financing Activities:			
Assumption of capital leases related to the acquisition of restaurants from franchisees	**$ —**	$ —	$ 8
Capital lease obligations incurred to acquire assets	**9**	7	13

Additionally, we assumed the full liability associated with capital leases of $95 million and short-term borrowings of $23 million when we acquired the remaining fifty percent ownership interest of our Pizza Hut United Kingdom unconsolidated affiliate (See Note 6). Previously, our fifty percent share of these liabilities were reflected in our Investment in unconsolidated affiliate balance under the equity method of accounting and were not presented as liabilities on our Consolidated Balance Sheet.

Pizza Hut United Kingdom Acquisition

On September 12, 2006, we completed the acquisition of the remaining fifty percent ownership interest of our Pizza Hut United Kingdom ("U.K.") unconsolidated affiliate for $187 million in cash, including transaction costs and prior to $9 million of cash assumed. This unconsolidated affiliate owned more than 500 restaurants in the U.K. The acquisition was driven by growth opportunities we see in the market and the desire of our former partner in the unconsolidated affiliate to refocus its business to other industry sectors. Prior to this acquisition, we accounted for our ownership interest under the equity method of accounting. Our Investment in unconsolidated affiliate balance for the Pizza Hut U.K. unconsolidated affiliate was $58 million at the date of this acquisition.

Subsequent to the acquisition we consolidated all of the assets and liabilities of Pizza Hut U.K. These assets and liabilities were valued at fifty percent of their historical carrying value and fifty percent of their fair value upon acquisition. We have preliminarily assigned fair values such that assets and liabilities recorded for Pizza Hut U.K. at the acquisition date were as follows:

Current assets, including cash of $9	$ 27
Property, plant and equipment	340
Intangible assets	19
Goodwill	117
Total assets acquired	503
Current liabilities, other than capital lease obligations and short-term borrowings	102
Capital lease obligation, including current portion	95
Short-term borrowings	23
Other long-term liabilities	38
Total liabilities assumed	258
Net assets acquired (cash paid and investment allocated)	$ 245

All of the $19 million in intangible assets (primarily reacquired franchise rights) are subject to amortization with a weighted average life of approximately 18 years. The $117 million in goodwill is not expected to be deductible for income tax purposes and will be allocated to the International Division in its entirety.

Under the equity method of accounting, we reported our fifty percent share of the net income of the unconsolidated affiliate (after interest expense and income taxes) as Other (income) expense in the Consolidated Statements of Income. We also recorded a franchise fee for the royalty received from the stores owned by the unconsolidated affiliate. From the date of the acquisition through December 4, 2006 (the end of our fiscal year for Pizza Hut U.K.), we reported Company sales and the associated restaurant costs, general and administrative expense, interest expense and income taxes associated with the restaurants previously owned by the unconsolidated affiliate in the appropriate line items of our Consolidated Statements of Income. We no longer recorded franchise fee income for the restaurants previously owned by the unconsolidated affiliate nor did we report other income under the equity method of accounting. As a result of this acquisition, company sales and restaurant profit increased $164 million and $16 million, respectively, franchise fees decreased $7 million and G&A expenses increased $8 million compared to the year ended December 31, 2005. The impacts on operating profit and net income were not significant.

If the acquisition had been completed as of the beginning of the years ended December 30, 2006 and December 31, 2005, pro forma Company sales and franchise and license fees would have been as follows:

	2006	2005
Company sales	$ 8,886	$ 8,944
Franchise and license fees	$ 1,176	$ 1,095

The pro forma impact of the acquisition on net income and diluted earnings per share would not have been significant in 2006 and 2005. The pro forma information is not necessarily indicative of the results of operations had the acquisition actually occurred at the beginning of each of these periods nor is it necessarily indicative of future results.

7. Franchise and License Fees

	2006	2005	2004
Initial fees, including renewal fees	$ 57	$ 51	$ 43
Initial franchise fees included in refranchising gains	(17)	(10)	(10)
	40	41	33
Continuing fees	1,156	1,083	986
	$ 1,196	$ 1,124	$ 1,019

8. Other (Income) Expense

	2006	2005	2004
Equity income from investments in unconsolidated affiliates	$ (51)	$ (51)	$ (54)
Gain upon sale of investment in unconsolidated affiliate[a]	(2)	(11)	—
Recovery from supplier[b]	—	(20)	—
Contract termination charge[c]	8	—	—
Foreign exchange net (gain) loss and other	(6)	2	(1)
Other (income) expense	$ (51)	$ (80)	$ (55)

(a) Reflects net gains related to the 2005 sale of our fifty percent interest in the entity that operated almost all KFCs and Pizza Huts in Poland and the Czech Republic to our then partner in the entity, principally for cash. This transaction has generated net gains of approximately $13 million for YUM as cumulative cash proceeds (net of expenses) of approximately $27 million from the sale of our interest in the entity exceeded our recorded investment in this unconsolidated affiliate.

(b) Relates to a financial recovery from a supplier ingredient issue in mainland China totaling $24 million, $4 million of which was recognized through equity income from investments in unconsolidated affiliates. Our KFC business in mainland China was negatively impacted by the interruption of product offerings and negative publicity associated with a supplier ingredient issue experienced in late March 2005. During 2005, we entered into agreements with the supplier for a partial recovery of our losses.

(c) Reflects an $8 million charge associated with the termination of a beverage agreement in the United States segment.

9. Property, Plant and Equipment, net

	2006	2005
Land	$ 541	$ 567
Buildings and improvements	3,449	3,094
Capital leases, primarily buildings	221	126
Machinery and equipment	2,566	2,399
	6,777	6,186
Accumulated depreciation and amortization	(3,146)	(2,830)
	$ 3,631	$ 3,356

Depreciation and amortization expense related to property, plant and equipment was $466 million, $459 million and $434 million in 2006, 2005 and 2004, respectively.

Goodwill and Intangible Assets

The changes in the carrying amount of goodwill are as follows:

	U.S.	International Division	China Division	Worldwide
Balance as of December 25, 2004	$ 395	$ 100	$ 58	$ 553
Acquisitions	—	1	—	1
Disposals and other, net[a]	(11)	(5)	—	(16)
Balance as of December 31, 2005	$ 384	$ 96	$ 58	$ 538
Acquisitions	—	123	—	123
Disposals and other, net[a]	(17)	18	—	1
Balance as of December 30, 2006	**$ 367**	**$ 237**	**$ 58**	**$ 662**

(a) Disposals and other, net for the International Division primarily reflects the impact of foreign currency translation on existing balances. Disposals and other, net for the U.S. Division, primarily reflects goodwill write-offs associated with refranchising.

Intangible assets, net for the years ended 2006 and 2005 are as follows:

	2006		2005	
	Gross Carrying Amount	Accumulated Amortization	Gross Carrying Amount	Accumulated Amortization
Amortized intangible assets				
Franchise contract rights	**$ 153**	**$ (66)**	$ 144	$ (59)
Trademarks/brands	**220**	**(18)**	208	(9)
Favorable operating leases	**15**	**(10)**	18	(14)
Reacquired franchise rights[a]	**18**	**—**	—	—
Pension-related intangible[b]	**—**	**—**	7	—
Other	**5**	**(1)**	5	(1)
	$ 411	**$ (95)**	$ 382	$ (83)
Unamortized intangible assets				
Trademarks/brands	**$ 31**		$ 31	

(a) Increase is primarily due to the acquisition of the remaining fifty percent interest in our former Pizza Hut U.K. unconsolidated affiliate.
(b) Subsequent to the adoption of SFAS 158 a pension-related intangible asset is no longer recorded. See Note 2 for further discussion.

We have recorded intangible assets through past acquisitions representing the value of our KFC, LJS and A&W trademarks/brands. The value of a trademark/brand is determined based upon the value derived from the royalty we avoid, in the case of Company stores, or receive, in the case of franchise and licensee stores, for the use of the trademark/brand. We have determined that our KFC trademark/brand intangible asset has an indefinite life and therefore is not amortized. We have determined that our LJS and A&W trademarks/brands are subject to amortization and are being amortized over their expected useful lives which are currently thirty years.

On March 24, 2006, we finalized an agreement with Rostik's Restaurant Ltd. ("RRL"), a franchisor and operator of a chicken chain in Russia known as Rostik's, under which we acquired the Rostik's brand and associated intellectual property for $15 million. We will also provide financial support, including loans and guarantees, up to $30 million to support future development by RRL in Russia, an insignificant amount of which has been incurred as of December 30, 2006. This agreement also includes a put/call option that may be exercised, subject to certain conditions, between the fifth and seventh year whereby ownership of then existing restaurants would be transferred to YRI. The majority of the purchase price of $15 million was allocated to the trademarks acquired for the International Division and will be amortized over a period of seven years.

Amortization expense for all definite-lived intangible assets was $15 million in 2006, $13 million in 2005 and $8 million in 2004. Amortization expense for definite-lived intangible assets will approximate $17 million annually in 2007 through 2011.

Accounts Payable and Other Current Liabilities

	2006	2005
Accounts payable	$ **554**	$ 473
Accrued compensation and benefits	**302**	274
Dividends payable	**119**	32
Other current liabilities	**411**	477
	$ 1,386	$ 1,256

Short-term Borrowings and Long-term Debt

	2006	2005
Short-term Borrowings		
Unsecured Term Loans, expire January 2007	$ **183**	$ —
Current maturities of long-term debt	**16**	211
Other	**28**	—
	$ **227**	$ 211
Long-term Debt		
Unsecured International Revolving Credit Facility, expires November 2010	$ **174**	$ 180
Unsecured Revolving Credit Facility, expires September 2009	**—**	—
Senior, Unsecured Notes, due April 2006	**—**	200
Senior, Unsecured Notes, due May 2008	**251**	251
Senior, Unsecured Notes, due April 2011	**646**	646
Senior, Unsecured Notes, due July 2012	**399**	398
Senior, Unsecured Notes, due April 2016	**300**	—
Capital lease obligations (See Note 13)	**228**	114
Other, due through 2019 (11%)	**76**	77
	2,074	1,866
Less current maturities of long-term debt	**(16)**	(211)
Long-term debt excluding SFAS 133 adjustment	**2,058**	1,655
Derivative instrument adjustment under SFAS 133 (See Note 14)	**(13)**	(6)
Long-term debt including SFAS 133 adjustment	**$ 2,045**	$ 1,649

Selected Financial Data
YUM! Brands, Inc. and Subsidiaries

(in millions, except per share and unit amounts)

	2006	2005	2004	2003	2002
Summary of Operations					
Revenues					
Company sales	$ 8,365	$ 8,225	$ 7,992	$ 7,441	$ 6,891
Franchise and license fees	1,196	1,124	1,019	939	866
Total	9,561	9,349	9,011	8,380	7,757
Closures and impairment expenses[a]	(59)	(62)	(38)	(40)	(51)
Refranchising gain (loss)[a]	24	43	12	4	19
Wrench litigation income (expense)[b]	—	2	14	(42)	—
AmeriServe and other (charges) credits[c]	1	2	16	26	27
Operating profit	1,262	1,153	1,155	1,059	1,030
Interest expense, net	154	127	129	173	172
Income before income taxes and cumulative effect of accounting change	1,108	1,026	1,026	886	858
Income before cumulative effect of accounting change	824	762	740	618	583
Cumulative effect of accounting change, net of tax[d]	—	—	—	(1)	—
Net income	824	762	740	617	583
Basic earnings per common share	3.02	2.66	2.54	2.10	1.97
Diluted earnings per common share	2.92	2.55	2.42	2.02	1.88
Cash Flow Data					
Provided by operating activities	$ 1,302	$ 1,238	$ 1,186	$ 1,099	$ 1,112
Capital spending, excluding acquisitions	614	609	645	663	760
Proceeds from refranchising of restaurants	257	145	140	92	81
Repurchase shares of common stock	983	1,056	569	278	228
Dividends paid on common shares	144	123	58	—	—
Balance Sheet					
Total assets	$ 6,353	$ 5,797	$ 5,696	$ 5,620	$ 5,400
Long-term debt	2,045	1,649	1,731	2,056	2,299
Total debt	2,272	1,860	1,742	2,066	2,445
Other Data					
Number of stores at year end					
Company	7,736	7,587	7,743	7,854	7,526
Unconsolidated Affiliates	1,206	1,648	1,662	1,512	2,148
Franchisees	23,516	22,666	21,858	21,471	20,724
Licensees	2,137	2,376	2,345	2,362	2,526
System	34,595	34,277	33,608	33,199	32,924
U.S. Company blended same store sales growth[e]	—	4%	3%	—	2%
International Division system sales growth[f]					
Reported	7%	9%	14%	13%	6%
Local currency[g]	7%	6%	6%	5%	7%
China Division system sales growth[f]					
Reported	26%	13%	23%	23%	25%
Local currency[g]	23%	11%	23%	23%	25%
Shares outstanding at year end	265	278	290	292	294
Cash dividends declared per common share	$ 0.865	$ 0.445	$ 0.30	—	—
Market price per share at year end	$ 58.80	$ 46.88	$ 46.27	$ 33.64	$ 24.12

Fiscal years 2006, 2004, 2003 and 2002 include 52 weeks and fiscal year 2005 includes 53 weeks.

Fiscal years 2006 and 2005 include the impact of the adoption of Statement of Financial Accounting Standards ("SFAS") No. 123R (Revised 2004), "Share Based Payment" ("SFAS 123R"). This resulted in a $39 million and $38 million decrease in net income, or a decrease of $0.14 and $0.13 to both basic and diluted earnings per share for 2006 and 2005, respectively. If SFAS 123R had been effective for prior years presented, reported basic and diluted earnings per share would have decreased $0.12 and $0.12, $0.12 and $0.12, and $0.14 and $0.13 per share for 2004, 2003 and 2002, respectively, consistent with previously disclosed pro-forma information. See Note 2 to the Consolidated Financial Statements.

From May 7, 2002, results include Long John Silver's ("LJS") and A&W All-American Food Restaurants ("A&W"), which were added when we acquired Yorkshire Global Restaurants, Inc.

The selected financial data should be read in conjunction with the Consolidated Financial Statements and the Notes thereto.

(a) See Note 4 to the Consolidated Financial Statements for a description of Closures and Impairment Expenses and Refranchising Gain (Loss) in 2006, 2005 and 2004.

(b) See Note 4 to the Consolidated Financial Statements for a description of Wrench litigation in 2006, 2005 and 2004.

(c) See Note 4 to the Consolidated Financial Statements for a description of AmeriServe and other (charges) credits in 2006, 2005 and 2004.

(d) Fiscal year 2003 includes the impact of the adoption of SFAS No. 143, "Accounting for Asset Retirement Obligations," which addresses the financial accounting and reporting for legal obligations associated with the retirement of long-lived assets and the associated asset retirement costs.

(e) U.S. Company blended same-store sales growth includes the results of Company owned KFC, Pizza Hut and Taco Bell restaurants that have been open one year or more. LJS and A&W are not included.

(f) International Division and China Division system sales growth includes the results of all restaurants regardless of ownership, including Company owned, franchise, unconsolidated affiliate and license restaurants. Sales of franchise, unconsolidated affiliate and license restaurants generate franchise and license fees for the Company (typically at a rate of 4% to 6% of sales). Franchise, unconsolidated affiliate and license restaurant sales are not included in Company sales we present on the Consolidated Statements of Income; however, the fees are included in the Company's revenues. We believe system sales growth is useful to investors as a significant indicator of the overall strength of our business as it incorporates all our revenue drivers, Company and franchise same store sales as well as net unit development. Additionally, as previously noted, we began reporting information for our international business in two separate operating segments (the International Division and the China Division) in 2005 as a result of changes in our management structure. Segment information for periods prior to 2005 has been restated to reflect this reporting.

(g) Local currency represents the percentage change excluding the impact of foreign currency translation. These amounts are derived by translating current year results at prior year average exchange rates. We believe the elimination of the foreign currency translation impact provides better year-to-year comparability without the distortion of foreign currency fluctuations.

Pier 1 imports®

2006 Annual Report

Item 6. *Selected Financial Data.*

FINANCIAL SUMMARY

| | \multicolumn{5}{c}{Year Ended} |
	2006	2005	2004	2003	2002
		($ in millions except per share amounts)			
SUMMARY OF OPERATIONS*:					
Net sales	$1,776.7	1,825.3	1,806.1	1,703.4	1,505.1
Gross profit	$ 601.7	703.6	760.9	736.4	636.9
Selling, general and administrative expenses	$ 588.3	549.6	526.1	487.0	435.7
Depreciation and amortization	$ 56.2	55.8	48.9	44.7	41.2
Operating income (loss)	$ (42.8)	98.2	186.0	204.8	160.0
Nonoperating (income) and expenses, net	$ (0.9)	(0.9)	(1.0)	(0.6)	(0.1)
Income (loss) from continuing operations before income taxes	$ (41.9)	99.1	187.0	205.6	160.1
Income (loss) from continuing operations, net of tax	$ (27.5)	62.8	117.7	129.6	101.3
Income (loss) from discontinued operations, net of tax	$ (12.3)	(2.3)	0.3	(0.3)	(1.1)
Net income (loss)	$ (39.8)	60.5	118.0	129.4	100.2
PER SHARE AMOUNTS:					
Basic earnings (loss) from continuing operations	$ (.32)	.72	1.32	1.40	1.07
Diluted earnings (loss) from continuing operations	$ (.32)	.71	1.29	1.36	1.05
Basic earnings (loss) from discontinued operations	$ (.14)	(.03)	.00	(.00)	(.01)
Diluted earnings (loss) from discontinued operations	$ (.14)	(.03)	.00	(.00)	(.01)
Basic earnings (loss) consolidated	$ (.46)	.69	1.32	1.39	1.06
Diluted earnings (loss) consolidated	$ (.46)	.68	1.29	1.36	1.04
Cash dividends declared	$ .40	.40	.30	.21	.16
Shareholders' equity	$ 6.81	7.63	7.66	6.93	6.20
OTHER FINANCIAL DATA:					
Working capital	$ 486.1	387.4	433.0	432.3	408.6
Current ratio	2.7	2.3	2.5	2.8	3.0
Total assets	$1,169.9	1,075.7	1,052.2	972.7	867.3
Long-term debt	$ 184.0	19.0	19.0	25.0	25.4
Shareholders' equity	$ 590.0	664.4	683.6	643.9	585.7
Weighted average diluted shares outstanding (millions)	86.6	88.8	91.6	95.3	96.2
Effective tax rate	34.5%	36.7	37.1	37.0	36.7
Return on average shareholders' equity	(4.4%)	9.3	17.7	21.1	18.1
Return on average total assets	(2.4%)	5.9	11.6	14.1	12.6
Pre-tax return on sales	(2.4%)	5.4	10.4	12.1	10.6

* Amounts are from continuing operations unless otherwise specified.

Item 8. *Financial Statements and Supplementary Data.*

REPORT OF INDEPENDENT REGISTERED PUBLIC ACCOUNTING FIRM

To the Board of Directors of Pier 1 Imports, Inc.

We have audited the accompanying consolidated balance sheets of Pier 1 Imports, Inc. as of February 25, 2006 and February 26, 2005, and the related consolidated statements of operations, shareholders' equity, and cash flows for each of the three years in the period ended February 25, 2006. These financial statements are the responsibility of the Company's management. Our responsibility is to express an opinion on these financial statements based on our audits.

We conducted our audits in accordance with the standards of the Public Company Accounting Oversight Board (United States). Those standards require that we plan and perform the audit to obtain reasonable assurance about whether the financial statements are free of material misstatement. An audit includes examining, on a test basis, evidence supporting the amounts and disclosures in the financial statements. An audit also includes assessing the accounting principles used and significant estimates made by management, as well as evaluating the overall financial statement presentation. We believe that our audits provide a reasonable basis for our opinion.

In our opinion, the financial statements referred to above present fairly, in all material respects, the consolidated financial position of Pier 1 Imports, Inc. at February 25, 2006 and February 26, 2005, and the consolidated results of its operations and its cash flows for each of the three years in the period ended February 25, 2006, in conformity with U.S. generally accepted accounting principles.

As discussed in Note 2 of the Notes to Consolidated Financial Statements, the Company corrected its classification of non-monetary transactions related to its beneficial interest in securitized receivables on the consolidated statements of cash flows. The prior periods presented have been restated for this correction.

We also have audited, in accordance with the standards of the Public Company Accounting Oversight Board (United States), the effectiveness of Pier 1 Imports, Inc.'s internal control over financial reporting as of February 25, 2006, based on criteria established in Internal Control — Integrated Framework issued by the Committee of Sponsoring Organizations of the Treadway Commission and our report dated April 25, 2006 expressed an unqualified opinion thereon.

/s/   Ernst & Young LLP

Fort Worth, Texas
April 25, 2006

Pier 1 Imports, Inc.

CONSOLIDATED STATEMENTS OF OPERATIONS
(In thousands except per share amounts)

	Year Ended		
	2006	2005	2004
Net sales	$1,776,701	$1,825,343	$1,806,092
Operating costs and expenses:			
Cost of sales (including buying and store occupancy costs)	1,175,011	1,121,697	1,045,180
Selling, general and administrative expenses	588,273	549,635	526,060
Depreciation and amortization	56,229	55,762	48,869
	1,819,513	1,727,094	1,620,109
Operating income (loss)	(42,812)	98,249	185,983
Nonoperating (income) and expenses:			
Interest and investment income	(3,510)	(2,635)	(2,724)
Interest expense	2,610	1,735	1,688
	(900)	(900)	(1,036)
Income (loss) from continuing operations before income taxes	(41,912)	99,149	187,019
Provision (benefit) for income taxes	(14,441)	36,384	69,315
Income (loss) from continuing operations	(27,471)	62,765	117,704
Discontinued operations:			
Income (loss) from discontinued operations (including write down of assets held for sale of $7,441 in 2006)	(17,583)	(2,308)	297
Income tax benefit	(5,250)	—	—
Income (loss) from discontinued operations	(12,333)	(2,308)	297
Net income (loss)	$ (39,804)	$ 60,457	$ 118,001
Earnings (loss) per share from continuing operations:			
Basic	$ (.32)	$ .72	$ 1.32
Diluted	$ (.32)	$ .71	$ 1.29
Earnings (loss) per share from discontinued operations:			
Basic	$ (.14)	$ (.03)	$ .00
Diluted	$ (.14)	$ (.03)	$ .00
Earnings (loss) per share:			
Basic	$ (.46)	$ .69	$ 1.32
Diluted	$ (.46)	$ .68	$ 1.29
Dividends declared per share:	$ .40	$ .40	$ .30
Average shares outstanding during period:			
Basic	86,629	87,037	89,294
Diluted	86,629	88,838	91,624

The accompanying notes are an integral part of these financial statements.

Pier 1 Imports, Inc.

CONSOLIDATED BALANCE SHEETS
(In thousands except share amounts)

	2006	2005
ASSETS		
Current assets:		
Cash and cash equivalents, including temporary investments of $238,463 and $178,289, respectively	$ 246,115	$ 185,722
Beneficial interest in securitized receivables	50,000	35,690
Other accounts receivable, net of allowance for doubtful accounts of $1,119 and $82, respectively	13,916	11,089
Inventories	368,978	365,767
Income tax receivable	18,011	—
Assets held for sale	32,359	39,815
Prepaid expenses and other current assets	45,544	40,864
Total current assets	774,923	678,947
Properties, net	298,922	320,138
Other noncurrent assets	96,016	76,664
	$1,169,861	$1,075,749
LIABILITIES AND SHAREHOLDERS' EQUITY		
Current liabilities:		
Accounts payable	$ 105,916	$ 108,132
Gift cards and other deferred revenue	63,835	60,844
Accrued income taxes payable	4,763	11,716
Liabilities related to assets held for sale	16,841	15,163
Other accrued liabilities	97,493	95,723
Total current liabilities	288,848	291,578
Long-term debt	184,000	19,000
Other noncurrent liabilities	107,031	100,802
Shareholders' equity:		
Common stock, $1.00 par, 500,000,000 shares authorized, 100,779,000 issued	100,779	100,779
Paid-in capital	132,075	141,850
Retained earnings	582,221	656,692
Cumulative other comprehensive loss	(583)	(1,426)
Less — 13,761,000 and 14,459,000 common shares in treasury, at cost, respectively	(222,254)	(233,526)
Less — unearned compensation	(2,256)	—
	589,982	664,369
Commitments and contingencies	—	—
	$1,169,861	$1,075,749

The accompanying notes are an integral part of these financial statements.

38

Pier 1 Imports, Inc.

CONSOLIDATED STATEMENTS OF CASH FLOWS
(In thousands)

	Year Ended		
	2006	**2005** (As restated, See Note 2)	**2004** (As restated, See Note 2)
Cash flow from operating activities:			
Net income (loss)	$(39,804)	$ 60,457	$118,001
Adjustments to reconcile to net cash (used in) provided by operating activities:			
Depreciation and amortization	78,781	75,624	64,606
Loss (gain) on disposal of fixed assets	1,781	315	(316)
Loss on impairment of fixed assets	6,024	741	459
Write-down of assets held for sale	7,441	—	—
Deferred compensation	11,402	7,710	6,573
Lease termination expense	4,176	2,243	3,258
Deferred income taxes	(14,496)	2,035	184
Sale of receivables in exchange for beneficial interest in securitized receivables	(74,550)	(91,071)	(83,931)
Tax benefit from options exercised by employees	760	3,668	4,897
Other	(524)	(222)	4,894
Change in cash from:			
Inventories	882	(6,860)	(40,520)
Other accounts receivable, prepaid expenses and other current assets	(22,778)	(11,302)	(16,927)
Income tax receivable	(18,011)	—	—
Accounts payable and accrued expenses	7,369	21,572	34,410
Income taxes payable	(6,966)	(14,116)	184
Other noncurrent assets	(2,558)	336	(2,027)
Other noncurrent liabilities	(3,226)	—	—
Net cash (used in) provided by operating activities	(64,297)	51,130	93,745
Cash flow from investing activities:			
Capital expenditures	(50,979)	(99,239)	(121,190)
Proceeds from disposition of properties	1,401	3,852	34,450
Proceeds from sale of restricted investments	3,226	—	—
Purchase of restricted investments	(3,500)	(10,807)	(8,752)
Collections of principal on beneficial interest in securitized receivables	60,240	99,712	78,788
Net cash provided by (used in) investing activities	10,388	(6,482)	(16,704)
Cash flow from financing activities:			
Cash dividends	(34,667)	(34,762)	(26,780)
Purchases of treasury stock	(4,047)	(58,210)	(76,009)
Proceeds from stock options exercised, stock purchase plan and other, net	7,641	12,473	15,709
Issuance of long-term debt	165,000	—	—
Notes payable borrowings	86,500	—	—
Repayment of notes payable	(86,500)	—	(6,390)
Debt issuance costs	(6,739)	(169)	(584)
Purchase of call option	(9,145)	—	—
Net cash provided by (used in) financing activities	118,043	(80,668)	(94,054)
Change in cash and cash equivalents	64,134	(36,020)	(17,013)
Cash and cash equivalents at beginning of period (including cash held for sale of $3,359, $6,148 and $6,506, respectively)	189,081	225,101	242,114
Cash and cash equivalents at end of period (including cash held for sale of $7,100, $3,359 and $6,148, respectively)	$253,215	$189,081	$225,101
Supplemental cash flow information:			
Interest paid	$ 8,136	$ 868	$ 1,791
Income taxes paid	$ 21,342	$ 45,655	$ 63,788

The accompanying notes are an integral part of these financial statements.

Pier 1 Imports, Inc.

CONSOLIDATED STATEMENTS OF SHAREHOLDERS' EQUITY
(In thousands except per share amounts)

| | Common Stock | | Paid-in Capital | Retained Earnings | Cumulative Other Comprehensive Income (Loss) | Treasury Stock | Unearned Compensation | Total Shareholders' Equity |
	Outstanding Shares	Amount						
Balance March 1, 2003	90,685	$100,779	$144,247	$539,776	$(2,210)	$(138,656)	$ —	$643,936
Comprehensive income:								
Net income	—	—	—	118,001	—	—	—	118,001
Other comprehensive income:								
Minimum pension liability adjustments, net of tax	—	—	—	—	(1,033)	—	—	(1,033)
Currency translation adjustments	—	—	—	—	4,910	—	—	4,910
Comprehensive income								121,878
Purchases of treasury stock	(3,758)	—	—	—	—	(76,009)	—	(76,009)
Exercise of stock options, stock purchase plan and other	1,300	—	1,137	—	—	19,469	—	20,606
Cash dividends ($.30 per share) ..	—	—	—	(26,780)	—	—	—	(26,780)
Balance February 28, 2004	88,227	100,779	145,384	630,997	1,667	(195,196)	—	683,631
Comprehensive income:								
Net income	—	—	—	60,457	—	—	—	60,457
Other comprehensive income (loss), net of tax:								
Minimum pension liability adjustments	—	—	—	—	(4,780)	—	—	(4,780)
Currency translation adjustments	—	—	—	—	1,687	—	—	1,687
Comprehensive income								57,364
Purchases of treasury stock	(3,225)	—	—	—	—	(58,210)	—	(58,210)
Exercise of stock options, stock purchase plan and other	1,238	—	(3,534)	—	—	19,880	—	16,346
Cash dividends ($.40 per share) ..	—	—	—	(34,762)	—	—	—	(34,762)
Balance February 26, 2005	86,240	100,779	141,850	656,692	(1,426)	(233,526)	—	664,369
Comprehensive income (loss):								
Net loss	—	—	—	(39,804)	—	—	—	(39,804)
Other comprehensive income (loss), net of tax:								
Minimum pension liability adjustments	—	—	—	—	1,149	—	—	1,149
Currency translation adjustments	—	—	—	—	(306)	—	—	(306)
Comprehensive loss								(38,961)
Purchases of treasury stock	(250)	—	—	—	—	(4,047)	—	(4,047)
Restricted stock grant and amortization	203	—	(386)	—	—	3,278	(2,256)	636
Exercise of stock options, stock purchase plan and other	746	—	(3,640)	—	—	12,041	—	8,401
Cash dividends ($.40 per share) ..	—	—	—	(34,667)	—	—	—	(34,667)
Purchase of call option, net of tax ..	—	—	(5,749)	—	—	—	—	(5,749)
Balance February 25, 2006	86,939	$100,779	$132,075	$582,221	$ (583)	$(222,254)	$(2,256)	$589,982

The accompanying notes are an integral part of these financial statements.

NOTES TO CONSOLIDATED FINANCIAL STATEMENTS

NOTE 1 — SUMMARY OF SIGNIFICANT ACCOUNTING POLICIES

Organization — Pier 1 Imports, Inc. and its consolidated subsidiaries (the "Company") is one of North America's largest specialty retailers of imported decorative home furnishings, gifts and related items, with retail stores located primarily in the United States, Canada, Puerto Rico and Mexico. On March 20, 2006, the Company sold its subsidiary based in the United Kingdom, The Pier Retail Group Limited ("The Pier"). At fiscal 2006 year end, The Pier was classified as held for sale and included in discontinued operations for all years presented. In the fourth quarter of fiscal 2006, the Company recorded an impairment charge of $7,441,000 to write goodwill and long-lived assets related to The Pier down by $918,000 and $6,523,000, respectively, to fair value less selling costs. *See Note 3 of the Notes to Consolidated Financial Statements for further discussion.*

Basis of consolidation — The consolidated financial statements of the Company include the accounts of all subsidiary companies except Pier 1 Funding, LLC, which is a non-consolidated, bankruptcy remote, securitization subsidiary. *See Note 4 of the Notes to Consolidated Financial Statements.* Material intercompany transactions and balances have been eliminated.

Segment information — The Company is a specialty retailer that offers a broad range of products in its stores and conducts business as one operating segment. The Company's domestic operations provided 93.0%, 93.7% and 94.1% of its net sales, with 6.7%, 6.0% and 5.7% provided by stores in Canada, and the remainder from royalties received from Sears Roebuck de Mexico S.A. de C.V. during fiscal 2006, 2005 and 2004, respectively. As of February 25, 2006 and February 26, 2005, $8,765,000 and $8,888,000, respectively, of the Company's long-lived assets were located in Canada. There were no long-lived assets in Mexico during either period.

Use of estimates — Preparation of the financial statements in conformity with U.S. generally accepted accounting principles requires management to make estimates and assumptions that affect the amounts reported in the financial statements and accompanying notes. Actual results could differ from those estimates.

Reclassifications — Certain reclassifications have been made in the prior years' consolidated financial statements to conform to the fiscal 2006 presentation. These reclassifications had no effect on net income and shareholders' equity with minimal effects on total assets and total liabilities. During the fourth quarter of fiscal 2006, the Company determined that a reclassification within its consolidated statements of cash flows was required to properly reflect the exchanges of securitized receivables as non-monetary transactions in the operating activities section of the Company's consolidated statements of cash flows. This reclass required a restatement for fiscal years 2005 and 2004. *See Note 2 of the Notes to Consolidated Financial Statements for further discussion.*

Fiscal periods — The Company utilizes 5-4-4 (week) quarterly accounting periods with the fiscal year ending on the Saturday nearest the last day of February. Fiscal 2006 ended February 25, 2006, fiscal 2005 ended February 26, 2005 and fiscal 2004 ended February 28, 2004, all of which contained 52 weeks.

Cash and cash equivalents — The Company considers all highly liquid investments with an original maturity date of three months or less to be cash equivalents, except for those investments that are restricted and have been set aside in a trust to satisfy pension obligations. As of February 25, 2006 and February 26, 2005, the Company's short-term investments classified as cash equivalents included investments in money market mutual funds totaling $238,463,000 and $178,289,000, respectively. The effect of foreign currency exchange rate fluctuations on cash is not material.

Translation of foreign currencies — Assets and liabilities of foreign operations are translated into United States dollars at fiscal year-end exchange rates. Income and expense items are translated at average exchange rates prevailing during the year. Translation adjustments arising from differences in exchange rates from period to period are included as a separate component of shareholders' equity and are included in other comprehensive income (loss). As of February 25, 2006, February 26, 2005 and

NOTES TO CONSOLIDATED FINANCIAL STATEMENTS — (Continued)

February 28, 2004, the Company had cumulative other comprehensive income balances of $4,990,000, $5,296,000, and $3,609,000, respectively, related to cumulative translation adjustments. The adjustments for currency translation during fiscal 2006, 2005 and 2004 resulted in other comprehensive income (loss) of ($306,000), $1,687,000, and $4,910,000, respectively. During fiscal 2006 and 2005, the Company provided deferred taxes of $531,000 and $703,000, respectively, on the portion of its cumulative currency translation adjustment considered not to be permanently reinvested abroad. Taxes on this portion of cumulative currency translation adjustments were insignificant in fiscal 2004.

Concentrations of risk — The Company has some degree of risk concentration with respect to sourcing the Company's inventory purchases. However, the Company believes alternative sources of products could be procured over a relatively short period of time. Pier 1 sells merchandise imported from over 40 different countries, with 35% of its sales derived from merchandise produced in China, 14% derived from merchandise produced in India, 13% derived from merchandise produced in the United States and 33% derived from merchandise produced in Indonesia, Brazil, Italy, Thailand, the Philippines, Vietnam and Mexico. The remaining 5% of sales was from merchandise produced in various Asian, European, Central American, South American and African countries.

Financial instruments — The fair value of financial instruments is determined by reference to various market data and other valuation techniques as appropriate. There were no assets or liabilities with a fair value significantly different from the recorded value as of February 25, 2006 and February 26, 2005.

From time to time, the Company purchases auction rate securities with the intention to hold them for short periods of time and considers them to be trading securities. The cash flows from the purchases and sales of these securities are reported in cash provided by operating activities. The Company had no auction rate securities outstanding at either February 25, 2006 or February 26, 2005.

Risk management instruments: The Company may utilize various financial instruments to manage interest rate and market risk associated with its on- and off-balance sheet commitments.

The Company hedges certain commitments denominated in foreign currencies through the purchase of forward contracts. The forward contracts are purchased only to cover specific commitments to buy merchandise for resale. The Company also uses contracts to hedge its exposure associated with the repatriation of funds from its Canadian operations. At February 25, 2006, there were no outstanding contracts to hedge exposure associated with the Company's merchandise purchases denominated in foreign currencies or the repatriation of Canadian funds. For financial accounting purposes, the Company does not designate such contracts as hedges. Thus, changes in the fair value of both types of forward contracts would be included in the Company's consolidated statements of operations. Both the changes in fair value and settlement of these contracts are included in cost of sales for forwards related to merchandise purchases and in selling, general and administrative expense for the contracts associated with the repatriation of Canadian funds.

The Company enters into forward foreign currency exchange contracts with major financial institutions and continually monitors its positions with, and the credit quality of, these counterparties to such financial instruments. The Company does not expect non-performance by any of the counterparties, and any losses incurred in the event of non-performance would not be material.

Beneficial interest in securitized receivables — The Company securitizes its entire portfolio of proprietary credit card receivables. During fiscal 2006, 2005 and 2004, the Company sold all of its proprietary credit card receivables, except those that failed certain eligibility requirements, to a special-purpose wholly owned subsidiary, Pier 1 Funding, LLC ("Funding"), which transferred the receivables to the Pier 1 Imports Credit Card Master Trust (the "Master Trust"). Neither Funding nor the Master Trust is consolidated by the Company and the Master Trust meets the requirements of a qualifying special-purpose entity under Statement of Financial Accounting Standards ("SFAS") No. 140. The Master Trust issues beneficial interests that represent undivided interests in the assets of the Master Trust consisting of

NOTES TO CONSOLIDATED FINANCIAL STATEMENTS — (Continued)

the transferred receivables and all cash flows from collections of such receivables. The beneficial interests include certain interests retained by Funding, which are represented by Class B Certificates, and the residual interest in the Master Trust (the excess of the principal amount of receivables held in the Master Trust over the portion represented by the certificates sold to a third-party investor and the Class B Certificates). Gain or loss on the sale of receivables depends in part on the previous carrying amount of the financial assets involved in the transfer, allocated between the assets sold and the retained interests based on their relative fair value at the date of transfer.

The beneficial interest in the Master Trust is accounted for as an available-for-sale security and is recorded at fair value. The Company estimates fair value of its beneficial interest in the Master Trust, both upon initial securitization and thereafter, based on the present value of future expected cash flows using management's best estimates of key assumptions including credit losses and payment rates. As of February 25, 2006 and February 26, 2005, the Company's assumptions used to calculate the present value of the future cash flows included estimated credit losses of 4.75% and 5%, respectively, of the outstanding balance, expected payment within a six-month period and a discount rate representing the average market rate the Company would expect to pay if it sold securities representing ownership in the excess receivables not required to collateralize the Class A Certificates. A sensitivity analysis performed assuming a hypothetical 20% adverse change in both interest rates and credit losses resulted in an immaterial impact on the fair value of the Company's beneficial interest. Although not anticipated by the Company, a significant deterioration in the financial condition of the Company's credit card holders, interest rates, or other economic conditions could result in other than temporary losses on the beneficial interest in future periods. *See Note 4 of the Notes to Consolidated Financial Statements for further discussion.*

Inventories — Inventories are comprised of finished merchandise and are stated at the lower of average cost or market, cost being determined on a weighted average inventory method. Cost is calculated based upon the actual landed cost of an item at the time it is received in the Company's warehouse using actual vendor invoices, the cost of warehousing and transporting product to the stores and other direct costs associated with purchasing products.

The Company recognizes known inventory losses, shortages and damages when incurred and maintains a reserve for estimated shrinkage since the last physical count, when actual shrink was recorded. The reserves for estimated shrink at the end of fiscal years 2006 and 2005 were $8,218,000 and $4,711,000, respectively. The increase was a result of timing of physical counts and not of an increase in rates of shrink.

Properties, maintenance and repairs — Buildings, equipment, furniture and fixtures, and leasehold improvements are carried at cost less accumulated depreciation. Depreciation is computed using the straight-line method over estimated remaining useful lives of the assets, generally thirty years for buildings and three to ten years for equipment, furniture and fixtures. Depreciation of improvements to leased properties is based upon the shorter of the remaining primary lease term or the estimated useful lives of such assets. Depreciation related to the Company's distribution centers is included in cost of sales. All other depreciation costs are included in depreciation and amortization. Depreciation costs were $54,870,000, $54,404,000 and $47,514,000 in fiscal 2006, 2005 and 2004, respectively.

Expenditures for maintenance, repairs and renewals that do not materially prolong the original useful lives of the assets are charged to expense as incurred. In the case of disposals, assets and the related depreciation are removed from the accounts and the net amount, less proceeds from disposal, is credited or charged to income.

Long-lived assets are reviewed at the store level for impairment at least annually and whenever an event or change in circumstances indicates that its carrying value may not be recoverable. If the carrying value exceeds the sum of the expected undiscounted cash flows, the asset is impaired. Expected cash flows are estimated based on management's estimate of changes in sales, merchandise margins, and expenses over the remaining expected terms of the leases. Impairment is measured as the amount by which the

43

NOTES TO CONSOLIDATED FINANCIAL STATEMENTS — (Continued)

carrying value of the asset exceeds the fair value of the asset. Fair value is determined by discounting expected cash flows. Impairment, if any, is recorded in the period in which the impairment occurred. Impairment charges were $5,601,000, $370,000 and $459,000 in fiscal 2006, 2005 and 2004, respectively, and included in selling, general and administrative expenses.

Goodwill and intangible assets — The Company applies the provisions of SFAS No. 142, "Goodwill and Intangible Assets." Under SFAS No. 142, goodwill and intangible assets with indefinite useful lives are not amortized, but instead are tested for impairment at least annually. In accordance with SFAS No. 142, the Company's reporting units were identified as components, and the goodwill assigned to each represents the excess of the original purchase price over the fair value of the net identifiable assets acquired for that component. The Company completed the annual impairment tests as of February 25, 2006 and February 26, 2005 for fiscal 2006 and 2005, respectively. The impairment tests were conducted by performing analyses of discounted future cash flows for the applicable reporting units. The analysis resulted in a write-down of intangible assets of $239,000, included in selling, general and administrative expenses, in fiscal 2006. No impairment loss was recognized in fiscal 2005 or fiscal 2004. *See Note 6 of the Notes to Consolidated Financial Statements for additional discussion of goodwill and intangible assets.*

Revenue recognition — Revenue is recognized upon customer receipt or delivery for retail sales, net of sales tax, including sales under deferred payment promotions on the Company's proprietary credit card. A reserve has been established for estimated merchandise returns based upon historical experience and other known factors. The reserves for estimated merchandise returns at the end of fiscal years 2006 and 2005 were $3,060,000 and $3,330,000, respectively. The Company's revenues are reported net of discounts and returns, and include wholesale sales and royalties received from franchise stores and Sears Roebuck de Mexico S.A. de C.V. Amounts billed to customers for shipping and handling are included in net sales and the costs incurred by the Company for these items are recorded in cost of sales.

Gift cards — Revenue associated with gift cards is recognized upon redemption of the gift card. Gift card breakage is estimated and recorded as income based upon an analysis of the Company's historical redemption patterns and represents the remaining unused portion of the gift card liability for which the likelihood of redemption is remote.

Leases — The Company leases certain property consisting principally of retail stores, warehouses, and material handling and office equipment under leases expiring through fiscal 2021. Most retail store locations are leased for primary terms of 10 to 15 years with varying renewal options and rent escalation clauses. Escalations occurring during the primary terms of the leases are included in the calculation of the minimum lease payments, and the rent expense related to these leases is recognized on a straight-line basis over this lease term. Prior to fiscal 2005, the Company recognized straight-line rent expense for store leases beginning on the earlier of the rent commencement date or the store opening date, which had the effect of excluding the build-out period of its stores from the calculation of the period over which it expenses rent. During the fourth quarter of fiscal 2005, the Company revised its accounting practices to extend the lease term to include this free rent period prior to the opening of its stores. This revision in practice resulted in a cumulative pre-tax charge of $6,264,000 for leases entered into prior to fiscal 2005, which was not material to any previously reported fiscal year. This cumulative adjustment had no effect on historical or future cash flows from operations or the timing of payments under the related leases. The portion of rent expense applicable to a store before opening is included in selling, general and administrative expenses. Once opened for business, rent expense is included in cost of sales. Certain leases provide for additional rental payments based on a percentage of sales in excess of a specified base. This additional rent is accrued when it appears that the sales will exceed the specified base. Construction allowances received from landlords are initially recorded as lease liabilities and amortized as a reduction of rental expense over the primary lease term. The Company's lease obligations are considered operating leases under SFAS No. 13.

NOTES TO CONSOLIDATED FINANCIAL STATEMENTS — (Continued)

NOTE 5 — PROPERTIES

Properties are summarized as follows at February 25, 2006 and February 26, 2005 (in thousands):

	2006	2005
Land	$ 18,778	$ 19,627
Buildings	95,056	98,184
Equipment, furniture and fixtures	271,702	297,034
Leasehold improvements	217,795	218,006
Computer software	60,208	63,515
Projects in progress	5,673	6,394
	669,212	702,760
Less accumulated depreciation and amortization	370,290	382,622
Properties, net	$298,922	$320,138

NOTE 6 — GOODWILL AND OTHER INTANGIBLE ASSETS

The Company's intangible assets at February 25, 2006 and February 26, 2005 included the right to do business within certain geographical markets where franchise stores were previously granted exclusive rights to operate, favorable operating leases acquired from a third party and goodwill related primarily to the acquisition of Pier 1 Kids. These intangible assets were included in other noncurrent assets in the Company's consolidated balance sheets. Amortization expense for fiscal 2006, 2005 and 2004 was $1,654,000, $1,656,000 and $1,493,000, respectively. The following is a summary of the Company's intangible assets at February 25, 2006 and February 26, 2005 (in thousands):

	2006	2005
Geographic market rights, gross	$ 14,926	$ 15,023
Accumulated amortization	(13,088)	(11,639)
Geographic market rights, net	$ 1,838	$ 3,384
Acquired operating leases, gross	$ 1,615	$ 1,975
Accumulated amortization	(463)	(257)
Acquired operating leases, net	$ 1,152	$ 1,718
Goodwill, not amortized	$ 4,088	$ 4,088

Estimated future amortization expense related to intangible assets at February 25, 2006 is as follows (in thousands):

Fiscal Year	Amortization Expense
2007	$1,530
2008	617
2009	155
2010	153
2011	129
Thereafter	406
Total future amortization expense	$2,990

Item 9. *Changes in and Disagreements with Accountants on Accounting and Financial Disclosure.*

None.

Item 9A. *Controls and Procedures.*

REPORT OF MANAGEMENT ON INTERNAL CONTROL OVER FINANCIAL REPORTING

Management is responsible for establishing and maintaining a system of internal control over financial reporting designed to provide reasonable assurance that transactions are executed in accordance with management authorization and that such transactions are properly recorded and reported in the financial statements, and that records are maintained so as to permit preparation of the financial statements in accordance with U.S. generally accepted accounting principles. Because of its inherent limitations, internal control over financial reporting may not prevent or detect misstatements. Management has assessed the effectiveness of the Company's internal control over financial reporting utilizing the criteria set forth by the Committee of Sponsoring Organizations of the Treadway Commission in *Internal Control — Integrated Framework.* Management concluded that based on its assessment, Pier 1 Imports, Inc.'s internal control over financial reporting was effective as of February 25, 2006. Management's assessment of the effectiveness of the Company's internal control over financial reporting as of February 25, 2006 has been audited by Ernst & Young LLP, an independent registered public accounting firm, as stated in their report which is included in this Annual Report on Form 10-K.

/s/ Marvin J. Girouard
_____

Marvin J. Girouard
Chairman of the Board and
Chief Executive Officer

/s/ Charles H. Turner
_____

Charles H. Turner
Executive Vice President, Finance,
Chief Financial Officer and Treasurer

Appendix D

Time Value of Money: Future Value and Present Value

The following discussion of future value lays the foundation for our explanation of present value in Chapter 8 but is not essential. For the valuation of long-term liabilities, some instructors may wish to begin on page 809 of this appendix.

The term *time value of money* refers to the fact that money earns interest over time. *Interest* is the cost of using money. To borrowers, interest is the expense of renting money. To lenders, interest is the revenue earned from lending. We must always recognize the interest we receive or pay. Otherwise, we overlook an important part of the transaction. Suppose you invest $4,545 in corporate bonds that pay 10% interest each year. After 1 year, the value of your investment has grown to $5,000. The difference between your original investment ($4,545) and the future value of the investment ($5,000) is the amount of interest revenue you will earn during the year ($455). If you ignored the interest, you would fail to account for the interest revenue you have earned. Interest becomes more important as the time period lengthens because the amount of interest depends on the span of time the money is invested.

Let's consider a second example, this time from the borrower's perspective. Suppose you purchase a machine for your business. The cash price of the machine is $8,000, but you cannot pay cash now. To finance the purchase, you sign an $8,000 note payable. The note requires you to pay the $8,000 plus 10% interest 1 year from the date of purchase. Is your cost of the machine $8,000, or is it $8,800 [$8,000 plus interest of $800 ($8,000 × .10)]? The cost is $8,000. The additional $800 is interest expense and not part of the cost of the machine.

Future Value

The main application of future value is the accumulated balance of an investment at a future date. In our first example above, the investment earned 10% per year. After 1 year, $4,545 grew to $5,000, as shown in Exhibit D-1.

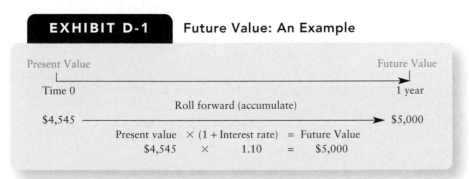

EXHIBIT D-1 Future Value: An Example

If the money were invested for 5 years, you would have to perform 5 such calculations. You would also have to consider the compound interest that your investment is earning. *Compound interest* is not only the interest you earn on your principal amount, but also the interest you receive on the interest you have already earned. Most business applications include compound interest. The following table shows the interest revenue earned on the original $4,545 investment each year for 5 years at 10%:

End of Year	Interest	Future Value
0	—	$4,545
1	$4,545 × 0.10 = $455	5,000
2	5,000 × 0.10 = 500	5,500
3	5,500 × 0.10 = 550	6,050
4	6,050 × 0.10 = 605	6,655
5	6,655 × 0.10 = 666	7,321

Earning 10%, a $4,545 investment grows to $5,000 at the end of 1 year, to $5,500 at the end of 2 years, and $7,321 at the end of 5 years. Throughout this appendix we round off to the nearest dollar.

Future-Value Tables

The process of computing a future value is called *accumulating* because the future value is *more* than the present value. Mathematical tables ease the computational burden. Exhibit D-2, Future Value of $1, gives the future value for a single sum (a present value), $1, invested to earn a particular interest rate for a specific number of periods. Future value depends on 3 factors: (1) the amount of the investment, (2) the length of time between investment and future accumulation, and (3) the interest rate. Future-value and present-value tables are based on $1 because unity (the value 1) is so easy to work with.

EXHIBIT D-2   Future Value of $1

Future Value of $1

Periods	4%	5%	6%	7%	8%	9%	10%	12%	14%	16%
1	1.040	1.050	1.060	1.070	1.080	1.090	1.100	1.120	1.140	1.160
2	1.082	1.103	1.124	1.145	1.166	1.188	1.210	1.254	1.300	1.346
3	1.125	1.158	1.191	1.225	1.260	1.295	1.331	1.405	1.482	1.561
4	1.170	1.216	1.262	1.311	1.360	1.412	1.464	1.574	1.689	1.811
5	1.217	1.276	1.338	1.403	1.469	1.539	1.611	1.762	1.925	2.100
6	1.265	1.340	1.419	1.501	1.587	1.677	1.772	1.974	2.195	2.436
7	1.316	1.407	1.504	1.606	1.714	1.828	1.949	2.211	2.502	2.826
8	1.369	1.477	1.594	1.718	1.851	1.993	2.144	2.476	2.853	3.278
9	1.423	1.551	1.689	1.838	1.999	2.172	2.358	2.773	3.252	3.803
10	1.480	1.629	1.791	1.967	2.159	2.367	2.594	3.106	3.707	4.411
11	1.539	1.710	1.898	2.105	2.332	2.580	2.853	3.479	4.226	5.117
12	1.601	1.796	2.012	2.252	2.518	2.813	3.138	3.896	4.818	5.936
13	1.665	1.886	2.133	2.410	2.720	3.066	3.452	4.363	5.492	6.886
14	1.732	1.980	2.261	2.579	2.937	3.342	3.798	4.887	6.261	7.988
15	1.801	2.079	2.397	2.759	3.172	3.642	4.177	5.474	7.138	9.266
16	1.873	2.183	2.540	2.952	3.426	3.970	4.595	6.130	8.137	10.748
17	1.948	2.292	2.693	3.159	3.700	4.328	5.054	6.866	9.276	12.468
18	2.026	2.407	2.854	3.380	3.996	4.717	5.560	7.690	10.575	14.463
19	2.107	2.527	3.026	3.617	4.316	5.142	6.116	8.613	12.056	16.777
20	2.191	2.653	3.207	3.870	4.661	5.604	6.728	9.646	13.743	19.461

In business applications, interest rates are always stated for the annual period of 1 year unless specified otherwise. In fact, an interest rate can be stated for any period, such as 3% per quarter or 5% for a 6-month period. The length of the period is arbitrary. For example, an investment may promise a return (income) of 3% per quarter for 6 months (2 quarters). In that case, you would be working with 3% interest for 2 periods. It would be incorrect to use 6% for 1 period because the interest is 3% compounded quarterly, and that amount differs from 6% compounded semiannually. *Take care in studying future-value and present-value problems to align the interest rate with the appropriate number of periods.*

Let's see how a future-value table like the one in Exhibit D-2 is used. The future value of $1.00 invested at 8% for 1 year is $1.08 ($1.00 × 1.080, which appears at the junction of the 8% column and row 1 in the Periods column). The figure 1.080 includes both the principal (1.000) and the compound interest for 1 period (0.080).

Suppose you deposit $5,000 in a savings account that pays annual interest of 8%. The account balance at the end of 1 year will be $5,400. To compute the future value of $5,000 at 8% for 1 year, multiply $5,000 by 1.080 to get $5,400. Now suppose you invest in a 10-year, 8% certificate of deposit (CD). What will be the future value of the CD at maturity? To compute the future value of $5,000 at 8% for 10 periods, multiply $5,000 by 2.159 (from Exhibit D-2) to get $10,795. This future value of $10,795 indicates that $5,000, earning 8% interest compounded annually, grows to $10,795 at the end of 10 years. Using Exhibit D-2, you can find any present amount's future value at a particular future date. Future value is especially helpful for computing the amount of cash you will have on hand for some purpose in the future.

Future Value of an Annuity

In the preceding example, we made an investment of a single amount. Other investments, called *annuities*, include multiple investments of an equal periodic amount at fixed intervals over the duration of the investment. Consider a family investing for a child's education. The Dietrichs can invest $4,000 annually to accumulate a college fund for 15-year-old Helen. The investment can earn 7% annually until Helen turns 18—a 3-year investment. How much will be available for Helen on the date of the last investment? Exhibit D-3 shows the accumulation—a total future value of $12,860.

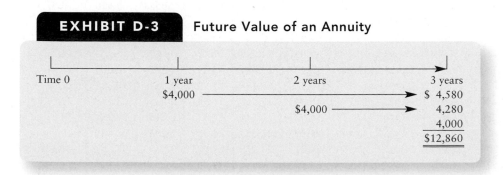

EXHIBIT D-3 **Future Value of an Annuity**

The first $4,000 invested by the Dietrichs grows to $4,580 over the investment period. The second amount grows to $4,280, and the third amount stays at $4,000 because it has no time to earn interest. The sum of the 3 future values

($4,580 + $4,280 + $4,000) is the future value of the annuity ($12,860), which can also be computed as follows:

End of Year	Annual Investment	Interest	Increase for the Year	Future Value of Annuity
0	—	—	—	0
1	$4,000	—	$4,000	$ 4,000
2	4,000	+ ($4,000 × 0.07 = $280) =	4,280	8,280
3	4,000	+ ($8,280 × 0.07 = $580) =	4,580	12,860

These computations are laborious. As with the Future Value of $1 (a lump sum), mathematical tables ease the strain of calculating annuities. Exhibit D-4, Future Value of Annuity of $1, gives the future value of a series of investments, each of equal amount, at regular intervals.

What is the future value of an annuity of 3 investments of $1 each that earn 7%? The answer, 3.215, can be found at the junction of the 7% column and row 3 in Exhibit D-4. This amount can be used to compute the future value of the investment for Helen's education, as follows:

Amount of each periodic investment	×	Future value of annuity of $1 (Exhibit C-4)	×	Future value of investment
$4,000	×	3.215	×	$12,860

EXHIBIT D-4   Future Value of Annuity of $1

Future Value of Annuity of $1

Periods	4%	5%	6%	7%	8%	9%	10%	12%	14%	16%
1	1.000	1.000	1.000	1.000	1.000	1.000	1.000	1.000	1.000	1.000
2	2.040	2.050	2.060	2.070	2.080	2.090	2.100	2.120	2.140	2.160
3	3.122	3.153	3.184	3.215	3.246	3.278	3.310	3.374	3.440	3.506
4	4.246	4.310	4.375	4.440	4.506	4.573	4.641	4.779	4.921	5.066
5	5.416	5.526	5.637	5.751	5.867	5.985	6.105	6.353	6.610	6.877
6	6.633	6.802	6.975	7.153	7.336	7.523	7.716	8.115	8.536	8.977
7	7.898	8.142	8.394	8.654	8.923	9.200	9.487	10.089	10.730	11.414
8	9.214	9.549	9.897	10.260	10.637	11.028	11.436	12.300	13.233	14.240
9	10.583	11.027	11.491	11.978	12.488	13.021	13.579	14.776	16.085	17.519
10	12.006	12.578	13.181	13.816	14.487	15.193	15.937	17.549	19.337	21.321
11	13.486	14.207	14.972	15.784	16.645	17.560	18.531	20.655	23.045	25.733
12	15.026	15.917	16.870	17.888	18.977	20.141	21.384	24.133	27.271	30.850
13	16.627	17.713	18.882	20.141	21.495	22.953	24.523	28.029	32.089	36.786
14	18.292	19.599	21.015	22.550	24.215	26.019	27.975	32.393	37.581	43.672
15	20.024	21.579	23.276	25.129	27.152	29.361	31.772	37.280	43.842	51.660
16	21.825	23.657	25.673	27.888	30.324	33.003	35.950	42.753	50.980	60.925
17	23.698	25.840	28.213	30.840	33.750	36.974	40.545	48.884	59.118	71.673
18	25.645	28.132	30.906	33.999	37.450	41.301	45.599	55.750	68.394	84.141
19	27.671	30.539	33.760	37.379	41.446	46.018	51.159	63.440	78.969	98.603
20	29.778	33.066	36.786	40.995	45.762	51.160	57.275	72.052	91.025	115.380

This one-step calculation is much easier than computing the future value of each annual investment and then summing the individual future values. In this way, you can compute the future value of any investment consisting of equal periodic amounts at regular intervals. Businesses make periodic investments to accumulate funds for equipment replacement and other uses—an application of the future value of an annuity.

Present Value

Often a person knows a future amount and needs to know the related present value. Recall Exhibit D-1, in which present value and future value are on opposite ends of the same time line. Suppose an investment promises to pay you $5,000 at the *end* of 1 year. How much would you pay *now* to acquire this investment? You would be willing to pay the present value of the $5,000 future amount.

Like future value, present value depends on 3 factors: (1) the *amount of payment* (*or receipt*), (2) the length of *time* between investment and future receipt (or *payment*), and (3) the *interest rate*. The process of computing a present value is called *discounting* because the present value is *less* than the future value.

In our investment example, the future receipt is $5,000. The investment period is 1 year. Assume that you demand an annual interest rate of 10% on your investment. With all 3 factors specified, you can compute the present value of $5,000 at 10% for 1 year:

$$\text{Present value} = \frac{\text{Future value}}{1 + \text{Interest rate}} = \frac{\$5,000}{1.10} = \$4,545$$

By turning the data around into a future-value problem, we can verify the present-value computation:

Amount invested (present value)	$4,545
Expected earnings ($4,545 × 0.10)...	455
Amount to be received one year from now (future value)..............	$5,000

This example illustrates that present value and future value are based on the same equation:

$$\text{Future value} = \text{Present value} \times (1 + \text{Interest rate})$$

$$\text{Present value} = \frac{\text{Future value}}{1 + \text{Interest rate}}$$

If the $5,000 is to be received 2 years from now, you will pay only $4,132 for the investment, as shown in Exhibit D-5. By turning the data around, we verify that $4,132 accumulates to $5,000 at 10% for 2 years:

Amount invested (present value)	$4,132
Expected earnings for first year ($4,132 × 0.10).........................	413
Value of investment after 1 year..	4,545
Expected earnings for second year ($4,545 × 0.10)	455
Amount to be received 2 years from now (future value)..............	$5,000

You would pay $4,132—the present value of $5,000—to receive the $5,000 future amount at the end of 2 years at 10% per year. The $868 difference between the amount invested ($4,132) and the amount to be received ($5,000) is the return on the investment, the sum of the 2 interest receipts: $413 + $455 = $868.

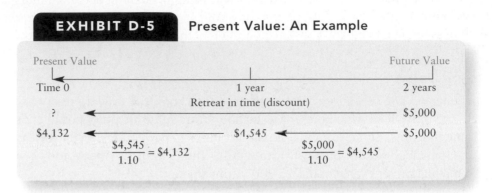

EXHIBIT D-5   Present Value: An Example

Present-Value Tables

We have shown the simple formula for computing present value. However, figuring present value "by hand" for investments spanning many years is time-consuming and presents too many opportunities for arithmetic errors. Present-value tables ease our work. Let's reexamine our examples of present value by using Exhibit D-6, Present Value of $1, given below.

EXHIBIT D-6   Present Value of $1

Present Value of $1

Periods	4%	5%	6%	7%	8%	10%	12%	14%	16%
1	0.962	0.952	0.943	0.935	0.926	0.909	0.893	0.877	0.862
2	0.925	0.907	0.890	0.873	0.857	0.826	0.797	0.769	0.743
3	0.889	0.864	0.840	0.816	0.794	0.751	0.712	0.675	0.641
4	0.855	0.823	0.792	0.763	0.735	0.683	0.636	0.592	0.552
5	0.822	0.784	0.747	0.713	0.681	0.621	0.567	0.519	0.476
6	0.790	0.746	0.705	0.666	0.630	0.564	0.507	0.456	0.410
7	0.760	0.711	0.665	0.623	0.583	0.513	0.452	0.400	0.354
8	0.731	0.677	0.627	0.582	0.540	0.467	0.404	0.351	0.305
9	0.703	0.645	0.592	0.544	0.500	0.424	0.361	0.308	0.263
10	0.676	0.614	0.558	0.508	0.463	0.386	0.322	0.270	0.227
11	0.650	0.585	0.527	0.475	0.429	0.350	0.287	0.237	0.195
12	0.625	0.557	0.497	0.444	0.397	0.319	0.257	0.208	0.168
13	0.601	0.530	0.469	0.415	0.368	0.290	0.229	0.182	0.145
14	0.577	0.505	0.442	0.388	0.340	0.263	0.205	0.160	0.125
15	0.555	0.481	0.417	0.362	0.315	0.239	0.183	0.140	0.108
16	0.534	0.458	0.394	0.339	0.292	0.218	0.163	0.123	0.093
17	0.513	0.436	0.371	0.317	0.270	0.198	0.146	0.108	0.080
18	0.494	0.416	0.350	0.296	0.250	0.180	0.130	0.095	0.069
19	0.475	0.396	0.331	0.277	0.232	0.164	0.116	0.083	0.060
20	0.456	0.377	0.312	0.258	0.215	0.149	0.104	0.073	0.051

For the 10% investment for 1 year, we find the junction of the 10% column and row 1 in Exhibit D-6. The figure 0.909 is computed as follows: 1/1.10 = 0.909. This work has been done for us, and only the present values are given in the table. To figure the present value for $5,000, we multiply 0.909 by $5,000. The result is $4,545, which matches the result we obtained by hand.

For the 2-year investment, we read down the 10% column and across row 2. We multiply 0.826 (computed as 0.909/1.10 = 0.826) by $5,000 and get $4,130, which confirms our earlier computation of $4,132 (the difference is due to rounding in the present-value table). Using the table, we can compute the present value of any single future amount.

Present Value of an Annuity

Return to the investment example near the bottom of page 809 of this appendix. That investment provided the investor with only a single future receipt ($5,000 at the end of 2 years). *Annuity investments* provide multiple receipts of an equal amount at fixed intervals over the investment's duration.

Consider an investment that promises *annual* cash receipts of $10,000 to be received at the end of 3 years. Assume that you demand a 12% return on your investment. What is the investment's present value? That is, what would you pay today to acquire the investment? The investment spans 3 periods, and you would pay the sum of 3 present values. The computation follows.

Year	Annual Cash Receipt	Present Value of $1 at 12% (Exhibit C-6)	Present Value of Annual Cash Receipt
1	$10,000	0.893	$ 8,930
2	10,000	0.797	7,970
3	10,000	0.712	7,120
Total present value of investment...............			$24,020

The present value of this annuity is $24,020. By paying this amount today, you will receive $10,000 at the end of each of the 3 years while earning 12% on your investment.

This example illustrates repetitive computations of the 3 future amounts, a time-consuming process. One way to ease the computational burden is to add the 3 present values of $1 (0.893 + 0.797 + 0.712) and multiply their sum (2.402) by the annual cash receipt ($10,000) to obtain the present value of the annuity ($10,000 × 2.402 = $24,020).

An easier approach is to use a present-value-of-an-annuity table. Exhibit D-7 shows the present value of $1 to be received periodically for a given number of periods. The present value of a 3-period annuity at 12% is 2.402 (the junction of row 3 and the 12% column). Thus, $10,000 received annually at the end of each of 3 years, discounted at 12%, is $24,020 ($10,000 × 2.402), which is the present value.

EXHIBIT D-7 Present Value of Annuity of $1

Present Value of Annuity of $1

Periods	4%	5%	6%	7%	8%	10%	12%	14%	16%
1	0.962	0.952	0.943	0.935	0.926	0.909	0.893	0.877	0.862
2	1.886	1.859	1.833	1.808	1.783	1.736	1.690	1.647	1.605
3	2.775	2.723	2.673	2.624	2.577	2.487	2.402	2.322	2.246
4	3.630	3.546	3.465	3.387	3.312	3.170	3.037	2.914	2.798
5	4.452	4.329	4.212	4.100	3.993	3.791	3.605	3.433	3.274
6	5.242	5.076	4.917	4.767	4.623	4.355	4.111	3.889	3.685
7	6.002	5.786	5.582	5.389	5.206	4.868	4.564	4.288	4.039
8	6.733	6.463	6.210	5.971	5.747	5.335	4.968	4.639	4.344
9	7.435	7.108	6.802	6.515	6.247	5.759	5.328	4.946	4.608
10	8.111	7.722	7.360	7.024	6.710	6.145	5.650	5.216	4.833
11	8.760	8.306	7.887	7.499	7.139	6.495	5.938	5.453	5.029
12	9.385	8.863	8.384	7.943	7.536	6.814	6.194	5.660	5.197
13	9.986	9.394	8.853	8.358	7.904	7.103	6.424	5.842	5.342
14	10.563	9.899	9.295	8.745	8.244	7.367	6.628	6.002	5.468
15	11.118	10.380	9.712	9.108	8.559	7.606	6.811	6.142	5.575
16	11.652	10.838	10.106	9.447	8.851	7.824	6.974	6.265	5.669
17	12.166	11.274	10.477	9.763	9.122	8.022	7.120	6.373	5.749
18	12.659	11.690	10.828	10.059	9.372	8.201	7.250	6.467	5.818
19	13.134	12.085	11.158	10.336	9.604	8.365	7.366	6.550	5.877
20	13.590	12.462	11.470	10.594	9.818	8.514	7.469	6.623	5.929

Present Value of Bonds Payable

The present value of a bond—its market price—is the present value of the future principal amount at maturity plus the present value of the future stated interest payments. The principal is a *single amount* to be paid at maturity. The interest is an *annuity* because it occurs periodically.

Let's compute the present value of the assumed 9% 5-year bonds of **Southwest Airlines** (discussed on pages 428–429). The face value of the bonds is $100,000, and they pay 4½% stated (cash) interest semiannually (that is, twice a year).[1] At issuance, the market interest rate is expressed as 10% annually, but it is computed at 5% semiannually. Therefore, the effective interest rate for each of the 10 semiannual periods is 5%. We thus use 5% in computing the present value (PV) of the maturity and of the interest. The market price of these bonds is $96,149, as follows:

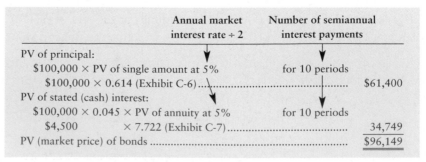

	Annual market interest rate ÷ 2	Number of semiannual interest payments	
PV of principal:			
$100,000 × PV of single amount at 5%		for 10 periods	
$100,000 × 0.614 (Exhibit C-6)			$61,400
PV of stated (cash) interest:			
$100,000 × 0.045 × PV of annuity at 5%		for 10 periods	
$4,500 × 7.722 (Exhibit C-7)			34,749
PV (market price) of bonds			$96,149

---

[1]For a definition of stated interest rate, see page 425.

The market price of the Southwest bonds shows a discount because the contract interest rate on the bonds (9%) is less than the market interest rate (10%). We discuss these bonds in more detail on pages 424–435.

Let's consider a premium price for the 9% Southwest bonds. Assume that the market interest rate is 8% (rather than 10%) at issuance. The effective interest rate is thus 4% for each of the 10 semiannual periods:

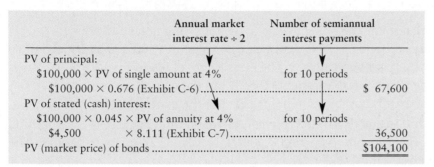

	Annual market interest rate ÷ 2	Number of semiannual interest payments	
PV of principal:			
$100,000 × PV of single amount at 4%		for 10 periods	
$100,000 × 0.676 (Exhibit C-6)			$ 67,600
PV of stated (cash) interest:			
$100,000 × 0.045 × PV of annuity at 4%		for 10 periods	
$4,500 × 8.111 (Exhibit C-7)			36,500
PV (market price) of bonds			$104,100

We discuss accounting for these bonds on pages 432–435. It may be helpful for you to reread this section ("Present Value of Bonds Payable") after you've studied those pages.

Capital Leases

How does a lessee compute the cost of an asset acquired through a capital lease? (See page 442 for the definition of *capital leases*.) Consider that the lessee gets the use of the asset but does *not* pay for the leased asset in full at the beginning of the lease. A capital lease is therefore similar to an installment purchase of the leased asset. The lessee must record the leased asset at the present value of the lease liability. The time value of money must be weighed.

The cost of the asset to the lessee is the sum of any payment made at the beginning of the lease period plus the present value of the future lease payments. The lease payments are equal amounts occurring at regular intervals—that is, they are annuity payments.

Consider a 20-year building lease that requires 20 annual payments of $10,000 each, with the first payment due immediately. The interest rate in the lease is 10%, and the present value of the 19 future payments is $83,650 ($10,000 × PV of annuity at 10% for 19 periods, or 8.365 from Exhibit D-7). The lessee's cost of the building is $93,650 (the sum of the initial payment, $10,000, plus the present value of the future payments, $83,650). The lessee would base its accounting for the leased asset (and the related depreciation) and for the lease liability (and the related interest expense) on the cost of the building that we have just computed.

Appendix Problems

PD-1. For each situation, compute the required amount.
a. **Kellogg Corporation** is budgeting for the acquisition of land over the next several years. Kellogg can invest $100,000 today at 9%. How much cash will Kellogg have for land acquisitions at the end of 5 years? At the end of 6 years?
b. Davidson, Inc., is planning to invest $50,000 each year for 5 years. The company's investment adviser believes that Davidson can earn 6% interest without taking on too much risk. What will be the value of Davidson's investment on the date of the last deposit if Davidson can earn 6%? If Davidson can earn 8%?

PD-2. For each situation, compute the required amount.
a. **Intel Corporation** operations are generating excess cash that will be invested in a special fund. During 20X2, Intel invests $5,643,341 in the fund for a planned

advertising campaign on a new product to be released 6 years later, in 20X8. If Intel's investments can earn 10% each year, how much cash will the company have for the advertising campaign in 20X8?

b. Intel will need $10 million to advertise a new type of chip in 20X8. How much must Intel invest in 20X2 to have the cash available for the advertising campaign? Intel's investments can earn 10% annually.

c. Explain the relationship between your answers to *a* and *b*.

PD-3. Determine the present value of the following notes and bonds:

1. Ten-year bonds payable with maturity value of $500,000 and stated interest rate of 12%, paid semiannually. The market rate of interest is 12% at issuance.
2. Same bonds payable as in number 1, but the market interest rate is 14%.
3. Same bonds payable as in number 1, but the market interest rate is 10%.

PD-4. On December 31, 20X1, when the market interest rate is 8%. Libby, Libby, & Short, a partnership, issues $400,000 of 10-year, 7.25% bonds payable. The bonds pay interest semiannually.

❙ Required

1. Determine the present value of the bonds at issuance.
2. Assume that the bonds are issued at the price computed in Requirement 1. Prepare an effective-interest-method amortization table for the first 2 semiannual interest periods. (p. 429)
3. Using the amortization table prepared in Requirement 2, journalize issuance of the bonds and the first 2 interest payments and amortization of the bonds. (p. 427–432)

PD-5. St. Mere Eglise Children's Home needs a fleet of vans to transport the children to singing engagements throughout Normandy. **Renault** offers the vehicles for a single payment of 630,000 euros due at the end of 4 years. **Peugeot** prices a similar fleet of vans for 4 annual payments of 150,000 euros at the end of each year. The children's home could borrow the funds at 6%, so this is the appropriate interest rate. Which company should get the business, Renault or Peugeot? Base your decision on present value, and give your reason.

PD-6. American Family Association acquired equipment under a capital lease that requires 6 annual lease payments of $40,000. The first payment is due when the lease begins, on January 1, 20X6. Future payments are due on January 1 of each year of the lease term. The interest rate in the lease is 16%.

❙ Required

Compute the association's cost of the equipment. (p. 442)

Answers

PD-1	a. 5 yrs. $153,900		
	6 yrs. $167,700		
	b. 6% $281,850		
	8% $293,350		
PD-2	a. $10,000,000		
	b. $5,640,000		
PD-3	1. $500,100	2. $446,820	3. $562,360
PD-4	1. $379,455	2. Bond	
	carry. amt. at 12-31-X2 $380,838		
PD-5	Renault PV €498,960		
	Peugeot PV €519,750		
PD-6	Cost $170,960		

Appendix E

Typical Charts of Accounts for Different Types of Businesses

A Simple Service Corporation

Assets	Liabilities	Stockholders' Equity
Cash	Accounts Payable	Common Stock
Accounts Receivable	Notes Payable, Short-Term	Retained Earnings
Allowance for Uncollectible Accounts	Salary Payable	Dividends
Notes Receivable, Short-Term	Wages Payable	**Revenues and Gains**
Interest Receivable	Payroll Taxes Payable	
Supplies	Employee Benefits Payable	Service Revenue
Prepaid Rent	Interest Payable	Interest Revenue
Prepaid Insurance	Unearned Service Revenue	Gain on Sale of Land (Furniture,
Notes Receivable, Long-Term	Notes Payable, Long-Term	Equipment, or Building)
Land		**Expenses and Losses**
Furniture		
Accumulated Depreciation—Furniture		Salary Expense
Equipment		Payroll Tax Expense
Accumulated Depreciation—Equipment		Employee Benefits Expense
Building		Rent Expense
Accumulated Depreciation—Building		Insurance Expense
		Supplies Expense
		Uncollectible Account Expense
		Depreciation Expense—Furniture
		Depreciation Expense—Equipment
		Depreciation Expense—Building
		Property Tax Expense
		Interest Expense
		Miscellaneous Expense
		Loss on Sale (or Exchange) of Land
		(Furniture, Equipment, or Building)

Service Partnership

Same as service corporation, except for owners' equity

Owners' Equity

Partner 1, Capital
Partner 2, Capital
.
.
.
Partner N, Capital

Partner 1, Drawing
Partner 2, Drawing
.
.
.
Partner N, Drawing

A Complex Merchandising Corporation

Assets

Cash
Short-Term Investments
Accounts Receivable
Allowance for Uncollectible
    Accounts
Notes Receivable, Short-Term
Interest Receivable
Inventory
Supplies
Prepaid Rent
Prepaid Insurance
Notes Receivable, Long-Term
Investments in Subsidiaries
Investments in Stock
    (Available-for-Sale
    Securities)
Investments in Bonds (Held-to-
    Maturity Securities)
Other Receivables, Long-Term
Land
Land Improvements
Furniture and Fixtures
Accumulated Depreciation—
    Furniture and Fixtures
Equipment
Accumulated Depreciation—
    Equipment
Buildings
Accumulated Depreciation—
    Buildings
Franchises
Patents
Leaseholds
Goodwill

Liabilities

Accounts Payable
Notes Payable, Short-Term
Current Portion of Bonds
    Payable
Salary Payable
Wages Payable
Payroll Taxes Payable
Employee Benefits Payable
Interest Payable
Income Tax Payable
Unearned Sales Revenue
Notes Payable, Long-Term
Bonds Payable
Lease Liability
Minority Interest

Stockholders' Equity

Preferred Stock
Paid-in Capital in Excess of
    Par—Preferred
Common Stock
Paid-in Capital in Excess of
    Par—Common
Paid-in Capital from Treasury
    Stock Transactions
Paid-in Capital from
    Retirement of Stock
Retained Earnings
Unrealized Gain (or Loss)
    on Investments
Foreign Currency Translation
    Adjustment
Treasury Stock

Revenues and Gains

Sales Revenue
Interest Revenue
Dividend Revenue
Equity-Method Investment
    Revenue
Unrealized Holding Gain on
    Trading Investments
Gain on Sale of Investments
Gain on Sale of Land
    (Furniture and Fixtures,
    Equipment, or Buildings)
Discontinued Operations—
    Gain
Extraordinary Gains

Expenses and Losses

Cost of Goods Sold
Salary Expense
Wage Expense
Commission Expense
Payroll Tax Expense
Employee Benefits Expense
Rent Expense
Insurance Expense
Supplies Expense
Uncollectible Account Expense
Depreciation Expense—Land
    Improvements
Depreciation Expense—
    Furniture and Fixtures
Depreciation Expense—
    Equipment
Depreciation Expense—
    Buildings
Organization Expense
Amortization Expense—
    Franchises
Amortization Expense—
    Leaseholds
Amortization Expense—
    Goodwill
Income Tax Expense
Unrealized Holding Loss on
    Trading Investments
Loss on Sale of Investments
Loss on Sale (or Exchange) of
    Land (Furniture and
    Fixtures, Equipment, or
    Buildings)
Discontinued Operations—
    Loss
Extraordinary Losses

A Manufacturing Corporation

Same as merchandising corporation, except for Assets

Assets

Inventories:
    Materials Inventory
    Work-in-Process Inventory
    Finished Goods Inventory
Factory Wages
Factory Overhead

Appendix F

Summary of Generally Accepted Accounting Principles (GAAP)

Every technical area has professional associations and regulatory bodies that govern the practice of the profession. Accounting is no exception. In the United States, generally accepted accounting principles (GAAP) are influenced most by the Financial Accounting Standards Board (FASB). The FASB has 7 full-time members and a large staff. Its financial support comes from professional associations such as the American Institute of Certified Public Accountants (AICPA).

The FASB is an independent organization with no government or professional affiliation. The FASB's pronouncements, called *Statements of Financial Accounting Standards*, specify how to account for certain business transactions. Each new *Standard* becomes part of GAAP, the "accounting law of the land." In the same way that our laws draw authority from their acceptance by the people, GAAP depends on general acceptance by the business community. Throughout this book, we refer to GAAP as the proper way to do financial accounting.

The U.S. Congress has given the Securities and Exchange Commission (SEC), a government organization that regulates the trading of investments, ultimate responsibility for establishing accounting rules for companies that are owned by the general investing public. However, the SEC has delegated much of its rule-making power to the FASB. Exhibit F-1 outlines the flow of authority for developing GAAP.

EXHIBIT F-1 Flow of Authority for Developing GAAP

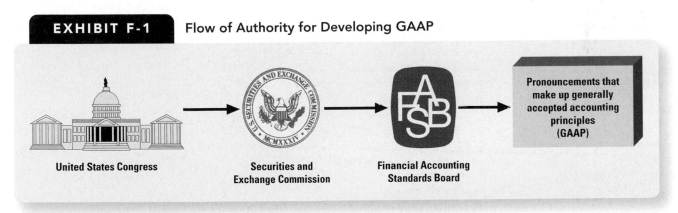

United States Congress → Securities and Exchange Commission → Financial Accounting Standards Board → Pronouncements that make up generally accepted accounting principles (GAAP)

The Objective of Financial Reporting

The basic objective of financial reporting is to provide information that is useful in making investment and lending decisions. The FASB believes that accounting information can be useful in decision making only if it is *relevant, reliable, comparable*, and *consistent*.

Relevant information is useful in making predictions and for evaluating past performance—that is, the information has feedback value. For example, PepsiCo's disclosure of the profitability of each of its lines of business is relevant for investor evaluations of the company. To be relevant, information must be timely. *Reliable* information is free from significant error—that is, it has validity. Also, it is free from the bias of a particular viewpoint—that is, it is verifiable and neutral. *Comparable* and *consistent* information can be compared from period to period to help investors and creditors track the entity's progress through time. These characteristics combine to shape the concepts and principles that make up GAAP. Exhibit F-2 summarizes the concepts and principles that accounting has developed to provide useful information for decision making.

| EXHIBIT F-2 | Summary of Important Accounting Concepts, Principles, and Financial Statements |

Concepts, Principles, and Financial Statements	Quick Summary	Text Reference
Concepts		
Entity concept	Accounting draws a boundary around each organization to be accounted for.	Chapter 1, page 38
Going-concern concept	Accountants assume the business will continue operating for the foreseeable future.	Chapter 1, page 39
Stable-monetary-unit concept	Accounting information is expressed primarily in monetary terms that ignore the effects of inflation.	Chapter 1, page 39
Time-period concept	Ensures that accounting information is reported at regular intervals.	Chapter 3, page 140
Conservatism concept	Accountants report items in the financial statements in a way that avoids overstating assets, owners' equity, and revenues and avoids understating liabilities and expenses.	Chapter 6, page 321
Materiality concept	Accountants perform strictly proper accounting only for items that are significant to the company's financial statements.	
Principles		
Reliability (objective) principle	Accounting records and statements are based on the most reliable data available.	Chapter 1, page 38
Cost principle	Assets and services, revenues and expenses are recorded at their actual historical cost.	Chapter 1, page 39
Revenue principle	Tells accountants when to record revenue (only after it has been earned) and the amount of revenue to record (the cash value of what has been received).	Chapter 3, page 140
Matching principle	Directs accountants to (1) identify and measure all expenses incurred during the period and (2) match the expenses against the revenues earned during the period. The goal is to measure net income.	Chapter 3, page 141
Consistency principle	Businesses should use the same accounting methods from period to period.	Chapter 6, page 321
Disclosure principle	A company's financial statements should report enough information for outsiders to make informed decisions about the company.	Chapter 6, page 321
Financial Statements		
Balance sheet	Assets = Liabilities + Owners' Equity at a point in time.	Chapter 1
Income statement	Revenues and gains − Expenses and losses = Net income or net loss for the period.	Chapters 1 and 11
Statement of cash flows	Cash receipts − Cash payments = Increase or decrease in cash during the period, grouped under operating, investing, and financing activities.	Chapters 1 and 12
Statement of retained earnings	Beginning retained earnings + Net income (or − Net loss) − Dividends = Ending retained earnings.	Chapters 1 and 11
Statement of stockholders' equity	Shows the reason for the change in each stockholders' equity account, including retained earnings.	Chapter 11
Financial statement notes	Provide information that cannot be reported conveniently on the face of the financial statements. The notes are an integral part of the statements.	Chapter 11

Appendix G

Check Figures for Assignment Materials

Chapter 1 (NCF=No check figures)

S1-1	a. $300,000; b. $200,000; c. $100,000
S1-2	NCF
S1-3	NCF
S1-4	NCF
S1-5	NCF
S1-6	NCF
S1-7	NCF
S1-8	Net inc. $70 mil.
S1-9	RE bal., end. $260 mil.
S1-10	Total assets $140,000 RE $35,000
S1-11	Net cash-oper. $60,000 Cash bal. 12/31/10 $34,000
S1-12	NCF

E1-13	NCF
E1-14	NCF
E1-15	Apple $17 bil.; PepsiCo $18 bil.; FedEx $12 bil.
E1-16	1. SE $109 mil. 2. $411 mil.
E1-17	1. $7 mil. 2. $10 mil. 3. $(2) mil.
E1-18	1. $528,000 2. $400,000
E1-19	NCF
E1-20	Total assets $400 mil. SE $37 mil.
E1-21	1. Net inc. $9 mil. 2. Div. $3 mil.
E1-22	Net cash-oper. $360,000 End. cash bal. $125,000
E1-23	Net inc. $9,100 RE 7/31/X9 $7,100
E1-24	Total assets $45,300
E1-25	Net cash-oper. $11,100 Net increase in cash $8,100
E1-26	NCF
E1-27	NCF

Q1-28	a	Q1-36	d
Q1-29	d	Q1-37	b
Q1-30	c	Q1-38	a
Q1-31	a	Q1-39	c
Q1-32	b	Q1-40	c
Q1-33	d	Q1-41	a
Q1-34	b	Q1-42	c
Q1-35	b		

P1-43A	1. Net inc. $24,000
P1-44A	1. Diamond: Beg. RE $25 mil. End. Assets $83 mil. Lance: End. RE $17 mil. Rev. $153 mil. Berger: Beg. Assets $7 mil. End. liab. $3 mil. Exp. $19 mil.
P1-45A	1. Total assets $143,700 SE $90,700
P1-46A	1. Total assets $170,000 RE $81,000
P1-47A	1. Net inc. $83,000 2. RE, end. $152,000 3. Total assets $206,000
P1-48A	1. Net cash-oper. $5,900 mil.
P1-49A	(Thousands) b. $1,300 d. $3,950 j. $1,070 m. $540 p. $4,430 s. $13,010 x. $950 z. $1,380
P1-50B	1. Net inc. $18 bil.
P1-51B	Samurai: End. Assets $340 mil. Net inc. $40 mil. Peking: Begin. Assets $20 mil. Expenses $14 mil. Osaka: Begin. Liab. $17 mil. Rev. $61 mil.; Div. $5 mil.
P1-52B	1. Total assets $78,000 SE $57,000
P1-53B	1. Total assets $200,000 RE $104,000
P1-54B	1. Net inc. $68,000 2. RE, end. $28,000 3. Total assets $173,000
P1-55B	1. Net cash-oper. $300 mil. Net increase in cash $100 mil.
P1-56B	b. $7,700 d. $17,200 h. $37,600 j. $300 m. $2,400 p. $19,100 w. $42,100 z. $400 r. $17,900 v. $19,400

DC1	NCF
DC2	1. Net inc. $5,000; Total assets $48,000
FOF	3. Total resources $6,353 mil. Stockholders owned $1,437 mil.
FOA	1. Total liab. $580 mil., SE $590 mil.

Chapter 2 (NCF=No check figures)

S2-1	NCF
S2-2	a. $12,000 b. $2,000
S2-3	Cash bal. $23,000
S2-4	NCF
S2-5	NCF
S2-6	2. A/P bal. $2,000
S2-7	Balances: Cash $2,500; A/R $1,500; Service Rev. $4,000
S2-8	T/B total $41 mil. Net inc. $12 mil.
S2-9	1. $95,000 2. $39,000 3. $38,000
S2-10	NCF
S2-11	NCF
S2-12	3. Total dr. = Total cr. = $160,000

E2-13	Total assets $310,000
E2-14	NCF
E2-15	NCF
E2-16	2. a. $66,300 c. $11,000 d. $55,300
E2-17	NCF
E2-18	NCF
E2-19	3. Total assets $27,400 Total SE $26,700
E2-20	NCF
E2-21	1. T/B total $69,200 2. Net inc. $12,300
E2-22	T/B total $94,200
E2-23	Cash bal. $4,300; A/P bal. $400
E2-24	1. T/B total $23,700 2. Net inc. $5,000
E2-25	4. T/B total $14,400
E2-26	a. $85,000 b. $52,000 c. $17,000
E2-27	1. T/B out of bal. $2,200 2. a. $42,900 c. $4,800
E2-28	Rogers: June Med. Exp. $20,000; June 30 Cash $25,000; A/P $20,000 Providence: June Service Rev. $20,000; June 30 Cash $0; A/R $20,000

Q2-29	c	Q2-32	a
Q2-30	d	Q2-33	d
Q2-31	c	Q2-34	b

Q2-35	c	Q2-42	b
Q2-36	a	Q2-43	a
Q2-37	b	Q2-44	d
Q2-38	d	Q2-45	c
Q2-39	d	Q2-46	b
Q2-40	c	Q2-47	a
Q2-41	a	Q2-48	b

P2-49A NCF
P2-50A 2. Net inc. $7,900
3. RE 6/30/X8 $8,800
4. Total assets $21,800
P2-51A 3. Cash bal. $5,400
A/P bal. $4,000
P2-52A 2. Total assets $57,500
P2-53A 3. Cash bal. $15,800
Total owed $25,600
P2-54A 3. T/B total $35,100
4. Total resources $31,100
Net inc. $2,300
P2-55A 3. T/B total $128,200
P2-56B NCF
P2-57B 2. Net inc. $7,300
3. RE 5/31/X1 $17,900
4. Total assets $64,400
P2-58B 3. Cash bal. $33,000
A/P bal. $4,800
P2-59B 2. Total assets $54,600
P2-60B 3. Cash bal. $20,400
Total owed $30,900
P2-61B 3. T/B total $27,900
4. Total resources $24,100
Net inc. $5,300
P2-62B 3. T/B total $174,300

DC1 3. T/B total $27,900
4. Net inc. $6,400
DC2 Net inc. $3,000
Total assets $21,000
FOF 3. Cash bal. $319 mil.; Accts. and Notes Rec. bal. $220 mil.; Invy. bal. $93 mil.
5. Net inc. $824 mil.
FOA 2. LT debt created by new borrowing $165 mil.
3. Net sales decreased 1.6%

Chapter 3 (NCF=No check figures)

S3-1 Net inc. $50 mil.
End. cash $90 mil.
S3-2 Inc. State.: Interest Exp. $1.0 mil.
Bal. Sheet: Notes Pay. $4.1 mil. and Interest Pay. $0.2 mil.
S3-3 NCF
S3-4 a. Prepaid Rent bal. $2,000
b. Supplies bal. $500
S3-5 3. Book value $20,000

S3-6 Inc. State.: Salary Exp. $42 mil.
Bal. Sheet: Salary Pay. $2 mil.
S3-7 3. Debit Interest Pay. $1,500
S3-8 3. Credit Interest Rec. $1,500
S3-9 b. Debit Unearned Sub. Rev. $40,000
S3-10 Prepaid Rent:
a. $6,000 b. $4,000
Rent Exp.: c. $0 d. $2,000
S3-11 NCF
S3-12 (Thousands)
Net inc. $3,500; RE 3/31/X4 $4,800; Total assets $97,900
S3-13 RE bal. 3/31/X4 $4,800
S3-14 1. 1.24 2. 0.69
S3-15 1. a. 1.43 b. 0.62
2. a. 1.29 b. 0.65

E3-16 NCF
E3-17 a. $110,000 b. $80,000
E3-18 NCF
E3-19 NCF
E3-20 NCF
E3-21 2. Net inc. overstated by $20,200
E3-22 Journal entry 1. Debit Supplies $800 2. Credit Supplies $3,600
E3-23 f. Book value $48,000
E3-24 Unearned Service Rev. bal. $100
Service Rev. bal. $15,700
E3-25 Net inc. $4,000; RE 12/31/X6 $6,800
Total assets $22,200
E3-26 Sales rev. $20,900 mil.; Insurance exp. $330 mil.; Other oper. exp. $4,200 mil.
E3-27 Mo.Frances' I/S: Service rev. $1,500
B/S: Unearned service rev. $1,500
E3-28 2. I/S: Service rev. £ 470 mil.
B/S: Unearned service rev. £ 100 mil.
E3-29 Net inc. $1,200
E3-30 NCF
E3-31 1. Total assets $39,100; Total SE $20,300
2. Current ratio 1.26; Debt ratio 0.48
E3-32 Current ratio: a. 1.43 b. 1.50
Debt ratio: a. 0.44 b. 0.33
E3-33 7. Net inc. $1,500; Total assets $12,800
9. Current ratio 0.56; Debt ratio 0.57
E3-34 Current ratio 12/31/08 1.87; 12/31/09 2.20
E3-35 a. $108,000 b. $158,000
d. $145,000

Q3-36	b	Q3-45	d
Q3-37	b	Q3-46	b
Q3-38	a	Q3-47	c
Q3-39	b	Q3-48	a
Q3-40	d	Q3-49	d
Q3-41	d	Q3-50	c
Q3-42	c	Q3-51	$4,800
Q3-43	a	Q3-52	d
Q3-44	c		

P3-53A 1. $27 mil. 3. $6 mil.
4. $8 mil.
P3-54A 2. Cash basis $(700); Accrual basis $3,300
P3-55A NCF
P3-56A a. Debit Insurance Exp. $3,400
d. Debt Supplies Exp. $6,600
P3-57A 2. Net inc. $6,000; RE 1/31/X2 $15,000; Total assets $54,000
P3-58A 2. Total assets $68,600; Total equity $61,200; Net inc. $4,100
P3-59A 1. Net inc. $39,200; RE 12/31/X6 $16,200; Total assets $47,000 2. Debt ratio 0.55
P3-60A 2. RE bal. 3/31/X3 $47,300
P3-61A 1. Total assets $83,300; Total SE $56,400 2. Current ratio 1.60; Debt ratio 0.32
P3-62A 1. Current ratio 1.68; Debt ratio 0.46
2. a. Current ratio 2.37; Debt ratio 0.37 b. Current ratio 2.01; Debt ratio 0.51
P3-63B 1. $15 mil. 3. $5 mil.
4. $6 mil.
P3-64B 2. Cash basis $(2,700); Accrual basis $1,100
P3-65B NCF
P3-66B c. Debit Supplies Exp. $11,400
f. Debit Insurance Exp. $2,700
P3-67B 2. Net inc. $20,200; RE 10/31/X2 $36,600; Total assets $62,000
P3-68B 2. Total assets $30,400; Total equity $15,700; Net inc. $25,500
P3-69B 1. Net inc. $88,600; RE 12/31/X1 $60,900; Total assets $109,000
2. Debt ratio 0.33
P3-70B 2. RE bal. 12/31/X5 $16,800
P3-71B 1. Total assets $55,000; Total SE $31,800
2. Current ratio 1.71; Debt ratio 0.42
P3-72B 1. Current ratio 1.36; Debt ratio 0.68
2. a. Current ratio 1.73; Debt ratio 0.61 b. Current ratio 2.73; Debt ratio 0.78

DC1	1. T/B out of bal. $2,000	P4-43A	1. Adj. bal. $6,090
	2. T/B total $57,900	P4-44A	1. Adj. bal $1,593.33
	3. Current ratio 0.87	P4-45A	NCF
DC2	Net inc. $7,000; RE 10/31/X4	P4-46A	1. (New financing needed)
	$4,000; Total assets $32,000		$(3,700) thou.
DC3	1. Your price $260,000	P4-47A	NCF
	2. Williams' price $222,000	P4-48B	NCF
FOF	5. 2006: Current ratio 0.52;	P4-49B	NCF
	Debt ratio 0.77	P4-50B	1. Adj. bal. $5,960
FOA	NCF	P4-51B	1. Adj. bal $8,239.00
GP	Net inc. $2,460; Total assets	P4-52B	NCF
	$2,400	P4-53B	1. (New financing needed)
			$(5,490)
		P4-54B	NCF

Chapter 4 (NCF=No check figures)

S4-1	NCF
S4-2	NCF
S4-3	NCF
S4-4	NCF
S4-5	Adj. bal. $3,005
S4-6	NCF
S4-7	NCF
S4-8	NCF
S4-9	NCF
S4-10	NCF
S4-11	Cash available $1 mil.
S4-12	NCF

E4-13	NCF
E4-14	NCF
E4-15	NCF
E4-16	NCF
E4-17	NCF
E4-18	NCF
E4-19	Adj. bal. $1,150
E4-20	Adj. bal $1,780
E4-21	NCF
E4-22	NCF
E4-23	NCF
E4-24	(New financing needed) $(64) mil.
E4-25	NCF
E4-26	7.37%
E4-27	NCF
E4-28	1. Cash available $45 thou. 2. Current ratio 1.60; Debt ratio 0.50

Q4-29	c	Q4-35	b
Q4-30	b	Q4-36	c
Q4-31	a	Q4-37	d
Q4-32	d	Q4-38	a
Q4-33	d	Q4-39	d
Q4-34	a	Q4-40	c

P4-41A	NCF
P4-42A	NCF

DC1	Bookkeeper stole $1,000
DC2	NCF
FOF	1. Adj. bal. $319 mil.
FOA	NCF

Chapter 5 (NCF=No check figures)

S5-1	NCF
S5-2	NCF
S5-3	Dr. Unrealized Loss $6,000
S5-4	NCF
S5-5	2. A/R, net $62,000
S5-6	Dr. Uncollect.-Acct. Exp. $15,000
S5-7	3. A/R, net $167,000
S5-8	d. Uncollect.-Acct. Exp. $9,000
S5-9	3. A/R, net $43,000
S5-10	b. Dr. Cash $104,000
S5-11	3. $104,500
S5-12	c. Dr. Cash $6,540
S5-13	c. Nothing to report d. Interest rev. $225
S5-14	1. 0.96 2. 32 days
S5-15	2. Net inc. $4,424 thou. 3. 1.60

E5-16	3. B/S: Short-term invest. $63,000 I/S: Unrealized gain $8,000
E5-17	I/S: Div. rev. $500; Unrealized (loss) $(7,000)
E5-18	Unrealized Loss on Invest. $2,000 Gain on Sale of Invest. $3,000
E5-19	NCF
E5-20	A/R, net $91,000
E5-21	3. A/R, net $41,000
E5-22	2. A/R, net $44,300
E5-23	3. A/R, net $224,850
E5-24	B/D Exp. $150; Write offs $148
E5-25	Dec. 31 Dr. Interest Rec. $852
E5-26	I/S: Interest rev. $1,200 for 20X8 and $400 for 20X9
E5-27	NCF

E5-28	a. 0.99 b. 32 days		
E5-29	1. 5 days		
E5-30	Expected net inc. w/bank cards $129,800		
E5-31	a. $21 mil. b. $34,663 mil.		

Q5-32	a	Q5-40	c
Q5-33	c	Q5-41	b
Q5-34	d	Q5-42	a
Q5-35	b	Q5-43	a
Q5-36	$201,000	Q5-44	*
Q5-37	d	Q5-45	a
Q5-38	b	Q5-46	c
Q5-39	$1,000	Q5-47	c

*Dr. Cash $10,450

P5-48A	3. $7,500 4. Div. rev. $320; Unrealized (loss) on invest. $(1,500)
P5-49A	NCF
P5-50A	5. I/S: Uncollect.-acct. exp. $323
P5-51A	3. A/R, net: 20X7 $221,000; 20X6 $207,800
P5-52A	2. Corrected ratios: Current 1.50; Acid-test 0.78 3. Net inc., corrected $82,000
P5-53A	2. 12/31/X8 Note rec. $25,000; Interest rec. $123
P5-54A	1. 2009 ratios: a. 2.02 b. 1.17 c. 31 days
P5-55B	3. 34,000 4. Div rev. $1,200; Unrealized gain on invest. $4,000
P5-56B	NCF
P5-57B	5. I/S: Uncollect.-acct. exp. $335 thou.
P5-58B	3. A/R, net: 20X4 $109,200; 20X3 $107,300
P5-59B	2. Corrected ratios: Current 1.30; Acid-test 0.77 3. Net inc., corrected $74,000
P5-60B	2. 12/31/X8 Note rec. $20,000; Interest rec. $247
P5-61B	1. 20X3 ratios: a. 1.83 b. 0.83 c. 32 days

DC1	Net inc. $223,000
DC2	20X7: Days' sales in rec. 26 days; Cash collections $1,456 thou.
FOF	2. Customers owed YUM $238 mil. in 2006 3. Collected $9,563 mil.
FOA	1. Customers owed Pier 1 $15,035 thou. 2. % doubtful .0744 in 2006

Chapter 6 (NCF=No check figures)

S6-1	NCF
S6-2	Gross profit $160,000
S6-3	COGS: Avg. $3,760; FIFO $3,740; LIFO $3,800
S6-4	Net inc.: Avg. $3,060; FIFO $3,100; LIFO $3,000
S6-5	Inc. tax exp: Avg. $1,224; FIFO $1,240; LIFO $1,200
S6-6	NCF
S6-7	COGS $421,000
S6-8	GP% 0.551; Invy TO 8.7 times
S6-9	$100,000
S6-10	c. $1,190 mil. d. $510 mil.
S6-11	1. Correct GP $5.6 mil. 2. Correct GP $3.2 mil.
S6-12	NCF

E6-13	2. Gross profit $1,100 thou.
E6-14	3. Gross profit $4,340
E6-15	1. COGS: (a) $2,190 (b) $2,210 (c) $2,160 (d) $2,260
E6-16	$40
E6-17	2. Net inc. $210
E6-18	1. GP: FIFO $0.8 mil.; LIFO $1.7 mil.
E6-19	NCF
E6-20	NCF
E6-21	Gross profit $45,000
E6-22	a. $475 c. $56 f. $2 g. $3 Krispy Kreme (net loss) $(136) mil.
E6-23	Krispy Kreme GP% 0.125; Invy. TO 17.9 times
E6-24	1. FIFO GP% 0.38; Invy. TO 4.5 times
E6-25	$1,272 mil.
E6-26	$34,000
E6-27	Net inc.: 20X5 $46,000; 20X4 $51,000
E6-28	NCF
E6-29	1. $141,000 2. $147,000
E6-30	20X7 ratios: GP% 0.197 Invy. TO 3.7 times

Q6-31	b	Q6-40	d
Q6-32	b	Q6-41	a
Q6-33	d	Q6-42	d
Q6-34	d	Q6-43	d
Q6-35	d	Q6-44	c
Q6-36	a	Q6-45	a
Q6-37	c	Q6-46	c
Q6-38	b	Q6-47	c
Q6-39	a		

P6-48A	3. Net inc. $502,500

P6-49A	2. Gross profit $2,409 3. $2,437
P6-50A	1. COGS: Avg. $7,299; FIFO $7,200; LIFO $7,440 3. Net inc. $1,861
P6-51A	1. GP: Avg. $60,286; FIFO $60,785; LIFO $59,845
P6-52A	NCF
P6-53A	1. Krispy Kreme: GP% 12.5%; Invy. TO 17.9 times
P6-54A	1. $872,000 2. GP $1,472,000
P6-55A	1. $771,000 2. Net inc. $160,000
P6-56A	1. Net inc. each yr. $2 mil.
P6-57B	3. Net inc. $1,128,000
P6-58B	2. Gross profit $1,173 3. $340
P6-59B	1. COGS: Avg. $40,937; FIFO $40,530; LIFO $41,550 3. Net inc. $8,070
P6-60B	1. GP: Avg. $291,571; FIFO $299,500; LIFO $278,500
P6-61B	NCF
P6-62B	1. Hewlett-Packard: GP% 25.0%; Invy. TO 7.5 times
P6-63B	1. $2,442,000 2. GP $3,432,000
P6-64B	1. $802,000 2. $160,000
P6-65B	1. Net inc. (thou): 2007 $150; 2006 $320; 2005 $50

DC1	1. Net inc.: FIFO $249,000; LIFO $213,000
DC2	NCF
FOF	3. $2,557 mil. 4. GP% 2006 69.5% 5. Invy. TO 29 times
FOA	1. c. $1,178 mil. 3. $1,180 mil. 5. GP% 2006 33.9%; Invy. TO 3.20 times

Chapter 6 Appendix A

S6A-1	NCF
S6A-2	2. $90,000 3. GP $50,000

E6A-3	COGS: Specific $2,890; Avg. $2,863; FIFO $2,800; LIFO $2,930
E6A-4	4. $2,930

P6A-5	2. GP $3,174
P6A-6	2. GP $1,680 thou.

Chapter 7 (NCF=No check figures)

S7-1	2. Book value $10,770 mil.
S7-2	NCF

S7-3	Dr. Land $60,000, Bldg. $60,000, Equip. $30,000
S7-4	NCF
S7-5	2. BV: SL $21,000,000 UOP $22,000,000 DDB $15,000,000
S7-6	a. $4,000,000 b. $5,000,000 c. $3,600,000
S7-7	2. $2,400,000
S7-8	a. €1,250,000 b. €2,800,000 c. €2,857,143
S7-9	Depr. Exp. $18,000
S7-10	2. Loss on Sale $1,000,000
S7-11	3. Book value $57.5 bil.
S7-12	1. $3,500,000
S7-13	Net inc. $2,100,000
S7-14	Net cash (used) $(115) mil.

E7-15	Land $310,500; Land improve. $81,400; Bldg. $1,050,000
E7-16	Gain on sale $3,300
E7-17	NCF
E7-18	2. Bldg., net $712,250
E7-19	Depr. 20X4: SL $3,000; UOP $2,400; DDB $0
E7-20	I/S: Depr. exp.—bldg. $8,000 B/S: Bldg., net $202,000
E7-21	$5,775
E7-22	Depr. Exp., Yr. 21 $30,000
E7-23	Loss on sale $1,154
E7-24	$325,000
E7-25	BV $336,000
E7-26	Part 2 Amortiz. Exp. $200,000
E7-27	1. $17 mil.
E7-28	a. Sale of bldg. $600,000
E7-29	2,000 hours
E7-30	(Loss) on sale $(73) mil.
E7-31	$56 mil.
E7-32	Net inc. Yr. 4 €1.5 mil. overstated

Q7-33	c	Q7-41	d
Q7-34	a	Q7-42	b
Q7-35	c	Q7-43	b
Q7-36	b	Q7-44	Gain $700
Q7-37	d	Q7-45	BV $7,050
Q7-38	a	Q7-46	c
Q7-39	d	Q7-47	a
Q7-40	b		

P7-48A	1. Land $294,600; Land Improve. $103,000; Sales Bldg. $579,100; Garage Bldg. $114,200; Furn. $81,200 2. Depr. Exp.— Land Improve. $3,433
P7-49A	2. A/D: Bldg. $358,000; Equip. $298,000

P7-50A   12/31 Depr. Exp.—Equip. $56,333 Depr. exp.—Bldgs. $1,050
P7-51A   NCF
P7-52A   3. Net inc. advantage of SL $31,200
          Cash flow advantage of DDB $20,800
P7-53A   1. Book value $2,712 mil.
P7-54A   2. Net inc. $292,800
P7-55A   1. (Loss) on sale $(0.1) bil.
          2. BV $0.7 bil.
P7-56B   1. Land $143,250; Land Improve. $118,300; Office Bldg. $654,100; Garage $63,600; Furn. $62,800
          2. Depr. Exp.—Land Improve. $4,436
P7-57B   2. A.D: Bldg. $52,000; Security equip. $442,500
P7-58B   12/31 On Nov. 4 purchase: Depr. Exp.—Comm. Equip. $4,000 Depr. Exp.—Tel. Equip. $1,333
P7-59B   NCF
P7-60B   3. Net inc. advantage of SL $9,316
          Cash flow advantage of DDB $5,017
P7-61B   1. Book value $6,463 mil.
P7-62B   2. Net inc. $900,000
P7-63B   1. (Loss) on sale $(0.2) bil.
          2. BV $6.8 bil.

DC1   1. Net inc.: LaPetite $95,400; Burgers $72,600
DC2   NCF
FOF   NCF
FOA   1. BV of assets sold $3,182 thou.
          4. % of assest used up 2006 55.3%

Chapter 8 (NCF=No check figures)

S8-1   3/31/X8 Debits include Interest Exp. $250
S8-2   2. Interest exp. $250
S8-3   2. Est. Warranty Pay. bal. $13,000
S8-4   NCF
S8-5   NCF
S8-6   a. $897,500 b. $551,875
S8-7   NCF
S8-8   12/31/00 Interest Exp. $163
S8-9   1. 7/31/X9 Bond carry. amt. $88,302
S8-10   3. Interest exp. 20X9 $3,934
S8-11   1. $4,700 4. $177.50
S8-12   b. Interest Exp. $188
S8-13   EPS: A $2.46; B $1.80

S8-14   Times-int.-earned ratio 2.8
S8-15   Total liab. $451,000

E8-16   2. Warranty exp. $9,000 Est. warranty pay. $7,600
E8-17   Unearned subscr. rev. $1,000
E8-18   P/R tax exp. $13,500; P/R tax pay. $900
E8-19   3. Interest exp. ea. yr. $2,400
E8-20   Income tax pay. $165,000 Income tax exp. $315,000
E8-21   2. Debt ratio 0.76
E8-22   Est. Loss $2,000,000
E8-23   Total current liab. $87,750
E8-24   12/31 Interest Exp. $3,000
E8-25   3. and 4. $316,000
E8-26   1. 12/31/10 Bond carry. amt. $376,509
E8-27   1. 6/30/10 Bond carry. amt. $330,255
E8-28   12/31/X5 Bond carry. amt. $600,000
E8-29   1. Carry. amt. $397,000
          2. Pd.-in Cap. in X/S of Par $377,000
E8-30   Kroger ratios: Current 0.89; Debt 0.77; Times-int.-earned 4.6
E8-31   1. EPS: A $7.66; B $3.97
E8-32   Pay off $1 bil.
E8-33   1. Gain on Retirement $37 mil.
          3. Debt ratio after 0.68
E8-34   5. 3/15/09 Bond carry. amt. $97,632

Q8-35	c	Q8-45	c
Q8-36	d	Q8-46	d
Q8-37	b	Q8-47	Interest Exp. $7,650
Q8-38	b	Q8-48	Interest Exp. $2,550
Q8-39	a	Q8-49	e
Q8-40	c	Q8-50	d
Q8-41	a	Q8-51	a
Q8-42	d	Q8-52	c
Q8-43	f	Q8-53	c
Q8-44	a		

P8-54A   e. Note pay. due in 1 yr. $20,000 Interest pay. $6,000
P8-55A   12/31/X5 Warranty Exp. $3,800 4/30/X6 Interest Exp. $1,500
P8-56A   2. Interest pay. $2,917 Bonds pay. $500,000
P8-57A   4. Interest pay. $5,667 Bonds pay., net $194,250
P8-58A   2. $486,500
          3. a. $20,750 b. $20,000
P8-59A   2. 12/31/Yr. 4 Bond carry. amt. $589,001

P8-60A   1. 12/31/X9 Bond carry. amt. $474,920
          3. Convert. bonds pay., net $284,952
P8-61A   NCF
P8-62A   1. Total current liab. $129,000 Total LT liab. $714,000
          3. Times-int.-earned ratio 4.3
P8-63B   e. Note pay. due in 1 yr. $20,000; Interest pay. $2,500
P8-64B   12/31/X8 Warranty Exp. $18,000
          6/30/X9 Interest Exp. $9,000
P8-65B   2. Interest pay. $20,000 Bonds pay. $1,000,000
P8-66B   4. Interest pay. $7,000 Bonds pay., net $289,000
P8-67B   2. $95,200 3. a. $4,600 b. $4,000
P8-68B   2. 12/31/Yr. 4 Bond carry. amt. $483,439
P8-69B   1. 12/31/X8 Bond carry. amt. $314,688
          3. Convert. bonds pay., net $157,344
P8-70B   NCF
P8-71B   1. Total current liab. $53,900 Total LT liab. $512,000
          3. Times-int.-earned ratio 2.7

DC1   1. Ratios after: Debt 0.93 Times-int.-earned 1.3
DC2   1. EPS: A $4.28 B $4.07; C $4.10
FOF   4. Debt ratio 0.77
FOA   1. Debt ratio 0.50
          3. 13.7%

Chapter 9 (NCF=No check figures)

S9-1   NCF
S9-2   NCF
S9-3   NCF
S9-4   NCF
S9-5   HP: Dr. Cash $17,993 mil.
S9-6   NCF
S9-7   Total SE $821 thou.
S9-8   a. $585 thou. b. $3,011 thou. c. $3,832 thou.
S9-9   Overall, SE decreased $21 mil.
S9-10   RE increased $50,000
S9-11   1. $150,000 4. Pfd. $450,000
S9-12   Cr. PIC in X/S of Par $63,000
S9-13   BV per share $61.40
S9-14   NCF
S9-15   ROA 1.5%; ROE 4.1%
S9-16   NCF

E9-17	NCF
E9-18	2. Total SE $92,500
E9-19	Total SE $143,000
E9-20	Total PIC $950,000
E9-21	Total SE $1,084 thou.
E9-22	Overall increase in SE $13,300
E9-23	NCF
E9-24	Total SE $12,471 mil.
E9-25	3. 515 mil. shares
	4. $136 mil. 5. $25.50
E9-26	20X4: Pfd. $9,000; Com. $41,000
E9-27	2. Total SE $7,939,000
E9-28	a. Decrease SE $80 mil.
E9-29	Total SE $2,606 mil.
E9-30	1. $10.40 2. $10.27
E9-31	ROA 0.116; ROE 0.183
E9-32	ROA 0.062; ROE 0.100
E9-33	NCF
E9-34	NCF
E9-35	NCF
E9-36	Div. $1,407 mil.
E9-37	12/31/X6 Total equity $72 mil.

Q9-38	c	Q9-48	d
Q9-39	c	Q9-49	e
Q9-40	d	Q9-50	b
Q9-41	c	Q9-51	a
Q9-42	b	Q9-52	c
Q9-43	e	Q9-53	a
Q9-44	a	Q9-54	a
Q9-45	c	Q9-55	d
Q9-46	b	Q9-56	b
Q9-47	a	Q9-57	c

P9-58A	NCF
P9-59A	2. Total SE $323,800
P9-60A	Total SE $540,000
P9-61A	NCF
P9-62A	Total SE $4,006,000
P9-63A	4. $183,700
P9-64A	2. Total SE $121,600
P9-65A	NCF
P9-66A	1. Total assets $554,000
	Total SE $290,000
	2. ROA 0.090; ROE 0.107
P9-67A	NCF
P9-68B	NCF
P9-69B	2. Total SE $207,500
P9-70B	Total SE $663,000
P9-71B	NCF
P9-72B	Total SE $7,280,000
P9-73B	4. $22,500
P9-74B	2. Total SE $92,800
P9-75B	NCF
P9-76B	1. Total assets $439,000
	Total SE $309,000
	2. ROA 0.089; ROE 0.125
P9-77B	NCF

DC1	3. Total SE: Plan 1 $220,000
	Plan 2 $230,000
DC2	NCF
DC3	3. Debt ratio, adjusted 0.87
FOF	4. ROE 57.1%; ROA 16.1%
FOA	1. Avg. price paid $16.19
	Avg. price rec'd $11.26
	3. RE bal. 2/25/06 $582,221 thou.

Chapter 10 (NCF=No check figures)

S10-1	1. Unrealized Loss on Invest. $900 2. LT avail.-for-sale invest. $5,100
S10-2	1. Gain on sale $600
S10-3	3. LT Invest. bal. $426 mil.
S10-4	(Loss) on sale $(73) mil.
S10-5	NCF
S10-6	NCF
S10-7	2. Cash interest $70,000
	4. Interest rev. $68,000
S10-8	c. Dr. Interest Rev. $1,000
S10-9	Nov. 10 FC Transaction Gain $1,000
S10-10	Aug. 28 FC Transaction Gain $2,000
S10-11	NCF
S10-12	NCF

E10-13	d. Loss on Sale $3,600
E10-14	2. Unrealized Loss $36,625
	3. LT investments $212,025
E10-15	Invest. end. bal. $1,055,000
E10-16	Gain on sale $1,645,000
E10-17	2. LT investment, at equity $525,000
E10-18	2. Consol. total SE $321,000
E10-19	3. Interest rec. $325 LT invest. in bonds $19,430
E10-20	1. 4/30 FC Transaction Loss $3,000
E10-21	FC translation adj. $47,000
E10-22	Net cash (used)-invest. $(11.8) mil.
E10-23	NCF
E10-24	3. c. LT invest., at equity $755,000
E10-25	3. Accum. other comp. (loss) $(40) mil.

Q10-26	a	Q10-32	d
Q10-27	d	Q10-33	b
Q10-28	Gain on Sale $8,000	Q10-34	a
		Q10-35	b
Q10-29	b	Q10-36	d
Q10-30	c	Q10-37	c
Q10-31	a		

P10-38A	2. B/S: LT invest. at equity $523,300
	I/S: Equity-method invest. rev. $178,500; Div. rev. $240; Unrealized (loss) $(2,600)
P10-39A	2. LT Invest. in MSC bal. $659,000
P10-40A	3. Consol. debt ratio 0.90
P10-41A	Consol. total assets $907,000
P10-42A	2. B/S: LT invest. in bonds $628,500
	I/S: Interest rev. $22,500
P10-43A	1. I/S: FC transaction (loss), net $(40)
P10-44A	1. FC translation adj. $298,000
P10-45A	NCF
P10-46B	2. B/S: LT invest., at equity $526,300
	I/S: Equity-method invest. rev. $87,500; Div. rev. $750; Unrealized (loss) $(3,300)
P10-47B	2. LT Invest. in Affil. bal. $535,000
P10-48B	3. Consol. debt ratio 0.891
P10-49B	Consol. total assets $976,000
P10-50B	2. B/S: LT invest. in bonds $482,156
	I/S: Interest rev. $29,656
P10-51B	1. I/S: FC transaction gain $5,800
P10-52B	1. FC translation adj. $207,000
P10-53B	NCF

DC1	NCF
DC2	2. Gain on sale $6,200
	3. Gain on sale $80,000
FOF	NCF
FOA	NCF

Chapter 11 (NCF=No check figures)

S11-1	NCF
S11-2	NCF
S11-3	Net inc. $21,000 thou.
S11-4	EPS for net inc. $1.50
S11-5	Comp. inc. $24,000
S11-6	Est. value $39.33
S11-7	NCF
S11-8	2. Net inc. $66,000 Deferred tax liab. $8,000
S11-9	RE, 12/31/X1 $201,000
S11-10	1. $85,000 3. Sold TS for $11,000

E11-11	Net inc. $1,150 thou.
E11-12	1. EPS for net inc. $3.69 2. $45.57
E11-13	NCF

E11-14	5.1%
E11-15	$5.25
E11-16	EPS for net inc. $0.93
E11-17	Net inc. $360,000
	Deferred tax liab. $20,000
E11-18	2. $100,000 3. $60,000
E11-19	RE, 12/31/X2 $401 mil.
E11-20	Total SE 12/31/X5 $2,080,000
E11-21	1. Total SE 12/31/X9 $6,950 thou. 2. 41.8%
	4. $6.09 per share
E11-22	NCF

Q11-23	b	Q11-29	c
Q11-24	b	Q11-30	d
Q11-25	d	Q11-31	a
Q11-26	a	Q11-32	b
Q11-27	b	Q11-33	d
Q11-28	c	Q11-34	c

P11-35A	1. Net inc. $41,400
	EPS for net inc. $1.77
P11-36A	RE, 12/31/X8 $63,400
P11-37A	Est. value $600,000
	Current mkt. value $640,000
P11-38A	1. EPS for net inc. $1.41
	2. Est. value at 6% $26.17
P11-39A	Comp. inc. $91,200
	EPS for net inc. $2.34
P11-40A	1. $120,000
	2. Cr. Deferred Tax Liab. $4,000
	3. Net inc. $78,000
P11-41A	1. $900 mil. 2. $1 per share
	3. $10.20 per share
	4. Increase in SE $20 mil.
	5. 10%
P11-42B	1. Net inc. $71,000
	EPS for net inc. $2.54
P11-43B	RE, 4/30/X3 $150,000
P11-44B	Est. value $1,016,667
	Current mkt. value $1,200,000
P11-45B	1. EPS for net inc. $0.92
	2. Est. value at 7% $15.71
P11-46B	Comp. inc. $67,200
	EPS for net inc. $1.22
P11-47B	1. $185,000
	2. Cr. Deferred Tax Liab. $6,000
	3. Net inc. $120,000
P11-48B	1. $600 mil. 2. $1 per share
	3. $3.77 per share
	4. Increase in SE $20 mil.
	5. 10%

DC1	Use $0.59
DC2	NCF
FOF	2. Est. value at 5% $60.40
FOA	3. Est. value at 6% $12.00

Chapter 12 (NCF=No check figures)

S12-1	NCF
S12-2	NCF
S12-3	Net cash-oper. $70,000
S12-4	NCF
S12-5	Net cash-oper. $54,000
S12-6	Net cash-oper. $54,000
	Net increase in cash $53,000
S12-7	a. $60,000 b. $20,000
S12-8	a. New borrowing $10,000
	b. Issuance $8,000
	c. Dividends $146,000
S12-9	Net cash-oper. $110,000
	Net (decrease) in cash $(20,000)
S12-10	Net cash-oper. $13,000
S12-11	Net cash-oper. $13,000
	Net increase in cash $12,000
S12-12	a. $699,000 b. $326,000
S12-13	a. $68,000 b. $134,000

E12-14	NCF
E12-15	NCF
E12-16	NCF
E12-17	Net cash-oper. $11,000
E12-18	Net cash-oper. $48,000
E12-19	1. Net cash-oper. $99,000
	Net increase in cash $27,000
	Noncash inv. and fin. $50,000
E12-20	NCF
E12-21	a. $500 b. $11,000
E12-22	NCF
E12-23	NCF
E12-24	Net cash-oper. $21,000
E12-25	NCF
E12-26	1. Net cash-oper. $102,000
	Net increase in cash $29,000
E12-27	a. $50,000 b. $113,000
E12-28	(Thousands)
	a. $24,637 b. $18,134
	c. $3,576 d. $530 e. $73
	f. $1,294
E12-29	1. Gain $120 thou.
	2. $240 thou.

Q12-30	c	Q12-40	b
Q12-31	a	Q12-41	a
Q12-32	b	Q12-42	c
Q12-33	b	Q12-43	a
Q12-34	d	Q12-44	a
Q12-35	c	Q12-45	a
Q12-36	c	Q12-46	d
Q12-37	*	Q12-47	d
Q12-38	c	Q12-48	a
Q12-39	d	Q12-49	a

*financing operating

P12-50A	NCF
P12-51A	1. Net inc. $51,667 2. Total assets $396,667 3. Net cash-oper. $(49,000); Net increase in cash $90,000
P12-52A	Net cash-oper. $63,200
	Net increase in cash $16,000
	Noncash inv. and fin. $160,000
P12-53A	1. Net cash-oper. $76,900
	Net (decrease) in cash $(4,100)
	Noncash inv. and fin. $101,000
P12-54A	1. Net cash-oper. $80,000
	Net increase in cash $12,300
P12-55A	1. Net cash-oper. $95,700
	Net (decrease) in cash $(2,700)
	Noncash inv. and fin. $79,400
P12-56A	1. Net inc. $51,667 2. Total assets $396,667 3. Net cash-oper. $(49,000); Net increase in cash $90,000
P12-57A	Net cash-oper. $80,000
	Net increase in cash $12,300
P12-58A	1. Net cash-oper. $55,800
	Net (decrease) in cash $(2,000)
	Noncash inv. and fin. $99,100
P12-59A	1. Net cash-oper. $73,200
	Net increase in cash $20,000
	Noncash inv. and fin. $19,000
P12-60B	NCF
P12-61B	1. Net inc. $157,333 2. Total assets $340,333 3. Net cash-oper. $81,000; Net increase in cash $191,000
P12-62B	Net cash-oper. $74,500
	Net (decrease) in cash $(5,700)
	Noncash inv. and fin. $290,4000
P12-63B	1. Net cash-oper. $68,700
	Net increase in cash $16,300
	Noncash inv. and fin. $30,000
P12-64B	1. Net cash-oper. $90,600
	Net increase in cash $13,100
P12-65B	1. Net cash-oper. $30,000
	Net increase in cash $7,600
	Noncash inv. and fin. $142,800
P12-66B	1. Net inc. $157,333 2. Total assets $340,333 3. Net cash-oper. $81,000; Net increase in cash $191,000
P12-67B	1. Net cash-oper. $90,600
	Net increase in cash $13,100
P12-68B	1. Net cash-oper. $77,200
	Net (decrease) in cash $(4,600)
	Noncash inv. and fin. $83,200
P12-69B	1. Net cash-oper. $40,400
	Net increase in cash $4,100
	Noncash inv. and fin. $48,300

DC1   (Thousands)
       1. Net cash-oper. $132
          Net (decrease) in cash $(46)
DC2   NCF
FOF   1. a. $9,577 mil.
       b. $2,476 mil.
FOA   4. BV sold $3,182 thou.
       5. $38,714 thou.

Chapter 13 (NCF=No check figures)

S13-1   2007 Net inc. (decrease) (2.0)%
S13-2   2009 Sales trend 107%
S13-3   20X4 Cash 2.1%
S13-4   Net inc. % Porterfield 6.2%
S13-5   20X4 Current ratio 1.21
S13-6   1. 2005 Acid-test ratio 0.27
S13-7   a. 29 times b. 8.7 days
S13-8   1. 0.774 2. 8.2
S13-9   a. 8.6% b. 16.1% c. 57.1%
S13-10 1. EPS $4.85; P/E 16
S13-11 (a) $3,855 thou. (d) $873 thou.
S13-12 (a) $562 thou. (d) $3,768 thou.
        (e) $1,294 thou.
S13-13 $570 thou.

E13-14 2007 WC (decrease) (5.4)%
E13-15 Net inc. decreased 5.8%
E13-16 Yr. 4 Net inc. trend 147%
E13-17 Current assets 24.6%
        Total liab. 41.7%
E13-18 Net inc. 20% both years
E13-19 NCF
E13-20 a. 1.67 b. 0.83 c. 4.42
        d. 9.5 e. 38 days
E13-21 20X9 ratios: a. 2.07 b. 0.91
        c. 0.47 d. 4.13

E13-22 20X8 ratios: a. 0.098 b. 0.132
        c. 0.151 d. $0.67
E13-23 20X7 ratios: a. 17.3 b. 0.014
        c. $6.00
E13-24 Amazon $100 mil.
E13-25 Total assets $20,000 mil.
        Current liab. $6,800 mil.
E13-26 Sales $6,400 mil.
        Net inc. $720 mil.

Q13-27	b	Q13-33	b
Q13-28	c	Q13-34	c
Q13-29	a	Q13-35	a
Q13-30	b	Q13-36	a
Q13-31	d	Q13-37	d
Q13-32	c	Q13-38	d

P13-39A 1. 20X8 trends: Net sales
         186%; Net inc. 169%; Total
         assets 155%
         2. 20X8 0.074
P13-40A 1. Net inc. 10.7%
         Current assets 77.1%
P13-41A NCF
P13-42A 1. Current ratio before 1.74
         2. a. Current ratio after 1.84
P13-43A 1. 20X6 ratios: a. 1.41 b. 2.24
         c. 4.32 d. 0.173 g. 11.9
P13-44A 1. Video: a. 060 b. 2.16
         c. 100 d. 0.68 f. 0.196
         2. Video $30,000
P13-45A NCF
P13-46B 1. 2008 trends: Net rev. 134%;
         Net inc. 205%; SE 147%
         2. 2008 0.111

P13-47B Net inc. 5.3%
         Current assets 75.0%
P13-48B NCF
P13-49B 1. Current ratio before 1.54
         2. a. Current ratio after 1.44
P13-50B 1. 20X9 ratios a. 2.04 b. 2.77
         c. 10.8 d. 0.315 f. 16
P13-51B 1. Thrifty Nickel: a. 0.78
         b. 2.32 c. 40 d. 0.41 h. 10.6
         2. Thrifty Nickel $34,000
P13-52B NCF

DC1   NCF
DC2   NCF
DC3   NCF
FOF   2006 trend: Total rev. 114%;
       Net inc. 134%;
       Net cash-oper. 118%
FOA   2006 trend: Net sales 118%;
       Net (loss) (40)%

Appendix C

PC-1   a. 5 yrs. $153,900
       b. 6% $281,850
PC-2   a. $10,000,000
       b. $5,640,000
PC-3   1. $500,100 2. $446,820
       3. $562,360
PC-4   1. $379,455 2. 12/31/X2
       Bond carry. amt. $380,838
PC-5   Renault €498,960
       Peugeot €519,750
PC-6 $170,960

Company Index

Glindex

A Combined Glossary and Subject Index